THE GUINNESS BOOK OF RECORDS 1991

EDITOR
Donald McFarlan

FOUNDING EDITOR
Norris D. McWhirter

AMERICAN EXECUTIVE EDITOR
Michelle Dunkley McCarthy

AMERICAN EDITOR (NEW YORK)
Mark Young

Facts On File
New York • Oxford

Grateful acknowledgment is made to the individuals, organizations and governing bodies who have helped in our research.

We would like to give special thanks to the editor and staff of the *Facts On File World News Digest*.

The Guinness Book of Records wishes to thank:

DEPUTY EDITORS
Sheila Goldsmith
Nicholas Heath-Brown
Michael G. Laraque
Maria Morgan
Stewart Newport

SPORTS EDITOR
Peter J. Matthews

CORRESPONDENCE EDITOR
Martin Day

DESIGN MANAGER
David L. Roberts
Jo Stein

ASSISTANT DESIGNER
Amanda Sedge

Additional design
Jon Lucas

PICTURE EDITOR
Alex P. Goldberg

Picture Assistant
Julie O'Leary

INFORMATION SYSTEMS MANAGER
Alex E. Reid

PRODUCTION MANAGER
Chris Lingard
Olivia McKean

EDITORIAL ASSISTANTS
Marion R. Casey
Denise Ling

SECRETARIAL SUPPORT
Debbie Bigmore
Maria Kashioulis
Muriel Ling

PRESS OFFICER
Cathy Brooks

INDEX
Ann Hall

JACKET DESIGN
Julia King

ARTWORK, MAPS AND DIAGRAMS
Ad Vantage Studios
Kathy Aldridge
Matthew Hillier
Pat Gibbon
Peter Harper
Neil Randon.

Facts On File, Inc.
460 Park Avenue South
New York, NY 10016
USA

World Copyright Reserved
Copyright © 1990 by Guinness Publishing Ltd

Facts On File books are available at special discounts when purchased in bulk quantities for businesses, associations, institutions or sales promotions. Please contact the Special Sales Department of our New York office at 212/683-2244 (dial 800/322-8755 except in NY, AK or HI).

ISBN 0-8160-2439-1

ISSN 0300-1679

'Guinness International' is a registered trademark of Guinness Publishing Ltd.

Text design by Guinness Publishing Ltd, Enfield
Composition by Guinness Publishing Ltd, Enfield
Manufactured by Arcata Graphics Company
Printed in the United States of America

This book is printed on acid-free paper.

CONTENTS

EDITORIAL POLICY

The Guinness Book of Records is the authoritative source for facts, feats and exploits of the world and its inhabitants. This collection of records covers all fields of human, and non-human, endeavor; however, it is not a compendium of every record set, but rather a subjective selection of those that the editors find to be the most significant. Records in our sense have to be both measurable and comparable. Novel events, unique occurrences and fascinating idiosyncrasies are not necessarily records. We are likely to publish only those records that improve upon previously published records. We reserve the right to determine at our sole discretion the records to be published.

Guidance regarding the breaking of records is available from this office upon written application and receipt of a business-size self-addressed stamped envelope, and should be sought at least one month before completing plans for a record attempt. Send your application to:

Guinness Book of Records
Facts On File, Inc.
460 Park Avenue South
New York, NY 10016

THE HISTORY OF THE GUINNESS BOOK

First published in the United Kingdom in fall 1955, *The Guinness Book of Records* quickly established itself as an annual bestseller. The brainchild of Sir Hugh Beaver (1890–1967), managing director of Guinness Ltd., the book was produced by Norris and Ross McWhirter. The worldwide expansion of the Guinness tradition began with the publication of the first US edition in 1956. There are currently 262 editions in 35 languages. The first Soviet edition was published in 1990. In November 1974 *The Guinness Book of Records* gained a place within its own pages, becoming the top-selling copyright book in publishing history, with sales of 23·9 million. In 1989 global sales surpassed the 60 million mark.

This 29th US edition is the first for Facts On File, Inc. This edition also marks the first time that it has been printed in full color throughout. The editors have updated world records and added many American records never previously published. The editors would like to thank the many people who have been contacted by our research staff and have provided us with the information needed to produce an accurate account of the world and its records.

THE HUMAN BEING

Origins

Dimensions

Reproductivity

Longevity

Physiology

Anatomy

Most complete Hominid skeleton ● Dr Donald C. Johanson (far left) with his co-researchers displaying the complete collection of hominid fossils which were found by the Awash River, Hadar, Ethiopia on 30 Nov 1974. The most famous of the find was the the earliest hominid skeleton of 'Lucy' (40 percent complete). (Photo: Science Photo Library)

Origins

EARLIEST MAN

SCALE OF TIME *If the age of the Earth-Moon system (latest estimate 4·45 billion years) is likened to a single year, Hominids appeared on the scene at about 4:15 P.M. on 31 December the Christian era began about 14 seconds before midnight and the life span of a 120-year-old person would be about three-quarters of a second. Present calculations indicate that the Sun's increased heat as it becomes a 'red giant,' will make life on Earth insupportable in about 5·5 billion years. Meanwhile there may well be colder epicycles. The period of 1 billion years is sometimes referred to as an eon.*

Man (homo sapiens) is a species in the subfamily Homininae of the family Hominidae of the superfamily Hominoidea of the suborder Simiae (or Anthropoidea) of the order Primates of the infraclass Eutheria of the subclass Theria of the class Mammalia of the subphylum Vertebrata (Craniata) of the phylum Chordata of the subkingdom Metazoa of the animal kingdom.

Earliest Primate ■ These appeared in the Paleocene epoch about 69 million years ago. The earliest members of the suborder Anthropoidea are known from both Africa and South America in the early Oligocene, 34–30 million years ago, when the two infra-orders, Platyrrhini and Catarrhini, from the New and Old Worlds respectively, were already distinct. New finds from the Fayum, in Egypt, are being studied and

Most complete Hominid skeleton ● Dr Donald C. Johanson (far left) with his co-researchers displaying the complete collection of hominid fossils which were found by the Awash River, Hadar, Ethiopia on 30 Nov 1974. The most famous of the find was the earliest hominid skeleton of 'Lucy' (40 percent complete). (Photo: Science Photo Library)

may represent primates from the Eocene period, as old as 38 million years ago.

Earliest Hominoid ■ Recent hominoid remains from Salonika in Greece are claimed to be 25 million years old and thought to provide a link between man and his ape ancestors. These finds, however, require more intensive research.

Earliest Hominid ■ Characteristics typical of the Hominidae such as the large brain and bipedal locomotion (walking on two legs) do not appear until much later. The earliest undoubted hominid relic found is an Australopithecine jaw–bone with two molars 2 in long found by Kiptalam Chepboi near Lake Baringo, Kenya in February 1984 and dated to 4 million years ago by associated fossils and to 5·6–5·4 million years ago through rock correlation by potassium-argón dating.

The most complete of the earliest hominid skeletons is that of 'Lucy' (40 percent complete) found

by Dr Donald C. Johanson and T. Gray at Locality 162 by the Awash River, Hadar, in the Afar region of Ethiopia on 30 Nov 1974. She was estimated to be *c.* 40 years old when she died 3 million years ago, and she was 3½ ft tall. New 'human' remains from southwest China found in 1989 are claimed to be up to 500,000 years older than the African hominids, but not enough details are yet known to confirm these finds.

Parallel tracks of hominid footprints extending over 80 ft were first discovered at Laetoli, Tanzania in 1978, by Paul Abell, in volcanic ash dating to 3·5 million years ago. The height of the smallest of the seemingly three individuals was estimated to be 3 ft 11 in.

Earliest genus–*Homo* ■ The earliest species of this genus is *Homo habilis*, or 'Handy Man,' so named by Professor Raymond Arthur Dart (1893-1988) in 1964.

The greatest age attributed to fossils of this genus is 1·9 million years for the skull KNM-ER (Kenya National Museum-East Rudolf) 1470 discovered in 1972 by Bernard Ngeneo at Koobi Fora by Lake Turkana, northern Kenya. It was reconstructed by Dr Maeve Leakey (nee Epps).

The earliest stone tools are abraded core-choppers dating from *c.* 2·5 million years ago. They were found at Hadar, Ethiopia in November–December 1976 by Hélène Roche (France). Finger–held (as opposed to fist–held) quartz slicers found by Roche and Dr John Wall (New Zealand) close to the Hadar site by the Gona River are also dated to *c.* 2.5 million years ago.

Earliest *Homo erectus* ■ This species (upright man), the direct ancestor of *Homo sapiens*, was discovered by Kamoya Kimeu on the surface at the site of Nariokotome III to the west of Lake Turkana, Kenya in August 1985. The skeleton of this 5 ft 5 in 12-year-old boy is the most complete of this species ever found; only a few small pieces are missing. It is dated to 1·6 million years ago.

Earliest Americans ■ Over 500 artifacts 11,000 to 16,000 years old were found in Washington County, PA in April 1973 after being brought to the attention of the University of Pittsburgh by Albert Miller, whose family owned the land. The dig, led by Dr James Adovasio, started in June 1973 and lasted until June 1983. The artifacts consist mainly of unfluted lanceolate projectile points (either spearheads or darts), an assortment of bifacial and unifacial tools (knives and scrappers), polyhedral blade cores (long thin flakes from which blades are made), and blades struck from this core. These items are all made from chert, a flint–like rock.

The site dates to the Pre-Clovis Paleo-Indian Culture and it is believed that the *Homo sapien* Paleo-Indians were the initial inhabitants of the site. The tools dated by the Mass Accelerator Spectrometer Technique (MAS), which measures the carbon content present in the amino acids at the time of death, resembled tools found in Manchuria. This supports theories that North America was first inhabited by peoples coming across a natural land–bridge between Siberia and Alaska, that is now deep beneath the Bering Sea.

In 1968 a burial site containing bones of two individuals believed to be an infant and a adolescent were uncovered by construction workers in Wilsall, MT. The Anzick Burial site also contained 120 artifacts with a red ocher covering believed to be grave offerings. These were mainly flint and stone bifacial (flaked by percussion along both sides of the chopping edge) tools and the remains of spear shafts.

The bones were dated by the MAS Technique to

not less than 10,600 years ago. The remains are believed to be of members of the Paleo-Indian Culture, with the artifacts in the style of the Clovis Age.

Dimensions

GIANTS

The true height of human giants is frequently obscured by exaggeration and commercial dishonesty. The only admissible evidence on the actual height of giants is that collected since 1870 under impartial medical supervision. Unfortunately even medical authors themselves are not always blameless and can include fanciful, as opposed to measured, heights.

The assertion that Goliath of Gath (c. 1060 B.C.) stood 6 cubits and a span (9 ft 6½ in) suggests a confusion of units or some over-zealous exaggeration by the Hebrew chroniclers.

The Jewish historian Flavius Josephus (born A.D. 37/38, died c. A.D. 100) and some of the manuscripts of the Septuagint (the earliest Greek translation of the Old Testament) attribute to Goliath the wholly credible height of 4 Greek cubits and a span (6 ft 10 in).

Giants exhibited in circuses and exhibitions are routinely under contract not to be measured and are, almost traditionally, billed by their promoters at heights up to 18 in excess of their true heights. The most recent example is Haji Mohammad Alam Channa (b. 1953) of Sehwan, Pakistan, who allegedly measured 8 ft 2 ¾ in. On 21 Aug 1987 he was measured in New York, NY and found to be 7 ft 8 in.

TALLEST MEN

Earliest opinion is that the tallest man in medical history of whom there is irrefutable evidence was Robert Pershing Wadlow born at 6:30 A.M. on 22 Feb 1918 in Alton, IL. Weighing 8 ½ lb at birth his abnormal growth started at the age of 2 following a double hernia operation. On his 13th birthday he stood 7 ft 1 ¾ in tall and at the age of 17 had reached 8 ft ½ in.

On 27 Jun 1940 Dr C.M. Charles, Associate professor of anatomy at Washington University's School of Medicine in St Louis, MO, and Dr Cyril MacBryde measured Robert Wadlow at 8 ft 11·1 in (arm-span 9 ft 5¾ in) in St Louis. Wadlow died 18 days later at 1:30 A.M. on 15 Jul 1940 weighing 439 lb in a hotel in Manistee, MI as a result of a septic blister on his right ankle caused by a poorly fitting brace. He was buried in Oakwood Cemetery, Alton, IL in a casket measuring 10 ft 9 in.

Because of his rapid growth he had limited feeling in his legs below the knees. Wadlow was still growing during his terminal illness and would probably have ultimately reached or just exceeded 9 ft in height if he had survived for another year. His greatest recorded weight was 491 lb on his 21st birthday. His shoes were size 37AA (18½ in) and his hands measured 12¾ in from the wrist to the tip of the middle finger (cf. the depth of this page at 11 ¼ in).

Living ■ The acromegalic giant, Haji Mohammad Alam Channa (b. 1953) of Bachal Channa, Sehwan Sharif, Pakistan stands 7 ft 8 in. When he was 10 years old his abnormal growth was noted by his family and it continued until he reached the age of 26 years. In 1989 he married Naseem and is currently working at the shrine of the great mystic saint Hazrat Lal Shahbaz Qalandar at Sehwan.

TALLEST WOMEN

The tallest woman in history was the acromegalic giantess Zeng Jinlian (b. 26 Jun 1964) of

---

ROBERT WADLOW

Weighing 8 ½ lb at birth, the abnormal growth of Robert Wadlow started at the age of 2 following a double hernia operation. His height progressed as follows:

AGE	HEIGHT		WEIGHT
	ft	in	lb
5	5	4	105
8	6	0	169
9	6	2 ¼	180
10	6	5	210
11	6	7	–
12	6	10 ½	–
13	7	1 ¾	255
14	7	5	301
15	7	8	355
16	7	10 ¼	374
17	8	0 ½	315[1]
18	8	3 ½	–
19	8	5 ½	480
20	8	6 ¾	–
21	8	8 ¼	491
22·4[2]	8	11¹/₁₀	439

[1] Following severe influenza and infection of the foot.

[2] Still growing during his terminal illness.

Yujiang village in the Bright Moon Commune, Hunan Province, central China who was 8 ft 1¾ in when she died on 13 Feb 1982. This figure, however, represented her height with assumed normal spinal curvature because she suffered from severe scoliosis (curvature of the spine) and could not stand up straight. She began to grow abnormally from the age of 4 months and stood 5 ft 1½ in before her 4th birthday (cf. 5 ft 4 in for Robert Wadlow at the age of 5) and 7 ft 1½ in when she was 13. Her hands measured 10 in and her feet 14 in in length. Both her parents and her brother are of normal size.

The giantess Ella Ewing (1875–1913) of Gorin, MO was billed at 8 ft 2 in, but this height was exaggerated. She measured 7 ft 4 ½ in at the age of 23, and may have attained 7 ft 6 in by the time of her death.

Living ■ The world's tallest woman is Sandy Allen (b. 18 Jun 1955) in Chicago, IL and now working as a secretary in Indianapolis, IN. A 6 ½ lb baby, her abnormal growth began soon after birth. At 10 years of age she stood 6 ft 3 in and measured 7 ft 1 in when she was 16. On 14 Jul 1977 this acromegalic giantess underwent a pituitary gland operation which inhibited further growth at 7 ft 7 ¼ in. She now weighs 462 lb and takes a size 16 EEE shoe.

Twins ■ The world's tallest identical twins are Michael and James Lanier (b. 27 Nov 1969) from Troy, MI. They measured 7 ft 1 in at the age of 14 years and both now stand 7 ft 4 in. Their sister Jennifer is 5 ft 2 in tall.

Identical twin sisters Heidi and Heather Burge (b. 11 Nov 1971) from Palos Verdes, CA both measure 6 ft 4¾ in tall.

Married couple ■ Anna Hanen Swan (1846–88) of Nova Scotia, Canada was billed at 8 ft 1 in but actually measured 7 ft 5½ in. At St Martin-in-the-Fields, London, United Kingdom on 17 Jun 1871 she married Martin van Buren Bates (1845–1919) of Whitesburg, Letcher County, KY, who stood 7 ft 2½ in, making them the tallest married couple on record.

DWARFS

The strictures that apply to giants apply equally

GIANTS

The only other people for whom heights of 8 ft or more have been reliably reported are the eleven listed below. In seven cases, gigantism was followed by acromegaly, a disorder which causes an enlargement of the nose, lips, tongue, lower jaw, hands and feet, due to renewed activity and increase in growth hormone by an already swollen pituitary gland, which is located at the base of the brain.

Robert Wadlow (1918-1940), of Alton, IL [1] .... 8 ft 11 1/10 in.
John William Rogan (1871–1905), of Gallatin, TN [2] .... 8 ft 8 in.
John F. Carroll (1932–69) of Buffalo, NY [3] .... 8 ft 7 ¾ in.
Välnö Myllyrinne (1909–63) of Helsinki, Finland [4] .... 8 ft 3 in.
Don Koehler (1925–81) of Denton, MO, later of Chicago [5] .... 8 ft 2 in.
Bernard Coyne (1897–1921) of Anthon, IO [6] .... 8 ft 2 in.
Zeng Jinlain (1964–1982) of Yujiang, China [7] .... 8 ft 1 ¾ in.
Patrick Cotter (O'Brien) (1760–1806) of Kinsale, County Cork, Republic of Ireland [8] .... 8 ft 1 in.
'Constantine' (1872–1902) of Reutlingen, West Germany [9] .... 8 ft 0·8 in.
Gabriel Estavao Monjane (1944–1990) of Monjacaze, Mozambique [10] .... c. 8 ft ¾ in.
Sulaimān 'Ali Nashnush (b. 1943–fl. 1968) of Tripoli, Libya [11] .... 8 ft 0·4 in.

[1] See above.

[2] Measured in a sitting position. Unable to stand owing to ankylosis (stiffening of the joints through the formation of adhesions) of the knees and hips. Weighed only 175 lb.

[3] Severe kyphoscoliosis (two-dimensional spinal curvature). The figure represents his height with assumed normal spinal curvature, calculated from a standing height of 8 ft measured on 14 Oct 1959. His standing height was 7 ft 8¼ in shortly before his death.

[4] Stood 7 ft 3½ in at the age of 21 years. Experienced a second phase of growth in his late thirties and measured 8 ft 1·2 in at the time of his death. In 1931 he reportedly weighed 434 lb.

[5] Abnormal growth started at the age of 10. He had a twin sister who is 5 ft 9 in tall. His father was 6 ft 2 in and his mother 5 ft 10 in.

[6] Eunuchoidal giant (Daddy long-legs syndrome). Rejected by Army in 1918 when 7 ft 9 in. Still growing at time of death.

[7] Measurement based on assumed normal spianl curvature because she suffered from severe scoliosis and could not stand up straight.

[8] Revised height based on skeletal remeasurement after bones exhumed on 19 Dec 1972.

[9] Eunuchoidal. Height estimated, as both legs were amputated after they turned gangrenous. He claimed a height of 8 ft 6 in.

[10] Died in January 1990 after a fall at his home.

[11] Operation to correct abnormal growth successfully carried out in Rome in 1960.

Note: fl is the abbreviation for floruit, Latin for living at the relevant date.

EXAGGERATED HEIGHTS

The following lists a number of well-known giants whose heights have been exaggerated.

NAME	DATES	COUNTRY	HEIGHT		
			CLAIMED		ACTUAL
			ft in		ft in
Edouard Beaupre	1881–1904	Canada	8 3	....	7 8
Muhammad Aalam Channa¹	1956–fl. 1989	Pakistan	8 2¾	....	7 8
Fernard (Atlas) Bacheland	1923–76	Belgium	9 2	....	7 8¼
Joachim Eleizegue	1822–fl. 1845	Spain	7 10	....	7 8
Chang Wu-Gow	1846–93	China	9 2	....	7 8
Johann Petrussen	1914–fl. 1986	Iceland	8 8	....	7 7
Max Palmer	1928–fl. 1986	USA	8 0½	....	7 7
Rigardus Riynhout	1922–fl. 1955	Netherlands	9 1½	....	7 6½
Baptiste Hugo	1879–1916	France	8 10	....	7 6½
Bernardo Gigli	1736–62	Italy	8 0	....	7 6½
James Toller	1795–1819	England	8 6	....	7 6
Eddie Carmel²	1938–72	Israel	9 0½	....	7 6
Daniel Cajanus	1724–49	Finland	9 3½	....	7 3½
Patrick Murphy	1834–62	Ireland	8 10	....	7 3½
Jakop Loll	1783–1839	USSR	8 4½	....	7 3
Paul Henoch	1852–76	Germany	8 3	....	7 2

¹ Channa was medically assessed in New York on 21 Aug 1987 and found to measure 7 ft 8 in (7 ft 10 in in his shoes).
² The height of Eddie Carmel was estimated from photographs and that of Cajanus from evidence by bones. Each of the other actual heights was obtained from independent medical authority. The embalmed body of Beaupre in the anatomical museum of the University of Montreal measures 7 ft 1 ⅜ in in length.

Tallest identical female twins ● Heidi and Heather Burge play basketball for the Univ. of Virginia. (Photo: Michael Harrison/Daily Progress)

to dwarfs, except that exaggeration gives way to understatement. In the same way as 9 ft may be regarded as the limit towards which the tallest giants tend, so 23 in must be regarded as the limit towards which the shortest adult dwarfs or midgets tend (cf. the average length of new-born babies is 18–20 in). In the case of child dwarfs, their *ages* are often enhanced by their agents or managers.

There are many forms of human dwarfism, but those suffering from ateliosis (midgets) are generally the shortest. They have essentially normal proportions but suffer from growth hormone deficiency. Such dwarfs tended to be more diminutive in the past due to lower nutritional standards.

Shortest female ■ The shortest mature human of whom there is independent evidence was Pauline Musters ('Princess Pauline'), a Dutch dwarf. She was born at Ossendrecht, on 26 Feb 1876 and measured 11·8 in at birth. At 9 years of age she was 21·65 in tall and weighed only 3 lb 5 oz. She died on 1 Mar 1895 in New York City at the age of 19, of pneumonia, with meningitis, her heart weakened from alcoholic excesses. Although she was billed at 19 in, she had earlier been medically assessed and found to be 23·2 in tall. A postmortem examination showed her to be exactly 24 in (there was some elongation after death). Her mature weight varied from 7½ to 9 lb and her 'vital statistics' were 18½–19–17 in, which suggests she was overweight.

In 1979 a height of 19·68 in and a weight of 4 lb 6 oz were reported for a 9-year-old Greek girl named Stamatoula (b. Sep 1969; length 5·9 in). When she died on 22 Aug 1985 at the Lyrion Convent, Athens, Greece she measured 26·4 in and weighed 11 lb. The child, believed to be the survivor of twins, suffered from Seckel's syndrome, also known as 'bird-headed dwarfism,' because victims have prominent eyes and noses.

Shortest male ■ The shortest recorded adult male dwarf was Calvin Phillips, born on 14 Jan 1791 in Bridgewater, MA. He weighed 2 lb at birth and stopped growing at the age of 5. When he was 19 he measured 26½ in and weighed 12 lb with his clothes on. He died 2 years later, in April 1812, from progeria, a rare disorder characterised by dwarfism and premature senility.

In 1938 a height of 19 in was attributed to Paul Del Rio (b. Madrid, 1920) by *Life* magazine when he visited Hollywood, but the fact that his presence created no great impression among other dwarfs in the film capital and that he weighed as much as 12 lb suggests that he was closer to 26 in tall.

William E. Jackson, *alias* 'Major Mite,' born 2 Oct 1864 in Dunedin, New Zealand, measured 9 in long and weighed 12 oz at birth. In November 1880 he stood 21 in and weighed 9 lb. He died in New York City on 9 Dec 1900, when he measured 27 in.

The Portuguese dwarf Antonio Ferreiro, a former holder of the 'shortest human' title (29 ½ in) died in Lisbon on 11 Feb 1989 at age 44. He was a drummer in a pop group.

The most famous midget in history was Charles Sherwood Stratton, alias 'General Tom Thumb,' born on 4 Jan 1838. When he joined up with Phineas T. Barnum the famous American showman his birth date was changed to 4 Jan 1832 so that when billed at 30½ in at the age of 18 he was in fact 12.

At the age of 25 he married Lavinia Warren (2 ft 8 in) on 10 February 1863 while she was also in P. T. Barnum's Circus. Two thousand people attended the wedding at New York City's Grace Episcopal Church. At the hotel reception that followed the bridal couple stood on top of a piano to greet the guests, then cut into a wedding cake that weighed more than they did together. Later, President Lincoln gave a reception for them at the White House and they went on to 20 years of married life.

Tom died of apoplexy on 15 Jul 1885 at his birthplace, Bridgewater, CT, aged 45 (not 51) and was 3 ft 4 in (70 lb).

Living ■ The world's shortest known mobile living adult human is believed to be Nelson de la Rosa Aquino (b. June 1968), of Santo Domingo, Dominican Republic, who suffers from Seckel's syndrome. On 2 Apr 1987 he was examined by the head of the Dominican Republic Medical Association who revealed that this tiny prodigy measured 28·3 in in height and weighed only 15 lb. (Compare 7½ lb for an average baby at birth.) Other statistics include a 17½ in chest and 16 in waist. The doctor also reported that Nelson had stopped growing. The rest of his family are all of normal size.

Madge Bester (b. 26 Apr 1963) of Johannesburg, South Africa is only 25·5 in tall, but she suffers from *Osteogenesis imperfecta* and is confined to a wheelchair. In this disease there is an inherited abnormality of collagen, which, with calcium salts, provides the rigid structure of bones. It is characterized by brittle bones and other deformities of the skeleton. Her mother, Winnie, is not much taller, measuring 27·5 in, and she too is confined to a wheelchair.

Twins ■ The shortest twins ever recorded were the primordial dwarfs Matjus and Bela Matina (b. 1903–fl. 1935) of Budapest, Hungary, who later became naturalized Americans. They both measured 30 in.

The world's shortest living twins are John and Greg Rice (b. 3 Dec 1951) of West Palm Beach, FL who both measure 34 in.

The shortest identical twin sisters are Dorene Williams of Oakdale and Darlene McGregor of Almeda, CA (b. 1949) who both stand 4 ft 1 in.

Oldest ■ There are only two centenarian dwarfs on record. The older was Hungarian-born Miss Susanna Bokoyni ('Princess Susanna') of Newton, NJ, who died at age 105 on 24 Aug 1984. She was 3 ft 4 in tall and weighed 37 lb.

The other was Miss Anne Clowes of Matlock, United Kingdom, who died on 5 Aug 1784 aged 103 years. She was 3 ft 9 in tall and weighed 48 lb.

Most variable stature ■ Adam Rainer, born in Graz, Austria in 1899, measured 3 ft 10.45 in at the age of 21. He then suddenly started growing at a rapid rate, and by 1931 he had reached 7 ft 1¾ in. He became so weak as a result that he was bedridden for the rest of his life. At the time of his death at age 51 on 4 Mar 1950 he measured 7 ft 8 in and was the only person in medical history to have been both a dwarf and a giant.

Most dissimilar couple ■ On 30 Jun 1984, 6 ft 7 in Nigel Wilks (b. 1963) of Kingston upon Hull, United Kingdom married 3 ft 11 in Beverly Russell, (b. 1963) who suffers from a skeletal disorder. Their son Daniel, 9 lb 5 oz, was born by cesarean section on 22 Mar 1986.

TRIBES

Tallest ■ The tallest major tribes in the world are the slender Tutsi (also known as the Watusi) of Rwanda and Burundi, Central Africa, and the Dinka of the Sudan. In the case of the Tutsi, average adult males and females stand 6 ft 5 in and 5 ft 10 in respectively.

The Tehuelches of Patagonia, Argentina, long regarded as of gigantic stature, i.e. 7–8 ft, have in fact an average height (males) of 5 ft 10 in and apparently do not exceed 6 ft 6 in.

Shortest ■ The smallest pygmies are the Mbuti of the Ituri forest, Zaïre, Central Africa with an average height of 4 ft 6 in for men and 4 ft 5 in for women, with some groups averaging only 4 ft 4 in for men and 4 ft 1 in for women.

WEIGHT

People suffering from the Prader-Willi syndrome, a rare brain disorder that makes them constantly crave for food, have been known to get so fat that they die from asphyxiation.

Heaviest men ■ The heaviest in medical history was Jon Brower Minnoch (b. 29 Sep 1941) of Bainbridge Island, WA, who had suffered from obesity since childhood. The 6 ft 1 in tall former taxi driver was 392 lb in 1963, 700 lb in 1966 and 975 lb in September 1976.

Eighteen months later, in March 1978, Minnoch was rushed to University Hospital, Seattle, saturated with fluid and suffering from heart and respiratory failure. It took a dozen firemen and an improvised stretcher to move him from his home to a ferryboat. When he arrived at the hospital he was put in two beds lashed together. It took 13 people just to roll him over. By extrapolating his intake and elimination rates, consultant endocrinologist Dr Robert Schwartz calculated that Minnoch must have weighed more than 1,387 lb when he was admitted, a great deal of this was water accumulation due to his congestive heart failure. After nearly 2 years on a 1,200-calories-a-day diet the choking fluid had gone, and he was discharged at 476 lb. But the weight crept back again, and in October 1981 he had to be readmitted, after putting on 197 lb. When he died on 10 Sep 1983 he weighed more than 798 lb.

Living ■ The heaviest living man is T. J. Albert Jackson (b. Kent Nicholson), also known as 'Fat Albert' of Canton, MS (see table). He recently tipped the scales at 891 lb. He has a 120 in chest, a 116 in waist, 70 in thighs and a 29½ in neck.

Albert Pernitsch of Grafkorn, Austria also claims to be the world's heaviest man, but the greatest weight recorded for him so far is 869 lb.

When an attempt was made to weigh Walter Hudson (b. November 1944) of New York, NY on an industrial scale that registered up to 995 lb the machine broke down, but the 5 ft 10 in tall super-heavyweight was later found to weigh 1,190 lb. He measured 106 in around the chest and 110 in around the waist. On 14 Sep 1987 he made the headlines when he became wedged in his bedroom doorway and had to be rescued by firemen. It took nine men to carry him back to the reinforced bed in which he had been a virtual prisoner for 27 years. Hudson, a foodaholic since his early childhood, is now on a special weight–loss program and by June 1988 had lost 630 lb.

Weight Loss ■ Jon Brower Minnoch (1941–83) had reduced to 476 lb by July 1979 thus indicating a weight loss of at least 924 lb in 2 years.

Michael Hebranko (b. 14 May 1953) of Brooklyn,

<table>
<tr><td colspan="2" align="center">SUPER HEAVYWEIGHTS</td></tr>
<tr><td>Jon Brower Minnoch (1941–83) Bainbridge, WA 6 ft 1 in</td><td>1,400 lb</td></tr>
<tr><td>Walter Hudson (b. 1944) New York, NY 5 ft 10 in</td><td>1,197 lb</td></tr>
<tr><td>Michael Walker né Francis Lang (b. 1934) Clinton, IA 6 ft 2 in [1]</td><td>1,187 lb</td></tr>
<tr><td>Robert Earl Hughes (1926–58) Monticello, MO 6 ft ½ in</td><td>1,069 lb</td></tr>
<tr><td>Mike Parteleno (b. 1958) USA 6 ft</td><td>1,022 lb</td></tr>
<tr><td>Mills Darden (1798–1857) Henderson County, TN 7 ft 6 in</td><td>1,020 lb</td></tr>
<tr><td>Michael Edelman (b. 1964) USA</td><td>994 lb</td></tr>
<tr><td>John Finnerty (b. 1952) USA</td><td>1,000 lb</td></tr>
<tr><td>'Big Tex' (1902–fl 1956) USA 6 ft 1½ in</td><td>924 lb</td></tr>
<tr><td>Mickey Mounds (b. 1953) USA</td><td>910 lb [2]</td></tr>
<tr><td>John Hanson Craig (1856–94) Danville, IN 6 ft 5 in [3]</td><td>907 lb</td></tr>
<tr><td>Michael Hebranko (b. 1954) Brooklyn, NY 6 ft</td><td>905 lb [4]</td></tr>
<tr><td>Arthur Knorr (1914–60) USA 6 ft 1 in</td><td>900 lb [5]</td></tr>
<tr><td>T. J. Albert Jackson (b. 1941) Canton, MS 6 ft 4 in</td><td>891 lb</td></tr>
</table>

[1] Peak weight attained in 1971 as a result of drug-induced bulimia. Reduced to 365 lb by February 1980.

[2] Reduced to 364 lb by February 1989.

[3] Won $1,000 in a 'Bonny Baby' contest in New York City in 1858.

[4] Reduced to 224 lb by June 1989

[5] Gained 295 lb in the last 6 months of his life.

NY in July 1987 weighed 905 lb. Within 15 months he lost over 500 lb, and by June 1989 weighed 217 lb, having shed a total of 688 lb within a period of less than 24 months. His waist measurement was 115 in but is now 36-38 in, a reduction of 79 in.

Paul M. Kimelman (b. 1943) of Pittsburgh, PA reduced from 487 lb to 130 lb between 1 Jan 1967 and 3 Aug 1967, a loss of 350 lb in 215 days.

Richard Stephens of Birmingham, AL, went from 467 lb to 305 ¾ lb in 157 days between 12 Apr and Sep 1985.

On 14 Mar 1982 surgeons at a hospital in New York City, NY removed 140 lb of adipose tissue from the abdominal wall of a 798 lb man. They had to use a hoist to lift the layers of fat as they were removed.

Ron Allen (b. 1947) sweated off 21 ½ lb of his 239 lb in Nashville, TN in 24 hours in August 1984.

Women ■ The circus fat lady Mrs Celesta Geyer (b. 1901), alias Dolly Dimples, went from 546 lb to 141 lb in 1950–51, a loss of 392 lb in 14 months. Her 'vital statistics' diminished from 79–84–84 in to a svelte 34–28–36 in. Her book *How I Lost 392 lbs* was not a best-seller perhaps because of the difficulty of would-be readers

---

identifying themselves with the dressmaking and other problems of losing more than 392 lb when 4 ft 11 in tall. In December 1967 she was reportedly down to 110 lb.

In February 1961 Mrs. G. Levandowski (b.1893) of Burnips, MI, underwent a protracted operation for the removal of an ovarian cyst which reduced her weight from 616 lb to 308 lb.

Weight gaining ■ Jon Minnoch (see above) in October 1981 when readmitted to University of Washington Hospital, Seattle, WA had regained 196 lb in seven days.

Arthur Knorr gained 294 lb in the last six months of his life.

Miss Doris James of San Francisco, CA is alleged to have gained 325 lb in the 12 months before her death in August 1965, aged 38, at a weight of 675 lb. She was only 5 ft 2 in tall.

Greatest differential ■ The greatest weight difference recorded for a married couple is *c.* 1,300 lb in the case of Jon Brower Minnoch and his 110 lb wife Jeannette in March 1978.

Heaviest women ■ When Mrs Percy Pearl Washington, who suffered from polydipsia (excessive thirst), died in a hospital in Milwaukee on 9 Oct 1972 the scales registered only up to 800 lb, but she was credited with a weight of 880 lb. She was 6 ft tall and wore a size 62 dress.

In 1888 a weight of 850 lb was also reported for an unnamed woman living in Boston, MA, but further details are lacking.

Ida Maitland (1898–1932) of Springfield, MS reportedly weighed 911 lb, but this claim has never been substantiated.

Living ■ The heaviest woman ever recorded was probably Rosie Carnemolla (b. 1944) of Poughkeepsie, ND, who registered a peak weight of 850 lb on 13 Mar 1988. A week later she was put on a carefully controlled diet that reduced her weight by 250 lb in 6 months, and then underwent an operation to reduce the size of her stomach. By September 1988 the former food addict was down to 350 lb, during which time her waistline had declined from 98 in to 46 in and her dress size from 70 to 46. Her target weight is 150 lb.

Heaviest twins ■ Billy Leon and Benny Loyd (b. 7 Dec 1946) McCrary, alias McGuire, of Hendersonville, NC were normal in size until the age of 6 when they both contracted German measles. In November 1978 they weighed 743 lb (Billy) and 723 lb (Benny) and had 84 in waists. As professional tag wrestling performers they were *billed* at weights up to 770 lb. Billy died at Niagara Falls, Ontario, Canada on 13 Jul 1979 after a mini-motorcycle accident.

Lightest ■ The lightest adult was Lucia Zarate (b. San Carlos, Mexico 1863–89), an emaciated Mexican dwarf of 26½ in, who weighed 4·7 lb at the age of 17. She 'fattened up' to 13 lb by her 20th birthday. At birth she weighed 2½ lb.

The thinnest recorded adults of normal height are those suffering from anorexia nervosa. Losses up to 65 percent of the original body weight have been recorded in females, with a 'low' of 45 lb in the case of Emma Shaller (b. 1868–90) of St Louis, MO, who stood 5 ft 2 in.

It is reported that the American performer Rosa Lee Plemons (b. 1873) weighed 27 lb at the age of 18.

Edward C. Hagner (1892–1962), alias Eddie Masher (US) is alleged to have weighed only

48 lb at a height of 5 ft 7 in. He was also known as 'Skeleton Dude.'

In August 1825 the biceps measurement of Claude-Ambroise Seurat (1797–1826) of Troyes, France was 4 in and the distance between his back and his chest was less than 3 in. According to one report he stood 5 ft 7½ in and weighed 78 lb, but in another account he was described as being 15 ft 4 in and only 36 lb.

Reproductivity

MOTHERHOOD

Most children ■ The greatest officially recorded number of children born to one mother is 69, by the first of the two wives of Feodor Vassilyev (b. 1707-*fl*.1782), a peasant from Shuya, 150 miles east of Moscow, USSR. In 27 confinements she gave birth to 16 pairs of twins, 7 sets of triplets and 4 sets of quadruplets. The case was reported by the Monastery of Nikolskiy on 27 Feb 1782 to Moscow. At least 67 survived infancy were born in the period *c.* 1725-65.

It was reported on 31 Jan 1989 that farmer's wife

> **Most premature child** ● Now a lively and healthy 3 year old, James Elgin Gill was born on 30 May 1987 128 days premature and weighing 1 lb 6 oz.

Mrs. Maria Olivera (b. 1939) of San Juan, Argentina, gave birth to her 32nd child. They are all still alive.

United States ■ Women in the United States average 1·9 children — well below the world average of 3·6. The highest annual birthrate is Rwanda's (East Africa) which averages 8·5, and the lowest is Italy's at 1·5.

Oldest mother ■ The oldest recorded mother for whom the evidence satisfied medical verification was Mrs Ruth Alice Kistler (nee Taylor), formerly Mrs Shepard (1899–1982), of Portland, OR. A birth certificate indicated that she gave birth to a daughter, Suzan, at Glendale, near Los Angeles, CA, on 18 Oct 1956, when her age was 57 years 129 days.

In the *Gazette Médicale de Liége* (1 Oct 1891) Dr E. Derasse reported the case of one of his patients who gave birth to a healthy baby at the age of 59 years 5 months. He had managed to obtain her birth certificate. The woman already had a married daughter aged 40 years.

Longest and shortest pregnancy ■ Claims up to 413 days have been widely reported but accurate data are bedeviled by the increasing use of oral contraceptive pills, which is a cause of amenorrhea (abnormal absence of menstration). *The US Medical Investigator* of 27 Dec 1884 reported a case of 15 months 20 days and the *Histoire de l'Académie* of 1751 the most extreme case of 36 months.

In May 1961 a Burmese woman aged 54 was delivered by cesarean section in Rangoon (now known as Yangon) of a 3 lb calcified fetus after 25 years' gestation. She had gone into labour in 1936, but no child was born.

Premature - Living ■ James Elgin Gill was born to his parents, Brenda and James, on 20 May 1987 in Ottawa, Ontario, Canada 128 days premature and weighing 1 lb 6 oz.

Joanne and Mark Holding (nonidentical twins) were born on 28 Feb 1988 in Portsmouth, United Kingdom 105 days premature, Joanne weighed 1 lb 15 oz and Mark was 1 lb 8 oz.

Tina Piper of St Leonards-on-Sea, United Kingdom, was delivered of quadruplets on 10 Apr 1988, at exactly 26 weeks' term. Oliver, 2 lb 9 oz, (d.February 1989), Francesca 2 lb 2 oz, Charlotte 2 lb 4 ½ oz and Georgina 2 lb 5 oz were all born at The Royal Sussex County Hospital, Sussex, United Kingdom.

United States ■ Ernestine Hudgins was born on 8 Feb 1983 in San Diego, CA about 18 weeks premature and weighing 17 oz.

BABIES

Heaviest ■ Big babies (i.e., over 10 lb) are usually born to mothers who are large, overweight or have some medical problem such as diabetes. The heaviest of a healthy mother were boys of 22 lb 8 oz born to Signora Carmelina Fedele of Aversa, Italy in September 1955 and by Cesarean section to Mrs Christina Samane at Sipetu Hospital, Transkei, South Africa on 24 May 1982. The latter boy, named Sithandawe, who suffers from Weaver's syndrome (excessive growth in children because of abnormalities in the parents' genes), weighed 154 lb and stood 5 ft 5 in on his 6th birthday.

Mrs Anna Bates (nee Swan; 1846–88), the 7 ft 5½ in Canadian giantess (see also p 7), gave birth to a boy weighing 23 lb 12 oz (length 30 in) at her home in Seville, OH on 19 Jan 1879, but the baby died 11 hours later. Her first child, an 18 lb girl (length 24 in) was stillborn in 1872.

On 9 Jan 1891 Mrs Florentin Ortega of Buenos Aires, Argentina produced a stillborn boy weighing 25 lb.

In May 1939 a deformed baby weighing 29 lb 4 oz was born in a hospital at Effingham, IL, but died 2 hours later.

Lightest ■ The lowest birth weight recorded for a surviving infant, of which there is definite evidence, is 10 oz in the case of Mrs Marian Taggart (nee Chapman; b. 5 June 1938, d. 31 May 1983). This baby was born six weeks premature in South Shields, United Kingdom. She was born unattended (length 12 in) and was nursed by Dr D. A. Shearer, who fed her hourly for the first 30 hours with brandy, glucose and water through a fountain-pen filler. At 3 weeks she weighed 1 lb 13 oz and by her first birthday 13 lb 14 oz. Her weight on her 21st birthday was 106 lb.

MULTIPLE BIRTHS

HIGHEST NUMBER REPORTED AT SINGLE BIRTH
World
10 (decaplets) (2 male, 8 female) Bacacay, Brazil, 22 Apr 1946 (also report from Spain, 1924 and China, 12 May 1936).

HIGHEST NUMBER MEDICALLY RECORDED
9 (nonuplets) (5 male, 4 female) to Mrs Geraldine Brodrick at Royal Hospital, Sydney, Australia on 13 June 1971. 2 males stillborn. Richard (12 oz) survived 6 days.
9 (all died) to patient at University of Pennsylvania, Philadelphia, PA 29 May 1972.
9 (all died) reported from Bagerhat, Bangladesh, c. 11 May 1977 to 30-year-old mother.
United States
7 (Septuplets) to Patti Jorgenson (Mrs Frustaci) on 21 May 1985. The three babies who survived ranged in weight from 1 lb upwards.

HIGHEST NUMBER SURVIVING[1]
World
6 out of 6 (3 males, 3 females) to Mrs Susan Jane Rosenkowitz (*née* Scoones) (b. Colombo, Sri Lanka, 28 Oct 1947) at Mowbray, Cape Town, South Africa on 11 Jan 1974. In order of birth they were: David, Nicolette, Jason, Emma, Grant and Elizabeth. They totalled 24 lb 1 oz.
6 out of 6 (4 males, 2 females) to Mrs Rosanna Giannini (b. 1952) at Careggi Hospital, Florence, Italy on 11 Jan 1980. They are Francesco, Fabrizio, Giorgio Roberto, Letizia and Linda.
Heaviest
25 lb Mrs Lui Saulien, Chekiang, China, 7 Jun 1953.
25 lb Mrs Kamalammal, Pondicherry, India, 30 Dec 1956.
World Most Sets
No recorded case of more than a single set.

QUADRUPLETS
World Heaviest
22 lb 13 oz Mrs Ayako Takeda, Tsuchihashi Maternity Hospital, Kagoshima, Japan, 4 Oct 1978 (4 girls).
World Most Sets
4 Mde Feodor Vassilyev, Shuya, Russia (d. *ante* 1770).

TRIPLETS[2] *World Heaviest*
26 lb 6 oz (unconfirmed) Iranian case (2 male, 1 female) 18 Mar 1968.
World Most Sets
15 Maddalena Granata, Italy (1839–*fl.* 1886).

TWINS *World Heaviest*
27 lb 12 oz (surviving) Mrs J. P. Haskin, Fort Smith, AR, 20 Feb 1924.
World Most Sets
16 Mde Vassilyev (see above). *Note also* Mrs Barbara Zulu of Barbeton, South Africa bore 3 sets of girls and 3 mixed sets in 7 years (1967–73).

[1] The South African press were unable to verify the birth of 5 babies to Mrs Charmaine Craig (*née* Peterson) in Cape Town on 16 Oct 1980 and a 6th on 8 Nov. The reported names were Frank, Salome, John, Andrew, William and belatedly Deborah.
[2] Mrs Anna Steynvaait of Johannesburg, South Africa produced 2 sets within 10 months in 1960.

A weight of 8 oz was reported on 20 Mar 1938 for a baby born prematurely to Mrs John Womack, after she had been knocked down by a truck in East St Louis, IL. The baby was taken alive to St Mary's Hospital but died a few hours later.

On 23 Feb 1952 it was reported that a 6 oz baby only 6½ in long lived for 12 hours in a hospital in Indianapolis, IN. A twin was stillborn.

Coincident birthdates ■ It should be mentioned that births are not completely random. There are some days of the year on which more births are recorded than others. It is also true that within families there are tendencies toward births occurring at approximately the same (general) time, if not specific day.

The only verified example of a family producing 5 single children with coincident birthdays is that of Catherine (1952), Carol (1953), Charles (1956), Claudia (1961) and Cecilia (1966), born to Carolyn and Ralph Cummins of Clintwood, VA, all on 20 February. The random odds against five single siblings sharing a birthdate would be one in 17,797,577,730—more than 3½ times the world's population.

The three children of the Henriksen family of Andenes, Norway, Heidi (b. 1960), Olav (b. 1964) and Lief-Martin (b. 1968), all celebrate their birthday infrequently, because these all fall on Leap Day – February 29.

Ralph Bertram Williams was born on 4 July 1982 in Wilmington, NC. His father, grandfather and, in 1876, his great-grandfather were also born on 4 July.

Rosemary and Leo Dignan of Palos Heights, IL became grandparents of 2 girls and 1 boy within 2 hours between 11:15 A.M. and 1:04 P.M. on 25 Aug 1989. The 3 babies were born to 2 sons and one daughter of the Dignans. The mothers did not know that they were in hospital having babies at the same time.

Most southerly birth ■ Emilio Marcos Palma (Argentina), born 7 Jan 1978 at the Sargento Cabral Base, Antarctica, is the only person alive who can claim to be the first born on any continent. This mother was flown from Argentina at government expense.

Test-tube baby ■ Louise Brown (5 lb 12 oz) was delivered by cesarean section from Lesley Brown, aged 31, in Oldham General Hospital, United Kingdom at 11:47 P.M. on 25 Jul 1978. Louise was externally conceived on 10 Nov 1977.

United States ■ Elizabeth Carr (5 lb 12 oz) was delivered by cesarean section from Judy Carr, age 28, in Norfolk General Hospital, VA on 28 December 1981. Elizabeth was externally conceived on 15 April 1981. Dr Howard Jones of Eastern Virginia Medical School performed the in-vitro procedure.

First birth from frozen-embryo ■ Zoe (last name unknown) was delivered by cesarean section weighing 5 lb 13 oz on 28 March 1984 in Melbourne, Australia. Scientists from Monash University announced the birth.

United States ■ A boy (9 lb 8 oz) was delivered by cesarean section on 4 Jun 1986 from Monique, age 36, in Cottage Hospital, Santa Barbara, CA. A second child was born on 23 Oct 1989 by the same procedure and it is believed that this is the only case of siblings from frozen embryo. Dr. Richard Marrs was in charge of the procedure.

MULTIPLE BIRTHS

Lightest twins ■ Mary, 16 oz, and Margaret, 19 oz, were born on 16 Aug 1931 to Mrs Florence Stimson, Old Fletton, Peterborough, Cambridgeshire, United Kingdom.

'Siamese' twins ■ Conjoined twins derived the name 'Siamese' from the celebrated Chang and Eng Bunker ('Left' and 'Right' in Thai) born at Meklong on 11 May 1811 of Chinese parents. They were joined by a cartilaginous band at the chest and they married the Misses Sarah and Adelaide Yates of Wilkes County, NC in April 1843 and fathered 10 and 12 children respectively. They died within three hours of each other on 17 Jan 1874, aged 62.

The rarest form of conjoined twins is Dicephales tetrabrachius dipus (two heads, four arms and two legs). The only known examples are Masha and Dasha Krivoshlyapovy born in the USSR on 4 Jan 1950 and Catherine and Eilish Holton of County Kildare, Republic of Ireland born on 24 August 1988 at Coombe Hospital, Dublin.

The earliest successful separation of Siamese twins was performed on xiphopagus (joined at the sternum) girls at Mt Sinai Hospital, Cleveland, OH by Dr Jac S. Geller on 14 Dec 1952.

Nadir and Juraci Climerio de Oliverra of Santo Amaro de Purifcacao, Bahia, Brazil, born on 2 Jun 1957.

An unnamed pair were separated in a 10-hour operation in Washington, DC on 23 Jun 1977.

Fonda Michelle and Shannon Elaine Beaver of Forest City, NC were born on 9 Feb 1980 and successfully separated in February 1981.

Another successful separation was carried out on Viet and Duc (b. 1981) at a hospital in Ho Chi Minh City (formerly Saigon), Vietnam on 4 Oct 1988.

The oldest surviving unseparated twins are the craniopagus (heads are fused at the crown) pair, Yvonne and Yvette McCarther (b. 1949) of Los Angeles, CA. They have rejected an operation to separate them.

Most twins ■ In Chungchon, South Korea it was reported in September 1981 that there were unaccountably 38 pairs in only 275 families-the highest ratio ever recorded.

Longest separated twins ■ Through the help of New Zealand's television program *Missing* on 27 Apr 1989, Iris (nee Haughie) Johns and Aro (nee Haughie) Campbell (b. 13 Jan 1914) were reunited after 75 years' separation.

United States ■ Identical twins Lloyd Ecre and Floyd Ellswerk Clark were born on 15 Feb 1917 in Nebraska. They were separated when only 4 months' old and lived under their adopted names, Dewayne William Gramly (Lloyd) and Paul Edward Forbes (Floyd). Both men knew that they had been born twins but it wasn't until 16 Jun 1986 that they were reunited, after having been separated for over 69 years.

Fastest triplet birth ■ Bradley, Christopher and Carmon were born naturally to Mrs James E. Duck of Memphis, TN in two minutes on 21 Mar 1977.

Septuplets ■ Septuplets were born on 21 May 1985 to Patti Jorgenson (Mrs) Frustaci of Orange, CA, a 30-year-old English teacher who had been taking a fertility drug. One baby was stillborn and the living infants ranged from 1 lb upwards in weight. In the weeks that followed, three more babies died but three have survived.

First test-tube quintuplets ■ Alan, Brett, Connor, Douglas and Edward were born to Linda and Bruce Jacobssen at University College Hospital, London on 26 Apr 1985.

Quindecaplets ■ It was announced by Dr Gennaro Montanino of Rome that he had removed by hysterotomy after 4 months of the pregnancy the fetuses of 10 girls and 5 boys from the womb of a 35-year-old housewife on 22 Jul 1971. A fertility drug was responsible for this unique instance of quindecaplets.

Longest interval between twins ■ Mrs Danny Berg (b. 1953) of Rome, Italy, who had been on hormone treatment after suffering two miscarriages, gave birth normally to a baby girl, Diana, on 23 Dec 1987, but she was not delivered of the other twin, Monica, by cesarean, until 30 Jan 1988.

DESCENDANTS

In polygamous countries, the number of a person's descendants can become incalculable. The last Sharifian Emperor of Morocco, Moulay Ismail (1672–1727), known as 'The Bloodthirsty,' was reputed to have fathered a total of 525 sons and 342 daughters by 1703 and achieved a 700th son in 1721.

In April 1984 the death was reported of Adam Borntrager, aged 96, of Medford, WI, who had 707 direct descendants of whom all but 32 were living. The total comprised 11 children, 115 grand-, 529 great-grand- and 20 great-great-grandchildren.

Mrs Peter L. Schwartz (1902–88) had 14 children, 13 of whom are still living, 175 grandchildren, 477 great-grandchildren and 20 great-great-grandchildren. Both families are of the Amish sect, and eschew cars, telephones, electric light and higher education.

Seven-generation family ■ Augusta Bunge (nee Pagel; b. 13 Oct 1879); of Wisconsin, learned that her great-great-great-grand-daughter had become a mother by receiving news of her great-great-great-great-grandson, Christopher John Bollig (b. 21 Jan 1989).

Great-grandmother ■ Harriet Holmes of Newfoundland, Canada (b. 17 Jan 1899) became the youngest living great-great-great-grand-mother on 8 Mar 1987 at the age of 88 years 50 days.

Most living ascendants ■ Megan Sue Austin (b. 16 May 1982) of Bar Harbor, ME had a full set of grandparents and great-grandparents and five great-great-grandparents, making 19 direct ascendants.

Longevity

No single subject is more obscured by vanity, deceit, falsehood and deliberate fraud than human longevity. Claims are generally made on behalf of the very aged rather than *by* them. Apart from the traces left by accidental 'markers' (e.g. the residial effects of established dated events such as the Chernoby incident), there is no known scientific method of checking the age of any part of the living body.

Many hundreds of claims throughout history have been made for persons living well into their second century and some, insulting to the intelligence, for people living even into their third. Centenarians surviving beyond their 113th year are in fact of the extremest rarity and the present absolute proven limit of human longevity does not yet admit of anyone living to celebrate any birthday after his or her 120th.

Several claimed ages of more than 110 year old are believed to have been double lives (father and son, relations with the same names or successive bearers of a title). The most famous example was Christian Jakobsen Drackenberg who alleged to have been born in Stavanger, Norway on 18 Nov 1626 and to have died in Aarhus, Denmark at age 145 yr 326 days on 9 Oct 1772. From data on documented centenarians, actuaries have shown that only one 115-year-life can be expected in 2·1 billion lives (cf. world population was estimated to be *c*. 5·3 billion by mid-1990).

The height of credulity was reached on 5 May 1933, when a news agency filed a story from China with a Beijing dateline that Li Chung-yun, the 'oldest man on Earth,' born in 1680, had just died after 256 years (*sic*).

The most extreme case of longevity recently claimed in the USSR has been 168 years for Shirali 'Baba' Muslinov of Barzavu, Azerbaijan, who died on 2 Sep 1973 and was reputedly born on 26 Mar 1805. No interview with this man was ever permitted to any Western journalist or scientist. He was even said to have celebrated, in 1966, the 100th birthday of his third wife, Hartun, and that of one of his grandchildren in August 1973. It was reported in 1979 that 241 centenarians had been found in the Abkhazian Republic of Georgia (pop 520,000), USSR, where aged citizens are invested with an almost saint-like status. 2·58 percent of the population were aged over 90–24 times the proportion in the United States.

Dr Zhores Aleksandrovich Medvedev (b. Tbilisi, 14 Nov 1925), the Russian gerontologist who was refused a visa to return to the USSR in 1973, referring to USSR claims in Washington, DC, on 30 Apr 1974 stated, 'The whole phenomenon looks like a falsification' adding, 'He [Stalin] liked the idea that [other] Georgians lived to be 100 or more. Local officials tried hard to find more and more cases for Stalin.' He points out (a) the *average* life span in the regions claiming the highest incidence of centenarians is lower than the USSR average and (b) unlike to the rest of the world, the incidence of centenarians claimed in the Caucasus had declined rapidly from 8,000 in 1950 to 4,500 in 1970.

The latest census in China revealed 3,800 centenarians, of whom two-thirds were women. According to a 1985 census carried out in the Chinese province of Xinjiang Urgur, there were 850 centenarians in the area, four between the ages of 125 and 103. In the United States as of 1 July 1989 the figure was 61,000. Birth and death

Youngest great-great-great-grandmother
● Seen here with her family is Harriet Holmes of Newfoundland, Canada who became a great-great-great-grandmother to Brian Bursey on 8 Mar 1987, when she was aged 88 years 50 days. (Photo: Herb Parsons)

registration, however, became complete only in 1933 and was only 30·9 percent by 1915.

According to research carried out by scientists at the Scripps Institution of Oceanography at La Jolla, CA, in 1979, it is now possible to work out a person's age within a 10 percent margin of error by examining the amino acids in teeth and eyes.

Oldest authentic centenarian ◼ The greatest *authenticated* age to which any human has ever lived is a unique 120 years 237 days in the case of Shigechiyo Izumi of Asan on Tokunoshima, an island 820 miles southwest of Tokyo, Japan. He was born at Asan on 29 Jun 1865 and recorded as a 6-year-old in Japan's first census of 1871.

He died in his ranch house at 12:15 GMT on 21 Feb 1986 after developing pneumonia.

Oldest living ◼ The oldest living person in the world whose date of birth can be reliably authenticated is Carrie C. White (nee Joyner) who was born in Gadsden, FL on 18 Nov 1874. She now lives in a nursing home in Palatka, FL.

AUTHENTIC NATIONAL LONGEVITY RECORDS

	Years	Days		Born		Died	
Japan	120	237	Shigechiyo Izumi	29 Jun	1865	21 Feb	1986
United States[1]	115		Carrie White (Mrs) (nee Joyner)	18 Nov	1874	fl. Mar	1990
United Kingdom[2]	114	208	Anna Eliza Williams (Mrs) (nee Davies)	2 Jun	1873	27 Dec	1987
France	114		Jeanne Louise Calment	21 Feb	1875	fl. Mar	1990
Canada[3]	113	124	Pierre Joubert	15 Jul	1701	16 Nov	1814
Australia	112	330	Caroline Maud Mockridge	11 Dec	1874	6 Nov	1987
Spain[4]	112	228	Josefa Salas Mateo	14 Jul	1860	27 Feb	1973
Norway	112	61	Maren Bolette Torp	21 Dec	1876	20 Feb	1989
Morocco	>112		El Hadj Mohammed el Mokri (Grand Vizier)		1844	16 Sep	1957
Poland	112	+	Roswlia Mielczarak (Mrs)		1868	7 Jan	1981
Ireland	111	327	The Hon. Katherine Plunket	22 Nov	1820	14 Oct	1932
Scotland[5]	111	238	Kate Begbie (Mrs)	9 Jan	1877	5 Sep	1988
South Africa[6]	111	151	Johanna Booyson	17 Jan	1857	16 Jun	1968
Czechoslovakia	111	+	Marie Bernatkova	22 Oct	1857	fl. Oct	1968
Netherlands[7]	111		Christina van Druten-Hoogakker	20 Jan	1876	8 Dec	1987
Germany[8]	111		Maria Corba	15 Aug	1878	fl. Mar	1990
Channel Islands, Guernsey	110	321	Margaret Ann Neve (nee Harvey)	18 May	1792	4 Apr	1903
Northern Ireland	110	234	Elizabeth Watkins (Mrs)	10 Mar	1863	31 Oct	1973
Sweden[9]	110	200+	Wilhelmine Sande (Mrs)	24 Oct	1874	21 Jan	1986
Yugoslavia	110	150+	Demitrius Philipovitch	9 Mar	1818	fl. Aug	1928
Greece[10]	110	+	Lambrini Tsiatoura (Mrs)		1870	19 Feb	1981
USSR[11]	110	+	Khasako Dzugayev	7 Aug	1860	fl. Aug	1970
Italy	110	+	Damiana Sette (Sig)		1874	25 Feb	1985
Denmark	109	265	Maria Louise Augusta Bramsen	4 May	1878	23 Jan	1988
Finland	109	182	Andrei Akaki Kuznetsoff	17 Oct	1873		1984
Tasmania (State of)	109	179	Mary Ann Crow (Mrs)	2 Feb	1836	31 Jul	1945
Belgium	108	327	Mathilda Vertommen-Hellemans	12 Aug	1868	4 Jul	1977
Iceland	108	45	Halldóra Bjarndóttir	14 Oct	1873	28 Nov	1981
Portugal[12]	108	+	Maria Luisa Jorge	7 Jun	1859	fl. Jul	1967
Malaysia	106	+	Hassan Bin Yusoff	14 Aug	1865	fl. Jan	1972
Luxembourg	105	228	Nicolas Wiscourt	31 Dec	1872	17 Aug	1978

[1] Ex-slave Mrs Martha Graham died at Fayetteville, NC on 25 Jun 1959 reputedly aged 117 or 118. Census researches by Eckler show that she was seemingly born in Dec 1844 and hence aged 114 years 6 months. Mrs Rena Glover Brailsford died in Summerton, SC on 6 Dec 1977 reputedly aged 118 years. Mrs Rosario Reina Vasquez who died in California on 2 Sep 1980 was reputedly born in Sonora, Mexico on 3 Jun 1866, which would have made her 114 years 93 days. The 1900 US Federal Census for Crawfish Springs Militia District of Walker County, GA, records an age of 77 for a Mark Thrash. If the Mark Thrash (reputedly born in Georgia in December 1822) who died near Chattanooga, TN on 17 Dec 1943 was he, and the age attributed was accurate, then he would have survived for 121 years.

[2] British-born Miss Isabella Shepheard was allegedly 115 years old when she died at St Asaph, Clwyd, United Kingdom, on 20 Nov 1948, but her actual age was believed to have been 109 years 90 days.

[3] Mrs Ellen Carroll died in North River, Newfoundland, Canada on 8 Dec 1943, reputedly aged 115 years 49 days.

[4] Senor Benita Medrana of Avila died on 28 Jan 1979 allegedly aged 114 years 335 days.

[5] Lachlen McDonald, who died 7 Jun 1858 in Harris, United Kingdom, was recorded as being '110 years' on his death certificate.

[6] Mrs Susan Johanna Deporter of Port Elizabeth, South Africa, was reputedly 114 years old when she died on 4 Aug 1954. Mrs Sarah Lawrence, Cape Town, South Africa was reputedly 112 on 3 Jun 1968.

[7] Thomas Peters was recorded to have been born on 6 Apr 1745 in Leeuwarden, UK and died aged 111 years 354 days on 26 Mar 1857 in Arnhem, UK.

[8] Mrs W Sande was born in present-day Norway.

[9] West Germany: an unnamed female died in 1979 aged 112 years and an unnamed male died, aged also 112 years, in 1969. The Austrian record is 108 years (female d. 1975) and the Swiss record is also 108 years (female d. 1967).

[10] The claim that Liakon Efdokia died 17 Jan 1982 aged 118 years 13 days is not substantiated by the censuses of 1971 or 1981. Birth registration before 1920 was fragmentary.

[11] There are allegedly 21,700 centenarians in the USSR (cf. 54,000 in the US). Of these 21,000 are ascribed to the Georgian SSR, i.e. one in every 232. In July 1962 it was reported that 128, mostly male, were in the one village of Medini.

[12] Senhora Jesuina da Conceicao of Lisbon was reputedly 113 years old when she died on 10 Jun 1965.

Note: fl. is the abbreviation for *floruit*, Latin for he (or she) was living at the relevant date.

Mrs. Birdie May (nee Musser) was 112 on 3 Aug 1988. She was married on 10 Nov 1929 and now resides in a retirement village in Miami, FL.

Oldest quadruplets ■ The Ottman quads of Munich, West Germany, Adolf, Anne-Marie, Emma and Elisabeth, celebrated their 77th birthday on 5 May 1989.

Oldest triplets ■ Faith, Hope and Charity Caughlin were born at Marlboro, MA on 27 Mar 1868. The first to die was Mrs (Ellen) Hope Daniels, at age 93, on 2 Mar 1962.

Oldest twins ■ Eli Shadrack and John Meshak Phipps were born on 14 Feb 1803 at Affinghton, VA. Eli died at Hennessey, OK on 23 Feb 1911 at the age of 108 years 9 days, on which day John was still living in Shenandoah, IA.

On 17 Jun 1984, identical twin sisters Mildred Widman Philippi and Mary Widman Franzini of St Louis, MO celebrated their 104th birthday. Mildred died on 4 May 1985, 44 days short of the twins' 105th birthday. The chances of identical twins both reaching 100 are now probably about one in 50 million.

Oldest siblings ■ The oldest living siblings on record in the United States are Lewis A. Kelly (b. 18 Feb 1887), Winona Dee Methany (b. 31 Jul 1888) and Wayne Kelly (b. 29 Jan 1890). They were born in Saunders County, NE. Winona has spent her entire life in Nebraska, while Wayne now lives in Seattle and Lewis lives in Arizona.

Oldest mummy ■ Mummification (from the Persian word *mūm*, wax) dates from 2600 B.C. or the 4th dynasty of the Egyptian pharaohs. The oldest known mummy is that of a high-ranking young woman who was buried *c.* 2600 B.C. on a plateau near the Great Pyramid of Cheops at Gaza, or Al-Gizeh, Egypt. Her remains, which appear to represent the first attempts at mummification, were discovered in a 6 ft deep excavation on 17 Mar 1989, but only her skull was intact. She is believed to have lived in the lost kingdom of Ankh Ptah.

The oldest surviving mummy is of Wati, a court musician of *c.* 2400 B.C. from the tomb of Nefer in Saqqara, Egypt, found in 1944.

Anatomy and Physiology

Hydrogen (63 percent) and oxygen (25·5 percent) constitute the commonest of the 24 elements normally regarded as being in the human body. Carbon, sodium, potassium, calcium, sulfur, chlorine (as chlorides), iron and zinc are all present in significant quantities. Present in 'trace' quantities, but generally regarded as normal in a healthy body (even if their 'essentiality' is a matter of controversy) are: phosphorus, iodine, fluorine, copper, cobalt, chromium, manganese, selenium, molybdenum, vanadium (probably), nickel (probably), silicon (probably) tin (probably) and arsenic.

HANDS, FEET AND HAIR

Touch ■ The extreme sensitivity of the fingers is such that a vibration with a movement of 0·02 of a micron can be detected.

Longest fingernails ■ Finger nails grow about 0·02 in a week—four times faster than toenails.

The aggregate measurement of those of Shridhar Chillal (b. 1937) of Pune, India, on 25 Mar 1990 was 173 in for the 5 nails on his left hand (thumb 40 in, first finger 30 ½ in, second finger and third fingers 34 in, and the fourth 34 ½ in). He last cut his nails in 1952. As he is now having trouble with sleeping, he is willing to sell his nails.

Least toes ■ The two-toed syndrome exhibited by some members of the Wadomo tribe of the Zambezi Valley, Zimbabwe and the Kalanga tribe of the eastern Kalahari Desert, Botswana is hereditary via a single mutated gene. These 'ostrich people,' as they are known, are not handicapped by their deformity, and can walk great distances without discomfort.

Largest feet ■ If cases of elephantiasis are excluded, then the biggest feet known are those of Haji Mohammad Alam Channa of Pakistan, who wears a size 22 sandal.

Longest hair ■ Human hair grows at the rate of about 0·5 in in a month. If left uncut it will usually grow to a maximum of 2–3 ft. In 1780 a head of hair measuring 12 ft in length and dressed in a style known as the Plica Polonica (hair closely matted together) was sent to Dresden after adorning the head of a Polish peasant woman for 52 years. The braid of hair was 11·9 in in circumference.

Swami Pandarasannadhi, the head of the Tirudaduturai monastery, Tanjore district, Madras, India, was reported in 1949 to have hair 26 ft in length but no photographic or scientific evidence has ever been supplied in order to support this extreme measurement.

In March 1989 a length of 21 ft was claimed for the hair of 74-year-old Mata Jagdamba, a Yogin living in Ujjain, North India.

The length of hair of Miss Skuldfrid Sjorgren (b. Stockholm) was reported from Toronto, Canada in 1927 to have reached twice her height at 10 ft 6 in.

The hair of Diane Witt of Worcester, MA measured 11 ft in May 1990. She last cut her hair 9 years ago.

Most valuable hair ■ On 18 Feb 1988 a bookseller from Cirencester, Gloucestershire, United Kingdom, paid £5,575 for a lock of hair belonging to Lord Nelson (1758–1805) at an auction held at Crewkerne, Somerset, United Kingdom.

Longest beard ■ The beard of Hans N. Langseth (b. 1846 near Eidsroll, Norway) measured 17½ ft at the time of his burial at Kensett, IA in 1927 after 15 years' residence in the United States. It was presented to the Smithsonian Institution, Washington, DC, in 1967.

The beard of the bearded lady Janice Deveree (b. Bracken Co., KY, 1842) was measured at 14 in in 1884.

The beard of Mlle Hélène Antonia of Liège, Belgium, a 17th-century exhibitionist, was said to have reached to her hips.

Longest mustache ■ The mustache of Birger Pellas (b. 21 Sep 1934) of Malmö, Sweden, grown since 1973 reached 9 ft 6 in on 25 Apr 1990.

Karna Ram Bheel (1928–87) was granted permission by a New Delhi prison governor in February 1979 to keep the 7 ft 10 in mustache, which he had grown since 1949 during his life sentence. He used mustard, oil, butter and cream to keep it in trim.

DENTITION

Earliest ■ The first deciduous or milk teeth normally appear in infants at 5–8 months, these being the mandibular and maxillary first incisors. There are many records of children born with teeth, the most distinguished example being Prince Louis Dieudonné, later Louis XIV of France, who was born with two teeth on 5 Sep 1638. Molars usually appear at 24 months, but in Pindborg's case published in Denmark in 1970, a 6-week premature baby was documented with 8 natal teeth, of which 4 were in the molar region. Shaun Keaney of Newbury, United Kingdom was born on 10 Apr 1990 with 12 teeth.

Tooth enamel is the only part of the body which remains unchanged (i.e., cells are not replaced) throughout life. It is also the hardest substance in the body with a Knoop number of over 300.

Most ■ Cases of the growth in late life of a third set of teeth have been recorded several times. A reference to a case in France of a fourth dentition, known as Lison's case, was published in 1896. A triple row of teeth was noted in 1680 by Albertus Hellwigius.

Most dedicated dentist ■ Brother Giovanni Battista Orsenigo of the Ospedale Fatebenefratelli, Rome, a religious dentist, conserved all the teeth he extracted in three enormous cases during the time he exercised his profession from 1868 to 1904. In 1903 the number was counted and found to be 2,000,744 teeth, indicating an average of 185 teeth, or nearly six total extractions, a day.

Most valuable tooth ■ In 1816 a tooth belonging to Sir Isaac Newton (1643–1727) was sold in London for £730. It was purchased by a nobleman who had it set in a ring, which he wore constantly.

Earliest false teeth ■ From discoveries made in Etruscan tombs, partial dentures of bridgework type were being worn in what is now Tuscany, Italy as early as 700 B.C. Some were permanently attached to existing teeth and others were removable.

OPTICS

Highest visual acuity ■ The human eye is capable of judging relative position with remarkable accuracy, reaching limits of between 3 and 5 sec of arc.

In April 1984 Dr Dennis M. Levi of the College of Optometry, University of Houston, TX, repeatedly identified the position of a thin white line within 0·85 sec of arc. This is equivalent to a displacement of some ¼ in at a distance of 1 mile.

Color sensitivity ■ The unaided human eye, under the best possible viewing conditions, comparing large areas of color, in good illumination, using both eyes, can distinguish 10,000,000 different color surfaces. The most accurate photoelectric spectrophotometers possess a precision probably only 40 percent as good as this. About 7·5 percent of men and 0·1 percent of women are color blind. The most extreme form, monochromatic vision, is very rare. The highest rate of red–green color blindness is in Czechoslovakia and the lowest rate among Fijians and Brazilian Indians.

Earliest Dentition ● There are many cases of children born with teeth. Prince Louis Dieudonné, who became Louis XIV of France, was born with two teeth.

BONES

Longest ■ Excluding a variable number of sesamoids (small rounded bones), there are 206 bones in the adult human body, compared with 300 for children (as they grow, some bones fuse together). The thigh bone or *femur* is the longest. It constitutes usually 27½ percent of a person's stature, and may be expected to be 19 ¾ in long in a 6 ft tall man. The longest recorded bone was the femur of the German giant Constantine, who died in Mons, Belgium, on 30 Mar 1902, at the age of 30. It measured 29·9 in. The femur of Robert Wadlow, the tallest man ever recorded, measured an estimated 29·5 in. (see p. 7).

Smallest ■ The *stapes* or stirrup bone, one of the three auditory ossicles in the middle ear, measures from 0·10 to 0.17 in in length and weighs from 0.03 – 0·065 grains.

MUSCLES

Largest ■ Muscles normally account for 40 percent of the body weight; the bulkiest of the 639 named muscles in the human body is usually the *gluteus maximus* or buttock muscle, which extends the thigh. However, in pregnant women the uterus or womb can increase its weight from about 1 oz to over 2·2 lb and becomes larger than even the most successful body builder's buttock.

Smallest ■ The *stapedius*, which controls

the *stapes* (see p.15), an auditory ossicle in the middle ear, is less than 0·05 in long.

Longest ■ The longest muscle in the human body is the *sartorius* which is a narrow ribbon-like muscle which runs from the pelvis and across the front of the thigh to the top of the tibia below the knee. It's action is to draw the lower limb into the cross-legged sitting position, proverbially associated with tailors. (Latin: *sartor* = a tailor). As other, stronger, muscles in the body exist to perform this action the *sartorius* could be regarded as an 'optional extra' of doubtful merit as it is extremely painful if torn.

Strongest ■ The strongest muscle in the human body is the masseter (one on each side of the mouth) which is responsible for the action of biting. In August 1986, Richard Hofmann (b. 1949) of Lake City, FL, achieved a bite strength of 975 lb for approximately 2 seconds in a research test using a gnathodynamometer at the College of Dentistry, University of Florida. This figure is over 6 times the normal biting strength.

Longest name ■ The muscle with the longest name is the *levator labii superioris aloeque nasi* which runs inwards and downwards on the face, with one branch running to the upper lip and the other to the nostril. It is the muscle which everts or curls the upper lip and its action was particularly well demonstrated in the performances of the late Elvis Presley.

Largest chest measurements ■ The largest are among endomorphs (those with a tendency towards globularity). In the extreme case of Hughes this was 124 in, and T. J. Albert Jackson, currently the heaviest living man (see p. 9) has a chest measurement of 120 in.

This was exceeded by Jamie Reeves (b. 1962) of Sheffield, South Yorkshire, United Kingdom, who has a chest measurement of 60 in with a height of 6 ft 4 in; he weighs 322 lb.

Vasiliy Alekseyev (b.1942), the 6 ft 1 ¼ in Russian super-heavyweight weight-lifting champion, had a 60 ½ in chest at his top weight of 350 lb.

Power-lifter Rick Brown (b. 4 Apr 1960) of Los Angeles, CA, known to his friends as 'Grizzly,' has a chest measurement of 66 in at a bodyweight of 365 lb.

The largest muscular chest measurement recorded so far is that of another American power-lifter named Isaac 'Dr Size' Nesser (b. 21 Apr 1962) of Greensburg, PA, who measures 68·06 in. He stands 5 ft 10 in and weighs 351 lb.

'Gentleman Dan' Bernhardt of Salt Lake City, UT, had a 70 in expanded chest in 1977.

Largest and smallest biceps ■ Isaac 'Dr Size' Nesser has biceps of 26⅛ in cold (not pumped).

WAISTS

Largest ■ The largest waist ever recorded was that of Walter Hudson, which measured 119 in at his peak weight of 1,197 lb.

Smallest ■ Queen Catherine de Medici (1519–89) decreed a waist measurement of 13·77 in for ladies of the French court, but this was at a time when females were more diminutive.

The smallest recorded waist among women of normal stature in the 20th century is a reputed 13 in in the case of the French actress Mlle Polaire (real name Emile Marie Bouchand)(1881–1939).

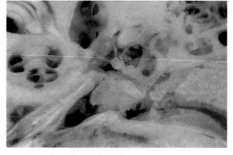

Smallest bone ● The *stapes* or stirrup bone is seen here in a cross-sectional slice of the inner ear. (Photo: St Mary's Hospital, United Kingdom)

Mrs Ethel Granger (1905–82) of Peterborough, Cambridge, United Kingdom reduced from a natural 22 in to 13 in over the period 1929–39.

NECKS

Longest ■ The maximum measured extension of the neck by the successive fitting of copper coils, as practiced by the women of the Padaung or Kareni tribe of Myanmar (formerly Burma), is 15 ¾ in. When the rings are removed, the muscles developed to support the head and neck shrink to their normal length.

BRAINS

Heaviest ■ In normal brains there is no correlation between intelligence and size. The brain of an average adult male (i.e., 20–55 years) weighs 3 lb 2·2 oz, decreasing gradually to 3 lb 1·1 oz with advancing age.

The heaviest brain ever recorded was that of a 50-year-old male which weighed 4 lb 8·29 oz reported by Dr Thomas F. Hegert, chief medical examiner for District 9, State of Florida, on 23 Oct 1975.

Human brains are getting heavier. Examination of postmortem records shows that the average male brain weight has increased from 3 lb 0·4 oz in 1860 to 3 lb 2·2 oz today. Women's brains have also put on weight, from 2 lb 11·8 oz to 2 lb 12·6 oz and in recent years have been growing almost as fast as men's.

Human computer ● Jaime Garcia Serrano made the fastest extraction of a 13th root from a 100-digit number on 24 May 1989 in a record time of 0·15 seconds.

Most expensive skull ■ The skull of Emanuel Swedenborg (1688–1772), the Swedish philosopher and theologian, was bought in London by the Royal Swedish Academy of Sciences for £5,500 on 6 Mar 1977. It is kept in the Session Room of the Academy.

Human computer ■ The fastest extraction of a 13th root from a 100-digit number was achieved by Jaime Garcia Serrano of Bogotá, Colombia in a time of 0.15 sec on 24 May 1989 at the Hilton Hotel, Colombia.

Mrs Shakuntala Devi of India demonstrated the multiplication of two 13-digit numbers randomly selected 7,686,369,774,870 × 2,465,099,745,779 by the Computer Department of Imperial College, London on 18 Jun 1980, in 28 seconds. Her answer, which was correct, was 18,947,668,177,995,426,462,773,730. Some experts on calculating prodigies refuse to give credence to Mrs Devi on the grounds that her achievements are so vastly superior to the calculating feats of any other invigilated prodigy that the invigilation must have been defective.

Memory ■ Bhandanta Vicitsara recited 16,000 pages of Buddhist canonical texts in Yangon (formerly known as Rangoon), Myanmar (formerly Burma) in May 1974.

Gon Yang-ling, 26, has memorized more than 15,000 telephone numbers in Harbin, China according to the Xinhua News Agency. Rare instances of eidetic memory—the ability to re-project and hence 'visually' recall material—are known to science.

George Uhrin of Houston, TX memorized a random sequence of thirty separate packs of cards (1,560) that had been all shuffled together on a single sighting with two errors at the Texas Commerce Tower, Houston, TX on 16 Jul 1989.

The greatest number of places of π ■ Hideaki Tomoyori (b. 30 Sep 1932) of Yokohama, Japan recited 'pi' from memory to 40,000 places in 17 hr 21 min including 4 hr 15 min breaks on 9–10 Mar 1987 at the Tsukuba University Club House. On a Japanese TV program, Mr Tomoyori also demonstrated his ability to recite correctly the 20 consecutive digits following a randomly selected string of digits from within the sequence of numbers.

VOICE

Highest and lowest ■ Before this century the extremes were a staccato E in *alt altissimo*

(e^{iv}) by Ellen Beach Yaw (1869–1947) in Carnegie Hall, NY on 19 Jan 1896, and an A_1 (55 Hz [cycles per sec]) by Kasper Foster (1617–73).

Madeleine Marie Robin (1918–60), the French operatic coloratura, could produce and sustain the B above high C in the Lucia mad scene in Donizetti's *Lucia di Lammermoor*. Since 1950 singers have achieved high and low notes far beyond the hitherto accepted extremes. However, notes at the bass and treble extremities of the register tend to lack harmonics and are of little musical value.

Fraulein Marita Gunther, trained by Alfred Wolfsohn, has covered the range of the piano from the lowest note, A_{11} to c^v. Of this range of 7¼ octaves, 6 octaves were considered to be of musical value.

Roy Hart, also trained by Wolfsohn, has reached notes below the range of the piano.

Barry Girard of Canton, OH in May 1975 reached the E (4,340 Hz) above the piano's top note. The highest note put into song is G^{iv} first occurring in Mozart's *Popoli di Tessaglia*.

The lowest vocal note in the classical repertoire is in Mozart's *Die Entführung aus dem Serail* in Osmin's aria which calls for a low D (73·4 Hz).

Dan Britton reached the fourth E below middle C at 20·6 Hz at Anoka County Fair, MN on 31 Jul 1984.

Stefan Zucker sang A in *alt altissimo* for 3·8 sec in the tenor role of Salvini in the premiere of Bellini's *Adelson e Salvini* in New York on 12 Sep 1972.

Greatest range ■ The normal intelligible outdoor range of the male human voice in still air is 600 ft. The *silbo*, the whistled language of the Spanish-speaking Canary Island of La Gomera, is intelligible across the valleys, under ideal conditions, at 5 miles. There is a recorded case, under freak acoustic conditions, of the human voice being detectable at a distance of 10½ miles across still water at night. It was said that Mills Darden could be heard 6 miles away when he bellowed at the top of his voice.

Screaming ■ The highest scientifically measured emission has been one of 128 dbA by the screaming of Simon Robinson of McLaren Vale, South Australia at the Guinness Challenge at the Australian Grand Prix, Adelaide, on 11 Nov 1988.

Shouting ■ Donald H. Burns of St George's, Bermuda achieved 119 decibels in shouting while appearing on Fuji TV filming of the Japanese program *Narvhodo the World* at Liberty State Park, NJ on 18 Jan 1989.

Lowest detectable sound ■ The intensity of noise or sound is measured in terms of pressure. The pressure of the quietest sound that can be detected by a person of normal hearing at the most sensitive frequency of *c.* 2,750 Hz is 2×10^{-5} pascal. One-tenth of the logarithm to this standard provides a unit termed a decibel (dbA). A noise of 30 dbA is negligible.

Highest noise levels ■ Prolonged noise above 150 decibels will cause permanent deafness while above 192 dbA a lethal overpressure shock-wave can be formed. Equivalent continuous sound levels (LEQ) above 90 dbA are impermissible in factories in many countries, but this compares with 125 emitted by racing cars and 130 by amplified music.

Highest detectable pitch ■ The upper limit is reckoned to be 20,000 Hz (cycles per sec), although it has been alleged that children with

Longest necks ● The Padaugs or Kareni women of Burma wear coils of copper which are very rarely removed. If they are removed it would be for a great occasion such as a wedding, and the 'victim' would have to lie still in bed helpless until refitted. (Photo: HOA-QUI)

asthma can detect sounds of 30,000 Hz. Bats emit pulses at up to 90,000 Hz. It was announced in February 1964 that experiments in the USSR had conclusively proved that oscillations as high as 200,000 Hz can be detected if the oscillator is pressed against the skull.

Fastest talker ■ Few people are able to speak *articulately* at a sustained speed above 300 words per minute. The fastest broadcaster has been regarded as Gerry Wilmot (b. Victoria, BC, Canada, 6 Oct 1914), the ice hockey commentator in the late forties.

In public life the highest speed recorded was a burst in excess of 300 words per min in a speech made in December 1961 by President John Fitzgerald Kennedy (1917–63).

John Moschitta (USA) recited 545 words in 55·8 sec, or 586 words per minute, on 24 May 1988 in Los Angeles, CA.

Backwards Talking ■ Steve Briers of Kilgetty, Dyfed, United Kingdom recited the entire lyrics of Queen's album *A Night at the Opera* at the British Broadcasting Corporation North-West Radio 4's *Cat's Whiskers* on 6 Feb 1990 in a time of 9 min 58·44 sec.

United States ■ David Fuhrer of California recited the entire lyrics of Queen's album *A Night at the Opera* at Trax Recording Studio, CA on 28 Jul 1989 in a time of 10 min 19 sec.

BLOOD

Groups ■ The preponderance of one blood group varies greatly from one locality to another. On a world basis Group O is the most common (46 percent), but in some areas, for example Norway, Group A predominates.

The rarest type in the world is a type of Bombay blood (subtype h-h) found so far only in a Czechoslovak nurse in 1961 and in a brother (Rh positive) and sister (Rh negative) named Jalbert in Massachusetts reported in February 1968.

United States ■ The commonest subgroup in the United States is O+, which is found in 39 percent of the population. The rarest generic blood group is AB-, which occurs in only 0·6 percent of persons in the United States.

Richest natural resources ■ Joe Thomas of Detroit, MI was reported in August 1970 to have the highest known level of Anti-Lewis B, the rare blood antibody. A biological supply firm pays him $1,500 per quart. The Internal Revenue Service regards this income as a taxable liquid asset.

Donor and recipient ■ From Sep 1966 to Feb 1989, Allen Doster, a self-employed beautician, has made a total of 1,037 platelet donations by both manual and machine plasmapheresis at Roswell Park Memorial Institute, NY. The current limit in America on machine plateletpheresis donations is 24 per year.

A 50-year-old haemophiliac Warren C. Jyrich required 2,400 donor units (1,900 pints of blood) when undergoing open-heart surgery at the Michael Reese Hospital, Chicago in December 1970.

Largest vein ■ The largest is the *inferior vena cava*, which returns the blood from the lower half of the body to the heart.

Largest artery ■ The largest is the *aorta* which is 1.18 in in diameter where it leaves the heart. By the time it ends at the level of the fourth lumbar vertebra it is about 0·68 in in diameter.

Most alcoholic subject ■ California University Medical School, Los Angeles, reported in December 1982 the case of a confused but conscious 24-year-old female who was shown to have a blood alcohol level of 1,510 mg per 100 ml. After two days she discharged herself.

Tommy Johns of Brisbane, Queensland, Austra-

lia died in April 1988 from a brain tumor at the age of 66 years, after having been arrested nearly 3,000 times for being drunk and disorderly in a public place. (See Chapter 10, Most Appearances).

William Pitt the Younger (1759–1806), the British prime minister, once allegedly drank 574 bottles of claret, 854 bottles of Madeira and 2,410 bottles of Port in a single year!

BODY TEMPERATURE

Highest ■ Willie Jones, 52, was admitted to Grady Memorial Hospital, Atlanta, GA on 10 Jul 1980 with heatstroke on a day when the temperature reached 90° F: with 44 percent humidity. His temperature was found to be 115·7° F. After 24 days he was discharged 'at prior baseline status.'

Lowest ■ There are three recorded cases of patients surviving body temperatures as low as 60·8° F. The first is Dorothy Mae Stevens (1929–74), who was found in an alley in Chicago, IL on 1 Feb 1951 and whose pulse dropped to 12 beats per min; the second is Vickie Mary Davis, aged 2 years 1 month, in an unheated house in Marshalltown, IA on 21 Jan 1956; and the third is 2-year-old Michael Troke, in the snow near his home in Milwaukee, WI on 19 Jan 1985.

People may die of hypothermia with body temperatures of 95°F.

ILLNESS AND DISEASE

Commonest ■ The commonest non-contagious disease is periodontal disease, such as *gingivitis* (inflammation of the gums), which subclinically afflicts some 80 percent of the US population.

The commonest contagious disease in the world is coryza (*acute nasopharyngitis*), or the common cold.

Infestation with pinworm (*Enterobius vermicularis*) approaches 100 percent in some tropical areas of the world.

United States ■ The greatest reported loss of working time in the United States, as reported by the Bureau of Labor Statistics, is from sprains and strains. In 1987 63·3 days per 100 employees were lost to illness or injury in the private sector. In 1988 76·1 days were lost.

Rarest ■ Medical literature periodically records hitherto undescribed diseases. A disease as yet undiagnosed but predicted by a Norwegian doctor is podocytoma of the kidney–tumor of the epithelial cells lining the glomerulus of the kidney.

The last case of endemic smallpox was recorded in Ali Maow Maalin in Merka, Somalia on 26 Oct 1977.

Kuru, or laughing sickness is now believed to be extinct and was only ever found among the Fore tribe of Papua New Guinea. It is believed that the virus was transmitted during ritual mourning when the brain of the dead was handled by women and children.

Most infectious and most fatal ■ The pneumonic form of plague, as evidenced by the Black Death of 1347–51, had a mortality rate of killing everyone who caught it, a quarter of the population of Europe.

Highest mortality ■ Rabies in humans has been regarded as uniformly fatal when associated with the hydrophobia symptom (a pathological fear of drinking fluids because of painful spasms while swallowing). A 25-year-old woman, Candida de Sousa Barbosa of Rio de Janeiro, Brazil, following surgery by Dr Max Karpin, was believed to be the first ever survivor of the disease in November 1968.

Some sources prefer the case of an unnamed 7-year-old boy living near Tampa, FL who, on 23 Jun 1953, was bitten on the chest by a rabid common vampire bat (*Desmodus rotundus*). The boy was put on a course of prophylactic immunization and eventually made a full recovery.

While the *disease* rabies is regarded as being almost universally fatal, this is not to be confused with being bitten by a rabid animal. With immediate treatment the virus can be prevented from invading the nervous system and chances of survival can be as high as 95 percent.

The virus AIDS (Acquired Immune Deficiency Syndrome) was first reported in 1981. The Human Immunodeficiency Virus (HIV), which causes AIDS, was jointly discovered in January 1983 by Luc Montagnier, Françoise Barré Sinoussi and Jean-Claude Chermann at the Institute Pasteur, Paris and Robert Gallo and co-workers at the National Institute of Health, Bethesda as a Human T-lymphotrophic Type III (HTLV III) virus. The World Health Organization reported 237,110 cases HIV positive worldwide by 1 Apr 1990. These are actual diagnosed cases as reported by member countries. It is believed that there are three times as many cases that have not been reported. There have not as yet been any cases of a recovery from AIDS.

By April 1990 the total number of HIV positive cases in the United States was 128,319. This total included 126,127 adults and 2,192 children under 13. The total number of deaths was 78,341, with 77,159 adults and 1,182 children.

AIDS STATISTICS

State	Number of Cases
New York	28,611
California	24,826
Florida	10,562
Texas	8,806
New Jersey	8,456

City	Number of Cases
New York City	24,935
Los Angeles	8,739
San Fransisco	7,894
Houston	3,746
Newark	3,595

Data: Center for Disease Control Atlanta, GA (April 1990)

Leading cause of death ■ In industrialized countries arteriosclerosis (thickening of the arterial wall) underlies much coronary and cerebrovascular disease. In 1987, deaths from diseases of the circulatory system in the United States totaled 988,568 (including heart, cerebrovascular, and chronic obstructive pulmonary diseases). There were 476,927 deaths from cancer, and accidents claimed 95,020 lives.

Most notorious carrier ■ The most publicized of all typhoid carriers has been Mary Mallon (real name Maria Anna Caduff), known as Typhoid Mary, who was born in Graubunden, Switzerland in 1855 and arrived as an immigrant in New York City, NY, on 11 Jan 1868. In her job as a cook she was the source of 53 outbreaks, including the 1903 epidemic of 1,400 cases in Ithaca, NY and 3 deaths. She was placed under permanent detention at Riverside Hospital on North Brother Island, East River from 1915 until her death from bronchopneumonia on 11 Nov 1938.

MEDICAL EXTREMES

Postmortem birth ■ The longest gestation interval in a postmortem birth was one of 84 days in the case of a baby girl born on 5 Jul 1983 from a clinically brain dead woman in Roanoke, VA who had been kept on life support since April.

Heart stoppage ■ The longest is 4 hr in the case of a Norwegian fisherman, Jan Egil Refsdahl (b. 1936), who fell overboard in the icy waters off Bergen on 7 Dec 1987. He was rushed to nearby Haukeland Hospital after his body temperature fell to 77° F and his heart stopped beating, but he made a full recovery after he was connected to a heart–lung machine normally used for heart surgery.

United States ■ On 9 Oct 1986, Allen Smith, aged 2, fell into the swollen waters of the Stanislaus River at Oakdale, CA. He was spotted 90 minutes later and rushed to Modesto Memorial Hospital, where 2 hours later his heart began beating again spontaneously.

Pulse rates ■ A normal adult rate is 70–72 beats per min at rest for males and 78–82 for females. Rates increase to 200 or more during violent exercise.

Longest coma ■ Elaine Esposito (b. 3 Dec 1934) of Tarpon Springs, FL, never stirred after an appendectomy on 6 Aug 1941, when she was 6, in Chicago, IL, and died on 25 Nov 1978 aged 43 years 357 days, having been in a coma for 37 years 111 days.

Dreams ■ Dreaming sleep is characterised by rapid eye movements known as REM, first described in 1953 by William Dement of the University of Chicago. The longest recorded period of REM is one of 2 hr 23 min on 15 Feb 1967 at the Department of Psychology, University of Illinois, Chicago on Bill Carskadon, who had had his previous sleep interrupted. In July 1984 the Sleep Research Centre, Haifa, Israel recorded nil REM in a 33-year-old male who had a shrapnel brain injury.

Longest in 'iron lung' ■ Mrs Laurel Nisbet (1912–85) of La Crescenta, CA, was in an 'iron lung' for 37 years 58 days continuously until her death.

Fastest nerve impulses ■ The results of experiments published in 1966 have shown that the fastest messages transmitted by the human nervous system can travel at 180 mph. With advancing age, impulses are carried 15 percent more slowly.

Heaviest organ ■ The skin is medically considered to be an organ. It weighs around 5·9 lb in an average adult. The heaviest internal organ is the liver at 3·3 lb. This is 4 times heavier than the heart.

Hiccupping ■ The longest recorded attack of hiccupping is that afflicting Charles Osborne (b. 1894) of Anthon, IA for the past 68 years from 1922. He contracted it when slaughtering a hog and has been unable to find a cure, but leads a reasonably normal life in which he has had two wives and fathered eight children. He has admitted, however, that he cannot keep in his false teeth. In July 1986 he was reported to be hiccupping at 20–25 per minute from his earlier high of 40.

Sneezing ■ The longest lasting fit ever recorded is that of Donna Griffiths (b. 1969) of Pershore, Hereford and Worcester, United Kingdom. She started sneezing on 13 Jan 1981 and surpassed the previous duration record of 194 days on 27 Jul 1981. She sneezed an estimated million times in the first 365 days. She achieved her first sneeze-free day on 16 Sep 1983–the 978th day.

The highest speed at which expelled particles have ever been measured to travel is 103·6 mph.

Snoring ■ The highest sound level recorded by any chronic snorer is peaks of 90 decibels measured at the Department of Medicine, University of British Columbia, Vancouver, Canada, during the evening of 3 Nov 1987. The meter was placed 2 ft above the head of Mark Thompson Hebbard (b. 28 Feb 1947) of Richmond, British Columbia, Canada, who maintained an overall level of 85 decibels. As a Vancouver city traffic bylaw for acceptable noise is set at 80 decibels, he wonders if he is legally entitled to sleep there.

Sleeplessness ■ Research indicates that on the Circadian (from Latin: *circa* = around and *dies* = a day) cycle for the majority peak efficiency is attained between 8 and 9 P.M. and the low point comes at 4 A.M. The longest recorded period for which a person has voluntarily gone without sleep is 453 hr 40 min by Robert McDonald of California in a rocking chair from 14 Mar to 2 Apr 1986 (see Chapter 9). Victims of the very rare condition chronic colestites (total insomnia) have been known to go without definable sleep for many years. Jesus de Frutos (b. 1925) of Segovia, Spain asserts that he has only dozed since 1954.

Motionlessness ■ The longest that anyone has continuously remained motionless is 24 hours—by William Fuqua at Glendale, CA, on 17-18 May 1985 while sitting on a motorcycle.

Antonio Gomes dos Santos of Zare, Portugal, continuously stood motionless for 15 hr 2 min 55 sec on 30 Jul 1988 at the Amoreiras Shopping Center, Lisbon, Portugal.

The longest recorded case of being made to stand at attention was when Corporal Everett D. Reamer of the 60th Coast Artillery Regiment AA Battery F FFE was so punished in Camp No 1, Osaka, Japan for 132 consecutive hours from 8:00 A.M. 15 Aug until 8:00 P.M. 20 Aug 1944.

Fire breathers and extinguishers ■ Reg Morris blew a flame from his mouth to a distance of 31 ft at the Miner's Rest, Chasetown, Staffordshire, United Kingdom on 29 Oct 1986. On 25 June 1988 Reg Morris also extinguished 22,888 torches of flame in his mouth in 2 hr at Yew Tree School, Walsall, West Midlands, United Kingdom.

On 26 Jul 1986 at Port Lonsdale, Victoria, Australia, Sipra Ellen Lloyd set a female record by extinguishing 8,357 torches. *Fire-eating is potentially a highly dangerous activity.*

Human salamanders ■ The highest dry-air temperature endured by naked men in the US Air Force experiments in 1960 was 400° F and for heavily clothed men 500° F. Steaks require only 325° F to cook. Temperatures of 284° F have been found quite bearable in saunas.

Swallowing ■ The worst reported case of compulsive swallowing involved an insane female, Mrs H. aged 42, who complained of a 'slight abdominal pain.' She proved to have 2,533 objects, including 947 bent pins, in her stomach.

These were removed by Drs Chalk and Foucar in June 1927 at the Ontario Hospital, Canada. In a more recent case 212 objects were removed from the stomach of a man admitted to Groote Schuur Hospital, Cape Town, South Africa in May 1985. They included 53 toothbrushes, 2 telescopic aerials, 2 razors and 150 handles of disposable razors.

Sword ■ Edward 'Count Desmond' Benjamin (b. 1941) of Binghamton, NY swallowed thirteen 23 in long blades to below his xiphisternum (the lowermost part of the breastbone which is sword shaped; from Greek: *xiphos* = a sword) and injured himself in the process. *No further claims will be published.*

Hunger strike ■ Doctors estimate a well-nourished individual can survive without medical consequences on a diet of sugar and water for 30 days or more. The longest period for which anyone has gone without solid food is 382 days by Angus Barbieri (b. 1940) of Tayport, Fife, United Kingdom, who lived on tea, coffee, water, soda water and vitamins in Maryfield Hospital, Dundee, Angus, United Kingdom from June 1965 to July 1966. His weight declined from 472 lb to 178 lb. *Records claimed, unless there is continuous medical surveillance, are inadmissible.*

The longest recorded case of survival without food *and* water is 18 days by Andreas Mihavecz, then 18, of Bregenz, Austria who was put into a holding cell on 1 Apr 1979 in a local government building in Höchst, Austria but was totally forgotten by the police. On 18 Apr 1979 he was discovered close to death having had neither food nor water. He had been a passenger in a crashed car.

Under water ■ The world record for voluntarily staying under water is 13 min 42·5 sec by Robert Foster, then aged 32, an electronics technician of Richmond, CA, who stayed under 10 ft of water in the swimming pool of the Bermuda Palms Motel at San Rafael, CA on 15 Mar 1959. He hyperventilated with oxygen for 30 min before his descent. *Underwater record-breaking of this kind is an extremely dangerous activity.*

In 1986 2-year-old Michelle Funk of Salt Lake City, UT, made a full recovery after spending 66 minutes under water. The toddler fell into a swollen creek near her home while playing. When she was eventually discovered rescue workers found she had no pulse or heartbeat.

> **Black Death** ● This pneumonic form of plague ravaged Europe between 1347–51. Whole communities and families were annihilated at all levels of society. (Photo: Archiv Für Kunst und Geschichte)

Her life was saved by the first successful bypass machine which warmed her blood, which had dropped to 66° F. Doctors at the hospital described the time she had spent under water as the 'longest documented submergence with an intact neurological outcome.'

G forces ■ The highest g value endured on a water-braked rocket sled is 82·6 g for 0·04 of a sec, by Eli L. Beeding, Jr at Holloman Air Force Base, NM, on 16 May 1958. He was hospitalized for 3 days.

A land diver of Pentecost Island, Vanuatu (formerly the New Hebrides) dived from a platform 81 ft 3 in high with liana vines attached to his ankles on 15 May 1982. The body speed was 50 ft per sec (34 mph). The jerk transmitted a momentary g force in excess of 110.

Longest stay in hospital ■ Miss Martha Nelson was admitted to the Columbus State Institute for the Feeble-Minded in Ohio in 1875. She died in January 1975 at the age of 103 years 6 months in the Orient State Institution, OH after spending more than 99 years in institutions.

Pill-taking ■ The highest recorded total of pills swallowed by a patient is 565,939 between 9 Jun 1967 and 19 Jun 1988 by C. H. A. Kilner (1926–88) of Bindura, Zimbabwe.

Most injections ■ A diabetic, Mrs Evelyn Ruth Winder (b. 1921) of Invercargill, New Zealand gave an estimated 61,123 insulin injections to herself over 59 years to May 1990.

Most tattoos ■ Bernard Moeller of Pennsylvania claimed to have 8,960 individual tattoos at 4 Dec 1989 and Walter Stiglitz of New Jersey claims 5,488 separate tattoos by 6 different artists.

The world's most decorated woman is strip artiste 'Krystyne Kolorful' (b. 5 Dec 1952, Alberta, Canada). Her 95 percent body suit took 10 years to complete and cost $15,000.

OPERATIONS

Longest ■ The most protracted reported operation, for surgical as opposed to medical control purposes, has been one of 96 hr performed on Mrs Gertrude Levandowski during the period 4–8 Feb 1951 in Chicago, IL. The patient suffered from a weak heart and surgeons had to exercise the utmost caution during the operation.

Most ■ Padmabhushan Dr M. C. Modi, a pioneer of mass eye surgery in India since 1943, together with assistants, has performed as many as 833 cataract operations in one day, visited 45,416 villages and 10,094,632 patients, making a total of 595,019 operations to February 1990.

Dr Robert B. McClure (b. 1901) of Toronto, Canada performed a career total of 20,423 major operations from 1924 to 1978.

On 2 Mar 1977 Mr Jens Kjaer Jension (b. 1914) of Hoven, Denmark, was discharged from a local hospital after having had 32,131 thorns removed from his body over a period of six years and 248 visits. In 1967 he had tripped and fallen into a pile of spiky berberry cuttings in his garden and was rushed unconscious to the hospital. Even today he is still troubled by thorns working their way out through the skin of his legs.

Oldest patient ■ The greatest recorded age at which anyone has undergone an operation is 111 years 105 days in the case of James Henry Brett, Jr (1849–1961) of Houston, TX. He underwent a hip operation on 7 Nov 1960.

Earliest appendectomy ■ The earliest recorded successful appendix operation was per-

formed in 1736 by Claudius Amyand (1680–1740). He was Serjeant Surgeon to King George II (reigned 1727–60).

Earliest general anesthesia ■ The earliest recorded operation under general anesthesia was for the removal of a cyst from the neck of James Venable by Dr Crawford Williamson Long (1815-78), using diethyl ether ($C_2H_5)_20$, in Jefferson, GA on 30 Mar 1842.

Most durable cancer patient ■ The longest recorded case of survival from diagnosed cancer is that of Mrs Winona Mildred Melick (née Douglass) (b. 22 Oct 1876) of Long Beach, CA. She had four cancer operations in 1918, 1933, 1966 and 1968 but died from pneumonia on 28 Dec 1981, 67 days after her 105th birthday.

Fastest amputation ■ The shortest time recorded for a leg amputation in the pre-anesthetic era was 13–15 sec by Napoleon's chief surgeon, Dominique Larrey. There could have been no ligation of blood vessels.

Largest tumor ■ The largest tumor ever recorded was Spohn's case of an ovarian cyst weighing 328 lb taken from a woman in Texas in 1905. She made a full recovery.

Surgical instruments ■ The largest instruments are robot retractors used in abdominal surgery, introduced by Abbey Surgical Instruments of Chingford, Essex, United Kingdom in 1968 and weighing 11 lb. Some bronchoscopic forceps measure 23½ in in length.

The smallest is Elliot's eye trephine, which has a blade 0·078 in in diameter and 'straight' stapes picks with a needle-type tip or blade 0·013 in long.

TRANSPLANTS

Heart ■ The first operation was performed on Louis Washkansky, age 55, at the Groote Schuur Hospital, Cape Town, South Africa between 1 A.M. and 6 A.M., on 3 Dec 1967, by a team of 30 headed by Professor Christiaan Neethling Barnard (b. Beaufort West, South Africa 8 Oct 1922). The donor was Miss Denise Ann Darvall, age 25. Washkansky lived for 18 days.

United States ■ The first operation was performed on a 2½- week-old baby boy at Maimonides Hospital,Brooklyn, NY on 6 December 1967 by a team of 22 headed by Dr Adrian Kantrowitz. The donor was a newborn infant. The baby boy lived 6½ hours.

The first adult transplant took place at the Stanford Medical Center in Palo Alto, CA on 6 January 1968 by Dr Norman E Shumway and was performed on Mike Kasperak, age 54. Mr Kasperak, a retired steelworker, lived 14 days.

From Dec 1967 until Feb 1990 there have been 7,831 heart transplants. In 1989 there was a total of 1,621 transplants.

Double heart transplant ■ The first operation in the United States was performed on Darrell Hammarley, age 56, at the Stanford Medical Center in Palo Alto, CA on 20 November 1968 by Dr Norman E. Shumway. The first heart implanted failed to beat steadily and was replaced by a second transplant two hours later.

Longest surviving ■ William George van Buuren of California (b. 24 May 1929), who received an unnamed person's heart at the Stanford Medical Center, Palo Alto, CA on 3 Jan 1970. The surgeon who performed the operation was Dr Edward Stinson.

Youngest ■ Paul Holt of Vancouver, British Columbia, Canada underwent a heart transplant at Loma Linda Hospital in California on 16 Oct

1987 at the age of 2 hr 34 min. He was born 6 weeks premature at 6 lb 6 oz.

First transplantee to give birth ■ Betsy Sneith, 23, gave birth to a baby girl, Sierra (7 lb 10 oz), at Stanford University, CA on 17 Sep 1984. She had received a donor heart in February 1980.

Animal-to-human transplant ■ The first operation in the United States was carried out on 23 Jan 1964 at the University of Mississippi Medical Center in Jackson, MS by a team of 12 headed by Dr James D. Hardy. The patient, age 64, received the heart of a chimpanzee, which beat for 90 minutes.

Five-organ ■ Tabatha Foster (1984–1988) of Madisonville, KY, at 3 years 143 days of age, received a transplanted liver, pancreas, small intestine, portions of stomach and large intestine in a 15-hour operation at the Children's Hospital, Pittsburgh on 31 Oct 1987. Before the operation, she had never eaten solid food.

Heart–lung–liver ■ The first triple transplant took place on 17 Dec 1986 at Papworth Hospital, Cambridge, Cambridgeshire, United Kingdom when Mrs Davina Thompson (b. 28 Feb 1951) of Rawmarsh, South Yorkshire, United Kingdom, underwent surgery for 7 hours by a team of 15 headed by chest surgeon Dr John Wallwork and Professor Sir Roy Calne.

Artificial heart ■ On 1–2 Dec 1982 at the Utah Medical Center, Salt Lake City, UT Dr Barney B. Clark, 61, of Des Moines, WA was the first recipient of an artificial heart. The surgeon was Dr William C. DeVries. The heart was a Jarvik 7 designed by Dr Robert K. Jarvik (b Midland, MI 11 May 1946). Dr Clark died on 23 Mar 1983, 112 days later. William J. Schroeder survived 620 days in Louisville, KY from 25 Nov 1984 to 7 Aug 1986.

The Food and Drug Administration (FDA) recalled the Jarvik-7 on 11 Jan 1990. At the time of the recall it was the only artificial heart approved by the FDA and thus the only one allowed in the United States.

First synthetic heart implant ■ Haskell Karp, aged 47, of Skokie, IL received the first synthetic heart implant on 4 April 1969, at St. Luke's Episcopal Hospital, Houston, TX. Dr Denton A. Cooley led the team of doctors, which included the developer of the heart, Dr Domingo Liotta. The artifical heart was replaced by a human transplant on 7 April.

Kidney ■ Dr Richard H. Lawler (b. 1895) (USA) performed the first transplant of the kidney in a human at Little Company of Mary Hospital, Chicago, IL, on 17 June, 1950.

United States ■ The first successful kidney transplant operation was performed at Peter Bent Brigham Hospital (now Brigham and Women's Hospital) in Boston, MA on 23 Dec 1954 by a team of surgeons headed by Dr John P. Merrill. The patient, Richard Herrick, aged 23, received a kidney from his identical twin, Richard.

On 19 Oct 1967 Mary Lowndes (nee Taylor) (b. 7 Jun 1944) received a kidney from her father, Rev. Herbert Taylor (b. 11 April 1927), of Florida. The operation was performed at the Methodist Hospital, Rochester, MN.

Lung ■ The first transplant operation in the United States took place on 11 June 1963 at the University of Mississippi Medical Center at Jackson. The surgery, which was headed by Dr James D. Hardy lasted, three hours and involved the replacement of the patient's left lung. The patient, John Richard Russell, survived 18 days.

THE LIVING WORLD

Largest lizard ● The largest of all lizards is the Komodo monitor or Ora (*Varanus komodoensis*), a dragonlike reptile found on the Indonesian islands of Komodo, Rintja, Padar and Flores. Adult males average 7 ft 5 in in length and weigh about 130 lb. Lengths up to 29·98 ft have been claimed for this species, but the largest specimen to be accurately measured was a male presented to an American zoologist in 1928 by the Sultan of Bima which measured 10 ft 0·8 in. In 1937 this animal was put on display in St Louis Zoological Gardens, MO for a short period. It then measured 10 ft 2 in in length and weighed 365 lb. (Photo: Harvey Mann)

Animal Kingdom General Records

Noisiest ■ The noisiest land animals in the world are the Howling monkeys (*Alouatta*) of Central and South America. The males have an enlarged bony structure at the top of the windpipe that enables the sound to reverberate, and their fearsome screams have been described as a cross between the bark of a dog and the bray of an ass increased 1,000-fold. Once they are in full voice they can clearly be heard for distances up to 10 miles away.

Most fertile ■ It has been calculated that a single cabbage aphid (*Brevicoryne brassica*) can give rise in a year to a mass of descendants weighing 906 million tons, more than three times the total weight of the world's human population. Fortunately the mortality rate is tremendous!

Strongest ■ In proportion to their size the strongest animals are the larger beetles of the Scarabaeidae, which are found mainly in the tropics. In tests carried out on a rhinoceros beetle (*Dynastinae*) it was found that it could support 850 times its own weight on its back (cf. 25 percent of its body weight for an adult elephant). A dorbeetle (*Geotrupes stercorosus*) shifted a load weighing 2·82 oz or 400 times its own body weight, from one point to another and also managed to lift 3 ½ oz.

Strongest bite ■ Experiments carried out with a Snodgrass gnathodynamometer (sharkbite meter) at the Lerner Marine Laboratory in Bimini, Bahamas revealed that a 6 ft 6¾ in long dusky shark (*Carcharhinus obscurus*) could exert a force of 132 lb between its jaws. This is equivalent to a pressure of 22 tons/in² at the tips of the teeth.

Suspended animation ■ In 1846 two specimens of the desert snail *Eremina desertorum* were presented to the British Museum (Natural History) as dead exhibits. They were glued to a small tablet and placed on display. Four years later, in March 1850, the Museum staff, suspecting that one of the snails was still alive, removed it from the tablet and placed it in tepid water. The snail moved and later began to feed. This hardy little creature lived for a further two years before it fell into a torpor and died.

Regeneration ■ The sponge (*Porifera*) has the most remarkable powers of regeneration of lost parts of any animal, and it can regrow its entire body from a tiny fragment of itself. If a sponge is squeezed through a fine-meshed silk gauze, each piece of separated tissue will live as an individual.

Most dangerous ■ The world's most dangerous animals (excluding man) are the malarial parasites of the genus *Plasmodium* carried by mosquitoes of the genus *Anopheles,* which, if excluding wars and accidents, have probably been responsible directly or indirectly for 50 percent of all human deaths since the Stone Age. Even today, despite major campaigns to eradicate it, at least 200 million people are afflicted by the disease each year, and more than one million babies and children die annually from malaria in Africa alone.

Fastest land mammal ● Seen here in full flight in the Masai Mara Reserve, Kenya, the cheetah or hunting leopard (*Acinonyx jubatus*) of the open plains of East Africa, Iran, Turkmenia and Afghanistan can attain a speed of 60–63 mph over distances of up to 1,641 ft on suitably level ground. (Photo: Ace)

Largest colonies ■ The black-tailed prairie dog (*Cynomys ludovicianus*) of the western United States and northern Mexico builds the largest colonies. One single 'town' discovered in 1901 was estimated to cover an area measuring 24,000 miles². It contained about 400 million individuals.

Greatest concentration ■ The greatest concentration of animals ever recorded was an unbelievably huge swarm of Rocky Mountain locusts (*Melanoplus spretus*) that passed over Nebraska on 15–25 Aug 1875. According to one local scientist, who watched their movements for five days, these locusts covered an area of 198,600 miles² as they flew over the American state. If he overestimated the size of the swarm by 50 percent (most locusts do not fly at night) it still covered an area of 99,300 miles², which is approximately the area of Colorado or Oregon. It has been calculated that this swarm of Rocky Mountain locusts contained at least 12·5 trillion insects weighing 27·5 million tons. For reasons unexplained this pest mysteriously disappeared in 1902 and has not been seen since.

Most prodigious eater ■ The larva of the Polyphemus moth (*Antheraea polyphemus*) of North America consumes an amount equal to 86,000 times its own birth weight in the first 48 hours of its life. In human terms, this would be equivalent to a 7 lb baby taking in 301 tons of nourishment!

Champion dieter ■ During the seven-month lactation period a 132 ton female blue whale (*Balaenoptera musculus*) can lose up to 25 percent of her body weight nursing her calf.

Most valuable ■ The most valuable animals in cash terms are thoroughbred racehorses. The most paid for a yearling is $13·1 million on 23 Jul 1985 at Keeneland, KY by Robert

Sangster and partners for *Seattle Dancer* (see Chapter 11, Horseracing).

Size difference ■ Although many differences exist in the animal world between the male and female of any species, the most striking difference in size can be seen in the marine worm *Bonellia viridis*. The females of this species are 3·9–39 in long compared with just 0·039–0·19 in for the male, making the females millions of times heavier than the males.

Slowest growth ■ The slowest growth in the Animal Kingdom is that of the Deep-sea clam *Tindaria callistisormis* of the North Atlantic which takes *c.* 100 years to reach a length of 0·31 in.

Mammals
Mammalia

Largest and heaviest ■ The longest and heaviest mammal in the world, and the largest animal ever recorded, is the blue or sulphur-bottom whale (*Balaenoptera musculus*), also called Sibbald's rorqual. The longest specimen ever recorded was a female landed at the Compañia Argentina de Pesca, Grytviken, South Georgia in 1909 that measured 110 ft 2½ in in length. Another female measuring 90 ft 6 in caught in the Southern Ocean by the Soviet Slava whaling fleet on 20 Mar 1947 weighed 209 tons. Its tongue and heart weighed 4·7 tons and 1,540 lb respectively.

Blue whales inhabit the colder seas and migrate to warmer waters in the winter for breeding. Observations made in the Antarctic in 1947–48 showed that a blue whale can maintain a speed of 20 knots for ten minutes when frightened. It has been calculated that a 90 ft blue whale traveling at 20 knots would develop 520 hp. Newborn calves measure 21 ft 3½ in–28 ft 6 in in length and weigh up to 6,614 lbs.

The barely visible ovum of the blue whale calf weighing a fraction of a 1/480th of an oz troy grows to a weight of *c.* 29 tons in 22¾ months made up of 10¾ months' gestation and the first 12 months of life. This is equivalent to an increase of 30 billion.

The low-frequency pulses made by blue whales when communicating with each other have been measured up to 188 decibels, making them the loudest sounds emitted by any living source. They have been detected 530 miles away.

It has been estimated that there are only about 10–12,000 blue whales roaming the world's oceans today as a result of over-hunting. This compares with a peak estimate of *c.* 220,000 at the turn of the century. The species has been protected de jure since 1967, although nonmember countries of the International Whaling Commission, e.g. Panama, Taiwan, South Korea and the

---

Tallest land mammal ● The giraffe (*Giraffa camelopardalis*), which is now found only in the dry savannah and semidesert areas of Africa south of the Sahara, is the tallest living animal, reaching an overall height of 18 ft. The tallest ever recorded was a Masai bull (*G. camelopardalis tippelskirchi*) named George, received at Chester Zoo, Lancashire, United Kingdom on 8 Jan 1959 from Kenya. His 'horns' *almost* grazed the roof of the 20 ft high Giraffe House when he was nine years old. George died on 22 Jul 1969. Despite its awkward appearance, because of its long stride the giraffe is surprisingly swift and can attain speeds of about 30 mph at a gallop. (Photo: HOA-QUI)

Philippines, are not bound by this agreement. An indefinite worldwide ban on commercial whaling came into force at the start of the 1985/86 season, but Japan, Norway and Iceland are still slaughtering minke, fin and sei whales (*Balaenoptera acutorostrata*, *B. physalus* and *B. borealis*) under the guise of 'research whaling.' In 1988 Iceland caught 68 fin whales and ten sei whales and 300 minke whales were captured by Japanese whalers in the southern ocean. The ban on commercial whaling will be reassessed in July 1990.

Deepest dive ■ On 14 Oct 1955 a 47 ft bull sperm whale (*Physeter catodon = macrocephalus*) was found at a depth of 3,720 ft, its jaw entangled with a submarine cable running between Santa Elena, Ecuador and Chorillos, Peru. At this depth the whale withstood a pressure of 1,680 lb/in^2 of body surface. In 1970 American scientists, by triangulating the location clicks of sperm whales, calculated that the *maximum* depth reached by this species was 8,202 ft. However on 25 Aug 1969 another bull sperm whale was killed 100 miles south of Durban after it had surfaced from a dive lasting 1 hr 52 min, and inside its stomach were found two small sharks that had been swallowed about an hour earlier. These were later identified as *Scymnodon* sp., a type of dogfish found only on the seafloor. At this point from land the depth of water is in excess of 9,876 ft for a radius of 30–40 miles, which suggests that the sperm whale sometimes descends to a depth of over 9,840 ft when seeking food and is limited by pressure of time rather than by pressure of pressure.

Largest on land ■ The largest living land animal is the African bush elephant (*Loxodonta africana*). The average adult bull stands 10 ft 6 in at the shoulder and weighs 6·3 tons. The

1. COMMON DOLPHIN (*Delphinus delphis*)

1.COMMON DOLPHIN (*Delphinus delphis*)-this dolphin can hear frequencies as high as 280kHz (cf 20 kHz for the adult human limit). **2.COMMERSON'S DOLPHIN** (*Cephalorhynchus commersonii*)-probably the smallest totally marine mammal in terms of weight. In one series of six adult specimens the weights ranged from 50·7 lb to 77·1 lb. **3.FRANSCISCANA** (*Pontoporia blainvillei*)-this dolphin has the longest beak in proportion to its body length of any small cetacean. This species is found in the shallow coastal waters of South America from Valdés Peninsula and La Plata delta, Argentina to São Paulo, Brazil. **4.VAQUITA** (*Phocoena sinus*)-one of the rarest marine mammals. It has not been sighted since 1980, and may be extinct. Hundreds of thousands have been accidentally caught in gill nets in the last 45 years. **5.BOTTLENOSE DOLPHIN** (*Tursiops truncatus*)-this species is probably the most familiar to visitors of oceanariums and dolphinariums and is arguably the most intelligent cetacean if the theory of encephalisation (the larger the brain in relation to body size, the greater the creature's biological intelligence) is considered. **6.KILLER WHALE** (*Orcinus orca*)-the fastest marine mammal. On 12 Oct 1958 a bull Killer whale measuring an estimated 20–25 ft in length was timed at 30 knots (34·2 mph) in the east Pacific. The Killer whale is also the most widely distributed of all cetaceans and is the largest of the dolphins, males reaching a length of 31·16 ft. **7.DALL'S PORPOISE** (*Phocoenoides dalli*)-speeds of up to 30 knots (34·2 mph) in short bursts have also been reported for Dall's porpoise in the North Pacific. It is also claimed that this species never sleeps at all.

7. DALL'S PORPOISE (*Phocoenoides dalli*)

6. KILLER WHALE (*Orcinus orca*)

3. FRANCISCANA *(Pontoporia blainvillei)*

4. VAQUITA *(Phocoena sinus)*

2. COMMERSON'S DOLPHIN
(Cephalorhynchus commersonii)

5. BOTTLENOSE DOLPHIN
(Tursiops truncatus)

DOLPHINS & PORPOISES

(Artwork: Matthew Hillier/Guinness Publishing)

largest specimen ever recorded was a bull shot 25 miles north–northeast of Mucusso, southern Angola on 7 Nov 1974. Lying on its side this elephant measured 13 ft 8 in in a projected line from the highest point of the shoulder to the base of the forefoot, indicating that its standing height must have been about 13 ft. Other measurements included an overall length of 35 ft (tip of extended trunk to tip of extended tail) and a forefoot circumference of 5 ft 11 in. The weight was computed to be 13·5 tons.

The endangered desert elephant of Damaraland (reduced to 84 individuals in August 1981) is the tallest species in the world because it has proportionately longer legs than other elephants, and this particular animal weighed an estimated 8·8 tons.

The tallest elephant ever recorded was a bull shot south of Sesfontein in Damaraland, Namibia on 4 Apr 1978 after it had allegedly killed 11 people and caused widespread crop damage. Lying on its side, this mountain of flesh measured 14 ft 6 in in a projected line from the shoulder to the base of forefoot, indicating that its standing height must have been about 13 ft 10 in. Other measurements included an overall length of 34 ft 1 in, and a forefoot circumference of 5 ft 2 in.

Toothed mammal ■ The largest toothed mammal ever recorded is the sperm whale (*Physeter catodon*), also called the cachalot. In the summer of 1950 a record-sized bull measuring 67 ft 11 in was captured off the Kurile Islands, northwest Pacific, by a Soviet whaling fleet. Bulls of much larger size were reported in the early days of whaling. The 16 ft 4¾ in long lower jaw of a sperm whale exhibited in the British Museum (Natural History) belonged to a bull measuring nearly 84 ft, and similar lengths have been reported for other outsized individuals killed.

Tallest land ■ The giraffe (*Giraffa camelopardalis*), which is now found only in the dry savannah and semidesert areas of Africa south of the Sahara, is the tallest living animal. The tallest ever recorded was a Masai bull (*G. camelopardalis tippelskirchi*) named George, received at Chester Zoo, Lancashire, United Kingdom on 8 Jan 1959 from Kenya. His 'horns' *almost* grazed the roof of the 20 ft high Giraffe House when he was nine years old. George died on 22 Jul 1969. Less credible heights of up to 23 ft (between pegs) have been claimed for bulls shot in the field.

Smallest land mammal ■ The endangered Kitti's hog-nosed bat (*Craseonycteris thonglongyai*), also called the bumblebee bat, is confined to about 21 limestone caves (population more than 2,000) on the Kwae Noi River, Kanchanaburi, Thailand, and mature specimens (both sexes) have a wingspan of *c.* 6·29 in and weigh 0·062–0·071 oz.

Insectivore ■ Mature specimens of Savi's white-toothed pygmy shrew (*Suncus etruscus*), also called the Etruscan shrew, which is found along the coast of the Mediterranean and southwards to Cape Province, South Africa have a head and body length of 1·32–2·04 in, a tail length of 0·94–1·14 in and weigh between 0·052 and 0·09 oz.

Smallest marine ■ In terms of weight, the smallest totally marine mammal is probably Commerson's dolphin (*Cephalorhynchus commersonii*), also known as Le Jacobite, which is found in the waters off the southern tip of South America. In one series of six adult speci-

mens the weights ranged from 50·7 lb to 77·1 lb. The sea otter (*Enhydra lutris*) of the north Pacific is of comparable size (55–81·4 lb), but this species sometimes comes ashore during storms.

Rarest land ■ A number of mammals are known only from a single or type specimen. One of these is the small-toothed fruit bat (*Neopteryx frosti*), collected from Tamalanti, West Celebes, in 1938.

The thylacine or tasmanian wolf or tiger (*Thylacinus cynocephalus*), feared extinct since the last captive specimen died in Beaumaris Zoo, Hobart, Tasmania on 7 Sep 1936, was possibly identified in July 1982 when a wildlife ranger claimed he saw one of these predatory marsupials in the spotlight of his parked car. Since then, however, there have been no more positive sightings.

The red wolf (*Canis rufus*) of the southeast United States became extinct in the wild in the early 1970s, but there are now over 50 individuals (not all of them genetically pure) held by the US Fish and Wildlife Service. In June 1988 it was announced that two pairs released in North Carolina by the captive breeding program had produced cubs.

The black-footed ferret (*Mustela nigripes*) of the northern United States is also extinct in the wild, but in 1988 the captive population (25), housed in a special center in Cheyenne, WY, more than doubled when the second breeding season produced 38 pups. The ferret will be reintroduced in Wyoming in the early 1990s.

Rarest marine ■ Longman's beaked whale (*Indopacetus pacificus*) is known only from two skulls. The type specimen was discovered on a beach near MacKay, Queensland, Australia in 1922, and the second near Muqdisho, Somalia, east Africa in 1955. The vaquita or gulf porpoise (*Phocoena sinus*) has not been sighted since 1980, and may now be extinct. Many hundreds of thousands have been accidentally killed by gillnet fishing in the last 45 years.

Fastest land ■ Over a short distance (i.e. up to 1,800 ft) the cheetah or hunting leopard (*Acinonyx jubatus*) of the open plains of East Africa, Iran, Turkmenia and Afghanistan has a probable maximum speed of 60–63 mph on suitably level ground. Speeds of 71, 84 and 90 mph have been claimed for this animal, but these figures must be considered exaggerated. Tests in London in 1937 showed that on an oval greyhound track over 1,035 ft a female cheetah's average speed over three runs was 43·4 mph (cf. 44·91 mph for the fastest racehorse, see Chapter 11), but this specimen was not running flat out and had great difficulty negotiating the bends.

The fastest land animal over a sustained distance (i.e. 3,000 ft or more) is the pronghorn antelope (*Antilocapra americana*) of the western United States. Specimens have been observed to travel at 35 mph for 4 miles, at 42 mph for 1 mile and 55 mph for half a mile.

Fastest marine ■ On 12 Oct 1958 a bull killer whale (*Orcinus orca*) measuring an estimated 20–25 ft in length was timed at 30 knots in the east Pacific. Speeds of up to 30 knots in short bursts have also been reported for Dall's porpoise (*Phocoenoides dalli*).

Slowest ■ The ai or three-toed sloth (*Bradypus tridactylus*) of tropical South America has an average ground speed of 6–8 ft a minute (0·068–0·098 mph), but in the trees it can 'accelerate' to 15 ft a minute (0·17 mph) (cf. these figures with the 0·03 mph of the common garden snail and the 0·17 mph of the giant tortoise).

Sleepiest ■ Some armadillos (*Dasypodidae*), opossums (*Didelphidae*) and sloths (*Bradypodidae*) spend up to 80 percent of their lives sleeping or dozing, while it is claimed that Dall's porpoise (*Phocoenoides dalli*) never sleeps at all.

Longest hibernation ■ The barrow ground squirrel (*Spermophilus parryi barrowensis*) of Point Barrow, AK hibernates for nine months of the year. During the remaining three months it feeds, breeds and collects food for storage in its burrow.

Oldest ■ No other mammal can match the extreme proven 120 years attained by man (*Homo sapiens*) (see Chapter 1). It is probable that the closest approach is made by the Asiatic elephant (*Elephas maximus*). The greatest age that has been verified with absolute certainty is 78 years in the case of a cow named 'Modoc,' who died at Santa Clara, CA on 17 Jul 1975. She was imported into the United States from Germany in 1898 at the age of two years.

Nepal's royal elephant 'Prem Prasad' was reportedly 81 when he died at Kasra, Chitwan, on 27 Feb 1985, but his actual age was believed to have been 65–70 years.

Sri Lanka's famous bull elephant 'Rajah,' who had led the annual Perahera procession through Kandi carrying the Sacred Tooth of the Buddha since 1931, died on 16 Jul 1988 allegedly aged 81 years.

Highest living ■ The yak (*Bos grunniens*), of Tibet and the Sichuanese Alps, China, occasionally climbs to an altitude of 20,000 ft when foraging.

Largest herds ■ The largest herds on record were those of the springbok (*Antidorcas marsupialis*) during migration across the plains of the western parts of southern Africa in the 19th century. In 1849 John (later Sir John) Fraser observed a *trekbokken* that took three days to pass through the settlement of Beaufort West, Cape Province. Another herd seen moving near Nels Poortje, Cape Province in 1888 was estimated to contain 100 million head, although 10 million is probably a more realistic figure. A herd estimated to be 15 miles wide and more than 100 miles long was reported from Karree Kloof, Orange River, South Africa in July 1896.

Longest gestation period ■ The Asiatic elephant (*Elephas maximus*) has an average gestation period of 609 days or just over 20 months and a maximum of 760 days—more than two and a half times that of a human. By 1981 only *c.* 35,000 survived.

Shortest gestation period ■ The gestation periods of the American opossum (*Didelphis marsupialis*), also called the Virginian opossum, the rare water opossum or yapok (*Chironectes minimus*) of central and northern South America, and the eastern native cat (*Dasyurus viverrinus*) of Australia are all normally 12–13 days but they can be as short as eight days.

Largest litter ■ The greatest number of young born to a *wild* mammal at a single birth is 31 (30 of which survived) in the case of the tailless tenrec (*Tenrec ecaudatus*) found in Madagascar and the Comoro Islands. The normal litter size is 12–15, although females can suckle up to 24.

Youngest breeder ■ The streaked tenrec (*Hemicentetes semispinosus*) of Madagascar is weaned after only five days, and females can breed 3–4 weeks after birth.

CARNIVORES

Largest living terrestrial carnivore

■ The average adult male Kodiak bear (*Ursus arctos middendorffi*), which is found on Kodiak Island and the adjacent Afognak and Shuyak islands in the Gulf of Alaska, has a nose-to-tail length of 8 ft (tail about 4 in). It stands 52 in at the shoulder and weighs between 1,050 lb and 1,175 lb. In 1894 a weight of 1,656 lb was recorded for a male shot at English Bay, Kodiak Island, whose *stretched* skin measured 13 ft 6 in from the tip of the nose to the root of the tail. This weight was exceeded by a 'cage-fat male' in the Cheyenne Mountain Zoological Park, Colorado Springs, CO, which scaled 1,670 lb at the time of its death on 22 Sep 1955.

In 1981 an unconfirmed weight of over 2,000 lb was reported for a peninsula giant bear (*Ursus a. gyas*) from Alaska on exhibition at the Space Farms Zoological Park at Beemerville, NJ.

Weights in excess of 2,000 lb have been reported for the polar bear (*Ursus maritimus*), but the average adult male weighs 850–900 lb and measures 7 ft 9 in nose-to-tail.

In 1960 a polar bear allegedly weighing 2,210 lb was shot at the polar entrance to Kotzebue Sound, northwest Alaska. In April 1962 the 11 ft 1¼ in tall mounted specimen was put on display at the Seattle World's Fair.

Smallest ■ The smallest living member of the order Carnivora is the least weasel (*Mustela rixosa*), also called the dwarf weasel, which is circumpolar in distribution. Four races are recognized, the smallest of which is *M. r. pygmaea* of Siberia. Mature specimens have an overall length of 6·96–8·14 in and weigh between 1¼–2½ oz.

Largest feline ■ The largest member of the cat family (Felidae) is the protected long-furred Siberian tiger (*Panthera tigris altaica*), also called the Amur or Manchurian tiger. Adult males average 10 ft 4 in in length (nose to tip of extended tail), stand 39–42 in at the shoulder and weigh about 585 lb. In 1950 a male weighing 846·5 lb was shot in the Sikhote-Alin Mts, Maritime Territory, USSR.

An outsized Indian tiger (*Panthera tigris tigris*) shot in northern Uttar Pradesh in November 1967 measured 10 ft 7 in between pegs (11 ft 1 in over the curves) and weighed 857 lb (cf. 9 ft 3 in and 420 lb for an average adult male). It is now on display in the Museum of Natural History, Smithsonian Institution, Washington, DC.

The largest tiger ever held in captivity, and the heaviest 'big cat' on record, is a nine-year-old Siberian male named Jaipur, owned by animal trainer Joan Byron-Marasek of Clarksburg, NJ. This specimen measures 10 ft 11 in in total length and tipped the scales at 932 lb in October 1986.

The average adult African lion (*Panthera leo*) measures 9 ft overall, stands 36–38 in at the shoulder and weighs 400–410 lb. The heaviest wild specimen on record was one weighing 690 lb shot just outside Hectorspruit in the eastern Transvaal, South Africa in 1936.

In July 1970 a weight of 826 lb was reported for a black-maned lion named Simba (b. Dublin Zoo, 1959) at Colchester Zoo, Essex, United Kingdom. He died on 16 Jan 1973 at the now defunct Knaresborough Zoo, North Yorkshire, United Kingdom, where his stuffed body had been on display.

An adult male Litigon (an Indian lion/Tigon

cross) named Cubanacan at Alipore Zoological Gardens, Calcutta, India, is also believed to weigh at least 800 lb. This animal stands 52 in at the shoulder (cf. 44 in for the lion 'Simba') and measures a record 11 ft 6 in in total length.

Smallest feline ■ The smallest member of the cat family is the rusty-spotted cat (*Felis rubiginosa*) of southern India and Sri Lanka. The average adult male has an overall length of 25–28 in (tail 9–10 in) and weighs about 3 lb.

PINNIPEDS Seals, Sea-lions, Walruses

Largest ■ The largest of the 34 known species of pinniped is the southern elephant seal (*Mirounga leonina*), which inhabits the sub-Antarctic islands. Adult bulls average 16½ ft in length (tip of inflated snout to the extremities of the outstretched tail flippers), 12 ft in maximum bodily girth and weigh about 5,000 lb. The largest accurately measured specimen on record was a bull killed in Possession Bay, South Georgia on 28 Feb 1913 that measured 21 ft 4 in after flensing (original length about 22½ ft) and probably weighed at least 4·4 tons. There are old records of bulls measuring 25–30 ft and even 35 ft but these figures must be considered exaggerated. Adult cows are much smaller, averaging 10 ft in length and weighing about 1,500 lb.

Smallest ■ The smallest pinnipeds are the ringed seal (*Phoca hispida*) of the Arctic and the closely-related Baikal seal (*P. sibirica*) of Lake Baikal and the Caspian seal (*P. caspica*) of the Caspian Sea, USSR. Adult specimens (males) measure up to 5 ft 6 in in length and reach a maximum weight of 280 lb. Females are about two-thirds this size.

Most abundant ■ In 1978 the total population of the Crabeater seal (*Lobodon carcinophagus*) of Antarctica was believed to be nearly 15 million.

Rarest ■ The last reliable sighting of the Caribbean or West Indian monk seal (*Monachus tropicalis*) was on Serranilla Bank off the coast of Mexico's Yucatan peninsula in 1952. In 1974 two seals were seen near Cay Verde and Cay Burro, southeast Bahamas, but a search in 1979

found nothing. It has been suggested that these sightings (and others) may have been Californian sea lions (*Zalophus californianus*) which had escaped from captivity and have been recorded in the Gulf of Mexico on several occasions.

Fastest ■ The highest swimming speed recorded for a pinniped is a 25 mph short spurt by a Californian sea lion. The fastest-moving pinniped on land is the crabeater seal, which has been timed at speeds up to 11·8 mph.

Deepest dive ■ In *c*. May 1988 a team of scientists from the University of California at Santa Cruz tested the diving abilities of the northern elephant seal (*Mirounga anguistirostris*) off Ano Nuevo Point, CA. One female reached a record depth of 4,135 ft, and another one remained under water for 48 minutes. Similar experiments carried out by Australian scientists on southern elephant seals in the Southern Ocean recorded a dive of 3,720 ft, and other dives lasting nearly two hours were observed. It was also discovered that the seals regularly swam down to about 2,500 ft and when they surfaced again apparently had no 'oxygen debt.'

Oldest ■ A female gray seal shot at Shunni Wick in the Shetland Islands, United Kingdom, on 23 Apr 1969 was believed to be 'at least 46 years old' based on a count of dentine rings. The captive record is an estimated 41 years for a bull gray seal 'Jacob' held in Skansen Zoo (1901–42).

Smallest ● The smallest known monkey is the pygmy marmoset (*Cebuella pygmaea*) of the upper Amazon basin. Average adults have a head and body length of 6 in and weigh about 3 oz. (Photo: Jacana)

BATS

Largest ■ The only flying mammals are bats (order Chiroptera), of which there are about 950 living species. That with the greatest wingspan is the Bismarck flying fox (*Pteropus neohibernicus*) of the Bismarck Archipelago and New Guinea. One specimen preserved in the American Museum of Natural History has a wing spread of 5 ft 5 in, but some unmeasured bats probably reach 6 ft.

United States ■ Mature specimens of the large mastiff bat (*Eumops perotis*), found in southern Texas, California, Arizona and New Mexico, have a wingspan of 22·04 in.

Smallest ■ The smallest bat in the world is Kitti's hog-nosed bat.

United States ■ The smallest native bat is the Western pipistrelle (*Pipistrellus hesperus*), found in the western United States. Mature specimens have a wingspan of 0·79 in.

Rarest ■ At least three species of bat are known only from the type specimen. They are: the small-toothed fruit bat (*Neopteryx frosti*) from Tamalanti, West Celebes (1938/39); *Paracoelops megalotis* from Vinh, Vietnam (1945); and

Latidens salimalii from the High Wavy Mountains, southern India (1948).

Fastest ■ Because of the great practical difficulties little data on bat speeds have been published. The greatest velocity attributed to a bat is 32 mph in the case of a Mexican free-tailed bat, but this may have been wind-assisted. In one American experiment using an artificial mine tunnel and 17 different kinds of bat, only four of them managed to exceed 13 mph in level flight.

Oldest ■ The greatest age reliably reported for a bat is 32 years for a banded female little brown bat (*Myotis lucifugus*) in the United States in 1987.

Highest detectable pitch ■ Because of their ultrasonic echolocation, bats have the most acute hearing of any terrestrial animal. Vampire bats (*Desmodontidae*) and fruit bats (*Pteropodidae*) can hear frequencies as high as 120–210 kHz compared with 20 kHz for the adult human limit but 280 kHz for the common dolphin (*Delphinus delphis*).

Largest colonies ■ The largest concentration of bats found living anywhere in the world today is that of the Mexican free-tailed bat (*Tadarida brasiliensis*) in Bracken Cave, San Antonio, TX, where up to 20 million animals assemble after migration.

Deepest ■ A little brown bat has been recorded at a depth of 3,805 ft in a zinc mine in New York. The mine serves as winter quarters for 1,000 members of this species, which normally roost at a depth of 656 ft.

PRIMATES

Largest living ■ The average adult male eastern lowland gorilla (*Gorilla g. graueri*) of the lowland forests of eastern Zaïre and south-western Uganda, stands 5 ft 9 in tall and weighs 360 lb.

The mountain gorilla (*Gorilla g. beringei*) of the volcanic mountain ranges of western Rwanda, south-western Uganda and eastern Zaïre is also of comparable size, i.e. 5 ft 8 in and 343 lb, and most of the exceptionally large gorillas taken in the field have been of this race.

The greatest height (top of crest to heel) recorded for a gorilla in the wild is 6 ft 2 in for a bull of the mountain race shot in the eastern Congo (Zaïre) *c*. 1920. The tallest gorilla ever kept in captivity is reportedly an eastern lowland male named Colossus (b. 1966), who is currently on display at a zoo in Gulf Breeze, FL. He allegedly stands 6 ft 2 in tall and weighs 575 lb, but these figures have not yet been confirmed.

A western lowland gorilla called Baltimore Jack, who was received at Baltimore Zoo, MD in 1956 and later sold to Phoenix Zoo, AZ, had exceptionally long legs for a gorilla. He reportedly stood 6 ft 3 in tall, but his actual height was somewhere between 5 ft 7 in and 5 ft 9 in (weight 300 lb). He died in 1972.

The heaviest gorilla ever kept in captivity was a male of the mountain race named N'gagi, who died in San Diego Zoo, CA on 12 Jan 1944 at the age of 18. He scaled 683 lb at his heaviest in 1943, and weighed 635 lb at the time of his death. He was 5 ft 7¾ in tall and boasted a record chest measurement of 78 in.

Smallest ■ Adult specimens of the rare pen-tailed shrew (*Ptilocercus lowii*) of Malaysia, have a total length of 9–13 in (head and body 3·93–5·51 in; tail 5·1–7·5 in) and weigh 1·23–1·76 oz.

The pygmy marmoset (*Cebuella pygmaea*) of the upper Amazon basin and the lesser mouse lemur (*Microcebus murinus*) of Madagascar are also of comparable length but heavier, adults weighing 1·76–2·64 oz and 1·58–2·82 oz respectively.

Rarest ■ The greater bamboo broad-nosed gentle lemur (*Hapalemur simus*) of Madagascar reportedly became extinct in the early 1970s, but in 1986 a group consisting of 60–80 individuals was discovered living in a remote rain forest near Ranomafana in the southeastern part of the island by an expedition from Duke University, Durham, NC.

The golden-rumped tamarin (*Leontopithecus chrysopygus*), which is now restricted to two areas of forest in the state of São Paulo, southeast Brazil, is also on the verge of extinction, with only 75–100 surviving in 1986.

Oldest ■ The greatest irrefutable age reported for a non-human primate is *c.* 59 years in the case of a male orangutan (*Pongo pygmaeus*) named Guas, who died in Philadelphia Zoological Garden, PA on 9 Feb 1977. When he was received on 1 May 1931 he was at least 13 years of age.

The oldest chimpanzee (*Pan troglodytes*) on record was a male named Jimmy, at Seneca Zoo, Rochester, NY who died on 17 Sep 1985 at the age of 55 years 6 months.

The famous western lowland gorilla 'Massa' (b. July 1931) died on 30 Dec 1984 at the age of 53 years 5 months.

The oldest female gorilla on record was 'Carolyn' (b. 1939) of New York Zoological Park (Bronx Zoo), NY who died on 27 Sep 1986 at the age of 47.

Strongest ■ In 1924 Boma, a 165 lb male chimpanzee at the New York Zoological Park (Bronx Zoo), NY recorded a right-handed pull (feet braced) of 847 lb on a dynamometer (cf. 210 lb for a man of the same weight).

On another occasion an adult female chimpanzee named Suzette (estimated weight 135 lb) at the same zoo registered a right-handed pull of 1,260 lb while in a rage.

An American record of a 100 lb chimpanzee achieving a two-handed dead lift of 600 lb with ease suggests that a male gorilla could, with training, raise 2,000 lb.

MONKEYS

Largest ■ The only species of monkey reliably credited with weights of more than 100 lb is the mandrill (*Mandrillus sphinx*) of equatorial West Africa. The greatest reliable weight recorded is 119 lb for a captive male but an unconfirmed weight of 130 lb has been reported. (Adult females are about half the size of males.)

Smallest ■ The smallest known monkey is the pygmy marmoset (*Cebuella pygmaea*) of the upper Amazon basin. (See Primates, Smallest.)

Oldest ■ The world's oldest monkey, a male white-throated capuchin (*Cebus capucinus*) called Bobo, died on 10 Jul 1988 at age 53 following complications related to a stroke. He was originally imported from South America and donated to the Mesker Park Zoo in Evansville, IN on 1 Jan 1935. When the zoo disbanded its monkey colony he was given to Dr Raymond T. Bartus, founder of the Geriatric Research Program at Lederle Laboratories, American Cyanamid Co., Pearl River, NY, and lived in the geriatric monkey colony from 31 Oct 1981 until his death.

RODENTS

Largest ■ The capybara (*Hydrochoerus hydrochaeris*), also called the carpincho or water hog, of tropical South America, has a head and body length of 3¼–4½ ft and can weigh up to 250 lb (cage-fat specimen).

Smallest ■ The northern pygmy mouse (*Baiomys taylori*) of central Mexico and southern Arizona and Texas, measures up to 4·3 in in total length and weighs 0·24–0·28 oz.

Largest pinniped ● The largest of the 34 known species of pinniped is the southern elephant seal (*Mirounga leonina*), which inhabits the sub-Antarctic islands. Adult bulls average 16½ ft in length (tip of inflated snout to the extremities of the outstretched tail flippers), 12 ft in maximum bodily girth and weigh about 5,000 lb. The largest accurately measured specimen on record was a bull killed in Possession Bay, South Georgia, South Atlantic on 28 Feb 1913 that measured 21 ft 4 in after skinning (original length about 22½ ft) and probably weighed at least 4·4 tons. Adult cows are much smaller, averaging 10 ft in length and weighing about 1,500 lb. The specimen seen here is accompanied by a Californian sea lion (*Zalophus californianus*). (Photo: Klaus Paysan)

Rarest ■ The rarest rodents in the world are Garrido's hutia (*Capromys garridoi*) of the Canarreos Archipelago, Cuba, and the little earth hutia (*C. sanfelipensis*) of Juan Garcia Cay, an islet off southern Cuba. The latter species has not been recorded since its discovery in 1970.

Oldest ■ The greatest reliable age reported for a rodent is 27 years, 3 months for a Sumatran crested porcupine (*Hystrix brachyura*), which died in National Zoological Park, Washington, DC on 12 Jan 1965.

Fastest breeder ■ The female meadow vole (*Microtus agrestis*), found in Britain, can reproduce from the age of 25 days and have up to 17 litters of 6–8 young in a year.

INSECTIVORES

Largest ■ The moon rat (*Echinosorex gymnurus*), also known as Raffles' gymnure, which is found in Myanmar (formerly Burma), Thailand, Malaysia, Sumatra and Borneo, has a head and body length of 10·43–17·52 in, a tail measuring 7·87–8·26 in and weighs up to 3·08 lb.

Although the much larger anteaters (families *Tachyglossidae* and *Myrmecophagidae*) feed on

termites and other soft-bodied insects, they are not insectivores, but belong to the orders *Mono-tremata* and *Edentata* ('without teeth').

Smallest ◼ The smallest insectivore is Savi's white-toothed pygmy shrew (*Suncus etruscus*). (See Mammals, Smallest.)

Oldest ◼ The greatest reliable age recorded for an insectivore is 16+ years for a lesser hedgehog-tenrec (*Echinops telfairi*), which was born in Amsterdam Zoo, Netherlands in 1966 and was later sent to Jersey Zoo, NJ. It died on 27 Nov 1982.

ANTELOPES

Largest ◼ The rare giant eland (*Taurotragus derbianus*) of western and central Africa may surpass 2,000 lb.

The common eland (*T. oryx*) of eastern and southern Africa has the same shoulder height of up to 5 ft 10 in but is not quite so massive, although there is one record of a 5 ft 5 in bull shot in Malawi *c.* 1937 that weighed 2,078 lb.

Smallest ◼ Mature specimens of the royal antelope (*Neotragus pygmaeus*) of western Africa measure 10–12 in at the shoulder and weigh only 7–8 lb, which is the size of a large brown hare (*Lepus europaeus*).

Salt's dik-dik (*Madoqua saltina*) of northeastern Ethiopia and Somalia weighs only 5–6 lb when adult, but this species stands about 14 in at the withers.

Rarest ◼ Until recently, the Arabian oryx (*Oryx leucoryx*) had not been reported in the wild since 1972 when three were killed and four others captured on the Jiddat-al-Harasis plateau, South Oman. Between March 1980 and August 1983 a total of 17 antelopes from the World Herd at San Diego Zoo, CA were released into the open desert in South Oman under the protection of a nomadic tribe. Since then there have been at least 43 live births, and at the beginning of 1989, the wild herd totaled 60. The Arabian oryx has also been successfully reintro-duced into the Shaumari Reserve in Jordan, where there are now 90 of these animals.

Oldest ◼ The greatest reliable age recorded for an antelope is 25 years 4 months for an Addax (*Addax nasomaculatus*) that died in Brookfield Zoo, Chicago, IL on 15 Oct 1960.

DEER

Largest ◼ The largest deer is the Alaskan moose (*Alces alces gigas*). Adult bulls average 6 ft at the shoulder and weigh *c.* 1,100 lb. A bull standing 7 ft 8 in between pegs and weighing an estimated 1,800 lb was shot on the Yukon River in the Yukon Territory, Canada in September 1897. Unconfirmed measurements of up to 8 ft 6 in at the shoulder and estimated weights of up to 2,600 lb have been claimed.

The record antler spread or 'rack' is 78½ in (skull and antlers 91 lb). They were taken from a moose killed near the headwaters of the Stewart River in the Yukon, Canada in October 1897 and are now on display in the Field Museum, Chicago, IL.

Smallest ◼ The smallest true deer (family Cervidae) is the Northern pudu (*Pudu mephisto-pheles*) of Ecuador and Colombia. Mature speci-mens measure 13–14 in at the shoulder and weigh 16–18 lb.

The smallest ruminant is the Lesser Malay chevrotain (*Tragulus javanicus*) of Southeast Asia, Sumatra and Borneo. Adult specimens measure 8–10 in at the shoulder and weigh 6–7 lb.

Rarest ◼ Until recently, Fea's muntjac (*Muntiacus feae*) was known only from two specimens collected on the borders of southern Myanmar (formerly Burma) and western Thai-land. In December 1977 a female was received at Dusit Zoo, Bangkok, followed by two females in 1981 and three males and three females from Xizang, Tibet from February 1982–April 1983.

Oldest ◼ The world's oldest recorded deer is a red deer (*Cervus elaphus scoticus*) named Bambi (b. 8 Jun 1963), owned by the Fraser family of Kiltarlity, Beauly, Highland, United Kingdom.

The greatest reliable age recorded for a deer is 26 years 8 months for a red deer (*Cervus elaphus scoticus*) that died in Milwaukee Zoo, WI on 28 Jun 1954.

Oldest ● The red deer (*Cervus elaphus*) named Bambi (b. 8 Jun 1963), owned by the Fraser family of Kiltarlity, Beauly, Highland, United Kingdom, reached the greatest reliably recorded age for a deer in February 1990.

MARSUPIALS

Largest ◼ The adult male red kangaroos (*Macropus rufus*) of central, southern and east-ern Australia stand up to 7 ft tall, measure up to 8 ft ½ in in total length and weigh up to 187 lb.

Smallest ◼ The smallest known marsupial is the rare long-tailed planigale (*Planigale ingrami*), a flat-skulled mouse, of northeastern and northwestern Australia. Adult males have a head and body length of 2·16–2·48 in, a tail length of 2·24–2·36 in and weigh 0·13–0·19 oz.

Oldest ◼ The greatest reliable age recorded for a marsupial is 26 years 22 days for a common wombat (*Vombatus ursinus*) that died in London Zoo, United Kingdom on 20 Apr 1906.

Fastest speed ◼ The highest speed recorded for a marsupial is 40 mph for a mature female eastern gray kangaroo. One large male red kangaroo died from his exertions after being paced for 1 mile at 35mph.

Highest jump ◼ A captive eastern gray once cleared an 8 ft fence when a car backfired and there is also a record of a hunted red kangaroo clearing a stack of timber 10 ft high.

Longest jump ◼ During the course of a chase in New South Wales in January 1951 a female red kangaroo made a series of bounds that included one of 42 ft. There is also an unconfir-med report of an eastern gray kangaroo jumping nearly 44 ft 8½ in on the flat.

TUSKS

Longest ◼ The longest recorded elephant tusks (excluding prehistoric examples) are a pair from Zaïre preserved in the National Collection of Heads and Horns kept by the New York Zoological Society in Bronx Park, NY. The right tusk measures 11 ft 5½ in along the outside curve and the left 11 ft. Their combined weight is 293 lb. A single tusk of 11 ft 6 in has been reported. Ivory rose from $2·30 to $34/lb in the period 1970–80.

Heaviest ◼ A pair of tusks in the British Museum (Natural History) that were collected from an aged bull shot by an Arab with a muzzle-loading gun at the foot of Mt Kiliman-jaro, Kenya in 1897, originally weighed 240 lb (length 10 ft 2½ in) and 225 lb (length 10 ft 5½ in) respectively, giving a total weight of 465 lb, but their combined weight today is 440½ lb. A single elephant tusk collected in Benin, West Africa and exhibited at the Paris Exposition in 1900 weighed 258 lb.

HORNS

Longest ◼ The longest horns grown by any living animal are those of the water buffalo (*Bubalus arnee = B. bubalis*) of India. One huge bull shot in 1955 had horns measuring 13 ft 11 in from tip to tip along the outside curve across the forehead. The longest single horn on record was one measuring 81¼ in on the outside curve found on a specimen of domestic ankole cattle (*Bos taurus*) near Lake Ngami, Botswana.

The largest spread recorded for a Texas long-horn steer is 10 ft 6 in. They are currently on exhibition at the Hermitage Museum, Big Springs, TX.

HORSES AND PONIES

The world's equine population is estimated to be 75 million. For record horse prices see Agricul-ture, Chapter 7.

Earliest domestication ◼ The first dom-estication of the horse reportedly occurred in what is now the Ukraine, USSR *c.* 6,500 years ago when paleolithic hunters tamed some for their flesh and milk.

Largest ◼ A 19·2-hand purebred red roan Belgian (Brabant) stallion named Brooklyn Supreme (1928–48) owned by C. G. Good of Ogden, IA weighed 3,200 lb at its heaviest in 1938 and had a chest girth of 102 in. Each of his 7½ lb shoes measured 14 in across and required 30 in of iron (cf. 22 in for 'Wandle Goliath;' see below).

In April 1973 a weight of 3,218 lb was reported for an 18·2-hand Belgian (Brabant) mare named Wilma du Bos (foaled 15 Jul 1966) shortly before she was shipped from Antwerp to her new owner, Virgie Arden of Reno, NV, but at the time she was heavily in foal (maximum girth 12 ft). When this horse arrived in New York she scaled 3,086 lb, but after foaling her weight returned to her normal 2,400–2,500 lb.

Tallest ◼ The tallest documented horse on record was the shire gelding Sampson (later renamed Mammoth) bred by Thomas Cleaver of Toddington Mills, United Kingdom. This horse (foaled in 1846) measured 21·2½ hands in 1850 and was later said to have weighed 3,360 lb.

Smallest ◼ The falabela of Argentina was developed over a period of 70 years by inbreeding and crossing a small group of undersized horses originally discovered in the southern part of the country. Most adult specimens stand less than 30 in and average 80–100 lb.

The smallest mature horse bred by Julio Fal-abela of Recco de Roca before he died in 1981 was a mare that stood 15 in and weighed 26¼ lb.

ANTELOPES

Smallest antelope ● Mature specimens of the tiny royal antelope (*Neotragus pygmaeus*), which is found alone or in pairs in the dense forests of West Africa, measure 10 in at the shoulder and weigh only 7–8 lb. (Artwork: Matthew Hillier for Guinness Publishing)

Largest antelope ● The distinctive giant, or Derby, eland (*Taurotragus derbianus*) of western and central Africa can attain a height of 6 ft at the shoulder and weigh over 2,000 lb. As this scale drawing shows, the royal antelope might be ill-advised to venture out of its dense forest and on to the open plains or lightly wooded areas that serve as the 'land of the giants.' (Artwork: Matthew Hillier for Guinness Publishing)

On 30 Nov 1975 Dr T. H. Hamison of the Circle Veterinary Center, Spartenburg, SC certified that the stallion 'Little Pumpkin' (foaled 15 Apr 1973) owned by J. C. Williams, Jr of Della Terra Mini Horse Farm, Inman, SC, stood 14 in and weighed 20 lb.

Oldest ■ The greatest reliable age recorded for a horse is 62 years in the case of 'Old Billy' (foaled 1760), believed to be a cross between a Cleveland and eastern blood, who was bred by Edward Robinson of Wild Grave Farm in Woolston, Lancashire, United Kingdom. In 1762 or 1763 he was sold to the Mersey and Irwell Navigation Company and remained with them in a working capacity (i.e. marshaling and towing barges) until 1819 when he was retired to a farm at Latchford, near Warrington, United Kingdom, where he died on 27 Nov 1822. The skull of this horse is preserved in the Manchester Museum, United Kingdom, and his stuffed head (fitted with false teeth) is now on display in Bedford Museum, United Kingdom.

The greatest reliable age recorded for a pony is 54 years for a stallion owned by a farmer in central France (*fl.* 1919).

A roan pony named Bonnie Lass, owned by twin sisters Sylvia Moore and Marion Atkinson of Old Harlow, Essex, United Kingdom, died on 2 May 1987 aged 42 years.

Exactly a year to the day later, a moorland pony called Joey belonging to June and Rosie Osborne of the Glebe Equestrian Centre, Wickham Bishop, Essex, United Kingdom died at the age of 44.

The greatest age recorded for a thoroughbred racehorse is 42 years, in the case of the chestnut gelding 'Tango Duke' (foaled 1935), owned by Mrs Carmen J. Koper of Barongarook, Victoria, Australia. The horse died on 25 Jan 1978.

Strongest ■ The greatest load ever hauled by a pair of draught horses was allegedly one weighing 144 tons, which two Shires with a combined weight of 3,500 lb pulled on a sled litter for a distance of 1,320 ft along a frozen road at the Nester Estate near Ewen, MI on 26 Feb 1893, but this tonnage was exaggerated. The load, which comprised 50 logs of white pine scaling 36,055 board feet, actually weighed in the region of 47 tons.

On 23 Apr 1924 a shire gelding named Vulcan, owned by Liverpool Corporation, United Kingdom, registered a pull equal to a starting load of 32.5 tons on a dynamometer at the British Empire Exhibition, and a pair of shires *easily* pulled a starting load of 56 tons, the maximum registered on the dynamometer.

Largest mules ■ Apollo (b. Tennessee 1977) and Anak (b. Kentucky 1976) owned by Herbert L. Mueller of Chicago, IL are the largest mules on record. Apollo measures 19·1-hands (6·5 ft) and weighs 2,200 lb and Anak is 18·3-hands (6·2 ft) and 2,100 lb, giving a combined weight of 4,300 lb. Both are the hybrid offspring of Belgian mares and mammoth jacks.

DOGS

The American canine population for 1989 is estimated by the Pet Food Institute at 50·5 million dogs in 33·5 million households, or 36·2 percent of the population, compared with 6·6 million for the United Kingdom and 400 million for the world.

In 1989, American dog owners bought 6·6 billion pounds of dog food at a cost of $3·3 billion.

Heaviest ■ The heaviest breed of domestic dog (*Canis familiaris*) are the Old English mastiff and the St. Bernard, both of which (males) regularly weigh 170–200 lb at maturity. The heaviest (and longest) dog ever recorded is Aicama Zorba of La-Susa (whelped 26 Sep 1981), an Old English mastiff owned by Chris Eraclides of London, United Kingdom. In September 1987 this canine super-heavyweight tipped the scales at 319 lb (shoulder height 35 in). Despite his enormous size, however, he does not carry any surplus weight because his diet is strictly controlled. Unfortunately, in March 1989, 'Zorba' was left in the charge of a relative who overfed him and he ballooned to 338 lb but he is now back to his ideal weight. Other statistics include a chest girth of 57 in, a 36½ in neck, and a nose to tail length of 8 ft 3 in. One of his sons Chandor (whelped 6 Aug 1987), weighed 266 lb at the age of 18 months (cf. 238 lb for Zorba at two years).

The heaviest St. Bernard on record is Benedictine Jr. Schwarzwald Hof (whelped 1982) owned by breeders Thomas and Anne Irwin of Grand Rapids, MI. His last recorded weight was 310 lb (height at shoulder 39 in).

Tallest ■ The Great Dane and the Irish wolfhound both can exceed 39 in at the shoulder. In the case of the Great Dane the extreme recorded example was Shamgret Danzas (whelped in 1975), owned by Mr and Mrs Peter Comley of Milton Keynes, Buckinghamshire, United Kingdom. He stood 41½ in or 42 in when his hackles went up and weighed up to 238 lb. He died on 16 Oct 1984.

The Irish wolfhound Broadbridge Michael (1920–29), owned by Mary Beynon of Sutton-at-Hone, Kent, United Kingdom, stood 39½ in at the age of two years.

Smallest ■ *Miniature* versions of the Yorkshire terrier, the chihuahua and the toy poodle have been known to weigh less than 16 oz when adult.

The smallest mature dog on record was a matchbox-sized Yorkshire terrier owned by Arthur Marples of Blackburn, Lancashire, United Kingdom, a former editor of *Our Dogs.* This tiny atom, which died in 1945 aged nearly two years, stood 2½ in at the shoulder and measured 3¾ in from the tip of its nose to the root of its tail. Its weight was an incredible 4 oz.

The smallest living adult dog is a miniature chihuahua named Peanuts (whelped 23 Sep 1986) owned by Floyd and Grace Parker of Wilson's Mills, NC. She measures 9·84 in head to tail, 5·5 in at the shoulder and tipped the scales at 18 oz on 25 Oct 1988.

Oldest ■ Most dogs live between 8 and 15 years, and authentic records of dogs living over 20 years are rare. They are generally the smaller breeds. The greatest reliable age recorded for a dog is 29 years 5 months for an Australian cattle-dog named Bluey, owned by Les Hall of Rochester, Victoria, Australia. The dog was obtained as a puppy in 1910 and worked among cattle and sheep for nearly 20 years. He was put to sleep on 14 Nov 1939.

Longest trail ■ The 1,049 mile Iditarod Trail from Anchorage to Nome, AK has existed since 910 and as the course of an annual race from 1967. The fastest time was set by Susan Butcher (winner in 1986–87–88–90) in 1987 with 11 days 2 hr 5 min 13 sec. Her fourth win, in the 1990 race, equaled the record set by Rick Swenson between 1977 and 1982.

On 8 Feb 1988 the Rev Donald Ewen McEwen, owner-musher of Nekanesu Kennels, Eldorado, Ontario, Canada drove a 76-dog sled for 2 miles single-handedly on the ice and about the shore of Lingham Lake. The team, consisting of 25 Siberian huskies and 51 Alaskan huskies, was assembled for the filming of an British TV commercial.

Rarest ■ At the last count (18 March 1988) there were only 70 living examples of the American hairless terrier, 68 of them owned by Willie and Edwin Scott of Trout, LA.

Guide dog ■ The longest period of *active service* reported for a guide dog is 14 years 8 months (August 1972–March 1987) in the case of a labrador retriever bitch

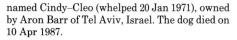
named Cindy–Cleo (whelped 20 Jan 1971), owned by Aron Barr of Tel Aviv, Israel. The dog died on 10 Apr 1987.

Largest litter ■ Lena, an American foxhound bitch owned by Commander W. N. Ely of Ambler, PA produced a litter of 23 on 19 Jun 1944. All the puppies survived.

On 6–7 Feb 1975 Careless Ann, a St. Bernard owned by Robert and Alice Rodden of Lebanon, MO, also produced a litter of 23, 14 of which survived.

The same number (16 survived) was thrown by Shalimar Bootsie, a Great Dane owned by Marjorie Harris of Little Hall, Essex, United Kingdom in June 1987.

Most prolific ■ The greatest sire of all time was the champion greyhound Low Pressure, nicknamed 'Timmy,' whelped in September 1957 and owned by Mrs Bruna Amhurst of Regent's Park, London, United Kingdom. From December 1961 until his death on 27 Nov 1969 he fathered 2,414 registered puppies, with at least 600 others unregistered.

Most valuable ■ In 1907 Mrs Clarice Ashton Cross of Ascot, Berkshire, United King- dom turned down an offer of £32,000 from the American financier and industrialist J. Pierpont Morgan for her famous pekingese Ch. Ch'êrh of Alderbourne (1904–14). Mr Morgan then came back with an 'open' cheque, but again she turned him down. The largest legacy devoted to a dog was by Miss Ella Wendel of New York who bequeathed her

standard poodle Toby the sum of £15 million in 1931.

Highest jump ■ The canine 'high jump' record for a leap and a scramble over a smooth wooden wall (without ribs or other aids) is held by a German shepherd dog named Volse, who scaled 11 ft 9 in at a demonstration in Avignon, France in November 1989. The dog is owned by Phillipe Clement of Aix-en-Provence.

Duke, a three-year-old German shepherd dog, handled by Cpl Graham Urry of Royal Air Force Newton, Nottinghamshire, United Kingdom, scaled a ribbed wall with regulation shallow slats to a height of 11 ft 9 in on the British TV program *Record Breakers* on 11 Nov 1986.

Longest jump ■ A greyhound named Bang jumped 30 ft while coursing a hare at Brecon Lodge, Gloucestershire, United Kingdom in 1849. He cleared a 4 ft 6 in gate and landed on a hard road, but despite a damaged pastern bone he still managed to kill the hare.

Ratting ■ During the five-year period 1820–24 a 26 lb 'bull and terrier' dog named Billy dispatched 4,000 rats in 17 hr, a remarkable feat considering that he was blind in one eye. His most notable feat was the killing of 100 rats in 5 min 30 sec at the Cockpit in Tufton Street, Westminster, London on 23 Apr 1825. He died on 23 Feb 1829 at the age of 13. James Searle's famous 'bull and terrier' bitch Jenny Lind was another outstanding ratter. On 12 Jul 1853 she was backed to kill 500 rats in under 3 hr at The Beehive in Old Crosshall Street, Liverpool, United Kingdom, and completed the job in 1 hr 36 min.

Tracking ■ In 1925 a Dobermann pins cher named Sauer, trained by Detective-Sergeant Herbert Kruger, tracked a stock thief 100 miles across the Great Karroo, South Africa by scent alone.

In 1923 a collie dog named Bobbie, lost by his owners while on holiday in Wolcott, IN, turned up at the family home in Silverton, OR six months later, after covering a distance of some 2,000 miles. The dog, later identified by householders who had looked after

him along the route, had apparently traveled back through the states of Illinois, Iowa, Nebraska and Colorado before crossing the Rocky Mountains in the depths of winter.

Top show dogs ■ The greatest number of challenge certificates won by a dog is the 78 compiled by the famous chow chow Ch. U'Kwong King Solomon (whelped 21 Jun 1968). Owned and bred by Mrs Joan Egerton of Bramhall, Cheshire, United Kingdom, 'Solly' won his first CC at the Cheshire Agricultural Society Championship Show on 4 Jun 1969, and his 78th CC was awarded at the City of Birmingham Championship Show on 4 Sep 1976. He died on 3 Apr 1978.

The greatest number of Best-in-Show awards won by any dog in all-breed shows is the career total of 203 compiled by the Scottish terrier bitch Ch. Braeburn's Close Encounter (whelped 22 Oct 1978) up to 10 Mar 1985. She is owned by Sonnie Novick of Plantation Acres, FL.

Ch. Clayfield's Mon Ami, a German shepherd bitch whelped in 1973, won a unique ten dog show championships on four continents from 1975 to 1987. She is owned by Neal, Sharon, Buffy and Holly Leas of West Des Moines, IA.

Largest show ■ At the Ladies' Kennel Association Show (LKA) held at the Birmingham National Exhibition Centre, United Kingdom on 14–15 Dec 1984 there were 21,212 entries and a total of 14,611 dogs exhibited.

Top trainer ■ The most successful dog

Tallest dog/Smallest horse ● The tallest known Great Dane, standing 41 ½in at the shoulder, was almost three times taller than the 15 in horse bred by Julio Falabella, the pioneer of miniature-horse breeding, or the tiny stallion shown in the photo on the right. (Artwork: Matthew Hillier for Guinness Publishing)

Smallest ● The falabella of Argentina was developed over a period of 70 years by inbreeding and crossing a small group of undersized horses originally discovered in the southern part of the country. Most adult specimens stand less than 30 in high and average 80–100 lb. Rayford Ely, founder of the Worldwide Miniature Horse Association, can be seen here with 'Playboy,' one of his eight miniature horses. (Photo: Retna)

trainer in the world was Mrs Barbara Woodhouse (1910–88) of Rickmansworth, Hertfordshire, United Kingdom, who trained 19,000 dogs to obey the basic commands during the period 1951 to her retirement in 1985 following a stroke.

Will Markham of the Corley Dog Training Centre in Coventry, United Kingdom trained 140 dogs in five basic obedience commands in 6 hours 55 mins on 3 Dec 1989.

United States ■ The fastest trainer is Mr Armand Rabuttinio of Aston, PA. His highest total for a single day (9 A.M.–6 P.M.) is 132 dogs at a training marathon held at Upland, PA on 12 Jun 1982.

Drug sniffing ■ The greatest drug-sniffing dogs on record are a pair of Malinoises called Rocky and Barco. These Belgian sheepdogs (whelped 1984) are members of an American stop-and-search team that patrols the Rio Grande Valley ('Cocaine Alley') along the southern Texas border. In 1988 alone they were involved in 969 seizures of drugs worth $182 million, and they are so proficient at their job that Mexican drug smugglers have put a $30,000 price on their heads. Rocky and Barco were recently awarded honorary titles of sergeant major and always wear their stripes when they are on duty.

The only drug-sniffing dog with a 100 percent arrest record was a German shepherd of the US Army called General. During the period April 1974 to March 1976 this canine detective and his handler, SP4 Michael R. Harris of the 591st Military Police Company in Fort Bliss, TX, carried out 220 searches for narcotics, arrested 220 people for possession and uncovered 330 caches of drugs.

The German shepherd 'Blue' of the Los Angeles Police Department was reported in January 1986 to have assisted in apprehending 253 suspected felons.

In October 1988 another German shepherd owned by the Essex Police sniffed out 2·2 tons of cannabis worth £6 million when it was sent into a remote cottage on the outskirts of Harlow, Essex, United Kingdom.

CATS

United States feline population for 1989 was 57·9 million, in 27·7 million homes, or 30·0 percent of the population. Cat owners bought 5·5 billion pounds of cat food at a cost of $2·6 billion.

Largest ■ The largest of the 330 breeds of cat is the ragdoll with males weighing 15–20 lb. In the majority of domestic cats (*Felis catus*), the average weight of the male (tom) at maturity is 8·6 lb, compared with 7·2 lb for the adult female or queen. Neuters and spays average out somewhat heavier.

The heaviest domestic cat on record was a neutered male tabby named Himmy, owned by Thomas Vyse of Redlynch, Cairns, Queensland, Australia. At the time of his death (from respiratory failure) on 12 Mar 1986 aged 10 years 4 months he weighed 46 lb 15¼ oz (neck 15 in, waist 33 in, length 38 in).

In Feb 1988 an unconfirmed weight of 48 lb was reported for a cat named Edward Bear, owned by Miss Jackie Fleming of Sydney, New South Wales, Australia.

Smallest ■ The smallest breed of domestic cat is the Singapura or 'Drain Cat' of Singapore. Adult males average 6 lb in weight and adult females 4 lb.

A male Siamese cross named Ebony-Eb-Honey Cat owned by Miss Angelina Johnston of Boise,

ID tipped the scales at only 1 lb 12 oz in February 1984 when aged 23 months.

Oldest ■ Cats are generally longer-lived than dogs. The average life expectancy of entire well-fed males raised under household conditions, and receiving good medical attention, is 13–15 years (15–17 years for intact females), but neutered males and females live on the average one to two years longer.

The oldest cat ever recorded was probably the tabby Puss, owned by Mrs T. Holway of Clayhidon, Devon, United Kingdom, who celebrated his 36th birthday on 28 Nov 1939 and died the next day.

A more recent and better-documented case was that of the female tabby Ma, owned by Mrs Alice St George Moore of Drewsteignton, Devon, United Kingdom. This cat was put to sleep on 5 Nov 1957 aged 34.

Oldest twins ■ The oldest twin cats on record were Beau and Bubbles (b. 17 Oct 1963) owned by Diane Phelps of Dearborn, MI. Bubbles died on 29 Apr 1985 aged 21 years 6 months and Beau was put to sleep on 28 Dec 1985 aged 22 years 2 months. They were longhair and part Persian.

Largest litter ■ A litter of 19 kittens (four stillborn) was delivered by cesarean section to Tarawood Antigone, a four-year-old brown Burmese, on 7 Aug 1970. Her owner, Valerie Gane of Church Westcote, Oxfordshire, United Kingdom, said it was the result of a mis-mating with a half-Siamese. Of the 15 survivors, 14 were males and one female.

The largest live litter (all of which survived) was one of 14 kittens born in December 1974 to a Persian cat named Bluebell, owned by Elenore Dawson of Wellington, Cape Province, South Africa.

Most prolific ■ A tabby named Dusty (b. 1935) living in Bonham, TX produced 420 kittens during her breeding life. She gave birth to her last litter (a single kitten) on 12 Jun 1952.

In May 1987 Kitty, owned by George Johnstone of Croxton, Staffordshire, United Kingdom, produced two kittens at the age of 30 years, making her the oldest feline mother on record. She died in June 1989, just short of her 32nd birthday, having given birth to a known total of 218 kittens.

Most valuable ■ In 1988 Carl Mayes, a breeder in Atlanta, GA turned down an offer of $10,000 for his male Singapura, Bull, the best-known example of its breed in the United States.

When Mrs Grace Alma Patterson of Joplin, MO died in Jan 1978, she left her entire estate worth $250,000 to her 18 lb white alley cat Charlie Chan. When the cat dies, the estate, which includes a three-bedroom house, a 7–acre pet cemetary and a collection of valuable antiques,

will be auctioned off and the proceeds donated to humane societies.

Best climber ■ On 6 Sep 1950 a four-month-old kitten belonging to Josephine Aufdenblatten of Geneva, Switzerland followed a group of climbers up to the top of the 14,691 ft Matterhorn in the Alps.

Mousing champion ■ A female tortoise-shell named Towser (b. 21 Apr 1963) owned by Glenturret Distillery Ltd near Crieff, Tayside, United Kingdom notched up an estimated lifetime score of 28,899. She averaged three mice per day until her death on 20 Mar 1987.

RABBITS AND HARES

Largest ■ The largest breed of domestic rabbit (*Oryctolagus cuniculus*) is the Flemish giant. Adults weigh 15·4–18·7 lb (average toe-to-toe length when fully stretched 36 in), but weights up to 25 lb have been reliably reported for this breed.

In April 1980 a five-month-old French Lop doe weighing 26·45 lb was exhibited at the Reus Fair, northeast Spain.

The heaviest recorded wild rabbit (av. weight 3½ lb) was one of 8 lb 4 oz, killed by Norman Wilkie of Markinch, Fife, United Kingdom while ferreting on 20 Nov 1982.

Smallest ■ The Netherland dwarf and the Polish both have a weight range of 2–2½ lb when fully grown. In 1975 Jacques Bouloc of Coulommière, France announced a new cross of the above breeds that weighed 14 oz.

Most prolific ■ The most prolific domestic breeds are the New Zealand white and the Californian. Does (female rabbits) produce 5–6 litters a year, each containing 8–12 kittens during their breeding life (cf. five litters and three to seven young for the wild rabbit).

Longest ears ■ The longest ears are found in the Lop family (four strains), and in particular the English Lop. The ears of a typical example measure about 24 in from tip to tip (taken across the skull), and 5·51 in in width. In 1901 a specimen was exhibited in Britain that had 30·5 in ears; it is not known, however, if this was a natural attainment or if weights had been used to stretch the ears and left the veins inside badly varicosed.

Largest hare ■ In November 1956 a Brown hare weighing 15 lb 1 oz was shot near Welford, Northamptonshire, United Kingdom. The average adult weight is 8 lb.

> **Oldest caged rat** ● 'Rodney,' (right) born in January 1983 and owned by Rodney Mitchell of Tulsa, OK, is the world's longest lived domestic rat.

CAGED PET LONGEVITY

Animal/Species	Name (Owner), etc.	Years	Months
RABBIT	*Flopsy* caught 6 Aug 1964 d.29 Jun 1983 (L.B. Walker) Longford, Tasmania, Australia	18	10 ¾
GUINEA PIG	*Snowball* d. 14 Feb 1979 (M. A. Wall) Bingham, United Kingdom	14	10 ½
GERBIL Mongolian	*Sahara* May 1973–4 Oct 1981 (Aaron Milstone) Lathrup Village, MI	8	4 ½
MOUSE House	*Fritzy* 11 Sep 1977–24 April 1985 (Bridget Beard) West House School, Birmingham, United Kingdom	7	7
RAT Common	*Rodney* b. January 1983 (Rodney Mitchell) Tulsa, OK	7	1

LARGEST PET LITTERS

Animal/Breed	No.	Owner	Date	
CAT *Burmese/Siamese*	15[1]	Mrs Valerie Gane, Church Westcote, United Kingdom	Aug	1970
DOG *American foxhound*	23[2]	Cdr W. N. Ely, Ambler, PA	Jun	1944
DOG *St. Bernard*	23[3]	R. and A. Rodden, Lebanon, MO	Feb	1975
DOG *Great Dane*	23[4]	Mrs Marjorie Harris, Little Hall, Essex, United Kingdom	Jun	1987
RABBIT *New Zealand white*	24	Joseph Filek, Sydney, Cape Breton, Nova Scotia, Canada		1978
GUINEA PIG (CAVY)	12	Laboratory specimen		1972
HAMSTER *Golden*	26[5]	L. and S. Miller, Baton Rouge, LA	Feb	1974
MOUSE *House*	34[6]	Marion Ogilvie, Blackpool, United Kingdom	Feb	1982
GERBIL *Mongolian*	14[7]	Sharon Kirkman, Bulwell, Nottingham, United Kingdom	May	1983
DOMESTIC FERRET	15	John Cliff, Denstone, Uttoxeter, United Kingdom		1981

[1] 4 stillborn [2] all survived [3] 14 survived [4] 16 survived [5] 18 killed by mother [6] 33 survived [7] Litter of 15 recorded 1960s by George Meares, geneticist-owner of gerbil breeding farm, St. Petersburg, FL. Used special food formula.

Birds *Aves*

Largest ratite ■ The largest living bird is the North African ostrich (*Struthio c. camelus*), which is found in reduced numbers south of the Atlas Mountains from Upper Senegal and Niger across to the Sudan and central Ethiopia. Male examples (adult hens are smaller) of this flightless or ratite subspecies have been recorded up to 9 ft in height and 345 lb in weight.

Largest carinate ■ The world's heaviest flying birds are the Kori bustard or Paauw (*Ardeotis kori*) of eastern South Africa and the great bustard (*Otis tarda*) of Europe and Asia. Weights up to 40 lb have been reported for the former shot in South Africa, and there is an isolated record of 46·2 lb for a cock bird shot in Manchuria that was too heavy to fly. The heaviest great bustard on record weighed 35 lb.

The mute swan (*Cygnus olor*), which is resident in Britain, can reach 40 lb on very rare occasions, and there is a record from Poland of a cob weighing 49·6 lb that had temporarily lost the power of flight.

Bird of prey ■ The heaviest bird of prey is the Andean condor (*Vultur gryphus*), adult males averaging 20–25 lb. A weight of 31 lb has been claimed for an outsized male California condor (*Gymnogyps californianus*) now preserved in the California Academy of Sciences at Los Angeles. This species is appreciably smaller than the Andean condor and rarely exceeds 23 lb.

Largest wingspan ■ The Wandering albatross (*Diomedea exulans*) of the southern oceans has the largest wingspan of any living bird, adult males averaging 10 ft 4 in with wings tightly stretched. The largest recorded specimen was a very old male 11 ft 11 in caught by members of the Antartic research ship USNS *Eltanin* in the Tasman Sea on 18 Sep 1965. Unconfirmed measurements up to 13 ft 10 in have been claimed for this species.

The only other bird reliably credited with a wingspan in excess of 11 ft is the vulture-like marabou stork (*Leptoptilus crumeniferus*) of tropical Africa. In 1934 an extreme measurement of 13 ft 4 in was reported for a male shot in central Africa by naturalist Richard Meinertzhagen (1879–1967), but this species rarely exceeds 9 ft.

Smallest ■ The smallest bird in the world is the bee hummingbird (*Mellisuga helenae*) of Cuba and the Isle of Pines. Adult males (females are slightly larger) measure 2·24 in in total length, half of which is taken up by the bill and tail. It weighs 0·056 oz, which means it is lighter than a privet hawkmoth (*Sphinx ligustri*) 0·084 oz (see smallest nest).

The smallest bird of prey is the 1·23 oz white-fronted falconet (*Microhierax latifrons*) of north-western Borneo, which is sparrow-sized.

The smallest seabird is the least storm petrel (*Halocyptena microsoma*), which breeds on many of the small islands in the Gulf of California, northwestern Mexico. Adult specimens average 5½ in in total length and weigh *c.* 1 oz.

The world's smallest species of duck is the Indian cotton teal, or Indian pygmy goose (*Nettapus coromandelianus*), found in freshwater habitats of tropical Asia and northeastern Australia. The adult bird is 12–14 in and the drake weighs on average 13·4 oz. In September 1989 the first ever captive breeding of this duck was achieved at the Pensthorpe Waterfowl Trust in Fakenham, Norfolk, United Kingdom when two eggs, removed to the safety of an incubator after being laid in the same tree hole as the eggs of the related African pygmy goose, were successfully hatched.

United States ■ The smallest American bird is the calliope hummingbird (*Stellula calliope*). Adult specimans measure 2 ¾–3 ½ in from bill to tail with a wingspan of 4 ½ in and an approximate weight of 1/10th of an ounce. The calliope is found in the western United States.

Most abundant ■ *Wild bird* ■ The Red-billed quelea (*Quelea quelea*), a seed-eating weaver of the drier parts of Africa south of the Sahara, has an estimated adult breeding population of 1·5 billion and at least 1 billion of these 'feathered locusts' are slaughtered annually without having any impact on the population. One huge roost in the Sudan contained 32 million birds.

Seabird ■ The most abundant is probably the very small Wilson's storm petrel (*Oceanites oceanicus*), which breeds on the Antarctic continent and adjacent sub-Antarctic islands. No population estimates have been published, but the numbers must run into hundreds of millions.

Domesticated bird ■ The most abundant species is the chicken, the tame version of the wild red jungle fowl (*Gallus gallus*) of Southeast Asia. According to the FAO (Food and Agriculture Organization of the United Nations), the world's chicken population stood at 8,295,760,000 in 1985, which means there are 1·6 chickens for every member of the human race.

United States ■ The red-winged blackbird (*Agelaius phoeniceus*) had a population of 25·6 million birds as of Jan 1983. The US Fish & Wildlife Office estimates the current total is at least 30 million. The blackbird is found throughout the country, except for desert and mountainous regions.

Largest ratite ● The largest living bird is the North African ostrich (*Struthio camelus camelus*). The average adult male (seen here with the black-and-white plumage) of this flightless or ratite subspecies can reach 9 ft in height and weigh up to 345 lb. In spite of its bulk, a startled ostrich can run at up to 40 mph and delivers a vicious kick if cornered. (Photo: Jacana)

Rarest ■ The number of threatened bird species worldwide has risen in the past 10 years from 290 to 1,029 as a result of human activity, according to a survey published in October 1988. Because of the practical difficulties in assessing bird populations in the wild, it is virtually impossible to establish the identity of the world's rarest living bird.

The world's rarest, most restricted and most endangered bird is now probably the Aldabra brush warbler (*Nesillas aldabrabus*). Not discovered until 1967, five individuals (three males and two females) were ringed between July 1974 and February 1977. One of the males was re-sighted in 1978 and again in September 1983, but this was the last confirmed record. This species is restricted to a coastal strip 1·24 miles

long and 162 ft wide on the northern tip of Aldabra Atoll in the Indian Ocean.

The strongest contender, up until very recently, was the dusky seaside sparrow (*Ammospiza nigrescens*), formerly of Titusville Marshes, FL, but the last known example (a male) died at Discovery Island, Disney World, Orlando, FL on 16 May 1987. Some of its tissue has been frozen in the hope that future technology might allow a pure strain of dusky seaside sparrow to be resurrected through genetic cloning.

The Guam flycatcher (*Myiagra freycineti*) and the Rufous fantail (*Rhipidura rufifrons*), also of Guam, were last seen in 1984 and may now also be extinct.

The Guam rail (*Rallus owstons*) has only been sighted three times since 1985.

The oa (*Moho braccatus*) of Kauai in the Hawaiian Islands, reportedly extinct, was rediscovered in 1960 in the mountain rain forests of the Alahari swamp. Its nest was found in 1979 and it was seen again in 1981. It is now protected and there may be one or two pairs left.

The crested shellduck (*Tadorna cristata*) is known from only three specimens. The last sighting was in 1971 but it may still survive in

the remoter Japanese coastal regions or in adjacent waters.

The imperial woodpecker (*Campephilus imperiali*) of Mexico has not been sighted since 1958 on the Sonora-Chihuahua border, but there were unconfirmed reports from southwest Chihuahua in 1977.

The Socorro dove (*Zenaida graysoni*) of Socorro Island off the west coast of Mexico is now extinct in the wild and survives only in captivity.

The Itombwe owl is known only from the type specimen collected in 1951 while sleeping in long grass high in the Itombwe mountains, eastern Zaïre, and the Kibale groundthrush (*Turdus kibalensis*) of western Uganda is known only from two males collected in 1966.

The sea-cliff swallow (*Hirunda perdita*) is known only from a dead specimen found on an islet off Port Sudan in 1984 and has not been recorded since.

In 1979 the Chatham Island black robin (*Petroica traversi*) was another bird on the verge of extinction, with only five surviving. By a pioneering method of cross-fostering the chicks of this wild songbird with local tom tits, however, members of the New Zealand Wildlife Service managed to increase the population to 38 by 1984. There are now over 100 of these robins spread throughout several islands. Another remarkable fact is that every living example of this species is descended from the female known as 'Old Blue.' She lived for *c.* 14 years (over twice the normal lifespan) and remained fertile right to the end. The death of this amazing little bird was officially announced in New Zealand Parliament and her body has been preserved in a museum.

Spix's macaw (*Cyanopsitta spixii*) of Brazil, the world's most endangered parrot, became extinct in the wild *c.* 1988. There are only ten left in captivity, eight of them in Brazil.

United States ■ Under the California Condor Recovery Program administered by the US Fish & Wildlife Service, all condors were captured and placed in captivity. Seven birds were captured between 25 Jun 1985 and 19 Apr 1987, with the last wild California condor (*Gymnogyps californianus*) captured in Kern County, CA, to join 26 others held for captive breeding in San Diego Wildlife Park and Los Angeles Zoo. On 29 Apr 1988 the first California condor ever born in captivity was successfully hatched out at San Diego Wildlife Park and the chick was fed successfully for six months with condor hand puppets. As of March 1990 there were 35 specimens in captivity. It is hoped that these birds can be released back into the wild at some point.

The ivory-billed woodpecker and the Bachman's warbler have not been seen in at least three decades but are not yet considered extinct.

The Eskimo curlew has not had a verifiable sighting in several decades, but there have been unverified reports at regular intervals in recent years.

After more than three decades, federal officials may remove the bald eagle from the endangered species list, as the official symbol of the nation is no longer in immediate risk of extinction. In 1974 there were fewer than 791 nesting pairs in the lower 48 states; as of March 1990 there are now more than 2,660 pairs. A 1989 survey by the National Wildlife Federation lists the bald eagle population, including immature birds, at 11,610. The US government has spent about $25 million helping the bald eagle recover. The five states which would move the bald eagle to the threat-

ened list, one step down from endangered, include Washington, Oregon, Minnesota, Wisconsin, and Michigan.

Fastest flying ■ The fastest creature on the wing is the peregrine falcon (*Falco peregrinus*) when stooping from great heights during territorial displays. In one series of German experiments, a velocity of 168 mph was recorded at a 30° angle of stoop, rising to a maximum of 217 mph at an angle of 45°.

The white-throated spinetail swift (*Hirundapus caudacutus*) of Asia and the alpine swift (*Apus melba*) are also extremely fast during courtship display flights, and the former has been timed at speeds up to 105·6 mph in tests carried out in the USSR.

The fastest fliers in level flight are found among the ducks and geese (*Anatidae*), and some powerful species such as the red-breasted merganser (*Mergus serrator*), the eider (*Somateria mollissima*), the canvasback (*Aythya valisineria*) and the spur-winged goose (*Plectropterus gambiensis*) can probably exceed an air speed of 65 mph.

Air speeds up to 70 mph have been claimed for the golden plover (*Pluvialis apricaria*) fed flushed, but it is very doubtful whether this rapid-flying bird can exceed 50–55 mph — even in an emergency.

United States ■ America's fastest bird is the white-throated swift (*Aeronautes saxatilis*), which has been estimated to fly at speeds of 200 mph. The peregrine falcon (*Falco peregrinus*) has been credited with a speed of 175 mph while in a dive. The dunlin (*Calidris alpina*) has been clocked from a plane at 110 mph.

Slowest flying ■ Probably at least 50 percent of the world's flying birds cannot exceed an air speed of 40 mph in level flight. The slowest flying bird is the American woodcock (*Scolopax minor*), which has been timed at 5 mph without sinking during courtship flights.

Fastest Running ■ It is claimed that the wild turkey (*Meleagris gallopavo*) can reach speeds of 30 mph.

Fastest wing beat ■ The wing beat of the horned sungem (*Heliactin cornuta*) of tropical South America has a rate of 90 beats per sec.

Longest-lived ■ The greatest irrefutable age reported for any bird is 80+ years for a male sulphur-crested cockatoo (*Cacatua galerita*) named Cocky, who died at London Zoo, United Kingdom in 1982. He was presented to the zoo in 1925, and had been with his previous owner since 1902 when he was already fully mature.

In 1987 an unconfirmed age of *c.* 82 years was reported for a male Siberian white crane (*Crus leucogeranus*) named Wolfe at the International Crane Foundation, Baraboo, WI. The bird was said to have hatched out in a zoo in Switzerland *c.* 1905. He died in late 1988 after breaking his bill while repelling a visitor near his pen.

In 1964 the death was reported of a male Andean

condor called Kuzya at Moscow Zoo, USSR, aged 72+ years. As this bird was already fully grown when it was received in 1892, it must have been at least 77.

The oldest ringed seabird on record is a female royal albatross (*Diomedea epomophora*) named Grandma ('Blue White'), who laid another egg at Taiaroa Head, near Dunedin, South Island, New Zealand in November 1988, aged 60 years. She was banded for the first time in 1937 when she was a breeding adult, and such birds do not start breeding until they are nine years old. Since then she has raised ten chicks of her own and fostered three others. Her mate, Green White Green, is 47.

Longest flights ■ The greatest distance covered by a ringed bird is 14,000 miles by an arctic tern (*Sterna paradisea*), which was banded as a nestling on 5 Jul 1955 in the Kandalaksha Sanctuary on the White Sea coast and was captured alive by a fisherman 8 miles south of Fremantle, Western Australia on 16 May 1956. The bird had flown south via the Atlantic Ocean and then circled Africa before crossing the Indian Ocean. It did not survive to make the return journey. There is also another report of an arctic tern flying from Greenland to Australasia, but further details are lacking.

In 1990 six foraging Wandering albatrosses (*Diomedea exulans*) were tracked across the Indian Ocean by satellite via radio transmitters fitted by Pierre Jouventin and Henri Weimerskirch of the National Centre for Scientific Research at Beauvoir, France. Results showed that the birds covered between 2,237 and 9,321 miles in a single feeding trip and that they easily maintained a speed of 35 mph over a distance of more than 498 miles, with the males going to sea for up to 33 days while their partners remained ashore to incubate the eggs.

Highest flying ■ Most migrating birds fly at relatively low altitudes (i.e. below 300 ft) and it is only a few dozen species that fly higher than 3,000 ft.

The highest acceptable altitude recorded for a bird is 37,000 ft for a Ruppell's vulture (*Gyps rueppellii*), which collided with a commercial aircraft over Abidjan, Ivory Coast, West Africa, on 29 Nov 1973. The impact damaged one of the aircraft's engines, causing it to shut down, but the plane landed safely without further incident. Sufficient feather remains of the bird were recovered to allow the Museum of Natural History to make a positive identification of this high-flier, which is rarely seen above 20,000 ft.

United States ■ The highest verified altitude record for a bird in America is 21,000 ft for a mallard (*Meleagris gallopavo*) that collided with a commericial jet on 9 Jul 1963 over Nevada. The jet crashed killing all aboard.

Most airborne ■ The most aerial of all

Rarest bird ● The last wild California condor (*Gymnogyps californianus*) was captured on 19 Apr 1987 in Kern County, CA to join 26 others held for captive breeding in San Diego Wildlife Park and Los Angeles Zoo. On 29 Apr 1988 the first California condor born in captivity was hatched out at San Diego Wildlife Park and the chick was fed successfully for six months by handlers using condor hand puppets to simulate the parent birds. (Photo: Jacana)

birds is the sooty tern (*Sterna fuscata*), which, after leaving the nesting grounds, remains continuously aloft from three to ten years as a sub-adult, before returning to land to breed.

The most aerial land bird is the common swift (*Apus apus*), which remains airborne for two to three years, during which time it sleeps, drinks, eats and even mates on the wing.

Fastest swimmer ■ The gentoo penguin (*Pygoscelis papua*) has a maximum burst speed of *c*. 17 mph.

Deepest dive ■ In 1969 a depth of 870 ft was recorded for a small group of ten emperor penguins (*Aptenodytes forsteri*) at Cape Crozier, Antarctica by a team of American scientists. One bird remained submerged for 18 minutes.

Vision ■ Birds of prey (Falconiformes) have the keenest eyesight in the avian world, and large species with eyes similar in size to those of man have visual acuity at least two times stronger than human vision. It has also been calculated that a large eagle can detect a target object at a distance 3–8 times greater than that achieved by man.

Thus the golden eagle (*Aquila chrysaetos*) can detect an 18 in-long hare at a range of 2 miles in good light and against a contrasting background, and a peregrine falcon (*Falco peregrinus*) can spot a pigeon at a range of over 5 miles.

In experiments carried out on the Tawny owl (*Strix aluco*) at the University of Birmingham, West Midlands, United Kingdom in 1977, it was revealed that the bird's eye on average was only 2½ times more sensitive than the human eye. It was also discovered that the Tawny owl sees perfectly adequately in daylight and that its visual acuity is only slightly inferior to that of the human.

G force ■ American experiments have revealed that the beak of the red-headed woodpecker (*Melanerpes erythrocephalus*) hits the bark of a tree with an impact velocity of 13 mph. This means that when the head snaps back the brain is subject to a deceleration of about 0.35 oz.

Longest feathers ■ The longest feathers grown by any bird are those of the phoenix fowl or Onagadori (a strain of red junglefowl *Gallus gallus*), which has been bred in southwestern Japan since the mid-17th century. In 1972 a tail covert measuring 34 ft 9½ in was reported for a rooster owned by Masasha Kubota of Kochi, Shikoku, Japan.

Among flying birds the tail feathers of the male crested pheasant (*Rheinhartia ocellata*) of Southeast Asia regularly reach 5 ft 8 in in length and 5 in wide, and the central tail feathers of the Reeves' pheasant (*Syrmaticus reevesi*) of central and northern China have exceptionally reached 8 ft.

Most and least feathers ■ In a series of 'feather counts' on various species of bird a Whistling swan (*Cygnus columbianus*) was found to have 25,216 feathers, 20,177 of which were on the head and neck. The ruby-throated hummingbird (*Archilochus colubris*) has only 940.

Largest egg ■ The average ostrich (*Struthio camelus*) egg measures 6–8 in in length,

Fastest flying ● The fastest creature on the wing is the endangered peregrine falcon (*Falco peregrinus*) when stooping from great heights during territorial displays. A velocity of 168 mph at a 30° angle of stoop, rising to a maximum of 217 mph at 45° was registered in a series of German experiments carried out *c*. 1968. (Photo: Jacana)

4–6 in in diameter and weighs 3·63–3·88 lb (around two dozen hens' eggs in volume). It requires about 40 min for boiling. The shell, though 0·059 in thick, can support the weight of a 279.9 lb man.

On 28 Jun 1988 a two-year-old cross between a northern and a southern ostrich (*Struthio c. camelus*) × (*Struthio c. australis*) laid an egg weighing a record 5·07 lb at the Kibbutz Ha'on collective farm, Israel.

United States ■ The largest egg laid by any bird on the American list is that of the trumpeter swan, which measures 4·3 in in length, and 2·8 in in diameter. The average California condor egg measures 4·3 in in length, 2·6 in diameter and weighs 9·5 oz.

Smallest egg ■ The smallest egg laid by any bird is that of the vervain hummingbird (*Mellisuga minima*) of Jamaica. Two specimens measuring less than 0·39 in in length weighed 0·0128 oz and 0·0132 oz respectively.

United States ■ The smallest egg laid by a bird on the American list is that of the Costa hummingbird (*Calypte coastae*), which measures 0·48 in in length , 0·33 in in diameter and weighs 0·017 oz.

Longest incubation ■ The longest normal incubation period is that of the wandering albatross (*Diomedea exulans*), with a normal range of 75–82 days.

There is an isolated case of an egg of the mallee fowl (*Leipoa ocellata*) of Australia taking 90 days to hatch against its normal incubation of 62 days.

Shortest incubation ■ The shortest incubation period is the 10 days of the Great spotted woodpecker (*Dendrocopus major*) and the Blackbilled cuckoo (*Coccyzus erythropthalmus*).

The idlest of cock birds include hummingbirds (family Trochilidae), eider duck (*Somateria mollissima*) and golden pheasant (*Chrysolophus pictus*), among which the hen bird does 100 percent of the incubation, whereas the female Common kiwi (*Apteryx australis*) leaves this to the male for 75–80 days.

Longest bills ■ The bill of the Australian pelican (*Pelicanus conspicillatus*) measures 13·3–18·5 in long.

The longest bill in relation to overall body length is that of the sword-billed hummingbird (*Ensifera ensifera*) of the Andes from Venezuela to Bolivia. It measures 4 in in length and is longer than the bird's actual body if the tail is excluded.

Shortest bills ■ The shortest bills in relation to body length are found among the smaller swifts (*Apodidae*) and in particular that of the glossy swiftlet (*Collocalia esculenta*), which is almost nonexistent.

Bird-watcher ■ The world's leading bird-watcher or 'twitcher' is Harvey Gilston (b. 12 Oct 1922) of Lausanne, Switzerland, who had logged 6,713 of the 9,016 known species by 10 Apr 1990.

The greatest number of species spotted in a 24-hour period is 342, by Kenyans Terry Stevenson, John Fanshawe and Andy Roberts on day two of the Birdwatch Kenya '86 event held on 29–30 Nov.

The 48-hour record is held by Don Turner and David Pearson of Kenya, who spotted 494 species at the same event.

Peter Kaestner of Washington, DC was the first person to see at least one species of each of the world's 159 bird families. He saw his final family on 1 Oct 1986. Since then Dr Ira Abramson of North Miami, FL and Dr Martin Edwards have also succeeded in this achievement.

Largest nest ■ A nest measuring 9½ ft wide, 20 ft deep was built by a pair of bald eagles (*Haliaeetus leucocephalus*) and possibly their successors near St. Petersburg, FL. It was examined in 1963 and was estimated to weigh more than 2.2 tons.

The golden eagle (*Aquila chrysaetos*) also constructs huge nests, and one 15 ft deep was reported from Scotland in 1954. It had been used for 45 years.

The incubation mounds built by the mallee fowl (*Leipoa ocellata*) of Australia are much larger, having been measured up to 15 ft in height and 35 ft across, and it has been calculated that the

nest site may involve the mounding of 900 ft³ of matter weighing 330 tons.

Smallest nest ■ The smallest nests are built by hummingbirds (*Trochilidae*). That of the vervain hummingbird (*Mellisuga minima*) is about half the size of a walnut, while the deeper one of the bee hummingbird (*M. helenea*) is thimble-sized.

DOMESTICATED BIRDS

Earliest ■ The earliest domesticated bird was the greylag goose (*Anser*) of the Neolithic period (20,000 years ago) of southeastern Europe and Asia Minor.

Oldest ■ The longest-lived domesticated bird (excluding the ostrich, which has lived up to 68 years) is the domestic goose (*Anser anser domesticus*), which normally lives about 25 years. On 16 Dec 1976 a gander named George, owned by Florence Hull of Thornton, Lancashire, United Kingdom died aged 49 years 8 months. He was hatched out in April 1927.

The longest-lived small cagebird is the canary (*Serinus canaria*). The oldest example on record was a 34-year-old cock bird named Joey, owned by Mrs K. Ross of Hull, United Kingdom. The bird was purchased in Calabar, Nigeria in 1941 and died on 8 Apr 1975.

The oldest budgerigar (*Melopsittacus undulatus*) was a hen bird named Charlie, owned by Miss J. Dinsey of Stonebridge, London, United Kingdom, which died on 20 Jun 1977 aged 29 years 2 months.

Most talkative ■ A number of birds are renowned for their talking ability (i.e. the reproduction of words) but the African gray parrot (*Psittacus erythacus*) reigns supreme in this department.

A female specimen named Prudle, formerly owned by Lyn Logue (died January 1988) and now in the care of Iris Frost of Seaford, East Sussex, United Kingdom, won the Best Talking Parrot-like Bird title at the National Cage and Aviary Bird Show in London, United Kingdom each December for 12 consecutive years (1965–76). Prudle, who has a vocabulary of nearly 800 words, was taken from a nest at Jinja, Uganda in 1958. She retired undefeated.

Reptiles *Reptilia*

(Crocodiles, snakes, turtles, tortoises, lizards)

CROCODILIANS

Largest ■ The largest reptile in the world is the estuarine or saltwater crocodile (*Crocodylus porosus*) of Southeast Asia, the Malay Archipelago, Indonesia, northern Australia, Papua New Guinea, Vietnam and the Philippines. Adult males average 14–16 ft in length and scale about 900–1,150 lb.

At the present time there are four protected estuarine crocodiles at the Bhitarkanika Wildlife Sanctuary, Orissa State, eastern India that measure more than 19 ft 8 in in length. The largest individual is over 23 ft long.

Captive ■ The largest crocodile ever held in captivity is an estuarine/Siamese hybrid named Yai (b. 10 Jun 1972) at the Samutprakarn Crocodile Farm and Zoo, Thailand. He measures 19 ft 8 in in length and weighs 2,465 lb.

Smallest ■ Osborn's dwarf crocodile (*Osteolaemus osborni*), found in the upper region of the Congo River, West Africa rarely exceeds 3 ft 11 in in length.

Oldest ■ The greatest age authenticated for a crocodilian is 66 years for a female American alligator (*Alligator mississipiensis*) which arrived at Adelaide Zoo, South Australia, on 5 Jun 1914 as a two-year-old, and died there on 26 Sep 1978 aged 66 years.

Another female of this species named Smiley at the Maritime Museum Aquarium, Gothenburg, Sweden, died on 10 Feb 1987 aged 65 years after the electricity heating its pool was accidentally turned down.

Rarest ■ The total population of the protected Chinese alligator (*Alligator sinensis*) of the lower Chang Jiang (Yangtse Kiang) River of Anhui, Zhejiang and Jiangsu Provinces, is currently estimated at 700–1,000 individuals.

LIZARDS

Largest ■ The largest of all lizards is the Komodo monitor or Ora (*Varanus komodoensis*), a dragonlike reptile found on the Indonesian islands of Komodo, Rintja, Padar and Flores. Adult males average 7 ft 5 in in length and weigh about 130 lb. Lengths up to 30 ft (*sic*) have been claimed for this species, but the largest specimen to be accurately measured was a male presented to an American zoologist in 1928 by the Sultan of Bima that measured 10 ft 0·8 in. In 1937 this animal was put on display in St Louis Zoological Gardens, MO for a short period. It then measured 10 ft 2 in in length and weighed 365 lb.

The longest lizard in the world is the slender Salvadori monitor (*Varanus salvadori*) of Papua New Guinea, which has been reliably measured up to 15 ft 7 in. Nearly 70 percent of the total length, however, is taken up by the tail.

Smallest ■ *Sphaerodactylus parthenopion*, a tiny gecko indigenous to the island of Virgin Gorda, one of the British Virgin Islands, is believed to be the world's smallest lizard. It is known only from 15 specimens, including some gravid females found between 10 and 16 Aug 1964. The three largest females measured 0·67 in from snout to vent, with a tail of approximately the same length.

It is possible that another gecko, *S. elasmorhynchus*, may be even smaller. The only known specimen was an apparently mature female with a snout-vent length of 0·67 in and a tail of the same measurement. It was found on 15 Mar 1966 among the roots of a tree in the western part of the Massif de la Hotte in Haiti.

Oldest ■ The greatest age recorded for a lizard is more than 54 years for a male slow worm (*Anguis fragilis*) kept in the Zoological Museum in Copenhagen, Denmark from 1892 until 1946.

Fastest ■ The highest speed measured for any reptile on land is 18 mph for a six-lined race runner (*Cnemidophorus sexlineatus*) near McCormick, SC, in 1941.

CHELONIANS

Largest ■ The largest living chelonian is the leatherback turtle (*Dermochelys coriacea*), which is circumglobal in distribution. The average adult measures 6–7 ft from the tip of the beak to the end of the tail (carapace 5–5½ ft), about 7 ft across the front flippers and weighs anything up to 1,000 lb.

The greatest weight reliably recorded is 1,908 lb for a male captured off Monterey, CA on 29 Aug 1961, which measured 8 ft 4 in overall.

The largest leatherback turtle ever recorded is a male found washed ashore at Harlech, Gwynedd, United Kingdom on 23 Sep 1988. It measured 9 ft 5½ in in total length over the carapace (nose to tail), 9 ft across the front flippers, and tipped the scales at an astonishing 2,016 lb. It was put on public display at the National Museum of Wales, in Cardiff, United Kingdom on 16 Feb 1990. Most museums refuse to exhibit large turtles because they can drip oil for up to 50 years.

Tortoise ■ The largest living tortoise is the Aldabra giant tortoise (*Geochelone gigantea*) of the Indian Ocean islands of Aldabra, Mauritius and the Seychelles (introduced 1874).

A male named Esmerelda, a longtime resident on Bird Island in the Seychelles, recorded a weight of 657 lb on 26 Feb 1989.

Smallest ■ The smallest marine turtle in the world is the Atlantic ridley (*Lepidochelys kempii*), which has a shell length of 19·7–27·6 in and does not exceed 80 lb.

Longest lived ■ The greatest authentic age recorded for a tortoise is over 152 years for a male Marion's tortoise (*Testudo sumeirii*), brought from the Seychelles to Mauritius in 1766 by the Chevalier de Fresne, who presented it to the Port Louis army garrison. This specimen (it went blind in 1908) was accidentally killed in 1918.

The greatest proven age of a continuously observed tortoise is more than 116 years for a Mediterranean spur-thighed tortoise (*Testudo graeca*).

The oldest turtle on record was an alligator snapping turtle (*Macrochelys temminckii*) at Philadelphia Zoo, PA. When it was accidentally killed on 7 Feb 1949 it was 58 years 9 months 1 day.

Fastest ■ The highest speed claimed for any reptile in water is 22 mph by a frightened Pacific leatherback turtle.

Slowest ■ In a recent 'speed' test carried out in the Seychelles a male giant tortoise (*Geochelone gigantea*) could cover only 15 ft in 43·5 sec (0·23 mph) despite the enticement of a female.

Deepest dive ■ In May 1987 it was reported by Dr Scott Eckert that a leatherback turtle (*Dermochelys coriacea*) fitted with a pressure-sensitive recording device had dived to a depth of 3,973 ft off the Virgin Islands in the West Indies.

Rarest ■ The world's rarest chelonian is the protected short-necked swamp tortoise (*Pseudemydura umbrina*), which is confined to Ellen Brook and Twin reserves near Perth, Western Australia. The total wild population is now only 20–25, with another 22 held at Perth Zoo.

SNAKES

Longest ■ The reticulated python (*Python reticulatus*) of Southeast Asia, Indonesia and the Philippines, regularly exceeds 20 ft 6 in. In 1912 a specimen measuring 32 ft 9½ in was shot near a mining camp on the north coast of Celebes in the Malay Archipelago.

Captive ■ The longest (and heaviest) snake ever held in captivity was a female reticulated python named Colossus who died in Highland Park Zoo, PA on 15 Apr 1963. She measured 28 ft 6 in in length, and scaled 320 lb at her heaviest.

United States ■ Three species in the Southeast have average measurements of 8 ft 6 in. These include the indigo snake (*Drymarchon corais*) the eastern coachwhip (*Masticophis flagellum*) and the black ratsnake (*Elaphe obsoleta*). The indigo snake has been measured at 8 ft 7½ in.

Shortest ■ The shortest snake in the world is the very rare thread snake (*Leptotyphlops bilineata*), which is known only from the islands

of Martinique, Barbados and St Lucia in the West Indies. In one series of eight specimens the two longest both measured 4·25 in.

Heaviest ■ The anaconda (*Eunectes murinus*) of tropical South America and Trinidad is nearly twice as heavy as a reticulated python (*Python reticulatus*) of the same length. A female shot in Brazil *c.* 1960 was not weighed, but as it measured 27 ft 9 in in length with a girth of 44 in it must have scaled nearly 500 lb. The average adult length is 18–20 ft.

The heaviest venomous snake is probably the eastern diamondback rattlesnake (*Crotalus adamanteus*) of the southeastern United States. One specimen measuring 7 ft 9 in in length weighed 34 lb. Adult examples average 5–6 ft in length and scale 12–15 lb.

The western diamondback rattlesnake (*C. atrox*) of the southwestern United States is second to the eastern diamondback in terms of size and a 7 ft 5 in example weighed 24 lb.

The West African gaboon viper (*Bitis gabonica*) of the tropical rain forests is probably bulkier than this rattlesnake, but its average length is only 4–5 ft. A 6 ft long female weighed 25 lb and another female measuring 5 ft 8½ in scaled 18 lb with an empty stomach.

In Feb 1973 a posthumous weight of 28 lb was reported for a 14 ft 5 in long king cobra (*Ophiophagus hannah*) at New York Zoological Park (Bronx Zoo), NY. It had been ill for some time.

Oldest ■ The greatest irrefutable age recorded for a snake is 40 years 3 months and 14 days for a male Common boa (*Boa constrictor constrictor*) named Popeye who died at Philadelphia Zoo, PA on 15 Apr 1977.

Fastest ■ The fastest-moving land snake is probably the slender black mamba (*Dendroaspis polylepis*) of the eastern part of tropical Africa. It is thought that speeds of 10–12 mph may be possible for short bursts over level ground.

Most venomous ■ The sea snake (*Hydrophis belcheri*) has a myotoxic venom a hundred times as toxic as that of the Australian taipan (*Oxyuranus scutellatus*). The snake abounds round Ashmore Reef in the Timor Sea, off the coast of northwest Australia.

The most venomous land snake is the 6 ft 6¾ in long smooth-scaled snake (*Parademansia micro-*

Heaviest ● The giant anaconda, or great water boa (*Eunectus murinus*), can be almost twice as heavy as a reticulated python (*Python reticulatus*) of the same length. A female shot in Brazil *c.* 1960 was not weighed but, as it measured 27 ft 9 in in length with a girth of 44 in, it must have scaled nearly 500 lb. This specimen was captured near the Xingu River, Brazil by members of the Suia tribe. (Photo: ZEFA)

lepidotus) of the Diamantina River and Cooper's Creek drainage basins in Channel County, Queensland and western New South Wales, which has a venom nine times as toxic as that of the tiger snake (*Notechis scutatus*) of South Australia and Tasmania. One specimen yielded 0·00385 oz of venom after milking, a quantity sufficient to kill 125,000 mice, but so far no human fatalities have been reported.

More people die of snakebite in Sri Lanka than any comparable area in the world. An average of 800 people are killed annually on the island by snakes, and and more than 95 percent of the fatalities are caused by the common krait (*Bungarus caeruleus*), the Sri Lankan cobra (*Naja naja naja*) and Russell's viper (*Vipera russelli pulchella*).

The saw-scaled or carpet viper (*Echis carinatus*) bites and kills more people in the world than any

Rarest ● The total population of the St. Lucia racer (*Liophis ornatus*), which now inhabits only Maria Island (24·71 acres), off St. Lucia, West Indies, following the introduction of rats and mongooses on St Lucia itself, was estimated to be 50–100 in 1989. (Photo: Dr David Corke)

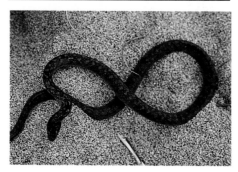

other species. Its geographical range extends from West Africa to India.

United States ■ The most venomous snake in the United States is the coral snake (*Micrurus fulvius*). In a standard LD99-100 test, which kills 99-100 percent of all mice injected with the venom, it takes 0·55 grain of venom per 2·2 lbs of mouse weight injected intravenously. In this test, the smaller the dosage, the more toxic the venom. However, the teeth of the coral snake point back into its mouth, and its venom cannot be injected until the snake has a firm hold on its victim.

Longest venomous ■ The longest venomous snake in the world is the king cobra (*Ophiophagus hannah*), also called the Hamadryad, of Southeast Asia and the Philippines, which has an average adult length of 12–15 ft. An 18 ft 2 in specimen, captured alive near Fort Dickson in the state of Negri Sembilan, Malaya in April 1937, later grew to 18 ft 9 in in London Zoo, United Kingdom. It was destroyed at the outbreak of war in 1939.

Shortest venomous ■ The Namaqua dwarf adder (*Bitis schneider*) of Namibia, Southwest Africa has an average adult length of 7·87 in.

Longest fangs ■ The longest fangs of any snake are those of the highly venomous gaboon viper (*Bitis gabonica*) of tropical Africa. In a 6 ft long specimen they measured 1·96 in. On 12 Feb 1963 a gaboon viper under severe stress sank its fangs into its own back at Philadelphia Zoo, PA and died as a result from traumatic injury to a vital organ. It did not, as has been widely reported, succumb to its own venom.

Rarest ■ Following a successful conservation campaign and captive breeding of the keel-scaled boa of Round Island, its place as the world's rarest snake has been taken by the St Lucia racer or couresse (*Liophis ornatus*), which inhabits only Maria Island, off St Lucia, West Indies. Estimates by Dr David Corke of the Polytechnic of East London, United Kingdom put its population at under 100 in 1989, with no specimens held in captivity.

The Round Island boa (*Bolyeria multicarinata*) is only known from two specimens collected in the past 40 years and probably became extinct in 1980.

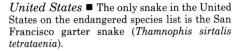

United States ■ The only snake in the United States on the endangered species list is the San Francisco garter snake (*Thamnophis sirtalis tetrataenia*).

Amphibians
Amphibia

Largest ■ The largest species of amphibian is the Chinese giant salamander (*Andrias davidianus*), which lives in northeastern, central and southern China. The average adult measures 3 ft 9 in in length and weighs 55–66 lb. One specimen collected in Hunan province measured 5 ft 11 in in length and scaled 143 lb.

Smallest ■ The smallest known amphibian is the tiny Cuban frog *Sminthillus limbatus*, which is less than ½ in long.

Oldest ■ The greatest authentic age recorded for an amphibian is 55 years for a Japanese giant salamander that died in Amsterdam Zoo, Netherlands in 1881.

Longest gestation ■ The viviparous alpine black salamander (*Salamandra atra*) has a gestation period of up to 38 months at altitudes above 4,600 ft in the Swiss Alps, but this drops to 24–26 months at lower altitudes.

Rarest ■ Only five specimens of the Israel painted frog (*Discoglossus nigriventer*) of Lake Huleh have been reported since 1940.

Highest and lowest ■ The greatest altitude at which an amphibian has been found is 26,246 ft for a common toad (*Bufo bufo*) collected in the Himalayas. This species has also been found at a depth of 1,115 ft in a coal mine.

Most poisonous ■ The most active known poison is the batrachotoxin derived from the skin secretions of the golden poison-dart frog (*Phyllobates terribilis*) of western Colombia, which was not discovered until 1973. Its skin secretions are at least 20 times more toxic than those of any other known dart-poison frog (human handlers have to wear thick gloves), and an average adult specimen contains enough poison (0·000067 oz) to kill nearly 1,500 people. Rather surprisingly, this species is preyed upon by the frog-eating snake (*Leimadophis epinephelus*), which is thought to be immune to its poison.

Largest frog ■ The largest known frog is the rare African giant frog or goliath frog (*Conrana goliath*) of Cameroon and Equatorial Guinea. A specimen captured in April 1989 on the Sanaga River, Cameroon by Andy Koffman of Seattle, WA had a snout-to-vent length of 14·5 in (34·5 in overall with legs extended) and weighed 129 oz on 30 Oct 1989.

Smallest frog ■ The smallest frog in the world is *Sminthillus limbatus* of Cuba. (See Smallest amphibian.)

Longest jump ■ (*Competition frog jumps are invariably the aggregate of three consecutive leaps.*)

The greatest distance covered by a frog in a triple jump is 33 ft 5½ in by a South African sharp-nosed frog (*Ptychadena oxyrhynchus*) named Santjie at a frog derby held at Lurula Natal Spa, Paulpietersburg, Natal, South Africa on 21 May 1977.

At the annual Calaveras Jumping Jubilee held at Angels Camp, CA on 18 May 1986, an American bullfrog (*Rana catesbeiana*) called Rosie the Ribeter, owned and trained by Lee Giudicci of Santa Clara, CA, leapt 21 ft 5¾ in. Santjie would have been ineligible for this contest because entrants must measure at least 4 in 'stem to stern.'

Largest toad ■ The largest known toad is the marine toad (*Bufo marinus*) of tropical South America and Queensland, Australia (introduced). An average adult specimen weighs 1 lb.

The largest toad ever recorded was a female marine toad (*Bufo marinus*) nicknamed Totally Awesome (Toad A) owned by Blank Park Zoo, Des Moines, IA. She was purchased from an animal dealer in Miami, FL on 11 May 1983, when she weighed about 2 lb, and attained a peak 5 lb 1½ oz (snout-vent length 9½ in) on 19 Nov 1987. She died on 8 Apr 1988, most probably from old age.

Smallest toad ■ The smallest toad in the world is the short-headed toad. (See Smallest amphibian.)

Fishes *Gnathostomata, Agnatha*

Largest marine ■ The largest fish in the world is the rare plankton-feeding whale shark (*Rhincodon typus*), which is found in the warmer areas of the Atlantic, Pacific and Indian Oceans. The longest scientifically measured one on record was a 41½ ft specimen captured off Baba Island near Karachi, Pakistan on 11 Nov 1949. It measured 23 ft around the thickest part of the body and weighed an estimated 16·53 tons.

Carnivorous ■ The largest carnivorous fish (excluding plankton-eaters) is the comparatively rare great white shark (*Carcharodon carcharias*), also called the 'man-eater.' Adult specimens (females are larger than males) average 14–15 ft in length and generally scale between 1,150–1,700 lb, but larger individuals have been recorded. The length and weight record is held by a 21 ft female caught off Castillo de Cojimar, Cuba in May 1945. It weighed 7,302 lb and yielded a 1,005 lb liver.

On 17 Apr 1987 a female great white shark with a 'linear' measurement of 23 ft 5 in and an estimated weight of 6,613 lb was caught off Malta by Alfred Cutajar. Unfortunately the preserved jaws do not confirm this extreme measurement. A formula based on the size of the shark's teeth and the perimeter measurement of its upper jaw indicate a more acceptable measurement of 17½–18 ft.

Bony ■ The longest of the bony or 'true' fishes (Pisces) is the oarfish (*Regalecus glesne*), also called the 'King of the Herrings,' which has a worldwide distribution.

In *c.* 25 ft-long example weighing 600 lb was caught by fishermen off Pemaquid Point, ME. Another oarfish, seen swimming off Asbury Park, NJ by a team of scientists from the Sandy Hook Marine Laboratory on 18 Jul 1963, was estimated to measure 50 ft in length.

The heaviest bony fish in the world is the ocean sunfish (*Mola mola*), which is found in all tropical, subtropical and temperate waters. On 18 Sep 1908 a specimen was accidentally struck by the SS *Fiona* off Bird Island about 40 miles from Sydney, New South Wales, Australia and towed to Port Jackson. It measured 14 ft between the anal and dorsal fins and weighed 4,927 lb.

Largest freshwater ■ The largest fish that spends its whole life in fresh or brackish water is the rare Pla beuk (*Pangasianodon gigas*). It is confined to the Mekong River and its major tributaries in China, Laos, Cambodia and Thailand. The largest specimen, captured in the River Ban Mee Noi, Thailand was reportedly 9 ft 10¼ in long and weighed 533·5 lb. This *was* exceeded by the European catfish or wels (*Silurus glanis*) in earlier times (in the 19th century lengths up to 15 ft and weights up to 720 lb were reported for Russian specimens), but today anything over 6 ft and 200 lb is considered large.

The arapaima (*Arapaima glanis*), also called the pirarucu, found in the Amazon and other South American rivers and often claimed to be the largest freshwater fish, averages 6½ ft and 150 lb. The largest 'authentically recorded' measured 8 ft 1½ in in length and weighed 325 lb. It was caught in the Rio Negro, Brazil in 1836.

In September 1978, a Nile perch (*Lates niloticus*) weighing 416 lb was netted in the eastern part of Lake Victoria, Kenya.

Smallest marine ■ The shortest recorded marine fish — and the shortest known verte-

Oldest goldfish ● These lion-headed fish represent one of the many varieties of goldfish (*Carassius auratus*), specimens of which have been reported to live for over 50 years. (Photo: Bruce Coleman)

brate — is the dwarf goby *Trimmatom nanus* of the Chagos Archipelago, central Indian Ocean. In one series of 92 specimens collected by the 1978–9 Joint Services Chagos Research Expedition of the British Armed Forces the adult males averaged 0·338 in in length and the adult females 0·35 in.

The lightest of all vertebrates and the smallest catch possible for any fisherman is the dwarf goby *Schindleria praematurus* from Samoa, which measures 0·47–0·74 in. Mature specimens have been known to weigh only 0·03 grain, which is equivalent to 14·175 to the oz.

Shark ■ The spined pygmy shark (*Squaliolus laticaudus*) of the western Pacific matures at 5·9 in in length.

Smallest freshwater ■ The shortest and lightest freshwater fish is the dwarf pygmy goby *Pandaka pygmaea*, a colorless and nearly transparent species found in the streams and lakes of Luzon in the Philippines. Adult males measure only 0·28–0·38 in in length and weigh 0·00014–0·00018 oz.

The world's smallest commercial fish is the now endangered sinarapan (*Mistichthys luzonensis*), a goby found only in Lake Buhi, Luzon, Philippines. Adult males measure 0·39–0·51 in in length, and a dried 1 lb fish cake contains about 70,000 of them!

Fastest ■ The maximum swimming speed of a fish is dependent on its length and temperature. The cosmopolitan sailfish (*Istiophorus platypterus*) is considered to be the fastest species of fish over short distances, although the practical difficulties of measuring make data extremely difficult to secure. In a series of speed trials carried out at the Long Key Fishing Camp, FL, one sailfish took out 300 ft of line in 3 sec, which is equivalent to a velocity of 68 mph (compare 60 mph for the cheetah).

Some American fishermen believe that the bluefin tuna (*Thunnus thynnus*) is the fastest fish in the sea, and burst speeds up to 56 knots have been claimed for this species, but the highest speed recorded so far is 43·4 mph in a 20-second dash. The yellowfin tuna (*Thunnus albacares*) and the wahoo (*Acanthocybium solandri*) are also extremely fast, having been timed at 46·35 mph and 47·88 mph respectively during 10–20 second sprints.

Oldest ■ Aquaria are of too recent origin to be able to establish with certainty which species of fish can be regarded as being the longest lived. Early indications are, however, that it may be the lake sturgeon (*Acipenser fulvescens*) of North America. In one study of the growth rings (annuli) of 966 specimens caught in the Lake Winnebago region, WI between 1951 and 1954, the oldest sturgeon was found to be a male (length 6 ft 7 in), which gave a reading of 82 years and was still growing.

The perch-like marine fish *Notothenia neglecta* of the Antarctic Ocean, whose blood contains a natural antifreeze, is reported to live up to 150 years, but this claim has not yet been verified.

In July 1974 a growth ring count of 228 years (*sic*) was reported for a female koi fish, a form of fancy carp, named Hanako living in a pond in Higashi Shirakawa, Gifu Prefecture, Japan, but the greatest authoritatively accepted age for this species is 'more than 50 years.'

In 1948 the death was reported of an 88-year-old female European eel (*Anguilla anguilla*) named Putte in the aquarium at Hälsingborg Museum, southern Sweden. She was allegedly born in the Sargasso Sea, in the North Atlantic, in 1860, and was caught in a river as a three-year-old elver.

Oldest goldfish ■ Goldfish (*Carassius auratus*) have been reported to live for over 50 years in China.

Shortest-lived ■ The shortest-lived fishes are probably certain species of the suborder Cyprinodontei (Killifish), found in Africa and South America, which normally live about eight months.

Most abundant ■ The most abundant species is probably the 3 in long deepsea bristlemouth (*Cyclothone elongata*), which has a worldwide distribution. It would take about 500 of them to weigh 1 lb.

Deepest ■ The greatest depth from which a fish has been recovered is 27,230 ft in the Puerto Rico Trench (27,488 ft) in the Atlantic by Dr Gilbert L. Voss of the US research vessel *John Elliott* who took a 6½ in long *Bassogigas profundissimus* in April 1970. It was only the fifth such brotulid ever caught.

Dr Jacques Piccard and Lt Don Walsh of the US Navy reported seeing a sole-like fish about 1 ft long (tentatively identified as *Chascanopsetta lugubris*) from the bathyscaphe *Trieste* at a depth of 35,820 ft in the Challenger Deep (Marianas Trench) in the western Pacific on 24 Jan 1960. This sighting, however, has been questioned by some authorities, who still regard the brotulids of the genus *Bassogigas* as the deepest-living vertebrates.

Most eggs ■ The ocean sunfish (*Mola mola*) produces up to 30 million eggs, each of them measuring about 0·05 in in diameter, at a single spawning.

Least eggs ■ The mouth-brooding cichlid *Tropheus moorii* of Lake Tanganyika, East Africa, produces seven eggs or less during normal reproduction.

Most valuable ■ The world's most valuable fish is the Russian sturgeon (*Huso huso*). One 2,706 lb female caught in the Tikhaya Sosna River in 1924 yielded 541 lb of best-quality caviar, which would be worth £189,350 on today's market.

The 30 in long Ginrin Showa koi, which won supreme championship in nationwide Japanese koi shows in 1976, 1977, 1979 and 1980, was sold two years later for 17 million yen. In March 1986 this ornamental carp was acquired by Derry Evans, owner of the Kent Koi Centre near Sevenoaks, Kent, United Kingdom for an undisclosed sum, but the 15-year-old fish died five months later. It has since been stuffed and mounted to preserve its beauty.

Most venomous ■ The most venomous fish in the world are the stonefish (Synanceidae) of the tropical waters of the Indo-Pacific, and in particular *Synanceja horrida,* which has the largest venom glands of any known fish. Direct contact with the spines of its fins, which contain a strong neurotoxic poison, often proves fatal.

Most ferocious ■ The razor-toothed piranhas of the genera *Serrasalmus, Pygocentrus* and *Pygopristis* are the most ferocious freshwater fish in the world. They live in the sluggish waters of the large rivers of South America, and will attack any creature, regardless of size, if it is injured or making a commotion in the water. On 19 Sep 1981 more than 300 people were reportedly killed and eaten when an overloaded passenger-cargo boat capsized and sank as it was docking at the Brazilian port of Obidos. According to one official, only 178 of the estimated people aboard the boat survived.

Most electric ■ The most powerful electric fish is the electric eel (*Electrophorus electricus*), which is found in the rivers of Brazil, Colombia,

Venezuela and Peru. An average-sized specimen can discharge 400 volts at 1 ampere, but measurements up to 650 volts have been recorded.

Starfishes *Asteroidea*

Largest ■ The largest of the 1,600 known species of starfish in terms of total arm span is the very fragile brisingid *Midgardia xandaros*. A specimen collected by the Texas A & M University research vessel *Alaminos* in the southern part of the Gulf of Mexico in the late summer of 1968 measured 54·33 in tip to tip, but the diameter of its disc was only 1·02 in. Its dry weight was 2·46 oz.

The heaviest species of starfish is the five-armed *Thromidia catalai* of the western Pacific. One specimen collected off Ilot Amédée, New Caledonia on 14 Sep 1969 and later deposited in Nouméa Aquarium weighed an estimated 13·2 lb (total arm span 24·8 in).

Smallest ■ The smallest known starfish is the asterinid sea star *Patiriella parvivipara* discovered by Wolfgang Zeidler on the west coast of the Eyre peninsula, South Australia in 1975. It has a maximum radius of only 0·18 in and a diameter of less than 0·35 in.

Most destructive ■ The crown of thorns (*Acanthaster planci*) of the Indo-Pacific region and the Red Sea can destroy 46·5–62 in² of coral a day.

Deepest ■ The greatest depth from which a starfish has been recovered is 24,881 ft for a specimen of *Porcellanaster ivanovi* collected by the USSR research ship *Vityaz* in the Marianas Trench, in the west Pacific, c. 1962.

Crustaceans
Crustacea

(Crabs, lobsters, shrimps, prawns, crawfish, barnacles, water fleas, fish lice, woodlice, sandhoppers, krill, etc.)

Largest marine ■ The largest of all crustaceans (although not the heaviest) is the Takashigani or giant spider crab (*Macrocheira kaempferi*), also called the stilt crab, which is found in deep waters off the southeastern coast of Japan. Mature specimens usually have a body measuring 10 × 12 in and a claw span of 8–9 ft, but unconfirmed measurements up to 19 ft have been reported. A specimen with a claw span of 12 ft 1½ in weighed 41 lb.

The largest species of lobster, and the heaviest of all crustaceans, is the American or North Atlantic lobster (*Homarus americanus*). On 11 Feb 1977 a specimen weighing 44 lb 6 oz and measuring 3 ft 6 in from the end of the tail fan to the tip of the largest claw was caught off Nova Scotia, Canada, and later sold to a New York restaurant owner.

Smallest ■ Water fleas of the genus *Alonella* may measure less than 0·0098 in in length. They are found in British waters.

The smallest known lobster is the Cape lobster (*Homarus capensis*) of South Africa, which measures 3·9–4·7 in in total length.

The smallest crabs in the world are the aptly named pea crabs (family Pinnotheridae). Some species have a shell diameter of only 0·25 in, including *Pinnotheres pisum*, which is found in British waters.

Oldest ■ Very large specimens of the American lobster (*Homarus americanus*) may be as much as 50 years old.

Most destructive starfish ● The crown of thorns starfish (*Acanthaster planci*) of the Indo-Pacific region and the Red Sea has between 12 and 19 arms and can measure up to 24 in in diameter. It feeds on coral polyps and can destroy 46·5–62 in² of coral in one day. (Photo: Bruce Coleman)

Right: Largest ● The largest of all crustaceans (although not the heaviest) is the Takashigani or giant spider crab (*Macrocheira kaempferi*), also called the stilt crab, which is found in deep waters off the southeastern coast of Japan. Mature specimens usually have a body measuring 10 × 12 in and a claw span of 8–9 ft. (Photo: Bruce Coleman)

Deepest ■ The greatest depth from which a crustacean has been recovered is 34,450 ft for *live* amphipods from the Challenger Deep, Marianas Trench, West Pacific by the US research vessel *Thomas Washington* in November 1980. Amphipods and isopods have also been collected in the Ecuadorean Andes at a height of 13,300 ft.

Largest concentration ■ The largest single concentration of crustaceans ever recorded was an enormous swarm of krill (*Euphausia superba*) estimated to weigh 11 million tons and tracked by US scientists off Antarctica in March 1981.

Arachnids *Arachnida*

SPIDERS (order Araneae)

Largest ■ The world's largest known spider is the goliath bird-eating spider (*Theraphosa leblondi*) of the coastal rainforests of Suriname, Guyana (formerly British Guyana) and French Guiana, northeastern South America; isolated specimens have also been reported from Venezuela and Brazil. In February 1985 Charles J. Seiderman of New York City, NY captured a huge female just north of Paramarido, Suriname. This spider had a maximum leg span of 10½ in (total body length 4 in), 1 in long fangs and weighed a peak 4·3 oz before its death from moulting problems in Jan 1986.

An outsized male example collected by members of the Pablo San Martin Expedition at Rio Cavro, Venezuela in April 1965 had a leg span of 11·02 in; the female is built on much heavier lines.

United States ■ The *Rhecosticta california*, a type of tarantula, found in the Southwest, is the heaviest spider and has the longest body. However, its leg span is equaled by the orb web spider (*Nephila clavipes*) of the family *Araneidae*, found in the southern Gulf States, and the wolf spider (*Lycosa carolinensis*) of the family *Lycosidae*, found in the Southeast.

Smallest ■ The smallest known spider is *Patu marplesi* (family Symphytognathidae) of Western Samoa in the Pacific. The type specimen (male) found in moss at *c.* 2,000 ft in Madolelei,

Upolu, Western Samoa in Jan 1965 measured 0·017 in overall, which means that it was about the size of a period on this page.

United States ■ The *Troglonata paradoxum* of the family *Mysmmenidae* is the smallest spider in the United States.

Most common ■ The crab spiders (family *Thomisidae*) have a worldwide distribution.

United States ■ The house spider (*Archaearanea tepidariorum*), of the family *Theridiidae*, has been sighted throughout the United States.

Rarest ■ The most elusive of all spiders are the rare Trapdoor spiders of the genus *Liphistius*, which are found in southeast Asia.

United States ■ The most elusive spiders in the United States are the *Nesticus Dilutus*, one specimen found by T. S. Barr at Grassy Creek Cave, TN, and the *Nesticus Valentines*, one specimen found by J. M. Valentine at Mont Eagle Saltpeter Cave, TN.

Oldest ■ The longest-lived of all spiders are the primitive *Mygalomorphae* (tarantulas and allied species). One female therasophid collected in Mexico in 1935 lived for an estimated 26–28 years.

United States ■ The longest-lived species of American spider is the *Rhecosticta californica* of the family *Theraphosidae*, which has an average life span of 25 years.

Fastest ■ The fastest-moving arachnids are the long-legged sun spiders of the genus *Solpuga*, which live in the arid semidesert regions of Africa and the Middle East. They feed on geckos and other lizards and can reach speeds of over 10 mph.

Largest webs ■ Aerial webs spun by the tropical orb weavers of the genus *Nephila* have been measured up to 18 ft 9¾ in in circumference.

Smallest webs ■ The smallest webs are spun by spiders such as *Glyphesis cottonae* which cover about 0·75 in².

Most venomous ■ The world's most venomous spiders are the Brazilian wandering spiders of the genus *Phoneutria*, and particularly *P. fera*, which has the most active neuro-

toxic venom of any living spider. These large and highly aggressive creatures frequently enter human dwellings and hide in clothing or shoes. When disturbed they bite furiously several times, and hundreds of accidents involving these species are reported annually. Fortunately an effective antivenin is available, and when deaths do occur they are usually children under the age of seven.

SCORPIONS (Scorpiones)

Largest ■ The largest of the 800 or so species of scorpion is the tropical emperor *Pandinus imperator* of Guinea, adult males of which can attain a body length of 7 in or more. Its black coloring is indicative of species found in moist or higher mountain habitats.

Smallest ■ The smallest scorpion in the world is *Microbothus pusillus* from the Red Sea coast, which measures about 0·5 in in total length.

Most venomous ■ The most venomous scorpion in the world is the Palestine yellow scorpion (*Leiurus quinquestriatus*), which ranges from the eastern part of North Africa through the Middle East to the shores of the Red Sea. Fortunately, the amount of venom it delivers is very small (0·000009 oz) and adult lives are seldom endangered, but it has been responsible for a number of fatalities among children under the age of five.

Insects *Insecta*

Heaviest ■ The heaviest living insects are the goliath beetles (family Scarabaeidae) of equatorial Africa. The largest members of the group are *Goliathus regius*, *G. goliathus* (= *G. giganteus*) and *G. druryi*, and in one series of fully-grown males (females are smaller) the lengths from the tips of the small frontal horns to the end of the abdomen measured up to 4·33 in and the weights ranged from 2·5–3·5 oz.

The elephant beetles (*Megasoma*) of Central America and the West Indies attain the greatest dimensions in terms of volume, but they lack the massive build-up of heavy chiton forming the thorax and anterior sternum of the goliaths, and this gives them a distinct weight advantage.

Largest scorpion ● The largest of the 800 or so species of scorpion is the black *Pandinus imperator* of Guinea, which can attain a body length of 7 in and over. (Life size artwork: Matthew Hillier for Guinness Publishing)

Fastest wing beat ■ The fastest wing beat of any insect under natural conditions is 62,760 per min by a tiny midge of the genus *Forcipomyia*. In experiments with truncated wings at a temperature of 98·6° F the rate increased to 133,080 beats/min. The muscular contraction-expansion cycle in 0·00045 or 1/2218th of a sec further represents the fastest muscle movement ever measured.

Slowest wing beat ■ The slowest wing beat of any insect is 300 per min by the swallowtail butterfly (*Papilio machaon*). The average is 460–636 per min.

Largest termite mound ■ In 1968 W. Page photographed a specimen south of Horgesia, Somalia estimated to be 28·5 ft tall.

DRAGONFLIES (Odonata)

Largest ■ *Megaloprepus caeruleata* of Central and South America has been measured up to 4·72 in across the wings and 7·52 in in body length.

United States ■ The giant green darner (*Anax Walsinghami*), found in the West, has a body length of up to 4 ½ in.

Smallest ■ The smallest dragonfly in the world is *Agriocnemis naia* of Myanmar (formerly Burma). A specimen in the British Museum (Natural History) had a wing expanse of 0·69 in and a body length of 0·71 in.

United States ■ The smallest insect is the elfin skimmer (*Nannothaemis Bella*), which has a body length of 4/5 in.

FLEAS (Siphonaptera)

Largest ■ Siphonapterologists recognize 1,830 varieties, of which the largest known is *Hystrichopsylla schefferi*, which was described from a single specimen taken from the nest of a mountain beaver (*Aplodontia rufa*) at Puyallup, WA in 1913. Females measure up to 0·31 in in length, which is the diameter of a pencil.

Longest jump ■ The champion jumper among fleas is the common flea (*Pulex irritans*). In one American experiment carried out in 1910 a specimen allowed to leap at will performed a long jump of 13 in and a high jump of 7¾ in. In jumping 130 times its own height a flea subjects itself to a force of 200 *g*.

BUTTERFLIES AND MOTHS

Largest ■ The largest known butterfly is the protected Queen Alexandra's birdwing (*Ornithoptera alexandrae*) which is restricted to the Popondetta Plain in Papua New Guinea. Females may have a wingspan exceeding 11·02 in and weigh over 0·88 oz.

The largest moth in the world (although not the heaviest) is the Hercules moth (*Cosdinoscera hercules*) of tropical Australia and New Guinea. A wing area of up to 40·8 in² and a wingspan of 11 in have been recorded. In 1948 an unconfirmed measurement of 14·17 in was reported for a female captured near the post office at the coastal town of Innisfail, Queensland, Australia, now in the Oberthur collection.

The rare owlet moth (*Thysania agrippina*) of Brazil has been measured up to 12·16 in wingspan in the case of a female taken in 1934 and now in the collection of John G. Powers in Ontario, Canada.

Largest cockroach ■ The world's largest cockroach is *Megaloblatta longipennis* of Colombia. A preserved female in the collection of Akira Yokokura of Yamagata, Japan measures 3·81 in in length and 1·77 in across.

Longest ■ The longest insect in the world is the giant stick-insect (*Pharnacia serratipes*) of Indonesia, females of which have been measured up to 13 in.

The longest known beetle (excluding antennae) is the Hercules beetle (*Dynastes hercules*) of Central and South America, which has been measured up to 7·48 in. More than half the length, however, is taken up by the prothoracic horn.

Smallest ■ The smallest insects recorded so far are the 'feather-winged' beetles of the family Ptiliidae (Trichopterygidae) and the 'battledore-wing fairy flies' (parasitic wasps) of the family Mymaridae, which are smaller than some species of protozoa (single-celled animals).

The male bloodsucking banded louse (*Enderleinellus zonatus*) and the parasitic wasp (*Caraphractus cinctus*) may each weigh as little as 5,670,000 to an oz. Eggs of the latter each weigh 141,750,000 to an oz.

Rarest ■ It is estimated that there may be as many as 30 million species of insect — more than all other phyla and classes put together — but thousands are known only from a single or type specimen.

Fastest flying ■ Experiments have proved that the widely publicized claim by an American scientist in 1926 that the deer botfly (*Cephenemyia pratti*) could attain a speed of 818 mph (sic) at an altitude of 12,000 ft was widely exaggerated. If true, the fly would have had to develop the equivalent of 1·5 hp and consume 1 ½ times its own weight in food per second to acquire the energy that would be needed, and even if this were possible it would still be crushed by the air pressure and incinerated by the friction. Acceptable modern experiments have now established that the highest maintainable air speed of any insect including the deer botfly, hawkmoths (*Sphingidae*), horseflies (*Tabamis bovinus*) and some tropical butterflies (*Hesperiidae*) is 24 mph, rising to a maximum of 36 mph for the Australian dragonfly *Austrophlebia costalis*, for short bursts.

Fastest moving ■ The fastest moving insects are large tropical cockroaches (*Dictyoptera*), and specimens measuring about 1·18 in in length have been timed at 47–51 in/sec, 2·68–2·90 mph or 40–43 body lengths per second.

Highest g force ■ The click beetle (*Athous haemorrhoidalis*) averages 400 *g* when 'jackknifing' into the air to escape predators. One example measuring 0·47 in in length and weighing 0·00014 oz that jumped to a height of 11¾ in was calculated to have 'endured' a peak brain deceleration of 2,300 *g* by the end of the movement.

Oldest ■ The most primitive insect known is the unidentified species of springtail (order Collembola). Widely distributed throughout the world, these wingless insects date back 300 million years and range in size from 0·04–0·4 in.

The longest-lived insects are the splendor beetles (Buprestidae). On 27 May 1983 a *Buprestis aurulenta* appeared from the staircase timber in the home of Mr W. Euston of Prittlewell, Essex, United Kingdom after 47 years as a larva.

Loudest ■ The loudest of all insects is the male cicada (family Cicadidae). At 7,400 pulses/min its tymbal organs produce a noise (officially described by the US Department of Agriculture as 'Tsh-ee-EEEE-e-ou') detectable more than a quarter of a mile distant.

United States ■ The largest *native* butterfly in the United States is the giant swallowtail (*Papilio cresphontes*), found in the eastern states.

Smallest ■ The females of many species of moth are wingless but, to compensate for this, their bodies are always larger and heavier than those of their male counterparts.

The smallest of the 140,000 known species of Lepidoptera is *Stigmella ridiculosa*, which has a wingspan of 0·079 in with a similar body length and is found in the Canary Islands.

United States ■ The smallest butterfly in the United States is the pygmy blue (*Brephidium exilis*) found in the Southeast.

Rarest ■ The birdwing butterfly *Ornithopteria* (*Troides*) *allottei* of Bougainville, Solomon Islands is known from less than a dozen specimens. A male from the collection of C. Rousseau Decelle was auctioned for £750 in Paris on 24 Oct 1966.

United States ■ The State's rarest butterfly (30 species) is the Schaus swallowtail (*Papilio aritodemus*).

Most acute sense of smell ■ The most acute sense of smell exhibited in nature is that of the male emperor moth (*Eudia pavonia*), which, according to German experiments in 1961, can detect the sex attractant of the virgin female at the almost unbelievable range of 6·8 miles upwind. This scent has been identified as one of the higher alcohols ($C_{16}H_{29}OH$), of which the female carries less than 0·0000015 grain.

Largest butterfly farm ■ The Stratford-upon-Avon Butterfly Farm, United Kingdom can accommodate 2,000 exotic butterflies in authentic rain forest conditions. The total capacity of all flight areas at the farm, which opened on 15 Jul 1985, is over 141,528 ft³. The complex also includes insect and plant houses and educational facilities.

United States ■ Butterfly World, in Coconut Creek, FL, accommodates between 2,000 and 3,000 butterflies in authentic conditions. About 80 species of butterfly can be seen at any one time, and in the course of a year up to 300 species are shown in the 37 screened enclosures.

The museum, founded by Mr. Boender, Clive Farrell, and John Chalk, cost $1·5 million and was built in five months to open 23 Mar 1988.

Centipedes *Chilopoda*

Longest ■ The longest known species of centipede is a large variant of the widely distributed *Scolopendra morsitans*, found on the Andaman Islands in the Bay of Bengal. Specimens have been measured up to 13 in in length and 1·5 in in breadth.

United States ■ *Tomotaemia parviceps*, found in California and Washington, has been measured up to 5·9 in in length and 0·1 in in diameter.

Shortest ■ The shortest recorded centipede is an unidentified species that measures only 0·19 in.

United States ■ *Nampabius georgianus*, found in Georgia, measures up to 0·19 in in length and 0·03 in in diameter.

Poaaphilus keywinus, found in Iowa, is smaller in diameter at 0·007 in, but has a length of 0·25 in.

Most legs ■ *Himantarum gabrielis*, found in

southern Europe, has 171–177 pairs of legs (342–354 legs) when adult.

Fastest ■ The fastest centipede is probably *Scrutigera coleoptrata* of southern Europe, which can travel at 1·1 mph.

Millipedes *Diplopoda*

Longest ■ Both *Graphidostreptus gigas* of Africa and *Scaphistostreptus seychellarum* of the Seychelles in the Indian Ocean have been measured up to 11·02 in in length and 0·78 in in diameter.

United States ■ *Orthoporus ornatus*, found in Texas and Arizona, measures up to 7·28 in in length and 0·55 in in diameter.

Shortest ■ The shortest millipede in the world is the British species *Polyxenus lagurus*, which measures 0·082–0·15 in.

United States ■ *Polyxenus fasciculatus*, found in the Southeast, measures only 0·07 in in length and 0·03 in in diameter.

The next shortest millipede is *Buotus carolinus*, found in North Carolina and Virginia, which has been measured 0·11 in in length and only 0·01 in in diameter.

Most legs ■ The greatest number of legs reported for a millipede is 375 pairs (750 legs) for *Illacme plenipes* of California.

Segmented Worms *Annelida*

Longest ■ The longest known species of earthworm is *Microchaetus rappi* (*M. microchaetus*) of South Africa. In *c.* 1937 a giant measuring 22 ft in length when naturally extended and 0·78 in in diameter was collected in the Transvaal.

Shortest ■ *Chaetogaster annandalei* measures less than 0·019 in in length.

Mollusks *Mollusca*

(Squids, octopuses, shellfish, snails, etc.)

Largest invertebrate ■ The Atlantic giant squid, *Architeuthis dux*, is the world's largest known invertebrate. The heaviest ever recorded was a 2·2 ton monster that ran aground in Thimble Tickle Bay, Newfoundland, Canada on 2 Nov 1878.

There are numerous types of squids, ranging in size from 0·75 in to the longest ever recorded — a 57 ft giant *Architeuthis longimanus* that was washed up on Lyall Bay, Cook Strait, New Zealand in October 1887. Its two long slender tentacles each measured 49 ft 3 in.

Largest octopus ■ The largest octopus known to science is *Octopus apollyon* of the coastal waters of the North Pacific. One huge individual caught single-handedly by skin diver Donald E. Hagen in Lower Hoods Canal, Puget Sound, WA on 18 Feb 1973 had a relaxed radial spread of 23 ft and weighed 118 lb 10 oz.

Largest eye ■ The Atlantic giant squid has the largest eye of any animal — living or extinct. It has been estimated that the one recorded at Thimble Tickle Bay had eyes 15·75 in in diameter — almost the width of this open book!

Oldest mollusk ■ The longest-lived mollusk is the ocean quahog (*Arctica islandica*), a thick-shelled clam found in the mid-Atlantic. A specimen with 220 annual growth rings was collected in 1982.

SHELLS

Largest ■ The largest of all existing bivalve shells is the marine giant clam *Tridacna gigas*, found on the Indo-Pacific coral reefs. An outsized specimen measuring 45·2 in in length and weighing 734 lb was collected off Ishigaki Island, Okinawa, Japan in 1956 but was not scientifically examined until August 1984. It probably scaled just over 750 lb when alive (the soft parts weigh up to 20 lb). Another giant clam collected at Tapanoeli (Tapanula) on the northwest coast of Sumatra before 1817 and now preserved at Arno's Vale, measures 54 in in length and weighs 507 lb.

Smallest ■ The smallest known shell-bearing species is the gastropod *Ammonicera rota*, which is found in British waters. It measures 0·02 in in diameter.

The smallest bivalve shell is the coinshell *Neolepton sykesi*, which is known only from a few examples collected off Guernsey, Channel Islands, United Kingdom and western Ireland. It has an average diameter of 0·047 in.

Most expensive ■ The value of a seashell does not necessarily depend on its rarity or its prevalence. Some rare shells are inexpensive because there is no demand for them, while certain common shells fetch high prices because they are not readily accessible. In theory the most valuable shells in the world should be some of the unique examples collected in deepsea

trawls, but these shells are always dull and unattractive and hold very little interest for the collector. The most sought-after shell at present is probably *Cypraea fultoni*. In 1987 two live specimens were taken by a Russian trawler off Mozambique in the Indian Ocean. The larger of the two was later sold in New York to collector Dr Massilia Raybaudi of Italy for $24,000. The other was put up for sale at $17,000. A third, *C. fultoni*, went for $6,600 in June 1987 to a Carmel, CA collector. This collector also purchased a *C. teramachii* for $6,500 in a one-week buying spree. Another *C. fultoni*, in the American Museum of Natural History, NY, was valued at $14,000 a few years ago.

GASTROPODS

Largest ■ The largest known gastropod is the trumpet or baler conch (*Syrinx aruanus*) of Australia. One outsized specimen collected off Western Australia in 1979 and now owned by Don Pisor (who bought it from a fisherman in Kaohsiung, Taiwan in November 1979) of San Diego, CA measures 30·39 in in length and has a maximum girth of 39·76 in. It weighed nearly 40 lb when alive.

The largest known land gastropod is the African giant snail (*Achatina* sp.). A specimen named Gee Geronimo owned by Christopher Hudson (1955–79) of Hove, East Sussex, United Kingdom measured 15½ in from snout to tail when fully extended (shell length 10¾ in) in December 1978 and weighed exactly 2 lb. The snail was collected in Sierra Leone in June 1976.

Fastest ■ The fastest-moving species of land snail is possibly the common garden snail (*Helix aspersa*). On 21 Feb 1990 a garden snail named Verne completed a 12·2 in course at West Middle School in Plymouth, MI in a record 2 min 13 sec. On 9 Jul 1988 another garden snail called Hercules dragged a 8·5 oz stone for 18½ in across a table in 10 min in the Basque town of Val de Trapagua, Spain.

It is probable, however, that the carnivorous (and cannabalistic) snail *Euglandina risea* could out-run other snails in its hunt for prey. The snail-racing equivalent of a four minute mile is 24 in in 3 min or a 5½ day mile.

Ribbon Worms
Nemertina

Longest ■ The longest of the 550 recorded species of ribbon worm, also called nemertines (or nemerteans), is the 'boot-lace' worm (*Lineus longissimus*), which is found in the shallow waters of the North Sea. A specimen washed ashore at St Andrews, Fife, United Kingdom in 1864 after a severe storm measured more than 180 ft in length.

Immolation ■ Some ribbon worms absorb themselves when food is scarce. One specimen under observation digested 95 percent of its own body in a few months without apparently suffering any ill effects. As soon as food became available the lost tissue was restored.

Jellyfishes and Corals *Cnidaria*

Largest jellyfish ■ The largest jellyfish is the arctic giant jellyfish (*Cyanea capillata arctica*) of the northwestern Atlantic. One washed up in Massachusetts Bay had a bell diameter of 7 ft 6 in and tentacles stretching 120 ft.

Most venomous cnidarian ■ The beautiful but deadly Australian sea wasp (*Chironex fleckeri*) is the most venomous jellyfish in the world. Its cardiotoxic venom has caused the deaths of 66 people off the coast of Queensland since 1880, with victims dying within 1–3 minutes if medical aid is not available. One effective defense is women's panty hose, outsize versions of which are now worn by Queensland lifesavers at surfing tournaments.

Coral ■ The world's greatest stony coral structure is the Great Barrier Reef off Queensland, northeast Australia. It stretches 1,260 miles and covers 80,000 miles².

The world's largest reported known example of discrete coral is a stony colony of *Galaxea fascicularis* found in Sakiyama Bay off Irimote Island, Okinawa on 7 Aug 1982 by Dr Shohei Shirai of the Institute for Development of Pacific Natural Resources. It has a long axis measurement of 23 ft 9 in, a height of 13 ft 1½ in and a maximum circumference of 59 ft 5 in.

Sponges *Porifera*

Largest ■ The largest known sponge is the barrel-shaped loggerhead sponge (*Spheciospongia vesparium*) of the West Indies and the waters off Florida. Individuals measure up to 3 ft 6 in in height and 3 ft in diameter.

Neptune's cup or goblet (*Poterion patera*) of Indonesia grows to 4 ft in height, but it is a less bulky animal.

In 1909 a wool sponge (*Hippospongia canaliculatta*) measuring 6 ft in circumference was collected off the Bahamas. When first taken from the water it weighed between 80–90 lb but after it had been dried and relieved of all excrescences it scaled 12 lb. (This sponge is now preserved in the US National Museum, Washington, DC.)

Smallest ■ The widely distributed *Leucosolenia blanca* measures 0·11 in in height when fully grown.

Deepest ■ Sponges have been recovered from depths of up to 18,500 ft.

Extinct Animals

The first dinosaur to be scientifically described was *Megalosaurus bucklandi* ('great fossil lizard') in 1824. The remains of this bipedal flesh-eater were found by workmen before 1818 in a slate quarry near Woodstock, Oxfordshire, United Kingdom and later placed in the University Museum, Oxford, United Kingdom. The first fossil bone of *Megalosaurus* was actually illustrated in 1677, but its true nature was not realized until much later. It was not until 1841 that the name Dinosauria ('terrible lizards') was given to these newly discovered giants.

Disappearance ■ No wholly satisfactory theory has been offered for the dinosaurs' sudden extinction, but one school of thought is that 65 million years ago an asteroid hit the earth, thus triggering volcanic activity and producing lethal doses of acid rain over a period of 10,000 years.

Earliest known ■ The earliest dinosaur is believed to be the *Herrerasaurus*, which is known from an almost complete skeleton discovered in 1989 in the foothills of the Andes in Argentina by an expedition led by Paul Sereno of the University of Chicago, IL. This specimen is thought to date from 230 million years ago and is named after Victorino Herrera, a fossil hunter

who discovered fragments of bone years earlier. The *Herrerasaurus* was a carnivore that stood about 6 ½–8 ft and weighed over 220 lb, and its importance in the evolutionary process is suggested by its dual-hinged jaw, a feature that did not appear in other dinosaurs for another 50 million years. Other early dinosaurs from the Jurassic age are known from incomplete remains found in Brazil, Argentina, Morocco, India and Scotland.

Largest ■ The largest terrestrial vertebrates of all time were the brachiosaurs ('arm lizards') of the Tendaguru and Morrison Formations of Africa and North America respectively, which lumbered across the landscape 150 million years ago. Estimated weights up to 209 tons have been published for the biggest members of this family (Brachiosauridae), but such weights are unlikely. Present estimates range from 33–88 tons for *Brachiosaurus*. Most of the brachiosaurs discovered so far weighed a more acceptable 38–44 tons, but they could have been up to 33 percent heavier in prime fat-bearing condition.

The largest (and tallest) species for which the whole skeleton is known is the gracile *Brachiosaurus (Giraffatitan) brancai* from the famous Tendaguru site in Tanzania, which was excavated by a German expedition during the period 1909–11. The bones were later shipped back to the Humboldt Museum für Naturkunde in East Berlin, Germany for preparation and assembly and the specimen (a composite of several partial skeletons of different sizes) was finally put on display in 1937. As it stands today the world's largest mounted dinosaur measures 72 ft 9½ in overall length (height at shoulder 19 ft 8 in) and has a raised head height of 46 ft. It weighed an estimated 34·7 tons.

The isolated fibula of another *Brachiosaurus* in the same museum is 13 percent larger than its equivalent in the mounted skeleton and it has been calculated that the bone must have come from a sauropod measuring 82 ft in total length (shoulder height 22 ft 3½ in) and has an estimated height of 52½ ft to the top of its raised head. It weighed 49·6 tons.

Brachiosaurus (B) altithorax from western Colorado was also in the same class but heavier-bodied, and probably weighed about 55 tons in lean condition.

Three large sauropods were described from the Uncompahgre Plateau of western Colorado in 1985 and 1986. *Dystylosaurus edwini* ('two beam lizard'), found in 1979, is based on a single giant vertebra, and it is probably a brachiosaurid, like *Ultrasaurus macintoshi* ('extreme lizard'), also found in 1979. The latter is said to have had a body length of 98 ft and a body weight of 110–143 tons.

Supersaurus vivianae ('super lizard'), found in the same general area in 1972, has shoulder bones and neck vertebrae that suggest a height of 54 ft and a total body length of 82–98 ft. *Supersaurus* is probably a diplodicid.

Trackways are also a good indication of size, and the print named *Breviparopus*, found at Taghbalout, Morocco, together with those of the brachiosaur *Pleurocoelus* from the Paluxy River, TX, suggest that they were also in the very large size class, i.e., 55 tons.

Titanosaurs ■ A small number of titanosaurs ('giant lizards') have also been described as super-sized, and *Antarctosaurus giganteus* ('Antarctic lizard') of South America, India and Kazakhstan probably rivaled the largest brachiosaurs in terms of weight. There is also an enormous incomplete femur (original length at least 8 ft) in the Museum of La Plata, Argentina that must have come from a titanosaur (*A. giganteus*) massing about 60·6 tons.

Diplodocid ■ In 1985 the remains of a huge diplodocid said to be 'the largest dinosaur ever known' (*sic*) were excavated from a site near Albuquerque, NM. According to Dr David Gillette, a paleontologist at the New Mexico Museum of Natural History, this giant sauropod, informally dubbed *Seismosaurus* ('earthquake lizard'), measured an estimated 100–140 ft in total length and weighed at least 49·2 tons, but it is doubtful whether this new species was as heavy as *Supersaurus vivianae*.

Size limits ■ The largest known sauropods appear to weigh around the 55–110 ton mark, but this doesn't necessarily represent the ultimate weight limit for a land vertebrate. Theoretical calculations suggest that some dinosaurs approached the maximum body weight possible for a terrestrial animal, namely 132 tons. At weights greater than that, the legs would have to be so massive to support the bulk that the dinosaur could not have moved!

Longest ■ Up until very recently the longest dinosaurs on record were believed to be certain attenuated diplodocids. A complete reconstruction of a *Diplodocus carnegii* in the Carnegie Museum of Natural History in Pittsburgh, PA measures 87 ft 6 in in total length — head and body 22 ft, body 15 ft, tail 50 ft 6 in — and has a mounted height of 11 ft 9 in at the pelvis, the highest point on the body. But this giant was a lightweight, relatively speaking, and only weighed an estimated 11·8 tons.

By comparison, *Supersaurus vivianae* (see page 46) measured an estimated 82–98 ft in total length, while *Breviparopus* (see page 46) attained the astonishing length of 157 ft — making it the longest vertebrate on record! Note, however, that this estimate is based on footprints only.

Largest land predator ■ The largest flesh-eating dinosaur recorded so far is *Tyrannosaurus rex* ('king tyrant lizard'), which, 70 million years ago, stalked across what are now the states of Montana, Wyoming and Texas and the provinces of Alberta and Saskatchewan in Canada. A composite skeleton of this nightmarish beast in the American Museum of Natural History, NY has a bipedal height of 18 ft 6 in (total length 34 ft 9 in), and weighed an estimated 6·3 tons (close to 7·7 tons with large fat reserves). This individual, however, may have been a sub-adult, because the upper jawbone (maxilla) of another *Tyrannosaurus* in the Museum of Paleontology at the University of California, Berkeley is 29 percent longer (35·4 in) than the one in the American Museum of Natural History. This indicated a 44 ft theropod weighing anything up to 13·2 tons!

Its Mongolian relative *Tarbosaurus bataar* ('alarming lizard'), known from 13 skeletons, had a longer skull than *Tyrannosaurus* but was less heavily built. It measured 33–46 ft in total length while *Dynamosaurus imperiosus* ('dynamic lizard') of Shandong Province, China, was also in the same size league, measuring up to 46 ft overall (bipedal length 20 ft), but these tyrannosaurids were not as heavily built as their North American relative.

Allosaurs ■ Some of the allosaurs ('other lizards') of North America, Africa, Australia and China also reached exceptional sizes, and one individual excavated near Kenton, OK in 1934 measured 42 ft in total length and had a bipedal height of 16 ft. It was built on even more massive lines than the tyrannosaurids and was named *Saurophagus maximus* 'lizard eater.' Later, however, the bones were reexamined and found to be those of a large allosaur, or an *Acrocanthosaurus* ('very spiky reptile'), which measured about 39 ft overall. Seven skeletons of this terrifying meateater have been found in Oklahoma since 1950.

Recent collections of the allosaur *Epanterias amplexus* from Masonville, CO have suggested to Dr Robert Bakker of the University of Colorado that this theropod reached a length of 50 ft and a weight of 4·4 tons, but remains are incomplete.

Another allosaur from China, *Yangchuanosaurus magnus*, has been described as the largest non-tyrannosaurid carnosaur so far recorded, with a skull even more massive than that of *T. rex*. It measured over 34 ft in length overall.

Spinosaurus aegyptiacus ('thorn lizard') of Niger and Egypt was even longer than the largest known tyrannosaurid, with a total length of *c.* 49 ft, and combined its tremendous length with 5 ft 3 in-long blade-like spines running down its back, but it was a much more lightly built theropod than the tyrannosaurids and probably did not exceed 4·4 tons.

Ornithomimosaurs ■ Most of the ornithomimosaurs ('ostrich mimic lizard') were of modest size, but one giant form, *Deinocheirus mirificus* ('terrible hand'), is represented by a pair of arms each 8 ft long, from Mongolia. These suggest a total body size of 24 ft or more.

The megalosaurids ('great lizards') also produced some enormities, including *Megalosaurus ingens* from the Tendaguru site in Tanzania, and *Bahariasaurus* from Egypt and Algeria, both of which were nearly as large as *T. rex*.

Smallest ■ The chicken-sized *Compsognathus* ('pretty jaw') of southern West Germany and southeast France, and an undescribed plant-eating fabrosaurid from Colorado measured 29·5 in from the snout to the tip of the tail and weighed about 15 lb.

Juvenile dinosaurs are even smaller: a *Psittacosaurus* from the late Cretaceous of Mongolia was smaller than a pigeon (9–10 in long); a *Mussaurus* from the late Triassic of Argentina was the size of a kitten (8 in long); and an embryo of Orodromeus, reported in 1988 from the late Cretaceous of Montana, still in its egg, was only 4 in long.

Longest neck ■ The sauropod *Mamenchisaurus* ('mamenchi lizard') of the Late Jurassic of Sichuan, south-central China, has the longest neck of any animal that has ever lived. It measures 36 ft or half the total length of the dinosaur.

Longest trackway ■ In 1983 a series of four *Apatosaurus* (*Brontosaurus*) trackways that ran parallel for a distance of over 705 ft were recorded from 145-million-year-old Morrison strata in southeast Colorado.

Fastest ■ Trackways can be used to estimate dinosaur speeds, and one from the Late Morrison of Texas discovered in 1981 indicated that a carnivorous dinosaur had been moving at 25 mph. Some of the ornithomimids (ostrich dinosaurs) were even faster, and the large-brained 220 lb *Dromiceiomimus* ('emu mimic') of the late Cretaceous of southern Alberta, Canada could probably outsprint an ostrich, which has a top speed of 45 mph.

Largest footprints ■ In 1932 the gigantic footprints of a large bipedal hadrosaurid (duckbill) measuring 53·5 in in length and 31·8 in wide were discovered at Salt Lake City, UT, and other reports from Colorado and Utah refer to footprints 37·4–39·4 in wide. Footprints attributed to the largest brachiosaurids also range up to 39·3 in wide for the hind feet.

Most brainless ■ *Stegosaurus* ('plated lizard'), which roamed across the states of Colo-

Earliest known ● The earliest and most primitive known dinosaur is the *Herrerasaurus* discovered in 1989 at the foot of the Andes in Argentina by an expedition led by Paul Sereno of the University of Chicago, IL. Named after Victorino Herrera, a fossil hunter responsible for the discovery of fragments of bone many years earlier, this bipedal carnivore is believed to be nearly 230 million years old. The almost complete skeleton suggested that this predator stood 6 ½–8 ft tall and weighed over 220 lb. Despite its otherwise primitive features, the *Herrerasaurus* had a dual-hinged jaw, which did not appear in other dinosaurs for another 50 million years, anticipating a turning point in the evolutionary process. (Artwork: Matthew Hillier for Guinness Publishing)

rado, Oklahoma, Utah and Wyoming about 150 million years ago, measured up to 30 ft in total length but had a walnut-sized brain weighing only 2½ oz. This represented 0·004 of 1 percent of its computed body weight of 1·9 tons (cf. 0·074 of 1 percent for an elephant and 1·88 percent for a human).

Largest eggs ■ The largest known dinosaur eggs are those of *Hypselosaurus priscus* ('high ridge lizard'), a 40 ft-long titanosaurid that lived about 80 million years ago. Some examples found in the valley of the Durance near Aix-en-Provence, southern France in October 1961 would have had, uncrushed, a length of 12 in and a diameter of 10 in (capacity 5·8 pt).

Largest claws ■ The therizinosaurids ('scythe lizards') from the Late Cretaceous of the Nemegt Basin, southern Mongolia, had the largest claws of any known animal, and in the case of *Therizinosaurus cheloniformis* measured up to 36 in around the outer curve (cf. 8 in for *T. rex*). It has been suggested that these sickle claws were designed for grasping and tearing apart large victims, but this creature had a feeble skull partially or entirely lacking teeth and probably lived on termites.

Largest skull ■ The skulls of the long-frilled ceratopsids were the largest of all known land animals and culminated in the long-frilled *Torosaurus sp.* ('piercing lizard'). This herbivore, which measured *c.* 25 ft in total length and weighed up to 8·8 tons, had a skull measuring up to 9 ft 10 in in length (including fringe) and weighing up to 2·2 tons. It ranged from Montana to Texas.

Largest flying creature ■ The largest flying creature was the pterosaur *Quetzalcoatlus northropi* ('feathered serpent'), which, about 70 million years ago, glided over what is now Texas, Wyoming and New Jersey in the United States, Alberta in Canada, Senegal in Africa, and Jordan. Partial remains discovered in Big Bend National Park, western Texas in 1971 indicate that this reptile must have had a wingspan of 36–39 ft and weighed about 250 lb.

Largest marine reptile ■ *Kronosaurus queenslandicus*, a short-necked pliosaur from the Early Cretaceous (135 million years ago) of Australia, had a 10 ft-long skull containing 80 massive teeth and measured up to 50 ft in length.

Largest crocodile ■ The largest known crocodile was the euschian *Deinosuchus riograndensis* ('terrible crocodile'), which lived in the lakes and swamps of what is now the state of Texas about 75 million years ago. Fragmentary remains discovered in Big Bend National Park, western Texas indicate a hypothetical length of 52 ft 6 in, compared with the 50 ft of the huge gharial *Rhamphosuchus* of northern India (2 million years ago) and the 46 ft of *Sarcosuchus imperator* of Niger.

Largest chelonians ■ The largest prehistoric chelonian was *Stupendemys geographicus*, a pelomedusid turtle that lived about 5 million years ago. Fossil remains discovered by Harvard University paleontologists in northern Venezuela in 1972 indicate that this turtle had a carapace (shell) measuring 7 ft 2 in–7 ft 6½ in in mid-line length and measured 9 ft 10 in in overall length. It had a computed weight of 4,500 lb in life.

Largest tortoise ■ The largest prehistoric tortoise was probably *Geochelone (Colossochelys) atlas*, which lived in what is now northern India, Myanmar (formerly Burma), Java, the Celebes and Timor, about 2 million years ago. In 1923 the fossil remains of a specimen with a carapace 5 ft 11 in long (7 ft 4 in over the curve) and 2 ft 11 in high were discovered near Chandigarh in the Siwalik Hills, India. This animal had a total length of 8 ft and is computed to have weighed 2,100 lb when it was alive.

Longest snake ■ The longest prehistoric snake was the python-like *Gigantophis garstini*, which inhabited what is now Egypt about 38 million years ago. Parts of a spinal column and a small piece of jaw discovered at Fayum in the Western Desert indicate a length of *c.* 37 ft. Another huge fossil snake from Middle Eocene in Mali was originally credited with a length of 75 ft (sic), but this measurement was overestimated. It was actually 30 ft.

Largest amphibian ■ The largest amphibian ever recorded was the gharial-like *Prionosuchus plummeri*, which lived 270 million years ago. In 1972 the fragmented remains of a specimen measuring an estimated 30 ft in life were discovered in northern Brazil.

Largest fish ■ No prehistoric fish larger than living species has yet been discovered. The claim that the great shark (*Carcharodon megalodon*), which abounded in Miocene seas some 15 million years ago, measured 80 ft in length, based on ratios from fossil teeth has now been shown to be in error. The modern estimate is that this shark did not exceed 43 ft.

Largest insect ■ The largest prehistoric insect was the dragonfly *Meganeura monyi*, which lived about 300 million years ago. Fossil remains (i.e., impressions of wings) discovered at Commentry, central France, indicate a wing extending up to 27·5 in.

Largest bird ■ The largest prehistoric bird was the flightless *Dromornis stirtoni*, a huge emu-like creature that lived in central Australia 11 million years ago. Fossil leg bones found near Alice Springs in 1974 indicate that the bird must have stood *c.* 10 ft in height and weighed *c.* 1,100 lb.

The giant moa *Dinornis maximus* of New Zealand was even taller, attaining a maximum height of 12 ft, but it weighed only about 500 lb.

Flying bird ■ The largest known flying bird was the giant teratorn (*Argentavis magnificens*) which lived in Argentina about 6 million years ago. Fossil remains discovered at a site 100 miles west of Buenos Aires, Argentina in 1979 indicate that this gigantic vulture had a wingspan of 23–25 ft and weighed about 265 lb.

Seabird ■ In 1987 an expedition from the Charleston Museum of South Carolina discovered the fossil remains of a 30 million-year-old giant seabird (*Pseudodontornis sp.*), which was related to the pelicans and cormorants. It had a wingspan of *c.* 19 ft and weighed about 90 lb.

Largest land mammal ■ The largest land mammal ever recorded was *Paraceratherium* (*Baluchitherium*), a long-necked hornless rhinocerotid that roamed across western Asia and Europe (Yugoslavia) about 35 million years ago. A restoration in the American Museum of Natural History, NY measures 17 ft 9 in to the top of the shoulder hump and 37 ft in total length, and this particular specimen must have weighed about 22 tons. The bones of this gigantic browser were first discovered in the Bugti Hills in east Baluchistan, Pakistan in 1907–8.

Largest marine mammal ■ The serpentine *Basilosaurus* (*Zeuglodon*) *cetoides*, which swam in the seas over modern-day Arkansas and Alabama 50 million years ago, measured up to 70 ft in length.

Largest mammoth ■ The largest prehistoric elephant was the steppe mammoth *Mammuthus (Parelephas) trogontherii*, which roamed over what is now central Europe a million years ago. A fragmentary skeleton found in Mosbach, West Germany indicates a shoulder height of 14 ft 9 in.

Largest primate ■ The largest known primate was *Gigantopithecus*, of the Middle Pleistocene of what is now northern Vietnam and southern China. Males would have stood an estimated 9 ft tall and weighed about 600 lb. It is risky, however, to correlate tooth size and jaw depth of primates with their height and bodyweight, and *Gigantopithecus* may have had a disproportionately large head, jaws and teeth for his body size. The only remains that have been discovered so far are three partial lower jaws and more than 1,000 teeth.

Antlers ■ The prehistoric giant deer (*Megaloceros giganteus*), which lived in northern Europe and northern Asia as recently as 8000 B.C., had the longest horns of any known animal. One specimen recovered from an Irish bog had greatly palmated antlers measuring 14 ft across, which correspond to a shoulder height of 6 ft and a weight of 1,100 lb.

Tusks ■ The longest tusks of any prehistoric animal were those of the straight-tusked elephant *Paleoloxodon antiquus germanicus*, which lived in northern Germany about 300,000 years ago. The average length in adult bulls was 16 ft 5 in.

A single tusk of a woolly mammoth (*Mammuthus primigenius*) preserved in the Franzens Museum at Brno, Czechoslovakia measures 16 ft 5½ in along the outside curve.

In *c.* August 1933, a single tusk of an imperial mammoth (*Mammuthus imperator*) measuring 16 + ft (anterior end missing) was unearthed near Post, Gorza County, TX. In 1934 this tusk was presented to the American Museum of Natural History in New York.

The heaviest single fossil tusk on record is one weighing 330 lb with a maximum circumference of 35 in now preserved in the Museo Civico di Storia Naturale in Milan, Italy. The specimen (in two pieces) measures 11 ft 9 in in length.

The heaviest recorded fossil tusks are a pair belonging to a 13 ft 4 in tall Columbian mammoth (*Mammuthus columbi*) in the State Museum, Lincoln, NE, which have a combined weight of 498 lb and measure 13 ft 9 in and 13 ft 7 in respectively. They were found near Campbell, NE in April 1915.

Plant Kingdom
Plantea

PLANTS

Oldest ■ 'King Clone,' the oldest known clone of the Creosote plant (*Larrea tridentata*), found in southwest California, was estimated in February 1980 by Professor Frank C. Vasek to be 11,700 years old. It is possible that crustose lichens in excess of 19·6 in in diameter may be as old. In 1981 it was estimated that Antarctic lichens of more than 3·9 in in diameter are at least 10,000 years old.

Rarest ■ Plants thought to be extinct are rediscovered each year and there are thus many plants of which specimens are known in but a single locality. The last surviving specimen (a female) of the Cycad *Encephalartos woodii*, a palm-like tropical plant of a group known to have existed for between 65 and 225 million years, is held at the Royal Botanic Gardens at Kew, Surrey, United Kingdom. It is possible that this plant is a hybrid of the specimen *Encephalartos allensteinii*, also at Kew. (See Oldest pot plant.)

Pennantia baylisiana, a tree found in 1945 on Three Kings Island, off New Zealand also only exists as a female and cannot fruit.

In May 1983 it was reported that there was a sole surviving specimen of the lady's slipper orchid (*Cypripedium calceolus*) in Britain.

Northernmost ■ The yellow poppy (*Papaver radicatum*) and the Arctic willow (*Salix arctica*) survive, the latter in an extremely stunted form, on the northernmost land (83° N).

Southernmost ■ Lichens resembling *Rhinodina frigida* have been found in Moraine Canyon in 86°09'S 157°30'W in 1971 and in the Horlick Mountain area, Antarctica in 86°09'S 131°14'W in 1965.

The southernmost recorded flowering plant is the Antarctic hair grass (*Deschampsia antarctica*), which was found in latitude 68°21'S on Refuge Island, Antarctica on 11 Mar 1981.

Highest ■ The greatest certain altitude at which any flowering plants have been found is 21,000 ft on Kamet (25,447 ft) by N. D. Jayal in 1955. They were *Ermania himalayensis* and *Ranunculus lobatus*.

Roots ■ The greatest reported depth to which roots have penetrated is a calculated 400 ft in the case of a wild fig tree at Echo Caves, near Ohrigstad, eastern Transvaal, South Africa.

An elm tree root of at least 360 ft was reported from Auchencraig, Largs, Ayrshire *c.* 1950.

A single winter rye plant (*Secale cereale*) has been shown to produce 387 miles of roots in 1·83 ft³ of earth.

Worst weeds ■ The most intransigent weed is the mat-forming water weed *Salvinia auriculata*, found in Africa. It was detected on the filling of Kariba Lake in May 1959 and within 11 months had choked an area of 77 miles² rising by 1963 to 387 miles².

The world's worst land weeds are regarded as purple nut sedge, Bermuda grass, Barnyard grass, jungle-rice, goose grass, Johnson grass, Guinea grass, Cogon grass and lantana.

United States ■ The most damaging and widespread weed in America is the purple nutsedge (*Cyperus rotundas*), primarily found in the southern states. Its seeds can germinate at 95°F and will withstand temperatures of −68°F for two hours and remain viable. The purple nutsedge will grow to 39 in in height and speeds underground through its system of rhyzones and tubers. It remains domant underground in extreme weather conditions.

Tallest weeds ■ The tallest weed in the United States is the Melaleuca tree (*Melaleuca quinquenervia*) introduced to the Florida and Gulf Coasts from Australia in 1900. Growing to an average of 39 ft, the weed has infested 3·7 acres of the 4·7 acres of Florida wetlands. Very dense and resistant to fire, the crowns are destroyed but the stem survives. It is a fire hazard in that it contains 'essential' oils that spread fire quickly.

Most spreading ■ The greatest area covered by a single clonal growth is that of the wild box huckleberry (*Gaylussacia brachyera*), a mat-forming evergreen shrub first reported in 1796. A colony covering about 100 acres was found on 18 July 1920 near the Juniata River,

Oldest pot plant ● The oldest known potted plant (and one of the world's rarest plants) is a single specimen of the palmlike cycad *Encephalartos allensteinii*, brought from South Africa in 1775 and now housed at the Royal Botanic Gardens, Kew, Surrey, United Kingdom.

PA. It has been estimated that this colony began 13,000 years ago.

Smallest flowering and fruiting ■ The floating flowering aquatic duckweed (*Wolffia angusta*) of Australia, described in 1980, is only 0·00236 in in length and 0·00129 in in width. It weighs about 1,190,000th of an oz, its fruit resembling a minuscule fig weighing 400,000 to the oz.

United States ■ The smallest plant regularly flowering in the United States is *Wolffia globosa*, which is found in the San Joaquin Valley, central California, and rivers draining the Sierra Nevada Mountains. The plant weighs about 150 micrograms, and is listed as 0·015 in to 0·027 in in length, and 0·011 in in width.

Fastest growing ■ The case of a *Hesperoyucca whipplei* of the family Liliaceae growing 12 ft in 14 days was reported from Tresco Abbey, Isles of Scilly, United Kingdom in July 1978.

Slowest flowering ■ The slowest flowering of all plants is the rare *Puya raimondii*, the largest of all herbs, discovered at 13,000 ft in Bolivia in 1870. The panicle emerges after about 80–150 years of the plant's life. One planted near sea level at the University of California's Botanical Garden, Berkeley in 1958 grew to 25 ft and bloomed as early as August 1986 after only 28 years. It then dies. (See also Largest blooms.)

Oldest pot plant ■ The world's oldest, and probably rarest, pot plant is the single cycad *Encephalartos allensteinii* brought from South Africa in 1775 and now housed at the Royal Botanic Gardens at Kew, Surrey, United Kingdom. (See Rarest plant.)

Biggest collection ■ Dr Julian A. Steyermark (d. 15 Oct 1988) of the Missouri Botanical Garden, St Louis, MO, had by Oct 1988 made an unrivaled total of 138,000 collections, of which 132,223 were his own continuous number series.

Largest aspidistra ■ The biggest aspidistra in the world measures 56 in and belongs to Cliff Evans of Kiora, Moruya, New South Wales, Australia.

Earliest flower ■ A flower believed to be 120 million years old was identified in 1989 by Dr Leo Hickey and Dr David Taylor of Yale University, CT from a fossil discovered near Melbourne, Victoria, Australia. The flowering angiosperm, which resembles a modern black pepper plant, had two leaves and one flower and is known as the Koonwarra plant.

United States ■ The oldest fossil of a flowering plant with palm-like imprints in America was found in Colorado in 1953 and dated about 65 million years old.

Largest cactus ■ The largest of all cacti is the Saguaro (*Cereus giganteus* or *Carnegiea gigantea*), found in Arizona, southeastern California and Sonora, Mexico. The green fluted column is surmounted by candelabra-like branches rising to a height of 57 ft 11 ¾ in in the case of a specimen discovered in the Maricopa Mountains, 11 miles east of Gila Bend, AZ on 17 Jan 1988 by J. D. and R. M. Fairfield, and R. N. and D. J. Wells. They have waxy white blooms that are followed by edible crimson fruit.

An armless cactus 78 ft in height was measured in April 1978 by Hube Yates in Cave Creek, AZ. It was toppled in a windstorm in July 1986 at an estimated age of 150 years.

Mosses ■ The smallest of mosses is the microscopic pygmy moss (*Ephemerum*) and the longest is the brook moss (*Fontinalis*), which forms streamers up to 3 ft long in flowing water.

SEAWEED

Largest ■ The longest species of seaweed is the Pacific giant kelp (*Macrocystis pyrifera*), which, although it does not exceed 196 ft in length, can grow 18 in in a day.

Deepest ■ The greatest depth at which plant life has been found is 884 ft by Mark and Diane Littler (USA) off San Salvadore Island, Bahamas in October 1984. These maroon-colored algae survived though 99·9995 percent of sunlight was filtered out.

VINES AND VINEYARDS

Largest vine ■ This was planted in 1842 at Carpinteria, CA. By 1900 it was yielding more than 9·9 tons of grapes in some years, and averaging 7·7 tons per year. It died in 1920. A single bunch of grapes (Red Thomson seedless) weighing 20 lb 11½ oz was weighed in Santiago, Chile in May 1984.

Largest vineyard ■ The world's largest vineyard extends over the Mediterranean facade between the Rhône and the Pyrenees in the departments of Hérault, Gard, Aude and Pyrénées-Orientales in an area of 2,075,685 acres, of which 52·3 percent is *monoculture viticole*.

United States ■ The largest continuous vineyard in the US is Minor Thornton Ranch in Fresno, CA. Owned by the Golden State Vintners Corp., the vineyard is 5,200 acres and produces 6,500 tons of grapes each year.

Most northerly vineyard ■ A vineyard at Sabile, Latvia, USSR is just north of Lat. 57° N.

Most southerly vineyard ■ The most southerly commercial vineyards are to be found in central Otago, South Island, New Zealand south of Lat. 45° S.

Renton Burgess Vineyard, south of Alexandra, South Island, New Zealand, is in Lat. 44°36'S.

UNITED STATES FRUIT, VEGETABLES, FLOWERS

TYPE	SIZE (Weight/Dimensions)	GROWER	LOCATION	YEAR
APPLE[1]	17 ½ in	Mr & Mrs H. Spitler	Arcanum, OH	1985
BEET	45 ½ lb	R. Meyer	Brawley, CA	1974
BEGONIA[2]	6 ft tall	T. Worrall	Fort Collins, CO	-
CANTALOUPE	55 lb	G. Daughtridge	Rocky Mount, NC	1982
COLLARD	35 ft tall	B. Rackley	Rocky Mount, NC	1980
CORN	31 ft high	D. Radda	Washington, IA	1946
DAHLIA	16 ft 5 in	S. & P Barnes	Chattahoochee, FL	1982
EGGPLANT	5 lb 5·4 oz	J. & J Charles	Summerville, SC	1984
GARLIC[3]	2 lb 12 oz	R. Kirkpatrick	Eureka, CA	1985
GOURD	93 ½ in long	B.W. Saylor	Licking, MT	1986
GOURD (weight)[4]	78 lb	L. Childers	Stinesville, IN	86
GRAPEFRUIT	6 lb 8 ½ oz	J. & A. Sosnow	Tucson, AZ	1984
KOHLRABI	36 lb	E. Krejci	Mout Clemens, MI	1979
LEMON	8 lb 8 oz	C. & D. Knutzen	Whittier, CA	1983
LIMA BEAN	14 in	N. McCoy	Hubert, NC	1979
MARIGOLD	8 ½ ft	G. Auert-Brown	Palm Beach Gardens, FL	1987
OKRA STALK[5]	17 ft 6 ¼ in	C. H. Wilber	Crane Hill, AL	1983
ONION[6]	7 ½ lb	N. W. Hope	Tempe, AZ	1984
PEANUT	3 11/16 in	B. Senkbeil	Sylvester, GA	1987
PEPPER	13 ½ in	J. Rutherford	Hatch, NM	1975
PEPPER PLANT	8 ft 1 in	R. Allen	Gillespie, IL	1987
PETUNIA	13 ft 8 in	B. Lawrence	Windham, NY	1985
PHILODENDRON	1,114 ft	F. J. Francis	U. of Massachusetts	1984
PUMPKIN[7]	671 lb	R. Gancarz	Jacobstown, NJ	1986
RUTABAGA[8]	39 lb	R. & J. Towns	Gresgham, OR	1979
SQUASH	743 lb	L. B. Stellpflug	Honeoye Falls, NY	1989
SWEET POTATO	40 ¾ b	O. Harrison	Kite, GA	1982
TOMATO	7 lb 12 oz	G. Graham	Edmond, OK	1986
TOMATO PLANT	53 ft 6 in	G. Graham	Edmond, OK	1985
TOMATO YIELD[9]	342 lb 2 oz	C. H. Wilber	Crane Hill, AL	1985
TOMATO (CHERRY)	28 ft 7 in	C. H. Wilber	Crane Hill, AL	1985
WATERMELON	279 lb	B. Rogerson	Robersonville, NC	1988
ZUCCHINI[10]	19·92 lb	W. C. Nicholas	Hatley, WI	1984

[1] An apple weighing 3 lb 1 oz was reported by V. Loveridge of Ross-on-Wye, UK in 1965.
[2] Single stalk plant. A begonia plant 5 ft 2 in tall was grown by Ralph Wettstein of Islington, Ontario, Canada, in 1987.
[3] Elephant garlic variety. The garlic had a circumference of 18 ½ in.
[4] A gourd weighing 196 lb was grown in Herringfleet, Suffolk, UK by J. Leather in 1846.
[5] This record was tied in 1986 by Buddy and Evelyn Crosby of Brooksville, FL.
[6] A speciman weighing 9 lb 11 ½ oz was grown by V. Throup in Silsden, United Kingdom in 1989.
[7] A pumpkin weighing 755 lb was grown by Gordon Thomson of Hemmingford, Quebec, Canada in 1989.
[8] A rutabaga weighing 51 lb was reported from Alaska in 1981, but this has not been substantiated.
[9] It was reported at the Tsukba Science Expo of 1988 that a single plant produced 16,897 tomtatoes.
[10] A speciman weighing 36 lb 3 oz was grown by M. M. Ricci of Montreal, Canada in 1982.

The heaviest orange ever reported is one weighing 5 lb 8 oz exhibited in Nelspruit, South Africa on 19 Jun 1981. It was the size of a human head, and was soon stolen.

BLOOMS AND FLOWERS

Largest ■ The largest of all blooms are the parasitic stinking corpse lily (*Rafflesia arnoldii*). They attach themselves to the cissus vines of the jungle in Southeast Asia and measure up to 3 ft across and ¾ in thick, and attain a weight of 15 lb. True to name, the plant is extremely offensive in scent.

Inflorescence ■ The largest known inflorescence as distinct from the largest of all blooms is that of *Puya raimondii*, a rare Bolivian monocarpic member of the Bromeliaceae family with an erect panicle (diameter 8 ft) that emerges to a height of 35 ft. Each of these bears up to 8,000 white blooms (see also Slowest flowering plant). The flower-spike of an agave was in 1974 measured to be 52 ft long in Berkeley, CA.

Blossoming plant ■ The giant Chinese wisteria (*Wisteria sinensis*) at Sierra Madre, CA was planted in 1892 and now has branches 500 ft long. It covers nearly an acre, weighs 248 tons and has an estimated 1·5 million blossoms during its blossoming period of five weeks, when up to 30,000 people pay admission to visit it.

Most valuable ■ The Burpee Co. $10,000 prize offered in 1954 for the first all-white marigold was won on 12 Aug 1975 by Alice Vonk of Sully, IA.

Largest arrangement ■ The largest arrangement of a single variety of flower was made by Johan Weisz, floral designer of Amsterdam, and 15 assistants at the City Hall, Aalsmeer, Netherlands from 23–25 Sep 1986. It consisted of 35,000 'Zurella' roses and measured 71 ft 6 in in length, 25 ft 2 in in width and 24 ft 11 in high.

Largest bouquet ■ Thirty-six people took 335 hr to make an 36 ft 10 in high bouquet of 9,299 flowers at Annecy, France on 19 Sep 1986.

Largest wreath ■ A wreath built by the Clemsonville Christmas Tree Farm of Union Bridge, MD in December 1988 measured 113 ft in diameter and weighed 8,120 lb.

Longest daisy chain ■ The longest daisy chain, made in 7 hr and measuring 6,980 ft 7 in, was made by villagers of Good Easter, Chelmsford, Essex, United Kingdom on 27 May 1985. The team is limited to 16.

Largest rhododendron ■ Examples of the scarlet *Rhododendron arboreum* reach a height of 65 ft on Mt Japfu, Nagaland, India.

The cross-section of the trunk of a *Rhododendron giganteum*, reputedly 90 ft high, from Yunnan, China, is preserved at Inverewe Gardens, Highland, United Kingdom.

Largest chrysanthemum ■ François Santini of Laboratoire Algochimie, Château Renault, Indre-et-Loire, France grew an 8·2 ft tall chrysanthemum with a total of 4,041 blooms.

Longest philodendron ■ A 735 ft long philodendron grows in the home of Mr M. J. Linhart in Thornton, Leicestershire, United Kingdom.

Largest rose tree ■ A Lady Banks rose tree at Tombstone, AZ has a trunk 40 in thick, stands 9 ft high and covers an area of 5,380 ft[2] supported by 68 posts and several thousand feet of piping. This enables 150 people to be seated under the arbor. The cutting came from Scotland in 1884.

Smallest sunflower ■ A fully mature sunflower measuring a mere 2·2 in tall was grown by Michael Lenke in Lake Oswego, OR in 1985 using a patented bonsai technique.

ORCHIDS

Tallest ■ The largest of all orchids is *Grammatophyllum speciosum*, native to Malaysia. Specimens have been recorded up to 25 ft in height.

United States ■ The tallest of all American orchids is the *Eulophia ecristata*, with a recorded height of 5·6 ft. There are five species of vanilla orchids that are vines and can spread to almost any length depending on the environment. These include *Phaeantha*, *Planifolia*, *Inodora*, *Dilliana*, and *Barbellata*. These orchids root in the ground and will grow in any direction over their surroundings.

Largest flower ■ The largest orchid flower is that of *Phragmipedium caudatum*, found in tropical areas of America. Its petals grow up to 18 in long, giving it a maximum outstretched diameter of 3 ft. The flower is, however, much less bulky than that of the stinking corpse lily (see above).

Galeola foliata, a saprophyte of the vanilla family, has been recorded at a height of 49 ft. It grows in the decaying rain forests of Queensland, Australia but is not freestanding.

United States ■ The largest flowering orchid in America is the yellow ladyslipper (*Cypripedium calceolus*) of the Pubsecens variety. Its petals grow up to 7 in long.

Smallest ■ The smallest orchid is *Platystele jungermannoides*, found in Central America. Its flowers are 0·04 in across.

United States ■ The smallest orchid is *Lepanthopsis melanantha*, with a petal spread of 0·02 in and a maximum height of 1·6 in.

Most expensive ■ The highest price ever paid for an orchid is 1,150 guineas (£1,207·50), paid by Baron Schröder to Sanders of St. Albans, United Kingdom for an *Odontoglossum crispum* (variety *pittianum*) at an auction by Protheroe & Morris of Bow Lane, London, United Kingdom on 22 Mar 1906.

A cymbidium orchid called Rosanna Pinkie was sold in the United States for $4,500 in 1952.

FRUITS AND VEGETABLES

Most nutritive ■ An analysis of the 38 commonly eaten raw (as opposed to dried) fruits shows that the one with the highest calorific value is avocado (*Persea americana*), with 741 calories per edible lb. Avocados probably originated in Central and South America and also contain vitamins A, C and E and 2·2 percent protein.

Least nutritive ■ That with the lowest calorific value is cucumber, with 73 calories per lb.

Asparagus ■ Joaquin Calvo Peligros of Madrid, Spain found a 7·15 ft-long asparagus with a 0·78 in diameter on La Maraña hill, Carveña, Madrid on 1 May 1988.

Chilli ■ A 21 ft 7 in chilli plant was grown by Shri Kishan Joshi of Almora, India in 1985–86.

Cucumber ■ Mrs Eileen Chappel of Bowen Hills, Queensland, Australia grew a cucumber weighing 66 lb in April 1989.

Pineapple ■ A pineapple weighing 17 lb 8 oz was harvested by Dole Philippines Inc. at South Cotabato, Philippines in November 1984. Pineapples up to 28·6 lb were reported in 1978 from Tarauaca, Brazil.

Potato display ■ A record display of 369 varieties of potato (*Solanum tuberosum*) was mounted on British Broadcasting Corporation *Record Breakers* by Donald MacLean on 16 Sep 1984.

HERBS

Herbs are not botanically defined but consist of plants whose leaves or roots are of culinary or medicinal value.

Most heavily consumed ■ The most heavily consumed is coriander (*Coriandrum sativum*). It is used in curry powder, confectionery, in bread and in gin.

FERNS

Largest ■ The largest of all the more than 6,000 species of fern is the tree fern (*Alsophila excelsa*) of Norfolk Island, in the South Pacific, which attains a height of up to 60 ft.

United States ■ The highest in America is the giant fern (*Acrostichum danaeaefolium*) of the Gulf Coast, which measures up to 16·4 ft. However, the bracken fern (*Pteridium aquilinum*) is the largest fern plant. It grows to a height of 4·9 ft above ground, but grows giant clones or stem systems underground that can reach up to a quarter of a mile. This fern is found throughout the United States.

Smallest ■ The world's smallest ferns are *Hecistopteris pumila*, found in Central America, and *Azolla caroliniana*, which is native to the United States and has fronds down to ½ in.

GRASSES

Commonest ■ The world's commonest grass is *Cynodon dactylon* or Bermuda grass. The Callie hybrid, selected in 1966, grows as much as 6 in a day and stolons reach 18 ft in length.

United States ■ The most common grasses in America include Kentucky bluegrass (*Poa pratensis*), Canada bluegrass (*Poa compressa*) and annual brome grass (*Bromus tectorum*).

Fastest growing ■ Some species of the 45 genera of bamboo have been measured to grow at up to 36 in per day (0·00002 mph).

Tallest ■ A thorny bamboo culm (*Bambusa arundinacea*) felled at Pattazhi, Travancore, India in November 1904 measured 121½ ft.

United States ■ The tallest grass native to America is the giant cane (*Arundinaria gigantea*), which reaches a height of 30 ft.

Shortest ■ In the United States, the shortest grass is false buffalo grass (*Munroa squarrosa*), which has a maximum growing height of 0·8 in, but on average the grass, which is found throughout the states, grows only to a height of 0·4 in.

LEAVES

Largest ■ The largest leaves of any plant belong to the raffia palm (*Raphia raffia*) of the Mascarene Islands in the Indian Ocean, and the Amazonian bamboo palm (*R. toedigera*) of South

Largest ● The largest seeds in the world are those of the double coconut or coco-der-mer (*Lodoicea seychellarum*), that grows only in the Seychelles and bears a single-seeded fruit which may weigh 40 lb. (Photo: Picturepoint Ltd)

America, whose leaf blades may measure up to 65 ft in length with petioles up to 13 ft.

The largest undivided leaf is that of *Alocasia macrorrhiza*, found in Sabah, East Malaysia. One found in 1966 was 9 ft 11 in long and 6 ft 3½ in wide, with a unilateral area of 34·2 ft².

A specimen of the water lily *Victoria amazonica* (longwood hybrid) in the grounds of the Stratford-upon-Avon Butterfly Farm, United Kingdom measured 8 ft in diameter on 2 Oct 1989.

United States ■ The largest outdoor leaves in America are those of the climbing fern (*Lygodium japonicum*), found in the Gulf Coast, with leaves of 23 ft.

Fourteen-leafed clover ■ A fourteen-leafed white clover (*Trifolium repens*) was found by Randy Farland near Sioux Falls, SD on 16 Jun 1975. A fourteen-leafed red clover (*Trifolium pratense*) was also reported by Paul Haizlip, at the age of 12 at Bellevue, WA on 22 Jun 1987.

SEEDS

Largest ■ The largest seed in the world is that of the double coconut or coco-de-mer (*Lodoicea seychellarum*), the single-seeded fruit of which may weigh 40 lb. This grows only in the Seychelles, in the Indian Ocean.

Smallest ■ The smallest seeds are those of epiphytic orchids, at 35 million to the oz (cf. grass pollens at up to 6 billion grains/oz).

A single plant of the American ragweed can generate 8 billion pollen grains in five hours.

Most viable ■ The most protracted claim for the viability of seeds is that made for the arctic lupine (*Lupinus arcticus*) found in frozen silt at Miller Creek in the Yukon, Canada in July 1954

by Harold Schmidt. The seeds were germinated in 1966 and were dated by the radiocarbon method of associated material to at least 8000 B.C. and more probably to 13,000 B.C.

HEDGES

Tallest ■ The Meikleour beech hedge in Perthshire, United Kingdom was planted in 1746 and has now attained a trimmed height of 85 ft. It is 1,800 ft long. Some of its trees now exceed 105 ft.

Tallest yew ■ A yew hedge in Earl Bathurst's Park, Cirencester, Gloucestershire, United Kingdom was planted in 1720, and runs for 510 ft, reaches 36 ft, is 15 ft thick at its base and takes 20 man-days to trim.

Tallest box ■ The tallest box hedge is 35 ft in height, at Birr Castle, County Offaly, Republic of Ireland, dating from the 18th century.

TREES AND WOOD

Most massive ■ The most massive living thing on Earth is the biggest known giant sequoia (*Sequoiadendron giganteum*) named the 'General Sherman,' standing 274·9 ft tall, in the Sequoia National Park, CA. It has a true girth of 82·3 ft (1989) (at 4·5 ft above the ground). The General Sherman has been estimated to contain the equivalent of 600,120 board feet of timber, sufficient to make 5 billion matches. The foliage is blue-green, and the red-brown tan bark may be up to 24 in thick in parts. Estimates place its weight, including its root system, at 2,756 tons but the timber is light (18 lb/ft³).

The largest known petrified tree is one of this species with a 295 ft trunk near Coaldale, NV.

The seed of a 'big tree' weighs only 1/6000th of an oz. Its growth at maturity may therefore represent an increase in weight of 13×10^{11}.

The tree canopy covering the greatest area is the great banyan *Ficus benghalensis* in the Indian Botanical Garden, Calcutta with 1,775 prop or supporting roots and a circumference of 1,350 ft. It covers overall some 3 acres and dates from *ante* 1787. However, it is reported that a 550-year-

at Watts River, Victoria, Australia, reported in 1872 by trained forester William Ferguson. It measured 435 ft and almost certainly measured over 500 ft originally.

A *Eucalyptus regnans* at Mt Baw Baw, Victoria, Australia is believed to have measured 470 ft in 1885. The closest measured rivals to these champions have been:

415 ft Douglas fir *Pseudotsuga menziesii*, Lynn Valley, British Columbia, 1902.

393 ft Mineral Douglas fir *Pseudotsuga menziesii*, WA, 1905.

380 ft Nisqually fir *Pseudotsuga menziesii*, Nisqually River, WA, 1899.

375 ft Cornthwaite mountain ash *Eucalyptus regnans*, Thorpdale, Victoria, Australia, 1880.

367·6 ft Coast redwood *Sequoia sempervirens*, Guerneville, CA, 1873. This tree was felled for timber in 1875.

The tallest tree currently standing is the Dyerville giant of the coast redwood species *Sequoia sempervirens* at Humboldt Redwood State Park in Humbolt County, CA which measured 362 ft according to data supplied by The American Forestry Association.

The tallest standing broadleaf tree is a mountain ash (*Eucalyptus regnans*) in the Styx Valley, Tasmania at 312 ft.

Christmas ■ The world's tallest cut Christmas tree was a 221 ft tall Douglas fir (*Pseudosuga menziesii*) erected at Northgate Shopping Center, Seattle, WA in December 1950.

Oldest ■ The oldest recorded tree was a bristlecone pine (*Pinus longaeva*) designated WPN-114, which grew at 10,750 ft above sea level on the northeast face of Mt Wheeler, eastern Nevada. It was found to be 5,100 years old.

The oldest known *living* tree is the bristlecone pine named Methuselah at 10,000 ft in the California side of the White Mountains, confirmed as 4,700 years old. In March 1974 it was reported that this tree had produced 48 live seedlings. Dendrochronologists estimate the *potential* life span of a bristlecone pine at nearly 5,500 years, while the greatest age shown by a ring count carried out on a California big tree (*Sequoia giganteum*) is 3,500 years. No single cell lives more than 30 years.

United States ■ The oldest species is the bristlecone pine, which grows in the desert regions of South California and Nevada. The exact date of the oldest tree is not known, however some living species are believed to be at least 4,000 years old.

Earliest species ■ The earliest species of tree still surviving is the maidenhair tree (*Ginkgo biloba*), of Zhexiang, China, which first appeared about 160 million years ago, during the Jurassic era. It was 'rediscovered' by Kaempfer (Netherlands). It has been grown in Japan since *c.* 1100, where it was known as *ginkyō* ('silver apricot') and is now known as *icho*.

Most leaves ■ Little work has been done on the laborious task of establishing which species has most leaves. A large oak has perhaps 250,000 but a cypress may have some 45–50 million leaf scales.

Remotest ■ The tree believed to be the remotest from any other is a Norwegian spruce, the only one on Campbell Island, Antarctica. Its nearest companion would be over 120 miles away on the Auckland Islands.

Most expensive ■ The highest price ever

old banyan tree (known as 'Thimmamma Marrimanu') in Gutibayalu village near Kadiri Taluk, Andrha Pradesh, India spreads over 5·2 acres.

Greatest girth ■ 'El Arbol del Tule,' in the state of Oaxaca, in Mexico is a 135 ft tall Montezuma cypress (*Taxodium mucronatum*) with a girth of 117·6 ft at a height of 5 ft above the ground in 1982.

Measurements up to 180 ft in circumference have been attributed to baobab trees (*Adansonia digitata*).

United States ■ A Coast Douglas fir at Olympic National Park, Washington has a girth of 44·5 ft at a height of 4 ½ ft.

Fastest growing ■ Discounting bamboo, which is not botanically classified as a tree but as a woody grass, the fastest rate of growth recorded is 35 ft 3 in in 13 months by an *Albizzia falcata* planted on 17 Jun 1974 in Sabah, Malaysia.

The youngest recorded age for a tree to reach 100 ft is 64 months for one of the species planted on 24 Feb 1975, also in Sabah.

The world's most productive forest is a plan-

tation of eucalypts (*Eucalyptus grandis*) at Aracruz, Brazil, where the average growth rate is 2,472 ft³ per 2·5 acres.

Slowest growing ■ The speed of growth of trees depends largely upon conditions, although some species, such as box and yew, are always slow-growing. The extreme is represented by the *Dioon edule* (Cycadaceae) measured in Mexico in 1981–6 by Dr Charles M. Peters. He found the average annual growth rate to be 0·03 in and a 120-year old specimen of 3·9 in tall.

The growing of miniature trees or *bonsai* is an oriental cult mentioned as early as *c.* 1320.

Tallest ■ According to the researches of Dr A. C. Carder, the tallest tree ever measured was an Australian eucalyptus (*Eucalyptus regnans*)

Most massive ● The Sequoia National Park in California is the home of the largest trees in the world, including the most massive living thing on Earth, the giant sequoia (*Sequoiadendron giganteum*) known as General Sherman which stands 275 ft tall and has a true girth of 83 ft measured 4 ½ ft above the ground. (Photo: Bruce Coleman)

TALLEST TREES IN THE UNITED STATES
(By species)

			ft
ASH (Black)	Adrian, MI		155
ASH (Green)	Cass County, MI		131
ASPEN (Bigtooth)	Marquette, MI		132
BEECH (American)	Ashtabula County, OH		130
BUCKEYE (Ohio)	Liberty, KY		144
BUCKEYE (Painted)	Chattahoochee National Forest, GA		144
BUCKEYE (Yellow)	Great Smokey Mountain National Park, TN		145
CEDAR (Incense)	Marble Mountain Wilderness, CA		152
CEDAR (Port-Orford)	Siskiyou National Forest, OR		219
COTTONWOOD (Black)	Willamette Mission State Park, OR		155
DOUGLAS FIR (Bigcone)	Angeles National Forest, CA		145
DOUGLAS FIR (Coast)	Olympic National Park, WA		298
DOUGLAS FIR (Rocky Mountain)	Ochoco National Forest, OR		158
ELM (September)	Colbert County, AL		150
EUCALYPTUS (Bluegum)	Fort Ross State Historic Park, Sonoma, CA		165
EUCALYPTUS (Longbeak)	Kern County, CA		171
FIR (Bristlecone)	Los Padres National Forest, CA		182
FIR (California Red)	Sierra National Forest, CA		180
FIR (Grand)	Olympic National Park, WA		251
FIR (Noble)	Mount St. Helens National Monument, WA		272
FIR (Pacific Silver)	Forks, WA		203
FIR (Shasta Red)	Rogue River National Forest, OR		228
FIR (White)	Meridan, CA		192
HEMLOCK (Western)	Olympic National Park, WA		241
HICKORY (Mockernut)	Humpreys County, MS		156
HICKORY (Nutmeg)	Lowndes County, AL		145
HICKORY (Pignut)	Robbinsville, NC		190
HICKORY (Red)	Great Smokey National Park, TN		140
HICKORY (Shagbark)	Henry County, SC		153
LARCH (Western)	Libby, MT		175
MAPLE (Red)	St. Clair County, MI		179
OAK (Overcup)	Lewiston-Woodville, Bertie County, NC		156
OAK (Scarlet)	Colbert County, AL		150
OAK (Swamp Chestnut)	Fayette County, AL		200
OAK (Swamp White)	Wayne County, MI		144
OAK (Valley)	South of Covelo, CA		163
PECAN	Cocke County, TN		143
PINE (Digger)	Redding, CA		161
PINE (Eastern White)	Marquette, MI		201
PINE (Jeffrey)	Stanislaus National Forest, CA		197
PINE (Ponderosa)	Plumas, CA		223
PINE (Red)	Watersmeet, MI		154
PINE (Slash)	Collton, County, SC		150
PINE (Sugar)	North Fork of Stanislaus River, CA		216
PINE (Western White)	El Dorado National Forest, CA		157
RED CEDAR (Western)	Forks, WA		178
REDWOOD (Coast)	Humboldt Redwoods State Park, CA		362
SEQUOIA (Giant)	Sequoia National Park, CA		275
SPRUCE (Brewer)	Siskiyou National Forest, OR		170
SPRUCE (Engelmann)	Payette Lake, ID		179
SPRUCE (Sitka)	Seaside, OR		206
YELLOW POPLAR (Tuliptree)	Bedford, VA		146

Data supplied by The American Forestry Association, 1990

paid for a tree is $51,000 for a single starkspur golden delicious apple tree from near Yakima, WA, bought by a nursery in Missouri in 1959.

Largest forest ■ The largest afforested areas in the world are the vast coniferous forests of the northern USSR, lying between latitude 55°N and the Arctic Circle. The total wooded area amounts to 2·7 billion acres (25 percent of the world's forests), of which 38 percent is Siberian larch. The USSR is 34 percent afforested.

The largest area of forest in the tropics remains the Amazon Basin, amounting to some (81·5 million acres).

United States ■ The largest forest in the United States is the Tongass National Forest (16·7 million acres), in Alaska. The United States is 32·25 percent afforested.

A figure of 190 ft in circumference was recorded for the pollarded European chestnut (*Castanea sativa*) known as the 'Tree of the 100 Horses'

(Castagno di Cento Cavalli) on Mount Etna, Sicily, Italy in 1770 and 1780. It is now in three parts widely separated.

Longest avenue ■ The longest avenue of trees has been the now partly felled private avenue of 1,750 beeches in Savernake Forest near Marlborough, Wiltshire, United Kingdom. It measures 3·6 miles.

Heaviest wood ■ Black ironwood (*Olea laurifolia*), also called South African ironwood, has a specific gravity of up to 1·49, and weighing up to 93 lb/ft³.

United States ■ The heaviest American wood is the lead wood tree (*Krugiodendron ferreum*), with a specific gravity of 1·34:1·42.

Lightest wood ■ The lightest wood is *Aeschynomene hispida*, found in Cuba, which has a specific gravity of 0·044 and a weight of only 2¾ lb/ft³.

The wood of the balsa tree (*Ochroma pyramidale*)

is of very variable density — between 2½ and 24 lb/ft³.

The density of cork is 15 lb/ft³.

United States ■ The lightest American wood is pithe wood (*Moscheutos*) with a specific gravity of 0·5 or less.

Kingdom Protista

Protista were first discovered in 1676 by Antonie van Leeuwenhoek of Delft (1632–1723), a Dutch microscopist. Among Protista are characteristics common to both plants and animals. The more plant-like are termed Protophyta (protophytes), including unicellular algae, and the more animal-like are placed in the phylum Protozoa (protozoans), including amoeba and flagellates.

Largest ■ The largest protozoans in terms of volume that are known to have existed were calcareous foraminifera (Foraminiferida) belonging to the genus *Nummulites*, a species which in the Middle Eocene rocks of Turkey, attained 8·6 in in diameter.

The largest existing protozoan, a species of the fan-shaped *Stannophyllum* (Xenophyophorida), can exceed this in length (9·8 in has been recorded) but not in volume.

Smallest protophytes ■ The marine microflagellate alga *Micromonas pusilla* has a diameter of less than 2 microns or micrometers 0·00008 in.

Fastest ■ The protozoan *Monas stigmatica* has been measured to move a distance equivalent to 40 times its own length in a second. No human can cover even seven times his own length in a second.

Fastest reproduction ■ The protozoan *Glaucoma*, which reproduces by binary fission, divides as frequently as every three hours. Thus in the course of a day it could become a great-great-great-great-great-great grandparent and the progenitor of 510 descendants.

Kingdom Fungi

Largest ■ Marcia Wallgren of Yellow Springs, OH found a puff ball (*Calvatia gigantea*) 77 in in circumference in 1988.

A 72 lb example of the edible mushroom (*Polyporus frondosus*) was reported by Joseph Opple near Solon, OH in September 1976.

The largest recorded tree fungus is a specimen of the bracket fungus *Rigidoporus ulmarius* growing from dead elm wood in the grounds of the C.A.B International Mycological Institute at Kew, Surrey, United Kingdom. This perennial species measured 57·9 x 47·7 in with a circumference of 161 in on 28 Dec 1989 and is still growing.

Most poisonous toadstool ■ The yellowish-olive death cap (*Amanita phalloides*), which may be found in England, is regarded as the world's most poisonous fungus. From 6–15 hours after tasting, the effects are vomiting, delirium, collapse and death. Among its victims was Cardinal Giulio de' Medici, Pope Clement VII (b. 1478) on 25 Sep 1534.

Aeroflora ■ Fungi were once classified in the subkingdom Protophyta of the kingdom Protista. The highest total fungal spore count was 5,686,860·6/ft³ near Cardiff, United Kingdom

on 21 Jul 1971. A plane tree pollen count of 76,278·24/ft³ was recorded near London on 9 May 1971. The lowest counts of airborne allergens are nil.

Kingdom Procaryota

BACTERIA

Antonie van Leeuwenhoek (1632–1723) was the first to observe bacteria, in 1675. The largest of the bacteria is the sulfur bacterium *Beggiatoa mirabilis*, which is 16–45 μm in width.

The bacteria *Thermoactinomyces vulgaris* have been found alive in cores of mud taken from the bottom of Windermere, Cumbria, United Kingdom and have been dated to 1,500 years before the present.

Smallest free-living entity ■ The smallest of all free-living organisms are pleuro-pneumonia-like organisms (PPLO) of the *Mycoplasma*. One of these, *Mycoplasma laidlawii*, first discovered in sewage in 1936, has a diameter during its early existence of only 10^{-7} m. Examples of the strain known as H.39 have a maximum diameter of 3×10^{-7} m and weigh an estimated 10^{-16} g. Thus a 209·4 ton blue whale would weigh 1·9 quadrillion times as much.

Highest ■ In April 1967 the US National Aeronautics and Space Administration (NASA) reported that bacteria had been discovered at an altitude of 135,000 ft (25·56 miles).

Oldest ■ The oldest deposits from which living bacteria are claimed to have been extracted are salt layers near Irkutsk, USSR, dating from about 600 million years ago, but the discovery was not accepted internationally.

The US Dry Valley Drilling Project in Antarctica claimed resuscitated rod-shaped bacteria from caves up to one million years old.

Fastest ■ The rod-shaped bacillus *Bdellovibrio bacteriovorus*, by means of a polar flagellum rotating 100 times/sec, can move 50 times its own length of 2μm per sec. This would be the equivalent of a human sprinter reaching 200 mph or a swimmer crossing the English Channel in 6 min.

Toughest ■ The bacterium *Micrococcus radiodurans* can withstand atomic radiation of 6·5 million röntgens or 10,000 times that fatal to the average man.

In March 1983 John Barras (University of Oregon) reported bacteria from sulfurous seabed vents thriving at 583°F in the East Pacific Rise at Lat. 21°N.

VIRUSES

Largest ■ Dmitriy Ivanovsky (1864–1920) first reported filterable objects in 1892 but Martinus Willem Beijerink (1851–1931) first confirmed the nature of viruses in 1898. These are now defined as aggregates of two or more types of chemical (including either DNA or RNA) that are infectious and potentially pathogenic.

The longest known is the rod-shaped *Citrus tristeza* virus with particles measuring 2×10^{-5} m.

Smallest ■ The smallest known viruses are the nucleoprotein plant viruses, such as the satellite of tobacco *Necrosis virus* with spherical particles 17 nm in diameter.

A putative new infectious submicroscopic organism but without nucleic acid, named a

Largest ● The largest recorded tree fungus is a specimen of the bracket fungus *Rigidoporus ulmarius* growing from dead elm wood in the grounds of the C.A.B. Mycological Institute at Kew, Surrey, United Kingdom. This perennial species measured 58 × 47 in with a circumference of 161 in in December 1989 and is still growing. (Photo: Mycological Institute)

'prion,' was announced from the University of California in February 1982.

Viroids (RNA cores without protein coating) are much smaller than viruses. They were discovered by Theodor O. Diener (USA) in February 1972.

Dr Rohwer of Bethesda, MD stated in September 1984 that scrapie-specific protein was smaller than the concept of a 'yet to be identified prion.'

Parks, Zoos, Oceanaria, Aquaria

PARKS

Largest ■ The Wood Buffalo National Park in Alberta, Canada (established 1922), has an area of 11,172,000 acres (17,560 miles²).

United States ■ The largest public park in the United States is Wrangell-St. Elias National Park and Preserve (13·2 million acres) in Alaska.

ZOOS

It has been estimated that throughout the world there are some 757 zoos with an estimated annual attendance of 350 million.

Largest game reserve ■ The world's largest zoological reserve is the Etosha National Park, Namibia. Established in 1907 its area has grown to 38,427 miles².

Oldest zoo ■ The earliest known collection of animals was that set up by Shulgi, a 3rd-dynasty ruler of Ur from 2097–2094 B.C. at Puzurish in southeast Iraq.

The oldest known zoo is that at Schönbrunn, Vienna, Austria, built in 1752 by the Holy Roman Emperor Franz I for his wife Maria Theresa.

The oldest existing public zoological collection in the world is that of the Zoological Society of London, United Kingdom, founded in 1826. Its collection, housed partly in Regent's Park, London (36 acres) and partly at Whipsnade Zoo, Bedfordshire, United Kingdom (541 acres) (opened 23 May 1931), is the most comprehensive in the United Kingdom. The stocktaking on 1 Jan 1989 accounted for a total of 11,108 specimens. These comprised 2,628 mammals, 1,916 birds, 489 reptiles, 175 amphibians, an estimated total of 2,300 fish and an estimated total of 3,600 invertebrates excluding some common species. The

record annual attendances are 3,031,571 in 1950 for Regent's Park and 756,758 in 1961 for Whipsnade Zoo.

United States ■ The Philadephia Zoo received its charter from the state of Pennsylvania in 1859, but did not open to the public until 1874. Lincoln Park Zoo, a 60-acre public park owned by the city of Chicago, received a gift of two swans from Central Park, NY in 1868. By 1870 a 'small barn and paddocks' had been built to house further animals that had been donated by the public. The current facility is 35 acres.

According to the American Association of Zoological Parks and Aquariums, the top zoo for attendance is Lincoln Park Zoo with 4·5 million visitors per year. The next largest total is San Diego Zoo, which hosts 3·8 million visitors per year.

Earliest without bars ■ The earliest zoo without bars was that at Stellingen, near Hamburg, West Germany. It was founded in 1907 by Carl Hagenbeck (1844–1913), who made use of deep pits and large pens instead of cages to separate the exhibits from visitors.

OCEANARIA

Earliest ■ The world's first oceanarium is Marineland of Florida, opened in 1938 at a site 18 miles south of St Augustine, FL. Up to 5·8 million gal of seawater are pumped daily through two major tanks, one rectangular (100 ft long by 40 ft wide by 18 ft deep) containing 375,000 gal, and one circular (233 ft in circumference and 12 ft deep) containing 330,000 gal. The tanks are seascaped, including coral reefs and even a shipwreck.

AQUARIA

Largest aquarium ■ In terms of the volume of water held, The Living Seas Aquarium opened in 1986 at the EPCOT Center in Florida is the world's largest, with a total capacity of 6·25 million gal. It contains over 3,000 fish representing 90 species.

The largest in terms of marine life is the Monterey Bay Aquarium opened on 20 Oct 1984 in California at a cost of $55 million, which houses 6,500 specimans (525 species) of flora and fauna in its 95 tanks. The aqaurium, which sits on 2·2 acres of land, has a capacity of 750,000 gallons. The two largest tanks hold 335,000 and 326,000 gallons respectively.

THE
NATURAL
WORLD &
SPACE

The Natural World and Space

THE EARTH

The Earth is not a true sphere, but flattened at the poles and hence an oblate spheroid. The polar diameter of the Earth, which is 7,899·806 miles, is 26·575 miles less than the equatorial diameter (7,926·381 miles). The Earth has a pear-shaped asymmetry with the north polar radius being 148 ft longer than the south polar radius. There is also a slight ellipticity of the equator since its long axis (about longitude 37° W) is 522 ft greater than the short axis. The greatest departures from the reference ellipsoid are a protuberance of 240 ft in the area of Papua New Guinea and a depression of 344 ft south of Sri Lanka, in the Indian Ocean.

The greatest circumference of the Earth, at the equator, is 24,901·46 miles, compared with 24,859·73 miles at the meridian.

The area of the surface is estimated to be 196,937,400 miles^2.

The period of axial rotation, i.e., the true sidereal day, is 23 hr 56 min 4·0996 sec, mean time.

The mass of the Earth was first assessed by Dr Nevil Maskelyne (1732–1811) in Perthshire, United Kingdom in 1774. The modern value is 6·6 sextillion tons and its density is 5·515 times that of water.

The volume is an estimated 0·26 trillion miles^3.

The Earth picks up cosmic dust but estimates vary widely, with 33 tons a year being the upper limit. Modern theory is that the Earth has an outer shell or lithosphere 50 miles thick, then an outer and inner rock layer or mantle extending 1,745 miles deep, beneath which there is an iron-rich core of radius 2,164 miles. If the iron-rich core theory is correct, iron would be the most abundant element in the Earth. At the center of the core, the estimated density is 0·47 lb/in^3, the temperature 8,132° F and the pressure 26,432 tons f/in^2.

Structure and Dimensions

OCEANS

The area of the Earth covered by water is estimated to be 139·8 million miles^2 or 70·98 percent of the total surface.

The mean depth of the hydrosphere was once estimated to be 12,450 ft, but recent surveys suggest a lower estimate of 11,660 ft.

The total weight of the water is estimated to be 1·45 quintillion tons, or 0·022 percent of the Earth's total weight.

The volume of the oceans is estimated to be 323·9 million miles^3 compared to 8·4 million miles^3 of fresh water.

Largest ■ The largest ocean in the world is the Pacific. Excluding adjacent seas, it represents 45·9 percent of the world's oceans and covers 64·2 million miles^2 in area. The average depth is 13,740 ft.

Clearest sea ● The Weddell Sea, 71° S, 15° W off Antarctica, has the clearest water of any sea. A Secchi disc was visible to a depth of 262 ft on 13 Oct 1986, as measured by Dutch researchers of the German Alfred-Wegener Institute. Such clarity corresponds to what scientists consider attainable in distilled water. This shot shows broken pack ice in the Weddell Sea. (Photo: Science Photo Library)

The shortest navigable transpacific distance from Guayaquil, Ecuador to Bangkok, Thailand is 10,905 miles.

Deepest ■ The deepest part of the ocean was first pinpointed in 1951 by the British Survey Ship *Challenger* in the Mariana Trench in the Pacific Ocean. The depth was measured by wide-band sounding at 35,639 ft. Subsequent visits have resulted in slightly deeper measurements. A survey by the Soviet research ship *Vityaz* in 1957 produced a depth that was later refined to 36,200 ft, and on 23 Jan 1960 the US Navy bathyscaphe *Trieste* descended to the bottom at 35,813 ft. A more recent visit produced a figure of 35,839 ft ± 33 ft, from data obtained by the survey vessel *Takuyo* of the Hydrographic Department, Japan Maritime Safety Agency in 1984, using a narrow multi-beam echo sounder.

A metal object, for example a 2·2 lb ball of steel, dropped into water above this trench would take nearly 64 min to fall to the seabed, where hydrostatic pressure is over 18,000 lb/in^2.

United States ■ Defining US territorial waters as within 200 nautical miles of any US territory (Economic Exclusive Zone [EEZ]), the deepest point in American waters is Challenger D in the Mariana Trench in the Pacific Ocean. Challenger D is 5,973 fathoms (10,924 miles) deep, 170 nautical miles SW of Guam at 11° 22·4 N, 142° 35·5 E.

The deepest point from an American state is the Vega Basin in the Aleutian Trench, which is 4,198 fathoms (7,679 miles) deep at 50° 51 N, 177° 11 E, 60 nautical miles south of the Aleutian Islands, AK.

Largest sea ■ The largest of the world's seas is the South China Sea, with an area of 1·1 million miles^2.

Waves ● Right: The area of the Earth covered by sea is estimated to be 139,781,000 miles^2 or 70·98 percent of the total surface. Excluding adjacent seas, the Pacific represents 45·9 percent of the world's oceans and covers 64,185,600 miles^2 in area. (Photo: Vince Cavataio/All-Sport)

Largest gulf ■ The largest gulf in the world is the Gulf of Mexico, with an area of 580,000 miles^2 and a shoreline of 3,100 miles from Cape Sable, FL to Cabo Catoche, Mexico.

Largest bay ■ The largest bay in the world measured by shoreline length is Hudson Bay, northern Canada, with a shoreline of 7,623 miles and with an area of 317,500 miles^2.

The area of the Bay of Bengal is, however, 839,000 miles^2.

Longest fjord ■ The world's longest fjord is the Nordvest Fjord arm of the Scoresby Sound in eastern Greenland, which extends inland 195 miles from the sea.

The longest Norwegian fjord is the Sognefjord, which extends 126·8 miles inland from the island of Sogneoksen to the head of the Lusterfjord arm at Skjolden. Its width ranges from 1½ miles at its narrowest up to 3¼ miles at its widest. Its deepest point is 4,252 ft.

The longest Danish fjord is Limfjorden (100 miles).

Highest sea mountain ■ The highest known submarine mountain, or seamount, is one discovered in 1953 near the Tonga Trench, between Samoa and New Zealand. It rises 28,500 ft from the seabed, with its summit 1,200 ft below the surface.

Remotest spot from land ■ The world's most distant point from land is a spot in the South Pacific, approximately 48° 30′ S, 125° 30′ W, which is about 1,660 miles from the nearest points of land, namely Pitcairn Island, Ducie Island and Cape Dart, Antarctica. Centered on this spot, therefore, is a circle of water with an area of about 8·6 million miles^2—about 7,000 miles^2 larger than the USSR, the world's largest country.

Most southerly ■ The most southerly part of the oceans is 85° 34′ S, 154° W, at the snout of

Waves ● The area of the Earth covered by sea is estimated to be 362 033 000 km² *139 781 000 miles²* or 70·98 per cent of the total surface. Excluding adjacent seas, the Pacific represents 45·9 per cent of the world's oceans and covers 166 241 000 km² *64 185 600 miles²* in area. (Photo: Vince Cavataio/All-Sport)

the Robert Scott Glacier, 305 miles from the South Pole.

Temperature ■ The temperature of the water at the surface of the sea varies from 28·5° F in the White Sea to 96° F in the shallow areas of the Persian Gulf in summer. Ice-focused solar rays have been known to heat lake water to nearly 80° F. The normal Red Sea temperature is 71·6° F.

The highest temperature recorded in the ocean is 759° F, for a spring measured by an American research submarine some 300 miles off the American West Coast, in an expedition under the direction of Professor Jack Diamond of Oregon State University in 1985. Remote probes measured the temperature of the spring, which was kept from vaporizing by the weight of water above it.

Clearest ■ The Weddell Sea, 71° S, 15° W off Antarctica, has the clearest water of any sea. A Secchi disc was visible to a depth of 262 ft on 13 Oct 1986, as measured by Dutch researchers at the German Alfred-Wegener Institute. Such clarity corresponds to what scientists consider attainable in distilled water.

STRAITS

Longest ■ The longest straits in the world are the Tatarskiy Proliv or Tartar Straits between Sakhalin Island and the USSR mainland, running from the Sea of Japan to Sakhalinsky Zaliv—497 miles, thus marginally longer than the Malacca Straits.

Broadest ■ The broadest named straits in the world are the Davis Straits between Green-land and Baffin Island, Canada, with a minimum width of 210 miles.

The Drake Passage between the Diego Ramirez Islands, Chile and the South Shetland Islands is 710 miles across.

Narrowest ■ The narrowest navigable straits are those between the Aegean island of Euboea and the mainland of Greece. The gap is only 131 ft wide at Khalkis.

WAVES

Highest ■ The highest officially recorded sea wave was calculated at 112 ft from trough to crest; it was measured by Lt Frederic Margraff, USN, from the USS *Ramapo* proceeding from Manila, Philippines to San Diego, CA on the night of 6–7 Feb 1933, during a 68-knot hurricane.

The highest instrumentally measured wave was one 86 ft high, recorded by the British ship *Weather Reporter*, in the North Atlantic on 30 Dec 1972 in Lat. 59° N, Long. 19° W. It has been calculated on the statistics of the Stationary Random Theory that one wave in more than 300,000 may exceed the average by a factor of four.

On 9 Jul 1958 a landslip caused a 100 mph wave to wash 1,720 ft high along the fjord-like Lituya Bay in Alaska.

Highest seismic ■ The highest estimated height of a *tsunami* (often wrongly called a tidal wave) was one of 278 ft, which appeared off Ishigaki Island, Ryukyu Chain on 24 Apr 1771. It tossed a 826·7 ton block of coral more than 1·3 miles. Tsunami (a Japanese word: *nami*, a

wave; *tsu*, overflowing) have been observed to travel at 490 mph.

Evidence for a 1,000-ft ocean wave having occurred about 100,000 years ago was reported on 4 Dec 1984. This is believed to have broken on the southern shore of Lanai, Hawaiian Islands and was due to a meteorite, a volcanic eruption or a submarine landslide.

CURRENTS

Greatest ■ The greatest current in the oceans is the Antarctic Circumpolar Current or West Wind Drift Current, which was measured in 1969 in the Drake Passage between South America and Antarctica to be flowing at a rate of 9,500 million ft³ per sec—nearly treble that of the Gulf Stream. Its width ranges from 185–1,240 miles and has a proven surface flow rate of ⁴/₁₀ of a knot.

Strongest ■ The world's strongest currents are the Nakwakto Rapids, Slingsby Channel, British Columbia, Canada (Lat. 51° 05′ N, Long. 127° 30′ W), where the flow rate may reach 16 knots .

TIDES

Extreme tides are due to lunar and solar gravitational forces affected by their perigee, perihelion and syzygies. Barometric and wind effects can superimpose an added 'surge' element. Coastal and seafloor configurations can accentuate these forces. The normal interval between tides is 12 hr 25 min.

Greatest ■ The greatest tides occur in the Bay of Fundy, which divides the peninsula of Nova Scotia, Canada from the United States'

Narrowest straits ● The narrowest navigable straits in the world are those between the Aegean island of Euboea and the mainland of Greece. This satellite image of the area shows the Aegean Sea at the top and right, with Euboea almost joined to the mainland. The gap here is only 131 ft wide at the town of Khalkis. The color coding is red and pink for vegetation and cultivated areas, and light blue-gray for centers of urbanization and industrialization. (Photo: Science Photo Library)

northeasternmost state of Maine and the Canadian province of New Brunswick.

Burncoat Head in the Minas Basin, Nova Scotia, has the greatest mean spring range, with 47 ft 6 in. A range of 54 ft 6 in was recorded at springs in Leaf Basin, in Ungava Bay, Quebec, Canada in 1953. Tahiti experiences virtually no tide.

ICEBERGS
Largest and tallest ■ The largest iceberg on record was an antarctic tabular iceberg of over 12,000 miles², 208 miles long and 60 miles wide sighted 150 miles west of Scott Island, in the South Pacific Ocean, by the USS *Glacier* on 12 Nov 1956.

The 200-ft thick arctic ice island T.1 (140 miles²), discovered in 1946, was tracked for 17 years.

The tallest iceberg measured was one of 550 ft reported off western Greenland by the US icebreaker *East Wind* in 1958.

Most southerly arctic ■ The most southerly arctic iceberg was sighted in the Atlantic by a USN weather patrol in Lat. 28° 44′ N, Long. 48° 42′ W in April 1935.

Most northerly antarctic ■ The most northerly antarctic iceberg was a remnant sighted in the Atlantic by the ship *Dochra* at Lat. 26° 30′ S, Long. 25° 40′ W, on 30 Apr 1894.

LAND
There is satisfactory evidence that at one time the Earth's land surface comprised a single primeval continent of 80 million miles², now termed Pangaea, and that this split about 190 million years ago, during the Jurassic period, into two supercontinents, which are termed Laurasia (Eurasia, Greenland and North America) and Gondwanaland (Africa, Arabia, India, South America, Oceania and Antarctica), named after Gondwana, India, which itself split 120 million years ago. The South Pole was apparently in the area of the Sahara as recently as the Ordovician period of *c.* 450 million years ago.

ROCKS
The age of the Earth is generally considered to be within the range of 4,500 ± 70 million years, based on the lead isotope systematics. However, no rocks of this great age have yet been found on the Earth since geological processes have presumably destroyed them.

Oldest ■ The greatest reported age for any scientifically dated rock is 3·962 billion years in the case of Acasta Gneisses found in May 1984. The rocks were discovered approximately 200 miles north of Yellowknife, Northwest Territories, Canada by Dr Samuel Bowring as part of an ongoing Canadian geology survey mapping project. When the samples were analyzed in June 1989, Dr Bowring and scientists from Australian National University in Canberra established their age using a machine called SHRIMP (Sensitive High-mass Resolution Ion MicroProbe).

Older minerals have been identified that are not rocks. Some zircon crystals discovered by Bob Pidgeon and Simon Wilde in the Jack Hills, 435 miles north of Perth, Western Australia in 1984 were found to be 4·276 billion years old, again using SHRIMP. These are the oldest fragments of the Earth's crust discovered so far.

United States ■ The oldest rocks in the United States are the Morton Gneisses, found in 1935 by G. A. Phiel and C. E. Dutton scattered over an area of 50 miles from New Ulm, Brown County to Renville County in Minnesota. In 1980 these rocks were dated at 3·6 billion years old by Sam Goldrich of the US Geological Survey in Denver, CO, using the Uranium-Lead Dating method.

Largest ■ The largest monolith in the world is Ayers Rock, which rises 1,143 ft above the surrounding desert plain in Northern Territory, Australia. It is 1·5 miles long and 1 mile wide. The nearest major town is Alice Springs, which is 250 miles to the northeast.

It was estimated in 1940 that La Gran Piedra, a volcanic plug located in the Sierra Maestra, Cuba, weighs 75,747 tons.

CONTINENTS
Largest ■ Of the Earth's surface 41·25 percent, or 81·2 million miles², is covered by continental masses of which only about two-thirds or 29·02 percent of the Earth's surface (57·2 million miles²) is land above water, with a mean height of 2,480 ft above sea level. The Eurasian landmass is the largest, with an area (including islands) of 20·7 million miles². The Afro-Eurasian landmass, separated artificially only by the Suez Canal, covers an area of 32·7 million miles² or 57·2 percent of the Earth's landmass.

Smallest ■ The smallest continent is the Australian mainland, with an area of 2·9 million miles², which, together with Tasmania, New Zealand, New Guinea and the Pacific Islands, is described sometimes as Oceania.

Land remotest from the sea ■ The point of land remotest from the sea is at Lat. 46° 16·8′ N, Long. 86° 40·2′ E in the Dzoosotoyn Elisen (desert), northern Xinjiang Uygur Zizhiqu (Sinkiang), China's most northwesterly province. It was visited by Nicholas Crane and Dr Richard Crane on 27 Jun 1986 and is at a straight-line distance of 1,645 miles from the nearest open sea.

Peninsula ■ The world's largest peninsula is Arabia, with an area of about 1·25 million miles².

ISLANDS
Largest ■ Discounting Australia, which is usually regarded as a continental landmass, the largest island in the world is Greenland (renamed Kalaallit Nunaat on 1 May 1979), with an area of about 840,000 miles². There is evidence that Greenland is in fact several islands overlaid by an ice cap without which it would have an area of 650,000 miles².

The largest sand island in the world is Fraser Island, Queensland, Australia with a 75-mile long sand dune.

Freshwater ■ The largest island sur-

Northernmost land ● The northernmost land is Oodaq Ø, which is 4,434 ft north of Kaffeklubben Ø off Pearyland, Kalaallit Nunaat (formerly Greenland) in Lat. 83° 40′ 32·5″ N, Long. 30° 40′ 10·1″ W. It was first observed on 26 Jul 1978 by Uffe Petersen of the Danish Geodetic Institute. It is 438·9 miles from the North Pole. (Photo: Geodetic Institute, Denmark)

rounded by fresh water (18,500 miles²) is the Ilha de Marajó in the mouth of the River Amazon, Brazil.

The world's largest inland island (i.e., land surrounded by rivers) is Ilha do Bananal, Brazil (7,000 miles²).

The largest island in a lake is Manitoulin Island (1,068 miles²) in the Canadian section of Lake Huron.

Remotest ■ The remotest island in the world is Bouvet Øya (formerly Liverpool Island), discovered in the South Atlantic by J. B. C. Bouvet de Lozier on 1 Jan 1739, and first landed on by Capt George Norris on 16 Dec 1825. Its position is 54° 26′ S, 3° 24′ E. This uninhabited Norwegian dependency is about 1,050 miles from the nearest land—the uninhabited Queen Maud Land coast of eastern Antarctica.

The remotest inhabited island in the world is Tristan da Cunha, discovered in the South Atlantic by Tristão da Cunha, a Portuguese admiral, in March 1506. It has an area of 38 miles² (habitable area — 12 miles²). The first permanent inhabitant was Thomas Currie, who landed in 1810. The island was annexed by the United Kingdom on 14 Aug 1816. After evacuation in 1961 (due to volcanic activity), 198 islanders returned in November 1963. The nearest inhabited land to the group is the island of St Helena, 1,320 miles to the northeast. The nearest continent, Africa, is 1,700 miles away.

Greatest archipelago ■ The world's greatest archipelago is the 3,500-mile long crescent of more than 13,000 islands that forms Indonesia.

Highest rock pinnacle ■ The world's highest rock pinnacle is Ball's Pyramid near Lord Howe Island in the Pacific, which is 1,843 ft high, but has a base axis of only 660 ft. It was first scaled in 1965.

Northernmost land ■ On 26 Jul 1978 Uffe Petersen of the Danish Geodetic Institute observed the islet of Oodaq Ø 100 ft across, 0·8 miles north of Kaffeklubben Ø off Pearyland, Greenland at Lat. 83° 40′ 32·5″ N, Long. 30° 40′ 10·1″ W. It is 438·9 miles from the North Pole.

Southernmost land ■ The South Pole, unlike the North Pole, is on land. The Amundsen–Scott south polar station was built there at an altitude of 9,370 ft in 1957. It is drifting bodily with the ice cap 27–30 ft per year in the direction 43° W and was replaced by a new structure in 1975.

Newest ■ The world's newest island is the lava islet of Fukuto Kuokanoba near Iwo Jima in the Pacific reported in January 1986. It measures 2,132 × 1,476 ft and is 40 ft above sea level.

Largest atoll ■ The largest atoll in the world is Kwajalein in the Marshall Islands, in the central Pacific Ocean. Its slender 176-mile long coral reef encloses a lagoon of 1,100 miles².

The atoll with the largest land area is Christmas Atoll, in the Line Islands, in the central Pacific Ocean. It has an area of 248 miles², of which 125 miles² is land. Its principal settlement, London, is only 2½ miles distant from another settlement, Paris.

Longest reef ■ The Great Barrier Reef off Queensland, northeastern Australia, is 1,260 statute miles in length. Between 1959 and 1971 a large section between Cooktown and Townsville was destroyed by the crown-of-thorns starfish (*Acanthaster planci*).

DEEPEST CAVES BY COUNTRIES

Depth (ft)		
5,256	Réseau Jean Bernard	France
4,947	Shakta Pantjukhina	USSR
4,728	Sistema del Trave	Spain
4,439	Sistema Huautla	Mexico
3,999	Schwersystem	Austria
3,986	Complesso Fighiera Corchia	Italy
3,930	Veliko Fbrego	Yugoslavia
3,802	Anou Ifflis	Algeria
3,346	Siebenhengste System	Switzerland

Deepest caves ● Right: The deepest cave in the world is in France. In a ranking of countries by the deepest cave in each country, the USSR would come next, followed by Spain, Mexico, Austria and Italy. This photograph shows the lower streamway in the Complesso Fighiera Corchia cave in Italy, which is 3,986 ft deep. (Photo: Dr A C Waltham)

DEPRESSIONS

Deepest ■ The deepest depression so far discovered is the bedrock in the Bentley subglacial trench, Antarctica at 8,326 ft below sea level.

The greatest submarine depression is an area of the northwest Pacific floor that has an average depth of 15,000 ft.

The deepest exposed depression on land is the shore surrounding the Dead Sea, now 1,312 ft below sea level. The deepest point on the bed of this saltiest of all lakes is 2,388 ft below sea level. The rate of fall in the lake surface since 1948 has been 13·78 in per year.

The deepest part of the bed of Lake Baikal in Siberia, USSR is 4,872 ft below sea level.

United States ■ The lowest-lying area in the United States is in Death Valley, CA at 282 ft below sea level.

Largest ■ The largest exposed depression in the world is the Caspian Sea basin in the Azerbaijan, Russian, Kazakh and Turkmen Republics of the USSR and northern Iran. It is more than 200,000 miles², of which 143,550 miles² is lake area. The preponderant land area of the depression is the Prikaspiyskaya Nizmennost, lying around the northern third of the lake and stretching inland for a distance of up to 280 miles.

CAVES

Longest ■ The most extensive cave system in the world is that under the Mammoth Cave National Park, KY, first entered in 1799. Explorations by many groups of cavers have revealed and interconnected the cave passages beneath the Flint, Mammoth Cave and Toohey Ridges to make a system with a total mapped length that is now 348 miles.

Largest ■ The world's largest cave chamber is the Sarawak Chamber, Lubang Nasib Bagus, in the Gunung Mulu National Park, Sarawak, discovered and surveyed by the 1980 British-Malaysian Mulu Expedition. Its length is 2,300 ft; its average width is 980 ft; and it is nowhere less than 230 ft high. It would be large enough to garage 7,500 buses.

Greatest descent ■ The world depth

record was set by the Groupe Vulcain in the Gouffre Jean Bernard, France at 5,256 ft in 1989. However, this cave, explored via multiple entrances, has never been entirely descended, so the 'sporting' record for the greatest descent into a cave is recognized as 4,947 ft in the Shakta Pantjukhina in the Russian Caucasus Mountains by a team of Ukrainian cavers in 1988.

Longest stalactite ■ The longest known stalactite in the world is a wall-supported column extending 195 ft from roof to floor in the Cueva de Nerja, near Málaga, in Spain.

Probably the longest free-hanging stalactite in the world is one of 21·5 ft, in the Poll an Ionain cave in County Clare, Republic of Ireland.

Tallest stalagmite ■ The tallest known stalagmite in the world is believed to be one in the Krásnohorska cave in Czechoslovakia, which is generally accepted as being about 105 ft tall.

The tallest cave column is considered to be the 128 ft high Flying Dragon Pillar in Nine Dragons Cave (Daji Dong), Guizhou (Kweichow), China.

Deepest ■ The deepest cave in the United States is Columbine Crawl in Wyoming at 1,550 ft. The second deepest cave is Lechuguilla Cave in Carlsbad Caverns, Carlsbad, NM, which currently measures 1,510 ft. This cave is still being surveyed and it could overtake the Columbine cave when measurement is complete.

MOUNTAINS

Highest ■ An eastern Himalayan peak of 29,028 ft above sea level on the Tibet–Nepal border (in an area first designated Chu-mu-langma on a map of 1717) was discovered to be the world's highest mountain in 1852 by the Survey Department of the Government of India, from theodolite readings taken in 1849 and 1850. In 1860 its height was computed to be 29,002 ft. On 25 Jul 1973 the Chinese announced a height of 29,029 ft 3 in. It was named Mt Everest after Col.

Sir George Everest, (1790–1866), formerly surveyor-general of India.

Everest's status as the world's highest mountain, maintained for 135 years (1852–1987), was most recently challenged by K2 (formerly Godwin Austen), also known as Chogori, in the disputed Kashmiri Northern Areas of Pakistan, in an announcement on 6 Mar 1987 by the US K2 Expedition. Their satellite transit surveyor yielded altitudes of between 29,064–29,228 ft as against the hitherto official 19th-century figure of 28,250 ft, and the 20th-century proposed height of 28,740 ft. However, on 13 Aug 1987 the Chinese reaffirmed their heights of 29,029 ft 3 in for Everest and 28,250 ft for K2. The Research Council in Rome announced on 23 Oct 1987 that new satellite measurements restored Everest to primacy, at 29,078 ft, and put K2 down to 28,238 ft. It was on 31 Jul 1954 that K2 was first climbed, by A. Compagnoni and L. Lacedelli of Italy, 14 months after the summit of Everest had been reached. (For details of Everest ascents, see under Mountaineering in Chapter 11.)

The mountain whose summit is farthest from the Earth's center is the Andean peak of Chimborazo (20,561 ft), 98 miles south of the equator in Ecuador, South America. Its summit is 7,057 ft further from the Earth's center than the summit of Mt Everest.

The highest mountain on the equator is Volcán Cayambe (19,285 ft), Ecuador, in Long. 77° 58′ W. A mountaineer on the summit would be moving at 1,038 mph relative to the Earth's center due to the Earth's rotation.

The highest insular mountain in the world is Puncak Jayak (formerly Puncak Sukarno, formerly Carstensz Pyramide) in Irian Jaya, Indonesia. A survey by the Australian Universities' Expedition in 1973 yielded a height of 16,023 ft. Ngga Pula, now 15,950 ft, was in 1936 possibly c. 16,110 ft before the melting of its snow cap.

United States ■ The highest mountain in the United States is Mount McKinley in Alaska, with a highest point of 20,320 ft. McKinley, so named in 1896, was called Denali (Great One) in the Athabascan language of North American Indians.

Unclimbed ■ The highest unclimbed summit is Lhotse Middle Peak (27,657 ft) in the Khumbu district of the Nepal Himalaya. It is the tenth highest individually recognized summit in the world, Lhotse being the fourth highest mountain.

Tallest ■ The world's tallest mountain measured from its submarine base (3,280 fathoms) in the Hawaiian Trough to its peak is Mauna Kea (Mountain White) on the island of

---

Greatest plateau ● The most extensive high plateau in the world is the Tibetan Plateau in Central Asia. The average altitude is 16,000 ft and the area is 77,000 miles^2. (Photo: Spectrum)

Hawaii, with a combined height of 33,476 ft, of which 13,796 ft are above sea level.

Another mountain whose dimensions, but not height, exceed those of Mt Everest is the volcanic Hawaiian peak of Mauna Loa (Mountain Long) at 13,680 ft. The axes of its elliptical base, 16,322 ft below sea level, have been estimated at 74 miles and 53 miles.

It should be noted that Cerro Aconcagua (22,834 ft) is more than 38,800 ft above the 16,000-ft deep Pacific abyssal plain or 42,834 ft above the Peru-Chile Trench, which is 180 miles distant in the South Pacific.

Greatest ranges ■ The world's greatest land mountain range is the Himalaya-Karakoram, which contains 96 of the world's 109 peaks of over 24,000 ft. *Himalaya* derives from the Sanskrit *him*, snow; *alaya*, home.

The greatest of all mountain ranges is, however, the submarine Indian/East Pacific Oceans Cordillera extending 19,200 miles from the Gulf of Aden to the Gulf of California by way of the seabed between Australia and Antarctica with an average height of 8,000 ft above the base ocean depth.

Longest lines of sight ■ Vatnajökull (6,952 ft), Iceland has been seen by refracted light from the Faeroe Islands 340 miles distant. In Alaska, Mt McKinley (20,320 ft) has been sighted from Mt Sanford (16,237 ft): a distance of 230 miles.

Greatest plateau ■ The most extensive high plateau in the world is the Tibetan Plateau in Central Asia. The average altitude is 16,000 ft and the area is 77,000 miles^2.

Sheerest wall ■ Mt Rakaposhi (25,498 ft), rises 3·72 miles from the Hunza Valley, Pakistan in 6·21 miles with an overall gradient of 31°.

The 3,200 ft wide northwest face of Half Dome, Yosemite, California is 2,200 ft high but nowhere departs more than 7 degrees from the vertical. It was first climbed (Class VI) in 1957 by Royal Robbins, Jerry Gallwas and Mike Sherrick.

Highest halites ■ Along the northern shores of the Gulf of Mexico for 1,725 miles there exist 330 subterranean 'mountains' of salt, some of which rise more than 60,000 ft from bedrock and appear as the low salt domes first discovered in 1862.

WATERFALLS

Highest ■ The highest waterfall (as opposed to vaporized bridal-veil fall) in the world is the Salto Angel in Venezuela, on a branch of the River Carrao, an upper tributary of the Caroni, with a total drop of 3,212 ft—the longest single drop is 2,648 ft. The Angel Falls were named after the United States pilot Jimmy Angel (d. 8 Dec 1956), who recorded them in his log book on 14 Nov 1933. The falls, known by the Indians as Cherun-Meru, were first reported by Ernesto Sanchez La Cruz in 1910.

United States ■ The tallest continuous waterfall in the United States is Ribbon Falls in Yosemite National Park in California, with a drop of 1,612 ft. This is a seasonal waterfall and is generally dry from late July to early September.

Yosemite Falls, also in Yosemite National Park, has the greatest *total* drop at 2,425 ft, but actually consists of three distinct waterfalls. These are the Upper (1,430 ft), Middle (675 ft) and Lower falls (320 ft).

Greatest ■ On the basis of the average annual flow, the greatest waterfalls in the world are the Boyoma (formerly Stanley) Falls in Zaïre with 600,000 cusec.

The flow of the Guaíra (Salto das Sete Quedas) on the Alto Paraná river between Brazil and Paraguay has at times attained a peak rate of 1·75 million cusec.

It has been calculated that a waterfall 26 times greater than the Guaíra and perhaps 2,625 ft high was formed, when some 5·5 million years ago the Mediterranean basins began to be filled from the Atlantic through the Straits of Gibraltar.

Widest ■ The widest waterfalls in the world are the Khône Falls (50–70 ft high) in Laos, with a width of 6·7 miles and a flood flow of 1·5 million cusec.

RIVERS

Longest ■ The two longest rivers in the world are the Nile (Bahr-el-Nil), flowing into the Mediterranean, and the Amazon (Amazonas), flowing into the South Atlantic. Which is the longer is more a matter of definition than simple measurement.

The length of the Nile watercourse, as surveyed by M. Devroey (Belgium) before the loss of a few miles of meanders due to the formation of Lake Nasser, behind the Aswan High Dam, was 4,145 miles. This course is unitary from a hydrological standpoint and runs from the source in Burundi of the Luvironza branch of the Kagera feeder of the Victoria Nyanza via the White Nile (Bahrel-Jebel) to the delta in the Mediterranean.

The true source of the Amazon was discovered in 1953 to be a stream named Huarco, deriving from the Misuie Glacier (17,715 ft) in the Arequipa Andes of Peru. This stream progressively becomes the Toro, then the Santiago, then the Apurimac, which in turn is known as the Ene and then the Tambo before its confluence with the Amazon prime tributary, the Ucayali. The length of the Amazon from this source to the South Atlantic via the Canal do Norte was measured in 1969 and found to be 4,007 miles (usually quoted to the rounded-off figure of 4,000 miles).

If, however, a vessel navigating down the river follows the 'arm' (carrying 10 percent of the river's water) to the south of Ilha de Marajó through the Furo Tajapuru and Furo dos Macacos into the Pará, the total length of the watercourse becomes 4,195 miles. The Rio Pará is *not*, however, a tributary of the Amazon, being hydrologically part of the basin of the Tocantins, which itself, however, flows into the Bahía de Marajó and out into the South Atlantic.

United States ■ The longest river in the United States is the Mississippi, with a length of 2,348 miles. It flows from its source at Lake Itasca, MN through 31 states before reaching the Gulf of Mexico.

Shortest ■ As with the longest river, two rivers could also be considered to be the shortest river with a name, depending on exactly where the measurement is taken from, plus factors such as tides and weather conditions. The D River, in Lincoln City, OR, which connects Devil's Lake to the Pacific Ocean, and the Roe River, near Great Falls, MT, which flows into the Missouri River, have both been measured on different occasions, and lengths varying from 200 ft down to 58 ft have been recorded.

Largest basin ■ The largest river basin in the world is that drained by the Amazon (4,007 miles), which covers about 2·7 million miles². It has about 15,000 tributaries and subtributaries, of which four are more than 1,000 miles long. These include the Madeira, the longest of all tributaries, with a length of 2,100 miles, which is surpassed by only 14 rivers in the world.

Longest sub-tributary ■ The longest sub-tributary is the Pilcomayo (1,000 miles) in South America. It is a tributary of the Paraguay (1,500 miles long), which is itself a tributary of the Paraná (2,500 miles).

Longest estuary ■ The world's longest estuary is that of the often frozen Ob', in the northern USSR, at 550 miles. It is up to 50 miles wide.

Largest delta ■ The world's largest delta is that created by the Ganges (Ganga) and Brahmaputra in Bangladesh and West Bengal, India. It covers an area of 30,000 miles².

Greatest flow ■ The greatest flow of any river in the world is that of the Amazon, which discharges an average of 4·2 million cusec into the Atlantic Ocean, increasing to more than 7 million cusec in full flood. The lowest 900 miles of the Amazon average 300 ft in depth.

Submarine ■ In 1952 a submarine river 250 miles wide, known as the Cromwell Current, was discovered flowing eastward 300 ft below the surface of the Pacific for 3,500 miles along the equator. Its volume is 1,000 times that of the Mississippi.

Subterranean ■ In August 1958 a cryptoriver was tracked by radio isotopes flowing under the Nile with six times its mean annual flow or 20 trillion ft³.

Largest swamp ■ The world's largest tract of swamp is in the basin of the Pripyat River— a tributary of the Dnieper in the USSR. These swamps cover an estimated area of 18,125 miles².

RIVER BORES
The bore on the Ch'ient'ang'kian (Hangchow city) in eastern China is the most remarkable of the 60 in the world. At spring tides the wave attains a height of up to 25 ft and a speed of 13–15 knots. It is heard advancing at a range of 14 miles.

The annual downstream flood wave on the Mekong sometimes reaches a height of 46 ft.

The greatest volume of any tidal bore is that of the Canal do Norte (10 miles wide) in the mouth of the Amazon.

LAKES AND INLAND SEAS
Largest ■ The largest inland sea or lake in the world is the Kaspiyskoye More (Caspian Sea) in the southern USSR and Iran. It is 760 miles long and its total area is 143,550 miles². Of the total area, some 55,280 miles² (38·5 percent) are in Iran, where it is named the Darya-ye-Khazar. Its maximum depth is 3,360 ft and its surface is 93 ft below sea level. Its estimated volume is 21,500 miles³ of saline water. Its surface has varied between 105 ft (11th century) and 72 ft (early 19th century) below sea level.

United States ■ The largest lake in the United States is Lake Michigan, with an area of 22,400 miles², a length of 321 miles and a maximum depth of 923 ft. Both Lake Superior and Lake Huron have a larger area, but these straddle the Canadian/American border.

Deepest ■ The deepest lake in the world is Ozero (Lake) Baikal in central Siberia, USSR. It is 385 miles long and between 20–46 miles wide. In 1957 the lake's Olkhon Crevice was measured to be 6,365 ft deep and hence 4,872 ft below sea level.

United States ■ The deepest lake in the United States is the 6-mile long Crater Lake, in Crater Lake National Park in the Cascade Mountains of Oregon. Its surface is 6,176 ft above sea level and its extreme depth is 1,932 ft, with an average depth of 1,500 ft. The lake has neither inlets nor outlets, instead it is filled and maintained solely by precipitation.

Highest ■ The highest navigable lake in the world is Lake Titicaca (maximum depth 1,214 ft), with an area of about 3,200 miles² in South America (1,850 miles² in Peru and 1,350 miles² in Bolivia). It is 130 miles long and is situated 12,506 ft above sea level.

There are higher lakes in the Himalayas, but most are glacial and of a temporary nature only. A survey of the area carried out in 1984 showed a lake at a height of 17,762 ft named Panch Pokhri that was 1 mile long.

Freshwater ■ The freshwater lake with the greatest surface area is Lake Superior, one of the Great Lakes of North America. The total area is 31,800 miles², of which 20,700 miles² are in Minnesota, Wisconsin and Michigan and 11,100 miles² in Ontario, Canada. It is 1,600 ft above sea level.

The freshwater lake with the greatest volume is Lake Baikal in Siberia, USSR, with an estimated volume of 5,520 miles³.

Lake in a lake ■ The largest lake in a lake is Manitou Lake (41·09 miles²) on the world's largest lake island, Manitoulin Island (1,068 miles²), in the Canadian part of Lake Huron. The lake itself contains a number of islands.

Underground ■ Probably the world's largest underground lake is that in the Drachenhauchloch cave in Namibia, discovered in 1986. Its surface has an area of 5¼ acres, and lies 200 ft underground, over water 300 ft deep.

United States ■ Reputedly the United States' largest underground lake is the Lost Sea, 300 ft subterranean in the Craighead Caverns, Sweetwater, TN, measuring 4½ acres and discovered in 1905.

Largest lagoon ■ Lagoa dos Patos in southernmost Brazil is 158 miles long and extends over 4,110 miles².

OTHER FEATURES
Desert ■ Nearly an eighth of the world's land surface is arid with a rainfall of less than 9·8 in per year. The Sahara in North Africa is the largest in the world. At its greatest length it is 3,200 miles from east to west. From north to south it is between 800 and 1,400 miles. The area covered by the desert is about 3·25 million miles². The land level varies from 436 ft below sea level in the Qattâra Depression, Egypt to the mountain Emi Koussi (11,204 ft) in Chad. The daytime temperature range in the western Sahara may be more than 80° F.

United States ■ The largest desert in the

Longest glaciers ● The longest single glacier in the Himalayas is the Siachen, which is 47 miles long, in the Karakoram range. (Photo: Bruce Coleman)

United States is the Mojave Desert in southeast California. It covers an area of 115,000 miles² and has an average rainfall of 5 in.

Sand dunes ■ The world's highest measured sand dunes are those in the Saharan sand sea of Isaouane-N-Tifernine of east-central Algeria in Lat. 26° 42′ N, Long. 6° 43′ E. They have a wavelength of 3·1 miles and attain a height of 1,410 ft.

Largest mirage ■ The largest mirage on record was that sighted in the Arctic at 83° N 103° W by Donald B. MacMillan in 1913. This type of mirage, known as the Fata Morgana, appeared as the same 'hills, valleys, snow-capped peaks extending through at least 120 degrees of the horizon' that Peary had misidentified as Crocker Land six years earlier.

On 17 Jul 1939 a mirage of Snaefells Jokull (4,715 ft) on Iceland was seen from the sea at a distance of 335–350 miles.

Largest gorge ■ The largest land gorge in the world is the Grand Canyon on the Colorado River in north-central Arizona. It extends from Marble Gorge to the Grand Wash Cliffs, over a distance of 217 miles. It varies in width from 4–13 miles and is some 5,300 ft deep.

The submarine Labrador Basin canyon is c. 2,150 miles long.

Deepest canyon ■ The deepest canyon is El Cañón de Colca, Peru, reported in 1929, which is 10,574 ft deep. It was first traversed by the

---

Deepest permafrost ● The deepest recorded permafrost is more than 4,500 ft, reported from the upper reaches of the Viluy River, Siberia, USSR in February 1982. Permafrost can give rise to spectacular crevasses, such as this one being negotiated by a climber in the Antarctic Peninsula. (Photo: Doug Allan/Science Photo Library)

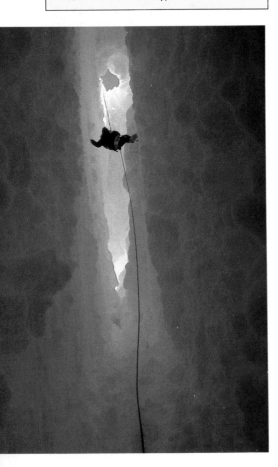

Polish Expedition CANOANDES' 79 kayak team from 12 May–14 Jun 1981.

A stretch of the Kali River in central Nepal flows 18,000 ft below its flanking summits of the Dhaulagiri and Annapurna mountain groups.

The deepest submarine canyon yet discovered is one 25 miles south of Esperance, Western Australia, which is 6,000 ft deep and 20 miles wide.

United States ■ The deepest canyon in the United States is Kings Canyon, East Fresno, CA, which runs through Sierra and Sequoia National Forests. The deepest point, which measures 8,200 ft, is in the Sierra National Park Forest section of the canyon.

The deepest canyon in low relief territory is Hell's Canyon, dividing Oregon and Idaho. It plunges 7,900 ft from the Devil Mountain down to the Snake River.

Cliffs ■ The highest sea cliffs yet pinpointed anywhere in the world are those on the north coast of east Moloka'i, HI near Umilehi Point, which descend 3,300 ft to the sea at an average gradient of more than 55°.

Natural arches ■ The longest natural arch in the world is the Landscape Arch in the Arches National Park, 25 miles north of Moab in Utah. This natural sandstone arch spans 291 ft and is set about 100 ft above the canyon floor. In one place erosion has narrowed its section to 6 ft.

Larger, however, is the Rainbow Bridge, UT discovered on 14 Aug 1909, which although only 278 ft long, is more than 22 ft wide.

Longest glaciers ■ It is estimated that 6·02 million miles², or 10·5 percent of the Earth's land surface, is permanently glaciated. The world's longest known glacier is the Lambert Glacier, discovered by an Australian aircraft crew in Australian Antarctic Territory in 1956–57. It is up to 40 miles wide and, with its upper section, known as the Mellor Glacier, it measures at least 250 miles in length. With the Fisher Glacier limb, the Lambert forms a continuous ice passage about 320 miles long.

The longest Himalayan glacier is the Siachen (47 miles) in the Karakoram range, though the Hispar and Biafo combine to form an ice passage 76 miles long.

The fastest-moving major glacier is the Quarayaq in Greenland, flowing 65–80 ft per day.

United States ■ The largest glacier in the United States is the Malaspina glacier, 30 miles north of Yakutut, AK. It measures 850 miles² and is part of the 2,000-miles² Malaspina Glacier Complex.

Thickest ice ■ The greatest recorded thickness of ice is 2·97 miles measured by radio echo soundings from a US Antarctic research aircraft at 69° 9′ 38″ S 135° 20′ 25″ E 250 miles from the coast in Wilkes Land on 4 Jan 1975.

Deepest permafrost ■ The deepest recorded permafrost is more than 4,500 ft, reported from the upper reaches of the Viluy River, Siberia, USSR in February 1982.

Natural Phenomena

EARTHQUAKES ■ (Seismologists record all dates with the year *first*, based not on local time but on Universal Time/Greenwich Mean Time).

Greatest ■ It is estimated that each year there are some 500,000 detectable seismic or microseismic disturbances of which 100,000 can be felt and 1,000 cause damage. The deepest recorded hypocenters are of 447 miles in Indonesia in 1933, 1934 and 1943.

The most commonly used scale to measure the size of earthquakes is Richter's magnitude scale (1954). It is named after Dr Charles Richter (1900–85) and the most commonly used form is M_s, based on amplitudes of surface waves, usually at a period of 20 sec. The largest reported magnitudes on this scale are about 8·9, but the scale does not properly represent the size of the very largest earthquakes, above M_s about 8, for which it is better to use the concept of seismic moment, M_o, devised by K. Aki in 1966. Moment can be used to derive a 'moment magnitude,' M_w, first used by Hiroo Kanamori in 1977. The largest recorded earthquake on the M_w scale is the Chilean shock of 1960 May 22, which had $M_w = 9·5$, but only 8·3 on the M_s scale. For the largest events such as the Chilean shock of 1960, the energy released is more than 10^{19} joules.

United States ■ The strongest earthquake in American history was near Prince William Sound, AK (80 miles east of Anchorage) on 27 Mar 1964, which measured 8·4 on the Richter Scale, killed 117 people and caused an estimated $750 million in damage. It caused a tsunami 50 feet high that traveled 8,445 miles at 450 mph. The town of Kodiak was destroyed, and tremors were felt in California, Hawaii and Japan.

Worst death toll ■ The greatest chronicled loss of life occurred in the earthquake that rocked every city of the Near East and eastern Mediterranean c. July 1201. Contemporary accounts estimate the loss of life at 1·1 million.

Less uncertain is the figure of 830,000 fatalities in a prolonged earthquake (*ti chen*) in the Sheanxi, Shanxi and Henan provinces of China, of 1556 Feb 2 (new style; Jan 23 old style).

The highest death toll in modern times has been in the Tangshan earthquake (Mag. 7·9) in eastern China on 1976 Jul 27 (local time was 3 A.M. July 28). The first figure published on 4 Jan 1977 revealed 655,237 killed, later adjusted to 750,000. On 22 Nov 1979 the New China News Agency unaccountably reduced the death toll to 242,000.

United States ■ The highest death toll for the United States is 700 in the Great San Francisco Earthquake of 8 Apr 1906, which measured an estimated 8·3 on the Richter Scale. Accurate records were not kept at this time, and some experts believe the 700 deaths to be a low calculation. There was also no Richter Scale and this measurement, although the consensus, is debated.

Material damage ■ The greatest physical devastation was in the earthquake on the Kanto plain, Japan, of 1923 Sept 1 (Mag. 8·2, epicenter in Lat. 35° 15′ N, Long. 139° 30′ E); in Sagami Bay the sea bottom in one area sank 1,310 ft. The official total of persons killed and missing in this *shinsai* or great 'quake and the resultant fires was 142,807. In Tokyo and Yokohama 575,000 dwellings were destroyed. The cost of the damage was estimated at 1 billion pounds sterling (now 17 billion pounds sterling).

VOLCANOES

The total number of known active volcanoes in the world is 1,343, of which many are submarine. The greatest active concentration is in Indonesia, with some 200 volcanoes. The name volcano derives from the now dormant Vulcano Island (from the god of fire Vulcanus) in the Mediterranean.

Greatest explosion ■ The greatest explosion in historic times (possibly since Santoriní in the Aegean Sea, 60 miles north of Crete, in 1628 B.C.) occurred at *c.* 10 A.M. (local time), or 3:00 A.M. GMT, on 27 Aug 1883, with an eruption of Krakatoa, an island (then 18 miles²) in the Sunda Strait, between Sumatra and Java, in Indonesia. One hundred and sixty-three villages were wiped out, and 36,380 people killed by the wave it caused. Pumice was thrown 34 miles high and dust fell 3,313 miles away 10 days later. The explosion was recorded four hours later on the island of Rodrigues, 2,968 miles away, as 'the roar of heavy guns,' and was heard over $\frac{1}{13}$ of the surface of the globe. This explosion, estimated to have had about 26 times the power of the greatest H-bomb test (by the USSR), was still only a fifth of the Santoriní cataclysm.

Greatest eruption ■ The total volume of matter discharged in the eruption of Tambora, a volcano on the island of Sumbawa, in Indonesia, 5–7 Apr 1815, was 93·3–111·9 miles. The energy of this 1,395 mph eruption, which lowered the height of the island by 4,100 ft from 13,450 ft to 9,350 ft, was $8·4 \times 10^{19}$ joules. A crater seven miles in diameter was formed. Some 90,000 were killed or died as a result of the subsequent famine. This compares with a probable 37–40 miles³ejected by Santoriní (see above) and 12·5 miles³ ejected by Krakatoa (see above). The internal pressure at Tambora has been estimated at 20·76 tons/in².

The ejecta in the Taupo eruption in New Zealand *c.* A.D. 130 has been estimated at 33 billion tons of pumice moving at one time at 400 mph. It flattened 6,180 miles² (over 26 times the devastated area of Mount St Helens, which erupted in Washington State on 18 May 1980). Less than 20 percent of the 15·4 billion tons of pumice ejected in this most violent of all documented volcanic events fell within 125 miles of the vent.

Longest lava flow ■ The longest lava flow in historic times is a mixture of pahoehoe ropey lava (twisted cord-like solidifications) and aa blocky lava, resulting from the eruption of Laki in 1783 in southeast Iceland that flowed 40·5–43·5 miles. The largest known prehistoric flow is the Roza basalt flow in North America *c.* 15 million years ago, which had an unsurpassed length 300 miles, area 15,400 miles² and volume 300 miles³.

Largest active ■ Mauna Loa in Hawaii has a dome 75 miles long and 31 miles wide (above sea level) with lava flows that occupy more than 1,980 miles² of the island. Its pit crater, Mokuaweoweo, measures 4 miles² and is 500–600 ft deep. It rises 13,677 ft and has averaged one eruption every 3½ years since 1832, although none since 1984.

Highest active ■ The highest volcano regarded as active is Ojos del Salado (which has fumaroles), at a height of 22,595 ft, on the frontier between Chile and Argentina.

Highest potentially active ■ The highest potentially active volcano is Volcán Llullaillaco (22,057 ft), also on the frontier between Chile and Argentina.

Northernmost and southernmost ■ The northernmost volcano is Beeren Berg (7,470 ft) on the island of Jan Mayen (71° 05′ N) in the Greenland Sea. It erupted on 20 Sep 1970 and the island's 39 inhabitants (all male) had to be evacuated. It was possibly discovered by

Largest active volcano ● Mauna Loa in Hawaii has a dome 75 miles long and 64 miles wide, with a lava flow that occupies more than 2,000 miles² of the island. Its pit crater, Mokuaweoweo, measures 4 miles² and is 500–600 ft deep. It rises 13,677 ft and has averaged one eruption every 3 ½ years since 1832, although none since 1984. (Photo: Peter Menzell/Science Photo Library)

Henry Hudson the English navigator and explorer (d. 1611) in 1607 or 1608, but was definitely visited by Jan Jacobsz Mayen (Netherlands) in 1614. It was annexed by Norway on 8 May 1929. The Ostenso seamount (5,825 ft) 346 miles from the North Pole in Lat. 85° 10′ N, Long. 133° W was volcanic. The most southerly known active volcano is Mt Erebus (12,450 ft) on Ross Island (77° 35′ S), in Antarctica. It was discovered on 28 Jan 1841 by the expedition of Captain (later Rear-Admiral Sir) James Clark Ross of the British Navy (1800–62), and first climbed at 10 A.M. on 10 Mar 1908 by a British party of five, led by Professor (later Lieut-Col Sir) Tannatt William Edgeworth David (1858–1934).

Largest crater ■ The world's largest *caldera* or volcano crater is that of Toba, north-central Sumatra, Indonesia covering 685 miles².

AVALANCHES
Greatest ■ The greatest natural avalanches, though rarely observed, occur in the Himalayas but no estimates of their volume have been published. It was estimated that 120 million ft³ of snow fell in an avalanche in the Italian Alps in 1885. The 250 mph avalanche triggered by the Mount St Helens eruption in on 18 May 1980 was estimated to measure 96 billion ft³ (see Accidents and Disasters, Chapter 10).

GEYSERS
Tallest ■ The Waimangu (Maori 'black

WORLD'S STRONGEST EARTHQUAKES
Progressive list of instrumentally recorded earthquakes

Kanamori Scale Magnitudes M$_w$	Richter Scale Magnitude M$_s$	Location	Date	
8·8	8·6	Ecuador	1906	31 Jan
9·0	8 ¼	Kamchatka, USSR	1952	4 Nov
9·1	7 ¾	Andreanof Islands, Aleutian Islands	1957	9 Mar
9·2	8·4	Alaska	1964	27 Mar
9·5	8·3	Chile	1960	22 May

$\log E = 1 \cdot 5M + 4 \cdot 8$ (joules)

water') geyser, in New Zealand, erupted to a height in excess of 1,500 ft in 1904, but has not been active since it erupted violently at 6:20 A.M. on 1 Apr 1917 and killed four people.

Currently the world's tallest active geyser is the US National Parks' Service Steamboat Geyser, in Yellowstone National Park, WY. During the 1980s it erupted with intervals ranging from 19 days to more than four years, although there were occasions in the 1960s when it erupted as frequently as every four to ten days. The maximum height ranges from 195–380 ft.

The greatest measured water discharge was an estimated 740,000–1,000,000 gallons by the Giant Geyser, also in Yellowstone National Park. However, this estimate, made in the 1950s, was only a rough calculation.

The *Geysir* ('gusher') near Mt Hekla in south-central Iceland, from which all others have been named, spurts, on occasions, to 180 ft, while the adjacent Strokkur, reactivated by drilling in 1963, spurts at 10–15 min intervals.

Weather

The meteorological records given below necessarily relate largely to the last 140–160 years, since data before that time are both sparse and often unreliable. Reliable registering thermometers were introduced as recently as *c.* 1820. The longest continuous observations have been maintained at the Radcliffe Observatory, Oxford, United Kingdom since 1815, though discontinuous records have enabled the Chinese to assert that 903 B.C. was a very bad winter.

It is believed that 1·2 million years ago the world's air temperature averaged 95° F.

Most equable temperature ■ The location with the most equable recorded temperature over a short period is Garapan, on Saipan, in the Mariana Islands, Pacific Ocean. During the nine years from 1927 to 1935, inclusive, the lowest temperature recorded was 67·3° F on 30 Jan 1934 and the highest was 88·5° F on 9 Sep 1931, giving an extreme range of 21·2° F.

Between 1911 and 1966 the Brazilian offshore island of Fernando de Noronha had a minimum temperature of 65·5° F on 17 Nov 1913 and a maximum of 89·6° F on 2 Mar 1965, an extreme range of 24·1° F.

Greatest temperature ranges ■ The greatest recorded temperature ranges in the world are around the Siberian 'cold pole' in the eastern USSR. Temperatures in Verkhoyansk (67° 33′ N, 133° 23′ E) have ranged 192° F from −94° F (unofficial) to 98° F.

The greatest temperature variation recorded in

Cloud extremes ● The highest standard cloud form is cirrus, 27,000 ft and above. A cirrus cloud at 26,500 ft contains unfrozen but super-cooled water at −31° F. (Photo: Science Photo Library)

a day is 100° F (a fall from 44° F to −56° F) at Browning, MT on 23–24 Jan 1916.

The most freakish rise was 49° F in 2 min at Spearfish, SD, from −4° F at 7:30 A.M. to 45° F at 7:32 A.M. on 22 Jan 1943.

Upper atmosphere ■ The lowest temperature ever recorded in the atmosphere is −225·4° F at an altitude of about 50–60 miles, during noctilucent cloud research above Kronogård, Sweden from 27 Jul to 7 Aug 1963.

Most intense rainfall ■ Difficulties attend rainfall readings for very short periods, but the figure of 1½ in in one min at Barst, Guadeloupe on 26 Nov 1970 is regarded as the most intense recorded in modern times.

Humidity and discomfort ■ Human comfort or discomfort depends not merely on temperature but on the combination of temperature, humidity, radiation and wind speed. The United States Weather Bureau uses a Temperature-Humidity Index, which equals two-fifths of the sum of the dry and wet bulb thermometer readings plus 15. A THI of 98·2 has been twice recorded in Death Valley, CA—on 27 Jul 1966 (119° F and 31 percent) and on 12 Aug 1970

(117° F and 37 percent). A person driving at 45 mph in a car without a windshield in a temperature of −45° F would, by the chill factor, experience the equivalent of −125° F, i.e., within 3·6° F of the world record.

Hurricanes ■ The most commonly used scale to measure the size of a hurricane is the Saffir-Simpson Scale, which rates hurricanes on a scale of one to five, five being the most severe.

The most damaging hurricane in the United States was Hurricane Hugo, which hit the US mainland 21–22 Sep 1989 after devastating a number of islands in the Caribbean. The storm made landfall at Sullivan Island, northeast of Charleston, SC. On crossing the mainland, Hugo measured four on the Saffir-Simpson Scale. Winds measured 135 mph and the 28 people were killed.

The most fatalies from an American hurricane is an estimated 6,000 deaths on 8 Sep 1900 in Galveston Island, TX. The second highest death toll was 1,836 people killed by a hurricane that hit Lake Okeechobee, FL on 17 Sep 1928. Both hurricanes measured category four on the Saffir–Simpson Scale.

Lightning ■ The visible length of lightning strokes varies greatly. In mountainous regions, when clouds are very low, the flash may be less than 300 ft long. In flat country with very high clouds, a cloud-to-earth flash may measure 4 miles, though in the most extreme cases such flashes have been measured at 20 miles. The intensely bright central core of the lightning channel is extremely narrow. Some authorities suggest that its diameter is as little as ½ in. This core is surrounded by a 'corona envelope' (glow discharge), which may measure 10–20 ft in diameter.

The speed of a discharge varies from 100–1,000 miles/sec for the downward leader track, and reaches up to 87,000 miles/sec (nearly half the speed of light) for the powerful return stroke.

Every few million strokes there is a giant discharge, in which the cloud-to-earth and return strokes flash from and to the top of the thunderclouds. In these 'positive giants' energy of up to 3 billion joules (3×10^{16} ergs) has been recorded. The temperature reaches about 54,032 ° F, which is more than that of the surface of the Sun.

Highest waterspout ■ The highest waterspout of which there is a reliable record was one observed on 16 May 1898 off Eden, New South Wales, Australia. A theodolite reading from the shore gave its height as 5,014 ft. It was about 10 ft in diameter.

Cloud extremes ■ The highest standard cloud form is cirrus, averaging 27,000 ft and above, but the rare nacreous, or mother-of-pearl formation sometimes reaches nearly 80,000 ft (see also Noctilucent clouds, p. 68). A cirrus cloud at 26,500 ft contains unfrozen but super-cooled water at −31° F. The lowest is stratus, below 3,500 ft. The cloud form with the greatest vertical range is cumulonimbus, which has been observed to reach a height of nearly 68,000 ft in the tropics.

Highest shade temperature ■ The highest ever recorded shade temperature is 136·4° F at al'Azīzīyah, Libya (alt. 367 ft) on 13 Sep 1922.

United States ■ The highest temperature in

EXTREME TEMPERATURES
(Progressive recordings)

HIGH

127·4°F	Ouargla, Algeria	27 Aug	1884
130°F	Amos, CA	17 Aug	1885
130°F	Mammoth Tank, CA	17 Aug	1885
134°F	Death Valley, CA	10 Jul	1913
136·4°F	Al'Aziziyah (el-Azizia), Libya*	13 Sep	1922

Obtained by the US National Geographical Society but not officially recognized by the Libyan Ministry of Communications.

A reading of 140°F at Delta, Mexico, in August 1953 is not now accepted because of overexposure to roof radiation. The official Mexican record of 136·4°F at San Luis, Sonora on 11 Aug 1933 is not internationally accepted.

A freak heat flash reported from Coimbra, Portugal, in September 1933 said to have caused the temperature to rise to 158°F for 120 sec is apocryphal.

LOW

−73°F	Floeberg Bay, Ellesmere I., Canada		[1] 1852
−90·4°F	Verkhoyansk, Siberia, USSR	3 Jan	1885
−90·4°F	Verkhoyansk, Siberia, USSR	5 & 7 Feb	1892
−90·4°F	Oymyakon, Siberia, USSR[2]	6 Feb	1933
−100·4°F	South Pole, Antarctica	11 May	1957
−102·1°F	South Pole, Antarctica	17 Sep	1957
−109·1°F	Sovietskaya, Antarctica	2 May	1958
−113·3°F	Vostok, Antarctica	15 Jun	1958
−114·1°F	Sovietskaya, Antarctica	19 Jun	1958
−117·4°F	Sovietskaya, Antarctica	25 Jun	1958
−122·4°F	Vostok, Antarctica	7–8 Aug	1958
−124·1°F	Sovietskaya, Antarctica	9 Aug	1958
−125·3°F	Vostok, Antarctica	25 Aug	1958
−126·9°F	Vostok, Antarctica	24 Aug	1960
−128·6°F	Vostok, Antarctica	21 Jul	1983

[1] *The earliest recorded occasion that mercury froze (at −40°F) was by M. V. Lomonosov, near Moscow c. 1750.*

[2] *Population in 1986 reported to be 4,000—the world's coldest inhabited place.*

Maximum sunshine ● At Yuma, AZ the annual average sunshine figure is just over 90 percent (approximately 4,000 hours). The picture shows a cloudless sky at a farm in the area. (Photo: Gamma)

the United States was 134°F at Greenland Ranch, Death Valley, CA on 10 Jul 1913.

Lowest screen temperature ■ A record low of −128·6°F was registered at Vostok, Antarctica (alt. 11,220 ft) on 21 Jul 1983.

The coldest permanently inhabited place is the Siberian village of Oymyakon (pop. 4,000) 63°16′N, 143°15′E, (2,300 ft) in the USSR, where the temperature reached −89·9°F in 1933.

United States ■ The lowest temperature in the United States was −79·8°F on 23 Jan 1971 in Prospect Creek, AK.

The lowest temperature in the continental United States was −69·7°F in Rogers Pass, MT on 20 Jan 1954.

Greatest rainfall ■ A record 73·62 in of rain fell in 24 hours in Cilaos (alt. 3,937 ft), La Réunion, Indian Ocean on 15 and 16 Mar 1952. This is equal to 8,327 tons of rain per acre.

For a calendar month, the record is 366·14 in, at Cherrapunji, Meghalaya, India in July 1861.

The 12-month record was also at Cherrapunji, with 1,041·78 in between 1 Aug 1860 and 31 Jul 1861.

United States ■ In the United States, the 24 hour record is 19 inches at Alvin, TX, on 25–26 Jul 1979. Over a 12 month period, 739 inches fell at Kukui, Maui, HI from Dec 1981 – Dec 1982.

Wettest place ■ By average annual rainfall, the wettest place in the world is Tutunendo, in Colombia, with 463·4 in per year.

Greatest snowfall ■ 1,224½ in of snow fell over a 12 month period from 19 Feb 1971 to 18 Feb 1972 at Paradise, Mt Rainier, in Washington State. The record for a single snowstorm is 189 in at Mt Shasta Ski Bowl, CA from 13–19 Feb 1959. And for a 24 hr period it is 76 in at Silver Lake, CO on 14–15 Apr 1921. The greatest depth of snow on the ground was 37 ft 7 in at Tamarack, CA in March 1911.

The highest average snowfall in the United States for 1989 was 240·8 inches in Blue Canyon, CA.

Maximum sunshine ■ The annual average at Yuma, AZ is 90 percent (over 4,000 hours). St Petersburg, FL, recorded 768 consecutive sunny days from 9 Feb 1967 to 17 Mar 1969.

Minimum sunshine ■ At the South Pole there is nil sunshine for 182 days every year and at the North Pole the figure is nil for 176 days.

Barometric pressure ■ The highest barometric pressure ever recorded was 32 in, at Agata, Siberia, USSR (alt. 862 ft) on 31 Dec 1968.

The lowest sea-level pressure was 25·69 in in Typhoon Tip, 300 miles west of Guam, Pacific Ocean, at Lat. 16°44′N, Long. 137°46′E on 12 Oct 1979.

Highest surface wind speed ■ A surface wind speed of 231 mph was recorded at Mt Washington (6,288 ft), NH on 12 Apr 1934.

The highest speed at low level was registered on 8 Mar 1972 at the USAF base at Thule, Greenland (145 ft), when a peak speed of 207 mph was recorded.

The highest speed measured to date in a tornado is 280 mph at Wichita Falls, TX on 2 Apr 1958.

Thunder-days ■ Tororo, Uganda recorded an average of 251 days of thunder per year for the 10-year period 1967–76.

Between Lat. 35°N and 35°S there are some 3,200 thunderstorms each 12 nighttime hours, some of which can be heard at a range of 18 miles.

Hottest place ■ On an annual mean basis, with readings taken over a six-year period from 1960 to 1966, the temperature at Dallol, in Ethiopia, was 94°F.

In Death Valley, CA, maximum temperatures of over 120°F were recorded on 43 consecutive days, between 6 Jul and 17 Aug 1917.

At Marble Bar, Western Australia (maximum 121°F), 162 consecutive days with maximum temperatures of over 100°F were recorded between 30 Oct 1923 and 8 Apr 1924.

At Wyndham, also in Western Australia, the temperature reached 90°F or more on 333 days in 1946.

Coldest place ■ Polus Nedostupnosti, Pole of Inaccessibility (78°S, 96°E), Antarctica is the coldest place in the world, with an extrapolated annual mean of −72°F.

The coldest measured mean is −70°F, at Plateau Station, Antarctica.

Most rainy days ■ Mt Wai-'ale-'ale (5,148 ft), Kauai, HI has up to 350 rainy days per year.

Driest place ■ The annual mean rainfall in the Desierto de Atacama, near Calama, Chile is nil.

Longest drought ■ Desierto de Atacama, in Chile, experienced a drought for some 400 years up to 1971.

Heaviest hailstones ■ The heaviest hailstones on record, weighing 2¼ lb, are reported to have killed 92 people in the Gopalganj district of Bangladesh on 14 Apr 1986.

Longest sea-level fogs ■ Sea-level fogs—with visibility less than 3,000 ft—persist for weeks on the Grand Banks, Newfoundland, Canada, with the average being more than 120 days per year.

Windiest place ■ The Commonwealth Bay, George V Coast, Antarctica, where gales reach 200 mph, is the world's windiest place.

Gems, Jewels and Precious Stones

DIAMOND

Largest. 3,106 carats. Found on 25 Jan 1905 in the Premier Mine, Pretoria, South Africa and named *The Cullinan* after the mine's discoverer, Sir Thomas Cullinan. Presented to King Edward VII in 1907. Currently the largest uncut stone is of 599 carats, found near Pretoria, South Africa in July 1986 and revealed by De Beers on 11 Mar 1988. It is expected to yield a 350–carat cut stone.

Largest cut. 530·2 carats. A 74-facet pear-shaped gem named *The Star of Africa*, cleaved from *The Cullinan* by Jak Asscher and polished by Henri Koe in Amsterdam in 1908. Now in the Royal Sceptre, United Kingdom.

Largest natural intense fancy blue. 136·25 carats. The 'Queen of Holland' cushion-shaped brilliant cut diamond was found in 1904. It was cut by F. Freedman & Co. in Amsterdam, and was exhibited at the Paris Exhibition in 1925. It was then sold to an Indian maharaja, but its current owners are unknown.

Largest natural intense fancy green. 41 carats. This is located in the Green Vaults in Dresden, East Germany.

Smallest. 0·0001022 carat. D. Drukker & Zn NV of Amsterdam, Netherlands have produced a 57-facet brilliant with a diameter of 0·009 in.

Rarest color. Blood red. The largest is a 5·05 carat flawless stone found in Tichtenburg, South Africa in 1927 and now in a private collection in the United States.

Highest priced. $9,130,000. The flawless pear-shaped 85·91–carat–stone, sold to Laurence Graff of London at Sotheby's New York on 19 Apr 1988. The record per carat is $975,068 for a 0·95–carat purplish red stone at Christie's, New York in April 1988. A record price of $10 million was paid for a rough uncut diamond by Chow Tai Fook of Hong Kong on 4 Mar 1989.

RUBY

Largest star. 2,475 carats. *Rajarathna*, India, displays an animated star of six lines and is cut as a cabochon.

Largest double star. 1,370 carats. A cabochon cut gem, *Neelanjahi*, owned by G. Vidyaraj, Bangalore, India, displays 12 star lines and measures 3 in in height and 2 in in diameter.

Largest. 8,500 carats. In July 1985 jeweler James Kazanjian of Beverly Hills, CA displayed a 5 ½ in tall red corundum (Al_2O_3) carved to resemble the Liberty Bell.

Highest priced. $4,620,000. This ruby and diamond ring made by Chaumet, in Paris, France weighs 32·08 carats and was sold at Sotheby's, New York on 26 Oct 1989. The record per carat is $227,300 for a ruby ring with a stone weighing 15·97 carats, which was sold at Sotheby's, New York on 18 Oct 1988.

EMERALD

Largest cut. 86,136 carats. This natural beryl was found in Carnaiba, Brazil in August 1974. It was carved

Highest priced diamond ● This flawless pear-shaped 85·91 carat diamond was sold to Laurence Graff of London at Sotheby's in New York for $9·1 million on 19 Apr 1988. (Photo: Sotheby's)

by Richard Chan in Hong Kong and valued at £718,000 in 1982.

Largest single crystal. 7,025 carats. The largest single emerald crystal of gem quality was found in 1969 at the Cruces Mine, near Gachala, Colombia, and is owned by a private mining concern. Larger Brazilian and Russian stones do exist, but of low quality.

Highest priced. $3,080,000. (Single lot of emeralds). This emerald and diamond necklace made by Cartier, London, United Kingdom in 1937 (a total of 12 stones weighing 108·74 carats) was sold at Sotheby's, New York on 26 Oct 1989. The highest price for a single emerald is $2,126,646, for a 19·77–carat emerald and diamond ring made by Cartier in 1958, which was sold at Sotheby's, Geneva, Switzerland on 2 Apr 1987. This also represented the record price per carat for an emerald, at $107,569.

SAPPHIRE

Largest carved. 2,302 carats. Found at Anakie, Queensland, Australia in *c.* 1935, this corundum (Al_2O_3) was carved into a 1,318–carat head of Abraham Lincoln and is now in the custody of the Kazanjian Foundation of Los Angeles, CA.

Largest star sapphire. 9,719·50 carats. This stone cut in London, United Kingdom in November 1989 has

Largest topaz ● This 22,892·5 carat rectangular, cushion-cut *American Golden Topaz* with 172 facets and an overall width of 5 ⅞ in, has been on display at the Smithsonian Institution, Washington, DC since 4 May 1988. (Photo: Smithsonian Institution)

been named *The Lone Star* and is owned by Harold Roper.

Highest priced. $2,791,723. A step-cut stone of 62·02 carats was sold as a sapphire and diamond ring at Sotheby's, St Moritz, Switzerland on 20 Feb 1988.

CRYSTAL BALL

Largest. 106·75 lb. The world's largest flawless rock crystal ball is 13 in in diameter, and was cut in China from Burmese rough material. It is now in the Smithsonian Institution in Washington, DC.

OPAL

Largest. 26,350 carats. The largest single piece of gem quality white opal was found in July 1989 at the Jupiter Field at Coober Pedy in South Australia. It has been named *Jupiter-Five* and is in private ownership.

Largest black opal. 1,520 carats. A stone found on 4 Feb 1972 at Lightning Ridge in Australia produced this finished gem, called the *Empress of Glengarry*. It measures 4 ¾ × 3 ⅛ × ⅝ in, and is owned by Peter Gray.

Largest rough black opal. 2,020 carats. The largest gem quality uncut black opal was also found at Lightning Ridge, on 3 Nov 1986. After cleaning, it weighs 2,020 carats and measures 4 × 2 ⅝ × 2 ½ in. It has been named *Halley's Comet* and is owned by a team of opal miners known as The Lunatic Hill Syndicate.

PEARL

Largest. 14 lb 1 oz. The *Pearl of Lao-tze* (also known as *the Pearl of Allah*) was found at Palawan, Philippines on 7 May 1934 in the shell of a giant clam. The property of Wilburn Dowell Cobb until his death, this 9 ½-in long by 5 ½-in diameter molluscan concretion was bought at auction on 15 May 1980 in San Francisco, CA by Peter Hoffman and Victor Barbish for $200,000. An appraisal by the San Francisco Gem Laboratory in May 1984 suggested a value of $40–42 million.

Largest cultured pearl. 138·25 carats. A 1 ½-in round cultured pearl weighing 1 oz was found near Samui Island, off Thailand, in January 1988. The stone is owned by the Mikimoto Pearl Island Company, Japan.

Highest priced. $864,280. *La Régente*, an egg-shaped pearl weighing 302·68 grains and formerly part of the French crown jewels, was sold at Christie's, Geneva, Switzerland on 12 May 1988.

TOPAZ

Largest. 22,892·5 carats. The rectangular, cushion-cut *American Golden Topaz* with 172 facets and 5 ⅞ in in overall width has been on display at the Smithsonian Institution, Washington, DC since 4 May 1988.

JADE

Largest. 291 tons. A single boulder of nephrite jade was found in northeast China in March 1990. It measured 23 × 20 × 16 ft.

AMBER

Largest. 33 lb 10 oz. The 'Burma Amber' is located in the Natural History Museum, London, United Kingdom. Amber is a fossil resin derived from extinct coniferous trees, and often contains trapped insects.

GOLD

Largest nugget. 7,560 oz. The *Holtermann Nugget* found on 19 Oct 1872 in the Beyers & Holtermann Star of Hope mine, Hill End, New South Wales, Australia contained some 220 lb of gold in a 630–lb slab of slate.

Largest pure nugget. The *Welcome Stranger* found at Moliagul, Victoria, Australia in 1869 yielded 2,248 troy oz of pure gold from 2,280 ¼ oz.

The Universe & Space

LIGHT-YEAR—that distance traveled by light (speed 186,282·397 miles/sec or 670·7 million mph in vacuo) in one tropical year (365·24219878 mean solar days at January 0·12 hours Ephemeris time in A.D. 1900) and is equivalent to 5·9 trillion miles. The unit was first used in March 1888 and fixed at this constant in October 1983. MAGNITUDE — a measure of stellar brightness such that the light of a star of any magnitude bears a ratio of 2·511886 to that of a star of the next megnitude. Thus a fifth magnitude star is 2·511886 times as bright, while one of the first magnitude is exactly 100 (or 2·511 886^5) times as bright, as a sixth magnitude star. In the case of such exceptionally bright bodies as Sirius, Venus, the Moon (magnitude — 12·71) or the Sun (magnitude — 26·78), then magnitude is expressed as a minus quantity. PROPER MOTION—that component of a star's motion in space which, at right angles to the line of sight, constitutes an apparent change of position of the star in the celestial sphere.

METEOROIDS

Meteoroids are of cometary or asteroidal origin. A meteor is the light phenomenon caused by a meteoroid's entry into the Earth's atmosphere.

Meteor shower ■ The greatest shower on record occurred on the night of 16–17 Nov 1966, when the Leonid meteors (which recur every 33¼ years) were visible between western North America and eastern USSR. It was calculated that meteors passed over Arizona, at a rate of 2,300 per min for a period of 20 min from 5 A.M. on 17 Nov 1966.

METEORITES

Meteorites ■ When a *meteoroid* (consisting of broken fragments of cometary or asteroidal origin and ranging in size from fine dust to bodies several miles in diameter) penetrates the Earth's surface, the remnant, which could be either aerolite (stony) or siderite (metallic), is described as a *meteorite*. Such events occur about 150 times per year over the whole land surface of the Earth.

The most anxious time of day for meteorophobes should be 3 P.M. In historic times, the only recorded person injured by a meteorite was Mrs Ann Hodges of Sylacauga, AL. On 30 Nov 1954 a 9 lb stone, some 7 in in length, crashed through the roof of her home, hitting Mrs Hodges on the arm and bruising her hip. The physician who examined her, Dr Moody D. Jacobs, declared her fit but she was subsequently hospitalised as a result of the attendant publicity.

Oldest ■ A revision by T. Kirsten in 1981 of the estimates of the ages of meteorites which have remained essentially undisturbed after their formation suggest that the oldest which has been dated with accuracy is the Krahen-

Largest meteorite ● Found in 1920 at Hoba West in Southwest Africa, it is estimated to weigh 130,000 lb and is 93 percent iron and 7 percent nickel. (Photo: Bruce Coleman)

berg meteorite at 4,600 ± 20 million years which predates the Solar System by about 70 million years.

It was reported in August 1978 that dust grains in the Murchison meteorite which fell in Australia in September 1969 may also be older than the Solar System.

Largest ■ There was a mysterious explosion of 12½ megatons in Lat. 60° 55′ N, Long. 101° 57′ E, in the basin of the Podkamennaya Tunguska River, 40 miles north of Vanavar, in Siberia, USSR, at 00 hrs 17 min 11 sec UT on 30 June 1908. The cause was variously attributed to a meteorite (1927), a comet (1930), a nuclear explosion (1961) and to antimatter (1965). This devastated an area of about 1,500 miles^2 and the shock was felt as far as 600 miles away. The theory is now favored that this was the terminal flare of stony debris from a comet, possibly Encke's comet, at an altitude of only or less than 20,000 ft.

The largest known meteorite was found in 1920 at Hoba West, near Grootfontein in Southwest Africa and is a block 9 ft long by 8 ft broad, estimated to be 65 tons.

The largest meteorite exhibited by any museum is the 'Tent' meteorite, weighing 68,085 lb, found in 1897 near Cape York, on the west coast of Greenland, by the expedition of Commander (later Rear-Admiral) Robert Edwin Peary (1856–1920). It was known to the Inuits as the Abnigh-

ito and is now exhibited in the Hayden Planetarium in New York City.

The largest piece of stony meteorite recovered is a piece of 3,902 lb, part of a 4·4 ton shower that struck Jilin (formerly Kirin), China on 8 Mar 1976.

Craters ■ It has been estimated that some 2,000 asteroid-Earth collisions have occurred in the last 600 million years. One hundred and two collision sites or astroblemes have been recognized.

A crater 150 miles in diameter and ½ mile deep was postulated in 1962 in Wilkes Land, Antarctica. It would be caused by a 14·33 billion ton meteorite striking at 44,000 mph. Soviet scientists reported in December 1970 an astrobleme with a 60-mile diameter and a maximum depth of 1,300 ft in the basin of the River Popigai.

There is a crater-like formation or astrobleme 275 miles in diameter on the eastern shore of the Hudson Bay, Canada, where the Nastapoka Islands are just off the coast.

One of the largest and best-preserved craters is the Coon Butte or Barringer Crater, discovered in 1891 near Canyon Diablo, Winslow, northern Arizona. It is 4,150 ft in diameter and now about 575 ft deep, with a parapet rising 130–155 ft above the surrounding plain.

It has been estimated that an iron-nickel mass of some 2·2 million tons and diameter of 200–260 ft gouged this crater in c. 25,000 B.C.

Evidence was published in 1963 discounting a meteoric origin for the crypto-volcanic Vredefort Ring (diameter 26 miles), to the southwest of Johannesburg, South Africa, but this has now been reasserted.

The New Quebec (formerly the Chubb) 'Crater,' first sighted on 20 June 1943 in northern Ungava, Canada, is 1,325 ft deep and measures 6·8 miles around its rim.

Tektites ■ The largest of which details have been published has been of 7·04 lb found in 1932 at Muong Nong, Saravane Province, Laos and now in the Louvre Paris Museum. Eight SNC meteorites named after their find sites at Shergotty, India; Nakla, Egypt and Chassigny, France, are believed to have emanated from Mars.

Fireball ■ The brightest ever photographically recorded was by Dr Zdenek Ceplecha over Sumava, Czechoslovakia on 4 Dec 1974 with a momentary magnitude of −22 or 10,000 times brighter than a full Moon.

AURORAE

Most frequent ■ Polar lights, known since 1560 as aurora borealis or northern lights in the northern hemisphere, and since 1773 as aurora australis in the southern, are caused by electrical solar discharges in the upper atmosphere and occur most frequently in high latitudes. Aurorae are visible at some time on *every* clear dark night in the polar areas within 20 degrees of the magnetic poles.

The extreme height of aurorae has been measured at 620 miles, while the lowest may descend to 45 miles.

The most recent great display in northwest Europe was that of 4–5 Sep 1958.

Lowest latitudes ■ Extreme cases of displays in very low latitudes are Cuzco, Peru (2 Aug 1744); Honolulu, HI (1 Sep 1859); and, questionably, Singapore (25 Sep 1909).

Noctilucent clouds ■ These remain sunlit long after sunset owing to their great altitude, and are thought to consist of ice crystals or meteoric dust. Regular observations (at heights of *c.* 52 miles) in Western Europe date only from 1964, since when the record high and low number of nights on which these phenomena have been observed have been 43 (1979) and 15 (1970).

THE MOON

The Earth's closest neighbor in space and its only natural satellite is the Moon, which has an average diameter of 2,159·3 miles and a mass of $8·1 \times 10^{19}$ tons or 0·0123 Earth masses so the density is 3·344 times that of water.

The Moon orbits at a mean distance of 238,854·5 miles center-to-center, although the center of mass is displaced from the center of figure by 1·1 miles towards the Earth so that the distance surface-to-surface is 233,813 miles. In the present century the closest approach (smallest perigee) was 221,441 miles center-to-center on 4 Jan 1912 and the farthest distance (largest apogee) was 252,718 miles on 2 Mar 1984.

The orbital period (sidereal month) is 27·321661 days, giving an average orbital velocity of 2,289 mph.

The currently accepted 'giant impact' theory of the lunar origin suggests that the Moon was formed just outside of the Earth's Roche Limit (about 11,500 miles from the Earth's center) from the debris resulting from a glancing collision between the Earth and a Mars-size planetesimal. That this event must have occurred in the early history of the Solar System is indiciated by the fact that the oldest lunar rocks and soils brought back to Earth by the Apollo program crews are of a similar age to the oldest known meteorites (about 4·5 billion years).

The first direct hit on the Moon was achieved at 2 min 24 sec after midnight (Moscow time) on 14 Sep 1959, by the Soviet space probe *Lunar II* near the Mare Serenitatis.

The first photographic images of the hidden side were collected by the USSR *Lunar III* from 6:30 A.M. on the 7 Oct 1959, from a range of up to 43,750 miles and transmitted to the Earth from a distance of 292,000 miles .

Crater ■ Only 59 percent of the Moon's surface is directly visible from the Earth because it is in 'captured rotation,' i.e., the period of rotation is equal to the period of orbit. The largest wholly visible crater is the walled plain Bailly, towards the Moon's South Pole, which is 183 miles across, with walls rising to 14,000 ft. The Orientale Basin, partly on the averted side, measures more than 600 miles in diameter.

The deepest crater is the Newton Crater, with a floor estimated to be between 23,000–29,000 ft below its rim and 14,000 ft below the level of the plain outside. The brightest directly visible spot on the Moon is Aristarchus.

Highest mountains ■ In the absence of a sea level, lunar altitudes are measured relative to an adopted reference sphere of radius 1,079·943 miles. Thus the greatest elevation attained on this basis by any of the 12 US astronauts has been 25,688 ft on the Descartes Highlands by Capt John Watts Young, USN and Major Charles M. Duke, Jr on 27 Apr 1972.

Temperature extremes ■ When the Sun is overhead the temperature on the lunar equator reaches 243° F (31 ° F above the boiling point of water). By sunset the temperature is 58° F but after nightfall it sinks to −261° F.

THE SUN
Distance extremes ■ The true distance of the Earth from the Sun is 1·00000102 astronomical units or 93 million miles. The orbit is elliptical and the distance of the Sun varies between a minimum (perihelion) of 91·5 million miles and a maximum (aphelion) of 94·5 million miles. Based on an orbital circumference of 58·4 million miles and an orbital period (sidereal year) of 365·256366 days, then the average orbital velocity is 66,620 mph, but this varies between a minimum of 65,500 mph at aphelion and a maximum of 67,750 mph at perihelion.

Temperature and dimensions ■ The Sun has a stellar classification of a *yellow dwarf* type G2, although its mass at 2 octillion tons is 332,946·04 times that of the Earth and represents over 99 percent of the total mass of the Solar System. The solar diameter at 865,040 miles leads to a density of 1·408 times that of water.

The Sun has a central temperature of about 15,400,000 K and a core pressure of 1·65 billion tons and uses up about 4·4 million tons of hydrogen per sec, equal to an energy output of 3·85 x 10²⁶ watts, although it will take 10 billion years to exhaust its energy supply (about 5 billion years from the present).

The luminous intensity of the Sun is 2·7 octillion candela, which is equal to a luminance of 290,000 candela/in².

Sunspots ■ To be visible to the protected naked eye, a sunspot must cover about one two-thousandth part of the Sun's disc and thus have an area of about 0·5 billion miles². The largest sunspot ever noted was in the Sun's southern hemisphere on 8 Apr 1947. Its area was about 7 billion with an extreme longitude of 187,000 miles and an extreme latitude of 90,000 miles. Sunspots appear darker because they are more than 2,732 ° F cooler than the rest of the Sun's surface temperature of 9,945 ° F.

In October 1957 a smoothed sunspot count showed 263, the highest recorded index since records started in 1755 (cf. previous record of 239 in May 1778). In 1943 one sunspot lasted for 200 days from June to December.

ECLIPSES
Earliest recorded ■ For the Middle East, lunar eclipses have been extrapolated to 3450 B.C. and solar ones to 4200 B.C.

The oldest recorded total solar eclipse is on a clay tablet found in 1948 among the ruins of the ancient city of Ugarit (now in Syria).

A reassessment in 1989 suggests that this records the eclipse of the 5 Mar 1223 B.C. No center of the path of totality for a solar eclipse crossed London, United Kingdom for the 575 years from 20 Mar 1140 to 3 May 1715.

Longest duration ■ The maximum *possible* duration of an eclipse of the Sun is 7 min 31 sec.

The longest actually *measured* was on 20 Jun 1955 (7 min 8 sec), seen from the Philippines. One of 7 min 29 sec should occur in mid-Atlantic on 16 Jul 2186, which will then be the longest for 1,469 years.

Most and least frequent ■ The highest number of eclipses possible in a year is seven, as in 1935, when there were five solar and two lunar eclipses; or four solar and three lunar eclipses, as occurred in 1982.

The lowest possible number in a year is two, both of which must be solar, as in 1944 and 1969.

COMETS
Earliest recorded ■ Records date from the seventh century B.C. The speeds of the estimated two million comets vary from 700 mph in outer space to 1·25 million mph when near the Sun. The successive appearances of Halley's Comet have been traced back to 467 B.C. It was first depicted in the Nuremberg Chronicle of A.D. 684.

The first prediction of its return by Edmund Halley (1656–1742) proved true on Christmas Day 1758, 16 years after his death. On 13–14 Mar 1986, the European satellite *Giotto* (launched 2 Jul 1985) penetrated to within 335 miles of the nucleus of Halley's Comet. It was established that this was 9·3 miles in length and velvet black in color.

Closest approach ■ On 1 Jul 1770, Lexell's Comet, traveling at a speed of 23·9 miles/sec (relative to the Sun), came to within 745,000 miles of the Earth. However, the Earth is believed to have passed through the tail of Halley's Comet, most recently on 19 May 1910.

Largest ■ The tail of the brightest of all comets, the Great Comet of 1843, trailed for 0·2 billion miles.

The bow shock of Holmes Comet of 1892 once measured 1·5 million miles in diameter.

Shortest period ■ Of all the recorded periodic comets (these are members of the Solar System), the one which most frequently returns is Encke's Comet, first identified in 1786. Its period of 1,206 days (3.3 years) is the shortest established. Not one of its 53 returns (including that of 1983) has been missed by astronomers. Now increasingly faint, it is expected to die by February 1994.

The most frequently observed comets are Schwassmann-Wachmann I, Kopff and Oterma, which can be observed every year between Mars and Jupiter.

Longest period ■ At the other extreme is Delavan's Comet of 1914, whose path was not accurately determined. It is not expected to return for perhaps 24 million years.

PLANETS
Largest ■ The nine major planets (including the Earth) are bodies within the Solar System that revolve round the Sun in definite orbits.

Jupiter, with an equatorial diameter of 88,846 miles and a polar diameter of 83,082 miles is the largest of the nine major planets, with a mass 317·828 times, and a volume 1,323·3 times, that of the Earth. It also has the shortest period of rotation resulting in a Jovian day of only 9 hr 50 min 30·003 sec in the equatorial zone.

Smallest, coldest and outermost ■ Pluto was first recorded by Clyde William Tombaugh (b. 4 Feb 1906) at Lowell Observatory, Flagstaff, AZ on 18 Feb 1930 from photographs he took on 23 and 29 Jan. His find was announced on 13 March.

Pluto's companion Charon was announced on 22 Jun 1978 from the US Naval Observatory, Flagstaff, AZ. Pluto, with a mass of about 1/500th of that of the Earth, has a diameter of 1,429 miles, while Charon has a diameter of 737 miles. Their mean distance from the Sun is 3·7 billion miles, with a period of revolution of 248·54 years. Because of their orbital eccentricity they will have been temporarily closer to the Sun than Neptune in the period from 23 Jan 1979 to 15 Mar 1999. The lowest observed surface temperature of any natural body in the Solar System is 391° F in the case of Neptune's large moon *Triton*, although the true surface temperature of Pluto and Charon remain to be measured.

Fastest ■ Mercury, which orbits the Sun at an average distance of 0·4 million miles, has a period of revolution of 87·9686 days, so giving the highest average speed in orbit of 107,030 mph.

Hottest ■ For Venus a surface temperature of 864°F has been estimated from measurements made from the USSR *Venera* and US *Pioneer* surface probes.

Nearest ■ The fellow planet closest to the Earth is Venus, which is, at times, only 26 million miles inside the Earth's orbit, compared with Mars' closest approach of 35 million miles outside the Earth's orbit.

Mars, known since 1965 to be cratered, has temperatures ranging from 85° F to −190° F.

Surface features ■ By far the highest and most spectacular is Olympus Mons (formerly Nix Olympica) in the Tharsis region of Mars, with a diameter of 310–370 miles and a height of 75,450–95,150 ft above the surrounding plain.

Venus has a canyon 21,000 ft deep and 250 miles long, some 1,000 miles south of Venusian equator.

The ice cliff on the Uranian moon Miranda is 65,000 ft high.

Brightest and faintest ■ Viewed from the Earth, by far the brightest of the five planets visible to the naked eye is Venus, with a maximum magnitude of −4·4.

Uranus, the first to be discovered by telescope when it was sighted by Sir William Herschel from his garden at 19 New King St, Bath, United Kingdom on 13 Mar 1781, is only marginally visible with a magnitude 5·5.

The faintest planet is Pluto, with a magnitude of 15·0.

Densest and least dense ■ Earth is the densest planet, with an average figure of 5·515 times that of water, while Saturn has an average density only about one-eighth of this value or 0·685 times that of water.

Conjunctions ■ The most dramatic recorded conjunction (coming together) of the other seven principal members of the Solar System (Sun, Moon, Mercury, Venus, Mars, Jupiter and Saturn) occurred on 5 Feb 1962, when 16° covered all seven during an eclipse in the Pacific area. It is possible that the sevenfold conjunction of September 1186 spanned only 12°.

The next notable conjunction will take place on 5 May 2000.

Largest scale model ■ The largest scale model of the Solar System was inaugurated by the Futures' Museum, Falun, Sweden on 29 Nov 1986. A model of the Earth of diameter ½ in was placed in the museum. The Sun, 5 ft, and the planets, which ranged from 0·13 in to 5 ½ in, were positioned at the nearby city of Borlange some 10 miles away. *Proxima Centauri* was positioned at the Museum of Victoria, Melbourne, Australia.

SATELLITES

Most ■ Of the nine major planets, all but Venus and Mercury have satellites. The planet with the most is Saturn, with at least 17 satellites.

The Earth and Pluto are the only planets with a single satellite. The distance from their parent planets varies from the 5,827 miles of *Phobos* from the center of Mars to the 15 million miles of Jupiter's outer satellite *Sinope* (Jupiter IX).

The Solar System has a total of 60 established satellites.

Largest and smallest ■ The largest and heaviest satellite is *Ganymede* (Jupiter III), which is 2·017 times heavier than the Earth's Moon and has a diameter of 3,273 miles.

Of satellites that have been measured, the smallest is *Deimos*, the outermost moon of Mars. Although irregularly shaped it has an average diameter of 7·8 miles. The diameter of *Leda* (Jupiter XIII) is estimated to be less than 9 miles.

Largest asteroids ■ In the belt that lies between Mars and Jupiter, there are some 45,000 (about 4,600 numbered to October 1990) minor planets or asteroids that are, for the most part, too small to yield to diameter measurement.

The largest and first discovered (by G. Piazzi at Palermo, Sicily on 1 Jan 1801) of these is *Ceres*, which has a diameter of 582 miles.

The only one visible to the naked eye is asteroid 4 *Vesta* (diameter 322 miles), discovered on 29 Mar 1807 by Dr Heinrich Wilhelm Olbers (1758–1840), a German amateur astronomer.

The closest approach to the Earth by an asteroid is 430,000 miles, by 1989 FC on the 22 Mar 1989. Although probably less than 1,311 ft in diameter impact would have resulted in a crater up to 4 miles in diameter.

The most distant detected is 2,060 *Chiron*, found between Saturn and Uranus on 18–19 Oct 1977, by Charles T. Kowal from the Hale Observatory, CA.

STARS

Largest and most massive ■ The variable star *Eta Carinae*, which is 9,100 light-years distant in the Carina Nebula in our own galaxy, has a mass at least 200 times greater than our own Sun.

Betelgeux (top left star of Orion) has a diameter of 400 million miles or about 500 times greater than the Sun. In 1978 it was found to be surrounded not only by a dust 'shell' but also an outer tenuous gas halo up to $5·3 \times 10^{11}$ miles in diameter, over 1,100 times the diameter of the star. The light from *Betelgeux* left in A.D. 1680.

Smallest and lightest ■ A mass of 0·014 that of the Sun is estimated for the very faint star RG 0058.8−2807, which was discovered by I. Neill Reid and Gerard Gilmore using the British Schmidt telescope and was announced in April 1983.

The white dwarf star L362-81 has an estimated diameter of 3,500 miles or only 0·0040 that of the Sun.

Brightest ■ Sirius A (*Alpha Canis Majoris*), also known as the Dog Star, is apparently the brightest star of the 5,776 stars of naked eye visibility in the heavens, with an apparent magnitude of −1·46. It is in the constellation *Canis Major* and is visible in the winter months of the northern hemisphere, being due south at midnight on the last day of the year.

Sirius is 8·64 light-years distant and has a luminosity 26 times as much as that of the Sun. It has a diameter of 1·45 million miles and a mass of 4·7 octillion tons.

The faint white dwarf companion Sirius B has a diameter of only 6,000 miles but is 350,000 times heavier than the Earth. The magnitude of Sirius should rise to a maximum of −1·67 by c. A.D. 61,000.

Farthest ■ The Solar System, with its Sun's nine principal planets, 60 satellites, asteroids and comets, is located in the outer regions of our Milky Way Galaxy, orbiting at a mean distance of 29,700 light-years and with an orbital eccentricity of 0·07. The present distance from the center is 27,700 light-years and it will reach the minimum distance of 27,600 light-years (perigalacticon) in about 15 million years' time.

The galaxy has a diameter of about 70,000 light-years so the most distant star will be at 66,700 light-years when the Solar System is farthest from the center (apogalacticon), while at present the most distant stars are at 62,700 light-years.

The present orbital velocity of the Sun and a large number of nearby stars have been averaged to 492,000 mph (the 'Local Standard of Rest'), which would lead to an orbital period of 237 million years. However, the Sun's actual velocity is 60,400 mph faster than this average.

Nearest ■ Excepting the special case of our own Sun (*q.v.* above), the nearest star is the very faint *Proxima Centauri*, discovered in 1915, which is 4·22 light-years (25 trillion miles) away.

The nearest star visible to the naked eye is the southern hemisphere binary *Alpha Centauri*, or *Rigel Kentaurus* (4·35 light-years distant), with an apparent magnitude of −0·29. It was discovered by Nicolas L. da Lacaille (1713–62) in c. 1752. In A.D. 29,700 this binary will reach a minimum distance of 2·84 light-years and should then be the second brightest star, with an apparent magnitude of −1·20.

Most and least luminous ■ If all the stars could be viewed at the same distance, the most luminous would be the variable *Eta Carinae* (see Most Massive Star), which now has a total luminosity 6,500,000 times that of the Sun but at its peak brightness in 1843 was at least ten times more luminous than this.

The visually brightest star is the hypergiant *Cygnus OB2 No.12*, 5,900 light-years distant, which has an absolute visual magnitude of −9·9 and is therefore visually 810,000 times more luminous than the Sun. This brightness may be matched by the supergiant IV b 59 in the nearby galaxy Messier 101.

In 1843 the variable *Eta Carinae* had an absolute brightness 70 million times that of the Sun.

The faintest star detected is the recently discovered RG 0058.8−2807 (see Lightest Star), which has a total luminosity only 0·00021 that of the Sun and an absolute visual magnitude of 20·2, so that the visual brightness is less than one millionth that of the Sun.

Brightest and latest supernova ■ The brightest ever seen by historic man is believed to be SN 1006 in April 1006 near *Beta Lupi*, which flared for two years and attained a magnitude of −9 to −10. The remnant is believed to be the radio source G.327·6 + 14·5 nearly 3,000 light-years distant.

Others have occurred in 1054, 1604, 1885 and most recently on 23 Feb 1987 when Ian Shelton sighted that designated − 69,202 in the Large Magellanic Cloud 170,000 light-years distant. This supernova was visible to the naked eye when at its brightest in May 1987. A claim to have detected a fast spinning pulsar at the center of the supernova debris was withdrawn in February 1990.

Constellations ■ The largest of the 89 constellations is *Hydra* (the Sea Serpent), which covers 1,302·844 °² or 6·3 percent of the hemisphere and contains at least 68 stars visible to the naked eye (to 5·5 mag.).

The constellation *Centaurus* (Centaur), ranking ninth in area, however, embraces at least 94 such stars.

The smallest constellation is *Crux Australis* (Southern Cross) with an area of only 0·16 percent of the whole sky *viz* 68·477 deg² compared with the 41,252·96 deg² of the whole sky.

Stellar planets ■ All claims to have discovered planetary systems around other stars must be treated with suspicion since there appears to be a confusion with small, dim stellar companions known as 'brown dwarfs,' which are failed stars since they are too cool to trigger the fusion of hydrogen.

Of the nine possible candidates announced by Bruce Campbell, Gordon Walker, and Stephenson Yang of the University of Victoria, British Columbia, Canada in August 1988, the most promising appears to be the inferred existence of a planet one and a half times the mass of Jupiter orbiting the bright star 36 Ursae Majoris A with an orbital period of three years.

Longest name ■ *Shurnarkabtishashutu* is the Arabic for 'under the southern horn of the bull.'

Black Holes ■ The concept of superdense bodies was first adumbrated by the Marquis de LaPlace (1749–1827). This term for a star that has undergone complete gravitational collapse was first used by Prof John Archibald Wheeler at an Institute for Space Studies meeting in New York City on 29 Dec 1967.

THE MOST DISTANT MEASURED HEAVENLY BODIES

The possible existence of galaxies external to our own Milky Way system was mooted in 1789 by Sir William Herschel (1738–1822). These extra-galactic nebulae were first termed 'island universes.' Sir John Herschel (1792–1871) opined as early as 1835 that some might be more than 250 quadrillion miles distant. The first direct measurement of any body outside our Solar System was in 1838. Distances in the table below assume that the edge of the observable Universe is at a distance of 14 billion light years.

Estimated Distance in Light-years[1]	Object	Method	Astronomers	Observatory	Date
about 6 (now 11·08)	61 Cygni	Parallax	F. Bessel	Königsberg, Germany	1838
>20 (now 26)	Vega	Parallax	F. G. W. Struve	Dorpat (now Tartu), Estonia	1840
c. 200	Limit	Parallax			by 1900
900,000 (now 2·31 million)[2]	Galaxy M31	Cepheid variable	E. P. Hubble (1889–1953)	Mt. Wilson, CA	1924

Millions of Light–Years	Recession Speed % of c	Object	Redshift[3]	Astronomers	Observatory	Date
c.200	1·4	NGC 7619		M. L. Humason	Mt. Wilson, CA	early 1928
>2,100	>15·0	Ursa Major No. 2		Humason & E. P. Hubble	Mt. Wilson, CA	by 1936[4]
4,600	32·6	Cluster 1448	0·403		Palomar, CA	1956
5,100	36·2	3C 295 in Boötes	0·461	R. Minkowski	Palomar, CA	June 1960
5,700	41·0	QSO 3C 147	0·545	M. Schmidt & T. A. Matthews	Palomar, CA	Feb 1964[5]
11,200	80·1	QSO 3C 9	2·01	M. Schmidt	Palomar, CA	Apr 1965
11,400	81·3	QSO 0106 +01	2·11	E. M. Burbidge et al.	Palomar, CA	Dec 1965
11,400	81·4	QSO 1116 +12	2·12	C. R. Lynds & A. N. Stockton	Steward, AZ	Mar 1966
				M. Schmidt	Palomar, CA	Mar 1966
11,500	82·4	QSO Pks 0237 −23	2·22	H. C. Arp et al.	Palomar, CA	Dec 1966
11,700	83·7	QSO 4C 25.05	2·36	E. T. Olsen & M. Schmidt	Palomar, CA	Dec 1967[6]
12,300	87·5	QSO 4C 05.34	2·88	R. Lynds & D. Wills	Kitt Peeak, AZ	Mar 1970
12,600	90·2	QSO OH 471	3·40	R. F. Carswell & P. A. Strittmatter	Steward, AZ	Mar 1973
12,700	90·7	QSO OQ 172	3·53	E. J. Wampler et al.	Lick, CA	May 1973
12,800	91·6	QSO Pks 2000 −330	3·78	B. A. Peterson et al.	Siding Spring, NSW, Australia	Apr 1982[7]
12,800	91·7	QSO Pks 1208 +1011	3·80	C. Hazard et al	Siding Spring, NSW, Australia	Feb 1986[8]
12,900	92·3	QSO 0046 −293	4·01	S.J.Warren et al	Siding Spring, NSW, Australia	Sept 1986[8]
12,900	92·4	QSO PC0910 +5625	4·04	M. Schmidt et al	Palomar, CA	June 1987
13,000	92·6	QSO 0000 −2620	4·11	C. Hazard et al	Siding Spring, NSW, Australia	Aug 1987[8]
13,100	93·4	QSO 0051 −279	4·43	S. J. Warren et al	Siding Spring, NSW, Australia	Nov 1987[8]
13,200	94·1	QSO PC 1158 +4635	4·73	D. P. Schneider et al	Palomar, CA	Aug 1989

Note: c is the notation for the speed of light (see page 67). [1] Term first utilised in March 1888. [2] Re-estimate by M.Rowan-Robinson in March 1988. [3] Discovered by Vesto Slipher (1875–1969) from Flagstaff, AZ, 1920. Redshift, denoted by z, is the measure of the speed of recession indicated by the ratio resulting from the subtraction of the rest wavelength of an emission line from the observed wavelength divided by the rest wavelength. [4] In 1934 Hubble opined that the observable horizon would be 3 billion light-years. [5] In Dec 1963 Dr I. S. Shklovsky's (USSR) suggestion that QS0 3C2 was more distant was subsequently confirmed with a value of 0·612c. [6] In Oct 1968 Dr Margaret Burbidge published a tentative redshift of 2·38 for QSO 5C 2.56. [7] Anglo-Australian telescope. [8] United Kingdom Schmidt telescope.

The first tentative identification of a Black Hole was announced in December 1972 in the binary-star X-ray source Cygnus X-1.

The best candidate is LMC X–3 of 10 solar masses and 180,000 light-years distant reported in Jan 1983. The critical size has been estimated to be as low as a diameter of 3·67 miles. One at the center of the Seyfert galaxy, NGC 4151 in *Canes Venatici*, was estimated by Michael Preston in Oct 1983 to be of between 50–100 million solar masses or up to $2 \times 2\cdot2$ decillion tons.

THE UNIVERSE

Outside the Milky Way galaxy, which is part of the so-called Local Group of galaxies moving at a speed of 1·4 million mph relative to the microwave background radiation in a direction offset 44° from the center of the Virgo cluster, there exist 10 billion other galaxies.

In November 1989 Margaret Geller and John Huchra of the Harvard-Smithsonian Center for Astrophysics, Cambridge, Massachusetts, announced the discovery of a 'Great Wall' in space, a concentration of galaxies in the form of a 'crumpled membrane' with a minimum extent of 200 million light-years by 500 million light-years ($2\cdot9 \times 10^{21}$ miles) and a depth of at least 15 million light-years.

Farthest visible object ■ The remotest heavenly body visible with the *naked eye* is the Great Galaxy in *Andromeda* (mag. 3·47), known as Messier 31. First noted by Simon Marius (1570–1624) from Germany, it is a rotating nebula in spiral form, and its distance from the Earth is about 2,309,000 light-years, or 13 million trillion miles, and is moving towards us. It is just possible, however, that under ideal seeing conditions, Messier 33, the Spiral in Triangulum (mag. 5·79), can be glimpsed by the naked eye of keen-sighted people at a distance of 2·36 million light-years.

Quasars ■ An occultation of 3C-273, observed from Australia on 5 Aug 1962, enabled the existence of quasi-stellar radio sources ('quasars' or QSOs) to be announced by Maarten Schmidt (b. Netherlands 1929). The red shift proved to be z = 0·158.

Quasars have immensely high luminosity for bodies so distant and of such small diameter. It was announced in May 1983 that the quasar S5 0014 + 81 had a visual luminosity 1·1 quadrillion times greater than that of the Sun.

The first double quasar (0957 + 56) among 1,500 known quasars, was announced in May 1980.

Pulsars ■ The earliest observation of a pulsating radio source or 'pulsar' CP 1919 (now PSR 1919 + 21) by Dr Jocelyn Burnell (nee Bell, 1943) was announced from the Mullard Radio Astronomy Observatory, Cambridge, United Kingdom on 24 Feb 1968. It had been detected on 28 Nov 1967.

For pulsars whose spin rates have been accurately measured, the fastest spinning is PSR 1937 + 214, which was discovered by a group led by Donald C Backer in November 1982. It is in the minor constellation Vulpecula (the Little Fox), 16,000 light-years distant, and has a pulse period of 1·557806449 millisec, which is equivalent to a spin rate of 641·9282708 revolutions per sec.

The pulsar that has the slowest spin down rate and is therefore the most accurate stellar clock is PSR 1855 + 09 at only $2\cdot1 \times 10^{-20}$ sec per sec.

Remotest object ■ Both the interpretation of the very large red shifts exhibited by quasars and the estimation of equivalent distances remain controversial. The record red shift of $Z = 4\cdot43$ for quasar 0051-279 (see Table) was announced by Stephen Warren et al. on November 1987 from analysis of plates from the UK Schmidt telescope, Siding Spring, New South Wales, Australia. Assuming an 'observable horizon,' where the speed of recession very closely approaches the speed of light c. 14 billion light years or 82·3 million trillion miles, this quasar would be more than 13·1 billion light-years distant. The 3 K background radiation or primordial hiss discovered in 1965 by Arno Penzias and Robert Wilson of Bell Laboratories appears to be moving at a velocity of 99·9998 percent of the speed of light.

Work in the near infrared spectrum by Richard Elston and George H and Marcia J Rieke, from April 1987 at the University of Arizona's Steward Observatory, revealed two very dim, fuzzy, protogalaxies, seemingly living beyond the most distant quasars. It was suggested in February 1988 that these might have a high red shift value of $Z = 6$ has not yet been confirmed.

Age of the Universe ■ For the age of the Universe a consensus value of 143 eons or gigayears (an eon or gigayear being 1 billion light-years) is obtained from various cosmological techniques. The equivalent value of the Hubble constant based on a Friedman model of the Universe without cosmological constant is Mpc43 ± 9 m/s. In 1973 an *ex nihilo* creation was postulated by Edward P. Tryon (US). Modified versions of the Inflationary Model, originally introduced by Alan Guth (US) in 1981, now complement the Big Bang theory of creation.

Telescopes

Earliest ■ It is not known when the first telescopes were made. The refractive properties of lenses were certainly known in ancient times, and spectacles were in use in the 13th century. Roger Bacon (*c.* 1214–92) in England wrote extensively about lenses, and claims have been made on behalf of various others, notably the Elizabethan scientists Diggs and Dee. However, the first telescope of which we have definite knowledge was made by H. Lippershey in Holland in 1608. The first astronomical observations with telescopes were made shortly afterwards, notably in 1609 by Thomas Harriot, who even drew a telescopic map of the Moon — though the first really systematic telescopic observations were made by Galileo from January 1610.

Largest Reflector ■ *Metal-Mirror* ■ This was the 72-in reflector made by the third Earl of Rosse, and set up at Birr Castle, Republic of Ireland in 1845. The mirror was of speculum metal (an alloy of copper and tin). With it, Lord Rosse discovered the spiral forms of the galaxies. It was last used in 1909.

The altazimuth-mounted 236·2-in reflector is sited on Mount Semirodniki, near Zelenchukskaya in the Caucasus Mountains, USSR, at an altitude of 6,830 ft and was completed in 1976. It is much the largest single mirror telescope in the world but has never performed up to its highest expectations. The largest satisfactory single-mirror telescope is the 200 in Hale reflector at Mount Palomar, CA. Though the Hale was completed in 1948, it is now much more efficient than it was then, as it is used with electronic devises that are much more sensitive than photographic plates. The CCD (Charged-Coupled Device) increases the sensitivity by a factor of around one hundred.

Largest planned ■ The Keck Telescope on Mauna Kea now being constructed will have a 393·70-in mirror, made up of 36 segments fitted together to produce the correct curve. However, the largest telescope of the century should be the VLT or Very Large Telescope being planned by the European Southern Observatory; it will consist of four 26·24-ft telescopes working together, providing a light-grasp equal to a single 52·49-ft mirror. It is hoped to have the first units working by 1995, and the complete telescope by 2000. It will be set up in the Atacama Desert of Northern Chile.

Solar ■ The McMath Solar Telescope at Kitt Peak (Arizona) has a 6·88-ft primary mirror; the light is sent to it via 32-degree inclined tunnel, from a coelostat (movable mirror) at the top end.

Multiple-Mirror ■ The Multiple-Mirror Telescope (MMT), at the Whipple Observatory at Mount Hopkins, AZ uses six 600·3-in mirrors together, giving a light-grasp equal to a single 176-in mirror. There are, however, considerable operational problems.

Infrared ■ The United Kingdom's reflector on Mauna Kea, HI is the largest having a 147 in mirror. It is however, so good that it can be used for visual work as well as infrared.

Southern ■ The largest southern telescope is the 157·87-in reflector at Cerro Tololo in the Atacama Desert. The Anglo-Australian Telescope (AAT) at Siding Spring in the New South Wales has a 153·14-in mirror.

Submillimeter ■ The James Clerk Maxwell telescope on Mauna Kea, HI has a 49·21-ft paraloloid primary, and is used for studies of the submillimeter part of the electromagnetic spectrum (0·01–0·03 in). It does not produce a visual image.

Largest refractor ■ The 62-ft long 40-in telescope completed in 1897 is situated at the Yerkes Observatory, Williams Bay, WI and belongs to the University of Chicago, IL. A larger 59·05-in refractor was built in France and shown at the Paris Exhibition in 1900, but was a failure and never used for scientific work.

Largest radio dish ■ Radio waves from the Milky Way were first detected by Karl Jansky of Bell Telephone Laboratories, Holmdel, NJ in 1931 when he was investigating static with an improvised 100-ft aerial. The only intentional radio telescope built before the outbreak of the war in 1939 was made by an amateur, Grote Reber, who detected radio emissions from the Sun. The diameter of the dish was 31·16 ft.

The world's largest dish radio telescope is the partially steerable ionospheric assembly built over a natural bowl at Arecibo, Puerto Rico, completed in November 1963 at a cost of about $9,000,000. The dish has a diameter of 1,000 ft and covers 18½ acres. Its sensitivity was raised by a factor of 1,000 and its range to the edge of the observable Universe at some 15 billion light-years by the fitting of new aluminum plates at a cost of $8·8 million. Rededication was on 16 Nov 1974.

The world's largest fully steerable dish is the 328-ft diameter, 3,360-ton assembly at the Max Planck Institute for Radio Astronomy of Bonn in the Effelsberger Valley, West Germany; it was completed in 1971.

Largest radio installation ■ It was reported in October 1986 that radio astronomers first linked the NASA deep-space installation at Tidbinbilla, Australia with the tracking stations at Usuda and Kashima, Japan, and with the TDRS (Tracking and Data Relay Satellite), which is in a geosynchronous orbit. It includes dishes at Parkes (210 ft), Siding Spring (72 ft) and Culgoora (72 ft). This has now been developed to create a radio telescope with an effective diameter of 2·16 Earth diameters (17,102 miles).

The VLA (Very Large Array) of the US National Science Foundation is Y-shaped, with each arm 13 miles long with 27 mobile antennae (each of 82 ft diameter) on rails. It is 50 miles west of Socorro in the Plains of San Augustin, NM. It was completed on 10 Oct 1980.

First telescope to use active optics ■ Active optics involves automatic correction of the mirror curve as the telescope is moved around. It gives a great increase in resolution. The first major telescope to use active optics was the New Technology Telescope (NTT) at La Siila in the Atacama Desert of Chile, the observing site of the ESO (European Southern Observatory). The NTT has a altazimuth mount, and is probably the most effective telescope in the world today.

Observatory ■ *Oldest* ■ The oldest building extant is 'Tower of the Winds' used by Andronichus of Cyrrhus in Athens, Greece *c.* 100 B.C., and equipped with sundials and clepsydra.

Highest ■ The High Altitude Observatory at Denver, CO is at 14,100 ft and was opened in 1973. The main instrument is a 24 in reflector. It is slightly higher than the observatory at the summit of Mauna Kea, in Hawaii.

First space ■ This was the Orbiting Solar Observatory 0504 launched on 18 Oct 1967.

Lowest ■ The lowest 'observatory' is at Homestake Mine, SD, where the 'telescope' is a tank of cleaning fluid (perchioroethylene), which contains chlorine, and can trap neutrinos from the Sun. The installation is 1·56 miles below ground level, in the shaft of a gold mine; the detector has to be at this depth, as otherwise the experiments would be confused by cosmic rays. The Homestake Observatory has been operating since 1964 and has provided results of tremendous value, as the solar neutrinos are far less numerous than had been predicted by theory.

Planetaria ■ The ancestor of the planetarium is the rotatable Gottorp Globe, built by Andreas Busch in Denmark about 1660. It was 34·6 ft in circumference, weighed nearly 3·9 tons and is now preserved in Leningrad, USSR. The stars were painted on the inside. The first modern-type planetarium was opened 1923 at Jena, East Germany; it was designed by Walther Bauersfelt of the Zeiss company.

The world's largest planetarium is in Miyazaki, Japan. Construction was completed on 30 Jun 1987 and the dome has a diameter of 88 ft 7 in.

United States ■ The Rueben H. Fleet Space Theater & Science Center in San Diego, CA and The Ethyl Universe Planetarium & Space Theater in Richmond, VA both have dome diameters of 75·5 ft.

The American Museum–Hayden Planetarium, New York City has a dome diameter of 75·1 ft, but has the largest seating capacity in the United States with 650 seats.

The Adler Planetarium in Chicago, IL, which opened on 12 May 1930, is the oldest planetarium in the United States. Its dome is 68 ft in diameter and it seats 450 people.

Space telescope ■ *Largest* ■ The largest is $1·5 billion NASA Edwin P Hubble Space Telescope of 12 tons and 43 ft in overall length with a 94·5-in reflector placed in orbit at 381 miles altitude aboard a US Space Shuttle. The cost of maintaining it and its staff after the launch postponement of October 1986 has been $230,000 per day.

First ■ The Hubble Space Telescope (HST) was launched from Cape Canaveral, FL on 25 April 1990. It has a 94·48-ft mirror, and should have a lifetime of at least 15 years.

SCIENCE & TECHNOLOGY

Most complex object in mathematics? ● The Mandelbrot Set, named after Benoît Mandelbrot, is represented by a unique pattern plotted from complex number coordinates. (A number is described as complex if it takes the form:

$$a + b \sqrt{(-1)}$$

where *a* and *b* are real numbers). A mathematical description of the shape's outline would require an infinity of information and yet the pattern can be generated from a few lines of computer code. Used in the study of chaotic behaviour, Mandelbrot's work has found applications in fields such as fluid mechancis, economics and linguistics. (Photo: Science Photo Library)

Elements

All known matter in, on and beyond the Earth is made up of chemical elements. It is estimated that there are 10^{87} electrons in the known Universe. The total of naturally occurring elements is 94, comprising, at ordinary temperatures, 2 liquids (Bromide and Mercury), 11 gases and 81 solids (including 72 metals). The so-called 'fourth state' of matter is plasma, when negatively charged electrons and positively charged ions are in flux.

Lightest and heaviest sub-nuclear particles

■ By April 1988 the existence was accepted of 31 'stable' particles, 64 meson resonance multiplets, and 52 baryon resonance multiplets, representing the eventual discovery of 247 particles and an equal number of anti-particles.

The heaviest stable particles fully accepted is the neutral weak gauge boson, the Z°, of mass 92·4 GeV, which was discovered in May 1983 by the UA1 Collaboration, CERN, Geneva, Switzerland led by Prof Carlo Rubbia using the 540 GeV Super Proton Synchrotron proton-antiproton beam collider.

The heaviest hadron accepted is the upsilon (6S) meson resonance of mass 11·02 GeV and lifetime $8·3 \times 10^{-24}$ sec., which consists of a bottom or beauty quark and its anti-quark, and which was first identified in October 1984 by two groups using the electron storage ring facilities at Cornell University, Ithaca, NY. Subatomic concepts require that the masses of the graviton, photon and neutrino should all be zero. Based on the sensitivities of various cosmological theories, upper limits for the masses of these particles are $7·6 \times 10^{-67}$ g for the graviton, $5·3 \times 10^{-60}$ g for the photon, and $3·2 \times 10^{-32}$ g for the neutrino (cf. electron mass $9·10939 \times 10^{-28}$ g).

Most and least stable

■ The 'grand unified' theory of the weak, electromagnetic, and strong forces predicts that the proton will not be stable. However, experiments reported in 1986 indicate that the lifetime of the most likely decay mode (to a positron and a neutral pion) has a lower limit of $3·1 \times 10^{32}$ years, which is over 40 times longer than the maximum lifetime predicted by the theory.

The least stable or shortest-lived particles are the two baryon resonances N(2220) and N(2600), both with $1·6 \times 10^{-24}$ sec, although the *predicted* lifetimes of both the weak gauge bosons, the $W^{\pm}$ and Z°, are $2·6 \times 10^{-25}$ sec.

Newest particle

■ The newest particles are the chi (2P) meson resonances, announced in 1987 by a joint Columbia University–State University of New York at Stony Brook, who used the electron storage ring facilities at Cornell University, Ithaca, NY. The mesons consist of a mixture of a bottom quark and its anti-quark and have masses of 10·235 GeV(^{10}), 10·255 GeV(^{11}) and 10·269 GeV (^{12}).

Smelliest substance

■ The most evil, of the 17,000 smells so far classified, must be a matter of opinion but ethyl mercaptan (C_2H_5SH) and butyl seleno-mercaptan (C_4H_9SeH) are pungent claimants, each with a smell reminiscent of a combination of rotting cabbage, garlic, onions, burned toast and sewer gas.

Most expensive perfume

■ Retail prices tend to be fixed with an eye to public relations rather than levels solely dictated by the market cost of ingredients and packaging. The Chicago-based firm Jōvan marketed from March 1984 a cologne called Andron that contains a trace of the attractant pheromone androstenol, which has a cost of $2,750 per oz.

Most potent poison

■ The rickettsial disease, Q-fever, can be instituted by a *single* organism though it is fatal in only 1 in 1,000 cases. About 10 organisms of *Francisella tularenesis* (formerly *Pasteurella tularenesis*) can institute tularemia, variously called alkali disease, Francis disease or deerfly fever. This is fatal in upwards of 10 cases in 1,000.

Most powerful nerve gas

■ VX, 300 times more toxic than phosgene ($COCl_2$) used in World War I, was developed at the Chemical Defence Experimental Establishment, Porton Down, Wiltshire, United Kingdom in 1952. Patents were applied for in 1962 and published in February 1974, showing it to be ethyl S-2-diisopropylaminoethylmethylphosphonothiolate. The lethal dosage is 10 mg-minute/m³ airborne or 0·3 mg orally.

Most absorbent substance

■ The US Department of Agriculture Research Service announced on 18 Aug 1974 that 'H-span' or Super Slurper, composed of one-half starch derivative and one-fourth each of acrylamide and acrylic acid can, when treated with iron, retain water 1,300 times its own weight.

Finest powder

■ The ultimate is solid helium, which was first postulated to be a monatomic powder as early as 1964.

Most lethal man-made chemical

■ TCDD (2,3,7,8-tetrachlorodibenzo-p-dioxin), the most deadly of the 75 known dioxins, is admitted to be 150,000 times more deadly than cyanide, at 3·1 trillion moles/kg.

Most refractory substance

■ Tantalum carbide $TaC_{0.88}$ melting at 3,990°C.

Least dense substances

■ These are the silica aerogels in which tiny spheres of bonded silicon and oxygen atoms are joined into long strands with pockets of air separating them. In February 1990 the lightest of these areogels, with a density of only 5 oz/ft³, was produced at the Lawrence Livermore Laboratory, CA. The main use will be in space to collect micrometeoroids and the debris present in comets' tails.

Highest superconducting temperature

■ In March 1988 bulk superconductivity with a transition to zero resistance at −234°F was obtained at the IBM Almaden Research Center, San Jose, CA for a mixed oxide of thallium, calcium, barium and copper — $Tl_2Ca_2Ba_2Cu_3O_x$.

Most acidic solution

■ pH values of a normal solution of perchloric acid $HClO_4$ tends towards 0, although the most powerful acid based on its power as a hydrogen-ion donor is a solution of antimony pentafluoride SbF_5 in fluorosulfonic acid FSO_3H.

Most Alkaline solution

■ pH values of normal solutions of sodium hydroxide (caustic soda) $NaOH$, potassium hydroxide (caustic potash) KOH, and tetramethylammonium hydroxide $N(CH_3)_4 OH$ tend towards 14.

Sweetest substance

■ Talin from arils of katemfe (*Thaumatococcus Daniellii*), discovered in West Africa, is 6,150 times as sweet as a 1% sucrose solution.

Bitterest substance

■ Vilex (denatonium benzoate) leaves a lingering bitter taste even with a dilution of one part in 100 million.

The 109 Elements

There are 94 naturally occuring elements, while to date a further 15 transuranic elements (elements 95 to 109) have been claimed, of which 10 are undisputed. By 1984 6,845,000 chemical compounds had been produced from these elements, of which some 65,000 were in common use.

Commonest

■ *Extraterrestrial:* ■ Hydrogen (H) accounts for 90% of all known matter in the Universe and 70·68% by mass in the Solar System.

Earth's Lithosphere: ■ Oxygen (0) at 46·40% by weight.

Atmosphere: ■ Nitrogen (N) at 78·08% by volume (75·52% by mass).

Rarest (of the 94)

■ *Earth's Lithosphere:* ■ Only 0·0056 oz of astatine (At) is present in the Earth's crust, of which the isotope astatine 215 (At 215) (discovered by B. Karlik and T. Bernert of Austria in 1943) accounts for only $1·6 \times 10^{10}$ oz.

Atmosphere: ■ Radon (Rn) at 6×10^{-20} parts per million by volume. This is only 5·3 lb overall, but concentration of this radioactive gas in certain granitic areas has been blamed for a number of cancer deaths. The total amount of radon in the Earth's crust available to replenish the atmosphere is estimated to be 160 tons.

Density

■ *Solid* ■ The lightest element at room temperature is the metal lithium (Li) at 33·30 lb/ft³, although the density of solid hydrogen at its melting point of −498·54°F is only 5·44 lb/ft³. The heaviest solid at room temperature is osmium (Os) at 1,410 lb/ft³.

Gas ■ At NTP (Normal Temperature and Pressure, 32°F and one atmosphere) the lightest gas is hydrogen (H) at 0·005612 lb/ft³, while the heaviest gas is radon (Rn) at 0·6274 ln/ft³.

Melting/Boiling point

■ *Highest* ■ Metallic tungsten (W) melts at 6,188°F and boils at 10,580°F. On the assumption that graphite transforms to carbonous forms above 4,172°F, then the nonmetal with the highest melting and boiling points would be carbon (C) at 6,386°F and 6,998°F respectively. However, this is disputed, and an alternative suggestion is that graphite remains stable at high temperatures and sublimes directly to vapor at 6,728°F and cannot be obtained in a liquid form unless the temperature exceeds 8,546°F and the pressure 100 atm (10 MPa).

Lowest ■ Helium (He) cannot be obtained as a solid atmospheric pressure — the minimum pressure being 24·985 atm (2·532 MPa), which occurs at a temperature of −522·27°F. The boiling point of helium is −516·07°F. Monatomic hydrogen (H) is expected to be a non-liquifiable superfluid gas. The metal with the lowest melting and boiling points is mercury (Hg), at −37·836°F and 673·9°F respectively.

Thermal Expansion

■ At room temperature, the metal with the highest expansion is cesium (Cs), at 94×10^{-6} per °C, while the diamond allotrope of carbon (C) has the lowest expansion at $1·0 \times 10^{-6}$ per °C.

Hardest substance

■ The carbon (C) allotrope diamond has a Knoop value of 8,400.

Most ductile

■ 1 oz of gold (Au) can be drawn to 43 miles.

Purest

■ In April 1978, P. V. E. McClintock of the University of Lancaster, United Kingdom, reported on the success in obtaining the isotope helium 4 (He 4) with impurity levels at less than 2 parts in 10^{15}.

Most expensive

■ For commercially available elements, californium (Cf) was sold in 1970 for $10 per microgram.

Newest ■ The discovery of element 108 or unniloctium (Uno) (provisional I.U.P.A.C. name) was announced in April 1984 by G. Münzenberg *et al* and was based on the observations of only three atoms at the Gesellschaft für Schwerionenforschung (GSI), Darmstadt, Federal Republic of Germany. A less-substantiated claim was made in June of the same year by Yu. Ts. Oganessian *et al* of the Joint Institute for Nuclear Research, Dubna, USSR. The single atom of unnilennium (Une) produced at GSI on 29 Aug 1982 counts as the highest atomic number (109) and the heaviest atomic mass (266) obtained; a tentative Soviet claim to have detected element 110 or ununnillium (Uun) with a probable mass of 272 has not been substantiated.

Isotopes ■ *Most* ■ 36 each for both xenon (Xe) (9 stable isotopes identified by F. W. Aston [United Kingdom] between 1920 and 1922, and 27 radioactive identified between 1939 and 1981) and cesium (Cs) (1 stable, identified by Aston in 1921, and 35 radioactive identified between 1935 and 1983).

Least ■ Three confirmed isotopes for hyrdogen (H) including two stable (identified by Aston in 1920 [protium] and by H. C. Urey, F. G. Brickwedde and G.M. Murphy [US] in 1931) and one radioactive (tritium) first identified by M. L. E. Oliphant, P. Harteck and Lord Rutherford (United Kingdom) in 1934 but characterized as a radioactive isotope by L. W. Alvarez and R. Cornog (US) in 1939.

Most stable ■ The most stable radioactive is the double-beta decaying tellurium 128 (Te 128) with a half-life of 1.5×10^{24} years. It was first identified as being naturally occuring by F. W. Aston (United Kingdom) in 1924 and confirmed as being the longest living by E. C. Alexander, Jr., B. Srinivasan and O. K. Manuel (US) in 1968. The alpha-decay record 8×10^{15} years for samarium 148 (Sm 148) and the beta-decay record 9×10^{15} years for cadmium 113 (Cd 113). Both isotopes were identified as being naturally occuring by Aston in 1933 and 1924 respectively, while proof of their radioactivity was first obtained by T. R. Wilkins and A. J. Dempster (US) in 1938 for Sm 148, and by D. E. Watt and R. N. Glover (United Kingdom) in 1961 for Cd 113.

Least stable ■ Lithium 5 (Li5), with a lifetime of 4.4×10^{-22} sec — first characterized by E. W. Titterton and T. A. Brinkley (Australia/United Kingdom) in 1950.

Toxic ■ The most stringent restriction placed on a non-radioactive element is for beryllium (Be), with a Threshold Limit Value in air of only 2 micrograms/m³. For radioactive isotopes which occur naturally or are produced in nuclear installations and have ecologically significant half-lives (i.e., in excess of 6 months), then the severest restriction in air is placed on thorium 228 (Th228 or radiothorium, first observed by O. Hahn [Germany] in 1905) at 2.4×10^{16} grams/m³ (equivalent radiation itensity 0·0074 Becquerel/m³), while the severest restriction in water is placed on radium 228 (Ra228 or mesothorium 1 discovered by Hahn in 1907) at 1.1×10^{-13} grams/liter (equivalent radiation intensity 1·1 Becquerel/liter).

Numbers

In dealing with large numbers, scientists use the notation of 10 raised to various powers to eliminate a profusion of zeros. For example, 19·16 trillion miles would be written 1.916×10^{12} miles. Similarly, a very small

Mendeleyev ● Element 101 is named after Dimitry Ivanovich Medeleyev (1834-1907), the Russian chemist who formulated the 'Periodic Table' of the elements between 1868-71. By grouping the 62 then known elements in order of increasing atomic weight he demonstrated a recurrence of properties and predicted the properties of elements which 'ought' to exist but which had not then been discovered. His system did not gain wide acceptance at first but the discovery of the 'missing' elements, with the properties which he had predicted, helped validate his theory which is now part of the framework of chemistry. (Photo: Science Photo Library)

The metallic element with lowest melting point ● Is that of Mercury (Hg) at $-37.836°$ F. In this photograph Mercury's greater cohesion compared with water (stained red) is demonstrated. (Photo: Science Photo Library)

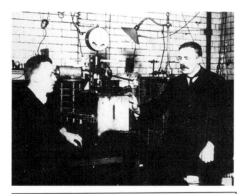

Elements ● Ernest Rutherford (1871-1937) right and Hans Geiger (1882-1945) in their laboratory at Manchester University, Manchester, United Kingdom in about 1908. They are seen with the instrumentation they used to detect and count alpha particles from a radio active source. The experiment led to Rutherford identifying alphas particles as helium ions, later shown to be helium *nuclei*. (Photo: Science Photo Library)

number, for example 0·0000154324 of a gram, would be written 1.54324×10^{-5}. Of the prefixes used before numbers the smallest is 'atto' from the Danish or Norwegian *atten*, for 18, symbol a, indicating 10^{-18} of a unit. The highest is 'exa' *(Greek, hexa, six, i.e. six groups of three zeros)*, symbol E, indicating 10^{18}.

Highest numbers ■ The highest lexicographically accepted named number in the system of successive powers of ten is the centillion, first recorded in 1852. It is the hundredth power of a million, or one followed by 600 zeros. The number 10^{100} is designated a Googol. The term was suggested by the nine–year–old nephew of Dr Edward Kasner (US) (d. 1955). Ten raised to the power of a Googol is described as a Googolplex. Some conception of the magnitude of such numbers can be gained when it is said that the number of electrons in some models of the observable Universe does not exceed 10^{87}. The highest named number outside the decimal notation is the Buddhist *asankhyeya*, which is equal to 10^{140} and mentioned in Jain works of *c.* 100 B.C.

The highest number ever used in a mathematical proof is a bounding value published in 1977 and known as Graham's number. It concerns bichromatic hypercubes and is inexpressible without the special 'arrow' notation, devised by Knuth in 1976, extended to 64 layers.

Largest factored number ■ Computer scientists, using more than 400 linked computers, have found the factors of a 100–digit number. The calculation took 26 days, and threatens the security of many modern crytographic systems.

Prime numbers ■ A prime number is any positive integer (excluding unity 1) having no integral factors other than itself and unity, e.g. 2, 3, 5, 7 or 11. The lowest prime number is thus 2. The highest *known* prime number is $391,581 \times 2^{216193} - 1$, discovered on 6 Aug 1989 by a team, known as 'Amdahl Six.' The number contains 65,087 digits and was found on an Amdahl 1200 supercomputer in Santa Clara, CA. The 'team' also discovered the largest known twin primes:
$$1,706,595 \times 2^{11235} - 1$$
$$\text{and } 1,706,595 \times 2^{11235} + 1.$$
The lowest non-prime or composite number (excluding 1) is 4.

Perfect numbers ■ A number is said to be perfect if it is equal to the sum of its divisors other than itself, e.g. $1 + 2 + 4 + 7 + 14 = 28$. The lowest perfect number is $6 (= 1 + 2 + 3)$. The highest known and the 31st so far discovered, is $(2^{216091} - 1) \times 2^{216090}$. It is a consequence of the largest Mersenne prime (also the second largest prime known) being $2^{216091} - 1$.

Newest mathematical constant ■ The study of turbulent water, the weather, and other chaotic phenomena has revealed the existence of a new universal constant, the Feigenbaum number, named after its discoverer. It is equal to approximately 4·669201609102990.

Most-proved theorem ■ A book published in 1940 contained 370 different proofs of Pythagoras' theorem, including one by President Garfield.

Longest proof ■ The proof of the classification of all finite simple groups is spread over more than 14,000 pages, in nearly 500 papers in mathematical journals, contributed by more than 100 mathematicians over a period of more than 35 years.

Oldest mathematical puzzle ■ dating from 1650 B.C.. This is an English version.

As I was going to St Ives, I met a man with seven wives. Every wife had seven sacks, and every sack had seven cats. Kitten, cats, sacks and wives; how many were going to St Ives?

Most prolific mathematician ■ Leonard Euler, (Switzerland) (1707–83) was so proli-

fic that his papers were still being published for the first time more than 50 years after his death. His collected works have been printed bit by bit since 1910 and will eventually occupy more than 75 large quarto volumes.

Greatest mathematical prodigy ■ Blaise Pascal (1623–62), the French philosopher and mathematician, discovered Pascal's theorem at the age of 16.

Largest prize ever offered ■ Dr Paul Wolfskell left prize money in his will for the first person to solve Pierre Fermat's (1601–65) last theorem. This prize was worth 100,000 deutsche marks in 1908. As a result of inflation, the prize is now just over 10,000 deutsche marks.

Longest computer computation for a yes–no answer ■ The twentieth Fermat number $2^{2^{20}} + 1$, was tested on a CRAY-2 supercomputer in 1986 to see if it was a prime number. After 10 days of calculation the answer was NO.

Most innumerate ■ The Nambiquara of the northwest Matto Grosso of Brazil lack any system of numbers. They do, however, have a verb that means 'they are alike.'

Most accurate and most inaccurate version of 'pi' ■ In 1989 the greatest number of decimal places to which *pi* (π) has been calculated is 1,011,196,691 by David and Gregory Chudnovsky at Columbia University, NY. The calculation was performed twice on an IBM 3090 mainframe and on a CRAY-2 supercomputer, and the results matched.

In 1897 the General Assembly of Indiana enacted in House Bill No. 246 that *pi* was *de jure* 4. Places 762 – 767 comprise six consecutive '9's.

In 1853 William Shanks published his calculation of π to 707 decimal places, all calculated by hand. Ninety-two years later, in 1945, it was discovered that the last 180 digits were in fact all wrong.

Earliest measures ■ The earliest known measure of weight is the *beqa*, of the Amratian period of Egyptian civilization c. 3800 B.C., found at Naqada, Egypt. The weights are cylindrical, with rounded ends from 6·65–7.45 oz.

The unit of length used by the megalithic tomb-builders in northwestern Europe c. 3500 B.C. appears to have been 2·72 ± 0·003 ft. This was deduced by Professor Alexander Thom (1894–1985) in 1966.

Time measure ■ Owing to variations in the length of a day, which is estimated to be increasing irregularly at the average rate of about a millisecond per century due to the Moon's tidal drag, the second has been redefined. Instead of being 1/86 400th part of a mean solar day, it has, since 1960, been reckoned as 1/315569259747th part of the solar (or tropical) year at A.D. 1900, January 0·12 hr, Ephemeris time. In 1958 the second of Ephemeris time was computed to be equivalent to 9,192,631,770 ± 20 cycles of the radiation corresponding to the transition of cesium 133 atoms when unperturbed by exterior fields. The greatest diurnal change recorded has been 10 milliseconds on 8 Aug 1972, due to the most violent solar storm recorded in 370 years of observations.

The accuracy of the cesium beam frequency standard approaches eight parts in 10^{14}, compared to two parts in 10^{13} for the methane-stabilized helium-neon laser and six parts in 10^{13} for the hydrogen maser.

The longest measure of time is the *kalpa* in Hindu chronology. It is equivalent to 4,320 million years. In astronomy a cosmic year is the period of rotation of the Sun around the center of the Milky Way galaxy, i.e., 225 million years. In the Late Cretaceous Period of c. 85 million years ago, the Earth rotated faster, resulting in 370·3 days per year, while in Cambrian times, some 600 million years ago, there is evidence that the year extended over 425 days.

Physical Extremes

Smallest optical prism ■ Researchers at the National Institute of Standards and Technology laboratories in Boulder, CO have created a glass prism of sides 0.001 in barely visible to the naked eye; this should find application in fiber optics research and instrumentation.

Highest temperature ■ Those produced in the center of a thermonuclear fusion bomb are of the order of 540,032,000 – 720,032,000 °F. Of controllable temperatures, the highest effective laboratory figure reported is 392,000,000 °F achieved in the Tokamak Fusion Test Reactor at the Princeton Plasma Physics Laboratory, Princeton, NJ in June 1986.

Lowest temperature ■ The absolute zero of temperature, 0 K, on the Kelvin scale corresponds to −459·67° F. The lowest temperature reached is 2×10^{-9} Kelvin, i.e., two billionths of a degree above absolute zero. This was achieved at the Low Temperature Laboratory, Helsinki University of Technology, Finland, in a nuclear demagnetization device by a team led by Professor Olli V. Lounasmaa, including Dr Pertii Hakonen of Helsinki University and Dr Shi Yin of Michigan State University and was announced in October 1989.

Smallest thermometer ■ Dr Frederich Sachs, a biophysicist at the State University of New York at Buffalo, has developed an ultra-microthermometer for measuring the temperature of single living cells. The tip is one micron in diameter, about one-fiftieth the diameter of a human hair.

Largest barometer ■ A water barometer 39 ft in height was constructed in 1987 by Bert Bolle, curator of the Barometer Museum, Maartensdijk, Netherlands, where the instrument is situated.

Highest pressures ■ A sustained laboratory pressure of 1·70 megabars (12,320 tons force/in²), was achieved in the giant hydraulic diamond-faced press at the Carnegie Institution's Geophysical Laboratory, Washington, DC and reported in June 1978. This laboratory announced solid hydrogen achieved at 57 kilobars pressure on 2 Mar 1979. If created, metallic hydrogen is expected to be silvery white but soft, with a density of 0·04 lb/in³. The pressure required for the transition is estimated by H. K. Mao and P. M. Bell to be 1 megabar at 77° F. Using dynamic methods and impact speeds of up to 18,000 mph, momentary pressures of 75 million atmospheres (548,800 tons/in²) were reported from the US in 1958.

Highest velocity ■ The highest velocity at which any solid visible object has been projected is 335,000 mph, in the case of a plastic disc at the Naval Research Laboratory, Washington DC reported in August 1980.

Finest balance ■ The Sartorius Model 4108 manufactured in Göttingen, West Germany can weigh objects of up to an accuracy of 0·01 μg or 0·00000001 g, equivalent to little more than one sixtieth of the weight of the ink on this period.

Largest bubble chamber ■ The $7 million installation, completed in October 1973 at Weston, IL, is 15 ft in diameter. It contains 8,712 gallons of liquid hydrogen at a temperature of −476° F and has a superconducting magnet of 3 tesla.

Fastest centrifuge ■ Ultra-centrifuges were invented by Theodor Svedberg (b. 30 Aug 1884; Sweden) in 1923.

The highest man-made rotary speed ever achieved, and the fastest speed of any earthbound object is 4,500 mph by a swirling tapered 6 in-carbon fiber rod in a vacuum at Birmingham University, United Kingdom, reported on 24 Jan 1975.

Finest cut ■ The $13 million Large Optics Diamond Turning Machine at the Lawrence Livermore National Laboratory, CA was reported in June 1983 to be able to sever a human hair 3,000 times lengthwise.

Longest echo ■ The longest echo in any building is one of 15 sec following the closing of the door of the Chapel of the Mausoleum, Hamilton, United Kingdom, built 1840–55.

Most powerful electric current ■ If fired simultaneously, the 4,032 capacitors comprising the Zeus capacitor at the Los Alamos Scientific Laboratory, NM would produce, for a few microseconds, twice as much current as that generated elsewhere on Earth.

Hottest flame ■ Carbon subnitride (C_4N_2), at one atmosphere pressure, can produce a flame calculated to reach 5,261 K.

Highest measured frequency ■ The highest *directly* measured frequency is a visible yellow-green light at 520·2068085 terahertz (a terahertz being a trillion hertz or cycles per second) for the o-component of the 17–1 P(62) transition line of iodine 127.

The highest measured frequency determined by precision metrology is a green light at 582·491703 terahertz for the b_{21} component of the R(15) 43–0 transition line of iodine 127. However, with the decision on 20 Oct 1983 by the Conférence Générale des Poids et Mesures (CGPM) to define exactly the meter (m) in terms of the velocity of light (c) such that 'the meter is the length of the path traveled by light in vacuum during a time interval of 1/299792458 of a second' then frequency (f) and wavelength (λ) are exactly interchangeable through the relationship $f\lambda = c$.

Lowest friction ■ The lowest coefficient of static and dynamic friction of any solid is 0·02, in the case of polytetrafluoroethylene ($[C_2F_4]n$), called PTFE—equivalent to wet ice on wet ice. It was first manufactured in quantity by E. I. du Pont de Nemours & Co Inc. in 1943, and is marketed from the United States as Teflon.

In the centrifuge at the University of Virginia a 30-lb rotor magnetically supported has been spun at 1,000 rev/sec in a vacuum of 10^{-6} mm of mercury pressure. It loses only one revolution per second per day, thus spinning for years.

Smallest hole ■ A hole of 40 Å was shown visually using a JEM 100C electron microscope and Quantel Electronics devices at the Department of Metallurgy, Oxford University, United Kingdom on 28 Oct 1979. To find such a hole is equivalent to finding a pinhead in a haystack with sides of 1·2 miles.

An electron microscope beam on a sample of sodium beta-alumina at the University of Illinois in May 1983 accidentally bored a hole 6·5 billion ft in diameter.

Most powerful laser beams ■ The first

illumination of another celestial body was achieved on 9 May 1962, when a beam of light was successfully reflected from the Moon by the use of a laser (light amplification by stimulated emission of radiation) attached to a 48-in telescope at Massachusetts Institute of Technology, Cambridge, Massachusetts. The spot was estimated to be 4 miles in diameter on the Moon. The device was propounded in 1958 by the American Dr Charles Hard Townes (b. 1915). Such a flash for 1/5000th of a second can bore a hole through a diamond by vaporization at 18,032° F, produced by 2×10^{23} photons. The 'Shiva' laser was reported at the Lawrence Livermore Laboratory, CA to be concentrating $2 \cdot 6 \times 10^{13}$ watts into a pinhead-sized target for $9 \cdot 5 \times 10^{-11}$ sec in a test on 18 May 1978.

Brightest light ■ The brightest artificial sources are 'laser' pulses generated at the US Los Alamos National Laboratory, NM, announced in March 1987 by Dr Robert Graham. An ultraviolet flash lasting 1 picosecond (1 trillionth sec) is intensified to an energy of 5×10^{15} watts.

Of continuously burning sources, the most powerful is a 313 kW high-pressure argon arc lamp of 1,200,000 candlepower, completed by Vortek Industries Ltd of Vancouver, British Columbia, Canada in March 1984.

The most powerful searchlight ever developed was one produced during World War II by the General Electric Company Ltd at the Hirst Research Centre in Wembley, London, United Kingdom. It had a consumption of 600 kW and gave an arc luminance of 300,000 candles/in² and a maximum beam intensity of 2·7 billion candles from its parabolic mirror (diameter 10 ft).

Shortest light pulse ■ Charles Z. Shank and colleagues of the AT & T Laboratories, Murray Hill, NJ achieved a light pulse of 8 femtoseconds (8×10^{-15} sec) announced in April 1985. The pulse comprised only four or five wavelengths of visible light or 2·4 micrometers long.

Most durable light ■ The average bulb lasts for 750–1,000 hr. There is some evidence that a 5 watt carbide filament bulb made by the Shelby Electric Co and presented by Mr Bernell in the Fire Department, Livermore, South Alameda County, CA was first shedding light in 1901.

Heaviest magnet ■ That in the Joint Institute for Nuclear Research at Dubna, near Moscow, USSR for the 10 GeV synchrophasotron, measuring 196 ft in diameter, and weighing 39,683 tons.

Largest Electromagnet ■ The world's largest electromagnet is part of the L3 detector, another experiment on LEP. The octagonal-shaped magnet consists of 6,400 tons of low carbon steel yoke and 1,100 tons of aluminum coil. The yoke elements, welded pieces of up to 30 tons each, were manufactured in the Soviet Union. The coil was manufactured in a modular technique in Switzerland and consists of 168 turns welded together to form an eight-sided frame. Thirty thousand amperes of current flow through the aluminum coil to creat a uniform magnetic field of 5 kilogauss. The magnet is higher than a four-story building with a volume of approximately 39·37 ft x 39·3 ft x 39·37 ft. The total weight of the magnet, including the frame, coil and inner support tube, is 7,810 tons. The L3 magnet is composed of more metal than the Eiffel Tower.

Magnetic fields ■ The strongest conti-

Most powerful particle accelerator ● This exposure was taken from the 16th floor of the Fermi National Accelerator Laboratory (Fermilab) at Illinois. The Tevatron is 6,562 ft in diameter and contains two accelerators, one above the other. The top accelerator uses ordinary magnets and accelerates protons to 150 GeV. It then passes them to the lower accelerator, with superconducting magnets, which accelerates them up to 1,000 GeV (1 TeV). (Photo: Science Photo Library)

nuous field strength achieved was a total of 35·3 ± 0·3 teslas at the Francis Bitter National Magnet Laboratory, Massachusetts Institute of Technology, Cambridge, MA on 26 May 1988, employing a hybrid magnet with holmium pole pieces. This had the effect of enhancing the central magnetic field generated in the heart and brain.

The weakest magnetic field measured is one of 8×10^{-15} tesla in the heavily shielded room at the same laboratory. It is used by Dr David Cohen for research into the very weak magnetic field generated in the heart and brain.

Most powerful microscope ■ The scanning tunneling microscope (STM) invented at the IBM research laboratory in Zürich, Switzerland in 1981 has the magnifying ability of 100 million and is capable of resolving down to one-hundredth the diameter of an atom (3×10^{-10} m). The fourth generation of the scanning tunneling microscope now being developed is said to be 'about the size of a finger tip.'

By using field ion microscopy the tips of probes of scanning tunneling microscopes have been

Particle accelerator ● A section of the tunnel of the Super-Proton-Synchrotron accelerator at CERN, Geneva, Switzerland during its construction in 1974. (Photo: Science Photo Library)

shaped to end in a single atom — the last three layers constituting the world's smallest man-made pyramid consisting of 7, 3 and 1 atoms. It was announced in January 1990 that D. M. Eigler and E. K. Schweizer of the IBM Almaden Research Center, San Jose, CA had used an STM to move and reposition single atoms of xenon on a nickel surface in order to spell out the word 'IBM.'

Loudest noise ■ The loudest in a laboratory has been 210 decibels, or 400,000 acoustic watts, reported by NASA from a 48-ft steel and concrete test bed for the Saturn V rocket static with 60-ft deep foundations at Marshall Space Flight Center, Huntsville, AL in October 1965. Holes could be bored in solid material by this means, and the audible range was in excess of 100 miles.

Smallest microphone ■ Professor Ibrahim Kavrak of Bogazici University, Istanbul, Turkey developed a microphone for a new technique of pressure measurement in fluid flow in 1967. It has a frequency response of 10 Hz to 10 KHz and measures 0·06 in × 0·03 in.

Highest note ■ A laser beam striking a sapphire crystal at the Massachusetts Institute of Technology, Cambridge, MA in September 1964 generated a note of 60 gigahertz.

Most powerful particle accelerator ■ The 6,562-ft diameter proton synchrotron at the Fermi National Accelerator Laboratory east of Batavia, IL is the highest energy 'atomsmasher' in the world. On 14 May 1976 an energy of 500 giga electron volts (5×10^{11}) was achieved for the first time. On 13 Oct 1985 a center of mass energy of 1·6 tera electron volts ($1 \cdot 6 \times 10^{11}$ electron volts) was achieved by colliding beams of protons and antiprotons. This involves 1,000 superconducting magnets maintained at a temperature of − 452° F by means of the world's largest 1,188 gallons per hour helium liquefying plant, which began operating on 18 Apr 1980.

The aim of CERN (*Conseil Européen pour la Recherche Nucléaire*) to collide beams of protons and antiprotons in their Super Proton Synchroton (SPS) near Geneva, Switzerland at 270 GeV × 2 = 540 GeV was achieved at 4:55 A.M. on 10 Jul 1981. This was the equivalent of striking a fixed target with protons at 150 TeV or 150,000 GeV. However, the largest scientific instrument so far is the 16·57-mile circumference electron-positron storage ring 'LEP' at CERN, which began operations on 13 Aug 1989. The

This is equivalent to depopulating (baseball-sized) molecules from 1 yard to 50 miles.

Lowest viscosity ■ The California Institute of Technology first announced on 1 Dec 1957 that there was no measurable viscosity, i.e., perfect flow, in liquid helium II, which exists at temperatures close to absolute zero ($-459.67°$ F).

Highest voltage ■ The highest ever potential difference obtained in a laboratory has been $32 ± 1.5$ million volts by the National Electrostatics Corporation at Oak Ridge, TN on 17 May 1979.

Borings & Mines

Deepest ■ Man's deepest penetration into the Earth's crust is a geological exploratory drilling near Zapolarny, Kola peninsula, USSR begun in 1970. By 1987 a depth of 8.07 miles (42,650 ft) was surpassed. Progress has understandably greatly slowed to 1,640 ft per year as the eventual target of 49,212 ft in 1990 is neared. The drill bit is mounted on a turbine driven by a mud pump. The temperature at 6.83 miles was already 392° F. The West Germans announced the test drilling of the Erbendorf hole, Upper Bavaria on 9 Oct 1986. The planned depth of the £ 150 million project is 8.6 miles (45,900 ft).

Ocean drilling ■ The deepest recorded drilling into the seabed by the *Glomar Challenger* of the US Deep Sea Drilling Project is one of 5,709 ft off northwest Spain in 1976.

The deepest site is now 23,077 ft below the surface on the western wall of the Mariana Trench in May 1978.

The deepest drilling in the North Sea is in 2,611 ft of water on 11–12 Jun 1986 by the *Sovereign Explorer*, a propulsion-assisted semi-submersible drilling unit operated by Scotdrill Offshore Company, Aberdeen, United Kingdom and contracted to Chevron Petroleum.

Ice-core drilling ■ The deepest borehole in ice was drilled during the course of the 30th Soviet Antarctic Expedition in 1985 when a depth of 7,225 ft was achieved at the Vostok station in central Antarctica. The 18th Expedition drilled the deepest 'dry' borehole (without antifreeze) in 1972, which reached 3,125 ft.

Oil fields ■ In 1989 the world's largest oil producer was the USSR, with 12.5 million barrels per day, followed by the United States, with 7.5 million.

The world's largest oil field is the Ghawar field, Saudi Arabia, developed by ARAMCO, which measures 150 x 22 miles.

United States ■ The largest oil field in the United States is Permian Basin, which covers approximately 100,000 miles² in Southeast New Mexico, Western and Northwestern Texas.

In 1989, the United States imported 7,979,000 barrels of oil per day.

Gas deposits ■ The largest gas deposit in the world is at Urengoi, USSR, with an eventual production of 261.6 billion yd³ per year through six pipelines from proved reserves of 9.156 trillion yd³. The trillionth (10^{12}) cubic meter was produced on 23 Apr 1986.

Oil platforms *Heaviest* ■ The world's heaviest oil platform is the *Gullfaks C* in the North Sea, built and operated by the Norwegian oil company Statoil. The platform is of the

tunnel 12.5-ft in diameter, runs between 164 and 492-ft under the Earth's surface, and is accessible through 18 vertical shafts. Over 60,000 tons of technical equipment have been installed in the tunnel and its eight underground work zones. It is intended to be a 'Z° factory' producing up to 10,000 of these neutral weak gauge bosons every day in order to obtain a deeper understanding of the subatomic nature of matter. The aim is that by 1992 the electron and positron beams will have energies of 96 GeV each.

The US Department of Energy set up a study for the $6 billion Super Superconductivity Collider (SSC) 1995 with two 20 TeV proton and antiproton colliding beams on 16 Aug 1983 with a diameter of 52 miles. White House approval was announced on 30 Jan 1987.

Largest Scientific Instrument ■ CERN, the European Laboratory for Particle Physics Research, has announced the completion of its Large Electron-Positron Collider (LEP). It is the result of an eight-year cooperative program by CERN's 14 member states and is housed in a 16.7-mile long underground tunnel, running in a circle under the French-Swiss border near Geneva.

Quietest place ■ The 'dead room,' measuring 35 ft×28 ft in the AT&T Bell Laboratory, Murray Hill, NJ, is the most anechoic room in the world, eliminating 99.98 percent of reflected sound.

Sharpest objects and smallest tubes ■ The sharpest objects yet made are glass micropipette tubes used in intracellular work on living cells. Techniques developed and applied by Professor Kenneth T. Brown and Dale G. Flaming of the Department of Physiology, University of California, San Francisco achieved by 1977 beveled tips with an outer diameter of 0.02 μm and 0.01 μm inner diameter.

The latter is smaller than the smallest known nickel tubing by a factor of 340 and is 6,500 times thinner than human hair.

Highest vacuum ■ Those obtained at the IBM Thomas J. Watson Research Center, Yorktown Heights, NY in October 1976 in a cryogenic system with temperatures down to $-452°$ F in scientific research are of the order of 10^{-14} torr.

MINE RECORDS

EARLIEST *World* ● 41,250 B.C. ± 1,600 Lion Cavern, Haematite (red iron ore) at Ngwenya, Hhohho, Swaziland.

DEEPEST *World*[1] ● 11,749 ft Gold, Western Deep Levels (temp 131°F) at Carletonville, South Africa.

FASTEST DRILLING
The most footage drilled in one month is 34,574 ft of a hole drilled during June 1988 by Harkins & Company Rig Number 13 while drilling four wells in McMullen County, TX.

COPPER *Deepest open pit* ● 2,625 ft Bingham Canyon (begun 1906), Location near Salt Lake City, UT.
Largest underground ● 356 miles tunnels, San Manuel Mine, Magma Copper Co in AZ.

LEAD *Largest* ● >10 percent of world output Viburnum Trend in southeast Missouri.

GOLDMINING *Area* ● >51 percent of world output, 38 mines of the Witwatersrand Discovery, South Africa, in 1886.

GOLD *Largest*[2] ● 12,100 acres East Rand Proprietary Mines Ltd at Boksburg, Transvaal, South Africa.
Richest ● 49·4 million fine oz, Crown Mines (all-time yield) in Transvaal, South Africa.

IRON *Largest* ● 22·4 billion tons rich ore Lebedinsky (45–65% ore), Kursk region, USSR.

PLATINUM *Largest* ● 30·8 tons per annum, Rustenburg Platinum Mines Group, Rustenburg Platinum, Mine Location Western Transvaal, South Africa.

TUNGSTEN *Largest* ● 2,205 tons per day, Union Carbide Mount Morgan mine, near Bishop, CA.

URANIUM *Largest* ● 5,600 tons of uranium oxide, Rio Tinto Zinc open cast pit at Rössing, Namibia.

SPOIL DUMP *Largest* ● 275 million yd[3] New Cornelia Tailings at Ten Mile Wash, AZ.

QUARRY *Largest* ● 2·81 miles[2]. 3,698 million tons extracted. Bingham Canyon, UT.

COAL, OPEN CAST MINE ● 1,103 ft deep 8 mile[2] area Fortuna-Garsdorf (lignite) (begun 1955), near Bergheim, West Germany.

COAL MINE *Oldest, US*[3] ● c. 1750 at James River coalfield near Richmond, VA. This site is now abandoned.

[1] *Sinking began in July 1957. Scheduled to reach 12,370 ft by 1992, with 14,000 ft or 2·65 miles regarded as the limit. No. 3 vertical ventilation shaft is the world's deepest shaft at 9,675 ft. This mine requires 141,150 tons of air per day and refrigeration, which uses the energy it would take to make 41,440 short tons of ice. An underground shift comprises 11,150 men. The deepest exploratory coal–mining shaft is one reaching 6,700 ft near Thorez in the Ukrainian Donbas field, USSR in August 1983.*

[2] *The world's most productive gold mine may be Muruntau, Kyzyl Kum, Uzbekistan, USSR. According to one Western estimate it produces 88 tons of gold in a year. It has been estimated that South Africa has produced in 96 years (1886–1982) 40,768 tons or more than 31 percent of all gold mined since 3900 B.C.*

[3] *The first recorded discovery of coal in the United States was in 1679 by French explorers, who reported a 'coal mine' on the Illinois River.*

WORST US OIL SPILLS

SPILL	LOCATION	BARRELS LOST	DATE
Ranger TX (Drilling Rig)	Gulf of Mexico, off Texas coast	326,000	6 Nov 1985
Exxon Valdez (Tanker)	Prince William Sound, AK	258,000	24 March 1989
Burmah Agate (Tanker)	Gulf of Mexico, 5 miles south of Galveston, TX	255,000	1 Nov 1979
Texaco Oklahoma (Tanker)	Atlantic Ocean, 120 miles northeast of Cape Hatteras, NC	220,000	March 1971

US Coast Guard, 1990

Condeep type, with a steel deck and modules on top of a concrete gravity base. Total dry weight of the £1·3 billion structure is 932·5 tons. Total height is 115·82 ft. The gravity base is built by Norwegian Contractors, Stavanger and the deck by Aker, Stord.

Tallest ■ The world's tallest production platform stands in water 1,760 ft deep about 100 miles off the Louisiana Coast. It is operated by Conoco and co-owned by Conoco, Texas and Occidental Petroleum.

Gusher ■ The greatest wildcat ever recorded blew at Alborz No 5 well, near Qum, Iran on 26 Aug 1956. The uncontrolled oil gushed to a height of 170 ft at 120,000 barrels per day at a pressure of 9,000 lb/in². It was closed after 90 days' work by B. Mostofi and Myron Kinley of Texas.

The Lake View No 1 gusher in California on 15 Mar 1910 may have yielded 125,000 barrels in its first 24 hours.

Oil spills ■ The slick from the Mexican marine blow-out beneath the drilling rig *Ixtoc I* in the Gulf of Campeche, Gulf of Mexico, on 3 Jun 1979 reached 400 miles by 5 Aug 1979. It was eventually capped on 24 Mar 1980 after a loss of 3 million barrels (599,200 tons).

The *Exxon Valdez* in Prince William Sound, AK struck a reef on 24 Mar 1989 spilling 10 million gallons of crude slick spread over 2,600 miles².

The worst oil spill in history was of 260,142·8 tons of oil from two supertankers, *Atlantic Empress* and *Aegean Captain*, when they collided off Tobago on 19 Jul 1979.

Flare ■ The greatest gas fire was that which burned at Gassi Touil in the Algerian Sahara from noon on 13 Nov 1961 to 9:30 A.M. on 28 Apr 1962. The pillar of flame rose 450 ft and the smoke 600 ft. It was eventually extinguished by Paul Neal ('Red') Adair (b. 1932), of Houston, TX using 550 lb of dynamite. His fee was understood to be about $1 million plus expenses.

Water well ■ The world's deepest water bore is the Stensvad Water Well 11-W1 of 7,320 ft drilled by the Great Northern Drilling Co Inc in Rosebud County, MT in October–November

Worst oil spill ● The worst oil spill in history was of 260,142·8 tons of oil from two super-tankers *Atlantic Empress* and *Aegean Captain* when they collided off Tobago on 19 Jul 1979. (Photo: Gamma/Lochon).

US OIL IMPORTS TOP FIVE

Country	Barrels of Oil Per Day
Saudi Arabia	1,224,000
Canada	910,000
Venezuela	867,000
Nigeria	809,000
Mexico	763,000

American Petroleum Institute 1990

1961. The Thermal Power Co geothermal steam well begun in Sonoma County, CA in 1955 is down to 9,029 ft.

Power

Largest power plant ■ Currently, the most powerful installed power station is the Grand Coulee, WA, with 7·4 million kilowatt hours (ultimately 10,830 MW), which began operating in 1942.

The $11-billion Itaipu power station on the Paranā River by the Brazil-Paraguay border began generating power formally on 25 Oct 1984 and will attain 13,320 kW from 18 turbines. Construction began in 1975 with a work force reaching 28,000. A 20,000-MW power station project on the Tunguska River, USSR was announced in February 1982.

The world's largest coal-fired power complex at Ekibastuz, Kazakhstan, USSR began generating in May 1982.

Earliest atomic pile ■ The world's first atomic pile was built in a disused doubles squash court at Stagg Field, University of Chicago, IL. It went 'critical' at 3:25 P.M. on 2 Dec 1942.

Nuclear power station ■ The first nuclear power station producing electricity was the ERR-1 in the United States on 20 Dec 1951.

The world's largest nuclear power station with 10 reactors and an output of 9,096 MW is the station in Fukushima, Japan.

Nuclear reactor ■ The largest single nuclear reactor in the world is the 1,450-MW (net) reactor at the Ignalina station, Lithuania, USSR, put on full power in January 1984.

The largest under construction is the CHOOZ-B1 reactor in France, which is scheduled for operation in 1991 and will have a net capacity of 1,457 MW.

Fusion power ■ Tokamak-7, the experimental thermonuclear apparatus, was declared in January 1982 by USSR academician Velikhov to be operating 'reliably for months on end.' An economically featured thermonuclear reactor is not anticipated in 1990 until 'about 2030.'

The recent temperature attained in the Joint European Torus (JET) at Culham, Oxfordshire, United Kingdom was 180 million° F on 10 Oct 1988.

Largest windmill ● The £12 million 3,000kW aerogenerator LS-1 with a 196 ft 10 in diameter rotor is equivalent to a Jumbo Jet's wingspan. It is situated on Burgar Hill, Orkney, United Kingdom and was built by the Wind Engergy Group (a Taylor Woodrow, British Aerospace and GEC consortium). It will generate about 9 million kWh per year. (Photo: Taylor Woodrow Group)

Most windmills ● Wind Energy Group Ltd commercial windfarm at Altamont, Pasadena, California is the world's largest area of wind energy usage. (Photo: Spectrum)

Solar power plant ■ The largest solar furnace in the world is the $141-million 10 megawatt 'Solar I,' 12 miles southeast of Barstow, CA, first tested in April 1982. It comprises 1,818 mirrors in concentric circles focused on a boiler at the top of a 255-ft high tower. Sunlight from 222 heliostats is concentrated on a target 114 ft up in the power tower.

The $30-million thermal solar energy system at Pakerland Packing Co, Bellevue Plant, Green Bay, WI completed in January 1984 comprises 9,750 4x8 ft collectors covering 7·16 acres. It will yield up to 8 billion BTUs a month.

Tidal power station ■ The world's first major station is the *Usine marémotrice de la Rance*, officially opened on 26 Nov 1966 at the Rance estuary in the Golfe de St-Malo, Brittany, France. It was built in five years at a cost of 420 million francs, and has a net annual output of 544 million kWh. The 2,640 ft barrage contains 24 turbo alternators.

The $1-billion Passamaquoddy project for the Bay of Fundy in Maine, and New Brunswick, Canada, remains a project. The $46 million pilot Annapolis River project for the Bay of Fundy was begun in 1981.

Largest boiler ■ The largest boilers ever designed are those ordered in the United States from Babcock & Wilcox (US), with a capacity of 1,330 MW, involving the evaporation of 9·33 million lb of steam per hour.

Largest generator ■ Generators in the 2 million-kW (or 2,000-MW) range are now in the planning stages both in the United States and the United Kingdom.

The largest operational is a turbogenerator of 1,450 MW (net) being installed at the Ignalina Atomic Power Station in Lithuania .

Largest turbines ■ The largest hydraulic are those rated at 815,000 kW (equivalent to 1·1 million hp), 32 ft in diameter with a 449-ton runner and a 350-ton shaft installed by Allis-Chalmers at the Grand Coulee 'Third Powerplant,' WA.

Pump ■ The world's largest reversible pump-turbine is that made by Allis-Chalmers for the Bath County project, VA. It has a maximum rating of 457 MW as a turbine and maximum operating head of 1,289 ft. The impeller/runner diameter is 20 ft 9 in, with a synchronous speed of 257·1 rpm.

Gas ■ The largest gas turbine is type GT 13 E from BBC Brown Boveri AG, with a maximum output of 140MW. The first machine is being installed in Holland in order to increase the general output of a 500MW steam-powered plant (Hemweg 7) by more than 46 percent.

Battery *Largest* ■ The 10 MW lead-acid battery at Chino, CA has a design capacity of 40 MWh. It will be used at an electrical substation for leveling peak demand loads. This $13 million project is a cooperative effort by Southern California Edison Company, Electric Power Research Institute, and International Lead Zinc Research Organization Inc.

Longest-lasting ■ The zinc foil and sulfur dry-pile batteries made by Watlin and Hill of London in 1840 have powered ceaseless tintinnabulation inside a bell jar at the Clarendon Laboratory, Oxford, United Kingdom, since that year.

Biggest black-out ■ The greatest power failure in history struck seven northeastern states and Ontario, Canada on 9–10 Nov 1965. About 30 million people in 80,000 miles^2 were plunged into darkness. Only two were killed.

In New York City the power failed at 5:27 P.M. and was not fully restored for 13½ hr.

The total consequential losses in the 52-min New York City power failure of 13 Jul 1977, including looting, was put at $1 billion.

Windmill ■ The earliest recorded windmills are those used for grinding corn in Iran in the seventh century A.D.

Tallest ■ De Noord windmill in Schiedam, Netherlands, at 109 ft 4 in, is the tallest in Europe.

Largest ■ The world's first 3,000-kW wind generator was the 492-ft tall turbine, built by Grosse Windenergie-Anlage, which was set up in 1982 on the Friesian coast of West Germany.

The $14·2-million GEC MOD-5A installation on the north shore of Oahu, HI will produce 7,300 kW when the wind reaches 32 mph with 400-ft rotors. Installation was started in March 1984.

Engineering

Oldest machinery ■ The earliest mechanisms still in use are the *dâlu*—a water-raising instrument known to have been in use in the Sumerian civilization, which originated *c.* 3500 B.C. in what is now lower Iraq, and that are thus even earlier than the *saqiyas* on the Nile.

Blast furnace ■ The noncommunist world's largest blast furnace has an inner volume of 185,224 ft^3 and a 49-ft diameter hearth at ZBF at the Oita Works, Kyūshū, Japan, completed in October 1976 with 4·82 million tons annual capacity.

Cat cracker ■ The world's largest catalyst cracker is Exxon's Bayway Refinery plant at Linden, NJ, with a fresh feed rate of 5·04 million gals per day.

Concrete pumping ■ The world-record distance for pumping ready-mixed concrete without a relay pump is 4,986 ft, set on the Lake Chiemsee, Bavaria sewage tunnels project in the summer of 1989.

Conveyor belt ■ The world's longest single-flight conveyor belt is one of 18 miles in Western Australia installed by Cable Belt Ltd of Camberley, Surrey, United Kingdom.

The world's longest multi-flight conveyor is one of 62 miles between the phosphate mine near Bucraa and the port of El Aaiún, Morocco, built by Krupps and completed in 1972. It has 11 flights of between 5·6–6·8 miles and was driven at 10·06 mph but has since been closed down.

Most powerful crane ■ The most powerful cranes are the two aboard the semisubmersible vessel *Micoperi 7000* (623·35 ft in length and 292 ft in breadth) operated by Officine Meccaniche Reggiane designed by American Hurst & Derrick Company, built by Monfalcone, Gorizia, Italy and launched 15 Dec 1986. Each has a capacity of 7,716 tons. In its first six months of operation it achieved a record lift of 6,283 tons.

Gantry crane ■ The 92·3-ft wide Rahco (R. A. Hanson Disc. Ltd) gantry crane at the Grand Coulee Dam Third Powerplant was tested to lift a load of 2,570·5 tons in 1975. It lowered a 1,972-ton generator rotor with an accuracy of 1/32 in.

Tallest mobile crane ■ The 893-ton Rosenkranz K10001, with a lifting capacity of 1,102 tons, and a combined boom and jib height of 663 ft, is carried on 10 trucks each limited to a length of 75 ft 8 in and an axle weight of 130 tons. It can lift 33 tons to a height of 525 ft.

The Taklift 4 craneship of the Smit International fleet based in Rotterdam, Netherlands, has boom jib reaching a height of 312 ft.

Most powerful diesel engines ■ Five 12RTA84 type diesel engines have been constructed by Sulzer Brothers of Winterthur, Switzerland for containerships built for the American President Lines. Each 12-cylinder power unit gives a maximum continuous output of 41,920 kW (57,000 bhp) at 95 rev/min. The first of these ships, the *President Truman*, was handed over in April 1988 and the most recent in September of that year.

Most powerful rocket engine ■ The most powerful rocket engine was built in the USSR by Scientific Industrial Corporation of Energetic Engineering during 1980. The engine has a thrust of 2,645·5 tons in open space and a thrust of 4,409 tons at the Earth surface. The RD-170 has a turbopump of 190 MW and burns liquid oxygen and kerosene.

Dragline ■ The Ural Engineering Works (named after Ordzhonikidze) in Sverdlovsk, USSR, completed in March 1962, has a dragline known as the ES-25(100), with a boom of 328 ft and a bucket with a capacity of 848 ft^3.

The world's largest walking dragline is 'Big Muskie,' the Bucyrus-Erie 4250W with an all-up weight of 13,227 tons and a bucket capacity of 5,933 ft^3 on a 310 ft boom. This is the largest mobile land machine and is now operating on the Central Ohio Coal Company's Muskingum site in Ohio.

Earthmover ■ The giant wheeled loader developed for open-air coal mining in Australia by SMEC, a consortium of 11 manufacturers in Tokyo, Japan is 55·1 ft in length, weighs 198 tons and its rubber tires are 11·5 ft in diameter. The bucket has a capacity of 671 ft^3.

Escalator ■ The term was registered in the United States on 28 May 1900, but the earliest 'Inclined Escalator' was installed by Jesse W. Reno on the pier at Coney Island, NY in 1896.

The escalators on the Leningrad underground, USSR at Lenin Square have 729 steps and a vertical rise of 195 ft 9½ in.

The world's longest *ride* is on the four-section outdoor escalator at Ocean Park, Hong Kong,

which has an overall length of 745 ft and a total vertical rise of 377 ft.

The world's longest 'moving sidewalks' are those installed in 1970 in the Neue Messe Centre, Dusseldorf, West Germany, which measure 738 ft between comb plates.

The ultimate in absurdity to weary shoppers can be found at the Shopping Mall at Kawaski-shi, Japan. It has a vertical height of 32·83 in and was installed by Hitachi Ltd.

Excavator ■ The world's largest excavator is the 14,330 ton bucket wheel excavator being assembled at the open-cast ligmite mine of Hambach, West Germany, with a rating of 2·15 million ft^2 per 20 hr working day. It is 690 ft in length and 269 ft tall. The wheel is 222 ft in circumference with 16 ft buckets.

Forging ■ The largest forging on record is one of a 225-ton, 55-ft long generator shaft for Japan, forged by the Bethlehem Steel Corp of Pennsylvania in October 1973.

Fork lift truck ■ Kalmar LMV of Sweden manufactured in 1985 ten counterbalanced fork-lift trucks capable of lifting loads up to 88 tons at a load center of 90·5 in. They were built to handle the large-diameter pipeline in the Libyan Great Manmade River Project.

Lathe ■ The largest is the 460-ton, 126-ft long giant lathe built by Waldrich Siegen of West Germany in 1973 for the South African Electricity Supply Commission at Rosherville with a capacity for 330-ton workpieces and swing-over beds of 16 ft 5 in in diameter.

Greatest lift ■ The heaviest lifting operation in engineering history was the raising of the entire 0·745-mile long offshore Ekofisk complex in the North Sea, owing to subsidence of the seabed. The complex consists of eight platforms weighing some 44,092 tons. During 17–18 Aug 1987 it was raised 21 ft 4 in by 122 hydraulic jacks requiring a computer-controlled hydraulic system developed and supplied by the Dutch Mannesmann-Texroth company: Hydraudyne Systems & Engineering bv of Boxtel, Netherlands.

Slowest machine ■ A nuclear environmental machine for testing stress corrosion has been developed by Nene Instruments of Wellingborough, United Kingdom that can be controlled at a speed as slow as one million millionth of a millimeter per minute, or 3·28 ft in about 2 billion years.

Oil tank ■ The largest oil tanks ever constructed are the five ARAMCO 1½-million-barrel storage tanks at Ju'aymah, Saudi Arabia. They are 72 ft tall with a diameter of 386 ft and were completed in March 1980.

Passenger lift ■ The fastest domestic passenger lifts in the world are the express lifts to the 60th floor of the 787·4-ft tall 'Sunshine 60' building, Ikebukuro, in Tōkyō, Japan completed 5 Apr 1978. Built by Mitsubishi Corp, they operate at a speed of 2,000 ft/min or 22·72 mph.

Much higher speeds are achieved in the winding cages of mine shafts. A hoisting shaft 6,800 ft deep, owned by Western Deep Levels Ltd in South Africa, winds at speeds of up to 40·9 mph (3,595 ft per min). Otitis-media (popping of the ears) presents problems much above even 10 mph.

Pipelines *Oil* ■ The world's earliest pipeline, of 2-in diameter cast iron, laid at Oil Creek, PA in 1863, was torn up by Luddites.

The longest crude oil pipeline in the world is the

Interprovincial Pipe Line Company's installation from Edmonton, Alberta, Canada to Buffalo, NY, a distance of 1,775 miles. Along the length of the pipe, 13 pumping stations maintain a flow of 8·3 million gals of oil per day.

The eventual length of the Trans-Siberian Pipeline will be 2,319 miles, running from Tuimazy through Omsk and Novosibirsk to Irkutsk. The first 30-mile section was opened in July 1957.

Gas ■ The world's longest submarine pipeline is that of 264 miles for natural gas from the Union Oil Platform to Rayong, Thailand opened on 12 Sep 1981.

The longest natural gas pipeline in the world is the Trans-Canada Pipeline, which by 1974 had 5,654 miles of pipe up to 42 in diameter.

The Tyumen–Chelyabinsk–Moscow–Brandenburg gasline stretches 2,690 miles.

The large-caliber Urengoi-Uzhgorod line to Western Europe, begun in November 1982, stretches 2,765 miles and was completed on 25 Jul 1983. It has a capacity of 1·13 trillion ft³ per year.

Water ■ The world's longest water pipeline runs a distance of 350 miles to the Kalgoorlie gold fields from near Perth in Western Australia. Engineered in 1903, the system has since been extended fivefold by branches.

Most expensive ■ The world's most expensive pipeline is the Alaska Pipeline, running 798 miles from Prudhoe Bay to Valdez. By completion of the first phase in 1977, it had cost at least $6 billion. The pipe is 48 in in diameter and will eventually carry up to 2 million barrels of crude oil per day.

Press ■ The world's two most powerful production machines are forging presses in the United States. The Loewy closed-die forging press, in a plant leased from the US Air Force by the Wyman-Gordon Company at North Grafton, MA weighs 10,438 tons and stands 114 ft 2 in high, of which 66 ft is sunk below the operating floor. It has a rated capacity of 49,163 tons and became operational in October 1955.

Largest excavator ● This 14,330-ton bucket wheel excavator is in use at the open-cast ligmite mine of Hambach, West Germany. It is operated by a crew of five and can move up to 3,884,592·2 cubic feet of coal or earth every day. Because of its vast size it was constructed on the site and took around two years to complete. (Photo: Science Photo Library)

The other similar press is at the plant of the Aluminum Company of America in Cleveland, OH.

In January 1986 ASEA's QUINTUS Dept delivered a sheet metal forming press to BMW AG, Munich, West Germany. This press, which is the largest in the world in terms of forming pressure and press force is a QUINTUS Fluid Cell Press with a press force of 116,844 tons. The Bêché and Grohs counter-blow forging hammer, manufactured in West Germany is rated at 66,138 tons.

Printer ■ The world's fastest printer is the Radiation Inc electro-sensitive system at the Lawrence Radiation Laboratory, Livermore, CA. High-speed recording of up to 30,000 lines, each containing 120 alphanumeric characters, per minute is attained by controlling electronic pulses through chemically-impregnated recording paper which is rapidly moving under closely-spaced fixed styli. It can thus print the wordage of the whole Bible (773,692 words) in 65 seconds; 3,306 times as fast as the world's fastest typist.

Radar installation ■ The largest of the three installations in the US Ballistic Missile Early Warning System (BMEWS) is that near Thule, in Kalaallit Nunaat (Greenland), 931 miles from the North Pole. It was completed in 1960 at a cost of $500 million.

Its sister stations are one at Cape Clear, AK, which was completed in 1961 and the $115 million radar installation at Fylingdales Moor, North Yorkshire, United Kingdom, which was completed in June 1963.

The largest scientific radar installation is the 21-acre ground array at Jicamarca, Peru.

Ropeway or téléphérique ■ The longest ropeway in the world is the Compagnie Minière de l'Ogoouè, or COMILOG, installation built in 1959–62 for the Moanda manganese mine in Gabon, which extends 47·2 miles. It has 858 towers and 2,800 buckets with 96·3 miles of wire rope running over 6,000 idler pulleys.

The highest and longest passenger-carrying aerial ropeway in the world is the Teleférico Mérida (Mérida téléphérique) in Venezuela, from Mérida City (5,379 ft) to the summit of Pico Espejo (15,629 ft), a rise of 10,250 ft. The ropeway is in four sections, involving three car changes in the 8 mile ascent in 1 hr. The fourth span is 10,070 ft in length. The two cars work on the pendulum system—the carrier rope is locked and the cars are hauled by means of three pull ropes powered by a 233 cv motor. They have a maximum capacity of 45 persons and travel at 32 ft per sec (21·8 mph).

The longest single-span ropeway is the 13,500-ft span from the Coachella Valley to Mt San Jacinto (310,821 ft), in California, inaugurated on 12 Sep 1963.

Shovel ■ The Marion 6360 has a reach of 236·75 ft, a dumping height of 153 ft and a bucket capacity of 4,860 ft³. Manufactured in 1964 by the Marion Power Shovel Company, OH, it weighs 24·3 million lb and uses 20 electric motors that generate 45,000 horse power to operate its 220·5-ft long boom arm. It is operated for open-cast coal mining near Percy in Illinois by the Arch Mineral Corporation .

Snow plow blade ■ A blade measuring 32 ft 3 in in length was designed and constructed by Thomas Sedgwick Construction Co. Inc. of Syracuse, NY for use at Hancock International Airport. With a 6-in snowfall the plow can push away 229,506 ft³ of snow in one hour.

Transformer ■ The world's largest single-phase transformers are rated at 1·5 million kVA, of which eight are in service with the American Electric Power Service Corporation. Of these, five step down from 765 to 345 kV.

Transmission lines ■ The longest span between pylons of any power line in the world is that across the Sogne Fjord, Norway, between Rabnaberg and Fatlaberg. Supplied in 1955 by Whitecross of Warrington, Cheshire, United Kingdom, and projected and erected by A. S. Betonmast of Oslo as part of the high-tension power cable from Refsdal power station at Vik, it has a span of 16,040 ft and a weight of 13·3 tons. In 1967 two further high-tensile steel/aluminum lines 16,006 ft long, and weighing 36·4 tons, manufactured by Whitecross and BICC, were erected here.

Highest ■ The world's highest are those across the Straits of Messina, with towers of 675 ft (Sicily side) and 735 ft (Calabria) and 11,900 ft apart.

Highest voltages ■ The highest voltages now carried are 1,330,000 volts for 1,224 miles on the DC Pacific Inter-tie in the United States. The Ekibastuz DC transmission lines in Kazakhstan, USSR are planned to be 1,490 miles long with 1·5 million volt capacity.

Valve ■ The world's largest valve is the 32-ft in diameter, 187-ton butterfly valve designed by Boving & Co Ltd of London for use at the Arnold Air Force Base engine test facility in Tennessee.

Wire ropes ■ The longest wire ropes in the world are the four made at British Ropes Ltd, Wallsend, Tyne and Wear, United Kingdom, each measuring 14·9 miles. The ropes are 1·3 in in diameter, weigh 120 tons each and were ordered by the CEGB for use in the construction of the 2,000-MW cross-Channel power cable.

The thickest ever made are spliced crane strops from wire ropes 11¼ in thick made of 2,392 individual wires in March 1979 by British Ropes Ltd of Doncaster at Willington Quay, also Tyne and Wear, United Kingdom, designed to lift loads of up to 3,307 tons.

The suspension cables on the Seto Grand Bridge, Japan, completed in 1988, are 41 in in diameter.

The heaviest ever wire ropes (four in number) are each of 143 tons, made for the twin shaft system of Western Deep Levels Gold Mine, South Africa, by Haggie Rand Ltd of Johannesburg.

Wind tunnels ■ The world's largest wind tunnel is that on the NASA-Ames Research Center in Mountain View, Palo Alto, CA reopened on 11 Dec 1987 with a 40 × 80 ft tunnel powered by six 22,500 hp motors enabling a best speed of 345 mph.

TIME PIECES

Largest sundial ■ The world's largest sundial is the Samrat Yantra, with gnomon height of 88·5 ft and a vertical height of 118 ft, built in 1724 at Jaipur, India.

Most accurate time measurer ■ The most accurate timekeeping devices are the twin atomic hydrogen masers installed in 1964 in the US Naval Research Laboratory, Washington, DC. They are based on the frequency of the hydrogen atom's transition period of 1,420,450,751,694 cycles/sec. This enables an accuracy to within 1 sec in 1·7 million years.

Clock ■ *Oldest* ■ The earliest mechanical clock, that is, one with an escapement, was completed in China in A.D. 725 by I Xing and Liang Lingzan.

The oldest surviving working clock in the world is the faceless clock dating from 1386, or possibly earlier, at Salisbury Cathedral, Wiltshire, United Kingdom, which was restored in 1956, having struck the hours for 498 years and ticked more than 500 million times. Earlier dates, ranging back to c. 1335, have been attributed to the weight-driven clock in Wells Cathedral, Somerset, United Kingdom, but only the iron frame is original.

A model of Giovanni de Dondi's heptagonal astronomical clock of 1348–64 was completed in 1962.

Largest ■ The world's most massive clock is the Astronomical Clock in the Cathedral of St-Pierre, Beauvais, France, constructed between 1865 and 1868. It contains 90,000 parts and measures 40 ft high, 20 ft wide and 9 ft deep.

The Su Sung Clock, built in China at Kaifeng in 1088–92, had a 23-ton bronze armillary sphere for 1·7 tons of water. It was removed to Beijing in 1126 and was last known to be working in its 40-ft high tower in 1136.

'Timepiece,' which measures 51 ft × 51 ft × 51 ft, is suspended over five stories in the atrium of the International Square building in Washington, DC. Computer-driven and accurate to within 1/100th of a second, it weighs 2·3 tons. It is lit by 400 ft of neon tube lighting and requires 1,500 ft of cable and wiring. Twelve tubes at its base light to tell the hour and the minute. The clock, designed by the sculptor John Safer, also indicates when the sun is at its zenith in twelve international cities.

Clock faces ■ The world's largest is that of the floral clock at 68 ft 10 ¾ in in diameter, manufactured by Seiko for Koryu Fujisho Com-

pany and installed in June 1988 inside the Rose Building in the city of Hokkaido, Japan. The large hand of the clock is 27 ft 10 ½ in long.

The largest four-faced clock in the world is that on the building of the Allen Bradley Company of Milwaukee, WI. Each face has a diameter of 40 ft 3½ in with a minute hand 20 ft in overall length.

The digital, electronic, two-sided clock that revolves on top of the Texas Building in Fort Worth, TX, has dimensions of 44 × 44 × 28 ft.

The largest vertical outdoor clockface is the octagonal Colgate Clock in Jersey, NJ, with a diameter of 50 ft and a minute hand 27 ft 3 in length. In 1989 it was dismantled from the position it has occupied since 1908 at the top of the company's factory, which is being redeveloped. It is planned to relocate it at another site.

The tallest four-faced clock in the world is that of the Williamsburgh Savings Bank in Brooklyn, New York City. It is 430 ft above street level.

Most accurate mechanical ■ The Olsen Clock, completed for Copenhagen Town Hall, Denmark in December 1955 has more than 14,000 units, and took 10 years to make; the mechanism functions in 570,000 different ways. The celestial pole motion will take 25,753 years to complete a full circle and is the slowest-moving designed mechanism in the world. The clock is accurate to 0·5 sec in 300 years—50 times more accurate than the previous record.

Most expensive ■ The highest price paid for any clock is £880,000 for a Thomas Tompion (1639–1713) unrecorded miniature longcase, known as a 'night clock,' at the auction house Christies, London, United Kingdom, on 6 Jul 1989.

Pendulum ■ The longest pendulum in the world is 73 ft 9¾ in, on the water-mill clock installed by Hattori Tokeiten Company in the Shinjuku NS building in Tokyo, Japan in 1983.

Watch ■ *Oldest* ■ The portable clockwork timekeeper is one made of iron by Peter Henlein in Nürnberg (Nüremberg), Bavaria, Germany, c. 1504.

The earliest wristwatches were those of Jacquet-Droz and Leschot of Geneva, Switzerland, dating from 1790.

Largest ■ The largest watch is a 'Swatch,' 531 ft 6 in long and 65 ft 7½ in in diameter, made by D. Thomas Feliu, was set up on the Bank of Bibao building, Madrid, Spain from 7—12 Dec 1985.

The Eta 'watch' on the Swiss pavilion at Expo 86 in Vancouver, British Columbia from May–October weighed 38·5 tons and stood 80 ft high.

Smallest ■ Those produced by Jaeger le Coultre of Switzerland. Equipped with a 15-jeweled movement measure just over ½ in long and ³⁄₁₆ in in width. Movement and case weigh under 0·25 oz.

Thinnest ■ The wristwatches of the Swiss Concord Delirium IV measure 0·0385 in thick and retailed for $16,000 (including 18-carat gold strap) in June 1980.

Astronomical ■ The entirely mechanical Planetarium Copernicus, made by Ulysse Nardin of Switzerland, is the only wristwatch that indicates the time of the day, the date, phases of the Moon, the astronomical position of the Sun, Earth, Moon and the planets known in Copernicus' day. It also represents the Ptolemaic universe showing the astrological 'aspects' at any given time.

A special version of 65 Planetaria is being

produced with the face cut from the meteorite found by Admiral R. E. Peary in Cape York, Greenland in 1897.

Most expensive ■ The record price paid for a watch is £16,004,392 at Habsbury Feldman, Geneva, Switzerland on 9 Apr 1989 for a Patek Philippe Calibre '89 with 1,728 separate parts.

Excluding watches with jeweled cases, the most expensive standard man's pocket watch is *Heaven at Hand*, known to the connoisseurs as *the Packard* and made in 1922 by Patek Philippe for the American automobile magnate James Packard. The timepiece is the most outstanding example of a 'complicated' pocket watch in the world, and was bought back by Patek Philippe in September 1988 for £750,000. To satisfy Packard's eccentric demands, Patek Philippe created a perfect celestial chart in enamel on the watch and housed it in one of the gold casings, to show the heavens as they moved over Packard's hometown of Warren, OH—in fact exactly as he could see them from his bedroom window.

COMPUTERS

Earliest ■ The earliest programmable electronic computer was the 1,500-valve Colossus formulated by Prof Max H. A. Newman (1897–1985) and built by T. H. Flowers. It was run in December 1943 at Bletchley Park, Buckinghamshire, United Kingdom to break the German coding machine Enigma. It arose from a concept published in 1936 by Dr Alan Mathison Turing (1912–54), in his paper *On Computable Numbers with an Application to the Entscheidungsproblem*. Colossus was declassified on 25 Oct 1975.

The world's first stored-program computer was the Mark I, at Manchester University, United Kingdom, which incorporated the Williams storage cathode ray tube (pat. 11 Dec 1946). It ran its first program, by Prof Tom Kilburn (b. 1921), for 52 min on 21 Jun 1948.

The concept of the integrated circuit, which has enabled micro-miniaturization, was first published on 7 May 1952 by Geoffrey W. A. Dummer (b. 1909) in Washington, DC.

The microcomputer was achieved in 1969–73 by M. E. Hoff, Jr of Intel Corporation with the production of the microprocessor chip '4004.'

Most powerful and fastest ■ The world's most powerful and fastest computer is the liquid-cooled CRAY-2, named after Seymour R. Cray of Cray Research, Inc, Minneapolis, MN. Its memory has a capacity of 256 million 64-bit words, resulting in a capacity of 32 million bytes of main memory. (N.B. a 'byte' is a unit of storage comprising 8 'bits,' which are collectively equivalent to one alphabetic symbol or two numericals.) It attains speeds of 250 million floating point operations per second. The cost of a mid-range system was quoted in October 1985 at $17 million.

Sondia National Laboratory, NM on 18 Mar 1988 announced a 'massively parallel' hypercube computer with 1,024 parallel processors, which, by breaking down problems into parts for simultaneous solution, proved 1,019 times faster than a conventional mainframe computer.

In May 1988 NEC (Nippon Electric Co.) announced a £1·6 billion research program to attain a fifth-generation computer able to read handwriting and understand speech in many languages and incorporating superconduction and Josephson functions.

Smallest modem ■ Modems are devices that allow electron signals to be transmitted over large distances, by MOdulating the signal at one end, and DEModulating the signal back to

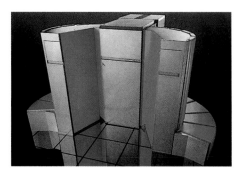

Most accurate and complicated clock ● Above: Designed and built by Jens Olsen the Olsen Clock was set in motion at Copenhagen Town Hall, Denmark on 15 Dec 1955. (Photo: Lars Høj Madsen).

Computer ● The CRAY Y-MP/832 computer system is the top of the line supercomputer of Cray Research Inc, Minneapolis, MN. It contains eight central processors and 32 million 64-bit words of memory. (Photo: Paul Shambroom/Cray Research.)

Largest sundial ● The Jaipur sundial is part of an observatory built in 1724. Its polar-directed gnomon is a stairway 118 ft long, whose shadow on the half-ring shaped equatorial dial moves about a foot in five minutes. This type of dial has the Indian name of Samrat Yantra. (Photo: Spectrum)

its original form at the destination. The smallest is the SRM-3A: length of 2·.4 in; width 1·2 in; height 0·8 in and weighing 1·1 oz. It is currently manufactured by RAD Data Communications Ltd of Tel Aviv, Israel.

Smallest word processor ■ The Easi-Text 1350 was introduced by Minimicro of Huntington, North Yorkshire, United Kingdom in April 1986. It is based on the Sharp PC-1350 computer that measures $7·2 \times 2·8 \times 0·6$ in, and the entire system, including a letter-size Epson P-80 printer, fits into an executive briefcase.

Megabits ■ The megabit barrier was broken in February 1984, with the manufacture of a 1,024K-bit integrated circuit the size of a thumb-tack head and as thin as a human hair, by four Japanese companies, Hitachi, NEC, NTT Atsugi Electrical Communications and Toshiba. Toshiba announced that manufacture of an 80-picosecond LSI (large-scale integration) chip of gallium arsenide had started in 1985–86.

Fastest Transistor ■ A transistor capable of switching 230 billion times per second was announced by Illinois State University on 5 Oct 1986.

TELECOMMUNICATIONS

Telephone ■ There were approximately 423,618,819 telephones in the world on 1 Jan 1989, it was estimated by the American Telephone and Telegraph Co. The country with the greatest number of lines is the United States with 118,400,662.

The territory with fewest reported telephone lines is Pitcairn Island, with 24.

The city with the most telephones is Tokyo, Japan, with 5,511,000. In the United States, New York City had the most telephones, with 4,589,000 as of 1 Jan 1989. In 1983 Washington, DC reached the level of 1,730 telephones per 1,000 people.

The greatest total of calls made in any country is in the United States, with 421,022 million. These calls were broken down into 369,714 million local calls, 51,744 million long distance calls, and 364·07 million international calls. In 1988 there were 1,707,527 payphones in the United States.

Longest telephone cable ■ The world's longest submarine telephone cable is ANZCAN, which runs for 9,415 miles (8,181 nautical miles) from Port Alberni, Canada to Auckland, New Zealand and Sydney, Australia via Fiji and Norfolk Island. It cost some $379 million and was inaugurated by Her Majesty Queen Elizabeth II in November 1984.

Longest terrestrial call ■ A telephone call around the world, over an estimated 98,700 miles, was made on 28 Dec 1985 from, and back to, the Royal Institution, London, United Kingdom, during one of the Christmas lectures given by David Pye, Professor of Zoology, Queen Mary College, London, United Kingdom. The international telecommunications 'rule,' that only one communication satellite be used at a time, was suspended for the demonstration so that both geostationary Intelsats, one over the Indian Ocean and one over the Pacific, could be employed. The two 'telephonists,' Anieka Russell and Alison Risk, experienced a delay in their conversation of 530 milliseconds.

Telephone directories ■ The world's most difficult directory to tear in half would be that for Houston, TX, which runs to 2,889 pages for 939,640 listings. It is now issued in two sections.

The easiest would be that for Knippa, TX — 221 listings on two pages.

The directory for Anguilla in 1972 was of 26 numbers in typescript.

Largest and smallest telephone ■ The smallest operational telephone was created by Jeff Smith of GTE Northwest, Everett, WA in 1988 and measured 4 ⅛ in × ¾ in × 1 ½ in.

The world's largest operational telephone was exhibited at a festival on 16 Sep 1988 to celebrate the 80th birthday of Centraal Beheer, an insurance company based in Apeldoorn, Netherlands. It was 8 ft 1 in high and 19 ft 11 in long, and weighed 3·8 tons. The handset, being 23 ft 5 in long, had to be lifted by crane in order to make a call.

Busiest telephone exchange ■ GPT (GEC Plessey Telecommunications Ltd) demonstrated the ability of the 'System X' telephone exchange to handle 1,558,000 calls in an hour through one exchange at Beeston, Nottingham, United Kingdom on 27 Jun 1989.

Largest switchboard ■ The world's biggest switchboard is that in the Pentagon, Washington, DC, with 25,000 lines handling over 200,000 calls per day through 100,000 miles of telephone cable.

ROCKETRY AND MISSILES

Earliest uses ■ War rockets, propelled by gun-powder charcoal-saltpeter-sulfur, were described by Zeng Kung Liang of China in 1042. This early form of rocket became known in Europe by 1258.

The first launching of a liquid-fueled rocket (patented 14 Jul 1914) was by Dr Robert Hutchings Goddard (1882–1945) of the USA, at Auburn, MA, on 16 Mar 1926, when his rocket reached an altitude of 41 ft and traveled a distance of 184 ft.

The USSR's earliest rocket was the semiliquid fueled GIRD-IX (Gruppa Izucheniya Reaktivnogo Dvizheniya), begun in 1931 and tested on 17 Aug 1933.

Longest ranges ■ On 16 Mar 1962, Nikita Khrushchev, then prime minister of the USSR, claimed in Moscow that the USSR possessed a 'global rocket' with a range of about 19,000 miles, i.e., more than the Earth's semicircumference and therefore capable of hitting any target from either direction.

Highest velocity ■ The first space vehicle to achieve the Third Cosmic velocity sufficient to break out of the Solar System was *Pioneer 10* (see table p.OO). The Atlas SLV-3C launcher with a modified Centaur D second stage and a Thiokol Te-364-4 third stage left the Earth at an unprecedented 32,114 mph on 2 Mar 1972.

Closest approach to the Sun by a rocket ■ The research spacecraft *Helios B* approached within 27 million miles of the Sun, carrying both US and West German instrumentation on 16 Apr 1976.

Remotest man-made object ■ *Pioneer 10*, launched from Cape Canaveral, FL, crossed the mean orbit of Pluto on 17 Oct 1986, then at a distance of 3·670 billion miles. It was beyond the furthest extension of Pluto's April 1989 and will continue into space at 30,450 mph. In A.D. 34,593 it will make its nearest approach to the star *Ross 248*, 10·3 light-years distant. *Voyager 1*, traveling faster, will surpass *Pioneer 10* in remoteness from the Earth.

The spacecraft carries a plaque designed to communicate with any possible interstellar humanoids. This shows a man and a woman and, diagramatically, where the spacecraft comes from in our Solar System and how our Sun relates to the pulsars whose rates are given in digital code.

SPACEFLIGHT

The physical laws controlling the flight of artificial satellites were first propounded by Sir Isaac Newton (1642–1727) in his *Philosophiae Naturalis Principia Mathematica* (*Mathematical Principles of Natural Philosophy*), begun in March 1686 and first published in July 1687.

The first artificial satellite was successfully put into orbit at an altitude of 142/588 miles and a velocity of more than 17,750 mph from Baikonur, north of Tyuratam, 170 miles east of the Aral Sea on the night of 4 Oct 1957. This spherical satellite *Sputnik* ('Fellow Traveller') *1*, officially designated 'Satellite 1957 Alpha 2,' weighed 184·3 lb, with a diameter of 22·8 in, and its lifetime is believed to have been 92 days, ending on 4 Jan 1958. The 96 ft 8 in SL-4 launcher was designed under the direction of former Gulag prisoner Dr Sergey Pavlovich Korolyov (1907-66).

Earliest manned satellite ■ The earliest manned space flight ratified by the world governing body, the Fédération Aéronautique Internationale (FAI, founded 1905), was by Cosmonaut Flight Major (later Colonel) Yuri Alekseievich Gagarin (1934–68) in *Vostok 1* on 12 Apr 1961.

Details filed showed takeoff to be from the Baikonur Cosmodrome at 6:07 A.M. GMT and the landing near Smelovka, near Engels, in the Saratov region, USSR, 108 minutes later.

The maximum altitude during *Vostok I*'s 25,394·5 miles flight was listed at 203·2 miles, with a maximum speed of 17,560 mph.

Colonel Gagarin, invested a Hero of the Soviet Union and awarded the Order of Lenin and the Gold Star Medal, was killed in a jet plane crash near Moscow on 27 Mar 1968.

United States ■ On 5 May 1961, aboard *Mercury 3*, Alan B. Shepard, Jr. became the first American to man a space flight. The sub-orbital flight, which lasted 15½ minutes, covered 302 miles and reached an altitude of 116·5 miles.

John H. Glenn was the first American to orbit the earth. His flight aboard *Mercury 6*, (*Friendship 7*), was launched at 9:47 A.M. EST on 20 Feb 1962 and splashed down into the Atlantic Ocean at 2:43 P.M. EST that same day. Glenn completed 3 orbits of the earth and traveled approximately 81,000 miles.

First woman in space ■ The first woman to orbit the Earth was Junior Lieutenant (now Lt-Col Eng) Valentina Vladimirovna Tereshkova (b. 6 Mar 1937), who was launched in *Vostok 6* from Tyuratam, USSR, at 9:30 A.M. GMT on 16 Jun 1963, and landed at 8:16 A.M. on 19 Jun, after a flight of two days 22 hr 50 min, during which she completed over 48 orbits (1·23 million miles) and passed momentarily within 3 miles of *Vostok 5*.

United States ■ The first American woman in space was Sally Ride, who was launched in *US Space Shuttle Challenger STS-7* on 18 Jun 1983, and returned to earth 24 June.

Space fatalities ■ The greatest published number to perish in any of the 134 attempted spaceflights to 30 Apr 1990 is seven (five men and two women) aboard the *Challenger* 5IL on 28 Jan

Remotest spacecraft ● A member of the Voyager Mission imaging team processing data from the Voyager 2 spacecraft to produce a full-color image of the planet Neptune at NASA's Jet Propulsion Laboratory (JPL) in Pasadena, CA. (Science Photo Library)

1986 when an explosion occurred 73 sec after lift off at a height of 47,000 ft.

First 'walk' in space ■ Lt-Col (now Maj-Gen) Aleksey Arkhipovich Leonov (b. 20 May 1934) from *Voskhod 2* was the first person to engage in 'extravehicular activity' on 18 Mar 1965. Capt Bruce McCandless II (b. 8 Jun 1937) USN, from the space shuttle *Challenger*, was the first to engage in untethered EVA, at an altitude of 164 miles above Hawaii, on 7 Feb 1984. His MMU (Manned Manoeuvering Unit) back-pack cost $15 million to develop.

United States ■ The first American to 'walk' in space was Edward H. White II (1930–67) from the spacecraft *Gemini 4* on 3 Jun 1965. Between 3–7 June, White and James McDivitt completed 62 circuits in orbit around the earth, and it was during the third orbit that White left the capsule and, using a 25-ft lifeline, maneuvered for 20 minutes in space.

The first American woman to 'walk' in space was Kathryn D. Sullivan, on 11 Oct 1984 as part of the Space Shuttle *Challenger* mission 5–13 Oct 1984.

Astronaut ■ *Oldest* ■ The oldest astronaut of the 228 people in space was Karl Gordon Henize (US), age 58 while on the 19th Space Shuttle mission aboard the *Challenger* on 29 Jul 1985.

■ The youngest has been Major (later Lt-Gen) Gherman Stepanovich Titov (b. 11 Sep 1935), who was 25 years 329 days when launched in *Vostok 2* on 6 Aug 1961.

The youngest American astronaut was Sally Ride (b. 26 May 1951), who, on 18 Jun 1983, at the age of 32 years 169 days, was launched in the space shuttle *Challenger*.

Longest manned space flight ■ Col Vladimir Georgeyevich Titov (b. 1 Jan 1951) and flight engineer Musa Khiramanovich Manarov (b. 22 Mar 1951) launched to the Mir space station aboard *Soyuz* TM4 on 21 Dec 1987, landed, in *Soyuz* TM6 (with French spationaut Jean-Loup Chrétien), at a secondary recovery

PROGRESSIVE ROCKET ALTITUDE RECORDS

HEIGHT (MILES)	ROCKET	PLACE	LAUNCH DATE
0·71	A 3 in rocket	Hackney, London, United Kingdom	Apr 1750
1·24	Reinhold Tiling[1] (Germany) solid fuel rocket	Osnabruck, Germany	Apr 1931
3·1	GIRD-X semi-liquid fuel (USSR)	Moscow, USSR	25 Nov 1933
8·1	USSR 'Stratosphere' rocket	USSR	1935
52·46	A.4 rocket (Germany)[2]	Peenemünde, Germany	3 Oct 1942
c. 85	A.4 rocket (Germany)[2]	Heidelager, Poland	early 1944
118	A.4 rocket (Germany)[2]	Heidelager, Poland	mid 1944
244	V-2/W.A.C. Corporal (2-stage) Bumper No. 5 (US)	White Sands, NM	24 Feb 1949
318	Geophysical rocket V-5-V (USSR)	Tyuratam, USSR	1950–52
682	Jupiter C (US)	Cape Canaveral, FL	20 Sep 1956
>800	ICBM test flight R-7 (USSR)	Tyuratam, USSR	Aug 1957
>2,700	Farside No. 5 (4-stage) (US)	Eniwetok Atoll	20 Oct 1957
70,700	Pioneer 1-B Lunar Probe (US)	Cape Canaveral, FL	11 Oct 1958
215,300,000*	Luna 1 or Mechta (USSR)	Tyuratam, USSR	2 Jan 1959
242,000,000*	Mars 1 (USSR)	USSR	1 Nov 1962
3,666,000,000[3]	Pioneer 10 (US) (see page 85)	Kennedy Space Center, Cape Canaveral, FL	2 Mar 1972

*Apogee in solar orbit.
[1] There is some evidence that Tiling may shortly after have reached 5·90 miles with a solid fuel rocket at Wangerooge, East Friesian Islands, West Germany.
[2] The A4 was latterly referred to as the V2 rocket, a code for second revenge weapon (vergeltungswaffe) following upon the V1 'flying bomb.'
[3] Distance on crossing Pluto's orbit on 17 Oct 1986. It is much deeper into space and will be surpassed by Voyager 1.

site near Dzhezkazgan, Kazakhstan, USSR, on 21 Dec 1988, after a spaceflight lasting 365 days 22 hr 39 min 47 sec.

The most experienced space traveler is Col Yuri Romanenko (b. 1944) who has clocked up 430 days 18 hr 20 min on three spaceflights, in 1977–78, 1980 and 1987.

United States ■ Gerald P. Carr, Edward G. Gibson and Willia R. Pogue manned the longest American flight aboard *Skylab SL–4*, which was launched 16 Nov 1974 and splashed down 8 Feb 1975, after 2,017 hrs 15 min 32 sec in space.

Most journeys ■ Capt John Watts Young (b. 24 Sep 1930) (USN ret) completed his sixth space flight on 8 Dec 1983 when he relinquished command of *Columbia* STS 9/Spacelab after a space career of 34 days 19 hr 42 min 13 sec.

Largest crew ■ The most crew on a single space mission is eight. This included one female and was launched on Space Shuttle STS 61A, *Challenger 9*, the 22nd shuttle mission, on 30 Oct 1985, carrying the West German Spacelab D1 laboratory. The mission, commanded by Hank Warren Hartsfield, lasted 7 days 44 min 51 sec.

Most in space ■ The greatest number of people in space at any one time is 11: five Americans aboard a Shuttle and five Russians and an Indian aboard *Salyut 7* in April 1984; the eight STS 61A astronauts above and three Russians aboard *Salyut 7* in October 1985; and the five STS 27 astronauts and five Soviet cosmonauts and one Frenchman aboard *Mir* in December 1988.

Lunar conquest ■ Neil Alden Armstrong (b. 5 Aug 1930), command pilot of the *Apollo 11* mission, became the first man to set foot on the Moon, on the Sea of Tranquility, at 02:56 and 15 sec GMT on 21 Jul 1969. He was followed out of the Lunar Module *Eagle* by Col Edwin Eugene Aldrin, Jr, USAF (b. 20 Jan 1930), while the Command Module *Columbia* piloted by Lt Col Michael Collins, USAF (b. 31 Oct 1930) orbited above.

Eagle landed at 20:17 and 42 sec GMT on 20 Jul and lifted off at 17:54 GMT on 21 Jul, after a stay of 21 hr 36 min. *Apollo 11* had blasted off from Cape Canaveral, FL at 13:32 GMT on 16 Jul and was a culmination of the US space program,

which, at its peak, employed 376,600 people and attained in 1966–67 a record budget of $5·9 trillion.

There is evidence that Pavel Ivanovich Belyayev was the cosmonaut selected by the USSR for a manned circumlunar flight in *Zond 7* on 9 Dec 1968, 12 days before the *Apollo 8* flight, but no launch took place.

Most powerful rocket ■ The USSR's *Energia,* first launched on 15 May 1987 from the Baikonur Cosmodrome, when fully loaded weighs 2,646 tons and has a thrust of over 4,410 tons. It is capable of placing 154 tons into low Earth orbit and measures 193·56 ft tall with a maximum diameter of 52·5 ft. It comprises a core stage powered by four liquid oxygen and liquid hydrogen engines – the first cryogenic units flown by the Russians. There are also four strap-on boosters powered by single RD 170 engines burning liquid oxygen and kerosene. A six-strap version with an upper stage could place up to 198 tons into low Earth orbit, take 35 tons to the Moon or 30 tons to Venus or Mars.

Altitude ■ The greatest altitude attained by man was when the crew of the ill-fated *Apollo 13* were at apocynthion (i.e., their furthest point) 158 miles above the lunar surface and 248,655 miles above the Earth's surface at 1:21 A.M. GST on 15 Apr 1970. The crew were Capt James Arthur Lovell, Jr, USN (b. 25 Mar 1928) Fred Wallace Haise, Jr (b. 14 Nov 1933) and John L. Swigert (1931–82).

The greatest altitude attained by a woman is 381 miles by Astronaut Kathryn D. Sullivan during her flight in Space Shuttle *Discovery* on 24 Apr 1990.

Speed ■ The fastest speed at which humans have traveled is 24,791 mph when the Command Module of *Apollo 10* carrying Col (now Brig Gen) Thomas Patten Stafford, USAF (b. 17 Sep 1930), and Cdr Eugene Andrew Cernan (b. 14 Mar 1934) and Cdr (now Capt) John Watts Young, USN (b. 24 Sep 1930) reached this maximum value at the 400,000 ft altitude interface on its trans-Earth return flight on 26 May 1969.

The highest speed ever attained by a woman is 17,470 mph by Jnr Lt (now Lt Col) Valentina Vladimirovna Tereshkova (b. 6 Mar 1937) of the USSR in *Vostok 6* on 16 June 1963.

Duration record on the Moon ■ The crew of *Apollo 17* collected a record 253 lb of rock and soil during their longest 'extravehicular activity' of 22 hr 5 min. They were Capt Eugene A. Cernan, USN (b. 14 Mar 1934) and Dr Harrison H. (Jack) Schmitt (b. 3 Jul 1935), who became the 12th man on the Moon. The crew were on the lunar surface for 74 hr 59 min during this longest of lunar missions, which took 12 days 13 hr 51 min on 7–19 Dec 1972.

First extraterrestrial vehicle ■ The first wheeled vehicle landed on the Moon was *Lunakhod I*, which began its Earth-controlled travels on 17 Nov 1970. It moved a total of 6·54 miles on gradients up to 30° in the Mare Imbrium and did not become nonfunctioning until 4 Oct 1971.

The lunar speed and distance record was set by the *Apollo 16* Rover, with 11·2 mph downhill and 22·4 miles.

Heaviest and largest space object ■ The heaviest object orbited is the Saturn V third stage with *Apollo 15* (spacecraft), which, prior to translunar injection in parking orbit, weighed 309,690 lb.

The 442-lb US RAE (Radio Astronomy Explorer) B or *Explorer 49* launched on 10 Jun 1973 had, however, antennae 1,500 ft from tip to tip.

Most expensive project ■ The total cost of the US manned space program up to and including the lunar mission of *Apollo 17* has been estimated to be $25,541,400,000. The first 15 years of the USSR space program from 1958 to September 1973 have been estimated to have cost $45 billion. The cost of the NASA Shuttle program was $9·9 billion to the launch of *Columbia* on 12 Apr 1981.

First Reusable Spacecraft ■ The US space shuttle *Colombia STS–1*, the world's first reusable spacecraft, lifted off from its launch pad at Cape Canaveral, FL, on 12 Apr 1981 at 7 A.M. EST. After 36 orbits and 54 hours in space, the craft glided to a perfect landing on a dry lake bed at Edwards Air Force Base in the Mojave Desert, CA on 14 Apr at 1:21 P.M. EST. The craft was manned by John W. Young and Robert L. Crippen.

BUILDINGS & STRUCTURES

Offices

Housing

Buildings for Entertainment

Towers & Masts

Bridges

Canals

Dams

Tunnels

Specialized Structures

Tallest monument ● The stainless steel Gateway to the West arch in St. Louis, MO, rises to a height and span of 630 ft. It was designed by Eero Saarinen and was completed on 28 Oct 1965. (Photo: Spectrum)

EARLIEST STRUCTURES

World ■ The earliest known human structure is a rough circle of loosely piled lava blocks found on the lowest cultural level at the Lower Paleolithic site at Olduvai Gorge in Tanzania, revealed by Dr Mary Leakey in January 1960. The structure was associated with artifacts and bones on a work-floor, dating from *c.* 1,750,000 B.C.

The earliest evidence of *buildings* yet discovered is that of 21 huts with hearths or pebble-lined pits and delimited by stake-holes found in October 1965 at the Terra Amata site in Nice, France, thought to belong to the Acheulian culture of *c.* 400,000 years ago. Excavation carried out between 28 Jun and 5 Jul 1966 revealed one hut with palisaded walls with axes of 49 ft and 20 ft. The remains of a 20-ft high stone tower originally built into the walls of Jericho have been excavated and are dated to 5000 B.C. The foundations of the walls themselves have been dated to as early as 8350 B.C.

The oldest free-standing structures in the world are now believed to be the megalithic temples at Mgarr and Skorba in Malta. With those at Ggantija in Gozo, they date from *c.* 3250 B.C.

Buildings for Working

LARGEST

Construction project ■ The Madinat Al-Jubail Al-Sinaiyah project in Saudi Arabia is believed to be the largest public works project in modern times. Construction started in 1976 for the new industrial city covering 250,705 acres. At the peak of construction, nearly 52,000 workers were employed, representing 62 nation-alities. The total earth-moving and dredging volume by 1988 had reached 953·5 billion ft³, enough to construct a belt around the Earth at the equator 23 ft wide x 3·3 ft high.

The seawater cooling system is believed to be the world's largest canal system, bringing 353 million ft³ of seawater per day to cool the industrial establishment.

Industrial ■ The largest industrial plant in the world is the Nizhniy Tagil Railroad Car and Tank Plant, 85 miles northwest of Sverdlovsk, USSR, which has 204·3 acres of floor space. It has an annual capacity to produce 2,500 T-72 tanks.

Commercial ■ The greatest ground area covered by any commercial building in the world under one roof is the flower auction building of the Co-operative VBA (Verenigde Bloemenveilingen Aalsmeer, Aalsmeer), the Netherlands, built with dimensions of 2,546 × 2,070 ft. The floor surface of 84·82 acres was extended in 1986 to 91·05 acres.

The building with the largest cubic capacity in the world is the Boeing Company's main assembly plant at Everett, WA, completed in 1968 with a capacity of 200 million ft³.

Scientific ■ The most capacious is the Vehicle Assembly Building (VAB) at Complex 39, the selected site for the final assembly and launching of the Apollo Moon spacecraft on the Saturn V rocket, at the John F. Kennedy Space Center (KSC) on Merritt Island, Cape Canaveral, FL. Construction began in April 1963 by the Ursum Consortium. It is a steel-framed building measuring 716 ft in length, 518 ft in width and 525 ft high. The building contains four bays, each with its own door 460 ft high. Its floor area is 343,500 ft² and its capacity is 129·5 million ft³. The building was 'topped out' on 14 Apr 1965 at a cost of $108,700,000.

Administrative ■ The largest ground area covered by any office building is that of the Pentagon, in Arlington, VA. Built to house the US Defense Department's offices it was completed on 15 Jan 1943 and cost an estimated $83 million. Each of the outermost sides is 921 ft long and the perimeter of the building is about 4,500 ft. Its five stories enclose a floor area of 6·5 million ft². The corridors measure 17 miles in length and there are 7,748 windows to be cleaned. Twenty-nine thousand people work in the building, which has over 44,000 telephones connected by 160,000 miles of cable. Two hundred and twenty staff handle 280,000 calls a day. Two restaurants, six cafeterias, ten snack bars and a staff of 675 form the catering department.

Office ■ Those with the largest rentable space are the World Trade Center in New York City with a total of 4·37 million ft² in each of the twin towers of which the taller Tower Two (formerly B) is 1,362 ft 3¼ in. The tip of the TV antenna on Tower One is 1,710 ft above street level and is thus 151 ft taller than the antennae on top of the Sears Tower (see p. 89).

TALLEST

The tallest office building in the world is the Sears Tower, national headquarters of Sears, Roebuck & Co in Wacker Drive, Chicago, IL with 110 stories rising to 1,454 ft and begun in August 1970. Its gross area is 4·4 million ft². It was 'topped out' on 4 May 1973, having surpassed the World Trade Center in New York City in height at 2:35 P.M. on 6 Mar 1973 with the first steel column reaching to the 104th story. The addition of two TV antennae brought the total

THE WORLD'S TALLEST STRUCTURES—PROGRESSIVE RECORDS

HEIGHT ft	STRUCTURE	LOCATION	MATERIAL	BUILDING OR COMPLETION DATES
204	Djoser Step Pyramid (earliest Pyramid)	Saqqâra, Egypt	Tura limestone casing	*c.* 2650 B.C.
300·8	Pyramid of Meidum	Meidum, Egypt	Tura limestone casing	*c.* 2600 B.C.
331·6	Snefru Bent pyramid	Dahshûr, Egypt	Tura limestone casing	*c.* 2600 B.C.
342	Snefru North Stone pyramid	Dahshûr, Egypt	Tura limestone casing	*c.* 2600 B.C.
480·9[1]	Great Pyramid of Cheops (Khufu)	El Gizeh, Egypt	Tura limestone casing	*c.* 2580 B.C.
525[2]	Lincoln Cathedral, Central Tower	Lincoln, England	lead sheathed wood	*c.* 1307–1548
489[3]	St Paul's Cathedral spire	City of London, England	lead sheathed wood	1315–1561
465	Minster of Notre Dame	Strasbourg, France	Vosges sandstone	1420–1439
502[4]	St Pierre de Beauvais spire	Beauvais, France	lead sheathed wood	–1568
475	St Nicholas Church	Hamburg, Germany	stone and iron	1846–1847
485	Rouen Cathedral spire	Rouen, France	cast iron	1823–1876
513	Köln Cathedral spires	Cologne, W. Germany	stone	–1880
555[5]	Washington Monument	Washington, D.C.	stone	1848–1884
985·9[6]	Eiffel Tower	Paris, France	iron	1887–1889
1,046	Chrysler Building	New York City	steel and concrete	1929–1930
1,250[7]	Empire State Building	New York City	steel and concrete	1929–1930
1,572	KWTV Television Mast	Oklahoma City	steel	Nov 1954
1,610[8]	KSWS Television Mast	Roswell, NM	steel	Dec 1956
1,619	WGAN Television Mast	Portland, ME	steel	Sept 1959
1,676	KFVS Television Mast	Cape Girardeau, MO	steel	Jun 1960
1,749	WTVM & WRBL Television Mast	Columbus, GA	steel	May 1962
1,749	WBIR-TV Mast	Knoxville, TN	steel	Sept 1963
2,063	KTHI-TV Mast	Fargo, ND	steel	Nov 1963
2,120·6	Warszawa Radio Mast	Plock, Poland	galvanised steel	22 July 1974

[1] *Original height. With loss of pyramidion (topmost stone) height now 449 ft 6 in.*
[2] *Fell in a storm.*
[3] *Struck by lightning and destroyed 4 June 1561.*
[4] *Fell April 1573, shortly after completion.*
[5] *Sinking at a rate of 0·0047 ft a year or 5 in since 1884.*
[6] *Original height. With addition of TV antenna in 1957, now 1,052 ft.*
[7] *Original height. With addition of TV tower on 1 May 1951, now 1,472 ft. Exterior is clad in limestone from the Empire Quarry, Indiana.*
[8] *Fell in gale in 1960.*

height to 1,707 ft. The building's population is 16,700, served by 103 elevators and 18 escalators. It has 16,000 windows.

SHALLOWEST

The shallowest commercial building is the 6-ft wide, 100-ft long Sam Kee Building at 8 West Pender, Vancouver, Canada. It was erected in 1912.

HABITATIONS

Greatest altitude ■ The highest inhabited buildings in the world are those in the Indo–Tibetan border fort of Bāsisi by the Māna Pass (Lat. 31° 0 4′ N, Long. 79° 24′ E) at *c.* 19,700 ft.

In April 1961, however, a three-room dwelling was discovered at 21,650 ft on Cerro Llullaillaco (22,057 ft), on the Argentine–Chilean border, believed to date from the late pre-Columbian period *c.* 1480. A settlement on the T'e-li-mo trail in southern Tibet is sited at an apparent altitude of 19,800 ft.

Northernmost ■ The Danish Scientific station set up in 1952 in Pearyland, northern Kalaallit Nunaat (Greenland), is over 900 miles north of the Arctic Circle. Inuit hearths dated to before 1000 B.C. were discovered in Pearyland in 1969. Polar Inuits were discovered in Inglefield Land, NW Greenland in 1818.

The USSR's drifting research station 'North Pole 15' passed within 1¼ miles of the North Pole in December 1967.

The most northerly continuously inhabited place is the Canadian Department of National Defense outpost at Alert on Ellesmere Island, Northwest Territories in Lat. 82° 30′ N, Long. 62° W, set up in 1950.

Southernmost ■ The most southerly permanent human habitation is the United States' Amundsen–Scott South Polar Station (see Chapter 9), completed in 1957 and replaced in 1975.

EMBASSIES AND CIVIC BUILDINGS

Largest ■ The USSR embassy on Bei Xiao Jie, Beijing, China, in the northeastern corner of the northern walled city, occupies the whole 45-acre area of the old Orthodox Church Mission (established 1728), now known as the *Beiguan.* It was handed over to the USSR in 1949.

United States ■ The largest American embassy is in Bonn, West Germany. It is 285,416 ft² in size.

EXHIBITION CENTRES

Largest ■ The International Exposition Center in Cleveland, OH, the world's largest, is situated on a 175 acre site adjacent to Cleveland Hopkins International Airport in a building that measures 2·5 million ft². An indoor terminal provides direct rail access and parking for 10,000 cars.

INDUSTRIAL STRUCTURES

Tallest chimneys ■ The $5·5 million Inter-

Tallest office building ● Dominating the New York skyline are the two gleaming towers of the World Trade Center. Cleaning the 43,600 windows is not such a grueling task as imagined as there are fewer pollutants in the air at the top and rain washes dirt from the upper windows and deposits it on the lower ones. (Photo: ZEFA)

national Nickel Company's stack is 1,245 ft 8 in tall at Copper Cliff, Sudbury, Ontario, Canada, completed in 1970. It was built by Canadian Kellogg Ltd in 60 days and the diameter tapers from 116·4 ft at the base to 51·8 ft at the top. It weighs 42,996 tons and became operational in 1971.

The world's most massive chimney is one of 1,148 ft at Puentes de Garcia Rodriguez, northwest Spain, built by M. W. Kellog Co. It contains 549,840 ft³ of concrete and 2·9 million lb of steel and has an internal volume of 6·7 million ft³.

Cooling towers ■ The largest is that adjacent to the nuclear power plant at Uentrop, West Germany, which is 590 ft tall, completed in 1976.

HANGARS

Largest ■ Hangar 375 ('Big Texas') at Kelly Air Force Base, San Antonio, TX, completed on 15 Feb 1956, has four doors, each 250 ft wide, 60 ft high and weighing 670 tons. The high bay area measures 2,000 × 300 × 90 ft and is surrounded by a 44-acre concrete apron.

Delta Airlines' jet base on a 140-acre site at Hartsfield International Airport, Atlanta, GA has 36 acres under roof.

GRAIN ELEVATOR

Largest ■ The single-unit elevator operated by the C-G-F Grain Company at Wichita, KS, consists of a triple row of storage tanks, 123 on each side of the central loading tower or 'head house.' The unit is 2,717 ft long and 100 ft wide. Each tank is 120 ft high, with an inside diameter of 30 ft giving a total storage capacity of 20 million bushels of wheat.

The largest collection of elevators in the world are the 23 in Thunder Bay, Ontario, Canada, on Lake Superior, with a total capacity of 103·9 million bushels.

SEWAGE WORKS

Largest ■ The West-Southwest Treatment Plant, opened in 1940 on a site of 501 acres in Chicago, IL, serves an area containing 2,940,000 people. The plant treated an average of 835 million gal of waste per day in 1973 and the capacity of its sedimentation and aeration tanks is 45·2 trillion ft³.

WOODEN BUILDING

Largest ■ The two US Navy airship hangars built in 1942–43 at Tillamook, OR are now used by the Louisiana-Pacific Corporation as a sawmill. They measure 1,000 ft long, 170 ft high at the crown and 296 ft wide at the base.

AIR-SUPPORTED BUILDING

Largest ■ That of the 80,600 capacity octagonal Pontiac Silverdome Stadium, MI was 522 ft wide and 722 ft long. The air pressure was 5 lb/in² supporting the 10-acre translucent 'Fiberglas' roofing. The structural engineers were Geiger-Berger Associates of New York City.

The largest standard size air hall was one 860 ft long, 140 ft wide and 65 ft high. One was first sited at Lima, OH, made by Irvin Industries of Stamford, CT.

Buildings for Living

WOODEN BUILDINGS

Oldest ■ The oldest extant wooden buildings in the world are those comprising the Pagoda, Chumanar gate and the Temple of Horyu (Horyu-ji), at Nara, Japan, dating from c. A.D. 670 and completed in 715. The wood used were beams from 1,000-year-old Hinoki trees. The nearby Daibutsuden, built in 1704–11, once measured 285·4 ft long, 167·3 ft wide and 153·3 ft tall. Presently the dimensions are 188 × 165·3 × 159·4 ft.

CASTLES

Earliest ■ The castle at Gomdan, in the Yemen, originally had 20 stories and dates from before A.D. 100.

Largest ■ The largest inhabited castle in the world is the royal residence of Windsor Castle at New Windsor, Berkshire, United Kingdom. It is primarily of twelfth century construction and is in the form of a waisted parallelogram 1,890 x 540 ft.

Forts ■ The largest ancient castle in the world is Hradčany Castle, Prague, Czechoslovakia, originating in the ninth century. It is an oblong irregular polygon with an axis of 1,870 ft and an average traverse diameter of 420 ft with a surface area of 18 acres.

Thickest walls ■ Urnammu's city walls at Ur (now Muqayyar, Iraq), destroyed by the Elamites in 2006 B.C., were 88½ ft thick in mud brick.

PALACES

Largest ■ The Imperial Palace (Gu gong) in the center of Beijing, the 'northern capital,' China, covers a rectangle 3,150 x 2,460 ft, an area of 177·9 acres. The outline survives from the construction of the third Ming emperor, Yung Lo of 1402–24, but due to constant rearrangements

most of the intramural buildings are 18th-century. These consist of five halls and 17 palaces, of which the last occupied by the last empress until 1924 was the Palace of Accumulated Elegance (Chu xia gong).

The Palace of Versailles, 14 miles southwest of Paris, has a facade with 375 windows, 1,902 ft in length. The building, completed in 1682 for Louis XIV, occupied over 30,000 workmen under Jules Hardouin-Mansert (1646–1708).

Residential ■ The palace (Istana Nurul Iman) of H.M. the Sultan of Brunei in the capital Bandar Seri Begawan and completed in January 1984 at a reported cost of £300 million is the largest in the world, with 1,788 rooms and 257 lavatories. The underground garage accommodates the sultan's 110 cars.

Largest moat ■ From plans drawn by French sources it appears that those which surround the Imperial Palace in Beijing (see above) measure 162 ft wide and have a total length of 10,800 ft. In all, the city's moats total 23½ miles.

HOTELS

Largest ■ The Excalibur Hotel/Casino, NV built on a 117-acre site, was opened in April 1990. Comprising 4,032 deluxe rooms and employing 4,000 staff, the facilities include seven themed restaurants and a total of eleven food outlets throughout the hotel/casino.

The Hotel Rossiya in Moscow opened in 1967 with 3,200 rooms, but owing to its proportion of dormitory accommodation, it is not now internationally listed among the largest hotels.

The Izmailovo Hotel complex opened in July 1980 for the XXIInd Olympic Games in Moscow was designed to accommodate 9,500 people.

The Las Vegas Hilton, NV, built on a 63-acre site in 1974–81, has 3,174 rooms, 13 international restaurants and a staff of 3,600. It has a 10-acre rooftop recreation deck, a 48,000 ft² pillar-free ballroom and 125,000 ft² of convention space.

Largest lobby ■ The lobby at the Hyatt Regency, San Francisco, is 350 ft long, 160 ft wide, and at 170 ft is the height of a 17-story building.

Tallest ■ Measured from street level of its main entrance to the top, the 741·9 ft tall 73-story Westin Stamford in Raffles City, Singapore was topped out in March 1985. The $235 million hotel is operated by Westin Hotel Company and owned by Raffles City Pte Ltd. However, their Detroit Plaza, measuring from the rear entrance level, is 748 ft tall.

Smallest ■ Punta Grande Hotel, Las Puntas, Hierro Island, Tenerife in the Canaries has a total area of 6,459 ft². There are four double bedrooms looking onto a small terrace, a lounge, a bar–restaurant and a solarium. Rebuilt in 1987, the building is more than 150 years old.

Most expensive ■ The roof-top Royal Suite in the Marbella–Dinamar, Puerto Banus, Marbella, Spain costs 500,000 pesetas per day excluding tax. It has two halls, two dining rooms, five double bedrooms, seven bathrooms, a kitchen, a service area, a study/library/office, a lounge, a 26·24-ft heated swimming pool with a massage system, two solariums, a sauna and an 18-hole putting green.

In May 1989 the Hotel Bel-Air in Los Angeles was sold for a record $1·2 million per room to the Sekitei Kaihatsu Company of Tokyo, Japan.

HIGHEST STRUCTURES IN THE UNITED STATES

Feet	Stories	Tower	Year
1,454	110	Sears Tower, Chicago, IL	1974
1,368	110	World Trade Center (North), New York, NY	1972
1,362	110	World Trade Center (South), New York, NY	1973
1,250	102	Empire State Building, New York, NY	1931
1,136	80	Amoco Building, Chicago, IL	1973
1,127	100	John Hancock Center, Chicago, IL	1968
1,046	77	Chrysler Building, New York, NY	1930
1,012	75	Library Square Tower, Los Angeles, CA	UC89
1,000	79	Texas Commerce Plaza, Houston, TX	1982
970	71	Allied Bank Plaza, Houston, TX	1983

Council of Tall Buildings and Urban Habitat
Lehigh University, Bethlehem, PA

Most mobile ■ The three-story brick Hotel Fairmount (built 1906) in San Antonio, TX, which weighed 1,600 tons, was moved on 36 dollies with pneumatic tires over city streets approximately five blocks and over a bridge, which had to be reinforced. The move by Emmert International of Portland, OR took four days, 30 Mar–2 Apr 1985, and cost $650,000.

Spas ■ The largest, measured by number of available hotel rooms, is Vichy, Allier, France, with 14,000 rooms.

Spas are named after the watering place in the Liège province of Belgium, where hydropathy was developed from 1626.

The highest French spa is Barèges, Hautes-Pyrénées, at 4,068 ft above sea level.

HOUSING
According to the National Association of Realtors, the median price of existing homes sold in the 83 largest metropolitan areas in the United States during the first quarter of 1990 was $95,900. The city with the highest median price was Honolulu, HI, at $290,400.

Largest house ■ The 250-room Biltmore House in Asheville, NC, is owned by George and William Cecil, grandsons of George Washington Vanderbilt II (1862–1914). The house was built between 1890 and 1895 on an 2,000 acre estate of 119,000 acres at a cost of $4·1 million and is now valued at $55 million.

Most expensive ■ The most expensive private house ever built is the Hearst Ranch at San Simeon, CA. It was built from 1922–39 for William Randolph Hearst (1863–1951), at a total cost of more than $30 million. It has more than 100 rooms, a 104-ft long heated swimming pool, an 83-ft long assembly hall and a garage for 25 limousines. The house required 60 servants to maintain it.

Largest non–palatial residence ■ St Emmeram Castle, Regensburg, West Germany, valued at more than $177 million, contains 517 rooms with a floor space of 231,000 ft². Only 95 rooms are personally used by its owner, Prince Johannes von Thurn und Taxis, and his family.

Longest continuous home construction ■ Winchester House is San Jose, CA has been under construction for 38 years. The original house was an eight-room farmhouse with separate barn on the 161-acre estate of Oliver Winchester, who did not invent the Winchester

rifle, but owned its patent. Sarah Winchester, widowed in 1886, consulted a physic in Boston, who told her that she alone could balance the ledger for those killed by Winchester firearms by never stopping construction of the estate.

Mrs Winchester moved to California, where she transformed the farmhouse into a mansion, which now has 13 bathrooms, 52 skylights, 47 fireplaces, 10,000 windows, 40 staircases, 2,000 doorways and closets opening into blank walls, secret passageways, trap doors and three $10,000 elevators. The house remodeling is intended to confuse the resident ghosts.

APARTMENTS
Tallest ■ The tallest apartment is the 716-ft Metropolitan Tower on West 57th Street, NY. Of its 78 stories, the upper 48 are residential.

Mobile ■ The Cudecom Building, an eight-story apartment block in Bogota, Colombia, South America weighing 8,490 tons was moved intact 95 ft by Antionio Paez–Restrepo & Cia., S. en C on 6 Oct 1974 to make way for a road.

Buildings for Entertainment

STADIUM
Largest ■ The open Strahov Stadium in Prague, Czechoslovakia was completed in 1934 and can accommodate 240,000 spectators for mass displays of up to 40,000 Sokol gymnasts.

Soccer ■ The Maracaña Municipal Stadium in Rio de Janeiro, Brazil, has a normal capacity of 205,000, of whom 155,000 may be seated.

Outdoor ■ America's largest outdoor stadium is the Rose Bowl, Pasadena, CA, which has a current seating capacity of 102,083.

Covered ■ The Azteca Stadium, Mexico City, Mexico, opened in 1968, has a capacity of 107,000— nearly all seats are under cover.

The world's largest retractable roof covers the 54,000-seat capacity SkyDome stadium near the CN Tower, Toronto, Ontario, Canada, completed in June 1989. The diameter is 679 ft.

Indoor ■ The 13-acre, $173 million, 273-ft tall Superdome in New Orleans, LA was completed in May 1975. Its maximum seating capacity for conventions is 97,365 or 76,791 for football. Boxes rent for $35,000 excluding the price of admission. A gondola with six 26-ft TV screens produces instant replay.

Largest roof ■ The transparent acryl glass 'tent' roof over the Munich Olympic Stadium, West Germany measures 914,940 ft² in area, resting on a steel net supported by masts.

The roof of longest span in the world is the 680-ft diameter of the Louisiana Superdome. The major axis of the elliptical Texas Stadium completed in 1971 at Irving, TX is, however, 787 ft 4 in.

Amusement resort *Largest* ■ Disney World is set in 28,000 acres of Orange and Osceola counties, 20 miles southwest of Orlando in central Florida. It was opened on 1 Oct 1971 with a $400 million investment. The attendance in 1988 was 22·5 million.

Most attended ■ Disneyland, Anaheim, CA (opened 1955) received its 250 millionth visitor on 24 Aug 1985 at 9:52 A.M. Disneyland welcomed its 300 millionth visitor in 1989.

Largest pleasure beach ■ Virginia Beach, VA has 28 miles of beachfront on the Atlantic and 10 miles of estuary frontage. The area embraces 255 miles² and 134 hotels and motels.

Piers *Origins* ■ The origin of piers goes back to the origin of man-made harbors. That at Caesarea reportedly had the first free-standing breakwaters in 13 B.C. However, it is possible that the structures associated with the 'great harbors' of the ancient world at places like Crete, Alexandria and Carthage predate this.

Longest ■ The longest pleasure pier in the world is Southend Pier at Southend-on-Sea in Essex, United Kingdom. It is 1·34 miles in length and it was first opened in August 1889 with final extensions made in 1929. In 1949–50 the pier had a peak 5·75 million visitors.

The pier railroad closed in October 1978, and reopened on 2 May 1986.

Most piers ■ The resort with the most piers is Atlantic City, NJ, with seven. Currently only

Record attendance ■ 64,218,770 attended Expo 70, held on a 815-acre site at Osaka, Japan from March to September 1970. It made a profit of 19,439,402,017 yen.

Ferris wheel ■ The original Ferris Wheel, named after its constructor, George W. Ferris (1859–96), was erected in 1893 at the Midway, Chicago, IL at a cost of $385,000. It was 250 ft in diameter, 790 ft in circumference, weighed 1,200 tons and carried 36 cars, each seating 60 people, making a total of 2,160 passengers. The structure was removed in 1904 to St Louis, MO and was eventually sold as scrap for $1,800.

The largest diameter wheel now operating is the Cosmoclock 21 at Yokohama City, Japan. It is 344·48 ft high and 328 ft in diameter, with 60 gondolas, each with eight seats. With such features as illumination by laser beams and acoustic effects by sound synthesizers, the 60 arms holding the gondalas each serve as a second hand for the 42·65-ft long electric clock mounted at the hub.

Roller coaster ■ The maximum speeds claimed for roller coasters, scenic railroads or switchbacks have in the past been exaggerated for commercial reasons.

Longest ■ The longest roller coaster in the world is *The Beast* at Kings Island near Cincinnati, OH. Measurements at the bottom of its 141-ft high drop returned a speed of 64·77 mph on 5 Apr 1980. The run of 1·40 miles incorporates 800 ft of tunnels and a 540-degree banked helix.

Highest vertical drop ■ The $8 million Magnum XL-200, opened early 1989 at Cedar Point Park, Sandusky, OH has a vertical drop of 194 ft 8 in on which a speed of 72 mph is reached. Cedar Point has nine coasters making its total more than any other Park.

Tallest ■ The tallest is the *Moonsault Scramble* at the Fujikyu Highland Park, near Kawaguchi Lake, Japan opened on 24 Jun 1983. It is 246 ft tall (with a speed of 65·2 mph).

Largest looping ■ At its highest point 188 ft above the ground the *Viper* at Six Flags Magic Mountain, Valencia, CA sends riders upside-down 7 times over a 3,830 ft track reaching speeds of up to 70 mph.

Longest slide ■ The Bromley Alpine Slide on Route 11 in Peru, VT, has a length of 4,600 ft and a vertical drop of 820 ft.

Largest harem ■ The Winter Harem of the Grand Seraglio at Topkapi, Istanbul, Turkey was completed in 1589 with 400 rooms. By the time of the deposing of Abdul Hamid II in 1909 the number of *carge* (those who serve) had dwindled from 1,200 to 370 odalisques with 127 eunuchs.

Night club ■ The earliest night club (*boîte de nuit*) was 'Le Bal des Anglais' at 6 rue des Anglais, Paris, France. Founded in 1843, it closed c. 1960.

Largest ■ 'Gilley's Club', built in 1955, was extended in 1971 on Spencer Highway, Houston, TX with a seating capacity of 6,000 under one roof covering 4 acres.

In the more classical sense the largest night club in the world is 'The Mikado' in the Akasaka district of Tokyo, Japan with a seating capacity of 2,000. It is manned by 1,250 hostesses. Binoculars are essential to an appreciation of the floor show.

Lowest ■ The 'Minus 206' in Tiberias, Israel on the shores of the Sea of Galilee. It is 676 ft below sea level. An alternative candidate is the

Amusement resort ● One of the many attractions that can be seen by the thousands of visitors who flock to Disney World at Florida. (Photo: Images)

Roller coaster ● The Magnum XL–200 at Cedar Point Park, OH is one of nine coasters at the park. It has a vertical drop of 194 ft 8 in and reaches speeds of up to 72 mph. (Photo: Gamma/Liaison).

five remain, namely the Garden Pier (1912), Million Dollar (1906), Auditorium (1900), now the Steeplechase, Steel (1898) and Applegates (1883), now known as Central.

FAIRS

Largest ■ The site of the St Louis, MO, Louisiana Purchase Exposition covered 1,271·76 acres and drew an attendance of 19,694,855. It also staged the 1904 Olympic Games.

often-raided 'Outer Limits,' opposite the Cow Palace, San Francisco, CA. It has been called 'The Most Busted Joint' and 'The Slowest to Get the Message.'

Restaurants *Earliest* ■ The 'Casa Botin' was opened in 1725 in Calle de Cuchilleros 17, Madrid, Spain.

Highest ■ The highest restaurant in the world is at the Chacaltaya ski resort, Bolivia, at 17,519 ft.

Largest ■ The 'Tump Nak' Thai restaurant in Bangkok consists of 65 adjoining houses built on 10 acres. A thousand waiters are available to serve the 3,000 potential customers.

BARS

Largest *World* ■ The largest beer-selling establishment in the world is the 'Math-äser,' Bayerstrasse 5, Munich, West Germany, where the daily sale reaches 84,470 pts. It was established in 1829, was demolished in World War II and rebuilt by 1955, and now seats 5,500 people.

Beer consumption at the Dube beer halls in the Bantu township of Soweto, Johannesburg, South Africa may, however, be higher on some Saturdays when the average daily consumption of 48,000 pts is far exceeded.

Tallest bar ■ Humperdink's Seafood and Steakhouse Bar at Dallas, TX is 25 ft 3 in high with two levels of shelving containing over 1,000 bottles. The lower level has four rows of shelving approximately 40 ft across and can be reached from floor level. If an order is requested from the upper level, which has five rows of shelving, it is reached by climbing a ladder.

Longest bars ■ The world's longest permanent bar is the 340-ft long bar in 'Lulu's Roadhouse,' Kitchener, Ontario, Canada opened on 3 Apr 1984. The 'Bar at Erickson's,' on Burnside Street, Portland, OR in its heyday (1883–1920) possessed a bar that ran continuously around and across the main saloon measuring 684 ft. The chief bouncer, Edward 'Spider' Johnson, had an assistant named 'Jumbo' Reilly who weighed 322 lb and was said to resemble 'an ill-natured orangutan.' Beer was 5 cents for 16 fluid ounces. Temporary bars have been erected of greater length.

Towers and Masts

TALLEST STRUCTURES

World ■ The tallest structure in the world, the guyed Warszawa Radio mast at Konstanty-now near Gabin and Plock, 60 miles northwest of the capital of Poland, is 2,120⅔ ft tall or more than four-tenths of a mile. It was completed on 18 Jul 1974 and put into operation on 22 Jul 1974. It was designed by Jan Polak and weighs 606 tons. The mast is so high that anyone falling off the top would reach their terminal velocity and hence cease to be accelerating before hitting the ground. Work was begun in July 1970 on this tubular steel construction, with its 15 steel guy ropes. It recaptured for Europe, after 45 years, a record held in the United States since the Chrysler Building surpassed the Eiffel Tower in 1929.

TALLEST TOWERS

The tallest tower built before the era of television masts is the Eiffel Tower in Paris, France, designed by Alexandre Gustav Eiffel (1832–1923) for the Paris Exhibition and completed on 31

Tallest bar ● Paul Ellinson designed and constructed this steel structured bar for Humperdink's Seafood and Steakhouse, Dallas, TX, which can hold over 1,000 bottles. The top shelf can only be reached by climbing a library-type ladder and stepping onto a balcony. Some of the most exclusive liquors are purposely placed on the top shelf and patrons get a kick out of sending staff up there.

Mar 1889. It was 985 ft 11 in tall, now extended by a TV antenna to 1,052⅓ ft, and weighs 8,090 tons. The maximum sway in high winds is 5 in. The whole iron edifice, which has 1,792 steps, took two years, two months and two days to build and cost 7,799,401 francs 31 centimes.

The tallest self-supporting tower (as opposed to a guyed mast) in the world is the $44 million CN Tower in Metro Center, Toronto, Canada, which rises to 1,815 ft 5 in. Excavation began on 12 Feb 1973 for the 143,300-ton structure of reinforced, post-tensioned concrete topped out on 2 Apr 1975. The 416-seat restaurant revolves in the Sky Pod at 1,140 ft, from which the visibility extends to hills 74½ miles distant. Lightning strikes the top about 200 times (30 storms) per year.

Bridges

Oldest ■ Arch construction was understood by the Sumerians as early as 3200 B.C. and a reference exists to a Nile bridge in 2650 B.C.

The oldest surviving datable bridge in the world is the slab stone single-arch bridge over the River Meles in Smyrna (now Izmir), Turkey, which dates from *c.* 850 B.C.

LONGEST

Cable suspension ■ The world's longest bridge span is the main span of the Humber Estuary Bridge, Humberside, United Kingdom, at 4,626 ft. Work began on 27 Jul 1972, after a decision announced on 22 Jan 1966. The towers are 533 ft 1⅛ in tall from datum and are 1⅜ in

out of parallel, to allow for the curvature of the Earth. Including the Hessle and the Barton side spans, the bridge stretches 1·37 miles. It was structurally completed on 18 Jul 1980 at a cost of £96 million and was opened by Queen Elizabeth II on 17 Jul 1981. Tolls range between 70 pence for motorcycles and £10·90 for heavy vehicles; pedestrians and pedal cyclists are toll-free.

The Akashi-Kaikyo double-deck road bridge linking Honshu and Shikoku, Japan was started in 1988 and completion is planned for 1998. The main span will be 5,839 ft in length with an overall suspended length with side spans totaling 11,680 ft.

The Seto-Ohashi double-deck road and rail bridge linking Kojima, Honshu with Sakaide, Shikoku, Japan opened on 10 Apr 1988 at a cost of £4·9 billion and 17 lives. The tolls for cars are £24 each way for the 7·9 miles on spans and viaducts.

Work on the Messina Bridge linking Sicily with Calabria on the Italian mainland is due to start in 1991. The single span will be the world's largest by far at 10,892 ft. The escalating cost of such a project was estimated already to have passed the £10·25 billion mark.

The longest cable-stayed bridge in the world is the Annacis bridge in British Columbia, Canada, with a span of 1,526 ft, slightly longer than the Dao Kanong bridge over the Chao Phya in Bangkok, which at 1,476 ft is the longest single-plane cable-stayed bridge.

United States ■ The longest suspension bridge in the United States is the Verrazano–Narrows Bridge, which measures 4,260 ft. The bridge spans Lower New York Bay and connects Staten Island to Brooklyn. Construction was completed in 1964

Cantilever ■ The Quebec Bridge (Pont de Québec) over the St Lawrence River in Canada has the longest cantilever truss span of any in the world—1,800 ft between the piers and 3,239 ft overall. It carries a railroad track and two

WORLD BRIDGE RECORDS

Assuming the average length of a Japanese car to be 5 metres, a bumper-to-bumper jam from one end of the Akashi Kaikyo bridge to the other would comprise 4272 cars in six lanes.

(Bridge widths are exaggerated for the purposes of this diagram).

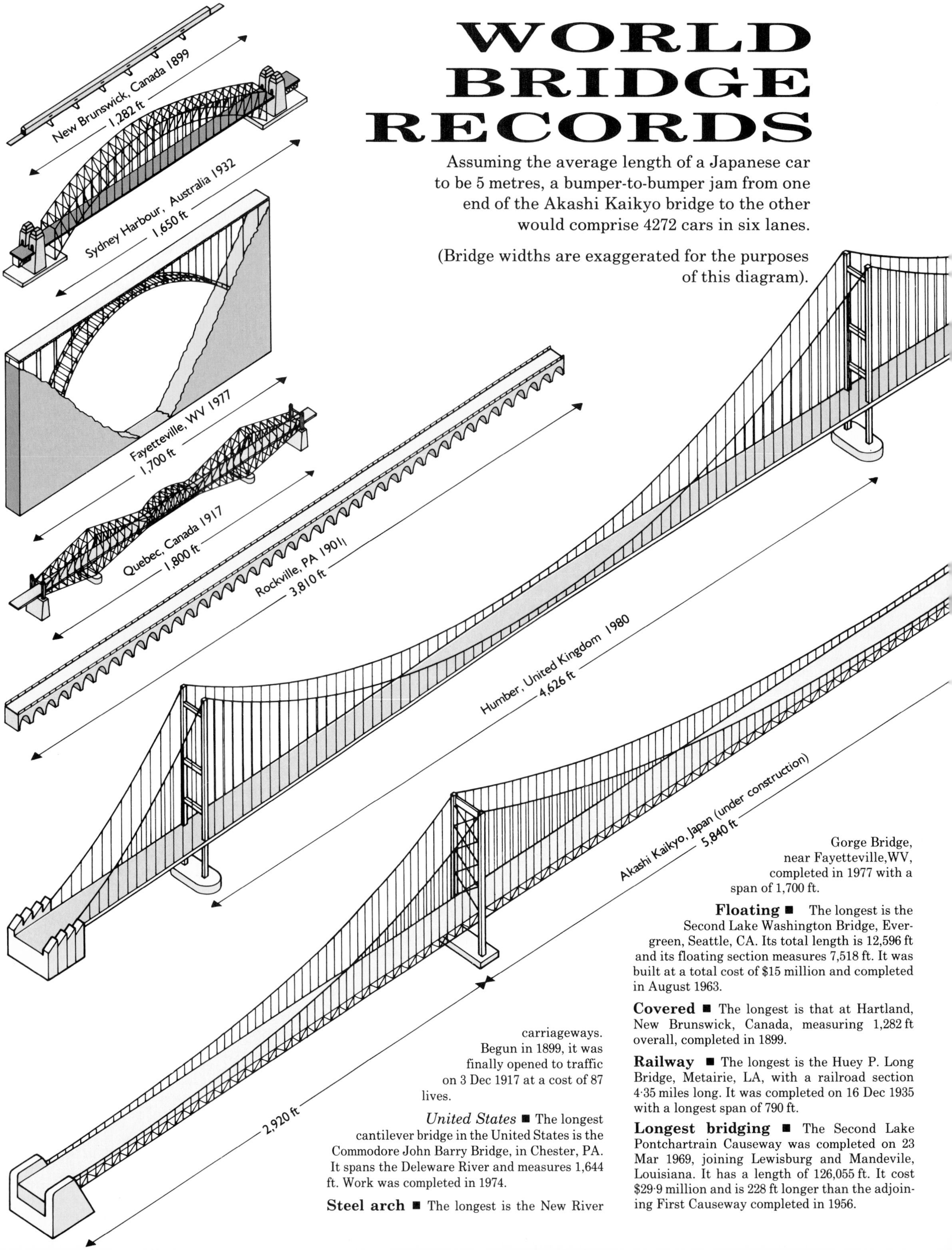

New Brunswick, Canada 1899
1,282 ft

Sydney Harbour, Australia 1932
1,650 ft

Fayetteville, WV 1977
1,700 ft

Quebec, Canada 1917
1,800 ft

Rockville, PA 1901
3,810 ft

Humber, United Kingdom 1980
4,626 ft

Akashi Kaikyo, Japan (under construction)
5,840 ft

2,920 ft

carriageways. Begun in 1899, it was finally opened to traffic on 3 Dec 1917 at a cost of 87 lives.

United States ■ The longest cantilever bridge in the United States is the Commodore John Barry Bridge, in Chester, PA. It spans the Deleware River and measures 1,644 ft. Work was completed in 1974.

Steel arch ■ The longest is the New River

Gorge Bridge, near Fayetteville,WV, completed in 1977 with a span of 1,700 ft.

Floating ■ The longest is the Second Lake Washington Bridge, Evergreen, Seattle, CA. Its total length is 12,596 ft and its floating section measures 7,518 ft. It was built at a total cost of $15 million and completed in August 1963.

Covered ■ The longest is that at Hartland, New Brunswick, Canada, measuring 1,282 ft overall, completed in 1899.

Railway ■ The longest is the Huey P. Long Bridge, Metairie, LA, with a railroad section 4·35 miles long. It was completed on 16 Dec 1935 with a longest span of 790 ft.

Longest bridging ■ The Second Lake Pontchartrain Causeway was completed on 23 Mar 1969, joining Lewisburg and Mandevile, Louisiana. It has a length of 126,055 ft. It cost $29·9 million and is 228 ft longer than the adjoining First Causeway completed in 1956.

Longest ■
The Volga-Baltic
Canal opened in April
1965 runs 1,850 miles from
Astrakhan up the Volga, via
Kuybyshev, Gorki and Lake Ladoga,
to Leningrad, USSR.

The longest canal of the ancient world was the Grand Canal of China from Beijing to Hangzhou. It was begun in 540 B.C. and not completed until A.D. 1327, by which time it extended (including canalized river sections) for 1,107 miles. The estimated work force c. A.D. 600 reached 5 million on the Bian section. Having been allowed by 1950 to silt up to the point that it was nowhere more than 6 ft deep, it is now, however, plied by vessels of up to 2,205 tons.

The Beloye More (White Sea) Baltic Canal from Belomorsk to Povenets, in the USSR, is 141 miles long with 19 locks. It was completed with the use of forced labor in 1933. It cannot accommodate ships of more than 16 ft in draught.

The world's longest big ship canal is the Suez Canal linking the Red and Mediterranean Seas, opened on 16 Nov 1869 but inoperative from June 1967 to June 1975. The canal was planned by the French diplomatist Comte Ferdinand de Lesseps (1805–94) and work began on 25 Apr 1859. It is 100·6 miles in length from Port Said lighthouse to Suez Roads, and 197 ft wide. The work force consisted of 8,213 men and 368 camels.

The largest vessel to transit has been SS *Settebello*, of 355,432 tons dwt (length 1,110·3 ft; beam 188·1 ft at a maximum draft of 73·3 ft). This was southbound in ballast on 6 Aug 1986. USS *Shreveport* transited southbound on 15–16 Aug 1984 in a record 7 hr 45 min.

HIGHEST
The highest bridge in the world is over the Royal Gorge of the Arkansas River in Colorado, which is 1,053 ft above the water level. It is a suspension bridge with a main span of 880 ft and was constructed in six months, ending on 6 Dec 1929.

Railway ■ The highest railroad bridge in the world is the Mala Rijeka Viaduct of Yugoslav Railways at Kolasin on the Belgrade-Bar line. It is 650 ft high and was opened on 1 Jun 1976. It consists of steel spans mounted on concrete piers.

Road ■ The road bridge at the highest altitude in the world, 18,380 ft, is the 98·4-ft long Bailey Bridge designed and constructed by Lt Col S. G. Vombatkere and an Indian Army team in Aug 1982 near Khardung-La, in Ladakh, India.

TALLEST
The tallest bridge in the world is the Golden Gate Bridge, which connects San Francisco and Marin County, CA. The towers of this suspension bridge extend 745 ft above the water. Completed in 1937, the bridge has an overall length of 9,266 ft.

AQUEDUCTS
Longest ancient ■ The greatest of ancient aqueducts was the Aqueduct of Carthage in Tunisia, which ran 87·6 miles from the springs of Zaghouan to Djebel Djougar. It was built by the Romans during the reign of Publius Aelius Hadrianus (Hadrian) (A.D. 117–138). By 1895, 344 arches still survived. Its original capacity has been calculated at 7 million gal per day.

The tallest of the 14 arches of Aguas Livres Aqueduct, built in Lisbon, Portugal in 1784, is 213 ¼ ft .

Longest modern ■ The world's longest aqueduct, in the non-classical sense of water conduit, excluding irrigation canals, is the California State Water Project aqueduct, completed in 1974, having a length of 826 miles, of which 385 miles is canalized.

Canals

Earliest ■ Relics of the oldest canals in the world, dated by archaeologists c. 4000 B.C., were discovered near Mandali, Iraq early in 1968.

Longest railroad viaduct ■
The longest railroad viaduct in the world is the rock-filled Great Salt Lake Railroad Trestle, carrying the Southern Pacific Railroad 11·85 miles across the Great Salt Lake, UT. It was opened as a pile and trestle bridge on 8 Mar 1904, but converted to rock fill in 1955–60.

Stone arch ■ The longest stone arch bridge is the 3,810-ft long Rockville Bridge north of Harrisburg, PA, with 48 spans containing 216,051 tons of stone and completed in 1901.

Stone arch span ■ The longest stone arch span is the 295-ft Planen Bridge in East Germany.

Concrete arch ■ The longest concrete arch is the Jesse H. Jones Memorial Bridge, which spans the Houston Ship Canal in Texas. Completed in 1982, the bridge measures 1,500 ft.

Widest ■ The widest long-span bridge is the 1,650-ft Sydney Harbor Bridge, Australia (160 ft wide). It carries two electric overhead railroad tracks, eight lanes of roadway and a cycle and footway. It was officially opened on 19 Mar 1932.

The Crawford Street Bridge in Providence, RI has a width of 1,147 ft.

Bridge building ■ British Soldiers from the 35th Engineer Regiment based at Hameln, West Germany constructed a bridge across an 26 ft gap using a five-bay single-story medium girder bridge in 8 min 31 sec at Quebec Barricks, Osnabruck, West Germany on 17 Oct 1989.

Cycleway bridge ■ The longest cycleway bridge is over the 17 railroad tracks of Cambridge Station, Cambridgeshire, United Kingdom. It has a 114·82-ft high tower and two 164-ft long approach ramps, and is 779·52 ft in length.

~ 2,920 ft

Longest aqueduct ● The greatest of the ancient aqueducts is that of Carthage in Tunisia. Built by the Romans its original capacity has been calculated at 7 million gal per day. (Photo: Spectrum Colour Library)

United States ■ The longest canal in the United States is the Erie Barge Canal, connecting the Hudson River at Troy, NY with Lake Erie at Buffalo, NY. It is 365 miles long, 150 ft wide and 12 ft in depth. The Erie Barge is part of the main waterway of the New York State Barge Canal System, which covers a distance of 525 miles.

Busiest ■ The busiest big ship canal is the Kiel Canal linking the North Sea with the Baltic Sea in West Germany, with over 45,000 transits recorded in 1987.

Next comes the Suez Canal, with over 20,000 transits, and third the Panama Canal, with over 10,000 transits.

Busiest in terms of tonnage of shipping using it is the Suez Canal with nearly 440 million grt.

Longest seaway ■ The St Lawrence Seaway (189 miles long) along the New York State–Ontario border from Montreal to Lake Ontario enables ships up to 728 ft long and 26·2 ft draught, some of which are of 29,100 tons, to sail 2,342 miles from the North Atlantic up the St Lawrence estuary and across the Great Lakes to Duluth, MN on Lake Superior (602 ft above sea level). The project, begun in 1954, cost $470 million and was opened on 25 Apr 1959.

Longest irrigation ■ The Karakumskiy Kanal stretches 528 miles from Haun-Khan to Ashkhabad, Turkmenistan, USSR. In September 1971 the 'navigable' length reached 280 miles. The length of the £370 million project will reach 930 miles

LOCKS

Largest ■ The Berendrecht Lock, which links the river Scheldt with docks at the port of

---

Largest hydro-electric dam ● If measured by power output the Itaipu power station by the Brazil-Paraguay border is the largest in the world. Its 18 turbines can attain 13,320 kW. (Photo: Gamma/Sampers).

Antwerp, Belgium, is the largest sea lock in the world. First used in April 1989, it has a length of 1 640·41 ft, a width of 223 ft and a sill level of 44·29 ft. Each of its four sliding lock gates weigh 1,653·5 tons and the total cost of construction was approximately 12 billion Beligan francs.

Deepest ■ The Zaporojie on the Dnieper-bug, USSR can raise or lower barges at 128 ft and the Carrapatelo Lock on the Douro, Portugal is 114 ft.

United States ■ The John Day Dam lock on the River Columbia, in Oregon and Washington State, was completed in 1963. It can raise or lower barges 113 ft, served by a 1,100-ton gate.

Highest rise and longest flight ■ The world's highest lock elevator overcomes a head of 225 ft at Ronquières on the Charleroi–Brussels Canal, Belgium. The two 236-wheeled caissons, each able to carry 1,510 tons, take 22 min to cover the 4,698-ft long inclined plane.

Largest cut ■ The Corinth Canal, which opened in 1893, was 2,073 ft long, 26·24 ft deep, with an average depth of cutting of 1,003 ft over some 26 miles, and an extreme depth of 1,505 ft. The Gaillard Cut (known as 'the Ditch') on the Panama Canal is 270 ft deep between Gold Hill and Contractor's Hill, with a bottom width of 500 ft. In one day in 1911 as many as 333 dirt trains each carrying 357 tons left this site.

Dams

Earliest ■ The earliest known dams were those uncovered by the British School of Archaeology in Jerusalem in 1974 at Jawa in Jordan. These stone-faced earth dams are dated to *c.* 3200 B.C.

Most massive ■ Measured by volume the earth and rock filled Pati Dam on the Paraná river, Argentina has a volume of 8·4 billion ft³. It is 108·6 miles in length and 118 ft high. The Chapetón Dam also on the Paraná, is planned to have a volume of 10·4 billion ft³ and a crest length of 139 miles. Both will be surpassed in volume by the Syncrude Tailings Dam in Canada with 19 billion ft³.

Largest concrete ■ The Grand Coulee Dam on the Columbia River, WA was begun in 1933 and became operational on 22 Mar 1941. It was completed in 1942 at a cost of $56 million. It has a crest length of 4,173 ft and is 550 ft high, with a capacity of 285 million ft³ of concrete, and weighs approximately 21·5 million tons.

Highest ■ This will be the 1,098-ft high Rogunsky earthfill dam across the river Vakhsh, Tadzhikistan, USSR, with a crest length of only 1,975 ft and a volume of 3·002 billion ft³. Under construction since 1973, the completion date is set for 1990.

Meanwhile the tallest completed is the 984 ft high Nurek dam, USSR, of 2·05 billion ft³ volume.

United States ■ The embankment–earthfill Oroville Dam is the United States' highest dam, reaching 754 ft and spanning the Feather River of California. It was completed in 1968.

Longest ■ The 134½-ft high Yacyreta Apipe Dam across the Paraná on the Paraguay-Argentina borders will extend for 24·7 miles, it is due for completion in 1992.

The Kiev Dam across the Dnieper, Ukraine completed in 1964, has a crest length of 256 miles. The Chapeton Dam under construction on the Paraná river, Argentina will have a crest length of 139 miles and is due to be completed in 1996.

In the early 17th century an impounding dam of moderate height was built in Lake Hungtze, Jiangsu, China, to a reputed length of 62 miles.

The longest sea dam in the world is the Afsluitdijk, stretching 20·195 miles across the mouth of the Zuider Zee in two sections of 1·553 miles (mainland of North Holland to the Isle of Wieringen) and 18·641 miles from Wieringen to Friesland. It has a sea-level width of 293 ft and a height of 24 ft 7 in.

Strongest ■ Upon completion, this will be the 793-ft high Sayano-Shusenskaya Dam on the River Yenisey, USSR, which is designed to bear a load of 19·8 million tons from a fully filled reservoir of 1·1 trillion ft³ capacity.

Largest reservoir ■ The most voluminous man-made reservoir is the Bratskoe Reservoir, USSR, on the Angara River in Siberia, with a volume of 2,111·967 miles². It extends for 31 miles in length with a width of 33½ miles. It was filled in 1961–67.

The world's largest artificial lake measured by surface area is Lake Volta, Ghana, formed by the Akosombo Dam completed in 1965. By 1969 the lake had filled to an area of 3,275 miles², with a shoreline 4,500 miles in length.

The completion in 1954 of the Owen Falls Dam near Jinja, Uganda, across the northern exit of the White Nile from the Victoria Nyanza marginally raised the level of that natural lake by adding 218·9 million acre-feet, and technically turned it into a reservoir with a surface area of 17·2 million acres.

The $4-billion Tucurui Dam in Brazil of 2·27 billion ft³, had, by 1984, converted the Tocantins River into a 1,180 mile long chain of lakes.

United States ■ The largest wholly artificial reservoir in the United States is Lake Mead in Nevada. It was formed by the Hoover Dam, which was completed in 1936. The lake has a capacity of 1,241,445 million ft³ and a surface area of 28·255 million acre-ft.

Largest polder (*Reclaimed land*) ■ Of the five great polders in the old Zuider Zee,

Netherlands, will be the 149,000 acre (232·8 miles ^{2}) Markerwaard. Work on the 66 mile long surrounding dike was begun in 1957. The water area remaining after the erection of the 1927–32 dam (20 miles in length) is called IJssel meer, which will have a final area of 487½ miles ^{2}.

Largest levees ■ The most massive ever built are the Mississippi levees begun in 1717 but vastly augmented by the US federal government after the disastrous floods of 1927. These extend for 1,732 miles along the main river from Cape Girardeau, MO to the Gulf of Mexico and comprise more than 27 billion ft ^{3} of earthworks. Levees on the tributaries comprise an additional 2,000 miles.

The Pine Bluff, AR to Venice, LA segment of 650 miles is continuous.

Tunnels

LONGEST

Rail ■ The 33·46-mile long Seikan Rail Tunnel has been bored 787 ft beneath sea level and 328 ft below the seabed of the Tsugaru Strait between Tappi Saki, Honshu, and Fukushima, Hokkaido, Japan. Tests started on the subaqueous section (14½ miles) in 1964 and construction in June 1972. It was holed through on 27 Jan 1983 after a loss of 34 lives. The cost by the completion of tunneling after 20 years 10 months in March 1985 and subsequent maintenance to February 1987 was 700 billion yen. The first test run took place on 13 Mar 1988.

Proposals for a Brenner Base Tunnel between Innsbruck, Austria and Italy envisage a rail tunnel between 36 and 39 miles long.

United States ■ The longest main–line tunnel railroad in the United States is the Moffat Tunnel, which cuts through a 6·2-mile section of the Rocky Mountains in Colorado. Tunnel construction was completed in 1928.

Continuous subway ■ The Moscow Metro underground railroad line from Belyaevo to Medvedkovo is *c.* 19·07 miles long and was completed in 1978/9.

Road tunnel ■ The 10·14 mile long two-lane St Gotthard Road Tunnel from Göschenen to Airolo, Switzerland, opened to traffic on 5 Sep 1980. Nineteen lives were lost during its construction, begun in fall 1969, at a cost of 686 million Swiss francs.

United States ■ The longest road tunnel in the United States is the 2·5-mile Lincoln Tunnel, linking New York City and New Jersey. The tunnel was dug beneath the Hudson River and completed in 1937.

Largest ■ The largest diameter road tunnel in the world is that blasted through Yerba Buena Island, San Francisco, CA. It is 76 ft wide, 58 ft high and 540 ft long. More than 80 million vehicles pass through on its two decks every year.

Water supply tunnel ■ The longest tunnel of any kind is the New York City–West Delaware water-supply tunnel, begun in 1937 and completed in 1944. It has a diameter of 13½ ft and runs for 105 miles from the Rondout Reservoir into the Hillview Reservoir, on the border of Yonkers and New York City.

Hydroelectric irrigation ■ The 51½-mile long Orange-Fish Rivers Tunnel, South Africa, begun in 1967 at an estimated cost

of £ 60 million. The boring was completed in April 1973. The lining to a minimum thickness of 9 in will give a completed diameter of 17½ ft .

The Majes project in Peru involves 60·9 miles of tunnels for hydroelectric and water-supply purposes. The dam is at an altitude of 13,780 ft.

Sewerage ■ The Chicago TARP (Tunnels and Reservoir Plan) in Illinois involves 120 miles of sewerage tunneling. The Viikinmäki Central Treatment Plant in Helsinki, Finland is the world's first major wastewater plant to be built underground. It will involve the excavation of nearly 35,314 ft ^{3} of rock before its completion in 1993.

Bridge-tunnel ■ The Chesapeake Bay Bridge-Tunnel, extending 17·65 miles from Eastern Shore, VA Peninsula to Virginia Beach, VA. It cost $200 million and was completed after 42 months and opened to traffic on 15 Apr 1964.

The longest bridged section is Trestle C (4·56 miles long) and the longest tunnel is the Thimble Shoal Channel Tunnel (1·09 miles).

Longest and largest canal-tunnel ■ The Rove Tunnel on the Canal de Marseille au Rhône in the south of France was completed in 1927 and is 23,359 ft long, 72 ft wide and 37 ft high. Built to be navigated by seagoing ships, it was closed in 1963 following a collapse of the structure and has not been reopened.

Oldest navigable ■ The Malpas Tunnel on the Canal du Midi in southwest France was completed in 1681 and is 528 ft long. Its completion enabled vessels to navigate from the Atlantic Ocean to the Mediterranean Sea via the river Garonne to Toulouse and the Canal du Midi to Sète.

Tunneling ■ The longest unsupported example of a machine-bored tunnel is the Three Rivers Water Tunnel driven 9·37 km30 769 linear feet with a 3·2 m10·5 ft diameter for the city of Atlanta, GA from April 1980 to February 1982.

Specialized Structures

Largest lego statue ■ The sculpture of Indian chief Sitting Bull at the Legoland Park, Billund, Denmark measures 25 ft to the top of the feather. The largest statue ever constructed from Lego, it required 1·5 million bricks individually glued together to withstand the weather.

Highest advertising signs ■ The four Bank of Montreal logos at the top of the 72-story 935-ft tall First Canadian Place, Toronto, Canada. Each sign, built by Claude Neon Industries Ltd, measures 20 × 22 ft and was lifted by helicopter.

Largest ■ The most conspicuous sign ever erected was the electric Citroën sign on the Eiffel Tower, Paris. It was switched on on 4 Jul 1925, and could be seen 24 miles away. It was in six colors with 250,000 lamps and 56 miles of electric cables. The letter 'N' that terminated the name 'Citroën' between the second and third levels measured 68 ft 5 in in height was dismantled in 1936. (For the largest ground sign see Chapter 8, Largest letter.)

Neon signs *Longest* ■ The letter 'M' installed on the Great Mississippi River Bridge is 1,800 ft long and comprises 200-high intensity lamps.

The largest neon sign measures 210 × 55 ft built for Marlboro cigarettes at Hung Hom, Kowloon, Hong Kong in May 1986. It contains 35,000 ft of neon tubing and weighs approximately 126 tons.

An interior lit fascia advertizing sign in Clearwater, FL completed by Adco Sign Corp in April 1983 measures 1,168 ft 6½ in in length.

Billboards ■ Bassat Ogilvy Promotional Campaigns erected the world's largest billboard for Ford Espana, measuring 475 ft 9 in in length and 78 ft 9 in in wide at Plaza de Toros Monumental de Barcelona, Barcelona, Spain.

Illuminated sign ■ The largest illuminated sign is the name VOLVO LEX extending 190 ft 1 in installed by Herbert & Sons Signs Ltd of Surrey, United Kingdom at Lex, a Volvo dealer in London, United Kingdom.

Animated sign ■ The world's most massive is reputed to be that outside the Circus Circus Hotel, Reno, NV named Topsy the Clown. It is 127 ft tall and weighs over 45 tons, with 1·4 miles of neon tubing. His smile measures 14 ft across.

Longest airborne sign ■ Reebok International Ltd of Massachusetts, flew a banner from a single seater plane which read 'Reebok Totally Beachin.' The banner measured 50 ft in height and 100 ft in length, it was flown from 13–16 and 20–23 March 1990 for 4 hr each day.

Largest bonfire ■ This was constructed in Espel, in the Noordoost Polder, Netherlands. It stood 91 ft 5 in high with a base circumference of 276 ft 11 in and was lit on 19 Apr 1987.

Longest breakwater ■ The world's longest breakwater is that which protects the Port of Galveston, TX. The granite South Breakwater is 6·74 miles in length.

Buildings demolished by explosives ■ The largest has been the 21-story Traymore Hotel, Atlantic City, NJ on 26 May 1972 by Controlled Demolition Inc of Towson, MD. This 600-room hotel had a cubic capacity of 6·5 million ft³.

The tallest chimney ever demolished by explosives was the Matla Power Station chimney, Kriel, South Africa on 19 Jul 1981. It stood 902 ft and was brought down by the Santon (Steeplejack) Co Ltd of Greater Manchester, United Kingdom.

Cemetery *Largest* ■ The Piskarevskoe cemetery in Leningrad contains over 470,000 victims of the German army's seige of 1941–44. It is 64·2 acres extent. The greatest number of victims were buried on 20 Feb 1942 and that day reached 10,043 bodies.

The United States' largest cemetary is the Arlington National Cemetary, which is situated on the Potomac River in Virginia, directly opposite Washington, D.C. It is 612 acres in extent and has more than 200,000 servicemen interred there. Presidents' William Howard Taft and John Fitzgerald Kennedy are also buried there.

Tallest ■ The permanently illuminated Memorial Cemiferio Ecuméncio, São Paulo, Brazil is 10-storys high, occupying an area of 4·448 acres. When full, the final capacity of spaces will be 20,000.

Tallest columns ■ The 36 90-ft tall fluted pillars of Vermont marble in the colonnade of the Education Building, Albany, NY State. Their base diameter is 6½ ft.

The tallest load-bearing stone columns in the world are those measuring 69 ft in the Hall of Columns of the Temple of Amun at Karnak, opposite Thebes on the Nile, the ancient capital of Upper Egypt. They were built in the 19th dynasty in the reign of Rameses II c. 1270 B.C.

Crematorium ■ The largest crematorium in the world is at the Nikolo-Arkhangelskoye Cemetery, East Moscow, USSR with seven twin cremators of British design, completed in March 1972. It has several Halls of Farewell for atheists.

Largest dome ■ The Louisiana Superdome, New Orleans has a diameter of 680 ft. (See p. 91 for further details.)

The largest dome of ancient architecture is that of the Pantheon, built in Rome in A.D. 112, with a diameter of 142½ ft.

Doors *Largest* ■ The four doors in the Vehicle Assembly Building near Cape Canaveral, FL have a height of 460 ft (see p. 91).

Heaviest ■ Leading to the laser target room at Lawrence Livermore National Laboratory, CA. It weighs 360 tons, is up to 8 ft thick and was installed by Overly.

Largest dry dock ■ With a maximum shipbuilding capacity of 1·34 million tons deadweight, the Daewoo Okpo No 1 Dry Dock, Koje Island in South Korea measures 1,738·84 ft long by 430 ft wide and was completed in 1979. The dock gates, 46 ft high and 32·8 ft thick at the base, are the world's largest.

Largest earthworks ■ Prior to the mechanical era were the Linear Earth Boundaries of the Benin Empire in the Bendel state of Nigeria. These were first reported in 1900 and partially surveyed in 1967. In April 1973 it was estimated by Patrick Darling that the total length of the earthworks was probably between 4,000 and 8,000 miles, with the amount of earth moved estimated at from 13·4 –16 billion ft³.

Fence *Longest* ■ The dingo-proof wire fence enclosing the main sheep areas of Australia is 6 ft high, 1 ft underground and stretches for 3,437 miles. The Queensland State Government discontinued full maintenance in 1982 but 310 miles is now being repaired.

Tallest ■ The world's tallest fences are security screens 65·6 ft high erected by Harrop-Allin of Pretoria, South Africa in November 1981 to protect fuel depots and refineries at Sasolburg, South Africa.

Tallest flagpole ■ Erected outside the Oregon Building at the 1915 Panama-Pacific International Exposition in San Francisco, CA, and trimmed from a Douglas fir, the flagpole stood 299 ft 7 in in height and weighed 51·8 tons.

The tallest unsupported flagpole in the world is the 282-ft tall steel pole weighing 120,000 lb, which was erected on 22 Aug 1985 at the Canadian Expo 86 exhibition in Vancouver, British Columbia and supports a gigantic ice hockey stick 205 ft in length. Mr Sherrold Haddad of Flag Chevrolet Oldsmobile Ltd was instrumental in moving and reconstructing the flagstaff where it has been relocated at the company's premises in 104th Avenue, Surrey, British Columbia, Canada.

Tallest fountain ■ The Fountain at Fountain Hills, AZ built at a cost of $1·5 million for McCulloch Properties Inc. At full pressure of 375 lb/in² and at a rate of 5,828 imp. gal/min, the 560-ft tall column of water weighs more than 8·8 tons. The nozzle speed achieved by the three 600 hp pumps is 146·7 mph.

Largest fumigation ■ Carried out during the restoration of the Mission Inn complex in Riverside, CA on 28 Jun–1 Jul 1987 to rid the buildings of termites. It was performed by Fume Masters Inc of Riverside with over 350 tarpaulins weighing up to 350 lb and involved completely covering the 70,000 ft² site and buildings — domes, minarets, chimneys and balconies — some of which exceeded 100 ft in height.

SEVEN WONDERS

The Seven Wonders of the World were first designated by Antipater of Sidon in the second century B.C. They included the Pyramids of Giza, built by three Fourth-dynasty Egyptian pharaohs, Khwfw (Khufu or Cheops), Kha-f-Ra (Khafre, Khefren or Chepren) and Menkaure (Mycerinus) near El Giza (El Gizeh), southwest of El Qâhira (Cairo) in Egypt.

THE GREAT PYRAMID

The 'Horizon of Khufu' was finished under Rededef c. 2580 B.C. Its original height was 480 ft 11 in (now, since the loss of its topmost stones and the pyramidion, reduced to 449 ft 6 in) with a base line of 756 ft and thus covering slightly more than 13 acres. It has been estimated that a permanent work force of 4,000 required 30 years to maneuver into position the 2·3 million limestone blocks averaging 2·76 tons each, totaling about 6,437,432 tons and a volume of 90·7 million ft³. Some blocks weighed 15 tons. A costing exercise published in December 1974 indicated that it would require 405 men six years at a cost of $1·13 billion.

FRAGMENT REMAINS OF:

The Temple of Artemis (Diana) of the Ephesians, built c. 350 B.C. at Ephesus, Turkey (destroyed by the Goths in A.D. 262); The Tomb of King Mausolus of Caria, at Halicarnassus, now Bodrum, Turkey, c. 325 B.C.

NO TRACE REMAINS OF:

The Hanging Gardens of Semiramis, at Babylon, Iraq c. 600 B.C.; The statue of Zeus (Jupiter), by Phidias (fifth century B.C.) at Olympia, Greece (lost in a fire at Istanbul) in marble, gold and ivory and 40 ft tall ;
The figure of the god Helios (Apollo), the 117-ft tall statue by Chares of Lindus called the Colossus of Rhodes (sculptured 292–280 B.C., destroyed by an earthquake in 224 B.C.);

The 400-ft tall world's earliest lighthouse, built by Sostratus of Cnidus (c. 270 B.C.) as a pyramidicallyshaped tower of white marble (destroyed by earthquake in A.D. 1375), on the island of Pharos (Greek, pharos=lighthouse), off the coast of El Iskandariya (Alexandria), Egypt.

Largest garbage dump ■ Reclamation Plant No. 1, Fresh Kills, Staten Island, NY, opened in March 1974, is the world's largest sanitary landfill. In its first four months, 503,751 tons of refuse from New York City was dumped on the site by 700 barges.

Largest gas tank ■ The gas tanks at Fontaine l'Évêque, Belgium, where disused mines have been adapted to store up to 17·6 billion ft³ of gas at ordinary pressure.

Longest deep-water jetty ■ The Quai Hermann du Pasquier at Le Havre, France, with a length of 5,000 ft, is part of an enclosed basin and has a constant depth of water of 32 ft on both sides.

Tallest lamppost ■ The tallest lighting columns are the four made by Petitjean & Cie of Troyes, France and installed by Taylor Woodrow at Sultan Qaboos Sports Complex, Muscat, Oman, they stand 208 ft 4 in high.

Lighthouse ■ *Tallest* ■ The 348 ft steel tower near Yamashita Park in Yokohama, Japan has a power of 600,000 candles and a visibility range of 20 miles.

United States ■ Cape Hatteras Lighthouse on the Cape Hatteras National Seashore, NC stands 191 ft tall.

Highest ■ The highest lighthouse above sea level in the United States is the Cape Mendocino Lighthouse in Cape Mendocino, CA. It stands 515 ft above sea level.

Greatest range ■ The lights with the greatest range are those 1,092 ft above the ground on the Empire State Building, New York City. Each of the four-arc mercury bulbs has a rated candlepower of 450 million, visible 80 miles away on the ground and 300 miles away from aircraft. They were switched on on 31 Mar 1956.

Oldest ■ The oldest lighthouse in the United States is Boston Lighthouse in Boston, MA. It was first lighted in 1716. The oldest lighthouse in continuous service is Sandy Hook Lighthouse in Sandy Hook, NJ. It was first lighted in 1764.

Largest marquee ■ Covering an area of 188,368 ft² (4·32 acres) and erected by the firm of Deuter from Augsburg, West Germany, for the 1958 'Welcome Expo' in Brussels, Belgium.

Maze ■ The oldest datable representation of a labyrinth is that on a clay tablet from Pylos, Greece from *c.* 1200 B.C.

The world's largest hedge maze is that at Longleat, near Warminster, Wiltshire, United Kingdom, designed for Lord Weymouth by Greg Bright, which has 1·69 miles of paths flanked by 16,180 yew trees. It was opened on 6 Jun 1978 and measures 381 × 187 ft.

'Il Labirinto' at Villa Pisani, Stra, Italy, in which Napoleon was 'lost' in 1807, had 4 miles of pathways.

Menhir ■ The tallest found is the 418·8-ton Grand Menhir Brisé, now in four pieces, which originally stood 69 ft high at Locmariaquer, Brittany, France. Recent research suggests possible 75-ft high menhir, in three pieces, weighing 280 tons, also at Locmariaquer.

Monuments *Tallest* ■ The stainless steel Gateway to the West arch in St Louis, MO, completed on 28 Oct 1965 to commemorate the westward expansion after the Lousiana Purchase of 1803 is a sweeping arch spanning 630 ft

and rising to the same height of 630 ft and costing $29 million . It was designed in 1947 by the Finnish-American architect Eero Saarinen (d.1961).

Tallest column ■ Constructed from 1936–39, at a cost of $1·5 million, the tapering column that commemorates the Battle of San Jacinto (21 Apr 1836), on the bank of the San Jacinto River near Houston, TX, is 570 ft tall, 47 ft square at the base, and 30 ft square at the observation tower, which is surmounted by a star weighing 220 tons. It is built of concrete, and is faced with buff limestone, having a weight of 35,150 tons.

Tallest statue ● This statue called 'Motherland' commemorates the victory of the Battle of Stalingrad (1942–3) and stands on Mamayev Hill outside Volgograd, USSR. (Photo: Gamma/Novosti)

The largest trilithons exist at Stonehenge, to the south of Salisbury Plain, Wiltshire, United Kingdom, with single sarsen blocks weighing over 49·6 tons and requiring over 550 men to drag them up a 9° gradient. The earliest stage of the construction of the ditch has been dated to 2800 B.C. Whether Stonehenge was built as

a temple or place of worship, a lunar calendar, an eclipse-predictor or a navigation school is still debated.

Largest artificial mound ■ The gravel mound built as a memorial to the Seleucid King Antiochus I (reigned 69–34 B.C.) stands on the summit of Nemrud Dagi (8,205 ft) southeast of Malatya, eastern Turkey. This measures 197 ft tall and covers 7·5 acres.

Naturist resort *Oldest and largest*■ The oldest resort is Der Freilichtpark, Klingberg, West Germany, established in 1903.

The largest in area in the world is the Beau Valley Country Club, Warmbaths, South Africa, extending over 988 acres, with up to 20,000 visitors a year.

However, 100,000 people visit the smaller center Helio-Marin at Cap d'Agde, southern France, which covers 222 acres. The appellation 'nudist camp' is deplored by naturists.

Largest standing obelisk (monolithic) ■ The skewer or spit (from the Greek *obeliskos*) of Tuthmosis III brought from Aswan, Egypt by Emperor Constantius in the spring of A.D. 357 was repositioned in the Piazza San Giovanni in Laterane, Rome on 3 Aug 1588. Once 118·1 ft tall, it now stands 107·6 ft and weighs 501·5 tons.

The unfinished obelisk, probably commissioned by Queen Hatshepsut *c.* 1490 B.C., at Aswan, is 136·8 ft in length and weighs 1,287 tons.

The longest an obelisk has remained *in situ* is that still at Heliopolis, near Cairo, erected by Senwosret I *c.* 1750 B.C.

Tallest ■ The world's tallest obelisk is the Washington Monument in Washington D.C. Situated in a 106 acre site and standing 555 ft 5⅛ in in height, it was built to honor George Washington (1732-99), first President of the United States.

Longest pier *(Commercial)* ■ The Dammam Pier, Saudi Arabia, on the Persian Gulf with an overall length of 6·79 miles, was begun in July 1948 and completed on 15 Mar 1950. The area was subsequently developed by 1980 into the King Abdul Aziz Port, with 39 deep-water berths. The original causeway, much widened and the port extend for 7·95 miles.

Largest pyramid ■ The largest pyramid, and the largest monument ever constructed, is the Quetzacóatl at Cholula de Rivadabia, 63 miles southeast of Mexico City. It is 177 ft tall and its base covers an area of nearly 45 acres. Its total volume has been estimated at 116·5 million ft³ compared with 88·2 million ft³ for the Pyramid of Cheops (Khufu: see Seven Wonders of the World). The pyramid-building era here was between the second and sixth centuries A.D.

Oldest pyramid ■ The Djoser Step Pyramid at Saqqâra, Egypt, constructed by Imhotep to a height of 204 ft, originally with a Tura limestone casing *c.* 2650 B.C.

The largest known single block comes from the Third Pyramid (Pyramid of Mycerinus) and weighs 320 tons.

The oldest New World pyramid is that on the island of La Venta in southeastern Mexico built by the Olmec people *c.* 800 B.C. It stands 100 ft tall with a base dimension of 420 ft.

Scaffolding ■ The largest free-standing scaffolding is believed to be that erected for the restoration of the antenna at Goldstone, CA. It was 170 ft high, 70 ft deep and went 180 ft around the circumference of the structure.

Scarecrow ■ The tallest was 'Stretch II,' constructed by the Speers family of Paris, Ontario, Canada and a crew of 15 at the Paris Fall Fair on 2 Sep 1989. It measured 103 ft 6¾ in in height.

Snow and ice constructions ■ A snow palace 87 ft high, and one of four structures that spanned 702·7 ft wide, was unveiled on 7 Feb 1987 at Asahikawa City, Hokkaido, Japan.

The world's largest ice construction was the Ice Palace built in January 1986 using 9,000 blocks of ice at St Paul, MN during the Winter Carnival. Designed by Ellerbe Associates Inc., it stood 128 ft 9 in high — the equivalent of a 13-story building.

Snowman ■ 'Super Frosty,' built by a team in Anchorage, AK led by Myron L. Ace between 20 Feb and 5 Mar 1988, stood 63·56 ft.

Longest stairway ■ The service staircase for the Niesenbahn funicular rises to 7,759 ft near Spiez, Switzerland. It has 11,674 steps and a bannister. The stone-cut Taichan temple stairs of 6,600 steps in the Shandong Mountains, China ascend 4,700 ft.

The longest spiral staircase is one 1,103 ft deep with 1,520 steps installed in the Mapco-White County Coal Mine, Carmi, IL by Systems Control Inc in May 1981.

Longest statue ■ Near Bamiyan, Afghanistan there are the remains of the recumbent Sakya Buddha, built of plastered rubble, which was 'about 1,000 ft' long and is believed to date from the third or fourth century A.D.

Tallest statue ■ A full-figure statue, that of 'Motherland,' an enormous prestressed concrete female figure on Mamayev Hill, outside Volgograd, USSR, designed in 1967 by Yevgeni Vuchetich, to commemorate victory in the Battle of Stalingrad (1942–43). The statue from its base to the tip of the sword clenched in her right hand measures 270 ft.

United States ■ The Statue of Liberty, originally named Liberty Enlightening the World, is the tallest statue in the United States. Designed and built in France to commemorate the friendship of the two countries, the 152-ft statue was shipped to New York, where its copper sheets were assembled. President Grover Cleveland accepted the statue for the United States on 28 Oct 1886.

The statue, which became a national monument in 1924, stands on Liberty Island in Upper New York Bay. The base of the statue is an eleven–point star; a 150-ft pedestal is made of concrete faced with granite. The statue was closed to the public on 23 Jun 1985 in order to complete restoration work, at a cost of $698 million. The statue was officially reopened by President Ronald Reagan on 4 Jul 1986 during a weekend–long celebration of the statue's 100th birthday.

Tallest swing ■ A glider swing 30 ft high was constructed by Kenneth R. Mack, Langenburg, Saskatchewan, Canada for Uncle Herb's Amusements. The swing is capable of taking its four sides 25 ft off the ground.

Largest tomb ■ The Mount Li tomb, belonging to Zeng, the first emperor of China, dates to 221 B.C. and is situated 25 miles east of Xianyang. The two walls surrounding the grave measure 7,129 × 3,195 ft and 2,247 × 1,896 ft. Several pits in the tomb contained a vast army of an estimated 8,000 life-size terracotta soldiers.

A tomb housing 180,000 Second World War dead on Okinawa, Japan was enlarged in 1985 to accommodate another 9,000 bodies thought to be buried on the island.

Tallest totem pole ■ A 173 ft tall pole was raised on 6 Jun 1973 at Alert Bay, British Columbia, Canada. It tells the story of the Kwakiutl and took 36 man-weeks to carve.

Vats *Largest* ■ The largest wooden wine cask in the world is the Heidelberg Tun, that was completed in 1751, in the cellar of the Friedrichsbau Heidelberg, West Germany. Its capacity is 40,790 gal.

'Strongbow,' used by H.P. Bulmer Ltd, the English cider makers of Hereford, measures 64½ ft in height and 75½ ft in diameter, with a capacity of 1·6 million gal.

Oldest ■ The world's oldest is that in use since 1715 at Hugel et Fils (founded 1639) Riquewihr, Haut-Rhin by the most recent of the 12 generations of the family.

Longest wall ■ The Great Wall of China has a main-line length of 2,150 miles — nearly three times the length of Britain. Completed during the reign of Qin Shi Huangdi (221–210 B.C.), it has a further 1,780 miles of branches and spurs. Its height varies from 15–39 ft and it is up to 32 ft thick. It runs from Shanhaikuan, on the Gulf of Bohai, to Yumenguan and Yang-guan and was kept in repair up to the 16th century. Some 32 miles of the wall have been destroyed since 1966 and part of the wall was blown up to make way for a dam in July 1979. On 6 Mar 1985 a report from China stated that a five-year-long survey proved that the total length had been 6,200 miles.

Water tower ■ The Union at New Jersey, built in 1965, rises to a height of 210 ft, with a capacity of 250,000 gal. The tower is owned and operated by the Elizabethtown Water Company.

Largest waterwheel ■ The Mohammadieh Noria wheel at Hamah, Syria has a diameter of 131 ft and dates from Roman times.

Largest window ■ The largest sheet of glass ever manufactured was one of 538·2 ft², or 65 ft 7 in by 8 ft 2¼ in, exhibited by the Saint Gobin Company in France at the *Journées Internationales de Miroiterie* in March 1958.

The largest single windows in the world are those in the Palace of Industry and Technology at Rondpoint de la Défense, Paris, France with an extreme width of 715·2 ft and a maximum height of 164 ft.

The largest sheet of tempered glass (safety) ever processed was one made by P. T. Sinar Rasa Kencana of Jakarta, Indonesia, which measures 22·96 ft long by 7·02 ft wide and is 0·05 in thick.

Largest wine cellar ■ The cellars at Paarl, those of the Ko-operative Wijnbouwers Vereeniging, known as KWV, near Cape Town, in the center of the wine-growing district of South Africa, cover an area of 25 acres and have a capacity of 30 million gal.

The Cienega Winery of the Almaden Vineyards in Hollister, CA covers 4 acres and can house 37,300 oak barrels containing 1·83 million gallons of wine.

Largest ziggurat ■ The largest (from the Assyrian *ziqqurati*, summit, height) ever built was by the Elamite King Untash *c.* 1250 B.C. known as the Ziggurat of Choga Zanbil, 18·6 miles from Haft Tepe, Iran. The outer base was 344 ft and the fifth 'box' 91·8 ft, nearly 164 ft above.

The largest surviving ziggurat is the Ziggurat of Ur (now Muquyyar, Iraq) with a base 200 × 150 ft built to three stories surmounted by a summit temple. The first and part of the second stories now survive to a height of 60 ft . It was built in the reign of Ur-nammu (*c.* 2113-2096 B.C.).

TRANSPORT

Ships
Road Vehicles
Roads
Railroads
Aircraft

Largest commercial jet airliner ● The first 747-400 was put into service on 26 Jan 1988 with a wing span of 213 ft and theoretically a seating capacity for 516 passengers. (Photo: Spectrum)

Ships

EARLIEST SEAGOING BOATS

Aborigines are thought to have been able to cross the Torres Strait from New Guinea to Australia, then at least 43½ miles across, as early as 40,000 B.C. They are believed to have used double canoes.

The earliest *surviving* 'vessel' is a pinewood dugout found in Pesse, Netherlands and dated to *c.* 275 B.C., now in the Provincial Museum, Assen.

The earliest representation of a boat is disputed between possible rock-art outlines of Mesolithic skin-boats in Høgnipen, Norway (*c.* 8000–7000 B.C.); Minateda, Spain (7000–3000 B.C.); and Kobystan, USSR (8000–6000 B.C.).

A 18 in long paddle was found at the Star Carr site in North Yorkshire, United Kingdom, discovered in 1948. It has been dated to *c.* 7600 B.C. and is now in the Cambridge Museum of Archaeology.

The oldest surviving boat is a 27-ft long 2½-ft wide wooden eel-catching canoe discovered at Tybrind Vig on the Baltic Island of Fünen that is dated to *c.* 4490 B.C.

The oldest shipwreck ever found is one of a Cycladic trading vessel located off the islet of Dhókós, near the Greek island of Hydra, reported in May 1975 and dated to 2450 B.C.

A wreck about 2,400 years old is currently being excavated in the crater of a live volcano off the northern coast of Sicily. The cargo includes large quantities of classic Greek pottery.

Earliest power ■ Propulsion by steam engine was first achieved when in 1783 the Marquis Claude-François-Dorothée Jouffroy d'Abbans (1751–1832) ascended a reach of the river Saône near Lyon, France, in the 198-ton paddle wheeler *Pyroscaphe*.

The tug *Charlotte Dundas* was the first successful power-driven vessel. She was a stern paddle-wheeler built for the Forth and Clyde Canal in 1801–02 by William Symington (1763–1831), using a double-acting condensing engine constructed by James Watt (1736–1819).

The screw propeller was invented and patented by a Kent farmer, Sir Francis Pettit Smith (1808–71), on 31 May 1836 (British Patent Number 7104).

The world's oldest active steamship is the paddle wheeler *Skibladner*, which has plied Lake Mjøsa, Norway since 1856. She was built in Motala, Sweden and has had two major refits.

WARSHIPS

Largest battleships ■ The 887¾-ft long USS *New Jersey*, with a full-load displacement of 63,933 tons, was the last fire-support ship on active service off the Lebanon coast, with her nine 16-in guns, from 14 Dec 1983 to 26 Feb 1984.

The $405-million refit of the USS *Iowa* was completed in May 1984. On 19 April 1989 she was damaged by an explosion on board killing 47 crew. The Navy has so far spent $26 million in repairs but it was announced in January 1990 that both the *Iowa* and *New Jersey* would be 'mothballed' in reserve. Sister ships the USS *Missouri* and *Wisconsin* will remain in commission.

The USS *Missouri* and USS *Wisconsin* were recommissioned in 1986 and 1988 respectively. The 16-inch projectiles of 2,700 lb can be fired 23 miles.

The Japanese battleships *Yamato* (completed on 16 December 1941 and sunk southwest of Kyushu, Japan by US planes on 7 Apr 1945) and *Musashi* (sunk in the Philippine Sea by 11 bombs and 16 torpedoes on 24 Oct 1944) were the largest battleships ever commissioned, each with a full load displacement of 81,545 tons. With an overall length of 863 ft, a beam of 127 ft and a full-load draught of 35½ ft, they mounted nine 18·1-in guns in three triple turrets. Each gun weighed 181·5 tons and was 75 ft in length, firing a 3,200-lb projectile.

Fastest warship ■ The hovercraft, the 78-ft long 110-ton US Navy test vehicle SES-100B achieved a speed of 91·9 knots (105·8 mph.) (See Hovercrafts, fastest).

Fastest destroyer ■ The highest speed attained by a destroyer was 45·25 knots (51·83 mph) by the 3,120-ton French destroyer *Le Terrible* in 1935. She was built in Blainville, France and powered by four Yarrow small-tube boilers and two Rateau geared turbines giving 100,000 shaft horsepower. She was removed from the active list at the end of 1957.

AIRCRAFT CARRIERS

Largest ■ The warships with the largest full load displacement in the world are the Nimitz class US Navy aircraft carriers USS *Nimitz, Dwight D. Eisenhower, Carl Vinson, Theodore Roosevelt* and *Abraham Lincoln* at 100,846 tons. They are 1,092 ft in length overall, with 4½ acres of flight deck, and have a speed well in excess of 30 knots from their four nuclear-powered 260,000 shp geared steam turbines. They have to be refueled after about 900,000 miles' steaming. Their complement is 5,684.

The USS *Enterprise* is, however, 1,102 ft long, and thus still the longest warship ever built.

Most landings ■ The greatest number on an aircraft carrier in one day was 602, achieved by Marine Air Group 6 of the United States Pacific Fleet Air Force aboard the USS *Matanikau* on 25 May 1945 between 8 A.M. and 5 P.M.

Battleship ● The Aircraft Carrier USS Theodore Roosevelt was first launched in 1984 at a cost of $2·3 billion and is now based at Norfolk, VA. The 16-inch projectiles of 2,700 lb can be fired 23 miles. (Photo: US Navy)

Deepest submarine ● The *Trieste II* is one of two USN vessels able to descend 12,000 ft. It was reconstructed from the bathyscape *Trieste*, but without the Krupp-built sphere, which enabled it to descend to 35,813 ft. (Photo: US Navy)

SUBMARINES

Largest ■ The world's largest submarines are of the USSR Typhoon class. The launch of the first at the secret covered shipyard at Severodvinsk in the White Sea, USSR was announced by NATO on 23 Sep 1980. They are believed to have a dived displacement of 27,557 tons, measure 557·6 ft overall and be armed with 20 SS NX 20 missiles with a 4,800 nautical mile range, each with seven warheads. By late 1987 two others built in Leningrad, USSR were operational, each deploying 140 warheads.

The longest dived and unsupported submarine patrol is 111 days by H M Submarine *Warspite* (Cdr J. G. F. Cooke RN) in the South Atlantic from 25 Nov 1982 to 15 Mar 1983. She sailed 30,804 nautical miles.

Fastest ■ The Russian Alfa-class nuclear-powered submarines have a reported maximum speed of 42 knots plus. With use of titanium alloy, they are believed to be able to dive to 2,500 ft. A US spy satellite over Leningrad's naval yard on 8 Jun 1983 showed they were being lengthened and are now 260·1 ft long.

Deepest ■ The two USN vessels able to descend 12,000 ft are the three-man *Trieste II* (DSV I) of 340 tons (recommissioned in November 1973) and the deep submergence vessel USS *Alvin* (DSV 2). The *Trieste II* was reconstructed from the record-breaking bathyscape *Trieste*, but without the Krupp-built sphere, that enabled it to descend to 35,820 ft. (See Chapter 3, Greatest ocean descent.)

PASSENGER LINERS

Largest ■ By tonnage, the 73,192 grt Norwegian cruise ship *Sovereign of the Seas*. Built at the French shipyard Chantiers de l'Atlantique at St-Nazaire, she entered service from Miami in January 1988.

Longest ■ The *Norway*, at 70,202 grt and 1,035 ft 7½ in in overall length, with a capacity of 2,400 passengers. She was built as the *France* in 1961 and renamed after purchase in June 1979 by Knut Kloster of Norway. Her second maiden voyage was from Southampton, Hampshire, United Kingdom on 7 May 1980. Based in Miami, she is normally employed on cruises in the Caribbean. Work undertaken during an extensive refit, including two new decks during the Autumn of 1990 increased the *Norway's* tonnage to about 75,000 grt thus making her the largest, as well as the longest, passenger ship in the world.

The RMS *Queen Elizabeth* (finally 82,998 but formerly 83,673 gross tons), of the Cunard fleet,

Marine Circumnavigation Records

(Compiled by Nobby Clarke and Richard Boehmer)

Strictly speaking, a circumnavigation involves someone passing through a pair of antipodal points. Of the records listed below, only those with an asterisk against them are actually known to have met this requirement. A non-stop circumnavigation is entirely self-maintained; no water supplies, provisions, equipment or replacements of any sort may be taken aboard en route. Vessel may anchor, but no physical help may be accepted apart from passing mail or messages.

CATEGORY	VESSEL	SKIPPER	START	FINISH
* EARLIEST	*Vittoria* Expedition of Fernão de Magalhães (Ferdinand Magellan)	Juan Sebastián de Elcano or del Cano (d. 1526) and 17 crew	Seville 20 Sep 1519	San Lucar 6 Sep 1522 30,700 miles
EARLIEST WOMAN	*Etoile* (Storeship for Bougainville's *La Boudeuse*)	Crypto-female valet of M. de Commerson, named Jeanne Baret	St Malo 1766	1769 (revealed as female on Hawaii)
EARLIEST FORE-AND-AFT RIGGED VESSEL	*Union* 98 tons (Sloop)	John Boit Junior, aged 19–21, (American) and 22 crew	Newport, RI 1794 (via Cape Horn westabout)	Newport, RI 1796
EARLIEST YACHT	*Nancy Dawson* (Schooner)	Robert Shedden (British) and crew (died in Mexico, 1849)	Thames 1847	Thames 1850
EARLIEST YACHT OWNERS	*Sunbeam* 170 ft 3-masted Topsail schooner	Lord and Lady Brassey (British), passengers and crew	Cowes, Isle of Wight 1876	Cowes, Isle of Wight 1877
* EARLIEST SOLO	*Spray* 36 ¾ ft Gaff yawl	Capt Joshua Slocum, 51, (American) (a non-swimmer)	Newport, RI, via Magellan Straits 24 Apr 1895	3 Jul 1898 46,000 miles (100 mpd)
* EARLIEST TRIMARAN	*Victress* 40 ft Bermudan ketch	Nigel Tetley (British) (b. South Africa)	Plymouth 1968 (W–E via Cape Horn)	1969 (trimaran sank after circumnavigation was completed)
EARLIEST SOLO CATAMARAN	*Amon-Re* 26 ft 2 in Bermudan sloop	Alan Butler (Canadian)	Barbados 1980 (E–W via Panama)	Barbados 1986 (also smallest catamaran to circumnavigate)
EARLIEST MOTOR BOAT	*Speejacks* 98 ft	Albert Y. Gowen (American) wife and crew	New York City 1921	New York City 1922
EARLIEST SOLO MOTOR BOAT	*Mabel E. Holland* 42 ft (no sails)	David Scott Cowper (British)	Plymouth 1984 (via Panama Canal)	Plymouth 170 days 2 hr 15 min (165·7 mpd)
EARLIEST WOMAN SOLO	*Mazurek* 31 ft 2 in Bermudan sloop	Krystyna Chojnowska-Liskiewicz (Polish)	Las Palmas 28 Mar 1976 (westabout via Panama)	Tied knot 21 Mar 1978
* EARLIEST NON-STOP SOLO Port to Port	*Suhaili* 32·4 ft Bermudan ketch	Robin Knox Johnston (British)	Falmouth 14 Jun 1968	22 Apr 1969 (312 days)
EARLIEST WOMAN NON-STOP SOLO	*First Lady* 37 ft Bermudan sloop	Kay Cottee (Australian)	Sydney 1987 (W–E via Cape Horn)	Sydney 1988 (approx 127 mpd)
MOST NON-STOP SOLO CIRCUMNAVIGATIONS	*Parry Endeavour* 44 ft Bermudan sloop	Jon Sanders (Australian)	Fremantle 25 May 1986	Fremantle 13 Mar 1988 (3 circumnavigations in 657 days)
SMALLEST BOAT	*Acrohc Australis* 11 ft 10 in Bermudan sloop	Serge Testa (Australian)	Brisbane 1984	Brisbane 1987 (500 sailing days)
EARLIEST SUBMERGED	*Triton* US Submarine	Capt Edward L. Beach USN plus 182 crew	New London, Connecticut 16 Feb 1960	10 May 1960 39,708 miles
EARLIEST SOLO IN BOTH DIRECTIONS	*Solitaire* 34 ft Bermudan sloop	Leslie Thomas Powles (British)	Falmouth 1975 (E–W) Lymington 1980 (W–E)	(via Panama) Lymington 1978 (via Cape Horn) Lymington 1981
EARLIEST SOLO IN BOTH DIRECTIONS (via Cape Horn)	*Ocean Bound* 41 ft Bermudan sloop	David Scott Cowper (British)	Plymouth 1979 (W–E) Plymouth 1981 (E–W)	Plymouth 1980 Plymouth 1982
EARLIEST SOLO ROUND THREE TIMES (same yacht)	*Tarmin* 24 ft 7 in Bermudan sloop	John Sowden (American)	Various ports 1966, 1974, 1983	1970, 1977, 1986
MOST SOLO CIRCUMNAVIGATIONS	*Perie Banou* 33 ft 7 in and *Parry Endeavour* (see above)	Jon Sanders (Australian)	Fremantle 1981 Fremantle 1986	Fremantle 1982 (twice) Fremantle 1988 (thrice)
MOST CIRCUMNAVIGATIONS ALONE BY HUSBAND/WIFE	*Myonie* 36 ft Gaff ketch	Al Gehrman (American), Helen (wife) (no passengers or crew)	Florida 1961, 1966, 1972, 1979	Florida 1964, 1970, 1976, 1983
FASTEST SAIL NON-STOP W–E Solo in monohull	*Ecureuil d'Aquitaine II* 60 ft ULDB cutter	Titouan Lamazou (French)	Les Sables (VCG) 26 Nov 1989	Les Sables (via 5 capes) 16 Mar 1990 109 days 8 hr 48 min 50 sec (205·7 mpd)
* FASTEST SAIL WITH STOPS W–E Solo in multihull	*Un Autre Regard* 75 ft trimaran	Olivier de Kersauson (French)	Brest 28 Dec 1988	Brest (via 5 capes and 2 stops) 5 May 1989 125 d 19 h 32 m 33 s + 2 days in port
FASTEST SAIL WITH STOPS W–E Solo in monohull	*Crédit Agricole (III)* 60 ft ULDB cutter	Philippe Jeantot (French)	Newport, RI (BOC) 30 Aug 1986	Newport, RI (via 3 capes and 3 stops) 7 May 1987 134 d 5 h 23 m 56 s + 115 d 17 h 26 m in port
* FASTEST SAIL WITH STOPS W–E Non-solo in monohull	*UBS Switzerland* 80 ft IOR sloop	Pierre Fehlmann (Swiss)	Portsmouth (WRWR) 28 Sep 1985	Portsmouth (via 4 capes and 3 stops) 9 May 1986 117 d 14 h 31 m 42 s + 105 d 5 h 49 m 58 s in port
FASTEST SAIL WITH STOP W–E Clippership	*James Baines* 266 ft 3-masted ship	Charles McDonnell (British)	Liverpool 10 Dec 1854	Liverpool (via Melbourne) 20 May 1855 133 days + 28 days in port
FASTEST SAIL WITH STOPS E–W Solo in monohull	*Ocean Bound* 41 ft Bermudan sloop	David Scott Cowper (British)	Plymouth 22 Sep 1981	Plymouth (via 5 capes and 3 stops) 17 May 1982 221 days + 16 days in port

Eduard Roditi, author of *Magellan of the Pacific*, advances the view that Magellan's slave, Enrique, was the first circumnavigator. He had been purchased in Malacca and it was shown that he already understood the Filipino dialect Vizayan, when he reached the Philippines from the east. He 'tied the knot' off Limasawa on 28 Mar 1521. The first to circumnavigate in both directions was Capt Tobias Furneaux, RN (1735–81) as second lieutenant aboard the *Dolphin* from/to Plymouth, United Kingdom east to west via the Magellan Straits from 1766–68 and as captain of the *Adventure* from/to Plymouth, United Kingdom west to east via Cape Horn in 1772–4. ULDB = Ultra-light displacement boat. VCG = Vendée Globe Challenge Race. BOC = British Oxygen Corp. Challenge Around Alone Race. IOR = International Offshore Rule. WRWR = Whitbread Round World Race. All mileages are nautical miles.

TRANSATLANTIC MARINE RECORDS

(Compiled by Nobby Clarke and Richard Boehmer)

CATEGORY	VESSEL	SKIPPER	START	FINISH	DURATION	DATE
EARLIEST CRUISE	Lively 140-ton Brig	Shuttleworth (British) guests + 25 crew	UK Hudson Bay	Florida UK	420 days	1783–84
EARLIEST SOLO SAILING E–W	15-ton gaff sloop	Josiah Shackford (American)	Bordeaux, France	Surinam (Guiana)	35 days	1786
EARLIEST ROWING	Ship's boat c. 20 ft	John Brown & 5 British deserters from garrison	St Helena (10 Jun)	Belmonte, Brazil (fastest ever row)	28 days (83 mpd)	1799
EARLIEST CROSSING (2 men)	Charter Oak 43 ft	C. R. Webb & 1 crew (American)	New York	Liverpool	35 days 15 hr	1857
EARLIEST TRIMARAN (Raft)	Non Pareil 25 ft	John Mikes & 2 crew (American)	New York	Southampton	51 days	1868
EARLIEST SOLO SAILING W–E	Centennial 20 ft	Alfred Johnson (American)	Shag Harbor, ME.	Wales	46 days	1876
EARLIEST WOMAN (with US husband)	New Bedford 20 ft (Bermudan ketch)	Mrs Joanna Crapo (b. Scotland) (Thomas Crapo)	Chatham, MA.	Newlyn, Cornwall	51 days (Earliest with Bermudan rig)	1877
EARLIEST SINGLE-HANDED RACE	Sea Serpent 15 ft	J. W. Lawlor (American) (winner)	Boston (21 Jun)	Coverack, Cornwall	45 days	1891
EARLIEST ROWING BY 2 MEN (fastest 2-crew)	Fox 18 ½ ft	Georg Harboe & Frank Samuelsen (Norwegian)	New York (6 Jun)	Isles of Scilly (1 Aug)	55 days (56 mpd) (see solo rows)	1897
EARLIEST MOTOR-BOAT	Abiel Abbott Low 38 ft (Engine: 10hp kerosene)	William C. Newman (American) Edward (son)	New York	Falmouth	36 days (83·3 mpd)	1902
EARLIEST OUTBOARD	Trans-Atlantic 26 ft (2·65 hp Evinrudes)	Al Grover (American) Dante (son)	St Pierre, NF (via Azores)	Lisbon	34 days (88 mpd approx)	1985
EARLIEST CANOE (with sail)	Deutscher Sport 21 ½ ft	Franz Romer (German)	Las Palmas	St Thomas	58 days (47 mpd)	1928
EARLIEST WOMAN SOLO E–W	Felicity Ann 23 ft	Ann Davison (British)	Las Palmas (20 Nov 1952)	Dominica	65 days	1952–53
EARLIEST WOMAN SOLO W–E	Lugger 18 ft	Gladys Gradeley (American)	Nova Scotia	Hope Cove, Devon	60 days	1903
EARLIEST WOMAN SOLO (both directions)	Ultima Ratio 35 ft (trimaran)	Ingeborg von Heister (German)	Las Palmas Bermuda	Barbados Gibraltar	33 days 46 days	1969 1970
EARLIEST WOMAN SOLO (across 2 oceans)	Zama Zulu 43 ft (ferroconcrete hull)	Anna Woolf (South African)	Cape Town	Bowling, Scotland	8,920 miles in 109 days	1976
SMALLEST W–E	God's Tear 8 ft 11 in	Wayne Dickinson (American)	Allerton, Mass. (30 Oct)	Aranmore Is. NW Ireland (20 Mar)	142 days	1982–83
SMALLEST E–W (Southern)	Toniky-Nou 5 ft 10 ½ in (barrel)	Eric Peters (British)	Las Palmas (25 Dec)	St Françoise, Guadeloupe (8 Feb)	46 days	1982–83
OLDEST SOLO ROWING	Khaggavisana 19 ¾ ft	Sidney Genders (51 years) (British)	Penzance, Cornwall	Miami, Florida via Antigua	160 days 8 hr	1970
YOUNGEST SOLO ROWING	Finn Again 20 ft 6 in	Sean Crowley (25 years 306 days) (British)	Halifax, NS (17 Jun)	Co. Galway (21 Sep)	95 days 22 hr	1988
EARLIEST ROW BOTH DIRECTIONS	QE III 19 ft 10 in	Don Allum (British)	Canaries St John's, NF	Nevis Ireland	114 days 77 days	1986 1987
EARLIEST SOLO ROWING E–W	Britannia 22 ft	John Fairfax (British)	Las Palmas (20 Jan)	Ft Lauderdale, Florida (19 Jul)	180 days	1969
EARLIEST SOLO ROWING W–E	Super Silver 20 ft	Tom McClean (Irish)	St John's, NF	Black Sod Bay, Ireland (27 Jul)	70·7 days	1969
YOUNGEST SOLO SAILING	Sea Raider 35 ft	David Sandeman (British) (17 years 176 days)	Jersey, CI	Newport, RI	43 days	1976
OLDEST SOLO SAILING	Tawny Pipit 25 ft	Stefan Szwarnowski (British) (76 years 165 days)	New Jersey (2 Jun)	Bude (13 Aug)	72 days	1989
SMALLEST RAFT	L'Egaré 17 ft (Cedar logs)	Henri Beaudout (French) & 2 crew	Halifax, NS	Falmouth	87 days	1956
FASTEST POWER W–E	Gentry Eagle 110 ft	Tom Gentry (American)	Ambrose Light Tower 1349 BST 24 Jul 1989	Bishop Rock Light 0356 BST 27 Jul 1989	2 days 14 hr 7 min 47 sec (45·7 knots smg)	1989
FASTEST SAIL W–E Non-solo in multihull	Jet Services 5 75 ft catamaran	Serge Madec (French)	Ambrose Light Tower 24 May 1988	Lizard Lighthouse 31 May 1988	7 days 6 hr 30 min (16·6 knots smg)	1988
FASTEST SAIL W–E Non-solo in monohull	Phocea 243 ft ULDB schooner	Philippe Morinay (French)	Ambrose Light Tower 26 Jun 1988	Lizard Lighthouse 3 Jul 1988	8 days 3 hr 29 min (14·8 knots smg)	1988
FASTEST SAIL W–E Solo in multihull	Ericsson 74 ft catamaran	Bruno Peyron (French)	Ambrose Light Tower 7 Apr 1987	Lizard Lighthouse 19 Apr 1987	11 days 11 hr 4 min (10·5 knots smg)	1987
FASTEST SAIL W–E Clippership	Red Jacket 251 ft 3-masted ship	Asa Eldridge (American)	Sandy Hook, NJ 11 Jan 1854	Liverpool Bar 23 Jan 1854	12 days (approx 260 mpd ave.)	1854
FASTEST SAIL E–W Non-solo in multihull	Royale (II) 85 ft catamaran	Loic Caradec (French)	Plymouth (2STAR) 8 Jun 1986	Newport, RI 21 Jun 1986	13 days 6 hr 12 min 30 sec (9·1 knots smg)	1986
FASTEST SAIL E–W Non-solo in monohull	Faram Serenissima 67 ft ULDB sloop	Bruno Bacilieri (Italian)	Plymouth (2STAR) 6 Jun 1981	Newport, RI 22 Jun 1981	16 days 1 hr 25 min (7·5 knots smg)	1981
FASTEST SAIL E–W Solo in multihull	Fleury Michon (IX) 60 ft trimaran	Philippe Poupon (French)	Plymouth (STAR) 5 Jun 1988	Newport, RI 15 Jun 1988	10 days 9 hr 15 min 9 sec (11·6 knots smg)	1988
FASTEST SAIL E–W Solo in monohull	Thursday's Child 60 ft ULDB cutter	Warren Luhrs (American)	Plymouth (STAR) 2 Jun 1984	Newport, RI 19 Jun 1984	16 days 22 hr 27 min (7·1 knots smg)	1984
FASTEST SAIL E–W Clippership	Andrew Jackson 220 ft 3-masted ship	W.S. Johnson (American)	Liverpool 3 Nov 1860	New York 18 Nov 1860	15 days (approx 210 mpd ave.)	1860

N.B. ULDB = Ultra-light displacement boat. All mileages are nautical miles. STAR and 2STAR are Transatlantic races. smg = speed made good.

was the largest passenger vessel ever built and had the largest displacement of any liner in the world. She had an overall length of 1,031 ft, was 118 ft 7 in in breadth and was powered by steam turbines that developed 168,000 hp. Her last passenger voyage ended on 15 Nov 1968. In 1970 she was removed to Hong Kong to serve as a floating marine university and renamed *Seawise University*. She was burned out on 9 Jan 1972 when three *simultaneous* outbreaks of fire strongly pointed to arson. The gutted hull had been cut up and removed by 1978. *Seawise* was a pun on the owner's initials — C. Y. Tung (1911–82).

TANKERS

Largest ■ The largest tanker and ship of any kind in service is the 611,832·7-ton deadweight *Hellas Fos*, a steam turbine tanker built in 1979. Of 254,583 gross registered tonnage and 227,801 net registered tonnage, she is Greek-owned by the Bilinder Marine Corporation of Athens.

The *Happy Giant*, formerly the *Seawise Giant*, is 622,511·7 tons deadweight. She is 1,504 ft long overall, with a beam of 225 ft 11 in, and has a draught of 80 ft 9 in. She was lengthened by Nippon Kokan in 1980 by adding an 265-ft 8-in midship section. She was attacked by Iraqi Mirage jets off Larak Island in the Persian Gulf on 22 Dec 1987 and was severely damaged in another attack on 14 May 1988. Despite severe damage, she has been bought by an owner in Norway, and is to be returned to service after refitting in South Korea. A new diesel engine in place of her steam turbines will result in her deadweight tonnage being reduce to approximately 420,000.

CARGO VESSELS

Largest ■ Carrying dry cargo is the Norwegian ore carrier *Berge Stahl* of 402,082·6 tons dwt, built in South Korea for the Norwegian owner Signora Bergesen. It has a length of 1,125 ft, a beam measuring 208 ft and was launched on 5 Nov 1986.

Largest whale factory ■ The USSR's *Sovietskaya Ukraina* (35,878 tons), with a summer deadweight of 51,519 tons, was completed in October 1959. She is 714½ ft in length and 84 ft 7 in in the beam.

Barges ■ The world's largest RoRo (roll-on, roll-off) ships are four El Rey class barges of 18,408 tons and 580 ft in length. They were built by the FMC Corp of Portland, OR and are operated by Crowley Maritime Corp of San Francisco between Florida and Puerto Rico with tri-level lodging of up to 376 truck-trailers.

Largest containership ■ Shipborne containerization began in 1955 when the tanker *Ideal X* was converted by Malcom McLean. She carried containers only on deck.

The 12 built for United States Lines in Korea in 1984–85 are capable of carrying 4,482 TEU (20-ft equivalent units—20-ft containers) and have a gross tonnage of 57,075. They were named *American Alabama, California, Illinois, Kentucky* etc. Following the financial collapse of United States Lines, the fleet was sold and the 12 ships now have names such as *Sea-Land Atlantic, Sea-Land Achiever, Commitment, Integrity* etc, while others carry names either with the prefix 'Nedlloyd' (*Nedlloyd Holland*) or the suffix 'Bay' (*Galveston Bay*). Their new owners have decided to limit their capacity to 3,456 TEU in normal operation. American President Lines has built three ships in Germany, *Presidents Adams, Jackson* and *Polk,* which are termed post-

Panamax, being the first container vessels built too large for transit of the Panama Canal. They are 902·69 ft in length and 129·29 ft in beam; the maximum beam for the Panama transit is 105·97 ft. These vessels have a quoted capacity of 4,300 TEU; they have in fact carried in excess of this in normal service.

Most powerful tugs ■ The *Nikolay Chiker* and *SB–134,* commissioned in April/May 1989, built by Hollming Ltd of Sweden to V/O Sudoiport, USSR, of 24,480 horsepower and 250 tons bollard pull at full power, is 324·80 ft long and 63·81 ft wide.

Largest car ferries ■ The world's largest car and passenger ferry is the 46,398 grt *Cinderella,* which entered service across the Baltic between Helsinki, Finland and Stockholm, Sweden in 1989. Operated by the Viking Line, she can carry 2,500 passengers and 480 cars or 60 buses.

Fastest ■ The 24,065 grt gas turbine-powered *Finnjet.* Built in 1977, it operates in the Baltic between Helsinki, Finland and Travemunde, West Germany and is capable of exceeding 30 knots.

Largest rail ferry ■ The 9,700-dwt 21-knot *Railship II* went into service on the Baltic run in November 1984. She can carry 65 ft 7 in long railcars, is 611 ft 10 in overall and was built for HM Gehrckens of Hamburg, West Germany.

Largest propeller ■ The largest propeller ever made is the triple-bladed screw of 36-ft 1-in diameter made by Kawasaki Heavy Industries on 17 Mar 1982 for the 233,787-ton bulk carrier *Hoei Maru* (now renamed *New Harvest*).

Largest hydrofoil ■ The 212-ft long *Plainview* (347 tons full load) naval hydrofoil was launched by the Lockheed Shipbuilding and Construction Co at Seattle, WA on 28 June 1965. She has a service speed of 50 knots.

Three 185-ton Supramar PTS 150 Mk III hydrofoils carry 250 passengers at 40 knots across the Öre Sound between Malmö and Copenhagen. They were built by Westermoen Hydrofoil Ltd of Mandal, Norway.

A 560-ton wing ground effect vehicle capable of carrying 1,008 tons has been reported in the USSR.

River boat ■ The world's largest inland boat is the 382-ft *Mississippi Queen* designed by James

Gardner of London, United Kingdom. The vessel was commissioned on 25 Jul 1976 in Cincinatti, OH and is now in service on the Mississippi River.

Fastest building ■ The fastest times in which complete ships of more than 10,000 tons were ever built were achieved at Kaiser's Yard, Portland, OR during the wartime program for building 2,742 Liberty ships in 18 yards from 27 Sep 1941. In 1942 No. 440, named *Robert E. Peary,* had her keel laid on 8 November, was launched on 12 November and was operational after 4 days 15 ½ hr on 15 November. She was broken up in 1963.

Most powerful icebreakers ■ The most powerful purpose-built icebreaker is the 28,000 ton, 460-ft long *Rossiya,* powered by 75,000 hp nuclear engines, built in Leningrad, USSR and completed in 1985.

A $Can 500 million, 100,000 hp 636-ft long Polar icebreaker of the Class 8 was ordered by the Canadian Government in October 1985.

The largest *converted* icebreaker was the 1,007-ft long SS *Manhattan* (43,000 shp), which was converted by the Humble Oil Co into a 168,000-ton icebreaker with an armored prow 69 ft 2 in long. She made a double voyage through the Northwest Passage in arctic Canada from 24 Aug to 12 Nov 1969.

The Northwest Passage was first navigated by Roald Engebereth Gravning Amundsen (Norway) (1872–1928) in the sealing sloop *Gjöa* on 11 Jul 1906.

Yacht *Most expensive* ■ The fitting out of the 470-ft Saudi Arabian royal yacht *Abdul Aziz,* built in Denmark, was completed on 22 Jun 1984 at Vospers Yard, Hampshire, United Kingdom. It was estimated in September 1987 to be worth more than $100 million.

Longest ■ The private (non-royal) 282-ft yacht *Nabila,* originally costing some $29 million. She was sold in September 1987 by the Sultan of Brunei to New York property dealer Donald

Most expensive yacht ● The 470 ft royal yacht owned by the King of Saudi Arabia *Abdul Aziz* built in Denmark is estimated to be worth more than $100 million. (Photo: Gamma/Siccoli.)

TRANSPACIFIC AND OTHER MARINE RECORDS

(Compiled by Nobby Clarke and Richard Boehmer)

CATEGORY	VESSEL	SKIPPER	START	FINISH	DURATION	DATE
EARLIEST SOLO (Woman)	*Sea Sharp II* 31 ft	Sharon Sites Adams (American)	Yokohama, Japan	San Diego, CA.	75 days (5,911 miles)	1969
EARLIEST ROWING	*Britannia II* 35 ft	John Fairfax (British) Sylvia Cook (British)	San Francisco 26 Apr 1971	Hayman I., Australia 22 Apr 1972	362 days	1971–72
EARLIEST ROWING SOLO	*Hele-on-Britannia* 32 ft	Peter Bird (British)	San Francisco 23 Aug 1982	Gt Barrier Reef, Australia 14 Jun 1983	294 days *9,000 miles*	1982–83
EARLIEST SOLO (Legally Blind)	*Dark Star* 25 ft 7 in (BM Sloop)	Hank Dekker (American)	San Francisco 27 Jul 1983	Honolulu 19 Aug 1983	23 days (Braille charts, compass and loran)	1983
EARLIEST RAFT (shore to shore)	*La Balsa* 42 ft (Balsa logs)	Vital Alsar (Spanish) & 3 crew	Guayaquil Ecuador	Mooloolaba Australia	160 days	1970
FASTEST SAIL CALIFORNIA–HAWAII Non-solo in multihull	*Aikane X-5* 63 ft catamaran	Rudy Choy (American)	Los Angeles 17 Aug 1989	Honolulu 24 Aug 1989	6 days 22 hr 41 min 12 sec (13·3 knots smg)	1989
FASTEST SAIL CALIFORNIA–HAWAII Non-solo in monohull	*Merlin* 67 ft ULDB sloop	Bill Lee (American)	Los Angeles (TransPac) 2 Jul 1977	Honolulu 10 Jul 1977	8 days 11 hr 1 min 45 sec (11·0 knots smg)	1977
FASTEST SAIL CALIFORNIA–HAWAII Solo in multihull	*Bullfrog Sunblock* 40 ft trimaran	Ian Johnston (Australian)	San Francisco (SoloTP) 14 Jun 1986	Kauai 24 Jun 1986	10 days 10 hr 3 min 43 sec (8·5 knots smg)	1986
FASTEST SAIL CALIFORNIA–HAWAII Solo in monohull	*Intense* 30 ft ULDB sloop	Bill Strange (American)	San Francisco (SoloTP) 25 Jun 1988	Kauai 7 Jul 1988	11 days 15 hr 21 min (7·6 knots smg)	1988
FASTEST SAIL AUSTRALIA–HORN Clippership	*Lightning* 243 ft 3-masted ship	James Forbes (British)	Melbourne 20 Aug 1854	Cape Horn 8 Sep 1854	19 days (approx 315 mpd ave.)	1854
GOLD RUSH ROUTE Multihull	*Great American* 60 ft trimaran	Georgs Kolesnikovs (Canadian)	New York 10 Mar 1989	San Francisco 26 May 1989	76 days 23 hr 20 min (7·36 knots smg)	1989
GOLD RUSH ROUTE Monohull	*Thursday's Child* 60 ft ULDB cutter	Warren Luhrs (American)	New York 24 Nov 1988	San Francisco 12 Feb 1989	80 days 18 hr 39 min (includes 3 day stop)	1988–89
GOLD RUSH ROUTE Clippership	*Flying Cloud* 229 ft 3-masted ship	Josiah Creesy (American)	New York 21 Jan 1854	San Francisco 20 Apr 1854	88 days 19 hr (approx. 155 mpd ave.)	1854
BRITISH TEA ROUTE Solo in multihull	*Elle & Vire* 60 ft trimaran	Philippe Monnet (French)	off Foo Chow 8 Dec 1989	London 13 Feb 1990	67 days 10 hr 26 min 5 sec (8·34 knots smg)	1989–90
BRITISH TEA ROUTE Clippership	*Zingra*	W. Gould	Shanghai 26 Dec 1863	Liverpool 20 Mar 1864	85 days (approx. 165 mpd ave.)	1863–64
AROUND AUSTRALIA Multihull	*Steinlager I* 60 ft trimaran	Peter Blake (New Zealander)	Sydney (AA) 8 Aug 1988	Sydney (7 stops) 13 Oct 1988	33 days 17 hr 42 min 7 sec (+ 32 days in port)	1988
AROUND AUSTRALIA Monohull	*NBL Technovator* 53 ft ULDB sloop	Peter Neale (Australian)	Sydney (AA) 8 Aug 1988	Sydney (7 stops) 18 Oct 1988	45 days 3 hr 35 min 23 sec (+ 25 days in port)	1988
AROUND BRITISH ISLES Power	*Ilan Voyager* 70 ft trimaran	Mark Pridie (British)	Brighton 9 May 1989	Brighton 12 May 1989	3 days 0 hr 42 min (21·6 knots smg)	1989
AROUND BRITISH ISLES Multihull	*Saab Turbo* 75 ft catamaran	François Boucher (French)	Plymouth (RB & I) 18 Jun 1989	Plymouth (4 stops) 3 Jul 1989	7 days 7 hr 30 min (+ 8 days in port)	1989
AROUND BRITISH ISLES Monohull	*Voortreckker II* 60 ft ULDB sloop	Bertie Reed (South African)	Plymouth (RB & I) 10 Jul 1982	Plymouth (4 stops) 29 Jul 1982	10 days 16 hr 10 min (+ 8 days in port)	1982
ROUND THE HORN 50–50 Sailing ship	*Brenhilda* length unknown, bark	James Learmont (British)	49° 50' S 65° 05' W noon 9 Jul 1902	50° 20' S 75° 44' W noon 14 Jul 1902	5 days 1 hr	1902
BEST DAY'S RUN Non-solo in multihull	*Formule TAG* 80 ft catamaran	Mike Birch (Canadian)	49·181° N 40·424° W 2259 GMT 25 Aug 1984	52·170° N 27·796° W 2241 GMT 26 Aug 1984	511·7 nm/23 hr 42 min (21·6 knots smg)	1984
BEST DAY'S RUN Non-solo in monohull	*Phocea* 243 ft ULDB schooner	Philippe Morinay (French)	during transatlantic record run in 1988		490 nm/24 hr (20·4 knots smg)	1988
BEST DAY'S RUN Non-solo in monohull, < 200 ft	*Fortuna Extra Lights* 77 ft ULDB sloop	Jose Santana (Spanish)	48° 11' S 70° 15' E 1338 GMT 16 Nov 1989	45° 35' S 79° 23' E 1316 GMT 17 Nov 1989	405·4 nm (GCD)/23 hr 38 min (17·2 knots smg)	1989
BEST DAY'S RUN Solo in multihull	*Laiterie Mont St Michel* 60 ft trimaran	Olivier Moussy (French)	50° 13' N 11° 30' W 1818 GMT 6 Jun 1988	48° 18' N 23° 30' W 2117 GMT 7 Jun 1988	430·8 nm (GCD)/24 hr (18·0 knots smg)	1988
BEST DAY'S RUN Clippership	*Champion of the Seas* 252 ft 3-masted ship	Alex Newlands (British)	47° 01' S 88° 31' E noon 11 Dec 1854	49° 58' S 99° 15' E noon 12 Dec 1854	461·5 nm (GCD)/23 hr 17 min (19·8 knots smg)	1854
BEST DAY'S RUN Sailboard	*Fanatic board* Gaastra sail	Françoise Canetos (French)	Sète, France 13 Jul 1988	14 Jul 1988	227 nm/24 hr (9·46 knots smg)	1988
ENGLISH CHANNEL 2 X Multihull	*Fleury Michon (VIII)* 75 ft trimaran	Philippe Poupon (French)	Calais Dec 1986	Calais via Dover Dec 1986	2 hr 21 min 57 sec (18·6 knots smg)	1986
ENGLISH CHANNEL 2 X Sailboard	*Hi Fly Board* Gaastra sail	Pascal Maka (French)	Cape Blanc-Nez 1985	Cape Gris-Nez via Dover 1985	1 hr 59 min 57 sec (18·5 knots smg)	1985
ONE NAUTICAL MILE Multihull	*Crédit Agricole (II)* 74 ft catamaran	Philippe Jeantot (French)	Martinique January 1985		2 min 13 sec (27·1 knots smg)	1985

N.B.—The earliest single-handed Pacific crossings were achieved East–West by Bernard Gilboy (American) in 1882 in the 18 ft double-ender *Pacific* to Australia and West–East by Fred Rebel (Latvia) in the 18 ft Elaine, (from Australia) and Edward Miles (American) in the 36 ¾ ft Sturdy II (from Japan) both in 1932, the latter via Hawaii. ULDB = Ultra-light displacement boat. AA = Around Australia Race. RB & I = Round Britain & Ireland Race. GCD = Great circle distance. smg = speed made good. All mileages are nautical miles.

J. Trump (b. 1946) for close to this price and renamed *Trump Princess.* Her original owner was Adnan Kashoggi, who installed a helicopter pad and an operating theater.

Dredger most powerful ■ The 468·4-ft long *Prins der Nederlanden* of 10,586 grt can dredge 19,700 tons of sand from a depth of 115 ft via two suction tubes in less than an hour.

Wooden ship Heaviest ■ The *Richelieu,* 333 ⅔ ft long and 8,534 tons was launched in Toulon, France on 3 Dec 1873.

HM battleship *Lord Warden,* completed in 1869, displaced 7,940 tons.

Longest ■ Of modern wooden ships ever built the longest was the New York-built *Rochambeau* (1867–72), formerly the *Dunderberg,* measuring 377 ft 4 in overall.

It should be noted that the biblical length of Noah's ark was 300 cubits or, at 18 in to a cubit, 450 ft.

Largest human-powered ■ The giant ship *Tessarakonteres,* a three-banked catamaran galley with 4,000 rowers, built for Ptolemy IV c. 210 B.C. in Alexandria, Egypt, measured 420 ft with up to eight men to an oar of 38 cubits (57 ft) in length.

Longest canoe ■ The 117-ft long 20-ton Kauri wood Maori war canoe *Nga Toki Matawhaorua* was built by adzes at Kerikeri Inlet, New Zealand in 1940 for a crew of 70 or more.

The 'Snake Boat' *Nadubhagóm,* 135 ft long, from Kerala, southern India, has a crew of 109 rowers and nine 'encouragers.'

SAILING SHIPS

Largest ■ The largest vessel ever built in the era of sail was the *France II* (5,806 gross tons), launched at Bordeaux, France in 1911. The *France II* was a steel-hulled, five-masted barque (square-rigged on four masts and fore-and-aft rigged on the aftermost mast). Her hull measured 418 ft overall. Although principally designed as a sailing vessel with a stump topgallant rig, she was also fitted with two steam engines. She was wrecked off New Caledonia on 13 Jul 1922.

The only seven-masted sailing schooner ever built was the 375·6-ft long *Thomas W. Lawson* (5,218 gross tons) built at Quincy, MA in 1902 and wrecked off the Isles of Scilly, United Kingdom on 15 Dec 1907.

Largest in service ■ Is the 385½-ft *Sedov* built in 1921 in Kiel and used for training in the USSR. She is 48 ft in width and has a sail area of

45,123 ft² and a displacement of 6,300 tons and gross registered tonnage of 3,556 tons.

The world's only surviving First Rate Ship-of-the-Line is the Royal Navy's 104-gun battleship HMS *Victory,* laid down at Chatham, Kent, United Kingdom on 23 Jul 1759 and constructed from the wood of some 2,200 oak trees. She bore the body of Admiral Nelson from Gibraltar to Portsmouth, arriving 44 days after serving as his victorious flagship at the Battle of Trafalgar of 21 Oct 1805. In 1922 she was moved to No 2 dock, Portsmouth—site of the world's oldest graving dock. The length of her cordage (both standing and running rigging) is 19·12 miles.

Oldest active ■ The oldest active square-rigged sailing vessel in the world is the restored *SV Maria Asumpta,* formerly the *Ciudad de Inca,* built near Barcelona, Spain in 1858. She is 125 ft overall with a grt of 142·3 tons. She was restored in 1981–82 and is used for film work, promotional appearances at regattas and sail training. She is operated by The Friends of *Maria Asumpta* of Lenham, Kent, United Kingdom.

Longest ■ The longest is the 613-ft long French-built *Club Med 1,* with five aluminum masts. The 2,500-ft² polyester sails are computer-controlled. It is operated as a Caribbean cruise vessel for 425 passengers for Club Med.

Largest junks ■ The largest on record was the seagoing *Cheng Ho,* flagship of Admiral Cheng Ho's 62 treasure ships, of c. 1420, with a displacement of 3,472 tons and a length variously estimated up to 538 ft, and believed to have had nine masts.

A river junk 361 ft long, with treadmill-operated paddle wheels, was recorded in A.D. 1161.

In c. A.D. 280 a floating fortress 600 ft square, built by Wang Zhün on the Yangtze, took part in the Qin-Wu river war. Present-day junks do not, even in the case of the Jiangsu traders, exceed 170 ft in length.

Longest day's run under sail ■ Calculated for any commercial vessel under sail the longest day's run was one of 462 nautical miles by the clipper *Champion of the Seas* (3,048·7 tons) of the Liverpool Black Ball Line running before a

> **Largest sailing ship** ● The *Sedov* is the largest, measuring 385 ½ ft in length. She was launched in 1921 and used for training in the USSR with a full crew of 65 and 120 officer trainees. She is 48 ft in width and has a sail area of 45,123 ft². (Photo: Gamma/Caoudal)

Tallest single masted yacht ● The *Velsheda,* a Class J sailing vessel measures from heel fitting to the mast truck 169 ft 3 in in height.

northwesterly gale in the south Indian Ocean under the command of Capt Alex Newlands in 1854. The elapsed time between the fixes was 23 hr 17 min, giving an average of 19·97 knots (see Chapter 11, Yachting for sporting record).

Largest sails ■ Sails are known to have been used for marine propulsion since 3500 B.C. The largest spars ever carried were those in H.M. Battleship *Temeraire,* completed at Chatham, Kent, United Kingdom, on 31 Aug 1877. She was broken up in 1921. The fore and main yards measured 115 ft in length. The foresail contained 5,100 ft of canvas, weighing 2·23 tons and the total sail area was 25,000 ft².

H.M. Battleship *Sultan* was ship-rigged when completed at Chatham, Kent, United Kingdom on 10 Oct 1871 and carried 34,100 ft² of sails plus 15,300 ft² of stunsails. She was broken up in 1946.

Tallest mast ■ The *Velsheda,* a J-Class sailing vessel is the tallest known single-masted yacht in the world. Measured from heel fitting to the mast truck she is 169¼ ft in height. Built in 1933, the second of the four British J-Class yachts, she was unusual in that she was the only one ever built that was not intended to race for the America's Cup. With a displacement of 160 tons, she supports a sail area of 80,731·97 ft.

Largest wreck ■ The 312,186 dwt VLCC (Very Large Crude Carrier) *Energy Determination* blew up and broke in two in the Straits of Hormuz on 12 Dec 1979. Her full value was $58 million.

The largest wreck removal was carried out in 1979 by Smit Tak International, which removed the remains of the French tanker *Betelguese,* 120,000 tons, from Bantry Bay, Ireland, within 20 months.

Most massive collision ■ The closest approach to an irresistible force striking an immovable object occurred on 16 Dec 1977, 22 miles off the coast of southern Africa, when the tanker *Venoil* (330,954 dwt) struck her sister ship *Venpet* (330,869 dwt).

OCEAN CROSSINGS

Earliest Atlantic ■ The earliest crossing of the Atlantic by a power vessel, as opposed to an auxiliary-engined sailing ship, was a 22-day voyage begun in April 1827, from Rotterdam, Netherlands to the West Indies, by the *Curaçao*. She was a 127-ft wooden paddle boat of 490·5 tons, built as the *Calpe* in Dover, Kent, United Kingdom in 1826 and purchased by the Dutch Government for the West Indian mail service.

The earliest Atlantic crossing entirely under steam (with intervals for desalting the boilers) was by HMS *Rhadamanthus,* from Plymouth, Devon, United Kingdom to Barbados in 1832.

The earliest crossing under continuous steam power was by the condenser-fitted packet ship *Sirius,* 787 tons, from Queenstown (now Cóbh), Ireland to Sandy Hook, NJ, in 18 days 10 hr, on 4–22 Apr 1838.

Fastest Atlantic ■ This was made by the *United States* (then 51,988, now 38,216, gross tons), former flagship of the United States Lines. On her maiden voyage between 3 and 7 Jul 1952 from New York to Le Havre, France and Southampton, United Kingdom, she averaged 35·39 knots, or for 3 days 10 hr 40 min (6:36 P.M. GMT, 3 July to 5:16 A.M., 7 July) on a route of 2,949 nautical miles from the Ambrose Light Vessel to the Bishop Rock Light, Isles of Scilly, United Kingdom. During this run, on 6–7 Jul 1952, she steamed the greatest distance ever covered by any ship in a day's run (24 hr) —868 nautical miles, hence averaging 36·17 knots. The maximum speed attained from her 240,000-shp engines was 38·32 knots in trials on 9–10 Jun 1952.

Fastest Pacific ■ From Yokohama to Long Beach, CA (4,840 nautical miles) in 6 days 1 hr 27 min (30 Jun–6 Jul 1973) by the containership *Sea-Land Commerce,* 56,353 tons, at an average of 33·27 knots.

Water speed ■ The highest speed ever achieved on water is an estimated speed of 300 knots (345 mph) by Kenneth Peter Warby (b. 9 May 1939) on the Blowering Dam Lake, New South Wales, Australia on 20 Nov 1977 in his unlimited hydroplane *Spirit of Australia.*

The official world water speed record is 277·57 knots (319·627 mph) set on 8 Oct 1978 by Warby on Blowering Dam Lake.

Fiona Countess of Arran (b. 1918) drove her 15-ft three-point hydroplane *An Stradag* (Gaelic for The Spark), to the first world water speed record for electrically propelled powerboats at a speed of 51·973 mph, at the National Water Sports Centre, Holme Pierrepoint, Nottingham, United Kingdom on 22 Nov 1989.

MERCHANT SHIPPING

Total ■ The world total of merchant shipping, excluding vessels of less than 100 gross tonnage, sailing vessels and barges, was 410,480,693 gross tonnage on 1 Jul 1989.

United States ■ As of 1 Feb 1990, there were 404 privately owned deep draught merchant ships with a gross tonnage of 1,000 or more in the United States. These ships are either ocean going or Great Lakes carriers. Their carrying capacity is 23 million dead weight tons.

Largest fleet ■ The largest merchant fleet in the world as at mid-1989 was that under the flag of Liberia, with a fleet totaling 47,892,529 gross tonnage.

PORTS

Largest ■ Physically, the largest port in the world is the Port of New York and New Jersey. The port has a navigable waterfront of 755 miles (295 miles in New Jersey), stretching over 92 miles ^{2}. A total of 261 general cargo berths and 130 other piers gives a total berthing capacity of 391 ships at one time. The total warehousing floor space is 422·4 acres.

Busiest ■ The world's busiest port and largest artificial harbor is Rotterdam-Europoort in the Netherlands, which covers 38 miles ^{2}, with 76 miles of wharfs. It handled 300·7 million tons of seagoing cargo in 1988, an increase of almost 7 percent on its 1987 figure.

Although the port of Singapore handled less tonnage, in terms of numbers of ships it was busier, with 36,000 ships calling there during 1988.

United States ■ The busiest port in the United States is New Orleans, LA, which handled 1·755 billion tons of cargo in 1988.

HOVERCRAFT (skirted air-cushion vehicles)

Fastest ■ The world's fastest warship-hovercraft is the 78-ft long 110·2-ton US Navy test vehicle SES-100B. She attained a world record 91·9 knots (105·8 mph) on 25 Jan 1980 on the Chesapeake Bay Test Range, MD. As a result of the success of this test craft, a 3,307-ton US Navy Large Surface Effect Ship (LSES) was built by Bell Aerospace under contract from the Department of Defense in 1977–81.

Longest journey ■ The longest hovercraft journey was one of 5,000 miles, under the leadership of David Smithers, through eight West African countries in a Winchester Class SRN6, between 15 Oct 1969 and 3 Jan 1970, by the British Trans-African Hovercraft Expedition.

Highest ■ The greatest altitude at which a hovercraft is operating is on Lake Titicaca, Peru,

BUSIEST AMERICAN PORTS TOP FIVE

Port	Total Tonnage
New Orleans, LA	175,500,858
New York	155,061,783
Houston, TX	124,886,883
Valdez Harbor, AK	107,144,515
Baton Rouge, LA	78,857,473

Waterborne Commerce Statistics Center, 1990

where since 1975 an HM2 Hoverferry has been hovering 12,506 ft above sea level.

Road Vehicles

COACHING

The longest horse-drawn procession was a cavalcade of 68 carriages that measured 'nose to tail' 3,018 ft, organized by the Spies Traveling Company of Denmark on 7 May 1986. It carried 810 people through the woods around Copenhagen to celebrate the coming of spring.

MOTOR CARS

Earliest automobiles *Model* ■ The earliest automobile of which there is record is a two-foot-long steam-powered model constructed by Ferdinand Verbiest (d. 1687), a Belgian Jesuit priest, and described in his *Astronomia Europaea.* His model of 1668 was possibly inspired either by Giovanni Branca's description of a steam turbine, published in his *La Macchina* in 1629, or by writings on 'fire carts' or *Nan Huai-Zen* in the Rhu dynasty (c. 800 B.C.).

Passenger-carrying ■ The earliest full-scale automobile was the first of two military steam tractors, completed at the Paris Arsenal in 1769 by Nicolas-Joseph Cugnot (1725–1804). This reached 2 ¼ mph. Cugnot's second, larger tractor, completed in May 1771, today survives in the Conservatoire nationale des arts et métiers in Paris.

The world's first passenger-carrying automobile was a steam-powered road vehicle carrying eight passengers and built by Richard Trevithick (1771–1833). It first ran on 24 Dec 1801 in Camborne, Cornwall, United Kingdom.

Internal combustion ■ The Swiss, Isaac de

Desert, NV, in his 17,000 lb thrust Rolls Royce 302 jet-powered *Thrust 2*, designed by John Ackroyd (see table).

The highest reputed land speed is 739·666 mph or Mach 1·0106 by Stan Barrett (US) in *The Budweiser Rocket*, a rocket-engined three-wheeled car at Edwards Air Force Base, CA on 17 Dec 1979 (see table).

The highest land speed recorded by a woman is 524·016 mph by Mrs Kitty Hambleton, nee O'Neil, in the 48,000-hp rocket-powered three-wheeled S.M.1 *Motivator* over the Alvard Desert, OR on 6 Dec 1976. Her official two-way record was 512·710 mph and she probably touched 600 mph momentarily.

Diesel engined ■ The prototype 230 hp 3-liter Mercedes C 111/3 attained 203·3 mph in tests on the Nardo Circuit, southern Italy on 5–15 Oct 1978, and in April 1978 averaged 195·398 mph for 12 hours, so covering a world record 2,399·76 miles.

Rocket-powered sleds ■ The highest speed recorded on ice is 247·93 mph by *Oxygen* driven by Sammy Miller (b. 15 Apr 1945) on Lake George, NY on 15 Feb 1981.

Electric car ■ The Land Speed Record was last broken in an electric car by Camille Jenatzy in *La Jamais Contente* in April 1899, with a speed of 65·79 mph over a flying kilometer in one direction. Ninety years later this was beaten by D. J. S. Lambert in a replica of the original car with a speed of 67·62 mph, on 25 Mar 1989 at RAF Elvington, North Yorkshire, United Kingdom.

Steam car ■ On 19 Aug 1985 Robert E. Barber broke the 79-year-old record for a steam car driving No 744 *Steamin' Demon*, built by the Barber-Nichols Engineering Co, 145·607 mph at Bonneville Salt Flats, UT.

Road cars ■ Various detuned track cars have been licensed for road use but are not for-sale production models. Manufacturers of very fast and very expensive models understandably limit speed tests to stipulated engine revs.

LARGEST CARS

Of cars produced for private road use, the largest was the Bugatti 'Royale' type 41, known in

---

Pedal car ● Six drivers working in shifts together with a back-up team left Marble Arch, London, United Kingdom on 27 May 1989 and pedalled their way to Dover, boarded a ferry and docked at Calais. They continued their journey until they arrived at L'Arch De Triomphe in France, having covered a distance of 249 miles in a time of 23 hr 21 min 27 sec.

Rivaz (d. 1828), built a carriage powered by his 'explosion engine' in 1805. The first practical internal-combustion-engined vehicle was that built by the British Samuel Brown (Patent 5350, 25 Apr 1826) whose 4 hp two-cylinder atmospheric gas 88-liter engined carriage climbed Shooters Hill, Blackheath, Kent, United Kingdom in May 1826.

The first successful gasoline-fueled car, the Motorwagen, built by Karl-Friedrich Benz (1844–1929) of Germany, ran at Mannheim, Germany in late 1885. It was a 3 cwt three-wheeler reaching 8–10 mph. Its single-cylinder engine (bore 3·6 in, stroke 6·3 in) delivered 0·85 hp at 400 rpm. It was patented on 29 Jan 1886. Its first 0·62 mile road test was reported in the local newspaper, the *Neue Badische Landeszeitung*, of 4 Jun 1886, under the heading 'Miscellaneous.'

Registrations *Earliest* ■ The world's first plates were probably introduced by the Parisian police in 1893.

Licence plate No 8 was sold at a Hong Kong government auction for HK$5 million on 13 Feb 1988 to Law Ting-pong, a textile manufacturer. The number 8 is considered a lucky number.

United States ■ In 1988 there were 188,187,000 cars registered in the United States. As of 1 May 1990, it was estimated that there were 193,045,000 registered cars.

FASTEST CARS

Land speed ■ The *official* one-mile land-speed record is 633·468 mph set by Richard Noble (b. 1946) on 4 Oct 1983 over the Black Rock

---

Fastest car ● The highest *tested* speed for a standard production model is 202 mph in a Lamborghini Diablo. Its satanic swiftness comes from a 5729 cc V12 engine of 492 bhp and a drag coefficient of only 0·31. (Photo: Lamborghini)

Longest car ● The ultimate in cars - owned by Jay Ohrberg of California, this 100 ft monster is made to drive as one piece or it can be made to bend in the middle. It has two cad engines and moves along with 26 wheels, among its special features are a swimming pool with diving board, a king size water bed and a helicopter landing base, plus many items which are now part of our modern technology and essentials in the office and kitchen.

Britain as the 'Golden Bugatti,' of which only six were assembled (although it is *believed* that seven were built) at Molsheim, France by the Italian Ettore Bugatti. First built in 1927, this machine has an 8-cylinder engine of 12·7 liters capacity, and measures over 22 ft in length. The bonnet is over 7 ft long.

Largest engines ■ The largest car ever used was the 'White Triplex,' sponsored by J. H. White of Philadelphia, PA. Completed early in 1928, after two years' work, the car weighed about 4·5 tons and was powered by three Liberty V12 aircraft engines with a total capacity of 81,188 cc, developing 1,500 bhp at 2,000 rpm. It was used to break the world speed record but crashed at Daytona, FL on 13 Mar 1929.

Most powerful *Production car* ■ The highest engine capacity of a production car was 824 in³, for the US Pierce-Arrow 6–66 Raceabout of 1912–18, the US Peerless 6–60 of 1912–14 and the Fageol of 1918.

The most powerful current production car is the Ferrari F40, which develops 478 hp; it is reported that approximately 770 will be built.

Heaviest ■ The heaviest car in production today (four to five made annually) appears to be the Soviet-built Zil limousine, which weighs 3·3 tons. The 'stretched' Zil used by Mikhail S. Gorbachev weighs 6·6 tons and is made of 3-inch armor-plated steel. The 8-cylinder, 7-liter engine guzzles fuel at the rate of 6 miles to the gallon.

Longest ■ A 100 ft long 26-wheeled limo was designed by Jay Ohrberg of Burbank, CA. It has many features, including a swimming pool and

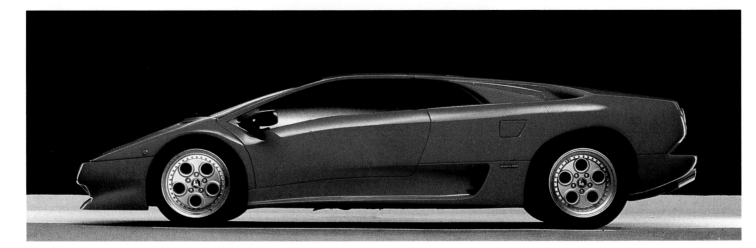

FASTEST CARS

CATEGORY	MPH	CAR	DRIVER	PLACE	DATE
JET ENGINED *official*	633·468	Thrust 2	Richard Noble (British)	Black Rock Desert, NV	4 Oct 1983
ROCKET ENGINED *official*	622·287	Blue Flame	Gary Gabelich (US)	Bonneville, UT	23 Oct 1970
*unofficial**	739·666	Budweiser Rocket	Stan Barrett (US)	Edwards Air Force Base,CA	17 Dec 1979
WHEEL DRIVEN *turbine*	429·311	Bluebird	Donald Campbell (British)	Lake Eyre, Australia	17 Jul 1964
multi piston engine	418·504	Goldenrod	Robert Summers (US)	Bonneville, UT	12 Nov 1965
single piston engine	397·996	Speed O Motive	Al Teague (US)	Bonneville, UT	9 Nov 1989

* This published speed of Mach 1·0106 is *not* officially sanctioned by the USAF whose Digital Instrumented Radar was not calibrated or certified. The radar information was *not* generated by the vehicle directly but by an operator aiming the dish by means of a TV screen. To claim a speed to six significant figures appears quite unsustainable.

diving board and a king-size water bed. It is designed to drive as one piece or it can be changed to bend in the middle. Its main purpose is for use in films and exhibitions.

CARS MISCELLANEOUS

Highest mileage ■ The highest recorded mileage for a car was 1·2 million authenticated miles by August 1978 for a 1957 Mercedes 180 D owned by Robert O'Reilly of Olympia, WA. Its subsequent fate is unknown.

Longest in production ■ The Morgan 4/4 celebrated its 54th birthday on 27 Dec 1989. Built by the Morgan Motor Car Co of Malvern, Hereford and Worcester, United Kingdom (founded 1910), there is still a four year waiting list.

Amongst mass-production models, both the Citroen 2CV and Volkswagen 'Beetle' date from 1938. The Citroen ceased production in July 1990.

Lightest ■ Louis Borsi of London, United Kingdom has built and driven a 21-lb car with a 2·5cc engine. It is capable of 15 mph.

Longest in production ● First produced in 1935 the Morgan 4/4 still employs traditional construction with a separate chassis and an ash frame clad in either sheet steel or aluminum panels. It also has a unique sliding pillar front suspension system, designed when H.S.F. Morgan built his first car in 1910. (Photo: Morgan Motor Company Ltd)

MOST EXPENSIVE

Special ■ The most expensive car ever built was the US Presidential 1969 Lincoln Continental Executive delivered to the US Secret Service on 14 Oct 1968. It has an overall length of 21 ft 6·3 in with a 13-ft 4-in wheelbase and with the addition of 2·2 tons of armor plate, weighs 6 tons (12,000 lb). The estimated cost of research, development and manufacture was $500,000, but it is rented at $5,000 per year. Even if all four tires were shot out it can travel at 50 mph on inner rubber-edged steel discs.

Carriage House Motor Cars of New York in March 1978 completed four years' work on converting a 1973 Rolls-Royce, including lengthening it by 30 in. The price tag was $500,000.

Collections ■ The unrivaled collector of Rolls-Royces was Bhagwan Shri Rajneesh (1931–90),the Indian mystic of Rajneeshpuram, OR. His disciples bestowed 93 of these upon him before his deportation in November 1985.

Used ■ The greatest price paid for any used car is £10 million in November 1989 for a red left-hand drive Ferrari 250 GTO, one of the 36 models made between 1962 and '64, built for the Le Mans 24-hour classic, although this particular car never raced. The buyer was an anomymous Japanese tycoon and the deal was made privately through Supercar International of Sutton, Surrey, United Kingdom.

United States ■ The greatest price paid for any used car in the United States is $8·1 million for the 1931 Berline de Voyage Royale, one of six Bugatti Royales, by Thomas Monaghan of Ann Arbor, MI. The car, formerly part of the William F. Harrah collection, was first sold to property developer Jerry Moore for $6·5 million when the collection was cut down from 1,700 to 1,300 cars in June 1986, then on to Mr Monaghan some months later.

Most inexpensive ■ The cheapest car of all time was the 1922 Red Bug Buckboard, built by Briggs and Stratton Co of Milwaukee, WI, listed at $150–$125. It had a 62-in wheel base and weighed 245 lb. Early models of the King Midget cars were sold in kit form for self-assembly for as little as $100 as late as 1948.

DRIVING

Around the world ■ The fastest circumnavigation embracing more than an equator's length of driving (24,901·47 road miles) is one of 69 days 19 hr 5 min by Mohammed Salauddin, *alias* Saloo Choudhury, and his wife, Neena, of Calcutta, India from 9 Sep to 17 Nov 1989 in a Hindustan 'Contessa Classic' 1989 car. Their epic journey started and finished at Delhi after traveling through six continents and 25 countries. The distance covered was 25,187·8 miles.

Manfred Müller and Paul-Ernst Luhrs drove around the world in their 1963 Citroen 2CV, covering 83 countries and 217,490 miles. They started and finished in Bremerhaven, West Germany.

Amphibious circumnavigation ■ The only circumnavigation by an amphibious vehicle was by Ben Carlin (Australia) (d. 7 Mar 1981) in an amphibious jeep, *Half-Safe*. He completed the last leg of the Atlantic crossing (the English Channel) on 24 Aug 1951. He arrived back in Montreal, Canada on 8 May 1958, having completed a circumnavigation of 39,000 miles over land and 9,600 miles by sea and river. He was accompanied on the transatlantic stage by his ex-wife Elinore (US) and on the long transpacific stage (Tokyo to Anchorage) by Broye Lafayette De-Mente (b. Missouri, 1928).

One-year duration record ■ The greatest distance ever covered in one year is 354,257 miles, by 2 Opel Rekord 2-liter passenger sedans that both covered this distance between 18 May 1988 and the same date in 1989 without any major mechanical breakdowns. The vehicles were manufactured by Delta Motor Corporation, Port Elizabeth, South Africa, and were driven on tar and gravel roads in the Northern Cape by a team of Company drivers from Delta. The entire undertaking was monitored by the Automobile Association of South Africa.

Trans-Americas ■ Garry Sowerby (Canada), with Tim Cahill (US) as co-driver and navigator, drove a 1988 GMC Sierra K3500 four-wheel-drive pickup truck powered by a 6·2 liter V8 Detroit diesel engine from Ushuaia, Tierra del Fuego, Argentina to Prudhoe Bay, AK, a distance of 14,739 miles, in a total elapsed

time of 23 days 22 hr 43 min from 29 Sep to 22 Oct 1987. The vehicle and team were surface-freighted from Cartagena, Colombia to Balboa, Panama so as to bypass the Darién Gap.

This was first traversed by the Land Rover *La Cucaracha Carinosa* (The Affectionate Cockroach) of the Trans-Darién Expedition 1959–60, crewed by Richard E. Bevir (United Kingdom) and engineer Terence John Whitfield (Australia). They left Chepo, Panama on 3 Feb 1960 and reached Quibdó, Columbia on 17 Jun, averaging 660 ft per hour of indescribable difficulty.

Cape to Cape ■ The first traverse of the world's greatest land mass (Afro-Eurasia) was achieved by Richard Pape, who left the North Cape in an Austin A90 on 28 Jul and arrived in Cape Town on 22 Oct 1955 with the milometer recording 17,500 miles after 86 days. The speed record was set by Ken Langley and Gerry Sowerby of Canada driving north in 28 days 13 hr 10 min for 12,531 miles from 4 Apr–2 May 1984.

Cape to London ■ The record time for the 11,674-mile road route from Cape Town, South Africa to London is 14 days 19 hr 26 min, set by husband-and-wife team Brig John and Dr Lucy Hemsley from 8 to 22 Jan 1983 in a Range Rover. Apart from the Channel crossing, they were the first to drive entirely overland from Cape Town, South Africa, to London, United Kingdom.

Gasoline Consumption ■ An experimental Japanese vehicle achieved the equivalent of 6,409 mpg in the Shell Mileage Marathon at Silverstone, Nothamptonshire, United Kingdom on 30 Jun 1988.

Longest fuel range ■ The greatest distance driven without refueling on a single fuel fill in a standard vehicle (40·7 gal carried in factory optional twin fuel tanks) is 1,300·9 miles by a Toyota Land Cruiser diesel pickup driven by Ewan Kennedy and Ray Barker with John Windass (Observer newspaper) from Sydney, Australia to a point on the Eyre Highway west of Wirrulla in South Australia in 31 hr 8 min in May 1988. The average speed was 41·8 mph giving 31·9 mpg .

Driving in reverse ■ Charles Creighton (1908–70) and James Hargis of Maplewood, MO drove their Ford Model A 1929 roadster in reverse from New York 3,340 miles to Los Angeles, CA from 26 Jul–13 Aug 1930 without once stopping the engine. They arrived back in New York in reverse on 5 September, so completing 7,180 miles in 42 days.

Brian 'Cub' Keene and James 'Wilbur' Wright drove their Chevrolet Blazer 9,031 miles in 37 days (1 Aug–6 Sep 1984) through 15 US states and Canada. Though it was prominently named 'Stuck in Reverse,' law-enforcement officers in Oklahoma refused to believe it and insisted they drove in reverse reverse, i.e. forwards, out of the state.

PROGRESSIVE SPEED RECORDS

Speed mph	Person and Vehicle	Place	Date
25	Sledging	Heinola, Finland	c.6500 B.C.
35	Horse-riding	Anatolia, Turkey	c.1400 B.C.
45	Mountain Sledging	Island of Hawaii (now USA)	*ante* A.D. 1500
50	Ice Yachts (earliest patent)	Netherlands	A.D. 1600
56·75	Grand Junction Railway 2–2–2: *Lucifer*	Madeley Banks, United Kingdom	13 Nov 1830
87·8	Tommy Todd, downhill skier	La Porte, CA	Mar 1873
90·0	Midland Railway 4–2–2 2·36 m *7 ft 9 in* single	Ampthill, United Kingdom	Mar 1897
130·61	Siemens and Halske electric engine	Marienfeld-Zossen, near Berlin	27 Oct 1903
c.150	Frederick H. Marriott (fl. 1957) Stanley Steamer *Wogglebug*	Ormond Beach, FL	26 Jan 1907
210·64	Sadi Lecointe (France) Nieuport-Delage 29	Villesauvage, France	25 Sep 1921
415·2	Flt Lt (Later Wing Cdr) George Hedley Stainforth AFC *Supermarine S.6B*	Lee-on-Solent, United Kingdom	29 Sep 1931
623·85	Flugkapitan Heinz Dittmar *Me. 163V–1*	Peenemunde, Germany	2 Oct 1941
670	Capt Charles Elwood Yeager, USAF *Bell XS–1*	Muroc Dry Lake, CA	14 Oct 1947
967	Capt Charles Elwood Yeager, USAF *Bell XS–1*	Muroc Dry Lake, CA	26 Mar 1948
2,905	Major Robert M. White, North American *X–15*	Muroc Dry Lake, CA	7 Mar 1961
17,560	Flt Maj Yuriy Alekseyevich Gagarin, *Vostok 1*	Earth orbit	12 Apr 1961
24,226	Col Frank Borman, USAF, Capt James Arthur Lovell, Jr, USN, Major William A. Anders, USAF *Apollo VIII*	Trans-lunar injection	21 Dec 1968
24,790·8	Cdrs Eugene Andrew Cernan and John Watts Young, USN and Col Thomas P. Stafford, USAF *Apollo X*	Re-entry after lunar orbit	26 May 1969

A complete progressive table comprising entries from prehistoric times to date was published in the 1977 edition.

—WORLD— BUS TRIP

Between 6 Nov 1988 and 3 Dec 1989
Hughie Thompson (28), John Weston (28)
and Richard Steel (27) visited 18 countries
in their red double-decker bus covering
a distance of 54,289 miles

(Photos : Hughie Thompson)

The crew in Delaware, USA

Tire changing on Autobahn, Switzerland

Roadside in Pakistan

Cappodocia, Central Turkey

New York, New York

Central Chile

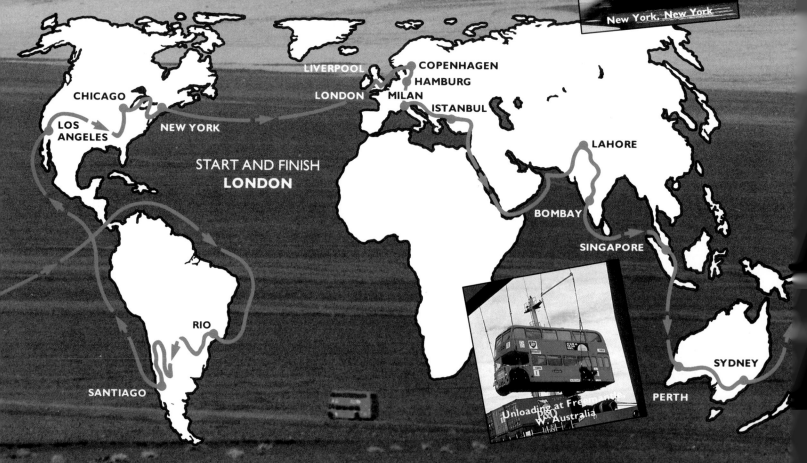

LIVERPOOL
COPENHAGEN
HAMBURG
LONDON
MILAN
ISTANBUL

CHICAGO

LOS ANGELES
NEW YORK

START AND FINISH
LONDON

LAHORE

BOMBAY

SINGAPORE

RIO

SANTIAGO

SYDNEY

PERTH

Unloading at Fremantle, W. Australia

> **Drive Round The World ●** Manfred Müller amd Paul-Ernst Luhrs spent 20 years driving their 1963 Citroen 2cv through 83 countries and covering a distance of 217,490 miles.

The highest average speed attained in any nonstop reverse drive exceeding 500 miles was achieved by Gerald Hoagland, who drove a 1969 Chevrolet Impala 501 miles in 17 hr 38 min at Chemung Speed Drome, NY on 9–10 Jul 1976 to average 28·41 mph.

Two side-wheel driving *Car* ■ Bengt Norberg (b. 23 Oct 1951) of Äppelbo, Sweden drove a Mitsubishi Colt GTi-16V on two side wheels nonstop for a distance of 192·873 miles in a time of 7 hr 15 min 50 sec; he also achieved a distance of 30·328 miles in one hour at Rattvik Horse Track, Sweden on 24 May 1989.

Carlos Cunha (34) achieved a speed of 96·836 mph on the two wheels of a Kadette GS at the Interlagos Racing Circuit in São Paulo, Brazil on 30 Apr 1989.

Truck ■ Gilbert Bataille of Paris, France drove a Leyland T45 Road Runner Truck on two wheels for a distance of 2·864 miles at the British Truck Grand Prix, Silverstone, Northamptonshire, United Kingdom on 17 Aug 1986.

Wheelie ■ Steve Murty drove a Multi-Part Skytrain truck on its rear wheels for 1,353 ⅓ ft at Mondello Park, Co. Kildare, Republic of Ireland on 23 Aug 1987. The 66-ton truck was powered by a 500 bhp Cummins turbocharged 14-liter engine and had a ZF-Ecomat hp 600 five-speed automatic gearbox.

Most durable driver ■ The Goodyear Tire and Rubber Co. test driver Weldon C. Kocich drove 3,141,946 miles from 5 Feb 1953 to 28 Feb 1986, so averaging 95,210 miles per year.

Oldest driver ■ Roy M. Rawlins (b. 10 Jul 1870) of Stockton, CA was warned for driving at 95 mph in a 55 mph zone in June 1974. On 25 Aug 1974 he was awarded a California State license valid until 1978, but Mr Rawlins died on 9 Jul 1975, one day short of his 105th birthday.

Mrs Maude Tull of Inglewood, CA who took to driving at age 91 after her husband died, was issued a renewal on 5 Feb 1976 at age 104.

Driving tests ■ The world's easiest tests have been those in Egypt, in which the ability to drive 19·64 ft forward and the same in reverse has been deemed sufficient. In 1979 it was reported that accurate reversing had been added between two rubber traffic cones. 'High cone attrition' soon led to the substitution of white lines.

SERVICES

Car parks ■ The world's largest is the West Edmonton Mall, Edmonton, Alberta, Canada, which can hold 20,000 vehicles. There are overflow facilities on an adjoining lot for 10,000 more cars.

Garage ■ The largest private garage is one of two stories built outside Bombay for the private collection of 176 cars owned by Pranlal Bhogilal (b. 1939).

The KMB Overhaul Centre operated by the Kowloon Motor Bus Co (1933) Ltd, Hong Kong, is the world's largest multistoried service center. Purpose-built for doubledecker buses, its four floors occupy in excess of 11·6 acres.

Filling stations ■ The largest concentration of pumps are 204—96 of them are Tokheim electronic Unistar and 108 are Tokheim Explorer (Mechanical)—in Jeddah, Saudi Arabia.

The highest in the world is at Leh, Ladakh, India, at 12,001 ft, operated by the Indian Oil Corporation.

Unleaded gasoline ■ Under the provisions of the Clean Air Act (1970), the Environmental Protection Agency (EPA) was given a mandate to set a timetable for the introduction of unleaded gasoline to service stations throughout the United States. On 22 Feb 1972, the EPA announced proposed regulations that required all large service stations to carry low octane 'non-leaded' gas with a maximum lead content of 0·05 grams per gallon. On 27 Dec 1972, the EPA set a deadline of 1 Jul 1974 for stations to carry 'non-leaded' gas.

Tires *Largest* ■ The world's largest ever manufactured were by the Goodyear Tire & Rubber Co. for giant dump trucks. They measure 12 ft in diameter, weigh 12,500 lb and cost $74,000. A tire 17 ft in diameter is believed to be the limitation of what is practical.

Fattest ■ The widest tire in normal production is the Pirelli P Zero, with 335/35Z5R17 dimensions.

Skid marks ■ The skid marks made by the jet-powered *Spirit of America*, driven by Norman Craig Breedlove, after the car went out of control at Bonneville Salt Flats, UT, on 15 Oct 1964, were nearly 6 miles long.

Tow ■ The longest on record was one of 4,759 miles from Halifax, Nova Scotia to Canada's Pacific coast, when Frank J. Elliott and George A. Scott of Amherst, Nova Scotia, Canada persuaded 168 passing motorists in 89 days to tow their Model T Ford (in fact engineless) to win a $1,000 bet on 15 Oct 1927.

After his 1969 MGB, TJN 405H broke down in the vicinity of Moscow, USSR, the late Eddie McGowan of Chipping Warden, Oxfordshire, United Kingdom was towed a distance 1,456 miles from Moscow to West Berlin on a 7 ft single nylon tow rope from 12–17 Jul 1987.

VEHICLES

Largest ambulance ■ The world's largest are the 59 ft ½-in long articulated Alligator Jumbulances Mark VI, VII and VIII and IX, operated by The ACROSS Trust to convey the sick and handicapped on holidays and pilgrimages across Europe. They are built by Van Hool of Belgium with Fiat engines, cost £200,000 and convey 44 patients and staff.

Crawler ■ The most massive vehicle ever constructed is the Marion eight-caterpillar crawler used for conveying *Saturn V* rockets to their launchpads at Cape Canaveral, FL. It measures 131 ft 4 in x 114 ft, and the two built cost $12,300,000. The loaded train weight is 9,000 tons.

The windshield wipers are 42-in blades and are the world's largest.

Land ■ The most massive automotive land vehicle is 'Big Muskie,' the 12,004-ton mechanical shovel built by Bucyrus Erie for the Musk mine. It is 487 ft long, 151 ft wide and 222 ft high, with a grab capacity of 364 tons.

Longest ■ The Arctic Snow Train owned by the world-famous wire-walker Steve McPeak (US) has 54 wheels and is 572 ft long. It was built by R.G. Le Tourneau Inc of Longview, TX for the US Army. Its gross train weight is 441 tons, with a top speed of 20 mph, and it was driven by a crew of six when used as an 'overland train' for the military. McPeak repaired it and every punctured wheel single-handedly in often sub-zero temperatures in Alaska. It generates 4,680 shp and has a fuel capacity of 6,522 gal.

Buses *Earliest* ■ The first municipal motor omnibus service in the world was inaugurated on 12 Apr 1903 between Eastbourne railroad station and Meads, East Sussex, United Kingdom.

Longest ■ The 23,957-lb, 76-ft articulated buses, with 121 passenger seats and room also for 66 'strap-hangers,' built by the Wayne Corporation of Richmond, IN for use in the Middle East.

The longest rigid single bus is 49 ft long, carrying 69 passengers, built by Van Hool of Belgium.

Largest fleet ■ The world's largest bus fleet is the 6,580 single-deck buses in Rio de Janeiro, Brazil.

Longest route ■ The longest regularly scheduled bus route is by 'Across Australia Coach Lines,' who inaugurated a regular scheduled service between Perth and Brisbane on 9 Apr 1980. The route is 3,389 miles, taking 75 hr 55 min.

Campers *Longest journey* ■ The continuous caravan journey of 143,716 miles by

Harry B. Coleman and Peggy Larson in a Volkswagen Camper from 20 Aug 1976 to 20 Apr 1978 through 113 countries.

Saburo Ouchi (b. 7 Feb 1942) of Tokyo, Japan drove 167,770 miles in 91 countries from 2 Dec 1969 to 10 Feb 1978.

Fastest ■ The world speed record for a camper is 124·91 mph by an Alpha 14 towed by a Le Mans Aston Martin V8 saloon driven by Robin Hamilton at RAF Elvington, North Yorkshire, United Kingdom on 14 Oct 1980.

Dump truck ■ The world's largest is the Terex Titan 33–19 manufactured by the Terex Division of General Motors Corporation. It has a loaded weight of 604·7 tons and a capacity of 350 tons. When tipping its height is 56 ft. The fuel tank holds 1,300 gal and the 16-cylinder engine delivers 3,500 hp.

Fire engine ■ The world's most powerful fire appliance is the 860 hp 8-wheel Oshkosh fire-truck used for aircraft fires. It can discharge 41,600 gal of foam through two turrets in just 150 sec. It weighs 66 tons.

Fastest ■ The fastest on record is the Jaguar XJ12 - 'Chubb Firefighter,' which on 2 Nov 1982 attained a speed of 130·57 mph in tests when servicing the *Thrust 2* land speed record trials.

Go-Karts ■ The highest mileage recorded in 24 hours on a closed circuit driven by a four-man team is 1,018 laps of a mile at Erbsville Kartway, Waterloo, Ontario, Canada. The 5-hp 140-cc Honda-engined go-kart was driven by Owen Nimmo, Gary Ruddock, Jim Timmins and Danny Upshaw on 4–5 Sep 1983.

The greatest distance recorded in a 48-hour marathon is 1,696·3 miles by Denis Wedes, Stephen Mantle, Len Nicholson and Janice Bennett, driving a Yamaha RC100SE go-kart powered by a KT100J 100 cc engine at Mount Sugarloaf Circuit, Newcastle, New South Wales, Australia on 25–27 Mar 1983.

Lawn mowers ■ The widest gang mower in the world is the 5·6-ton 60-ft wide 27-unit 'Big Green Machine' used by the sod farmer Jay Edgar Frick of Monroe, OH. It mows an acre in 60 sec.

Longest distance ■ The longest drive on a lawn mower was 3,034 miles, when Ian Ireland of Harlow, Essex, United Kingdom drove a Iseki SG 15 from Harlow, Essex to Southend Pier, United Kingdom from 13 Aug to 7 Sep 1989. He was assisted by members from 158 Round Table Luton, Bedfordshire, United Kingdom and raised over £15,000 in aid of the Leukaemia Research Fund.

Pedal car ■ The record from London, United Kingdom to the Arc de Triomphe, Paris, France, including a channel crossing by ferry, is 23 hr 21 min 27 sec, a distance of 249 miles, by six members of Lea Manor High School and Community College, Luton, Bedfordshire, United Kingdom on 27–28 May 1989.

Snowmobiles ■ Tony Lenzini of Duluth, MN, drove his 1986 Arctic Cat Cougar snowmobile a total of 7,211 miles in 60 riding days between 28 Dec 1985 and 20 Mar 1986.

Solar powered ■ The highest speed attained by a solely solar-powered land vehicle is 48·71 mph by Molly Brennan driving the General Motors *Sunraycer* at Mesa, AZ on 24 Jun 1988. On the same day *Sunraycer* also attained a top speed of 80·2 mph, using both solar and battery power. In November 1987 *Sunraycer* won the 1,950 mile solar challenge race in Australia,

Longest taxi fare ● On 19 Aug 1988 a taxi with passengers set off from Buckingham Palace, London, United Kingdom, to start the longest journey. After travelling through 14 countries and covering a distance of 13,670 miles, they arrived at Sydney Opera House in Australia on 27 October having raised £250,000 along the way for charities. The fare on the meter read an amazing £31,446. (Photo: Paul Chelow)

finishing two and a half days ahead of its nearest competitor.

Taxis ■ The largest taxi fleet is that in Mexico City, Mexico, with 60,000 'normal' taxis, *pesaros* (communal fixed route taxis) and *settas* (airport taxis).

The city with the largest taxi fleet in the United States is New York City, which on 1 May 1990 had 11,787 registered yellow medallion cabs and 42,000 drivers. There are approximately another 40,000 driver hire car services vehicles in New York City.

The longest fare on record is £31,446—13,670 miles with the meter running. Ned Kelly and a team of five, including taxi driver Guy Smith, left London on 19 Aug 1988 traveling through 14 countries and arrived in Australia on 27 Oct 1988. A sum of £ 250,000 was raised for charities in Ireland, the United Kingdom, Singapore and Australia.

Oldest taxi driver ■ Carmen Fasanella (b. 19 Feb 1903) was continuously licensed as a taxicab owner and driver in the Borough of Princeton, NJ for 68 years 243 days from 1 Feb 1921 to 2 Nov 1989.

Tractor ■ The world's largest tractor is the $459,000 US Department of Agriculture Wide Tractive Frame Vehicle completed by Ag West of Sacramento, CA in June 1982. It measures 33 ft between its wheels, which are designed to run on permanent paths, and weighs 24·5 tons.

The sport of tractor-pulling was put on a national US championship basis in 1967 at Bowl-

ing Green, OH, where the winner was 'The Purple Monster' built and driven by Roger E. Varns. Today there are 12 classes ranging up to '12,200 lb unlimited.'

Trams ■ *Longest journey* ■ The longest now possible is from Krefeld St Tönis to Witten Annen Nord, West Germany. With luck at the eight interconnections the 65·5 mile trip can be achieved in 5½ hr.

By late 1987 there were more than 320 tramway systems surviving of which the most extensive is that of Leningrad, USSR, with 2,500 cars on 53 routes.

Most powerful truck ■ A 1987 Ford L T L 9000 truck, owned and driven by Ken Warby of Cincinnati, OH, is equipped with a General Electric J 79 tuned to produce 20,000 lbf of thrust. Weighing 4·8 tons, it has achieved 210·2 mph in 7·7 sec over a quarter-mile standing start.

Wrecker ■ The world's most powerful wrecker is the Twin City Garage and Body Shop's 22·7-ton 36-ft long 1969 International M6-23 'Hulk' stationed at Scott City, MO. It can lift in excess of 325 tons on its short boom.

ROAD LOADS

Heaviest load ■ On 14–15 Jul 1984 John Brown Engineers & Contractors BV moved the Conoco Kotter Field production deck with a roll-out weight of 325 tons for the Continental Netherlands Oil Company of Leidsenhage, Netherlands.

MODEL CAR

Nonstop duration ■ A scalextric Jaguar X58 ran nonstop for 866 hr 7 min 55 sec and covered a distance of 1,762·8 miles from 2 May to 7 Jun 1989. The event was organized by the Reverend Bryan G. Apps, MA and church members of Southbourne, United Kingdom.

MOTORCYCLES

In 1989, there were an estimated 4,376,000 motorcycles registered in the United States.

Earliest ■ The earliest internal combustion-engined motorized bicycle was a wooden-framed machine built at Bad Cannstatt in Oct–Nov 1885 by Gottlieb Daimler (1834–1900) of Germany and first ridden by Wilhelm Maybach (1846–1929). It had a top speed of 12 mph and developed *one-half of one horsepower* from its single-cylinder 264-cc four-cycle engine at 700 rpm. Known as the 'Einspur,' it was lost in a fire in 1903.

The earliest factory, which made motorcycles in quantity, was opened in 1894 by Heinrich and Wilhelm Hildebrand and Alois Wolfmüller at Munich, West Germany. In its first two years this factory produced over 1,000 machines, each having a water-cooled 1488-cc twin-cylinder four-cycle engine developing about 2·5-bhp at 600 rpm—the highest capacity motorcycle engine ever put into production.

Fastest racing machine ■ There is no satisfactory answer to the identity of the fastest track machine other than to say that the current Honda, Suzuki and Yamaha machines have all been geared to attain speeds marginally in excess of 186·4 mph under race conditions.

Highest speeds ■ Official world speed records must be set with two runs over a measured distance made in opposite directions within a time limit—1 hr for FIM records and 2 hr for AMA records.

Donald A. Vesco (US; b. 8 Apr 1939), riding his 21-ft long *Lightning Bolt* streamliner, powered by two 1016 cc Kawasaki engines on Bonneville Salt Flats, UT on 28 Aug 1978 set AMA and FIM absolute records with an overall average of 318·598 mph and had a fastest run at an average of 318·66 mph.

The world record for 0·62 miles from a standing start is 16·68 sec by Henk Vink (b. 24 Jul 1939) (Netherlands) on his supercharged 984-cc four-cylinder Kawasaki, at Elvington Airfield, North Yorkshire, United Kingdom on 24 Jul 1977. The faster run was made in 16·09 sec.

The world record for 1,320 ft from a standing start is 8·805 sec by Henk Vink on his supercharged 1132-cc four-cylinder Kawasaki at Elvington Airfield, North Yorkshire, United Kingdom on 23 Jul 1977. The faster run was made in 8·55 sec.

The fastest time for a single run over 1,320 ft from a standing start is 7·08 sec by Bo O'Brechta (US) riding a supercharged 1200-cc Kawasaki-based machine at Ontario Speedway, CA in 1980.

The highest terminal velocity recorded at the end of a 1,320-ft run from a standing start is 199·55 mph by Russ Collins (US) at Ontario Speedway on 7 Oct 1978.

Smallest ■ Simon Timperley and Clive Williams of Progressive Engineering Ltd, Ashton-under-Lyne, United Kingdom designed and constructed a motorcycle with a wheelbase of 4·25 in, a seat height of 3¾ in and with a wheel dimension of 0·75 in for the front and 0·950 in for the back in diameter. Simon rode the bike a distance of 3·2, ft reaching a speed of 2 mph.

Duration ■ The longest time a solo motorcycle has been kept in nonstop motion is 560 hr by Norberto Naummi, Foppiani Maurizio and Roberto Ghillani, who covered 18,000 miles at an average speed of 33·69 mph in Varano do Melegari, Italy from 16 Aug–8 Sep 1986.

Wheelie *Distance* ■ Doug Domokos on the Alabama International Speedway, Talladega on 27 Jun 1984 covered 145 miles nonstop on the rear wheel of his Honda XR 500. He stopped only when the gas ran out.

Two-wheel sidecar riding ■ Graham John Martin drove a distance of 198·9 miles on a Yamaha XS 1100-cc bike in a time of 3 hr 5 min at Gerotek Test Track, Pretoria, South Africa on 21 Aug 1988.

Most on one machine ■ The record for the most people on a single machine is for 46 members of the Illawarra Mini Bike Training Club, New South Wales, Australia. They rode on a 1000-cc motorcycle and traveled a distance of 1 mile on 11 Oct 1987.

BICYCLES

Earliest ■ The first design for a machine propelled by cranks and pedals with connecting rods has been attributed to Leonardo da Vinci (1452–1519), or one of his pupils, dated *c.* 1493.

The earliest such design actually built was in 1839–40 by Kirkpatrick Macmillan (1810–78) of Dumfries. It is now in the Science Museum, Kensington and Chelsea, London, United Kingdom.

The first practical bicycle was the *vélocipède* built in March 1861 by Pierre and his son Ernest Michaux of Rue de Verneuil, Paris, France.

In 1870, James Starley, in Coventry, United Kingdom, constructed the first 'penny-farthing' or ordinary bicycle. It had wire-spoked wheels for lightness and was available with an optional speed gear.

Bicycle parade ■ The greatest participation is one involving 2¾ percent of the entire population of San Juan, Puerto Rico (1,816,300) on 17 Apr 1988. It was organized by TV personality 'Pacheco' a.k.a. Joaquín Monserrat.

Trishaw ■ The longest trishaw parade on record was when 177 trishaw peddlers rode in single convoy in Penang, Malaysia on 23 Nov 1986.

Longest ■ The longest true tandem bicycle ever built (i.e., without a third stabilizing wheel) is one of 66 ft 11 in for 35 riders built by the Pedaalstompers Westmalle of Belgium. They rode *c.*195 ft in practice on 20 Apr 1979. The machine weighs 2,425 lb.

Terry Thessman of Pahiatua, New Zealand designed and built a bike measuring 72·96 ft long, and weighing 154 lb, which was ridden a distance of 807·08 ft on 27 Feb 1988.

Smallest ■ The world's smallest wheeled ridable bicycle is one with wheels of 0·76-in diameter that was ridden by its constructor, Neville Patten of Gladstone, Queensland, Australia, for a distance of 13 ft 5½ in on 25 Mar 1988.

Jacques Puyoou of Pau, Pyrénées-Atlantiques, France has built a tandem 14·1-in wheel diameter ridden by him and Madame Puyoou.

Largest ■ The largest bicycle as measured by the front wheel diameter is 'Frankencycle,' built by Dave Moore of Rosemead, CA and first ridden by Steve Gordon of Moorpark, CA on 4 Jun 1989. The wheel diameter is 10 ft and it is 11 ft 2 in high.

HPV's *Fastest Land* ■ The world speed records for human-powered vehicles (HPVs) 656 ft flying start (single rider) are 65·484 mph by Fred Markham at Mono Lake, CA on 11 May 1986 and 62·92 mph (multiple riders) by Dave Grylls and Leigh Barczewski at the Ontario Speedway, CA on 4 May 1980. The 1-hour standing start (single rider) is held by Fred Markham, riding Garner Martin's *Gold Rush,* averaging a speed of 45·366 mph on 15 Sep 1989 at Michigan International Speedway, Brooklyn Michigan.

Water ■ The Men's 6,562 ft (single ride) is 12·84 mph in *Flying Fish* by Steve Hegg at Long Beach, CA on 20 Jul 1987.

Unicycles ■ The tallest unicycle ever mastered is one 101 ft 9 in tall ridden by Steve McPeak (with a safety wire or mechanic suspended by an overhead crane) for a distance of 376 ft in Las Vegas in October 1980. The freestyle riding of ever taller unicycles (i.e., without any safety harness) must inevitably lead to serious injury or fatality.

Largest big-wheel unicycle ■ A unicycle with a 73-in wheel was constructed by Steve

Gordon and Dave Moore of Moorpark, CA in 1989.

Smallest ■ Peter Rosendahl of Las Vegas, NV rode a unicycle with a wheel diameter of 5 in in a circle with a radius of 4 ft for 30 sec at Circus Circus Hotel, NV on 16 Mar 1990.

Endurance ■ Deepak Lele of Maharashtra, India unicycled 3,963 miles from New York to Los Angeles from 6 Jun–25 Sep 1984.

The sprint record from a standing start over 100 meters (328 ft) is 13·71 sec by John Foss of Westbury, NY, in Tokyo, Japan on 1 Aug 1987. Takayuki Koike of Kanagawa, Japan set a record for 100 miles in 6 hr 44 min 21·84 sec on 9 Aug 1987.

Underwater tricycling ■ A team of 32 divers pedaled a distance of 116·66 miles in 75 hr 20 min on a standard tricycle at Diver's Den, Santa Barbara, CA on 16–19 Jun 1988 to raise money for the Muscular Dystrophy Association.

Roads

ROADS
Traffic volume ■ The most heavily traveled stretch of road is Route 10, Junction 13·80, Normandie Avenue Interchange, in California, with a peak-hour traffic volume of 18,000 vehicles.

The territory with the highest traffic density in the world is Hong Kong. By 1 Jan 1987 there were 300,000 motor vehicles on 867 miles of serviceable roads, giving a density of 13·6 ft per vehicle.

Bridge ■ The world's busiest bridge is the Howrah Bridge across the river Hooghly in Calcutta. In addition to 57,000 vehicles a day it carries an incalculable number of pedestrians across its 1,500-ft long 72-ft wide span.

Longest traffic jams ■ The longest ever reported was that of 16 Feb 1980 which stretched northwards from Lyon 109·3 miles towards Paris, France. A record traffic jam was reported for 1½ million cars crawling bumper-to-bumper over the East-West German border on 12 Apr 1990.

Square *Largest* ■ Tiananmen (Gate of Heavenly Peace) Square in Beijing, described as the navel of China, extends over 98 acres.

The Maiden e Shah in Isfahan, Iran extends over 20·1 acres.

Parking meters ■ The earliest ever installed, put in the business district of Oklahoma City, OK on 19 Jul 1935, were the invention of Carl C. Magee (US).

Worst driver ■ It was reported that a 75-year-old male driver received ten traffic tickets, drove on the wrong side of the road four times, committed four hit-and-run offenses and caused six accidents, all within 20 minutes, in McKinney, TX on 15 Oct 1966.

Street *Longest* ■ The longest designated street in the world is Yonge Street, running north and west from Toronto, Canada. The first stretch, completed on 16 Feb 1796, ran 34 miles. Its official length now extended to Rainy River at the Ontario-Minesota border, is 1,178·3 miles.

Most winding ■ Lombard Street, the steep one-way street in San Francisco, has eight consecutive 90-degree turns of 20-ft radius.

Narrowest ■ The world's narrowest street is in the village of Ripatransone in the Marche region of Italy. It is called Vicolo della Virilita (Virility Alley) and is 16·9 in wide.

Shortest ■ The title of 'The Shortest Street in the World' is claimed by Bacup in Lancashire, United Kingdom, where Elgin Street, situated by the old market ground, measures just 17 ft 0 in.

Steepest ■ The steepest street in the world is Baldwin Street, Dunedin, New Zealand, which has been surveyed to have a maximum gradient of 1 in 1·266.

Road *Mileages* ■ The country with the greatest length of road is the United States (all 50 states), with 3·89 million miles of graded roads at 31 Dec 1988.

Regular driving licenses are issuable to 15-year-olds without a driver-education course only in Hawaii and Mississippi. Thirteen US states issue restricted juvenile licenses at 14.

Longest motorable road ■ The Pan-American Highway, from northwest Alaska to Santiago, Chile, then eastward to Buenos Aires, Argentina and terminating in Brasilia, Brazil. There remains a gap known as the Tapon del Darién, in Panama and the Atrato Swamp, Colombia.

Longest road ● The Pan-American Highway run from north-west Alaska to Santiago, Chile, then eastwards to Buenos Aires, Argentina and terminates in Brazil. There is a gap known as the Tapon del Daríen in Panama. Seen here is Garry Sowerby who with Tim Cahill set the Trans-Americas record (Photo: Garry Sowerby)

Highest roads ■ The highest trail in the world is a 8-mile stretch of the Gangdi-su between Khaleb and Xinji-fu, Tibet, which in two places exceeds 20,000 ft.

The highest carriageable road in the world is one 733·2 miles long between Tibet and southwestern Xinjiang, completed in October 1957, which takes in passes of an altitude up to 18,480 ft above sea level.

Lowest roads ■ The lowest road runs along the Israeli shores of the Dead Sea, 1,290 ft below sea level.

The world's lowest 'pass' is Rock Reef Pass, Everglades National Park, FL, which is 3 ft above sea level.

Widest roads ■ The Monumental Axis running for 1½ miles from the Municipal Plaza to the Plaza of the Three Powers in Brasilia, the capital of Brazil. The six-lane boulevard was opened in April 1960 and is 820·2 ft wide.

The San Francisco-Oakland Bay Bridge Toll Plaza has 23 lanes (17 westbound) serving the Bridge in Oakland, CA.

Railroads

TRAINS
Earliest ■ The first practical electric rail-

road was Werner von Siemens' oval meter-gauge demonstration track, about 984 ft long, at the Berlin Trades Exhibition on 31 May 1879.

Fastest ■ The highest speed attained by a railed vehicle is 6,121 mph or Mach 8 by an unmanned rocket sled over the 9½-mile long rail track at White Sands Missile Range, NM on 5 Oct 1982.

The world's fastest speed with passengers in a non-railed vehicle is 249 mph by the Maglev (magnetic levitation) MLU-001 test train over the 4·3-mile long JNR experimental track at Miyazaki, Japan on 4 Feb 1987.

The highest speed recorded on any national rail system is 320 mph, by the French SNCF high-speed train TGV-OSE on trial in May 1990. The TGV (Train à Grande Vitesse) inaugurated on 27 Sep 1981 by September 1983 had reduced its scheduled time for the Paris-Lyon run of 264 miles to 2 hr exactly, so averaging 132 mph. The peak attained was 186 mph.

Longest nonstop ■ Steam Locomotive No. 4472, *Flying Scotsman*, completed a nonstop run hauling 590 tons between Parkes and Broken Hill in New South Wales, Australia on 6 Aug 1989. The total distance covered was 422 miles in a time of 9 hr 25 min 15 sec.

Most powerful ■ The world's most powerful steam locomotive, measured by tractive effort, was No.700, a triple-articulated or triplex 2-8-8-8-4, six-cylinder engine built by the Baldwin Locomotive Works in 1916 for the Virginian Railroad. It had a tractive force of 166,300 lb working compound and 199,560 lb working simple.

Probably the heaviest train ever hauled by a single engine was one of 17,135 tons made up of 250 freight cars stretching 1·6 miles by the *Matt H. Shay* (No 5014), a 2-8-8-8-2 engine, which ran on the Erie Railroad from May 1914 until 1929.

Greatest load ■ The heaviest single pieces of freight ever conveyed by rail are limited by the capacity of the rolling stock.

The world's strongest rail carrier with a capacity of 838 tons is the 36-axle 301 ft 10 in long 'Schnabel' built for a US railroad by Krupp, West Germany, in March 1981.

The heaviest load ever moved on rails is the 11,971-ton Church of the Virgin Mary built in 1548 in the village of Most, Czechoslovakia, in October–November 1975, because it was in the way of coal workings. It was moved 2,400 ft at 0·0013 mph over 4 weeks at a cost of £ 9 million.

Freight trains ■ The world's longest and heaviest freight train on record with the largest number of wagons recorded, was a run on the 3 ft 6 in gauge Sishen-Saldanha railroad in South Africa on 26–27 Aug 1989. The train consisted of 660 wagons each loaded to 105 tons gross, a tank car and a caboose, moved by nine 50 kV electric and 7 diesel-electric locomotives distributed along the train. The train was 4 ½ miles long and weighed 77,720 tons excluding locomotives. It traveled a distance of 535 miles.

United States ■ The longest and heaviest freight on record was about 4 miles in length. It comprised 500 coal cars with three 3,600-hp diesels pulling and three more in the middle, on the Iaeger, WV, to Portsmouth, OH stretch of 157 miles on the Norfolk and Western Railway on 15 Nov 1967. The total weight was nearly 47,040 tons.

TRACKS
Longest ■ The world's longest run is one of 5,864½ miles on the Trans-Siberian line from Moscow to Nakhodka, USSR, in the Soviet Far

East. There are 97 stops on the journey, which takes 8 days 4 hr 25 min.

The 1,954 mile Baikal-Amur main line (BAM), begun with forced labour in 1938, was restarted in 1974 and put into service on 27 Oct 1984. A total of 13·5 billion ft³ of earth had to be moved and 3,901 bridges built in this £ 8 billion project.

Longest straight ■ The Commonwealth Railways Trans-Australian line over the Nullarbor Plain from Mile 496 between Nurina and Loongana, Western Australia, to Mile 793 between Ooldea and Watson, South Australia, is 297 miles dead straight, although not level.

Widest and narrowest gauge ■ The widest in standard use is 5 ½ ft. This width is used in Spain, Portugal, India, Pakistan, Bangladesh, Sri Lanka, Argentina and Chile.

The narrowest gauge on which public services are operated is 10¼ in on the Wells Harbor (0·7 mile) and the Wells-Walsingham Railways (4 miles) in Norfolk, United Kingdom.

Highest line ■ At 15,806 ft above sea level the standard gauge (4 ft 8½ in) track on the Morococha branch of the Peruvian State Railways at La Cima is the highest in the world.

Lowest line ■ The world's lowest line is in the Seikan Tunnel between Honshu and Hokkaido, Japan. The rails are 786 ft below the Tsugaro Straits. The tunnel was opened on 13 Mar 1988. It is 33·4 miles long.

Steepest gradient ■ The world's steepest standard gauge gradient by adhesion is 1:11, between Chedde and Servoz on the meter-gauge SNCF Chamonix line, France.

Busiest system ■ The railroad carrying the largest number of passengers is the East Japan Railway Company, which in 1988 carried 14,660,000 passengers daily. Among articles lost in 1988 were 377,712 umbrellas, 141,200 clothing items, 143,761 books and stationery items, 4,359 accessories and 89,799 purses.

Greatest length of railroads ■ The country with the greatest length of railroad is the United States, with 184,235 miles of track.

RAIL TRAVEL
Most countries in 24 hours ■ The number of countries traveled through entirely by train in 24 hours is 10, by Aaron Kitchen on 16–17 Feb 1987. His route started in Yugoslavia and continued through Austria, Italy, Liechtenstein, Switzerland, France, Luxembourg, Belgium and the Netherlands, arriving in West Germany 22 hr 42 min later.

Handpumped railcars ■ A speed of 40 mph for a 984-ft course was achieved by Gold's Gym, Surrey, British Columbia at the Annual World Championship Handcar Races, Port Moodby, British Columbia, Canada by the five-man team (one pusher, four pumpers) in a time of 32·71 sec on 2 Jul 1988.

STATIONS
Largest ■ The world's largest is Grand Central Terminal, Park Avenue and 42nd Street, New York City, built 1903–13. It covers 48 acres on two levels with 41 tracks on the upper level and 26 on the lower. On average more than 550 trains and 180,000 people per day use it.

Highest ■ Condor station in Bolivia at 15,705 ft on the meter-gauge Rio Mulato to Potosi line.

Waiting rooms ■ The world's largest waiting rooms are the four in Beijing Station, Chang'an Boulevard, Beijing, China, opened in September 1959, with a total standing capacity of 14,000.

Platform ■ The longest railroad platform in the world is the Kharagpur platform, West Bengal, India, which measures 2,733 ft in length.

The State Street Center subway platform staging on 'The Loop' in Chicago, IL measures 3,500 ft in length.

The two platforms comprising the New Misato railroad station on the Musashino line, Saitama, Japan are 984 ft apart and are connected by a bridge.

SUBWAYS

Most extensive ■ The subway with most stations in the world is the New York City Metropolitan Transportation Authority subway (first section opened on 27 Oct 1904) with a total of 231·73 route miles, 468 stations and 1·05 billion passengers in 1989.

Traveling *New York subway* ■ The record for traveling the whole system is 26 hr 21 min 08 sec set by Kevin Foster on 25–26 Oct 1989.

Moscow metro ■ The record transit on 9 Dec 1988 (all 123 named stations) was 9 hr 39 min 50 sec by Peter Altman of Edgware, Middlesex and Miss Jackie Smith of Bobblestock, Herefordshire, United Kingdom.

Busiest ■ The world's busiest metro system is that in Greater Moscow, USSR, with as many as 2·55 billion passengers per year. There are 132 stations (15 of which have more than one name, being transfer stations) and 140 miles of track. The 5 kopeck fare has not changed since the Metro first went into operation in 1935.

MODEL RAILWAYS

Smallest ■ The most miniature model railroad ever built is one of 1:1,000 scale by Jean Damery (b. 1923) of Paris, France. The engine ran on a 4½-volt battery and measures 5/16 in overall.

Aircraft

Note—The use of the Mach scale for aircraft speeds was introduced by Prof Ackeret of Zürich, Switzerland. The Mach number is the ratio of the velocity of a moving body to the local velocity of sound. This ratio was first employed by Dr Ernst Mach (1838–1916) of Vienna, Austria in 1887. Thus Mach 1·0 equals 760·98 mph at sea level at 15°C, and is assumed, for convenience, to fall to a constant 659·78 mph in the stratosphere, i.e. above 36,089 ft.

EARLIEST FLIGHTS

The first controlled and sustained power-driven flight occurred near the Kill Devil Hill, Kitty Hawk, NC, at 10:35 A.M. on 17 Dec 1903, when Orville Wright (1871–1948) flew the 12-hp chain-driven *Flyer I* for a distance of 120 ft at an air speed of 30 mph, a ground speed of 6·8 mph and an altitude of 8–12 ft for about 12 sec, watched by his brother Wilbur (1867–1912), four men and a boy. Both brothers, from Dayton, OH, were bachelors because, as Orville put it, they had not the means to 'support a wife as well as an airplane.' The *Flyer* is now in the National Air and Space Museum at the Smithsonian Institution, Washington D.C.

The first hop by a man-carrying airplane entirely under its own power was made when Clément Ader (1841–1925) of France flew in his *Eole* for about 164 ft at Armainvilliers, France on 9 Oct 1890. It was powered by a lightweight steam engine of his own design, which developed about 20 hp (15kW).

The earliest 'rational design' for a flying machine, according to the Royal Aeronautical Society, was that published by Emanuel Swedenborg (1688–1772) in Sweden in 1717.

Jet-engined ■ Proposals for jet propulsion date back to Captain Marconnet (1909) of France, and Henri Coanda (1886–1972) of Romania, and to the turbojet proposals of Maxime Guillaume in 1921.

The first flight by an airplane powered by a turbojet engine was made by the Heinkel He 178, piloted by Flug Kapitan Erich Warsitz, at Marienehe, Germany, on 27 Aug 1939. It was powered by a Heinkel He S3b engine (834 lb as installed with long tailpipe) designed by Dr Hans 'Pabst' von Ohain and first tested in August 1937.

Supersonic flight ■ The first was achieved on 14 Oct 1947 by Capt (later Brig Gen) Charles ('Chuck') Elwood Yeager, (b. 13 Feb 1923), over Edwards Air Force Base, Muroc, CA, in a Bell XS-1 rocket plane ('Glamorous Glennis'-named for Yeager's wife) with Mach 1·015 (670 mph) at an altitude of 42,000 ft.

Trans-Atlantic ■ The first crossing of the North Atlantic by air was made by Lt Cdr (later Rear Admiral) Albert Cushion Read (1887–1967) and his crew (Stone, Hinton, Rodd, Rhoads and Breese) in the 84-knot US Navy/Curtiss flying boat NC-4 from Trepassey Harbor, Newfoundland, Canada, via the Azores, to Lisbon, Portugal, from 16–27 May 1919. The whole flight of 4,717 miles, originating from Rockaway Air Station, Long Island, NY, on 8 May, required 53 hr 58 min, terminating at Plymouth, Devon, United Kingdom, on 31 May. The Newfoundland–Azores flight of 1,200 miles took 15 hr 18 min at 81·7 knots.

Non-stop ■ The first nonstop transatlantic flight was achieved 18 days later at 4:13 P.M. GMT on 14 Jun 1919, from Lester's Field, St John's, Newfoundland, Canada 1,960 miles to Derrygimla Bog near Clifden, Co. Galway, Republic of Ireland, at 8:40 A.M. GMT, 15 Jun, when the pilot, Capt John William Alcock (1892–1919), and the navigator, Lt Arthur Whitten Brown (1886–1948), flew across in a Vickers Vimy, powered by two 360-hp Rolls-Royce Eagle VIII engines.

Solo ■ The 79th man to achieve a transatlantic flight but the first to do so solo was Capt (later Brig) Charles Augustus Lindbergh (1902–74) who took off in his 220-hp Ryan monoplane *Spirit of St Louis* at 12:52 P.M. GMT on 20 May 1927 from Roosevelt Field, Long Island, NY. He landed at 10:21 P.M. GMT on 21 May 1927 at Le Bourget Airfield, Paris, France. His flight of 3,610 miles lasted 33 hr 29½ min and he won a prize of $25,000 . The *Spirit of St Louis* is now in the National Air and Space Museum at the Smithsonian Institution, Washington DC.

Most flights ■ Between March 1948 and his retirement on 1 Sep 1984 Flight Service Manager Charles M. Schimpf logged a total of 2,880 Atlantic crossings—a rate of 6·4 per month.

Trans-Pacific ■ The first nonstop flight was by Major Clyde Pangborn and Hugh Herndon in the Bellanca cabin plane *Miss Veedol*, from Sabishiro Beach, Japan 4,558 miles to Wenatchee, WA, in 41 hr 13 min from 3–5 Oct 1931. (For earliest crossing see Circumnavigational flights below.)

Circumnavigational flights ■ Strict circumnavigation requires passing through two antipodal points, thus with a minimum distance of 24,859·75 miles.

Earliest ■ The earliest such flight of 26,345 miles was by two US Army Douglas DWC amphibians in 57 'hops.' The *Chicago* was piloted by Lt Lowell H. Smith and Lt Leslie P. Arnold and the *New Orleans* by Lt Erik H. Nelson and Lt John Harding between 6 Apr and 28 Sep 1924, beginning and ending at Seattle, WA.

Fastest ■ The fastest flight under the FAI rules, which permit flights that exceed the length of the Tropic of Cancer or Capricorn (22,858·754 miles), was that of the 23,125 mile eastabout flight of 36 hr 54 min 15 sec by the Boeing 747 SP 'Friendship One' (Capt. Clay Lacy) from Seattle, WA with 141 passengers on 28–30 Jan 1988. The plane reached 803 mph over the Atlantic and refueled only in Athens, Greece, and Taipei, Taiwan.

First without refueling ■ Dick Rutan and Jeana Yeager, in their specially constructed aircraft, *Voyager 1990*, designed by Dick's brother Burt Rutan, flew from Edwards Air Force Base, CA, from 14–23 Dec 1986. Their first flight took 9 days 3 min 44 sec and they covered a distance of 24,986·665 miles averaging 115·64 mph. The plane, with a wingspan of 110·8 ft, was capable of carrying 1,240 gal of fuel weighing 8,934 lb. It took over two years and 22,000 man-hours to construct. The pilot flew from a cockpit measuring 5·6 x 1·8 ft and the off-duty crew member occupied a cabin 7½ x 2 ft. *Voyager* is now in the National Air and Space Museum at the Smithsonian Institution, Washington DC, WA.

First circumpolar ■ Achieved by Capt Elgen M. Long, 44, in a Piper Navajo from 5 Nov–3 Dec 1971. He covered 38,896 miles in 215 flying hours. The cabin temperature sank to −40° F over Antarctica.

First single-engined flight ■ Richard Norton, an American airline captain, and Calin Rosetti, head of satellite navigation systems at the European Space Agency, made the first single-engined circumpolar flight in a Piper PA-46-310P Malibu. This began and finished at Le Bourget Airport, Paris, France, from 21 Jan–15 Jun 1987. They traveled 34,342 miles in a flying time of 185 hr 41 min. The so-called 'Flight of the Arctic Tern' also set 16 other point-to-point records.

Largest wingspan ■ The aircraft with the largest wingspan ever constructed is the $40-million Hughes H.4 Hercules flying boat ('Spruce Goose'), which was raised 70 ft into the air in a test run of 3,000 ft, piloted by Howard Hughes (1905–76) off Long Beach Harbor, CA, on 2 Nov 1947. The eight-engined 212-ton aircraft had a wingspan of 319 ft 11 in and a length of 218 ft 8 in, and never flew again. In a brilliant engineering feat she was moved bodily by Goldcoast Corp, aided by the US Navy barge crane YD-171, on 22 Feb 1982 to her final resting place 6 miles across the harbor under a 415-ft diameter, clear–span aluminum dome, the world's largest.

Among current aircraft, the Soviet Antonov An-124 has a span of 240 ft 5¾ in and the Boeing 747-400 one of 213 ft.

A modified six-engine version of the An-124, dubbed An-225 and built to carry the Soviet space shuttle *Buran*, has a wingspan of 290 ft 0 in (see heaviest below).

The $34-million Piasecki Heli-Stat, comprising a framework of light alloy and composite materials, to mount four Sikorsky SH-34J helicopters and the envelope of a Goodyear ZPG-2 patrol airship, was exhibited on 26 Jan 1984 at Lakehurst, NJ. Designed for use by the US Forest Service and designated Model 94-37J Logger, it had an overall length of 343 ft and was intended

Heaviest Bomber ● Above: The B-52H Strato-fortress has eight-jet swept wings with a maximum take-off weight of 242·51 tons. Its wing span is 185 ft and 157 ft 6 ³/₄ in in length. (Photo: US Air Force)

Fastest Bomber ● Right: A top view of an FB-111A aircraft of the 509th Bombardment wing, one of the world's fastest bombers with a maximum speed of Mach 2·5. (Photo: US Air Force).

to carry a payload of 24 tons. It crashed on 1 Jul 1986.

Heaviest ■ The aircraft with the highest standard maximum takeoff weight is the Antonov An-225 *Myriya* (Dream) at 560 tons. This aircraft lifted a payload of 344,579 lb to a height of 40,715 ft on 22 Mar 1989. This flight was achieved by Capt Alexander Galunenko and his crew of 7 pilots. The flight was made along the route Kiev-Leningrad-Kiev without landing at a range of 1,305 miles for 3 hr 47 min. One hundred and nine world aviation records have been fixed for this flight.

Electric plane ■ The MB-E1 is the first electrically propelled aircraft. A Bosch 8-kW motor 10·7 hp is powered by Varta FP25 nickel-cadmium 25 Ah batteries. The plane, with a wingspan of 39·4 ft is 23 ft long and weighs 882 lb. It was designed by the model aircraft constructor American Fred Militky and made its maiden flight on 21 Oct 1973.

Solar-powered ■ The *Solar Challenger*, designed by a team led by Dr Paul MacCready, was flown for the first time entirely under solar power on 20 Nov 1980. On 7 Jul 1981, piloted by Steve Ptacek (US), the *Solar Challenger* became the first aircraft of this category to cross the English Channel. Taking off from Pontois-Cormeilles, Paris, France, the 163 mile journey to Manston, Kent, United Kingdom was completed in 5 hr 23 min at a maximum altitude of 11,000 ft. The aircraft has a wingspan of 47 ft.

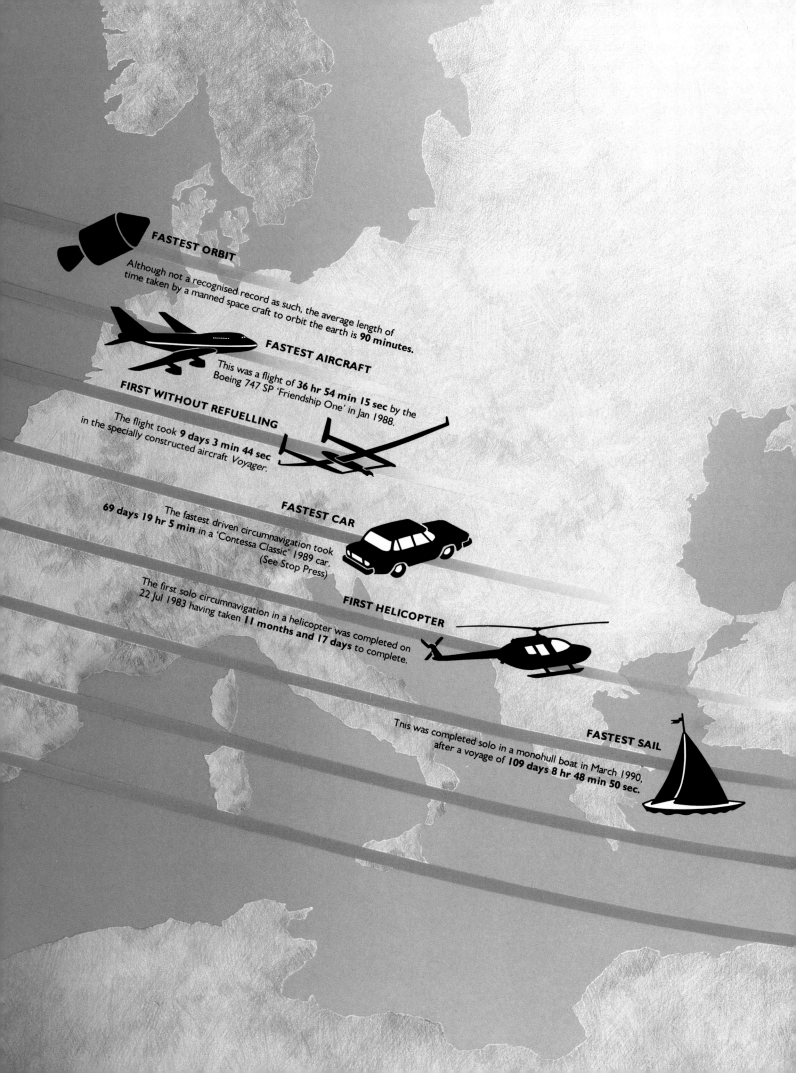

FASTEST ORBIT

Although not a recognised record as such, the average length of time taken by a manned space craft to orbit the earth is **90 minutes.**

FASTEST AIRCRAFT

This was a flight of **36 hr 54 min 15 sec** by the Boeing 747 SP 'Friendship One' in Jan 1988.

FIRST WITHOUT REFUELLING

The flight took **9 days 3 min 44 sec** in the specially constructed aircraft Voyager.

FASTEST CAR

The fastest driven circumnavigation took **69 days 19 hr 5 min** in a 'Contessa Classic' 1989 car. (See Stop Press)

FIRST HELICOPTER

The first solo circumnavigation in a helicopter was completed on 22 Jul 1983 having taken **11 months and 17 days** to complete.

FASTEST SAIL

This was completed solo in a monohull boat in March 1990, after a voyage of **109 days 8 hr 48 min 50 sec.**

CIRCUMNAVIGATION OF THE EARTH

Circumnavigation of the earth has been accomplished in a variety of ways. Compared here are the durations of some of the more diverse forms of transport.

DOUBLE DECKER BUS

This circumnavigation by bus included visiting 18 countries in a duration of 11 months.

WALKING

The first verified walk around the world took **4 years 3 months 15 days**, completed on 5 Oct 1974 by David Kunst.

Ultralight ■ On 3 Aug 1985 Anthony A. Cafaro (b. 30 Nov 1951) flew a ULA (max weight 245 lb, max speed 65 mph, fuel capacity 5 gal) single-seater Gypsey Skycycle for 7 hr 31 min at Dart Field, Mayville, NY. Nine fuel 'pickups' were completed during the flight.

Smallest ■ The smallest plane ever flown is the *Bumble Bee Two*, designed and built by Robert H. Starr of Arizona. It was 8 ft 10 in long, with a wingspan of 5 ft 6 in, and weighed 396 lb empty. The highest speed attained was 190 mph, On 8 May 1988 it flew to a height of approximately 400 ft, crashed and was totally destroyed.

The smallest jet is the 280 mph Silver Bullet, weighing 432 lb with a 17-ft wingspan, built by Bob Bishop (US).

Bombers *Heaviest* ■ The eight-jet swept-wing Boeing B-52H Stratofortress, which has a maximum takeoff weight of 242.5 tons, a wingspan of 185 ft and is 157 ft 6¾ in in length, with a speed of over 650 mph. The B-52 can carry 12 SRAM thermonuclear short-range attack missiles or 24 750-lb bombs under its wings and eight more SRAMs or 84 500-lb bombs in the fuselage.

The ten-engined Convair B-36J, weighing 204 tons, had a greater wingspan, at 230 ft, but it is no longer in service. Its top speed was 435 mph.

Fastest ■ The world's fastest operational bombers are the French Dassault Mirage IV, which can fly at Mach 2.2 (1,450 mph) at 36,000 ft.

The American variable-geometry or 'swing-wing' General Dynamics FB-111A has a maximum speed of Mach 2.5 and the Soviet swing-wing Tupolev Tu-22M known to NATO as 'Backfire' has an estimated over-target speed of Mach 2.0 but which may be as fast as Mach 2.5.

Largest airliner ■ The highest capacity jet airliner is the Boeing 747 'Jumbo Jet,' first flown on 9 Feb 1969 and having a capacity of from 385 to more than 500 passengers and a maximum speed of 602 mph. Its wingspan is 231.8 ft and its length 195.7 ft. It entered service on 22 Jan 1970. The first 747-400 entered service with Northwest Airlines on 26 Jan 1988 with a wingspan of 213 ft, a range exceeding 8,000 miles and a capacity for 422 passengers. Theoretical accommodation is available for 516 passengers seated ten abreast in the main cabin plus up to 69 in the stretched upper deck in the 747-300.

A stretched version of the McDonnell Douglas MD-11 airliner was being studied with accommodation for 515 passengers in the main cabin and up to 96 in a lower so-called panorama deck forward of the wing. This has given way to the MD-12 proposed in early 1990.

The greatest passenger load recorded was one of 306 adults, 328 children and 40 babies (total 674) from the cyclone-devastated Darwin to Sydney, New South Wales, Australia, on 29 Dec 1974.

Fastest airliner ■ The supersonic BAC/Aérospatiale Concorde, first flown on 2 Mar 1969, with a designed capacity of 128 passengers, cruises at up to Mach 2.2 (1,450 mph). It has a maximum takeoff weight of 408,000 lb. It flew at Mach 1.05 on 10 Oct 1969, exceeded Mach 2 for the first time on 4 Nov 1970, and became the first supersonic airliner on passenger services on 21 Jan 1976. In service with Air France and British Airways, Concorde has been laid out for 100 passengers. The New York–London record is 2 hr 54 min, set on 15 April 1990.

Most capacious ■ The Aero Spacelines Super Guppy has a cargo hold with a usable volume of 49,790ft³ and a maximum takeoff weight of 87.5 tons. Wingspan is 156 ft 3 in,

length 141 ft 3 in. Its cargo compartment measures 108 ft 10 in in length with a cylindrical section of 25 ft in diameter.

The Soviet Antonov An-124 *Ruslan* has a cargo hold with a usable volume of 35,800 ft³ and a maximum takeoff weight of 446 tons. It is powered by four Lotarev D-18T turbofans giving a cruising speed of up to 528 mph at 39,370 ft and a range of 2,796 miles. A special-purpose heavy-lift version of the An-124, dubbed An-225, has been developed with a stretched fuselage providing as much as 42,000 ft³ usable volume. A new wing center section carries an additional two engines, providing an estimated total 310,000 lb thrust. Having flown first on 21 Dec 1988, the aircraft was expected to be used to ferry large parts of the Soviet Energia launch vehicle on a complete *Buran* space shuttle.

Largest propeller ■ The largest ever used was the 22 ft 7½-in diameter Garuda propeller, fitted to the Linke-Hofmann R II built in Breslau, Germany (now Wroclaw, Poland), which flew in 1919. It was driven by four 260-hp Mercedes engines and turned at only 545 rpm.

Most flights by jet airliner ■ A survey of ageing airlines or so-called 'geriatric jets' in Flight International magazine for April 1990 reported a McDonnell Douglas DC-9 which had logged 90,914 flights in less than 21 years. This equates to ten flights a days and 11 daily flights at weekends, but after allowing for 'downtime' for maintenance the real daily average is higher.

Scheduled flights *Longest* ■ The nonstop flight of United Airlines and Qantas Los Angeles–Sydney — 14 hr 50 min in a Boeing 747 SP (Special Performance), over 7,487 miles.

The longest delivery flight by a commercial jet is 9,719 nautical miles from London to Sydney by a Qantas Boeing 747-400 *Longreach*, using 176.6 tons of specially formulated Shell Jet A-1 high-density fuel, in 20 hr 9 min on 16–17 Aug 1989. It is the first time this route has been completed nonstop by an airliner.

United Airlines provides the shortest scheduled flight by jet — a Boeing 727 between San Francisco and Oakland, CA. There are three round-trip flights daily, the flight time averaging 5 minutes for the 12-mile journey.

Gary W. Rovetto of Island Air on 21 Mar 1980 flew on the scheduled flight from Center Island to Decatur Island, WA in 41 sec.

London – New York ■ From central London to downtown New York City, by helicopter and Concorde, the record is 3 hr 59 min 44 sec, the return in 3 hr 40 min 40 sec, both by David J. Springbett and David Boyce on 8 and 9 Feb 1982.

Los Angeles–Washington ■ The record time from Los Angeles to Washington is 68 min 17 sec by Lieut Col Ed Yeilding, pilot, and Lieut Col J. T. Vida, reconnaissaance systems officer aboard the SR-71 Blackbird spy plane during its retirement flight on 7 Mar 1990. The Blackbird was refueled over the Pacific Ocean at 60,000 ft before heading east from the California coastline and crossing the finish line near Salisbury, MD. The plane flew at 2,153.24 mph between Los Angeles and Washington.

HIGHEST SPEED

Official record ■ The air speed record is 2,193.167 mph, by Capt Eldon W. Joersz and Maj George T. Morgan, Jr in a Lockheed SR-71A near Beale Air Force Base, CA, over a 15½-mile course on 28 Jul 1976.

Air-launched record ■ The fastest fixed-

wing aircraft in the world was the US North American Aviation X-15A-2, which flew for the first time (after modification from X-15A) on 25 Jun 1964 powered by a liquid oxygen and ammonia rocket-propulsion system. Ablative materials on the airframe once enabled a temperature of 3,000°F to be withstood. The landing speed was momentarily 242 mph. The highest speed attained was 4,520 mph (Mach 6.7) when piloted by Maj William J. Knight, USAF (b. 1930), on 3 Oct 1967.

An earlier version piloted by Joseph A. Walker (1920–66) reached 354,200 ft (67.08 miles) also over Edwards Air Force Base, CA, on 22 Aug 1963. The program was suspended after the final flight of 24 Oct 1968.

The US NASA Rockwell International Space Shuttle Orbiter *Columbia* was launched from the Kennedy Space Center, Cape Canaveral, FL, commanded by Cdr John W. Young, USN and piloted by Robert L. Crippen on 12 Apr 1981 after expenditure of $9.9 billion since 1972. *Columbia* broke all records for space by a fixed-wing craft, with 16,600 mph at main engine cutoff. After reentry from 75.8 miles, experiencing temperatures of 3,920°F, she glided home weighing 107 tons, with a landing speed of 216 mph, on Rogers Dry Lake, CA, on 14 Apr 1981.

Under a new FAI (Fédération Aéronautique Internationale) Category P for aerospacecraft, the *Columbia* is holder of the current absolute world record for duration — 10 days 7 hr 47 min 23 sec to main touchdown when launched on its sixth mission, STS 9 Spacelab 1, with six crewmen, on 28 Nov 1983. *Challenger* was destroyed soon after launch from Cape Canaveral on 28 Jan 1986 (see Chapter 4).

Discovery holds the Shuttle altitude record of 341 miles, achieved on 24 Apr 1990.

The greatest mass lifted by the Shuttle and placed in orbit was 261,679 lb by *Discovery* on STS 51A, launched on 8 Nov 1984.

Fastest jet ■ The USAF Lockheed SR-71, a reconnaissance aircraft, is the world's fastest jet (See Official record above). First flown on 22 Dec 1964, it was reportedly capable of attaining an altitude ceiling of close to 100,000 ft. It has a wingspan of 55.6 ft and a length of 107.4 ft and weighs 85 tons at takeoff. Its reported range was 2,982 miles at Mach 3 at 78,750 ft. At least 30 are believed to have been built and the plane has now been retired by the US Air Force.

It was reported on 15 Jan 1988 that the US Air Force was developing secretly a Mach 5 3,800-mph high-altitude (above 100,000 ft) stealth aircraft.

Fastest combat jet ■ The USSR Mikoyan MiG-25 fighter (NATO code name 'Foxbat'). The reconnaissance 'Foxbat-B' has been tracked by radar at about Mach 3.2 (2,110 mph). When armed with four large underwing air-to-air missiles known to NATO as 'Acrid,' the fighter 'Foxbat-A' is limited to Mach 2.8 (1,845 mph). The single-seat 'Foxbat-A' spans 45 ft 9 in, is 278 ft 2 in long and has an estimated maximum takeoff weight of 82,500 lb.

Fastest biplane ■ The Italian Fiat CR42B, with a 1010-hp Daimler-Benz DB601A engine, which attained 323 mph in 1941. Only one was built.

Fastest piston-engined aircraft ■ The fastest speed for a cut-down privately-owned Hawker Sea Fury which attained 520 mph in level flight over Texas, in August 1966. It was piloted by Mike Carroll (d. 1969) of Los Angeles.

The FAI accredited record for a piston-engined aircraft is 517·055 mph over Mojave, CA by Frank Taylor (US) in a modified North American P-51D Mustang powered by a 2,237 kW Packard Merlin, over a 15½ mile course, on 30 Jul 1983.

Fastest propeller-driven aircraft ■
The Soviet Tu-114 turboprop transport achieved a recorded speed of 545·076 mph carrying heavy payloads over measured circuits. It is developed from the Tupolev Tu-95 bomber, known in NATO as the 'Bear,' and has four 14,795-hp engines.

The turboprop-powered Republic XF-84H prototype US Navy fighter which flew on 22 Jul 1955 had a top *design* speed of 670 mph, but was abandoned.

McDonnell Douglas expects its projected MD-91X, powered by counter-rotating multi-bladed fans, to cruise at about Mach 0·78 514 mph. Testing during 1987–88 with an MD-80 experimentally fitted with a General Electric GE36 engine driving two fans (in place of one of the two standard Pratt & Whitney JT8D turbofans) attained a maximum speed of Mach 0·865.

Fastest transatlantic flight ■
The flight record is 1 hr 54 min 56.4 sec by Maj James V. Sullivan, 37, and Maj Noel F. Widdifield, 33, flying a Lockheed SR-71A eastwards on 1 Sep 1974. The average speed, slowed by refueling by a KC-135 tanker aircraft, for the New York–London stage of 3,461·53 miles was 1,806·963 mph.

The solo record (Gander to Gatwick) is 8 hr 47 min 32 sec by Capt John J. A. Smith in a Rockwell 685 on 12 Mar 1978.

Fastest climb ■
Heinz Frick of British Aerospace took a Harrier GR5 powered by a Rolls-Royce 11-61 Pegasus engine from a standing start to 39,370 ft in 126·63 sec at the Rolls-Royce flight test center, Bristol, Avon, United Kingdom on 15 Aug 1989.

Aleksandr Fedotov (USSR) in a Mikoyan E 266M (MiG-25) aircraft established the fastest climb record on 17 May 1975, reaching 98,425 ft in 4 min 11·7 sec after takeoff.

Duration ■
The record is 64 days 22 hr 19 min and 5 sec, set by Robert Timm and John Cook in a Cessna 172 'Hacienda.' They took off from McCarran Airfield, Las Vegas, NV just before 3:53 P.M. local time on 4 Dec 1958 and landed at the same airfield just before 2:12 P.M. on 7 Feb 1959. They covered a distance equivalent to six times around the world, with continued refuelings, without landing.

AIRPORTS

Largest ■
The world's £2·1 billion King Khalid International Airport outside Riyadh, Saudi Arabia covers an area of 86 miles². It was opened on 14 Nov 1983.

It also has the world's largest control tower, 243 ft in height.

The Hajj Terminal at the £2·8 billion King Abdul-Aziz Airport near Jeddah is the world's largest roofed structure, covering 370 acres.

The present six runways and five terminal buildings of Dallas/Fort Worth Airport, TX are planned to be extended to nine runways, 13 terminals, and 260 gates, with an ultimate capacity for 150 million passengers.

The world's largest airport terminal is Hartsfield Atlanta International Airport, GA, opened on 21 Sep 1980, with floor space covering 50½ acres. It has 138 gates handling nearly 50 million passengers a year but has capacity for 75 million.

The new airport planned for Denver, CO was expected to occupy an area of 45 miles², and in early 1988 was the only new major airport being planned. It was to have 12 runways. Construction of new homes within the expected 60 dB noise 'contour' was banned.

Busiest ■
The busiest airport in the world is the Chicago International Airport, O'Hare Field, with a total of 59,130,007 passengers and 780,658 aircraft operations in the year 1989. The next busiest is the Dallas/Fort Worth International Airport with a total of 47,579,046 passengers and 698,870 aircraft operations. The O'Hare total represents a takeoff or landing every 40·4 sec around the clock.

In terms of freight operations, New York City's Kennedy International Airport handled 1·18 tons in 1988, while Tokyo International Airport handled 1·12 tons of international freight.

Non-airline airport ■
Among airports served by very few airlines, Van Nuys in Southern California, is the busiest. In 1987, the airport saw 492,936 operations, of which less than 1 percent were scheduled airline, which equates to more than 55 non-airline takeoffs or landings per hour throughout the year.

Santa Ana, also in southern California, recorded 528,096 operations in 1989, but at least 20–25 percent were airline operations.

The busiest landing area ever has been Bien Hoa Air Base, South Vietnam, which handled approximately one million takeoffs and landings in 1970.

Helipad ■
The world's largest 'helipad' was An Khe, South Vietnam. The heliport at Morgan City, LA, one of a string used by helicopters flying energy-related offshore operations into the Gulf of Mexico, has pads for 46 helicopters.

Landing fields Highest ■
The highest is La Sa (Lhasa) Airport, People's Republic of China, at 14,315 ft.

Lowest ■
The lowest landing field is El Lisan on the east shore of the Dead Sea, 1,180 ft below sea level, but during World War II BOAC Short C-class flying boats operated from the surface of the Dead Sea 1,292 ft below sea level.

The lowest international airport is Schiphol, Amsterdam, the Netherlands, at 15 ft below sea level.

Farthest and nearest to city or capital ■
The airport farthest from the city center it allegedly serves is Viracopos, Brazil, which is 60 miles from São Paulo. Gibraltar Airport is a mere 2,625 ft from the city center.

Longest runway ■
The longest runway in the world, at 7 miles in length (of which 15,000 ft is concreted), is at Edwards Air Force Base on the bed of Rogers Dry Lake at Muroc, CA. The whole test center airfield extends over 65 miles². In an emergency, an auxiliary 12-mile strip is available along the bed of the Dry Lake. The *Voyager* aircraft, taking off on its round-the-world unrefueled flight (see Circumnavigational flights) used 14,200 ft of concrete runway at Edwards AFB.

The world's longest civil airport runway is one of 3·04 miles at Pierre van Ryneveld Airport, Upington, South Africa, constructed in five months from August 1975 to January 1976.

A paved runway 3·88 miles long appears on maps of Jordan at Abu Husayn.

The most southerly major runway (1·6 miles) in the world is at Mount Pleasant, East Falkland (Lat 51° 50′S), built in 16 months to May 1985.

Longest air ticket ■
This was one of 39 ft 4½ in issued for $4,500 to M. Bruno Leunen of Brussels, Belgium, in December 1984 for a 53,203-mile trip on 80 airlines with 109 layovers.

AIRLINE

Busiest ■
The country with the busiest airlines system is the United States, where the total number of passengers for large carriers (more than 60 seats) was 415·6 million in 1989. The total number of passengers, including small carriers (60 seats or less) was 443 million. Large carriers travelled a total of 328·4 billion miles, the total including small carriers was 333·2 billion miles.

Largest ■
The USSR state airline 'Aeroflot,' so named since 1932, was instituted on 9 Feb 1923. It operates a fleet of 1,650 aircraft over 620,000 miles of routes, employs 500,000 people and carried 119 million passengers and 3·3 million tons of freight in 1987. Seventy percent of its routes are international and it serves 160 passen-

ger routes and five cargo routes outside the country, making regular flights to 98 countries. Its domestic network covers 3,600 towns.

Oldest ■ Koninklijke-Luchtvaart-Maatschappij NV (KLM),the national airline of the Netherlands, opened its first scheduled service (Amsterdam-London) on 17 May 1920, having been established on 7 Oct 1919.

Delag (Deutsche Luftschiffahrt AG) was founded at Frankfurt am Main on 16 Nov 1909 and started a scheduled airship service in June 1910.

Chalk's International Airline has been flying amphibious planes from Miami, FL to the Bahamas since July 1919. Albert 'Pappy' Chalk flew from 1911 to 1975.

HELICOPTERS

Earliest ■ Leonardo da Vinci (1452–1519) proposed the idea of a helicopter-type craft, although it is believed that the Chinese had built helicopter toys before this time.

Igor Sikorsky built a helicopter in Russia in 1909, but the first practical machine was the Focke-Achgellis, first flown in 1936.

Fastest ■ Trevor Eggington, 53, averaged 249·10 mph over Somerset, United Kingdom, on 11 Aug 1986 in a Westland Lynx company demonstrator helicopter.

Largest ■ The Soviet Mil Mi-12 (NATO codename 'Homer'), also known as the V-12, is powered by four 6,500-hp turboshaft engines and has a span of 219 ft 10 in over its rotor tips, with a length of 121 ft 4½ in and weighing 114 tons.

Greatest load ■ On 3 Feb 1982 at Podmoscovnoé in the USSR, a Mil Mi-26 heavy-lift helicopter, crewed by G. V. Alfeurov and L. A. Indeyev (co-pilot), lifted a total mass of 62·5 tons to 6,560 ft.

Smallest ■ The Aerospace General Co one-man rocket-assisted minicopter weighs about 160 lb cruising 250 miles at 185 mph.

Highest altitude ■ The record for helicopters is 40,820 ft by an Aérospatiale SA315B *Lama*, over France on 21 Jun 1972.

The highest recorded landing has been at 23,000 ft below the southeast face of Everest in a rescue sortie in May 1971.

Longest hover ■ Doug Daigle, Brian Watts and Dave Meyer, of Tridair Helicopters, together with Rod Anderson of Helistream, Inc. of California, maintained a continuous hovering flight in a 1947 Bell B Model for 50 hr 50 sec between 13–15 December 1989.

Circumnavigation ■ H. Ross Perot and Jay Coburn, both of Dallas, TX, made the first helicopter circumnavigation in 'Spirit of Texas' on 1–30 Sep 1982.

The first solo around-the-world flight in a helicopter was completed by Dick Smith (Australia) on 22 Jul 1983. Flown from and to the Bell Helicopter facility at Fort Worth, TX, in a Bell Model 206L *Long Ranger III*, his unhurried flight began on 5 Aug 1982 and covered a distance of 35,258 miles.

AUTOGYROS

Earliest ■ The autogyro or gyroplane, a rotorcraft with an unpowered rotor turned by the airflow in flight, preceded the practical helicopter with engine-driven rotor.

Juan de la Cierva (Spain) made the first successful autogyro flight with his model C.4 (commercially named an *Autogiro*) at Getafe, Spain, on 9 Jan 1923.

Speed, altitude and distance records
■ Wing-Cdr Kenneth H. Wallis (GB) holds the straight-line distance record of 543·27 miles set in his WA-116F autogyro on 28 Sep 1975 nonstop from Lydd, Kent, United Kingdom to Wick in the Highlands.

On 20 Jul 1982, flying from Boscombe Down, Wiltshire, United Kingdom, he established a new autogyro altitude record of 18,516 ft in his WA-121/Mc.

Wing-Cdr Wallis also flew his WA-116, with a 72-hp McCulloch engine, to a record speed of 120½ mph over a 1·86 mile straight course on 18 Sep 1986.

It was reported that on 8 Apr 1931, Amelia Earhart (US) reached a height in excess of 19,000 ft at Pitcairn Aviation Field, PA.

FLYING BOAT
Fastest ■ The fastest flying boat ever built has been the Martin XP6M-1 Seamaster, the US Navy four-jet-engined minelayer flown in 1955–59 with a top speed of 646 mph. In September 1946 the Martin JRM-2 Mars flying boat set a payload record of 68,327 lb.

The official flying boat speed record is 566·69 mph, set up by Nikolay Andreievski and crew of two in a Soviet Beriev M-10, powered by two AL-7 turbojets, over a 9·3 to 15½-mile course on 7 Aug 1961.

The M-10 holds all 12 records listed for jet-powered flying boats, including an altitude of 49,088 ft set by Georgi Burianov and crew over the Sea of Azov on 9 Sep 1961.

AIRSHIPS
Earliest ■ The earliest flight in an airship was by Henri Giffard from Paris in his steam-powered coal-gas 88,300 ft[3] 144-ft long airship on 24 Sep 1852.

Largest *Rigid* ■ The 235-ton German *Graf Zeppelin II* (LZ 130), with a length of 803·8 ft and a capacity of 7·06 million ft[3]. She made her maiden flight on 14 Sep 1938 and in May and August 1939 made radar spying missions in British air space. She was dismantled in April 1940. Her sister ship *Hindenburg* was 5·6 ft longer.

Non-rigid ■ The largest ever constructed was the US Navy ZPG 3-W, which had a capacity of 1·5 million ft[3], was 403 ft long and 85·1 ft in diameter, with a crew of 21. She first flew on 21 Jul 1958, but crashed into the sea in June 1960.

Hot-air ■ The world altitude record of 10,365 ft is held by the Cameron D-38 hot-air airship flown at Cunderdin, Western Australia, on 27 Aug 1982 flown by R. W. Taaffe (Australia).

Oscar Lindstrom in a Colt AS 56 Hotair airship achieved a distance and duration record of 57·8 miles in a time of 3 hr 41 min 55 sec, from Stockholm to Tobo, Sweden on 20 Mar 1988.

Greatest passenger load ■ The most people ever carried in an airship was 207, in the US Navy *Akron* in 1931. The transatlantic record is 117 by the German *Hindenburg* in 1937.

Distance records ■ The FAI (Fédération Aéronautique Internationale) accredited straight-line distance record for airships is 3,967·1 miles, set up by the German *Graf Zeppelin*, captained by Dr Hugo Eckener, between 29 Oct and 1 Nov 1928.

The German Zeppelin L59 flew from Yambol, Bulgaria, to south of Khartoum, Sudan, and returned from 21–25 Nov 1917 to cover a minimum of 4,500 miles.

Duration record ■ The longest recorded flight by a non-rigid airship (without refueling) is 264 hr 12 min by a US Navy Goodyear-built ZPG-2 class ship (Cdr J. R. Hunt, USN) from South Weymouth NAS, MA from 4–15 Mar 1957, landing back at Key West, FL after having flown 9,448 miles.

BALLOONING
Earliest ■ The earliest recorded ascent was by a model hot-air balloon invented by Father Bartolomeu de Gusmão (ne Lourenço; 1685–1724), which was flown indoors at the Casa da India, Terreiro do Paço, Portugal on 8 Aug 1709.

Distance record ■ The record distance traveled by a balloon is 5,208·68 miles, by the Raven experimental helium-filled balloon *Double Eagle V* (capacity 399·053 ft[3]) from 9–12 Nov 1981, from Nagashima, Japan to Covello, CA. The crew for this first manned balloon crossing of the Pacific Ocean were Ben L. Abruzzo, 51, Rocky Aoki, 43 (Japan), Ron Clark, 41 and Larry M. Newman, 34.

Ex-USAF Colonel Joe Kittinger (see Parachuting) became the first man to complete a solo transatlantic crossing by balloon.

Accomplished in the 105,944 ft[3] helium-filled balloon *Rosie O'Grady* between 14–18 Sep 1984, Kittinger lifted off from Caribou, ME and completed a distance of approximately 3,543 miles before landing at Montenotte, Italy in 86 hr.

The first balloon crossing of the North Atlantic had been made during 12–17 Aug 1978 (137 hr 6 min) in the gas balloon *Double Eagle II,* crewed by Ben L. Abruzzo, Maxie L. Anderson and Larry M. Newman.

The first crossing of the United States was by the helium-filled balloon *Super Chicken III* (pilots Fred Gorell and John Shoecraft) 2,515 miles from Costa Mesa, CA, to Blackbeard's Island, GA from 9–12 Oct 1981.

Highest *Unmanned* ■ The altitude attained by an unmanned balloon was 170,000 ft by a Winzen balloon of 47·8 million ft[3] launched at Chico, CA in October 1972.

Manned ■ The greatest altitude reached in a manned balloon is an unofficial 123,800 ft by Nicholas Piantanida (1933–66) of Bricktown, NJ from Sioux Falls, SD on 1 Feb 1966. He landed in a cornfield in Iowa but did not survive.

The official record is 113,740 ft by Cdr Malcolm D. Ross, USNR and the late Lt Cdr Victor A. Prother, USN in an ascent from the deck of USS *Antietam* on 4 May 1961 over the Gulf of Mexico in a balloon of 12 million ft[3].

Owing to an oversight, Keith Lang and Harold Froelich, scientists from Minneapolis, ascended in an open gondola and without the protection of pressure suits to an altitude of 42,150 ft, just under 8 miles, on 26 Sep 1956. During their 6½-hour flight, at maximum altitude they observed the Earth without goggles and measured a temperature of −72°F.

Largest ■ The largest balloons built have an inflatable volume of 70 million ft[3] by Winzen Research Inc, MN. These stand 1,000 ft tall and are unmanned.

Hot-air ■ The modern revival in this form of ballooning began in the United States in 1961, and the first World Championships were held in Albuqerque, NM on 10–17 Feb 1973.

Most in a balloon ● On 17 Aug 1988 from Lelystad airport in the Netherlands, Henk Brink made a free flight of 656 ft in the 850,000 ft³ *Nashua Number One* carrying a total of 50 passengers and crew reaching an altitude of 328 ft. (Photo: Nashua).

Atlantic crossing ■ Richard Branson (United Kingdom) and his pilot Per Lindstrand (United Kingdom) were the first to cross the Atlantic in a hot-air balloon, on 2–3 Jul 1987 from Sugarloaf, ME to Limavady, County Londonderry Northern Ireland, a distance of 3,075 miles, in 31 hours 41 minutes. Their balloon, *Virgin Atlantic Challenger,* of 2·3 million ft³ capacity, was the largest ever flown and reached speeds in excess of 130 mph.

Altitude ■ Per Lindstrand (United Kingdom) achieved the altitude record of 64,996 ft in a Colt 600 hot-air balloon over Laredo, TX on 6 Jun 1988.

The FAI endurance and distance record for a gas and hot-air balloon is 96 hr 24 min and 2,074·817 miles by *Zanussi,* crewed by Donald Allan Cameron (United Kingdom) and Major Christopher Davey, which failed by only 103 miles to achieve the first balloon crossing of the Atlantic on 30 Jul 1978.

Highest tethered ■ *Miss Champagne* a balloon of 2·6 million ft³ capacity was built by Tom Handcock of Portland, ME. Tethered, it rose to height of 50 ft with 61 passengers on board on 19 Feb 1988.
The Dutch balloonist Henk Brink made a free flight of 656 ft in the 850,000 ft³ *Nashua Number One*, carrying a total of 50 passengers and crew. The flight, on 17 Aug 1988, lasted 25 min, commenced from Lelystad Airport, the Netherlands, and reached an altitude of 328 ft.

Highest number to jump from a Balloon ■ On 5 Apr 1990 12 members of the Red Devils Free Fall Parachute Team, free fell from a Cameron A210, G-BRVX Hot air balloon over Bath, Avon, United Kingdom, at a height of 6,000 ft in one flight.

PERSONAL AVIATION RECORDS

Oldest and youngest passengers ■ Airborne births are reported every year.

The oldest person to fly has been Mrs Jessica S. Swift (nee Anna Stewart, 17 Sep 1871), at age 110 yrs 3 months, from Vermont to Florida in Dec 1981.

Pilots ■ A wholly untutored James A. Stoodley at age 14 years 5 months took his 13-year-old brother John on a 29-minute joy ride in an unattended US Piper Cub trainer aircraft near Ludgershall, Wiltshire, United Kingdom in December 1942.

Oldest ■ The world's oldest pilot is Ed McCarty (b. 18 Sep 1885) of Kimberly, ID, who in 1979 was flying his rebuilt 30-year-old Ercoupe, at age 94.

Most flying hours *Pilot* ■ John Edward Long (US; b.10 Nov 1915) between 1 May 1933 to 7 Sep 1989 totaled 53,290 hr 5 min logged flights as a pilot, more than six years airborne.

Passenger ■ The record as a supersonic passenger is held by Fred Finn, who made his 654th Concorde crossing in May 1989.

Most takeoffs and landings ■ Al Yates and Bob Phoenix of Texas made 193 takeoffs and daylight landings at unduplicated airfields in 14 hr 57 min in a Piper Seminole, on 15 Jun 1979.

Most planes flown ■ James B. Taylor, Jr (1897–1942) flew 461 different types of powered aircraft during his 25 years as an active experimental test and demonstration pilot for the US Navy and a number of American aircraft manufacturing companies. The airplanes flown included the most advanced military fighter and attack aircraft of their day. He was one of the few pilots of the 1920s and 30s qualified to perform terminal velocity dives. During one dive in 1939, he may have become the first pilot in history to fly faster than 500 mph and live.

Human-powered flight ■ The Daedalus Project, centered on the Massachusetts Institute of Technology, achieved its goal of human-powered flight from Crete to the island of Santorini 74 miles distant on 23 Apr 1988 when Kanellos Kanellopoulos (b. 25 Apr 1957) averaged 18·5 mph in his 112-ft wingspan machine.

MODEL AIRCRAFT

Altitude, speed and duration ■ Maynard L. Hill (US), flying radio-controlled models, established the world record for altitude of 26,929 ft on 6 Sep 1970, and on 4 Jul 1983 set a closed-circuit distance record of 1,231 miles. The free-flight speed record is 213·70 mph by V. Goukoune and V. Myakinin (both USSR), with a radio-controlled model at Klementyevo, USSR, on 21 Sep 1971. The record duration flight is one of 32 hr 7 min 40 sec by Eduard Svoboda, flying a radio-controlled glider on 23–24 Aug 1980. An indoor model with a rubber motor designed by J. Richmond (US) set a duration record of 52 min 14 sec on 31 Aug 1979.

Largest glider ■ *Eagle III,* a radio-controlled glider weighing 14·5 lb with a wingspan of 32 ft 6 in was designed and constructed by Carlos Reńe Tschen and Carlos Reńe Tschen, Jr of Colonia San Łazaro, Guatemala.

Cross-Channel ■ The first model helicopter flight was achieved by an 11-lb model Bell 212 radio controlled by Dieter Zeigler for 32 miles between Ashford, Kent, United Kingdom and Ambleteuse, France on 17 Jul 1974.

Smallest ■ The smallest to fly is one weighing 0·004 oz powered by attaching a horsefly and designed by insectonaut Don Emmick of Seattle, WA, United States on 24 Jul 1979. One flew for 5 minutes at Kirkland, WA.

Paper aircraft ■ The flight duration record for a paper aircraft is 16·89 sec by Ken Blackburn in the Reynolds Coliseum, North Carolina State University on 29 Nov 1983. The indoor record with a 12-ft ceiling is 1 min 33 sec set in the Fuji TV studios, Tokyo, Japan on 21 Sep 1980. A paper plane was witnessed to have flown 1¼ miles by 'Chick' C. O. Reinhart from a tenth-story office window at 60 Beaver Street, New York City across the East River to Brooklyn in August 1933, helped by a thermal from a coffee-roasting plant. An indoor distance of 193 ft was recorded by Tony Felch at the La Crosse Center, WI on 21 May 1985.

Largest ■ The largest flying paper airplane was constructed by Werner Heise and Beat Schück at Kongresshaus, Zürich on 18 Dec 1988. With a wingspan of 10 ft it was launched from a 10-ft high platform and flown for a distance of 70 ft .

PARACHUTING RECORDS

It is estimated that the human body reaches 99 percent of its low-level terminal velocity after falling 1,880 ft, which takes 13–14 sec. This is 117–125 mph at normal atmospheric pressure in a random posture, but up to 185 mph in a head-down position.

FIRST ● Tower [1] ● Louis-Sébastien Lenormand (1757–1839), quasi-parachute, Montpellier, France, 1783.

Balloon ● André-Jacques Garnerin (1769–1823), 2,230 ft Monceau Park, Paris, France, 22 Oct 1797.

Aircraft ● Man; 'Captain' Albert Berry, an aerial exhibitionist, St. Louis, MI, 1 Mar 1912. *Woman*; Mrs Georgina 'Tiny' Broadwick (b. 1893), Griffith Park, Los Angeles, CA, 21 Jun 1913.

LONGEST DURATION FALL ● Lt Col Wm H. Rankin, USMC, 40 min due to thermals, NC, 26 Jul 1956.

LONGEST DELAYED DROP ● World ● *Man*; Capt Joseph W. Kittinger [2], 84,700 ft 16·04 miles, from balloon at 102,800 ft, Tularosa, NM, 16 Aug 1960. *Woman*; E. Fomitcheva (USSR) 48,556 ft over Odessa, USSR, 26 Oct 1977.

MID-AIR RESCUE ● Earliest ● Miss Dolly Shepherd (1886-1983) brought down Miss Louie May on her single 'chute from balloon at 11,000 ft, Longton, United Kingdom, 9 Jun 1908.

Lowest ● Gregory Robertson saved Debbie Williams (unconscious), collision at 9,000 ft, pulled her ripcord at 3,500 ft — 10 secs from impact, Coolidge, AZ, 18 Apr 1987.

HIGHEST ESCAPE ● Flt Lt J. de Salis, RAF and Fg Off P. Lowe, RAF, 56,000 ft, Moynash, Derby, United Kingdom, 9 Apr 1958.

Lowest ● S/Ldr Terence Spencer, RAF, 30–40 ft, Wismar Bay, Baltic, 19 Apr 1945.

HIGHEST LANDING ● Ten USSR parachutists [3], 23,405 ft, Lenina Peak, USSR May 1969.

LOWEST INDOOR JUMP ● Andy Smith and Phil Smith, 192 ft, Houston Astrodome, TX, 16–17 Jan 1982.

MOST SOUTHERLY ● T/Sgt Richard J. Patton (d. 1973), Operation Deep Freeze, South Pole, 25 Nov 1956.

MOST NORTHERLY ● Dr Jack Wheeler (US); pilot Capt Rocky Parsons, −25° F, in Lat. 90° 00′ N, 15 Apr 1981.

CROSS-CHANNEL (LATERAL FALL) ● Sgt Bob Walters with three soldiers and two Royal Marines, 22 miles from 25,000 ft, Dover, Kent, United Kingdom to Sangatte, France, 31 Aug 1980.

TOTAL SPORT PARACHUTING DESCENTS ● *Man*; Roch Charmet (France, d. 20 Feb 1989), 14,650, various locations. *Woman*; Valentina Zakoretskaya (USSR), 8,000, over USSR, 1964–Sep 1980.

24-HOUR TOTAL ● Dale Nelson (US), 301 (in accordance with United States Parachute Association rules), PA, 26–27 May 1988.

MOST TRAVELLED ● Kevin Seaman from a Cessna Skylane (pilot Charles E. Merritt), 12,186 miles, jumps in all 50 US States, 26 Jul–15 Oct 1972.

HEAVIEST LOAD ● US Space Shuttle *Columbia*, external rocket retrieval, 80 ton capacity, triple array, each 120 ft diameter, Atlantic, off Cape-Canaveral, FL, 12 Apr 1981.

HIGHEST COLUMN ● 24 Royal Marine Team, Dunkeswell, Devon, United Kingdom, 20 Aug 1986.

LARGEST FREE FALL FORMATION ● 144, held for 8·8 sec, from 16,000 ft, Quincy, IL, 11 Jul 1988.

OLDEST ● *Man*; Edwin C. Townsend (d. 7 Nov 1987), 89 years, Vermillion Bay, LA, 5 Feb 1986. *Woman*; Mrs Sylvia Brett (UK), 80 years 166 days, Cranfield, United Kingdom, 23 Aug 1986.

LONGEST FALL WITHOUT PARACHUTE ● World ● Vesna Vulovic (Yugoslavia), air hostess in DC-9 which blew up at 33,330 ft over Serbska Kamenice, Czechoslovakia, 26 Jan 1972.

[1] *The king of Ayutthaya, Siam in 1687 was reported to have been diverted by an ingenious athlete parachuting with two large umbrellas. Faustus Verancsis is reputed to have descended in Hungary with a framed canopy in 1617.*

[2] *Maximum speed in rarefied air was 625·2 mph at 90,000 ft—marginally supersonic.*

[3] *Four were killed.*

MILESTONES IN ABSOLUTE HUMAN ALTITUDE RECORDS

ft	Pilot	Vehicle	Place	Date
80*	Jean François Pilâtre de Rozier (1757–85) (France)	Hot Air Balloon (tethered)	Fauxbourg, Paris	15 & 17 Oct 1783
c.330	de Rozier and the Marquis d'Arlandes (1742–1809) (France)	Hot Air Balloon (free flight)	LaMuette, Paris [1]	21 Nov 1783
c.3,000	Dr Jacques-Alexandre-César Charles (1746–1823) and Ainé Robert (France)	Charlière Hydrogen Balloon	Tuileries, Paris	1 Dec 1783
c.9,000	Dr J.-A.-C. Charles (France)	Hydrogen Balloon	Nesles, France	1 Dec 1783
c.13,000	James Sadler (GB)	Hydrogen Balloon	Manchester, United Kingdom	May 1785
25,400 [2]	James Glaisher (1809–1903) (GB)	Hydrogen Balloon	Wolverhampton, United Kingdom	17 Jul 1862
31,500	Prof A. Berson (Germany)	Hydrogen Balloon Phoenix	Strasbourg, France	4 Dec 1894
36,565	Sadi Lecointe (France)	Nieuport Aircraft	Issy-les-Moulineaux, France	30 Oct 1923
51,961	Prof Auguste Piccard and Paul Kipfer (Switzerland)	FNRS 1 Balloon	Augsburg, Germany	27 May 1931
72,395	Capts Orvill A. Anderson and Albert W. Stevens (US Army Air Corps)	US Explorer II Helium Balloon	Rapid City, SD	11 Nov 1935
79,600	William Barton Bridgeman (US)	US Douglas D558–11 *Skyrocket*	California	15 Aug 1951
126,200	Capt Iven C. Kincheloe, Jr (USAF)	US Bell X-2 Rocket plane	California	7 Sep 1956
169,600	Joseph A. Walker (US)	US X-15 Rocket plane	California	30 Mar 1961
Statute miles				
203·2	Flt-Major Yuriy A. Gagarin (USSR) (1934–68)	USSR *Vostok I* Capsule	Orbital flight	12 Apr 1961
234,672	Col Frank Borman, USAF, Capt James Arthur Lovell, Jr, USN and Major William A. Anders, USAF	US *Apollo VIII* Command Module	Circum-lunar flight	25 Dec 1968
248,655	Capt James Arthur Lovell Jr, USN, Frederick Wallace Haise Jr and John L. Swigert Jr (1931–82)	US *Apollo XIII*	Abortive lunar landing mission	15 Apr 1970

* *There is some evidence that Father Bartolomeu de Gusmo flew in his hot-air balloon in his fourth experiment post August 1709 in Portugal.*

[1] *Duration c. 1:54 to 2:16 pm from Château de LaMuette to Butte aux Cailles, Paris 13e. Volume of the 70 ft high balloon was 60,000 'piedcubes' c. 60,034 ft³.*

[2] *Glaisher, with Henry Tracey Coxwell (1819–1900) claimed 37,000 ft from Wolverhampton, United Kingdom on 5 Sep 1862. Some writers accept 30,000 ft.*

A complete progressive table comprising entries from 1783 to date was published in the 1977 edition.

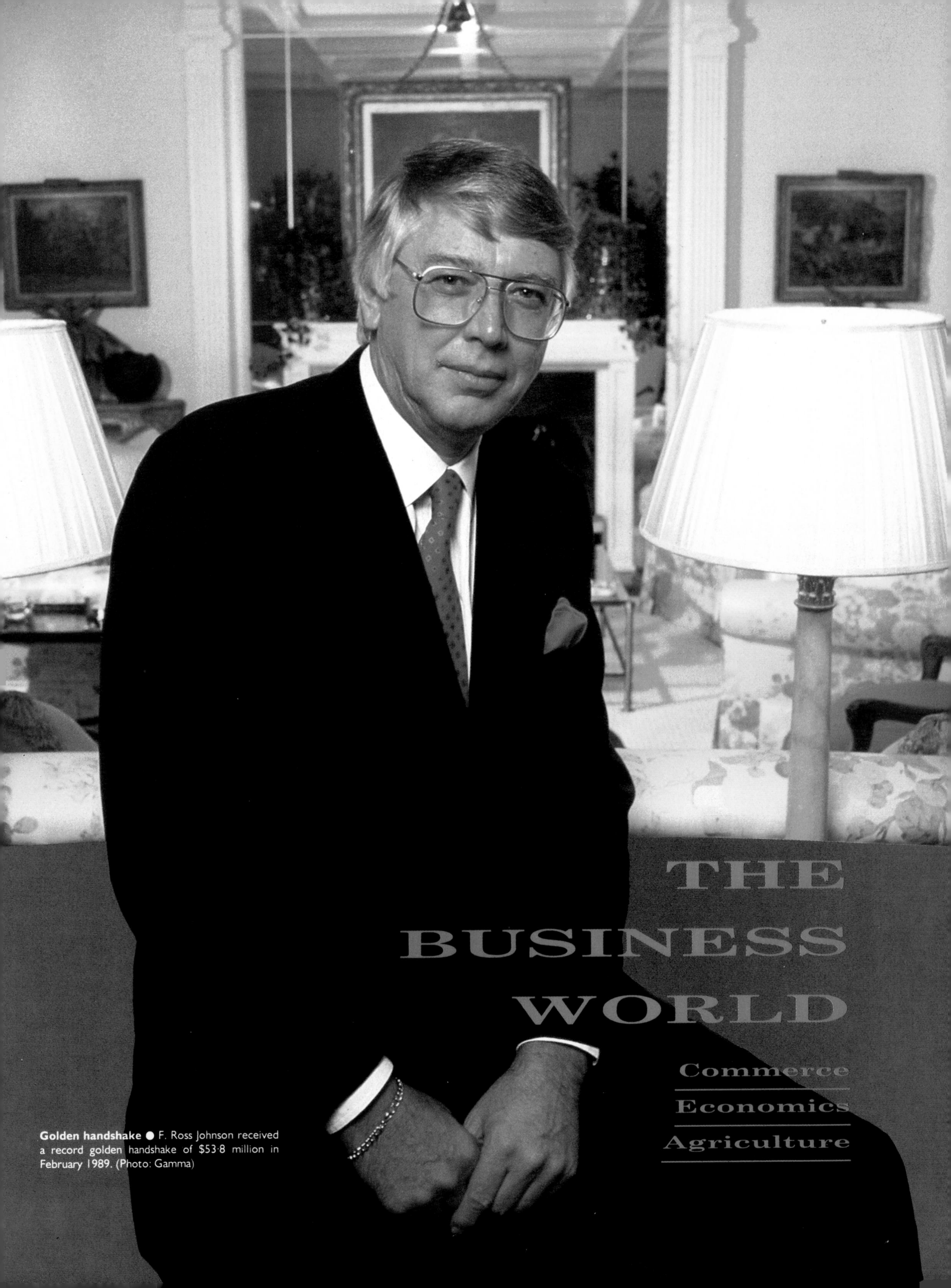

THE BUSINESS WORLD

Commerce
Economics
Agriculture

Golden handshake ● F. Ross Johnson received a record golden handshake of $53·8 million in February 1989. (Photo: Gamma)

Commerce

Oldest industry ■ The oldest known industry is flint knapping, involving the production of chopping tools and hand axes, dating from 2·5 million years ago in Ethiopia. The earliest evidence of trading in exotic stone and amber dates from c. 28,000 B.C. in Europe. Agriculture is often described as 'the oldest industry in the world,' whereas in fact there is no firm evidence yet that it was practiced before c. 11,000 B.C.

Oldest company ■ The Faversham Oyster Fishery Co. is referred to in the Faversham Oyster Fishing Act of 1930 as existing 'from time immemorial,' i.e., in British law, from before 1189.

Stora Kopparbergs Bergslags of Falun, Sweden is one of the world's oldest industrial enterprises and has been in continuous operation since the 11th century. It is first mentioned in historical records in the year 1288, when a Swedish Bishop bartered an eighth share in the enterprise. Originally concerned with the mining and processing of copper, it is today the largest privately-owned power producer in Sweden.

Greatest assets ■ The business with the greatest amount in physical assets was the Bell System, which comprised the American Telephone and Telegraph Co. (AT&T) and its subsidiaries. The Bell System's total assets on the consolidated balance sheet at the time of its divestiture and breakup into eight companies on 31 Dec 1983 reached $149·529 billion. The plant involved included more than 142 million telephones. The number of employees was 1,036,000. The company's market value of $59·4 billion was held among 3 million ordinary stockholders. A total of 20,109 stockholders attended the annual meeting in April 1961, setting a world record.

Currently the largest assets of any manufacturing corporation are the $83·2 billion of Exxon Corporation, the world's largest oil company, on 1 Jan 1989. They have 104,000 employees.

The first company to have assets in excess of $1 billion was the United States Steel (now USX) Corporation, with $1·5 billion at the time of its creation by merger in 1902.

The largest recorded rights issue was one of £ 921 million by Barclays Bank, London, United Kingdom announced on 7 Apr 1988.

Greatest profit ■ The greatest net profit ever made by a corporation in 12 months is $7·6 billion by American Telephone and Telegraph Co. from 1 Oct 1981 to 30 Sep 1982.

Greatest loss ■ The Argentine-government owned petroleum company YPF (Yacimientos Petroliferos) was reported to have made a trading loss of $4·6 billion in 1983.

Largest employer ■ The world's largest employer is Indian Railways, with 1,624,121 staff in 1988–89.

Greatest sales ■ The first company to surpass the $1 billion mark in annual sales was the United States Steel (now USX) Corporation in 1917. There are now 570 corporations with sales exceeding £1 billion, including 272 from the United States.

The *Fortune 500 List* of April 1990 is headed by the General Motors Corporation of Detroit, MI with sales of $127 billion for 1989.

Take-overs ■ The highest bid in a corporate takeover was $21 billion for RJR Nabisco Inc., the tobacco, food and beverage company, by the Wall Street leveraged buyout firm Kohlberg Kravis Roberts, which offered $90 a share on 24 Oct 1988. By 1 Dec 1988 the bid, led by Henry Kravis, had reached $109 per share to aggregate $25 billion.

Bankruptcies ■ Rajendra Sethia (b. 1950) was arrested in New Delhi on 2 Mar 1985 on charges including criminal conspiracy and forgery. He had been declared bankrupt by the High Court in London, United Kingdom on 18 Jan 1985 when Esal Commodities was said to be in debt for a record £ 170 million. His personal debts were estimated at £ 140 million. William G. Stern (b. Hungary, 1936) of London, United Kingdom, a US citizen since 1957, who set

---

> **Oldest company** ● Stora Kopparbergs Bergslags of Falun, Sweden, one of the world's oldest industrial enterprises, has been in continuous operation since the 11th century. It is first mentioned in historical records in the year 1288 (see the Deed of exchange below), when a Swedish Bishop bartered an eighth share in the enterprise. Originally concerned with the mining and processing of copper, today it is the largest privately-owned producer in Sweden. (Photo: Stora Foto)

up Wilstar Group Holding Co. in the London property market in 1971, was declared bankrupt for £ 104 million in February 1979. This figure rose to £ 143 million by February 1983. He was discharged for £ 500,000 suspended for 2½ years on 28 Mar 1983.

Directorships ■ The record for directorships was set by Hugh T. Nicholson (1914–85), formerly senior partner of Harmood Banner & Sons, London, United Kingdom, who, as a liquidating chartered accountant, became director of all 451 companies of the Jasper group in 1961 and had seven other directorships.

Accountants ■ The now merged Price Waterhouse Andersen jointly generated global revenues in 1988 of $4·8 billion.

Advertising ■ The largest advertising group in the world is WPP Group of London, United Kingdom. *Advertising Age* lists the group's billings for 1989 at $16·1 billion.

The largest advertising *agency* is Dentsu Inc. of Tokyo with billings for 1989 quoted as $10·1 billion by *Advertising Age*.

The world's biggest advertiser is Sears, Roebuck and Co., spending $1·3 billion in 1989, excluding its catalog.

Aerospace company ■ The world's largest aerospace company is the Boeing Co, with 1989 sales of $20·3 billion and a work force of 164,000 worldwide. Cessna Aircraft Company of Wichita, KS had total sales of $600·9 million in 1989. The company has produced more than 177,000 aircraft since Clyde Cessna's first was built in 1911.

Aluminum producer ■ The world's largest producer of primary aluminum is Alcan Aluminium Ltd of Montreal, Canada, with its affiliated companies. The company shipped 2·5 million tons in 1988.

Auctioneers ■ The largest and oldest firm of art auctioneers in the world is the Sotheby Group of London and New York, founded in 1744, although their trading until 1778 was primarily in books. Christie's held their first art auction in 1766. Sotheby's turnover in 1989 was a record £ 2·9 billion. A single session record of £ 342 million was set at Sotheby's of New York in November 1989.

Banks ■ The International Bank for Reconstruction and Development (founded 27 Dec 1945), the 'World Bank,' the world's largest multilateral development bank, at 1818 H Street NW, Washington DC, had an authorized share capital of $171·4 billion at 31 Dec 1988. There were 151 members with a subscribed capital of $102 billion at 31 Dec 1988 at which time the World Bank also had reserves and accumulated net income, unallocated, of $9·2 billion. The International Monetary Fund (IMF), also in Washington DC, had 152 members with total quotas of $119,568·93 million lion as of Feb 1990.

The world's biggest commercial bank is Dai-Ichi Kangyo Bank Ltd of Japan with assets on 31 Mar 1989 of $414·1 billion.

The largest commercial bank in the United States is Citibank, N.A., located in New York with total assets of $152·78 billion and deposits of $105·94 billion as of 30 Jun 1989.

The bank with most branches is the State Bank of India with 12,203 on 1 Jan 1990 and assets of £ 26·4 billion.

The oldest bank in the United States in conti-

nuous operation is The Bank of New York, founded in 1784 by Alexander Hamilton.

Bicycle manufacturers ■ The world's biggest manufacturer of bicycles is Hero Cycles of Ludhiana, Punjab, India, founded in 1956 by the Munjal brothers. In 1989 they turned out 2,936,073 units.

China is estimated to have 210 million bicycles.

Bookstore ■ The bookstore with most titles and the longest shelving (30 miles) in the world is W. & G. Foyle Ltd of London, United Kingdom. First established in 1904 in a small store, the company now has a site of 75,825 ft².

The most capacious individual bookstore in the world measured by square footage is Barnes & Noble Bookstore at 105 Fifth Ave at 18th Street, New York City, with 154,250 ft² and with 12·87 miles of shelving.

Brewers ■ The oldest brewery in the world is the Weihenstephan Brewery, Freising, near Munich, West Germany, founded in A.D. 1040.

The largest single brewing organization in the world is Anheuser-Busch Inc. of St Louis, MO, with 12 breweries in the United States. In 1989 the company sold 80·7 million barrels, the greatest annual volume ever produced by a brewing company. The company's St Louis plant covers 100 acres and after the completion of current modernization projects will have an annual capacity in excess of 468 million gallons.

The largest brewery on a single site is Coors Brewing Company of Golden, CO, where 550 million gallons were produced in 1989.

Brickworks ■ The largest brickworks in the world is the London Brick Company Ltd plant at Stewartby, Bedfordshire, United Kingdom. The works, established in 1898, now cover 221 acres and have a production capacity of 10·5 million bricks and brick equivalent each week.

Chemicals ■ The largest manufacturer of chemicals in the United States is E. I. Du Pont de Nemours & Co. Inc. of Wilmington, DE. *Forbes* Magazine lists 1989 sales at $35·2 billion, with 145,787 employees.

Computer company ■ The world's largest computer firm is International Business Machines (IBM) Corporation of New York. As of December 1989 assets were $78 billion and gross income was $63 billion. It has 383,220 employees worldwide and 815,580 stockholders.

Confectioners ■ The largest chocolate and confectionery factory is that built by Hershey Chocolate United States in Hershey, PA in 1903–5. It has 2 million ft² of floor space.

Department stores ■ Woolworth Corporation, which celebrated its centenary in 1979, now operates more than 8,000 stores worldwide. Frank Winfield Woolworth opened his first store 'The Great Five Cent Store' in Utica, NY on 22 Feb 1879. The net income for 1989 was $329 million.

The world's largest department store is R. H. Macy & Co. Inc. at Herald Square, New York City. It covers 50·5 acres and employs 14,000 staff handling 400,000 items. Total sales for the company's 150 stores in 1989 were $6·7 billion. Rowland Hussey Macy's sales on his first day at his fancy goods store on 6th Avenue, on 27 Oct 1858, were recorded as $11·06.

One of the largest department stores in the world

is Harrods Ltd of Knightsbridge, London United Kingdom, named after Henry Charles Harrod (1800–85), who opened a grocery in Knightsbridge Village in 1849. It has a total selling area of 22 acres with 50 lifts and 36 flights of stairs and escalators, employes 4,000–5,500 people depending on the time of year, and achieved record sales of over £ 312 million in the year ending 1 Feb 1987. The record for a day is £ 7 million in the January 1987 sale. Nearly £ 13 million was taken over the first four days of the 1990 January sale.

Distillers ■ The world's largest distilling company is the Seagram Company Ltd, of Canada, with sales in the year ending 31 Jan 1990 totaling $5·6 billion. The group employs about 17,600 people.

The largest blender and bottler of Scotch whiskey is United Distillers, the spirits company of Guinness plc, at their Shieldhall plant in Glasgow, United Kingdom, which has the capacity to fill an estimated 144 million bottles of Scotch a year. This is equivalent to approximately 24 million gal, most of which is exported. The world's best-selling brands of Scotch and Gin, Johnnie Walker Red Label and Gordon's, are both products of United Distillers.

Old Bushmills Distillery, County Antrim, United Kingdom, licensed in 1608, claims to have been in production in 1276.

Drug store ■ The largest chain of drug stores in the world is Rite Aid Corporation of Shiremanstown, PA which in 1989 had 2,353 stores throughout the United States. The Walgreen Company of Deerfield, IL has fewer stores but a larger volume of sales, with $5·3 billion in 1989.

Electronics ■ The largest manufacturer of electronics in the United States is General Electric Corporation of Fairfield, CT, which is listed by *Forbes* Magazine as having 1989 sales of $55·264 billion and 292,000 employees.

Employment agency ■ Blue Arrow became the world's largest employment group when on 5 Sep 1987 it bid successfully for the US company Manpower at £ 825 million.

Fisheries ■ The greatest catch ever recorded from a single throw is 2,724 tons by the purse seine-net boat M/S *Flømann* from Hareide, Norway in the Barents Sea on 28 Aug 1986. It was estimated that more than 120 million fish were caught in this shoal.

The catch record for a single trawler is £ 278,798 from a 41,776-ton catch by the Icelandic vessel *Videy* at Hull, United Kingdom on 11 Aug 1987.

Grocery stores ■ The largest grocery chain in the United States is the Kroger Co. with 1988 sales of $19·1 billion, and total current assets valued at $4·46 billion. Kroger operates 1,235 supermarkets, 958 convenience stores and employs 170,000 people.

Hoteliers ■ Following its acquisition of Holiday Inns North America in February 1990, Bass plc, the United Kingdom's top brewing company, also became the world's largest hotel operator. The company now owns, manages and franchises 1,697 hotels with 326,388 rooms in 50 countries.

Insurance ■ The company with the highest volume of insurance in force in the world is the Prudential Insurance Company of America of Newark, NJ, with $757 billion at 31 Dec 1988. The total consolidated assets are $153 billion.

The largest single association in the world is the

Blue Cross and Blue Shield Association, the US-based hospital insurance organization, with a membership of 72·5 million on 31 Dec 1989. Benefits paid out in 1989 totaled $50·7 billion.

The largest life insurance policy ever written was one for $44 million for a Calgary land developer Victor T. Uy in February 1982 by Transamerica Occidental Life Assurance Co. The salesman was local manager Lorenzo F. Reyes.

The highest payout on a single life was reported on 14 Nov 1970 to be some $18 million to Mrs Linda Mullendore, widow of an Oklahoma rancher. Her murdered husband had paid $300,000 in premiums in 1969.

The largest ever marine insurance loss was approximately $836 million for the Piper Alpha Oil Field in the North Sea, United Kingdom. On 6 Jul 1988 a leak from a gas compression chamber underneath the living quarters ignited and triggered a series of explosions that blew Piper Alpha apart. Of the 232 people on board, only 65 survived.

The largest sum claimed for consequential losses is £ 890 million against owning, operating and building corporations and Claude Phillips resulting from the 55 million gallon oil spill from M. T. *Amoco Cadiz* on the Brittany coast of France on 16 Mar 1978.

Jewelry auction ■ The world's largest jewelry auction, which included the Van Cleef and Arpels 1939 ruby and diamond necklace, brought £ 31,380,197 on 3 Apr 1987 when the Duchess of Windsor's (1896–1986) collection was auctioned at Sotheby's of Geneva, Switzerland.

Land ■ The world's largest landowner is the United States Government, with a holding of 728 million acres, which is bigger than the world's eighth largest country, Argentina, and 12 times larger than Indiana.

It has been suggested that the USSR government constitutionally owns all the land in the entire country, with the exception, perhaps, of that on which foreign embassies stand.

The world's largest *private* landowner is reputed to be International Paper Co, with 9 million acres.

The longest tenure is that by St Paul's Cathedral of land at Tillingham, Essex, United Kingdom, given by King Ethelbert before A.D. 616.

The most expensive piece of property quoted in October 1988 by the Japanese National Land Agency is around the central Tokyo retail food store Mediya Building at 358·5 million yen per ft² (then equivalent to $248,000).

The highest rentals in the world for prime offices, according to *World Rental Levels* by Richard Ellis of London, United Kingdom, are in Tokyo, Japan at $187 per ft² per year (January 1990). With added service charges and property taxes Tokyo is also top at $204 per ft².

A typical apartment in the newly opened commercial and residential Kioicho building in Akasaka, Japan costs over $17,000 per month — payable 10 months in advance!

The highest and lowest property taxes quoted by the Richard Ellis Survey are Manchester, United Kingdom at 41 percent and Frankfurt am Main, West Germany at 1 percent.

Law firms ■ The world's largest law firm is Baker & McKenzie, employing 1,428 lawyers, 478

of whom are partners, in 30 countries at 1 Oct 1989. Founded in Chicago, IL in 1949, the 50th office was recently opened in East Berlin, East Germany.

Greatest auction ■ The greatest auction was of the Hughes Aircraft Co. for $5 billion by General Motors of Detroit, MI on 5 Jun 1985.

Greatest barter deal ■ The biggest barter in trading history was 30 million barrels of oil valued at £ 900 million exchanged for ten Boeing 747s for the Royal Saudi Airline in July 1984.

Menswear store ■ The world's largest store selling only men's suits and accessories is Slater Menswear of Howard Street, Glasgow, United Kingdom with a weekly turnover in excess of 2,000 suits. The store covers 40,250 ft² and stocks over 17,000 suits at any one time.

Mineral water ■ The world's largest mineral water firm is Source Perrier, near Nîmes, France, with an annual production of more than 2·5 billion bottles, of which 1·1 billion now come from Perrier. The French drink about 152 pints of mineral water per person per year.

Motor car manufacturer ■ The largest manufacturing company in the world is General Motors Corporation of Detroit, MI, with operations throughout the world. Apart from its core business of motor vehicles and components, it produces defense and aerospace materials and provides computer and communication services. Its total revenue in 1989 was $127 million and assets at 31 Dec 1989 were valued at $97 billion. Its total 1989 payroll was $28·3 billion to an average of 775,000 employees. Dividends paid in 1989 were $4·2 billion.

Largest plant ■ The largest single automobile plant in the world is the Volkswagenwerk at Wolfsburg, West Germany, with 61,000 employees and a capacity for 4,600 vehicles daily. The factory buildings cover an area of 371 acres and the whole plant covers 1,878 acres, with 43·5 miles of rail sidings.

Salesmanship ■ The career record total for automobile salesmanship in units sold individually is 13,407 to March 1990 by Larry Merritt of Sandy Springs, GA.

Oil refineries ■ The world's largest refinery is the Amerada Hess refinery in St Croix, VI producing on average 379,000 barrels per day in 1988.

Paper company ■ The world's largest producer of paper, fiber and wood products is International Paper of Purchase, NY with sales in 1989 of $11·4 billion employing 63,500 workers.

Pharmaceuticals ■ The world's largest pharmaceutical company is Merck, NJ, with sales of $5·67 billion in 1988.

LARGEST AMERICAN CORPORATIONS

Corporation	Sales (1989) $ Millions
General Motors, MI	126,974·3
Ford Motor, MI	96,932·6
Exxon, NY	86,656·0
Int'l Business Machines, NY	63,438·0
General Electric, CT	55,264·0

Fortune 500 Directory, 1990

The world's largest health-care products company is Johnson & Johnson of New Brunswick, NJ, with sales of $9·8 billion in 1989.

Photographic store ■ The photographic store with the largest selling area is Jessop of Leicester Ltd's Photo Centre, Leicester, United Kingdom, opened in June 1979 with an area now of 27,000 ft².

Public relations ■ The world's largest public relations firm is Burson Marsteller with headquarters in New York and a 1988 net fee income of $154·3 million.

Hill and Knowlton Inc. has most offices worldwide, 56, including one in Beijing, China.

Publishing ■ The largest publisher is Time Warner of New York with sales in 1989 of $7·6 billion employing 35,000 workers.

Record store ■ HMV opened the world's largest record store at 150 Oxford Street, London, United Kingdom on 24 Oct 1986. Its trading area measures 36,684 ft².

Restaurateurs ■ The largest restaurant chain in the world is that operated by McDonald's Corporation of Oak Brook, IL, founded on 15 Apr 1955 in Des Plaines, Chicago by Ray A. Kroc, BH (Bachelor of Hamburgerology) (1902–84), after buying out the McDonald brothers' restaurants. 'Mac' McDonald, who with his brother Dick opened his first fast food drive-in outlet in Pasadena, CA in 1937, died in 1971. By 3 Apr 1989 the number of McDonald's restaurants licensed and owned in 50 countries and territories around the world reached 10,500, serving 22 million customers per day, with an aggregate throughput of 70 billion 100 percent pure beef hamburgers. Sales system-wide in 1988 surpassed $16·1 billion.

Fish and chip restaurant ■ The world's largest fish and chip store is Harry Ramsden's at White Cross, West Yorkshire, United Kingdom, with 140 staff serving 1 million customers per year, who consume 235 tons of fish and 392 tons of potatoes. On 30 Oct 1988, between 11: 30 A.M. and 10: 00 P.M., Harry Ramsden's celebrated their Diamond Jubilee by serving 10,182 servings of fish and chips at 1928 prices.

Retailer ■ The largest retailing firm in the world is Sears, Roebuck and Co. (founded by Richard Warren Sears in North Redwood, MN in 1886) of Chicago, IL. Worldwide revenues were $31·6 billion in the year ending 31 Dec 1989 when Sears Merchandise Group had 847 retail stores, 1,731 sales offices and 1,769 independent catalog merchants in the US. Total assets stood at $2·5 billion.

Savings and Loan Associations ■ The world's biggest lender is the Japanese government-controlled House Loan Corporation.

The largest Savings and Loan Association in the United States is Home Savings of America, FA, located in Irwindale, Los Angeles, CA, with total assets of $38·987 billion at the year end 1989.

Shipbuilding ■ Worldwide production completed in 1989 was 13·2 million gross tonnage of ships, excluding sailing ships, non-propelled vessels and vessels of less than 100 gross tonnage.

The figures for the USSR, Romania and the People's Republic of China are incomplete.

Japan completed 5·4 million gross tonnage (40·5 percent of the world total) in 1989.

The world's leading shipbuilder in 1989 was Hyundai of South Korea, which completed 25 ships of 1·4 million gross tonnage.

Shipping line ■ The largest shipping owners and operators are Exxon Corporation, whose fleets of owned/managed and chartered tankers in 1987 totaled a daily average of 9·3 million dwt tonnes .

Shopping centers ■ The world's first shopping center was built in 1896 at Roland Park, Baltimore, MD.

The world's largest is the $1·1 billion West Edmonton Mall in Alberta, Canada, which was opened on 15 Sep 1981 and completed four years later. It covers 5·2 million ft² on a 110-acre site and encompasses 828 stores and services as well as 11 major department stores. Parking is provided for 20,000 vehicles for more than 500,000 shoppers per week.

The world's largest wholesale merchandise mart is the Dallas Market Center on Stemmons Freeway, Dallas, TX, with nearly 9·3 million ft² in eight buildings. The complex covers 150 acres with some 3,400 permanent showrooms displaying merchandise of more than 26,000 manufacturers. The Center attracts 600,000 buyers each year to its 38 annual markets and trade shows.

The longest mall in the world can be found at the £ 40 million shopping center at Milton Keynes, Buckinghamshire, United Kingdom. It measures 2,133 ft.

Soft drinks ■ Pepsico of Purchase, NY topped the *Fortune 500* table for beverage companies in April 1990, with total sales for 1989 of $15·4 billion, compared with $9·8 billion for the Coca-Cola Company of Atlanta, GA. Coca-Cola is, however, the world's most popular soft drink, with sales in 1989 of over 448 million drinks per day, representing an estimated 45 percent of the world market.

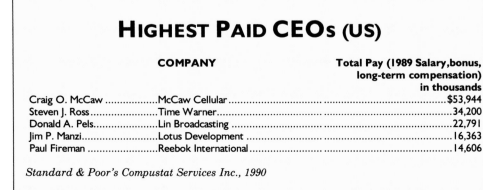

HIGHEST PAID CEOs (US)

COMPANY		Total Pay (1989 Salary, bonus, long-term compensation) in thousands
Craig O. McCaw	McCaw Cellular	$53,944
Steven J. Ross	Time Warner	34,200
Donald A. Pels	Lin Broadcasting	22,791
Jim P. Manzi	Lotus Development	16,363
Paul Fireman	Reebok International	14,606

Standard & Poor's Compustat Services Inc., 1990

Bank ● This 'drawn note' or check for £54,10s. 10d. (approx. $90) dated 1676 is believed to be the oldest example to survive with the corresponding ledger account. Drawn on C. Hoare & Co., the United Kingdom's oldest independent bank (founded 1672), it is shown here with a tankard made by the bank's founder, goldsmith Richard Hoare (1648–1718), together with the leather bottle used as the bank's logo and assorted gold and silver coins of the period. (Photo: C. Hoare & Co.)

Steel companies ■ The noncommunist world's largest producer of steel is Nippon Steel Corporation of Japan, which produced 9·92 million tons of crude steel in 1989.

The Pohang works of the Pohang Iron & Steel Co. Ltd (POSCO) of South Korea produced 32 million tons of crude steel in 1988, the highest amount produced by a single integrated works.

Sugar mills ■ The world's largest cane sugar refinery is that of the California & Hawaiian Sugar Co. founded in 1906 at Crockett, CA, with a capacity of 4,000 tons per day.

The highest recorded output for any sugar mill was set in 1966–67 by Ingenio de San Cristobal y Anexas, S.A., Veracruz, Mexico with a total of 277,648 tons of sugar refined from 3·3 million tons of cane.

Supermarkets ■ The world's first supermarket with a self-service format and checkouts was the Piggly Wiggly store opened in 1916 by Clarence Saunders (1881–1953) in Memphis, TN. Above 25,000 ft² net shopping area, stores are usually termed superstores, and above 50,000 ft² hypermarkets.

Tobacco plant ■ The world's largest and most automated cigarette plant is R. J. Reynolds Tobacco Co.'s $1 billion facility at Tobaccoville, NC, opened in September 1986, which produces more than 110 billion cigarettes annually.

Toy store ■ The world's biggest toy store is

Hamleys, founded in 1760 in Holborn, London, United Kingdom and removed to Regent Street, London in 1901. It has selling space of 45,000 ft² on six floors and employs over 400 staff during the Christmas season.

Undertakers ■ The world's largest undertaking business is SCI (Service Corporation International) of Houston, TX, with 551 funeral homes and 126 cemeteries. Its annual revenue in this most recession-proof of industries in the year ending 31 Dec 1989 was $519 million.

Vintners ■ The world's oldest champagne firm is Ruinart Père et Fils founded in 1729. The oldest cognac firm is Augier Frères & Cie, established in 1643.

Economics

MONETARY AND FINANCIAL

Largest budget ■ The greatest governmental expenditure ever made by any country has been $1·07 trillion by the United States government for the fiscal year 1988.

The highest ever revenue figure was $909·0 billion in the same US fiscal year.

The greatest fiscal surplus ever was $8,419,469,844 in the United States in 1947–48.

The worst deficit was the $221·4 billion in the US fiscal year 1986.

Foreign aid ■ The total net foreign aid given by the United States Government between 1 Jul 1945 and 1 Jan 1989 was $291·8 billion.

The country receiving most US aid in 1990 was Israel with $3 billion. Egypt was second with $2·3 billion. These totals are for both economic and military aid.

US foreign aid began with $50,000 to Venezuela for earthquake relief in 1812.

Least taxed ■ The lowest income-taxed sovereign countries in the world are Bahrain, Brunei, Kuwait and Qatar, where the rate, regardless of income, is nil.

No tax is levied on the Sarkese (inhabitants of Sark) in the Channel Islands, United Kingdom, or on the inhabitants of Tristan da Cunha.

Highest taxation rates ■ The country with the most confiscatory taxation is Norway, where in January 1974 the Labor Party and Socialist Alliance abolished the 80 percent limit. Some 2,000 citizens were then listed in the *Lignings Boka* as paying more than 100 percent of their taxable income. The shipping magnate Hilmar Reksten (1897–1980) was assessed at 491 percent.

The highest income tax rate in United States history was implemented in 1944 by the Individual Tax Act with a 91% bracket. The lowest income tax rate was 1% between 1913 and 1915. The current highest income tax bracket is 33%.

Balance of payments ■ The record deficit for any country for a fiscal year is $143·7 billion in 1987 by the US.

The record surplus is $96·4 billion in 1987 by Japan.

Highest tax demands ■ The highest recorded personal tax demand is one for $336 million on 70 percent of the estate of Howard Hughes.

National debt ■ The largest national debt of any country in the world is that of the United States, where the gross federal public debt of the federal government surpassed the trillion (10^{12}) dollar mark on 30 Sep 1981.

The total federal debt in the United States is estimated for the fiscal year ending 1990 at $3·113 trillion, with net interest payments of $175·6 billion, which is the highest national debt in US history. The lowest national debt figure was $33,533 in 1835.

Most foreign debt ■ The country most heavily in overseas debt in early 1990 was Brazil, with $111 billion.

Gross national product ■ The country with the largest gross national product is the United States, which, having reached $3 trillion ($3 \times 10^{12}$) in 1981, was running at $4·9 trillion at the end of the fiscal year 1988.

National wealth ■ The richest territory as listed in the 1989 rankings of the *World Bank Atlas* is Bermuda, which in 1987 had an average GNP per capita of $22,540.

The US, which had held the lead from 1910 to 1973, was third, behind Switzerland.

It has been estimated that the value of all physical assets in the United States on 1 Jan 1983 was $12·5 trillion ($12·5 \times 10^{12}$) per capita.

According to figures released by the Commerce Department's Bureau of Economic Analysis, in 1987 Connecticut enjoyed the highest per capita income level at 130·5% of the national average ($15,484), followed by New Jersey at 121·6% and New York at 109%.

Poorest country ■ Ethiopia had the lowest GNP per capita in 1987, with $130, although the *World Bank Atlas* has no publishable data for a number of socialist countries.

Gold and foreign currency reserves ■ The country with the greatest monetary gold reserve is the United States, whose Treasury had 261·87 million fine oz of the world's 944·76 million fine oz on hand at the end of 1988. Valued at $410 per fine oz, these amounts would translate to 107·4 billion and 387·4 billion respectively.

The United States Bullion Depository at Fort

Knox, 30 miles southwest of Louisville, KY, has been the principal federal depository of US gold since December 1936. Gold is stored in 446,000 standard mint bars of 400 troy ounces measuring $7 \times 3\frac{5}{8} \times 1\frac{5}{8}$ in. Gold's peak price was $850 on 21 Jan 1980.

Inflation ■ The United States Department of Labor measures changes in the Consumer Price Index (CPI) in twelve month periods ending in December. The Bureau of Labor Statistics first began keeping the Consumer Price Index in 1913. Since that time the change of the greatest magnitude was 20·4 % for the twelve month period ending December 1918, and the largest decline was −10·8 % in December 1921. The largest peacetime increase was recorded in December 1979 was a rate of 13·3 %. Figures are based on the United States city average CPI for all urban consumers.

Worst ■ The world's worst inflation occurred in Hungary in June 1946, when the 1931 gold pengö was valued at 130 million, trillion ($1·3 \times 10^{20}$) paper pengös. Notes were issued for 'Egymillard billion' (one sextillion or 10^{21}) pengös on 3 Jun and withdrawn on 11 Jul 1946. Vouchers for 1 billion trillion (10^{27}) pengös were issued for taxation payment only.

On 6 Nov 1923 the circulation of Reichsbank marks reached 400,338,326,350,700,000,000 and inflation was 755,700 million fold on 1913 levels.

The country with the highest inflation in 1989 was Argentina, where inflation was running at a monthly rate of 200 percent in July.

Least ■ The country with the least inflation over a year in recent times was Equatorial Guinea, which had a rate of −17·8 percent in 1986.

WEALTH AND POVERTY
The comparison and estimations of extreme personal wealth are beset with intractable diffi-

culties. Quite apart from reticence and the element of approximation in the valuation of assets, as Jean Paul Getty (1892–1976) once said: 'If you can count your millions you are not a billionaire.' The term millionaire was invented *c.* 1740 and billionaire in 1861. The earliest dollar centi-millionaire was Cornelius Vanderbilt (1794–1877), who left $100 million in 1877. The earliest billionaires were John Davison Rockefeller (1839–1937); Henry Ford (1863–1947) and Andrew William Mellon (1855–1937).

Richest men ■ Many of the riches of most of the world's 29 remaining monarchs are national rather than personal assets. The least fettered and most monarchical is HM Sir Muda Hassanal Bolkiah Mu'izzaddin Waddaulah (b. 15 Jul 1946) of Brunei. He appointed himself Prime Minister, Finance and Home Affairs Minister on 1 Jan 1984. *Fortune* Magazine reported in September 1989 that his fortune was $25 billion.

Forbes Magazine estimated in its 23 Jul 1990 issue that Yoshiaki Tsutsumi of Japan was the world's richest man, with assets of $16 billion. He controls his Seibu empire — consisting of an important railroad, Seibu Construction, the Seibu baseball Lions and a number of other companies — through Kokudo Keikaku Corp., a holding company of which he directly owns 40 percent.

Forbes Magazine reported in its 23 Oct 1989 issue that the richest man in the United States is John Kluge of Charlottesville, VA, with a personal fortune of $5·2 billion. Aged 75, Kluge is chairman of Metromedia. His $500 million estate in Charlottesville was described in *Town & Country* magazine as 'the most lavish of the century.'

Richest women ■ The title of the world's wealthiest woman has been wrongly conferred upon the recluse Hideko Osano (b. 1930), widow since October 1986 of the Japanese tycoon Kenji Osano. The US press first estimated her wealth at $25 billion. In fact much of her husband's wealth was diverted from her.

Queen Elizabeth II is asserted by some to be the wealthiest woman, and *The Sunday Times,* a

British newspaper, estimated in April 1990 that she had assets worth £ 6·7 billion. However, few of her assets under the perpetual succession of the Crown are either personal or disposable.

The cosmetician Madame C. J. Walker, nee Sarah Breedlove (b. 23 Dec 1867, d. 1919), is reputed to have become the first self-made millionairess. She was an uneducated black orphan whose fortune was founded on a hair relaxer.

Richest families ■ It has been tentatively estimated that the combined value of the assets nominally controlled by the Du Pont family of some 1,600 members may be of the order of $150 billion. The family arrived in the United States from France on 1 Jan 1800. Capital from Pierre du Pont (1730–1817) enabled his son Eleuthère Irénée du Pont to start his explosives company in the United States.

Youngest millionaires ■ The youngest person ever to accumulate a million dollars was the child film actor Jackie Coogan (b. Los Angeles 26 Oct 1914), co-star with Charles Chaplin (1889–1977) in *The Kid*, made in 1920.

The youngest millionairess was Shirley Temple (b. Santa Monica, CA 23 Apr 1928), formerly Mrs John Agar Jr, now Mrs Charles Black, who accumulated wealth exceeding $1 million before she was 10. Her childhood acting career spanned the years 1934–39.

Highest incomes ■ The greatest incomes derive from the collection of royalties per barrel by rulers of oil-rich sheikhdoms who have not abrogated personal entitlement. Shaikh Zayid ibn Sultan an-Nuhayan (b. 1918), head of state of the United Arab Emirates, arguably has title to some $9 billion of the country's annual gross national product.

Largest dowry ■ The largest recorded dowry was that of Elena Patiño, daughter of Don Simón Iturbi Patiño (1861–1947), the Bolivian tin millionaire, who in 1929 bestowed £ 8 million from a fortune at one time estimated to be worth £ 125 million.

Greatest miser ■ If meanness is measurable as a ratio between expendable assets and expenditure then Henrietta (Hetty) Howland Green (nee Robinson; 1835–1916), who kept a balance of over $31·4 million in one bank alone, was the all-time world champion. Her son had to have his leg amputated because of her delays in finding a *free* medical clinic. She herself ate cold porridge because she was too thrifty to heat it. Her estate proved to be of $95 million.

Return of cash ■ The largest amount of *cash* ever found and returned to its owners was $500,000 found by Lowell Elliott, 61, on his farm at Peru, IN. It had been dropped in June 1972 by a parachuting hijacker.

Jim Priceman, 44, assistant cashier at Doft & Co Inc., returned an envelope containing $37·1 million in *negotiable* bearer certificates found outside 110 Wall Street to A. G. Becker Inc. of New York on 6 Apr 1982. In announcing a reward of $250 Beckers were acclaimed as 'being all heart.'

Greatest bequests ■ The greatest bequest in the lifetime of a billionaire was that of Ryoichi Sasakawa, chairman of the Japanese Shipbuilding Industry Foundation, who made total donations of 644,699,912,000 yen ($5·16 billion) in the years 1962–88.

The largest single bequest in the history of philanthropy was the $500 million gift, announced on 12 Dec 1955, to 4,157 educational and other institutions by the Ford Foundation (established 1936) of New York.

Highest salary ■ It was reported by the US government that Michael Milken, the 'junk bond king' at Drexel Burnham Lambert Inc., earned $550 million in salary and bonuses in. 1987 (See also Fines, Chapter 10).

Highest fees ■ The highest-paid investment consultant in the world is Harry D. Schultz, who operates from Monte Carlo and Zurich, Switzerland. His standard consultation fee for 60 minutes is $2,400 on weekdays and $3,400 at weekends. Most popular are the five minute phone consultations at $200 (i.e., $40 a minute). His 'International Harry Schultz Letter,' instituted in 1964, sells at $50 per copy. A life subscription costs $2,400.

Golden handshake ■ *Business Week* magazine reported in May 1989 that the largest golden handshake ever given was one of $53·8 million, to F. Ross Johnson, who left RJR Nabisco as chairman in February 1989.

PAPER MONEY

Earliest ■ Paper money was an invention of the Chinese, first tried in A.D. 812 and prevalent by A.D. 970.

The world's earliest bank notes (*banco-sedler*) were issued in Stockholm, Sweden in July 1661, the oldest survivor being one of 5 dalers dated 6 Dec 1662.

Largest and smallest ■ The largest paper money ever issued was the 1-kwan note of the Chinese Ming dynasty issue of 1368–99, which measured 9 × 13 in. In October 1983 one sold for £ 340.

The smallest national note ever issued was the 10-bani note of the Ministry of Finance of Romania, in 1917. It measured (printed area) 1·09 × 1·49 in.

Of German *Notgeld* the smallest were the 1–3 pfg of Passau (1920–21) measuring 0·70 × 0·72 in.

Highest values ■ The highest value notes in circulation are US Federal Reserve bank notes for $10,000. They bear the head of Salmon Portland Chase (1808–73). None has been printed since July 1944 and the US Treasury announced in 1969 that no further notes higher than $100 would be issued; this note bears the head of Benjamin Franklin. Only 345 $10,000 bills remain in circulation or unretired.

The highest demomination ever issued by the US Federal Reserve System is a bank-note for $100,000 bearing the head of Woodrow Wilson, which is only used for transactions between Federal Reserve and the Treasury Department.

COINS

OLDEST

World: c. 670 B.C. electrum staters of King Gyges of Lydia, Turkey[1].

EARLIEST DATED

Samian silver tetradrachm struck in Zankle (now Messina), Sicily dated year I *viz* 494 B.C.—shown as 'A'. *Christian Era:* MCCXXXIIII (1234) Bishop of Roskilde coins, Denmark (6 known)

HEAVIEST

World: 43 lb 7 ¼ oz Swedish 10-daler copper plate 1644[2].

LIGHTEST AND SMALLEST

World: 14,000 to the oz Nepalese silver Jawa c. 1740.

MOST EXPENSIVE

World: $1,000,000 for a set of 1804 US coins (including the rare silver dollar), once presented to the King of Siam, by dealer Lester Merkin in 1979.

RAREST

World: Many 'singletons' known, e.g. the Axumite gold coin of Wazeba in the Bibliothèque Nationale, Paris and the Axumite ½ tremissis of Aphilas of *c.* A.D. 250 owned by Dr Bent Juel-Jensen of Oxford.

[1] Chinese uninscribed 'spade' money of the Zhou dynasty has been dated to *c.* 770 B.C.
[2] The largest coin-like medallion was completed on 21 Mar 1986 for the World Exposition in Vancouver, British Columbia, Canada, Expo 86—a $1,000,000 gold piece. Its dimensions were 37·5 in diameter and ³/₄ in thick and it weighed 365 lb 15 oz or 5,337 oz (troy) of gold.

Lowest values ■ The lowest value (and the lowest denomination) legal tender bank note is the 1-sen (or 1/100th of a rupiah) Indonesian note. Its exchange value in early 1990 was 175,000 to the dollar.

Bank note collection ■ R. Aguilar-Bolaños of the United Nations Industrial Development Organization in Vienna has amassed 173 bank notes, each from a different country, since he started collecting in 1965.

Largest check ● The largest check in the history of banking was £1·425 billion, issued on 11 Jul 1989. (Photo: Abbey National)

CHECKS AND COINS

Largest ■ The greatest amount paid by a single check in the history of banking was £ 1·425 billion. Issued on 11 Jul 1989 and signed by D. Gareth Jones, Abbey National Building Society Treasurer and Assistant General Manager, and Jonathan C. Nicholls, Abbey National Building Society Assistant Treasurer, the check represented a payment from the expiring Abbey National Building Society in favor of the newly created Abbey National plc.

A larger one, for $4,176,969,623·57, was drawn on 30 Jun 1954, although this was an internal US Treasury check.

Collections ■ The highest price ever paid for a coin collection was $25,235,360 for the Garrett family collection of US and colonial coins, which had been donated to Johns Hopkins University, Baltimore, MD. The sales were made at a series of four auctions held from 28–29 Nov 1979 and 25–26 Mar 1981 at the Bowers & Ruddy Galleries in Wolfeboro, NH. The collection was put together by members of the Garrett family between 1860 and 1942.

Most valuable ■ The most valuable coin collection formed by a single individual and sold at public auction was the Louis Eliasberg Collection of US gold coins. The collection, grouped into 1,074 lots, was sold by Bowers & Ruddy Galleries in New York City 27–29 Oct 1982 for $12·4 million. This is the highest total realized for a single coin auction. Eliasberg was a prominent Baltimore banker.

Auction price ■ The highest price paid at auction for a single coin is $990,000 for a US 1804 silver dollar (a Dexter-Bareford Class I) in proof condition at Rarcoa's, Chicago, IL on 7 Jul 1989 at the 'Auction '89' Sale.

Largest hoards ■ The most valuable hoard was one of about 80,000 aurei in Brescello near Modena, Italy in 1714, believed to have been deposited *c.* 37 B.C.

The numerically largest deliberately buried hoard ever found was the Brussels hoard of 1908 containing *c.* 150,000 coins.

The largest accidental hoard on record was the 1715 Spanish Plate Fleet, which sank off the coast of Florida. A reasonable estimate of its contents would be some 60 million coins, of which about half were recovered by Spanish authorities shortly after the event. Of the remaining 30 million pieces, perhaps 500,000 have been recovered by modern salvors. The other 29½ million coins are, presumably, still on the bottom of the sea, awaiting recovery.

Largest mint ■ The largest mint in the world is the US Treasury's mint built from 1965–69 on Independence Mall, Philadelphia, covering 11½ acres with an annual production capacity on a three-shift seven-day week of 15 billion coins. One new high-speed stamping machine can produce coins at a rate of 40,000 per hour.

Most popular coin ■ More than 250 billion pennies with Lincoln's head have been minted in the 80 years since its premiere issue in 1909 for the 100th anniversary of Lincoln's birth. If lined up, the 250 billion coins would stretch 2,808,586 miles and if piled up (17 to an inch) they would tower 220,851 miles into space.

Column of coins ■ The most valuable column of coins amassed for charity was worth £ 13,628 and was knocked over by Frankie Vaughan at Mecca's Club, Bolton, Lancashire, United Kingdom on 18 Aug 1984.

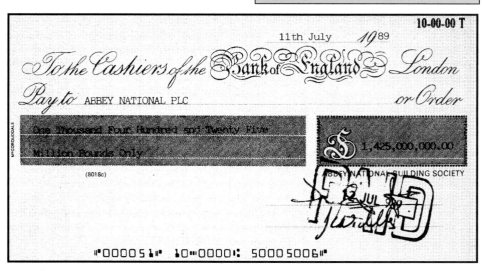

Line of coins ■ The highest-valued line of coins was (10 miles 5 ft 7 in) made up of 662,353 quarters to a value of $165,788 on 16 Mar 1985 at Central City Park, Atlanta, GA, and sponsored by the National Kidney Foundation of Georgia Inc.

A carpet of 1,945,223 Belgian 1 franc coins (0·83 in in diameter) and thus with a total length of 25·384 miles was laid in Geel, Belgium by members of Mepp-Stegeta on 25 Jun 1988.

Pile of coins ■ The Copper Mountain, devised by Terry Pitts Fenby for the National Society for the Prevention of Cruelty to Children at Selfridges, Oxford Street, London, United Kingdom consisted of over 3 million coins accumulated in 350 days (24 May 1984–7 May 1985), with a total value of £ 57,051·34.

LABOR

First trade union ■ The first officially recognised labor organization in the United States was formed by the Shoemakers and Coopers of Boston, MA. They were granted a three year charter by King Charles II in 1648. The charter was not renewed.

Largest trade union ■ The world's largest union is Professionalniy Soyuz Rabotnikov Agro-Promyshlennogo Kompleksa (Agro-Industrial Complex Workers' Union) in the Soviet Union, with 36,634,613 members at 1 Jan 1990.

United States ■ As of 31 Dec 1988 the largest union in the United States is the National Education Association (NEA), that has 1·9 million members. This is closely followed by the International Brotherhood of Teamsters, Chauffers, Warehousemen and Helpers of America, that has 1·7 million members.

Smallest trade union ■ The ultimate in small unions was the Jewelcase and Jewelry Display Makers Union (JJDMU) founded in 1894. It was dissolved on 31 Dec 1986 by its general secretary, Charles Evans. The motion was seconded by Fergus McCormack, its only surviving member.

Longest name ■ The union with the longest name is the International Association of Marble, Slate and Stone Polishers, Rubbers and Sawyers, Tile and Marble Setters' Helpers and Marble Mosaic and Terrazzo Workers' Helpers, or the IAMSSPRSTMSHMMTWH of Washington, D.C.

Earliest labor dispute ■ A labor dispute concerning monotony of diet and working conditions was recorded in 1153 B.C. in Thebes, Egypt. The earliest recorded strike was one by an orchestra leader named Aristos from Greece, in Rome *c.* 309 B.C. The cause was meal breaks.

Longest strike ■ The world's longest recorded strike ended on 4 Jan 1961, after 33 years. It concerned the employment of barbers' assistants in Copenhagen, Denmark. The longest recorded major strike was that at the plumbing fixtures factory of the Kohler Co in Sheboygan, WI, between April 1954 and October 1962. The strike is alleged to have cost the United Automobile Workers' Union about $12 million to sustain.

Lowest unemployment ■ In Switzerland in December 1973 (pop. 6·6 million), the total number of unemployed was reported to be 81.

Highest unemployment ■ The highest annual unemployment average in United States

history was 24·9 % in 1933 during the Great Depression and the lowest average was 1·2 % in 1944 during World War II. These figures are based on a labor force age of fourteen and older. Since 1948 the United States Department of Labor has kept statistics based on the Current Population Survey of households by a labor force age of sixteen and older. According to these figures, the highest annual unemployment average since 1948 was 9·7 % in 1982 and the lowest was 2·9 % in 1953.

The highest average number of people unemployed in United States history was 12,830,000 in 1933 and the lowest 670,000 in 1944. Again, these figures are based on a labor force age of fourteen and older. Since 1948 the highest average number of people unemployed was 10,717,000 in 1983 and the lowest was 1,834,000 in 1953 (based on a labor force age of sixteen and older).

Working career ■ The longest working life has been 98 years by Mr Izumi who began work goading draft animals at a sugar mill at Isen, Tokunoshima, Japan in 1872. He retired as a sugar cane farmer in 1970 aged 105.

Working week ■ A case of a working week of 142 hours (with an average each day of 3 hr 42 min 51 sec for sleep) was recorded in June 1980 by Dr Paul Ashton, 32, the anesthetics registrar at Birkenhead General Hospital, Merseyside, United Kingdom. He described the week in question as 'particularly bad but not untypical.' Some non-consultant doctors are contracted to work 110 hours a week or be available for 148 hours.

Some contracts for fully salaried university lecturers call for an eight-hr week or a 72-hr year spread over 24 weeks.

ENERGY CONSUMPTION

To express the various forms of available energy (coal, liquid fuels and water power etc., but omitting vegetable fuels and peat), it is the practice to convert them all into terms of coal.

The highest consumption in the world is in the Virgin Islands, with an average of 597·4 cwt (66,910·2 lb) per person per year. The highest in a sovereign state is 379·51 cwt (42,505·1 lb) in Qatar.

The lowest recorded average was in 1974 at 0·26 cwt (28·6 lb) per person in Rwanda.

STOCK EXCHANGES

The oldest stock exchange of the 138 listed throughout the world is that of Amsterdam, the Netherlands, founded in 1602 with dealings in printed shares of the United East India Company of the Netherlands in the Oude Zijds Kapel. The largest in trading volume in 1989 was Tokyo, with $1·45 trillion, ahead of New York City with $957 billion and London, United Kingdom with $282 billion.

Highest par value ■ The highest denomination of any share quoted in the world is a single share in Moeara Enim Petroleum Corporation, worth £ 52,480 on 17 Aug 1989.

US records ■ At the time of press, the highest index figure on the Dow Jones average (instituted 8 Oct 1896) of selected industrial stocks at the close of a day's trading was 2,935·19 on 4 Jun 1990, which was also the tenth record close in fifteen days of trading, during which the Dow Jones also broke the 2,900 level.

The old record trading volume in a day on the New York Stock Exchange of 16,410,030 shares

on 29 Oct 1929, the 'Black Tuesday' of the famous 'crash,' was unsurpassed until April 1968.

The Dow Jones industrial average, which reached 381·71 on 3 Sep 1929, plunged 30·57 points on 29 Oct 1929, on its way to the Depression's lowest point of 41·22 on 8 Jul 1932.

The largest decline in a day, 508·32 points (22·6 percent), occurred on 19 Oct 1987 and was also the largest point collapse in Wall Street history. It surpassed even the 12·9 % one day percentage decline in the 1929 crash that heralded the onset of the Great Depression.

The total lost in security values from 1 Sep 1929 to 30 Jun 1932 was $74 billion.

The greatest paper loss in a year was $210 billion in 1974.

The record daily increase of 69·89 on 3 Apr 1986 was most recently bettered on 21 Oct 1987 with 186·84 points to 2,027·85.

The record days trading was 608·12 million shares on 20 Oct 1987.

The largest stock trade in the history of the New York Exchange was a 48,788,800-share block of Navistar International Corporation stock at $10 in a $487,888,000 transaction on 10 Apr 1986.

The highest price paid for a seat on the New York Stock Exchange was $1·15 million in 1987.

The lowest 20th-century price was $17,000 in 1942.

The market value of stocks listed on the New York Stock Exchange reached an all-time high at the end of August 1987 — $2,946 billion.

Largest and smallest equity ■ The greatest aggregate market value of any corporation at year end was £ 26 billion for IBM on 31 Dec 1985.

Greatest personal loss ■ The highest recorded personal paper losses on stock values were incurred by the late Ray A. Kroc, chairman of McDonald's Corporation, with $65 million on 8 Jul 1974.

Largest flotation ■ The largest ever flotation in stock-market history was that of British Gas plc, with an equity offering producing proceeds of £ 7·75 billion to 4·5 million stockholders. Allotment letters were dispatched on 15 Dec 1986.

Largest investment house ■ The largest securities company in the US, and formerly the world's largest partnership, with 124 partners, before becoming a corporation in 1959, is Merrill, Lynch, Pierce, Fenner & Smith Inc. (founded 6 Jan 1914) of New York. Its parent, Merrill, Lynch and Co. Inc., had $64 billion in balance- sheet assets, held $336 billion in client assets and employed about 40,000 staff.

POSTAL SERVICES

The practice of numbering houses began on the Pont Notre Dame, Paris, France in 1463.

Largest mail ■ The country with the largest mail in the world is the United States, whose population posted 161·6 billion letters and packages in the year ending 30 Sep 1989, when the US Postal Service employed 763,743 people, with the world's largest civilian vehicle fleet of 182,533 cars and trucks.

The United States also takes first place in the average number of letters and packages each person posts during one year. The figure was 650 in the year ending 30 Sep 1989.

POSTAGE STAMPS

EARLIEST

Put on sale at GPO 1 May 1840. 1d Penny Black of Great Britain, Queen Victoria, 68,158,080 printed.

HIGHEST PRICE (TENDER)

$1·1 million. Lady McGill 2 cent local red-brown City Post stamp issued by AJ Dallas Co. in Pittsburgh, PA in 1852, sold by Marc Rousso's Coach Investments to a Japanese bank on 9 Oct 1987.

HIGHEST PRICE (AUCTION)

$1·1 million (including buyer's premium). 'Curtiss Jenny' plate block of four 24 cent stamps from 1918 with inverted image of an airplane, bought by an unnamed American executive at Christie's, NY on 12 Oct 1989. For a single stamp, *£615,000 (including buyer's premium).* Baden 9-kr black on blue-green color error from 1851 in the John R. Boker Jr collection, sold by Heinrich Köhler in Wiesbaden, West Germany on 16 Mar 1985.

LARGEST PHILATELIC PURCHASE

$11 million. Marc Haas collection of 3,000 US postal and pre-postal covers to 1869 by Stanley Gibbons International Ltd of London, United Kingdom in August 1979.

LARGEST (SPECIAL PURPOSE)

9¾×2¼ in. Express Delivery of China, 1913.

LARGEST (STANDARD POSTAGE)

6·3×4·33 in. Marshall Islands 75-cent issued 30 Oct 1979.

SMALLEST

0·31×0·37 in. 10-cent and 1-peso Colombian State of Bolivar, 1863–66.

HIGHEST DENOMINATION

£100. Red and black, George V of Kenya, 1925–7.

LOWEST DENOMINATION

3,000 pengö of Hungary. Issued 1946 when 150 trillion pengö = 1 cent.

RAREST

Unique examples include: British Guiana (now Guyana) 1-cent black on magenta of 1856; Swedish 3-skilling banco yellow color error of 1855. Gold Coast provisional of 1885 and the US post-master stamp from Boscowen, New Hampshire and Lockport, NY.

Agriculture

Origins ■ It has been estimated that, while about 21 percent of the world's land surface is cultivable, only 7·6 percent is actually under cultivation.

Evidence adduced in 1971 from Nok Nok Tha and Spirit Cave, Thailand tends to confirm that plant cultivation was part of the Hoabinhian culture *c.* 11,000 B.C., but it is still likely that hominids (humans and their human-like ancestors) probably survived for 99·93 percent of their known

Most expensive stamps ● The world record price for stamps at an auction is $1·1 million (including buyer's premium), for the 'Curtiss Jenny' plate block of four 24 cent stamps from 1918 with an inverted image of an aeroplane, bought by an unnamed American executive at Christie's, New York, on 12 Oct 1989. (Photo: Christie's New York)

history without cultivating plants or domesticating animals.

A new village site found near Nineveh, Iraq has been dated provisionally to 9000 B.C. and shows evidence of agricultural practices.

The growing of maize in the New World is now radiocarbon dated to *c.* 3600 B.C. at the Coxcatlan prehistoric cave sites in Mexico.

It has been suggested that reindeer (*Rangifer tarandus*) may have been domesticated as early as 18,000 B.C., but definite proof remains lacking.

The earliest known animals domesticated for food were probably descendants of the wild goat of Bezoar (*Capra aegagrus* = *hircus*), which were herded at Asiah, Iran *c.* 7700 B.C. Sheep (*Ovis aries*) have been dated *c.* 7200 B.C. at Argissa Magula in Thessaly, Greece, and pigs (*Sus domestica*) and cattle (*Bos primigenius* = *taurus*) *c.* 7000 B.C. at the same site.

The earliest definite date for the horse (*Equus caballus*) is *c.* 4350 B.C. from Dereiska, Ukraine, USSR, but crib-biting evidence from southern France indicates that horses may have been tethered earlier than 30,000 B.C. Human use of the camel may go back as far as 8,200 years, as indicated by dated charred bones found recently at the Shell-midden site of Sihi in Saudi Arabia.

Chickens were domesticated before 6000 B.C. in Indochina and by 5900–5400 B.C. had spread to north China, as shown by radiocarbon dating from a Neolithic site at Peiligan, near Zhengzou and also Cishan and Beixin.

FARMS

Largest ■ The largest farms in the world are the collective farms (*kolkhozes*) in the USSR. These have been reduced in number from 235,500 in 1940 to only 18,000 in 1980 and have been increased in size so that units of over 60,000 acres are not uncommon.

The pioneer farm owned by Laucidio Coelho near Campo Grande, Mato Grosso, Brazil *c.* 1901 covered 3,358 miles² and accommodated 250,000 head of cattle at the time of his death in 1975.

Cattle station ■ The world's largest cattle station is the 11,600 miles² Anna Creek station

in South Australia owned by the Kidman family. The biggest component is Strangway at 5,500 miles².

Until 1915 the Victoria River Downs Station in Northern Territory, Australia covered 35,000 miles².

Chicken ranch ■ The Croton Egg Farm in Ohio has 4·8 million hens laying some 3·7 million eggs daily.

Community garden ■ The largest such project is that operated by the City Beautiful Council and the Benjamin Wegerzyn Garden Center at Dayton, OH. It comprises 1,173 allotments, each measuring 812 ft².

Hop farm ■ The world's leading hop growers are John I. Haas Inc., with hop farms in Idaho, Oregon, Washington State, Tasmania and the United Kingdom covering a total net area of 5,163 acres. The largest field covers 1,715 acres near Toppenish, WA.

Mushroom farm ■ The world's largest mushroom farm is owned by Moonlight Mushroom Inc., founded in 1937 in a disused limestone mine near Worthington, PA. It employs over 900 in a maze of underground galleries 110 miles long, producing over 22,500 tons of mushrooms per year. The French annual consumption is unrivaled at 7 lb per capita.

Piggery ■ The world's largest piggery is the Sljeme pig unit in Yugoslavia, which can process 300,000 pigs per year.

Rice farm ■ The largest contiguous wild-rice (*Zizania aquatica*) farm in the world is Clearwater Rice Inc. at Clearbrook, MN, with 2,000 acres. In 1986 it yielded 577,000 lb, the largest amount to date.

Sheep station ■ The largest sheep station in the world is Commonwealth Hill in the northwest of South Australia. It grazes 60–70,000 sheep and 24,000 uninvited kangaroos in an area of 4,080 miles² enclosed by 119 miles of dog-proof fencing. The head count on Sir William Stevenson's 30,000 acres Lochinver Station in New Zealand was 133,231 on 1 Jan 1990.

The largest sheep move on record occurred when 27 horsemen moved a flock of 43,000 sheep 40 miles from Barcaldine to Beaconsfield Station in Queensland, Australia in 1886.

Turkey farm ■ The world's largest turkey farm is that of Bernard Matthews plc at Great Witchingham, United Kingdom, with 2,600 staff tending 9 million turkeys.

Field Mouse ■ 'Kernal Mickey Mouse' covering 520 acres was cultivated by the Pitzenberger family on a farm owned by the Buehlje family in Sheffield, IA as part of Mickey Mouse's 60th birthday celebrations in August 1988. The 220 acres of corn and the 300 acres of oats can be seen from a height of 30,000 ft.

CROP YIELDS

Beet ■ The highest recorded yield for sugar beet is 62·4 tons/acre by Andy Christensen and Jon Giannini in the Salinas Valley, CA.

Corn ■ A yield of 370 bushels (15½ percent moisture) from an acre was achieved by Herman Warsaw in Saybrook, IL in 1985.

Wheat ■ The largest single fenced field of wheat was one of 35,000 acres sown in 1951 southwest of Lethbridge, Alberta, Canada.

Baling ■ A rick of 40,400 bales of straw was completed from 22 Jul to 3 Sep 1982 by Nick and Tom Parsons with a gang of eight at Cuckoo-pen Barn Farm, Birdlip, United Kingdom. It measured 150 × 30 × 60 ft high and weighed some 784 tons. The team baled, hauled and ricked 24,200 bales in seven consecutive days from 22–29 Jul.

Svend Erik Klemmensen of Trustrup, Djursland, Denmark baled 220 tons of straw in 9 hr 54 min using a Hesston 4800 baling machine on 30 Aug 1989.

Combine harvesting ■ Philip Baker of West End Farm, Merton, Bicester, United Kingdom harvested 182·5 tons of wheat in 8 hr using a Massey Ferguson MF 38 combine on 8 Aug 1989.

Ploughing ■ The world championship (instituted 1953) has been staged in 18 countries and won by ploughmen from 12 nations, with the United Kingdom being the most successful with ten championships. The only person to take the title three times is Hugh B. Barr of Northern Ireland in 1954, 1955, 1956.

The fastest recorded time for ploughing an acre (minimum of 32 right-hand turns and to a depth of 9 in) is 9 min 49·88 sec by Joe Langcake, using a case IH 7140 Magnum tractor and a Kverneland four-furrow plough at Hornby Hall Farm, Penrith, Cumbria, United Kingdom on 21 Oct 1989.

The greatest recorded acreage ploughed with a six-furrow plough to a depth of 9 in in 24 hr is 165·7 acres by Mark Dunford and Alan Cook of Romsey Young Farmers, using a Massey Ferguson 3680 tractor at Manor Farm, East Tytherley, United Kingdom on 2–3 Sep 1989.

Ploughing ● The fastest recorded time for ploughing 1 acre under the rules of the United Kingdom's Society of Ploughmen Ltd is 9 min 49·88 sec by Joseph Langcake, using an IH 7140 Magnum tractor and a Kverneland four-furrow plough at Hornby Hall Farm, Penrith, Cumbria, United Kingdom on 21 Oct 1989. (Photo: Blacksykes Photographic)

LIVESTOCK PRICES

Some exceptionally high livestock auction prices are believed to result from collusion between buyer and seller to raise the ostensible price levels of the breed concerned. Others are marketing and publicity exercises with little relation to true market prices.

Cattle ■ The highest price ever paid was $2·5 million for the beefalo (a ⅜ Bison, ⅜ Charolais, ¼ Hereford) 'Joe's Pride' sold by D. C. Basalo of Burlingame, CA to the Beefalo Cattle Co. of Canada on 9 Sep 1974.

A 14-month-old Canadian Holstein bull 'Pickland Elevation B. ET' was bought by Premier Breeders of Stamfordham, Northumberland, United Kingdom for £233,000 in September 1982.

Cow ■ The highest price ever paid for a cow is $1·3 million for a Holstein at auction in East Montpelier, VT in 1985.

Goat ■ On 25 Jan 1985 an Angora buck bred by Waitangi Angoras of Waitangi, New Zealand was sold to Elliott Brown Limited, Waipu, New Zealand for New Zealand $140,000.

Horse ■ The highest price paid for a draught horse is $47,000 by C. G. Good of Ogden, IA (see

page 30) for the seven-year-old Belgian stallion 'Farceur' at Cedar Falls, IA on 16 Oct 1917.

A Welsh mountain pony stallion named Coed Coch Bari was sold to an Australian bidder in Wales in September 1978 for £22,050.

Pig ■ The highest price ever paid for a pig is $56,000 for a crossbred barrow named Bud owned by Jeffrey Roemisch of Hermleigh, TX and bought by E. A. 'Bud' Olson and Phil Bonzio on 5 Mar 1983.

Sheep ■ The highest price ever paid for a sheep is £32,000 for a Scottish Blackface lamb ram 'Old Sandy' sold by Michael Scott at Lanark, Strathclyde, United Kingdom on 14 Oct 1988.

Wool ■ The highest price ever paid for wool is Australian $3,008·5 per kg greasy wool for a bale of Tasmania superfine at the wool auction in Tasmania, Australia on 23 Feb 1989 by Fujii Keori Ltd of Osaka, Japan — top bidders since 1973.

Lowest priced ■ The lowest price ever realized for livestock was at a sale at Kuruman, Cape Province, South Africa in 1934, where donkeys were sold for less than 3 cents each.

CATTLE

Largest ■ The heaviest breed of cattle is the Chianini, which was brought to the Chiana Valley in Italy from the Middle East in pre-Roman times. Four types of the breed exist, the largest of which is the Val di Chianini found on the plains and low hills of Arezzo and Sienna. Mature bulls average 5 ft 8 in at the forequarters and weigh 2,865 lb (cows 1,873 lb), but Chianini oxen have been known to attain heights up to 6 ft

2¾ in. The sheer expense of feeding such huge cattle has put the breed under threat of extinction in Italy, but farmers in North America, Mexico and Brazil are still enthusiastic buyers of the breed.

The heaviest example on record was a Holstein-Durham cross named Mount Katahdin exhibited by A. S. Rand of Maine from 1906–10 and frequently weighed at an even 5,000 lb. He was 6 ft 2 in at the shoulder with a 13-ft girth, and died in a barn fire *c.* 1923.

Smallest ■ The smallest breed of domestic cattle is the Ovambo of Namibia, with mature bulls and cows weighing 496 lb and 353 lb respectively on average.

Cheese consumption ● The most enthusiastic cheese-eaters are the people of France, who, in addition to consuming an annual average of 43·6 lb per person, also produce 240 of the world's 450 named cheeses. (Photo: Spectrum)

Oldest ■ 'Big Bertha,' a Dremon owned by Jerome O'Leary of Blackwatersbridge, Co. Kerry, Republic of Ireland, was born on 17 Mar 1944 (See prolificacy).

Prolificacy ■ On 25 Apr 1964 it was reported that a cow named 'Lyubik' had given birth to seven calves at Mogilev, USSR.

Five short-lived and one stillborn calf were recorded from a Friesian at Te Puke, North Island, New Zealand on 27 Jul 1980.

A case of five live calves at one birth was reported in 1928 by T. G. Yarwood of Manchester, United Kingdom.

'Soender Jylland's Jens,' a Danish black and white bull, left 220,000 surviving progeny by artificial insemination when he was put down aged 11 in Copenhagen in September 1978. 'Bendalls Adema,' a Friesian bull, died at the age of 14 at Clondalkin, Dublin, Republic of Ireland on 8 Nov 1978, having sired an estimated 212,000 progeny by artificial insemination.

Birth weights ■ The heaviest recorded live birth weight for a calf is 225 lb from a British Friesian at Rockhouse Farm, Bishopston, Swansea, United Kingdom in 1961.

On 28 May 1986 a Holstein owned by Sherlene O'Brien of Simitar Farms, Henryetta, OK gave birth to a perfectly formed stillborn calf weighing 270 lb. The sire was an Aberdeen-Angus bull that had 'jumped the fence.'

The lowest live birth weight recorded for a calf is 17 lb 10 oz for a bull (breed not identified) born on Jan van Rensberg's farm at Kankus, Orange Free State, South Africa in August 1972. It stood 15·74 in at the hindquarters and measured 21·6 in overall.

Milk yields ■ The highest recorded world life-time yield of milk is 465,224 lb by the unglamorously named cow No. 289 owned by M. G. Maciel & Son of Hanford, CA to 1 May 1984.

The greatest recorded yield for one lactation (maximum 365 days) is 55,661 lb by the Holstein 'Beecher Arlinda Ellen' owned by Mr and Mrs

Butterfat yield ● The world record for 365 days is 3,126lb by 'Roybrook High Ellen,' a Holstein owned by Yashuhiro Tanaka of Tottori, Japan.

Beecher of Rochester, IN in 1975.

The highest reported milk yield in a day is 241 lb by 'Urbe Blanca' in Cuba on or about 23 Jun 1982.

Hand milking ■ Andy Faust at Collinsville, OK in 1937 achieved 83·2 gal in 12 hr.

Butter fat yields ■ The world record life-time yield is 16,370 lb by the US Holstein 'Breezewood Patsy Bar Pontiac' in 3,979 days.

The world record for 365 days is 3,126 lb by 'Roybrook High Ellen,' a Holstein owned by Yashuhiro Tanaka of Tottori, Japan.

Cheese ■ The oldest and most primitive cheeses are the Arabian *kishk*, made of dried curd of goats' milk. There are currently 450 named cheeses in 18 major varieties, but many are merely named after different towns and differ only in shape or the method of packing. France has 240 varieties.

The most active cheese-eaters are the people of France, with an annual average in 1983 of 43·6 lb per person. The world's biggest producer is the United States, with a factory production of 4·78 billion lb in 1980.

GOATS
Largest ■ The largest goat ever recorded was a British Saanen named Mostyn Moorcock

owned by Pat Robinson of Ewyas Harold, Hereford and Worcester, United Kingdom, which reached a weight of 400 lb (shoulder height 44 in and overall length of 66 in). He died in 1977 aged four.

Smallest ■ Some pygmy goats weigh only 33–44 lb.

Oldest ■ The oldest goat on record is a Toggenburg feral cross named 'Hongi' (b. August 1971), belonging to April Koch of Glenorchy, nr Otago, New Zealand, which was still alive mid-March 1989 aged 17 years 8 months.

Prolificacy ■ According to the British Goat Society at least one or two cases of quintuplets are recorded annually out of the 10,000 goats registered, but some breeders only record the females born.

On 14 Jan 1980 a Nanny named 'Julie' owned by Galen Cowper of Nampah, ID gave birth to septuplets, but they all died, including the mother.

Milk yields ■ The highest recorded milk yield for any goat is 7,714 lb in 365 days by 'Osory Snow-Goose,' owned by Mr and Mrs Jameson of Leppington, NSW, Australia in 1977.

'Snowball,' the goat owned by Don Papin of Tipton, CA, lactated continuously for 12 years 10 months between 1977 and 1989.

PIGS
Largest ■ The heaviest pig ever recorded was a Poland-China hog named Big Bill who was so obese that his belly dragged along the ground. 'Bill' scaled an astonishing 2,552 lb just before

he was put down after suffering a broken leg in an accident en route to the Chicago World Fair for exhibition in 1933. Other statistics included a shoulder height of 5 ft and a length of 9 ft. At the request of his owner, W. J. Chappall, this prized possession was mounted and put on display in Weekly County, TN until 1946, when he was acquired by a traveling carnival. On the death of the carnival's proprietor his family allegedly donated 'Big Bill' to a museum, but no trace has been found of him since.

Smallest ■ The smallest breed of pig is the 'Mini Maialino' developed by Stefano Morini of St Golo d'Enza, Italy after ten years of experimentation with Vietnam pot-bellied pigs. The piglets weigh 14 oz at birth and 20 lb at maturity.

Prolificacy ■ A breeding sow will live 12 years or more before it is slaughtered, but the maximum potential lifespan is 20 years.

The highest recorded number of piglets in one litter is 34, farrowed on 25–26 Jun 1961 by a sow owned by 'Aksel Egedee' of Denmark. In February 1955 a Wessex sow belonging to E. C. Goodwin of Paul's Farm, Leigh, nr Tonbridge, Kent, United Kingdom also had a litter of 34, of which 30 were stillborn. A litter of 32 piglets (eight stillborn) was farrowed in February 1971 by a British Saddleback owned by R. Spence of Toddington, Gloucestershire, United Kingdom.

A Large White owned by H. S. Pedlingham farrowed 385 pigs in 22 litters (Dec 1923–Sep 1934). During the period 1940–52 a Large Black sow belonging to A. M. Harris of Lapworth, Birmingham, United kingdom farrowed 26 litters. A Newsham Large White × Landrace sow of Meeting House Farm, Staintondale, Yorkshire,

United Kingdom had farrowed 189 piglets (seven stillborn) in nine litters up to 22 Mar 1988. Between 6 May 1987 and 9 Feb 1988 she gave birth to 70 piglets.

Birth weights ■ The average birth weight for a piglet is 3 lb. A Hampshire × Yorkshire sow belonging to the Rev. John Schroeder of Mountain Grove, MO farrowed a litter of 18 on 26 Aug 1979. Five were stillborn, including one male that weighed 5·25 lb.

The highest recorded weight for a piglet at weaning (eight weeks) is 81 lb for a boar, one of nine piglets farrowed on 6 Jul 1962 by the Landrace gilt 'Manorport Ballerina 53rd,' alias 'Mary,' and sired by a Large White named Johnny at Kettle Lane Farm, West Ashton, Trowbridge, Wiltshire, United Kingdom.

In Nov 1957 a total weight of 1,134 lb was reported at weaning for a litter of 18 piglets farrowed by an Essex sow owned by B. Ravell of Seaton House, Thorugumbald, United Kingdom.

POULTRY

Chicken *Largest* ■ The heaviest breed of chicken is the White Sully developed by Grant Sullens of West Point, CA by crossing and recrossing large Rhode Island Reds with other

varieties. One monstrous rooster named Weirdo reportedly weighed 22 lb in January 1973 and was so aggressive that he killed two cats and crippled a dog that ventured too close. The heaviest chicken is currently a White Ross 1 rooster named 'Bruno' owned by John Steele of Kirkhills Farms, Boyndie, Grampian. On 4 Jul 1989 this outsized bird recorded a weight of 22 lb 1 oz.

Prolificacy ■ The highest authenticated rate of egg-laying is by a White Leghorn chicken, No. 2988 at the College of Agriculture, University of Missouri, with 371 eggs in 364 days in an official test conducted by Prof. Harold V. Biellier ending on 29 Aug 1979.

The highest recorded annual average per bird for a flock is 313 eggs in 52 weeks from a flock of 1,000 Warren-Stadler SSL layers (from 21 weeks of age) by Eric Savage of White Lane Farm, Albury, Surrey, United Kingdom in 1974–75.

Largest egg ■ The heaviest hen's egg reported is one of 16 oz, with double yolk and double shell, laid by a White Leghorn at Vineland, NJ on 25 Feb 1956.

The largest ever recorded was one of 'nearly 12 oz' for a five-yolked egg measuring 12¼ in around the long axis and 9 in around the short, laid by a Black Minorca at Mr Stafford's Damsteads Farm, Mellor, Lancashire, United Kingdom in 1896.

Smallest egg ■ The lightest egg weighed 0·05 oz (1·06 × 0·86 in) and was laid by a Leghorn/Ranger cross named 'Obedience' owned by Verity Nicholson of Adstock Fields

Farm House, Buckinghamshire, United Kingdom on 12 Mar 1986.

The smallest egg measured just 0·98 × 0·66 in and was laid by a Black Orpington owned by Stephen Taylor of Lockington, Victoria, Australia on 22 Jan 1989.

Most yolks ■ The highest claim for the number of yolks in a chicken's egg is nine, reported by Diane Hainsworth of Hainsworth Poultry Farms, Mount Morris, NY in July 1971, and also from a hen in Kirgizya, USSR in August 1977.

Flying ■ 'Sheena,' a barnyard bantam owned by Bill and Bob Knox, flew 630 ft 2 in at Parkesburg, PA on 31 May 1985.

Duck *Prolificacy* ■ An Aylesbury duck belonging to Annette and Angela Butler of Princes Risborough, Buckinghamshire, United Kingdom laid 457 eggs in 463 days, including an unbroken run of 375 in as many days. The duck died on 7 Feb 1986.

Another duck of the same breed owned by Edmond Walsh of Gormanstown, Co. Kildare, Republic of Ireland laid eggs every year right up to her 25th birthday. She died on 3 Dec 1978 aged 28 years 6 months.

Goose *Largest egg* ■ The heaviest egg on record is one of 24 oz measuring 13·5 in around the long axis and with a maximum circumference of 9·5 in. It was laid on 3 May 1977 by a white goose named 'Speckle' owned by Donny Brandenberg of Goshen, OH. The average weight is 10–12 oz.

Turkey *Largest and most expensive* ■ The greatest dressed weight recorded for a turkey is 86 lb for a stag named 'Tyson' reared by Philip Cook of Leacroft Turkeys Ltd of Peterborough, United Kingdom. It won the annual 'heaviest turkey' competition held in London on 12 Dec 1989 and was auctioned for charity for a record £4,400. Stags of this size have been so overdeveloped for meat production that they are unable to mate because of their shape and the hens have to be artificially inseminated.

Chicken and turkey plucking ■ Ernest Hausen (1877–1955) of Fort Atkinson, WI died undefeated after 33 years as champion. On 19 Jan 1939 he was timed at 4·4 sec.

Vincent Pilkington of Cootehill, Co. Cavan, Republic of Ireland killed and plucked 100 turkeys in 7 hr 32 min on 15 Dec 1978. His record for a single turkey is 1 min 30 sec on RTE Television in Dublin on 17 Nov 1980.

SHEEP

Largest ■ The heaviest sheep ever recorded was an old Leicester longwool ram that scaled 472 lb.

Smallest ■ The smallest breed of sheep is the Soay, which is now confined to the island of Hirta in the St Kilda group, Outer Hebrides, United Kingdom. Adults weigh 55–60 lb.

Prolificacy ■ A case of eight lambs at a birth was reported by D. T. Jones of Priory Farm, Gwent, United Kingdom in June 1956 and also by Ken Towse of Buckton nr Bridlington, Humberside, United Kingdom in March 1981, but none lived.

A Border Leicester × Merino sheep owned by Roger Saunders gave birth to four ram and three ewe live lambs at Strathdownie, Victoria, Australia on 19 Jun 1984.

Seven live lambs (four rams and three ewes) were also reported for a Finn × Targhoe ewe owned by Elsward Meine of Crookston, MN on 24 Mar 1980.

Birth weights ■ The highest recorded birth weight for a single lamb is 38 lb at Clearwater, Sedgwick County, KS in 1975, but neither lamb nor ewe survived. Another lamb of the same weight was born on 7 Apr 1975 on the Gerald Neises Farm, Howard, SD but died soon afterwards.

On 13 Apr 1990 it was reported that a Kent ewe had given birth to a live lamb weighing 28 lb on the Belton estate nr Grantham, Lincolnshire, United Kingdom farmed by Les Baker.

A four-year-old Suffolk ewe owned by Gerry Watson of Augusta, KS gave birth to two live sets of triplets on 30–31 Jan 1982. The total weight of the lambs was 49½ lb.

The lowest live birth weight recorded for a lamb is 2 lb 4 oz for a ram named Tiny owned by Jeanette Fox of Daisy Bank Farm, Barthomley, Cheshire, United Kingdom in April 1980. It was nursed to full health.

Oldest ■ A crossbred sheep owned by Griffiths & Davies of Dolclettwr Hall, Taliesin, nr Aberystwyth, Dyfed, United Kingdom gave birth to a healthy lamb in the spring of 1988 at the grand old age of 28 after lambing successfully more than 40 times. She died on 24 Jan 1989 just one week away from her 29th birthday.

Shearing ■ The highest speed for sheep shearing in a working day was that recorded for John Fagan, who machine-sheared 804 lambs (average 89·3 per hour) in 9 hr at Hautora Rd, Pio Pio, New Zealand on 8 Dec 1980.

Peter Casserly of Christchurch, New Zealand achieved a solo blade (i.e., hand-shearing) record of 353 lambs in 9 hr on 13 Feb 1976.

Four men machine-sheared 2,519 sheep in 9 hr at Stewarts Trust, Waikaia, New Zealand on 11 Feb 1982.

In a 24-hour shearing marathon, Alan MacDonald and Keith Wilson machine-sheared 2,220 sheep at Warkworth, Auckland Province on 26 Jun 1988.

Lavor Taylor (1896–1989) of Ephraim, UT claimed to have sheared 515,000 sheep to May 1984.

Survival ■ On 24 Mar 1978 Alex Maclennan found one ewe still alive after he had dug out 16 sheep buried in a snowdrift for 50 days near the River Skinsdale on Mrs Tyser's Gordonbush Estate in Sutherland, Highland, United Kingdom after the great January blizzard. The sheep's hot breath creates air holes in the snow, and the animals gnaw their own wool for protein.

A Merino wether lost in the Benambra State Forest, NSW, Australia for five years produced 54 lb of wool from a fleece 18 in long.

Prizewinners ■ Seven Dorset Down sheep bred by Mr and Mrs Fowler of Highland Orchard Farm in Bromsgrove, Worcestershire, United Kingdom swept the board of 1st prizes in their classes at the 1989 Royal Agricultural Show held at Stoneleigh, Warwickshire, United Kingdom.

Sheep ● These Dorset Down sheep, bred by Mr and Mrs Fowler of Highland Orchard Farm, Bromsgrove, Worcestershire, United Kingdom, were awarded 1st Prize in all their eligible classes at the 1989 Royal Agricultural Show held in Stoneleigh, Warwickshire, United Kingdom, the first time that one breeder and exhibitor has swept the board at this most prestigious show.

THE ARTS & ENTERTAINMENT

Painting
Sculpture
Antiques
Language
Literature
Music
Recordings
Photography
Theatre
Cinema
Radio
Television

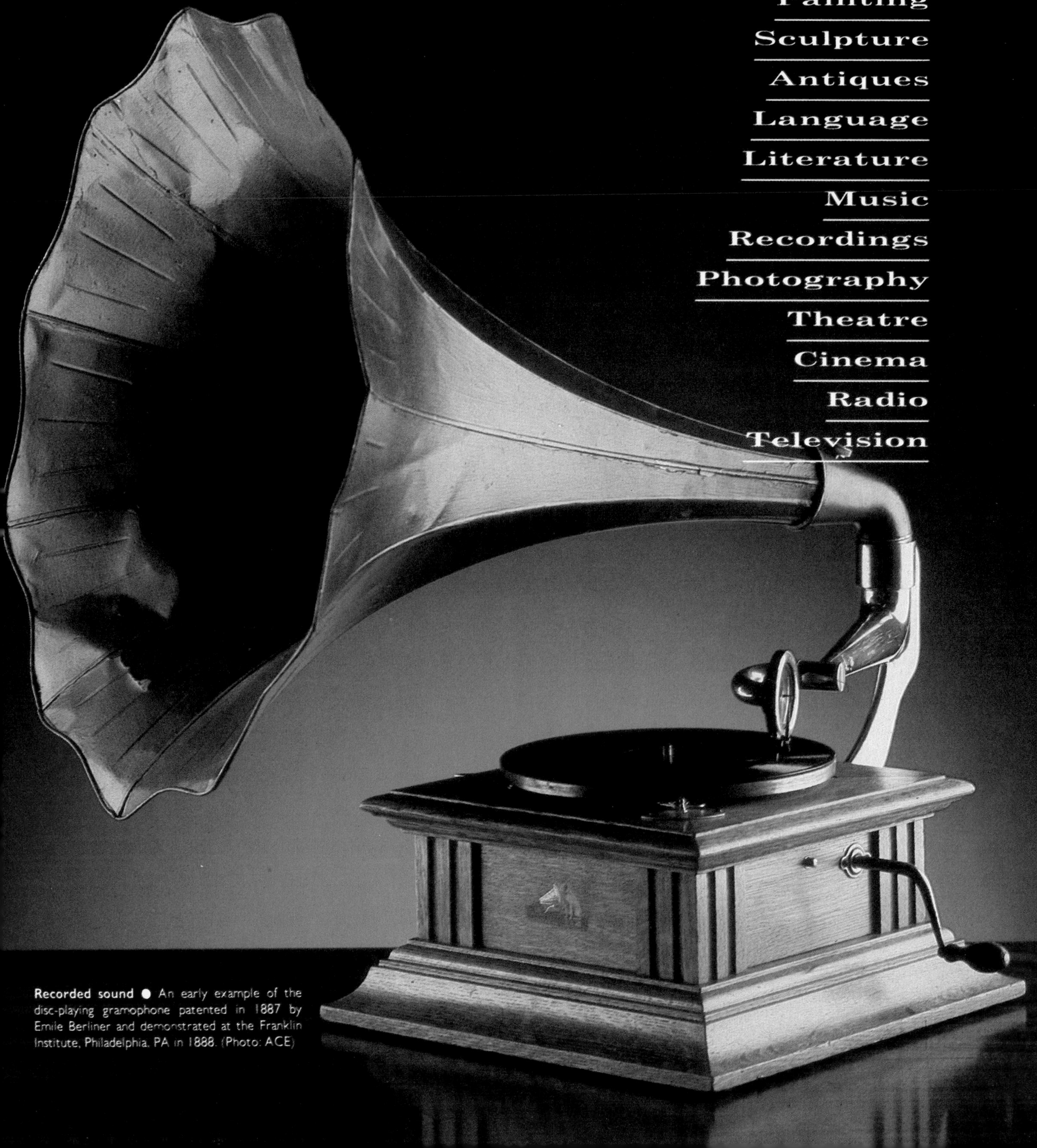

Recorded sound ● An early example of the disc-playing gramophone patented in 1887 by Emile Berliner and demonstrated at the Franklin Institute, Philadelphia, PA in 1888. (Photo: ACE)

Painting

Origins ■ Evidence of Paleolithic art was first found in 1833 at Veyrier, 3 miles southwest of Geneva, Switzerland, when François Mayor (1779–1854) found two harpoon-like objects decorated with geometric figures. Recently discovered pieces of bone with geometric engraved marks on them from an Old Stone Age site at Bilzingsleben, near Erfurt, East Germany could possibly be the world's oldest examples of art. They are dated to c. 350,000 years ago.

The oldest known dated examples of representational art come from La Ferrassie, near Les Eyzies in the Périgord, France, in layers dated to c. 25,000 B.C. Blocks of stone were found with engraved animals and female symbols; some of the blocks also had symbols painted in red ocher.

Pieces of ocher with ground facets have been found at Lake Mungo, New South Wales, Australia in a context *ante* 30,000 B.C. but there is no evidence whether these were used for body-painting or pictorial art.

Largest ■ The largest ever painting measured 72,437 ft² after allowing for shrinkage of the canvas. It is made up of brightly colored squares superimposed by a 'Smiley' face and was painted by students of Robb College at Armidale,

> **Largest poster** ● One of the world's largest posters, measuring 124,740 ft², was completed in two days by 12,000 members of the Saga City P.T.A. in celebration of the city's centennial and unveiled on the banks of the Kase River, Saga, Japan on 19 Nov 1989.

New South Wales, Australia aided by local schoolchildren and students from other neighboring colleges. The canvas was completed by its designer, Australian artist Ken Done, and unveiled at the University of New England at Armidale on 10 May 1990.

United States ■ *Panorama of the Mississippi,* completed by John Banvard (1815–91) in 1846, showing the river for 1,200 miles in a strip probably 5,000 ft long and 12 ft wide, was the largest painting in the world, with an area of more than 60,000 ft². The painting is believed to have been destroyed when the rolls of canvas, stored in a barn at Cold Spring Harbor, Long Island, NY, caught fire shortly before Banvard's death on 16 May 1891.

The Battle of Gettysburg, completed in 1883, after 2½ years of work, by Paul Philippoteaux (France) and 16 assistants, was 410 ft long, 70 ft high and weighed 6 tons. It depicts the climax of the battle, in southern Pennsylvania, on 3 Jul 1863. In 1964 it was bought by Joe King of

Winston-Salem, NC after being stored by E. W. McConnell in a Chicago warehouse since 1933, but, owing to deterioration, the sky was trimmed so decreasing the area.

Jackson Bailey's *Life of Christ* exhibited by Religious Art Institute of America Inc. of Atlanta, GA comprises 50 panels 11 × 20 ft and was complete by 1971 with an area of 11,000 ft².

'Old Master' ■ The largest 'Old Master' is *Il Paradiso,* by Jacopo Robusti, *alias* Tintoretto (1518–94), and his son Domenico (1565–1637) on the east wall of the Sala del Maggior Consiglio in the Palazzo Ducale (Doge's Palace) in Venice, Italy between 1587 and 1590. The work is 72 ft 2 in long and 22 ft 11½ in high and contains some 350 human figures.

Auction ■ The largest painting ever auctioned was Carl Larsson's *Midvinterblot,* painted in Stockholm, Sweden 1911–15 and sold at Sotheby's of London, United Kingdom on 25 Mar 1988 for £880,000 to the Umeda Gallery of Japan. The painting measured 44 × 9 ft.

Poster ■ A poster measuring 134,550 ft² was painted by 30,000 inhabitants of Miyazaki, Japan and unveiled on the banks of the Oyodo River to celebrate the '90 Himuka-no-Saiten Festival.

Most valuable ■ The 'Mona Lisa' (*La Gioconda*) by Leonardo da Vinci (1452–1519) in the Louvre, Paris, France was assessed for insurance purposes at $100 million for its move to Washington, D.C. and New York City for exhibition from 14 Dec 1962 to 12 Mar 1963. However, insurance was not concluded because the cost of the closest security precautions was less than that of the premiums. It was painted c. 1503–07 and measures 30·5 × 20·9 in.

It is believed to portray either Mona (short for Madonna) Lisa Gherardini, the wife of Francesco del Giocondo of Florence, or Constanza d'Avalos, coincidentally nicknamed La Gioconda, mistress of Giuliano de Medici. King Francis I of France bought the painting for his bathroom in 1517 for 4,000 gold florins, or 92 oz of gold.

Most prolific painter ■ Pablo Diego José Francisco de Paula Juan Nepomuceno Crispin Crispiano de la Santisima Trinidad Ruiz y Picasso (1881–1973) of Spain was the most prolific of all painters in a career that lasted 78 years. It has been estimated that Picasso produced about 13,500 paintings or designs, 100,000 prints or engravings, 34,000 book illustrations and 300 sculptures or ceramics. His life-time *oeuvre* has been valued at £500 million.

Most repetitious painter ■ William Allen Bixler (1876–1961) of Andersen, IN reproduced his painting *The Old Swimmin' Hole* over 5,000 times between the years 1912–18. The painting was inspired by James Whitcomb Riley's poem of the same name.

Largest galleries ■ The world's largest art gallery is the Winter Palace and the neighboring Hermitage in Leningrad, USSR. One has to walk 15 miles to visit each of the 322 galleries, which house nearly 3 million works of art and objects of archaeological interest.

The Georges Pompidou National Center for Art and Culture, Beauborg opened in Paris, France in 1977 with 183,000 ft² of floor space.

United States ■ The largest modern art gallery in the United States is the Museum of Modern Art in New York City, which was founded in 1929 and currently has 87,000 ft² of gallery space.

WORLD'S MOST EXPENSIVE PAINTINGS

TITLE	ARTIST	SALE PRICE	DATE
Portrait of Dr Gachet	Vincent van Gogh	$82·5 million	15 May 1990
Au Moulin de la Galette	P. A. Renoir	$78·1 million	17 May 1990
Irises*	Vincent van Gogh	$53·9 million	11 Nov 1987
The Marriage of Pierrette	Pablo Picasso	$51·3 million	Nov 1989
Yo Picasso	Pablo Picasso	$47·8 million	9 May 1989
Sunflowers	Vincent van Gogh	$39·9 million	30 Mar 1987
Acrobat and Young Harlequin	Pablo Picasso	$38·5 million	Nov 1985
Halberdier (Cosimo déMedici)	Jacopo Pontormo	$35·2 million	May 1989
Rue Mosnier, Paris, Decorated With Flags	Edouard Manet	$26·4 million	Nov 1989
Self Portrait	Vincent van Gogh	$26·4 million	May 1990

* Resold in March 1990, price not disclosed

Most heavily endowed museum ■ The most heavily endowed is the J. Paul Getty Museum at Malibu, CA, with an initial £ 700 million in January 1974, which now has an annual budget of £ 104 million for acquisitions to stock its 38 galleries.

Finest brush ■ The finest standard brush sold is the 000 in Series 7 by Winsor and Newton known as a 'triple goose.' It is made of 150–200 Kolinsky sable hairs weighing 0·000529 oz.

MURALS

Earliest ■ The earliest known murals on man-made walls are the clay relief leopards at Catal Hüyük in southern Anatolia, Turkey, discovered by James Malaart at level VII in 1961 and dating from *c.* 6200 B.C.

Largest ■ A mural on the 23-story Vegas World Hotel, Las Vegas, NV covers an area of 95,442 ft².

The longest recorded continuous mural is one stretching 1,633 ft on the walls of the Royal Liverpool Children's Hospital, Alder Hey, Liverpool, United Kingdom. It covers an area of 17,963 ft². *Future entries for this category will be assessed on overall area only.*

Largest mosaic ■ The world's largest mosaic is on the walls of the central library of the Universidad Nacional Autónoma de Mexico in Mexico City. Of the four walls, the two largest measure 12,949 ft², and the scenes on each represent the pre-Hispanic past.

HIGHEST PRICE

Most expensive painting ■ Following the collapse of Australian tycoon Alan Bond's business empire in 1989, he was forced to part with Vincent Van Gogh's *Irises*, which he had bought in 1987 for a then record price of $53·9 million. The sale followed reports that Sotheby's had loaned Mr Bond $27 million towards the purchase, a practice which the auction house has subsequently reviewed. *Irises* was re-sold to the Getty Museum for an undisclosed sum in March 1990. On 15 May 1990 this record was shattered again when another Van Gogh, *Portrait of Dr Gachet*, was sold within three minutes (including buyer's premium) at $82·5 at Christie's, New York. The painting depicts Van Gogh's physician and was completed only weeks before the artist's suicide in 1890. The new owner was subsequently identified as Ryoei Saito, Japan's second largest paper manufacturer.

Most expensive art collection ■ The most valuable art collection of a single owner sold at auction, realized $85,024,000 at Christie's, New York on 14 Nov 1988. The collection, consisting of 28 lots, was formed by William Gretz (b. 1887–d. 1969), a hollywood motion picture executive. Drawing the highest prices were 'Maternity,' 1901, oil on canvas by Pablo Picasso, $24·75 million; 'The Beach at Trouville,' 1870, oil on canvas by Claude Monet, $10·78 million; and 'After the Meal,' 1925, oil on canvas by Pierre Bonnard, $7·48 million.

Miniature ■ The highest price ever is the £ 352,000 paid by the Alexander Gallery, New York at a sale held by Christie's, London, United Kingdom on 7 Nov 1988 for a 2⅛ in high miniature of George Washington, painted by John Ramage (*c.* 1748–1802), an Irish-American miniaturist in 1789.

20th century painting ■ The record bid at auction for a 20th-century painting is $47·8 million for Picasso's (1881–1973) 1901 self-portrait *Yo Picasso* at Sotheby's, New York on 9 May 1989.

Largest mosaic ● The world's largest mosaic covers the walls of the Universidad Nacional Autónoma de Mexico in Mexico City. The two largest of its four walls each measure 12,950 ft² and the images represent the pre-Hispanic past. (Photo: Spectrum Colour Library)

Living artist ● The highest price paid for a contemporary painting is $20·68 million for Willem de Kooning's abstract *Interchange*, sold at Sotheby's, NY on 8 Nov 1989 and illustrated by the detail below. The purchaser was a Japanese dealer-cum-collector. (Photo: Sotheby's, NY)

Living artist ■ ■ The highest price paid at auction for a work by a living artist is $20·68 million for *Interchange*, an abstract by American Willem de Kooning (b. Rotterdam, Netherlands 1904) at Sotheby's, New York on 8 Nov 1989. Painted in 1955, it was bought by Japanese dealer-cum-collector Mr. Mountain Tortoise.

Print ■ The record price for a print at auction was £ 561,600 for a 1655 print of *Christ Presented to the People* by Rembrandt at Christie's, London, United Kingdom on 5 Dec 1985, sold by Chatsworth Settlement Trustees.

Drawing ■ The highest price ever paid for any drawing is £ 3,546,000 for a study of an apostle's head and hand for the *Transfiguration* in the Vatican by Raphael (Raffaello Santi 1483–1520) and sold for the 11th Duke of Devonshire (b. 1920) at Christie's, London, United Kingdom on 3 Jul 1984.

Poster ■ The record price for a poster is £ 62,000 for an advertisement for the 1902 Vienna Exhibition by Koloman Moser (b. 30 Mar 1868—d. 18 Oct 1918), sold at Christie's, London, United Kingdom on 1 Apr 1985.

Sculpture

Earliest ■ A piece of ox rib found in 1973 at Pech de l'Aze, Dordogne, France in an early Middle Paleolithic layer of the Riss glaciation c.105,000 B.C. has several engraved lines on one side, thought to be possibly intentional.

A churinga or curved ivory plaque rubbed with red ocher from the Middle Paleolithic Mousterian site at Tata, Hungary has been dated to 100,000 B.C. by the thorium/uranium method.The earliest known examples of sculpture date from the Aurignacian culture c. 28,000–22,000 B.C. and include the so-called Venus figurines from Austria and the numerous figurines from northern Italy and central France.

A carving in mammoth ivory from the Magdalenian culture of a horse 2½ in long was found in the Vogelherd cave in southwest Germany.

Most expensive ■ The highest price paid for the work of a sculptor during his lifetime is the $1,265,000 given at Sotheby Parke Bernet, New York on 21 May 1982 for the 75-in long elmwood *Reclining Figure* by Henry Moore (1898–1986).

The record price paid for a sculpture at auction is £ 6·82 million at Sotheby's, London, United Kingdom on 7 Dec 1989 for a bronze garden ornament *The Dancing Faun* made by Dutch-born Adrien de vries. London dealer Cyril Humphris bought the figure from an unnamed Brighton couple who had paid £ 100 for it in the 1950s and in whose garden it had stood unnoticed for 40 years.

Largest ■ The mounted figures of Jefferson Davis (1808–89), Gen Robert Edward Lee (1807–70) and Gen Thomas Jonathan (Stonewall) Jackson (1824–63), cover 1·33 acres on the face of Stone Mountain, near Atlanta, GA. They are 90 ft high. Roy Faulkner was on the mountain face for 8 years 174 days with a thermo-jet torch working with the sculptor Walker Kirtland Hancock and other helpers from 12 Sep 1963 to 3 Mar 1972.

If completed, the world's largest sculpture will be that of the Indian chief Tashunca-Uitco (c. 1849–77), known as Crazy Horse, of the Oglala tribe of the Dakota or Nadowessioux (Sioux) group, on horseback. The sculpture was begun on 3 Jun 1948 near Mount Rushmore, SD. A

projected 563 ft high and 641 ft long, it was the uncompleted life work of one man, Korczak Ziółkowski (1908–82). The horse's nostril is 50 ft deep and 35 ft in diameter. In 1985–86 another 44,800 tons of granite blasted off the mountain face brought the total to 9·2 million tons.

Ground figures ■ In the Nazca Desert, 185 miles south of Lima, Peru there are straight lines (one more than 7 miles long), geometric shapes and shapes of plants and animals drawn on the ground some time between 100 B.C. and A.D. 600 for an uncertain but probably religious, astronomical, or even economic purpose by a imprecisely identified civilization. They were first detected from the air c. 1928 and have also been described as the world's longest works of art.

Hill figures ■ In August 1968, a 330-ft tall figure was found on a hill above Tarapacá, Chile.

Most massive mobile ■ *White Cascade* weighing 8·8 tons and measuring 100 ft from top to bottom was installed on 24–25 May 1976 at the Federal Reserve Bank of Philadelphia, PA. It was designed by Alexander Calder (1898–1976), whose first mobiles were exhibited in Paris, France in 1932 and whose *Big Crinkley* sold for a record £ 555,572 at Sotheby's, New York on 10 May 1984.

Language

Earliest ■ The ability to speak is believed to be dependent upon physiological changes in the height of the larynx between *Homo erectus* and *Homo sapiens sapiens* as developed *ante* 45,000 B.C. A recent discovery of a hyoid bone (from the base of the tongue) shows that Neanderthal man from a cave site on Mt Carmel, Israel was capable of speech 60,000 years ago.

Oldest English words ■ It was first suggested in 1979 that languages ancestral to English and to Latvian (both Indo-European) split c. 3500 B.C. According to researches completed in 1989 about 40 words of a pre-Indo-European substrate survive in English, e.g. apple (apal), bad (bad), gold (gol) and tin (tin).

Commonest language ■ Today's world total of languages and dialects still spoken is about 5,000, of which some 845 come from India.

The language spoken by more people than any other is Mandarin, by an estimated 68 percent of China's population, hence 715 million people in 1988.

The so-called national language (*Guóyǔ*) is a standardized form of Northern Chinese (*Běifanghuà*) as spoken in the Beijing area. This was alphabetized into *zhùyīn fùhào* of 37 letters in 1913 by Wa Chih-hui (1865–1953).

On 11 Feb 1938 the *Hanyu-Pinyin-Fang'an* system, which is a phonetic pronunciation guide, was introduced.

The next most commonly spoken language, and the most widespread, is English, with an estimated 330 million native speakers and nearly twice as many using it as a second or third language.

Most languages ■ The former Australian territory of Papua New Guinea has, owing to so many isolated valleys, the greatest concentration of separate languages in the world, with more than 10 percent of the world's total of 5,000.

Most complex ■ The following extremes of complexity have been noted: Chippewa, the

North American Indian language of Minnesota, has the most verb forms, with up to 6,000; Haida, the North American Indian language, has the most prefixes, with 70; Tabassaran, a language of Daghestan, USSR, uses the most noun cases, 48, while Inuit uses 63 forms of the present tense and simple nouns have as many as 252 inflections.

In Chinese the 40-volume *Chung-wén Tà Tz'u-tiën* dictionary lists 49,905 characters. The fourth tone of 'i' has 84 meanings, varying as widely as 'dress,' 'hiccough' and 'licentious.' The written language provides 92 different characters of 'i⁴.'

The most complex written character in Chinese is that representing *xiè* consisting of 64 strokes, meaning 'talkative.'

The most complex in current use is *nang*, with 36 strokes, meaning a blocked-up nose.

Least irregular verbs ■ Esperanto was first published by its inventor Dr Ludwig Zamenhof (1859–1917) of Warsaw in 1887 without irregular verbs and is now estimated (by text book sales) to have a million speakers.

The even earlier interlanguage Volapük, invented by Johann Martin Schleyer (1831–1912), also has absolutely regular configuration.

The Turkish language has a single irregular verb — *olmak*, to be.

Most irregular verbs ■ According to *The Morphology and Syntax of Present-day English* by Professor Olu Tomori, English has 283 irregular verbs, 30 of which are merely formed with prefixes.

Rarest sounds ■ The rarest speech sound is probably that written ř in Czech, which occurs in very few languages and is the last sound mastered by Czech children.

In the southern Bushman language !xo there is a click articulated with both lips, which is written ⊙.

The *l* sound in the Arabic word *Allah*, in some contexts, is pronounced uniquely in that language.

Commonest sound ■ No language is known to be without the vowel *a* (as in the English *father*).

Vocabulary ■ The English language contains about 490,000 words plus another 300,000 technical terms, the most in any language, but it is doubtful if any individual uses more than 60,000.

The membership of the International Society for Philosophical Enquiry (no admission for IQs below 148) have an average vocabulary of 36,250 words.

Shakespeare employed a vocabulary of c. 33,000 words.

Greatest linguist ■ If the yardstick of ability to speak with fluency and reasonable accuracy is adhered to, it is doubtful whether any human could maintain fluency in more than 20–25 languages concurrently or achieve fluency in more than 40 in a lifetime.

The world's greatest linguist is believed to be George Campbell (b. 9 Aug 1912), who is retired from the British Broadcasting Corporation Overseas Service where he *worked* with 54 languages.

Powell Alexander Janulus (b. 1939) has *worked* with 41 languages in the Provincial Court of British Columbia, Vancouver, Canada.

The most multilingual living person is Derick Herning of Lerwick, Shetland, United Kingdom, winner of the inaugural 'Polyglot of Europe' contest organised by the Provinciaal Centrum voor Moderne Talen at Hasselt, Belgium and held in Brussels in May 1990. The minimum entry requirement was fluency in at least nine living spoken languages with a written form and contestants were judged by 'native speakers' in each language. Mr Herning's command of 22 languages defeated 19 other finalists.

The 1975 edition of *Who's Who in the United Nations* listed 'only' 19 languages for Georges Schmidt (b. Strasbourg, France, 28 Dec 1914), Chief of the UN Terminology Section in 1965–71 because he was then unable to find time to 'revive' his former fluency in 12 others.

Historically, the greatest linguists have been proclaimed as Cardinal Mezzofanti (1774–1849) of Italy (fluent in 26 or 27); Professor Rask (1787–1832) of Denmark, Sir John Bowring (1792–1872) of the United Kingdom and Dr Harold Williams of New Zealand (1876–1928), who were all fluent in 28 languages.

ALPHABET
Earliest ■ The earliest example of alphabetic writing has been found at Ugarit (now Ras Sharma), Syria, dated to c. 1450 B.C. It comprised a tablet of 32 cuneiform letters.

Oldest letter ■ The letter 'O' is unchanged in shape since its adoption in the Phoenician alphabet c. 1300 B.C.

Newest letters ■ The newest letters added to the English alphabet are 'j' and 'v,' which are of post-Shakespearean use c. 1630. Formerly they were used only as variants of 'i' and 'u.'

Speaking in tongues ● The 159 members of the United Nations gather to discuss global issues in a wide selection of the 4–5,000 languages still spoken. (Photo: Gamma/Ferry)

There are 65 alphabets now in use.

Longest ■ The language with most letters is Cambodian, with 72 (including some without any current use).

Shortest ■ Rotokas in central Bougainville Island has least letters with 11 (just a, b, e, g, i, k, o, p, ř, t and u).

Most and least consonants ■ The language with most distinct consonantal sounds is that of the Ubykhs in the Caucasus, with 80–85, and that with the least is Rotokas, which has only six consonants.

The English word 'latchstring' has six consecutive letters which are consonants, but the Georgian word *gvprtskvnis* (he is feeling us) has eight separately pronounced consonants.

Most and least vowels ■ The language with the most vowels is Sedang, a central Vietnamese language with 55 distinguishable vowel sounds, and that with the least is the Caucasian language Abkhazian with two.

The record in written English for consecutive vowels is six in the musical term *euouae*.

The Estonian word *jäääärne*, meaning the edge of the ice, has the same four consecutively.

The name of a language in Pará State, Brazil consists solely of seven vowels — *uoiauai*.

Largest letters ■ The largest permanent letters in the world are giant 600-ft letters spelling READYMIX on the ground in the Nullarbor Plain near East Balladonia, Western Australia. These were constructed in December 1971.

Smallest letters ■ In April 1990 the letters IBM were etched into a nickel crystal by an instrument called a scanning tunneling microscope to form a corporate logo measuring less than 2 nm (10^{-9}) long. It took physicists Donald Eigler and Erhard Schweizer at IBM's Almaden Research Center in San Jose, CA 22 hr to drag the 35 xenon atoms across the bumpy nickel surface, which had been chilled to near absolute zero. Their creation flew apart when the temperature rose to above $-380°$F.

WORDS
Longest ■ Lengthy concatenations and some compound or agglutinative words or nonce words are or have been written in the closed-up style of a single word, e.g. the 182-letter fricassee of 17 sweet and sour ingredients in Aristophanes' comedy *The Ecclesiazusae* in the 4th century B.C.

A compound 'word' of 195 Sanskrit characters (which transliterates into 428 letters in the Roman alphabet) describing the region near Kanci, Tamil Nadu, India appears in a 16th-century work by Tirumalāmbā, Queen of Vijayanagara.

English ■ The longest real word in the *Oxford English Dictionary* is *floccipaucinihilipilification* (alternatively spelled in hyphenated form with 'n' in seventh place), with 29 letters, meaning 'the action of estimating as worthless,'

first used in 1741, and later by Sir Walter Scott (1771–1832).

The longest factitious word in the *Oxford English Dictionary* is *pneumonoultramicroscopicsilicovolcanoconiosis (–koniosis),* with 45 letters – alleged to mean 'a lung disease caused by the inhalation of very fine silica dust.'

Webster's Third International Dictionary lists among its 450,000 entries: *pneumonoultramicroscopicsilicovolcanoconiosises* (47 letters), the plural of this disease.

The longest regularly formed English word is *praetertranssubstantiationalistically* (37 letters), used by Mark McShane in his 1963 novel *Untimely Ripped.* The medical term *hepaticocholangiocholecystenterostomies* (39 letters) refers to the surgical creations of new communications between gallbladders and hepatic ducts and between intestines and gallbladders.

The longest words in common use are *disproportionableness* and *incomprehensibilities* (21 letters).

Interdenominationalism (22 letters) is found in *Webster's Dictionary* and hence perhaps *interdenominationalistically* (28 letters) is permissible. Simon Proctor of Maidstone, Kent, United Kingdom has compiled 15,592 lesser words (excluding plurals) from its 28 letters.

Palindromes ■
The longest known palindromic word is *saippuakivikauppias* (19 letters), Finnish for a dealer in lye (i.e., caustic soda).

The longest in English is *tattarrattat* with 12 letters appearing in the *Oxford English Dictionary.*

The nine-letter word *Malayalam* is a proper noun given to the language of the Malayali people in Kerala, southern India, while *Kanakanak* near Dillingham, AK is a nine-lettered palindromic place-name.

The contrived chemical term *detartrated* has 11 letters.

Some baptismal fonts in Greece and Turkey bear the circular 25-letter inscription ΝΙΨΟΝ ΑΝΟΜΗ-ΜΑΤΑ ΜΗ ΜΟΝΑΝ ΟΨΙΝ meaning 'wash (my) sins not only (my) face.'

The longest palindromic composition devised is one of 100,000 words by Edward Benbow of Bewdley, Hereford and Worcester, United Kingdom. It begins 'Al, sign it, "Lover"!...' and hence predictably ends '.... revolting, Isla.'

The longest palindromic novel, *Dr Awkward and Olson in Oslo* contains 31,594 words and was written by Lawrence Levine, of New York in 1986.

Longest scientific name ■
The systematic name for deoxyribonucleic acid of the human mitochondria contains 16,569 nucleotide residues and is thus *c.* 207,000 letters long. It was published in key form in *Nature* on 9 Apr 1981.

Longest anagrams ■
The longest non-scientific English words that can form anagrams are the 19-letter transpositions *representationalism* and *misrepresentational.* The longest scientific transposals are *hydroxydesoxycorticosterone* and *hydroxydeoxycorticosterones,* with 27 letters.

Longest abbreviation ■
The longest known abbreviation is .'S.K.O.M.K.H.P.K.J.C. D.P.W.B., the initials of the Syarikat Kerjasama Orang-orang Melayu Kerajaan Hilir Perak Kerana Jimat Cermat Dan Pinjam-meminjam Wang Berhad. This is the Malay name for The

---

LONGEST WORDS

JAPANESE[1]
Chi-n-chi-ku-ri-n (12 letters)
a very short person (slang)

SPANISH
Superextraordinarisimo (22 letters)
extraordinary

FRENCH
Anticonstitutionnellement (25 letters)
anticonstitutionally

CROATIAN
Prijestolonasljednikovica (25 letters)
wife of an heir apparent

ITALIAN
Precipitevolissimevolmente (26 letters)
as fast as possible

PORTUGUESE
Inconstitucionalissimamente (27 letters)
with the highest degree of unconstitutionality

ICELANDIC
Haecstaréttarmálaflutningsmaður (29 letters)
supreme court barrister

RUSSIAN
Ryentgyenoelyektrokardiografichyeskogo
(33 Cyrillic letters, transliterating as 38)
of the X-ray electrocardiographic

HUNGARIAN
Megszentségtelenithetetlenségeskedéseitekért
(44 letters)
for your unprofanable actions

DUTCH[4]
Kindercarnavalsoptochtvoorbereidingswerkzaamheden
(49 letters)
preparation activities for a children's carnival procession

MOHAWK[2]
Tkanuhstasrihsranuhwe'tsraaksahsrakaratattsrayeri'
(50 letters)
the praising of the evil of the liking of the finding of the house is right

TURKISH[4]
Cekoslovakyalılastırabilemediklerimizlerdenmisiniz
(50 letters)
'are you not of that group of persons that we were said to be unable to Czechoslovakianise?'

GERMAN[3,4]
Donaudampfschiffahrtselectrizitaetenhauptbetriebs-werkbauunterbeamtengesellschaft (80 letters)
The club for subordinate officials of the head office management of the Danube steamboat electrical services (name of a pre-war club in Vienna)

SWEDISH[4]
Nordöstersjökustartilleriflygspaningssimulatoran-läggningsmaterielunderhållsuppföljningssystem-diskussionsinläggsförberedelsearbeten (130 letters)
Preparatory work on the contribution to the discussion on the maintaining system of support of the material of the aviation survey simulator device within the north-east part of the coast artillery of the Baltic

---

[1] Patent applications sometimes harbour long compound 'words.' An extreme example is one of 13 kana (Japanese syllabary) that transliterates into the 40-letter Kyūkitsūrohekimenfuchakunenry-ösekisanryö meaning 'the accumulated amount of fuel condensed on the wall face of the air intake passage.'
[2] Lengthy concatenations are a feature of Mohawk.
[3] The longest dictionary word in everyday usage is Rechtsschutz-versicherungsgesellschaften (39 letters) meaning 'insurance companies which provide legal protection.'
[4] Agglutinative words are limited only by imagination and are not found in standard dictionaries. The first 100-letter such word was published in 1975 by the late Eric Rosenthal in Afrikaans.

Cooperative Company of the Lower State of Perak Government's Malay People for Money Savings and Loans Ltd, in Teluk Anson, Perak, West Malaysia (formerly Malaya). The abbreviation for this abbreviation is Skomk.

The 55-letter full name of Los Angeles (El Pueblo de Nuestra Señora la Reina de los Angeles de Porciuncula) is abbreviated to L.A. or 3·63 percent of its length.

Longest acronym ■
The longest acronym is N I I O M T P L A B O P A R M B E T Z H E L B E T R A B S B O M O N I M O N K O N O T D T E K H S T R O M O N T with 56 letters (54 in Cyrillic) in the *Concise Dictionary of Soviet Terminology,* meaning: the laboratory for shuttering, reinforcement, concrete and ferroconcrete operations for composite-monolithic and monolithic constructions of the Department of the Technology of Building–assembly operations of the Scientific Research Institute of the Organization for building mechanization and technical aid of the Academy of Building and Architecture of the USSR.

Commonest words and letters ■
In written English the most frequently used words are, in order: *the, of, and, to, a, in, that, is, I, it, for* and *as.* The most used in conversation is *I.*

The commonest letter is 'e.' More words begin with the letter 's' than any other, but the most commonly used initial letter is 't' as in 'the,' 'to,' 'that' or 'there.'

Most meanings ■
The most overworked word in English is the word *set* that Dr Charles Onions of Oxford University Press gave 58 noun uses, 126 verbal uses and ten as a participial adjective.

Most succinct word ■
The most challenging word for any lexicographer to define briefly is the Fuegian (southernmost Argentina and Chile) word *mamihlapinatapai,* meaning 'looking at each other hoping that either will offer to do something which both parties desire but are unwilling to do.'

Most synonyms ■
The condition of being inebriated has more synonyms than any other condition or object. Delacourt Press of New York City has published a selection of 1,224 from 2,241 compiled by Paul Dickson of Garrett Park, MD.

Most homophones ■
The most homophonous sounds in English are *air* and *sol,* which, according to the researches of Dora Newhouse of Los Angeles, both have 38 homophones.

The homonym with most variant spellings is *air* with Aire, are, Ayer, Ayr, Ayre, err, e'er, ere, eyre and heir.

Shortest pangram (holoalphabetic sentence) ■
Pangrammists who endeavor to produce meaningful sentences of minimal length utilizing all the letters in the alphabet have now attained the ultimate of 26-letter brevity. The most intelligible example, with the help of a little punctuation, was devised by Paul Horn of New York and states that 'Mr Jock, T.V. quiz PhD, bags few lynx.' The number of ways 26 letters can be combined is $4·0329 \times 10^{26}$.

Most spellings ■
Mr B. Cook of Edinburgh, United Kingdom has recorded that in the period 1955–88 he has sighted 259 different spellings of the word isosceles. The word 'cushion' often found in old inventories and wills, has been noted by Adrian Room in some 400 guises ranging from 'coschen,' 'kushen,' 'quishin,' to 'whyssin.'

PERSONAL NAMES
Earliest ■
The earliest personal name that has survived is seemingly that of a predynastic king of Upper Egypt *ante* 3050 B.C., who is indicated by the hieroglyphic sign for a scorpion. It has been suggested that the name should be read as Sekhen.

Longest personal name ■ The longest name appearing on a birth certificate is that of Rhoshandiatellyneshiaunneveshenk Koyaanfsquatsiuty Williams born to Mr and Mrs James Williams in Beaumont, TX on 12 Sep 1984. On 5 Oct 1984 the father filed an amendment that expanded his daughter's first name to 1,019 letters and the middle name to 36 letters.

The longest Christian or given name on record is one of 622 letters given by Mr Scott Roaul Sör-Lökken of Missoula, Mont to his daughter Miss S. Ellen Georgina Sör-Lökken (b. 1979). The 'S' stands for a 598-letter name designed to overload the computers of federal bureaucracy. She is known as 'Snow Owl' for short or 'Oli' for shorter.

Most first names ■ John and Margaret Nelson of Chesterfield, Derbyshire, United Kingdom gave their daughter Tracy (b. 13 Dec 1985) a total of 139 other first names. In November 1986 the Registrar agreed to accommodate the names on a document separate from the birth certificate.

The great-great-grandson of Carlos III of Spain, Don Alfonso de Borbón y Borbón (1866–1934) had 94 first names, of which several were lengthened by hyphenation.

Shortest ■ The commonest single-letter surname is O, prevalent in Korea but with 52 examples in US telephone books (1973–81) and 12 in Belgium. This name causes most distress to those concerned with the prevention of cruelty to computers.

Every other letter, except Q, has been traced in US telephone books (used as a surname) by A. Ross Eckler.

Commonest family name ■ The Chinese name Chang is borne, according to estimates, by between 9·7 and 12·1 percent of the Chinese population, so indicating even on the lower estimate that there are at least some 104 million Changs—more than the entire population of all but seven of the 170 other sovereign countries of the world.

The commonest surname in the English-speaking world is Smith.

There were an estimated 2,382,509 Smiths in the United States.

Most versions ■ Edward A. Nedelcov of Regina, Saskatchewan, Canada has collected 1,201 versions of the spelling of his surname since January 1960. Mzilikazi of Zululand (b. c. 1795) had his name chronicled in 325 spellings, according to research by Dr R. Kent Rasmussen.

Most changed ■ Excluding members of the royal family the living monogamous woman who has most times changed her name is Lady Home of the Hirsel, formerly Lady Douglas-Home; Countess of Home; Lady Dunglass, and originally Miss Elizabeth Alington.

Most contrived ■ In the United States the determination to derive commercial or other benefit from being the last listing in the local telephone book has resulted in self-given names, starting with up to 9 Z's — an extreme example being Zachary Zzzzzzzzzra in the San Francisco book.

PLACE-NAMES

Earliest ■ The world's earliest known place-names are pre-Sumerian, e.g. Kish, Ur and the now lost Attara, and therefore earlier than c. 3600 B.C.

Longest ■ The official name for Bangkok, the capital city of Thailand, is Krungthep Mahanakhon. The full name is, however: Krungthep Mahanakhon Bovorn Ratanakosin Mahintharayutthaya Mahadilokpop Noparatratchathani Burirom Udomratchanivetmahasathan Amornpiman Avatarnsathit Sakkathattiyavisnukarmprasit (167 letters), which in its most scholarly transliteration emerges with 175 letters. Cauaiauaia in Angola has nine consecutive vowel letters.

The longest place-name now in use in the world is Taumatawhakatangihangakoauauotamateaturipukakapikimaungahoronukupokaiwhenuakitanatahu, the unofficial 85-letter version of the name of a hill (1,002 ft above sea level) in the Southern Hawke's Bay district of North Island, New Zealand. The Maori translation means 'The place where Tamatea, the man with the big knees, who slid, climbed and swallowed mountains, known as landeater, played his flute to his loved one.'

United States ■ The longest place-name in the United States is Chargoggagoggmanchauggagoggchaubunagungamaugg, the name of a lake in Webster, MA. It is a Nipmuck Indian name which translates as 'Fishing at the Boundary Neutral Fishing Grounds.'

Shortest ■ The shortest place-names in the world are the French village of Y (population 143), so named since 1241, the Danish village Å on the island Fyn, the Norwegian village of Å (pronounced 'Aw'), the Swedish place Å in Vikholandet, U in the Caroline Islands, Pacific Ocean, and the Japanese town of Sosei, which is alternatively called Aioi or O. There was once a '6' in West Virginia.

Most spellings ■ The spelling of the Dutch town of Leeuwarden has been recorded in 225 versions since A.D. 1046.

Literature

Oldest ■ The earliest written language discovered has been on Yangshao culture pottery from Paa-t'o, near Xi'an (Sian) in the Shaanxi (Shensi) province of China found in 1962. This bears proto-characters for the numbers 5, 7 and 8 and has been dated to 5000–4000 B.C.

The earliest dated pictographs are on clay tablets from Nippur, southern Iraq, from one of the lowest excavation levels equivalent to Uruk V/VI and dated in 1979 to c. 3400 B.C. Tokens or tallies from Tepe Asiab and Ganji-I-Dareh Tepe in Iran have however been dated to 8500 B.C.

The oldest surviving printed work is the Dharani scroll or *sutra* from wooden printing blocks found in the foundations of the Pulguk Sa pagoda, Kyŏngju, South Korea on 14 Oct 1966. It has been dated to no later than A.D. 704.

It was claimed in November 1973 that a 28-page book of Tang dynasty poems at Yonsei University, Korea was printed from metal type c. 1160.

Paper dating to between 71 B.C. and A.D. 21 have been found in northwest China, i.e. 100 years earlier than the previous presumed date for paper's invention.

The oldest medical literature, a small clay tablet in the Sumerian script from Nippur (now in Iraq), is dated to c. 2100 B.C. It is now in the University Museum of Philadelphia, PA and gives details of various ointments and plasters made of crushed turtle shell, nagasi plant, salt and mustard. Beer formed an ingredient of some of the ointments.

Oldest mechanically printed ■ It is widely accepted that the earliest mechanically printed full-length book was the 42-line per page Gutenberg Bible, printed in Mainz, West Germany, c. 1454 by Johann Henne zum Gensfleisch zur Laden, called 'zu Gutenberg' (c. 1398–1468).

Work on watermarks published in 1967 indicates a copy of a surviving printed 'Donatus' Latin grammar was made from paper of c. 1450.

The earliest exactly dated printed work is the Psalter completed on 14 Aug 1457 by Johann Fust (c. 1400–66) and Peter Schöffer (1425–1502), who had been Gutenberg's chief assistant.

The earliest printing by William Caxton (c. 1422–1491), though undated, would appear to be *The Recuyel of the Historyes of Troye* in Cologne in late 1473 to spring 1474.

Largest book ■ The *Super Book*, measuring 9 ft × 10 ft 2⅛ in when open, was published in Denver, CO in 1976. It consisted of 300 pages and weighed 557 lb. The entire Buddhist scriptures are inscribed on 729 marble slabs 5 × 3½ ft housed in 729 stupas in the Kuthodaw Pagoda, south of Mandalay, Myanmar (formerly Burma). They were incised in 1860–68.

Largest publication ■ The 1,112-volume set of *British Parliamentary Papers* was published by the Irish University Press in 1968–72. A complete set weighs 3·6 tons, costs £ 50,000 and would take six years to read at ten hours per day. The production involved the death of 34,000 Indian goats, and the use of £ 15,000 worth of gold ingots. The total print is 500 sets and the price per set in 1987 was £49,500.

The British Library has published its *General Catalogue of Printed Books to 1975* on a set of three CD-ROMs, priced at £ 9,000. Alternatively, readers can spent six months scanning 178,000 catalog pages in 360 volumes.

Largest dictionary ■ *Deutsches Wörterbuch* started by Jacob and Wilhelm Grimm in 1854 was completed in 34,519 pages and 33 volumes in 1971. Today's price is DM 5,425. *The Dictionary of Chinese Characters* (Sichuan and Huber) in eight volumes will contain 20 million characters when completed in 1989.

The largest English-language dictionary is the 20-volume *Oxford English Dictionary*, with 21,728 pages. The first edition, edited by Sir James Murray, was published between 1884 and 1928. A first Supplement of 964 pages appeared in 1932, and a second one in four volumes, edited by R. W. Burchfield, between 1972 and 1986. Work on the Second Edition prepared by J. A. Simpson and E. S. C. Weiner, began in 1984 and the work involved represented 500-person years. Published in March 1989, it defines a total of 616,500 word-forms, with 2,412,400 illustrative quotations, and approximately 350 million letters and figures. Now computerized, the *Dictionary* required 625 million bytes to store the text in machine-readable form. The longest entry in the Second Edition is that for the verb *set*, with over 75,000 words of text. The greatest outside contributor has been Marghanita Laski (1915–88) with a reputed 250,000 quotations from 1958 until her death.

The *New Grove Dictionary of Music and Musicians* edited by Stanley Sadie (b. 30 Oct 1930), published in 20 volumes by Macmillan in February 1981, contains over 22 million words and 4,500 illustrations and is the largest specialist dictionary. The price in 1987 was £ 1,100.

Smallest book ■ The smallest marketed bound printed book is one printed on 22 gsm paper measuring $\frac{1}{25} \times \frac{1}{25}$ in, comprising the children's story *Old King Cole!* and published in 85 copies in March 1985 by The Gleniffer Press of Paisley, United Kingdom. The pages can be turned (with care) only by the use of a needle.

Longest novel ■ The longest novel ever published is *Les hommes de bonne volonté* by Louis-Henri-Jean Farigoule (1885–1972), alias Jules Romains, of France, in 27 volumes in 1932–46.

The English version *Men of Good Will* was published in 14 volumes in 1933–46 as a 'novel-cycle.' The 4,959-page edition published by Peter Davies Ltd has an estimated 2,070,000 words, excluding a 100-page index.

The novel *Tokuga-Wa Ieyasu* by Sohachi Yamaoka has been serialized in Japanese daily newspapers since 1951. Now completed, it will require nearly 40 volumes.

Earliest encyclopedia ■ The earliest known encyclopedia was compiled by Speusippus (*post* 408–*c.* 338 B.C.), a nephew of Plato, in Athens *c.* 370 B.C.

Largest encyclopedia ■ The largest encyclopedia is *La Enciclopedia Universal Ilustrada Europeo-Americana* (J. Espasa & Sons, Madrid and Barcelona) totaling 105,000 pages and an annual supplement since 1935 comprising 165·2 million words. The number of volumes in the set in August 1983 was 104, and the price $2,325.

The largest encyclopedia ever compiled was the *Yung-lo ta tien* (the great thesaurus of the Yung-lo reign) of 22,937 manuscript chapters (370 still survive) in 11,095 volumes. It was written by 2,000 Chinese scholars in 1403–08.

Most comprehensive encyclopedia ■ The most comprehensive English-language encyclopedia is *The New Encyclopaedia Britannica*, first published in Edinburgh, United Kingdom in December 1768. A group of booksellers in the United States acquired reprint rights in 1898 and completed ownership in 1899. The current 32-volume 15th edition contains 32,330 pages and 44 million words from more than 4,000 contributors. It is now edited in Chicago, IL.

Longest index ■ The Tenth Collective Index of *Chemical Abstracts* completed in June 1983 contains 23,948,253 entries in 131,445 pages and 75 volumes, and weighs 380 lb.

Who's Who ■ The longest entry in *Who's Who* (founded 1848) was that of the Rt Hon. Sir Winston Leonard Spencer Churchill (1874–1965), who appeared in 67 editions from 1899 (18 lines) and had 211 lines by the 1965 edition.

Currently the longest entry in its wider format is that of Barbara Cartland, the romantic novelist, with 143 lines.

Apart from those who qualify for inclusion by hereditary title, the youngest entry has been Sir Yehudi Menuhin (b. New York City, 22 Apr 1916), the concert violinist, who first appeared in the 1932 edition aged 15.

The longest entry of the 66,000 entries in *Who's Who in America* is that of Dr Glenn T. Seaborg (b. 19 Apr 1912), with an all-time record of 100 lines.

Literary luncheons ■ Literary luncheons were inaugurated by Christina Foyle (Mrs Ronald Batty) in October 1930 at the Old Holborn Restaurant, London, United Kingdom.

Oldest map ■ A clay tablet depicting the river Euphrates flowing through northern Mesopotamia, Iraq, dates to *c.* 2250 B.C.

The earliest surviving product of English mapmaking is the Anglo-Saxon *mappa mundi*, known as the Cottonian manuscript, from the late 10th century.

The earliest printed map in the world is one of western China dated to 1115.

Largest map ■ A Giant Relief Map of California, by Reuben Hall, weighing 43 tons, was displayed in the Ferry Building, San Francisco, from 1924 until 1960. Now in storage in Hamilton Air Force Base, Novato, CA, it measures 450 × 18 ft. Known as *Paradise in Panorama* it required 29 man years and $147,000 to build.

HIGHEST PRICES

Most expensive book ■ The highest price paid for any book has been £ 8·14 million for the 226-leaf manuscript *The Gospel Book of Henry the Lion, Duke of Saxony* at Sotheby's, London, United Kingdom on 6 Dec, 1983. The book, 13½ × 10 in, was illuminated by the monk Herimann

Most expensive book ● The highest price paid for any book is £8·14 million for the long-lost manuscript *The Gospels of Henry the Lion, Duke of Saxony* at Sotheby's of London, United Kingdom on 6 Dec 1983. The 226-leaf book, which measures 13½ x 10 in, was illuminated by the Benedictine monk Herimann at Helmarshausen Abbey *c.* 1170 and bought by Hans Kraus for the West German Hermann Abs consortium. This is one of the 41 full-page miniature illustrations and shows the Coronation of Henry and Matilda by God. (Photo: Sotheby's)

c. 1170 at Helmershansen Abbey with 41 full-page illustrations, and was bought by Hans Kraus for the Hermann Abs consortium.

Printed book ■ The highest price ever paid for a printed book has been $5·39 million for an Old Testament (Genesis to the Psalms) of the Gutenberg Bible printed in 1455 in Mainz, Germany. It was bought by the Maruzen Co Ltd, Tokyo booksellers, at Christie's, New York on 22 Oct 1987.

The most expensive new book is the reproduc-

tion of the full set of ornithological prints *The Birds of America* by John James Audubon (1785–1851) by Abbeville Press, at $15,000.

Broadsheet ■ The highest price ever paid for a broadsheet was $412,500 for one of the 22 known copies of *The Declaration of Independence*, printed in Philadelphia, PA in 1776 by Samuel T. Freeman & Co, and sold to the Chapin Library, Williams College, Williamstown, MA at Christie's of New York on 22 Apr 1983.

Manuscript ■ The highest price ever paid for a complete manuscript has been £2·2 million by Armand Hammer at Christie's of London, United Kingdom on 12 Dec 1980 for Leonardo da Vinci's 36-page Codex Leicester illustrated manuscript on cosmology compiled *c.* 1507. It was sold by the trustees of the Holkham estate.

Musical ■ The auction record for a musical manuscript (including buyer's premium) is £2,585,000 for a 508-page 8½ × 6½ in bound volume of nine complete symphonies in Mozart's hand by London dealer James Kirkman at Sotheby's of London, United Kingdom on 22 May 1987. The seller was an anonymous European.

Scientific ■ The highest price paid for a scientific manuscript was $116 million for a 72-page document by Albert Einstein, that explained his theory of relativity, on 2 Dec 1987 at Sotheby's of New York.

Atlas ■ The highest price paid for an atlas has been £340,000 for a Gerardus Mercator atlas of Europe of *c.* 1571, sold at Sotheby's, London, United Kingdom on 13 Mar 1979.

BIBLE
Oldest ■ The earliest biblical texts are from two silver amulets found under the Scottish Church, Jerusalem in 1979 bearing Numbers Ch. 6 v. 22–27 dated to *c.* 587 B.C. In 1945 various papyrus texts were dicovered at Nag Hammodi, upper Egypt; they include gnostic gospels or secret books (apocrypha) ascribed to Thomas, James, John, Peter and Paul. They were buried *c.* 350 A.D. but the originals are thought to have been written *c.* A.D. 120–150.

The oldest Dead Sea Scrolls date from *c.* 225–200 B.C. Made of leather and papyrus and comprising fragments of Exodus and Samuel I, they were discovered in Cave 4 near Qumran, Jordan in 1952.

The oldest known bible is the *Codex Vaticanus* written in Greek *ante* A.D. 350 and preserved in the Vatican Museum, Rome.

The earliest complete bible *printed* in English was one edited by Miles Coverdale, Bishop of Exeter (*c.* 1488–1569), while living in Antwerp, and printed in 1535. William Tyndale's New Testament in English had, however, been printed in Cologne and in Worms, Germany in 1525 while John Wycliffe's first manuscript translation dates from 1382.

The first Bible printed in North America was in 1663. It is known as the Eliot Bible–named after the Puritan minister who translateed the scriptures into the language of the Massachusetts tribe of the Algonquin nation. The American Bible Society, New York City has the largest collection of Bibles in the United States, over 50,000 copies, including a copy of the Eliot Bible.

Longest and shortest book ■ The longest book in the Authorized (King James) Version of the Bible is the Book of Psalms, while the longest book including prose is the Book of the Prophet Isaiah, with 66 chapters.

The shortest is the Third Epistle of John has only 294 words in 14 verses. The Second Epistle of John has only 13 verses but 298 words.

Longest and shortest psalm ■ Of the 150 psalms, the longest is the 119th, with 176 verses, and the shortest is the 117th, with two verses.

Longest and shortest verse ■ The shortest verse in the Authorized (King James) Version of the Bible is verse 35 of Chapter XI of the Gospel according to St John, consisting of the two words 'Jesus wept.'

The longest is verse 9 of Chapter VIII of the Book of Esther, which extends to a 90-word description of the Persian empire.

Total letters and words ■ The total number of letters in the Bible is 3,566,480. The total number of words depends on the method of counting hyphenated words, but is usually given as between 773,692 and 773,746.

Longest name ■ The longest actual name in English-language bibles is the 18-letter Maher-shalal-hash-baz, the symbolic name of the second son of Isaiah (Isaiah, Chapter VIII, verses 1 and 3).

DIARIES AND LETTERS
Longest kept diary ■ Col. Ernest Loftus of Harare, Zimbabwe began his daily diary on 4 May 1896 at the age of 12 and continued it until his death on 7 Jul 1987 at the age of 103 years 178 days.

George C. Edler (b. 13 Dec 1889) of Bethesda, MD has kept a handwritten diary with no breaks since 20 Sep 1909, a total of 98 years.

Alisa Morris of New York, NY has a diary which comprised an estimated 14·4 million words in 228 volumes at April 1990.

The diary of T. C. Baskerville of Chorlton-cum-Hardy, Manchester, United Kingdom, maintained since 1939, comprises an estimated 5,650,000 words in 163 volumes occupying 36,000 pages.

Longest and most letters ■ The longest personal letter based on a word count is one of 1,402,344 words started on 3 Jan 1982 by Alan Foreman of New Barn, Dartford, Kent, United Kingdom and posted to his wife Janet on 25 Jan 1984.

Uichi Noda, former vice minister of treasury and minister of construction in Japan, from July 1961 until his bedridden wife Mitsu's death in March 1985, wrote her 1,307 letters amounting to 5 million characters during his overseas trips. These letters have been published in 25 volumes totaling 12,404 pages.

The Rev Canon Bill Cook and his fiancee, later wife, Helen of Diss, Norfolk, United Kingdom, exchanged 6,000 love letters during their 4½ year separation from March 1942–May 1946.

Longest letter to an editor ■ The *Upper Dauphin Sentinel* of Pennsylvania published a letter of 25,513 words over eight issues from August to November 1979, written by John Sultzbaugh of Lykens, PA.

Most letters to an editor ■ David Green, a solicitor, of Castle Morris, Dyfed, United Kingdom had 123 letters published in the main correspondence columns of *The Times* (London) by 17 Jul 1989. His record year was 1972 with 12.

Shortest correspondence ■ The short-est correspondence on record was that between Victor Marie Hugo (1802–85) and his publisher, Hurst and Blackett, in 1862. The author was on holiday and anxious to know how his new novel *Les Misérables* was selling. He wrote '?.' The reply was '!.'

The shortest letter to *The Times* (London) comprised the single abbreviated symbol 'Dr ²?' in the interrogative from R. S. Cookson of London, United Kingdom, on 30 Jul 1984, in a correspondence on the correct form of recording a plurality of academic doctorates.

On 8 Jan 1986 a letter was sent to *The Times* (London) by a seven-year-old girl from the Isle of Man. It read 'Sir, Yours faithfully Caroline Sophia Kerenhappuch Parkes.' The brief epistle was intended to inform readers of her unusual name, Kerenhappuch, mentioned in a letter the previous week from the Rev. John Ticehurst on the subject of uncommon 19th-century names.

Most personal mail ■ The highest confirmed mail received by any private citizen in a year is 900,000 letters by the baseball star Hank Aaron (b. 1934), reported by the US Postal Department in June 1974. About a third were letters of hate engendered by his bettering of 'Babe' Ruth's career record for 'home runs' set in 1927. (See Chapter 11.)

Pen pals ■ The longest sustained correspondence on record is one of 75 years from 11 Nov 1904 between Mrs Ida McDougall of Tasmania, Australia and Miss R. Norton of Sevenoaks, Kent, United Kingdom until Mrs McDougall's death on 24 Dec 1979.

Christmas card exchange ■ Warren Nord of Mesa, AZ and Thor (Tut) Andersen (d. 11 Sep 1988) of Ashtabula, OH exchanged the same Christmas card every year from 1930–87.

Christmas cards ■ The earliest known Christmas card was sent out by Sir Henry Cole (1808–82) in 1843 but did not become an annual ritual until 1862.

The greatest number of personal Christmas cards sent out is believed to be 62,824 by Mr Werner Erhard of San Francisco, CA in December 1975.

AUTOGRAPHS AND SIGNATURES
Earliest ■ The earliest surviving examples of an autograph are those made by scribes on cuneiform clay tablets from Tell Abu Salābīkh, Iraq dated to the early Dynastic III A *c.* 2600 B.C. A scribe named 'a-du' has added 'dub-sar' after his name thus translating to 'Adu, scribe.'

The earliest surviving signature on a papyrus is that of the scribe Amen-'aa dated to the Egyptian Middle Kingdom, which began *c.* 2130 B.C. and which is in the Leningrad Museum, USSR.

A signum exists for William I (the Conqueror) *c.* 1070. The earliest English sovereign whose handwriting is known to have survived is Edward III (1327–77). The earliest full signature extant is that of Richard II (dated 26 Jul 1386).

The Magna Carta does not bear even the mark of King John (reigned 1199–1216), but carries only his seal affixed on 19 Jun 1215.

Most expensive ■ The highest price ever paid on the open market for a single autograph letter signed was $360,000 paid on 29 Oct 1986 at Sotheby's, New York for a letter by Thomas Jefferson condemning prejudice against Jews in

1818. It was sold by Charles Rosenbloom of Pittsburgh, PA.

The highest price paid for an autograph letter signed by a living person is $12,500 at the Hamilton Galleries on 22 Jan 1981 for a letter from President Ronald Reagan praising Frank Sinatra.

A record $4,675 (including premium) was paid at a Hamilton sale on 12 Aug 1982 by Barry Hoffman for a signed portrait of Al Capone (1899–1947).

Rarest and most valuable ■ Only one example of the signature of Christopher Marlowe (1564–93) is known. It is in the Kent County Archives, Kent, United Kingdom on a will of 1583. It is estimated that a seventh Shakespearean signature, should it ever come to light would realize more than £1 million at auction.

The only known document that bears 10 US presidential signatures is a letter sent by President F. D. Roosevelt to Mr Richard C. Corbyn, then of Dallas (now of Amarillo, TX dated 26 Oct 1932. It was subsequently signed by Herbert Hoover, Harry Truman, Dwight Eisenhower, Gerald Ford, Lyndon Johnson, Jimmy Carter, Ronald Reagan and George Bush. Nixon's first signature was signed with an auto-pen but he later re-signed it.

AUTHORS

Most prolific ■ The champion of the goose quill era was Józef Ignacy Kraszewski (1812–87) of Poland, who produced more than 600 volumes of novels and historical works.

A lifetime output of 72–75 million words has been calculated for Charles Harold St John Hamilton, *alias* Frank Richards (1876–1961), the creator of Billy Bunter. In his peak years (1915–26) he wrote up to 80,000 words a week for the boys' school weeklies *Gem* (1907–39), *Magnet* (1908–40) and *Boys' Friend*.

Soho Tokutomi (1863–1957) wrote the history *Kinsei Nippon Kokuminshi* in 100 volumes of 42,468 pages and 19,452,952 letters in 35 years.

Most novels ■ The greatest number of novels published by an authoress is 904 by Kathleen Lindsay (Mrs Mary Faulkner) (1903–73) of Somerset West, Cape Province, South Africa. She wrote under two other married names and eight pen names. Baboorao Arnalkar (b. 9 Jun 1907) of Maharashtra State, India between 1936 and 1984 has published 1,092 short mystery stories in book form and several nonfiction books.

After receiving a probable record 743 rejection slips the British novelist John Creasey (1908–73), under his own name and 25 *noms de plume*, had 564 books totaling more than 40 million words published from 1932 to his death.

Enid Mary Blyton (1898–1968) (Mrs Darrell Waters) completed 700 titles of children's stories, many of them brief, with 59 in 1955.

Highest paid ■ In 1958 Mrs Deborah Schneider of Minneapolis, MN wrote 25 words to complete a sentence in a competition for the best blurb for Plymouth cars. She won from about 1.4 million entrants the prize of $500 every month for life. On normal life expectations she should collect $12,000 per word. No known anthology includes Mrs Schneider's deathless prose but it is in her deed box at her bank 'Only to be opened after death.' She passed $6,000 a word by 1983.

Greatest advance ■ The greatest advance paid for any book is $5 million for *Whirlwind* to James Clavell at auction in New York City on 11 Jan 1986 by William Morrow & Co and Avon Books, United Kingdom.

On 5 May 1988 Mary Higgins Clark (US) signed a contract for $10·1 million for four novels and a book of short stories.

On 11 Jul 1990 it was reported that Jeffrey Archer had signed a deal worth between $20 and $30 million with US publisher HarperCollins for two unwritten novels and a collection of short stories. The contract also includes film, television and audio rights.

Top selling ■ It was announced on 13 Mar 1953 that 672,058,000 copies of the works of Generalissimo Stalin (born Yózef Vissarionovich Dzhugashvili, 1879–1953), had been sold or distributed in 101 languages.

The top-selling authoress is currently Barbara Cartland, with global sales of over 500 million for 516 titles in 30 languages. She has averaged 23 titles per year for the last 14 years and received La Medaille de Vermeil de la Ville de Paris for selling 25 million books in France.

The all-time estimate of book sales for American Erle Stanley Gardner (1889–1970) to 1 Jan 1990 is 322,164,931 copies in 37 languages. An estimated 600 million copies of Belgian novelist Georges Simenon's (1903–89) works have been sold in 47 languages. His most famous character was the Parisian detective Inspector Maigret.

The top-selling lady crime writer has been Agatha Christie (nee Miller, later Lady Mallowan, 1890–1976) whose 78 crime novels sold an estimated 2 billion in 103 languages. Her famous Belgian detective, Hercule Poirot, features in 33 books and 56 stories, while his English counterpart, Miss Marple, has appeared in 12 books and 20 stories. Agatha Christie also wrote 19 plays and six romantic novels under the pseudonym Mary Westmacott. All 78 novels have been reissued to commemorate the centenary of her birth in 1990, and in 1989 Harper & Row paid $9·6 million for the rights to 33 titles. Present royalty earnings are estimated to be worth $4·25 per year.

Longest biography ■ The longest biography in publishing history is that of Sir Winston Churchill by his son Randolph (4,832 pages) and Martin Gilbert (16,745 pages) to date comprising some 9,244,000 words. Georges Simenon (b. 1903) wrote 22 autobiographical books from 1972.

Interviewer ■ The writer who has interviewed most heads of state and heads of government in the world is Brian Rossiter Crozier (b. 4 Aug 1918) of Britain with 64 in the period 1948–89.

Most rejections ■ The greatest number of publishers' rejections of a manuscript is 242 (by June 1990) for the 150,000-word *World Government Crusade*, written in 1966 by Gilbert Young (b. 1906) of Bath, Avon, United Kingdom. The record for rejections before publication is 176 (and non-acknowledgement from many other publishers) in the case of Bill Gordon's *How Many Books Do You Sell in Ohio?* from October 1983 to November 1985. The record was then spoiled by Mr Gordon's rejection of a written offer from publisher Aames-Allen.

Oldest authoress ■ The oldest authoress in the world was Mrs Alice Pollock (nee Wykeham-Martin, 1868–1971), of Haslemere, Surrey, United Kingdom, whose book *Portrait of My Victorian Youth* (Johnson Publications) was published in March 1971 when she was aged 102 years 8 months.

Longest literary gestation ■ The standard German dictionary *Deutsches Wörterbuch*, begun by the brothers Grimm in 1854, was finished in 1971. *Acta Sanctorum*, begun by Jean Bolland in 1643, arranged according to saints' days, reached the month of November in 1925 and an introduction for December was published in 1940.

Oxford University Press received back their proofs of *Constable's Presentments* from the Dugdale Society in December 1984. They had been sent out for correction 35 years earlier in December 1949.

Longest poem ■ The lengthiest poem ever published has been the Kirghiz folk epic *Manas*, which appeared in printed form in 1958 but which has never been translated into English. According to the *Dictionary of Oriental Literatures*, this three part epic runs to about 500,000 lines. Short translated passages appear in *The Elek Book of Oriental Verse*. In contrast, the 24-line Kamassian poem *Lament* is the only knwon literary work in this Samoyed language (distantly related to Hungarian), spoken in the Sayan Mountains near Lake Baikal, Siberia, USSR but on the verge of extinction. This short poem is chronicled in the Hungarian publication *Ancient Cultures of the Uralian Peoples* and is printed in International Phonetics because Kamassian has no written form of its own.

Roger Brien's (b. Montreal, 1910) *Prométhée-dialog des vivants et des morts* runs to 456,047 lines, written from 1964–81. Brien has written another 497,000 lines of French poetry in over 90 published works.

The longest poem ever written in the English language is one on the life of King Alfred by John Fitchett (1766–1838) of Liverpool, United Kingdom, which ran to 129,807 lines and took 40 years to write. His editor, Robert Riscoe, added the concluding 2,585 lines.

Rarest signatures ● The only known document bearing 10 US presidential signatures is a letter sent by Franklin D. Roosevelt to Mr Richard C. Corbyn of Amarillo, TX, dated 26 Oct 1932. It was subsequently signed by Presidents Herbert Hoover, Harry Truman, Dwight Eisenhower, Lyndon Johnson, Gerald Ford, Jimmy Carter, Ronald Reagan and George Bush. Nixon's first signature was signed with an auto-pen, but he later re-signed it. (Photo: R.C. & H. Corbyn)

Most successful poem ■ *If* by Joseph Rudyard Kipling (1865–1936), first published in 1910, has been translated into 27 languages and, according to Kipling, 'anthologized to weariness.'

HIGHEST PRINTINGS

The world's most widely distributed book is the Bible, which has been translated into 314 languages, and portions of it into a further 1,614 languages. This compares with 222 languages for the works of Lenin. It has been estimated that between 1815 and 1975 some 2·5 billion copies were printed, of which 1·5 billion were handled by Bible Societies.

In the period 1976–89 combined global sales of today's English Version (*Good News*) New Testament and Bible (which is copyright of the Bible Societies) exceeded 110 million copies.

Apart from the King James version (averaging some 13 million copies printed annually) there are at least 14 other copyrights on other versions of the Bible. The oldest publisher of bibles is the Cambridge University Press, which began with the Geneva version in 1591.

It has been reported that 800 million copies of the red-covered booklet *Quotations from the Works of Mao Tse-tung* were sold or distributed between June 1966, when possession became virtually mandatory in China, and September 1971 when

Largest library ● The British Library, housed in 18 buildings in London, United Kingdom and a 60 acre site at Boston Spa, West Yorkshire, is one of the largest in the world. The Document Supply Centre in Boston Spa operates the largest interlending service in the world, handling almost 3 million requests annually from libraries all over the world. Its music section, the National Sound Archive, holds over 1 million discs and 50,000 hours of recorded tape and the Newspaper Library contains 70,000 different titles. The famous Reading Room, situated in the main Great Russell St complex in central London, was designed by Sir Anthony Panizzi in 1854.

its promoter Marshal Lin Biao died in an air crash.

It is believed that in the United States, Van Antwerp Bragg and Co printed some 60 million copies of the 1879 edition of *The McGuffey Reader*, compiled by Henry Vail in the precopyright era for distribution to public schools.

The total disposal through noncommercial channels by Jehovah's Witnesses of *The Truth that Leads to Eternal Life* published by the Watchtower Bible and Tract Society of Brooklyn, NY on 8 May 1968, reached 106,865,672 in 117 languages by March 1989.

BEST-SELLING BOOKS

Excluding versions of the Bible, the world's all-time best-selling book is *The Guinness Book of Records*, first published in October 1955 by the Guinness Brewery and edited by Norris Dewar McWhirter (b. 12 Aug 1925) and his twin brother Alan Ross McWhirter (k. 27 Nov 1975). Global sales in 33 languages surpassed 63 million by mid 1990 and the book is now available in disk form on CD-Rom.

Best-seller lists ■ The longest duration on

FICTION BESTSELLERS OF THE 1980s*

TITLE (DATE)	AUTHOR
Clear and Present Danger (1989)	Tom Clancy
The Dark Half (1989)	Stephen King
The Tommyknockers (1987)	Stephen King
The Mammoth Hunters (1985)	Jean M. Auel
Daddy (1989)	Danielle Steel
Lake Wobegon Days (1985)	Garrison Keillor
The Cardinal of the Kremlin (1988)	Tom Clancy
Texas (1985)	James A. Michener
Red Storm Rising (1986)	Tom Clancy
It (1986)	Stephen King

*Rankings based on sales figures
Publishers Weekly, 5 Jan 1990

Best-selling author ● The world's favorite female crime writer is Agatha Christie (1890–1976), whose 78 novels have sold over 2 billion copies worldwide. Her most famous sleuths, Miss Marple and Hercule Poirot, are portrayed here by Margaret Rutherford (1892–1972) in the 1964 MGM film of *Murder Ahoy* and by Peter Ustinov in the 1978 version of *Death on the Nile*, which also featured David Niven (1909–83) and Bette Davis (1908–89). (Photo: Kobal Collection/Syndication International)

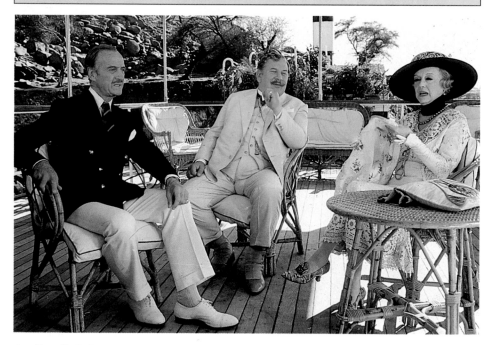

the *New York Times* best-seller list (founded 1935) has been for *The Road Less Traveled* by M. Scott Peck, which on 2 Oct 1988 had its 258th week on the list.

The longest running hardcover bestseller of 1989 was Amy Tan's *The Joy Luck Club* (Putnam) which spent 35 weeks on the fiction list. The longest running nonfiction bestseller of 1989 was Robert Fulghum's *All I Really Need to Know I Learned in Kindergarten* (Villard Books) which spent 51 weeks on the 1989 list and 7 weeks on the 1988 list. The longest running mass market paperback of 1989 was Rosamunde Pilcher's *The Shell Seekers* (Dell) which spent 43 weeks on the paperback bestseller list.

Fiction ■ The novel with the highest sales has been *Valley of the Dolls* (first published March 1966) by Jacqueline Susann (Mrs Irving

Mansfield) (1921–74) with a worldwide total of 28,712,000 to 30 Mar 1987. In the first six months Bantam sold 6·8 million copies. Alistair Stuart MacLean (1922–87) wrote 30 books that have been translated into 28 languages and 13 have been filmed. It has been estimated that a 'MacLean' novel is purchased every 18 seconds.

The Cruel Sea by Nicholas Monsarrat (1910–79), published in 1951 by Cassell, reached sales of 1·2 million in its original edition.

Fastest publisher ■ A thousand bound copies of Sir Frederick Mason's village history *Ropley – Past and Present* were produced in 12 hr 26 min from raw disk by publishers Scriptmate Editions in conjunction with printers Scan Laser Ltd.

Slowest seller ■ The accolade for the

world's slowest-selling book (known in US publishing as slooow sellers) probably belongs to David Wilkins' translation of the New Testament from Coptic into Latin, published by Oxford University Press in 1716 in 500 copies. Selling an average of one each 20 weeks, it remained in print for 191 years.

PUBLISHERS AND PRINTERS
Oldest publisher ■ Cambridge University Press has a continuous history of printing and publishing since 1584. The University received Royal Letters Patent to print and sell all manner of books on 20 Jul 1534.

In 1978 the Oxford University Press (OUP) celebrated the 500th anniversary of the printing of the first book in the City of Oxford in 1478. This was before OUP was itself in existence.

Most prolific publisher ■ Progress Publishers of Moscow, USSR prints over 750 titles in 50 languages annually. The company was founded in 1931 as Publishing Association of Foreign Workers in the USSR and is now the largest publishing house in the USSR, with a staff of 1,500.

Largest printer ■ The largest printers in the world are believed to be R. R. Donnelley & Sons Co. of Chicago, IL. The company, founded in 1864, has nearly 100 manufacturing facilities, offices, service centers and subsidiaries worldwide, turning out $3·12 million worth of work per year. However, Time Warner printers and publishers of New York had sales for 1989 of $7·64 billion, but this includes figures for Warner Communications acquired on 24 Jul 1989.

The largest printer under one roof is the United States Government Printing Office (founded 1861) in Washington D.C. Encompassing 34·4 acres of floor space, the central office processes an average of 1,954 print orders daily, and uses 98 million lb of paper annually. The Superintendent of Documents sells approximately $75·7 million worth of US government publications every year and maintains an inventory of over 16,500 titles in print, receiving 5,600 mail orders each day.

Largest print order ■ The initial print order for the 1990–91 Automobile Association (United Kingdom) *Members' Handbook* was 6,153,000 copies. Stacked on top of each other, this would be seven times the height of Mt Everest. The total print since 1908 is 97,673,000 and it is currently printed by Petty & Sons Ltd of Leeds, United Kingdom and Jarrolds Printing Ltd of Norwich, United Kingdom.

The aggregate print of *The Highway Code* (United Kingdom; instituted 1931) reached 109,539,339 at May 1990, with 2 million copies printed between April 1989 and May 1990.

LIBRARIES
Earliest ■ One of the earliest known collections of archival material was that of King Ashurbanipal at Nineveh (668–627 B.C.). He had clay tablets referring to events and personages as far back as the Dynasty of Agade *c.* 23rd century B.C.

Largest ■ The United States Library of Congress (founded on 24 Apr 1800), on Capitol Hill, Washington D.C. contains 88 million items, including 26 million volumes and pamphlets. The buildings contain 64·6 acres of floor space and 532 miles of shelving.

The largest non-statutory library in the world is the New York Public Library (founded 1895) on

Fifth Avenue, New York City, with a floor space of 525 276 ft² and 88 miles of shelving. Its collection including 82 branch libraries embraces 13,887,774 volumes, 18,349,585 manuscripts and 381,645 maps.

One of the largest libraries in the world is the British Library, dispersed among 18 buildings in London and a 60 acre site at Boston Spa, West Yorkshire, United Kingdom, with a total staff of some 2,500. The library contains over 18 million volumes. Stock increases involve over 8 miles of new shelving annually.

The greatest personal library ever amassed was that of Sir Thomas Phillipps. Dispersal began in 1886. The residue was bought largely unseen by the brothers Lionel Robinson and Philip Robinson for £100,000. Sales began on 1 Jul 1946.

Overdue books ■ The record for an unreturned and overdue library book was set when a book in German on the Archbishop of Bremen, published in 1609, was borrowed from Sidney Sussex College, Cambridge, United Kingdom by Colonel Robert Walpole in 1667–68. It was found by Professor Sir John Plumb in the library of the then Marquess of Cholmondeley at Houghton Hall, Norfolk, United Kingdom and returned 288 years later. No fine was exacted.

Oldest museum ■ The oldest museum still extant in the world is the Ashmolean Museum in Oxford built from 1679–83 and named after the collector Elias Ashmole (1617–92). Since 1924 it has housed an exhibition of historic scientific instruments.

Largest museum ■ The Smithsonian Institution, Washington D.C., comprises 14 museums with 6,000 employees, and contains over 137 million items.

One of the largest museums in the world is the British Museum (founded in 1753), which was opened to the public in 1759. The main building in London, United Kingdom was begun in 1823 and has a total floor area of 21·5 acres. In 1989, 4,396,138 people passed through its doors.

The American Museum of Natural History is situated between 77th and 81st Streets and Central Park West and Columbus Avenue in New York City. It was founded in 1869 and comprises 22 interconnected buildings. The buildings of the Museum and the Planetarium contain an area of 1·5 million ft² of floor space accommodating more than 36 million artifacts and specimens. Its exhibits are viewed by more than 2·6 million visitors each year.

Most popular ■ The highest attendance for any museum is that at the Smithsonian's National Air and Space Museum, Washington, D.C. opened in July 1976. The record-setting day in 1984 required the doors to be temporarily closed with an attendance of over 118,437.

NEWSPAPERS
Oldest ■ A copy has survived of a news pamphlet published in Cologne, West Germany in 1470.

The oldest existing newspaper in the world is the Swedish official journal *Post och Inrikes Tidningar*, founded in 1645. It is published by the Royal Swedish Academy of Letters.

The oldest existing commercial newspaper is the *Haarlems Dagblad/Oprechte Haarlemsche Courant*, published in Haarlem in the Netherlands. First issued as the *Weeckelycke Courante van Europa* on 8 Jan 1656, a copy of issue No. 1 survives.

United States ■ The oldest continuously published newspaper in the United States is the *Hartford Courant* established by Thomas Greene on 29 Oct 1764. Originally a weekly four-page newspaper, it had an estimated circulation of 8,000 during the American Revolution when it printed the full texts of both the Declaration of Independence and the Constitution. In 1836 the *Courant* became a daily newspaper and in 1913 started a Sunday edition. It was acquired by the Times Mirror organization in 1979 and has outlasted 40 other newspapers published at one time or another out of Hartford. Its current circulation figures are 230,358 daily and 316,792 Sunday papers, as of March 1990.

The oldest continuously published daily newspaper in the United States is the *New York Post* established as the *New York Evening Post* by Alexander Hamilton on 16 Nov 1801. Originally four pages, the newspaper had an estimated circulation of 600 in 1801. Its current circulation is 507,568, as of September 1989.

Largest newspapers ■ The most massive single issues of a newspaper have been of the *Sunday New York Times,* which by August 1987 had reached 14 lb with a prediction that 17 lb was a probability.

The largest page size ever used has been 51 in × 35 in for *The Constellation*, printed in 1859 by George Roberts as part of the 4th of July celebrations in New York City.

Smallest newspapers ■ The smallest original page size has been the 3 × 3¾ in of the *Daily Banner* (25 cents per month) of Roseberg, OR, issues of which, dated 1 and 2 Feb 1876, survive.

The British Library Newspaper Division has the *Watford News and Advertiser* of 1 Apr 1899 measuring 2·9 × 3·9 in.

Most ■ The United States had 1,657 English-language daily newspapers at 30 Sep 1986, with a combined net paid circulation of 62,766,232 copies per day.

The peak year for US newspapers was 1910, when there were 2,202.

The leading newspaper readers in the world are the people of Sweden, where 580 newspapers are sold for each 1,000.

Longest editorship ■ Sir Etienne Dupuch (b. 16 Feb 1899) of Nassau, Bahamas, editor-in-chief of *The Tribune* from 1 Apr 1919 to 1972, and contributing editor to the present time, entered his 71st year as an editor on 1 Apr 1989.

Most durable feature ■ Eric Hardy of Liverpool, United Kingdom is in his 63rd year as a regular natural history contributor to the *Daily Post* of Liverpool, United Kingdom, with a weekly 'Countryside' feature.

Most syndicated columnist ■ In 1987 Ann Landers (nee Eppie Lederer, b. 1920) appeared in over 1,200 newspapers with an estimated readership of 90 million. Her only serious rival was 'Dear Abby' (Mrs Pauline Phillips) her identical twin sister based in Beverly Hills, CA.

Earliest cartoon strip ■ 'The Yellow Kid' first appeared in the *New York Journal* on 18 Oct 1896.

Most syndicated cartoon strip ■ 'Peanuts' by Charles Schulz of Santa Rosa, CA has appeared in more than 2,000 newspapers in 68 countries in 26 languages since October 1950. In

1986 his income was estimated at $1 million per month.

Most durable cartoon strip ■ The most durable newspaper comic strip has been the 'Katzenjammer Kids' (Hans and Fritz) created by Rudolph Dirks and first published in the *New York Journal* on 12 Dec 1897.

Most misprints ■ The record for misprints in *The Times* (London) was set on 22 Aug 1978 when on page 19 there were 97 in 5½ single column inches. The passage concerned 'Pop' (Pope) Paul VI.

Most durable advertizer ■ The Jos Neel Co, a clothing store in Macon, GA (founded 1880) has run an 'ad' in the *Macon Telegraph* every day in the upper left corner of page 2 since 22 Feb 1889.

CIRCULATION
Earliest million ■ The first newspaper to achieve a circulation of 1 million copies was *Le Petit Journal*, published in Paris, France, which reached this figure in 1886, when selling at 5 cents.

Highest ■ The highest circulation for any newspaper in the world is that for the *Yomiuri Shimbun* (founded 1874) of Japan, which attained a figure of 14,811,181 copies on 1 Apr 1990. This is achieved by totaling the figures for editions published in various centers with a morning figure of 9,969,321 and an evening figure of 4,841,860. It reaches 24·58 percent of Japan's 40·56 million households and employs 7,996 staff in 132 bureaus. In Japan 569 newspapers are printed for each 1,000 people.

The eight-page weekly newspaper *Argumenty i Fakty* (founded 1978) of Moscow, USSR attained a figure of 33·4 million copies by May 1990. It has an estimated readership of 100 million.

Most read ■ The national newspaper that achieves the closest to a saturation circulation is the *Sunday Post*, established in Glasgow, United Kingdom in 1914. In 1989 its estimated readership in Scotland of 2,213,000 represented 54 percent of the entire population aged 15 and over. The *Arran Banner* (founded March 1974) is read by over 97 percent of the inhabitants of Britains 7th largest offshore island.

PERIODICALS
Oldest ■ The oldest continuing periodical in the world is *Philosophical Transactions of the Royal Society*, published in London, United Kingdom, which first appeared on 6 Mar 1665.

Curtis' *Botanical Magazine* has been in continuous publication since 1 Feb 1787, as several 'parts' a year forming a series of continuously numbered volumes.

Largest circulations ■ The peak circulation of any weekly periodical has been that of *TV Guide*, which in 1974 became the first magazine in history to sell a billion copies in a year.

The world's highest circulation magazine currently is *Modern Maturity*, with a figure in Jan–Jul 1988 of 17,924,783.

In its 39 basic international editions, *Reader's Digest* (established February 1922) circulates 28 million copies monthly in 15 languages, including a United States edition of more than 16·25 million copies and a United Kingdom edition (established 1939) of 1,527,560 copies (ABC July–December 1989).

Parade, the United States syndicated color magazine, is distributed with 333 newspapers

every Sunday. The circulation at July 1990 was 35 million.

Weightiest ■ The heaviest magazine ever published was the February/March 1990 issue of the US Conde Nast publication *Bride's*, which ran to 1,034 hernia-inducing pages.

Annual ■ *Old Moore's Almanack* has been published annually since 1697, when it first appeared as a broadsheet by Dr Francis Moore (1657–1715) of Southwark, London, United Kingdom to advertize his 'physiks.' The annual sale certified by its publishers, W. Foulsham & Co Ltd of Slough, Berkshire, United Kingdom, is 1 million copies, and its aggregate sale is estimated to be in excess of 108 million.

CROSSWORDS

First ■ A 25-letter acrostic of Roman provenance was discovered on a wall in Cirencester, Gloucestershire, United Kingdom in 1868.

The earliest known crossword was a 9 x 9 Double Diamond published in *St Nicholas* for September 1875 in New York City. This was discovered by Dr Kenneth Miller of Newcastle upon Tyne, Tyne and Wear, United Kingdom, inventor of the color crossword in 1983.

Largest published crossword ■ In July 1982 Robert Turcot of Québec, Canada compiled a crossword comprising of 82,951 squares. It contained 12,489 clues across, 13,125 down and covered 38·28 ft².

Fastest solution ■ The fastest recorded time for completing *The Times* (London) crossword under test conditions is 3 min 45 sec by Roy Dean of Bromley, Kent, United Kingdom in the British Broadcasting Corporation *Today* radio studio on 19 Dec 1970.

Dr John Sykes won *The Times* (London) championship nine times between 1972 and 1989, when he set a championship best time of 4 min 28 sec.

Slowest solution ■ In May 1966 *The Times* (London) received an announcement from a Fijian woman that she had just succeeded in completing their crossword No. 673 in the issue of 4 Apr 1932.

Most durable compilers ■ Adrian Bell (1901–1980) of Barsham, Suffolk, United Kingdom contributed a record 4,520 crosswords to *The Times* (London) from 2 Jan 1930 until his death.

The most prolific compiler is Roger F. Squires of Ironbridge, Shropshire, United Kingdom, who compiles 38 published puzzles singlehandedly each week. His total output to September 1990 was over 35,000 crosswords, and his millionth clue was published in the *Daily Telegraph* (London) on 6 Sep 1989.

ADVERTISING RATES

The world's highest newspaper advertising rate is 41·55 million yen for a full page in the morning edition and 32·37 million yen for the evening edition of the *Yomiuri Shimbun* of Tokyo (April 1989).

The highest ever price for a single page was $436,300 for a four-color back cover in *Parade* (circulation 33·2 million per week) in January 1989 (see above). The record for a four-color inside page is $421,400 in *Parade*, with a four-color back cover costing $492,900.

The advertising revenue from the November 1982 US edition of *Reader's Digest* was a peak $14,716,551.

TOP TEN ADVERTISERS, 1988	SPENDING ($millions)
Proctor & Gamble (US)	2,439·6
Philip Morris (US)	2,376·3
Unilever (Anglo-Dutch)	1,815·0
General Motors (US)	1,568·1
Nestle (Switzerland)	1,174·4
Sears, Roebuck (US)	1,045·2
RJR Nabisco (US)	911·3
Kellogg (US)	862·9
PepsiCo (US)	851·2
McDonald's (US)	828·1

Advertising Age

The highest expenditure ever incurred on a single advertisement in a periodical is $3 851 684 by Walt Disney Productions, celebrating Mickey Mouse's 60th birthday, on 7 Nov 1988 in *Time* magazine.

Music

Whistles and flutes made from perforated phalange bones have been found at Upper Paleolithic sites of the Aurignacian period (*c.* 25,000–22,000 B.C.), e.g. at Istallóskö, Hungary and in Moldova, USSR.

The world's earliest surviving musical notation dates from *c.* 1800 B.C.

A heptatonic scale deciphered from a clay tablet by Dr Duchesne-Guillemin in 1966–67 was found at a site in Nippur, Sumer, now Iraq.

An Assyrian love song, also *c.* 1800 B.C., to an Ugaritic god from a tablet of notation and lyric was reconstructed for an 11-string lyre at the University of California, Berkeley on 6 Mar 1974.

Musical history can, however, be traced back to the 3rd millennium B.C., when the yellow bell (*huang chung*) had a recognized standard musical tone in Chinese temple music.

INSTRUMENTS

Earliest piano ■ The earliest pianoforte in existence is one built in Florence, Italy in 1720 by Bartolommeo Cristofori (1655–1731) of Padua, and now preserved in the Metropolitan Museum of Art, New York City.

Grandest piano ■ The grandest grand piano was one of 1·4 tons and 11 ft 8 in in length made by Chas H. Challen & Son Ltd of London, United Kingdom in 1935. The longest bass string measured 9 ft 11 in, with a tensile strength of 33 tons.

Most expensive piano ■ The highest price ever paid for a piano was $390,000 at Sotheby Parke Bernet, New York on 26 Mar 1980 for a Steinway grand of *c.* 1888 sold by the Martin Beck Theater. It was bought by a non-pianist.

Smallest piano ■ The smallest playable piano is a ⅛ th scale model of a 1910 Knabe. It measures 7½ × 3⅜ × 6½ in and was built by Emil J. Cost.

Largest organ ■ The largest and loudest musical instrument ever constructed is the now

only partially functional Auditorium Organ in Atlantic City, NJ. Completed in 1930, this heroic instrument had two consoles (one with seven manuals and another movable one with five), 1,477 stop controls and 33,112 pipes, ranging in tone from ³/₁₆ of an inch to the 64 ft tone. It had the volume of 25 brass bands, with a range of seven octaves.

The world's largest fully functional organ is the six manual 30,067 pipe Grand Court Organ installed in the Wanamaker Store, Philadelphia, PA in 1911 and enlarged between then and 1930. It has a 64-ft tone gravissima pipe.

The world's most powerful electronic organ is Robert A. Nye's 7000-watt 'Golden Spirit' organ, designed by Henry N. Hunsicker. It has 700 speakers and made its public concert debut in Trump's Castle, Atlantic City, NJ on 9 Dec 1988.

The world's largest church organ is that in Passau Cathedral, West Germany. It was completed in 1928 by D. F. Steinmeyer & Co and has 16,000 pipes and five manuals.

The chapel organ at West Point US Military Academy, NY has, since 1911, been expanded from 2,406 to 18,200 pipes.

Loudest organ stop ■ The Ophicleide stop of the Grand Great in the Solo Organ in the Atlantic City Auditorium (see above) is operated by a pressure of water 3½ lb/in² and has a pure trumpet note of ear-splitting volume, more than six times the volume of the loudest locomotive whistles.

Largest pan pipes ■ The world's largest pan pipes created by Simon Desorgher and Lawrence Casserley consist of five contrabass pipes, each 4 in in diameter with lengths of 19 in, 16 in, 14 in, 12 in and 10 in respectively, and five bass pipes of 2 in diameter with lengths of 9·5 in, 8 in, 7 in, 6 in and 5 in. Their first public appearance was at Jubilee Gardens, London, United Kingdom on 9 Jul 1988.

Most durable musicians ■ Elsie Maude Stanley Hall (1877–1976) gave piano recitals for 90 years, giving her final concert in Rustenburg, Transvaal, South Africa at age 97.

The longest international career in the history of Western music was crowned by Mieczyslaw Horszowski (b. Poland, July 1892) with a recital of Bach, Chopin, Mozart and Schumann at the Aldeburgh Festival, Suffolk, United Kingdom on 15 Jun 1989. He played before Emperor Franz-Joseph in Vienna, Austria in 1899.

Norwegian pianist Reidar Thommesen (1889–1986) played over 30 hours a week in theater cafés when a nonagenarian.

Charles Bridgeman (1779–1873) of All Saints Parish Church, Hertford, United Kingdom, who was appointed organist in 1792, was still playing 81 years later in 1873.

Rolland S. Tapley retired as a violinist from the Boston Symphony Orchestra after reputedly playing for an unrivaled 58 years from February 1920 to 27 Aug 1978.

Yiannis Pipis (b. 25 Nov 1889) of Nicosia, Cyprus, a professional Folkloric violinist since 1912, continues to play even at the age of 100.

Largest brass instrument ■ The largest recorded brass instrument is a tuba standing 7½ ft tall, with 39 ft of tubing and a bell 3 ft 4 in across. This contrabass tuba was constructed for a world tour by the band of American composer John Philip Sousa (1854–1932), *c.* 1896–98. It is now owned by a circus promoter in South Africa.

Largest stringed instrument ■ The largest movable stringed instrument ever constructed was a pantaleon with 270 strings stretched over 50 ft² used by George Noel in 1767.

The greatest number of musicians required to operate a single instrument was the six required to play the gigantic orchestrion, known as the Apollonican, built in 1816 and played until 1840.

Largest guitar ■ The largest playable guitar in the world is 19·09 ft tall and was built by the Narrandera Country Music Association in 1989.

Most expensive standard sized guitar ■ A Fender Stratocaster belonging to legendary rock guitarist Jimi Hendrix (1942–70) was sold by his former drummer Mitch Mitchell to an anonymous buyer for £180,000 at Sotheby's, London, United Kingdom on 25 Apr 1990.

Largest double bass ■ A double bass measuring 14 ft tall, was built in 1924 in Ironia, NJ by Arthur K. Ferris, allegedly on orders from the Archangel Gabriel. It weighed 11·6 cwt with a sound box 8 ft across, and had leather strings totaling 104 ft. Its low notes could be felt rather than heard.

Sixteen musicians from Blandford, Dorset, United Kingdom played a double bass simultaneously (five fingering and eleven bowing) in a rendition of Strauss' *Perpetuum Mobile* at Blandford Town Hall on 6 Jun 1989.

Most valuable 'cello ■ The highest ever auction price for a violincello or any musical instrument is £682,000 at Sotheby's, London, United Kingdom on 22 Jun 1988 for a Stradivarius known as 'The Cholmondeley' made in Cremona, Italy *c.* 1698.

Most valuable violin ■ The Lady Blunt Stradivarius violin of 1721 failed at £820,000 to reach its undisclosed 'reserve' at Sotheby's, London, United Kingdom on 14 Nov 1985.

The highest price paid at auction for a violin is £572,000 for Joseph Guarneri del Gesu's Baron Heath violin, named after a diplomat who once owned it, made in 1743. It was sold at Sotheby's, London, United Kingdom on 23 Nov 1988. Stradivarius' (1644–1737) Alard violin was confirmed by Jacques Français to have been sold by private treaty by W. E. Hill for $1·2 million to a Singaporean.

Largest drum ■ A drum with a 13 ft diameter was built by the Supreme Drum Co, London, United Kingdom and played at the Royal Festival Hall, London on 31 May 1987.

Largest drum kit ■ A drum kit consisting of 81 pieces—45 drums, including six bass drums, 15 cymbals, five temple blocks, two triangles, two gongs, two sets of wind chimes, one solid bar chime, six assorted cowbells, a drum set tambourine, a vibra slap and an icebell, is owned by Darreld MacKenzie of Calgary, Alberta, Canada.

Longest alphorn ■ A 118-ft (excluding mouthpiece) horn weighing 183 lb was built by Swiss-born Peter Wutherich, of Boise, ID. The sound takes 105·7 milliseconds to emerge from the bowl after entry into the mouthpiece.

Highest and lowest notes ■ The extremes of orchestral instruments (excluding the organ) range between a handbell tuned to g^v (6,272 cycles/sec) and the sub-contrabass clarinet, which can reach C$_{11}$ or 16·4 cycles/sec.

The highest note on a standard pianoforte is c^v (4,186 cycles/sec), which is also the violinist's limit.

In 1873 a sub double bassoon able to reach B$_{111}$± or 14·6 cycles/sec was constructed but no surviving specimen is known.

The extremes for the organ are g^{vi} (the sixth G above middle C) (12·544 cycles/sec) and C$_{111}$ (8·12 cycles/sec) obtainable from ¾ in and 64 ft pipes respectively.

SONG

Oldest ■ The *shaduf* chant has been sung since time immemorial by irrigation workers on the man-powered pivoted-rod bucket raisers of the Nile water mills (or *saqiyas*) in Egypt.

The oldest known harmonized music performed today is the English song *Sumer is icumen in*, which dates from *c.* 1240.

National anthems ■ The oldest national anthem is the *Kimigayo* of Japan, the words which date from the 9th century, while the oldest music belongs to the Netherlands'.

The anthem of Greece constitutes the first two verses of the Solomos poem, which has 158 stanzas.

The shortest anthems are those of Japan, Jordan and San Marino, each with only four lines.

Of the 11 wordless national anthems, the oldest is that of Spain—dating from 1770.

Longest rendering ■ 'God Save the King' was played nonstop 16 or 17 times by a German military band on the platform of Rathenau railroad station, Brandenburg, Germany on the morning of 9 Feb 1909. The reason was that King Edward VII was struggling inside the train with the uniform of a German field marshal before he could emerge.

Top songs ■ The most frequently sung songs in English are *Happy Birthday to You* (based on the original *Good Morning to All*), by Kentucky Sunday School teachers Mildred Hill and Patty Smith Hill of New York (written in 1893 and copyrighted from 1935 to 2010); *For He's a Jolly Good Fellow* (originally the French *Malbrouk*), known at least as early as 1781, and *Auld Lang Syne* (originally the Strathspey *I Fee'd a Lad at Michaelmass*), some words of which were written by Robert Burns (1759–96). *Happy Birthday* was sung in space by the Apollo IX astronauts on 8 Mar 1969.

Top-selling sheet music ■ Sales of three non-copyright pieces are known to have exceeded 20 million, namely *The Old Folks at Home* by Stephen Foster (1855), *Listen to the Mocking Bird* (1855) and *The Blue Danube* (1867).

Of copyright material the two top sellers are *Let Me Call You Sweetheart* (1910, by Whitson and Friedman) and *Till We Meet Again* (1918, by Egan and Whiting) each with some 6 million sales by 1967. Other huge sellers have been *St Louis Blues*, *Stardust* and *Tea for Two*.

Most successful songwriters ■ The songwriters responsible for the most number-one singles are John Lennon (1940–80) and Paul McCartney (b. 18 Jun 1942). McCartney is credited as writer on 32 number-one hits in the US to Lennon's 26 (with 23 co-written).

In the United States Barry Gibb of the Bee Gees has written or cowritten 16 number-ones. The most successful female songwriter in the US is Carole King, (b. Carole Klein, 9 Feb 1942) with eight number-ones.

HYMNS

Earliest ■ There are more than 950,000 Christian hymns in existence.

The music and parts of the text of a hymn in the *Oxyrhynchus Papyri* from the second century are the earliest known hymnody.

The earliest exactly datable hymn is the *Heyr Himna Smiður* (*Hear, the Maker of Heaven*) from 1208 by the Icelandic bard and chieftain Kolbeinn Tumason (1173–1208).

Longest ■ The *Hora novissima tempora pessima sunt; vigilemus* by Bernard of Cluny (12th century), runs to 2,966 lines.

In English the longest is *The Sands of Time Are Sinking* by Mrs Anne Ross Cousin, nee Cundell (1824–1906), which is in full 152

lines, though only 32 lines in the Methodist Hymn Book.

Shortest ■ The shortest hymn is the single verse in long meter *Be Present at our Table Lord*, anonymous, but attributed to 'J. Leland.'

Most prolific hymnists ■ Mrs Frances (Fanny) Jane van Alstyne, (nee Crosby [US]; 1820–1915) wrote 8,500 hymns. She is reputed to have completed one hymn in 15 minutes.

Charles Wesley (1707–88) wrote about 6,000 hymns. The works of John Mason Neale (1818–66) appear 56 times in the 7th (1950) edition of *Hymns Ancient and Modern*.

BELLS

Oldest ■ The tintinnabulum found in the Babylonian Palace of Nimrod in 1849 by Mr (later Sir) Austen Henry Layard (1817–94) dates from *c.* 1100 B.C. The oldest known tower bell is one in Pisa, Italy dated MCVI (1106).

Heaviest ■ The Tsar Kolokol, cast on 25 Nov 1735 in Moscow weighs 216 tons, measures 19 ft 4½ in in diameter and 19 ft 3 in high, and its greatest thickness is 24 in. The bell was cracked in a fire in 1737 and a fragment, weighing about 12 tons, was broken from it. The bell has stood, unrung, on a platform in the Kremlin since 4 Aug 1836 with the fragment alongside.

The heaviest bell in use is the Mingun bell, weighing 101 tons with a diameter of 16 ft 8½ in at the lip, in Mandalay, The Union of Myanma (Burma) which is struck by a teak boom from the outside and it was cast at Mingun late in the reign of King Bodawpaya (1782–1819).

The heaviest swinging bell in the world is the Petersglocke in the southwest tower of Cologne Cathedral, West Germany, cast in 1923 with a diameter of 11 ft 1¾ in weighing 28 tons.

'Big Ben,' the bell in the tower of the House of Commons, London, United Kingdom was cast in 1858 and weighs 13 tons 10 cwt 3 qrs 15 lb. It is the most broadcast bell in the world and is note E.

Peals ■ A ringing peal is defined as a diatonic 'ring' of five or more bells hung for full-circle change ringing. Of 5,500 rings so hung only 70 are outside the United Kingdom and Ireland.

The heaviest ring in the world is that of 13 bells cast in 1938–39 for the Anglican Cathedral, Liverpool, United Kingdom. The total bell weight is 18·5 tons, of which Emmanuel, the tenor bell note A, weighs 82 cwt 11 lb.

Largest carillon ■ The largest carillon (minimum of 23 bells) in the world is the Laura Spelman Rockefeller Memorial Carillon in Riverside Church, New York City, with 74 bells weighing 102 tons. The bourdon, giving the note lower C, weighs 40,926 lb. This 18·27-ton bell, cast in England, with a diameter of 10 ft 2 in is the largest *tuned* bell in the world.

Bell ringing ■ Eight bells have been rung to their full 'extent' (40,320 unrepeated changes of Plain Bob Major) only once without relays. This took place in a bell foundry at Loughborough, Leicestershire, United Kingdom, beginning at 6:52 A.M. on 27 Jul 1963 and ending at 12:50 A.M. on 28 Jul, after 17 hr 58 min. The peal was composed by Kenneth Lewis of Altrincham, Manchester, United Kingdom, and the eight ringers were conducted by Robert B. Smith, aged 25, of Marple, Manchester, United Kingdom. Theoretically it would take 37 years 355 days to ring 12 bells (maximus) to their full extent of 479,001,600 changes.

The greatest number of peals (minimum of 5,040 changes, all in tower bells) rung in a year is 209, by Mark William Marshall of Ashford, Kent, United Kingdom in 1973.

The late George E. Fearn rang 2,666 peals from 1928 to May 1974. Matthew Lakin (1801–1899) was a regular bell-ringer at Tetney Church near Grimsby, Humberside, United Kingdom for 84 years.

ORCHESTRAS

Oldest Orchestra ■ The oldest orchestra in continuous existence is the Gewandhaus Orchestra in Leipzig founded in 1743.

United States ■ The oldest orchestra in the United States is the Philharmonic-Symphony Society of New York which was founded by Ureli Corelli Hill in 1842. It was established the same year as the Vienna Symphony Orchestra and both will celebrate their sesquicentennial 1992–93.

Largest orchestra ■ On 17 Jun 1872, Johann Strauss the younger (1825–99) conducted an orchestra of 987 pieces supported by a choir of 20,000, at the World Peace Jubilee in Boston, MA. The number of first violinists was 400.

Largest band ■ The most massive band ever assembled was one of 20,100 bandsmen at

Most prolific composer ● Despite his tragically short life, child prodigy Wolfgang Amadeus Mozart (1756–91) completed *c.* 1,000 major works, making him also one of the fastest composers. One of his later and most popular works is the opera *The Marriage of Figaro* , seen here performed at the Royal Opera House, Covent Garden, London, United Kingdom in 1987. (Photos: Internationale Stiftung Mozarteum/Dominic Photography/Catherine Ashmore)

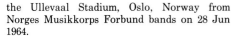

the Ullevaal Stadium, Oslo, Norway from Norges Musikkorps Forbund bands on 28 Jun 1964.

On 17 Apr 1982, 6,179 'musicians' congregated at Bay Shore Mall, Milwaukee, WI for a rendering of Sousa's 'Stars and Stripes Forever.' According to one music critic, the 'instruments' included 'kazoos, 7-Up bottles, one-man-band contraptions, coffee cans, bongo drums and anything-you-can-thump-on.' 'At times,' the report concluded, 'you could almost tell what they were playing.'

Largest marching band ■ The largest marching band was one of 4,524, including 1,342 majorettes, under the direction of Danny Kaye (1913–87) at Dodger Stadium, Los Angeles, CA on 15 Apr 1985.

Most successful bands ■ The most successful pipe band is the Shotts & Dykehead Caledonian Pipe Band, with their 10th world title in August 1980.

The City of Wellington Pipe Band Incorporated has won 26 Grade 1 New Zealand Championship titles since 1955.

Conductors ■ Austrian conductor Herbert von Karajan (1908–89), principal conductor of the Berlin Philharmonic Orchestra for 35 years before his retirement from the position shortly before his death, was the most prolific conductor ever, having made over 800 recordings of all the major works. Despite a reputation for being temperamental, Karajan had also led the Philharmonia of London, the Vienna State Opera and La Scala Opera of Milan. The Cork Symphony Orchestra of the Republic of Ireland performed under the baton of Dr Aloys Fleischmann for 54 seasons (1935–88).

Sir George Solti (b. 22 Oct 1912), the Hungarian born principal conductor of the Chicago Symphony Orchestra, has won a record 28 Grammy awards for his recordings.

United States ■ The Chicago Symphony Orchestra was directed by Frederick Stock (1872–1942) from 1905 until his death in 1942, a total of 37 seasons.

Largest choir ■ Excluding 'sing alongs' by stadium crowds, the greatest choir is one of 60,000, which sang in unison as a finale of a choral contest among 160,000 participants in Breslau, Germany on 2 Aug 1937.

Oldest choral society ■ The oldest active choral society in the United States is the Handel and Haydn Society of Boston which gave its first concert performance on Christmas Day 1815 at Stone Chapel (now King's Chapel). The Handel and Haydn Society also gave the first complete performance of *The Messiah* in the United States on 25 Dec 1818 at Boylston Hall, Boston. It celebrated its 175th anniversary during 1990.

ATTENDANCES

Classical ■ An estimated 800,000 attended a free open-air concert by the New York Philharmonic conducted by Zubin Mehta, on the Great Lawn of Central Park, NY on 5 Jul 1986, as part of the Statue of Liberty Weekend.

Pop festival ■ Estimating the size of audiences at open-air events where no admission is paid is often left to the police, media reporters, promoters and publicity agents. Estimates therefore vary widely and there is no way to check the accuracy of claims. The best claim is believed to be 725,000 for Steve Wozniak's 1983 US Festival in San Bernadino, CA. The Woodstock Music and Art Fair held on 15–17 Aug 1969 at Bethel, NY is thought to have attracted an audience of 300,000–500,000.

Solo performer ■ The largest paying audience ever attracted by a solo performer was an estimated 175,000 in the Maracaña Stadium, Rio de Janeiro, Brazil to hear Frank Sinatra (b. 1915) on 26 Jan 1980.

Jean-Michel Jarre entertained an estimated 1·2 million at downtown Houston, TX at a free concert on 5 Apr 1986.

Most successful concert tour ■ The Rolling Stones tour, which ended in December 1989, grossed an estimated $310 million. The Stones played to over 3·2 million people in 30 cities.

Stadium sell out ■ Michael Jackson sold out seven nights at Wembley Stadium, London, United Kingdom in the summer of 1988. The Stadium has a capacity of 72,000 so a total of 504,000 people saw Jackson perform on 14, 15, 16, 22, 23 Jul and 26, 27 Aug 1988.

COMPOSERS

Most prolific ■ The most prolific composer of all time was probably Georg Philipp Telemann (1681–1767) of Germany. He composed 12 complete sets of services (one cantata every Sunday) for a year, 78 services for special occasions, 40 operas, 600 to 700 orchestral suites, 44 Passions, plus concertos and chamber music.The most prolific symphonist was Johann Melchior Molter (c. 1695–1765) of Germany who wrote 169. Joseph Haydn (1732–1809) of Austria wrote 108 numbered symphonies, many of which are regularly played today.

Most rapid ■ Among composers of the classical period the most prolific was Wolfgang Amadeus Mozart (1756–91) of Austria, who wrote c. 1,000 operas, operettas, symphonies, violin sonatas, divertimenti, serenades, motets, concertos for piano and many other instruments, string quartets, other chamber music, masses and litanies, of which only 70 were published before he died aged 35. His opera *La Clemenza di Tito* (1791) was written in 18 days, and three symphonic masterpieces, Symphony No. 39 in E flat major, Symphony No. 40 in G minor and the Jupiter Symphony No. 41 in C major, were reputedly written in the space of 42 days in 1788. His overture *Don Giovanni* was written in full score at one sitting in Prague in 1787 and finished on the day of its opening performance.

Longest symphony ■ The longest of all single classical symphonies is the orchestral symphony No. 3 in D minor by Gustav Mahler (1860–1911) of Austria. This work, composed in 1896, requires a contralto, a women's and a boys' choir in addition to a full orchestra. A full performance requires 1 hr 40 min, of which the first movement alone takes between 30 and 36 min.

The Symphony No. 2 (the Gothic), composed from 1919–22 by William Havergal Brian (1876–1972), was played by over 800 performers (four brass bands) in the Victoria Hall, Hanley, Staffordshire, United Kingdom on 21 May 1978 (conductor Trevor Stokes). A recent broadcast required 1 hr 45½ min.

Brian wrote an even vaster work based on Shelley's 'Prometheus Unbound' lasting 4 hr 11 min, but the full score has been missing since 1961.

The symphony *Victory at Sea* written by Richard Rodgers and arranged by Robert Russell Bennett for NBC TV in 1952 lasted 13 hours.

Longest piano composition ■ The longest continuous non-repetitive piano piece ever published has been *The Well-Tuned Piano* by La Monte Young, first presented by the Dia Art Foundation at the Concert Hall, Harrison St, New York on 28 Feb 1980. The piece lasted 4 hr 12 min 10 sec.

Symphonic Variations, composed in the 1930s for piano and orchestra by the British-born Kaikhosru Shapurji Sorabji (1892–1988) on 500 pages of close manuscript in three volumes, would last for six hours at the prescribed tempo.

Longest silence ■ The longest interval between the known composition of a major composer and its performance in the manner intended is from 3 Mar 1791 until 9 Oct 1982 (over 191 years), in the case of Mozart's *Organ Piece for a Clock*, a fugue fantasy in F minor (K 608), arranged by the organ builders Wm Hill & Son and Norman & Beard Ltd at Glyndebourne, East Sussex, United Kingdom.

PERFORMERS

Highest-paid pianist ■ Wladziu Valentino Liberace (1917–87) earned more than $2 million each 26-week season, with a peak of $138,000 for a single night's performance at Madison Square Garden, New York in 1954.

The highest-paid classical concert pianist was Ignace Jan Paderewski (1860–1941), prime minister of Poland (1919–20), who accumulated a fortune estimated at $5 million, of which $500,000 was earned in a single season in 1922–23.

For concerts, Arthur Rubinstein (1887–1982) between 1937 and 1976 commanded 70 percent of the gross from his concerts.

Most successful singer ■ Of great fortunes earned by singers, the highest on record are those of Enrico Caruso (1873–1921), the Italian tenor, whose estate was about $9 million, and the Italian-Spanish coloratura soprano Amelita Galli-Curci (1889–1963), who received about $3 million.

The Irish tenor Count John Francis McCormack (1884–1945) gave up to ten concerts to capacity audiences in a single season in New York.

David Bowie drew a fee of $1·5 million for a single show at the US Festival in Glen Helen Regional Park, San Bernardino County, CA on 26 May 1983. The four-man rock band Van Halen attracted a matching fee.

The total attendance at Michael Jackson's world tour, Sep 1987–Dec 1988, brought in a tour gross revenue in excess of $124 million.

Singer's pulling power ■ In 1850, up to $653 was paid for a single seat at the United States concerts of Johanna ('Jenny') Maria Lind (1820–87), the 'Swedish night- ingale. She had a range from g to e''', of which the middle register is still regarded as unrivaled.

Worst singer ■ While no agreement exists as to the identity of history's greatest singer, there is unanimity on the worst. The excursions of the soprano Florence Foster Jenkins (1868–1944) into lieder and even high coloratura culminated on 25 Oct 1944 in her sell-out concert at the Carnegie Hall, New York. The diva's (already high) high F was said to have been made higher in 1943 by a crash in a taxi. It is one of the tragedies of musicology that Madame Jenkins' *Clavelitos*, accompanied by Cosme McMoon, was never recorded for posterity.

Fastest rapper ■ Daddy Freddy rapped 507 syllables in 60 sec on the British Broadcasting Corporation 'Record Breakers' program on 24

Most curtain calls ● Luciano Pavarotti sings the part of Nemorino in the 1990 Royal Opera House version of Donizetti's *L'Elisir d'Amore*, for which he received an unprecedented 165 curtain calls at the Deutsche Oper in Berlin, West Germany on 24 Feb 1988. (Photo: Dominic Photography/Richard Smith)

Nov 1989, beating his own record of 346 syllables set at the Capital Radio Music Festival, London, United Kingdom in June 1989.

OPERA

Longest ■ The longest of commonly performed operas is *Die Meistersinger von Nürnberg* by Wilhelm Richard Wagner (1813–83) of Germany. A normal uncut performance of this opera as performed by the Sadler's Wells company of London, United Kingdom between 24 Aug and 19 Sep 1968 entailed 5 hr 15 min of music.

The Heretics by Gabriel von Wayditch (1888–1969), a Hungarian-American, is orchestrated for 110 pieces and lasts 8½ hr.

Shortest ■ The shortest opera published was *The Deliverance of Theseus* by Darius Milhaud (1892–1972), first performed in 1928, which lasted for 7 min 27 sec.

Longest aria ■ The longest single aria, in the sense of an operatic solo, is Brünnhilde's immolation scene in Wagner's *Götterdämmerung*. A well-known recording of this has been precisely timed at 14 min 46 sec.

Largest opera houses ■ The Metropolitan Opera House, Lincoln Center, New York, completed in September 1966 at a cost of $45·7 million, has a capacity of 3,800 seats in an auditorium 451 ft deep. The stage is 234 ft wide and 146 ft deep.

The tallest opera house is one housed in a 42-story building on Wacker Drive in Chicago, IL.

The Teatro della Scala (La Scala) in Milan, Italy shares with the Bolshoi Theater in Moscow, USSR the distinction of having the greatest number of tiers. Each has six, with the topmost being nicknamed the *Galiorka* by Russians.

Youngest opera singers ■ Ginetta Gloria La Bianca, born in Buffalo, NY on 12 May 1934, sang Rosina in *The Barber of Seville* at the Teatro dell'Opera, Rome, Italy on 8 May 1950 aged 15 years 361 days, having appeared as Gilda in *Rigoletto* at Velletri 45 days earlier. Ginetta La Bianca was taught by Lucia Carlino and managed by Angelo Carlino.

Oldest opera singer ■ The tenor Giovanni Martinelli sang Emperor Altoum in *Turandot* in Seattle, WA on 4 Feb 1967 when aged 81.

Danshi Toyotake (b. 1 Aug 1891) has been singing *Musume Gidayu* for 91 years.

Longest encore ■ The longest operatic encore, listed in the *Concise Oxford Dictionary of Opera*, was of the entire opera *Il Matrimonio Segreto* by Domenico Cimarosa (1749–1801) at its premiere in 1792. This was at the command of the Austro-Hungarian Emperor Leopold II (reigned 1790–92).

Most curtain calls ■ On 24 Feb 1988 Luciano Pavarotti received 165 curtain calls and was applauded for 1 hr 7 min after singing the part of Nemorino in Gaetano Donizetti's *L'Elisir d'Amore* at the Deutsche Oper in West Berlin, West Germany.

BALLET

Fastest 'entrechat douze' ■ In the *entrechat* (a vertical spring from the fifth position with the legs extended criss-crossing at the lower calf), the starting and finishing position each count as one, such that in an *entrechat douze* there are *five* crossings and uncrossings. This was performed by Wayne Sleep for the British Broadcasting Corporation 'Record Breakers' program on 7 Jan 1973. He was in the air for 0·71 sec.

Grands jetés ■ On 28 Nov 1988, Wayne Sleep completed 158 grands jetés along the length of Dunston Staiths, Gateshead, Tyne and Wear, United Kingdom in 2 minutes.

Most turns ■ The greatest number of spins called for in classical ballet choreography is 32 *fouettés rond de jambe en tournant* in *Swan Lake* by Piotr Ilyich Tschaikovsky (1840–93). Miss Rowena Jackson (later Chatfield) (b.Invercargill, New Zealand 1925) achieved 121 such turns at her class in Melbourne, Victoria, Australia in 1940.

Most curtain calls ■ The greatest recorded number of curtain calls ever received is 89, by Dame Margaret Evelyn Arias, nee Hookham (born Reigate, Surrey, United Kingdom, 18 May 1919), *alias* Margot Fonteyn, and Rudolf Hametovich Nureyev (born on a train near Irkutsk, USSR, 17 Mar 1938), after a performance of *Swan Lake* at the Vienna Staatsoper, Austria in October 1964.

Recorded Sound

Origins ■ The phonograph was first conceived by Charles Cros (1842–88), a French poet

Japan marketed a microcassette recorder $4.2 \times 2 \times 0.55$ in weighing 4.4 oz.

Oldest records ■ The British Broadcasting Corporation record library contains over 1 million records, including 5,250 with no known matrix. The oldest records in the library are white wax cylinders dating from 1888. The world's largest private collection is believed to be that of Stan Kilarr (b. 1915) of Klamath Falls, OR, with some 500,000.

Smallest functional record ■ Six titles of $1^5/_{16}$ in diameter were recorded by HMV's studio at Hayes, Middlesex, United Kingdom on 26 Jan 1923 for Queen Mary's Dolls' House. Some 92,000 of these miniature records were pressed, including 35,000 of *God Save the King* (Bb 2439).

Phonographic identification ■ Dr Arthur B. Lintgen (b. 1932) of Rydal, PA, has an as yet unique and proven ability to identify the music on phonograph records purely by visual inspection without hearing a note.

Earliest jazz records ■ *Indiana* and *The Dark Town Strutters Ball* were recorded for the Columbia label in New York on or about 30 Jan 1917, by the Original Dixieland Jazz Band, led by Dominick (Nick) James La Rocca (1889–1961). This was released on 31 May 1917.

The first jazz record to be released was the ODJB's *Livery Stable Blues* (recorded 26 Feb), backed by *The Dixie Jass Band One-Step* (recorded 26 Feb), released by Victor on 7 Mar 1917.

Most successful solo recording artist ■ No independently audited figures have ever been published for Elvis Aron Presley (1935–77). In view of Presley's worldwide tally of over 170 major hits on singles and over 80 top-selling albums from 1956 continuing after his death, it may be assumed that it was he who must have succeeded Bing Crosby as the top-selling solo artist of all time.

On 9 Jun 1960 the Hollywood Chamber of Commerce presented Harry Lillis (*alias* Bing) Crosby Jr (1904–77) with a platinum disc to commemorate the alleged sale of 200 million records from the 2,600 singles and 125 albums he had recorded. On 15 Sep 1970 he received a second platinum disc when Decca claimed a sale of 300·6 million discs. No independently audited figures of his global lifetime sales have ever been published, and figures are considered exaggerated.

Most successful group ■ The singers with the greatest sales of any group have been The Beatles. This group from Liverpool, United Kingdom comprised George Harrison (b. 25 Feb 1943), John Ono (formerly John Winston) Lennon (b. 9 Oct 1940–k. 8 Dec 1980), James Paul McCartney (b. 18 Jun 1942) and Richard Starkey *alias* Ringo Starr (b. 7 Jul 1940). The all-time Beatles sales by May 1985 have been estimated by EMI at over 1 billion discs and tapes.

All four ex-Beatles sold many million further records as solo artists. Since their breakup in 1970, it is estimated that the most successful group in the world in terms of record sales is the Swedish foursome ABBA (Agnetha Faltskog, Anni-Frid Lyngstad, Bjorn Ulvaeus and Benny Andersson), with total sales of 215 million discs and tapes by May 1985.

Earliest golden discs ■ The first actual golden disc was one sprayed by RCA Victor for the US trombonist and band-leader Alton

'Glenn' Miller (1904–44) for his *Chattanooga Choo Choo* on 10 Feb 1942.

The earliest recorded piece eventually to aggregate a total sale of a million copies was of performances by Enrico Caruso (b. Naples, Italy, 1873, d. 2 Aug 1921) of the aria 'Vesti la giubba' ('On with the Motley') from the opera *I Pagliacci* by Ruggiero Leoncavallo (1858–1919), the earliest version of which was recorded with piano on 12 Nov 1902.

The first single recording to surpass the million mark was Alma Gluck's *Carry Me Back to Old Virginny* on the Red Seal Victor label on the 12-in single faced (later backed) record 74420.

Most golden discs ■ The only *audited* measure of gold, platinum and multiplatinum singles and albums within the United States is certification by the Recording Industry Association of America (RIAA) introduced 14 Mar 1958.

Out of the 2,582 RIAA awards made to 1 Jan 1985, The Beatles, with 47 (plus one with Billy Preston), have most for a group.

Paul McCartney has 27 more awards outside the group and with Wings (including one with Stevie Wonder and one with Michael Jackson).

The most awards to an individual is 51 to Elvis Presley (1935–77), spanning the period 1958 to 1 Jan 1986. Globally, however, Presley's total of million-selling singles has been authoritatively placed at 'approaching 80.'

Most recordings ■ In the period between February 1987 and August 1989, Genesis P. Orridge and his band Psychic TV released 14 live albums on Temple Records. The albums are part of a series of 23.

Biggest sellers (Singles) ■ The greatest seller of any phonograph record to date is *White Christmas* by Irving Berlin (b. Israel Bailin, at Tyumen, Russia, 11 May 1888, d. 22 Sep 1989), recorded by Bing Crosby on 29 May 1942. It was announced on Christmas Eve 1987 that North American sales alone reached 170,884,207 copies by 30 Jun 1987.

The highest claim for any 'pop' record is an unaudited 25 million for *Rock Around the Clock*, copyrighted in 1953 by James E. Myers under the name Jimmy DeKnight and the late Max C. Freedmann and recorded on 12 Apr 1954 by Bill Haley (1927–1981) and the Comets.

Biggest sellers (Albums) ■ The best-selling album of all time is *Thriller* by Michael Jackson (b. Gary, IN 29 Aug 1958), with global sales of over 40 million copies by May 1990.

The best-selling album by a group is Fleetwood Mac's *Rumours* with over 21 million sales to May 1990.

The best-selling album by a woman is *Whitney Houston* by Whitney Houston, released in 1985. It had sold over 14 million copies by May 1987, including over 9 million in America, 1 million in the United Kingdom, and a further million in Canada. This is also the best-selling debut album of all time.

The best-selling movie soundtrack is *Saturday Night Fever*, with sales of over 26·5 million to May 1987.

The charts (US Singles) ■ Singles record charts were first published by *Billboard* on 20 Jul 1940, when the No. 1 single was *I'll Never Smile Again* by Tommy Dorsey (1905–56).

Near You by Francis Craig stayed at the No. 1 spot for 17 weeks in 1947.

Longest opera ● The English National Opera performs Wagner's *Die Meistersinger von Nürnburg* in 1986. Lasting over five hours on average for an uncut version, this is the longest regularly performed opera. (Photo: Dominic Photography/ Catherine Ashmore)

and scientist, who described his idea in sealed papers deposited in the French Academy of Sciences on 30 Apr 1877.

However, the realization of a practical device was first achieved by Thomas Alva Edison (1847–1931) of the United States. The first successful wax cylinder machine was constructed by his mechanic, John Kruesi, on 4–6 Dec 1877, demonstrated on 7 Dec and patented on 19 Feb 1878.

The horizontal disc was introduced by Emile Berliner (1851–1929) and first demonstrated in Philadelphia on 18 May 1888.

Earliest recordings ■ The earliest voice recording is believed to be a speech made by Lord Stanley of Preston, Governor-General of Canada, during the opening of the Toronto Industrial Exhibition on 11 Sep 1888. Copies of this speech are held in the National Sound Archive, London, United Kingdom.

Tape recording ■ Magnetic recording was invented by Valdemar Poulsen (1869–1942) of Denmark with his steel wire Telegraphone in 1898 (US Pat. No. 661619). Fritz Pfleumer (German Patent 500900) introduced tape in 1928.

Plastic tapes were devised by BASF of Germany in 1932–35, but were not marketed until 1950 by Recording Associates of New York.

In April 1983 Olympic Optical Industry Co of

GRAMMY AWARDS
1958–1989

YEAR		TITLE	RECORDING ARTIST
1958	Record	Nel Blu Dipinto Bi Blu	Domenico Modugno
	Album	The Music from Peter Gunn	Henry Mancini
1959	Record	Mack the Knife	Bobby Darin
	Album	Come Dance With Me	Frank Sinatra
1960	Record	Theme from A Summer Place	Peroy Faith
	Album	Button Down Mind	Bob Newhart
1961	Record	Moon River	Henry Mancini
	Album	Judy at Carnegie Hall	Judy Garland
1962	Record	I Left My Heart In San Francisco	Tony Bennett
	Album	The First Family	Vaughn Meader
1963	Record	The Days of Wine And Roses	Henry Mancini
	Album	The Barbra Streisand Album	Barbra Streisand
1964	Record	The Girl From Ipanema	Stan Getz and Astrud Gilberto
	Album	Getz/Gilberto	Stan Getz & Joao Gilberto
1965	Record	A Taste Of Honey	Herb Albert & the Tijuana Brass
	Album	September of My years	Frank Sinatra
1966	Record	Strangers in the Night	Frank Sinatra
	Album	Sinatra: A Man And His Music	Frank Sinatra
1967	Record	Up, Up And Away	5th Dimension
	Album	Sgt. Pepper's Lonely Hearts Club Band	The Beatles
1968	Record	Mrs. Robinson	Simon and Garfunkel
	Album	By The Time I Get To Phoenix	Glen Campbell
1969	Record	Aquarius, Let The Sunshine In	5th Dimension
	Album	Blood, Sweat And Tears	Blood, Sweat And Tears
1970	Record	Bridge Over Troubled Water	Simon And Garfunkel
	Album	Bridge Over Troubled Water	Simon And Garfunkel
1971	Record	It's Too Late	Carole King
	Album	Tapestry	Carole King
1972	Record	The First Time Ever I Saw Your Face	Roberta Flack
	Album	The Concert For Bangladesh	George Harrison, et. Al
1973	Record	Killing Me Softly With His Song	Roberta Flack
	Album	Innervisions	Stevie Wonder
1974	Record	I Honestly Love You	Olivia Newton-John
	Album	Fulfillingness' First Finale	Stevie Wonder
1975	Record	Love Will Keep Us Together	Captain and Tennille
	Album	Still Crazy After All These Years	Paul Simon
1976	Record	This Masquerade	George Benson
	Album	Songs In The Key Of Life	Stevie Wonder
1977	Record	Hotel California	Eagles
	Album	Rumours	Fleetwood Mac
1978	Record	Just the Way You Are	Billy Joel
	Album	Saturday Night Fever	Bee Gees and album cast
1979	Record	What A Fool Believes	The Doobie Brothers
	Album	52nd Street	Billy Joel
1980	Record	Sailing	Christopher Cross
	Album	Christopher Cross	Christopher Cross
1981	Record	Bette Davis Eyes	Kim Carnes
	Album	Double Fantasy	John Lennon and Yoko Ono
1982	Record	Rosanna	Toto
	Album	Toto IV	Toto
1983	Record	Beat It	Michael Jackson
	Album	Thriller	Michael Jackson
1984	Record	What's Love Got To Do With It	Tina Turner
	Album	Can't Slow Down	Lionel Richie
1985	Record	We Are the World	USA for Africa
	Album	No Jacket Required	Phil Collins
1986	Record	Higher Love	Steve Winwood
	Album	Graceland	Paul Simon
1987	Record	Graceland	Paul Simon
	Album	The Joshua Tree	U2
1988	Record	Don't Worry Be Happy	Bobby McFerrin
	Album	Faith	George Michael
1989	Record	Wind Beneath My Wings	Bette Midler
	Album	Nick of Time	Bonnie Raitt

The National Academy of Recording Arts and Sciences, 1990

TOP MUSIC
VIDEOS 1989

TITLE	LABEL
$19.98 Home Vid	
Cliff'Em All! (Metallica)	Elektra
Def Leppard: Historia	Polygram
Moonwalker	CBS
Faith	CBS
Bruce Springsteen Anthology:	
1978-1988	CBS

Billboard 6 Jan 1990

The Charts (US Albums) ■ Billboard first published an album chart on 15 Mar 1945 when the No. 1 album was *King Cole Trio* featuring Nat 'King' Cole (1919–65). *South Pacific* was No. 1 for 69 weeks (non-consecutive) from May 1949.

Dark Side of the Moon by Pink Floyd enjoyed 730 weeks on the *Billboard* charts to April 1989.

The Beatles had the most No. 1s (15), Elvis Presley was the most successful male soloist (9), and Simon and Garfunkel the top duo with three. Elvis Presley has had the most hit albums (94 from 1956–April 1989).

The woman with the most No. 1 albums (6), and most hit albums in total (40 between 1963 and April 1989), is Barbra Streisand, 30 of whose albums have been certified gold (500,000 sales) or platinum (1 million sales) by the RIAA, making Streisand the best-selling female singer of all time.

Fastest-selling ■ The fastest-selling non-pop record of all time is *John Fitzgerald Kennedy—A Memorial Album* (Premium Albums), recorded on 22 Nov 1963, the day of Mr Kennedy's assassination, which sold 2·1 million copies at 99 cents in six days (7–12 Dec 1963), thus ironically beating the previous speed record set by the satirical LP *The First Family* in 1962–63.

Advance sales ■ The greatest advance sale for a single worldwide is 2·1 million for *Can't Buy Me Love* by the Beatles. Released 21 Mar 1964, it also holds the British record of 1 million jointly with another Beatles single, *I Want to Hold Your Hand*, released 29 Nov 1963.

Fastest live recording to retail ■ A limited edition of Midge Ure's *Dear God* single, including two live tracks *All Fall Down, United Kingdom* and *Strange Brew* on the B-side, was delivered to retail 81 hrs 15 min after the live performance at The Venue, Edinburgh, United Kingdom on 21 Nov 1988, at which the tracks were recorded.

Compact discs ■ Announced by Philips in 1978, and introduced by the same company in 1982, the compact disc (CD) increasingly challenges the LP and cassette as a recording medium.

The first CD to sell a million copies worldwide was Dire Straits' *Brothers in Arms* in 1986. It subsequently topped a record million sales in Europe alone.

Most Grammy awards ■ The all-time record of 28 awards is held by Sir Georg Solti, the British conductor born in Budapest, Hungary 22 Oct 1912, which he has won since 1958. The greatest number won in a year is eight by Michael Jackson in 1984.

The Beatles have had the most No. 1's (20), Conway Twitty the most Country No. 1's (35) and Aretha Franklin the most Rhythm & Blues No. 1s (20). Aretha Franklin is also the female solo artist with the most million-selling singles, with 14 between 1967 and 1973. Elvis Presley has had the most hit singles on *Billboard*'s Hot 100–149 from 1956 to May 1990. Bing Crosby's *White Christmas* spent a total of 72 weeks in the chart between 1942 and 1962, while *Tainted Love* by Soft Cell stayed on the chart for 43 *consecutive* weeks from January 1982.

Theater

Oldest ■ Theater in Europe has its origins in Greek drama performed in honor of a god, usually Dionysus. The earliest amphitheaters date from the 5th century B.C. The first stone-built theater in Rome, erected in 55 B.C., could accommodate 40,000 spectators.

Oldest indoor theater ■ The oldest indoor theater in the world is the Teatro Olimpico in Vicenza, Italy. Designed in the Roman style by Andrea di Pietro, *alias* Palladio (1508–80), it was begun three months before his death and finished by his pupil Vicenzo Scamozzi (1552–1616) in 1583. It is preserved today in its original form.

Largest ■ The world's largest building used for theater is the National People's Congress Building (*Ren min da hui tang*) on the west side of Tiananmen Square, Beijing, China. It was completed in 1959 and covers an area of 12·9 acres. The theater seats 10,000 and is occasionally used as such, as in 1964 for the play *The East Is Red.*

The highest capacity purpose-built theater is the Perth Entertainment Centre, Western Australia, completed at a cost of Austrialian $8·3 million in November 1976, with 8,003 seats. The stage area is 12,000 ft².

Smallest ■ The smallest regularly operated professional theater in the world is the Piccolo in Juliusstrasse, Hamburg, West Germany. It was founded in 1970 and has a maximum capacity of 30 seats.

Largest amphitheater ■ The Flavian amphitheater or Colosseum of Rome, Italy, completed in A.D. 80, covers 5 acres with a capacity of 87,000. It has a maximum length of 612 ft and a maximum width of 515 ft.

Largest stage ■ The largest stage in the world is in the Ziegfeld Room, Reno, NV, with 176 ft passerelle, three main lifts each capable of raising 1,200 show girls (72 tons), two 62½-ft circumference turntables and 800 spotlights.

Longest runs ■ The longest continuous run of any show in the world is *The Mousetrap* by Agatha Mary Clarissa Christie (nee Miller, later Lady Mallowan, 1890–1976). This thriller opened on 25 Nov 1952 at the Ambassadors Theatre (capacity 453) and moved after 8,862 performances to St Martin's Theatre next door on 25 Mar 1974. The 37th anniversary performance on 25 Nov 1989 was the 15,402nd. The 15,000th performance was on 9 Dec 1988, and the Box Office reached £15·5 million from more than 8 million attenders.

The Vicksburg Theater Guild, in Mississippi has been playing the melodrama *Gold in the Hills* by J. Frank Davis discontinuously but every season since 1936.

The audience participation comedy/murder-mystery show *Sheer Madness* reached its 4,000 performance on 23 Sep 1989 after having opened on 29 Jan 1980.

Revue ■ The greatest number of performances of any theatrical presentation is 47,250 (to April 1986) in the case of *The Golden Horseshoe Revue*—a show staged at Disneyland Park, Anaheim, CA. It started on 16 Jul 1955, closed on 12 Oct 1986 and has been seen by 16 million people. The three main performers were Fulton Burley, Dick Hardwick and Betty Taylor, who played as many as five houses a day in a routine that lasted 45 minutes.

Largest amphitheater ● The Flavian amphitheater or Colosseum of Rome, Italy covers 5 acres and originally could seat over 50,000 spectators. Construction began between A.D. 70 and 72 during the reign of Vespasian and the final story was added in A.D. 82, two years after the official opening by Titus. Although originally the scene of keen contests and fierce battles, Christians no longer fear this arena. (Photo: Spectrum Colour Library)

Broadway ■ *A Chorus Line* opened on 25 Jul 1975 and closed on 28 Apr 1990 after a record run of 6,137 performances and almost 15 complete seasons. It was created by Michael Bennet (1943–87) from a book coauthored by Nicholas Dante and James Kirkwood (1924–1989).

Musical shows ■ The off-Broadway musical show *The Fantasticks* by Tom Jones and Harvey Schmidt opened on 3 May 1960, and the total number of performances at the Sullivan Street Playhouse, Greenwich Village, NY to 7 Jun 1990 is 12,531.

London ■ *Cats* surpassed *Jesus Christ Superstar* on its eighth birthday at the New London Theatre, London, United Kingdom on 12 May 1989 (3,358 performances) when it was being played in ten centers simultaneously. The aggregate gross was estimated at £ 250 million.

Shortest runs ■ The shortest run on record was that of *The Intimate Revue* at the Duchess Theatre, London, United Kingdom, on 11 Mar 1930. Anything that could go wrong did. With scene changes taking up to 20 min apiece, the management scrapped seven scenes to get the finale on before midnight. The run was described as 'half a performance.'

The greatest loss sustained by a theatrical show was by the Royal Shakespeare Company's musical *Carrie*, which closed after five performances on Broadway on 17 May 1988 at a cost of $7 million.

Lowest attendance ■ The ultimate in low attendances was in December 1983, when the comedy *Bag* in Grantham, Lincolnshire, United Kingdom opened to a nil attendance.

Youngest Broadway producer ■ Margo Feiden (Margo Eden) (b. New York, 2 Dec 1944) produced the musical *Peter Pan*, which opened on 3 Apr 1961, when she was 16 years 5 months old. She wrote *Out Brief Candle*, which opened on 18 Aug 1962. She is now a leading art dealer.

One-man shows ■ The longest run of one-man shows is 849, by Victor Borge (b. Copenhagen, 3 Jan 1909) in his *Comedy in Music* from 2 Oct 1953 to 21 Jan 1956 at the Golden Theater, Broadway, New York City.

The world aggregate record for one-man shows is 1,700 performances of *Brief Lives* by Roy Dotrice (b. Guernsey, 26 May 1923), including 400 straight at the Mayfair Theatre, London, United Kingdom, ending on 20 Jul 1974. He was on stage for more than 2½ hr per performance of this 17th-century monologue and required 3 hr for makeup and 1 hr for removal of makeup, so aggregating 40 weeks in the chair.

Most durable actors and actresses ■ Kanmi Fujiyama (b. 1929) played the lead role in 10,288 performances by the comedy company Sochiku Shikigeki from November 1966 to June 1983.

Anna Neagle (1904–86) played the lead role in *Charlie Girl* at the Adelphi Theatre, London, United Kingdom for 2,062 of 2,202 performances between 15 Dec 1965 and 27 Mar 1971. She played the role a further 327 times in 327 performances in Australasia.

Frances Etheridge has played Lizzie, the housekeeper, in *Gold in the Hills* (see Longest runs) more than 660 times over a span of 47 years since 1936.

David Raven played Major Metcalfe in *The Mousetrap* on 4,575 occasions between 22 Jul 1957 and 23 Nov 1968.

Shakespeare ● The longest and most filmed of Shakespeare's 37 plays is *Hamlet*, with 4,042 lines and 29,551 words, including 11,610 spoken by the prince himself. John Barrymore (1882–1942) is seen here in the 1922 version staged in New York. (Photo: Kobal Collection)

Jack Howarth (1896–1984) was an actor on the stage and in television for 76 years from 1907 until his last appearance after 23 years as Albert Tatlock in *Coronation Street* on 25 Jan 1984. Lore Notto played The Boy's Father in *The Fantasticks* on 6,438 occasions between 3 May 1960 and 8 Jun 1986.

Advance sales ■ The Broadway record for advance sales was set in 1987 by *Phantom of the Opera* at $19 million. The London record for the opening day is £6·8 million on 25 May 1990 for the musical *Miss Saigon*.

Most roles ■ The greatest recorded number of theatrical, film and television roles is 3,385, from 1951 to March 1989 by Jan Leighton (US).

Most theatrical roles ■ Kanzaburo Nakamura (b. July 1909) has performed in 806 Kabuki titles from November 1926 to January 1987. As each title in this classical Japanese theatrical form lasts 25 days, he has therefore played 20,150 performances.

Shakespeare ■ The first all-amateur company to have staged all 37 plays was The Southsea Shakespeare Actors, Hampshire, United Kingdom (founded 1947) in October 1966 when, under K. Edmonds Gateley, they presented *Cymbeline*.

The longest is *Hamlet* with 4,042 lines and 29,551 words. Of Shakespeare's 1,277 speaking parts the longest is Hamlet with 11,610 words.

Longest chorus line ■ The longest chorus line in performing history numbered up to 120 in some of the early Ziegfeld's Follies. In the finale of *A Chorus Line* on the night of 29 Sep 1983, when it broke the record as the longest-running Broadway show ever, 332 top-hatted 'strutters' performed on stage.

Highest cabaret fee ■ Dolly Parton received up to $400,000 per live concert. Johnny Carson's fee for the non-televised Sears Roebuck Centenary Gala in October 1984 was set at $1 million.

Ice shows ■ Holiday on Ice Production Inc., founded by Morris Chalfen in 1945, stages the world's most costly live entertainment, with up to seven productions playing simultaneously in several of 75 countries. By 8 Mar 1988 the show had been seen by 250 million spectators. The total skating and other staff exceeds 900.

The most prolific producer of ice shows was Gerald Palmer (1908–83) with 137 since 1945, including 34 consecutive shows at the Empire Pool, London, United Kingdom with attendances up to 850,000.

Most ardent theatergoers ■ Dr H. Howard Hughes (b. 1902), Professor Emeritus of Texas Wesleyan College, Fort Worth, TX has attended 6,136 shows in the period 1956–87.

Arts festival ■ The world's largest arts festival is the annual Edinburgh Festival Fringe, Edinburgh, United Kingdom (instituted in 1947). In 1985, 510 groups gave 9,424 performances of 1,091 shows between 9 and 31 Aug.

Professor Gerald Berkowitz of Northern Illinois University attended a record 145 separate performances at the 1979 Festival from 15 Aug–8 Sep.

Fashion shows ■ The most prolific producer of fashion shows is Adalene Ross Riley of San Francisco, CA, with totals over 4,721 to April 1989.

Photography

CAMERAS

Earliest ■ The earliest veiled reference to a photograph on glass taken in a camera was in a letter dated 19 Jul 1822 from Joseph Nicéphore Niépce (1765–1833), a French scientist. It was a photograph of a copper engraving of Pope Pius VII taken at Gras, near Chalon-sur-Saône, France, and it was rediscovered in London, United Kingdom in February 1952 by the photo-historian Helmut Gernsheim after six years' research.

The world's earliest aerial photograph was taken in 1858 by Gaspard Félix Tournachon (1820–1910), *alias* Nadar, from a balloon near Villacoublay, on the outskirts of Paris, France.

Largest ■ The largest and most expensive industrial camera ever built is the 30 ton Rolls-Royce camera now owned by BPCC Graphics Ltd of Derby, United Kingdom commissioned in 1956. It measures 8 ft 10 in high, 8¼ ft wide and 46 ft long. The lens is a 63 in f 16 Cooke Apochromatic and the bellows were made by Camera Bellows Ltd of Birmingham, United Kingdom.

A pinhole camera was created from a Portakabin unit (PK31) measuring 34 x 9½ x 9 ft by photo-graphers John Kippen and Chris Wainwright at the National Museum of Photography, Film and Television at Bradford, United Kingdom on 25 Mar 1990. The unit produced a direct positive image measuring 33 x 6 ft.

Largest lens ■ The National Museum of Photography, Film and Television, Bradford, United Kingdom has the largest lens on display, made by Pilkington Special Glass Ltd, St Asaph, United Kingdom. Its dimensions are: focal length 333 in, diameter 54 in, weight 474 lb. Its focal length enables writing on the museum's walls to be read from a distance of 40 ft.

Smallest ■ Apart from cameras built for intra-cardiac surgery and espionage, the smallest that has been marketed is the circular Japanese 'Petal' camera, with a diameter of 1·14 in and a thickness of 0·65 in. It has a focal length of 0·47 in.

The smallest functional bellows camera is a model Edwardian field camera designed and built by William Pocklington of Ascot, United Kingdom in 1989, although the bellows were made by Camera Bellows Ltd. Constructed from matchsticks with brass fittings, when mounted for use on its collapsible tripod, this replica stands 5·8 in high and has a body measuring 1·3 in x 1·3 in x 2 in with bellows extended. When closed it measures just 1·3 in x 1·3 in x 0·7 in. Fitted with a reversing back for landscape and

Smallest camera ● This miniature Edwardian field camera was designed and built in 1989 by William Pocklington of Ascot, United Kingdom from matchsticks with brass fittings and bellows made by Camera Bellows Ltd of Birmingham, West Midlands, United Kingdom. When mounted on its collapsible tripod, the replica stands 0·06 in high and has a body measuring 0·13 x 0·13 x 0·07 in with bellows extended. Fitted with a reversing back for landscape or portrait format, the camera produces pictures measuring 0·08 x 0·07 in.

portrait format, the camera produces pictures measuring 0·8 in x 0·6 in.

Fastest ■ A camera built for research into high-power lasers by The Blackett Laboratory of Imperial College of Science and Technology, London, United Kingdom, registers images at a rate of 33 billion per sec.

Most expensive ■ The most expensive complete range of camera equipment in the world is that of Nikon Corporation of Tokyo, Japan, who marketed in April 1989 their complete range of 29 cameras with 83 lenses and 657 accessories. Fox Talbot of London, United Kingdom quoted £ 132,673·69 excluding tax as the price.

The highest auction price for an antique camera is £ 21,000 for a J. B. Dancer stereo camera, patented in 1856 and sold at Christie's, London, United Kingdom on 12 Oct 1977.

Longest negative ■ On 1 Jul 1988 Christopher Creighton of Port Hope, Ontario, Canada, using a 24-in focal length Turner-Reich lens, fitted to a Kodak 8 Cirkut camera, made a portrait of an estimated 1,500 inhabitants of Port Hope achieving a 355 degree view in a single shot. The resulting negative measured 11 ft 10½ in × 7¾ in.

Most expensive photograph ■ A photograph taken by Edward Weston in 1927 of a nautilus shell was sold at Sotheby's, New York in April 1989 for $115,000.

Cinema

FILMS
The earliest motion pictures ever taken were by Louis Aimé Augustin Le Prince (1842–90). He was attested to have achieved dim moving outlines on a whitewashed wall at the Institute for the Deaf, Washington Heights, NY as early as 1885–87. The earliest surviving film (sensitized 2⅛ in wide paper roll) is from his camera, patented in Britain on 16 Nov 1888, taken in early October 1888 of the garden of his father-in-law, Joseph Whitley, in Roundhay, Leeds, West Yorkshire, United Kingdom at 10 to 12 frames per second.

The first commercial presentation of motion pictures was at Holland Bros' Kinetoscope Parlor at 1155 Broadway, New York City on 14 Apr 1894. Viewers could see five films for 25 cents or 10 for 50 cents from a double row of Kinetoscopes developed by William Kennedy Laurie Dickson (1860–1935), assistant to Thomas Alva Edison (1847–1931) in 1889–91.

The earliest publicly presented film on a *screen* was *La Sortie des Ouvriers de l'Usine Lumière,* probably shot in August or September 1894 in Lyon, France. It was exhibited at 44 rue de Rennes, Paris, France on 22 Mar 1895 by the Lumière brothers, Auguste-Marie-Louis-Nicholas (1862–1954) and Louis-Jean (1864–1948).

Earliest 'talkie' ■ The earliest sound-on-film motion picture was achieved by Eugene-Augustin Lauste (1857–1935), who patented his process on 11 Aug 1906 and produced a workable system using a string galvanometer in 1910 at Benedict Road, Stockwell, London, United Kingdom.

The earliest public presentation of sound on film was by the Tri-ergon process at the Alhambra movie theater, Berlin, Germany on 17 Sep 1922.

Largest output ■ Indian production of feature-length films was a record 807 in 1987.

TOP EARNING FILMS*

FILM	EARNINGS
E. T. The Extra Terrestrial (United Artists, 1982)	$228 million
Star Wars (Fox, 1983)	$193 million
Return of the Jedi (Fox, 1983)	$168 million
Batman (Warner Brothers, 1989)	$150 million
The Empire Strikes Back (Fox, 1980)	$141 million

*Rankings based on domestic sales
Variety; 3 Jan 1990, 11-17 Jan 1989*

Most expensive film ■ The highest ever budgeted film has been $69 million for *Rambo III*, released in May 1988 starring Sylvester Stallone.

Cleopatra, starring Elizabeth Taylor and Richard Burton (1925–84), cost $44 million to produce in 1963, which translates to $176·5 million at 1990 rates.

Least expensive full-length feature film ■ The total cost of production for the 1927 film *The Shattered Illusion*, by Victorian Film Productions, was £ 300. It took 12 months to complete and included spectacular scenes of a ship being overwhelmed by a storm.

Most expensive film rights ■ The highest price ever paid for film rights was $9·5 million announced on 20 Jan 1978 by Columbia for *Annie*, the Broadway musical by Charles Strouse starring Andrea McCardle, Dorothy Loudon and Reid Shelton.

Longest film ■ The longest commercially-released film was Rainer Werner Fassbinder's 15

hr 21 min epic *Berlin Alexanderplatz*, which was shown in full at the Vista cinema, Hollywood, CA on 6–7 Aug 1983 with a two-hour break for dinner.

Fastest film production ■ The shortest time ever taken to make a feature-length film from the announcement of the title to the screening is 13 days for *Fast Forward*, produced by Russ Malkin and directed by John Gore. The all-star British cast, the crew, technicians and cinemagraphic suppliers accepted the charity challenge and the 75-minute thriller was given a gala premiere in London, United Kingdom on 27 May 1990 to raise money for the British Telethon '90.

Highest box office gross ■ In 1989 domestic box office receipts (US and Canada) passed the $5 billion mark to reach the highest gross in cinema history. It was also a record year for films earning $100 million at the box office, the industry milestone, with eight, the highest number ever. The film *Batman* (Warner Brothers) broke the three day weekend record by earning $40·49 million on 2,850 screens at its premier 23–25 Jun 1989. *Batman* was also the highest grossing film in 1989 domestic rentals earning $150·5 million (without reissues to make it unique in the top five all time highest grossing films — see chart).

Largest loss ■ Michael Cimino's 1980 production *Heaven's Gate* took $1·5 million in North American rentals against an estimated negative cost of $44 million and a total cost, including distribution and overheads, of $57 million.

Most expensive chase sequence ■ Over 150 vehicles, including two Cadillac Eldorados, two Chrysler Magnums, numerous boats, trucks and motorcycles and two Pitts high-performance airplanes, were wrecked in H. B. Halicki's 1982 film *The Junkman*.

Highest earnings ■ Jack Nicholson stood to receive up to $60 million for playing 'The Joker' in Warner Brothers' $50 million *Batman*, through a percentage of the film's receipts in lieu of salary.

The highest-paid actresses are Meryl Streep (b. Summit, NJ, 1949), with $4 million for *Out of Africa* and the same for *Heartburn*, and Barbra Streisand, with $5 million for *Nuts*.

Stuntman Dar Robinson was paid $100,000 for

Highest box office gross ● Paramount Pictures claimed *Indiana Jones and The Last Crusade*, starring Harrison Ford and Sean Connery, as the top-grossing film of 1989, based on *worldwide* figures of over $440·1 million, even though Warner's *Batman* topped the charts in the United Kingdom and the United States. (Photo: Kobal Collection)

the 1,100 ft leap from the CN Tower, Toronto, Canada in November 1979 for *High Point*. His parachute opened just 300 ft above ground. He died 21 Nov 1986 (aged 39).

Longest series still continuing ■ Japan's *Tora-San* films have now stretched from *Tora-San I* in August 1969 to *Tora-San XL* in 1988, with Kiyoshi Atsumi (b. 1929) starring in each for Shochiku Co.

Most portrayed character ■ The character most frequently recurring on the screen is Sherlock Holmes, created by Sir Arthur Conan Doyle (1859–1930). He has been portrayed by 70 actors in 197 films between 1900 and 1988.

In horror films the character most often portrayed is Count Dracula, created by the Irish writer Bram Stoker (1847–1912). Representations of the Count or his immediate descendants outnumber those of his closest rival, Frankenstein's monster, by 155 to 109.

Largest number of extras ■ It is believed that over 300,000 extras appeared in the funeral scene of Sir Richard Attenborough's *Gandhi* (1982).

Largest studios ■ The largest complex of film studios in the world is that at Universal City, Los Angeles, CA. The Back Lot contains 561 buildings and there are 34 sound stages on the 420-acre site.

Largest studio stage ■ The world's largest studio stage is the 007 stage at Pinewood Studios, Buckinghamshire, United Kingdom. It was designed by Ken Adam and Michael Brown and built in 1976 for the James Bond film *The Spy Who Loved Me*. It measures 336 × 139 × 41 ft and accommodated 1·2 million gallons of water, a full-scale 672,000 ton oil tanker and three nuclear submarines.

Largest film set ■ The largest film set ever built was the 1,312 × 754 ft Roman Forum designed by Veniero Colosanti and John Moore for Samuel Bronston's production of *The Fall of the Roman Empire* (1964). It was built on a 55-acre site outside Madrid, Spain. 1,100 workmen spent seven months laying the surface of the Forum with 170,000 cement blocks, erecting 22,000 ft of concrete stairways, 601 colums and 350 statues, and constructing 27 full-size buildings.

Longest directorial career ■ The directorial career of King Vidor (1894–1982) lasted for 66 years, beginning with the two-reel comedy *The Tow* and culminating in another short, a documentary called *The Metaphor*.

Oldest director ■ Joris Ivens (b. Netherlands 1898) directed the Franco-Italian co-production *Le Vent* in 1988 at the age of 89. He made his directorial debut with the Dutch film *De Brug* in 1928.

George Cukor (1899–1983) was Hollywood's oldest director. In October 1980, he was signed to MGM at the age of 81 to direct the film *Rich and Famous*, starring Jacqueline Bisset and Candice Bergen.

Most generations of screen actors in a family ■ There are four generations of screen actors in the Redgrave family. Roy Redgrave (1872–1922) made his screen debut in 1911 and continued to appear in Australian films until 1920. Sir Michael Redgrave married actress Rachel Kempson and their two daughters Vanessa and Lynn and son Corin all went into films. Vanessa's two daughters Joely and Natasha and Corin's daughter Jemma are already successful actresses with films such as *Wetherby*, *A Month in the Country* and *The Dream Demon* to their respective credit.

Largest number of costumes ■ The largest number of costumes for any one film was 32,000 for the 1951 film *Quo Vadis*.

Largest number of costume changes by one person ■ Elizabeth Taylor changed costume 65 times in *Cleopatra* (1963). The costumes were designed by Irene Sharaff and cost $130,000.

Most expensive costume ■ Constance

Most generations of screen actors ● Four generations of the Redgrave family have found fame as screen actors. Roy Redgrave (1872-1922), Australian star of the silent-screen, began a dynasty continued by his son Michael (1908–85), whose marriage to actress Rachel Kempson produced daughters Vanessa and Lynn and son Corin. Vanessa's daughters Joely and Natasha and Corin's daughter Jemma are already established actresses. Spot the family likeness between Roy in *In My Mind's Eye* (1911), Michael and Vanessa in *Behind the Mask* and Natasha in *A Month in the Country*. (Photos: Weidenfeld Publishers/National Film Archive/Warner Bros)

Bennett's sable coat in *Madam X* was valued at $50,000.

The most expensive costume designed and made specially for a film was Edith Head's mink and sequins dance costume worn by Ginger Rogers in *Lady in the Dark*. It cost Paramount $35,000.

Most expensive personal movie prop ■ The ruby slippers worn by Judy Garland in the 1939 film *The Wizard of Oz* were sold on 2 Jun 1988 to a mystery buyer at Christie's, New York for $165,000.

Longest screen kiss ■ The most prolonged osculatory marathon in movie theater history is one of 185 sec by Regis Toomey and Jane Wyman (b. Sarah Jane Faulks 4 Jan 1914, later Mrs Ronald Reagan) in *You're in the Army Now* released in 1940.

Most Oscars ■ Walter (Walt) Elias Disney (1901–66) won more 'Oscars'—the awards of the United States Academy of Motion Picture Arts and Sciences, instituted on 16 May 1929—than any other person. The physical count comprises 20 statuettes and 12 other plaques and certificates, including posthumous awards.

The only person to win four Oscars in a starring role has been Miss Katharine Hepburn, formerly Mrs Ludlow Ogden Smith (b. Hartford, Conn., 9 Nov 1909) in *Morning Glory* (1932–33), *Guess Who's Coming to Dinner* (1967), *The Lion in Winter* (1968) and *On Golden Pond* (1981). She has been nominated 12 times. Edith Head (Mrs

Wiard B. Ihnen, 1907–81) won eight individual awards for costume design.

Five actors have won two Oscars in starring roles — Frederic March in 1931–32 and 1946, Spencer Tracy in 1937 and 1938, Gary Cooper in 1941 and 1952, Marlon Brando in 1954 and 1972 and Dustin Hoffman in 1979 and 1988.

The film with most awards has been *Ben Hur* (1959) with 11. That with the highest number of nominations was *All About Eve* (1950) with 14. It won six (Best Supporting Actor: George Sanders; Best Picture, Best Costume Design; Edith Head, Charles Le Maire, Best Director; Joseph L. Mankiewicz, Best Sound Recording, Best Screenplay; Joseph L. Mankiewicz).

The youngest ever winner was Shirley Temple (b. 23 Apr 1928) at the age of five, with her honorary Oscar. The oldest recipients, George Burns (b. 20 Jan 1896) for *The Sunshine Boys* in 1976 and Jessica Tandy (b. 7 Jun 1909) for *Driving Miss Daisy* in 1990, were both 80 at the time of the presentation.

Versatility show-business awards ■ The only three performers to have won Oscar, Emmy, Tony and Grammy awards have been Helen Hayes (b. 1900) in 1932–1976; Richard Rodgers (1902–1979), composer of musicals, and Rita Moreno (b. 1931) in 1961–1977. Barbra Streisand (b. 24 Apr 1942 in Brooklyn, NY) received Oscar, Grammy and Emmy awards in addition to a special 'Star of the Decade' Tony award.

Most honored entertainer ■ The most honored entertainer in history is Bob Hope (ne Leslie Townes Hope, Eltham, London, United Kingdom; 29 May 1903). He has been uniquely awarded the USA's highest civilian honors – the Medal of Freedom (1969), Congressional Gold Medal (1963), Medal of Merit (1966), Distinguished Public Service Medal (1973), Distinguished Service Gold Medal (1971)—and is also an Hon CBE (1976) and was appointed Hon. Brigadier of the US Marine Corps. He also has 44 honorary degrees.

MOVIE THEATERS

Earliest ■ The earliest structure designed and exclusively used for exhibiting projected films is believed to be one erected at the Atlanta Show, GA in October 1895 to exhibit C. F. Jenkins' phantoscope.

Largest ■ The largest movie theater in the world is the Radio City Music Hall, New York City, opened on 27 Dec 1932 with 5,945 (now 5,874) seats.

Kinepolis, the first eight screens of which opened in Brussels, Belgium in 1988, is the world's largest movie theater complex. It has 24 screens and a total seating capacity of 7,000.

Most and least movie theaters ■ The country with the largest number of movie theaters in relation to population is San Marino, with one movie theater for every 3,190 inhabitants (a total of seven).

In comparison the United States has one movie theater for every 11,000 inhabitants and the United Kingdom has one movie theater for every 45,000 inhabitants.

Saudi Arabia (population 8 million) has no

movie theaters, the public presentation of films being illegal as contrary to strict Islamic belief.

Highest movie-theatergoing ■ The Chinese Ministry of Culture reported in September 1987 that there were 21 billion movie-theater attendances in 1986—or nearly 21 per person per year.

Biggest screen ■ The permanently installed movie-theater screen with the largest area is one of 92¾ ft × 70½ ft in the Keong Emas Imax Theater, Taman Mini Park, Jakarta, Indonesia opened on 20 Apr 1984. It was made by Harkness Screens Ltd at Borehamwood, Hertfordshire, United Kingdom.

A temporary screen 297 × 33 ft was used at the 1937 Paris Exposition.

Most films seen ■ Albert E. van Schmus (b. 1921) saw 16,945 films in 32 years (1949–1982) as a rater for the Motion Picture Association of America Inc.

Radio

The earliest patent for telegraphy without wires (wireless) was received by Dr Mahlon Loomis (US; 1826–86). It was entitled 'Improvement in Telegraphy' and was dated 20 Jul 1872 (US Pat. No. 129 971). He in fact demonstrated only potential differences on a galvanometer between two kites 14 miles apart in Loudoun County, VA in October 1866.

Earliest patent ■ The first patent for a system of communication by means of electromagnetic waves, numbered No. 12039, was granted on 2 Jun 1896 to the Italian-Irish Marchese Guglielmo Marconi (1874–1937).

A public demonstration of wireless transmission of speech was, however, given in the town square of Murray, KY in 1892 by Nathan B. Stubblefield. He died destitute on 28 Mar 1928.

The first permanent wireless installation was at The Needles on the Isle of Wight, United Kingdom, by Marconi's Wireless Telegraph Co Ltd, in November 1897.

Earliest broadcast ■ The world's first advertized broadcast was made on 24 Dec 1906 by the Canadian-born Professor Reginald Aubrey Fessenden (1868–1932) from the 420 ft mast of the National Electric Signalling Company at Brant Rock, MA. The transmission included Handel's *Largo*. Fessenden had achieved the broadcast of speech as early as November 1900 but this was highly distorted.

Transatlantic transmissions ■ The earliest claim to have received wireless signals (the letter S in Morse Code) across the Atlantic was made by Marconi, George Stephen Kemp and Percy Paget from a 10 kW station at Poldhu, Cornwall, United Kingdom, to Signal Hill, St John's, Newfoundland, Canada, at 12:30 P.M. on 12 Dec 1901.

Human speech was first heard across the Atlantic in November 1915 when a transmission from the US Navy station at Arlington, VA was received by US radiotelephone engineers on the Eiffel Tower.

Earliest radio-microphones ■ The radio-microphone, which was in essence also the first 'bug,' was devised by Reg Moores (GB) in 1947 and first used on 76 MHz in the ice show *Aladdin* at Brighton Sports Stadium, East Sussex, United Kingdom in September 1949.

Longest continuous broadcast ■ The longest continuous broadcast (excluding disc-jockeying) has been one of 484 hr (20 days 4 hr) by Larry Norton of WGRQ FM Buffalo, NY from 19 Mar–8 Apr 1981. *No further claims for the above category will be entertained.*

Radio Telefís Éireann transmitted an unedited reading of *Ulysses* by James Joyce (1882–1941) for 29 hr 38 min 47 sec on 16–17 Jul 1982.

Highest prize ■ Mary Buchanan, 15, on WKRQ, Cincinnati, won a prize of $25,000 for 40 years (*viz* $1 million) on 21 Nov 1980.

Most durable programs ■ CKNW's 'Roving Mike' program with Bill Hughes has been broadcast six days a week in New Westminster, British Columbia, Canada since 1944. On 8 Oct 1987, the program celebrated its 13,000th consecutive broadcast.

The weekly sports report 'The Tenpin Tattler' was first broadcast on WCFL, Chicago, IL on 24 Aug, 1935. Fifty-three years and 2,756 broadcasts later, it still continues on WGN, Chicago.

Rambling with Gambling, the early morning WOR-NY programme, began in March 1925 and has been continued by three generations of the Gambling family.

Earliest antipodal reception ■ Frank Henry Alfred Walker (b. 11 Nov 1904), on the night of 12 Nov 1924 at Crown Farm, Cuttimore Lane, Walton-on-Thames, Surrey, United Kingdom received on his home-made 2-valve receiver on 75 meters, signals from Marconi's yacht *Electra* (call sign ICCM) in Australian waters.

Most assiduous radio ham ■ The late Richard C. Spenceley of KV4AA at St Thomas, VI built his contacts (QSOs) to a record level of 48,100 in 365 days in 1978.

Most stations ■ The country with the greatest number of radio broadcasting stations is the United States, where there were 9,512 authorized broadcast stations as at April 1985, made up of both AM (amplitude modulation) and FM (frequency modulation). In the United States, as of January 1990, the most popular formats for listeners (18 years and older), per the Radio Advertising Bureau, were adult contemporary (18·9 %), contemporary hit radio–top 40 (18 %), country (17·7 %) and album oriented rock (12 %). The highest rated non-music format is news talk (8·2 %).

Smallest set ■ The Toshiba AM-FM RP-1070 with built-in loudspeaker measures 3·5 × 2·1 × 0·5 in and with battery weighs 2·5 oz.

Television

Invention ■ The invention of television, the instantaneous viewing of distant objects by electrical transmissions, was not an act but a process of successive and interdependent discoveries. The first commercial cathode ray tube was introduced in 1897 by Karl Ferdinand Braun (1850–1918), but was not linked to 'electric vision' until 1907 by Professor Boris Rosing (disappeared 1918) of Russia in St Petersburg (Leningrad).

A. A. Campbell Swinton (1863–1930) published the fundamentals of television transmission on 18 Jun 1908 in a brief letter to *Nature* entitled 'Distant Electric Vision.'

The earliest public demonstration of television was given on 27 Jan 1926 by John Logie Baird (1888–1946) of Scotland, United Kingdom using a development of the mechanical scanning system patented by Paul Gottlieb Nipkow (1860–1940) on 6 Jan 1884. He had achieved the transmission of a Maltese Cross over 10 ft in Hastings, East Sussex, United Kingdom by February 1924, and the first facial image (of William Taynton, 15) in London, United Kingdom on 30 Oct 1925. Taynton had to be bribed.

A patent application for the Iconoscope had been filed on 29 Dec 1923 by Dr Vladimir Kosma Zworykin (1889–1982) but was not issued until 20 Dec 1938. Kenjiro Takayanagi (b. 20 Jan 1899) succeeded in transmitting a 40-line electronic picture on 25 Dec 1926 with a Braun cathode ray tube and a Nipkow disc at Hamamatsu Technical College, Japan.

Baird launched his first television 'service' via a British Broadcasting Corporation transmitter on 30 Sep 1929 and marketed the first sets, Baird Televisors, at 26 guineas in May 1930.

Earliest service ■ The world's first high-definition (i.e., 405 lines) television broadcasting service was opened from Alexandra Palace, London, United Kingdom on 2 Nov 1936, when there were about 100 sets in the United Kingdom. The chief engineer was Mr Douglas Birkinshaw.

A television station in Berlin, Germany made a low-definition (180-line) transmission from 22 Mar 1935, but the transmitter burned out in August that year.

Transatlantic transmission ■ On 9 Feb 1928 the image of J. L. Baird and of a Mrs Howe was transmitted from Station 2 KZ at Coulsdon, Surrey, United Kingdom to Station 2 CVJ, Hartsdale, NY.

The earliest transatlantic transmission by satellite was achieved at 1 A.M. on 11 Jul 1962, via the active satellite *Telstar 1* from Andover, ME to Pleumeur Bodou, France. The picture was of Frederick R. Kappell, chairman of the American Telephone and Telegraph Company, which owned the satellite.

The first 'live' broadcast was made on 23 Jul 1962, and the first woman to appear was the *haute couturière* Ginette Spanier, directress of Balmain, the next day.

Longest telecast ■ The longest pre-scheduled telecast on record was a continuous transmission for 163 hr 18 min by GTV 9 of Melbourne, Australia, covering the Apollo XI moon mission from 19–26 Jul 1969.

The longest continuous TV transmission under a single director was a show hosted by Gerry Kaminski on Maclean Hunter Cable TV, Detroit, MI from 10–11 Jun 1989 for 40 hr 1 min 24 sec under the direction of Mark Dickson.

Earliest videotape recording ■ Alexander M. Poniatoff first demonstrated video-tape recording known as Ampex (his initials plus 'ex' for excellence) in 1956.

The earliest demonstration of a home video recorder was on 24 Jun 1963 at the British Broadcasting Corporation News Studio at Alexandra Palace, London, United Kingdom of the Telcan, developed by Norman Rutherford and Michael Turner of the Nottingham Electronic Valve Co.

Fastest video production ■ Tapes of the Royal Wedding of HRH Prince Andrew and Miss Sarah Ferguson on 23 Jul 1986 were produced by Thames Video Collection. Live filming ended with the departure of the honeymoon couple from Chelsea Hospital by helicopter at 4:42 P.M. The first fully edited and packaged VHS tapes were purchased 5 hr 41 min later by Fenella Lee and Lucinda Burland of West Kensing-

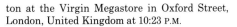

ton at the Virgin Megastore in Oxford Street, London, United Kingdom at 10:23 P.M.

Most durable shows ▪ The world's most durable TV show is NBC's *Meet the Press*, first transmitted on 6 Nov 1947 and weekly since 12 Sep 1948, originated by Lawrence E. Spivak, who appeared weekly as either moderator or panel member until 1975.

On 1 Jun 1986 Joe Franklin presented the 21,700th version of his show, started in 1951.

Since 1949 over 150,000 individual episodes of the TV show *Bozo the Clown*, by Larry Harmon Pictures, have been aired daily on 150 stations in the US and abroad.

The greatest number of hours on camera on US national commercial television is 10,037½ by the TV personality Hugh Down in over 43 years to 15 Apr 1988.

Most sets ▪ The global total of homes with television surpassed 500 million in 1987 led by the US with 89·13 million. However, on 15 Feb 1988 the new China News Agency announced that China's number of TV viewers has risen to 600 million from 100 million.

The US had, by January 1989, 90·4 million TV households, with 50·24 million on cable TV. The number of homes with color sets was 8·3 million (97 percent) by January 1989 and more than 60 percent of total households own two or more TV sets.

TV watching ▪ In June 1988 it was reported that the average American child sees at least 26,000 murders on TV by his or her 18th birthday. Between the ages of 2 and 11 the average viewing time is 31 hours 52 minutes per week.

There are 8,250 TV transmitting stations worldwide, of which 1,241 are in the US.

There are 364 TV sets per 1,000 people in the United States, compared with 348 in Sweden and 330 in Britain.

Greatest audience ▪ Estimated global audiences for the 1990 World Cup finals played in Italy from 8 Jun–8 Jul is 26·5 billion. Twenty-five billion are estimated to have tuned into the live and recorded transmissions of the XXIIIrd Olympic Games in Los Angeles, CA from 27 Jul to 13 Aug 1984. The American Broadcasting Co airing schedule comprised 187½ hours of coverage on 56 cameras.

The estimated viewership for the Live Aid concerts organized by Bob Geldof and Bill Graham, via a record 12 satellites, was 1·6 billion or nearly one-third of the world's population. The *Muppet Show* is the most widely viewed program in the world, with an estimated 235 million in 106 countries in August 1989.

The program that attracted the highest ever viewership was the Goodbye, Farewell and Amen final episode of M*A*S*H (the acronym for Mobile Army Surgical Hospital) transmitted by CBS on 28 Feb 1983 to 60·3 percent of all households in the United States. It was estimated that some 125 million people tuned in, taking a 77 percent share of all viewing.

Most expensive production ▪ *The Winds of War*, a seven-part Paramount World War II saga aired by ABC, was the most expensive ever TV production costing $42 million over 14 months' shooting. The final episode on 13 Feb 1983 attracted a rating of 41 percent (percentage of total number of viewers), and a share of 56 percent (percentage of total sets turned on that were tuned in).

Longest telecast ● On 10–11 Jun 1989 Mark Dickson directed a 40 hr 1 min 24 sec show on Maclean Hunter Cable TV of Detroit, MI. The photograph shows the host, Gerry Kaminski, being presented with a cake. (Photo: Maclean Hunter Cable TV)

Largest contracts ▪ The highest paid television performer currently is Bill Cosby, who was reported in September 1988 to have earned $92 million during the two-year period 1987–88 for his TV shows, concerts, albums and endorsements.

John William Carson (b. 23 Oct 1925), the host of *The Tonight Show*, has a contract with NBC reportedly calling for annual payment of $5 million for his one-hour evening shows aired four times weekly.

The highest-paid current affairs or news performer is Dan Rather of CBS, who reportedly signed an $8 million contract for five years from 1982.

Marie Osmond signed a contract worth $7 million for seven hours of transmission, paid by NBC on 9 Mar 1981. The figure includes talent and production costs.

Highest-paid entertainer ▪ It was reported by *Forbes* magazine in September 1988 that the world's highest-paid entertainer is Michael Jackson earning $97 million over a period of two years. A survey in *National Enquirer* published in February 1988 contended that the royalty income of Paul McCartney was running at $41 million per year and that his estimated personal fortune was $560 million.

Largest TV prizes ▪ On 24 Jul 1975 WABC-TV, New York City transmitted the first televised Grand Tier draw of the State Lottery, in which the winner took the grand prize of $1 million. This was, however, taxable.

Most successful telethon ▪ The world record for a telethon is $78,438,573 in pledges in 21½ hours by the 1989 Jerry Lewis Labor Day Telethon on 4 Sep.

The Comic Relief '89 Appeal in Britain, hosted by comedians Lenny Henry and Griff Rhys-Jones, raised over £26 million.

Biggest sale ▪ The greatest number of

episodes of any TV program ever sold has been 1,144 episodes of the British soap opera *Coronation Street* by Granada Television to CBKST Saskatoon, Saskatchewan, Canada, on 31 May 1971. This constituted 20 days 15 hr 44 min continuous viewing. A further 728 episodes (Jan 1974–Jan 1981) were sold to the Canadian Broadcasting Corporation (CBC) in August 1982.

Most prolific scriptwriter ▪ The most prolific television writer in the world is the Rt Hon. Lord Willis (b. 13 Jan 1918), who from 1949–90 has created 40 series, including the first seven years and 2·25 million words of *Dixon of Dock Green*, which ran on British Broadcasting Corporation television from 1955 to 1976, 34 stage plays and 39 feature films. He has had 26 plays produced and his total output since 1942 is estimated to be 19·6 million words.

TV producer ▪ Aaron Spelling (b. 1928) has produced more than 1,770 TV episodes totaling 2,250 hours of air time, as well as 207½ hours of TV movies and eight feature films. The total 2,467 broadcast hours is equal to 13·7 million ft of film and, projected 24 hours a day, it would take 103·9 days — just 3½ months — to screen it all. The average American TV is turned on six hours per day. At that rate, Spelling has produced enough film to last 374 days.

TOP RATED MOVIES SHOWN ON TV

TITLE	NIELSON RATING
Gone with the Wind (1976)	47·5
The Day After (1983)	46·0
Airport (1973)	42·3
Love Story (1972)	42·3
The Godfather, Part 2 (1974)	39·4
Jaws (1979)	39·1
Poseidon Adventure (1974)	39·0
True Grit (1972)	38·9
The Birds (1968)	38·9
Patton (1972)	38·5

Variety, 4-10 Jan 1990

Highest TV advertising rates ■ The highest TV advertising rate has been $600,000 per ½ min for NBC network prime time during the transmission of Super Bowl XXI on 25 Jan 1987, watched by a record 127 million viewers.

Most takes ■ The highest number of 'takes' for a TV commercial is 28 in 1973 by comedienne Pat Coombs, whose explanation was 'Every time we came to the punch line I just could not remember the name of the product.'

Commercial records ■ It was reported in March 1988 that Pepsi Cola had paid Michael Jackson £7 million to do four TV commercials for them.

Largest and smallest sets ■ The Sony Jumbo Tron color TV screen at the Tsukuba International Exposition '85 near Tokyo in March 1985 measured 80 ft × 150 ft.

Most expensive TV production ● *The Winds of War*, a World War II saga starring Robert Mitchum, Victoria Tennant, Ali MacGraw and Ralph Bellamy, was produced by Paramount for ABC at a cost of $42 million for seven episodes and filmed on location in California, Washington, Yugoslavia, Austria, Italy, Germany and England. (Photo: Kobal Collection)

The largest cathode ray tubes for color sets are 37 in models manufactured by Mitsubishi Electric of Japan.

The Seiko TV-Wrist Watch launched on 23 Dec 1982 in Japan has a 1·2 in screen and weighs only

2·8 oz. Together with the receiver unit and the headphone set the entire black and white system, costing 108,000 yen, weighs only 11·3 oz.

The smallest single-piece set is the Casio-Keisanki TV-10 weighing 11·9 oz with a 2·7 in screen, launched in Tokyo in July 1983.

The smallest color set is the liquid crystal display (LCD) Japanese Epson launched in 1985 with dimensions of 3 × 6¾ × 1⅛ in weighing, with batteries and its 52,800 crystals, only 16 oz.

ANTIQUE PRICE RECORDS

ANCIENT SCULPTURE

An 8-in 6,000-year-old Neolithic sculpture of a seated goddess from the estate of James Johnson Sweeney was sold at auction by Sotheby's, NY on 24 Nov 1986 for $1·32 million. The purchaser was Mrs Shelby White Levy, a New York financial writer.

ART NOUVEAU

The highest auction price for any piece of art nouveau is $1·78 million for a standard lamp in the form of three lotus blossoms by the Daum Brothers and Louis Majorelle of France sold at Sotheby's, NY on 2 Dec 1989.

BED

A 1930 black lacquer king-size bed made by Jean Durand was auctioned at Christie's, NY on 2 Oct 1983 for $75,000.

BLANKET

The most expensive blanket was a Navajo Churro hand-spun serape of c. 1852 sold for $115,500 (with premium) at Sotheby's, NY on 22 Oct 1983.

BOTTLE

A cobalt blue ink bottle made by the Isabella Glassworks of New Jersey c. 1855-65 was sold for $26,400 at the Robert W. Skinner Galleries in Bolton, MA on 7 Oct 1989.

CARPET

In 1946 the Metropolitan Museum in New York City privately paid $1 million for the 26·5 × 13·6 ft Anhalt Medallion carpet made in Tabriz or Kashan, Persia (Iran) c. 1590. The highest price ever paid at auction for a carpet is £384,230 for a Louis XV Savonnerie at Christie's, Monaco in June 1989.

CERAMICS

The highest auction price for any ceramic is £3·74 million for a Chinese Tang dynasty (A.D. 681–907) horse sold by the British Rail Pension Fund and bought by a Japanese dealer at Sotheby's, London, United Kingdom on 12 Dec 1989. The horse was stolen from a warehouse in Hong Kong on 14 Nov, but was recovered on 2 Dec in time for the sale.

CHAMBER POT

A 33-oz silver pot, made by David Willaume and engraved for the 2nd Earl of Warrington, was sold for £9,500 at Sotheby's, London, United Kingdom on 14 Jun 1984.

CIGARETTE CARD

The most valuable card is one of the six known

baseball series cards of Honus Wagner, who was a nonsmoker, which was sold in New York in December 1981 for $25,000.

DOLL

The highest price at auction for a doll is £90,200 for a 1909 bisque Kämmer and Reinhardt doll at Sotheby's, London, United Kingdom on 16 Feb 1989. It was purchased by Mme Dina Vierny.

FURNITURE

The highest price ever paid for a single piece of furiture is $15·1 million at Christie's, London, United Kingdom on 5 Jul 1990 for the 'Badminton Cabinet,' an 18th-century Italian cabinet, which was commissioned in Florence in the 1720s by the Duke of Beaufort. It was bought by Barbara Piasecka Johnson of Princeton, NJ. The highest price ever paid for a single piece of furniture in the United States is $12·1 million at Christie's, New York on 3 Jun 1989 for a mahogany desk cum bookcase made in the 1760s by master craftsman John Goddard of Newport, Rhode Island for the eminent statesman Nicholas Brown. It was bought by Israel Sack, one of New York's leading dealers in American furniture.

GLASS

The auction record is £520,000 for a Roman glass cage-cup of c. A.D. 300 measuring 7 in in diameter and 4 in in height, sold at Sotheby's, London, United Kingdom on 4 Jun 1979 to Robin Symes.

GOLD PLATE

The highest price for any gold artifact is £950,400 for the 22-carat font made by Paul Storr to the design of Humphrey Repton in 1797. It was sold at Christie's by Lady Anne Cavendish-Bentinck and bought by Armitage of London, United Kingdom on 11 Jul 1985.

GUNS

The highest price ever paid for a single gun is £125,000 given by the London dealers F. Partridge for a French flintlock fowling piece made for Louis XIII c. 1615 and attributed to Pierre le Bourgeoys of Lisieux, France (d. 1627). This piece was included in the collection of the late William Goodwin Renwick of the United States sold by Sotheby's, London, United Kingdom on 21 Nov 1972. It is now in the Metropolitan Museum of Art, NY. The highest price paid at auction for a pistol is $242,000 at Christie's, NY on 14 May 1987 for a .45 calibre Colt single-action army revolver, Serial No. 1 for 1873.

HAT

The highest price ever paid for a hat is $66,000 by the Alaska State Museum at a New York City auction in November 1981 for a Tlingit Kiksadi ceremonial frog helmet from c. 1600.

ICON

The record auction price for an icon is $150,000 paid at Christie's, NY on 17 Apr 1980 for the *Last Judgment* (from the George R. Hann collection, Pittsburgh) made in Novgorod, USSR in the 16th century.

JADE

The highest price ever paid for an item in jade is $396,000 (with premium) at Sotheby's, New York on 6 Dec 1983 for a mottled brownish yellow belt-hook and pendant mask of the Warring States Period (484–221 B.C.) of Chinese history.

JEWELRY

The highest auction price for individual items of jewelry is £2,825,000 (with buyer's premium) for two pear-shaped diamond drop earrings of 58·6 and 61 carats at Sotheby's, Geneva on 14 Nov 1980. Neither the buyer nor seller was disclosed.

MECHANICAL TOY

The auction record for a toy is £25,500 for a model train set of Stephenson's *Rocket* made by Marklin of Germany in tin plate in 1909, sold at Sotheby's, London, United Kingdom on 29 May 1984.

MUSICAL BOX

The highest price paid for a musical box is £20,900 (with premium) for a Swiss-made example made for a Persian prince in 1901, sold at Sotheby's, London, United Kingdom on 23 Jan 1985.

PLAYING CARDS

The highest price paid for a deck of playing cards is $143,352 (with premium) by the Metropolitan Museum of Art, New York at Sotheby's, London, United Kingdom on 6 Dec 1983.

SCIENTIFIC INSTRUMENT

The highest auction price for a scientific instrument is £385,000 for a 13 $\frac{1}{2}$-in Dutch gilt-brass astrolabe of 1559 by Walter Arsenius at Christie's, London, United Kingdom on 29 Sep 1988.

SILVER

The record for an item of silver is £982,581 paid by the three dealers Koopman, Phillips and Partridge in November 1989 at Sotheby's, New York for a pair of George II candelabra made by Kandler of London, United Kingdom in 1738. The record for a single piece of English silver is £770,000 for an epergne by de Lamerie sold at Christie's, London, United Kingdom by the Earl of Portarlington and bought by Jacques Koopman on 17 Dec 1986. The Treasury inkstand of Sir Robert Walpole, Prime Minister from 1715 to 1742, sold for £770,000 to the London dealers Spink and Armitage at Christie's, London, United Kingdom on 14 Dec 1988. The 100-piece Paul de Lamerie service made for the 7th Earl of Thanet c. 1745 was sold by Lord Hothfield at Sotheby's, London, United Kingdom on 22 Nov 1984 for £825,000 (with premium).

SNUFFBOX

The highest price ever paid for a snuff box is £764,826 in a sale at Christie's, Geneva, Switzerland on 11 Nov 1986 for a pale green chrysoprase and diamond gold box once owned by Frederick the Great of Prussia.

SPOONS

A Wiener Werkstätte spoon by Josef Hoffmann, Austria, c. 1905, was sold at Sotheby's, London, United Kingdom for £17,600 (with premium) on 28 Apr 1983. A set of 13 Henry VIII Apostle spoons owned by Lord Astor of Hever was sold for £120,000 on 24 Jun 1981 at Christie's, London, United Kingdom.

SWORD

The highest price paid for a sword is £823,045 for the Duke of Windsor's Royal Navy officer's sword (presented to him by King George V in 1913) at Sotheby's, Geneva, Switzerland on 3 Apr 1987.

TAPESTRY

The highest price paid for a tapestry is £550,000 for a Swiss medieval tapestry frieze in two parts dated 1468–1476 at Sotheby's, Geneva, Switzerland on 10 Apr 1981 by the Basle Historische Museum.

TEDDY BEAR

The highest price paid for a Teddy Bear at auction is £55,100 for a well-worn brown bear made by Steiff of Germany c. 1920 at Sotheby's, London, United Kingdom on 19 Sep 1989.

THIMBLE

The record auction price for a thimble is £8,000 paid by London dealer Winifred Williams at Christie's, London, United Kingdom on 3 Dec 1979 for a Meissen dentil-shaped porcelain piece of c. 1740.

TOY SOLDIER

The highest price paid for a single toy soldier is £1,200 for an extremely rare 70-mm scale figure of the colonel-in-chief, the Welsh Guards, at Phillips, London, United Kingdom on 9 Sep 1987.

TYPEWRITER

The highest price paid for an antique machine is £9,900 for an 1890 black enamel Guhl & Harbeck auctioned at Christie's, London, United Kingdom on 10 Aug 1989.

WALKING STICK

The highest auction price for a walking stick is $24,200 at Sotheby Parke Bernet, New York in 1983 for an octagonal whale ivory nobbed stick decorated by scrimshanders in 1845.

Most expensive chamber pot ● This traditional style silver pot, made by David Willaume of London, United Kingdom in 1744, fetched £9,500 at Sotheby's, London, United Kingdom on 14 Jun 1984. (Photo: Sotheby's)

HUMAN ACHIEVEMENTS

Endurance & Endeavour

Food & Drink

Manufactured Articles

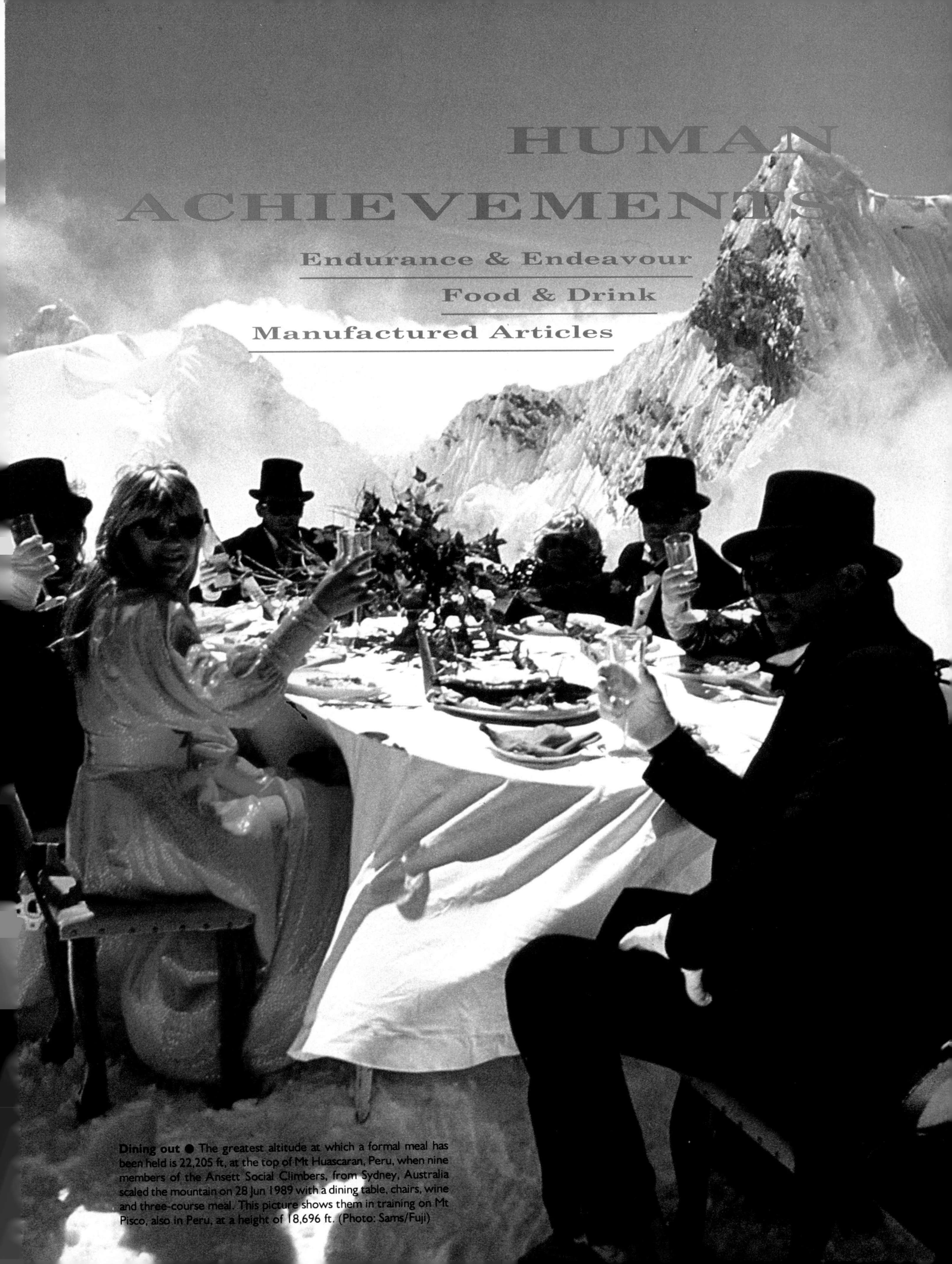

Dining out ● The greatest altitude at which a formal meal has been held is 22,205 ft, at the top of Mt Huascaran, Peru, when nine members of the Ansett Social Climbers, from Sydney, Australia scaled the mountain on 28 Jun 1989 with a dining table, chairs, wine and three-course meal. This picture shows them in training on Mt Pisco, also in Peru, at a height of 18,696 ft. (Photo: Sams/Fuji)

Endurance and Endeavor

Most traveled ■ The world's most traveled men are Parke G. Thompson, from Akron, OH and Giorgio Ricatto, from Turin, Italy, both of whom have visited all of the 170 sovereign countries and 61 of the 62 non-sovereign or other territories (see heading COUNTRIES, Chapter 10). Both men have yet to go to the Heard & McDonald Islands, an island group in the southern Indian Ocean.

The most traveled man in the era before motor vehicles was probably the Methodist preacher Bishop Francis Asbury (b. Handsworth, West Midlands, United Kingdom, 1745), who traveled 264,000 miles in North America from 1771 to 1815. During this time he preached some 16,000 sermons and ordained nearly 3,000 ministers.

Most isolated ■ The farthest any human has been removed from his nearest living fellow human is 2,233·2 miles in the case of the Command Service Module pilot Alfred M. Worden on the US *Apollo 15* lunar mission of 30 Jul–1 Aug 1971.

Longest walks ■ The first person reported to have 'walked round the world' is George Matthew Schilling (US) from 3 Aug 1897 to 1904, but the first verified achievement was by David Kunst (b. 1939) from 20 Jun 1970 to 5 Oct 1974.

Tomas Carlos Pereira (b. Argentina, 16 Nov 1942) spent ten years, 6 Apr 1968 to 8 Apr 1978, walking 29,825 miles around five continents. Steven Newman of Bethel, OH spent four years walking 22,500 miles around the world, 1 Apr 1983 to 1 Apr 1987, covering 20 countries and five continents.

Rick Hansen (b. Canada, 1957), who was paralyzed from the waist down in 1973 as a result of a motor accident, wheeled his wheelchair over 24,901·55 miles, through four continents and 34 countries. He started his journey from Vancouver, Canada on 21 Mar 1985 and arrived back on 22 May 1987.

George Meegan (b. 2 Oct 1952) from Rainham, Kent, United Kingdom walked 19,019 miles from Usuaia, the southern tip of South America, to Prudhoe Bay in northern Alaska, taking 2,426 days from 26 Jan 1977 to 18 Sep 1983, and thus completed the first traverse of the western hemisphere.

Sean Eugene Maguire (US; b. 15 Sep 1956) walked 7,327 miles from the Yukon River, north of Livengood, AK, to Key West, FL, in 307 days, 6 Jun 1978 to 9 Apr 1979.

The trans-Canada (Halifax to Vancouver) record walk of 3,764 miles is 96 days by Clyde McRae, 23, from 1 May to 4 Aug 1973.

John Lees (b. 23 Feb 1945) of Brighton, East Sussex, United Kingdom walked 2,876 miles across the United States from City Hall, Los Angeles, CA to City Hall, NY in 53 days 12 hr 15 min (average 53·75 miles a day) between 11 Apr and 3 Jun 1972.

North Pole conquest ■ The claim of neither of the two Arctic explorers Dr Frederick Albert Cook (1865–1940) and Cdr (later Rear-Ad.) Robert Edwin Peary (1856–1920) of the US Naval Civil Engineering branch in reaching the North Pole is subject to positive proof, and several recent surveys have produced conflicting conclusions.

On excellent pack ice and modern sleds, Wally Herbert's 1968–69 expedition (see heading Arctic crossing) attained a best day's route mileage of 23 miles in 15 hr. Cook claimed 26 miles twice, while Peary claimed a surely unsustainable average of 38 miles over eight consecutive days.

The first people definitely to have reached the

North Pole on ground level — the exact point Lat. 90° 00′ 00″ N (± 300 meters) — were Pavel Afanasevich Geordiyenko, Pavel Kononovich Sen'ko, Mikhail Mikhaylovich Somov and Mikhail Yemel'enovich Ostrekin (all USSR), on 23 Apr 1948. They arrived and departed by air.

The earliest indisputable attainment of the North Pole by surface travel over the sea-ice was at 3 P.M. (Central Standard Time) on 19 Apr 1968 by Ralph Plaisted (US) and three companions after a 42-day trek in four Skidoos (snowmobiles). Their arrival was independently verified 18 hr later by a US Air Force weather aircraft. The party returned by aircraft. The seabed is 13,410 ft below the North Pole.

Naomi Uemura (1941–84), the Japanese explorer and mountaineer, became the first person to reach the North Pole in a solo trek across the Arctic ice cap at 4:45 A.M. GMT on 1 May 1978. He had traveled 450 miles setting out on 7 Mar from Cape Edward, Ellesmere Island in northern Canada. He averaged nearly 8 miles per day with his sled 'Aurora' drawn by 17 huskies. He also left by aircraft.

Dr Jean-Louis Etienne, 39, was the first to reach the Pole solo and without dogs, on 11 May 1986 after 63 days.

On 20 Apr 1987 Fukashi Kazami, 36, of Tokyo, Japan reached the North Pole from Ward Hunt Island, northern Canada in 44 days, having started on his 250-cc motorcycle on 8 Mar. Both left by aircraft.

The first woman to set foot on the North Pole was Mrs Fran Phipps on 5 Apr 1971.

Galina Aleksandrovna Lastovskaya (b. 1941) and Lilia Vladislavovna Minina (b. 1959) were crew members of the USSR atomic icebreaker *Arktika*, which reached the Pole on 17 Aug 1977.

South Pole conquest ■ The first men to cross the Antarctic Circle (Lat. 66° 33′ S) were the 193 crew of the *Resolution* (509 tons) (Capt James Cook, RN [1728–79]) and *Adventure* (370 tons) (Lt Tobias Furneaux) on 17 Jan 1773 at 39° E.

The first person known to have sighted the Antarctic ice shelf was Capt Thaddeus Thadde-

---

Walking round the world ● The first verified walk round the world was by David Kunst (b. 1939) who left his home town of Waseca, MN on 20 Jun 1970 and arrived back there on 5 Oct 1974. His walk took him through America, Europe, Asia and Australia. At the start he was accompanied by his brother, John, but John was killed by bandits in Afghanistan and another brother, Peter, replaced him. Among the places that they visited were New York (left); Lisbon, in Portugal (right); New Delhi, in India (bottom left); and Perth, in Australia (bottom right). A total of four mules walked with them, one of which (Willie Makeit II) can be seen below with David and in the New Delhi picture. (Photos: David Kunst and Spectrum)

First man to walk to both poles ● The first man to walk to both the North Pole and South Pole was Robert Swan (Great Britain). He led the three-man Footsteps of Scott expedition, which reached the South Pole on 11 Jan 1986, and three years later headed the eight-man Icewalk expedition that arrived at the North Pole on 14 May 1989. The South Pole trek took the three British walkers 70 days, through what was described as 'the worst Antarctic winter for years.' The North Pole walk was an international expedition, with members from Australia, Canada, Great Britain, Japan, the Soviet Union, the US and West Germany. The walk represented just one part of the project, the second being a venture involving 22 students from 15 countries, who were carrying out environmental studies at the polar team base camp at Eureka on Canada's Ellesmere Island. (Photos: Roger Mear and Ben Olds)

vich Bellingshausen (Russia) (1778–1852) on 27 Jan 1820 from the vessels *Vostock* and *Mirnyi*.

The first known to have sighted the mainland of the continent was Capt William Smith (1790–1847) and Master Edward Bransfield, RN, in the brig *Williams.* They saw the peaks of Trinity Land 3 days later on 30 Jan 1820.

The South Pole (alt. 9,186 ft on ice and 336 ft bedrock) was first reached at 11 A.M. on 14 Dec 1911 by a Norwegian party of five men led by Capt Roald Engebereth Gravning Amundsen (1872–1928), after a 53-day march with dog sleds from the Bay of Whales, to which he had penetrated in the *Fram.* Subsequent calculations showed that Olav Olavson Bjaaland and Helmer Hanssen probably passed within 1,310–1,970 ft of the exact pole. The other two members

were Sverre H. Hassell (d. 1928) and Oskar Wisting (d. 1936). The first woman to set foot on Antarctica was Mrs Karoline Mikkelsen on 20 Feb 1935. No woman stood on the South Pole until 11 Nov 1969. On that day Lois Jones, Eileen McSaveney, Jean Pearson, Terry Lee Tickhill (all US), Kay Lindsay (Australia) and Pam Young (New Zealand) arrived by air.

First to see both poles ■ The first people

to see both poles were Roald Engebereth Amundsen and Oskar Wisting when they flew aboard the airship *Norse* over the North Pole on 12 May 1926, having previously been to the South Pole on 14 Dec 1911.

First to visit both poles ■ Dr Albert P. Crary (US; 1911–87) reached the North Pole in a Dakota aircraft on 3 May 1952. On 12 Feb 1961 he arrived at the South Pole by Sno Cat on a scientific traverse party from the McMurdo Station.

First to walk to both poles ■ The first man to walk to both the North and the South Pole was Robert Swan (b. 1956). He led the three-man Footsteps of Scott expedition, which reached the South Pole on 11 Jan 1986, and three years later headed the eight-man Icewalk expedition, which arrived at the North Pole on 14 May 1989.

Arctic crossing ■ The first crossing of the Arctic sea-ice was achieved by the British Trans-Arctic Expedition, which left Point Barrow, AK on 21 Feb 1968 and arrived at the Seven Island archipelago northeast of Spitzbergen, Svalbard 464 days later on 29 May 1969 after a haul of 2,920 statute miles and a drift of 700 miles, compared with the straight-line distance of 1,662 miles. The team comprised Wally Herbert (leader), 34, Major Ken Hedges, 34, RAMC, Allan Gill, 38, and Dr Roy Koerner (glaciologist), 36, and 40 huskies.

The only crossing achieved in a single season was that by Fiennes and Burton (see heading Polar circumnavigation) from Alert via the North Pole to the Greenland Sea in open snowmobiles. Both of these reached the North Pole and returned by land.

Antarctic crossing ■ The first surface crossing of the Antarctic continent was completed at 1:47 P.M. on 2 Mar 1958, after a trek of 2,158 miles lasting 99 days from 24 Nov 1957, from Shackleton Base to Scott Base via the Pole. The crossing party of 12 was led by Dr (now Sir) Vivian Ernest Fuchs (b. 11 Feb 1908).

The 2,600 mile trans-Antarctic leg from Sanae to Scott Base of the 1980–82 Trans-Globe Expedition was achieved in 66 days from 26 Oct 1980 to 11 Jan 1981, having passed through the South Pole on 23 Dec 1980. The three-man party on snowmobiles comprised Sir Ranulph Fiennes, Bt (b. 1944), Oliver Shepard and Charles Burton.

Polar circumnavigation ■ The first polar circumnavigation was achieved by Sir Ranulph Fiennes, Bt and Charles Burton of the British Trans-Globe Expedition, who traveled south from Greenwich (2 Sep 1979), via the South Pole (17 Dec 1980) and the North Pole (11 Apr 1982), and back to Greenwich, arriving after a 35,000 mile trek on 29 Aug 1982.

Longest sled journeys ■ The longest totally self-supporting polar sled journey ever made was one of 1,080 miles from west to east across Greenland (now Kalaallit Nunaat) from 18 Jun to 5 Sep 1934 by Capt M. Lindsay (1905–1981) (later Sir Martin Lindsay of Dowhill, Bt), Lt Arthur S. T. Godfrey, RE (later Lt Col, k. 1942), Andrew N. A. Croft (later Col,) and 49 dogs.

The Ross Sea Party of ten (three died) sleded over 2,000 miles in 300 days from 6 May 1915.

Greatest ocean descent ■ The record ocean descent was achieved in the Challenger Deep of the Mariana Trench, 250 miles southwest of Guam, in the Pacific Ocean, when the Swiss-built US Navy bathyscaphe *Trieste*, manned by Dr Jacques Piccard (Switzerland; b.

1914) and Lt Donald Walsh, USN reached a depth of 35,813 ft (6·78 miles) at 1:10 P.M. on 23 Jan 1960. The pressure of the water was 16 883 lbf/in² and the temperature 37·4° F. The descent took 4 hr 48 min and the ascent 3 hr 17 min.

Deep diving records ■ The record depth for the extremely dangerous activity of breath-held diving is 344 ft, by Jacques Mayol (France) off Elba, Italy, in December 1983. He descended on a sled in 104 seconds and ascended in 90 seconds.

The record for women is 246 ft ¾ in, by Rossana Majorca (Italy) off Syracuse, Sicily on 31 Jul 1987.

The record dive with scuba (self-contained underwater breathing apparatus) is 437 ft by John J. Gruener and R. Neal Watson (US) off Freeport, Grand Bahama on 14 Oct 1968.

For women it is 345 ft by Marty Dunwoody (US) off Bimini, Bahama Islands on 20 Dec 1987.

The record dive utilizing gas mixtures (nitrogen, oxygen and helium) is a simulated dive of 2,250 ft in a dry chamber by Stephen Porter, Len Whitlock and Erik Kramer at Duke University Medical Center in Durham, NC on 3 Feb 1981 in a 43-day trial in a sphere of 8 ft.

A team of six divers (four Comex and two French Navy) descended and worked efficiently during a period of six days to a depth of 1,706 ft off Marseilles, France as part of the Hydro VIII operation in ths spring of 1988. This involved the use of 'hydreliox,' a synthetic breathing mixture containing a high percentage of hydrogen.

Deepest under water escapes ■ The deepest under water rescue achieved was of the *Pisces III* in which Roger R. Chapman, 28, and Roger Mallinson, 35, were trapped for 76 hr when it sank to 1,575 ft, 150 miles southeast of Cork, Republic of Ireland on 29 Aug 1973. She was hauled to the surface by the cable ship *John Cabot* after work by *Pisces V*, *Pisces II* and the remote control recovery vessel US CURV on 1 Sep.

The greatest depth of an actual escape without any equipment has been from 225 ft by Richard A. Slater from the rammed submersible *Nekton Beta* off Catalina Island, CA on 28 Sep 1970.

The record for an escape with equipment was by Norman Cooke and Hamish Jones on 22 Jul 1987. During a naval exercise they escaped from a depth of 601 ft from the submarine HMS *Otus* in Bjornefjorden, off Bergen, Norway, wearing standard suits with a built-in lifejacket, from which air expanding during the ascent passes into a hood over the escaper's head.

Deepest salvage ■ The greatest depth at which salvage has been achieved is 16,500 ft by the bathyscaphe *Trieste II* (Lt Cdr Mel Bartels, USN), to attach cables to an 'electronic package' on the seabed 400 miles north of Hawaii on 20 May 1972.

The deepest salvage operation ever achieved with divers was on the wreck of HM cruiser *Edinburgh* sunk on 2 May 1942 in the Barents Sea off northern Norway inside the Arctic Circle in 803 ft of water. Twelve divers dived on the wreck in pairs using a bell from the *Stephaniturm* (1,594 tons) over 32 days under the direction of former RN officer Michael Stewart from 17 Sep to 7 Oct 1981. A total of 460 gold ingots (the only 100 percent salvage to date) was recovered, John Rossier being the first person to touch the gold.

High altitude diving ■ The record for high altitude diving is 16,200 ft in Lake Donag-Tsho in the Himalayas, Nepal by Frank B. Mee, Dr John Leach and Dr Andy McLean on 4 Mar 1989. They dived to a depth of 92 ft, having first of all cut through 5 ft of ice in temperatures of −18° F.

Greatest penetration into the earth ■ The deepest penetration made into the ground by human beings is in the Western Deep Levels Mine at Carletonville, Transvaal, South Africa, where a record depth of 11,749 ft was attained on 12 Jul 1977. The virgin rock temperature at this depth is 131° F.

Longest on a raft ■ The longest recorded survival alone on a raft is 133 days (4½ months) by Second Steward Poon Lim (b. Hong Kong) of the United Kingdom Merchant Navy, whose ship, the SS *Ben Lomond*, was torpedoed in the Atlantic 565 miles west of St Paul's Rocks in Lat. 00° 30′ N, Long. 38° 45′ W at 11:45 A.M. on 23 Nov 1942. He was picked up by a Brazilian fishing boat off Salinópolis, Brazil on 5 Apr 1943 and could walk ashore. In July 1943 he was awarded the BEM and now lives in New York.

Shaft-sinking record ■ The one-month (31 days) world record is 1,251 ft for a standard shaft 26 ft in diameter at Buffelsfontein Mine, Transvaal, South Africa, in March 1962.

Most marriages ■ The greatest number of marriages accumulated in the monogamous world is 27 by former Baptist minister Glynn 'Scotty' Wolfe (b. 25 Jul 1908) of Blythe, CA, who first married in 1927. His latest wife is Daisy Delgado (b. 29 Dec 1970), a Filipino from Liloan, Cebu. His previous oldest wife was 38. His total number of children is, he believes, 41.

The greatest number of monogamous marriages by a woman is 21, by Linda Lou Essex of Anderson, IN. She has been married to 15 different men since 1957, divorcing the last one in 1988.

The record for bigamous marriages is 104 by Giovanni Vigliotto, one of some 50 aliases used by either Fred Jipp (b. New York , 3 Apr 1936) or Nikolai Peruskov (b. Siracusa, Sicily, 3 Apr 1929) during 1949–81 in 27 states and 14 other countries. Four victims were aboard one ship in 1968 and two in London, United Kingdom. On 28 Mar 1983 in Phoenix, AZ he received 28 years for fraud, 6 for bigamy and was fined $336,000.

Oldest bride and bridegroom ■ The oldest recorded bridegroom has been Harry Stevens, 103, who married Thelma Lucas, 84, at the Caravilla Retirement Home, WI on 3 Dec 1984.

Longest engagement ■ The longest engagement on record was between Octavio Guillen and Adriana Martinez. They finally took the plunge after 67 years in June 1969 in Mexico City, Mexico. Both were then aged 82.

Longest marriage ■ The longest recorded marriages are of 86 years, one between Sir Temulji Bhicaji Nariman and Lady Nariman from 1853 to 1940 resulting from a cousin marriage when both were 5. Sir Temulji (b. 3 Sep 1848) died, aged 91 years 11 months, in August 1940 at Bombay, India.

Lazarus Rowe (b. Greenland, NH, 1725) and Molly Webber were recorded as marrying in 1743. He died first in 1829 after 86 years of marriage.

Golden weddings ■ The greatest number of golden weddings in a family is ten, the six sons

LOVE & MARRIAGE

Marriage records ● The greatest number of marriages accumulated in the monogamous world is 27 by former Baptist minister Glynn 'Scotty' Wolfe (b. 25 Jul 1908) of Blythe, CA, who first married in 1927. The largest mass wedding ceremony was one of 6,516 couples officiated over by Sun Myung Moon (b. 1920) of the Holy Spirit Association for the Unification of World Christianity at a factory near Seoul, South Korea on 30 Oct 1988. The most famous midget in history was Charles Sherwood Stratton alias General Tom Thumb (1838-83), who was 3 ft 4 in tall. He married Minnie Warren in 1865. (Photos: Gamma and Mary Evans Picture Library)

and four daughters of Joseph and Sophia Gresl of Manitowoc, WI all celebrating golden weddings between April 1962 and September 1988, and the six sons and four daughters of George and Eleonora Hopkins of Patrick County, VA all celebrating their golden weddings between November 1961 and October 1988.

Most married ■ Jack V. and Edna Moran of Seattle, WA have married each other 40 times since the original and only really necessary occasion on 27 Jul 1937 in Seaside, OR. Subsequent ceremonies have included those at Banff, Canada (1952), Cairo, Egypt (1966) and Westminster Abbey, London, United Kingdom (1975).

Youngest married ■ It was reported in 1986 that an 11-month-old boy was married to a 3-month-old girl in Bangladesh to end a 20-year feud between two families over a disputed farm.

Mass ceremony ■ The largest mass wedding ceremony was one of 6,516 couples officiated over by Sun Myung Moon (b. 1920) of the Holy Spirit Association for the Unification of World Christianity at a factory near Seoul, South Korea on 30 Oct 1988.

Most expensive wedding ■ The wedding of Mohammed, son of Shaik Rashid Bin Saeed Al Maktoum, to Princess Salama in Dubai in May 1981 lasted 7 days and cost an estimated £22 million in a purpose-built stadium for 20,000.

Oldest divorced ■ On 2 Feb 1984 a divorce was granted in Milwaukee, WI between Ida Stern, aged 91, and her husband Simon, 97.

Banquet ■ It was estimated that some 30,000 attended a military feast at Radewitz, Poland on 25 Jun 1730 thrown by King August II (1709–33).

The greatest number of people served indoors at

a single sitting was 18,000 municipal leaders at the Palais de L'Industrie, Paris on 18 Aug 1889. At the wedding of cousins Menachem Teitel baum, and Brucha Sima Melsels, both 18, con ducted by their grandfather Grand Rabbi Moses in Uniondale, Long Island, NY on 5 Dec 1984, the attendance of the Satmar sect of Hasidic Jews was estimated at between 17,000 and 20,000. Meal Mart of Brooklyn, a kosher caterer, pro vided the food including 2 tons of gefilte fish.

The most expensive menu ever served was for the main 5 ½ hr banquet at the Imperial Iranian 2,500th Anniversary gathering at Persepolis in October 1971. It comprised quail eggs stuffed with Iranian caviar, a mousse of crayfish tails in Nantua sauce, stuffed rack of rost lamb, with a main course of roast peacock stuffed with *foie gras*, fig rings and raspberry sweet champagne sherbet, with wines including *château Lafite-Rothschild* 1945 at £ 40 (now £ 235) per bottle from Maxime's, Paris, France.

Dining out ■ The world champion for eating out has been Fred E. Magel of Chicago, IL who since 1928 has dined out 46,000 times in 60 nations as a restaurant grader. He asserts the one which served largest helpings was Zehnder's Hotel, Frankenmuth, MI. Mr Magel's favorite dishes were South African rock lobster and mousse of fresh English strawberries.

The greatest altitude at which a formal meal has been held is 22,205 ft, at the top of Mt Huascaran, Peru, when nine members of the Ansett Social Climbers, from Sydney, Australia scaled the mountain on 28 Jun 1989 with a dining table, chairs, wine and three course meal. At the summit they put on top hats, thermal black ties and balldresses for their dinner party, which was marred only by the fact that the wine turned to ice.

Party giving ■ The 'International Year of the Child' children's party in Hyde Park, London, United Kingdom was attended by the British royal family and 160,000 children on 30–31 May 1979.

The world's biggest birthday party was attended by an estimated 35,000 people at Louisville, KY on 8 Sep 1979 to celebrate the 89th birthday of Colonel Harland Sanders, the founder of Ken tucky Fried Chicken.

The largest Christmas Party ever staged was that thrown by the Boeing Company in the 65,000-seat Kingdome, Seattle, WA, in two shows totaling 103,152 people on 15 Dec 1979.

During St Patrick's week of 11–17 Mar 1985, Houlihan's Old Place hosted St Pat's Parties at the 48 Kansas City, MO-based Gilbert–Robinson restaurants for a total of 206,854 documented guests.

Lecture fees ■ Dr Ronald Dante was paid $3,080,000 for lecturing students on hypnother apy at a two-day course held in Chicago on 1–2 Jun 1986. He was teaching for eight hours each day, and thus earned $192,500 per hour.

Longest pension ■ Miss Millicent Barclay was born on 10 Jul 1872, 3 months after the death of her father, Col William Barclay, and became eligible for a Madras Military Fund pension to continue until her marriage. She died unmarried on 26 Oct 1969, having drawn the pension for every day of her life of 97 years 3 months.

Medical families ■ The four sons and five daughters of Dr Antonio B. Vicencio of Los Angeles, CA all qualified as doctors during 1964–82.

Miscellaneous Endeavors

It is intended to gradually phase out many of the record categories in the 'Human Achievements' chapter where the duration of the event is the only criterion for inclusion. If you are planning an attempt on an endurance marathon you should contact us at a very early stage to check whether that category is likely to be retained in future editions of the book.

Abseiling ■ Wilmer Pérez and Luis Aulestia set an abseiling or rappeling record of 3,376 ft by descending from above the Angel Falls in Vene zuala down to its base on 24 Aug 1989. The descent took 1 ¼ hrs.

The longest descent down the side of a sky scraper is one of 805 ft 5 in, by Sgt Mick Herrick down the north tower of the Rialto Building in Melbourne, Victoria, Australia on 27 Nov 1988.

United States ■ The west face of Thor Peak, Baffin Island, northern Canada allowed an abseiling or rappeling record of 3,250 ft by a team of 16 led by Steve Holmes (US) in July 1982.

Accordion playing ■ Pieter van Logger enberg of Hoedspruit, Transvaal, South Africa played an accordion for 85 hr from 7–10 Jul 1987 as part of the Wildlife Festival of Hoedspruit.

Apple peeling ■ The longest single unbroken apple peel on record is one of 172 ft 4 in, peeled by Kathy Wafler of Wolcott, NY in 11 hr 30 min at Long Ridge Mall, Rochester, NY on 16 Oct 1976. The apple weighed 20 oz.

Apple picking ■ The greatest recorded performance is 15,830 lb, picked in 8 hr by George Adrian of Indianapolis, IN on 23 Sep 1980.

Auctioneering ■ The longest one-man auc tion on record is one of 60 hr, by Reg Coates at Gosport, Hampshire, United Kingdom from 9–11 Sep 1988.

Bag-carrying ■ The greatest nonstop bag carrying feat carrying 1 cwt of household coal in an open bag is 34 miles, by Neil Sullivan, 37, of Small Heath, Birmingham, United Kingdom, in 12 hr 45 min on 24 May 1986.

Bagpipes ■ The duration record pipe of 120 hr is held by Jordon Anderson, William Scannell, Frederick Côté and Andrew Belson at the Old Fort on St Helens' Island, Quebec, Canada, playing two at a time in shifts from 6–11 Aug 1988.

Balancing on one foot ■ The longest recorded duration for balancing on one foot is 34 hr, by N. Ravi in Sathyamangalam City, Tamil Nadu, India on 17–18 Apr 1982. The disengaged foot may not be rested on the standing foot nor may any object be used for support or balance.

Bale rolling ■ Michael Priestley and Marcus Stanley of Heckington Young Farmers Club rolled a 3 ft 11-in wide cylindrical bale over a 164-ft course in 18·06 sec at the Lincolnshire Federation of Young Farmers' Clubs annual sports day at Sleaford, Lincolnshire, United Kingdom on 25 Jun 1989.

Balloon release ■ The largest mass bal loon release ever was one of 1,429,643 balloons at Public Square in Cleveland, OH on 27 Sep 1986.

Band marathon ■ The longest recorded marathon is one of 108 hr by Alpha Connection at Bordon, Hampshire, United Kingdom from 29 Apr–4 May 1990.

Band, one-man ■ Rory Blackwell, aided by his double left-footed perpendicular percussion-pounder, plus his three-tier right footed horizontal 22-pronged differential beater, and his 12- outlet bellow-powered horn-blower, played 108 different instruments (19 melody and 89 percussion) simultaneously in Dawlish, Devon, United Kingdom on 29 May 1989. He also played 314 instruments in a single rendition in 1 min 23·07 sec, again at Dawlish, on 27 May 1985. Kalyanaraman Swaminathan of Eraiyur, Tamil Nadu, India played his one-man band (which must include at least three instruments played simultaneously) for 244 hr from 21 Aug–1 Sep 1989. Nicki Clarke of Chester, Cheshire, United Kingdom created the women's record of 100 hr 20 min from 24–28 Mar 1986 at the Hotel Leofric, Coventry, West Midlands, United Kingdom.

Barrel jumping on ice skates ■ The official distance record is 29 ft 5 in over 18 barrels, by Yvon Jolin at Terrebonne, Quebec, Canada on 25 Jan 1981.

The women's record is 20 ft 4½ in over 11 barrels, by Janet Hainstock in Michigan on 15 Mar 1980.

Barrel rolling ■ The record for rolling a full 36-gallon metal beer barrel over a measured mile is 8 min 7·2 sec, by Phillip Randle, Steve Hewitt, John Round, Trevor Bradley, Colin Barnes and Ray Glover of Haunchwood Col lieries Institute and Social Club, Nuneaton, Warwickshire, United Kingdom on 15 Aug 1982.

A team of 10 rolled a 140 lb barrel 150 miles in 30 hr 31 min in Chlumcany, Czechoslovakia on 27–28 Oct 1982.

Barrow pushing ■ The heaviest loaded one-wheeled barrow pushed for a minimum 200 level feet is one loaded with bricks weighing a gross 8,275 lb through 243 ft by John Sarich at London, Ontario, Canada on 19 Feb 1987.

Barrow racing ■ The fastest time attained in a 1 mile wheelbarrow race is 4 min 48·51 sec, by Piet Pitzer and Jaco Erasmus at the Trans valia High School, Vanderbijlpark, South Africa on 3 Oct 1987.

Baseball holding ■ Travis S. Johnson, age 16, of Elsberry, MO, held nine regulation baseballs in one hand without any adhesives on 14 Sep 1989.

Bathtub racing ■ The record for a 36 mile bathtub race is 1 hr 22 min 27 sec, by Greg Mutton at the Grafton Jacaranda Festival, New South Wales, Australia on 8 Nov 1987. Tubs are limited to 75 in and 6-hp motors.

The greatest distance for paddling a hand-propelled bathtub in 24 hr is 90·5 miles, by 13 members of Aldington Prison Officers Social Club, near Ashford, Kent, United Kingdom on 28–29 May 1983.

Baton twirling ■ Victor Cerda, Sol Lozano, Harry Little III (leader) and Manuel Rodriguez twirled batons for 122½ hours from 24–29 Jun 1984 in El Seveno, CA.

The greatest number of complete spins done between tossing a baton into the air and catch ing it is 10, by Donald Garcia, on the British Broadcasting Corporation 'Record Breakers' program on 9 Dec 1986.

The record for women is seven, by Lisa Fedick on the same program, Joanne Holloway, at the UK National Baton Twirling Association Cham pionships in Paignton, Devon, United Kingdom on 29 Oct 1987 and Rachel Hayes on 18 Sep 1988, also later shown on the British Broadcasting

Corporation 'Record Breakers' program.

Bed making ■ The pair record for making a bed with 1 blanket, 2 sheets, an undersheet, an uncased pillow, 1 bedspread and 'hospital' corners is 19·0 sec, by Sisters Jill Bradbury and Chris Humpish of Hammersmith Hospital, London, United Kingdom on 8 Oct 1985 on British Broadcasting Corporation TV's 'Record Breakers' program.

The record time for one person to make a bed, using the rigorous rules of the Australian Bedmaking Championships, is 28·2 sec, by Wendy Wall, 34, of Hebersham, Sydney, New South Wales on 30 Nov 1978.

Bed of nails ■ Ken Owen, 48, of Pontypridd, Mid Glamorgan, United Kingdom lay on a bed of nails for a total of 300 hr, including 132 hr 30 min without a break, from 3–14 May 1986, starting at Bridgend Hotel, Pontygwaith and concluding at the The Three Horse Shoes, Tonteg, Pontypridd. Much longer durations are claimed by uninvigilated *fakirs* — the most extreme case being *Silki* who claimed 111 days in São Paulo, Brazil ending on 24 Aug 1969.

Bed pushing ■ The longest recorded push of a normally sessile object is of 3,233 miles, in the case of a wheeled hospital bed by a team of nine employees of Bruntsfield Bedding Centre, Edinburgh, United Kingdom, 21 Jun–26 Jul 1979.

Bed race ■ The course record for the 10-mile Chew Valley Lake race (established 1977) in Avon, United Kingdom is 50 min, by the Westbury Harriers' three-man bed team.

Beer keg lifting ■ Tommy Gaskin raised a keg of beer weighing 137·79 lb above his head 656 times in the space of 6 hr at Newry, County Down, United Kingdom on 28 Oct 1989.

Beer mat flipping ■ Dean Gould of Felixstowe, Suffolk, United Kingdom flipped and caught a pile of 102 mats (490 gsm wood pulp board) through 180 degrees in Hamburg, West Germany on 18 Mar 1988.

Beer stein carrying ■ Barmaid Rosie Schedelbauer covered a distance of 49 ft 2½ in in 4 sec with five full steins in each hand in a televised contest at Königssee, West Germany on 29 Jun 1981.

Best man ■ The world champion 'best man' is Ting Ming Siong, from Sibu, Sarawak, in Malaysia, who officiated for the 561st time since 1976 in March 1990.

Bicycle, most mounting simultaneously ■ On 30 Jun 1988 at Semarang, Central Java, Indonesia, 19 members of the Jago Sport Club mounted and rode a single bicycle a distance of 656 ft 2 in.

Boat trot ■ The Luleå Sailing Society organized 437 sailboats belonging to members of their club to be moored into a double-ring pattern in the shape of a sunflower at Luleå, Sweden on 2 Jul 1988.

Boomerang throwing ■ The earliest mention of a word similar to *boomerang* is *wo-murrang* in Collins' *Acct. N. S. Wales Vocab.* 1798. The earliest Australian account of a returning boomerang (term established 1827) was in 1831 by Major (later Sir Thomas) Mitchell.

The greatest number of consecutive two-handed catches is 801, by Stéphane Marguerite (France) on 26 Nov 1989 at Lyon, France. The longest out and return distance is one of 440 ft 3 in by Jim

Cucumber slicing ● Norman Johnson of Blackpool, United Kingdom holds the record for fast cucumber slicing, with 264 slices in 13·4 sec. He is seen here demonstrating his skills at Covent Garden, London, United Kingdom.

Youngblood (US), on 12 Jun 1989 at Gaithersburg, MD.

The longest flight duration (with self-catch) is one of 2 min 59·94 sec by Dennis Joyce (US) at Bethlehem, PA on 25 Jun 1987. John Flynn (US) caught 70 boomerang throws in 5 min at Geneva, Switzerland on 20 Aug 1988. The juggling record — the number of consecutive catches with two boomerangs, keeping at least one boomerang aloft at all times — is 89 by Chet Snouffer (US) at Gunnison, CO on 20 Aug 1989.

Brick carrying ■ The greatest distance achieved for carrying a 9-lb brick in a nominated ungloved hand in an uncradled downward pincer grip is 61¾ miles by Reg Morris of Walsall, West Midlands, United Kingdom on 16 Jul 1985.

The women's record for a 9 lb 12 oz brick is 22½ miles by Wendy Morris of Walsall, West Midlands, United Kingdom on 28 Apr 1986.

Bricklifting ■ Russ Holland of Mansfield Woodhouse, Nottinghamshire, United Kingdom lifted 28 bricks on 24 Jul 1989. Before a standardized set of rules had been drawn up, Geoff Capes had also lifted 28 bricks, at Bidford-on-Avon, Warwickshire, United Kingdom on 18 Sep 1987.

Bricklaying ■ Robert Boll of Burbank, IL, laid 914 bricks in 60 min to win the first US Speed Bricklaying competition at Lansing, MI on 21 Feb 1987.

Brick throwing ■ The greatest reported distance for throwing a standard 5-lb building brick is 146 ft 1 in, by Geoff Capes at Braybrook School, Orton Goldhay, Cambridgeshire, United Kingdom on 19 Jul 1978.

Bubble ■ David Stein of New York created a 50-ft long bubble on 6 Jun 1988. He made the bubble using a bubble wand, dishwashing liquid and water.

Bubble gum blowing ■ The greatest reported diameter for a bubble gum bubble under the strict rules of this highly competitive activity is 22 in, by Susan Montgomery Williams of Fresno, CA in June 1985.

Burial alive ■ Voluntary burial alive claims (of which claims up to 217 days have been published) are inadmissible unless the depth of the coffin is a minimum 6 ft 6¾ in below ground; the coffin has a maximum cubic capacity of 54 ft³, and the single aperture for communication and feeding has a maximum dimension of 4 in. 'Country' Bill White, 50, was so buried from 31 Jul to 19 Dec 1981 (141 days) in Killeen, TX.

Camping out ■ The silent Indian *fakir* Mastram Bapu ('contented father') remained on the same spot by the roadside in the village of Chitra for 22 years from 1960–82.

Card throwing ■ Kevin St Onge threw a standard playing card 185 ft 1 in at the Henry Ford Community College Campus, Dearborn, MI on 12 Jun 1979.

Cardiopulmonary resuscitation ■ Three teams of two, consisting of David Bailey and Les Williams, Angie Drinkard and Rich Martel, and Michelle Tyler and Sherri Johnson, all completed CPR marathons (cardiopulmonary resuscitation — 15 — compressions alternating with two breaths) of 120 hr 6 min from 1–6 Sep 1988 at Melbourne, FL.

Carriage driving ■ The only man to drive 48 horses in a single hitch is Dick Sparrow of Zearing, IA, between 1972–77. The lead horses were on reins 135 ft long.

Car wrecking ■ The greatest number of cars wrecked in a stunting career is 1,997 to 1 Jun 1990 by Dick Sheppard of Gloucester, United Kingdom.

Catapulting ■ The greatest recorded distance for a catapult shot is 1,362 ft by James M. Pfotenhauer, using a patented 17 ft 1½-in Monarch IV Supershot and a 53-caliber lead musket ball on Ski Hill Road, Escanaba, MI on 10 Sep 1977.

Champagne cork flight ■ The longest distance from an untreated and unheated bottle 4 ft from level ground is 177 ft 9 in, reached by Professor Emeritus Heinrich Medicus, RPI, at the Woodbury Vineyards Winery, NY on 5 Jun 1988.

Champagne fountain ■ The greatest number of stories achieved in a champagne fountain, successfully filled from the top and using 10,404 traditional long-stem glasses, is 44 (height 24 ft 8 in), achieved by Pascal Leclerc at the Biltmore Hotel, Los Angeles, CA on 18 Jun 1984.

Cigar box balancing ■ Bruce Block balanced 212 ungimmicked cigar boxes on his chin for 13·5 sec at Rock Island, IL on 19 Feb 1990.

Clapping ■ The duration record for continuous clapping (sustaining an average of 160 claps per min audible at 120 yd) is 58 hr 9 min by V. Jeyaraman of Tamil Nadu, India from 12–15 Feb 1988.

Club swinging ■ Albert Rayner set a world record of 17,512 revolutions (4·9 per sec) in 60 min at Wakefield, West Yorkshire, United Kingdom on 27 Jul 1981. M. Dobrilla swung continuously for 144 hr at Cobar, New South Wales, Australia, finishing on 15 Sep 1913.

Coal shoveling ■ The record for filling a 1,120 lb hopper with coal is 29·4 sec, by Piet Groot at the Inangahua A and P Show, New Zealand on 1 Jan 1985.

Coin balancing ■ Hiem Shda of Kiriat Mozkien, Israel stacked a pyramid of 847 coins on the edge of a coin freestanding vertically on the base of a coin, which was on a table on 30 Jul 1989.

The tallest single column of coins ever stacked on the edge of a coin is 205 Canadian 25-cent pieces on top of a Canadian Olympic commemorative coin, by Bruce McConachy (b. 1963) of West Vancouver, BC, Canada for Fuji-TV in Tokyo, Japan on 24 Feb 1985.

Coin snatching ■ The greatest number of British 10 pence pieces (approximately the size of a quarter) clean-caught from being flipped from the back of a forearm into the same downward palm is 140 by Dean Gould in Hamburg, West Germany on 19 Mar 1988.

Cow chip tossing ■ The record distances in the sport of throwing dried cow chips depend on whether or not the projectile may be 'molded into a spherical shape.' The greatest distance achieved under the 'non-sphericalization and 100 percent organic' rule (established in 1970) is 266 ft, by Steve Urner at the Mountain Festival, Tehachapi, CA on 14 Aug 1981.

Crawling ■ The longest continuous voluntary crawl (progression with one or other knee in unbroken contact with the ground) on record is 28½ miles, by Reg Morris of Walsall, West Midlands, United Kingdom on 29 Jul 1988. The crawl took place on a measured course 1½ miles long. It took 9½ hours and 19 laps of the track to gain the record.

Over a space of 15 months ending on 9 Mar 1985, Jagdish Chander, 32, crawled 870 miles from Aligarh to Jamma, India to propitiate his favorite Hindu goddess, Mata.

Crochet ■ Barbara Jean Sonntag (b. 1938) of Craig, CO crocheted 330 shells plus five stitches (equivalent to 4,412 stitches) in 30 min at a rate of 147 stitches a minute on 13 Jan 1981.

Sybille Anthony completed a 120-hr crochet marathon at Toombul Shopping-town, Queensland, Australia on 7 Oct 1977.

Cucumber slicing ■ Norman Johnson of Blackpool College, Lancashire, United Kingdom set a record of 13·4 sec for slicing a 12 in cucumber, 1½ in in diameter, at 22 slices to the inch (total 264 slices) at *West Deutscher Rundfunk* in Cologne, West Germany on 3 Apr 1983.

Dancing dragon ■ The longest dancing dragon, created by schoolchildren and volunteers from St Helens, Merseyside, United Kingdom in June and July 1989, was 985 ft long. It was made from foil, paper, bamboo and cane and decorated with scales. Five hundred people then brought it to life in dance as part of the Mayor's Carnival in St Helens on 30 Jul 1989.

Debating ■ Students at University College, Dublin, Republic of Ireland debated the motion that 'Every Dog Should Have Its Day' for 503 hr 45 min, from 16 Nov–7 Dec 1988.

Demolition work ■ Fifteen members of the Black Leopard Karate Club demolished a seven-room wooden farmhouse west of Elnora, Alberta, Canada in 3 hr 18 min by foot and empty hand on 13 Jun 1982.

Domino stacking ■ David Coburn successfully stacked 291 dominoes on a single supporting domino on 19 Aug 1988 in Miami, FL.

Domino toppling ■ The greatest number set up single-handed and toppled is 281,581 out of 320,236 by Klaus Friedrich, 22, in Bayern, West Germany on 27 Jan 1984. The dominoes fell within 12 min 57·3 sec, having taken 31 days (10 hours daily) to set up.

Thirty students at Delft, Eindhoven and Tente Technical Universities in the Netherlands set up 1,500,000 dominoes depicting all of the European Community (EC) member countries. Of these, 1,382,101 were toppled by one push on 2 Jan 1988.

Drink round ■ Liam Fallon treated 1,613 people to a free drink at a charity fund-raising gathering on 4 Jul 1987 at Lord Byron's Wine Bar, Solihull, Warwickshire, United Kingdom.

Drumming ■ The world duration drumming record is 1,224 hr (51 days), by Trevor Mitchell at Scunthorpe, Humber side, United Kingdom from 20 Mar to 10 May 1990.

United States ■ The American record for drumming is 1,217 hr (50 days 17 hr) by Don Murphy at Fort Mill, SC from 28 May to 18 Jul 1989.

Ducks and drakes (stone skipping) ■ The record is 29 skips (14 plinkers and 15 pitty-pats), by Arthur Ring, 69, at Midway Beach, CA on 4 Aug 1984 and Jerdone 'Jerry' McGhee, 42, at Wimberley, TX on 18 Nov 1986.

Eating ■ Michel Lotito (b. 15 Jun 1950) of Grenoble, France, known as Monsieur Mangetout, has been eating metal and glass since 1959. Gastroenterologists have X-rayed his stomach and have described his ability to consume 2 lb of metal per day as unique. His diet since 1966 has included 10 bicycles, a supermarket trolley in 4½ days, 7 TV sets, 6 chandeliers and a low-calorie Cessna light aircraft, which he ate in Caracas, Venezuela. He is said to have provided the only example in history of a coffin (handles and all) ending up inside a man.

Egg and spoon racing ■ Dale Lyons of Meriden, West Midlands, United Kingdom ran 29·9 miles while carrying a dessert spoon with a fresh egg on it in 4 hr 18 min on 23 Apr 1990.

United States ■ Chris Riggio of San Francisco, CA completed a 28·5 mile fresh egg and dessert spoon marathon in 4 hr 34 min on 7 Oct 1979.

Egg dropping ■ The greatest height from which fresh eggs have been dropped (to earth) and remained intact is 650 ft, by David S. Donoghue from a helicopter on 2 Oct 1979 on a golf course in Tokyo, Japan.

Egg hunt ■ The greatest egg hunt on record involved 72,000 hard-boiled eggs and 40,000 candy eggs at the 26th annual Garrison Egg Hunt at Homer, GA on 7 Apr 1985.

Egg shelling ■ Two kitchen hands, Harold Witcomb and Gerald Harding, shelled 1,050 dozen eggs in a 7¼-hr shift at Bowyers, Trowbridge, Wiltshire, United Kingdom on 23 Apr 1971. Both were blind.

Egg throwing ■ The longest authenticated distance for throwing a fresh hen's egg without breaking it is 317 ft 10 in, by Risto Antikainen to Jyrki Korhonen at Siilinjarvi, Finland on 6 Sep 1981.

Escalator riding ■ The record for traveling a pair of 'up' and 'down' escalators is 101 hr, by David Beattie and Adrian Simons at Top Shop, Oxford Street, London, United Kingdom from 17–21 Jul 1989. They each traveled 133·19 miles.

Escapology ■ The most renowned of all escape artists has been Ehrich Weiss, *alias* Harry Houdini (1874–1926), who pioneered underwater escapes from locked, roped and weighted containers while handcuffed and shackled with irons.

A manufacturer of straitjackets acknowledges that an escapologist 'skilled in the art of bone and muscle manipulation' could escape from a standard jacket in seconds. There are, however, methods by which such circumvention can itself be circumvented. Nick Janson of Benfleet, Essex, United Kingdom has escaped from handcuffs locked on him by more than 1,300 different police officers since 1954.

Family tree ■ The farthest back the lineage of any family has been traced is that of K'ung Ch'iu or Confucius (551–479 B.C.). His great-great-great-great grandfather K'ung Chia is known from the eigth century B.C. This man's 85th lineal descendants Wei-yi (b. 1939) and Wei-ning (b. 1947) live today in Taiwan (Formosa).

Fashion show ■ The longest distance covered by female models is 71·1 miles from 19–21 Sep 1983 by Roberta Brown and Lorraine McCourt at Parke's Hotel, Dublin, Ireland.

Male model Eddie Warke covered a further 11·9 miles on the catwalk.

Faux pas ■ If measured by financial consequence, the greatest faux pas on record was that of the young multimillionaire James Gordon Bennett, committed on 1 Jan 1877 at the family mansion of his demure fiancée, one Caroline May, of Fifth Avenue, NY. Bennett arrived in a two-horse cutter late and obviously in wine. By dint of intricate footwork, he gained the portals to enter the withdrawing room, where he was the cynosure of all eyes. He mistook the fireplace for a plumbing fixture more usually reserved for another purpose. The May family broke the engagement and Bennett (1841–1918) was obliged to spend the rest of his foot-loose and fancy-free life based in Paris with the resultant noncollection of millions of tax dollars by the US Treasury.

Feminine beauty ■ Female pulchritude, being qualitative rather than quantitative, does not lend itself to records. It has been suggested that if the face of Helen of Troy (c. 1200 B.C.) was capable of launching 1,000 ships, a unit of beauty sufficient to launch one ship should be a milli-helen.

The first international beauty contest was staged by P. T. Barnum (with the public to be the judges) in the United States in June 1855.

The first Miss America contest was staged at Atlantic City, NJ in 1921 and was won by a thin blue-eyed blonde with a 30-in chest, Margaret Gorman.

The world's largest annual beauty pageants are the Miss World (inaugurated 1951) and Miss Universe (1952) contests. The most successful country in the latter contest has been the United States, with winners in 1954, '56, '60, '67, '80, '82. The greatest number of countries represented in the Miss Universe contest was 81 in 1983.

The country that has produced the most winners in the Miss World contest is the United Kingdom, with five. They were Rosemarie Frankland (1961); Ann Sidney (1964); Lesley Langley (1965); Helen Morgan (1974), who resigned, and Sarah-Jane Hutt (1983).

The maximum number of contestants was 84 in November 1988. The shortest reign was 18 hours, by Miss Germany (Gabriella Brum) in 1980.

Field gun pull ■ Three teams of eight members from 55 Ordnance Company (Volunteers) Royal Army Ordnance Corps pulled a 25-pounder field gun over a distance of 85·7 miles in 24 hours in Hounslow, Middlesex, United Kingdom on 15–16 Apr 1988.

Fine spinning ■ The longest thread of wool, hand-spun and plied to weigh 0·35 oz, was one with a length of 1,815 ft 3 in, achieved by Julitha Barber of Bull Creek, Western Australia, Australia at the International Highland Spin-In, Bothwell, Tasmania, Australia on 1 Mar 1989.

Fire pumping ■ The greatest gallonage stirrup-pumped by a team of eight in an 80-hr charity pump is 27,414 gal by fire fighters representing Grampian Fire Brigade, from 17–20 Aug 1989 at Aberdeen, Grampian, United Kingdom.

Fire pump manhandling ■ The longest unaided tow of a fire appliance in excess of 10 cwt in 24 hr on a closed circuit is 223 miles by a 32-man team of the Dublin Fire Brigade with an 1,144 lb fire pump on 20–21 Jun 1987.

Flute marathon ■ The longest recorded marathon by a flutist is 61 hr by Joseph Shury of the Sri Chinmoy Marathon Team, Toronto, Ontario, Canada from 21–23 Mar 1986.

Flying disc throwing (formerly Frisbee) ■ The World Flying Disc Federation distance records are, men: 623 ft 7 in by Sam Ferrans (US), 2 Jul 1988 at La Habra, CA; and women: 410 ft 5 in by Chris O'Cleary (US), 22 Jul 1988 at San Francisco, CA. The throw, run and catch records are, men: 303 ft 11 in by Hiroshi Oshima (Japan), 20 Jul 1988 at San Francisco, CA; and women: 196 ft 11 in by Judy Horowitz (US), 29 Jun 1985 at La Mirada, CA.

The 24-hour distance records for a pair are, men: 362·4 miles by Leonard Muise and Gabe Ontiveros (US), 21–22 Sep 1988 at Carson, CA; and women: 115·7 miles by Jo Cahow and Amy Berard (US), 30–31 Dec 1979 at Pasadena, CA.

The maximum time aloft records are, men: 16·72 sec by Don Cain (US), 26 May 1984 at Philadelphia, PA; and women: 11·75 sec by Anni Kreml (US), 21 Jul 1988 at San Francisco, CA.

Footbag ■ The world record for keeping a footbag airborne is 48,825 consecutive kicks or hacks by Ted Martin (US) at Memphis, TN on 4 Jun 1988. The women's record is held by Francine Beaudry (Canada), with 15,458 on 28 Jul 1987 at Golden, CO. The sport originated in Oregon in 1972 and was invented by John Stalberger (US).

Garbage collection ■ The greatest number of volunteers involved in collecting garbage on one day is 64,500, who cleaned up 2,900·03 miles of shoreline in the State of Florida on 23 Sep 1989 as part of the 'National Beach Clean–Up Campaign,' sponsored by the Center for Marine Conservation, a Washington, D.C.–based group.

Gladiatorial combat ■ Emperor Trajan of Rome (A.D. 98–117) staged a display involving 4,941 pairs of gladiators over 117 days.

Publius Ostorius, a freedman, survived 51 combats in Pompeii.

Gold panning ■ The fastest time for 'panning' eight planted gold nuggets in a 10-in diameter pan is 7·55 sec by Don Roberts of Diamond Bar, CA in the 27th World Gold Panning Championship on 16 Apr 1989 at Dahlonega, GA.

The female record is 10·03 sec, by Susan Bryeans of Fullerton, CA at the 23rd World Gold Panning Championship on 6 Mar 1983 at Knotts Berry Farm, Buena Park, CA.

Golf ball balancing ■ Lang Martin balanced seven golf balls vertically without adhesive at Charlotte, NC on 9 Feb 1980.

Grape catching ■ The greatest distance at

which a grape thrown from level ground has been caught in the mouth is 319 ft 8 in, by Arden Chapman at Northeast Louisiana University, Monroe on 18 Jul 1980.

Grave digging ■ It is recorded that Johann Heinrich Karl Thieme, sexton of Aldenburg, Germany, dug 23,311 graves during a 50-year career. In 1826 his understudy dug *his* grave.

Guitar playing ■ The longest recorded solo guitar-playing marathon is one of 300 hr by Vincent Paxton at the Lord Nelson public house, Winterslow, Wiltshire, United Kingdom from 23 Nov–6 Dec 1986. The fastest guitar playing ever was by Rick Raven (b. Gary Clarke), who played 5,400 notes in a minute at the Jacobean Nite Club, Stockport, Greater Manchester, United Kingdom on 27 Apr 1989.

Gum boot throwing ■ The longest recorded distance for 'Wellie wanging' (size 8 Challenger Dunlop Boot) is 173 ft, by Tony Rod-

gers of Warminster, Wiltshire, United Kingdom on 9 Sep 1978. Rosemary Payne established the women's record at Cannon Hill Park, Birmingham on 21 Jun 1975 with 129 ft 11 in.

Gum wrapper chain ■ The longest gum wrapper chain on record was 5,967 ft in length, and was made by Cathy Ushler of Redmond, WA between 1969 and 1987.

Gun running ■ The record for the Royal Tournament Naval Field Gun Competition (instituted 1907, with present rules since 1913) is 2 min 40·6 sec by the Portsmouth Command Field Gun crew at Earl's Court, London, United Kingdom on 19 Jul 1984. The barrel alone weighs 8 cwt. The wall is 5 ft high and the chasm 28 ft across.

Haggis hurling ■ The longest recorded distance for throwing a haggis (min. weight 1 lb 8 oz) is 180 ft 10 in, by Alan Pettigrew on Inchmurrin, Loch Lomond, Strathclyde, United Kingdom on 24 May 1984.

Hairdressing ■ Elie Algranti cut, set and styled hair continuously for 415 hr from 4–21 Feb 1989 in Mossel Bay, South Africa.

Hair splitting ■ The greatest reported

achievement in hair splitting has been that of the former champion cyclist and craftsman Alfred West (1901–85), who succeeded in splitting a human hair 17 times into 18 parts on eight occasions.

Handbell ringing ■ The longest recorded handbell-ringing recital has been one of 60 hr 3 min by 12 handbell ringers of Ecclesfield School, Sheffield, South Yorkshire, United Kingdom from 21–23 Oct 1989.

Handshaking ■ Rainer Vikström of Turku, Finland shook 19,592 different hands in 8 hours on 15 May 1988 during Turku's Fourth Annual Spring Market 'Manun Markkinat.'

The record number of hands shaken by a public figure at an official function was 8,513 by President Theodore Roosevelt (1858–1919) at a New Year's Day White House presentation in Washington, D.C. on 1 Jan 1907.

Hedge laying ■ John Williams of Sennybridge and David James of Llanwern, Brecon, United Kingdom hedged by the 'stake and pleach' method a total of 792 ft in 11 hr 24 min on 28 Apr 1986.

High diving ■ The highest regularly performed head-first dives are those of professional divers from La Quebrada ('The Break in the Rocks') at Acapulco, Mexico, a height of 87½ ft. The base rocks, 21 ft out from the takeoff, necessitate a leap of 27 ft out. The water is 12 ft deep.

The world record high dive is 176 ft 10 in, by Olivier Favre (Switzerland) at Villers-le-Lac, France on 30 Aug 1987.

The women's record is 120 ft, by Lucy Wardle (US) at Ocean Park, Hong Kong on 6 Apr 1985.

On 11 Feb 1968 Jeffrey Kramer, 24, leapt off the George Washington Bridge, 250 ft above the Hudson River, New York City, and survived.

Of the 696 identified people who have made 240-ft suicide dives from the Golden Gate Bridge, San Francisco, CA since 1937, 12 survived, of whom Todd Sharratt was the only one who managed to swim ashore unaided.

Col Harry A. Froboess (Switzerland) jumped 360 ft into the Bodensee from the airship *Graf Hindenburg* on 22 Jun 1936.

The greatest height reported for a dive into an air bag is 326 ft by stuntman Dan Koko from the top of Vegas World Hotel and Casino into a 20 × 40 × 14 ft target on 13 Aug 1984. His impact speed was 88 mph.

Kitty O'Neill dived 180 ft from a helicopter over Northridge, CA on 9 Sep 1979 onto an air cushion measuring 30 × 60 ft for a TV film stunt.

Hod carrying ■ Jim Ford of Bury, Lancashire, United Kingdom carried bricks totaling 355 lb up the minimum 12-ft ladder (17 rungs) on 28 Jun 1984 at Hever Castle, Kent, United Kingdom on the 'International Guinness TV Show' hosted by David Frost.

Eric Stenman of Jakobstad, Finland carried 74 bricks of 8·8 lb each, so totaling 651 lb, in a 8·8 lb hod 16·4 ft on the flat before ascending a runged ramp to a height of 7 ft on 25 Jul 1939.

Homework — longest on ice ■ In 1967, Thomas Litz, a teacher in Switzerland, set aside some homework, which he marked but forgot to return. It was only in 1988, while sorting through old papers, that he came across the exercises. One of the pupils, Mark Johnson, had by this time himself become a teacher at the school, and

on 1 Feb 1988 was given his homework back, 21 years late.

Hoop rolling ■ In 1968 it was reported that Zolilio Diaz (Spain) had rolled a hoop 600 miles from Mieres to Madrid, Spain and back in 18 days.

Hop-scotch ■ The longest recorded hop-scotch marathon is one of 101 hr 15 min by Mark Harrison and Tony Lunn at the Studio Night Club, Leicester, United Kingdom from 30 Sep to 4 Oct 1985.

United States ■ The longest recorded hop scotch marathon is one of 100 hr by Joellen Glass and Lesa Young of Seattle, WA between 1–5 Sept 1982.

House of cards ■ The greatest number of stories achieved in building freestanding houses of standard playing cards is 68, to a height of 12 ft 10 in, built by John Sain, 15, of South Bend, IN in May 1984.

Hula-Hooping ■ The highest claim for sustaining gyrating hoops between shoulders and hips is 81, by William Kleeman 'Chico' Johnson (b. 8 Jul 1939) on British Broadcasting Corporation TV's 'Record Breakers' on 18 Sep 1983. Three complete gyrations are mandatory.

The longest marathon for a single hoop is 90 hr, by Roxann Rose of Pullman, WA from 2–6 Apr 1987.

Human cannonball ■ The first human cannonball was Emilio Onra ne Maître jean at the Cirque d'Hiver, Paris, France on 21 Nov 1875.

The record distance for firing a human from a cannon is 175 ft, in the case of Emanuel Zacchini, son of the pioneer Hugo Zacchini, in the Ringling Bros. and Barnum & Bailey Circus, Madison Square Gardens, New York City in 1940. His muzzle velocity has been estimated at 54 mph. On his retirement the management was fortunate in finding that his daughter Florinda was of the same caliber.

An experiment on Yorkshire TV, United Kingdom on 17 Aug 1978 showed that when Miss Sue Evans, 17, was fired, she was ⅜ in shorter on landing.

Human centipede ■ The largest 'human centipede' to move 98 ft 5 in (with ankles firmly tied together) consisted of 1,004 members of the Singapore Armed Forces GI Army. Not one single person fell over in the course of the walk, which took place on 17 Jun 1990 at Marina Mall, Singapore.

Human fly ■ The longest climb achieved on the vertical face of a building occurred on 26 Jun 1986 when Daniel Goodwin, 30, of California climbed a record 1,125 ft up the outside of the 1,815 ft 5 in CN Tower in Toronto, Canada (the tallest self-supporting tower in the world) using neither climbing aids nor safety equipment.

Ironing ■ The duration record for ironing is 128 hr by Nigel Towning of Grantham, Lincolnshire, United Kingdom, from 3–8 Oct 1988.

Joke cracking ■ Felipe Carbonell of Lima, Peru told jokes for 72 hr at the Alfa Hotel, Lisbon, Portugal from 18–21 Mar 1988.

The duo record is 60 hr, by Derek Denniss and John Evans at Sandton City, Johannesburg, South Africa from 8–10 Sep 1988.

Jumble sale ■ The Cleveland Convention Center, OH White Elephant Sale (instituted 1933) on 18–19 Oct 1983 raised $427,935·21. The

greatest amount of money raised at a one-day sale is $170,139·76 at the 56th one-day rummage sale organized by the Winnetka Congregational Church, IL on 12 May 1988.

Kissing ■ Eddie Levin and Delphine Crha celebrated the breaking of the record for the longest ever kiss of 17 days 10½ hr in Chicago, IL on 24 Sep 1984 with a kiss.

James Whale kissed 4,525 women in 8 hr at the Yorkshire TV Telethon garden party in Leeds, West Yorkshire, United Kingdom on 30 May 1988, a rate of 1 every 6·36 sec.

Kite flying ■ The following records are all recognized by *Kite Lines* magazine:–

The longest kite flown was 2,313 ft in length, which was made and flown by Michel Trouillet, Pierre Agniel and Philippe Bertron, at Nîmes, France on 15 Nov 1987. The largest kite flown was one of 5,952 ft². It was first flown by a Dutch team on the beach at Scheveningen, Netherlands on 8 Aug 1981.

The classic record height is 31,955 ft by a train of eight kites over Lindenberg, Germany on 1 Aug 1919. The altitude record for a single kite is 12,471 ft, in the case of a kite flown by Henry Helm Clayton and A. E. Sweetland at Milton, MA on 28 Feb 1898.

The greatest number of kites flown on a single line is 2,233 by the Hiroshima Kite Club, at Futtsu, Chiba Prefecture, Japan under the direction of Kinji Tsuda on 15 Mar 1987. The fastest speed attained by a kite was 120 mph for a kite flown by Pete DiGiacomo at Ocean City, MD on 22 Sep 1989. The greatest lift by a single kite was one of 728 lb, achieved by a kite flown by G. William Tyrrell Jr, also at Ocean City, MD on 23 Sep 1984.

The longest recorded flight is one of 180 hr 17 min by the Edmonds Community College team at Long Beach, WA from 21–29 Aug 1982. Managing the flight of the J-25 parafoil was Harry N. Osborne.

Knitting ■ The world's most prolific hand-knitter of all time has been Mrs Gwen Matthewman of Featherstone, West Yorkshire, United Kingdom. She attained a speed of 111 stitches per min in a test at Phildar's Wool Shop, Central Street, Leeds, West Yorkshire, United Kingdom on 29 Sep 1980. Her technique has been filmed by the world's only Professor of Knitting — a Japanese.

The Exeter Spinners — Audrey Felton, Christine Heap, Eileen Lancaster, Majorie Mellis, Ann Sandercock and Maria Scott — produced a sweater by hand from raw fleece in 1 hr 55 min 50·2 sec on 25 Sep 1983 at British Broadcasting Corporation Television Centre, London, United Kingdom.

Knot-tying ■ The fastest recorded time for tying the six Boy Scout Handbook Knots (square knot, sheet bend, sheep shank, clove hitch, round turn and two half hitches, and bowline) on individual ropes is 8·1 sec by Clinton R. Bailey, Sr, 52, of Pacific City, OR on 13 Apr 1977.

Land rowing ■ Ashrita Furman covered a distance of 68 miles from the Outerbridge Crossing (Perth Amboy, NJ) to Independence Mall (Philadelphia, PA), using a landrowing machine on 17 Jul 1987.

Laundry ■ The greatest quantity of laundry washed in a nine-hour working day is 140,204 lb, by staff at Central Linen Service, Kilkenny, South Australia, Australia on 18 May 1989.

Leap-frogging ■ The greatest distance

covered was 888·1 miles by 14 members of the class of 1988 of Hanover High School, in Hanover, NH, who started leap-frogging on 10 Jun 1988 and stopped 189 hrs 49 mins later, on 18 Jun 1988.

Life saving ■ In November 1974 the city of Galveston, TX and the Noon Optimist Club unveiled a plaque to the deaf-mute lifeguard Leroy Colombo (1905–74) who saved 907 people from drowning in the waters around Galveston Island from 1917 to his death.

Lifting with teeth ■ Joe Ponder of Love Valley, NC raised a pumpkin weighing 606 lb 18 in off the ground with his teeth at Circleville, OH on 19 Oct 1985.

'Hercules' John Massis (b. Wilfried Oscar Morbée, 4 Jun 1940, d. 11 Jul 1988) of Oostakker, Belgium prevented a helicopter from taking off using only a tooth bit harness in Los Angeles, CA on 7 Apr 1979 for a 'Guinness Spectacular' TV show.

Lightning, most times struck ■ The only man in the world to be struck by lightning seven times is ex-park ranger Roy C. Sullivan (US), the human lightning conductor of Virginia. His attraction for lightning began in 1942 (lost big toenail), and was resumed in July 1969 (lost eyebrows), in July 1970 (left shoulder seared), on 16 Apr 1972 (hair set on fire), on 7 Aug 1973 (new hair refired and legs seared), on 5 Jun 1976 (ankle injured), and he was sent to Waynesboro Hospital with chest and stomach burns on 25 Jun 1977 after being struck while fishing. In September 1983 he died by his own hand, reportedly rejected in love.

Limbo ■ The lowest height for a bar (flaming) under which a limbo dancer has passed is 6⅛ in off the floor, by Marlene Raymond, 15, at the Port of Spain Pavilion, Toronto, Canada on 24 Jun 1973.

The record on roller skates is 5¼ in, first achieved by Denise Culp of Rock Hill, SC on 22 Jan 1984. This has since been equaled by Tracey O'Callaghan on 2 Jun 1984 and Sandra Siviour on 30 Mar 1985, both at Bexley North, New South Wales, Australia; Jessie Ball on 27 Jun 1985 at Beverley Hills, New South Wales; and Kelly Foley on 22 May 1987; Magdalena Petrik and Meegan Anderson, both on 13 Apr 1988; and Michelle Boyle, Donna Bray and Jessica McLeish, on 21 May 1988, all at Parramatta, New South Wales. On 28 Jun 1988 Erika Howell of Brunswick, GA equaled this height, as did Kellie Boyle at Burwood, New South Wales on 9 Aug 1989 and Bahar (Jenny) Sonmez at Gosford, New South Wales on 26 Nov 1989. Junior J. Renaud (b. 7 Jun 1954), Australia became the first Official World Limbo Champion at the inaugural International Limbo Competition on 19 Feb 1974 at Port of Spain, Trinidad.

Lion taming ■ The greatest number of lions mastered and fed in a cage by an unaided lion tamer was 40, by 'Captain' Alfred Schneider in 1925. Clyde Raymond Beatty handled more than 40 'cats' (mixed lions and tigers) simultaneously.

Beatty (b. Bainbridge, OH, 10 Jun 1903, d. Ventura, CA, 19 Jul 1965) was the featured attraction at every show he appeared in for more than 40 years. He insisted upon being called a lion-trainer. More than 20 lion tamers have died of injuries since 1900.

Logrolling ■ The record number of International Championships is 10, by Jubiel Wickheim of Shawnigan Lake, British Columbia, Canada, between 1956 and 1969. At Albany, OR on 4 Jul

Fastest magician ● Eldon D. Wigton, *alias* Dr Eldoonie, performed 118 different tricks in 2 min at Kilbourne, OH on 1 Mar 1990.

1956 Wickheim rolled on a 14-in log against Chuck Harris of Kelso, WA for 2 hr 40 min before losing.

The youngest international logrolling champion is Cari Ann Hayer (b. 23 Jun 1977), who won her first championship on 15 Jul 1984 at Hayward, WI.

Magician, fastest ■ Eldon D. Wigton, *alias* Dr Eldoonie, performed 118 different tricks in 2 min at Kilbourne, OH on 1 Mar 1990.

Mantle of bees ■ Danielle Goullet was covered by a mantle of an estimated 141,000 bees weighing 41·89 lb at Darra, Australia on 24 Sep 1988.

Merry-go-round ■ The longest merry-go-round marathon on record is one of 312 hr 43 min by Gary Mandau, Chris Lyons and Dana Dover in Portland, OR from 20 Aug–2 Sep 1976.

Message in a bottle ■ The longest recorded interval between drop and pickup is 73 years in the case of a message thrown from the SS *Arawatta* out of Cairns, Queensland, Australia on 9 Jun 1910 in a lotion bottle and reported to be found on Moreton Island on 6 Jun 1983.

Meteorological balloon inflation ■ The inflation of a standardized meteorological balloon to a diameter of 8 ft against time was achieved by Nicholas Berkeley Mason in 57 min 7 sec for a Fuji TV program in Tokyo, Japan on 9 Mar 1986.

Milk bottle balancing ■ The greatest distance walked by a person continuously balancing a full pint milk bottle on the head is 40·4 miles by Milind Deshmukh, from Pune to Lonavala, in India, on 22 Mar 1990.

United States ■ The greatest distance walked by a person continuously balancing a full pint milk bottle on the head in the United States is 32·9 miles by Ashrita Furman of New York at Phuket, Thailand on 23 Jan 1989.

Milk crate balancing ■ Frank Charles balanced 24 milk crates, with a total weight of

74 lb, on his chin for 19 sec at Leyton Youth Centre, London, United Kingdom on 30 Jul 1988.

Morse ■ The highest recorded speed at which anyone has received Morse code is 75·2 words per minute — over 17 symbols per second. This was achieved by Ted R. McElroy of the United States in a tournament at Asheville, NC on 2 Jul 1939.

The highest speed recorded for hand-key transmitting is 175 symbols a minute by Harry A. Turner of the US Army Signal Corps at Camp Crowder, MO on 9 Nov 1942.

Thomas Morris, a GPO operator, is reputed to have been able to send at 39–40 wpm *c.* 1919 but this is not verifiable.

Musical chairs ■ The largest game on record was one starting with 8,238 participants, ending with Xu Chong Wei on the last chair, which was held at the Anglo-Chinese School, Singapore on 5 Aug 1989.

Musical march ■ The longest recorded musical march was one of 42·5 miles at Wheeling, WV by the Wheeling Park High School Marching Band on 21 Oct 1989. Of the 69 members who started, 31 managed to complete the march, in 14 hr 53 min.

Needle threading ■ The record number of times that a strand of cotton has been threaded through a number 13 needle (eye ½ in × ¹⁄₁₆ in) in 2 hr is 6,062, set by Brajesh Shrivastava at Gautam Nagar, Bhopal, India on 21 Apr 1990.

United States ■ The record number of times that a strand of cotton has been threaded through a number 13 needle (eye ½ in × ¹⁄₁₆ in) in 2 hr is 5,370, set by Diane Sharp on 1 Aug 1987 at the Charitable Union's centenary event, Battle Creek, MI.

Noodle making ■ Mark Pi of the China Gate Restaurant, Columbus, OH made 2,048 noodle strings (over 5 ft) in 34·5 sec on 12 Feb 1983.

Omelet making ■ The greatest number of two-egg omelets made in 30 min is 427, by Howard Helmer at the International Poultry Trade Show held at Atlanta, GA on 2 Feb 1990.

Onion peeling ■ The record for peeling 50 lb of onions is 3 min 18 sec by Alan St Jean in Plainfield, CT on 6 Jul 1980.

Under revised rules stipulating a minimum of 50 onions, Alfonso Salvo of York, PA peeled 50 lb of onions (52 onions) in 5 min 23 sec on 28 Oct 1980.

Organ ■ The longest recorded electric organ marathon is one of 440 hr by Tony Peters at Sheppey Beach Social Club, Isle of Sheppey, Kent, United Kingdom from 20 Apr–8 May 1987.

The longest church organ recital ever sustained has been 119 hr, by Martin Stanley at St Mary the Virgin, Brixham, Devon, United Kingdom from 25–30 Aug 1986.

Oyster opening ■ The record for opening oysters is 100 in 2 min 21·65 sec, by Mike Racz in Invercargill, New Zealand on 26 Jun 1988.

Paddle boating ■ The longest recorded voyage is 2,226 miles in 103 days by the foot power of Mick Sigrist and Brad Rud down the Mississippi River from 4 Aug–11 Nov 1979.

Pancake tossing ■ The greatest number of times a pancake has been tossed in 2 minutes is 281, by Judith Aldridge on 27 Feb 1990 in the Merry Hill shopping center at Dudley, West Midlands, United Kingdom.

Piano playing ■ The record for piano playing is 1,218 hr (50 days 18 hr), playing 22 hr every day (with 5 min intervals each playing hour) from 7 May to 27 Jun 1982, by David Scott at Wagga Wagga League Football Club, New South Wales, Australia.

Pogo stick jumping ● Ashrita Furman of Jamaica, New York set a distance record of 13·06 miles in 5 hr 23 min on 15 Sep 1989 in New York.

Pipe smoking ■ The duration record for keeping a pipe (0·1 oz of tobacco) continuously alight with only an initial match under IAPSC (International Association of Pipe Smokers Clubs) rules is 126 min 39 sec by five-time champion William Vargo of Swartz Creek, MI at the 27th World Championships in 1975. The only other five-time champion is Paul T. Spaniola (US; 1951, 1966, 1970, 1973, 1977).

On 18 Aug 1984 Joe Oetli achieved 130 min 11 sec at the 15th Iowa State Fair contest using *two* matches. Longer durations have been recorded in less rigorously invigilated contests in which the foul practices of 'tamping' and 'gardening' are not unknown.

Plane pulling ■ Dave Gauder single-handedly pulled Concorde 40 ft across the tarmac at Heathrow Airport, London, United Kingdom on 11 Jun 1987.

Plate spinning ■ The greatest number of plates spun simultaneously is 84, by Dave Spathaky on British Broadcasting Corporation TV's 'Record Breakers' on 21 Oct 1986.

Pogo stick jumping ■ The greatest number of jumps achieved is 130,077, by Gary Stewart in Reading, OH on 8–9 Mar 1985.

Ashrita Furman of Jamaica, New York set a distance record of 13·06 miles in 5 hr 23 min on 15 Sep 1989 in New York .

Pole sitting ■ Modern records do not, in fact, compare with that of St Simeon the Younger (c. A.D. 521–597), called Stylites, a monk who spent his last 45 years up a stone pillar on the Hill of Wonders, near Antioch, Syria.

The 'standards of living' at the top of poles can vary widely. Mellissa Sanders lived in a shack measuring 6 ft × 7 ft at the top of a pole in Indianapolis, IN from 26 Oct 1986 to 24 Mar 1988, a total of 516 days.

Pat Bowen stayed in a barrel (max. capacity 150 gallons) at the top of a pole (18 ft) outside the Bull Hotel, Ludlow, Shropshire, United Kingdom for 40 days 1 hr from 28 May to 7 Jul 1986.

Pop/rock group ■ The duration record for a four-man group is 147 hr by the Dekorators at Becketts Bar, East Sussex, United Kingdom from 8–14 Jan 1984.

Postbox mounting ■ The record number to pile on top of or hang from a standard double mailbox (oval top of 6 ft²) is 32, all students of Wentworth College, York University, United Kingdom on 27 Feb 1985.

Potato peeling ■ The greatest amount of potatoes peeled by five people to an institutional cookery standard with standard kitchen knives in 45 min is 685 lb 4 oz (net) by Lia Sombroek, Marlene Guiamo, Walijem Kertoidjojo, Judith van Druenen and Wijna Scheringa at Emmeloord, Netherlands on 17 Sep 1987.

Pram pushing ■ The greatest distance covered in pushing a pram in 24 hr is 350·23 miles by 60 members of the Oost-Vlanderen branch of Amnesty International at Lede, Belgium on 15 Oct 1988.

A ten-man Royal Marine team from the Commando Training Centre, Lympstone, Devon, United Kingdom, with an adult 'baby,' covered 252·65 miles in 24 hr from 31 Mar to 18 Apr 1984.

Quizzes ■ The highest number of participants was 80,799 in the All-Japan High School Quiz Championship televised by NTV on 31 Dec 1983.

The most protracted contest was that lasting 110 hr in Long Hanborough, Oxfordshire, United Kingdom from 27 Mar to 1 Apr 1986. The 2 teams answered correctly 22,483 of the 37,310 questions.

Quoit throwing ■ The world record for rope quoit throwing is an unbroken sequence of 4,002 pegs, by Bill Irby, Sr of Australia in 1968.

Ramp jumping ■ The longest distance ever achieved for motorcycle long jumping is 246 ft, by Todd Seeley at a World of Wheels show in Tampa, FL on 28 Feb 1988.

The longest ramp jump in a car is one of 245 ft 2 in, by Kevin Major in a Ford Escort at Enstone Airfield, Oxfordshire, United Kingdom on 30 Oct 1989.

Riding in armor ■ The longest recorded ride in armor is one of 208 miles by Dick Brown, who left Edinburgh, Lothian on 10 Jun 1989 and arrived in his home town of Dumfries, Dumfries and Galloway, United Kingdom four days later. His total riding time was 35 hr 25 min.

Riveting ■ The world's record for riveting is 11,209 in 9 hr by John Moir at the Workman Clark Ltd shipyard, Belfast, Northern Ireland, in June 1918. His peak hour was his 7th, with 1,409, an average of nearly 23½ per min.

Rocking chair ■ The longest recorded 'Rockathon' is 453 hr 40 min by Robert McDonald at Mariposa, CA from 14 Mar–2 Apr 1986.

Rolling pin ■ The record distance for a woman to throw a 2 lb rolling pin is 175 ft 5 in by Lori La Deane Adams, 21, at Iowa State Fair, IA on 21 Aug 1979.

Safecracking ■ At the Associated Locksmiths of America convention in July 1988, Franklin 'Skip' Eckert (b. 7 Jun 1951) of Medina, OH opened a safe lock in 3 min 57 sec.

Sand castle ■ The tallest sand castle on record, using hands, buckets and shovels, was 17 ft 6 in high and was made by Pacific Northwest Sandshapers at Harrison Hot Springs, British Columbia, Canada on 14–15 Apr 1990.

The longest sand castle was 5·2 miles long, and was made by staff and pupils of Ellon Academy, near Aberdeen, United Kingdom on 24 Mar 1988.

Sand sculpturing ■ The longest sand sculpture ever made — with the sculpture meticulously carved out — was the 15,734-ft-long Totally in Sand 'Sand Stations 89,' which was constructed at Long Beach, WA on 23 Jul 1989 by 364 volunteers.

The tallest was the 'Invitation to Fairyland,' which was 56 ft 2 in high, and was built by 2,000 local volunteers at Kaseda, Japan on 26 Jul 1989 under the supervision of Gerry Kirk of Sand Sculptors International of San Diego and Shogo Tashiro of Sand Sculptors International of Japan.

See-saw ■ George Partridge and Tamara Marquez of Auburn High School, WA on a suspension see-saw completed 1,101 hr 40 min (indoor) from 28 Mar–13 May 1977.

Georgia Chaffin and Tammy Adams of Goodhope Junior High School, Cullman, AL completed 730 hr 30 min (outdoor) from 25 Jun–25 Jul 1975.

Sermon ■ The longest sermon on record was delivered by the Reverend Ronald Gallagher at the Baptist Temple, Appomattox, VA for 120 hr from 26 Jun–1 Jul 1983.

From 31 May to 10 June 1969 the 14th Dalai Lama (b. 6 Jul 1934 as Tenzin Gyalto), exiled ruler of Tibet, completed a sermon on Tantric Buddhism for 5–7 hr per day to total 60 hr, in India.

Shaving ■ The fastest barbers on record are Denny Rowe, who shaved 1,994 men in 60 min with a retractor safety razor in Herne Bay, Kent, United Kingdom on 19 Jun 1988, taking on average 1·8 sec per volunteer, and drawing blood four times and Gerry Harley, of Gillingham, Kent, United Kingdom who on 13 Aug 1984 shaved 235 even braver volunteers with a cut-throat razor, averaging 15·3 sec per face. He drew blood only once.

Sheaf tossing ■ The world's best performance for tossing an 8-lb sheaf for height is 64 ft 10¼ in by Trond Ulleberg of Skolleborg, Norway on 11 Nov 1978. Such pitchfork contests date from 1914.

Sheep to shoulder ■ At the International Wool Secretariat Development Centre, Ilkley, United Kingdom, a team of eight, using commercial machinery, produced a sweater from shearing sheep to the finished article in 2 hr 28 min 32 sec on 3 Sep 1986.

Shoe-shining ■ In this category (limited to a team of four teenagers; duration of 8 hr; shoes 'on the hoof') the record is 11,651 pairs by four members of the London Church of Christ at Covent Garden, London, United Kingdom on 18 Mar 1989.

Shorthand ■ The highest recorded speeds ever attained under championship conditions are: 300 words per min (99·64 percent accuracy) for 5 minutes and 350 wpm (99·72 percent accuracy, that is, two insignificant errors) for 2 minutes by Nathan Behrin (US) in tests in New York in December 1922. Behrin (b. 1887) used the Pitman system invented in 1837.

Morris I. Kligman, official court reporter of the US Court House, New York, has taken 50,000 words in 5 hr (a sustained rate of 166·6 wpm). Rates are much dependent upon the nature, complexity and syllabic density of the material.

Mr G. W. Bunbury of Dublin, Ireland held the unique distinction of writing at 250 wpm for 10 minutes on 23 Jan 1894.

Mr Arnold Bradley achieved a speed of 309 wpm without error using the Sloan-Duployan system, with 1,545 words in 5 minutes in a test in Walsall, West Midlands, United Kingdom on 9 Nov 1920.

Showering ■ The most prolonged continuous shower bath on record is one of 340 hr 40 min by Kevin McCartney of State University College at Buffalo, NY, from 29 Mar to 12 Apr 1985.

The women's record is 121 hr 1 min by Lisa D'Amato from 5–10 Nov 1981 at Harpur College, Binghamton, NY. Desquamation can be a positive danger.

Singing ■ The longest recorded solo singing marathon is one of 262 hr by Pastor S. Jeyaseelan at the Asian Glass House Building, Ramnad, India from 22 Apr–3 May 1989.

The marathon record for a choir is 80 hr 1 min by the Young Spirit of the Apache Junction High School, AZ from 2–5 Feb 1989.

Acharya Prem Bhikshuji (d. 18 Apr 1970) started chanting the Akhand Rama-Dhoon at Jamnagar, Gujarat, India on 31 Jul 1964 and devotees were still continuing in May 1990.

Skateboarding ■ 'World' championships have been staged intermittently since 1966. David Frank, 25, covered 270·5 miles in 36 hr 43 min 40 sec in Toronto, Canada on 11–12 Aug 1985.

The highest speed recorded on a skateboard under USSA rules is 71·79 mph on a course at Mt Baldy, CA in a prone position by Richard K. Brown, 33, on 17 Jun 1979. The stand-up record is 53·45 mph by John Hutson, 23, at Signal Hill, Long Beach, CA on 11 Jun 1978.

The high-jump record is 5 ft 5¾ in by Trevor Baxter (b. 1 Oct 1962) of Burgess Hill, East Sussex, United Kingdom at Grenoble, France on 14 Sep 1982. At the 4th US Skateboard Association Championship, at Signal Hill on 25 Sep 1977, Tony Alva, 19, jumped 17 barrels (17 ft).

Slinging ■ The greatest distance recorded for a slingshot is 1,434 ft 2 in using a 51 in long sling and a 2 oz stone by Lawrence L. Bray at Loa, UT on 21 Aug 1981.

Smoke ring blowing ■ The highest recorded number of smoke rings formed from the lips from a single pull of a cigarette (cheek-tapping is disallowed) is 355 by Jan van Deurs Formann of Copenhagen, Denmark, achieved in Switzerland in August 1979.

Snow shoeing ■ The USSSA record for covering 1 mile is 7 min 00·2 sec by Nick Akers at Edmonton, Alberta, Canada on 8 Jan 1989.

Spear throwing ■ The greatest distance achieved throwing a spear with the aid of a woomera is 326 ft 6 in by Bailey Bush on 27 Jun 1982 at Camden, New South Wales, Australia.

Spike driving ■ In the World Championship Professional Spike Driving Competition held at the Golden Spike National Historic Site in Utah, Dale C. Jones, 49, of Lehi, UT drove six 7-in railroad spikes in a time of 26·4 sec on 11 Aug 1984. He incurred no penalty points under the official rules.

Spinning by hand ■ The duration record for spinning a clock-balance wheel by unaided hand is 5 min 26·8 sec by Philip Ashley, 16, of Leigh, Lancashire, United Kingdom on 20 May 1968.

The record using 36 in of string with a 7¼ oz top is 58 min 20 sec by Peter Hodgson at Southend-on-Sea, Essex, United Kingdom on 4 Feb 1985.

Spitting ■ Randy Ober of Bentonville, AR spat a tobacco wad 47 ft 7 in at the Calico 5th Annual Tobacco Chewing and Spitting Championships north of Barstow, CA on 4 Apr 1982. The record for projecting a water-melon seed is 68 ft 9⅛ in by Lee Wheelis at Luling, TX on 24 Jun 1989. The furthest recorded distance for a cherry stone is 72 ft 7½ in, by Rick Krause, at Eau Claire, MI on 2 Jul 1988.

Square dance calling ■ Alan Covacic called for 26 hr 2 min for the Wheelers and Dealers Square Dance Club at RAF Halton, Aylesbury, United Kingdom from 18–19 Nov 1988.

Stair climbing ■ *These records can only be attempted in buildings with a minimum of 70 floors.*

The 100-floor record for stair climbing was set by Dennis W. Martz in the Detroit Plaza Hotel, Detroit, MI on 26 Jun 1978 at 11 min 23·8 sec.

Dale Neil, 22, ran a vertical mile on the stairs of the Peachtree Plaza Hotel, Atlanta, GA in continuous action of 2 hr 1 min 24 sec on 9 Mar 1984.

The record for the 1,760 steps (vertical height 1,122 ft) in the world's tallest free-standing structure, Toronto's CN Tower, Canada, is 7 min 52 sec by Brendan Keenoy on 29 Oct 1989. Robert C. Jezequel made 17 ascents (descending by lift) in 11 hr 20 min on 18 Oct 1981 for a vertical height of 19,074 ft.

The record for the 1,336 stairs of the world's tallest hotel, the Westin Stamford Hotel, Singapore is 6 min 55 sec by Balvinder Singh, in the 3rd Vertical Marathon on 4 Jun 1989.

Pete Squires raced up the 1,575 steps of the Empire State Building, NY on 12 Feb 1981 in 10 min 59 sec.

Stamp licking ■ John Kenmuir licked and affixed 328 stamps in 4 min at George Square Post Office, Glasgow, United Kingdom on 30 Jun 1989.

Standing ■ The longest period on record that anyone has continuously stood is for more than 17 years in the case of Swami Maujgiri Maharaj when performing the *Tapasya* or penance from 1955 to November 1973 in Shahjahanpur, Uttar Pradesh, India. When sleeping he would lean against a plank. He died aged 85 in September 1980.

Stilt-walking ■ The fastest stilt-walker on record is Masaharu Tatsushiro, who covered 328 ft on 1 ft high stilts in 14·15 sec in Tokyo, Japan on 30 Mar 1980. Over a long distance, the fastest is M. Garisoain of Bayonne, France who in 1892 walked the 4·97 miles from Bayonne to Biarritz on stilts in 42 min, at an average speed of 7·10 mph. The greatest distance ever walked on stilts is 3,008 miles, from Los Angeles, CA to Bowen, KY by Joe Bowen from 20 Feb to 26 Jul 1980.

In 1891 Sylvain Dornon stilt-walked from Paris, France to Moscow, USSR via Vilno in 50 stages for the 1,830 miles. Another source gives his time as 58 days. Either way, although Bowen's distance was greater, Dornon walked at a much higher speed. Even with a safety or Kirby wire, very high stilts are *extremely* dangerous — 25 steps are deemed to constitute 'mastery.'

The highest stilts ever mastered measured 40 ft 6½ in from ground to ankle, Eddy Wolf ('Steady Eddy') of Loyal, WI walking a distance of 27 steps without touching his safety handrail wires at Yokohama Dreamland Park, Yokohama, Japan on 9 Mar 1986. His aluminum stilts weighed 55 lb each. The heaviest stilts ever mastered weighed 56 lb each, Joe Long (b. Ken-

Stair climbing ● The record for climbing the 1,336 stairs of the Westin Stamford Hotel in Singapore—the world's tallest hotel—is 6 min 55 sec by Balvinder Singh, in the 3rd Vertical Marathon on 4 Jun 1989.

neth Caesar), who has suffered 5 fractures, mastering these at the British Broadcasting Corporation Television Centre, London, United Kingdom on 8 Dec 1978. They were 24 ft high.

Stowaway ■ The most rugged stowaway was Socarras Ramirez who escaped from Cuba on 4 Jun 1969 by stowing away in an unpressurised wheel well in the starboard wing of a Douglas DC8 from Havana, Cuba to Madrid, Spain in a 5,600 mile Iberian Airlines flight.

Stretcher bearing ■ The longest recorded carry of a stretcher case with a 140 lb 'body' is 142·3 miles in 38 hr 39 min by two four-man teams from 1 Field Ambulance, Canadian Forces Base, Calgary, Canada from 5–7 Apr 1989.

The record limited to Youth Organisations (under 20 years of age) and 8-hr carrying is 42·02 miles by 8 members of the Henry Meoles School, Moreton, Wirral, Cheshire, United Kingdom on 13 Jul 1980.

String ball, largest ■ The largest ball of string on record is one of 12 ft 9 in in diameter, 40 ft in circumference and weighing 11 tons, amassed by Francis A. Johnson of Darwin, MN between 1950–78.

Submergence ■ The *continuous* duration record (i.e. no rest breaks) for 'scuba' (i.e. self-contained and without surface air hoses) is 212 hr 30 min by Michael Stevens of Birmingham in a Royal Navy tank at the National Exhibition Centre, Birmingham, United Kingdom from 14–23 Feb 1986. Measures have to be taken to reduce the risk of severe desquamation in such endurance trials.

Suggestion boxes ■ The most prolific example on record of the use of any suggestion box scheme is that of John Drayton (1907–87) of Newport, Gwent, United Kingdom, who plied the British rail system with a total of 31,400 suggestions from 1924 to August 1987, of which over one in seven were adopted and 100 were accepted by London Transport. In 1983 he was presented with a chiming clock by British Rail to mark almost 60 years of suggestions.

Swinging ■ The record duration for continuous swinging in a hammock is 240 hr by John David Joyce of Bryan, TX from 29 Jul to 8 Aug 1986.

Switchback riding ■ The endurance record for rides on a roller coaster is 503 hr by M. M. Daniel Glada and Normand St-Pierre at Parc Belmont, Montreal, Canada from 18 Jul to 10 Aug 1983. The minimum qualifying average speed required is 25 mph.

Tailoring ■ The highest speed in which the manufacture of a three-piece suit has been executed from sheep to finished article is 1 hr 34 min 33·42 sec, by 65 members of the Melbourne College of Textiles, Pascoe Vale, Victoria, Australia on 24 Jun 1982. Catching and fleecing took 2 min 21 sec, and carding, spinning, weaving and tailoring occupied the remaining time.

Talking ■ The world record for talking is 360 hr by S.E. Jeyaraman at Madras, India from 8–23 Jun 1989.

The women's record was set by Mrs Mary E. Davis, who started on 2 Sep 1958 at a radio station in Buffalo, NY and talked for 110 hr 30 min 5 sec, finishing on 7 Sep in Tulsa, OK. (See also Filibusters, Chapter 10.)

The longest recorded after-dinner speech was one of 40 hr, by R. Meenakshisundaram at Madurai, Tamil Nadu, India, from 23–25 Jun 1989.

Historically the longest recorded after-dinner

Tightrope walking ● The greatest drop over which anyone has walked on a tightrope is 3,304 ft by Michel Menin, of France, above the Angel Falls, Venezuela on 1 Mar 1988. He repeated this feat the following day.

speech with *unsuspecting* victims was one of 3 hr by the Reverend Henry Whitehead (d. March 1896) at the Rainbow Tavern, Fleet Street, London, United Kingdom on 16 Jan 1874.

T-bone dive ■ The so-called T-bone dives or Dive Bomber crashes by cars off ramps over and onto parked cars are often measured by the number of cars but owing to their variable size and that their purpose is purely to cushion the shock, distance is more significant.

Stuart Cameron drove a Datsun 240Z for a record leap of 210 ft at Bovingdon Airfield, Hertfordshire, United Kingdom on 4 Sep 1988.

Throwing ■ The longest independently authenticated throw of any inert object heavier than air is 1,257 ft, for a flying ring, by Scott Zimmerman on 8 Jul 1986 at Fort Funston, CA.

Tightrope walking ■ The greatest 19th-century tightrope walker was Jean-François Gravelet, *alias* Charles Blondin (1824–97), of France, who made the earliest crossing of the Niagara Falls on a 3-in rope, 1,100 ft long, 160 ft above the Falls on 30 Jun 1859. He also made a crossing with Harry Colcord piggyback on 15 Sep 1860. Though other artistes still find it difficult to believe, Colcord was his agent.

The oldest wire walker was 'Professor' William Ivy Baldwin (1866–1953), who crossed the South Boulder Canyon, CO on a 320 ft wire with a 125-ft drop on his 82nd birthday on 31 Jul 1948.

The world tightrope endurance record is 185 days, by Henri Rochetain (b. 1926) of France, on a wire 394 ft long, 82 ft above a supermarket in Saint-Etienne, France from 28 Mar–29 Sep 1973. His ability to sleep on the wire has left doctors puzzled.

Ashley Brophy, of Neilborough, Victoria, Australia, walked 7·18 miles on a wire 147·64 ft long 32·81 ft high at the Adelaide Grand Prix, Australia on 1 Nov 1985 in 3½ hr.

Steve McPeak (b. 21 Apr 1945) of Las Vegas, NV ascended the 1·83-in diameter Zugspitzbahn cable for a vertical height of 2,313 ft in three stints aggregating 5 hr 4 min on 24/25/28 Jun 1981. The maximum gradient over the stretch of 7,485 ft was above 30 degrees.

The greatest drop over which anyone has walked on a tightrope is 3,304 ft, by Michel Menin, of France, above the Angel Falls, Venezuela on 1 Mar 1988. He repeated this feat the following day.

Tire supporting ■ The greatest number of motor tires supported in a free-standing 'lift' is 96, by Gary Windebank of Romsey, Hampshire, United Kingdom in February 1984. The total weight was 1,440 lb. The tires used were Michelin XZX 155 × 13.

Top spinning ■ A team of 25 from the Mizushima Plant of Kawasaki Steel Works in Okayama, Japan spun a giant top 6 ft 6¾ in tall and 8 ft 6¼ in in diameter, weighing 793·6 lb, for 1 hr 21 min 35 sec on 3 Nov 1986.

Train spotting ■ Bill Curtis of Clacton-on-Sea, Essex, United Kingdom is acknowledged as the world champion train spotter — or 'gricer' (after Richard Grice, the first champion). His totals include some 60,000 locomotives, 11,200 electric units and 8,300 diesel units, clocked up over a period of 40 years in a number of different countries.

Tree climbing ■ The fastest speed climb up a 100-ft fir spar pole and return to the ground is one of 24·82 sec by Guy German of Sitka, AK on 3 Jul 1988 at the World Championship Timber Carnival in Albany, OR.

The fastest time up a 29·5-ft coconut tree barefoot is 4·88 sec by Fuatai Solo, 17, in Sukuna Park, Fiji on 22 Aug 1980.

Tree sitting ■ The duration record for sitting in a tree is 431 days, by Timothy Roy at Golf n'Stuff Amusement Park, Norwalk, CA from 4 Jul 1982–8 Sep 1983.

Tree topping ■ Guy German climbed a 100-ft spar and sawed off the top in a record time of 53·35 sec at Albany, OR on 3 Jul 1989.

Typewriting ■ The world duration record for typewriting on an electric machine is 264 hr, by Violet Gibson Burns at the Royal Easter Show, Sydney, Australia from 29 Mar–9 Apr 1985.

The longest duration in a typing marathon on a manual machine is 123 hr, by Shambhoo Govind Anbhawane of Bombay, India, from 18–23 Aug 1986 on a Godrej Prima manual machine, aggregating 806,000 strokes.

Les Stewart of Mudjimba Beach, Queensland, Australia has typed the numbers 1 to 637,000 in *words* on 11,570 quarto sheets as of 15 Feb 1990. His target is to become a 'millionaire.'

The highest recorded speeds attained with a ten-word penalty per error on a manual machine are:

Five min: 176 wpm net, by Mrs Carole Forristall Waldschlager Bechen at Dixon, IL on 2 Apr 1959. One hour: 147 wpm net, by Albert Tangora (US) (Underwood Standard), 22 Oct 1923.

The official hour record on an electric machine is 9,316 words (40 errors) on an IBM machine, giving a net rate of 149 words per min, by Margaret Hamma, now Mrs Dilmore (US), in Brooklyn, NY on 20 Jun 1941.

In an official test in 1946, Stella Pajunas, now Mrs Garnard, attained a rate of 216 words in a minute on an IBM machine.

Mary Ann Morel (South Africa) set a numerical record at the CABEX '85 Exhibition in Johannesburg, South Africa on 6 Feb 1985 by typing spaced numbers from 1 to 781 in 5 min.

Unsupported circle ■ The highest recorded number of people who have demonstrated the physical paradox of all being seated without a chair is an unsupported circle of 10,323 employees of the Nissan Motor Company at Komazawa Stadium, Tokyo, Japan on 23 Oct 1982.

Walking on hands ■ The duration record for walking on hands is 871 miles, by Johann Hurlinger, of Austria, who in 55 daily 10-hr stints, averaged 1·58 mph from Vienna to Paris in 1900.

Shin Don-mok of South Korea completed a 54·68 yd inverted sprint in 17·44 sec at the Toda Sports Center, Saitama, Japan on 14 Nov 1986.

A four-man relay team of David Lutterman, Brendan Price, Philip Savage and David Scannel covered 1 mile in 24 min 48 sec on 15 Mar 1987 at Knoxville, TN. This compares with the record of 3 min 2 sec the right way up.

Walking on water ■ Wearing 11-ft water ski shoes, called Skijaks, and using a twin-bladed paddle, David Kiner walked 155 miles on the Hudson River from Albany to Battery Park, NY. His walk took him 57 hr, from 22–27 Jun 1987.

Rémy Bricka of Paris, France 'walked' across the Atlantic Ocean on 13-ft, 9-in long skis in 1988. Leaving Tenerife on 2 Apr 1988, he covered 3,502 miles, arriving at Trinidad on 31 May 1988.

Wall of death ■ The greatest endurance feat on a wall of death was 6 hr 7 min 38 sec, by Hugo Dabbert (b. Hildesheim, 24 Sep 1938) at Rüsselsheim, West Germany on 14 Aug 1980. He rode 6,841 laps on the 32·8-ft diameter wall on a Honda CM 400T averaging 21·8 mph for the 133·4 miles.

Whip cracking ■ The longest stock whip ever 'cracked' is one of 140 ft (excluding the handle) wielded by Garry Brophy at Adelaide, Australia on 31 Oct 1985.

Whistling ■ Roy Lomas achieved 122·5 decibels at 8·20 ft in the Deadroom at the British Broadcasting Corporation studios in Manchester, United Kingdom on 19 Dec 1983.

The marathon record is held by Vanka Ravindra Kumar of Guntur, Andhra Pradesh, India, who whistled for 45 hr 20 min from 10–12 Mar 1990.

Window cleaning ■ Keith Witt of Amarillo, TX cleaned three standard 42½ × 47 in office windows with a 11·8-in-long squeegee and 1·98 gal of water in 10·50 sec on 21 Jan 1990. The record was achieved at the International Window Cleaning Association's convention at Orlando, FL.

Wing walking ■ Cheryl 'Rusty' Butterworth flew on the wing of an aircraft for 3 hr 8 min on 4 Mar 1990, taking off from Ardmore Airfield, Auckland, New Zealand and landing at the same airfield after a flight over Auckland and many of the small towns in the area.

Winkling ■ Helen Kennedy picked 50 shells (with a straight pin) in 2 min 44·37 sec at Epping, Essex, United Kingdom on 16 Sep 1989.

Wire slide ■ The greatest distance recorded in a wire slide is from the London Weekend TV building to the barge *Driftwood* 370 ft below and 925 ft distant on the River Thames, London, United Kingdom on 27 Oct 1986. This 'death slide' set up by the Royal Marines was traversed by Lady Nourse, nee Lavinia Malim for charity. The estimated run length was 1,000 ft.

Wood cutting ■ The first recorded lumberjack sports competition was held in 1572 in the Basque region of Spain. The records set at the Lumberjack World Championships at Hayward, WI (founded 1960) are:

Power Saw	8·71 sec	
Ron Johnson (US)	1986	
One-Man Bucking	18·96 sec	
Rolin Eslinger (US)	1987	
Standing Block Chop	22·05 sec	
Melvin Lentz (US)	1988	
Underhand Block Chop	17·84 sec	
Laurence O'Toole (Australia)	1985	
Two-man Bucking	7·27 sec	
Jim Colbert (US), Mike Sullivan (US)	1988	
Springboard Choppping	1 min 18·45 sec	
Bill Youd (Australia)	1985	

Writing minuscule ■ In 1926 an account was published of Alfred McEwen's pantograph record in which the 56-word version of the Lord's Prayer was written by diamond point on glass in the space of 0·0016 × 0·0008 in.

Frederick C. Watts of Felmingham, Norfolk, United Kingdom demonstrated for photographers on 24 Jan 1968 his ability, without mechanical or optical aid, to write the Lord's Prayer 34 times (9,452 letters) within the size of a definitive United Kingdom postage stamp *viz* 0·84 × 0·71 in.

Pan Xixing of Wuxi, China wrote 'True friendship is like sound health, the value of which is seldom known until it be lost (Proverb)' twice on a human hair in March 1990.

Surendra Apharya of Jaipur, India succeeded in writing 638 characters (names of various countries, towns and regions) on a single grain of rice on 28 Jan 1990.

Writing under handicap ■ The ultimate feat in 'funny writing' appears to be the ability to write extemporaneously and decipherably backwards, upside down, laterally inverted (mirror-style), while blindfolded, with both hands simultaneously. Three claims to this ability, with both hands and feet simultaneously, by Mrs Carolyn Webb of Thirlmere, New South Wales, Australia, Mrs Judy Hall of Chesterfield, VA and Robert Gray of Toronto, Ontario, Canada, are outstanding.

Yard of ale ■ Peter Dowdeswell of Earls Barton, Northamptonshire, United Kingdom drank a yard of ale (2½ pints) in 5·0 sec at RAF Upper Heyford, Oxfordshire, United Kingdom on 4 May 1975.

Yodelling ■ The most protracted yodel on record was one of 30 hr 1 min by Jim Whitman of Washington, Tyne and Wear, United Kingdom on 16–17 Nov 1989. Yodeling has been defined as 'repeated rapid changes from the chest-voice to falsetto and back again.'

The most rapid recorded is five tones (three falsetto) in 1·9 sec by Donn Reynolds of Canada on 25 Jul 1984.

Yo-yo ■ A yo-yo was a toy in Grecian times and is depicted on a bowl dated 450 B.C. It was also a Filipino jungle fighting weapon recorded in the 16th century weighing 4 lb with a 20-ft thong. The word means 'come-come.' Though illustrated in a book in 1891 as a bandalore, the craze did not begin until it was started by Donald F. Duncan of Chicago, IL in 1926. The most difficult modern yo-yo trick is the 'whirlwind,' incorporating both inside and outside horizontal loop-the-loops.

The individual continuous endurance record is 130 hr 13 min by Jason Stremble and Scott Fletcher at Variety Village, Scarborough, Ontario, Canada from 17–22 Jul 1989. Dr Allen Bussey in Waco, TX on 23 Apr 1977 completed 20,302

loops in 3 hr and on 5 Nov 1988 Luis Salamanca of Bogotá, Colombia set a 1-hr speed record of 7,574 loops at the Channel 9 Studios in Artarmon, Sydney, Australia.

Circus and juggling records

CIRCUS RECORDS
The world's largest permanent circus is Circus Circus, Las Vegas, NV opened on 18 Oct 1968 at a cost of $15 million. It covers an area of 129,000 ft² capped by a tent-shaped flexiglass roof 90 ft high. The largest traveling circus is the Gold Unit of Ringling Bros. and Barnum & Bailey Circus. It seats 7,000 people and is 394 ft × 197 ft × 66 ft. It was first used for a show at Sapporo, Japan on 1 Jul 1988.

The largest circus crowd comprised 52,385 people attending a performance of The Greatest Show On Earth at the Superdome in New Orleans, LA on 14 Sep 1975.

Flying trapeze ■ Downward circles or 'muscle grinding' — 1,350 by Sarah Denu (age 14) (US) Madison, WI, 21 May 1983. Single-heel hang on swinging bar, Angela Revelle (Angelique), Australia, 1977.

Highest aerial act ■ Ian Ashpole (b. 15 Jan 1956) of Ross-on-Wye, Hereford and Worcester, United Kingdom performed a trapeze act suspended from a hot-air balloon between St Neots, Cambridgeshire, United Kingdom and Newmarket, Suffolk, United Kingdom at 16,420 ft on 16 May 1986.

Triple-twisting double somersault ■ Tom Robin Edelston to catcher John Zimmerman, Circus World, FL, 20 Jan 1981.

Full-twisting triple and the quadruple ■ Vasquez Troupe. Miguel Vasquez to catcher Juan Vasquez at Ringling Bros, Amphitheater, Chicago, IL in November 1981. On 20 Sep 1984 he performed a triple somersault in a layout position (no turn) to catcher Juan Vasquez at the Sports Arena, Los Angeles, CA.

Triple back somersault with 1½ twists ■ Terry Cavaretta Lemus (now Mrs St Jules). At Circus Circus, Las Vegas, NV in 1969.

Teeter board ■ A seven-person high perch pyramid was established by the Bulgarian 'Kehaiovi Troupe' at the Tower Circus, Blackpool, Lancashire, United Kingdom on 16 Jul 1986. It was finished off with a leap from the top by 13-year old member Magdelena.

Trampoline ■ Septuple twisting back somersault to bed and quintuple twisting back somersault to shoulders by Marco Canestrelli to Belmonte Canestrelli at Madison Square Garden, NY on 5 Jan and 28 Mar 1979. Richard Tison (France) performed a triple-twisting triple back somersault for television near Berchtesgaden, West Germany on 30 Jun 1981.

Flexible pole ■ Double full-twisting somersault to a 2-in diameter pole by Roberto Tabak (age 11) in Sarasota, FL in 1977. Triple full-twisting somersault by Corina Colonelu Mosoianu (age 13) at Madison Square Garden, NY on 17 Apr 1984.

Human pyramid (or tuckle) ■ Twelve (3 high) supported by a single under-stander. Weight: 1,700 lb by Tahar Douis of the Hassani Troupe at BBC TV Pebble Mill Studio, Birmingham, West Midlands, United Kingdom on 17 Dec 1979.

Nine high by top-mounter Josep-Joan Martínez Lozano, age 10, of the Colla Vella dels Xiquets, 39 ft tall on 25 Oct 1981 in Valls, Spain.

Oldest clown ■ Charlie Revel (b. Andrea Lassere, Spain, 24 Apr 1896) performed for 82 years (1899–1981).

JUGGLING RECORDS
8 clubs (flashed) ■ Anthony Gatto (US), 1989.

7 clubs (juggled) ■ Albert Petrovski (USSR), 1963; Sorin Munteanu (Romania), 1975; Jack Bremlov (Czechoslovakia), 1985; Albert Lucas (US), 1985; Anthony Gatto (US), 1988.

8 plates ■ Enrico Rastelli (Italy), 1896–1931; Albert Lucas (US), 1984.

10 balls ■ Enrico Rastelli (Italy), 1896–1931; Albert Lucas (US), 1984.

12 rings (flashed) ■ Albert Lucas (US), 1985.

11 rings (juggled) ■ Albert Petrovski (USSR), 1963–66; Eugene Belaur (USSR), 1968; Sergei Ignatov (USSR), 1973.

7 flaming torches ■ Anthony Gatto (US), 1989.

Bounce juggling ■ Tim Nolan (US), 10 balls, 1988.

Basketball spinning ■ Dave Davlin (US), 12 basketballs, 1989.

Duration: 5 clubs without a drop ■ 45 min 2 sec, Anthony Gatto (US), 1989.

Duration: 3 objects without a drop ■ Jas Angelo (Great Britain), 8 hr 57 min 31 sec, 1989.

7 ping-pong balls with mouth ■ Tony Ferko (Czechoslovakia), 1987.

5 balls inverted ■ Bobby May (US), 1953.

Most objects aloft ■ 524 jugglers kept 1,997 objects up in the air simultaneously, each person juggling at least three objects, 1989.

3 objects while running—juggling ■ Owen Morse (US), 100 m in 11·68 sec, 1989. Albert Lucas (US), 110 m hurdles in 20·36 sec and 400 m hurdles in 1 min 10·37 sec, 1989. Owen Morse, Albert Lucas, Tuey Wilson and John Wee (all US), 1 mile relay in 4 min 1·49 sec, 1989. Kirk Swenson (US), 1 mile in 4 min 43 sec, 1986 and 3·1 miles in 16 min 55 sec, 1986. Ashrita Furman (US), marathon — 26 miles 385 yd — in 3 hr 22 min 32·5 sec, 1988 and also 50 miles in 8 hr 52 min 7 sec, 1989.

5 objects while running—juggling ■ Owen Morse (US), 100 m in 13·8 sec, 1988. Bill Gillen (US), 1 mile in 7 min 41·01 sec, 1989 and 3·1 miles in 28 min 11 sec, 1989.

Dancing

Marathon dancing must be distinguished from dancing mania, or tarantism, which is a pathological condition. The worst outbreak of this was at Aachen, Germany in July 1374, when hordes of men and women broke into a frenzied and compulsive choreomania in the streets. It lasted for many hours until injury or complete exhaustion ensued.

Largest and longest dances ■ An estimated 25,000 attended a 'Moonlight Serenade' outdoor evening of dancing to the music of the Glenn Miller Orchestra in Buffalo, NY on 20 Jul 1984. An estimated total of 20,000 dancers took part in the National Square Dance Convention at Louisville, KY on 26 Jun 1983.

The most severe marathon dance staged as a public spectacle was one by Mike Ritof and Edith Boudreaux, who logged 5,148 hr 28½ min to win $2,000 at Chicago's Merry Garden Ballroom, Belmont and Sheffield, IL from 29 Aug 1930 to 1 Apr 1931. Rest periods were progressively cut from 20 to 10 to 5 to nil minutes per hour with 10-inch steps and a maximum of 15 seconds for closure of eyes.

'Rosie Radiator' (Rose Marie Ostler) led an ensemble of 14 dancers through the streets of San Francisco, CA on 18 Jul 1987, covering a distance of 7¾ miles.

> **Greatest assemblage of tap dancers** ● The greatest assemblage of tap dancers in a single routine is 4,877 in front of Macy's 34th St. department store in New York City on 13 Aug 1989 for the 11th annual Tap-o-Mania.

Ballroom *Marathon* ■ The individual continuous world record for ballroom dancing is 126 hr by Scott Michael, 31, a dancing instructor of Huntington Beach, CA on 20–25 Jun 1986 at the Dance Masters Ballroom Studio, Stanton, CA. Twenty-seven girls worked shifts as his partner.

Champions ■ The world's most successful professional ballroom dancing champions have been Bill Irvine and Bobbie Irvine, who won 13 world titles between 1960 and 1968. The oldest competitive ballroom dancer is Albert J. Sylvester (b. 24 Nov 1889) of Corsham, Wiltshire, United Kingdom who retired aged 94.

Belly dancing ■ The longest recorded belly dancing marathon was one of 106 hr by Eileen Foucher at Rush Green Hospital, Romford, Essex, United Kingdom from 30 Jul–3 Aug 1984.

Charleston ■ The charleston duration record is 110 hr 58 min by Vicky Huber, AKA 'Nitro,' of Lansdowne, PA from 15–20 Jan 1979.

Conga ■ The longest recorded conga was the Miami Super Conga, held in conjunction with Calle Ocho — a party to which Cuban-Americans invite the rest of Miami for a celebration of life together. Held on 13 Mar 1988, the conga consisted of 119,986 people.

The longest one in Britain comprised a 'snake' of 8,659 people from the South Eastern Region of the Camping and Caravanning Club of Great Britain and Ireland on 4 Sep 1982 at Brands Hatch, Kent, United Kingdom.

Country dancing ■ The most complex Scottish country dance ever held was a 256-some reel, choreographed by Ian Price, which took place on 24 Apr 1988 in Vancouver, Canada.

Disco ■ The longest recorded disco dancing marathon is one of 481 hr 30 min by V. R. P. Raman of Chandigarh, India from 7–27 Apr 1990.

Flamenco ■ The fastest flamenco dancer ever measured is Solero de Jerez, age 17, who in Brisbane, Australia in September 1967 in an electrifying routine attained 16 heel taps per second.

Jiving ■ The duration record for non-stop jiving is 110 hr 2 min by Jan Frenningsmoen (with a relay of partners) in Oslo, Norway from 27 Dec 1989–1 Jan 1990. Under the strict rules of the European Rock 'n' Roll Association the duration pair record is 24 hr 5 min by five couples at the Clayton Community Festival, Victoria, Australia from 11–12 Oct 1986.

Tap ■ The fastest *rate* ever measured for tap dancing is 32 taps per second by Stephen Gare of Sutton Coldfield at the Grand Hotel, Birmingham, West Midlands, United Kingdom on 28 Mar 1990. Roy Castle, the host of the BBC TV 'Record Breakers' program, achieved 1 million taps in 23 hr 44 min at the Guinness World of Records exhibition, London, United Kingdom on 31 Oct–1 Nov 1985.

United States ■ The fastest *rate* ever measured for tap dancing is 28 taps per second by Michael Flatley of Palos Park, IL on 9 May 1989.

The greatest ever assemblage of tap dancers in a single routine is 4,877 outside Macy's department store in New York City on 13 Aug 1989.

Drink

As from 1 Jan 1981 the strength of spirits has been expressed only in terms of percentage volume of alcohol at 68° F. Absolute or '100 percent vol' alcohol was formerly expressed to be 75·35° over proof or 75·35° OP.

In the United States proof is double the actual percentage of alcohol by volume at 60° F such that absolute alcohol is 200 percent proof spirit. 'Hangovers' are said to be aggravated by the presence of such toxic congenerics as amyl alcohol ($C_5H_{11}OH$).

Beer *Strongest* ■ Roger & Out brewed at the Frog & Parrott in Sheffield, South Yorkshire, United Kingdom from a recipe devised by W.R. Nowill and G.B. Spencer, has an alcohol volume of 16·9 percent. It was first brewed in July 1985 and has been on sale ever since.

The strongest lager is Samichlaus Dark 1987, brewed by Brauerei Hürlimann of Zürich, Switzerland. It is 14·93 percent alcohol by volume at 68° F.

Bottles *Largest* ■ A bottle 6 ft 11 in tall and 5 ft 4½ in in circumference was displayed at the Laidley Tourist Festival, Laidley, Queensland, Australia on 2 Sep 1989. The bottle was filled with 92 gal of Laidley Gold, a wheat beer only available in Laidley.

The largest bottles normally used in the wine and spirit trade are the Jeroboam (equal to 4 bottles of champagne or, rarely, of brandy and from 5 to 6½ bottles of claret according to whether blown or molded) and the double magnum (equal, since *c.* 1934, to 4 bottles of claret or, more rarely, red Burgundy). A complete set of champagne bottles would consist of a quarter bottle, through the half bottle, bottle, magnum, Jeroboam, Rehoboam, Methuselah, Salmanazar and Balthazar, to the Nebuchadnezzar, which has a capacity of 28·14 pt, and is equivalent to 20 bottles.

A bottle containing 58 pt of Château La Rose Maréchale 1985 equal in volume to 44 whole wine bottles was auctioned on 11 Oct 1988 in Copenhagen, Denmark.

Martell Cognac is available in a range of 21 bottle sizes from 0·05 pt to 6·6 pt.

Smallest ■ The smallest bottles of liquor now sold are of White Horse Scotch Whisky, which stand just over 2 in high and contain 22 minims. A mini case of 12 bottles costs £ 6·00, including tax, and measures 1·84 × 1·31 × 1·06 in. The distributors are Cumbrae Supply Co., Linwood, Strathclyde, Scotland, United Kingdom.

Most alcoholic drinks ■ During independence (1918–40) the Estonian Liquor Monopoly marketed 98 percent potato alcohol (196 proof US). In 31 US states *Everclear*, 190 proof or 95 percent vol alcohol, is marketed by the American Distilling Co. 'primarily as a base for home-made cordials.'

Royal Navy rum, introduced in 1655, was 40° OP (79 percent vol) before 1948, but was reduced to 4·5° UP (under proof) or 46 percent vol before its abolition on 31 July 1970. The Royal New Zealand Navy still issues Navy Rum at 4·5 UP and is the only Navy in the world that does.

Spirits *Most expensive* ■ The most expensive spirit is Springbank 1919 Malt Whisky, which is sold at Harrods in London, United Kingdom for £ 6,500 (including tax) per bottle.

Wine *Oldest* ■ The oldest datable wine ever found were two bottles from Xinyang, Hunan, China in 1980, from a tomb dated to 1300 B.C.

A wine jar recovered in Rome has been found to bear the label 'FAL MAS Q.LVTATIO C.MARIO COS,' meaning that it was pro-

duced in the consulship of Q. Lutatius and C. Marius, i.e., in 102 B.C.

The oldest bottle of wine to have been sold at an auction was a bottle of 1648 Johannisberger, which was bought by Scharlachberg brandy distillery for 19,720 DM (including buyer's premium) through Weichmann auctioneers at Wiesbaden, West Germany in December 1981. At the time this was equivalent to £ 4,085.

Most expensive ■ £ 105,000 was paid for a bottle of 1787 Château Lafite claret, sold to Christopher Forbes (US) at Christie's, London, United Kingdom on 5 Dec 1985. The bottle was engraved with the initials of Thomas Jefferson (1743–1826), 3rd President of the United States — 'Th J' — a factor that greatly affected the bidding. In November 1986 its cork, dried out by exhibition lights, slipped. Although the wine has not been tasted, it is assumed to be undrinkable as a result.

The record price for a half bottle of wine is FF180,000, for a 1784 Château Margaux, also bearing the initials of Thomas Jefferson, which was sold by Christie's at Vinexpo in Bordeaux, France on 26 Jun 1987.

The record price for a glass of wine is FF3,500, for the first glass of Beaujolais Nouveau 1989 released in Beaune, in the wine region of Burgundy, France. It was bought by Bernard Repolt at Pickwick's, a British pub in Beaune on 16 Nov 1989.

Auction ■ The largest single sale of wine was conducted by Christie's of London, United Kingdom on 10–11 Jul 1974 at Quaglino's Ballroom, London, United Kingdom, when 2,325 lots comprising 432,000 bottles realized £ 962,190.

Tasting ■ The largest ever reported was that staged by the Wine Institute at the St Francis Hotel, San Francisco, CA on 17 Jul 1980, with 125 pourers, 90 openers and a consumption of 3,000 bottles.

Food

Apple pie ■ The largest apple pie ever baked was that by ITV chef Glynn Christian in a 40 ft × 23 ft dish at Hewitts Farm, Chelsfield, Kent, United Kingdom from 25–27 Aug 1982. Over 600 bushels of apples were included in the pie, which weighed 30,115 lb. It was cut by Rear Admiral Sir John Woodward.

Banana split ■ The longest banana split

ever made was one of 4·55 miles in length made by residents of Selinsgrove, PA on 30 Apr 1988.

Barbecue ■ The record attendance at a one-day barbecue was 35,072, at the Iowa State Fairgrounds, Des Moines, IA on 21 Jun 1988.

The greatest meat consumption at a one-day barbecue was at the same event — 20,130 lb of pork in five hours.

The greatest quantity of meat consumed at any barbecue was 21,112 lb of beef at the Sertoma Club Barbecue, New Port Richey, FL from 7–9 Mar 1986.

Cakes ■ The largest cake ever created weighed 128,238 lb 8 oz, including 16,209 lb of icing. It was made to celebrate the 100th birthday of Fort Payne, AL, and was in the shape of Alabama. The cake was the idea of local newspaper editor Gary Gengozian, the first cut being made by 100-year old resident Ed Henderson on 18 Oct 1989. The tallest cake was 77 ft 8 in high, created by Mrs Nilasari with assistance from a team of 121 in Surabaya, Indonesia. Work started on the cake on 16 Feb 1989 and it was finished on 9 Apr 1989.

The 'Alimentarium,' a museum of food in Vevey, Switzerland, has on display the world's oldest cake, which was sealed and 'vacuum-packed' in the grave of Pepionkh, who lived in Ancient Egypt around 2200 B.C. The 4·3 in wide cake has sesame on it and honey inside, and possibly milk too.

Candy ■ The world's top-selling candy (candies) are Life Savers with nearly 35 billion rolls since 1913. A tunnel formed by the holes in the middle placed end to end would stretch to the Moon and back more than three times. Thomas Syta of Van Nuys, CA made one last 7 hr 10 min (with hole intact) on 15 Jan 1983.

The largest candy was a marzipan chocolate weighing 4,078·5 lb, made at the Ven International Fresh Market, Diemen, Netherlands on 11–13 May 1990.

Cheese ■ The largest cheese ever created was a cheddar of 40,060 lb, made on 13–14 Mar 1988 at Simon's Specialty Cheese, Little Chute,

Oldest cake ● The 'Alimentarium,' a museum of food in Vevey, Switzerland, has on display the world's oldest cake, which was sealed and 'vacuum-packed' in the grave of Pepionkh, who lived in Ancient Egypt around 2200 B.C. The 4·3 in wide cake has sesame on it and honey inside, and possibly milk too. (Photo: Alain Morvain/Gamma)

WI. It was subsequently taken on tour in a specially designed, refrigerated 'Cheesemobile.'

Cherry pie ■ The largest cherry pie ever made was one weighing a total of 28,355·17 lb and containing 25,890 lb of cherry filling. It measured 17 ft 6 in in diameter, 26 in in depth, and was baked by Chef Pierre Bakeries in conjunction with the Michigan Cherry Committee in Traverse City, MI on 25 Jul 1987.

Chocolate model ■ The largest chocolate model was one weighing 3,968·3 lb, of the 1992 Olympic Centre, Barcelona, Spain. It was made by Gremi Provincial de Pastigeria i Confiteria School, Barcelona in November 1985 and measured 32 ft 9½ in × 16 ft 4 ³/₅ in × 2 ft 4¾ in.

Cocktail ■ The largest cocktail on record was a 'Piña Colada' of 327 gal created by Kai Wulf, Ivano Birello and Axel Bornemann at Göttingen, West Germany on 26 Aug 1988.

United States ■ The largest cocktail on record in the United States was one of 300 gal created by Bacardi Imports in Miami, FL on 9 Mar 1989, and named 'Cuba Libre.'

Condiment, rarest ■ The world's most prized condiment is Cà Cuong, a secretion recovered in minute amounts from beetles in North Vietnam. Owing to war conditions, the price had risen to $100 per 1 oz before supplies virtually ceased in 1975.

Crepe ■ The largest crepe was 32 ft 11 in in diameter and 1 in deep. It was made and flipped at Dijkerhoek, Holten, Netherlands on 13 May 1990 and weighed 2,866 lb.

Dish ■ The largest menu item in the world is roasted camel, prepared occasionally for Bedouin wedding feasts. Cooked eggs are stuffed into fish, the fish stuffed into cooked chickens, the chickens stuffed into a roasted sheep's carcass and the sheep stuffed into a whole camel.

Doughnut ■ The largest doughnut ever made was a lemon-filled doughnut weighing 2,099 lb, with a diameter of 22 ft, baked by Ed Sanderson at Crystal River, FL on 10 Dec 1988.

Easter eggs ■ The heaviest Easter egg ever made was one weighing 7,561 lb 13½ oz, measuring 10 ft high, by Siegfried Berndt at 'Macopa' Patisserie, Leicester, United Kingdom, and completed on 7 Apr 1982. An egg 18 ft 11½ in tall was constructed by Tobler Suchard of Bedford, United Kingdom, on 10 Apr 1987.

Food, most expensive ■ The most expensively priced food (as opposed to spice) is First Choice Black Périgord truffle (*Tuber melanosporum*), which is sold at Harrods in London, United Kingdom for £ 17·50 per 0·44 oz jar. However, in January 1985 in the Hafr El-Baten market, Riyadh, Saudi Arabia local truffles sold for SR 5,000 for 6·6 lb, equivalent to £ 50·16 for 0·44 oz.

Fruit, most expensive ■ On 5 Apr 1977 John Synnott of Ashford, County Wicklow, Republic of Ireland sold 1 lb of strawberries (a punnet of 30 berries) to the restaurateur Leslie Cooke at auction by Walter L. Cole Ltd in the Dublin Fruit Market for £ 530 or £ 17·70 a berry.

Gingerbread house ■ A house 52 ft high and 32 ft square was built by David Sunken, Roger A. Pelcher and 100 volunteers on 2 Dec 1988. Over 2,000 sheets of gingerbread and 1,650 lb of icing were used in its construction.

Haggis ■ The largest haggis (a Scottish dish made from sheep's or calf's offal, oatmeal, suet and seasonings boiled in a skin made from the animal's stomach) was one weighing 603 lb made

for the ASDA Superstore, Corby, United Kingdom by David A. Hall Ltd of Broxburn, Lothian, United Kingdom on 6 Nov 1986.

Hamburger ■ The largest hamburger on record was one of 5,520 lb, made at the Outgamie County Fairgrounds, Seymour, WI on 5 Aug 1989.

Ice cream sundae ■ The largest ice cream sundae was one weighing 54,914·8 lb made by Palm Dairies Ltd under the supervision of Mike Rogiani in Edmonton, Alberta, Canada on 24 Jul 1988. It consisted of 44,689·5 lb of ice-cream, 9,688·1 lb of syrup and 537·2 lb of topping.

Jello ■ The world's largest jello, a 7,700 gal watermelon-flavored pink jello made by Paul Squires and Geoff Ross, worth $14,000, was set at Roma Street Forum, Brisbane, Queensland, Australia on 5 Feb 1981 in a tank by Pool Fab.

Kebab ■ The longest kebab ever was one 1,000 ft 8 in long, made by *The Natal Witness* newspaper under the supervision of Dave Erasmus and Daniel Anastasis at Pietermaritzburg, South Africa on 20 Aug 1989.

Easter egg ● The tallest Easter egg on record was 18 ft 11½ in tall, and was constructed by Tobler Suchard of Bedford, United Kingdom on 10 Apr 1987. It was made of milk chocolate and the hollow shell was approximately 1½ in thick.

Loaf ■ The longest loaf on record was one 2,357 ft 10 in long, baked by the Northlands Job Corps, Vergennes, VT on 3 Nov 1987. Some 35,840 lb of dough were required in the preparation of the loaf, and over 4,480 lb of charcoal and 4,700 ft of tin foil were used to bake it.

The largest pan loaf baked was one of 3,163 lb 10 oz, measuring 9 ft 10 in × 4 ft 1 in × 3 ft 7 in, by staff of Sasko in Johannesburg, South Africa on 18 Mar 1988.

Lollipop ■ The largest lollipop was one of 2,052·5 lb made by the Hyatt Regency Memphis Hotel, TN on 20 Feb 1986.

Meat pie ■ The largest meat pie on record weighed 19,908 lb and was the 9th in the series of Denby Dale pies. It was baked on 3 Sep 1988 to mark the bicentenary of Denby Dale pie making, the first one in 1788 having been made to celebrate King George III's return to sanity. The fourth (Queen Victoria's Jubilee, 1887) went a bit 'off' and had to be buried in quick-lime.

Milk shake ■ The largest milk shake was a chocolate one of 1,891·69 gal, made by Smith Dairy Products Company at Orrville, OH on 20 Oct 1989.

Omelet ■ The largest omelet in the world was one with an area of 706 ft 8 in², made of 54,763 eggs with 531 lb cheese in a skillet 30 ft in diameter. It was cooked by Michael McGowan, assisted by his staff and the Sunrise Jaycees of Las Vegas, NV on 25 Oct 1986.

Paella ■ The largest paella measured 52 ft 6 in in diameter and was made by Josep Gruges 'Pepitu' on 25 Aug 1987 in the Playa de Aro, Gerona, Spain. The ingredients included 8,140 lb of rice, 6,600 lb of meat, 3,300 lb of mussels, 1,540 lb each of beans and peppers, 440 lb of garlic and 88 gal of oil. The paella was eaten by 40,000 people who washed it all down with 8,000 bottles of Catalan champagne.

Pastry ■ The longest pastry in the world was the 'record' pastry 1,683 ft 2½ in in length made by chefs at the Hyatt Regency Ravinia, Atlanta, GA on 26 Jul 1986.

Pie ■ The largest and heaviest pie of any kind is a pecan pie weighing 40,266 lb with a diameter of 40 ft, baked 16 Jun 1989 for the Pecan Festival in Okmulgee, OK.

Pizza ■ The largest pizza ever baked was one measuring 111 ft 3 in in diameter, made by Pizza Hut at the World Trade Center in Singapore on 9 Jun 1990.

Popcorn ■ The largest container of popcorn was a box measuring 25 ft × 25 ft, which was filled at Jones High School, Orlando, FL on 15–17 Dec 1988. After popping, the average depth of the corn was 6·06 ft, giving a total volume of 3,787·5 ft³.

Popsicle ■ The world's largest popsicle was one of 5,750 lb constructed for the Westside Assembly of God Church, Davenport, IA on 7 Sep 1975.

Potato chips ■ The Pringle's Plant in Jackson, TN produced a pringle potato chip 23 in x 14½ in on 19 April 1990. Pringle potato chips are made from potato flour.

Salami ■ The longest salami on record was one 61 ft 3½ in long with a circumference of 24 in, weighing 1,202·5 lb, made by Kutztown Bologna Company, PA and displayed at the Lebanon Bologna Fest in Kutztown on 11–13 Aug 1989.

Sausage ■ The longest continuous sausage ever made was one of 13·125 miles, made at the premises of Keith Boxley at Wombourne, near Wolverhampton, United Kingdom in 15 hr 33 min on 18–19 Jun 1988.

Spice, most expensive ■ Prices for wild ginseng (root of *Panax quinquefolius*), from the Chan Pak Mountain area of China, thought to have aphrodisiac qualities, were reported in November 1977 to be as high as $23,000 per ounce in Hong Kong. Total annual shipments from Jilin Province do not exceed 140 oz a year. A leading medical journal in the United States has likened its effects to 'corticosteroid poisoning.'

Spice 'hottest' ■ The hottest of all spices is claimed to be Siling labuyo from the Philippines.

The chili pepper or capsicum known as Tepin, of southwest US, comes in pods ³/₈ in in diameter. A single dried gram will produce detectable 'heat' in 68·3 lb of bland sauce.

Strawberry bowl ■ The largest strawberry bowl ever picked had a net weight of 4,832 lb. The strawberries were picked at Walt Furlong's farm at New Ross, County Wexford, Republic of Ireland during the Enniscorthy Strawberry Fair on 9 Jul 1989.

Trifle ■ The largest sherry trifle on record was one weighing 2,513 lb including 22 gal of sherry made on 1 Feb 1989 by students of Seale-Hayne College, Newton Abbot, Devon, United Kingdom.

Manufactured Articles

Amplifier ■ The largest working guitar amplifier is 9·04 ft high, weighs 718 lb, houses 32 10-in speakers driven by 600 watts of all tube power. However, it can handle 1,400 watts' output. This Ampeg Mega SVT Bass Amp System was unveiled at the NAMM EXPO in Chicago, IL by St Louis Music of St Louis, MO.

Antique ■ The largest antique ever sold was London Bridge, in March 1968. The sale was made by Ivan F. Luckin of the Court of Common Council of the Corporation of London, United Kingdom to the McCulloch Oil Corporation of Los Angeles, CA for £ 1,029,000. The 10,230 tons of facade stonework were reassembled, at a cost of £ 3 million, at Lake Havasu City, AZ and 'rededicated' on 10 Oct 1971.

Armor ■ The highest auction price paid for a suit of armor was £ 1,925,000, by B. H. Trupin (US) on 5 May 1983 at Sotheby's, London, United Kingdom for a suit made in Milan by Giovanni Negroli in 1545 for Henri II of France. It came from the Hever Castle Collection in Kent, United Kingdom.

Basket ■ The biggest basket ever made was 15 ft tall, woven by Nineteenth Century Basket Company, Warren, OH in 1986.

Beds ■ In Bruges, Belgium, Philip, Duke of Burgundy had a bed 12½ ft × 19 ft erected for the perfunctory *coucher officiel* ceremony with Princess Isabella of Portugal in 1430.

A promotional 19 ft 8 in × 14 ft 5 in pinewood bed, accommodating 39 people, was exhibited by a French company in August 1986.

Beer cans ■ Beer cans date from a test marketing by Krueger Beer of Newark, NJ at Richmond, VA in 1935.

The largest collection has been made by John F. Ahrens of Mount Laurel, NJ, with nearly 15,000 different cans.

A Rosalie Pilsner can sold for $6,000 in the United States in April 1981. A collection of 2,502 unopened bottles and cans of beer from 103 countries was bought for $25,000 by the Downer Club ACT of Australia, at the Australian Associated Press Financial Markets Annual Charity Golf Tournament on 23 Mar 1990.

Beer labels (Labology) ■ Jan Solberg of Oslo, Norway had amassed 322,200 different labels from around the world by May 1990.

Beer mats (Tegestology) ■ The world's largest collection of beer mats is owned by Leo Pisker of Vienna, Austria, who had collected 130,600 different mats from 153 countries by April 1990.

Beer tankard ■ The largest tankard was made by the Selangor Pewter Co. of Kuala Lumpur, Malaysia and unveiled on 30 Nov 1985. It measures 6½ ft in height and has a capacity of 615 gal.

Blanket ■ The world's largest blanket was

Bottle caps ● At 13 May 1990 Helge Friholm's collection contained 59,180 different crown bottle caps from 167 countries, including one made for his 80th birthday by the Faxe-Jyske Brewery of Søborg, Denmark.

made by the people of Perth, Western Australia in a joint venture between the Living Stone Foundation Inc. and Radio 6PR. Comprising hand-knitted, machine-knitted and crocheted sections, it measured 27,976 ft² and was unveiled on 6 Aug 1989.

Bottle, gold ■ A gold bottle, appraised at $115,000, was created by Jewelry Designer Henry Dunay for Schenley Affiliated Brands Corps., Dallas, TX in May 1990. The 18-Karat Pinch Gold Bottle, crafted in the likeness of the three-cornered pinch 'dimple' bottle, took more than 200 man hours to complete and contains enough gold to make 2,000 wedding bands.

Bottle caps ■ Since 1950 Helge Friholm (b. 1910) of Søborg, Denmark has amassed 59,180 different bottle caps (to May 1990) from 167 countries.

Pyramid ■ A pyramid consisting of 263,810 bottle caps was constructed by 12 students of Nanyang Technological Institute, Singapore from 10–17 Jun 1990.

Bottle collections ■ David L. Maund of Upham, Hampshire, United Kingdom has a collection of unduplicated miniature Scotch whisky bottles amounting to 8,732. Over the past 30 years he has also collected 323 different miniature Guinness bottles.

George E. Terren of Southboro, MA had a collection of 29,508 miniature and distilled spirit and liquor bottles at 1 Mar 1988.

At 29 May 1990 Ted Shuler of Germantown, TN had a collection of 2,248 different bottled beers with specimens from 97 countries.

The world's greatest collection of whiskey bottles is one of 3,100 unduplicated, assembled by Signor Edward Giaccone at his *whiskeyteca*, Salo, Lake Garda, Italy.

The largest reported collection of spirits and liquers is 2,890 unduplicated bottles collected by Ian Boasman at Bistro French, Preston, Lancashire, United Kingdom by February 1990.

Cans ■ An stadium-shaped structure consisting of 2 million empty beverage cans was built in Verona, Italy by 150 members of AVIS–AIDO with the cooperation of Rail (producers of aluminum cans). It was completed on 1 Dec 1989 after 18,000 hours of work.

Candles ■ A candle 80 ft high and 8½ ft in diameter was exhibited at the 1897 Stockholm Exhibition by the firm of Lindahls. The overall height was 127 ft.

A candle constructed by Enham Industries at the Charlton Leisure Centre, Andover, Hampshire, United Kingdom on 2 Jul 1989 measured 101·7 ft high.

Cards ■ The world's largest greeting card was produced by seven members of Oceanway PTA, Jacksonville, FL. It measured 37 ft 3 in × 54 ft 9 in. It was delivered by the United States Postal Service to Oceanway Seventh Grade Center on 21 Apr 1989.

Craig Shergold of Carshalton, Surrey, United Kingdom had collected a record 16,250,692 get-well cards by May 1990.

Jarrod Booth of Salt Spring Island, British Columbia, Canada had a collection of 205,120 Christmas cards in February 1990.

Carpets and rugs ■ The earliest carpet known is a Seythian woolen pile-knotted carpet measuring 6 ft² and dating from the 4th–3rd centuries B.C. It was discovered by the Russian archaeologist Sergei Ivanovich Rudenko in 1947 in the Pazyryk Valley in southern Siberia and is now preserved in the Hermitage, Leningrad, USSR.

Of ancient carpets, the largest was a gold-enriched silk carpet of Hashim (dated A.D. 743) of the Abbasid caliphate in Baghdad, Iraq. It is reputed to have measured 180 × 300 ft. A 52,225 ft² or 31·4-ton red carpet was laid on 13 Feb 1982, by the Allied Corporation, from Radio City Music Hall to the New York Hilton along the Avenue of the Americas, New York, NY.

The most finely woven carpet known is one woven by five women having 3,716 per in², selected from 3,000 weaving specialists for Ozipek Halicilik A.S. of Hereke, Turkey. The project took five years to complete and the finished product, named *Hereke Treasure*, was

sold to Gandhara Carpet Japan Ltd, Tokyo in March 1988.

The most magnificent carpet ever made was the Spring carpet of Khusraw made for the audience hall of the Sassanian palace at Ctesiphon, Iraq. It was about 7,000 ft² of silk and gold thread, and encrusted with emeralds. It was cut up as booty by looters in A.D. 635 and from the known realization value of the pieces must have had an original value of some £ 100 million.

Chair ■ An enlarged version, 53 ft 4 in tall, of the chair George Washington sat in while presiding at the Constitutional Convention was made by the NSA and brought to Washington, DC for the 1989 Inauguration.

Chandeliers ■ The world's largest set of chandeliers was created by the Kookje Lighting Co. Ltd of Seoul, Korea. It is 39 ft high, weighs 11·8 tons and has 700 bulbs. Completed in November 1988, it occupies three floors of the Lotte Chamshil Department Store in Seoul.

Check ■ The largest check ever made measured 45 ft × 22 ft 6 in. Signed by Nick Shute and Richard Spencer of ANZ Bank, the check for £ 26,096·38p, in favor of the British Broadcasting Corporation's Children in Need Appeal, was presented to the British Broadcasting Corporation during the 'Children in Need' program on 17 Nov 1989.

Christmas cracker (party favor) ■ The largest functional cracker ever constructed was one measuring 120 ft 3 in long built by The Christmas Cracker Project. After two attempts, the cracker was pulled by London schoolchildren outside the Royal Festival Hall, London, United Kingdom on 25 Sep 1989.

Cigars ■ The largest cigar ever made measures 16 ft 8½ in in length and weighs 577 lb 9 oz, taking 243 hours and using 3,330 full tobacco leaves. It was made by Tinus Vinke and Jan Weijmer in February 1983 and is in the Tobacco Museum in Kampen, Netherlands.

The largest marketed cigar in the world is the 14-in Valdez Emperador manufactured by Fábrica de Puros Santa Clara of San Andrés Tuxtla, Veracruz, Mexico and exclusively distributed by Tabacos San Andrés.

The most expensive standard cigar in the world is the 9¼-in long Montecristo 'A,' which retails in Britain at £ 18·25.

Joseph Hruby of Lyndhurst, OH has the largest known collection of cigar bands with 202,434 different examples dating from c. 1895.

Cigarettes ■ World production in 1985 was 9·8 trillion cigarettes.

The people of China were estimated to consume 1·18 billion in 1985. In Senegal 80 percent of urban males smoke. In 1964, 53% of American men smoked; this number dropped to 29·5% in 1985. In 1964, 32% of American women smoked; 23·8% smoked cigarettes in 1985. The highest percentage of smokers were men age 35–44 (37% smokers). About two-thirds of smokers con-

sumed less than 25 cigarettes per day, while approximately 15% puffed two packs or more.

The longest cigarettes ever marketed were *Head Plays*, each 11 in long and sold in packets of five in the United States in about 1930, to save tax. The shortest were *Lilliput* cigarettes, each 1¼ in long and ⅛ in in diameter, made in Great Britain in 1956.

In the Philippines there is a brand with 1·1 grain nicotine per cigarette.

The world's largest collection of cigarettes is that of Robert E. Kaufman MD, of New York. In April 1989 he had 8,320 different cigarettes made in 172 countries. The oldest brand represented is *Lone Jack*, made in the United States c. 1885. Both the longest and shortest (see above) are represented.

Cigarette cards ■ The earliest known tobacco card is 'Vanity Fair' dated 1876, issued by Wm S. Kimball & Co, Rochester, NY. The earliest British example appeared c. 1883 in the form of a calendar issued by Allen & Ginter, of Richmond, VA, trading from Holborn Viaduct, City of London, United Kingdom. The largest known collection is that of Mr Edward Wharton-Tigar (b. 1913) of London, United Kingdom with more than 1 million cigarette and trade cards in about 45,000 sets. This collection has been accepted as a bequest by the British Museum, where it will eventually be available for public study.

On 30 Jul 1987, a complete set of Taddy's Clowns and Circus Artistes was sold at Phillips, London, United Kingdom for £ 15,500 (£ 17,050 including buyer's premium of £ 1,550), a record price for cigarette cards at auction. Only a handful of

complete sets of 20 are known. James Taddy & Co, a small London tobacco firm founded *c.* 1740, was renowned for its beautifully produced cards.

Cigarette lighters ■ The Leaders Lighthouse Table Lighter is made in 18-ct gold—designed in the shape of a lighthouse set on an island base of amethyst that alone weighs 1 cwt. It weighs 51·4 oz troy and the windows on the lighthouse stem are amethyst. Priced at £ 37,500, it was sold by Alfred Dunhill, St James's, London, United Kingdom in 1986.

Frans Van der Heijden of Vlijmen, Netherlands had collected over 13,515 different lighters by 1 May 1990.

Cigarette packets ■ The earliest surviving cigarette packet is a Finnish *Petit Canon* packet for 25, made by Tollander & Klärich in 1860, from the Ventegodt Collection. The rarest is the Latvian 700-year anniversary (1201–1901) *Riga* packet, believed to be unique, from the same collection. The largest verified private collection was one of 62,837 from over 150 countries owned by Vernon Young of Farnham, Surrey, United Kingdom.

Cigarette rolling paper booklets ■ The largest collection of cigarette rolling paper booklets is one of 2,366 owned by Peter Emmens of Kenley, Surrey, United Kingdom.

Credit cards ■ The largest collection of valid credit cards at May 1990 is one of 1,212 (all different) by Walter Cavanagh (b. 1943) of Santa Clara, CA. The cost of acquisition to 'Mr Plastic Fantastic' was nil, and he keeps them in the world's longest wallet—250 ft long weighing 35 lb and worth more than $1·6 million in credit.

Curtains ■ The largest curtain ever built was a bright orange-red 4·4-ton and 185-ft high curtain suspended 1,350 ft across the Rifle Gap, Grand Hogback, CO by Bulgarian-born sculptor Christo (ne Javacheff) on 10 Aug 1971. It blew apart in a 50 mph gust 27 hr later. The total cost involved in displaying this work of art was $750,000.

The world's largest functional curtain is one 550 ft × 65 ft in the Brabazon hangar at British Aerospace, Filton, Bristol, United Kingdom used to enclose aircraft in the paint-spraying bay. It is electrically drawn.

Dress ■ A wedding outfit created by Helene Gainville with jewels by Alexander Reza is believed to be worth $7,301,587·20 precisely. The dress is embroidered with diamonds mounted on platinum and was unveiled in Paris, France on 23 Mar 1989.

A robe for Emperor Field Marshal Jean-Bédel Bokassa with a 39-ft long train was encrusted with 785,000 pearls and 1·22 million crystal beads by Guiselin of Paris for £ 77,125. It was for his coronation at Bangui, Central African Empire (now Republic) on 4 Dec 1977 (see also Shoes).

The world's longest wedding dress train measured 97 ft 7 ¾ and was made by Margaret Riley of Thurnby Lodge, Leicestershire, United Kingdom for the blessing of the marriage of Diane and Steven Reid in Thurmaston, Leicestershire, United Kingdom on 6 May 1990.

Egg ■ The largest and most elaborate 'Easter Egg' stands 2 ft tall and was fashioned from 37 lb of gold studded with 20,000 pink diamonds. Designed by London jeweler, Paul Kutchinsky, the Argyle Library Egg took six British craftsmen 7,000 man-hours to create and has a price tag of £ 7 million. It was unveiled on 30 Apr 1990 before going on display at the Victoria and Albert Museum, London, United Kingdom.

Electric bulb ■ The smallest electric bulb is one 0·12 in long by 0·02 in in diameter made by the Hamai Electric Lamp Co, Tokyo, Japan.

Fabrics ■ The oldest surviving fabric discovered from Level VI A at atal Hüyük, Turkey has been radiocarbon dated to 5900 B.C.

The most expensive fabric is Vicuña cloth manufactured by Fujii Keori Ltd of Osaka, Japan, retailing at 1 million yen (£ 4,450) per meter in January 1988.

Fan ■ An intricately carved wooden fan measuring 10·9 ft when unfolded and 6 ft high was completed by Wang Xianbao of Shanghai, China in January 1987.

Fireworks ■ The largest firework ever produced has been Universe I Part II, exploded for the Lake Toya Festival, Hokkaido, Japan on 15 Jul 1988. The 1,543-lb shell was 1,354·7 in in diameter and burst to a diameter of 3,937 ft.

The longest firecracker display was produced by the Johor Tourism Department, the United Malaysian Youth Movement and Mr Yap Seng Hock, and took place on 20 Feb 1988 at Pelangi Garden, Johor Bahru, Johor, Malaysia. The total length of the display was 18,777 ft and consisted of 3,338,777 firecrackers and 1,468 lb of gunpowder. It burned for 9 hr 27 min.

Flags ■ The oldest known flag is one dated to *c.* 3000 B.C. found in 1972 at Khabis, Iran. It is of metal and measures 9 × 9 in and depicts an eagle, two lions and a goddess, three women and a bull.

The largest flag in the world, one of the Republic of China presented to the city of Kaohsiung, Taiwan by Unichamps Inpe'l Corp. on 9 Apr 1989, measured 413 x 275½ ft and weighed 1,807·7 lb.

The largest flag *flown* from a flagpole is a Brazilian national flag measuring 229 ft 8 in × 328 ft 1 in in Brasilia.

The study of flags is known as vexillology from

Dress ● This outfit, created by Helene Gainville with jewels by Alexander Reza, made its high-security appearance at the St James Club, Paris, France on 23 Mar 1989. The dress is embroidered with diamonds mounted on platinum, and the complete outfit is said to be worth $7,301,587·20. (Photo: Gamma/Darmigny)

Chandelier ● Right: The world's largest set of chandeliers was created by the Kookje Lighting Co. Ltd of Seoul, Korea. Completed in November 1988 and occupying three floors of the Lotte Chamshil Department Store in Seoul, the chandelier is 39 ft high, weighs 11·8 tons and has 700 bulbs consuming 54 kW of power. Spectacular *son et lumière* effects can be achieved by programming the supersonic-wave sensors fitted in the base.

Latin *vexillum*, a flag, and was coined by Dr Whitney Smith of Winchester, MA.

Float ■ The largest float was the 155-ft long, 24-ft wide 'Merry Christmas America' float bearing three double arches, a 17-ft Christmas tree, two 15-ft peppermint candy sticks and 5,380 ft² of wrapping paper, used at the 40th Annual Christmas Parade, Baton Rouge, LA on 5 Dec 1986.

Furniture ■ The largest item of furniture in the world is a wooden bench along the Masuhoura Beach, Ishikawa, Japan, which can seat over 1,400 people and measures 1,512 ft in length. It was completed by a team of 800 on 9 Mar 1987.

Garbage can ■ The world's largest garbage can was made by Glasdon UK Ltd of Blackpool, Lancashire, United Kingdom for 'Spring Clean Day' on 29 Mar 1990. The 18 ft 6 in tall replica of their standard 'Topsy' bin has a capacity of 5,719 gal.

Glass ■ The most priceless example of the art of glassmaking is usually regarded as the glass Portland Vase, which dates from late in the first century B.C. or first century A.D. It was made in Italy, and was in the possession of the Barberini family in Rome from at least 1642. It was eventually bought by the Duchess of Portland in 1792 but smashed while in the British Museum by William Lloyd on 7 Feb 1845.

The thinnest glass, type D263, has a minimum thickness of 0·00137 in and a maximum thickness of 0·0021 in. It is made by Deutsche Spezialglas AG, Grünenplan, West Germany for use in electronic and medical equipment.

Gold ■ The gold coffin of the 14th-century B.C.

> **Fan** ● An intricately carved wooden fan measuring 10·9 ft when unfolded and 6 ft high was completed by Wang Xianbao of Shanghai, China in January 1987.

Pharaoh Tutankhamun discovered by Howard Carter on 16 Feb 1923 in the Valley of the Kings, western Thebes, Egypt weighed 243 lb.

Hammock ■ A 145½ ft long hammock was woven by members of the Åboland Crafts Guild, Pargas, Finland in July 1988. The completed hammock was suspended between large oak trees and accommodated 21 people.

Jigsaw puzzles ■ The earliest jigsaw puzzles were made as 'dissected maps' by John Spilsbury (1739–69) in Russell Court off Drury Lane, London, United Kingdom c. 1762.

The world's largest jigsaw puzzle measured 9,739 ft². It comprised 1,085 pieces and was assembled on 26 Nov 1989 by the Prince George and District United Way of British Columbia, Canada.

In July 1986 'L'Association l'Arbre aux Mille Sources' constructed a jigsaw consisting of 150,000 pieces and measuring 25 × 82 × 48 ft.

Fujisankei Communications Group of Japan commissioned Yanoman Co. to produce a puzzle 10·63 × 19·29 ft with 61,752 pieces. Each piece was sold for charity.

Custom-made Stave puzzles made by Steve Richardson of Norwich, VT of 2,640 pieces cost $7,355 in March 1990.

Kettle ■ The largest antique copper kettle

---

was one standing 3 ft high with a 6 ft girth and a 20 gal capacity, built in Taunton, Somerset, United Kingdom, for the hardware merchants Fisher and Son c. 1800.

Knife ■ The penknife with the greatest number of blades is the Year Knife made by cutlers Joseph Rodgers & Sons, of Sheffield, South Yorkshire, United Kingdom whose trade mark was granted in 1682. The knife was made in 1822 with 1,822 blades and a blade was added every year until 1973 when there was no further space. It was acquired by Britain's largest hand tool manufacturers, Stanley Works (Great Britain) Ltd of Sheffield, South Yorkshire, United Kingdom in 1970.

Lego tower ■ The tallest Lego tower, 59 ½ ft , was built in Tel Aviv, Israel in May 1990 and consisted of 221,560 bricks.

Lantern ■ A 12 ft 1¾ in high lantern with a 39 ft 4 in circumference. It was made on 29 Apr 1989 by members of the Lotus Lantern International Buddhist Center and staff of the Seoul Hilton International Hotel, South Korea.

Matchbox labels ■ The oldest match label of accepted provenance is that of Samuel Jones c. 1830.

The finest collection of trademark labels (excluding any pub/bar or other advertizing labels) is some 280,000 pieces collected by the phillumenist Robert Jones of Indianapolis, IN.

Teiichi Yoshizawa (b. 1904) of Chiba-ken, Japan has amassed 712,118 matchbox labels (including advertizing labels) from 150 countries since 1925.

Garbage can ● 'Topsy', made by Glasdon UK Ltd of Blackpool, United Kingdom, stands 18 ft 6 in tall and has 305 times the capacity of a standard garbage can. Launched on Spring Clean Day on 29 Mar 1990, it is given the thumbs up by a conscientious passer-by in Blackpool. (Photo: Glasdon UK Ltd)

Flag ● The flag of the Republic of China presented to the city of Kaohsiung, Taiwan by Unichamps Inpe'l Corp. at the opening ceremony of the Kaohsiung Labourers' Athletic Meeting on 9 Apr 1989 measures 413 × 275 $\frac{1}{2}$ ft and weighs 1,807·7 lb.

Lantern ● Below: A handmade, 12 ft 1 $\frac{3}{4}$-in high lantern with a 39 ft 4 in circumference was completed on 29 Apr 1989, after 22 days' work, by members of the Lotus Lantern International Buddhist Center and staff of the Seoul Hilton International Hotel, South Korea.

Matchstick ■ The longest matchstick, made by Stichting 'De Langste Daag' at Tegelen, Netherlands on 25 Jun 1988, measured 61 ft 8 in, weighed 2,204 lb and burned for 6 hr 45 min 1 sec.

Needles ■ Needles made of bone have been found in sites of the Upper Paleolithic Aurignacian period in France dated c. 28,000–24,000 B.C.

The longest is one 6 ft 1 in long made by George Davies of Thomas Somerfield, Bloxwich, West Midlands, United Kingdom for stitching on mattress buttons lengthwise. One is preserved in the National Needle Museum at Forge Mill, Redditch, Worcestershire, United Kingdom.

Nylon ■ The finest denier nylon yarn ever produced is the 5 denier produced by Nilit Ltd of Tel Aviv, Israel. The sheerest stockings normally available are 9 denier. A hair from the average human head is about 50 denier.

Paper clip ■ An iron paper clip measuring 23 ft and weighing 1,328 lb was made by O. Mustad & Son of Norway and unveiled at the Norwegian School of Management in Sandvika in honor of Johan Våler, pioneer of the paper clip in 1899.

Pens ■ The most expensive writing pen is the 5003.002 CARAN D'ACHE 18-carat solid gold Madison slimline ballpoint pen incorporating white diamonds of 6·35 carats, exclusively distributed by Jakar International Limited of London, United Kingdom. Its recommended retail price in 1991 is £ 21,950 (incl. tax).

A Japanese collector paid 1·3 million French francs in Feb 1988 for the 'Anémone' fountain pen made by Réden, France. It was encrusted with 600 precious stones, including emeralds, amethysts, rubies, sapphires and onyx, and took skilled craftsmen over a year to complete.

The world's leading pen is the BiC Crystal, with daily global sales of 14 million by the BiC organization.

Pistol ■ In Dec 1983 it was reported that Ray Bily (US) owned an initialed gold pistol made for Adolf Hitler that was valued for insurance at $375,000.

The pistol with the largest magazine capacity is the .22LR M.100P, with 103 rounds of continuous firepower, manufactured by Calico, Bakersfield, CA.

Photographs with stars ■ Barbara Ann Thomas of Fredericksburg, VA has had her photograph taken with over 200 Hollywood stars. Husband John acts as photographer while they holiday at film locations in Hollywood, Los Angeles, CA.

Postcards ■ Deltiology is claimed to be the third largest collecting hobby next only to stamps and coins.

Austria issued the first cards in 1869, followed by Britain in 1872.

The highest price paid for a postcard was $4,400 for one of the five known Mucha Waverly Cycle postcards. It was sold by Susan Brown Nicholson of Lisle, IL in September 1984.

Pottery ■ The largest vase on record is one 11 ft in height, weighing 3,968 lb, thrown by Aksel Krog and Jorgen Hansen of Denmark on 10–13 Feb 1989. The Chinese ceramic authority Chingwah Lee of San Francisco, CA was reported in August 1978 to have appraised a unique 39 in Kang Hsi four-sided vase then in a bank vault in Phoenix, AZ at '$60 million.'

Quilt ■ The world's largest quilt was made by 7,000 citizens of North Dakota for the 1989 centennial of North Dakota. It measured 85 × 134 ft.

Ropes ■ The largest rope ever made was a coir fiber launching rope with a circumference of 47 in made in 1858 for the British liner *Great Eastern* by John and Edwin Wright of Birmingham, West Midlands, United Kingdom. It consisted of four strands, each of 3,780 yarns. The longest fiber rope ever made without a splice was one of 11·36 miles of 6½ in circumference manila by Frost Brothers (now British Ropes Ltd) in London, United Kingdom in 1874. (See also Wire ropes, Chapter 4.) The strongest cable-laid wire rope strop made is one 11·1 in in diameter with a breaking strain of 3,582 tons.

Scarf ■ The longest scarf ever knitted measured an amazing 20 miles 13 ft long. It was knitted by residents of Abbeyfield Houses for the Abbeyfield Society and was completed on 29 May 1988.

Shoes ■ James Smith, founder of James Southall & Co. of Norwich, Norfolk, United Kingdom introduced sized shoes in 1792. The firm began making 'Start-rite' children's shoes in 1923. Emperor Bokassa of the Central African Empire (now Republic) commissioned pearl-studded shoes from the House of Berluti, Paris, France for his self-coronation on 4 Dec 1977 at a cost of $85,000. The most expensive shoes are mink-lined golf shoes with 18-carat gold embellishments and ruby-tipped spikes made by Stylo Matchmakers International of Northampton, United Kingdom, which retail for $17,985 per pair in the US.

A pair of women's cream kid and braid high-heeled slap-soled shoes c. 1660 sold by Lord Hereford at Sotheby's, London, United Kingdom in September 1987 to Mrs Sonia Bata fetched £ 21,000. An export license was reportedly refused on 20 Jun 1988. Excluding cases of elephantiasis, the largest shoes ever sold are a pair size 42 built for the giant Harley Davidson of Avon, FL. The normal limit is size 14. For advertizing and display purposes facsimiles of shoes weighing up to 1·6 tons have been constructed.

Silver ■ The largest single pieces of silver are a pair of water jugs of 10,408 troy oz (4·77 cwt) made in 1902 for the Maharaja of Jaipur (1861–1922). They are 5 ft 3 in tall, with a circumference of 8 ft 1½ in, and have a capacity of 1,800 gallons. They are now in the City Palace, Jaipur, India. The silversmith was Gorind Narain.

Snuff ■ The most expensive snuff obtainable in Britain is 'Café Royale' sold by G. Smith and Sons (est. 1869) of 74 Charing Cross Road, London, United Kingdom. The price was £ 2·60 per oz in April 1990.

Soccer ball ■ The world's largest soccer ball measures 7¾ ft in diameter, weighs 80 lb and has 8,640 stitches requiring 425 ft of thread. It was made by Mitre Sports of Huddersfield, West Yorkshire, United Kingdom and it is hoped that the football will eventually be signed by each of the 92 English Football (Soccer) League Clubs.

Sofa ■ The longest standard sofa manufactured for market is the Augustus Rex Sofa, 12¼ ft in length made by Dodge & Son of Sherborne, Dorset, United Kingdom. In April 1990 a 21 ft 9 in long jacquard fabric sofa was specially manufactured by Mountain View Interiors of Collingwood, Ontario, Canada with an estimated value of $8,000.

Suit ■ EVA suits for extra-vehicular activity worn by Space Shuttle crews from 1982 have a unit cost of $3·4 million.

Table ■ The longest table was set up in Pesaro, Italy on 20 Jun 1988 by the US Libertas Scavolini Basketball team. It was 10,072 ft in length and was used to seat 12,000 people.

Table cloth ■ The world's largest tablecloth is one 986 ft long by 72 in wide made of damask by Tonrose Limited of Manchester, United Kingdom in June 1988.

Tapestry ■ The earliest known examples of tapestry woven linen are three pieces from the tomb of the Egyptian pharaoh Thutmose IV dated to 1483–1411 B.C.

The largest tapestry ever woven is the *History of Irak*, with an area of 13,370·7 ft². It was designed by the Yugoslavian artist Frane Delale and produced by the Zivtex Regeneracija Workshop in Zabok, Yugoslavia. The tapestry was completed in 1986 and it now adorns the wall of an amphitheater in Baghdad, Iraq. The famous Bayeux *Telle du Conquest, dite tapisserie de la reine Mathilde*, a hanging 19½ in wide by 231 ft in length, depicts events of 1064–66 in 72 scenes and was probably worked in Canterbury, Kent, United Kingdom c. 1086. It was 'lost' for 2½ centuries from 1476 until 1724. The Overlord Embroidery of 34 panels each 8 × 3 ft, commissioned by Lord Dulverton (b. 1915) from the Royal School of Needlework in London, United Kingdom, was completed in 1979 after 100 man-years of work and is 41 ft longer than the Bayeux. It has the largest area of any embroidery with 816 ft².

Tartan ■ The earliest evidence of tartan is the so-called Falkirk tartan, found stuffed in a jar of coins in Bells Meadow, Falkirk, Scotland. It is of a dark and light brown pattern and dates from c. A.D. 245. The earliest reference to a specific named tartan is to a Murray tartan in 1618, although Mackay tartan was probably worn earlier. There are 1,300 tartans known to the Museum of Scottish Tartans at Comrie, Perth, Tayside, United Kingdom. HRH Prince of Wales is eligible to wear 11, including the Balmoral, which has been exclusive to the royal family since 1852.

Ticket ■ The smallest ticket was one measuring 0·1 × 0·2 × 0·04 in for admission to the Asian-Pacific Exposition Fukuoka '89, Fukuoka, Japan. It was made of ceramic on which letters of 85–280 microns were printed.

Time capsule ■ The world's largest time capsule is the Tropico Time Tunnel of 10,000 ft³ in a cave in Rosamond, CA sealed by the Kern Antelope Historical Society on 20 Nov 1966 and intended for opening in A.D. 2866.

Toy ■ 'Lots-a-Lots-a-Legggggggs,' the 1,000-legged pink caterpillar, measures 250 ft and weighs 300 lb. It was created by Commonwealth Toy & Novelty Co., Inc, New York City.

Typewriters ■ The first patent for a typewriter was by Henry Mill in 1714 but the earliest known working machine was made by Pellegrine Turri (Italy) in 1808.

Wallet ■ The most expensive wallet ever made is a platinum-cornered, diamond-studded crocodile creation made by Louis Quatorze of Paris and Mikimoto of Tokyo selling in September 1984 at £ 56,000.

Wreath ■ The most expensive wreath on record was that presented to Sri Chinmoy in New York on 11 Jul 1983 by Ashrita Furman and Pahar Meltzer. It was handled by the Garland of Divinity's Love Florist, contained 10,000 flowers, and cost $3,500.

Yo-yo ■ The largest yo-yo ever constructed was one measuring 6 ft in diameter made by the woodwork class of Shakamak High School in Jasonville, IN. It weighed 820 lb and was launched from a 160-ft crane on 29 Mar 1990, when it 'yo-yoed' 12 times.

Zipper ■ The world's longest zipper was laid around the center of Sneek, Netherlands on 5 Sep 1989. The brass zipper, made by Yoshida (Netherlands) Ltd, is 9,353·56 ft long and consists of 2,565,900 teeth.

THE HUMAN WORLD

Politics
_____
Heads of State
_____
Royalty
_____
Government
_____
Awards
_____
Military
_____
Law
_____
Education
_____
Religion
_____

Oldest army ● The oldest army is the Pontifical Swiss Guard, founded before 1400. (Photo: Images)

Political & Social

Largest political division ■ The Commonwealth, a free association of 50 independent states and their dependencies, covers an area of 10,491,016 miles² with a population estimated in 1988 to be 1,213,601,000. The British Empire began to expand when Henry VII patented trade monopolies to John Cabot in March 1496 and when the East India Co. was incorporated on 31 Dec 1600.

COUNTRIES

The world comprises 170 sovereign countries and 62 separately administered non-sovereign or other territories, making a total of 232. Namibia became the 171st sovereign country when it achieved independence in March 1990, but the unification of North and South Yemen in May 1990 brought the number of sovereign countries back down to 170.

The United Nations still lists the *de jure* territories of East Timor (now incorporated into Indonesia), Western Sahara (now occupied by Morocco), the former mandated territory of Palestine and the uninhabited Canton and Enderbury Islands (now disputed between the United States and Kiribati) but does not list the three Baltic states of Estonia, Latvia and Lithuania, though their forcible incorporation into the USSR in 1940 has never been internationally recognized. Neither does it list the *de facto* territories of Taiwan, Mayotte or Spanish North Africa, the four Antarctic Territories or the Australian Territory of Coral Sea Islands and Heard and McDonald Islands.

Largest ■ The country with the greatest area is the Union of Soviet Socialist Republics (USSR), comprising 15 Union (constituent) Republics with a total area of 8,649,500 miles², or 15 percent of the world's total land area, and a total coastline (including islands) of 66,090 miles. The country measures 5,580 miles from east to west and 2,790 miles from north to south. Its population in mid-1989 was an estimated 289 million.

Smallest ■ The smallest independent country in the world is the State of the Vatican City (Stato della Città del Vaticano), which was made an enclave within the city of Rome, Italy on 11 Feb 1929. The enclave has an area of 108·7 acres. The maritime sovereign country with the shortest coastline is Monaco, with 3·49 miles, excluding piers and breakwaters.

The world's smallest republic is Nauru, less than 1 degree south of the equator in the western Pacific, which became independent on 31 Jan 1968. It has an area of 5,263 acres and a population of 8,900 (latest estimate 1988).

The smallest colony in the world is Gibraltar (since 1969, the City of Gibraltar), with an area of 2½ miles². However, Pitcairn Island, the only inhabited (49 people in March 1990) island of a group of four (total area 18½ miles²), has an area of 960 acres/1½ miles². It was named after the British Midshipman Robert Pitcairn of HMS *Swallow* in July 1767.

The official residence, since 1834, of the Grand Master of the Order of the Knights of Malta, totaling 3 acres and comprising the Villa del Priorato di Malta on the lowest of Rome's seven hills, the 151-ft Aventine, retains certain diplomatic privileges, as does 68 via Condotti. The Order has accredited representatives to foreign governments and is hence sometimes cited as the world's smallest 'state.'

Countries of the world ● The world comprises 170 sovereign countries and 62 separately administered non-sovereign or other territories, making a total of 232. Namibia became the 171st sovereign country when it achieved independence in March 1990, but the unification of North and South Yemen in May 1990 brought the number of sovereign countries back down to 170. The flag is of the new unified Yemen.

Flattest and most elevated ■ The country with the lowest highest point is Maldives, which attains 8 ft. The country with the highest lowest point is Lesotho. The egress of the Senqu (Orange) riverbed is 4,530 ft above sea level.

Longest and shortest frontier ■ The longest *continuous* frontier in the world is that between Canada and the United States, which (including the Great Lakes boundaries) extends for 3,987 miles (excluding 1,538 miles with Alaska).

The frontier which is crossed most frequently is that between the United States and Mexico. It extends for 1,933 miles and there are more than 120 million crossings every year.

The Sino-Soviet frontier, broken by the Sino-Mongolian border, extends for 4,500 miles, with no reported figure of crossings.

The 'frontier' of the Holy See in Rome measures 2·53 miles. The land frontier between Gibraltar and Spain at La Linea, closed between June 1969 and February 1985, measures 1 mile.

Most frontiers ■ China has the most land frontiers with 13 — Mongolia, USSR, North Korea, Hong Kong, Macau, Vietnam, Laos, Myanmar (formerly Burma), India, Bhutan, Nepal, Pakistan and Afghanistan. These extend for 14,900 miles. France, if all her *départements d'outre-mer* (overseas territories) are included, may, on extended territorial waters, have 20 frontiers.

Shortest coastline ● The maritime sovereign country with the shortest coastline is Monaco, with 3·49 miles, excluding piers and breakwaters. It is also the most densely populated sovereign country, with a population of 29,000 in 1989, in an area of just 473 acres, representing a density equal to 39,242 people per mile². (Photo: Images)

POPULATIONS

World ■ The average daily increase in the world's population is about 270,000 or an average of just under 200 per minute. There are, however, seasonal variations in the numbers of births and deaths throughout the year. For past, present and future estimates see table (page 202).

Matej Gaspar, born 11 Jul 1987 in Yugoslavia, was symbolically named the world's 5 billionth inhabitant by the United Nations Secretary-General.

United States ■ On 6 Mar 1990 the population of the United States reached the 250 million mark, according to the Census Bureau which also predicts that the country's population will reach 267 million by the year 2000. According to 1980 census figures, 60 percent of Americans have English, German and Irish ethnic origins. Afro-Americans are the largest non-white ethnic group with 20,965,000 persons counted in the 1980 census; there were 6,716,000 American Indians in 1980. The smallest ethnic group in the country at that time was Armenian with 213,000 people.

Most populous country ■ The most populated country is China, which in *pinyin* is written Zhongguo (meaning 'central land'). The

Flattest country ● The country with the lowest highest point is Maldives, in the Indian Ocean, which has a highest point of only 8 ft above sea level. (Photo: Picture Point)

Most densely populated territories ● Above: Hong Kong (400·5 miles²) is the most densely populated territory with an area of more than 386 miles². It contains an estimated 5·7 million people (1989), giving the territory a density of 14,232 per mile². (Photo: Spectrum Colour Library)

census of July 1982 was 1,008,175,288, and it was reported on 14 Apr 1989 that its population had reached 1·1 billion. The rate of natural increase in the People's Republic of China is now estimated to be 35,068 a day, or 12·8 million per year. The census of July 1982 required 5·1 million enumerators to work for 10 days. India is set to overtake China in size of population by A.D. 2050, with 1·59 billion against 1·554 billion.

Least populous ■ The independent state with the smallest population is the Vatican City (see Smallest country, above), with 750 inhabitants in 1989 and a recorded birth rate of zero.

Most densely populated ■ The most densely populated territory in the world is the Portuguese province of Macau, on the southern coast of China. It has an estimated population of 479,000 (1988) in an area of 6·5 miles², giving a density of 73,692 per mile².

The principality of Monaco, on the south coast of France, has a population of 29,000 (1989) in an area of just 473 acres, a density equal to 39,242 people per mile².

Of territories with an area of more than 386 miles², Hong Kong (400·5 miles²) contains an estimated 5·7 million (1989), giving the territory a density of 14,232/mile². Hong Kong is now the most populous of all colonies. The transcription of the name is from a local pronunciation of the Beijing dialect version of Xiang gang (meaning 'a port for incense').

The 1976 by-census showed that the west area of the urban district of Mong Kok on the Kowloon Peninsula had a density of 652,910/mile². In 1959, at the peak of the housing crisis, it was reported that in one house designed for 12 people the number of occupants was 459, including 104 in one room and four living on the roof.

SPECIES ON THE BRINK

The destruction of habitats spells extinction for millions of species within the lifetime of children being born today. Shown here are just five of these 'species on the brink.'

BLACK RHINOCEROS (below). Pictured here are a female black rhinoceros (*Diceros bicornis*) and her calf in the Ngorongoro Crater, Tanzania. A solitary inhabitant of open grassland, this is another species which falls prey to man's illegal hunting. (Photo: M Joseph/WWF UK)

SIBERIAN TIGER (above). An inhabitant of grassy or swampy regions, the endangered Siberian tiger (*Panthera tigris altaica*) shows its aptitude for swimming. (Photo: David Lawson/WWF UK)

SNOW LEOPARD (below). An inhabitant of Asia's highest mountain ranges, the Ounce or Snow leopard (*Panthera uncia*) spends its summers hunting along the snow line at an altitude of 13,000 ft. (Photo: David Lawson/WWF UK)

GIANT PANDA (below). Adopted as the symbol of WWF, the Giant Panda (*Ailuropoda melanoleuca*) inhabits bamboo forests and is found only in the mountains of central China and eastern Tibet. It is one of the rarest mammals in the world. The panda has been declared a 'national treasure' by the Chinese government, which has designated 10 areas in which they are protected. (Photo: WWF UK/Olwyn Sandbrook)

AFRICAN ELEPHANT (bottom). The threat to the African elephant (*Loxodonta africana*) is caused almost entirely by the illegal hunting of elephants for ivory. Some 70,000 elephants are killed every year and over half of Africa's elephants have disappeared since 1979, but recent bans and restrictions on ivory importation mean that the outlook for the elephant may be improving. (Photo: Storm Stanley/WWF UK)

WWF

The information and photographs for this feature were supplied by the World Wildlife Fund (WWF).

IN CRISIS

THREATENED HABITATS

Rainforests support half the planet's known living species and affect our weather. It is estimated that we are losing several species a day through the destruction of tropical rainforests alone. Fewer than 1·5 million of the Earth's estimated 30 million species have been scientifically described. At the present rate of extinction we will know nothing of the vast majority of all species before they become extinct. Conserving tropical rainforests is WWF's highest priority worldwide.

MEDICINAL PLANT TRAIL: Seen on the left are Kayapo Indians collecting medicinal plants. Of the 3,000 plants identified by the US National Cancer Institute as having anti-cancer properties, over 2,000 are from tropical rainforests. Yet less than one hundredth of known tropical rainforest plants have been screened for use in life-saving drugs. (Photo: WWF/Mauri Rautkari/Finland)

'The Earth is a wonderful and awe-inspiring place; it is full of great beauty that inspires some people to create wonderful works of art, and it gives others the insight to believe in a supreme being. For these reasons alone, surely this, our only planet, is worth our care, our thoughtfulness and our attention.'

HRH Prince Philip,
President, WWF.

•

'The world is in the midst of an environmental crisis beyond anything yet experienced; unless radical steps are taken to safeguard the planet, our future on it cannot be secured.'

Sen. Albert Gore (D-Ten), Chairman of the Subcommittee on Science, Technology and Space of the US Senate Commerce Committee.

Seen on the right (in Brazil) is the devastation that results from forest clearance for ranching. It is estimated by WWF that up to 50 million acres of forest are destroyed each year. This is an area equivalent to the State of Nebraska. (Photo: Janet Barber/WWF UK)

Almost as important as a habitat for a wide diversity of species are wilderness wetlands. These are threatened—from the Camargue, France (above) to Botswana (right)—by drainage, development and pollution. (Photos: Janet Barber/WWF UK)

Of countries over 1,000 miles² the most densely populated is Bangladesh, with a population of 112,757,000 (1989) living in 55,598 miles² at a density of 2,028 per mile². The Indonesian island of Java (with an area of 48,763 miles²) had a population of 100·3 million (1987), giving a density of 2,056 per mile².

WORLD POPULATION

Date	Millions	Date	Millions
8000 B.C.	c. 6	1970	3,698
A.D. 1	c. 255	1975	4,080
1000	c. 254	1980	4,450
1250	416	1981	4,528
1500	460	1982	4,607
1600	579	1983	4,684
1700	679	1984	4,760
1750	770	1985	4,854
1800	954	1986	4,917*
1900	1,633	1987	4,998*
1920	1,862	1988	5,096
1930	2,070	1989	5,194
1940	2,295	1990†	5,292
1950	2,515	2000†	6,251
1960	3,019	2025†	8,467

* The Population Institute of Washington, D.C. declared that the landmark of 5 billion was reached on 7 Jul 1987 whereas the UN nominated 11 Jul 1987 'Baby Five Billion Day.'

† These projections are from the latest UN publication 'World Population Prospects 1988.' This publication gives no projection beyond 2025. An earlier publication in 1984 forecast that the world population will not stabilise until 2095 at about 10·5 billion, but revised estimates in May 1988 said that it might be as high as 14 billion in 2050. Note: The all-time peak annual increase of 2·06 percent in the period 1965–70 had declined to 1·73 percent by 1985–90. By 2025 this should decline to 0·98 percent. In spite of the reduced percentage increase, world population is currently growing by 98 million people every year.

Using estimates made by the French demographer J. N. Biraben and others, A. R. Thatcher, a former Director of the Office of Population Censuses and Surveys, has calculated that the number of people who died between 40,000 B.C. and A.D. 1990 was nearly 60 billion. This estimate implies that the current world population is about one eleventh of those who have ever lived.

Most sparsely populated ■ Antarctica became permanently occupied by relays of scientists from October 1956. The population varies seasonally and reaches 2,000 at times.

The least populated territory, apart from Antarctica, is Kalaallit Nunaat (formerly Greenland), with a population of 54,600 (1988) in an area of 840,000 miles², giving a density of one person to every 15·38 miles². Some 84·3 percent of the island comprises an ice cap.

Emigration ■ More people emigrate from Mexico than from any other country. An estimated 800,000 illegally entered the United States in 1980 alone. The Soviet invasion of Afghanistan in December 1979 caused an influx of 2·9 million refugees into Pakistan and a further 2·2 million into Iran. By 1989 the number of Afghan refugees in Pakistan had increased to 3,622,000.

Immigration ■ The country that regularly receives the most legal immigrants is the United States. According to the 1980 Census, six percent of Americans (14,080,000) were born in a foreign country. Between 1981 and 1985 most immigrants came to America from the Caribbean, Mexico, Vietnam, the Philippines and Korea, accounting for more than 25 percent of the country's population increase. In addition, there are an estimated 20 million illegal immigrants in the United States.

In 1985, 95 percent of illegal aliens apprehended by the U.S. Immigration and Naturalization Service were from Mexico, but there are also undocumented immigrants from European countries such as Ireland. In 1989 a total of 954,119 illegal immigrants were arrested by US Border patrols.

Biggest demonstration ■ A figure of 2·7 million was published from China for the demonstration against the USSR in Shanghai on 3–4 Apr 1969 following the border clashes.

Most patient 'refusenik' ■ The USSR citizen who waited longest for an exit visa was Benyamin Bogomolny, who first applied in 1966. He arrived in Vienna, Austria on 14 Oct 1986.

The person who has currently been waiting the longest is Vladimir Raiz, who first applied to emigrate in February 1973.

Birthrate *Highest and lowest* ■ The crude birthrate—the number of births per thousand population—for the whole world was estimated to be 27·1 per 1,000 in 1985–90. The highest estimated by the UN is 53·9 per 1,000 for Kenya for 1985–90.

Excluding Vatican City, where the rate is zero (see page 199), the lowest recorded rate is 9·3 per 1,000 (1985) for San Marino.

United States ■ The crude birthrate for the United States was 15·7 per 100,000 persons or 3,809,394 people in 1987. The highest birthrate in one year was 4·3 million in 1957.

Death rate ■ The crude death rate—the number of deaths per thousand population of all ages—for the whole world was an estimated 9·9 per in 1985–90. The estimated death rate in Cambodia (formerly Kampuchea) of 40 per 1,000 from 1975–80 subsided to 16·6 in 1985–90. The estimated figure for Ethiopia from 1985–90 was 23·6.

The lowest of the latest available recorded rates is 2·8 deaths per 1,000 in Kuwait in 1985–90.

United States ■ The crude death rate for the United States in 1987 was 87·4 per 100,000 persons or 2,123,323 people.

Natural increase ■ The rate of natural increase for the whole world is estimated to be 17·2 (27·1 − 9·9) per 1,000 in 1985–90 compared with a peak 22 per 1,000 in 1965. The highest of the latest available recorded rates is 42·9 (53·9 − 11) from Kenya in 1985–90.

The lowest rate of natural increase in any major independent country is in West Germany with a negative figure of −1·3 per 1,000 (10·2 births and 11·5 deaths) for 1986.

Marriage and divorce ■ Of countries for which statistics are available, the USSR has the greatest number of marriages, with 2,776,568 in 1987—a rate of 9·8 per 1,000 population.

In the United States the average age at marriage in 1987 was 28 years (bridegrooms) and 25·9 years (brides). In 1983, 54 percent of all weddings were first time marriages for both the bride and groom.

As of 1987, there were 1,166,000 divorces in the United States, or 4·8 per 1,000 persons. The highest divorce rate was 5·3 per 1,000 persons in 1979 and 1981.

Sex ratio ■ There were estimated in 1981 to be 1,006·7 males in the world for every 1,000 females. The country with the largest recorded shortage of males is the USSR, with 1,132·1 females to every 1,000 males (1985 census). The country with the largest recorded woman shortage is Pakistan, with 906 to every

ILLEGAL IMMIGRATION TO THE US

Fiscal Year	Number Arrested
1986 (Nov 1985-Oct 1986)	1,615,854
1987 (Nov 1986-Oct 1987)	1,122,067
1988 (Nov 1987-Oct 1988)	943,063
1989 (Nov 1988-Oct 1989)	857,068

Dept. of Immigration, 1990

PROGRESSIVE LIST OF THE WORLD'S MOST POPULOUS URBAN SETTLEMENTS

Population	Name	Country	Date
>100	Dolní Věstonice	Czechoslovakia	c. 2,7000 B.C.
c. 150	Chemi Shanidar	Iraq	8900 B.C.
2,700	Jericho (Aríhā)	Occupied Jordan	7800 B.C.
c. 5,000	Ç atal Huyuk, Anatolia	Turkey	c. 6800 B.C.
> 5,000	Hierakonopolis (Nekhen)	Egypt	c. 3200 B.C.
50,000	Uruk (Erech) (now Warka) from 3800 B.C.	Iraq	3000 B.C.
250,000	Greater Ur (now Tell Muqayyar)	Iraq	2200 B.C.
350,000	Babylon (now al-Hillah)	Iraq	600 B.C.
500,000	Pataliputra (Patna) Bihăr	India	400–185 B.C.
600,000	Seleukia (near Baghdad)	Iraq	300 B.C.–165 A.D.
1,100,000	Rome (founded c. 510 B.C.)	Italy	133 B.C.
1,500,000	Angkor	Cambodia	900 B.C.
1·0–1·5 million	Hangchow (now Hangzhou)	China	1279
707,000	Peking (Cambaluc) (now Beijing)	China	1578
1,117,290	London	United Kingdom	1801
8,615,050	London (peak)	United Kingdom	1939
8,415,400	Tokyo[1]	Japan	1957

FOOTNOTE

[1] For up-to-date Tokyo population figure, see 'Most populous' below.

dating on specimens from the lowest levels reached by archaeologists indicates habitation there by perhaps 2,700 people as early as 7800 B.C.

The settlement of Dolní Věstonice, Czechoslovakia has been dated to the Gravettian culture c. 27,000 B.C.

The oldest capital city in the world is Dimashq (Damascus), Syria. It has been continuously inhabited since c. 2500 B.C.

Most populous ■ The most populous urban agglomeration in the world is the Tokyo-Yokohama Metropolitan Area or 'Keihin Metropolitan Area,' in Japan, which was listed in the United Nations *Prospects of World Urbanization, 1988* as having a population of 19·04 million in 1985.

The population of the Mexico City urban agglomeration in 1985 was given in the same publication as 16·65 million, but by 2000 it is expected to have a population of 24·44 million, against 21·32 million for Tokyo-Yokohama.

United States ■ The state capital with the largest population in 1987 was Phoenix, AZ with 853, 266 people; the smallest was Montpelier, VT with 8,167 people.

Largest in area ■ The world's largest town, in area, is Mount Isa, Queensland, Australia. The area administered by the City Council is 15,822 miles^2.

Highest ■ The highest capital in the world, before the occupation of Tibet by China, was Lhasa, at an elevation of 12,087 ft above sea level.

La Paz, administrative and *de facto* capital of Bolivia, stands at an altitude of 11,916 ft above sea level. Its airport, El Alto, is at 13,385 ft. The city was founded in 1,548 by Capt. Alonso de Mendoza on the site of an Indian village named Chuquiapu. It was originally called Ciudad de Nuestra Señora de La Paz (City of Our Lady of Peace), but in 1825 was renamed La Paz de Ayacucho, its present official name. Sucre, the legal capital of Bolivia, stands at 9,301 ft above sea level.

The new town of Wenzhuan, founded in 1955 on the Qinghai–Tibet road, north of the Tanglha range, is the highest in the world at 16,732 ft above sea level.

Lowest ■ The settlement of Ein Bokek (which has a synagogue), on the shores of the Dead Sea is the lowest in the world, at 1,291 ft below sea level.

Northernmost ■ The northernmost village is Ny Ålesund (78° 55′ N), a coal-mining settlement on King's Bay, Vest Spitsbergen, in the Norwegian territory of Svalbard, inhabited only during the winter season.

The northernmost capital is Reykjavik, Iceland in 64° 08′ N. Its population was estimated to be 95,800 in 1988.

Southernmost ■ The world's southernmost village is Puerto Williams (population about 350) on the north coast of Isla Navarino, in Tierra del Fuego, Chile, 680 miles north of Antarctica. Wellington, North Island, New Zealand, with a 1988 population of 325,200, is the southernmost capital city on 41° 17′ S.

The world's southernmost administrative center is Port Stanley, with a population of 1,200, (51° 43′ S) in the Falkland (Malvinas) Islands.

1,000 males in 1981. The figures are, however, probably under-enumerated due to *purdah* (keeping women in seclusion).

Infant mortality ■ The world infant mortality rate — the number of deaths at ages under one year per thousand live births — in 1987 was 80 per 1,000 live births. Based on deaths before one year of age, the lowest of the latest recorded rates is 5·0 in Japan in 1987.

In Ethiopia the infant mortality rate was unofficially estimated to be nearly 550/1,000 live births in 1969. The highest rate recently estimated is 172·1 per 1,000 in Afghanistan (1985–90).

United States ■ The infant mortality rate for the United States in 1987 was 10·1 per 100,000 live births or 34,408.

Expectation of life at birth ■ World expectation of life is rising from 47·4 years (1950–55) towards 64·5 years (1995–2000). In the decade 1890–1900 the expectation of life among the population of India was 23·7 years.

The highest average expectation of life is in Japan, with 81·9 years for women and 75·8 years for men in 1988. The lowest expectation of life at birth recently estimated is 39·4 years for males in Ethiopia and Sierra Leone, and 42 years for females in Afghanistan.

Housing ■ For comparison, dwelling units are defined as a structurally separated room or rooms occupied by private households of one or more people and having separate access or a common passageway to the street.

The first country to surpass 100 million housing units was India, in 1972. In 1981 the figure was 142,954,921.

United States ■ In March 1988 there were 91,066,000 households in the United States. Of these, 58,214,000 (63·9 percent) were owner occupied and 32,853,000 were rentals.

Physicians ■ The country with the most physicians is the USSR, with 1,232,300, or one for every 235 persons.

China had an estimated 1·4 million paramedical personnel, known as 'barefoot doctors,' by 1981.

Dentists ■ The country with the most dentists is the United States, where 145,800 were registered members of the American Dental Association in 1987.

Psychiatrists ■ The country with the most psychiatrists is the United States. The registered membership of the American Psychiatric Association (inst. 1894) was 32,000 in 1987. The membership of the American Psychological Association (inst. 1892) was 60,000 in 1987. The No. 1 city in the 1987 couch rankings is Boston, MA with one psychiatrist for 328 heads.

Largest hospital ■ The largest mental hospital in the world is the Pilgrim State Hospital, West Brentwood, Long Island, NY, with 3,618 beds. It formerly contained 14,200 beds. The largest psychiatric institute is at the University of California at Los Angeles (UCLA).

The busiest maternity hospital in the world has been the Mama Yemo Hospital, Kinshasa, Zaïre, with 41,930 deliveries in 1976. The record 'birthquake' occurred on a day in May 1976, with 175 babies born. The hospital had 599 beds.

STATES

Largest ■ The largest state in land area is Alaska, with 570,833 square miles. The largest of the 48 conterminous states is Texas, with 262,017 square miles of land.

Smallest ■ The smallest state is Rhode Island, with 1,055 square miles.

Most populous ■ The most populous state in the United States in 1987 was California, with 27·66 million people. The most populous urban area in 1987 was New York City with 17,678,100 people.

Least populous ■ The least populous state was Wyoming with 490,000 people in 1987. Salt Lake City, UT was the least populous urban area in 1987, with 1,041,400 people.

Thirteen original states ■ The thirteen original states were Connecticut, Delaware, Georgia, Maryland, Massachusetts, New Hampshire, New Jersey, New York, North Carolina, Pennsylvania, Rhode Island, South Carolina and Virgina.

Confederate states ■ Eleven states seceded from the union between December 1860 and June 1861. They were (in order of secession): South Carolina, Mississippi, Florida, Alabama, Georgia, Louisiana, Texas, Virginia, Arkansas, North Carolina and Tennessee.

TOWNS AND CITIES

Oldest ■ The oldest known walled town in the world is Arihā (Jericho). The radiocarbon

WORST DISASTERS IN THE WORLD

DISASTER	NUMBER KILLED	LOCATION	DATE
Pandemic	75,000,000	Eurasia: The Black Death (bubonic, pneumonic and septicaemic plague)	1347–51
Genocide	c. 35,000,000	Mongol extermination of Chinese peasantry	1311–40
Famine	c. 30,000,000[1]	Northern China	1959–61
Influenza	21,640,000	Worldwide	1918–19
Earthquake[2]	1,100,000	Near East and E. Mediterranean	c. July 1201
Circular Storm[2]	1,000,000	Ganges Delta Islands, Bangladesh	12–13 Nov 1970
Flood	900,000	Hwang-ho River, China	Oct 1887
Landslides (Triggered off by single earthquake)	180,000	Kansu Province, China	16 Dec 1920
Atomic Bomb	155,200	Hiroshima, Japan (including radiation deaths within a year)	6 Aug 1945
Conventional Bombing[3]	c. 140,000	Tokyo, Japan	10 Mar 1945
Volcanic Eruption	92,000	Tambora Sumbawa, Indonesia	5–7 Apr 1815
Avalanches	c. 18,000[4]	Yungay, Huascarán, Peru	31 May 1970
Marine (Single Ship)	c. 7700	Wilhelm Gustloff (28,540·8 tons) German liner torpedoed off Danzig by USSR submarine S-13 (only 903 survivors)	30 Jan 1945
Dam Burst	c. 5000[5]	Manchhu River Dam, Morvi, Gujarat, India	11 Aug 1979
Panic	c. 4000	Chungking (Zhong qing) China, air raid shelter	c. 8 Jun 1941
Industrial (Chemical)	3350	Union Carbide methylisocyanate plant, Bhopal, India	2–3 Dec 1984
Smog	2,850	London fog, United Kingdom (excess deaths)	5–13 Dec 1952
Tunnelling (Silicosis)	c. 2500	Hawk's Nest hydroelectric tunnel, West Virginia	1931–35
Explosion	1,963[6]	Halifax, Nova Scotia, Canada	6 Dec 1917
Fire[7] (Single Building)	1,670	The Theatre, Canton, China	May 1845
Mining[8]	1,572	Hinkeiko Colliery, China (coal dust explosion)	26 Apr 1942
Tornado	c. 1,300	Shaturia, Bangladesh	26 Apr 1989
Riot	c. 1,200	New York anti-conscription riots	13–16 Jul 1863
Mass Suicide[9]	960	Jewish Zealots, Masada, Israel	73
Railway	>800	Bagmati River, Bihar, India	6 Jun 1981
Fireworks	>800	Dauphin's wedding, Seine, Paris, France	16 May 1770
Aircraft (Civil)[10]	583	KLM-Pan Am Boeing 747 ground crash, Tenerife	27 Mar 1977
Man-eating Animal	436	Champawat district, India, tigress shot by Col. Jim Corbet (d. 1955)	1907
Terrorism	329	Bomb aboard Air-India Boeing 747, crashed into Atlantic south-west of Ireland. Sikh extremists suspected	23 Jun 1985
Hail	246	Moradabad, Uttar Pradesh, India	20 Apr 1888
Road[11]	176	Petrol tanker explosion inside Salang Tunnel, Afghanistan	3 Nov 1982
Offshore Oil Platform	167	Piper Alpha oil production platform, North Sea	6 Jul 1988
Submarine	130	Le Surcouf rammed by US merchantman Thomas Lykes in Caribbean	18 Feb 1942
Helicopter	54	Israel, military 'Sea Stallion', West Bank	10 May 1977
Ski Lift (Cable Car)	42	Cavalese resort, northern Italy	9 Mar 1976
Nuclear Reactor	31[12]	Chernobyl No. 4, Ukraine, USSR	26 Apr 1986
Mountaineering	23[13]	Mount Fuji, Japan	20 Mar 1972
Elevator (Lift)	23	Vaal Reefs gold mine lift fell 1·93 km 1·2 miles	27 Mar 1980
Lightning	21	Hut in Chinamasa Krael nr Mutari, Zimbabwe (single bolt)	23 Dec 1975
Yacht Racing	19	28th Fastnet Race—23 boats sank or abandoned in Force 11 gale	13–15 Aug 1979
Space Exploration	7	US Challenger 51L Shuttle, Cape Canaveral, FL	28 Jan 1986
Nuclear Waste Accident	high but undisclosed[14]	Venting of plutonium extraction wastes, Kyshtym, USSR	c. Dec 1957

FOOTNOTES

[1] It has been estimated that more than 5 million died in the post-World War I famine of 1920–21 in the USSR. The USSR government in July 1923 informed Mr (later President) Herbert Hoover that the ARA (American Relief Administration) had since August 1921 saved 20 million lives from famine and famine-related diseases.

[2] This figure published in 1972 for the Bangladeshi disaster was from Dr Afzal, Principal Scientific Officer of the Atomic Energy Authority Centre, Dacca. One report asserted that less than half of the population of the 4 islands of Bhola, Charjabbar, Hatia and Ramagati (1961 Census 1·4 million) survived. The most damaging hurricane recorded was Hurricane Gloria from 26-28 Sep 1985 with estimated insurance losses of £3·5 billion.

[3] The number of civilians killed by the bombing of Germany has been put variously at 593,000 and 'over 635,000' including some 35,000 deaths in the raids on Dresden, Germany from 13–15 Feb 1945. Total Japanese fatalities were 600,000 (conventional) and 220,000 (nuclear).

[4] A total of 18,000 Austrian and Italian troops was reported to have been lost in the Dolomite valleys of northern Italy on 13 Dec 1916 in more than 100 snow avalanches. Some of the avalanches were triggered by gun-fire.

[5] The dynamiting of a Yangtze Kiang dam at Huayuan Kow by the Kuomintang during the Sino-Japanese war in 1938 is reputed to have resulted in 900,000 deaths.

[6] Some sources maintain that the final death toll was over 3,000 on 6–7 Dec. Published estimates of the 11,000 killed at the BASF chemical plant explosion at Oppau, West Germany on 21 Sep 1921 were exaggerated. The best estimate is 561 killed.

[7] >200,000 killed in the sack of Moscow, as a result of fires started by the invading Tartars in May 1571. Worst ever hotel fire, killed 162, Hotel Daeyungak, Seoul, South Korea 25 Dec 1971. Worst circus fire killed 168 in Hartford, CT 6 Jul 1944.

[8] The worst gold mining disaster in South Africa was when 182 were killed in Kinross gold mine on 16 Sep 1986.

[9] As reported by the historian Flavius Josephus (c. 37–100). In modern times, the greatest mass suicide was on 18 Nov 1978 when 913 members of the People's Temple Cult died of mass cyanide poisoning near Port Kaituma, Guyana. 22,000 Japanese civilians jumped off a cliff to their deaths in June 1943 during the US Marines assault of the island of Tarawa (now in Kiribati).

[10] The crash of JAL's Boeing 747, flight 123, near Tokyo on 12 Aug 1985, in which 520 passengers and crew perished, was the worst single plane crash in aviation history.

[11] The global aggregate death toll in road accidents was put at 25 million by September 1975. The world's highest death rate is 29 per 100,000 in 1978 in Luxembourg and Portugal. The worst year for road deaths in the United States was 1969 (56,400).

[12] Explosion at 0123 hrs Soviet European time 26 Apr 1986. Moscow News reported on 8 Nov 1989 that at least 250 people working at Chernobyl or involved in the rescue operation had died in the 3 ½ years since the accident. The estimates for the eventual death toll vary between 200 and 600 by A.D. 2026 (per Nikolay Romanenko, Ukrainian Health Minister, on 4 Apr 1987) and 75,000 (per Dr Robert Gale, US bone transplant specialist).

[13] Some people have claimed that 40 mountaineers were killed in a Soviet expedition on Mount Everest in December 1952, but this is discounted by many authorities on the matter.

[14] More than 30 small communities in a 460 mile² area eliminated from USSR maps since 1958, with 17,000 people evacuated. Possibly an ammonium nitrate-hexone explosion.

Nuclear reactor disaster ● The worst nuclear reactor disaster was that at Chernobyl, USSR in April 1986. At the time reports quoted a figure of 31 dead, although estimates for the eventual death toll vary between 200 and 600 (a 1987 Soviet estimate) and 75,000 (an American estimate), and Moscow News reported on 8 Nov 1989 that at least 250 people working at Chernobyl or involved in the rescue operation had died in the 3 ½ years since April 1986. One of the major tasks following the accident was the decontamination of buildings. (Photo: Gamma/Novosti)

LARGEST US COUNTIES

County	Population (1987)
Los Angeles, CA	8,300,000
Cook, IL	5,300,000
Harris, TX	2,800,000
Brooklyn, NY	2,292,200
San Diego, CA	2,200,000

Almanac of American People

TEN MOST POPULOUS METROPOLITAN AREAS

Metropolitan Area	Population (1985)
New York, NY	17,678,100
Los Angeles, CA	13,074,800
Chicago, IL	8,116,100
San Francisco, CA	5,877,800
Philadelphia, PA	5,832,600
Detroit, MI	4,600,700
Boston, MA	4,055,700
Dallas, TX	3,655,300
Houston, TX	3,634,300
Washington, D.C.	3,563,000

Almanac of American People

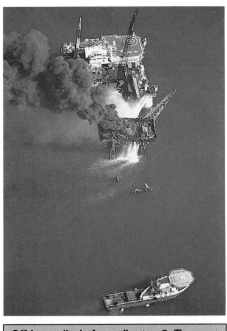

Offshore oil platform disaster ● The worst offshore oil platform disaster took place on 6 Jul 1988, when 167 men lost their lives in the Piper Alpha oil platform fire in the North Sea, United Kingdom. (Photo: Gamma/Tampyx)

Most remote from sea ■ The large town most remote from the sea is Wu-lu-mu-chi (formerly Ürümqi) in Xinjiang (formerly Tihwa, Sinkiang), capital of the Uighur autonomous region of China, at a distance of about 1,400 miles from the nearest coastline. Its population was estimated to be 947,000 in 1987.

Heads of State and Royalty

Head of State *Oldest and youngest* ■ The oldest head of state in the world is Olav V , King of Norway (b. 2 Jul 1903). The youngest is King Mswati III of Swaziland (b. 19 Apr 1968). (See below.)

First female president ■ Isabel Perón (b. 1931) of Argentina became the world's first female president when she succeeded her husband on his death on 1 Jul 1974. She held office until she was deposed in a bloodless coup on 24 Mar 1976. President Vigdis Finnbogadottir (b. 1930) of Iceland became the world's first democratically elected female head of state on 30 Jun 1980.

Oldest ruling house ■ The Emperor of Japan, Akihito (b. 23 Dec 1933), is the 125th in line from the first emperor, Jimmu Tenno or Zinmu, whose reign was traditionally from 660 to 581 B.C., but more probably from *c.* 40 B.C. to *c.* 10 B.C.

Reigns *Longest all-time* ■ The longest recorded reign of any monarch is that of Phiops II, or Neferkare, a Sixth Dynasty pharaoh of ancient Egypt. His reign began *c.* 2281 B.C., when he was age 6, and is believed to have lasted *c.* 94 years. Minhti, King of Arakan (now Myanmar, formerly Burma), is reputed to have reigned for 95 years between 1279 and 1374. Musoma Kanijo, chief of the Nzega district of western Tanganyika (now part of Tanzania), reputedly reigned

Longest-lived queen ● The longest-lived queen on record was Zita, Empress of Austria and Queen of Hungary, whose husband reigned as Emperor Charles I of Austria and King Charles IV of Hungary from 1916–18; she died on 14 Mar 1989 aged 96 years 309 days. (Photos: Gamma)

for more than 98 years from 1864, when aged 8, until his death on 2 Feb 1963.

The longest reign of any European monarch was that of Afonso I Henriques of Portugal, who ascended the throne on 30 Apr 1112 and died on 6 Dec 1185 after a reign of 73 years 220 days, first as a count and then as king.

Shortest ■ The Crown Prince Luis Filipe of Portugal was mortally wounded at the same time that his father was killed by a bullet that severed his carotid artery, in the streets of Lisbon on 1 Feb 1908. He was thus technically King of Portugal (Dom Luis III) for about 20 minutes.

Highest post-nominal numbers ■ The highest post-nominal number ever used to designate a member of a royal house was 75, briefly enjoyed by Count Heinrich LXXV Reuss zu Schleiz (1800–1). All male members of this branch of the German family are called Heinrich and are successively numbered from I upwards in three sequences — the first began in 1695 (and ended with Heinrich LXXV), the second began in 1803 (and ended with Heinrich XLVII) and the third began in 1910. These are purely *personal*

numbers and should not be confused with *regnal* numbers.

Longest-lived 'royals' ■ The longest life among the blood royal of Europe was that of the Princess Pauline Marie Madeleine of Croy (1887–1987), who celebrated her 100th birthday in her birthplace of Le Roeulx, Belgium on 11 Jan 1987.

The greatest age among European royal consorts is the 101 years 268 days of HSH Princess Leonilla Bariatinsky (b. Moscow, 9 Jul 1816), who married HSH Prince Louis of Sayn-Wittgenstein-Sayn and died in Ouchy, Switzerland on 1 Feb 1918.

The longest-lived queen on record was Zita, Empress of Austria and Queen of Hungary, whose husband reigned as Emperor Charles I of Austria and King Charles IV of Hungary from 1916–1918; she died on 14 Mar 1989 aged 96 years 309 days.

Youngest king and queen ■ Forty-six of the world's 170 sovereign states are not republics. They are headed by 1 emperor, 13 kings, 3 queens, 2 sultans, 1 grand duke, 2 princes, 3 emirs, an elected monarch, the pope, a president chosen from and by 7 hereditary sheiks, a head of state currently similar to a constitutional monarch, and 2 nominal non-hereditary 'princes' in one country. Queen Elizabeth II is head of state of 16 other Commonwealth countries.

The country with the youngest king is Swaziland, where King Mswati III was crowned on 25 Apr 1986 at age 18 years, 6 days. He was born Makhosetive, the 67th son of King Subhusa II.

The country with the youngest queen is Denmark, with Queen Margrethe II (b. 16 Apr 1940).

Heaviest monarch ■ The world's heaviest monarch is the 6 ft 3 in tall King Taufa'ahau of Tonga, who in September 1976 was weighed on the only adequate scales in the country at the airport, recording 462 lb. By 1985 he was reported to have slimmed down to 308 lb. His embassy car in London, United Kingdom has the licence plate '1 TON.'

Most prolific ■ The most prolific monogamous 'royals' have been Prince Hartmann of Liechtenstein (1613–86), who had 24 children, of whom 21 were live-born, by Countess Elisabeth zu Salm-Reifferscheidt (1623–88). HRH Duke Roberto I of Parma (1848–1907) also had 24 children, but by two wives.

One of his daughters, Zita, Empress of Austria and Queen of Hungary (1892–1989), was exiled on 23 Mar 1919, but visited Vienna, her titles intact, on 17 Nov 1982, reminding republicans that her father succeeded to the throne of Parma in 1854.

Legislatures

PARLIAMENTS — WORLD

Earliest and oldest ■ The earliest known legislative assembly or *ukkim* was a bicameral one in Erech, Iraq *c.* 2800 B.C. The oldest legislative body is the *Althing* of Iceland, founded in A.D. 930. This body, which originally comprised 39 local chieftains at Thingvellir, was abolished in 1800, but restored by Denmark to a consultative status in 1843 and a legislative status in 1874. The legislative assembly with the oldest continuous history is the Court of Tynwald in the Isle of Man, United Kingdom which celebrated its millennium in 1979.

Largest ■ The largest legislative assembly in the world is the National People's Congress of the People's Republic of China. The sixth congress, when convened in June 1983, had 2,978 members. Its standing committee has 197 members.

Smallest quorum ■ The House of Lords, (United Kingdom), the upper chamber of the British Parliament, has the smallest quorum, expressed as a percentage of eligible voters, of any legislative body in the world, namely less than one-third of one percent. The number of peers in 1988 was 1,244. To transact business there must be three peers present, including the Lord Chancellor or his deputy. The House of Commons' quorum of 40 MPs, including the Speaker or his deputy, is 20 times as exacting.

Longest membership ■ The longest span as a legislator was 83 years, by József Madarász (1814–1915). He first attended the Hungarian Parliament in 1832–36 as *oblegatus absentium* (*i.e.*, on behalf of an absent deputy). He was a full member in 1848–50 and from 1861 until his death on 31 Jan 1915.

Longest UN speech ■ The longest speech made in the United Nations has been one of 4 hr 29 min on 26 Sep 1960 by President Fidel Castro Ruz (b. 13 Aug 1927) of Cuba.

Oldest treaty ■ The oldest treaty still in force is the Anglo-Portuguese Treaty of Alliance, which was signed in London, United Kingdom over 617 years ago on 16 Jun 1373. The text

The Capitol ● The seat of the U.S. government at Washington, D.C., The Capitol is the city's dominating monument, built on an elevated site that was chosen by George Washington in consultation with Major Pierre L'Enfant. The building proper is over 750 ft long, including approaches c. 350 ft wide. (Photo: Imagen)

The Constitutional Convention ● In 1787 the Thirteen Colonies drew up one of the most influential documents in Western World history. George Washington was elected to preside and is represented in the painting depicted below. (Photo: Virginia Museum of Fine Arts)

was confirmed 'with my usual flourish' by John de Banketre, Clerk.

Constitutions ■ The world's oldest constitution still in existence is that of the United States of America, ratified by the necessary Ninth State (New Hampshire) on 21 Jun 1788 and declared to be in effect on 4 Mar 1789.

Women's suffrage ■ The earliest legislature with female voters was that of the Territory of Wyoming in 1869, followed by that of the Isle of Man, United Kingdom in 1881. The earliest country to have universal suffrage was New Zealand in 1893.

Fastest Amendment ■ The constitutional amendment that took the shortest time to ratify after congressional approval was the XXVI Amendment in 1971, which gave 18-year-olds the right to vote.

ELECTIONS — WORLD

Largest ■ The largest elections in the world were those beginning on 22 Nov 1989 for the Indian *Lok Sabha* (Lower House), which has 543 elective seats; 304,126,600 people out of an electorate of 498,647,786 cast their vote. Two hundred and ninety-one parties contested the elections, and there were more than 593,000 polling stations manned by 3½ million staff. As a result of the election a new government was formed under the leadership of Viswanath Pratap Singh of Janata Dal (People's Party).

Closest ■ The ultimate in close general elections occurred in Zanzibar (now part of Tanzania) on 18 Jan 1961, when the Afro-Shirazi Party won by a single seat, after the seat of Chake-Chake on Pemba Island had been gained by a single vote.

The narrowest recorded percentage win in an election would seem to be for the office of Southern District Highway Commissioner in Mississippi on 7 Aug 1979. Robert E. Joiner was declared the winner over W. H. Pyron, with 133,587 votes to 133,582. The loser got more than 49·9999 percent of the votes.

Most decisive ■ North Korea recorded a 100 percent turnout of electors and a 100 percent vote for the Workers' Party of Korea in the general election of 8 Oct 1962.

The next closest approach was in Albania on 14 Nov 1982, when a single voter spoiled national unanimity for the official (and only) Communist candidates, who thus obtained only 99·99993 percent of the poll in a 100 percent turnout of 1,627,968.

United States ■ In 1920 the XIX Amendment to the Constitution granted nation-wide suffrage to women.

UNITED STATES CONGRESS

Highest-paid legislators ■ The most highly paid of all the world's legislators are members of the US Congress.

The basic salary for members of the House of Representatives is $96,600, with an honoraria limit of $26,850. In addition, up to $1,021,167 per year is allowed for office help, with a salary limit of $50,000 for any one staff member (limited to 16 in number).

The basic salary for members of the Senate is $98,400, with an honoraria limit of $27,337. Senators are allowed up to $143,000 per year for an official office expense account from which official travel, telegram, long-distance telephone, air mail, postage, stationery, subscriptions to their newspapers and office expenses in home states are paid. They also command very low rates for filming, speech and radio transcriptions and, in the case of women senators, beauty treatment. When abroad they have access to 'counterpart funds.'

The President of the United States has a taxable salary of $200,000, and a lifetime pension of $107,300 per year, which is equivalent to level 1 of the US government's Executive Pay Schedule for Federal Employees.

Most roll calls ■ Senator William Proxmire (D-Wisconsin) did not miss a single one of the 9,695 roll calls from April 1966 to 27 Aug 1987. Rep William H. Natcher (D-Kentucky) has cast 12,268 consecutive roll call votes and responded in person to 4,175 recorded quorum calls, for a total of 16,443 votes. He has not missed a roll call or quorum call since being sworn in as a House member on 6 Jan 1954.

Filibusters ■ The longest continuous speech in the history of the United States Senate was that of Senator Wayne Morse (1900–74) of Oregon on 24–25 Apr 1953, when he spoke on the Tidelands Oil Bill for 22 hr 26 min without resuming his seat.

Interrupted only briefly by the swearing-in of a new senator, Senator Strom Thurmond (b. 1902) (R-South Carolina) spoke against the Civil Rights Bill for 24 hr 19 min on 28–29 Aug 1957.

The US national duration record is 43 hr by Texas State Senator Bill Meier against non-disclosure of industrial accidents in May 1977.

Most crooked ■ In the Liberian presidential election of 1927 President Charles D. B. King (1875–1961) was returned with a majority over his opponent, Mr Thomas J. R. Faulkner of the People's Party, officially announced as 234,000. President King thus claimed a 'majority' more than 15½ times greater than the entire electorate.

Highest personal majority ■ The highest ever personal majority for any politician has been 4,726,112 for Boris Yeltsin, the unofficial Moscow candidate, in the parliamentary elections held in the Soviet Union on 26 Mar 1989. Yeltsin received 5,118,745 votes out of the 5,722,937 that were cast in the Moscow constituency, his closest rival obtaining 392,633 votes.

In 1956 W. R. D. Bandaranaike achieved 91·82 percent of the poll, with 45,016 votes in Attanagalla constituency of Sri Lanka (then Ceylon).

Communist parties ■ The largest national Communist party outside the USSR (18·5 million members in 1987) and other communist states has been the Partito Comunista Italiano, with a membership of 2·3 million in 1946. The total was 1·6 million in 1986.

The membership in mainland China was estimated to be 44 million in 1987.

Largest ballot paper ■ There were 301 candidates for Belgaum City in the 5 Mar 1985 State Assembly (Vidhan Sabha) elections in Karnataka, India.

Most coups ■ Statisticians contend that Bolivia, since it became a sovereign country in 1825, had its 191st coup on 30 Jun 1984, when President Hernan Siles Zuazo, 70, was kidnapped from his official residence by more than 60 armed men.

PRESIDENTS AND STATESMEN

Oldest *President* ■ The oldest president was Ronald Wilson Reagan, who was 69 years

Highest majority ● The highest ever personal majority by any politician has been 4,726,112 by Boris Yeltsin, the unofficial Moscow candidate, in the parliamentary elections held in the Soviet Union on 26 Mar 1989. (Photo: Gamma/Shone)

349 days old when he took the oath of office on 20 Jan 1981. He was re-elected at age 74.

Statesmen ■ The longest-lived prime minister of any country was Naruhiko Higashikuni (Japan), who was born on 3 Dec 1887 and died on 20 Jan 1990, at age 102 years 48 days. He was his country's first prime minister after World War II, but held office for less than two months, resigning in October 1945.

El Hadji Muhammad el Mokri, Grand Vizier of Morocco, died on 16 Sep 1957 at a reputed age of 116 Muslim (*Hijri*) years, equivalent to 112½ Gregorian years.

The oldest age of first appointment has been 81, by Morarji Ranchhodji Desai of India (b. 29 Feb 1896) in March 1977.

Youngest *Presidents* ■ The youngest president to assume office was Theodore Roosevelt. Vice-President Roosevelt became president at the age of 42 years 10 months in 1901 when President McKinley was assassinated.

The youngest president ever elected was John Fitzgerald Kennedy, who took the oath of office at age 43 years 236 days in 1963.

Statesmen ■ Currently the youngest head of government is HM Druk Gyalpo ('dragon king') Jigme Singye Wangchuk of Bhutan (b. 11 Nov 1955), who has been head of government since

MOST COUPS

Most coups ● Statisticians contend that Bolivia, since it became a sovereign country in 1825, had its 191st coup on 30 June 1984 when President Hernan Siles Zuazo, 70, was kidnapped from his official residence by more than 60 armed men. In the July 1946 coup, revolutionaries stormed the presidential palace in La Paz—shown here—seized President Villarroel, and threw him from the balcony into the street below. The country was named after Simon Bolívar (below left). Currently the president is Jaime Paz Zamora (below right), who became president in August 1989 without the assistance of a coup. (Photos: Zefa/Gamma/ET Archives)

PRESIDENTIAL RECORDS

Article II of the Constitution provides for the office of the presidency. The President is head of all executive agencies, and has full responsibility for the execution of the laws, is commander in chief of the armed forces, conducts foreign affairs and with the advice and consent of Congress appoints cabinet members and any other executive officials. The Constitution sets the term of office at four years and requires that the position should be filled by election through the electoral college. The Twenty-second Amendment (1951) limits a President to two consecutive four-year terms. To be eligible for the presidency one must be a native born citizen, over 35 years old, and at least 14 years resident in the United States.

LONGEST TERM IN OFFICE	12 years 39 days	Franklin Delano Roosevelt	1933–45
SHORTEST TERM IN OFFICE	32 days	William Henry Harrison	4 Mar–4 Apr 1841
YOUNGEST TO ASSUME OFFICE	42 years 10 months	Theodore Roosevelt	1901–1909
YOUNGEST ELECTED	43 years 236 days	John Fitzgerald Kennedy	1961–63
OLDEST ELECTED	69 years 349 days	Ronald Wilson Reagan	1981–89
TALLEST	6 ft 4 in	Abraham Lincoln	1861–65
SHORTEST	5 ft 4 in	James Madison	1809–17
LONGEST LIVED	90 years 258 days	John Adams	1797–1801
MOST CHILDREN	14 or 15	John Tyler	1841–45
MOST CHILDREN (one spouse)	10	William Henry Harrison	1841
BACHELOR		James Buchanan	1857–61
IMPEACHED		Andrew Johnson	1865–69
RESIGNED		Richard M. Nixon	1969–74
ASSASSINATED	14 Apr 1865	Abraham Lincoln	1861–65
	2 Jul 1881	James A. Garfield	1881
	6 Sep 1901	William H. McKinley	1897–1901
	22 Nov 1963	John Fitzgerald Kennedy	1961–63

Presidental Assassination ● Right: James Abram Garfield (b.1831–d.81) was the 20th President of the United States (March–September 1881). Constantly harrassed by office seekers, President Garfield met his death after one of them, Charles J. Guiteau, shot the president on 2 Jul 1881. President Garfield died on 19 Sep 1881, and Chester A. Arthur succeeded to the presidency. (Photo: Picturepoint)

Oldest President ● Below: Ronald Wilson Reagan (1980–88) took the oath of office at 69 years 349 days on 20 Jan 1981. He was reelected at age 74. He left office in January 1989 with two-thirds of the American people approving his performance during his two terms. It was the highest rating for any retiring President since World War II. (Photo: London Features International)

PRESIDENTS OF THE UNITED STATES

PRESIDENT	TERM IN OFFICE	PARTY	BIRTH			DEATH		
George Washington *	1789–1797	Federalist	22 Feb	1732	14	Dec	1799
John Adams	1797–1801	Federalist	30 Oct	1735	4	Jul	1826
Thomas Jefferson	1801–1809	Dem-Rep	13 Apr	1743	4	Jul	1826
James Madison	1809–1817	Dem-Rep	16 Mar	1751	28	Jun	1836
James Monroe	1817–1825	Dem-Rep	28 Apr	1758	4	Jul	1831
John Quincy Adams	1825–1829	Dem-Rep	11 Jul	1767	23	Feb	1848
Andrew Jackson	1829–1837	Democratic	15 Mar	1767	8	Jun	1845
Martin Van Buren	1837–1841	Democratic	5 Dec	1782	24	Jul	1862
William H. Harrison †	1841	Whig	9 Feb	1773	4	Apr	1841
John Tyler	1841–1845	Whig	29 Mar	1790	18	Jan	1862
James K. Polk	1845–1849	Democratic	2 Nov	1795	15	Jun	1849
Zachary Taylor †	1849–1850	Whig	24 Nov	1784	9	Jul	1850
Millard Fillmore	1850–1853	Whig	7 Jan	1800	8	Mar	1874
Franklin Pierce	1853–1857	Democratic	23 Nov	1804	8	Oct	1869
James Buchanan	1857–1861	Democratic	23 Apr	1791	11	Jun	1868
Abraham Lincoln #	1861–1865	Republican	12 Feb	1829	15	Apr	1865
Andrew Johnson **	1865–1869	Union	29 Dec	1808	31	Jul	1875
Ulysses S. Grant	1869–1877	Republican	27 Apr	1822	23	Jul	1885
Rutherford B. Hayes	1877–1881	Republican	4 Oct	1822	17	Jan	1893
James A. Garfield #	1881	Republican	19 Nov	1831	19	Sep	1881
Chester A. Arthur	1881–1885	Republican	5 Oct	1829	18	Nov	1886
S. Grover Cleveland	1885–1889	Democratic	18 Mar	1837	24	Jun	1908
Benjamin Harrison	1889–1893	Republican	20 Aug	1833	13	Mar	1901
S. Grover Cleveland	1893–1897	Democratic	18 Mar	1837	24	Jun	1908
William McKinley #	1897–1901	Republican	29 Jan	1843	14	Sep	1901
Theodore Roosevelt	1901–1909	Republican	27 Oct	1858	6	Jan	1919
William H. Taft	1909–1913	Republican	15 Sep	1857	8	Mar	1930
T. Woodrow Wilson	1913–1921	Democratic	29 Dec	1856	3	Feb	1824
Warren G. Harding †	1921–1923	Republican	2 Nov	1865	2	Aug	1923
J. Calvin Coolidge	1923–1929	Republican	4 Jul	1872	5	Jan	1933
Herbert C. Hoover	1929–1933	Republican	10 Aug	1874	20	Oct	1964
Franklin D. Roosevelt †	1933–1945	Democratic	30 Jan	1882	12	Apr	1945
Harry S. Truman	1945–1953	Democratic	8 May	1884	26	Dec	1972
Dwight D. Eisenhower	1953–1961	Republican	14 Oct	1890	28	Mar	1969
John F. Kennedy #	1961–1963	Democratic	29 May	1917	22	Nov	1963
Lyndon B. Johnson	1963–1969	Democratic	27 Aug	1908	22	Jan	1973
Richard M. Nixon ‡	1969–1974	Republican	9 Jan	1913			
Gerald R. Ford	1974–1977	Republican	14 Jul	1913			
James E. Carter, Jr	1977–1981	Democratic	1 Oct	1924			
Ronald W. Reagan	1981–1989	Republican	6 Feb	1911			
George H. W. Bush	1989–	Republican	12 Jun	1924			

* There was no party system in place at the creation of the presidency, the system appeared during Washington's first term. † Died in office. # Assassinated. ** Impeached. ‡ Resigned.

March 1972. The youngest female head of government is Benazir Bhutto (b. 21 Jun 1953), who became Prime Minister of Pakistan in December 1988.

Term of office *Presidents* ■ Franklin Delano Roosevelt served 12 years 39 days (1933–45) as President of the United States. The shortest term in office was 32 days (4 Mar–4 Apr 1841) by William Henry Harrison.

Statesmen ■ The longest serving ᐧcurrent prime minister is Lee Kuan Yew, (b. 16 Sep 1923) of Singapore, who has been seven times reelected and remains in office after 30 years.

Marshal Kim Il Sung (ne Kim Sung Chu) (b. 15 Apr 1912) has been head of government or head of state of the Democratic People's Republic of Korea since 25 Aug 1948.

Andrei Andreievich Gromyko (1909–89) had been Minister of Foreign Affairs of the USSR since 15 Feb 1957, having been Deputy Foreign Minister since 1946, when he was elected President of the USSR in 2 Jul 1985, a position which he held until 30 Sep 1988.

Piotr Lomako (1904–90) has served in the government of the USSR as Minister for Non-Ferrous Metallurgy from 1940 to 1986. He was

relieved of his post after 46 years on 1 Nov 1986, aged 82, having served on the Central Committee of the CPSU since 1952.

Woman ■ Sirimavo Bandaranaike (b. 1916) of Ceylon (now Sri Lanka) became the first woman prime minister when her party, the Sri Lanka (Blessed Ceylon) Freedom Party, won the general election in July 1960.

POLITICAL OFFICE HOLDERS

Congressional Service ■ Carl Hayden (d. 25 Jan 1972; D-Arizona) holds the record for the longest Congressional service, a total of 56 consecutive years (1927–69), of which 42 years were spent as a Senator and the remainder as a Representative.

House of Representatives ■ The current longest serving member of the House of Representatives is Jamie L. Whitten (D-Mississippi). Whitten began his career as a Representative on 4 Nov 1941 and has served 25 consecutive two-year terms as of 1990.

Senate ■ The current longest serving member of the Senate is Strom Thurmond (R-South Carolina). Thurmond began his career in the Senate on 24 Dec 1954 and has served six consecutive six-year terms as of 1990. He was originally a Democrat but changed to the Republican Party in 1964.

Honors, Decorations and Awards

Oldest order ■ The earliest honor known was the 'Gold of Honour' for extraordinary valor awarded in the Eighteenth Dynasty *c.* 1440–1400 B.C. A statuette was found at Qan-el-Kebri, Egypt.

The oldest true order was the Order of St John of Jerusalem (the direct descendant of which is the Sovereign Military Order of Malta), legitimized in 1113.

Most titles ■ The most titled person in the world is the 18th Duchess of Alba (Alba de Tormes), Doña Maria del Rosario Cayetana Fitz-James Stuart y Silva. She is eight times a duchess, 15 times a marchioness, 21 times a countess and is 19 times a Spanish grandee.

Top jet ace ■ The greatest number of kills in jet to jet battles is 16, by Capt. Joseph Christopher McConnell, Jr, USAF (b. 30 Jan 1922) in the Korean War (1950–53). He was killed on 25 Aug 1954. It is possible that an Israeli ace may have surpassed this total in the period 1967–70, but the identity of Israeli pilots is subject to strict security.

Top woman ace ■ The record score for any woman fighter pilot is 12, by Jnr Lt Lydia Litvak (USSR) (b. 1921) on the Eastern Front between 1941 and 1943. She was killed in action on 1 Aug 1943.

Youngest award ■ The youngest age at which an official gallantry award has ever been won is eight years in the case of Anthony Farrer, who was given the Albert Medal on 23 Sep 1916 for fighting off a cougar at Cowichan Lake,

> **Female head of government** ● Benazir Bhutto (b. 21 Jun 1953) is currently the youngest female head of government, having become prime minister of Pakistan in December 1988 at the age of 35 years 5 months. (Photo: Gamma/Brynner)

Vancouver Island, Canada to save Doreen Ashburnham. She was also awarded the AM, which, in 1971, was exchanged for the George Cross.

United States ■ The highest US military decoration is the Congressional Medal of Honor. Five marines received both the Army and Navy Medals of Honor for the same deeds in 1918, and 15 officers and men received the medal on two occasions between 1864 and 1915 for two distinct acts. The Defense Department refuses to recognize any military hero as having the most awards, but various heroes have been nominated by unofficial groups. Since medals and decorations cannot be compared as to value, the title of most decorated can only be a matter of subjective evaluation.

General Douglas MacArthur (1880–1964), because of his high rank and his years of military service spanning three wars, would seem to hold the best claim to 'Most Decorated American Soldier.' In addition to the Congressional Medal of Honor, he also received 58 separate awards and decorations with 16 Oak Leaf Clusters, plus 18 campaign stars.

USSR ■ The USSR's highest award for valor is the Gold Star of a Hero of the Soviet Union. 12,709 Gold Stars have been awarded, 11,040 of which were in World War II. The only wartime triple awards were to Marshal Georgi Konstantinovich Zhukov (1896–1974) (subsequently awarded a fourth Gold Star) and to the leading air aces Guards Colonel (later Marshal of Aviation) Aleksandr Ivanovich Pokryshkin (1913–85) and Aviation Maj Gen Ivan Nikitovich Kozhedub (b. 8 Jun 1920) (Order of the Red Banner, seven times). Zhukov also uniquely had the Order of Victory (twice), the Order of Lenin (six times) and the Order of the Red Banner (three times).

The highest award of civil honor is the Gold Star of Socialist Labor, 20,424 of which have been awarded since it was established in 1983. There have been 15 awards of a third Gold Star of Socialist Labor. Leonid Ilyich Brezhnev (1906–1982) was four times Hero of the Soviet Union and Hero of Socialist Labor, Order of Victory (withdrawn in 1990), Order of Lenin (eight times) and Order of the Red Banner (twice).

Germany ■ The Knight's Cross of the Iron Cross with swords, diamonds and golden oak-leaves was uniquely awarded to Col. Hans Ulrich Rudel (1916–82) for 2,530 operational flying missions on the Eastern Front in the period 1941–45. He destroyed 519 Soviet armored vehicles.

Anti-submarine successes ■ The highest number of U-boat kills attributed to one ship in the Second World War was 15, to HMS *Starling* (Capt. Frederic John Walker). Captain Walker was in command at the sinking of a total of 25 U-boats between 1941 and the time of his death on 9 Jul 1944. The US Destroyer Escort *England* sank six Japanese submarines in the Pacific between 18 and 30 May 1944.

Most successful submarine captains ■ The most successful of all World War II submarine commanders was Lieutenant Otto Kretschmer, captain of the U.23 and U.99, who up to March 1941 sank one destroyer and 44 Allied merchantmen totaling 266,629 gross registered tons.

In World War I Lieutenant (later Vice Admiral) Lothar von Arnauld de la Périère, in the U.35 and U.139, sank 195 Allied ships totaling 458,856 gross tons.

Most decorated American soldier ● General Douglas MacArthur (1880–1964) has the strongest claim to be the most highly decorated American soldier, having received 59 separate awards and decorations with 16 Oak Leaf Clusters, plus 18 campaign stars. He was awarded the Medal of Honor in World War II. (Photos: City of Norfolk, Virginia)

The most successful boats were U.35, which in World War I sank 54 ships of 90,350 grt in a single voyage and 224 ships of 539,711 grt all told, and U.48, which sank 51 ships of 310,007 grt in World War II. The largest target ever sunk by a submarine was the Japanese aircraft carrier *Shinano* (66,131 tons) by USS *Archerfish* (Cdr Joseph F. Enright, USN) on 29 Nov 1944.

Most valuable annual prize ■ The value of each of the 1990 Nobel Prizes was Sw Kr 4 million. The ceremonial presentations for physics, chemistry, physiology or medicine, literature and economics take place in Stockholm, Sweden, and that for peace is in Oslo, Norway.

Most statues ■ The world record for raising statues to oneself was set by Generalissimo Dr Rafael Leónidas Trujillo y Molina (1891–1961), former president of the Dominican Republic. In March 1960 a count showed that there were 'over 2,000.' The country's highest mountain was named Pico Trujillo (later Pico Duarte). One province was called Trujillo and another Trujillo Valdez. The capital was named Ciudad Trujillo (Trujillo City) in 1936, but reverted to its old name of Santo Domingo de Guzmán on 23 Nov 1961. Trujillo was assassinated in a car ambush on 30 May 1961, and 30 May is now celebrated as a public holiday.

NOBEL PRIZES

Earliest 1901 for Physics, Chemistry, Physiology or Medicine, Literature and Peace.

Most Prizes The United States has won outright or shared 198 prizes, including most for Physiology or Medicine (67); Physics (53); Chemistry (35), Peace (18); Economics (15). France has most for Literature (12).

Oldest Laureate Professor Francis Peyton Rous (US; 1879–1970) in 1966 shared in Physiology or Medicine prize aged 87.

Youngest Laureates *At time of award:* Professor Sir Lawrence Bragg (1890–1971) 1915 Physics prize at 25 *At time of work:* Bragg, and Theodore W. Richards (US; 1868–1928) 1914 Chemistry prize at 23 *Literature:* Rudyard Kipling (United Kingdom; 1865–1936) 1907 prize at 41 *Peace:* Mrs Mairead Corrigan-Maguire (Republic of Ireland; b. 27 Jan 1944) 1976 prize (shared) at 32.

Most 3 Awards: International Committee of the Red Cross, Geneva (founded 1863) Peace 1917, 1944 and 1963 (shared); 2 Awards: Dr Linus Carl Pauling (US; b. 28 Feb 1901) Chemistry 1954 and Peace 1962; Mme Marja Sklodowska Curie (Polish-French; 1867–1934) Physics 1903 (shared) and Chemistry 1911; Professor John Bardeen (US; b. 23 May 1908) Physics 1956 (shared) and 1972 (shared); Professor Frederick Sanger (b. 13 Aug 1918) Chemistry 1958 and 1980 (shared); Office of the United Nations' High Commissioner for Refugees, Geneva (founded 1951) Peace 1954 and 1981.

Highest Prize Sw Kr 4,000,000 (for 1990).

Lowest Prize Sw Kr 115,000 (1923).

Most Nobel prizes ● The country which has won the most Nobel prizes is the USA, with 198 (outright or shared) up to and including the 1989 awards. It has particularly dominated the Physiology or Medicine prize, with 67 awards, 45 more than the next most successful country, Great Britain. The 1989 prize was shared by two Americans, and in 1988 the prize was awarded jointly to Sir James Black from Great Britain, and Gertrude Elion and George Hitchings from the USA, who are seen here at the Wellcome Research Laboratories, where they have spent over 40 years working together. The prize was awarded 'for their discoveries of important principles for drug treatment.' (Photo: Science Photo Library)

The man to whom most statues have been raised is Buddha (Siddhārtha Gautama). The 20th-century champion is Vladimir Ilyich Ulyanov, alias Lenin (1870–1924), busts of whom have been mass-produced, as also has been the case with Mao Zedang (1893–1976) and Ho Chi Minh (1890–1969).

Most honorary degrees ■ The greatest number of honorary degrees awarded to any individual is 118, given to Reverend Father Theodore M. Hesburgh (b. 1918), president of the University of Notre Dame, IN. These have been accumulated since 1954.

Military and Defense

WAR

Earliest conflict ■ The oldest known offensive weapon is a broken wooden spear found in April 1911 at Clacton-on-Sea, Essex, United Kingdom, by S. Hazzledine Warren. This is much beyond the limit of radiocarbon dating but is estimated to have been fashioned before 200,000 B.C.

Longest ■ The longest war was the Hundred Years War between England and France, which lasted from 1338 to 1453 (115 years), although it may be said that the nine Crusades from the First (1096–1104) to the Ninth (1270–91), extending over 195 years, comprised a single holy war.

Shortest ■ The shortest war on record was that between the United Kingdom and Zanzibar (now part of Tanzania) from 9:02 to 9:40 A.M. on 27 Aug 1896. The United Kingdom battle fleet under Rear-Admiral (later Admiral Sir) Harry

Rawson (1843–1910) delivered an ultimatum to the self-appointed sultan Sa'īd Khalid to evacuate his palace and surrender. This was not forthcoming until after 38 minutes of bombardment. Admiral Rawson received the Brilliant Star of Zanzibar (first class) from Hamud ibn Muhammad, the new sultan. It was proposed at one time that elements of the local populace should be compelled to defray the cost of the broadsides fired.

Bloodiest ■ By far the most costly war in terms of human life was World War II (1939–45), in which the total number of fatalities, including battle deaths and civilians of all countries, is estimated to have been 54·8 million, assuming 25 million Soviet fatalities and 7·8 million Chinese civilians killed. The country that suffered most was Poland, with 6,028,000 or 17·2 percent of its population of 35·1 million killed. The total combatant death toll from World War I was 9·7 million, compared with the 15·6 million from World War II.

In the Paraguayan war of 1864–70 against Brazil, Argentina and Uruguay, their population was reduced from 1·4 million down to 220,000 survivors, of whom only 30,000 were adult males.

Surgeon Major William Brydon (1811–1873) was the sole survivor of the seven-day retreat of 16,000 soldiers and camp followers from Kabul, Afghanistan. His horse died two days after his arrival at Jellalabad, India on 13 Jan 1842.

Modern **■** The battle with the greatest recorded number of *military* casualties was the first Battle of the Somme, France, from 1 Jul to 19 Nov 1916, with 1,043,896 — of these 623,907 were Allied and the rest German. The published German figure of *c.* 670,000 is not now accepted. Gunfire was heard in London, United Kingdom.

The greatest death toll in a battle has been estimated at *c.* 2·1 million in the Battle of Stalingrad, ending with the German surrender on 31 Jan 1943 by Field Marshal Friedrich von

Paulus (1890–1957). The Soviet garrison commander was Gen Vasiliy Chuikov. Additionally, only 1,515 civilians from a prewar population of more than 500,000 were found alive after the battle. The final invasion of Berlin by the Red Army from 16 Apr–2 May 1945 involved 3·5 million men, 52,000 guns and mortars, 7,750 tanks and 11,000 aircraft on both sides.

Civil **■** The bloodiest civil war in history was the *Taiping* ('Great Peace') rebellion, which was a revolt against the Chinese Ch'ing dynasty between 1851 and 1864. The rebellion was led by the deranged Hung Xiuquan (executed) who imagined himself to be a younger brother of Jesus Christ. His force was named Taiping Tianguo (Heavenly Kingdom of Great Peace). According to the best estimates, the loss of life was some 20 million, including more than 100,000 killed by government forces in the sack of Nanjing on 19–21 Jul 1864.

United States **■** The American Civil War (1861–65) is the bloodiest war fought on United States soil. The bloodiest battles between the Northern (Union) and the Southern (Confederate) forces were at Shiloh Church, near Pittsburg Landing in Hardin County, TN on 6–7 Apr 1862 when each side reported casualties of over 10,000; at Fredricksburg, VA on 13 Dec 1862 when Union casualties were over 12,000, more than double that of the Confederacy; and at Gettysburg, PA on 1–3 Jul 1863 when the Union reported casualties of 23,000 and the Confederacy 25,000 (a disputed figure). The American Civil War officially ended when the Confederate General Robert E. Lee surrendered to the Union General Ulysses S. Grant at Appomattox Courthouse on 9 Apr 1865.

Most costly ■ The material cost of World War II far transcended that of the rest of history's wars put together and has been estimated at $1·5 trillion. The total cost to the Soviet Union was estimated in May 1959 at 2·5 trillion roubles, while a figure of $530 billion has been estimated for the United States.

Greatest naval battle ■ The greatest number of ships and aircraft ever involved in a sea-air action was 231 ships and 1,996 aircraft in the Battle of Leyte Gulf, in the Philippines. It raged from 22 to 27 Oct 1944, with 166 Allied and 65 Japanese warships engaged, of which 26 Japanese and 6 US ships were sunk. In addition, 1,280 US and 716 Japanese aircraft were engaged.

The greatest purely naval battle of modern times was the Battle of Jutland on 31 May 1916, in which 151 Royal Navy warships were involved against 101 German warships. The British Royal Navy lost 14 ships and 6,097 men and the German fleet 11 ships and 2,545 men.

The greatest of ancient naval battles was the Battle of Salamis, Greece in September 480 B.C. There were an estimated 800 vessels in the defeated Persian fleet and 380 in the victorious fleet of the Athenians and their allies, with a possible involvement of 200,000 men. The death toll at the Battle of Lepanto on 7 Oct 1571 has been estimated at 33,000.

Greatest invasion *Seaborne* **■** The greatest invasion in military history was the Allied land, air and sea operation against the Normandy coasts of France on D-day, 6 Jun 1944. Thirty-eight convoys of 745 ships moved in on the first three days, supported by 4,066 landing craft, carrying 185,000 men, 20,000 vehicles and 347 minesweepers. The air assault comprised 18,000 paratroopers from 1,087 aircraft. The 42 available divisions possessed an air support from

13,175 aircraft. Within a month 1·1 million troops, 200,000 vehicles and 840,000 tons of stores were landed. The Allied invasion of Sicily from 10–12 Jul 1943 involved the landing of 181,000 men in three days.

Airborne ■ The largest airborne invasion was the Anglo-American assault of three divisions (34,000 men), with 2,800 aircraft and 1,600 gliders, near Arnhem, in the Netherlands, on 17 Sep 1944.

Greatest evacuation ■ The greatest evacuation in military history was that carried out by 1,200 Allied naval and civil craft from the beach-head at Dunkerque (Dunkirk), France between 27 May and 4 Jun 1940. A total of 338,226 British and French troops were taken off.

Worst sieges ■ The worst siege in history was the 880-day siege of Leningrad, USSR by the German Army from 30 Aug 1941 until 27 Jan 1944. The best estimate is that between 1·3 and 1·5 million defenders and citizens died. This included 641,000 people who died of hunger in the city and 17,000 civilians killed through shelling. More than 150,000 shells and 100,000 bombs were dropped on the city.

The longest recorded siege was that of Azotus (now Ashdod), Israel, which according to Herodotus was invested by Psamtik I of Egypt for 29 years in the period 664–610 B.C.

Chemical warfare ■ The greatest number of people killed through chemical warfare were the estimated 4,000 Kurds who died at Halabja, Iraq in March 1988 when President Hussein used chemical weapons against Iraq's Kurdish minority for the support it had given to Iran in the Gulf war.

DEFENSE SPENDING

In May 1988 it was estimated that the world's spending on armaments was running at the annual rate of some $660 billion. This represents 10 percent of the world's total production of goods and services. In 1987 there were 28,123,000 full-time armed force regulars or conscripts plus 40,289,400 reservists to total 68,412,400. The budgeted expenditure on defense by the US government for the fiscal year 1988 was $283,159 million.

The defense burden on the USSR has been estimated by official sources in the United States and the United Kingdom as between 13 and 17 percent of gross national product (GNP) and thus may be nearly treble the rate of that of the United States (5·9 percent of GNP in 1988).

ARMED FORCES

Largest ■ Numerically the largest regular armed force in the world is that of the USSR, with 4,258,000 (1989).

China's People's Liberation Army's strength in 1987 was estimated to be 3·2 million (comprising land, sea and air forces), with reductions continuing. China's reserves number around 4·4 million and its paramilitary forces of armed and unarmed militias are estimated by the International Institute of Strategic Studies, London, United Kingdom at 'some 12 million.'

The military manpower of the United States for 1988 was 2,138,000.

Navies *Largest* ■ The largest navy in the world in terms of manpower is the United States Navy, with a manpower of 583,800 and 199,600 Marines in mid-1987. The active strength in 1987 included five nuclear-powered aircraft carriers, with 10 non-nuclear carriers, three battleships,

92 nuclear attack submarines and four diesel attack submarines, 36 cruisers, 68 destroyers, 115 frigates and 60 amphibious warfare ships.

The USSR's navy has a larger submarine fleet of 375 vessels (including 127 nuclear attack). The Red Fleet has six aircraft carriers, 37 cruisers and 63 destroyers.

Longest-serving admiral ■ Admiral of the Fleet Sir Provo Wallis (1791–1892) first served on HMS *Cleopatra* in October 1804. Because of his service on HMS *Cleopatra* in 1805 against the French he was kept on the active list in 1870 for life. He thus was 87 years 4 months on paid active service, though he was earlier on the books as a volunteer from 1795–1804 for a further 9 years — a system by which even infants could gain seniority on joining.

Armies *Oldest* ■ The oldest army in the world is the 80–90 strong Pontifical Swiss Guard in the Vatican City, with a regular foundation dating back to 21 Jan 1506. Its origins, however, extend back before 1400.

Largest ■ Numerically, the world's largest army is that of the People's Republic of China, with a total strength of some 2·3 million in mid-1987.

The total size of the USSR's army in mid-1987 was estimated by the International Institute of Strategic Studies, London, United Kingdom at 2 million men believed to be organized into 209 divisions.

Oldest soldiers ■ The oldest soldier of all time was probably John B. Salling of the army of the Confederate States of America and the last accepted survivor of the US Civil War (1861–65). He died in Kingsport, TN on 16 Mar 1959, aged 113 years 1 day.

Youngest soldiers ■ Marshal Duke of Caxias (b. 25 Aug 1803, d. 7 May 1880), Brazilian military hero and statesman, entered his infantry regiment at the age of five in 1808.

Youngest conscripts ■ President Francisco Macias Nguema of Equatorial Guinea (deposed in August 1979) decreed in March 1976 compulsory military service for all boys aged between seven and 14. The edict stated that any parent refusing to hand over his or her son 'will be imprisoned or shot.'

Tallest soldiers ■ The tallest soldier of all time was Väinö Myllyrinne (1909–63), who was inducted into the Finnish Army when he was 7 ft 3 in and later grew to 8 ft 3 in.

Greatest mutiny ■ In the First World War 56 French divisions comprising some 650,000 men and their officers refused orders on the Western Front sector of General Robert Nivelle in April 1917 after the failure of his offensive.

Longest march ■ The longest march in military history was the famous Long March by the Chinese Communists in 1934–35. In 368 days, of which 268 days were days of movement, from October to October, their force of 90,000 covered 6,000 miles from Jiangxi to Yanan in Shaanxi via Yünnan. They crossed 18 mountain ranges and six major rivers and lost all but 22,000 of their force in continual rear-guard actions against nationalist Kuomintang (KMT) forces.

A team of the British 29th Commando Regiment, each man carrying a 40-lb pack, including a rifle, covered the Plymouth Marathon, Plymouth, Devon, United Kingdom in 4 hr 35 min 47·28 sec on 1 Nov 1987.

Army drill ■ On 8–9 Jul 1987 a 90-man squad of the Queen's Color Squadron, of the Royal Air Force (RAF), performed a total of 2,722,662 drill

movements (2,001,384 rifle and 721,278 foot) at RAF Uxbridge, Middlesex, United Kingdom from memory and without a word of command in 23 hr 55 min.

Air forces *Oldest* ■ The earliest autonomous air force is the British Royal Air Force (RAF), which can be traced back to 1878, when the War Office commissioned the building of a military balloon. The Royal Engineers Balloon Section and Depot was formed in 1890 and the Air Battalion of the Royal Engineers followed on 1 Apr 1911. On 13 May 1912 the Royal Flying Corps (RFC) was formed, with both Military and Naval Wings, the latter being renamed the Royal Naval Air Service (RNAS). The Royal Air Force was formed on 1 Apr 1918 from the RFC and the RNAS, and took its place alongside the Royal Navy and the Army as a separate service with its own Ministry. The Prussian Army used a balloon near Strasbourg, France as early as 24 Sep 1870.

Largest ■ The greatest air force of all time was the United States Army Air Corps (now the US Air Force), which had 79,908 aircraft in July 1944 and 2,411,294 personnel in March 1944. The US Air Force, including strategic air forces, had 605,805 personnel and 4,887 combat aircraft in mid-1986.

The USSR Air Force had 453,000 men in mid-1986. It had 5,150 aircraft. In addition the USSR's Offensive Strategic Rocket Forces had about 298,000 operational personnel in mid-1986.

BOMBS

Heaviest ■ The heaviest conventional bomb ever used operationally was the Royal Air Force's 'Grand Slam,' weighing 22,000 lb and measuring 25 ft 5 in long, dropped on Bielefeld railroad viaduct, Germany on 14 Mar 1945.

In 1949 the United States Air Force tested a bomb weighing 42,000 lb at Muroc Dry Lake, CA.

The heaviest known nuclear bomb was the MK 17 carried by US B-36s in the mid-1950s. It weighed 42,000 lb and was 24 ft 6 in long.

Atomic ■ The first atom bomb dropped on Hiroshima, Japan by the United States at 8:16 A.M. on 6 Aug 1945 had an explosive power equivalent to that of 12·5 kilotons of trinitrotoluene ($C_7H_5O_6N_3$), called TNT. Code-named 'Little Boy' it was 10 ft long and weighed 9,000 lb and burst *c.* 1,900 ft above the city center.

The most powerful thermonuclear device so far tested is one with a power equivalent to that of 57 megatons of TNT, detonated by the USSR in the Novaya Zemlya area at 8:33 A.M. GMT on 30 Oct 1961. The shock wave circled the world three times, taking 36 hr 27 min for the first circuit. Some estimates put the power of this device at between 62 and 90 megatons.

The largest US H-bomb tested was the 18–22 megaton 'Bravo' at Bikini Atoll, Marshall Islands on 1 Mar 1954.

On 9 Aug 1961, Nikita Khrushchev, then the Chairman of the Council of Ministers of the USSR, declared that the Soviet Union was capable of constructing a 100-megaton bomb, and announced the possession of one in East Berlin, East Germany on 16 Jan 1963. Such a device could make a crater in rock 355 ft deep and 1·8 miles wide and a fireball 8·7 miles in diameter.

Largest nuclear weapons ■ The most powerful ICBM (intercontinental ballistic missiles) are the USSR's SS-18s (Model 5), believed to be armed with 10,750-kiloton MIRVs (multiple independently targetable reentry vehicles).

Earlier models had a single 20-megaton warhead. The US Titan II carrying a W-53 warhead was rated at 5 to 9 megatons but is now withdrawn, leaving the 1–2 megaton W-56 as the most powerful US weapon.

Largest 'conventional' explosion ■

The largest use of conventional explosive was for the demolition of the fortifications and U-boat pens at Helgoland, Germany on 18 Apr 1947. A net charge of 7,122 tons gross was detonated by Commissioned Gunner E. C. Jellis of the British naval team headed by Lt F. T. Woosnam RN aboard HMS *Lasso* lying 9 miles out to sea.

TANKS

Earliest ■ The first tank was 'No. 1 Lincoln' modified to become 'Little Willie' built by William Foster & Co Ltd of Lincoln, United Kingdom. It first ran on 6 Sep 1915. Tanks were first taken into action by the Heavy Section, Machine Gun Corps, which later became the Royal Tank Corps, at the Battle of Flers-Courcelette in France on 15 Sep 1916. The Mark I Male tank, armed with a pair of 6-pounder guns and four machine guns, weighed 31·3 tons and was driven by a motor developing 105 hp, which gave it a maximum road speed of 3–4 mph.

Heaviest and fastest ■ The heaviest tank ever constructed was the German Panzer Kampfwagen Maus II, which weighed 211·6 tons. By 1945 it had only reached the experimental stage and research was not continued.

The heaviest operational tank used by any army was the 83 ton, 13-man French Char de Rupture 2C bis of 1922. It carried a 155-mm howitzer and had two 250 hp engines giving a maximum speed of 8 mph.

The world's most heavily armed tank since 1972 has been the Soviet T-72, with a 125-mm (4·92 in) high velocity gun. The British AVRE 'Centurion' has 165 mm (6.5 in) low-velocity demolition gun.

The world's fastest tank is the British Scorpion AFV, which can touch 50 mph with 75 percent payload.

GUNS

Earliest ■ Although it cannot be accepted as proven, the best opinion is that the earliest guns were constructed in both China and in North Africa in *c.* 1250.

The earliest antiaircraft gun was an artillery piece on a high-angle mounting used in the Franco-Prussian War of 1870 by the Prussians against French balloons.

Largest ■ The two most massive guns ever constructed were used by the Germans in the siege of Sevastopol on the Eastern Front in July 1942. They were of a caliber of 31½ in with barrels 94 ft 8½ in long and named Dore and Gustav. Their remains were discovered, one near Metzenhof, Bavaria in August 1945 and the other in the Soviet zone. They were built by Krupp as railroad guns carried on 24 cars, two of which had 40 wheels each. The whole assembly

> **Largest cannon** ● The highest-caliber cannon ever constructed is the 'Tsar Pushka' (King of Cannons), now housed in the Kremlin, Moscow, USSR. It was built in the 16th century with a bore of 36·2 in and a barrel 10 ft 5 in long. It weighs 44 tons. (Photo: Spectrum)

of the gun was 141 ft long and weighed 1,481·5 tons with a crew of 1,500. The range for an 8·9-ton projectile was 29 miles.

Greatest range ■ The greatest range ever attained by a gun was achieved by the HARP (High Altitude Research Project) gun consisting of two 16·5-in caliber barrels in tandem 119·4 ft long weighing 165 tons at Yuma, AZ. On 19 Nov 1966 an 185-lb projectile was fired to an altitude of 111·8 miles or 590,550 ft.

The static V3 underground firing tubes built in 50-degree shafts near Mimoyècques, near Calais, France to bombard London, United Kingdom were never operative. The famous long-range gun that shelled Paris in World War I was the 'Kaiser Wilhelm Geschütz,' with a caliber of 8·66 in, a designed range of 79½ miles and an achieved range of 76 miles from the Forest of Crépy in March 1918. The 'Big Berthas' were mortars of 16·53 in caliber and with a range of less than 9 miles.

Mortars ■ The largest mortars ever constructed were Mallet's mortar (Woolwich Arsenal, London, United Kingdom 1857) and the 'Little David' of World War II, made in the United States. Each had a caliber of 36¼ in, but neither was ever used in action.

The heaviest mortar used was the tracked German 23·6-in siege piece known as 'Karl' before Stalingrad, USSR in World War II.

Largest cannon ■ The highest-caliber cannon ever constructed is the 'Tsar Pushka' (King of Cannons), now housed in the Kremlin, Moscow, USSR. It was built in the 16th century with a bore of 36·2 in and a barrel 10 ft 5 in long, and it weighs 2,400 pounds.

The Turks fired up to seven shots per day from a bombard 26 ft long, with an internal caliber of 42 in against the walls of Constantinople (now Istanbul) from 12 Apr to 29 May 1453. It was dragged by 60 oxen and 200 men and fired a 1,200-lb stone cannonball.

Military engines ■ The largest military catapults, or onagers, could throw a missile weighing 60 lb a distance of 500 yd.

Conscientious objector ■ The only conscientious objector to be six times court-martialed in World War II was Gilbert Lane of Wallington, Surrey, United Kingdom. He served 31 months' detention and 183 days' imprisonment.

Nuclear delivery vehicles ■ As of mid-1987 the USSR deployed 2,511 strategic nuclear delivery vehicles, while the United States on the same date deployed 1,957 vehicles or 340 below the 2,250 SALT II limit.

The comparative number of warheads has been estimated by the International Institute for Strategic Studies, London, United Kingdom to be USSR: 11,044; United States: 13,873.

Judicial

LEGISLATION AND LITIGATION

Statutes *Oldest* ■ The earliest surviving judicial code was that of King Ur-Hammu during the third dynasty of Ur, Iraq, *c.* 2110 B.C.

Most inexplicable ■ Certain passages in several acts have always defied interpretation and the most inexplicable must be a matter of opinion. A judge of the Court of Session of Scotland once sent the Editor his candidate which reads: '*In the Nuts (unground), (other than ground nuts) Order, the expression nuts shall have reference to such nuts, other than ground*

The bail figure was reduced on 25 Feb by a Superior Court judge to a more affordable $500 but she was rearrested on 21 Mar 1988 for a fifth time. The Assistant District Attorney's comment was 'See what happens when you reduce a $5 billion bail.'

Best attended trial ■ The greatest attendance at any trial was that of Major Jesús Sosa Blanco, aged 51, for an alleged 108 murders. At one point in the 12½ hr trial (5:30 P.M. to 6 A.M., 22–23 Jan 1959), 17,000 people were present in the Havana Sports Palace, Cuba. He was executed on 18 Feb 1959.

Greatest damages *Personal injury* ■ The greatest personal injury damages ever awarded were $78 million to the model Marla Hanson, 26, on 29 Sep 1987, whose face was slashed with razors in Manhattan, NY in June 1987. The three men convicted and now serving 5–15 years have no assets and Miss Hanson is entitled to 10 percent of their post-prison earnings.

On 18 Jul 1986 a Bronx Supreme Court Jury awarded $65,086,000 to Mrs Agnes Mae Whitaker against the New York City Health and Hospitals Corporation for medical malpractice.

The compensation for the disaster in 1984 at the Union Carbide Corporation plant in Bhopal, India was agreed at $470 million. The Supreme Court of India passed the order for payment on 14 Feb 1989 after the settlement between the corporation and the Indian Government, which represented the interests of more than 500,000 claimants.

Civil damages ■ The largest damages awarded in legal history were $11·12 billion to Pennzoil Co against Texaco Inc. concerning the latter's allegedly unethical tactics in January 1984 to break up a merger between Pennzoil and Getty Oil Co, by Judge Solomon Casseb Jr in Houston, TX on 10 Dec 1985. The two leading counsels were Joe Jamail (Pennzoil) and Richard Miller (Texaco). An out-of-court settlement of $5·5 billion was reached after a 48-hour negotiation on 19 Dec 1987.

Defamation and libel ■ Richard A. Sprague, a prominent lawyer from Philadelphia, PA was awarded $34 million against the *Philadelphia Inquirer* on 3 May 1990 for a series of articles which the newspaper had published about him in 1973.

A sum of $16·8 million was awarded to Dr John J. Wild, 58, at the Hennepin District Court, MN on 30 Nov 1972 against The Minnesota Foundation and others for defamation, bad-faith termination of a contract, interference with a professional business relationship, along with $10·8 million in punitive damages. The Supreme Court of Minnesota granted an option of a new trial or a $1·5 million *remittitur* to Dr Wild on 10 Jan 1975. There was a no-disclosure clause in the settlement.

Magazine ■ The $39·6 million awarded in Columbus, OH on 1 Mar 1980 to Robert Guccione, publisher of *Penthouse*, against Larry Flynt, publisher of *Hustler*, for defamation, was reduced by Judge Craig Wright to $4 million on 17 Apr 1980.

A $640 million libel suit was brought by the California resort La Costa against *Penthouse* in March 1975. In May 1982 a jury exonerated the magazine of libel, but in July their verdict was set aside by a California judge, who was then removed from the case. Costs exceeded $10 million.

nuts, as would but for this amending Order not qualify as nuts (unground) (other than ground nuts) by reason of their being nuts (unground).'

Most protracted litigation ■ The longest contested lawsuit ever recorded ended in Poona, India on 28 Apr 1966, when Balasaheb Patloji Thorat received a favorable judgment on a suit filed by his ancestor Maloji Thorat 761 years earlier in 1205. The points at issue were rights of presiding over public functions and precedences at religious festivals.

Longest trial ■ The longest jury trial in legal history is *Kemner* v. *Monsanto Co.*, which started on 6 Feb 1984. The trial, at St Clair County Court House, Belleville, IL before Circuit Judge Richard P. Goldenhersh, ended on 22 Oct 1987. The testimony lasted 657 days, following which the jury deliberated for two months. The verdict was returned on 22 Oct when the plaintiffs secured sums of $1 nominal compensatory damage and $16,250,000 punitive damage in a case concerning an alleged toxic chemical spill in Sturgeon, MO in 1979.

Litigants in person ■ Dr Mark Feldman, a podiatric surgeon, of Lauderhill, FL became the first litigant in person to secure seven figures ($1 million) before a jury in compensatory and punitive damages in September 1980.

> **Supreme Court** ● The highest court in the United States, the Supreme Court was established in 1789 by Article 3 of the Constitution. Its judicial powers extend to all cases arising under the Constitution, laws and treaties of the United States; to cases concerning foreign diplomats and admirality practico; and to diversity cases (those between citizens of different states) and cases in which the United States or a state is a party. (Photo: All Sport/Morley)

The case concerned conspiracy and fraud alleged against six other doctors.

Highest bail ■ The world record for bail was set at $100 billion on Jeffrey Marsh, Juan Mercado, Yolanda Kravitz and Alvin Kravitz at the Dade County Courthouse, Miami, FL on 16 Oct 1989. The four defense attorneys in the case, concerning an armed robbery, stipulated the bail, and although a reduction was subsequently requested, this was denied. The presiding judge was David L. Tobin.

A bail of $5 billion was set by Judge J. Dominique Olcomendy of San Francisco Municipal Court, CA on Dorothy M. Toines, 25, for soliciting prostitution on 8 Feb 1988. She was unable to pay the 10 percent or $0·5 billion necessary for her release after repeated failures to appear in court.

Media Organization ■ The Supreme Court on 4 Apr 1988 let stand a $3,050,000 libel award against CBS Inc., its Chicago station WBBM and anchorman Walter Jacobsen. The damages awarded to Brown & Williamson Tobacco Corp. were the largest against a news media defendant in the United States.

The record libel award actually paid was $2·77 million by the *Pittsburgh Post-Gazette* to former judge Richard Disalle. Damages have been set by a Washington, PA jury in 1985, the Supreme Court declined to hear an appeal on 3 Jul 1988 and the award was paid on 11 Jul 1988.

Greatest compensation for wrongful imprisonment ■ Robert McLaughlin, 29, was awarded $1,935,000 in October 1989 for wrongful imprisonment as a result of a murder in New York City in 1979 which he did not commit. He had been sentenced to 15 years in prison and actually served six years, from 1980 to 1986, when he was released after his foster father succeeded in showing the authorities that he had nothing to do with the crime.

Greatest alimony suit ■ Belgian-born Sheika Dena Al-Fassi, 23, filed the highest ever alimony claim of $3 billion against her former husband, Sheik Mohammed Al-Fassi, 28, of the Saudi Arabian royal family, in Los Angeles, CA in February 1982. Attorney Marvin Mitchelson, explaining the size of the settlement claim, alluded to the Sheik's wealth, which included 14 homes in Florida alone and numerous private aircraft. On 14 Jun 1983 she was awarded $81 million and declared she would be 'very very happy' if she was able to collect.

Greatest divorce settlement ■ The reported settlement achieved in 1982 by the lawyers of Soraya Khashóggi was £0·5 billion plus property from her husband Adnan.

Mrs Anne Bass, former wife of Sid Bass of Texas, was reported to have rejected $535 million as inadequate to live in the style to which she had been made accustomed.

Patent case ■ On 13 Mar 1986 Hughes Tool Co of Houston, TX was awarded $205,381,259·40 in a suit involving Smith International Inc. over an infringement of their patent for the 'O' ring seal used in drilling. The inventor was Edward M. Galle.

Largest suit ■ The highest amount of damages ever sought to date is $675 trillion (then equivalent to 10 times the US national wealth) in a suit by Mr I. Walton Bader brought in the US District Court, NY on 14 Apr 1971 against General Motors and others for polluting all 50 states.

Highest costs ■ The McMartin Pre-School case in Los Angeles, CA is estimated to have cost $15 million. The trial, concerning the alleged abuse of children at the school in Manhattan Beach, CA, had begun with jury selection on 20 Apr 1987 and resulted with the acquittal on 18 Jan 1990 of the two defendants on 52 counts of child molestation and conspiracy. Peggy McMartin Buckey, the former director of the school, and her son Raymond, who had been a teacher's aide, had spent nearly two and five years in jail respectively since their arrest in 1984.

Longest lease ■ There is a lease concerning a plot for a sewage tank adjoining Columb Barracks, Mullingar, County Westmeath, Republic of Ireland, which was signed on 3 Dec 1868 for 10 million years. It is to be assumed that a future civil servant will bring up the matter for

review early in A.D. 10,001,868. Leases in Ireland lasting 'for ever' are quite common.

Greatest lien ■ The greatest lien by a court is 40 billion lire on 9 Apr 1974 upon Vittorio and Ida Riva in Milan for back taxes allegedly due on a chain of cotton mills around Turin, Italy.

Wills ■ The shortest valid will in the world is 'Vše zene,' the Czech for 'All to wife,' written and dated 19 Jan 1967 by Herr Karl Tausch of Langen, Hessen, West Germany.

Most durable judges ■ The oldest recorded active judge was Judge Albert R. Alexander (1859–1966) of Plattsburg, MO. He was the magistrate and probate judge of Clinton County until his retirement at age 105 years 8 months on 9 Jul 1965.

Youngest judge ■ No collated records on the ages of judicial appointments exist. However, David Elmer Ward had to await the legal age of 21 before taking office after nomination in 1932 as judge of the County Court at Fort Myers, FL.

Muhammad Ilyas passed the examination enabling him to become a civil judge in July 1952 at the age of 20 years 9 months, although formalities such as medicals meant that it was not until eight months later that he started work as a civil judge in Lahore, Pakistan.

Most judges ■ In *R.* v. *Canning* at the Old Bailey, London, United Kingdom in 1754 Elizabeth Canning was deported to Connecticut for willful perjury by 19 judges voting 10 to 9.

Most successful ■ Sir Lionel Luckhoo, senior partner of Luckhoo and Luckhoo of Georgetown, Guyana, succeeded in getting his 245th successive murder charge acquittal by 1 Jan 1985.

CRIME

Mass killings *China* ■ The greatest massacre ever imputed by the government of one sovereign nation against the government of another is that of 26·3 million Chinese during the regime of Mao Zedong between 1949 and May 1965. This accusation was made by an agency of the USSR government in a radio broadcast on 7 Apr 1969. The broadcast broke down the figure into four periods: 2·8 million (1949–52); 3·5 million (1953–57); 6·7 million (1958–60); and 13·3 million (1961–May 1965).

The Walker Report published by the US Senate Committee of the Judiciary in July 1971 placed the parameters of the total death toll within China since 1949 between 32·25 and 61·7 million. An estimate of 63·7 million was published by the *Figaro* magazine of 19–25 Nov 1978.

USSR ■ The total death toll in the Great Purge, or *Yezhovshchina*, in the USSR from 1936–38 has never been published. Evidence of its magnitude may be found in population statistics, which show a deficiency of people from *before* the outbreak of the 1941–45 war.

Nobel Prize-winner Alexander Solzhenitsyn estimated the loss of life from state repression and terrorism from October 1917 to December 1959 under Lenin, Stalin and Khrushchev at 66·7 million.

Nazi Germany ■ The best estimate of the number of Jewish victims of the Holocaust or the genocidal 'Final Solution' or *Endlösung* ordered by Adolf Hitler (1889–1945) in April 1941 and continuing into May 1945 is 5·8 million.

At the SS (*Schutzstaffel*) extermination camp (*Vernichtungslager*) known as Auschwitz-

Birkenau (Oświecim-Brzezinka), near Oświecim (Auschwitz) in southern Poland, where a minimum of 920,000 people (Soviet estimate is 4 million) were exterminated from 14 Jun 1940 to 18 Jan 1945, the greatest number killed in a day was 6,000.

Cambodia ■ As a percentage of a nation's total population the worst genocide appears to have been that in Cambodia, formerly Kampuchea. According to the Khmer Rouge Foreign Minister, Ieng Sary, more than a third of the 8 million Khmers were killed between 17 Apr 1975 and January 1979. The highest 'class' ideals induced indifference to individual suffering to the point of serving as a warrant for massacre. Under the rule of Saloth Sar *alias* Pol Pot, a founding member of the CPK (Communist Party of Kampuchea, formed in September 1960), towns, money and property were abolished and economical execution by bayonet and club introduced for such offenses as falling asleep during the day, asking too many questions, playing noncommunist music, being old and feeble, being the offspring of an 'undesirable' or being too well educated. Deaths at the Tuol Sleng interrogation center reached 582 in a day.

In Chinese history of the 13th–17th centuries there were three periods of wholesale massacre. The numbers of victims attributed to these events are assertions rather than reliable estimates. The figure put on the Mongolian invasions of northern China from 1210–19 and from 1311–40 are both of the order of 35 million, while the number of victims of the bandit leader Chang Hsien-chung (*c.* 1605–47), known as the 'Yellow Tiger,' from 1643–47 in the Siechuan province has been put at 40 million.

Saving of life ■ The greatest number of people saved from extinction by one man is an estimated 90,000 Jews in Budapest, Hungary from July 1944 to January 1945 by the Swedish diplomat Raoul Wallenberg (b. 4 Aug 1912). After escaping an assassination attempt by the Nazis, he was imprisoned without trial in the Soviet Union. On 6 Feb 1957 Andrei Gromyko, the Soviet Foreign Minister, said prisoner 'Wallenberg' had died in a cell in Lubyanka Jail, Moscow on 16 Jul 1947. Sighting reports within the Gulag system persisted for years after his disappearance. He was made an Honorary Citizen of the United States on 5 Oct 1981 and on 7 May 1987 a statue was unveiled to him in Budapest to replace an earlier one that had been removed.

Largest criminal organization ■ The largest syndicate of organized crime is the Mafia or La Cosa Nostra. The name 'Mafia' is thought to be derived from the first letters of each word of the slogan 'Morte alla Francia Italia anela' — 'Death to the French is Italy's cry.' It consists of some 3,000 to 5,000 individuals in 25 'families' federated under 'The Commission,' with an annual turnover in vice, gambling, protection rackets, tobacco, bootlegging, hijacking, narcotics, loan-sharking and prostitution that was estimated by *US News & World Report* in December 1982 at $200 billion and a profit estimated in March 1986 by the US District Attorney Rudolph Giuliani at $75 billion. Its origin in the United States dates from 1869 in New Orleans, LA.

The biggest Mafia killing was from 11–13 Sep 1931 when 40 mafiosi were liquidated following the murder in New York of Salvatore Maranzano, *Il Capo di Tutti Capi*, on 10 Sep. The greatest breaches of *omerta* (the vow of silence) were by Joseph Valachi who 'sang like a canary' in 1963, and by the much bereaved Tommaso

Buschetta, 56, in 1984. The latter's information led to 329 convictions and 2,655 years' imprisonment, and $9·6 million in fines plus 19 life sentences in the Sicilian Mafia or Cupola trial in Palermo from 10 Feb 1986 to 16 Dec 1987. Michele 'the Pope' and his brother Salvatore 'the Senator' Greco had been accused of slaying the Carabinieri General Dalla Chiesa in Palermo on 3 Sep 1982.

Murder rate *Highest and lowest* ■ The country with the highest recorded murder rate is Brazil, with 104 homicides for each 100,000 of the population in 1983, or 370 per day. The highest homicide rates recorded in New York City have been 58 in a week in July 1972 and 15 in a day in June 1989.

In the Indian state of Sikkim, in the Himalayas, murder is practically unknown, while in the Hunza area of Kashmir, in the Karakoram, only one definite case by a Hunzarwal has been recorded since 1900.

Most prolific murderers ■ It was established at the trial of Behram, the Indian Thug, that he had strangled at least 931 victims with his yellow and white cloth strip or *ruhmal* in the Oudh district between 1790 and 1840. It has been estimated that at least two million Indians were strangled by Thugs (*burtotes*) during the reign of the Thugee (pronounced tugee) cult from 1550 until its final suppression by the British raj in 1853.

The greatest number of victims ascribed to a murderess has been 650, in the case of Countess Erzsebet Bathory (1560–1614) of Hungary. At her trial, which began on 2 Jan 1611, a witness testified to seeing a list of her victims in her own handwriting totaling this number. All were alleged to be young girls from near her castle at Csejthe, where she died on 21 Aug 1614. She had been walled up in her room for 3½ years after being found guilty.

20th century ■ A total of 592 deaths was attributed to one Colombian bandit leader Teófilo ('Sparks') Rojas, 27, between 1948 and his death in an ambush near Armenia, Colombia on 22 Jan 1963. Some sources attribute 3,500 slayings to him during *La Violencia* of 1945–62.

In a drunken rampage lasting 8 hours on 26–27 Apr 1982, policeman Wou Bom-Kon, 27, killed 57 people and wounded 35 with 176 rounds of rifle ammunition and hand grenades in the Kyong Sang-Namdo province of South Korea. He blew himself up with a grenade.

Suicide ■ The estimated daily rate of suicides throughout the world surpassed 1,000 in 1965. The country with the highest suicide rate is the USSR, with a rate of 30 per 100,000 in 1984. The number in China rose to 382 per day, or 16 per hour, in 1987–88.

The country with the lowest recorded rate is Jordan, with just a single case in 1970 and hence a rate of 0·04 per 100,000.

Mass poisoning ■ On 1 May 1981 the first of more than 600 victims of the Spanish cooking oil scandal died. On 12 Jun it was discovered that this 8-year-old boy's cause of death was the use of 'denatured' industrial colza from rape seed. The trial of 38 defendants, including the manufacturers Ramón and Elias Ferrero, lasted from 30 Mar 1987 to 28 Jun 1988 on 586 counts, on which the prosecution demanded jail sentences totaling 60,000 years.

Robbery ■ The greatest robbery on record was that of the Reichsbank following Germany's collapse in April/May 1945. The Pentagon in

Washington described the event, first published in *The Guinness Book of Records* in 1957, as 'an unverified allegation.' *Nazi Gold* by Ian Sayer and Douglas Botting, published in 1984, however, finally revealed full details and estimated the total haul at current values as £2·5 billion.

Treasury Bills and certificates of deposit worth £292 million were stolen when a mugger attacked a money broker's messenger in London, United Kingdom on 2 May 1990. As details of the documents stolen were quickly flashed on the City's market dealing screens and given to central banks worldwide, the chances of anyone being able to benefit from the theft were considered to be very remote.

Art ■ It is arguable that the *Mona Lisa*, though never valued, is the most valuable object ever stolen. It disappeared from the Louvre, Paris, France on 21 Aug 1911. It was recovered in Italy in 1913 when Vincenzo Perruggia was charged with its theft.

On 18 Mar 1990, 11 paintings by Rembrandt, Vermeer, Degas, Manet and Flinck, plus a Chinese bronze beaker of about 1200 B.C., in total worth an estimated $200 million, were stolen from the Isabella Stewart Gardner Museum in Boston, MA. Although the paintings were insured against damage, none of them was insured against theft.

On 24 Dec 1985 140 'priceless' gold, jade and obsidian artifacts were stolen from the National Museum of Anthropology, Mexico City, Mexico. The majority of the stolen objects were recovered in June 1989 from the Mexico City home of a man described by officials as the mastermind of the theft.

Bank ■ During the extreme civil disorder prior to 22 Jan 1976 in Beirut, Lebanon, a guerrilla force blasted the vaults of the British Bank of the Middle East in Bab Idriss and cleared out safe deposit boxes with contents valued by former Finance Minister Lucien Dahadah at $50 million and by another source at an 'absolute minimum' of $20 million.

Train ■ The greatest recorded train robbery occurred between 3:03 A.M. and 3:27 A.M. on 8 Aug 1963, when a General Post Office mail train from Glasgow, United Kingdom was ambushed at Sears Crossing and robbed at Bridego Bridge near Mentmore, Buckinghamshire, United Kingdom. The gang escaped with about 120 mailbags containing £2,631,784 worth of bank notes being taken to London for destruction. Only £343,448 was recovered.

Jewels ■ The greatest recorded theft of jewels was from the bedroom of the 'well-guarded' villa of Prince Abdel Aziz bin Ahmed Al-Thani near Cannes, France on 24 Jul 1980 valued at $16 million.

Greatest kidnapping ransom ■ Historically the greatest ransom paid was that for Atahualpa by the Incas to Francisco Pizarro in 1532–33 at Cajamarca, Peru, which constituted a hall full of gold and silver, worth in modern money some $170 million.

The greatest ransom ever reported in modern times is 1,500 million pesos ($60 million) for the release of the brothers Jorge Born, 40, and Juan Born, 39, of Bunge and Born, paid to the left-wing urban guerrilla group Montoneros in Buenos Aires, Argentina on 20 Jun 1975.

The youngest person kidnapped has been Carolyn Wharton, born at 12:46 P.M. on 19 Mar 1955 in the Baptist Hospital, TX and kidnapped, by a woman disguised as a nurse, at 1:15 P.M. age 29 minutes.

Greatest hijack ransom ■ The highest amount ever paid to airplane hijackers has been $6 million, in the case of a JAL DC-8 at Dacca Airport on 2 Oct 1977 with 38 hostages. Six convicted criminals were also exchanged. The Bangladesh government had refused to sanction any retaliatory action.

Largest narcotics haul ■ The greatest drug haul ever achieved was on 28 Sep 1989, when cocaine with an estimated street value of $6–7 billion was seized in a raid on a warehouse in Los Angeles, CA. The haul of 22 tons was prompted by a tip-off from a local resident who had complained about heavy truck traffic and people leaving the warehouse 'at odd hours and in a suspicious manner.'

The bulkiest haul was 3,200 tons of Colombian marijuana in the 14-month-long 'Operation Tiburon,' concluded by the Drug Enforcement Administration (DEA) with the arrest of 495 people and the seizure of 95 vessels announced on 5 Feb 1982.

Greatest banknote forgery ■ The greatest forgery was the German Third Reich

Art robbery ● On 24 Dec 1985 140 'priceless' gold, jade and obsidian artifacts were stolen from the National Museum of Anthropology, Mexico City, Mexico, including this mask and the gold and turquoise pendant. The majority of the stolen objects were recovered in June 1989 from the home of a man described by officials as the mastermind of the theft. (Photos: Otis Imboden)

government's forging operation, code name 'Bernhard,' engineered by SS Sturmbannführer Alfred Naujocks of the Technical Dept of the German Secret Service Amt VI F in Berlin in 1940–41. It involved £ 150 million worth of £ 5 notes.

Biggest bank fraud ■ The Banca Nazionale del Lavoro, Italy's leading bank, admitted on 6 Sep 1989 that it had been defrauded of an estimated $3 billion, with the disclosure that its branch in Atlanta, GA had made unauthorized loan commitments to Iraq. Both the bank's chairman, Nerio Nesi, and its director general, Giacomo Pedde, resigned following the revelation.

Computer fraud ■ Between 1964 and 1973, 64,000 fake insurance policies were created on the computer of the Equity Funding Corporation in the United States involving $160 billion.

Stanley Mark Rifkin (b. 1946) was arrested in Carlsbad, CA by the FBI on 6 Nov 1978 charged with defrauding a Los Angeles bank of $10·2 million by manipulation of a computer system. He was sentenced to 8 years' imprisonment in June 1980.

Traffic citation ■ The youngest person ever to receive a traffic citation was Bobby De Sormier, age 23 months, who, on 23 May 1988, while driving on his bigwheel on the wrong side of the road, was hit by a neighbors car and dragged ten feet. Fortunately, Bobby was not seriously hurt.

Parking tickets ■ Mrs Silvia Matos of New York City has set what must be a world record in unpaid parking tickets, totaling $150,000. She collected the 2,800 tickets between 1985 and 1988, but authorities have been unable to collect a cent; she registered her car under 19 addresses and 36 licence plates and cannot be found.

Theft ■ The government of the Philippines announced on 23 Apr 1986 that they had succeeded in identifying $860·8 million 'salted' by the former President Ferdinand Edralin Marcos (1917–89) and his wife Imelda. It was asserted that the total since November 1965 was believed to be between $5 and $10 billion.

Largest object stolen by a single man ■ On a moonless night at dead calm high water on 5 Jun 1966, armed with only a sharp ax, N. William Kennedy slashed free the mooring lines at Wolfe's Cove, St Lawrence Seaway, Canada of the 10,639-dwt SS *Orient Trader* owned by Steel Factors Ltd of Ontario. The vessel drifted to a waiting blacked-out tug thus escaping a ban on any shipping movements during a violent wildcat waterfront strike. She sailed for Spain.

Maritime fraud ■ A cargo of 198,414 tons of Kuwaiti crude oil on the supertanker *Salem* at Durban was sold without title to the South African government in December 1979. The ship mysteriously sank off Senegal on 17 Jan 1980 leaving the government to pay £148 million to Shell International, who owned the shipment.

CAPITAL PUNISHMENT

Capital punishment is known to date at least from the Iron Age, as evidenced by the finding of Tollund man in Denmark. The countries in which capital punishment is still *prevalent* include China (hundreds of shootings per year), South Africa (about 100 hangings for rape, robbery and murder), Turkey, Iran, Saudi Arabia, Malaysia, US (reintroduced in 38 states since January 1983 for the most heinous murders) and the USSR (23 capital offenses, including profiteering, speculation and currency

offenses for which some 400 persons have been reportedly shot annually).

Through June 1990, 132 people have been put to death in the United States since the Supreme Court permitted states to restore the death penalty in 1976.

Capital punishment was first abolished *de facto* in 1798 in Liechtenstein.

Largest hanging ■ The most people hanged from one gallows were 38 Sioux Indians by William J. Duly outside Mankato, MN for the murder of unarmed citizens on 26 Dec 1862.

The Nazi Feldkommandant simultaneously hanged 50 Greek resistance men as a reprisal measure in Athens on 22 Jul 1944.

Last hangings ■ The last hanging in the United States occurred at Owensboro, KY in 1936.

Last from yardarm ■ The last naval execution at the yardarm was the hanging of Private John Dalliger, Royal Marines, aboard HMS *Leven* in Victoria Bay near Lu-da, China, on 13 Jul 1860. Dalliger had been found guilty of two attempted murders.

Last guillotinings ■ The last person to be publicly guillotined in France was the murderer Eugene Weidmann, before a large crowd at Versailles, near Paris, at 4:50 A.M. on 17 Jun 1939. The executioner was Henri Desfourneaux, who was succeeded by his nephew André Obrecht (1897–1983) in 1951, who was in turn succeeded by his niece's husband, Marcel Chevalier, in January 1978. Dr Joseph Ignace Guillotin (1738–1812) died a natural death. He had advocated the use of the machine designed by Dr Antoine Louis in 1789 in the French constituent assembly.

The last use before abolition on 9 Sep 1981 was on 10 Sep 1977 at Baumettes Prison, Marseille for torturer and murderer Hamida Djandoubi, 28.

Death Row ■ The longest sojourn on Death Row was the 39 years of Sadamichi Hirasawa (1893–1987) in Sendai Jail, Japan. He was convicted in 1948 of poisoning 12 bank employees with potassium cyanide to effect a theft of £ 100, and died at the age of 94.

Willie Jasper Darden, 54, survived a record six death warrants in 14 years on Death Row for the murder of a storekeeper in 1973. His final TV interview was interrupted by a power failure caused by a test of the Florida electric chair in which he died on 15 Mar 1988.

On 31 Oct 1987 Liong Wie Tong, 52, and Tan Tian Tjoen, 62, were executed for robbery and murder by firing squad in Jakarta, Indonesia after 25 years on Death Row.

Lynching ■ The worst year in the 20th century for lynchings in the United States has been 1901, with 130 lynchings, while the first year with no reported cases was 1952.

PRISON SENTENCES

Longest sentences ■ Chamoy Thipyaso, a Thai woman known as the queen of underground investing, and seven of her associates were each jailed for 141,078 years by the Bangkok Criminal Court, Thailand on 27 Jul 1989 for swindling the public through a multimillion dollar deposit-taking business.

For failing to deliver 42,768 letters, a sentence of 384,912 years, or nine years per letter, was *demanded* at the prosecution of Gabriel March

Grandos, 22, at Palma de Mallorca, Spain on 11 Mar 1972.

The longest sentence imposed on a mass murderer was 25 consecutive life terms in the case of Juan Corona, a Mexican-American, for killing 25 farm workers in 1970–71 around Feather River, Yuba City, CA. The sentence was passed at Fairfield, CA on 5 Feb 1973.

Longest time served ■ Paul Geidel (1894–1987) was convicted of second degree murder on 5 Sep 1911 as a 17-year-old porter in a New York hotel. He was released from the Fishkill Correctional Facility, Beacon, NY at age 85 on 7 May 1980, having served 68 years, 8 months and 2 days — the longest recorded term in US history. He first refused parole in 1974.

Oldest ■ Bill Wallace (1881–1989) was the oldest prisoner on record, spending the last 63 years of his life in Aradale Psychiatric Hospital, at Ararat, Victoria, Australia. He had shot and killed a man at a restaurant in Melbourne, Victoria in December 1925, and having been found unfit to plead, was transferred to the responsibility of the Mental Health Department in February 1926. He remained at Aradale until his death on 17 Jul 1989, shortly before his 108th birthday.

Most appearances ■ A record for arrests was set by Tommy Johns (1922–88) in Brisbane, Queensland, Australia on 9 Sep 1982 when he faced his 2,000th conviction for drunkenness since 1957. His total at the time of his last drink on 30 Apr 1988 was 'nearly 3,000.'

Greatest mass arrests ■ The greatest mass arrest reported in a non-communist country was of 15,617 demonstrators on 11 Jul 1988, rounded up by South Korean police to ensure security in advance of the 1988 Olympic Games in Seoul.

FINES

Heaviest ■ The largest fine ever was one of $650 million, which was imposed on the securities house Drexel Burnham Lambert in December 1988 for insider trading. This figure represented $300 million in direct fines, with the balance to be put into an account to satisfy claims of parties that could prove that they were defrauded by Drexel's actions.

The record for an individual is $200 million, which Michael Milken (see also Highest salary) agreed to pay on 24 Apr 1990. In addition, he agreed to settle civil charges filed by the Securities and Exchange Commission. The payments were in settlement of a criminal racketeering and securities fraud suit brought by the US government.

PRISONS

Most secure prison ■ After it became a maximum security federal prison in 1934, no convict was known to have lived to tell of a successful escape from the prison of Alcatraz Island in San Francisco Bay, CA. A total of 23 men attempted it but 12 were recaptured, five shot dead, one drowned and five presumed drowned. On 16 Dec 1962, just before the prison was closed on 21 Mar 1963, one man reached the mainland alive, only to be recaptured on the spot. John Chase held the record with 26 years there.

Most expensive prison ■ Spandau Prison, Berlin, West Germany, originally built in 1887 for 600 prisoners, was used solely for the Nazi war criminal Rudolf Hess (b. 26 Apr 1894, d. 17 Aug 1987) for the last twenty years of his life.

The cost of maintenance of the staff of 105 was estimated in 1976 to be $415,000 per year. On 19 Aug 1987 it was announced that Hess had strangled himself with a piece of electric cord and that he had left a note in old German script. He had remained in lone confinement at Spandau for a total of forty years. Two months after his death, the prison was demolished.

Longest escape ■ The longest recorded escape by a recaptured prisoner was that of Leonard T. Fristoe, 77, who escaped from Nevada State Prison on 15 Dec 1923 and was turned in by his son on 15 Nov 1969 at Compton, CA. He had had 46 years of freedom under the name of Claude R. Willis. He had killed two sheriff's deputies in 1920.

Greatest jail break ■ In February 1979 a retired US Army colonel, Arthur 'Bull' Simons, led a band of 14 to break into Gasre Prison, Tehran, Iran to rescue two fellow Americans. Some 11,000 other prisoners took advantage of this and the Islamic revolution in what became history's largest ever jail break.

In July 1971, Raoul Sendic and 105 other Tupamaro guerrillas escaped from a Uruguayan prison through a tunnel 298 ft long.

Education

Compulsory education was first introduced in 1819 in Prussia.

University *Oldest* ■ The Sumerians had scribal schools or *É-Dub-ba* soon after 3500 B.C.

The oldest existing educational institution in the world is the University of Karueein, founded in A.D. 859 in Fez, Morocco.

The University of Bologna, the oldest in Europe, was founded in 1088.

The oldest college in the United States is Harvard College founded in 1636 as Newtowne College and renamed in 1638 after its first benefactor, John Harvard. It was incorporated in 1650. The second oldest college in the United States is the College of William and Mary, at Williamsburg, VA. It was chartered in 1693, opened in 1694, and acquired university status in 1779. However, its antecendents were in the planned university at Henrico, VA (1619–22) which was postponed because of the Indian massacre of 1822.

Largest ■ The largest existing university building in the world is the M. V. Lomonosov State University on the Lenin Hills, south of Moscow, USSR. It stands 787 ft 5 in tall, has 32 stories and 40,000 rooms. It was constructed from 1949–53.

Most graduates in family ■ Mr and Mrs Harold Erickson of Naples, FL saw all of their 14 children—11 sons and three daughters—obtain university or college degrees between 1962 and 1978.

Youngest undergraduate and graduate ■ The most extreme recorded case of undergraduate juvenility was that of William Thomson (1824–1907), later Lord Kelvin, who entered Glasgow University, Glasgow, United Kingdom at age 10 years 4 months in October 1834 and matriculated on 14 Nov the same year.

Adragon Eastwood De Mello (b. 5 Oct 1976) of Santa Cruz, CA obtained his BA in Mathematics from the University of California in Santa Cruz on 11 Jun 1988 at the age of 11 years 8 months.

Youngest doctorate ■ On 13 Apr 1814 the mathematician Carl Witte of Lochau was made a

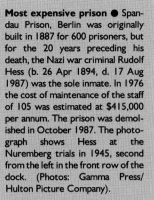

Doctor of Philosophy of the University of Giessen, Germany at age 12.

School *Most expensive* ■ The annual cost of keeping a pupil at the Gstaad International School, Gstaad, Switzerland (founded 1974) in

Youngest undergraduate ● The most extreme recorded case of undergraduate juvenility was that of William Thomson (1824–1907), later Lord Kelvin, who entered Glasgow University, Glasgow, United Kingdom at the age of 10 years 4 months in October 1834 and matriculated on 14 Nov the same year. (Photo: Science Photo Library)

1988/9 was 200,000 Swiss Francs. The school is run by Alain Souperbiet, its founder.

The annual cost of keeping a pupil at the most expensive school in the United States for the academic year 1990/91 is $26,250 at the Oxford Academy (founded 1906), in Westbrook, CT.

Youngest college president ■ The youngest president of a major college was Ellen Futter at age 31 who was appointed to head Barnard College in May 1981.

Most schools ■ The greatest documented number of schools attended by a pupil is 265, by Wilma Williams, now Mrs R. J. Horton, from 1933 to 1943 when her parents were in show business in the United States.

Highest endowment ■ The greatest single gift in the history of higher education has been $125 million, to Louisiana State University by C. B. Pennington in 1983.

Religions

Oldest ■ Human burial, which has religious connotations, is known from *c.* 60,000 B.C. among *Homo sapiens neanderthalensis* in the Shanidar cave, northern Iraq.

Largest ■ Religious statistics are necessarily only approximate. The test of adherence to a religion varies widely in rigor, while many individuals, particularly in the East, belong to two or more religions.

Christianity is the world's prevailing religion,

with some 1,669,520,000 adherents in 1988, or 32·9 percent of the world's population.

In 1989 there were 877,723,000 Roman Catholics, or 17·2 percent of the world's population in the same year.

The largest non-Christian religion is Islam, with some 880,555,000 followers in 1988.

Largest clergies ■ The world's largest religious organization is the Roman Catholic Church, with 150 cardinals, 744 archbishops, 3,181 bishops, 402,243 priests and 902,743 nuns in 1989.

Jews ■ The total of world Jewry is estimated to be 18·2 million. The highest concentration is in the United States with 5,944,000. The total in Israel is 3,537,000. The total in Tokyo, Japan is only 750.

PLACES OF WORSHIP

Earliest ■ Many archaeologists are of the opinion that the decorated Upper Paleolithic caves of Europe (c. 30,000–10,000 B.C) were used as places of worship or religious ritual. Claims have been made that the El Juyo cave, northern Spain contains an actual shrine, dated to c. 12,000 B.C.

The oldest surviving Christian church in the world is a converted house in Douro-Europos (now Qal'at es Salihiye) in eastern Syria, dating from A.D. 232.

Largest temple ■ The largest religious structure ever built is Angkor Wat (City Temple), enclosing 402 acres in Cambodia (formerly Kampuchea), Southeast Asia. It was built to the Hindu god Vishnu by the Khmer King Suryavarman II in the period 1113–50. Its curtain wall measures 4,199 × 4,199 ft and its population, before it was abandoned in 1432, was 80,000. The whole complex of 72 major monuments, begun c. A.D. 900, extends over 15 × 5 *miles.*

The largest Buddhist temple in the world is Borobudur, near Jogjakarta, Indonesia, built in the eighth century. It is 103 ft tall and 403 ft square.

The largest Mormon temple is the Salt Lake Temple, UT, dedicated on 6 Apr 1893 and with a floor area of 253,015 ft² or 5·80 acres.

Largest cathedral ■ The world's largest cathedral is the cathedral church of the Diocese of New York, St John the Divine, with a floor area of 121,000 ft² and a volume of 16,822,000 ft³. The cornerstone was laid on 27 Dec 1892, and work on the Gothic building was stopped in 1941. Work restarted in earnest in July 1979. The nave is the longest in the world at 601 ft in length, with a vaulting 124 ft in height.

The cathedral covering the largest area is that of Santa Mariá de la Sede in Sevilla (Seville), Spain. It was built in Spanish Gothic style between 1402 and 1519, and is 414 ft long, 271 ft wide and 100 ft high to the vault of the nave.

Smallest ■ The smallest church in the world designated as a cathedral is that of the Christ Catholic Church, Highlandville, MO. Consecrated in July 1983 it measures 14 × 17 ft and has seating for 18 people.

Largest church ■ The largest church in the world is the Basilica of St Peter, built between 1506 and 1614 in the Vatican City, Rome, Italy. Its length, including the walls of the apse and facade, is 717 ft 6 in. The area is 247,572 ft². The inner diameter of the famous dome is 139 ft

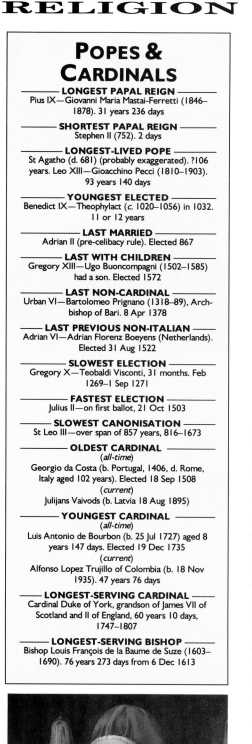

POPES & CARDINALS

LONGEST PAPAL REIGN
Pius IX—Giovanni Maria Mastai-Ferretti (1846–1878). 31 years 236 days

SHORTEST PAPAL REIGN
Stephen II (752). 2 days

LONGEST-LIVED POPE
St Agatho (d. 681) (probably exaggerated). ?106 years. Leo XIII—Gioacchino Pecci (1810–1903). 93 years 140 days

YOUNGEST ELECTED
Benedict IX—Theophylact (c. 1020–1056) in 1032. 11 or 12 years

LAST MARRIED
Adrian II (pre-celibacy rule). Elected 867

LAST WITH CHILDREN
Gregory XIII—Ugo Buoncompagni (1502–1585) had a son. Elected 1572

LAST NON-CARDINAL
Urban VI—Bartolomeo Prignano (1318–89), Archbishop of Bari. 8 Apr 1378

LAST PREVIOUS NON-ITALIAN
Adrian VI—Adrian Florenz Boeyens (Netherlands). Elected 31 Aug 1522

SLOWEST ELECTION
Gregory X—Teobaldi Visconti, 31 months. Feb 1269–1 Sep 1271

FASTEST ELECTION
Julius II—on first ballot, 21 Oct 1503

SLOWEST CANONISATION
St Leo III—over span of 857 years, 816–1673

OLDEST CARDINAL
(all-time)
Georgio da Costa (b. Portugal, 1406, d. Rome, Italy aged 102 years). Elected 18 Sep 1508
(current)
Julijans Vaivods (b. Latvia 18 Aug 1895)

YOUNGEST CARDINAL
(all-time)
Luis Antonio de Bourbon (b. 25 Jul 1727) aged 8 years 147 days. Elected 19 Dec 1735
(current)
Alfonso Lopez Trujillo of Colombia (b. 18 Nov 1935). 47 years 76 days

LONGEST-SERVING CARDINAL
Cardinal Duke of York, grandson of James VII of Scotland and II of England, 60 years 10 days, 1747–1807

LONGEST-SERVING BISHOP
Bishop Louis François de la Baume de Suze (1603–1690). 76 years 273 days from 6 Dec 1613

Fastest elected pope ● Julius II (1443–1513) was elected pope on the first ballot on 21 Oct 1503. His name is closely linked with artists such as Michelangelo and Raphael, and it was Raphael who painted this portrait of him as a pensive old man that hangs in the Uffizi gallery in Florence, Italy. (Photo: Picture Point)

8 in and its center is 393 ft 4 in high. The external height is 448 ft 1 in.

Taller, although not as tall as the Cathedral in Ulm, West Germany (see Tallest spire), is the Basilica of Our Lady of Peace (Notre Dame de la Paix) at Yamoussoukro, Ivory Coast completed in 1989. Including its golden cross, it is 519 ft high.

The elliptical Basilica of St Pius X at Lourdes, France, completed in 1957 at a cost of $2 million, has a capacity of 20,000 under its giant span arches and a length of 656 ft.

Longest ■ The crypt of the underground Civil War Memorial Church in the Guadarrama Mountains, 28 miles from Madrid, Spain, is 853 ft in length. It took 21 years (1937–58) to build, and is surmounted by a cross 492 ft tall.

Smallest church ■ The world's smallest church is the chapel of St Elizabeth of Hungary, in Colomares, a monument to Christopher Columbus at Benalmádena, Málaga, Spain. It is of irregular shape and has a total floor area of 21⅛ ft².

United States ■ The smallest church is the United States is Cross Island Chapel, at Oneida, NY, with a floor area of 29·1 ft² (6 ft 9 ½ in × 4 ft 3 ½ in).

Largest synagogue ■ The largest synagogue in the world is the Temple Emanu-El on Fifth Avenue at 65th Street, New York City. The temple, completed in September 1929, has a frontage of 150 ft on Fifth Avenue and 253 ft on 65th Street. The sanctuary proper can accommodate 2,500 people, and the adjoining Beth-El Chapel seats 350. When all the facilities are in use, more than 6,000 people can be accommodated.

Largest mosque ■ The largest mosque ever built was the now largely ruined al-Malawiya mosque of al-Mutawakil in Samarra, Iraq built from A.D. 842–52 and measuring 9·21 acres with dimensions of 784 × 512 ft.

The world's largest mosque in use is the Umayyad Mosque in Damascus, Syria, built on a 2,000-year-old religious site measuring 515 × 318 ft thus covering an area of 3·76 acres.

Tallest minaret ■ The tallest minaret in the world is that for the £ 218 million Great Hassan II Mosque, Casablanca, Morocco, measuring 576 ft. The Qutb Minar, south of New Delhi, India, built in 1194, is 238 ft tall.

Tallest and oldest pagoda ■ The world's tallest pagoda is the Phra Pathom Chedi at Nakhon Pathom, Thailand, which was built for King Mongkut from 1853–70. It rises to 377 ft.

The oldest pagoda in China is Sung-Yo Ssu in Henan built with 15 12-sided stories in A.D. 523, though the 326-ft tall Shwedagon Pagoda, Yangon (formerly known as Rangoon), Myanmar (formerly Burma) is built on the site of a 27-ft tall pagoda of 585 B.C.

Sacred object ■ The sacred object with the highest intrinsic value is the 15th-century gold Buddha in Wat Trimitr Temple in Bangkok, Thailand. It is 10 ft tall and weighs an estimated 6·06 tons. At the April 1990 price of £ 227 per fine ounce, its intrinsic worth was £ 21·1 million. The gold under the plaster exterior was found only in 1954.

Tallest spire ■ The tallest cathedral spire in the world is that of the Protestant Cathedral of Ulm in West Germany. The building is early Gothic and was begun in 1377. The tower, in the center of the west facade, was not finally completed until 1890 and is 528 ft high.

The world's tallest church spire is that of the Chicago Temple of the First Methodist Church on Clark Street, Chicago, IL. The building consists of a 22-story skyscraper (erected in 1924) surmounted by a parsonage at 330 ft, a 'Sky Chapel' at 400 ft and a steeple cross at 568 ft above street level.

Stained glass *Oldest* ■ Pieces of stained glass dated before A.D. 850, some possibly even to the seventh century, excavated by Professor Rosemary Cramp, were placed into a window of that date in the nearby St Paul's Church, Jarrow, County Durham, United Kingdom.

The oldest complete stained glass in the world represents the Prophets in a window of the Cathedral of Augsburg, Bavaria, West Germany, dating from the second half of the 11th century.

Largest ■ The largest stained-glass window is the complete mural of the Resurrection Mausoleum in Justice, IL, measuring 22,381 ft² in 2,448 panels, completed in 1971. Although not one continuous window, the Basilica of Our Lady of Peace (Notre Dame de la Paix) at Yamoussoukro, Ivory Coast contains a number of stained-glass windows covering a total area of 21,220 ft.

The tallest stained glass is the 135-ft-high back-lit glass mural, installed in 1979 in the atrium of the Ramada Hotel, Dubai, United Arab Emirates.

Brasses ■ The world's oldest monumental brass is that commemorating Bishop Yso von

Oldest pagoda ● The 326-ft tall Shwedagon Pagoda, Yangon (formerly Rangoon), Myanmar (formerly Burma) is built on the site of a 27-ft tall pagoda of 585 B.C. (Photo: Picture Point)

Wölpe in Andreaskirche, Verden, near Hanover, West Germany, dating from 1231. An engraved coffin plate of St Ulrich (d. 973), laid in 1187, was found buried in the Church of SS Ulrich and Afra, Augsburg, West Germany in 1979.

SAINTS

There are 1,848 'registered' saints (including 60 St Johns), of whom 628 are Italians, 576 French and 271 from the United Kingdom and Ireland. The total includes 79 popes.

The first United States citizen to be canonized as a Roman Catholic saint was Mother Francis Xavier Cabrini (1850–1917). She was born in Italy and sent by Pope Leo XIII to the United States in 1889 to aid Italian immigrants. From New York and Chicago she directed the establishment of hospitals, orphanages, nurseries, and schools throughout the country by her order, the Missionary Sisters of the Sacred Heart of Jesus. She was beatified in 1938 and

Tallest spire ● Below: The tallest cathedral spire in the world is that of the Protestant Cathedral of Ulm in West Germany. The building is early Gothic and was begun in 1377. The tower, in the center of the west facade, was not finally completed until 1890 and is 528 ft high. (Photo: Images/Erich Bach)

RELIGIOUS AFFILIATIONS

Religious Group   Members (1989)

Protestant and other	79,296,394
Roman Catholic	53,496,862
Jewish	5,943,700
Muslims	1,500,000
Other Catholic and Armenian Churches	829,007
Buddhists	100,000
Miscellaneous	192,065

The 1990 Almanac of American People

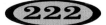

canonized on 7 July 1946, only 29 years after her death.

The first native-born American Roman Catholic saint is Mother Elizabeth Ann Bayley Seton (1774–1821), who was canonized on 14 Sep 1975. She was born in New York City, widowed with five young children in 1803, and converted to Catholicism in 1805. In 1809 at Emmitsburg, MD she opened the first Catholic free school, beginning the system of parochial education in America. She founded the first American congregation of the Sisters of Charity. She was beatified in 1963.

The first American male Roman Catholic saint is John Nepomucene Neumann (1811–60) who was canonized on 19 Jun 1977. He was born in Bohemia (Czechoslovakia) and emigrated to the United States in 1836. He was the fourth Bishop of Philadelphia (1851-60) and was also instrumental in the development of the American parochial school system.

Most rapidly canonized ▪ The shortest interval that has elapsed between the death of a saint and his canonization was in the case of St Peter of Verona, Italy, who died on 6 Apr 1252 and was canonized 337 days later on 9 Mar 1253. For the other extreme of 857 years see papal table.

CLERGY

Bishop *Youngest* ▪ The youngest bishop of all time was HRH the Duke of York and Albany, the second son of George III, who was elected Bishop of Osnabrück, through his father's influence as Elector of Hanover, at the age of 196 days on 27 Feb 1764. He resigned after 39 years' enjoyment.

The youngest serving bishop (excluding suffragans and assistants) in the Church of England is the Reverend Dr David Hope (b. 14 Apr 1940),

---

Largest crowd ● The greatest recorded number of human beings assembled with a common purpose was an estimated 15 million at the Hindu festival of Kumbh mela, at Prayag, Allahabad, in India on 6 Feb 1989. Kumbh mela is celebrated every three years, rotating between Prayag, Nasik, Haridwar and Ujjain, all in India. This shot shows the crowds at the 1986 festival. (Photo: Gamma/Poulet)

---

whose appointment to the See of Wakefield was announced on 2 Jul 1985.

When suffragans and assistants are counted, the youngest is Canon Michael Scott-Joynt, Bishop of Stafford, who at age 44 was appointed on 21 Apr 1987.

Oldest ▪ The oldest serving bishop (excluding suffragans and assistants) in the Church of England as of June 1987 was the Right Reverend Richard David Say, Bishop of Rochester, who was born on 4 Oct 1914.

The oldest Roman Catholic in recent years has been Bishop Angelo Teutonico, formerly Bishop of Aversa (b. 28 Aug 1874), who died age 103 years 276 days on 31 May 1978. He had celebrated mass about 24,800 times.

First ▪ The first consecrated Roman Catholic Bishop of the United States was John Carroll (1735–1815) of Baltimore, MD. In 1808, Carroll, a Jesuit, became the first Catholic Archbishop of the United States, with suffragan sees at Boston, New York City, Philadelphia and Baidstown, KY. Carroll also founded Georgetown University in 1789.

Oldest parish priest ▪ Father Alvaro Fernandez (b. 8 Dec 1880, d. 6 Jan 1988) served as a parish priest at Santiago de Abres, Spain from 1919 continuing into his 108th year.

The oldest Anglican clergyman, the Reverend

Clement Williams (b. 30 Oct 1879), died at age 106 years 3 months on 3 Feb 1986. He lined the route at Queen Victoria's funeral and was ordained in 1904.

Longest service ▪ Rev K. M. Jacob (b. 10 Jul 1880) was made a deacon in the Marthoma Syrian Church of Malabar in Kerala, southern India in 1897. He served his church until his death on 28 Mar 1984, 87 years later.

Longest-serving chorister ▪ John Love Vokins (1890–1989) was a chorister for 92 years. He joined the choir of Christ Church, Heeley, Sheffield, South Yorkshire, United Kingdom in 1895 and that of St Michael's, Hathersage, Derbyshire, United Kingdom 35 years later, and was still singing in 1987.

Sunday school ▪ Sunday schools were established by Congregationalists in Neath and Tirdwyncyn, Wales in 1697.

Roland E. Daab (b. 25 Mar 1914) now of St Paul United Church of Christ, Columbia, IL has attended for 3,700 consecutive Sundays without a miss for over 71 years to 22 Oct 1989.

Largest crowds ▪ The greatest recorded number of human beings assembled with a common purpose was an estimated 15 million at the Hindu festival of Kumbh mela, which was held at the confluence of the Yamuna (formerly called the Jumna), the Ganges and the invisible 'Saraswathi' at Allahabad, Uttar Pradesh, India on 6 Feb 1989. (See also Largest funerals).

Largest funerals ▪ The funeral of the charismatic C. N. Annadurai (d. 3 Feb 1969), Madras Chief Minister, was, according to a police estimate, attended by 15 million people.

The line at the grave of the Russian chansonnier and guitarist Vladimir Visotsky (d. 28 Jul 1980), stretched 6·2 miles.

SPORTS
& GAMES
Records for Sports
from Aerobactics
to Yachting

● (Photo: Vandystadt)

General Records

Origins ■ Sport stems from the time when self-preservation ceased to be the all-consuming human preoccupation. Archery, although a hunting skill in Mesolithic times (by *c.* 8000 B.C.), did not become an organized sport until later, possibly as early as *c.* 1150 B.C., as an archery competition is described in Homer's *Iliad*, and certainly by *c.* A.D. 300, among the Genoese. The earliest dated evidence is *c.* 2750–2600 B.C. for wrestling. Ball games by girls depicted on Middle Kingdom murals at Beni Hasan, Egypt have been dated to *c.* 2050 B.C.

Fastest ■ The highest speed reached in a nonmechanical sport is in skydiving, in which a speed of 185 mph is attained in a head-down free-falling position, even in the lower atmosphere. In delayed drops, speeds of 625 mph have been recorded at high, rarefied altitudes.

The highest projectile speed in any moving ball game is *c.* 188 mph, in pelota. This compares with 170 mph (electronically timed) for a golf ball driven off a tee.

Slowest ■ In wrestling, before the rules were modified towards 'brighter wrestling,' contestants could be locked in holds for so long that a single bout once lasted for 11 hr 40 min.

In the extreme case of the 2 hr 41 min pull in the regimental tug o' war in Jubbulpore, India, on 12 Aug 1889, the winning team moved a net distance of 12 ft at an average speed of 0·00084 mph.

Longest ■ The most protracted human-powered sporting event is the Tour de France cycling race. In 1926 this was over 3,569 miles, lasting 29 days, but the duration is now reduced to 21 days.

Largest playing field ■ For any ball game the largest playing field is 12·4 acres, for polo, or a maximum length of 900 ft and a width, without sideboards, of 600 ft. With boards the width is 480 ft.

Twice a year in the Parish of St Columb Major, Cornwall, United Kingdom, a game called hurling (not to be confused with the Irish game) is played on a 'pitch,' which consists of the entire parish, approximately 25 square miles.

World record breakers *Youngest* ■ The youngest age at which anybody has broken a nonmechanical world record is 12 yr 298 days, for Gertrude Caroline Ederle (US; b. 23 Oct 1906), with 13 min 19·0 sec for women's 880 yd freestyle swimming, at Indianapolis, IN on 17 Aug 1919.

Oldest ■ Gerhard Weidner (West Germany; b. 15 Mar 1933) set a 20-mile walk record on 25 May 1974, at age 41 yr 71 days, the oldest to set an official world record recognized by an international governing body. Lee Chin-yong (South Korea; b. 15 Aug 1925) was 62 yr 273 days when he broke the consecutive chins record on 14 May 1988.

Most prolific ■ Between 24 Jan 1970 and 1 Nov 1977 Vasily Alekseiev (USSR; b. 7 Jan 1942) broke 80 official world records in weightlifting.

Champion *Youngest* ■ The youngest successful competitor in a world title event was a French boy, whose name is not recorded, who coxed the Netherlands' Olympic pair at Paris, France on 26 Aug 1900. He was not more than ten and may have been as young as seven.

The youngest individual Olympic winner was Marjorie Gestring (US; b. 18 Nov 1922), who took the springboard diving title at the age of 13 yr 268 days at the Olympic Games in Berlin, Germany on 12 Aug 1936.

Oldest ■ Oscar Gomer Swahn (Sweden; 1847–1927) was 64 yr 258 days when he won a gold medal in the 1912 Olympic Running Deer team shooting competition.

Youngest international ■ The youngest age at which any person has won international honors is eight, in the case of Joy Foster, the Jamaican singles and mixed doubles table tennis champion in 1958.

Oldest competitor at major games ■ William Edward Pattimore (b. 1 Mar 1892) competed for Wales at bowls (lawn bowling) at the 1970 Commonwealth Games in Edinburgh, United Kingdom at the age of 78, the oldest competitor at such an international event open to competitors of all ages.

Most versatile ■ Charlotte 'Lottie' Dod (1871–1960) won the Wimbledon singles tennis title five times between 1887 and 1893, the British Ladies' Golf Championship in 1904, an Olympic silver medal for archery in 1908, and represented England at hockey in 1899. She also excelled at skating and tobogganing.

Mildred Ella 'Babe' Zaharias (nee Didrikson [US]; 1914–56) won two gold medals (80 m hurdles and javelin) and a silver (high jump) at the 1932 Olympic Games. She set world records in those three events in 1930–32. She was an All-American basketball player for three years and set the world record for throwing the baseball—296 ft. Switching to golf, she won the US Women's Amateur title in 1946 and the US Women's Open in 1948, 1950 and 1954. She also excelled at several other sports.

Charles Burgess Fry (Great Britain; 1872–1956) was probably the most versatile male sportsman at the highest level. On 4 Mar 1893 he equaled the world long jump record of 23 ft 6½ in. He represented England *v* Ireland at soccer (1901) and played first class rugby for the Barbarians. His greatest achievements, however, were at cricket, where he headed the English batting averages in six seasons and captained England in 1912. He was also an excellent fisherman and tennis player.

Longest reign ■ Jacques Edmond Barre (France; 1802–73) was a world champion for 33 years (1829–62) at court tennis.

Heaviest sportsman ■ Professional wrestler William J. Cobb of Macon, GA, who in 1962 was billed as 'Happy Humphrey,' weighed 802 lb.

The heaviest player of a ball-game was Bob Pointer, the 487-lb football tackle on the 1967 Santa Barbara High School team, CA.

Largest contract ■ In March 1990, the National Football League concluded a deal worth $3·64 billion for four years' TV coverage by the five major TV and cable networks, ABC, CBS, NBC, ESPN and TBS. This represented $26·1 million for each league team in the first year, escalating to $39·1 million in the fourth.

Largest crowd ■ The greatest number of live spectators for any sporting spectacle is the estimated 2·5 million who have lined the route of the New York Marathon. However, spread over three weeks, it is estimated that more than 10 million see the annual Tour de France cycling race.

Olympic ■ The total attendance at the 1984 Summer Games was given as 5,797,923 for all sports, including 1,421,627 for soccer and 1,129,465 for track and field athletics.

Single sporting venue ■ 'More than 400,000' travel to the annual Grand Prix d'Endurance motor race on the Sarthe circuit near Le Mans, France.

Stadium ■ A crowd of 199,854 attended the Brazil *v* Uruguay soccer match, in the Maracaña Municipal Stadium, Rio de Janeiro, Brazil on 16 Jul 1950.

Most participants ■ The Examiner Bay to Breakers 7·6-mile race in San Francisco, CA is contested annually by 100,000 runners. Including unregistered athletes, an estimated 110,000 took part on 15 May 1988.

The 1988 Women's International Bowling Congress Championship tournament attracted 77,735 bowlers for the 96-day event held 31 Mar–4 Jul at Reno/Carson City, NV.

Gymnastics / Aerobics display ■ The regular Czechoslovak Spartakiad features gymnastics displays by about 180,000 participants. Held at the Strahov Stadium, Prague, there are 200,000 spectators for each of the four days. On the 15-acre field there are markers for 13,824 gymnasts at a time.

Worst disasters ■ In recent history, the stands at the Hong Kong Jockey Club racetrack collapsed and caught fire on 26 Feb 1918, killing an estimated 604 people.

During the reign of Antoninus Pius (A.D. 138–161), 1,112 spectators were quoted as being killed when the upper wooden tiers in the Circus Maximus, Rome collapsed during a gladiatorial combat.

Aerobatics

Origins ■ The first aerobatic 'maneuver' is generally considered to be the sustained inverted flight in a Blériot of Célestin-Adolphe Pégoud (1889–1915), at Buc, France on 21 Sep 1913, but Lt Capt Petr Nikolayevich Nesterov (1887–1914), of the Imperial Russian Air Service, performed a loop in a Nieuport Type IV monoplane at Kiev, USSR on 27 Aug 1913.

World Championships ■ Held biennially since 1960 (except 1974), scoring is based on the system originally devised by Col. José Aresti of Spain. The competition consists of two compulsories and a free program. The men's team competition has been won a record six times by the USSR. Petr Jirmus (Czechoslovakia) is the only man to become world champion twice, in 1984 and 1986. Betty Stewart (US) won the women's competition in 1980 and 1982. Lyubov Nemkova (USSR) won a record five medals: first in 1986, second in 1982 and 1984 and third in 1976 and 1978. The oldest ever world champion has been Henry Haigh (US), at 60 in 1988.

Inverted flight ■ The duration record is 4 hr 9 min 5 sec by John 'Hal' McClain in a Swick Taylorcraft on 23 Aug 1980 over Houston International Raceways, TX.

Loops ■ On 21 Jun 1980, R. Steven Powell performed 2,315⅝ inside loops in a Bellanca Decathlon over Almont, MI.

Joann Osterud achieved 208 outside loops in a 'Supernova' Hyperbipe over North Bend, OR on 13 Jul 1989.

Archery

Origins ■ Though the earliest pictorial evidence of the existence of bows is seen in the Mesolithic cave paintings in Spain, archery as an organized sport appears to have developed in the third century A.D. Competitive archery may, however, date back to the 12th century B.C. The National Archery Association of America was established in 1879. The inaugural National Outdoor Target Championship was held in 1884. The world governing body is the Fédération Internationale de Tir à l'Arc (FITA), founded in 1931.

Highest championship scores ■ The highest scores achieved in either a world or Olympic championship for Double FITA rounds are: men, 2,617 points (possible 2,880) by Darrell Owen Pace (US; b. 23 Oct 1956) and Richard Lee McKinney (US; b. 12 Oct 1963) at Long Beach, CA on 21–22 Oct 1983; and women, 2,683 points by Kim Soo-nyung (South Korea; b. 5 Apr 1971) at Seoul, South Korea on 27–30 Sep 1988.

World championships ■ The most titles won by a man is four by Hans Deutgen (Sweden; b. 28 Feb 1917) in 1947–50 and by a woman is seven by Janina Spychajowa-Kurkowska (Poland; b. 8 Feb 1901) in 1931–34, 1936, 1939 and 1947. The United States has a record 14 men's and eight women's team titles.

Oscar Kessels (Belgium; 1904–68) participated in 21 world championships.

The most individual world titles by a US archer is three, by Richard McKinney: 1977, 1983 and 1985. Jean Lee, 1950 and 1952, is the only US woman to win two individual world titles. Luann Ryon (b. 13 Jan 1953) was Olympic women's champion in 1976 and also world champion in 1977.

World Archery Records Single FITA rounds

Event	Points	Name and Country	Possible	Year
		MEN		
FITA	1,342	Stanislav Zabrodskiy (USSR)	1440	1989
90 m	329	Yuriy Leontyev (USSR)	360	1988
70 m	344	Hiroshi Yamamoto (Japan)	360	1990
50 m	345	Richard McKinney (US)	360	1982
30 m	357	Takayoshi Matsushita (Japan)	360	1986
Final	342	Stanislav Zabrodskiy (USSR)	360	1989
Team	3,963	USSR (Stanislav Zabrodskiy, Vadim Shikarev, Vladimir Yesheyev)	4,320	1989
Final	999	USSR (Stanislav Zabrodskiy, Vadim Shikarev, Vladimir Yesheyev)	1,080	1989
		WOMEN		
FITA	1,368	Kim Soo-nyung (S. Korea)	1440	1989
70 m	341	Kim Soo-nyung (S. Korea)	360	1990
60 m	347	Kim Soo-nyung (S. Korea)	360	1989
50 m	336	Kim Soo-nyung (S. Korea)	360	1988
30 m	357	Joanne Edens (Great Britain)	360	1990
Final	343	Kim Soo-nyung (S. Korea)	360	1989
Team	4,025	S. Korea (Kim Soo-nyung, Wang Hee-nyung, Kim Kyung-wook)	4,320	1989
Final	1,010	S. Korea (Kim Soo-nyung, Wang Hee-nyung, Kim Kyung-wook)	4,320	1989

Indoor Double FITA rounds at 25 m

MEN	591	Erwin Verstegen (Holland)	600	1989
WOMEN	588	Yelena Marfel (USSR)	600	1985

Indoor FITA round at 18 m

MEN	591	Vladimir Yesheyev (USSR)	600	1989
WOMEN	587	Denise Parker (US)	600	1989

FLIGHT SHOOTING

CROSSBOW: 2,047 yd 2 in, Harry Drake (US; b. 7 May 1915), 'Smith Creek' Flight Range near Austin, NV, 30 Jul 1988.
UNLIMITED FOOTBOW: 1 mile 268 yd, Harry Drake, Ivanpah Dry Lake, CA, 24 Oct 1971.
RECURVE BOW: Men; 1,336 yd 1 ft 3 in, Don Brown (US), 'Smith Creek' Flight Range, 2 Aug 1987. Women; 1,039 yd 1 ft 1 in, April Moon (US), Wendover, UT, 13 Sep 1981.
CONVENTIONAL FOOTBOW: Men, 1,542 yd 2 ft 10 in, Harry Drake, Ivanpah Dry Lake, 6 Oct 1979. Women; 1,113 yd 2 ft 6 in, Arlyne Rhode (US; b. 4 May 1936), Wendover, UT, 10 Sep 1978.
COMPOUND BOW: Men; 1,159 yd 2 ft 6 in, Bert McCune Jnr (US), 'Smith Creek' Flight Range, 2 Aug 1987. Women (25 kg); 904 yd 4 in, April Moon, 'Smith Creek' Flight Range, 5 Oct 1989.
BROADHEAD FLIGHT BOWS Unlimited Compound Bow: Men; 658 yd 4 in, Roy Rodgers (US), Salt Lake City, UT, 24 Jun 1989. Women; 481 yd 4 in, April Moon, Salt Lake City, 29 Jun 1989.

Olympic Games ■ Hubert van Innis (Belgium; 1866–1961) won six gold and three silver medals at the 1900 and 1920 Olympic Games.

The most successful US archer at the Olympic Games has been Darrell Pace, gold medalist in 1976 and 1984. He was also world champion in 1975 and 1979.

US championships ■ The most US archery titles won is 17, by Lida Howell (nee Scott; 1859–1939), from 20 contested between 1883 and 1907. She won three Olympic gold medals in 1904, for Double National and Double Columbia rounds and for the US team.

The most men's titles is nine (3 individual, 6 pairs), by Richard McKinney, 1977, 1979–83, 1985–87. The greatest span of title winning is 29 years, by William Henry Thompson (1848–1918), who was the first US champion in 1879, and won his fifth and last men's title in 1908.

Greatest draw ■ Gary Sentman, of Roseberg, OR drew a longbow weighing a record 176 lb to the maximum draw on the arrow of 28¼ in at Forksville, PA on 20 Sep 1975.

24 hours – target archery ■ The highest recorded score over 24 hours by a pair of archers is 65,055 during 60 Portsmouth Rounds (60 arrows per round at 20 yd at 2 ft FITA targets) by Mick Brown and Les Powici at Guildford, Surrey, United Kingdom on 25–26 Mar 1989.

Paul Peters (US) set an individual record of 31,378 in 56 Portsmouth Rounds at Mukilteo, WA on 11–12 Nov 1989.

Auto Racing

Earliest races ■ There are various conflicting claims, but the first automobile race was the 201-mile Green Bay to Madison, WI run in 1878, won by an Oshkosh steamer. In 1887 Count Jules Félix Philippe Albert de Dion de Malfiance (1856–1946) won the La Vélocipéde 19·3 miles race in Paris, France in a De Dion steam quadricycle in which he is reputed to have exceeded 37 mph. The first 'real' race was from Paris to Bordeaux and back (732 miles) on 11–13 Jun 1895. The first to finish was Emile Levassor (1844–97) of France, in a Panhard-Levassor two-seater, with a 1·2-liter Daimler engine producing 3½ hp.

Most starts ● Italian Riccardo Patrese has started a record number of Grand Prix races but his successes have been few and far between. In his 13-year career he has won a mere three Grand Prix races: Monaco on 23 May 1982, South African on 16 Oct 1983 and most recently (pictured here) San Marino on 7 May 1990. (Photos: All-Sport/Pascal Rondeau)

His time was 48 hr 47 min (average speed 15·01 mph). The first closed circuit race was held over five laps of a mile dirt track at Narragansett Park, Cranston, RI on 7 Sep 1896. It was won by A. H. Whiting, driving a Riker electric.

The oldest race in the world still regularly run, is the Royal Automobile Club (RAC) Tourist Trophy, first staged on 14 Sep 1905 in the Isle of Man, United Kingdom. The French Grand Prix, was first held on 26–27 Jun 1906. The Coppa Florio, in Sicily, Italy has been irregularly held since 1906.

Fastest circuits ■ The highest average lap speed attained on any closed circuit is 250·958 mph in a time trial by Dr Hans Liebold (Germany; b. 12 Oct 1926) who lapped the 7·85 mile high-speed track at Nardo, Italy in 1 min 52·67 sec in a Mercedes-Benz C111-IV experimen-

tal coupé on 5 May 1979. It was powered by a V8 engine with two KKK turbochargers, with an output of 500 hp at 6,200 rpm.

The previous fastest road circuit was the Francorchamps circuit near Spa, Belgium, then 8·76 miles in length. It was lapped in 3 min 13·4 sec (average speed 163·086 mph) on 6 May 1973, by Henri Pescarolo (France; b. 25 Sep 1942) driving a 2,993-cc V12 Matra-Simca MS670 Group 5 sports car.

Fastest pit stop ■ Robert William 'Bobby' Unser (US; b. 20 Feb 1934) took 4 seconds to take on fuel on lap 10 of the Indianapolis 500 on 30 May 1976.

Fastest race ■ The fastest race is the Busch Clash at Daytona, FL over 50 miles on a 2½-mile 31-degree banked track. In 1987 Bill Elliott (b. 8 Oct 1955) averaged 197·802 mph in a Ford Thunderbird. Bill Elliott set the world record for a 500 mile race in 1985 when he won at Talladega, AL at an average speed of 186·288 mph.

WORLD CHAMPIONSHIP GRAND PRIX MOTOR RACING

Most successful drivers ■ The World Drivers' Championship, inaugurated in 1950, has been won a record five times by Juan-Manuel Fangio (Argentina; b. 24 Jun 1911) in 1951 and 1954–57. He retired in 1958, after having won 24 Grand Prix races (two shared) from 51 starts.

Alain Prost (France; b. 24 Feb 1955) holds the records for both the most Grand Prix points in a career, 633, and the most Grand Prix victories, 43, from 161 Grand Prix races, 1980–90. The most Grand Prix victories in a year is eight, by Ayrton Senna (Brazil; b. 21 Mar 1960) in 1988. The most Grand Prix starts is 200, by Riccardo Patrese (Italy; b. 4 Apr 1954) from 1977–90.

Two Americans have won the World Drivers' Championship, Phil Hill in 1961, and Mario Andretti, in 1978. Andretti has the most Grand Prix wins by a US driver; 12 in 128 races 1968–82.

Oldest and youngest ■ The youngest world champion was Emerson Fittipaldi (Brazil; b. 12 Dec 1946), who won his first World Championship on 10 Sep 1972 at age 25 yr 273 days. The oldest world champion was Juan-Manuel Fangio, who won his last World Championship on 4 Aug 1957 at age 46 yr 41 days.

The youngest Grand Prix winner was Bruce Leslie McLaren (1937–70) of New Zealand, who won the United States Grand Prix at Sebring, FL on 12 Dec 1959, at age 22 yr 104 days. Troy Ruttman (US) was 22 yr 80 days when he won the Indianapolis 500 on 30 May 1952, which was part of the World Championships at the time. The oldest Grand Prix winner (in pre-World Championship days) was Tazio Giorgio Nuvolari (Italy; 1892–1953), who won the Albi Grand Prix at Albi, France on 14 Jul 1946, at age 53 yr 240 days. The oldest Grand Prix driver was Louis Alexandre Chiron (Monaco; 1899–1979), who finished sixth in the Monaco Grand Prix on 22 May 1955, at age 55 yr 292 days. The youngest driver to qualify for a Grand Prix was Michael Christopher Thackwell (New Zealand; b. 30 Mar 1961) at the Canadian GP on 28 Sep 1980, at age 19 yr 182 days.

Manufacturers ■ Ferrari have won a record eight manufacturers' World Championships: 1961, 1964, 1975–77, 1979, 1982–83. Ferrari have 101 race wins in 463 Grand Prix, 1950–90.

The greatest dominance by one team was by McLaren in 1988, when they won 15 of the 16 Grands Prix. Ayrton Senna had eight wins and three seconds, Alain Prost had seven wins and seven seconds. The McLarens, powered by Honda engines, amassed over three times the points of their nearest rivals, Ferrari.

Fastest race ■ The fastest overall average speed for a Grand Prix race on a circuit in current use is 146·284 mph by Nigel Mansell (United Kingdom) in a Williams-Honda at Zeltweg in the Austrian Grand Prix on 16 Aug 1987. The qualifying lap record was set by Keke Rosberg (Finland) at 1 min 05·59 sec, an average speed of 160·817 mph, in a Williams-Honda at Silverstone in the British Grand Prix on 20 Jul 1985.

Closest finish ■ The closest finish to a World Championship race was when Ayrton Senna (Brazil) in a Lotus beat Nigel Mansell (United Kingdom) in a Williams by 0·014 sec in the Spanish Grand Prix at Jerez de la Frontera on 13 Apr 1986. In the Italian Grand Prix at Monza on 5 Sep 1971, 0·61 sec separated winner Peter Gethin (United Kingdom) from the fifth placed driver.

LE MANS

The greatest distance ever covered in the 24-hour Grand Prix d'Endurance (first held on 26–27 May 1923) on the old Sarthe circuit at Le Mans, France is 3,314·222 miles, by Dr Helmut Marko (Austria; b. 27 Apr 1943) and Gijs van Lennep (Netherlands; b. 16 Mar 1942), in a 4907-cc flat-12 Porsche 917K Group 5 sports car, on 12–13 Jun 1971. The record for the greatest distance ever covered for the current circuit is 3,313·241 miles (av speed 137·718 mph), by Jan Lammers (Holland), Johnny Dumfries and Andy Wallace (both from the United Kingdom) in a Jaguar XJR9 on 11–12 Jun 1988.

The race lap record (now 8·410-mile lap) is 3 min 21·27 sec (average speed 150·429 mph by Alain Ferté (France) in a Jaguar XRJ-9 on 10 Jun 1989. Hans Stück (West Germany) set the practice lap record of 3 min 14·8 sec (av. speed 156·62 mph) on 14 Jun 1985.

Most wins ■ The race has been won by Porsche cars twelve times, in 1970–71, 1976–77, 1979, 1981–87. The most wins by one man is six by Jacques Bernard 'Jacky' Ickx (Belgium; b. 1 Jan 1945), 1969, 1975–77 and 1981–82.

INDIANAPOLIS 500

The Indianapolis 500 mile race (200 laps) was inaugurated in the United States on 30 May 1911. Two drivers share the record for the most wins (4): Anthony Joseph 'A. J.' Foyt, Jr. (US; b. 16 Jan 1935) in 1961, 1964, 1967 and 1977; and Al Unser, Sr. (US; b. 29 May 1939), in 1970–71, 1978 and 1987. Foyt has also started in 33 Indianapolis 500 races (1959–90). The record time is 2 hr 41 min 18·248 sec (185·984 mph) by Arie Luyendyk (Netherlands) driving a 1990 Lola-Chevrolet on 27 May 1990.

The record average speed for four laps qualifying is 225·301 mph by Emerson Fittipaldi (Brazil) in a 1990 Penske-Cheverolet on 13 May 1990. On the same day he set the one-lap record of 225·575 mph. The track record is 228·502 mph by Al Unser, Jr. (US) on 11 May 1990. Rick Mears (US) has gained 5 poles in 1979, 1982, 1986, 1988 and 1989. The record prize fund is $6,325,803, and the individual prize record is $1,090,940, by Luyendyk, both in 1990.

INDY 500 Career Miles

Driver	Races	Miles
A.J. Foyt, Jr	32	11,237,50
Al Unser, Sr	24	9,427,50
Gordon Johncock	22	7,275,50
Johnny Rutherford	24	6,980,00
Bobby Unser	19	6,527,50

LAP LEADERS

Driver	Laps
Al Unser, Sr	811
A. J. Foyt, Jr	748
Ralph DePalma	613
Mario Andretti	521
Wilbur Shaw	508

TOP MONEY EARNERS

Driver	Victories	Earnings
Rick Mears	3—1979, 84, 88	$2,741,675
Al Unser, Sr	4—1970–71, 78, 87	$2,678,228
A. J. Foyt, Jr	4—1961, 64, 67, 77	$2,109,685
Mario Andretti	1—1969	$1,843,146
Johnny Rutherford	3—1974, 76, 80	$1,691,141

First woman driver ■ The first and only woman to compete in the Indianapolis 500 is Janet Guthrie (b. 7 Mar 1938). She passed her rookie test in May 1976, and earned the right to compete in the qualifying rounds, but was unable to win a place on the starting line when the Vollstedt-Offenhauser she drove was withdrawn from the race after repeated mechanical failures. In the 61st running of the Indianapolis 500, in 1977, Guthrie became the first woman to compete, although her car developed mechanical problems which forced her to retire after 27 laps. In 1978, she completed the race, finishing in ninth place after 190 laps.

Indy Car Championships (CART) ■ The first Indy Car Championship was held in 1909 and held under the authority of the American Automobile Association (AAA). In 1959 the United States Automobile Club (USAC) took over the running of the Indy series. Since 1979 Championship Auto Racing Teams Inc. (CART) have organized the Indy Championship, which since 1979 has been called the PPG Indy Car World Series Championship.

National Championships ■ The most successful driver in Indy car history is A. J. Foyt, Jr., who has won 67 races and seven championships (1960–61, 1963–64, 1967, 1975 and 1979). The record for the most victories in a season is 10 shared by two drivers: A. J. Foyt, Jr. (1964) and Al Unser, Sr. (1970). Mario Andretti holds the record for the most laps driven in Indy championships at 7,250 (as of June 1990); he also holds the record for most pole positions at 64.

As of June 1990, Rick Mears holds the career earnings mark for Indy drivers with $7,369,049. The single season earnings record was set at $2,166,078 in 1989 by Emerson Fittapaldi.

NASCAR (National Association for Stock Car Auto Racing) ■ The first NASCAR championship was held in 1949. Since 1971 the championship series has been called the Winston Cup Championship. The championship has been won a record seven times by Richard

has been won a record five times, by Shekhar Mehta (b. Kenya; 20 Jun 1945) in 1973, 1979–82.

Monte Carlo ■ The Monte Carlo Rally (first run 1911) has been won a record four times by: Sandro Munari (Italy; b. 27 Mar 1940) in 1972, 1975, 1976 and 1977; and Walter Röhrl (West Germany; b. 7 Mar 1947; with co-driver Christian Geistdorfer) in 1980, 1982–84, each time in a different car. The smallest car to win was an 851-cc Saab driven by Erik Carlsson (Sweden; b. 5 Mar 1929) and Gunnar Häggbom (Sweden; b. 7 Dec 1935) on 25 Jan 1962, and by Carlsson and Gunnar Palm on 24 Jan 1963.

World Championship ■ Two World Drivers' Championships (instituted 1979) have been won by Walter Röhrl, 1980 and 1982, Juha Kankkunen (Finland; b. 2 Apr 1959), 1986–87, and by Mikki Biasion (Italy) 1988–89. The most wins in World Championship races is 19, by Hannu Mikkola and Markku Alen (Finland) to April 1990.

DRAG RACING

Piston engined ■ The lowest elapsed time recorded by a piston-engined dragster from a standing start for 440 yd is 4·909 sec, by Darrell Gwynn (US; b. 1961) at Houston, TX on 3 Mar 1990. The highest terminal velocity reached at the end of a 440 yd run is 294·88 mph, by Gary Ormsby (US; b. 1941) at Ennis, Dallas, TX on 8 Oct 1989.

The lowest elapsed time for a women is 4·962 sec, by Shirley Muldowney (US; b. 1940) at Topeka,

---

First woman ● Shawna Robinson (b. 30 Nov 1954) was the first woman to win a NASCAR event, when she won the NASCAR Dash Series at Asheville, NC on 10 Jun 1988.

Lee Petty (US; b. 2 Jul 1937) - 1964, 1967, 1971–72, 1974–75 and 1979.

Petty won 200 NASCAR Winston Cup races in 1,107 starts from 1958 to 6 May 1990, and his best season was 1967, with 27 wins. Petty, on 1 Aug 1971, was the first driver to pass $1 million career earnings.

The NASCAR career money record is $10,538,178 to 20 May 1990, by Dale Earnhardt (b. 29 Apr 1952). Bill Elliott won a season record $2,383,187 in 1985. Geoff Bodine (b. 18 Apr 1949) won 55 races in NASCAR Modified racing in 1978.

Shawna Robinson (b. 30 Nov 1954) became the first woman to win a NASCAR race when she won an event in the NASCAR Dash Series at Asheville, NC on 10 Jun 1988.

Daytona 500 ■ The Daytona 500 has been held at the 2 ½ mile oval Daytona International Speedway in Daytona, FL since 1959. The race is the major event of the NASCAR season. Richard Petty has a record seven wins—1964, 1966, 1971, 1973–74, 1979 and 1981. The record average speed for the race is 177·602 mph by Buddy Baker in an Oldsmobile in 1980. The qualifying speed record is 210·364, by Bill Elliott in a Ford Thunderbird in 1987.

RALLYING

The earliest long rally, from Beijing, China to Paris, France, over about 7,500 miles from 10 Jun 1907, was promoted by the Parisian daily *Le Matin* . The winner, Prince Scipione Borghese (1872–1927) of Italy, arrived in Paris on 10 Aug 1907 in his 40-hp Itala accompanied by his chauffeur, Ettore, and Luigi Barzini.

Longest ■ The longest ever rally was the Singapore Airlines London—Sydney Rally over 19,329 miles from Covent Garden, London, United Kingdom on 14 Aug 1977 to Sydney Opera House, Sydney, Australia won on 28 Sep 1977 by Andrew Cowan, Colin Malkin and Michael Broad in a Mercedes 280E. The longest held annually is the Safari Rally (first run in 1953 as the Coronation Rally, through Kenya, Tanzania and Uganda, but now restricted to Kenya). The race has covered up to 3,874 miles, as in the 17th Safari held from 8–12 Apr 1971. It

---

Pikes Peak ● One of the country's oldest motor races is the Pikes Peak Auto Hill Climb, which began in 1916 (only the Indianapolis 500 is older). The course is 12·42 miles, rising from 9,402 ft to 14,110 ft through 156 turns. The winner in 1989 was Robby Unser, making a remarkable 30th victory for the Unser family. The first winner was Robby's great-uncle Louis in 1934, since then seven Unsers have won, with Robby's father, Bobby, winning a record 13 climbs between 1956 and 1974. (Photo: All-Sport/Tim DeFrisco)

Shortest time ● The lowest elapsed time to cover a quarter-mile, as officially recognised by the National Hot Rod Association, is 4·909 sec by Darrell Gwynn (b. 1961) at Houston, TX on 3 Mar 1990. (Photo: Leslie Lovett)

KS on 29 Sep 1989. For a gasoline-powered piston-engined car, the lowest elapsed time is 7·220 sec by Mark Pawuk (US; b. 1957), driving a Oldsmobile Cutlass at Houston, TX on 3 Mar 1990 and the highest terminal velocity is 191·32 mph, by Bob Glidden (b. 1944) in a Ford Thunderbird at Indianapolis, IN on 4 Sep 1987.

The lowest elapsed time for a gasoline-powered piston-engined motorcycle is 7·697 sec, by John Myers (US; b. 1958) at Gainesville, FL on 8 Mar 1990 and the highest terminal velocity is 176·47 mph, by John Mafaro (US; b. 1949) at Indianapolis on 4 Sep 1989.

Most wins ■ The greatest number of wins in National Hot Rod Association national events is 76 by Bob Glidden in Pro Stock, 1973–89.

Rocket or jet-engined ■ The highest terminal velocity recorded by any dragster is 392·54 mph, by Kitty O'Neil (US) at El Mirage Dry Lake, CA on 7 Jul 1977. The lowest elapsed time is 3·58 sec, by Sammy Miller in a Pontiac 'Funny Car' in 1986.

Highest speeds ■ The most successful land speed record breaker was Sir Malcolm Campbell (United Kingdom; 1885–1948). He broke the official record nine times between 25 Sep 1924, with 146·157 mph in a Sunbeam, and 3 Sep 1935, when he achieved 301·129 mph in the Rolls-Royce-engined Bluebird.

Badminton

Origins ■ A similar game was played in China in the second millennium B.C. The modern game may have evolved *c.* 1870 at Badminton Hall in Avon, United Kingdom, the seat of the Dukes of Beaufort, or from a game played in India. The first modern rules were codified in Pune (Poona), India in 1876.

World championships ■ Three Chinese players have won two individual world titles (instituted 1977): men's singles: Yang Yang 1987 and 1989; women's singles: Li Lingwei 1983 and 1989; Han Aiping 1985 and 1987. Li and Han won the women's doubles in 1985, and three titles

have been won by Park Joo-bong (South Korea), men's doubles 1985 and mixed doubles 1985 and 1989, and by Lin Ying (China), women's doubles 1983, 1987 and 1989. The most wins at the men's International Championship for the Thomas Cup (instituted 1948) is eight, by Indonesia (1958, 1961, 1964, 1970, 1973, 1976, 1979 and 1984).

The most wins at the women's International Championship for the Uber Cup (instituted 1956) is five, by Japan (1966, 1969, 1972, 1978 and 1981).

United States ■ The United States has never won the Thomas Cup, but won the Uber Cup on the first three occasions that it was contested, 1957, 1960 and 1963. Judy Hashman (nee Devlin [US]; b. 22 Oct 1935) was the only player on all three teams.

All-England Championships ■ Considered as the most prestigious championships, they were instituted in 1899. The men's singles have been won eight times by Rudy Hartono Kurniawan (Indonesia; b. 18 Aug 1948) in 1968–74 and 1976. The greatest number of titles won (including doubles) is 21, by George Alan Thomas (1881–1972), between 1903 and 1928. The women's singles were won ten times by Judy Hashman in 1954, 1957–58, 1960–64, 1966–67. She also equalled the greatest number of titles won of 17 by Meriel Lucas (later Mrs King Adams) from 1899 to 1910.

Most titles ■ Judy Hashman won a record number of 32 US titles: 12 women's singles, 1954,

WORLD SERIES RECORDS
AL American League, NL National League

Most wins	22	New York Yankees–AL	1923–78
Most series played	14	Lawrence Peter 'Yogi' Berra (New York Yankees–AL)	1947–63
Most series played by pitcher	11	Edward Charles 'Whitey' Ford (New York Yankees–AL)	1950–64

World Series career records

Batting average (min. 75 at bats)	·391	Louis 'Lou' Clark Brock (St Louis Cardinals–NL; 34 hits in 87 at bats, 3 series)	1964–68
Runs scored	42	Mickey Charles Mantle (New York Yankees–AL)	1951–64
Runs batted in (RBI's)	40	Mickey Mantle (New York Yankees–AL)	1951–64
Base hits	71	Yogi Berra (New York Yankees–AL)	1947–63
Home runs	18	Mickey Mantle (New York Yankees–AL)	1951–64
Victories pitching	10	Whitey Ford (New York Yankees–AL)	1950–64
Strikeouts	94	Whitey Ford (New York Yankees–AL)	1950–64

World Series single series records

Batting average (4 or more games)	·625	George Herman 'Babe' Ruth (New York Yankees–AL; 10 hits in 16 at bats)	1928
Runs scored	10	Reginald 'Reggie' Martinez Jackson (New York Yankees–AL)	1977
Runs batted in (RBI's)	12	Robert 'Bobby' Clinton Richardson (New York Yankees–AL)	1960
Base hits (7-game series)	13	Bobby Richardson (New York Yankees–AL)	1960
	13	Lou Brock (St Louis Cardinals–NL)	1968
	13	Martin Barrett (Boston Red Sox–AL)	1986
Home runs	5	Reggie Jackson (New York Yankees–AL; in 20 at bats)	1977
Victories pitching	3	Christy Matthewson (New York Yankees–AL; in five game series)	1905
	3	John Wesley 'Jack' Coombs (Philadelphia A's–AL; in five game series)	1910
		Ten other pitchers have won three games in more than five games	
Strikeouts	35	Robert 'Bob' Gibson (St Louis Cardinals–NL; in 7 games)	1968
	23	Sanford 'Sandy' Koufax (Los Angeles Dodgers–NL; in 4 games)	1963

World Series single game records

Home runs	3	Babe Ruth (New York Yankees–AL) v St Louis Cardinals	6 Oct 1926
	3	Babe Ruth (New York Yankees–AL) v St Louis Cardinals	9 Oct 1928
	3	Reggie Jackson (New York Yankees–AL) v Los Angeles Dodgers	18 Oct 1977
Runs batted in (RBI's) in a game	6	Bobby Richardson (New York Yankees–AL) v Pittsburgh Pirates	8 Oct 1960
Strikeouts by pitcher in game	17	Bob Gibson (St Louis Cardinals–NL) v Detroit Tigers	2 Oct 1968
Perfect game (9 innings)		Donald 'Don' James Larson (New York Yankees–AL) v Brooklyn Dodgers	8 Oct 1956

1956–63, 1965–67; 12 women's doubles, 1953–55, 1957–63, 1966–67 (11 with her sister Susan); and 8 mixed doubles, 1956–62, 1967.

Shortest game ■ In the 1969 Uber Cup in Tokyo, Japan, Noriko Takagi (later Mrs Nakayama;Japan) beat Poppy Tumengkol (Indonesia) in 9 min.

Longest rallies ■ In the men's singles final of the 1987 All-England Championships between Morten Frost (Denmark) and Icuk Sugiarto (Indonesia), there were two successive rallies of over 90 strokes.

Most shuttles ■ In the final of the Indian National Badminton Championships 1986, when Syed Modi beat Vimal Kumar 15–12, 15–12, 182 shuttles were used in the 66-minute period.

Baseball

Origins ■ In 1908 the Spalding Commission, sponsored by Albert G. Spalding, a sporting goods tycoon, concluded that the game of baseball has been invented by Abner Doubleday in 1839 at Cooperstown, NY and the legend of Doubleday's efforts has since become deeply embedded in American folklore. Despite its tradition, Spalding's official version of baseball history is disputed by sports historians. They argue that baseball in North America evolved from such English games as cricket, paddleball, trap ball and rounders. Printed references to 'base ball' in England date to 1700 and in the United States to the mid eighteenth century. Uncontested is that Alexander Cartwright, Jr formulated the rules of the modern game in 1845 and the first match under these rules was played on 19 Jun 1846 when the New York Nine defeated the New York Knickerbockers, 23–1, in four innings. On 17 Mar 1871 the National Association of Professional Base Ball Players was formed, the first professional league in the United States. Today there are two main professional baseball associations, the National League (organized 1876) and the American League (organized 1901, recognized 1903), that together form the major leagues, along with approximately 20 associations that make up the minor leagues. The champions of the two leagues first played for the World Series in 1903 and have played continuously since 1905. (For further details on World Series history see below.)

The first night game was played on 2 Jun 1883 (M.E. College *v* professionals from Quincy, IL). The major leagues were slow to adopt this change of program, then considered radical. The Cincinnati Reds were the first big-league team to play under lights when they hosted the Philadelphia Phillies on 24 May 1935. President Franklin D. Roosevelt pressed a button at the White House to flick the switch at Crosley Field.

WORLD SERIES
Origins ■ Played annually between the winners of the National League and the American League, the World Series was first staged unofficially in 1903, and officially from 1905. The most wins is 22, by the New York Yankees between 1923 and 1978 from a record 33 series appearances for winning the American League titles between 1921 and 1981. The most National League titles is 19, by the Dodgers—Brooklyn 1890–1957, Los Angeles 1958–88.

Most valuable player ■ The only men to have won the award twice are: Sanford 'Sandy' Koufax (b. 30 Dec 1935; Los Angeles (NL), 1963, 1965), Robert 'Bob' Gibson (b. 9 Nov 1935; St Louis (NL), 1964, 1967) and Reginald 'Reggie'

BASEBALL
MAJOR LEAGUE RECORDS
AL American League
NL National League

Career batting records

Batting average	·367	Tyrus 'Ty' Raymond Cobb (Detroit–AL, Philadelphia–AL)	1905–28
Runs scored	2,245	Ty Cobb	1905–28
Runs batted in (RBI's)	2,297	Henry Louis 'Hank' Aaron (Milwaukee, Atlanta–NL Milwaukee–AL)	1954–76
Base hits	4,256	Peter 'Pete' Edward Rose (Cincinnati–NL, Philadelphia–NL Montreal–NL)	1963–86
Total bases	6,856	Hank Aaron (Milwaukee, Atlanta–NL, Milwaukee–AL)	1954–76

Season batting records

Batting average	·440	Hugh Duffy (Boston–NL; 236 hits in 529 at bats)	1894
modern record (1900–present)	·426	Napoleon 'Nap' Lojoie (Philadelphia–AL; 232 hits in 544 at bats)	1901
Runs scored	192	William Robert Hamilton (Philadelphia–NL; in 131 games)	1894
modern record (1900–present)	177	George Herman 'Babe' Ruth (New York–AL; in 152 games)	1921
Runs batted in (RBI's)	190	Lewis Robert 'Hank' Wilson (Chicago–NL; in 155 games)	1930
Base hits	257	George Harold Sisler (St Louis–AL; 631 times at bat, 143 games)	1920
Singles	202	William H. 'Wee Willie' Keeler (Baltimore–NL; in 128 games)	1898
modern record(1900–present)	198	Lloyd James Waner (Pittsburgh–NL)	1927
Doubles	67	William Earl Webb (Boston–AL; in 151 games)	1931
Triples	36	John Owen Wilson (Pittsburgh–NL; in 152 games)	1912
Total bases	457	Babe Ruth (New York–AL)	1921
		85 singles, 44 doubles, 16 triples, 59 homes runs	

Single game batting records

Runs batted in (RBI's)	12	James LeRoy Bottomley (St Louis–NL) v Brooklyn	16 Sep 1924
Base hits	9	John Henderson Burnett (Cleveland–AL; in 18 innings)	10 Jul 1932
Total bases	18	Joseph Wilbur Adcock (Milwaukee–AL)	31 Jul 1954
		1 double, 4 home runs	

Career pitching records

Games won	511	Denton T. 'Cy(clone)' Young (in 906 games) (Cleveland, St Louis, Boston–NL and Cleveland, Boston–AL)	1890–1911
Shutouts	113	Walter Perry Johnson (Washington–AL; in 802 games)	1907–27
Stikeouts	*5,170	Lynn Nolan Ryan (New York–NL, California–AL Houston–NL, Texas–AL)	1968–89

*Through 1989 season

Season pitching records

Games won	60	Charles Gardner Radbourne (Providence–NL; and 12 losses)	1884
modern record(1900–present)	41	John Dwight 'Jack' Chesbro (New York–AL)	1904
Shutouts	16	George Washington Bradley (St Louis–NL; in 64 games)	1876
modern record (1900–present)	16	Grover Cleveland 'Pete' Alexander (Philadelphia–NL; 48 games)	1916
Strikeouts	513	Matthew Aloysius Kilroy (Baltimore–AL)	1886
modern record (1900–present)	383	Lynn Nolan Ryan (California–AL)	1973

Single game pitching records

Stikeouts (9 innings)	20	William Roger Clemens (Boston–AL) v Seattle	29 Apr 1986
Strikeouts in extra-innings	21	Thomas Edgar Cheney (Washington–AL) v Baltimore (16 innings)	12 Sep 1962

Most seasons leading the major leagues

				Between
Batting average	AL	12	Ty Cobb (Detroit)	1907–19
	NL	8	John Peter 'Honus' Wagner (Pittsburgh)	1900–19
Home Runs	AL	12	Babe Ruth (Boston, New York)	1918–31
	NL	8	Michael Jack Schmidt (Philadelphia)	1974–86
Runs batted in (RBI's)	AL	6	Babe Ruth (Boston, New York)	1919–28
	NL	4	Honus Wagner, Rogers Hornsby, Hank Aaron, Mike Schmidt	
Base hits	AL	8	Ty Cobb (Detroit)	1907–19
	NL	7	Pete Rose (Cincinnati, Philadelphia)	1965–81
Total bases	AL	6	Ty Cobb (Detroit)	1907–17
	AL	6	Babe Ruth (New York)	1919–28
	AL	6	Theodore Samuel 'Ted' Williams (Boston)	1939–51
	NL	8	Hank Aaron (Milwaukee, Atlanta)	1956–69
Stolen bases	AL	9	Luis Ernesto Aparicio (Chicago, Baltimore)	1956–64
	AL	9	Rickey Henderson (Oakland, New York)	1980–89
	NL	10	Max George Carey (Pittsburgh)	1913–25
Winning percentage	AL	5	Robert Moses 'Lefty' Grove (Philadelphia, New York)	1929–39
	NL	3	Edward Marvin Reulbach (Chicago)	1906–08
Earned Run Average	AL	8	'Lefty' Grove (Philadelphia, Boston)	1926–39
	NL	5	'Pete' Alexander (Philadelphia, Chicago)	1915–20
	NL	5	Sandy Koufax (Los Angeles)	1962–66
Strikeouts	AL	12	Walter Perry Johnson (Washington)	1910–24
	NL	7	Clarence Arthur 'Dazzy' Vance (Brooklyn)	1922–28

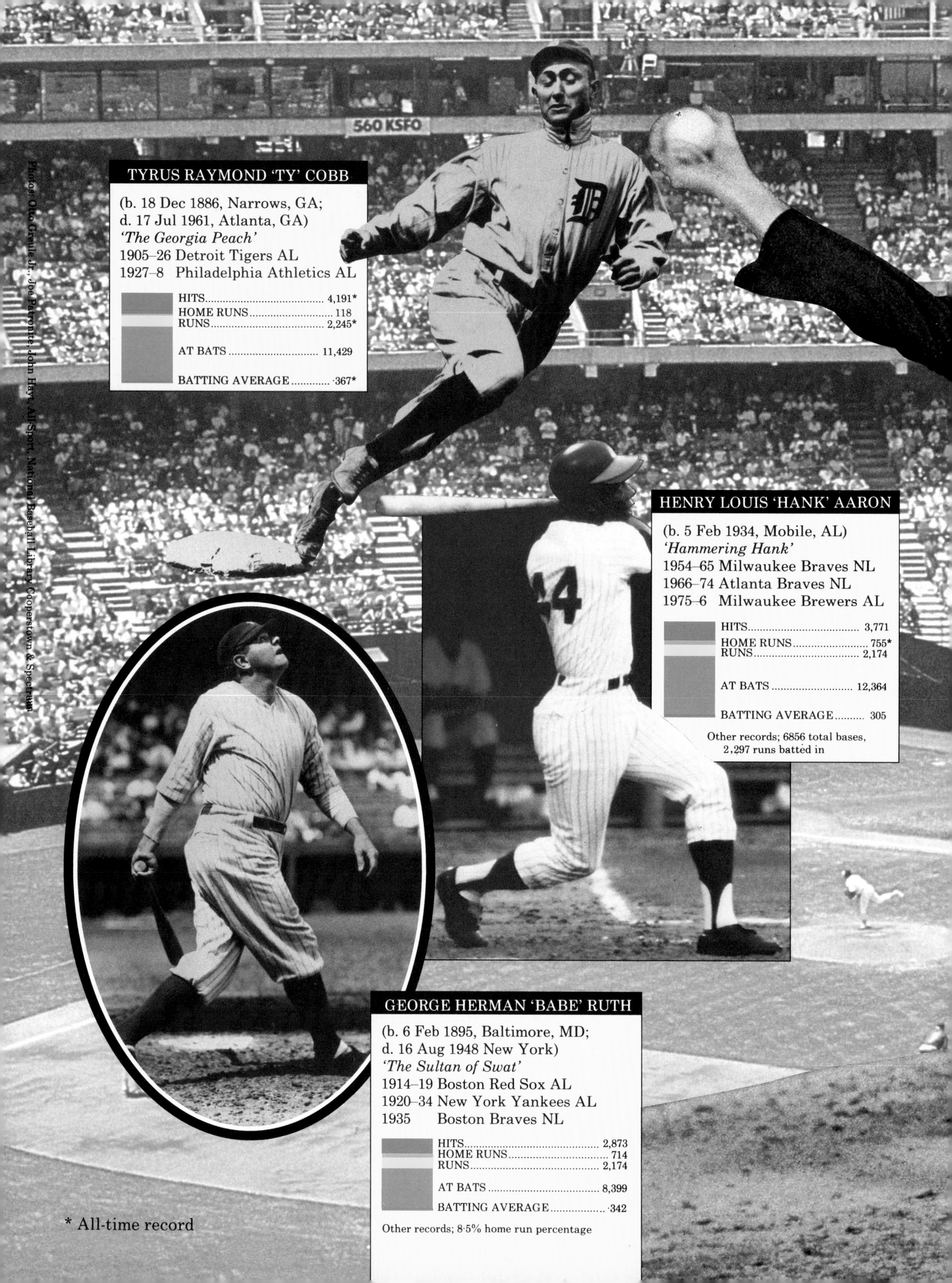

TYRUS RAYMOND 'TY' COBB

(b. 18 Dec 1886, Narrows, GA;
d. 17 Jul 1961, Atlanta, GA)
'The Georgia Peach'
1905–26 Detroit Tigers AL
1927–8 Philadelphia Athletics AL

HITS	4,191*
HOME RUNS	118
RUNS	2,245*
AT BATS	11,429
BATTING AVERAGE	·367*

HENRY LOUIS 'HANK' AARON

(b. 5 Feb 1934, Mobile, AL)
'Hammering Hank'
1954–65 Milwaukee Braves NL
1966–74 Atlanta Braves NL
1975–6 Milwaukee Brewers AL

HITS	3,771
HOME RUNS	755*
RUNS	2,174
AT BATS	12,364
BATTING AVERAGE	305

Other records; 6856 total bases, 2,297 runs batted in

GEORGE HERMAN 'BABE' RUTH

(b. 6 Feb 1895, Baltimore, MD;
d. 16 Aug 1948 New York)
'The Sultan of Swat'
1914–19 Boston Red Sox AL
1920–34 New York Yankees AL
1935 Boston Braves NL

HITS	2,873
HOME RUNS	714
RUNS	2,174
AT BATS	8,399
BATTING AVERAGE	·342

Other records; 8·5% home run percentage

* All-time record

Photos: Otto Greule Jr., Joe Patronite, John Hayt, All-Sport, National Baseball Library Cooperstown & Spectrum

BASEBALL
Aaron Cobb DiMaggio Ruth & Ryan

JOSEPH 'JOE' PAUL DIMAGGIO

(b. 25 Nov 1914, Martinez, CA)
'The Yankee Clipper'

1956-75 New York Yankees AL

HITS	2,214
HOME RUNS	361
RUNS	1,390
AT BATS	6,821
BATTING AVERAGE	·325

Other records; 56 games
consecutive hitting streak

◄ NOLAN RYAN, holds several of baseball's career pitching
records; most notably he has pitched 6 no-hitters, and has
struck out over 5,200 batters, a total that includes a season
record 383 in 1973. Born in Refugio, TX on 31 Jan 1947, he
bagan his career with the New York Mets (NL) in 1966. He
was traded to the California Angels (AL) in 1972 and
returned to the National League with the Houston Astros in
1980. In 1990, pitching for the Texas Rangers (AL), he became
the twentieth pitcher in baseball history to win 300 games.
Among his many other records he has pitched 12 one-hitters,
19 two-hitters and struck out ten or more players on 201
occasions, more than twice as many of his nearest rival.

Stolen bases ● Rickey Henley Henderson (b. 25 Dec 1958) of the Oakland Athletics, is renowned for his ability to steal bases and was the top exponent in the 1980s. He set a season's record of 130 steals in 1982 and is fast approaching the all-time record of Lou Brock. (Photo: All-Sport/Otto Greule Jr)

Martinez Jackson (b. 18 May 1946; Oakland (AL), 1973, New York (AL), 1977).

Attendance ■ The record attendance for a series is 420,784 for the six games when the Los Angeles Dodgers beat the Chicago White Sox 4–2 between 1 and 8 Oct 1959. The single game record is 92,706 for the fifth game of this series at the Memorial Coliseum, Los Angeles on 6 Oct 1959.

MAJOR LEAGUE

Most games played ■ Peter 'Pete' Edward Rose (b. 14 Apr 1941) played in a record 3,562 games with a record 14,053 at bats for the Cincinnati Reds (NL) 1963–78 and 1984–86, the Philadelphia Phillies (NL) 1979–83 and the Montreal Expos (NL) 1984. Henry Louis 'Lou' Gehrig (1903–41) played in 2,130 successive games for the New York Yankees (AL) from 1 Jun 1925 to 30 Apr 1939.

Most home runs *Career* ■ Henry Louis 'Hank' Aaron (b. 5 Feb 1934) holds the major league career record with 755 home runs from 12,364 at-bats; 733 for the Milwaukee (1954–65) and Atlanta (1966–74) Braves in the National League and 22 for the Milwaukee Brewers (AL) 1975–76. On 8 Apr 1974 he had bettered the previous record of 714 by George Herman 'Babe' Ruth (1895–1948).

Ruth hit his home runs from 8,399 times at bat, the highest home run percentage of 8·5%. Joshua Gibson (1911–47) of the Homestead Grays and Pittsburgh Crawfords, Negro League clubs, achieved a career total of nearly 800 homers,

including an unofficial record season's total of 75 in 1931.

Season ■ The major league record for home runs in a season is 61 by Roger Eugene Maris (1934–85) for the New York Yankees in 162 games and 590 at-bats in 1961. Babe Ruth hit 60 in 154 games in 1927 for the New York Yankees. The most official home runs in a minor league season is 72 by Joe Bauman of Roswell, NM in 1954.

Game ■ The most home runs in a major league game is four, first achieved by Robert Lincoln 'Bobby' Lowe (1868–1951) for Boston v Cinncinnati on 30 May 1894. The feat has been achieved an additional ten times since then.

Consecutive games ■ The most home runs hit in consecutive games is eight, by Richard Dale Long (b. 6 Feb 1926) for Pittsburgh (NL), 19–28 May 1956 and by Donald Arthur 'Don' Mattingly (b. 21 Apr 1961) for New York (AL) on 18 Jul 1987.

Grand Slams ■ Seven players have hit 2 grand slams in a single game. They are: Anthony M. Lazzeri for the New York Yankees (AL) on 24 May 1936, James R. Tabor for the Boston Red Sox (AL) on 4 Jul 1939, Rudolph York for the Boston Red Sox (AL) on 27 Jul 1946, James E. Gentile for the Baltimore Orioles (AL) on 9 May 1961, Tony L. Cloninger for the Atlanta Braves (NL) on 3 Jul 1966, James T. Northrup for the Detroit Tigers (AL) on 24 Jun 1968 and Frank Robinson for the Baltimore Orioles (AL) on 26 Jun 1970.

Don Mattingly of the New York Yankees (AL) hit 6 grand slams in 1987. Lou Gehrig hit 23 grand slams during his 16 seasons with the New York Yankees (AL), 1923–39.

Most career hits ■ The career record for most hits is 4,256, by Peter 'Pete' Edward Rose. He played 24 seasons with three teams: the Cincinnati Reds (NL) 1963–78, the Philadelphia Phillies (NL) 1979–83, the Montreal Expos (NL) 1984 and the Cincinnati Reds (NL) 1984–86. Rose's record hits total came from a record 14,053 at-bats, which gave him a career average of ·303.

Most consecutive hits ■ Michael Franklin 'Pinky' Higgins (1909–69) had 12 consecutive hits for the Boston Red Sox (AL) in a four game span, 19–21 Jun 1938. This was equaled by Walter 'Moose' Droppo (b. 30 Jan 1923) for the Detroit Tigers (AL) 14–15 Jul 1952. Joseph 'Joe' Paul DiMaggio (b. 25 Nov 1914) hit in a record 56 consecutive games for the New York Yankees (AL) in 1941; he went to bat 223 times, with 91 hits, totalling 56 singles, 16 doubles, 4 triples and 15 home runs.

Home runs and stolen bases ■ The first player to hit 40 or more home runs and have 40

stolen bases in a season was José Canseco (b. 2 Jul 1964) for the Oakland Athletics (AL) in 1988. His tallies were 42 and 40 respectively.

Walks ■ Babe Ruth holds the records for career walks, 2,056, and the single season record, 170 in 1923.

Two players share a record 6 walks for a single game: James 'Jimmy' E. Foxx of the Boston Red Sox (AL) set the mark on 16 Jun 1938 and Andre Thornton of the Cleveland Indians (AL) tied the record on 2 May 1984 in a game that went 18 innings.

Strikeouts ■ The batter with the career strikeout record is Reggie Jackson, with 2,597 in 21 seasons with four teams. The season record is 180, by Bobby Bonds, right fielder for the San Francisco Giants in 1970. The longest run of games without striking out is by Joe Sewell, while playing third base for the Cleveland Indians, who went to bat 437 times in 115 consecutive games in 1929. He had a record seven seasons batting at least 500 times yet with less than ten strikeouts, and struck out only 114 times in his 14-year career.

Most games won by a pitcher ■ Denton True 'Cy' Young (1876–1955) had a record 511 wins and a record 749 complete games from a total of 906 games and 815 starts in his career for Cleveland (NL) 1890–98, the St Louis Cardinals (NL) 1899–1900, the Boston Red Sox (AL) 1901–08, the Cleveland Indians (AL) 1909–11 and the Boston Braves (NL) 1911. He pitched a record total of 7,357 innings. The career record for most pitching appearances is 1,070 by James Hoyt Wilhem (b. 26 Jul 1923), for a total of nine teams between 1952 and 1969; he set the career record with 143 wins by a relief pitcher. The season's record is 106 appearances, by Michael Grant Marshall (b. 15 Jan 1943) for Los Angeles (NL) in 1974.

Most consecutive games won by a pitcher ■ Carl Owen Hubbell (1903–88) pitched for the New York Yankees (AL) (17 Jul 1936–27 May 1937) to win 24 consecutive games, 16 in 1936 and 8 in 1937.

Strikeouts ■ L. Nolan Ryan struck out a record 383 batters for the California Angels in 1973. He also holds the career strikeout record, with 5,173 strikeouts through 1 Jul 1990.

Shutouts ■ The record for the most shutouts in a career is 113, pitched by Walter P. Johnson in his 21 season career with the Washington Senators (AL), 1907–27. Donald 'Don' S. Drysdale pitched 6 consecutive shutouts for the Los Angeles Dodgers (NL) between 14 May and 4 Jun 1968. Orel Hershiser pitched a record 59 consecutive shutout innings for the Los Angeles Dodgers (NL) from 30 Aug to 28 Sep 1988

No-hitters ■ Nolan Ryan, playing for the Texas Rangers (AL) against the Oakland Athletics (AL), pitched his sixth no-hitter on 11 Jun 1990. John S. Vander Meer of the Cincinnati Reds (NL) is the only player in baseball history to have pitched consecutive no-hitters, 11–15 Jun 1938.

Perfect game ■ A perfect nine-inning game, in which the pitcher allows the opposition no hits, no runs and does not allow a man to reach first base, was first achieved by John Lee Richmond (1857–1929) for Worcester against Cleveland in the NL on 12 Jun 1880. There have been 13 subsequent perfect games, including one World Series game, over nine innings, but no pitcher has achieved this feat more than once.

On 26 May 1959 Harvey Haddix, Jr. (b. 18 Sep

LIFETIME ERA RECORDS

1·82 in 2,965 innings	Edward Augustine Walsh (b. 14 May 1881; 1904–17, Chicago–AL, Boston–NL)
1·89 in 2,327 innings	Adrian Joss (b. 12 Apr 1880; 1902–10, Cleveland, AL)
2·06 in 3,171 innings	Mordecai Peter Centennial 'Three Fingered' Brown (b. 19 Oct 1876: 1903–1916), St. Louis, NL (1903); Chicago, NL (1904–13); St. Louis & Brooklyn of Federal League (1915); Chicago, NL (1917)
2·10 in 2,462 innings	John Montgomery Ward (b. 3 Mar 1860; 1878–84) Providence, NL (1878–82); New York, NL (1883–84)
2·13 in 4,216 innings	Christopher 'Christy' Mathewson (b. 12 Aug 1880; 1900–16) New York, NL (1900–16); Cincinnati, NL (1916)
2·16 in 2,963 innings	George Edward 'Rube' Waddell (b. 13 Oct 1876; 1987, 1899–1910) Louisville, NL (1897–99); Pittsburgh, NL (1900–01); Chicago, NL (1901); Philadelphia, AL (1901–07); St Louis, AL(1908–10)
2·17 in 5,925 innings	Walter Perry 'Big Train' Johnson (b. 6 Nov 1887; 1907–27) Washington, AL (all)

1925) pitched a perfect game for 12 innings for the Pittsburgh Pirates against the Milwaukee Braves in the National League, but lost in the 13th.

Saves ■ Dave Righetti saved a record 46 games for the New York Yankees (AL) in 1986. The career record for saves is 341, by Roland 'Rollie' Fingers in his 18 seasons playing for the Oakland Athletics (AL), the San Diego Padres (NL) and the Milwaukee Brewers (AL), 1968–85. Fingers completed his record save total from 907 relief appearances.

Most Valuable Player ■ The most selections in the annual vote (instituted in 1931) of the Baseball Writers' Association for the Most Valuable Player of the Year in the major leagues is three, won by: National League: Stanley Frank Musial (b. 21 Nov 1920; St Louis), 1943, 1946, 1948; Roy Campanela (b. 19 Nov 1921; Brooklyn), 1951, 1953, 1955; Mike Schmidt (b. 27 Sep 1949; Philadelphia), 1980–81, 1986. American League: James Emory Foxx (1907–76; Philadelphia), 1932–33, 1938; Joe DiMaggio (New York), 1939, 1941, 1947; Yogi Berra (New York), 1951, 1954–55; Mickey Mantle (b. 20 Oct 1931; New York), 1956–57, 1962.

Cy Young award ■ Awarded from 1956 to the outstanding pitcher in each major league, the most wins is three: National League: George Thomas Seaver (b. 17 Nov 1944; New York), 1969, 1973, 1975; Stephen Norman Carlton (b. 22 Dec 1944; Philadelphia), 1977, 1980, 1982; Sanford 'Sandy' Koufax (b. 30 Dec 1935; Los Angeles), 1963, 1965–66: American League: James 'Jim' Alvin Palmer (b. 15 Oct 1945; Baltimore), 1973, 1975–76.

Dwight Gooden (b. 16 Nov 1964) of the New York Mets became the youngest pitcher to win the Cy Young Award in 1985 by unanimous vote of the 24 sportswriters who make the selection.

Managers ■ Connie Mack (b. Cornelius A. McGillicuddy; 1862–1956) managed in the major leagues for a record 53 seasons and he achieved a record 3,776 regular season victories (and a record 4,025 losses), 139 wins and 134 losses for the Pittsburgh Pirates (NL) 1894–96 and 3,627 wins and 3,891 losses for Philadelphia Athletics (AL), a team he later owned, 1901–50. The most successful in the World Series has been Charles Dillon 'Casey' Stengel (1890–1975), who managed the New York Yankees (AL) to seven wins in ten World Series, winning in 1949–53, 1956 and 1958, and losing in 1955, 1957 and 1960.

Joseph Vincent McCarthy (1887–1978) also managed the New York Yankees to seven wins, 1932, 1936–39, 1941 and 1942, and his teams lost in 1929 (Chicago) and 1942 (New York). Of mangers to have achieved at least 1,500 regular season wins, he has the highest winning percentage with 0·614%, 2,126 wins and 1,335 losses in his 24-year career, with the Chicago Cubs (NL) 1926–30, the New York Yankees (AL) 1931–46, the Boston Red Sox (AL) 1948–50. He never had an overall losing season.

Shortest games ■ The New York Giants (NL) beat the Philadelphia Phillies (NL), 6–1, in 9 innings in 51 min on 28 Sep 1919. (A minor league game, Atlanta *v* Mobile in the Southern Association on 19 Sep 1910 took only 33 min [see below].)

Longest games ■ The Brooklyn Dodgers (NL) and the Boston Braves (NL) played to a 1–1 tie after 26 innings on 1 May 1920. The Chicago White Sox (AL) played the longest ballgame in elapsed time—8 hours 6 min—before beating the Milwaukee Brewers, 7–6, in the 25th inning on 9 May 1984 in Chicago. The game started on

Tuesday night and was still tied at 3–3 when the 1 A.M. curfew caused suspension until Wednesday night.

The actual longest game was a minor league game in 1981 that lasted 33 innings. At the end of 9 innings the score was tied, 1–1, with the Rochester (NY) Red Wings battling the home team Pawtucket (RI) Red Sox. At the end of 21 innings it was tied, 2–2, and at the end of 32 innings, the score was still 2–2, when the game was suspended. Two months later, play was resumed and 18 minutes later, Pawtucket scored one run and won. The winning pitcher was the Red Sox Bob Ojeda.

Youngest player ■ Frederick Joseph Chapman (1872–1957) pitched for Philadelphia in the American Association at age 14 yr 239 days on 22 Jul 1887, but did not play again.

The youngest major league player of all time was the Cincinnati Reds (AL) pitcher Joseph Henry Nuxhall (b. 30 Jul 1928), who played one game in June 1944, at age 15 yr 314 days. He did not play again in the National League until 1952. The youngest player to play in a minor league game was Joe Louis Reliford (b. 29 Nov 1939) who played for the Fitzgerald Pioneers against Statesboro in the Georgia State League, at age 12 yr 234 days on 19 Jul 1952.

Oldest player ■ Leroy Robert 'Satchel' Paige (1906–82) pitched for the Kansas City A's (AL) at age 59 yr 80 days on 25 Sep 1965.

Shortest and tallest players ■ The shortest major league player was Eddie Gaedel, a 3 ft 7-in, 65 lb midget, who pinch hit for the St Louis Browns (AL) *v* the Detroit Tigers (AL) on 19 Aug 1951. Wearing number ⅛, the batter with the smallest ever major league strike zone walked on four pitches. Following the game, major league rules were hastily rewritten to prevent the recurrence of such an affair. The tallest major leaguer of all time is Randy Johnson (b. 10 Sep 1963) of Walnut Creek, CA, the Montreal Expos (NL) 6 ft 10-in pitcher, who played in his first game 15 Sep 1988.

Record attendances ■ The all-time season record for attendances for both leagues is 55,173,597 in 1989 (29,848,634 for the 14-team American League, including a record 3,375,573 for the home games of the Toronto Blue Jays and 25,324,963 for the 12-team National League).

An estimated 114,000 spectators watched a game between Australia and an American Services team in a demonstration event during the Olympic Games at Melbourne on 1 Dec 1956.

World Amateur Championships ■ Instituted in 1938, the most successful nation has been Cuba with 19 wins between 1939 and 1988. Baseball has been a demonstration sport at six Olympic Games, and American teams have won the tournament four times, 1912, 1956, 1964 and 1988.

COLLEGE BASEBALL

Various forms of college baseball have been played throughout the twentieth century, however, the NCAA did not organize a championship until 1947 and did not begin to keep statistical records until 1957.

NCAA Division I Regular Season

Hitting records ■ The most career home runs was 100, by Pete Incaviglia for Oklahoma State in three season, 1983–85. The most career hits was 118, by Phil Stephenson for Wichita State in four seasons, 1979–82.

Pitching records ■ Don Heinkel won 51

games for Wichita State in four seasons, 1979–82. Derek Patsumo struck out 541 batters for the University of Hawaii in three seasons, 1977–79.

College World Series ■ The first College World Series was played in 1947 at Kalamazoo, MI. The University of California at Berkeley defeated Yale University 8–7. Since 1950 the College World Series has been played continuously at Rosenblatt Stadium, Omaha, NE.

Most championships ■ The most wins in division one is 11 by the University of Southern California (USC) in 1948, 1958, 1961, 1963, 1968, 1970–74 and 1978.

Hitting records ■ The record for most home runs in a College World Series is 4 shared by three players: Bud Hollowell (University of Southern California), 1963; Pete Incaviglia (Oklahoma State), 1983–85; Ed Sprague (Stanford University), 1987–88. Keith Moreland of the University of Texas holds the record for the most hits in a College World Series career with 23 hits in three series, 1973–75.

Pitching records ■ The record for most wins in the College World Series is 4 games shared by nine players: Bruce Gardner (University of Southern California), 1958, 1960; Steve Arlin (Ohio State), 1965–66; Bert Hooton (University of Texas at Austin), 1969–70; Steve Rogers (University of Tulsa), 1969, 1971; Russ McQueen (University of Southern California), 1972–73; Mark Bull (University of Southern California), 1973–74; Greg Swindell (University of Texas), 1984–85; Kevin Sheary (University of Miami of Florida), 1984, 1985; Greg Brummett (Wichita State), 1988–89.

Carl Thomas of the University of Arizona struck out 64 batters in three College World Series, 1954–56.

LONGEST AND FASTEST

Longest home run ■ In a minor league game at Emeryville Ball Park, CA on 4 Jul 1929, Roy Edward 'Dizzy' Carlyle (1900–56) hit a home run measured at 618 ft.

In 1919 Babe Ruth hit a 587 ft homer in a Boston Red Sox *v* New York Giants exhibition match at Tampa, FL.

The longest measured home run in a regular-season major league game is 565 ft by Mickey Mantle (b. 20 Oct 1931) for the New York Yankees *v* Washington Senators on 17 Apr 1953, at Griffith Stadium, Washington, D.C.

Longest throw ■ Glen Edward Gorbous (b. Canada 8 Jul 1930) threw 445 ft 10 in on 1 Aug 1957.

Women ■ Mildred Ella 'Babe' Didrikson (later Mrs Zaharias; 1914–56) threw 296 ft at Jersey City, NJ on 25 Jul 1931.

Fastest base runner ■ The fastest time for circling bases is 13·3 sec by Ernest Evar Swanson (1902–73) at Columbus, OH in 1932, at an average speed of 18·45 mph.

Basketball

Origins ■ The game of 'Pok-ta-Pok' was played in the 10th century B.C., by the Olmecs in Mexico, and closely resembled basketball in its concept. 'Ollamalitzli' was a variation of this game played by the Aztecs in Mexico as late as the 16th century. If the solid rubber ball was put through a fixed stone ring the player was entitled to the clothing of all the spectators. Modern basketball was devised by the Canadian-born Dr James A. Naismith (1861–1939) at the Training School of the International

YMCA College at Springfield, MA in mid-December 1891. The first game played under modified rules was on 20 Jan 1892. The International Amateur Basketball Federation (FIBA) was founded in 1932; it has now dropped the word Amateur from its title.

Most titles *Olympic* ■ The United States has won nine men's Olympic titles. From the time the sport was introduced to the Games in 1936 until 1972 they won 63 consecutive matches in the Olympic Games, until they lost 50–51 to the USSR in the disputed final match in Munich, West Germany. They won eighth and ninth titles in 1976 and 1984.

The women's title was won by the USSR in 1976 and 1980, and by the United States in 1984 and 1988.

World ■ The USSR has won most titles at both the men's World Championships (instituted 1950) with three (1967, 1974 and 1982) and women's (instituted 1953), with six (1959, 1964, 1967, 1971, 1975 and 1983).

Highest score ■ In a senior international match Iraq scored 251 against Yemen (33) at New Delhi, India in November 1982 at the Asian Games.

Individual ■ Mats Wermelin, 13 (Sweden), scored all 272 points in a 272–0 win in a regional boys' tournament in Stockholm, Sweden on 5 Feb 1974.

Tallest players ■ Suleiman Ali Nashnush (b. 1943) was reputed to be 8 ft when he played for the Libyan team in 1962. Aleksandr Sizonenko (USSR) of Kuibyshev Stroitel is 7 ft 10 in tall. The tallest woman player was Iuliana Larionovna Semenova (USSR; b. 9 Mar 1952), at a reported 7 ft 2 in and weighing 281 lb.

Shooting speed ■ The greatest goal-shooting demonstration has been by Ted St Martin of Jacksonville, FL, who, on 25 Jun 1977, scored 2,036 consecutive free throws. Also at Jacksonville, he has scored 175 out of 185 free throws in 10 min on 27 Jan 1990, and 90 out of 97 attempts on 24 Feb 1990. Both records being achieved with one ball and one rebounder.

In 24 hours Jeff Liles scored 17,227 free throws from a total of 24,309 taken (70·86 percent) at Castleberry High School, Fort Worth, TX on 6–7 Apr 1990.

Steve Bontrager (US; b. 1 Mar 1959) of Polycell Kingston scored 21 points in a minute from seven positions in a demonstration for British Broadcasting Corporation TV's 'Record Breakers' on 29 Oct 1986.

Longest goal ■ Christopher Eddy (b. 13 Jul 1971) scored a field goal, measured at 90 ft 2¼ in, for Fairview High School *v* Iroquois High School at Erie, PA on 25 Feb 1989. The shot was made as time expired in overtime and won the game for Fairview, 51–50.

Olympic Games ■ Three men and two women have won two Olympic gold medals: Robert Albert 'Bob' Kurland (b. 23 dec 1924) in 1948 and 1952; William Marion 'Bill' Houghland (b. 20 Jun 1930) in 1952 and 1956; Burdette Eliele Haldorson (b. 12 Jan 1934) in 1956 and 1960; Anne Theresa Donovan (b. 1 Nov 1961) and Theresa Edwards, both in 1984 and 1988.

Dribbling ■ Peter del Masto (US) dribbled a basketball without 'traveling' from near Lee to Provincetown, MA, a distance of 265·2 miles, from 12–25 Aug 1989.

NBA RECORDS

Career records

Points	38,387	Kareem Abdul-Jabbar: Milwaukee Bucks, Los Angeles Lakers	1970–89
Field goal percentage	·599	Artis Gilmore: Chicago Bulls, San Antonio Spurs, Boston Celtics; min. 2,000 field goals	1977–88
Free throws made	7,694	Oscar Palmer Robertson: Cincinnati Royals, Milwaukee Bucks of 9,185 attempts	1961–74
Free throw percentage	·900	Rick Barry: San Francisco / Golden State Warriors, Houston Rockets; 3,818 from 4,243 attempts (technically ·89983)	1965–80
Field goals	15,837	Kareem Abdul-Jabbar	1970–89
Rebounds	23,924	Wilt Chamberlain: Philadelphia / San Francisco Warriors, Philadelphia 76ers, Los Angeles Lakers	1960–73
Assists	9,887	Oscar Robertson; in 1,040 games	1961–74
Steals	2,066	Maurice Cheeks: Philadelphia 76ers, San Antonio Spurs, New York Knicks	1979–90

Season's records

Points	4,029	Wilt Chamberlain: Philadelphia Warriors	1962
Field goal percentage	·727	Wilt Chamberlain: Los Angeles Lakers 426 of 586 attempts	1972
Free throws made	840	Jerry West: Los Angeles Lakers; of 977 attempts	1966
Free throw percentage	·958	Calvin Murphy: Houston Rockets; 206 of 215 attempts	1981
Rebounds	2,149	Wilt Chamberlain: Philadelphia Warriors	1961
Assists	1,134	John Stockton: Utah Jazz	1990
Steals	301	Alvin Robertson: San Antonio Spurs	1986

Single game records

Points	100	Wilt Chamberlain: Philadelphia Warriors v New York Knicks	2 Mar 1962
Field goals	36	Wilt Chamberlain	2 Mar 1962
Free throws made	28	Wilt Chamberlain	2 Mar 1962
	28	Adrian Dantley: Utah Jazz v Houston Rockets	5 Jan 1984
Rebounds	55	Wilt Chamberlain: Philadelphia Warriors v Boston Celtics	24 Nov 1960
Assists	29	Kevin Porter: New Jersey Nets v Houston Rockets;	24 Feb 1978
Steals	11	Larry Kenon: San Antonio Spurs v Kansas City Kings	26 Dec 1976

NBA PLAYOFF RECORDS

Most games played	237	Kareem Abdul-Jabbar: Milwaukee Bucks, Los Angeles Lakers	1970–89

Career records

Points	5,762	Kareem Abdul-Jabbar: (in 237 playoff games)	1970–89
Free throws made	1,213	Jerry West: Los Angeles Lakers (from 1,507 attempts)	1961–74
Assists	2,080	Earvin 'Magic' Johnson: Los Angeles Lakers	1980–90
Rebounds	4,104	Bill Russell: Boston Celtics	1957–69

Series records

Points	284	Elgin Baylor: Los Angeles Lakers (v Boston Celtics); in 7 games	1962
Field goals	113	Wilt Chamberlain: San Francisco (v St Louis); in 6 games	1964
Free throws made	86	Jerry West: Los Angeles Lakers (v Baltimore); in 6 games (in 6 games)	1965
Rebounds	220	Wilt Chamberlain: Philadelphia 76ers (v Boston Celtics) (in 7 games)	1965
Assists	115	John Stockton: Utah Jazz (v Los Angeles Lakers) (in 7 games)	1988

Single game records

Points	63	Michael Jordan: Chicago Bulls (v Boston Celtics) (incl two overtime periods)	20 Apr 1986
	61	Elgin Baylor: Los Angeles Lakers (v Boston Celtics)	14 Apr 1962
Field goals	24	Wilt Chamberlain Philadelphia 76ers v Syracuse Nationals; in 42 attempts	14 Mar 1960
	24	John Havelicek: Boston Celtics (v Atlanta Hawks) (in 36 attempts)	1 Apr 1973
	24	Michael Jordan: Chicago Bulls(v Cleveland Cavaliers) (45 attempts)	1 May 1988
Free throws made	30	Bob Cousy: Boston Celtics (v Syracuse Nationals) (incl four overtime periods; 32 attempts)	21 Mar 1953
	23	Michael Jordan: Chicago Bulls (v New York Knicks) (28 attempts)	14 May 1989
Rebounds	41	Wilt Chamberlain: Philadelphia 76ers (v Boston Celtics)	5 Apr 1967
Assists	24	Earvin 'Magic' Johnson Los Angeles Lakers (v Phoenix Suns)	15 May 1984
	24	John Stockton: Utah Jazz (v Los Angeles Lakers)	17 May 1988

NATIONAL BASKETBALL ASSOCIATION (NBA)

Origins ■ The Amateur Athletic Union (AAU) organized the first national tournament in the United States in 1897. The first professional league was the National Basketball League (NBL), founded in 1898, but this league only lasted two seasons. The American Basketball League was formed in 1925, but declined and the NBL was refounded in 1937. This organization merged with the Basketball Association of America in 1949 to form the National Basketball Association (NBA).

The Boston Celtics have won a record 16 NBA titles, in 1957, 1959–66, 1968–69, 1974, 1976, 1981, 1984, 1986.

Highest score ■ The highest aggregate score in an NBA game is 370, when the Detroit Pistons (186) beat the Denver Nuggets (184) at Denver, CO on 13 Dec 1983. Overtime was played after a 145–145 tie in regulation time. The record in regulation time is 318, when the Denver Nuggets beat the San Antonio Spurs 163–155 at Denver on 11 Jan 1984. The most points in a half is 97, by Atlanta in the second half at San Diego on 11 Feb 1970. The most points in a quarter is 58, by Buffalo at Boston (4th quarter) on 20 Oct 1972.

Individual scoring ■ Wilton Norman 'Wilt' Chamberlain (b. 21 Aug 1936) set an NBA record with 100 points for the Philadelphia Warriors *v* New York Knicks. The final result was 169 points to 147 at Hershey, PA on 2 Mar 1962. In this game, witnessed by 4,124 people Chamberlain made 36 field goals and 28 free throws (in 32 attempts) and a record 59 points in a half (the second). The free throws game record was equaled by Adrian Dantley (b. 28 Feb 1956) for the Utah Jazz *v* the Houston Rockets at Las Vegas, NV on 5 Jan 1984 (in 31 attempts). The most points scored in an NBA game in one quarter is 33, by George Gervin for San Antonio *v* New Orleans on 9 Apr 1978 (second quarter).

Most games ■ Kareem Abdul-Jabbar (formerly Ferdinand Lewis Alcindor; b. 16 Apr 1947) took part in a record 1,560 NBA regular season games over 20 seasons, totaling 57,446 minutes played, for the Milwaukee Bucks (1969–75) and the Los Angeles Lakers (1975–89). He also played a record 237 play-off games.

The most successive games is 906, by Randy Smith for Buffalo, the San Diego Clippers, the Cleveland Cavaliers and the New York Knicks from 18 Feb 1972 to 13 Mar 1983. The record for playing complete games in one season is 79, by Wilt Chamberlain for the Philadelphia Warriors in 1962, when he was on court for a record 3,882 minutes. Chamberlain went through his entire career of 1,945 games without fouling out.

Most points ■ Kareem Abdul-Jabbar set NBA career records with 38,387 points, including 15,837 field goals in regular season games, and 5,762 points, including 2,356 field goals in play-off games. The previous record holder, Wilt Chamberlain, had an average of 30·1 points per game for his total of 31,419 for the Philadelphia Warriors (1959–62), the San Francisco Warriors (1962–65), the Philadelphia 76ers (1964–68) and the Los Angeles Lakers (1968–73). He scored 50 or more points in 118 games, including 45 in 1961/2 and 30 in 1962/3 to the next best career total of 17, held by Elgin Baylor and Michael Jordan. Wilt Chamberlain set season's records for points and scoring average with 4,029 at 50·1 per game, and also for field goals, 1,597, for Philadelphia in 1961/2.

The highest career average for players exceeding 10,000 points is 32·8 by Michael Jordan (b. 17 Feb 1963), 14,106 points in 427 games for the Chicago Bulls, 1984–90. Jordan also holds the career scoring average record for play-offs at 35·4 for 1,309 points in 37 games 1984–90.

Leading scorer ■ Kareem Abdul-Jabbar (Milwaukee, Los Angeles) had a record nine seasons scoring more than 2,000 points: 1970–74, 1976–77, 1980–81; and 19 seasons scoring more than 1,000: 1970–88.

> **NBA career** ● Kareem Abdul–Jabbar retired at the end of the 1988–89 season and during his career with the Milwaukee Bucks (1969–75) and the Los Angeles Lakers (1975–89) set numerous NBA records. He retired on a high note taking part in his tenth NBA Finals series, against the Detroit Pistons. (Photo: All-Sport/Mike Powell)

Winning margin ■ The greatest winning margin in an NBA game was the 63 points, by which the Los Angeles Lakers, 162, beat the Golden State Warriors, 99, on 19 Mar 1972.

Most Valuable Player ■ Kareem Abdul-Jabbar was elected the NBA most valuable player a record six times, 1971–72, 1974, 1976–77 and 1980.

Steals ■ The most steals in an NBA game is 11, by Larry Kenon for the San Antonio Spurs at Kansas City on 26 Dec 1976. Alvin Robertson (b. 22 Jul 1962) set season's records for the San Antonio Spurs in 1985/6 with 301 at a record average of 3·67 per game.

Blocked shots ■ The record for most blocked shots in an NBA game is 17, by Elmore Smith for the Los Angeles Lakers *v* the Portland Trail Blazers at Los Angeles on 28 Oct 1973.

NCAA RECORDS
Through 1989–90 Season

Division 1 career records

Points	**3,667**	Peter 'Pistol Pete' Maravich: Louisiana State	1968–70
Field goals	**1,387**	Pistol Pete Maravich: Louisiana State	1968–70
Best percentage	**68·5**	Stephen Sheffler: Purdue	1987–90
Rebounds	**2,243**	Tom Gola: La Salle	1952–55
Assists	**960**	Shermon Douglas: Syracuse	1986–89

Division 1 season records

Points	**1,381**	Pistol Pete Maravich: Louisiana State	1970
Field goals	**522**	Pistol Pete Maravich: Lousiana State (from 1,168 attempts)	1970
Best percentage	**74·9**	Steve Johnson: Oregon State	1981
Three-point goals	**158**	Darrin Fitzgerald: Butler (in 362 attempts)	1987
Free throws	**355**	Frank Selvy: Furman (in 444 attempts)	1954
Best percentage	**95·9**	Craig Collins: Penn State	1985
Rebounds	**734**	Walt Dukes: Seton Hall (in 33 games)	1953
Assists	**406**	Mark Wade: Nevada–Las Vegas	1987
Blocked shots	**207**	David Robinson: Navy (in 35 games)	1986

Division 1 game records

Points	**100**	Frank Selvy: Furman	13 Feb 1954
Field goals	**41**	Frank Selvy: Furman	13 Feb 1954
Three-point goals	**14**	Dave Jamerson: Ohio (v Charleston)	21 Dec 1989
Free throws	**30**	Pistol Pete Maravich: Louisiana State (v Oregon State)	22 Dec 1969
Rebounds	**51**	Bill Chambers: William and Mary (v Virginia)	14 Feb 1953
Assists	**22**	Tony Fairly: Baptist (v Armstrong State)	9 Feb 1987
	22	Avery Johnson: Southern–B.R. (v Texas Southern)	25 Jan 1988
	22	Sherman Douglas: Syracuse (v Providence)	28 Jan 1989
Blocked shots	**14**	David Robinson: Navy (v North Carolina–Wilmington)	4 Jan 1986

Winning streak ■ Los Angeles Lakers won a record 33 NBA games in succession from 5 Nov 1971 to 7 Jan 1972, as during the 1971/2 season they won a record 69 games with 13 losses.

Youngest and oldest player ■ The youngest NBA player has been Bill Willoughby (b. 20 May 1957), who made his debut for the Atlanta Hawks on 23 Oct 1975 at 18 yr 156 days. The oldest NBA regular player was Kareem Abdul-Jabbar, who made his last appearance for the Los Angeles Lakers at age 42 yr 59 days in 1989.

Tallest player ■ Tallest in NBA history has been Manute Bol (Sudan; b. 16 Oct 1962) of the Washington Bullets and Golden State Warriors, at 7 ft 6 ¾ in, who made his pro debut in 1985.

Coaches ■ The most successful coach in NBA history has been Arnold 'Red' Auerbach (b. 1917), with 938 wins (1,037 including play-offs), Washington Capitols 1946–49 and Boston Celtics 1950–66. He led the Boston Celtics to nine NBA titles, including eight in succession 1959–66.

Record attendance ■ The Minnesota Timberwolves set an NBA record for total attendance of 1,072,572 during the 1989–90 season, the Timberwolves first in the league. The average crowd was 26,160 fans at the Metrodome in Minneapolis.

NCAA RECORDS

Championships ■ First contested in 1939, the record for most Division One titles is 10, by the University of California at Los Angeles (UCLA), 1964–65, 1967–73, 1975. The only player to have been voted the most valuable player in the NCAA final three times has been Lew Alcindor of UCLA in 1967–69. He subsequently changed his name to Kareem Abdul-Jabbar.

Points ■ The most points by an individual in an NCAA Division I game is 100 by Frank Selvy,

for Furman v Newberry on 13 Feb 1954, including a record 41 field goals. In Division II Clarence 'Bevo' Francis scored 113 points for Rio Grande v Hillsdale on 2 Feb 1954.

Career and season's scoring ■ Peter 'Pistol Pete' Maravich (1947–88) set unmatched NCAA scoring records while at Louisiana State University; 1,138 points, an average of 43·8 per

game, in 1968; 1,148 at 44·2 per game in 1969, and the season's record 1,381 at 44·5 per game in 1970—the three highest season's averages in NCAA history, for a total 3,667 points in 83 games. Maravich scored a career record 1,387 field goals and the career field goal percentage record (*minimum 400 scored*) is 67·8% by Steve Johnson, 828 from 1,222 attempts for Oregon State, 1976–81. In Division II competition Travis Grant of Kentucky State scored a record 4,045 points in 121 games, 1969–72 and a season's average record was set at 46·5 points by Clarence 'Bevo' Francis, with 1,255 points in 27 games for Rio Grande in 1954. In National Association of Intercollegiate Athletics (NAIA) competition, Philip Hutcheson of David Lipscomb University scored 4,064 points in his career, 1987–90.

Coaches ■ The man to have coached most victories in NCAA Division I competition is Adolph Rupp (1901–77) at Kentucky, with 875 wins (and 190 losses), 1931–72. John Wooden (b. 1910) coached UCLA to all their ten NCAA titles.

Record attendances ■ The highest paid attendance for a college game is 66,144 for Louisiana State's 82–80 victory over Georgetown at the Louisiana Superdome, New Orleans, LA on 28 Jan 1989.

The record for a women's college game is 24,563 in Knoxville, TN for a game between the University of Tennessee and the University of Texas on 9 Dec 1987.

Women's championships ■ First contested in 1982, the record for most Division One titles is three by the University of Southern California, 1983–84, Tennessee, 1987 and 1989 and Louisiana Tech University, 1982 and 1988.

The regular season match aggregate record is 261, when St Joseph's (Indiana) beat North Kentucky 131–130 on 27 Feb 1988. The most points by a woman in a college career is 4,061 by Pearl Moore of Francis Marion College, Florence, SC, 1975–79.

NCAA MEN'S CHAMPIONSHIP GAME RECORDS

Team records

Most championships	10	UCLA	1964–65, 1967–73, 1975
First championships		Oregon defeated Ohio State 46–33	1939
Most points	103	UNLV (v Duke)	1990
Most field-goals	41	UNLV (v Duke)	1990
Highest field-goal percentage	78·6%	Villanova (v Georgetown) (22–28)	1985
Most 3-point field-goals	10	Oklahoma (v Kansas)	1988
Rebounds	61	UCLA (v Purdue)	1969
Assists	24	UNLV (v Duke)	1990
Blocked shots	7	Louisville (v Duke)	1986
	7	Syracuse (v Indiana)	1987
Steals	16	UNLV (v Duke)	1990

Individual records

Most points	44	Bill Walton, UCLA (v Memphis State)	1973
Most field-goals	21	Bill Walton, UCLA (v Memphis State)	1973
Highest field-goal percentage	95·5%	Bill Walton, UCLA (v Memphis State) (21–22)	1973
3-point field-goals	7	Steve Alford, Indiana (v Syracuse)	1987
	7	Dave Sieger, Oklahoma (v Kansas)	1988
Rebounds	21	Bill Spivey, Kentucky (v Kansas State)	1951
Assists	9	Alvin Franklin, Houston (v Georgetown)	1984
	9	Michael Jackson, Georgetown (v Villanova)	1985
Blocked shots	3	Rony Seikaly, Syracuse (v Indiana)	1987
	3	Derrick Coleman, Syracuse (v Indiana)	1987
	3	Dean Garrett, Indiana (v Syracuse)	1987
Steals	7	Tommy Amaker, Duke (v Louisville)	1986
	7	Mookie Blaylock, Oklahoma (v Kansas)	1988

NCAA WOMEN'S CHAMPIONSHIP GAME RECORDS

Team records

Most championships	2	Louisiana Tech (1982, 1988), USC (1983–84), Tennessee (1987, 1989)	
First championships		Louisiana Tech defeated Cheyney State 76–62	1982
Most points	97	Texas (v USC)	1986
Most field-goals	40	Texas (v USC)	1986
Highest field-goal percentage	58·8%	Texas (v USC) (40–68)	1986
Most 3-point field-goals	11	Stanford (v Auburn)	1990
Rebounds	57	Old Dominion (v Georgia)	1985
Assists (since 1985)	22	Texas (v USC)	1986
Blocked shots (since 1988)	7	Tennessee (v Auburn)	1989
Steals (since 1988)	12	Louisiana Tech (v Auburn)	1988

Individual records

Most points	27	Cheryl Miller, USC (v Louisiana Tech)	1983
	27	Cynthia Cooper, USC (v Texas)	1987
	27	Bridgette Gordon, Tennessee (v Auburn)	1989
Most field-goals	12	Erica Westbrooks, Louisiana Tech (v Auburn)	1988
Highest field-goal percentage	88·9%	Jennifer White, Louisiana Tech (v USC) (8–9)	1983
Most 3-point field-goals (since 1988)	6	Katy Steding, Stanford (v Auburn)	1990
Rebounds	20	Tracy Claxton, Old Dominion (v Georgia)	1985
Assists (since 1985)	10	Kamie Ethridge, Texas (v USC)	1986
	10	Melissa McCray, Tennessee (v Auburn)	1989
Blocked shots (since 1988)	5	Sheila Frost, Tennessee (v Auburn)	1989
Steals (since 1988)	6	Erica Westbrooks, Louisiana Tech (v Auburn)	1988

Billiards

Origins ■ The earliest recorded mention of billiards was in France in 1429, and Louis XI, King of France 1461–83, is reported to have had a billiard table.

Most titles *World* ■ The greatest number of World Championships (instituted 1870) won by one player is eight, by John Roberts Jr (United Kingdom; 1847–1919), in 1870 (twice), 1871, 1875 (twice), 1877 and 1885 (twice). The record for world amateur titles is four, by Robert James Percival Marshall (Australia; b. 10 Apr 1910), in 1936, 1938, 1951 and 1962.

Youngest champion ■ The youngest winner of the world professional title is Mike Russell (b. 3 Jun 1969), aged 20 yr 49 days, when he won at Leura, Australia on 23 Jul 1989.

Highest breaks ■ Tom Reece (1873–1953) made an unfinished break of 499,135, including 249,152 cradle cannons (two points each) in 85 hr 49 min against Joe Chapman at Burroughes' Hall, Soho Square, London, United Kingdom between 3 Jun and 6 Jul 1907. This was not recognized because press and public were not continuously present.

The highest certified break made by the anchor cannon is 42,746 by William Cook (England) from 29 May to 7 Jun 1907.

The official world record under the then balkline rule is 1,784, by Joe Davis in the United Kingdom Championship on 29 May 1936.

Walter Albert Lindrum (Australia; 1898–1960) made an official break of 4,137 in 2 hr 55 min against Joe Davis at Thurston's on 19–20 Jan 1932, before the balkline rule was in force.

Davis had an unofficial personal best of 2,502 (mostly pendulum cannons) in a match against Tom Newman (England; 1894–1943) in Manchester, United Kingdom in 1930.

The highest break recorded in amateur competition is 1,149, by Michael Ferreira (India) at Calcutta, India on 15 Dec 1978.

Under the more stringent 'two pot' rule, restored on 1 Jan 1983, the highest break is Ferreira's 962 unfinished, in a tournament at Bombay, India on 29 Apr 1986.

Fastest century ■ Walter Lindrum made an unofficial 100 break in 27·5 sec in Australia on 10 Oct 1952. His official record is 100 in 46·0 sec set in Sydney, Australia in 1941.

3 CUSHION
Origins ■ This pocketless variation dates back to 1878. The world governing body, the Union Mondiale de Billiard (UMB), was formed in 1928.

Most titles ■ William F. Hoppe (US; 1887–1959) won 51 billiards championships in all forms, spanning the pre- and post-international era from 1906 to 1952.

UMB ■ Raymond Ceulemans (Belgium; b. 12 Jul 1935) has won 19 world three-cushion championships (1963–73, 1975–80, 1983, 1985).

Board Games

BACKGAMMON
Origins ■ Forerunners of the game have been traced back to a dice and a board game found in excavations at Ur, dated to 3000 B.C. Later the Romans played a game remarkably similar to the modern one. The name 'backgammon' is variously ascribed to Welsh 'little battle,' or Saxon 'back game.'

Shortest game ■ Alan Malcolm Beckerson (b. 21 Feb 1938) devised a game of just 16 throws in 1982.

CHECKERS
Origins ■ Checkers, known as draughts in Europe, was played in Egypt in the second millennium B.C. The earliest book on the game was by Antonio Torquemada of Valencia, Spain in 1547.

World champions ■ Walter Hellman (US) (1916–75) won a record eight world titles during his tenure as world champion 1948–75.

Dr Marion Tinsley (US; b. 3 Feb 1927), the current world champion, has been internationally undefeated in match play from 1947 to 1990.

Youngest and oldest national champion ■ Asa A. Long (b. 20 Aug 1904) became the youngest US national champion, aged 18 yr 64 days, when he won in Boston, MA on 23 Oct 1922. He became the oldest, at age 79 yr 334 days, when he won his sixth title in Tupelo, MS on 21 Jul 1984.

Most opponents ■ Charles Walker played a record 201 games simultaneously, winning 189 and drawing 12, at New Orleans Center, LA on 5 Nov 1988.

The largest number of opponents played without a defeat or draw is 172 by Nate Cohen of Portland, ME at Portland on 26 Jul 1981. This was not a simultaneous attempt, but consecutive play over a period of four hours.

Newell W. Banks (1887–1977) played 140 games simultaneously, winning 133 and drawing seven, in Chicago, IL in 1933. His playing time was 145 min, so averaging about one move per sec. In 1947 he played blindfolded for 4 hr per day for 45 consecutive days, winning 1,331 games, drawing 54 and losing only two, while playing six games at a time.

Longest and shortest games ■ In competition the prescribed rate of play is not less than 30 moves per hour, with the average game lasting about 90 min. In 1958 a game between Dr Marion Tinsley (US) and Derek Oldbury (United Kingdom) lasted 7 hr 30 min (played under the 5-minutes-a-move rule).

The shortest possible game is one of 20 moves composed by Alan Malcolm Beckerson (United Kingdom) in 1977.

CHESS
Origins ■ The game originated in ancient India under the name *chaturanga* (literally 'four-corps' – an army game). The name chess is derived from the Persian word *shah* (a king or ruler). The earliest reference is from the Middle Persian Karnamak (*c.* A.D. 590–628), though in December 1972, two ivory chessmen were found in the Uzbek Soviet Republic datable to A.D. 200. It reached Britain *c.* 1255. The Fédération Internationale des Echecs (FIDE) was established in 1924.

World championships ■ World champions have been generally recognized since 1886. The longest undisputed tenure was 26 yr 337 days, by Dr Emanuel Lasker (1868–1941) of Germany, from 1894 to 1921.

The women's world championship title was held by Vera Francevna Menchik-Stevenson (USSR, later United Kingdom; 1906–44) from 1927 until her death, and was successfully defended a record seven times.

The first American to be regarded as world champion was Paul Charles Morphy (1837–89) in 1858.

Team ■ The USSR has won the men's team title (Olympiad) a record 17 times and the women's title 11 times to 1988.

The United States has won the men's title five times: 1931, 1933, 1935, 1937 and 1976.

Youngest ■ Gary Kimovich Kasparov (USSR; b. 13 Apr 1963) won the title on 9 Nov 1985 at age 22 yr 210 days.

Maya Grigorievna Chiburdanidze (USSR; b. 17 Jan 1961) won the women's title in 1978 when only 17.

Oldest ■ Wilhelm Steinitz (Austria; 1836–1900) was 58 yr 10 days when he lost his title to Lasker on 26 May 1894.

Most active ■ Anatoliy Yevgenyevich Karpov (USSR; b. 23 May 1951) in his tenure as champion, 1975–85, averaged 45·2 competitive games per year, played in 32 tournaments and finished first in 26.

Highest rating ■ The highest rating ever attained on the officially adopted Elo System is 2,800, by Gary Kasparov (USSR) at the end of 1989.

The highest-rated woman player is Judit Polgar (Hungary; b. 25 Jul 1976), at 2,550.

Least games lost by a world champion ■ José Raúl Capablanca (Cuba; 1888–1942) lost only 34 games in his adult career, 1909–39. He was unbeaten from 10 Feb 1916 to 21 Mar 1924, and was world champion 1921–27.

US Championships ■ The most wins since the US Championships became determined by match play competition in 1888 is eight, by Robert James 'Bobby' Fischer (b. 9 Mar 1943), 1958–66. Fischer, world champion 1972–75, reached a rating on the Elo system of 2,785, the highest ever until surpassed by Gary Kasparov in 1989.

Most opponents ■ The record for most consecutive games played is 663, by Vlastimil Hort (Czechoslovakia; b. 12 Jan 1944) over 32½ hours at Porz, West Germany on 5–6 Oct 1984. He played 60–100 opponents at a time, scoring over 80 percent wins and averaging 30 moves per game. He also holds the record for most games simultaneously, 201 during 550 consecutive games, of which he only lost ten, in Seltjarnes, Iceland on 23–24 Apr 1977.

Eric G. J. Knoppert (Netherlands; b. 20 Sep 1959) played 500 games of 10-minute chess against opponents averaging 2,002 on the Elo scale on 13–16 Sep 1985. He scored 413 points (1 for win, ½ for draw), a success rate of 82·6 percent.

Slowest and longest games ■ The slowest reported moving (before modern rules) in an official event is reputed to have been by Louis Paulsen (Germany; 1833–91) against Paul Charles Morphy (US; 1837–84) on 29 Oct 1857. The game ended in a draw on move 56 after 15 hours of play, of which Paulsen used most of the allotted time.

Grand Master Friedrich Sämisch (Germany) (1896–1975) ran out of the allotted time (2 hr 30 min for 45 moves) after only 12 moves, in Prague, Czechoslovakia, in 1938.

The slowest move played, since time clocks were introduced, was at Vigo, Spain in 1980 when Francisco R. Torres Trois (b. 3 Sep 1946) took 2 hr 20 min for his seventh move *v.* Luis M. C. P. Santos (b. 30 Jun 1955).

The Master game with most moves on record was one of 269 moves, when Ivan Nikolic drew with Goran Arsovic in a Belgrade, Yugoslavia tournament on 17 Feb 1989. It took a total of 20 hr 15 min.

MONOPOLY

Monopoly, a real-estate trading game, of which Parker Brothers has sold in excess of 100 million copies worldwide in 23 languages (the most recent in Russian), was devised by Charles Darrow (1889–1967) of Germantown, PA, in 1923. While unemployed as a heating engineer during the depression, he created the game using the street names of Atlantic City, NJ, where he spent his vacations.

World Champions ■ The current holder of the World Monopoly Championship trophy and medal is Ikuo Hiyakuta of Japan. He won the eighth World Monopoly Tournament (held every three years under the auspices of Parker Brothers) at the Park Lane Hotel, London, United Kingdom in 1988 after two days of grueling play. his prize was $15,140 and a personal computer.

SCRABBLE®Crossword Game

Origins ■ The crossword game was invented by Alfred M. Butts in 1931 and was developed, refined and trademarked as Scrabble®Crossword Game by James Brunot in 1948.

Highest scores ■ The highest competitive game score is 1,049 by Phil Appleby (b. 9 Dec 1957) in June 1989. His opponent scord 253 and the margin of victory, 796 points, is also a record.

His score included a single turn of 374 for the word 'OXIDIZERS.' The highest competitive single turn score recorded, however, is 392, by Dr Saladin Karl Khoshnaw in Manchester, United Kingdom in April 1982. He laid down 'CAZIQUES,' which means 'native chiefs of West Indian aborigines.'

Most tournaments ■ Chuck Armstrong, a hospital worker from Saline, MI has won the most tournaments—65 to the end of 1989.

BIGGEST BOARD GAME

The world's biggest board game was a version of the game, Goose, and was organized by 'Jong Nederland.' It stretched for 2,090 ft and was played by 1,631 participants at Someren, Netherlands on 16 Sep 1989.

Bobsleigh and Tobogganing

BOBSLEDDING

Origins ■ The oldest known sled is dated *c.* 6500 B.C. and came from Heinola, Finland. The first known bobsleigh race took place at Davos, Switzerland in 1889. The International Federation of Bobsleigh and Tobogganing was formed in 1923, followed by the International Bobsleigh Federation in 1957.

Most titles ■ The Olympic four-man bob title (instituted 1924) has been won five times by Switzerland (1924, 1936, 1956, 1972 and 1988).

The United States (1932, 1936), Switzerland (1948, 1980), Italy (1956, 1968), West Germany (1952, 1972) and East Germany (GDR) (1976, 1984) have won the Olympic two-man bob (instituted 1932) event twice.

The most gold medals won by an individual is three, by Meinhard Nehmer (GDR; b. 13 Jun 1941) and Bernhard Germeshausen (GDR; b. 21 Aug 1951) in the 1976 two-man, 1976 and 1980 four-man events.

The most medals won is six (two gold, two silver, two bronze) by Eugenio Monti (Italy; b. 23 Jan 1928), 1956 to 1968.

World and Olympic ■ The world four-man bob title (instituted 1924) has been won 19 times by Switzerland (1924, 1936, 1939, 1947, 1954–57, 1971–73, 1975, 1982–83, 1986–90), including their five Olympic victories.

Italy won the two-man title 14 times (1954, 1956–63, 1966, 1968–69, 1971 and 1975).

Eugenio Monti was a member of 11 world championship crews, eight two-man and three four-man in 1957–68.

United States ■ Two American bobsledders have won two gold medals: driver William Mead Lindsley 'Billy' Fiske III (1911–40) and crewman Clifford Barton Grey (1887–1941) in 1928 and 1932. At age 16 yr 260 days in 1928, Fiske was America's youngest ever Winter Games gold medalist.

Oldest gold medalist ■ The oldest at which a gold medal has been won at any sport at the Winter Olympics is 49 yr 7 days, for James Jay O'Brien (US; 1883–1940) at four-man bob.

TOBOGGANING

Origins ■ The word *toboggan* comes from the Micmac American Indian word *tobaakan.* The St Moritz Tobogganing Club, Switzerland, founded in 1887, is the oldest toboggan club in the world. It is notable for being the home of the Cresta Run, which dates from 1884, and for the introduction of the one-man skeleton racing toboggan.

Cresta Run ■ The course is 3,977 ft long with a drop of 514 ft, and the record is 50·91 sec (av. 53·27 mph) by Franco Gansser of Switzerland on 22 Feb 1987. On 21 Feb 1986 Nico Baracchi (Switzerland) set a record from Junction (2,920 ft) of 41·58 sec.

The greatest number of wins in the Grand National (instituted 1885) is eight, by the 1948 Olympic champion Nino Bibbia (Italy; b. 9 Sep 1924) in 1960–64, 1966, 1968 and 1973. The greatest number of wins in the Curzon Cup (instituted 1910) is eight, by Bibbia in 1950, 1957–58, 1960, 1962–64, and 1969. He thus won the double in 1960 and 1962–64.

LUGEING

In lugeing the rider adopts a sitting, as opposed to a prone, position. Official international competition began at Klosters, Switzerland in 1881. The first European championships were at Reichenberg, Germany in 1914 and the first World Championships at Oslo, Norway in 1953. The International Luge Federation was formed in 1957. Lugeing became an Olympic sport in 1964.

Most titles ■ The most successful riders in the World Championships have been Thomas Köhler (GDR; b. 25 Jun 1940), who won the single-seater title in 1962, 1964 (Olympic), 1966 and 1967 and shared the two-seater title in 1967 and 1968 (Olympic), and Hans Rinn (GDR; b. 19 Mar 1953), Olympic champion two-seater 1976 and 1980 and world champion at single-seater 1973 and 1977, two-seater 1977 and 1980.

Margit Schumann (GDR; b. 14 Sep 1952) has won five women's titles, 1973–5, 1976 (Olympic) and 1977.

Steffi Walter (nee Martin [GDR]; b. 17 Sep 1962) became the first rider to win two Olympic single-seater luge titles, with victories at the women's event in 1984 and 1988.

Fastest speed ■ The highest recorded, photo-timed speed is 85·38 mph, by Asle Strand (Norway) at Tandådalens Linbana, Sälen, Sweden on 1 May 1982.

The maximum 900 for a three-game series was achieved by Glenn Richard Allison (b. 22 May 1930) at the La Habra Bowl in Los Angeles, CA on 1 Jul 1982, but this was not recognized by the ABC due to the oiling patterns on the boards. It has been recorded five times in unsanctioned games—by Leon Bentley at Lorain, OH on 26 Mar 1931; by Joe Sargent at Rochester, NY in 1934; by Jim Murgie in Philadelphia, PA on 4 Feb 1937; by Bob Brown at Roseville Bowl, CA on 12 Apr 1980; and by John Strausbaugh at York, PA on 11 Jul 1987. Such series must have consisted of 36 consecutive strikes (i.e., all pins down with one ball).

The record for consecutive strikes in sanctioned match play is 33, first achieved by John Pezzin (b. 1930) at Toledo, OH on 4 Mar 1976.

The highest number of sanctioned 300 games is 33 (to Jan 1990) by James Johnson, Jr (b. 17 Aug 1960) of Wilmington, DE and Robert Learn, Jr (b. 11 Apr 1962) of Erie, PA; the women's record is 17, by Jeanne Maiden.

The highest average for a season attained in sanctioned competition is 245·58, by Paul Geiger (b. 21 Apr 1966) of Jamestown, NY in 1989/90.

The women's record is 232, by Patty Ann of Bloomington, IL in 1983/4.

Juniors ■ Brentt Arcement, at age 16, bowled a three game bowling series of 888, the highest ever bowled in a league or tournament sanctioned by the Young American Bowling Alliance, which is the national organization serving junior bowlers, ages of 21 and under.

Youngest and oldest 300 shooters ■ The youngest bowler to score 300 is said to be Richard Daff, Jr of Crownsville, MD (b. 28 Aug 1978), who performed this feat at age 11, on 8 Apr 1990. The oldest bowler to score 300 is Leo Sites of Witchita, KS, who performed the feat on 10 Apr 1985 at age 80.

Largest bowling center ■ The Fukuyama Bowl, Osaka, Japan has 144 lanes. The Tokyo World Lanes Center, Japan, now closed, had 252 lanes.

United States ■ The largest bowling center in the United States is Showboat Lanes in Las Vegas, NV, with 106 lanes.

In the United States there were 8,103 bowling establishments with 153,403 lanes in 1988–89 and approximately 71 million bowlers.

Highest score—24 hours ■ A team of six called The Three Tornadoes scored 95,467 at the Taree Ten Pin Bowl, Australia on 18–19 Nov 1989.

United States ■ The individual bowling record for 24 hours is held by Mike Cernobyl, who scored 36,922 pins in 198 games on 25–26 Aug 1989.

PROFESSIONAL BOWLERS ASSOCIATION (PBA)

Most titles ■ Earl Anthony (b. 27 Apr 1938) of Dublin, CA has won a lifetime total of 41 PBA titles through 1986. The record number of titles won in one PBA season is 8, by Mark Roth (b. 10 Apr 1951) of North Arlington, NJ, in 1978.

Consecutive titles ■ Only three bowlers have ever won three consecutive professional tournaments—Dick Weber, (three times), in 1959, 1960 and 1961, Johnny Petraglia in 1971, and Mark Roth in 1977.

Bowling

Origins ■ The ancient German game of nine-pins (*Heidenwerfen* – 'knock down pagans') was exported to the United States in the early 17th century. In 1841 the Connecticut State Legislature prohibited the game and other states followed. Eventually a tenth pin was added to evade the ban; but there is some evidence of ten pins being used in Suffolk, United Kingdom about 300 years ago. The first body to standardize rules was the American Bowling Congress (ABC), established in New York City on 9 Sep 1895.

World Championships ■ The World (Fédération Internationale des Quilleurs) Championships were instituted for men in 1954 and for women in 1963.

The highest pinfall in the individual men's event is 5,963 (in 28 games) by Ed Luther (US) at Milwaukee, WI on 28 Aug 1971.

For the current schedule of 24 games the men's record is 5,261, by Richard Clay 'Rick' Steelsmith (b. 1 Jun 1964), and the women's record is 4,894, by Sandra Jo Shiery (US), both at Helsinki, Finland in June 1987.

Highest scores ■ The highest individual score for three sanctioned games (possible 900) is 899, by Thomas Jordan (US; b. 27 Oct 1966) at Union, NJ on 7 Mar 1989.

The record by a woman is 864, by Jeanne Maiden (b. 10 Nov 1957) at Solon, OH on 23 Nov 1986.

Perfect games ■ A total of 119 perfect (300-pin) games were bowled in PBA tournaments in 1979, the most ever for one year. Dick Weber rolled three perfect games in one tournament (Houston, TX) in 1965, as did Billy Hardwick of Louisville, KY (in the Japan Gold Cup competition) in 1968, John Wilcox (at Detroit, MI) in 1979, Norm Meyers of St Louis (at Peoria, IL). In 1979, Ray Shackelford of Hartwood, VA (at St Louis, MO) in 1982, Shawn Christensen of Denver (at Denver, CO) in 1984, and Amleto Monacelli of Venezuela (at Tuscon, AZ) in 1989.

Don Johnson of Las Vegas, NV, bowled at least one perfect game in 12 consecutive seasons, Amleto Monacelli rolled 7 perfect games on the 1989 tour and Guppy Troup of Savannah, GA, rolled 6 perfect games on the 1979 tour.

Highest earners ■ Marshall Holman (b. 29 Sep 1954) won a record $1,433,856 in Professional Bowlers Association (PBA) competitions through 1989. Earl Roderick Anthony (b. 27 Apr 1938) was the first to win $1 million and won a record 41 PBA titles to 1986.

Mike Aulby of Indianapolis, IN set a single season earnings mark in 1989 of $298,237.

Television bowling ■ Nelson Burton, Jr of St Louis, rolled the best series, 1,050, for four games (278–279–257–236) at Dick Weber Lanes in Florissant, MO, 11 Feb 1984.

AMERICAN BOWLING CONGRESS (ABC)

Highest score ■ The highest individual score for three games is 899 by Thomas Jordan (b. 27 Oct 1966) at Union, NJ on 7 Mar 1989. He followed with a 299, setting a 4-game series record of 1,198 pins. Glenn Allison (b. 1930) rolled a perfect 900 in a 3-game series in league play on 1 Jul 1982, at La Habra Bowl, Los Angeles, CA but the ABC could not recognize the record when an ABC inspector determined the lanes were improperly dressed. Highest 3-game team score is 3,858 by Budweisers of St Louis on 12 Mar 1958.

The highest season average attained in sanctioned competition is 245·63 by Doug Vergouven of Harrisonville, MO in the 1989–90 season.

The all-time ABC-sanctioned 2-man single-game record is 600, held jointly by the team of John Cotta (300) and Steve Lanson (300) on 1 May 1981, at the Manteca, CA, Bowling Association Tournament; and Jeff Marz and Dave Roney of Canton, OH on 8 Nov 1987 in the Ann Doubles Classic in Canton, OH and William Gruner and Dave Conway of Oceanside, CA on 27 Feb 1990. The 2-man team series record is 1,655 by Tom Jordan (899) and Ken Yorker, Jr (856) in Union, NJ on 7 Mar 1989.

Consecutive strikes ■ The record for consecutive strikes in sanctioned match play is 33 by John Pezzin (b. 1930) at Toledo, OH on 4 Mar 1976.

Perfect scores ■ The highest number of sanctioned 300 games is 33 by 2 bowlers: Bob Learn, Jr (b. 11 Apr 1962) of Erie, PA and Jim Johnson, Jr (b. 17 Aug 1960) of Wilmington, DE.

Two perfect games were rolled back-to-back *twice* by Al Spotts of West Reading, PA on 14 Mar 1982 and again on 1 Feb 1985.

The maximum 900 for a three-game series has been recorded 6 times in unsanctioned competition—by Leo Bentley at Lorain, OH, on 26 Mar 1931; by Joe Sargent at Rochester, NY, in 1934; by Bob Brown at Roseville Bowl, CA, on 12

Apr 1980; by Glenn Allison at Whittier, CA, on 1 Jul 1982, and by John Strausbaugh at Columbia, PA, on 11 Jul 1987.

Highest individual scores ■ Highest three-game series in singles is 813 by Paul Tetreault of Lebanon, NH in 1989. Best three-game total in any ABC event is 857 by Norm Duke of Albuquerque, NM in 1989. George Hall of Mundelein, IL holds the record for a nine-game All-events total with 2,227 (747–747–733) set in Wichita, KS in 1989.

ABC Hall of Famers Fred Bujack of Detroit, MI, Bill Lillard of Houston, TX and Nelson Burton, Jr of St Louis, MO, have won the most championships with eight each. Bujack shared in three team and four team All-Events titles between 1949 and 1955, and also won the individual All-Events title in 1955. Lillard bowled on regular and team All-Events champions in 1955 and 1956, the Classic team champions in 1962 and 1971, and won regular doubles and All-Events titles in 1956. Burton shared in three Classic team titles, two Classic doubles titles and has won Classic singles twice and Classic All-Events.

Highest doubles ■ The ABC national tournament record of 561 was set in 1989 by Rick McCardy and Steve Mesmer of Redford, MI. The record score in a doubles series is 1,499 set in 1989 by Gus Yannaras (757) and Gary Daroszewski (742) of Milwaukee, WI.

Perfect scores ■ Les Schissler of Denver scored 300 in the Classic team event in 1967, and Ray Williams of Detroit scored 300 in Regular team play in 1974, the first two perfect games bowled in team competition. In all, there have been only 97 perfect games in the ABC tournament through 1990.

Best finishes ■ Mike Newman of Buffalo, NY won the doubles, All-Events, and was on two winning teams in 1989 to tie Ed Lubanski of Detroit, MI and Bill Lillard of Houston, TX as the only men to win four ABC crowns in one year.

Youngest and oldest winners ■ The youngest champion was Ronnie Knapp of New London, OH, who was a member of the 1963 Booster team champions when he was 16 years old. The oldest champion was Joe Detloff of Chicago, IL who, at the age of 72, was a winner in the 1965 Booster team event. The oldest doubles team in ABC competition totaled 165 years in 1955: Jerry Ameling (83) and Joseph Lehnbeutter (82), both from St Louis.

Strikes and spares in a row ■ In the greatest finish to win an ABC title, Ed Shay set a record of 12 strikes in a row in 1958, when he scored a perfect game for a total of 733 in singles. Most strikes in a row is 20 by Lou Viet of Milwaukee, WI in 1977. The most spares in a row is 23 by Lt Hazen Sweet of Battle Creek, MI in 1950.

Most tournament appearances ■ Bill Doehrman of Fort Wayne, IN competed in 71 consecutive ABC tournaments, beginning in 1908. (No tournaments were held 1943–45.)

WOMEN'S INTERNATIONAL BOWLING CONGRESS (WIBC)

Highest score ■ Patty Ann of Appleton, WI, had a record five-year composite average of 225·4 through the 1987–88 season. She also had the best one-season average, 232, in the 1983–84 season.

Jeanne Maiden of Solon, OH, has rolled 17

perfect games to set the WIBC career record. She also set a record of 40 consecutive strikes in 1986 and rolled an 864 on games of 300–300–264.

The highest 5-woman team score for a 3-game series is 3,419 by Custom Decorators of St Louis, MO in the 1987–88 season. The highest game score by a 5-woman team is 1,244 by Chamberlain Wholesale, of Detroit, MI, in the 1987–88 season.

Championship Tournaments ■ The highest score for a 3-game series in the annual WIBC Championship Tournament is 746 by Linda Kelly of Huber Heights, OH in the 1987 doubles event.

The record for one game is 300 by Lori Gensch of Milwaukee, WI in the 1979 doubles event, by Rose Walsh of Pomona, CA in the 1986 singles event, and by Linda Kelly of Huber Heights, OH in the 1987 singles event.

Dorothy Miller of Chicago, IL has won 10 WIBC Championship Tournament events, the most by an individual. Millie Ignizo is the only one to have won 3 WIBC Queen Tournaments, 1967, 1970, and 1971.

The highest WIBC Championship Tournament lifetime average is 199·14 by Dorothy Fothergill of Lincoln, RI, who has bowled for 10 years, but is now inactive.

Oldest and youngest players ■ Mary Covell of Chicago, IL participated in her 58th WIBC tournament in 1989. The oldest participant was Ethel Brunnick (b. 30 Aug 1887) of Santa Monica, CA, at age 99 in 1987. Mary Ann Keiper of St Louis, MO was only 5 years old when she participated in the 1952 tournament. The youngest champion was Leila Wagner (b. 12 Jul 1960) of Annapolis, MD who was 18 when she was a member of the championship 5-woman team in 1979.

Perfect games ■ The most 300 games rolled in a career is 14 by Jeanne Maiden of Solon, OH. The oldest woman to bowl a perfect game (12 strikes in a row) was Helen Duval of Berkeley, CA, at age 65 in 1982. Of all the women who rolled a perfect game, the one with the lowest average was Diane Ponza of Santa Cruz, CA who had a 112 average in the 1977–78 season.

Consecutive strikes, spares and splits ■ The record for most consecutive strikes is 40 by Jeanne Maiden (see above). Mabel Henry of Winchester, KY, had 30 consecutive spares in the 1986–87 season. Shirley Tophigh of Las Vegas, NV, holds the unenviable record of rolling 14 consecutive splits.

Boxing

Origins ■ Boxing with gloves was depicted on a fresco from the Isle of Thera, Greece, which has been dated to 1520 B.C. The earliest prize-ring code of rules was formulated in England on 16 Aug 1743 by the champion pugilist Jack Broughton (1704–89), who reigned from 1734 to 1750. Boxing had, in 1867, come under the Queensberry Rules formulated for John Sholto Douglas, 8th Marquess of Queensberry (1844–1900). New York was the first state to legalize boxing in the United States in 1896. Today professional boxing is regulated in each state by athletic or boxing commissions.

Longest fights ■ The longest recorded fight with gloves was between Andy Bowen of New Orleans (1867–94) and Jack Burke at New Orleans, LA on 6–7 Apr 1893. It lasted 110 rounds, 7 hr 19 min (9:15 P.M.–4:34 A.M.), and was declared a no contest (later changed to a draw). Bowen won an 85-round bout on 31 May 1893.

The longest bare-knuckle fight was 6 hr 15 min between James Kelly and Jack Smith at Fiery Creek, Dalesford, Victoria, Australia on 3 Dec 1855.

The greatest number of rounds was 276 in 4 hr 30 min when Jack Jones beat Patsy Tunney in Cheshire, United Kingdom in 1825.

Shortest fights ■ There is a distinction between the quickest knockout and the shortest fight. A knockout in 10½ sec (including a 10 sec count) occurred on 23 Sep 1946, when Al Couture struck Ralph Walton while the latter was adjusting a gum shield in his corner at Lewiston, ME. If the time was accurately taken it is clear that Couture must have been more than half-way across the ring from his own corner at the opening bell.

The shortest fight on record appears to be one in a Golden Gloves tournament at Minneapolis, MN on 4 Nov 1947, when Mike Collins floored Pat Brownson with the first punch and the contest was stopped, without a count, 4 sec after the bell.

The shortest world title fight was 45 sec, when Lloyd Honeyghan (United Kingdom; b. 22 Apr 1960) beat Gene Hatcher (US) in an IBF welterweight bout at Marbella, Spain on 30 Aug 1987. Some sources also quote the Al McCoy (1894–1966) first round knockout of George Chip in a middleweight contest on 7 Apr 1914 as being in 45 sec.

The shortest ever heavyweight world title fight was the James J. Jeffries (1875–1953)–Jack Finnegan bout at Detroit, MI on 6 Apr 1900, won by Jeffries in 55 sec.

Eugene Brown, on his professional debut, knocked out Ian Bockes of Hull at Leicester, United Kingdom on 13 Mar 1989. The fight was officially stopped after '10 seconds of the first round.' Bockes got up after a count of six but the referee stopped the contest.

Tallest ■ The tallest boxer to fight professionally was Gogea Mitu (b. 1914) of Romania in 1935. He was 7 ft 4 in and weighed 327 lb.

John Rankin, who won a fight in New Orleans, LA in November 1967, was reputedly also 7 ft 4 in.

Jim Culley, 'The Tipperary Giant,' who fought as a boxer and wrestled in the 1940s is also reputed to have been 7 ft 4 in.

Most fights without loss ■ Edward Henry (Harry) Greb (US; 1894–1926) was unbeaten in a sequence of 178 bouts, but these included 117 'no decision,' of which five were unofficial losses, in 1916–23.

Of boxers with complete records, Packey McFarland (US; 1888–1936) had 97 fights (5 draws) in 1905–15 without a defeat.

Pedro Carrasco (Spain; b. 7 Nov 1943) won 83 consecutive fights from 22 April 1964 to 3 Sep 1970, drew once and had a further nine wins before his loss to Armando Ramos in a WBC lightweight contest on 18 Feb 1972.

Most knockouts ■ The greatest number of finishes classed as 'knockouts' in a career (1936–63) is 145 (129 in professional bouts), by Archie Moore (US; b. Archibald Lee Wright, 13 Dec 1913 or 1916).

The record for consecutive KO's is 44, by Lamar Clark (US; b. 1 Dec 1934) from 1958 to 11 Jan 1960.

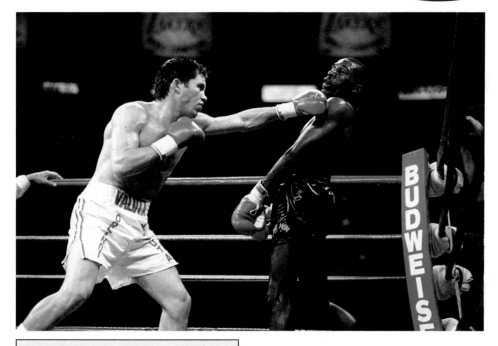

He knocked out six in one night (five in the first round) at Bingham, UT on 1 Dec 1958.

Largest purse ■ The total purse for the world heavyweight fight between Mike Gerard Tyson (US; b. 30 Jun 1966) and Michael Spinks (US; b. 22 Jul 1956) at Convention Hall, Atlantic City, NJ on 27 Jun 1988, was estimated as at least $35·8 million, $22 m for Tyson and $13·8 m for Spinks, who was knocked out after 1 min 31 sec of the first round.

Highest earnings in career ■ The greatest fortune amassed in a fighting career is an estimated $69 million by Cassius Clay (Muhammad Ali, US; b. 17 Jan 1942) from October 1960 to December 1981. This was from 61 fights (including exhibitions) comprising a total of 551 rounds.

Attendances *Highest* ■ The greatest paid attendance at any boxing fight has been 120,757 (with a ringside price of $27·50) for the Gene Tunney v Jack Dempsey world heavyweight title fight at the Sesquicentennial Stadium, Philadelphia, PA on 23 Sep 1926.

The indoor record is 63,350, at the Ali v Leon Spinks (b. 11 Jul 1956) fight in the Superdrome, New Orleans, LA on 15 Sep 1978.

The highest non-paying attendance is 135,132, at the Tony Zale v Billy Pryor fight at Juneau Park, Milwaukee, WI on 16 Aug 1941.

Lowest ■ The smallest attendance at a world heavyweight title fight was 2,434, at the Cassius (Muhammad Ali) Clay v Sonny Liston fight at Lewiston, ME on 25 May 1965.

WORLD HEAVYWEIGHT

Earliest title fight ■ Long accepted as the first world heavyweight title fight, with gloves and 3-min rounds, was that between John Lawrence Sullivan (1858–1918) and 'Gentleman' James John Corbett (1866–1933) in New Orleans, LA on 7 Sep 1892. Corbett won in 21 rounds. However the fight between Sullivan, then the

world bare-knuckle champion, and Dominick F. McCafferey in Chester Park, Cincinnati, OH on 29 Aug 1885 was staged under Queensberry Rules with the boxers wearing gloves over six rounds. The referee, Billy Tait, left the ring without giving a verdict, but when asked two days later said that Sullivan had won.

Reign *Longest* ■ Joe Louis (US; b. Joseph Louis Barrow, 1914–81) was champion for 11 years 252 days, from 22 Jun 1937, when he knocked out James Joseph Braddock in the eighth round at Chicago, IL, until announcing his retirement on 1 Mar 1949. During his reign Louis made a record 25 defenses of his title.

Shortest ■ 83 days for WBA champion James 'Bonecrusher' Smith (US; b. 3 Apr 1955), 13 Dec 1986 to 7 Mar 1987, and for Ken Norton (US; b. 9 Aug 1945), recognized by the WBC as champion from 18 Mar–9 Jun 1978. Tony Tucker (US; b. 28 Dec 1958) was IBF champion for 64 days, 30 May–2 Aug 1987.

Most recaptures ■ Muhammad Ali is the only man to regain the heavyweight championship twice. Ali first won the title on 25 Feb 1964, defeating Sonny Liston. He defeated George Foreman on 30 Oct 1974, having been stripped of the title by the world boxing authorities on 28 Apr 1967. He won the WBA title from Leon Spinks on 15 Sep 1978, having previously lost to him on 15 Feb 1978.

Undefeated ■ Rocky Marciano (b. Rocco Francis Marchegiano; 1923–69) is the only world champion at any weight to have won every fight of his entire professional career (1947–56); 43 of his 49 fights were by knockouts or stoppages.

Oldest successful challenger ■ Jersey Joe Walcott (US; b. Arnold Raymond Cream, 31 Jan 1914) was 37 yr 168 days when he knocked out Ezzard Mack Charles (1921–75) on 18 Jul 1951 in Pittsburgh, PA. He was also the oldest holder, at 38 yr 236 days, losing his title to Rocky Marciano on 23 Sep 1952.

Youngest ■ Mike Tyson (US) was 20 yr 144 days when he beat Trevor Berbick (US) to win the WBC version at Las Vegas, NV on 22 Nov 1986. He added the WBA title when he beat James 'Bonecrusher' Smith on 7 Mar 1987 at

20 yr 249 days. He became universal champion on 2 Aug 1987 when he beat Tony Tucker (US) for the IBF title.

Heaviest ■ Primo Carnera (Italy; 1906–67), the 'Ambling Alp,' who won the title from Jack Sharkey in New York City on 29 Jun 1933, scaled 260½ lb for this fight, but his peak weight was 270 lb. He had an expanded chest measurement of 54 in and the longest reach at 85½ in (fingertip to fingertip).

Lightest ■ Robert James 'Bob' Fitzsimmons (1863–1917), from Helston, Cornwall, United Kingdom weighed 167 lb when he won the title by knocking out James J. Corbett at Carson City, NV on 17 Mar 1897.

Tallest ■ There is uncertainty as to the tallest world champion. Ernest Terrell (US; b. 4 Apr 1939), WBA champion 1965–67, was reported to be 6 ft 6 in. Slightly higher figures had been given for earlier champions, but, according to measurements by the physical education director of the Hemingway Gymnasium, Harvard University, Cambridge, MA, Primo Carnera was 6 ft 5·4 in, although widely reported and believed to be up to 6 ft 8½ in. Jess Willard (1881–1968), who won the title in 1915, often stated to be 6 ft 6¼ in, was in fact 6 ft 5¼ in.

Shortest ■ Tommy Burns, world champion from 23 Feb 1906 to 26 Dec 1908, stood 5 ft 7 in and weighed between 168–180 lb.

Longest lived ■ Jack Dempsey, champion from 4 Jul 1919 to 23 Sep 1928, died at age 87 yr 341 days on 31 May 1983.

WORLD CHAMPIONS Any weight

Reign *Longest* ■ Joe Louis' heavyweight duration record of 11 yr 252 days stands for all divisions.

Shortest ■ Tony Cazonari (US; 1908–59) was world light welterweight champion for 33 days, 21 May to 23 Jun 1933, the shortest period for a boxer to have won and lost the world title in the ring.

Youngest ■ Wilfred Benitez (b. New York, 12 Sep 1958) of Puerto Rico, was 17 yr 176 days when he won the WBA light welterweight title in San Juan, Puerto Rico on 6 Mar 1976.

Oldest ■ Archie Moore, who was recognized as a light heavyweight champion up to 10 Feb 1962 when his title was removed, was then believed to be between 45 and 48.

Longest career ■ Bob Fitzsimmons had a career of over 31 years, from 1883 to 1914. He had his last world title bout on 20 Dec 1905 at the age of 42 yr 208 days. Jack Johnson (US; 1878–1946) also had a career of over 31 years, from 1897–1928.

Longest fight ■ The longest world title fight (under Queensberry Rules) was that between the lightweights Joe Gans (1874–1910), of the USA, and Oscar Matthew 'Battling' Nelson (1882–1954), the 'Durable Dane,' at Goldfield, NV on 3 Sep 1906. It was terminated in the 42nd round when Gans was declared the winner on a foul.

Most different weights ■ The first to have won world titles at four weight categories was Thomas Hearns (US; b. 18 Oct 1958), WBA welterweight in 1980, WBC super welterweight in 1982, WBC light heavyweight in 1987 and WBC middleweight in 1987. He added a fifth weight division when he won the super middleweight title recognized by the newly created World Boxing Organization (WBO) on 4 Nov 1988.

Most titles recognized by the WBA and the WBC ■ Sugar Ray Leonard (US; b. 17 May 1956) won world titles at his fourth and fifth weight categories, when he beat Donny Lalonde (Canada) on 7 Nov 1988, to annex both WBC light heavyweight and super middleweight titles. He had previously won the WBC welterweight in 1979 and 1980, WBA junior middleweight in 1981 and WBC middleweight in 1987.

The only man to hold world titles at three weights *simultaneously* was Henry 'Homicide Hank' Armstrong (US; 1912–88), at featherweight, lightweight and welterweight from August to December 1938. In recent years there has been a proliferation of weight categories and governing bodies but Armstrong was undisputed world champion at widely differing weights, which makes his achievement all the more remarkable.

Most recaptures ■ The only boxer to win a world title five times at one weight is 'Sugar' Ray Robinson (US; b. Walker Smith Jr, 1921–89), who beat Carmen Basilio (US) in Chicago Stadium, IL on 25 Mar 1958 to regain the world middleweight title for the fourth time.

The record number of title bouts in a career is 37, of which 18 ended in 'no decision,' by three-time world welterweight champion Jack Britton (US) (1885–1962) in 1915–22. The record containing no 'no decision' contests is 27 (all heavyweight), by Joe Louis between 1937–50.

Greatest weight difference ■ When Primo Carnera (Italy) 270 lb fought Tommy Loughran (US) 184 lb for the world heavyweight title at Miami, FL on 1 Mar 1934, there was a weight difference of 86 lb between the two fighters. Carnera won the fight on points.

Greatest 'tonnage' ■ The greatest 'tonnage' recorded in any fight is 700 lb, when Claude 'Humphrey' McBride (OK), 340 lb, knocked out Jimmy Black (Houston, TX), 360 lb, in the third round at Oklahoma City, OK on 1 Jun 1971.

The greatest 'tonnage' in a world title fight was 488 ¾ lb, when Carnera, then 259 ½ lb, fought Paolino Uzcudun (Spain), 229 ¼ lb, in Rome, Italy on 22 Oct 1933.

Most knockdowns in title fights ■ Vic Toweel (South Africa; b. 12 Jan 1929) knocked down Danny O'Sullivan of London 14 times in ten rounds in their world bantamweight fight at Johannesburg, South Africa on 2 Dec 1950, before the latter retired.

Twins ■ When Khaokor Galaxy (Thailand) won the WBA bantamweight title on 8 May 1988, he and his twin brother, Khaosai, were the first twins ever to be world boxing champions. Khaosai Galaxy had been WBA super flyweight champion since 21 Nov 1984.

AMATEUR

Most Olympic titles ■ Only two boxers have won three Olympic gold medals: southpaw László Papp (Hungary; b. 25 Mar 1926), middleweight winner in 1948, light-middleweight winner in 1952 and 1956; and Teofilo Stevenson (Cuba; b. 23 Mar 1952), heavyweight winner in 1972, 1976 and 1980.

The only man to win two titles in one celebration was Oliver L. Kirk (US), who won both bantam and featherweight titles in St Louis, MO in 1904, but he needed only one bout in each class.

Another record that will stand forever is that of the youngest Olympic boxing champion: Jackie

Fields (ne Finkelstein [US]; b. 9 Feb 1908), who won the 1924 featherweight title at 16 yrs 162 days. The minimum age for Olympic boxing competitors is now 17.

Oldest gold medalist ■ Richard Kenneth Gunn (United Kingdom; 1871–1961) won the Olympic featherweight gold medal on 27 Oct 1908 in London, United Kingdom at age 37 yr 254 days.

World Championships ■ Two boxers have won three world championships (instituted 1974): Teofilo Stevenson (Cuba), heavyweight winner in 1974, 1978 and super-heavyweight winner in 1986, and Adolfo Horta (Cuba; b. 3 Oct 1957), bantamweight winner in 1978, featherweight winner in 1982 and lightweight winner in 1986.

Most US titles ■ US Amateur Championships were first staged in 1888. The most titles won is five by middleweight W. Rodenbach, 1900–04.

Canoeing

The acknowledged pioneer of canoeing as a modern sport was John Macgregor (1825–92), a British barrister, in 1865. The Canoe Club was formed on 26 Jul 1866.

The oldest club in the United States is the New York Canoe Club, founded at St George, Staten Island, NY in 1871. The American Canoe Association was formed on 3 Aug 1880.

Most titles *Olympics* ■ Gert Fredriksson (Sweden; b. 21 Nov 1919) won a record six Olympic gold medals, 1948–60. He added a silver and a bronze for a record eight medals.

The most by a woman is three, by Lyudmila Iosifovna Pinayeva (nee Khvedosyuk [USSR]; b. 14 Jan 1936), 1964–72 and Birgit Schmidt (nee Fischer [GDR]; b. 25 Feb 1962), one in 1980 and two in 1988.

The most gold medals at one Games is three, by Vladimir Parfenovich (USSR; b. 2 Dec 1958) in 1980 and by Ian Ferguson (New Zealand; b. 20 Jul 1952) in 1984.

United States ■ The only American canoeist to have won two Olympic gold medals is Gregory Mark Barton (b. 2 Dec 1959), who won at K1 and K2 1,000 m events in 1988. He also has a US record three medals, as he took bronze at K1 1,000m in 1984.

World ■ Including the Olympic Games, a women's record 22 titles have been won by Birgit Schmidt, 1978–88.

The men's record is 13, by Gert Fredriksson, 1948–60, Rüdiger Helm (GDR; b. 6 Oct 1956), 1976–83, and Ivan Patzaichin (Romania; b. 26 Nov 1949), 1968–84.

Most US titles ■ Marcia Ingram Jones Smoke (b. 18 Jul 1941) won 35 US national titles between 1962 and 1981, as well as 24 North American Championships and three gold medals at the 1967 Pan-American Games. The men's record is 33 US titles by Ernest Riedel (b. 13 Jul 1901) between 1930 and 1948, mostly at kayak events.

Highest speed ■ The Hungarian four-man kayak Olympic champions in 1988 at Seoul, South Korea covered 1,000 m in 2 min 58·54 sec in a heat. This represents an average speed of 12·53 mph.

In this same race the Norwegian four achieved a 250 m split of 42·08 sec between 500 m and 750 m for a speed of 13·29 mph.

Longest journey ■ Father and son Dana

and Donald Starkell paddled from Winnipeg, Manitoba, Canada by ocean and river to Belem, Brazil, a distance of 12,181 miles, from 1 Jun 1980 to 1 May 1982. All portages were human powered.

Without portages or aid of any kind, the longest is one of 6,102 miles, by Richard H. Grant and Ernest 'Moose' Lassy, circumnavigating the eastern United States via Chicago, New Orleans, Miami, New York and the Great Lakes from 22 Sep 1930 to 15 Aug 1931.

Longest open sea voyage ■ Beatrice and John Dowd, Ken Beard and Steve Benson (Richard Gillett replaced him mid-journey) paddled 2,170 miles (of a total 2,192 miles) from Venezuela to Miami, FL, via the West Indies, 11 Aug 1977–29 Apr 1978 in two Klepper Aerius 20 kayaks.

Longest race ■ The Canadian Government Centennial Voyageur Canoe Pageant and Race from Rocky Mountain House, Alberta to the Expo 67 site at Montreal, Quebec was 3,283 miles. Ten canoes represented Canadian provinces and territories. The winner of the race, which took from 24 May to 4 Sep 1967, was the Province of Manitoba canoe *Radisson*.

24 hours *Men* ■ Zdzislaw Szubski paddled 157·1 miles in a Jaguar K1 canoe on the Vistula River, Wlocklawek to Gdansk, Poland, on 11–12 Sep 1987.

Women ■ Lydia Formentin paddled 97·2 miles on the Swan River, Western Australia in 1979.

Flat water ■ Thomas J. Mazuzan paddled, without benefit of current, 123·98 miles on the Barge Canal, NY State on 24–25 Sep 1986.

Open sea ■ Randy Fine (US) paddled 120·6 miles along the Florida coast on 26–27 Jun 1986.

Greatest lifetime distance ■ Fritz Lindner of Berlin, West Germany, totaled 64,278 miles from 1928 to 1987.

Highest altitude ■ In September 1976 Dr Michael Leslie Jones (1951–78) and Michael Hopkinson of the British Everest Canoe Expedition canoed down the River Dudh Kosi, Nepal from an altitude of 17,500 ft.

Eskimo rolls with paddle ■ Ray Hudspith (b. 18 Apr 1960) achieved 1,000 rolls in 34 min 43 sec at the Elswick Pool, Newcastle-upon-Tyne, United Kingdom on 20 Mar 1987.

Colin Hill completed 1,712 continuous rolls at Alsager Leisure Centre, Staffordshire, United Kingdom on 28 Feb 1990.

'Hand rolls' ■ Colin Brian Hill (b. 16 Aug 1970) achieved 1,000 rolls in 31 min 55·62 sec at Consett, County Durham, United Kingdom on 12 Mar 1987. He also achieved 100 rolls in 2 min 39·2 sec at Crystal Palace, London, United Kingdom on 22 Feb 1987. He completed 3,700 continuous rolls at Durham City Swimming Baths, County Durham, United Kingdom on 1 May 1989.

Canoe raft ■ A raft of 342 kayaks and canoes, held together by hands only, while free floating for 30 seconds, was established on the River Trent at Bridgeford, Nottinghamshire, United Kingdom on 26 May 1990, organized by the National Aociation of Boy's Clubs.

Card Games

CONTRACT BRIDGE
Origins ■ Bridge (a corruption of *biritch*, a now obsolete Russian word whose meanings include 'declarer') is thought either to be of Levantine origin, similar games having been played there in the early 1870s, or to have come from India.

Auction bridge (highest bidder names trump) was invented *c.* 1902. The contract principle, present in several games (notably the French game *plafond, c.* 1917), was introduced to bridge by Harold Sterling Vanderbilt (US; 1884–1970) on 1 Nov 1925 during a Caribbean voyage aboard the SS *Finland*. It became a worldwide craze after the United States *v.* Great Britain challenge match between Romanian-born Ely Culbertson (1891–1955) and Lt Col Walter Thomas More Buller (1887–1938) at Almack's Club, London, United Kingdom, in September 1930. The United States won the 200-hand match by 4,845 points.

Biggest tournament ■ The Epson World Bridge Championship, held on 8 Jun 1990, was contested by 88,000 players playing the same hands at centers in 90 countries.

Most world titles ■ The World Championship (Bermuda Bowl) has been won a record 13 times by Italy's Blue Team (Squadra Azzura), 1957–59, 1961–63, 1965–67, 1969, 1973–75 and by the US, 1950–51, 1953–54, 1970–71, 1976–77, 1979, 1981, 1983, 1985, 1987.

Italy also won the team Olympiad in 1964, 1968 and 1972.

Giorgio Belladonna (b. 7 Jun 1923) was in all the Italian winning teams.

The United States has a record five wins in the women's world championship for the Venice Trophy, 1974, 1976, 1978, 1987 and 1989, and three women's wins at the World Team Olympiad, 1976, 1980 and 1984.

Most world championship hands ■ In the 1987 Bermuda Bowl in Ocho Rios, Jamaica, Tony Forrester, from Bradford, United Kingdom, played a record 720 out of a possible 784 boards.

Most master points ■ In the latest ranking list based on Master Points awarded by the World Bridge Federation during the last ten years, the leading players in the world are (men) Robert Hamman (b. 1938) of Dallas, TX, with 597, and (women) Sandra Landy (United Kingdom), with 284.

The all-time leading Master Point winner was Giorgio Belladonna (Italy), with 1,821¼ points.

The world's leading woman player is Jacqui Mitchell (US), with 347 points.

Barry Crane of Los Angeles, CA led the American Contract Bridge League rankings from 1968 to his murder in 1985. He amassed a record total of 35,137·6 Master Points.

The current leader is Paul Soloway, with 32,772 to June 1990.

The most master points scored in a year is 3,270, by Grant Baze (US) in 1984.

The first man to win 10,000 Master Points was Oswald Jacoby (US; 1902–84), in October 1967. He had been a member of the winning World Championship team in 1935, and on 4 Dec 1983 became the oldest member of a winning team of a major open team championship, in the Curtis Reisinger Trophy.

Rika 'Rixi' Markus (Austria, later United Kingdom; b. 27 Jun 1910), one of the world leading players, has won numerous titles during an illustrious career and became the first woman World Grand Master in 1974.

Youngest Life Master ■ Dougie Hsieh (b. 23 Nov 1969) of New York City became the world's youngest ever Life Master in 1981 at 11 yr 306 days.

The youngest ever female Master is Patricia Thomas (b. 10 Oct 1968), at 14 yr 28 days in 1982.

Perfect deals ■ The mathematical odds against dealing 13 cards of one suit are 158,753,389,899 to 1, while the odds against a named player receiving a 'perfect hand' consisting of all 13 spades are 635,013,559,599 to 1. The odds against each of the four players receiving a complete suit (a 'perfect deal') are 2,235,197,406, 895,366,368,301,559,999 to 1.

Possible auctions ■ The number of possible auctions with North as dealer is 128,745,650,347, 030,683,120,231,926,111,609,371,363,122,697,557.

CRIBBAGE
Origins ■ The invention of the game (once called cribbidge) is credited to the English dramatist Sir John Suckling (1609–42).

Rare hands ■ Four maximum 29-point hands have been achieved by William E. Johnson of Waltham, MA, 1974–81, and by Mrs Mary Matheson of Springhill, Nova Scotia, Canada, 1974–85. Paul Nault of Athol, MA had two such hands within eight games in a tournament on 19 Mar 1977.

Most points in 24 hours ■ The most points scored by a team of four, playing singles in two pairs, is 111,201, by Christine and Elizabeth Gill, Jeanette MacGrath and Donald Ward at Grannie's Healin' Hame, Embo, Highland Region, United Kingdom on 2–3 May 1987.

Cricket

Origins ■ The earliest evidence of a game similar to cricket is from a drawing depicting two men playing with a bat and ball dated *c.* 1150. The game was played in Guildford, Surrey, United Kingdom, at least as early as 1550. The earliest major match of which the full score

Most runs ● In the 1989 calendar year, his first year of Test cricket, Mark Anthony Taylor (Australia; b. 27 Oct 1964) scored 1,219 runs. He played 20 innings at an average of 64·15, including 839 runs against England in six Tests (11 innings) – the 3rd highest total ever in a Test series. (Photo: All-Sport/ Pascal Rondeau)

survives was one in which a team representing England (40 and 70) was beaten by Kent (53 and 58 for 9) by one wicket at the Artillery Ground in Finsbury, London, United Kingdom on 18 Jun 1744. The first international match was played between Canada and the United States in 1844. Fifteen years later those countries were host to the first English touring team.

First-class records *Career* ■ The most runs scored in a career is 61,237, by Sir John Berry 'Jack' Hobbs (1882–1963) for Surrey and England, 1905–34. The most wickets taken by an individual is 4,187, by Wilfred Rhodes (1877–1973) for Yorkshire and England, 1898–1930. The most dismissals by a wicket-keeper is 1649, by Robert William Taylor (b. 17 Jul 1941) for Derbyshire and England, 1960–88. The most catches by a fielder is 1,018 by Frank Edward Wooley (1887–1978) for Kent and England, 1906–38.

TEST CRICKET

Origins ■ The first match, now considered as a Test match, was played at Melbourne, Australia on 15–19 Mar 1877 between Australia and England. Neither side was representative of their countries, and indeed such was the case for many matches, now accepted as Test matches, played over the next 50 years or so. Eight nations have played Test cricket; Australia, England, India, New Zealand, Pakistan, South Africa, Sri Lanka and West Indies.

Career records ■ The most runs scored by · an individual is 10,122, by Sunil Manohar Gavaskar (India; b. 10 Jul 1949), in 125 Tests, 1971–87. The most wickets taken by a bowler is 431, by Sir Richard John Hadlee (New Zealand; b. 3 Jul 1951) in 86 Tests, 1973–90. The most dismissals by a wicket-keeper is 355 by Rodney William Marsh (Australia; b. 11 Nov 1947), in 96 Tests, 1970–84. The most catches by a fielder is 125, by Allan Robert Border (Australia; b. 27 Jul 1955) in 115 Tests, 1978–90.

ONE-DAY INTERNATIONALS

The first 'limited overs' international was played at Melbourne Cricket Ground on 5 Jan 1971 between Australia and England. The Prudential (now Texaco) Trophy series of one-day internationals began in England in 1972, matches being of 55 overs per side. The Benson and Hedges World Cup Series has been held annually in Australia since 1979–80.

World Cup ■ The World Cup was held in England in 1975, 1979 and 1983, and in India and Pakistan in 1987. The West Indies are the only double winners, in 1975 and 1979. Matches were played at 60 overs per side (except at 50 overs in 1987).

One-day international records *Team* ■ The highest innings score by a team is 360–4 (50 overs), by the West Indies v Sri Lanka at Karachi, Pakistan on 13 Oct 1987. The lowest completed innings total is 45, by Canada v England at Old Trafford, United Kingdom on 14 Jun 1979. The largest victory margin is 232, by Australia v Sri Lanka (323–2 to 91), at Adelaide, Australia on 28 Jan 1985.

Individual ■ The highest individual score is 189 not out, by Isaac Vivian Alexander Richards (b. 7 Mar 1952) for the West Indies v England at Old Trafford, United Kingdom on 31 May 1984. The best bowling analysis is 7–51, by Winston Walter Davis (b. 18 Sep 1958) for the West Indies v Australia at Headingley, United Kingdom on

12 Jun 1983. The best partnership is 224, by Dean Mervyn Jones (b. 24 Mar 1961) and Allan Robert Border (b. 27 Jul 1955) for Australia v Sri Lanka at Adelaide, Australia on 28 Jan 1985

Career ■ The most matches played is 210, by Allan Border (Australia), 1979–90. The most runs scored is 6,501 (av. 47·80) by Vivian Richards (West Indies) in 179 matches, 1975–90. He has also taken most catches by a fielder, 99. The most wickets taken is 185 (av. 27·00), by Kapil Dev (India) in 157 matches, 1978–90. The most dismissals is 188 (170 catches, 18 stumpings), by Peter Jeffrey Leroy Dujon (West Indies; b. 28 Mar 1956) in 155 matches, 1981–90. Desmond Leo Haynes (West Indies; b. 15 Feb 1956) has scored a record 16 centuries in one day internationals, having played 174 matches, 1977–90.

Most extras ■ West Indies conceded 59 extras (8 byes, 10 leg byes 4 no balls and 37 wides) against Pakistan at Brisbane on 7 Jan 1989.

Croquet

Origins ■ Its exact origins are obscure, but croquet was probably derived from the French game *jeu de mail*, first mentioned in the 12th century. A game resembling croquet, possibly of foreign origin, was played in Ireland in the 1830s, and was introduced to Hampshire, United Kingdom 20 years later. The first club was formed in the Steyne Gardens, Worthing, West Sussex, United Kingdom in 1865.

International trophy ■ The MacRobertson International Shield (instituted 1925) has been won a record eight times by Great Britain, in 1925, 1937, 1956, 1963, 1969, 1974, 1982 and 1990.

A record six appearances have been made by John G. Prince (New Zealand), in 1963, 1969, 1975, 1979, 1982 and 1986; on his debut he was the youngest ever international, at 17 yr 190 days.

Cross-country Running

Origins ■ The earliest recorded international cross-country race took place over 9 miles 18 yd from Ville d'Avray, outside Paris, France on 20 Mar 1898 between England and France (England won by 21 points to 69).

World Championships ■ The inaugural International Cross-Country Championships took place at the Hamilton Park Racecourse, Scotland, United Kingdom on 28 Mar 1903.

The greatest margin of victory is 56 sec or 390 yd by John 'Jack' Thomas Holden (England; b. 13 Mar 1907) at Ayr Racecourse, Strathclyde, United Kingdom on 24 Mar 1934.

Since 1973 the events have been official world championships under the auspices of the International Amateur Athletic Federation.

The US has never won the men's team race, but Craig Steven Virgin (b. 2 Aug 1955) won the individual race twice, 1980–81.

Most wins ■ The greatest number of team victories has been by England, with 45 for men, 11 for junior men and seven for women.

The United States and USSR each have a record eight women's team victories.

The greatest team domination was by Kenya at Auckland, New Zealand on 26 March 1988. Their senior men's team finished eight men in the first nine, with a low score of 23 (six to score), and their junior men's team set a record low score, 11

(four to score) with six in the first seven. The greatest number of men's individual victories is four, by: Jack Holden (England) in 1933–35 and 1939; by Alain Mimoun-o-Kacha (France; b. 1 Jan 1921), in 1949, 1952, 1954 and 1956; by Gaston Roelants (Belgium; b. 5 Feb 1937) in 1962, 1967, 1969 and 1972; and by John Ngugi (Kenya; b. 10 May 1962), 1986–89.

The women's race has been won five times, by: Doris Brown-Heritage (US; b. 17 Sep 1942), 1967–71; and by Grete Waitz (nee Andersen [Norway]; b. 1 Oct 1953), 1978–81 and 1983.

US championship ■ First staged in 1890, the most wins in the mens race is eight, by Patrick Ralph Porter (b. 31 May 1959), 1982–89. The women's championship was first contested in 1972, and the most wins is four, by Lynn A. Jennings (b. 1 Jul 1960), 1985, 1987–89.

Most appearances ■ Marcel van de Wattyne (Belgium; b. 7 Jul 1924) ran in a record 20 races, 1946–65.

The women's record is 16 by Jean Lochhead (Wales; b. 24 Dec 1946), 1967–79, 1981, 1983–84.

Largest field ■ The largest recorded field in any cross-country race was 11,763 starters (10,810 finished), in the 18·6 miles Lidingöloppet, near Stockholm, Sweden on 3 Oct 1982.

Curling

Origins ■ Although a 15th-century bronze figure in the Florence Museum appears to be holding a curling stone, the earliest illustration of the sport was in one of the Flemish painter Pieter Bruegel's winter scenes *c.* 1560. The game was probably introduced into Scotland by Flemings in the 15th century. The earliest documented club is Muthill, Tayside, United Kingdom, formed in 1739. Organized administration began in 1838, with the formation in Edinburgh of the Grand (later Royal) Caledonian Curling Club, the international legislative body until the foundation of the International Curling Federation in 1966. Curling was first played indoors in Montreal, Canada in 1807.

The United States won the first Gordon International Medal series of matches, between Canada and the United States, at Montreal in 1884. Curling has been a demonstration sport at the Olympic Games of 1924, 1932, 1964 and 1988.

Most titles ■ Canada has won the men's World Championships (instituted 1959) 20 times, 1959–64, 1966, 1968–72, 1980, 1982–83, 1985–87, 1989–90.

The most Strathcona Cup (instituted 1903) wins is seven by Canada (1903, 1909, 1912, 1923, 1938, 1957, 1965) against Scotland.

The most women's World Championships (instituted 1979) is six, by Canada (1980, 1984–87, 1989).

The US has won the men's world title four times, with Bud Somerville skip on the first two winning teams, 1965 and 1974.

'Perfect' Game ■ Stu Beagle, of Calgary, Alberta, Canada, played a perfect game (48 points) against Nova Scotia in the Canadian Championships (Brier) at Fort William (now Thunder Bay), Ontario on 8 Mar 1960.

Bernice Fekete, of Edmonton, Alberta, Canada, skipped her rink to two consecutive eight-enders on the same ice at the Derrick Club, Edmonton on 10 Jan and 6 Feb 1973.

Two eight-enders in one bonspiel were scored at

World records ● Jeannie Longo (France) (b. 31 Oct 1958) is the current holder of a remarkable 11 cycling world records, both indoors and out. (Photo: All-Sport/Vandystadt)

the Parry Sound Curling Club, Ontario, Canada from 6–8 Jan 1983.

Fastest game ■ Eight curlers from the Burlington Golf and Country Club curled an eight-end game in 47 min 24 sec, with time penalties of 5 min 30 sec, at Burlington, Ontario, Canada on 4 Apr 1986, following rules agreed with the Ontario Curling Association. The time is taken from when the first rock crosses the near hogline until the game's last rock comes to a complete stop.

Longest throw ■ The longest throw of a curling stone was a distance of 576 ft 4 in, by Eddie Kulbacki (Canada) at Park Lake, Neepawa, Manitoba, Canada on 29 Jan 1989. The attempt took place on a specially prepared sheet of curling ice on frozen Park Lake, a record 1,200 ft long.

Largest bonspiel ■ The largest bonspiel (curling tournament) in the world is the Manitoba Curling Association Bonspiel, held annually in Winnipeg, Canada. In 1988 there were 1,424 teams of four men, a total of 5,696 curlers, using 187 sheets of curling ice.

Largest rink ■ The world's largest curling rink is the Big Four Curling Rink, Calgary, Alberta, Canada, opened in 1959. Ninety–six teams and 384 players are accommodated on two floors, each with 24 sheets of ice.

Cycling

Origins ■ The earliest recorded bicycle race was a velocipede race over 1·24 miles at the Parc de St Cloud, Paris on 31 May 1868, won by Dr James Moore (United Kingdom; 1847–1935) (later Chevalier de la Légion d'Honneur).

The first recorded cycle race in the United States was in September 1883 when G. M. Hendrie beat W. G. Rowe in a road race.

Highest speed ■ The highest speed ever achieved on a bicycle is 152·284 mph, by John Howard (US) behind a windshield at Bonneville Salt Flats, UT on 20 Jul 1985. It should be noted that considerable help was provided by the slipstreaming effect of the lead vehicle.

The 24 hr record behind pace is 860 miles 367 yd by Hubert Ferdinand Opperman (later the Hon. Sir; b. 29 May 1904) in Melbourne, Australia on 23 May 1932.

Most titles *Olympic* ■ The most gold medals won is three, by Paul Masson (France; 1874–1945) in 1896, Francisco Verri (Italy; 1885–

1945) in 1906; and Robert Charpentier (France; 1916–66) in 1936. Daniel Morelon (France) won two in 1968, and a third in 1972; he also won a silver in 1976 and a bronze medal in 1964. In the 'unofficial' 1904 cycling program, Marcus Latimer Hurley (US; 1885–1941) won four events.

Burton Cecil Down (1885–1929) won a record six medals at the 1904 Games, two gold, three silver and one bronze. The only US woman to win a cycling gold medal is Helen Constance 'Connie' Carpenter-Phinney (b. 26 Feb 1957), who won the individual road race in 1984. She became the first woman to compete in the winter and summer Olympics, as she had competed as a speed skater in 1972.

World ■ World Championships are contested annually. They were first staged for amateurs in 1893 and for professionals in 1895.

The most wins at a particular event is ten, by Koichi Nakano (Japan; b. 14 Nov 1955), professional sprint 1977–86.

The most wins at a men's amateur event is seven, by; Daniel Morelon (France; b. 28 Jul 1944), sprint 1966–67, 1969–71, 1973, 1975; and Leon Meredith (United Kingdom; 1882–1930), 100 km motor paced 1904–5, 1907–9, 1911, 1913.

The most women's titles is seven, by: Beryl Burton (United Kingdom; b. 12 May 1937), pur-

Most wins ● Wearing the distinctive yellow jersey, Eddy Merckx (Belguim) (b. 17 Jun 1945) leads the Tour de France. Merckx is one of three men to have won this famous race a record five times, winning in 1969–72 and 1974. (Photo: All-Sport)

suit 1959–60, 1962–63, 1966 and road 1960, 1967; Yvonne Reynders (Belgium), pursuit 1961, 1964–65 and road 1959, 1961, 1963, 1966; Jeannie Longo (France; b. 31 Oct 1958), pursuit 1986 and 1988–89 and road 1985–87 and 1989.

The most world titles won by a US cyclist is four, at women's 3 kilometers pursuit by Rebecca Twigg (b. 26 Mar 1963), 1982, 1984–85 and 1987. The most successful man has been Greg LeMond (b. 26 Jun 1960), winner of the individual road race in 1983 and 1989.

Tour de France ■ The greatest number of wins in the Tour de France (inaugurated 1903) is five, by Jacques Anquetil (France; 1934–1987), 1957, 1961–64; Eddy Merckx (Belgium; b. 17 Jun 1945), 1969–72 and 1974; and Bernard Hinault (France; b. 14 Nov 1954); 1978–79, 1981–82 and 1985.

Greg LeMond became the first American winner in 1986, and returned from serious injury to win in 1989 and 1990.

The closest race ever was in 1989 when after 2,030 miles over 23 days (1–23 Jul) Greg LeMond (US; b. 26 Jun 1960), who completed the Tour in 87 hr 38 min 35 sec, beat Laurent Fignon (France; b. 12 Aug 1960) in Paris by only 8 sec.

The fastest average speed was 24·16 mph by Pedro Delgado (Spain; b. 15 Apr 1960) in 1988.

The longest ever stage was the 486 km from Les Sables d'Olonne to Bayonne in 1919. The most participants was 204 starters in 1987

Six-day races ■ The most wins in six-day races is 88 out of 233 events, by Patrick Sercu (b. 27 Jun 1944), of Belgium, 1964–83.

Longest one-day race ■ The longest single-day 'massed start' road race is the 342–385 miles Bordeaux–Paris, France, event. Paced over all or part of the route, the highest average speed was 29·32 mph, by Herman van Springel (Belgium; b. 14 Aug 1943) for 363·1 miles in 13 hr 35 min 18 sec, in 1981.

Cross-America ■ The trans-America solo records recognized by the Ultra-Marathon Cycling Association for men is 8 days 8 hr 45 min, by Paul Selon at age 35 from Costa, CA to

WORLD RECORDS

Records are recognized by the Union Cycliste Internationale (UCI) for both professionals and amateurs on open air and indoor tracks for a variety of distances at unpaced flying and standing starts and for motor-paced. In this list only the best are shown, with a † to signify those records set by a professional rather than an amateur.

OPEN–AIR TRACKS

MEN

Distance	hr:min:sec	Name and country	Venue	Date
Unpaced standing start				
1 km	1:02·091	Maic Malchow (East Germany)	Colorado Springs, CO	28 Aug 1986
4 km	4:31·160	Gintautas Umaras (USSR)	Seoul, South Korea	18 Sep 1987
5 km	5:44·700	Gregor Braun (W. Germany)†	La Paz, Bolivia	12 Jan 1986
10 km	11:39·720	Francesco Moser (Italy)†	Mexico City, Mexico	19 Jan 1984
20 km	23:21·592	Francesco Moser (Italy)†	Mexico City, Mexico	23 Jan 1984
100 km	2:09:11·312	Kent Bostick (US)	Colorado Springs, CO	13 Oct 1989
1 hour	51·151 km	Francesco Moser (Italy)†	Mexico City, Mexico	23 Jan 1984
Unpaced flying start				
200 metres	10·118	Michael Hübner (East Germany)	Colorado Springs, CO	27 Aug 1986
500 metres	26·776	Philippe Boyer (France)†	La Paz, Bolivia	June 1989
1 km	58·269	Dominguez Rueda Efrain (Colombia)†	La Paz, Bolivia	13 Dec 1986
Motor-paced				
50 km	35:21·108	Aleksandr Romanov (USSR)	Tbilisi, USSR	6 May 1987
100 km	1:10:29·420	Giovanni Renosto (Italy)	Bassano del Grappa, Italy	16 Sep 1988
1 hour	85·067 km	Giovanni Renosto (Italy)	Bassano del Grappa, Italy	16 Sep 1988

WOMEN

Distance	hr:min:sec	Name and country	Venue	Date
Unpaced standing start				
1 km	1:14·249	Erika Salumyae (USSR)	Tashkent, USSR	17 May 1984
3 km	3:38·190	Jeannie Longo (France)	Mexico City, Mexico	5 Oct 1989
5 km	6:14·135	Jeannie Longo (France)	Mexico City, Mexico	27 Sep 1989
10 km	12:59·435	Jeannie Longo (France)	Mexico City, Mexico	1 Oct 1989
20 km	25:59·883	Jeannie Longo (France)	Mexico City, Mexico	1 Oct 1989
100 km	2:28:26·259	Francesca Galli (Italy)	Milan, Italy	26 Oct 1987
1 hour	46·35270km	Jeannie Longo (France)	Mexico City, Mexico	1 Oct 1989
Unpaced flying start				
200 metres	11·383	Isabelle Gautheron (France)	Colorado Springs, CO	16 Aug 1986
500 metres	30·59	Isabelle Gautheron (France)	Cali, Colombia	14 Sep 1986
1 km	1:10·463	Erika Salumyae (USSR)	Tashkent, USSR	15 May 1984

Many of the above venues, such as La Paz, Colorado Springs, Cali and Mexico City, are at high altitude. The UCI recognises separate world records for the classic one-hour event at venues below 600 metres. These are: MEN 49·80193 km Francesco Moser on 3 Oct 1986, WOMEN 43·58789 km Jeannie Longo on 30 Sep 1986, both at Milan.

INDOOR TRACKS

MEN

Distance	hr:min:sec	Name and country	Venue	Date
Unpaced standing start				
1 km	1:02·576	Aleksandr Kirichenko (USSR)	Moscow, USSR	2 Aug 1989
4 km	4:28·900	Vyachselav Yekimov (USSR)	Moscow, USSR	20 Sep 1986
5 km	5:39·316	Vyachselav Yekimov (USSR)	Moscow, USSR	25 Apr 1990
10 km	11:31·968	Vyachselav Yekimov (USSR)	Moscow, USSR	7 Jan 1989
20 km	23:14·553	Vyachselav Yekimov (USSR)	Moscow, USSR	3 Feb 1989
100 km	2:10:08·287	Beat Meister (Switzerland)	Stuttgart, W. Germany	22 Sep 1989
4 km team	4:10·877	(Vyacheslav Yekimov, Dmitriy Nelyubin, Mikhail Orlov, Yevgeniy Berzin)	Moscow, USSR	4 Aug 1989
1 hour	50·644 km	Francesco Moser (Italy)	Stuttgart, W. Germany	21 May 1988
Unpaced flying start				
200 metres	10·117	Nikolay Kovch (USSR)	Moscow, USSR	5 Feb 1988
500 metres	26·649	Aleksandr Kirichenko (USSR)	Moscow, USSR	29 Oct 1988
1 km	57·260	Aleksandr Kirichenko (USSR)	Moscow, USSR	25 Apr 1989
Motor-paced				
50 km	32:56·746	Aleksandr Romanov (USSR)	Moscow, USSR	21 Feb 1987
100 km	1:05:58·031	Aleksandr Romanov (USSR)	Moscow, USSR	21 Feb 1987
1 hour	91·131 km	Aleksandr Romanov (USSR)	Moscow, USSR	21 Feb 1987

WOMEN

Distance	hr:min:sec	Name and country	Venue	Date
Unpaced standing start				
1 km	1:13·377	Erika Salumyae (USSR)	Moscow, USSR	21 Sep 1983
3 km	3:43·490	Jeannie Longo (France)	Paris, France	14 Nov 1986
5 km	6:22·713	Jeannie Longo (France)	Grenoble, France	2 Nov 1986
10 km	12:54·26	Jeannie Longo (France)	Paris, France	19 Oct 1989
20 km	26:51·222	Jeannie Longo (France)	Moscow, USSR	29 Oct 1989
100 km	2:31:30·043	Mieke Havik (Netherlands)	Rotterdam, Netherlands	19 Sep 1983
1 hour	45·016 km	Jeannie Longo (France)	Moscow, USSR	29 Oct 1989
Unpaced flying start				
200 metres	11·170	Erika Salumyae (USSR)	Moscow, USSR	1 Aug 1989
500 metres	29·655	Erika Salumyae (USSR)	Moscow, USSR	6 Aug 1987
1 km	1:05·232	Erika Salumyae (USSR)	Moscow, USSR	30 May 1987
LONG DISTANCE BESTS (unpaced)				
24 hr	830·79 km	Michael L. Secrest (US)	Montreal, Canada	13–14 Mar 1985
1,000 km	32 hr 4 min	Herman de Munck (Belgium)	Keerbergen, Belgium	23–24 Sep 1983
1,000 miles	51:12:32	Herman de Munck (Belgium)	Keerbergen, Belgium	23–25 Sep 1983

New York, in the 1989 Race Across AMerica. Selon won the race while wearing a plastic neck brace. The women's record is 9 days 9 hr 9 min, by Susan Notorangelo at age 35, also in the 1989 Race Across AMerica. She clipped 16 hr 55 min off the previous ladies record.

The trans-Canada record is 13 days 15 hr 4 min, by Ronald J. Dossenbach of Windsor, Ontario, from Vancouver, BC to Halifax, Nova Scotia on 30 Jul–13 Aug 1988, a distance of 3,800 miles.

Daniel Buettner, Bret Anderson, Martin Engel and Anne Knabe cycled the length of the Americas, from Prudhoe Bay, AK to the Beagle Channel, Ushuaia, Argentina, from 8 Aug 1986–13 Jun 1987. They cycled a total distance of 15,266 miles.

Pete Penseyres and Len Haldeman of Harvard, IL, set a transcontinental tandem record of 7 days 14 hr 55 min in May 1987 from Huntington Beach, CA to Atlantic City, NJ. It was the fastest ever crossing on a bicycle.

Endurance ■ Thomas Edward Godwin (United Kingdom; 1912–75) in the 365 days of 1939, covered 75,065 miles, or an average of 205·65 miles per day. He then completed 100,000 miles in 500 days to 14 May 1940.

Jay Aldous and Matt DeWaal cycled 14,290 miles on an around-the-world trip from Place Monument, Salt Lake City, UT in 106 days, from 2 Apr–16 Jul 1984.

Nicholas Mark Sanders (b. 26 Nov 1957) of Glossop, Derbyshire, United Kingdom, circumnavigated the world (13,035 road miles) in 78 days 3 hr 30 min between 5 Jul and 21 Sep 1985.

Cycle touring ■ The greatest mileage amassed in a cycle tour was more than 402,000 miles, by the itinerant lecturer Walter Stolle (b. Sudetenland, 1926) from 24 Jan 1959 to 12 Dec 1976. He visited 159 countries, starting from Romford, Essex, United Kingdom.

From 1922 to 25 Dec 1973 Tommy Chambers (1903–84) of Glasgow, United Kingdom rode a verified total of 799,405 miles.

Visiting every continent, John W. Hathaway (United Kingdom; b. 13 Jan 1925) of Vancouver, Canada covered 50,600 miles from 10 Nov 1974 to 6 Oct 1976. Veronica and Colin Scargill, of Bedford, United Kingdom, traveled 18,020 miles around the world on a tandem, 25 Feb 1974–27 Aug 1975.

The most participants in a bicycle tour was 31,678 in the 56-mile London to Brighton Bike Ride (United Kingdom) on 19 Jun 1988.

The most participants in a tour in an excess of 1,000 km is 2,037 (from 2,157 starters) for the Australian Bicentennial Caltex Bike Ride from Melbourne to Sydney, from 26 Nov–10 Dec 1988.

Highest ■ Mark Merrony of Tenby, Dyfed, United Kingdom cycled at an altitude of 21,030 ft close to the relatively flat south summit of Mera Peak, Nepal on 7 May 1989.

CYCLO-CROSS
The greatest number of World Championships (instituted 1950) has been won by Eric de Vlaeminck (Belgium; b. 23 Aug 1945) with the Amateur and Open in 1966 and six Professional titles in 1968–73.

ROLLER CYCLING
James Baker (US) achieved a record speed of 153·2 mph at El Con Mall, Tucson, AZ on 28 Jan 1989.

Darts

Origins ■ Darts can be dated from the use by archers of heavily weighted 10-inch throwing arrows for self-defense in close-quarters fighting. The 'dartes' were used in Ireland in the 16th century and darts was played on the *Mayflower* by the Plymouth Pilgrims in 1620. The modern game dates from at least 1896, when Brian Gamlin of Bury, Lancashire, United Kingdom is credited with inventing the present numbering system on the board. The first recorded score of 180 was by John Reader at the Highbury Tavern in Sussex, United Kingdom in 1902.

Most titles ■ Eric Bristow (b. 25 Apr 1957) has most wins in the World Masters Championship (instituted 1974), with five, 1977, 1979, 1981 and 1983–84, the World Professional Championship (instituted 1978), with five, 1980–81 and 1984–86, and the World Cup Singles (instituted 1977), four, 1983, 1985, 1987 and 1989.

Seven men have won the annual *News of the World* Individual Championship twice; the most recent two-time winners have been Eric Bristow, 1983–84 and Mike Gregory (b. 16 Dec 1956), in 1987 and 1988.

John Lowe (b. 21 Jul 1945) is the only other man to have won each of the four major titles: World Masters, 1976 and 1980; World Professional, 1979 and 1987; World Cup Singles, 1981; and *News of the World*, 1981.

World Cup ■ The first World Cup was held at the Wembley Conference Centre, London, United Kingdom in 1977.

England has a record six wins at this biennial tournament. Eric Bristow and John Lowe played on all six teams.

A biennial World Cup for women was instituted in 1983 and has been won three times by England.

Record prize ■ John Lowe won £102,000 for achieving the first 501 scored with the minimum nine darts in a major event on 13 Oct 1984 at Slough in the quarter-finals of the World Matchplay Championships. His darts were six successive treble 20s, treble 17, treble 18 and double 18.

Speed records ■ The fastest time taken to complete three games of 301, finishing on doubles, is 1 min 47 sec, by Keith Deller on British Broadcasting Corporation TV's 'Record Breakers' on 22 Oct 1985.

The record time for going around the board clockwise in 'doubles' at arm's length is 9·2 sec, by Dennis Gower at the Millers Arms, Hastings, East Sussex, United Kingdom on 12 Oct 1975 and 14·5 sec in numerical order by Jim Pike (1903–60) at the Craven Club, Newmarket, Suffolk, United Kingdom in March 1944.

The record for this feat at the 9-ft throwing distance, retrieving own darts, is 2 min 13 sec, by Bill Duddy (b. 29 Sep 1932) at The Plough, Haringey, London, United Kingdom on 29 Oct 1972.

Least darts ■ Scores of 201 in four darts, 301 in six darts, 401 in seven darts and 501 in nine darts have been achieved on various occasions.

Roy Edwin Blowes (Canada; b. 8 Oct 1930) was the first person to achieve a 501 in nine darts, 'double-on, double-off,' at the Widgeons Pub, Calgary, Canada on 9 Mar 1987. His scores were; Bull, treble 20, treble 17, five treble 20s and a double 20 to finish.

The lowest number of darts thrown for a score of

1,001 is 19, by: Cliff Inglis (b. 27 May 1935) (160, 180, 140, 180, 121, 180, 40) at the Bromfield Men's Club, Devon, United Kingdom on 11 Nov 1975 and Jocky Wilson (140, 140, 180, 180, 180, 131, Bull) at The London Pride, Bletchley, Buckinghamshire, United Kingdom on 23 Mar 1989.

A score of 2,001 in 52 darts was achieved by Alan Evans (b. 14 Jun 1949) at Ferndale, Mid Glamorgan, United Kingdom on 3 Sep 1976.

A score of 3,001 in 73 darts was thrown by Tony Benson at the Plough Inn, Gorton, Manchester, United Kingdom on 12 Jul 1986.

Linda Batten (b. 26 Nov 1954) set a women's 3,001 record of 117 darts at the Old Wheatsheaf, Enfield, London, United Kingdom on 2 Apr 1986.

A score of 100,001 was achieved in 3,732 darts by Alan Downie of Stornoway, United Kingdom on 21 Nov 1986.

Equestrian Sports

Origins ■ Evidence of horse riding dates from a Persian engraving dated *c*. 3000 B.C. Pignatelli's academy of horsemanship at Naples dates from the 16th century. The earliest jumping competition was at the Agricultural Hall, London, United Kingdom, in 1869. Equestrian events have been included in the Olympic Games since 1912.

SHOW JUMPING
Olympic Games ■ The most Olympic gold medals won by a ride is five, by Hans-Günter Winkler (West Germany; b. 24 Jul 1926), four team in 1956, 1960, 1964 and 1972 and the individual Grand Prix in 1956. He also won team silver in 1976 and team bronze in 1968, for a record seven medals overall.

The most team wins in the Prix des Nations is six, by Germany in 1936, 1956, 1960, 1964 and as West Germany in 1972 and 1988. The lowest score obtained by a winner is no faults, by Frantisek Ventura (Czechoslovakia; 1895–1969) on Eliot, 1928, and Alwin Schockemöhle (West Germany; b. 29 May 1937) on Warwick Rex, 1976.

Pierre Jonquères d'Oriola (France; b. 1 Feb 1920), uniquely won the individual gold medal twice, 1952 and 1964.

United States ■ Two US riders have won individual gold medals: William Clark Steinkraus (b. 12 Oct 1925) won in 1968 and also won two silver and a bronze medal, 1952–68, and Joseph Halpin 'Joe' Fargis (b. 4 Feb 1948) won both individual and team gold medals in 1984 as well as team silver in 1988.

World Championships ■ The men's World Championships (instituted 1953) have been won twice by Hans-Günter Winkler (West Germany) (1954–55) and Raimondo d'Inzeo (Italy) (1956 and 1960).

The women's title (1965–74) was won twice by Jane 'Janou' Tissot (nee Lefebvre, [France]; b. Saigon, 14 May 1945) on Rocket (1970 and 1974).

President's Cup ■ The world team championship (instituted 1965) has been won a record 13 times by Great Britain, 1965, 1967, 1970, 1972–74, 1977–79, 1983, 1985–86, 1989.

World Cup ■ Instituted in 1979, the only double winners have been Conrad Homfeld (US; b. 25 Dec 1951), 1980 and 1985 and Ian Miller (Canada; b. 6 Jan 1947), 1988 and 1989.

Jumping records ■ The official Fédération Equestre Internationale records are: high jump, 8 ft 1¼ in, by Huasó, ridden by Capt Alberto Larraguibel Morales (Chile) at Viña del Mar, Santiago, Chile on 5 Feb 1949; long jump over water, 27 ft 6¾ in by, Something, ridden by André Ferreira (South Africa) at Johannesburg, South Africa on 25 Apr 1975.

THREE-DAY EVENT
Olympic Games & World Championships ■ Charles Ferdinand Pahud de Mortanges (Netherlands; 1896–1971), won a record four Olympic gold medals, team 1924 and 1928, individual (riding Marcroix) 1928 and 1932, He also won a team silver medal in 1932.

Bruce Oram Davidson (US; b. 13 Dec 1949) is the only rider to have won two world titles (instituted 1966), on Irish Cap in 1974 and Might Tango in 1978.

United States ■ The most medals won for the US is six, by John Michael Plumb (b. 28 Mar 1940); team gold 1976 and 1984, and four silver medals, team 1964, 1968 and 1972, and individual 1976. Edmund Sloane 'Tad' Coffin (b. 9 May 1955) is the one US rider to have won both team and individual gold medals in 1976.

DRESSAGE
Olympic Games & World Championships ■ Germany (West Germany post-1968) has won a record seven team gold medals, 1928, 1936, 1964, 1968, 1976, 1984 and 1988, and has most team wins, six, at the World Championships (instituted 1966). Dr Reiner Klimke (West Germany; b. 14 Jan 1936) has won a record six Olympic golds (team 1964–88, individual, 1984) and won individual bronze in 1976, for a record seven medals overall. He is the only rider to win two world titles, on Mehmed in 1974 and Ahlerich in 1982. Henri St Cyr (Sweden; 1904–79) won a record two individual Olympic gold medals, 1952 and 1956.

World Cup ■ Instituted in 1986, the only double winner is Christine Stückelberger (Switzerland) on Gauguin de Lully in 1987–88.

CARRIAGE DRIVING
World Championships were first held in 1972. Three team titles have been won by Great Britain, 1972, 1974 and 1980; Hungary 1976, 1978 and 1984; and the Netherlands, 1982, 1986 and 1988.

Two individual titles have been won by György Bárdos (Hungary), 1978 and 1980, and by Tjeerd Velstra (Netherlands), 1982 and 1986.

LONGEST RIDE ■ Henry G. Perry, a stockman from Mollongghip, Victoria, Australia rode 14,021 miles around Australia in 157 days, 1 May to 4 Oct 1985, with six horses.

Fencing

Origins ■ 'Fencing' (fighting with single sticks) was practiced as a sport, or as a part of a religious ceremony, in Egypt as early as *c.* 1360 B.C.

The modern foil was introduced in France as a practice weapon for the short court sword in the mid-17th century. In the late 19th century the épée was developed in France and the light fencing saber in Italy.

In the United States the Amateur Fencers League of America (AFLA) was founded on 22 Apr 1891 in New York City. This group assumed supervision of the sport in the United States. In June 1981 the AFLA changed its name to the United States Fencing Association (USFA).

Most titles *World* ■ The greatest number of individual world titles won is five, by Aleksandr Romankov (USSR; b. 7 Nov 1953), at foil 1974, 1977, 1979, 1982 and 1983, but Christian d'Oriola (France) won four world foil titles, 1947, 1949, 1953–54, as well as two individual Olympic titles.

Four women foilists have won three world titles: Hélène Mayer (Germany; 1910–53), 1929, 1931, 1937; Ilona Schacherer-Elek (Hungary; 1907–88), 1934–5, 1951; Ellen Müller–Preis (Austria; b. 6 May 1912), 1947, 1949–50; and Cornelia Hanisch (West Germany; b. 12 Jun 1952), 1979, 1981, 1985. Of these only Ilona Schacherer-Elek also won two individual Olympic titles (1936 and 1948). The longest span of winning a World/Olympic

---

Most international appearances ● Heiner Dopp (b. 27 Jun 1956) has represented West Germany a record 281 times, between 1975 and 1989, both indoors and out. (Photo: All-Sport/Simon Bruty)

title is 20 years, by Aladár Gerevich (Hungary; b. 16 Mar 1910) at saber, 1935–55.

Olympic ■ The most individual Olympic gold medals won is three, by Ramón Fonst (Cuba; 1883–1959), in 1900 and 1904 (two) and by Nedo Nadi (Italy; 1894–1952), in 1912 and 1920 (two). Nadi also won three team gold medals in 1920, making five gold medals at one celebration, the record for fencing and then a record for any sport.

Edoardo Mangiarotti (Italy; b. 7 Apr 1919), with six gold, five silver and two bronze, holds the record of 13 Olympic medals. He won them for foil and épée from 1936 to 1960.

The most gold medals won by a woman is four (one individual, three team), by Yelena Dmitryevna Novikova (nee Byelova, [USSR]; b. 28 Jul 1947), from 1968 to 1976, and the record for all medals is seven (two gold, three silver, two bronze), by Ildikó Sági (formerly Ujlaki, nee Retjö, [Hungary]; b. 11 May 1937), from 1960 to 1976.

United States ■ The only US Olympic champion was Albertson Van Zo Post (1866–1938), who won the men's single sticks and team foil (with two Cubans) at the 1904 Games.

United States National Championships ■ The most US titles won at one weapon is twelve at sabre, by Peter J. Westbrook, in 1974, 1975, 1978–86, 1988 and 1989. The women's record is ten at foil, by Janice Lee York Romany (b. 6 Aug 1928) in 1950–51, 1960–61, 1964–66 and 1968. Both York Romany and Norman Cudworth Armitage (ne Cohn; 1907–72), who won ten US titles at saber, competed at a record six Olympic Games (see Olympics).

The most individual épée championships won is seven, by Michael Marx in 1977, 1979, 1982, 1985–87 and 1990. L. G. Nunes won the most foil championships, with six, 1917, 1922, 1924, 1926, 1928 and 1932. Vincent Bradford won a record number of women's épée championships with four in 1982–84 and 1986.

Field Hockey

Origins ■ A representation of two players with curved snagging sticks apparently in an orthodox 'bully' position was found in Tomb No. 17 at Beni Hasan, Egypt, and has been dated to *c.* 2050 B.C. The modern game evolved in south London, United Kingdom in the 1870s.

The Fédération Internationale de Hockey was formed on 7 Jan 1924.

Most Olympic medals ■ India was Olympic champion from the reintroduction of Olympic hockey in 1928 until 1960, when Pakistan beat them 1–0 at Rome, Italy. They had their eighth win in 1980. Of the seven Indians who have won three Olympic team gold medals two have also won a silver medal – Leslie Walter Claudius (b. 25 Mar 1927), in 1948, 1952, 1956 and 1960 (silver), and Udham Singh (b. 4 Aug 1928), in 1952, 1956, 1964 and 1960 (silver).

A women's tournament was added in 1980, when Zimbabwe were the winners. The Netherlands won in 1984 and Australia in 1988.

United States ■ The US men won the bronze medal in 1932, but only three teams played that year, and the US women won the bronze in 1984.

World Cup ■ The World Cup for men was

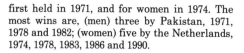 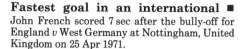 

first held in 1971, and for women in 1974. The most wins are, (men) three by Pakistan, 1971, 1978 and 1982; (women) five by the Netherlands, 1974, 1978, 1983, 1986 and 1990.

Champions' Trophy ■ First held in 1978 and contested annually since 1980 by the top six men's teams in the world; the most wins is four, by Australia, 1983–85, 1989. The first women's Champions' Trophy was won by the Netherlands in 1987. South Korea won in 1989.

MEN

The first international match was the Wales *v* Ireland match at Rhyl, Clywd, United Kingdom on 26 Jan 1895. Ireland won 3–0.

Highest international score ■ The highest score was when India defeated the United States 24–1 at Los Angeles, CA in the 1932 Olympic Games.

Most international appearances ■ Heiner Dopp (b. 27 Jun 1956) represented West Germany 283 times between 1975 and 1990, indoors and out.

Greatest scoring feats ■ The greatest number of goals scored in international hockey is 267, by Paul Litjens (Netherlands; b. 9 Nov 1947) in 177 games.

Fastest goal in an international ■ John French scored 7 sec after the bully-off for England *v* West Germany at Nottingham, United Kingdom on 25 Apr 1971.

Greatest goalkeeping ■ Richard James Allen (India; b. 4 Jun 1902) did not concede a goal during the 1928 Olympic tournament and a total of only three in the following two Olympics of 1932 and 1936. In these three Games India scored a total of 102 goals.

Longest game ■ The longest international game on record was one of 145 min (into the sixth period of extra time), when the Netherlands beat Spain 1–0 in the Olympic tournament at Mexico City, Mexico on 25 Oct 1968.

Club matches of 205 min have twice been recorded: the Hong Kong Football Club beat Prison Sports Dept as the first to score in a 'sudden death' play-off after 2–2 at full time on 11 Mar 1979, and Gore Court beat Hampstead in the first round of the English Club Championships in 1983.

WOMEN

The first national association was the Irish Ladies' Hockey Union founded in 1894.

The first international match was an England *v* Ireland game in Dublin in 1896. Ireland won 2–0.

Most international appearances ■ Valerie Robinson made a record 144 appearances for England, from 1963 to 1984.

Highest scores ■ The highest score in an international match was when England beat France 23–0 at Merton, London, United Kingdom on 3 Feb 1923.

Highest attendance ■ The highest attendance was 65,165 for the match between England and the United States at Wembley, London, United Kingdom on 11 Mar 1978.

Fishing

Oldest existing club ■ The Ellem fishing club was formed by a number of Edinburgh and Berwickshire gentlemen in Scotland, United Kingdom in 1829. Its first annual general meeting was held on 29 Apr 1830.

Largest single catch ■ The largest officially ratified fish ever caught on a rod was a man-eating great white shark (*Carcharodon carcharias*) weighing 2,664 lb and measuring 16 ft 10 in long, caught on a 130-lb test line by Alf Dean at Denial Bay, near Ceduna, South Australia on 21 Apr 1959. A great white shark weighing 3,388 lb was caught by Clive Green off Albany,

---

WORLD RECORDS; FRESHWATER AND SALTWATER

A selection of All-Tackle records ratified by the International Game Fish Association as at January 1990

Species	Weight lb oz	Name of Angler	Location	Date
BARRACUDA, GREAT	83 0	K. J. W. Hackett	Lagos, Nigeria	13 Jan 1952
BASS, EUROPEAN	20 11	Jean Baptiste Bayle	Saintes Maries de la Mer, France	6 May 1986
BASS, LARGEMOUTH	22 4	George W. Perry	Montgomery Lake, GA	2 Jun 1932
BASS, SMALLMOUTH	11 15	David L. Hayes	Dale Hollow Lake, KY	9 Jul 1955
BASS, STRIPED	78 8	Albert R. McReynolds	Atlantic City, NJ	21 Sep 1982
BLUEFISH	31 12	James M. Hussey	Hatteras, NC	30 Jan 1972
BONEFISH	19 0	Brian W. Batchelor	Zululand, South Africa	26 May 1962
CATFISH, FLATHEAD	98 0	William O. Stephens	Lewisville, TX	2 Jun 1986
COD, ATLANTIC	98 12	Alphonse J. Bielevich	Isle of Shoals, NH	8 Jun 1969
DOLPHIN	87 0	Manuel Salazar	Papagallo Gulf, Costa Rica	25 Sep 1976
HALIBUT (Pacific)	356 8	Gregory C. Olsen	Juneau, AK	8 Nov 1986
JACK, CREVALLE	54 7	Thomas F. Gibson, Jr	Port Michel, Gabon	15 Jan 1982
JEWFISH	680 0	Lynn Joyner	Fernandina Beach, FL	20 May 1961
MACKEREL, KING	90 0	Norton I. Thomton	Key West, FL	16 Feb 1976
MARLIN, BLACK	1,560 0	Alfred C. Glassell, Jr	Cabo Blanco, Peru	4 Aug 1953
MARLIN, BLUE (Atlantic)	1,282 0	Larry Martin	St Thomas, Virgin Islands	6 Aug 1977
MARLIN, BLUE (Pacific)	1,376 0	Jay Wm de Beaubien	Kaaiwi Point, Kona Coast, HI	31 May 1982
MARLIN, STRIPED	494 0	Bill Boniface	Tutukaka, New Zealand	16 Jan 1986
MARLIN, WHITE	181 14	Evandro Luiz Coser	Vitoria, Brazil	8 Dec 1979
MUSKELLUNGE	69 15	Arthur Lawton	St Lawrence River, NY	22 Sep 1957
PIKE, NORTHERN	55 1	Lothar Louis	Lake of Grefeern, West Germany	16 Oct 1986
SAILFISH (Atlantic)	128 1	Harm Steyn	Luanda, Angola	27 Mar 1974
SAILFISH (Pacific)	221 0	C. W. Stewart	Santa Cruz Island, Ecuador	12 Feb 1947
SALMON, ATLANTIC	79 2	Henrik Henriksen	Tana River, Norway	1928
SALMON, CHINOOK	97 4	Les Anderson	Kenia River, AK	17 May 1985
SALMON, COHO	33 4	Jerry Lifton	Pulaski, NY	27 Sep 1989
SHARK, HAMMERHEAD	991 0	Allen Ogle	Sarasota, FL	30 May 1982
SHARK, MAKO	1,115 0	Patrick Guillanton	Black River, Mauritius	16 Nov 1988
SHARK, PORBEAGLE	465 0	Jorge Potier	Padstow, Cornwall, United Kingdom	23 Jul 1976
SHARK, THRESHER	802 0	Dianne North	Tutukaka, New Zealand	8 Feb 1981
SHARK, TIGER	1,780 0	Walter Maxwell	Cherry Grove, SC	14 Jun 1964
SHARK, WHITE	2,664 0	Alfred Dean	Ceduna, South Australia	21 Apr 1959
SNAPPER, CUBERA	121 8	Mike Hebert	Cameron, LA	5 Jul 1982
SNOOK	53 10	Gilbert Ponzi	Parasmina Ranch, Costa Rica	18 Oct 1978
STURGEON	468 0	Joey Pallotta III	Benicia, CA	9 Jul 1983
SWORDFISH	1,182 0	L. Marron	Iquique, Chile	17 May 1953
TARPON	283 0	M. Salazar	Lake Maracaibo, Venezuela	19 Mar 1956
TROUT, BROOK	14 8	Dr W. J. Cook	Nipigon River, Ontario, Canada	Jul 1916
TROUT, BROWN	35 15	Eugenio Cavaglia	Nahuel Huapi, Argentina	16 Dec 1952
TROUT, LAKE	65 0	Larry Daunis	Great Bear Lake, NWT, Canada	8 Aug 1970
TROUT, RAINBOW	42 2	David Robert White	Bell Island, AK	22 Jun 1970
TUNA, BIGEYE (Pacific)	435 0	Dr Russel V. A. Lee	Cabo Blanco, Peru	17 Apr 1957
TUNA, BLUEFIN	1,496 0	Ken Fraser	Aulds Cove, Nova Scotia, Canada	26 Oct 1979
TUNA, YELLOWFIN	388 12	Curt Wiesenhutter	San Benedicto Island, Mexico	1 Apr 1977
WAHOO	149 0	John Pirovano	Cat Cay, Bahamas	15 Jun 1962
WALLEYE	25 0	Mabry Harper	Old Hickory Lake, TN	1 Apr 1960

Western Australia on 26 Apr 1976 but will remain unratified as whale meat was used as bait.

In June 1978 a great white shark measuring 20 ft 4 in in length and weighing over 5,000 lb was harpooned and landed by fishermen in the harbor of San Miguel, Azores.

The largest marine animal killed by hand harpoon was a blue whale 97 ft in length, by Archer Davidson in Twofold Bay, New South Wales, Australia in 1910. Its tail flukes measured 20 ft across and its jaw bone 23 ft 4 in.

The largest fish ever taken under water was an 804 lb giant black grouper or jewfish by Don Pinder of the Miami Triton Club, FL in 1955.

World Freshwater Championship ■ The Confédération Internationale de la Pêche Sportive (CIPS) championships were inaugurated as European championships in 1953 and recognized as World championships in 1957.

France won 12 times between 1956 and 1981 and Robert Tesse (France) took the individual title uniquely three times, 1959–60, 1965.

Casting ■ The longest freshwater cast ratified under ICF (International Casting Federation) rules is 574 ft 2 in, by Walter Kummerow (West Germany), for the Bait Distance Double-Handed 30 g event held at Lenzerheide, Switzerland in the 1968 Championships.

The currently contested weight of 17·7 g, known as 18 g Bait Distance, the longest Double-Handed cast is 457 ft ½ in by Kevin Carriero (US) at Toronto, Canada on 24 Jul 1984.

The longest Fly Distance Double-Handed cast is 319 ft 1 in by Wolfgang Feige (West Germany) at Toronto, Canada on 23 Jul 1984.

IGFA world records ■ The International Game Fish Association (IGFA) recognizes world records for game fish — both freshwater and saltwater—for a large number of species of fish. Their thousands of categories include all-tackle, various line classes and tippet classes for fly fishing. New records recognized by the IGFA reached an annual peak of 1,074 in 1984.

The heaviest freshwater category recognized by the IGFA is for the sturgeon — record weight of 468 lb, caught by Joey Pallotta on 9 Jul 1983 off Benicia, CA.

Longest fight ■ The longest recorded individual fight with a fish is 32 hr 5 min by Donal Heatley (New Zealand; b. 1938) with a black marlin (estimated length 20 ft and weight 1,500 lb) off Mayor Island off Tauranga, North Island, New Zealand on 21–22 Jan 1968. It towed the 13·2–ton launch 50 miles before breaking the line.

Football

Origins ■ On 6 Nov 1869 the universities of Princeton and Rutgers staged what is generally regarded as the first intercollegiate football game at New Brunswick, NJ. In October 1873 the Intercollegiate Football Association was formed (Columbia, Princeton, Rutgers and Yale), with the purpose of standardizing rules. At this point football was a modified version of soccer. The first significant move towards today's style of play came when Harvard accepted an invitation to play McGill University (Montreal, Canada) in

a series of three challenge matches, the first being in May 1874, under modified rugby rules. Walter Camp (1859–1925) is credited with organizing the basic format of the current game. Between 1880–1906, Camp sponsored the concepts of scrimmage lines, 11 men teams, reduction in field size, 'downs' and yards to gain' and a new scoring system. In 1902 the first Rose Bowl game was played at Pasadena, CA, and has been played continuously since 1916.

The first professional game was played on 31 Aug 1895 at Latrobe, PA, Latrobe defeating Jeannette (PA) 12-0. In 1920 the American Professional Football Association (APFA) was formed in Canton, OH. This organization was reorganized a number of times and in 1922 was renamed the National Football League (NFL). In 1944 the All-America Conference League was established, but eventually merged with the NFL in 1949. In 1959 the American Football League was formed and competed with the NFL until a merger was agreed in 1966, which led to the creation of the Super Bowl game, first played in January 1967. In 1970 the AFL and the NFL leagues merged to form the present NFL.

NATIONAL FOOTBALL LEAGUE (NFL) RECORDS
Championships ■ The Green Bay Packers have won a record 11 NFL titles, 1929–31, 1936, 1939, 1944, 1961–62, 1965–67.

Most consecutive wins ■ The Green Bay Packers have won 18 consecutive games twice in 1933–34 and 1941–42. The Miami Dolphins matched this mark in 1972–73. The most consecutive games without defeat is 25 by the Canton Bulldogs (22 wins and 3 ties) in 1921–23.

Most wins ● Above: A San Francisco 49ers helmet and the Vince Lombardi Trophy, awarded to the winners of the Super Bowl in memory of the man who coached the Green Bay Packers to the first two Super Bowl wins. (Photos: All-Sport/Steve Dunn)

Most wins ● Left: Joe Montana hands off to Roger Craig during the San Francisco 49ers' 55-10 rout of the Denver Broncos in Super Bowl XXIV. It was the highest team score and margin of victory in the history of Super Bowl and secured San Francisco's record-equalling fourth success. (Photo: All-Sport/Rick Stewart)

Most games played ■ George Blanda (b. 17 Sep 1927) played in a record 340 games in a record 26 seasons in the NFL, for the Chicago Bears (1948–58), the Baltimore Colts (1950), the Houston Oilers (1960–66) and the Oakland Raiders (1967–75).

The most consecutive games played is 282, by Jim Marshall for the Cleveland Browns (1960) and the Minnesota Vikings (1961–79).

Yards rushing ■ Walter Payton (b. 25 Jul 1954; Chicago Bears) had a record ten seasons rushing 1000 yards or more, 1976–81 and 1983–86. Eric Dickerson (b. 2 Sep 1960; Los Angeles Rams and Indianapolis Colts) had a record seven successive seasons, 1983–89, and reached a career total of 10,000 yards in fewest games, 91. Walter Payton had a record 77 games rushing 100 yards or more, and Orenthal James 'O.J.' Simpson (b. 9 Jul 1947; Buffalo Bills) had a record six games rushing 200 yards or more, 1973–76.

Yards passing ■ Dan Fouts (San Diego Chargers) had a record six seasons passing 3,000

NFL RECORDS

MOST POINTS

Career 2,002, George Blanda (Chicago Bears, Baltimore Colts, Houston Oilers, Oakland Raiders), 1949–75. **Season** 176, Paul Hornung (Green Bay Packers), 1960. **Game** 40, Ernie Nevers (Chicago Cardinals), 28 Nov 1929.

MOST TOUCHDOWNS

Career 126, Jim Brown (Cleveland Browns), 1957–65. **Season** 24, John Riggins (Washington Redskins), 1983. **Game** 6, Ernie Nevers (Chicago Cardinals), 28 Nov 1929; William 'Dub' Jones (Cleveland Browns) 25 Nov 1951; Gale Sayers (Chicago Bears), 12 Dec 1965.

MOST YARDS GAINED RUSHING

Career 16,726, Walter Payton (Chicago Bears), 1975–88. **Season** 2,105, Eric Dickerson (Los Angeles Rams), 1984. **Game** 275, Walter Payton (Chicago Bears), 20 Nov 1977. **Highest career average** 5·2 yds per game, Jim Brown (Cleveland Browns), 1957–65

MOST YARDS GAINED RECEIVING

Career 13,089, Steve Largent (Seattle Seahawks), 1976–90. **Season** 1,746, Charley Hennigan (Houston Oilers), 1961. **Game** 336, Willie 'Flipper' Anderson (Los Angeles Rams), 26 Nov 1989.

MOST YARDS GAINED PASSING

Career 47,003, Fran Tarkenton (Minnesota Vikings, New York Giants), 1961–78. **Season** 5,084, Dan Marino (Miami Dolphins), 1984. **Game** 554, Norm Van Brocklin (Los Angeles Rams), 28 Sep 1951.

PASSING ATTEMPTS

Career 6,467, Fran Tarkenton (Minnesota Vikings, New York Giants), 1961–78. **Season** 623, Dan Marino (Miami Dolphins), 1986. **Game** 68, George Blanda (Houston Oilers), 1 Nov 1964

MOST PASSES COMPLETED

Career 3,686, Fran Tarkenton (Minnesota Vikings, New York Giants), 1961–78. **Season** 378, Dan Marino (Miami Dolphins), 1986. **Game** 42 (from 59 attempts), Richard Todd (New York Jets), 21 Sep 1980. **Consecutive** 22, Joe Montana (San Francisco 49ers), 6 Dec 1987.

PASS RECEPTIONS

Career 819, Steve Largent (Seattle Seahawks), 1976–90. **Season** 106, Art Monk (Washington Redskins), 1984. **Game** 18, Tom Fears (Los Angeles Rams), 3 Dec 1950.

FIELD GOALS

Career 373, Jan Stenerud (Kansas City Chiefs, Green Bay Packers, Minnesota Vikings), 1967–85. **Season** 35, Ali Haji-Sheikh (New York Giants), 1983. **Game** 7, Jim Bakken (St Louis Cardinals), 24 Sep 1967; Rich Karlis (Minnesota Vikings), 5 Nov 1989. **Longest** 63 yds, Tom Dempsey (New Orleans Saints), 8 Nov 1970.

SACKS

Career 104, Lawrence Taylor (New York Giants), 1982–90. **Season** 22, Mark Gastineau (New York Jets), 1984. **Game** 6, Fred Dean (San Francisco 49ers v New Orleans Saints), 13 Nov 1983.

yards or more, 1979–81 and 1984–86. Dan Marino (b. 15 Sep 1961; Miami Dolphins) had a record four seasons at 4,000 yards or more, 1984–86, 1988. Dan Fouts had a record 51 games passing 300 yards or more and Dan Marino a record nine games passing 400 yards or more.

Longest run from scrimmage ■ Tony Dorsett competed a touchdown after a run of 99 yards for the Dallas Cowboys v the Minnesota Vikings on 3 Jan 1983.

Longest field goal ■ 63 yards by Tom Dempsey for the New Orleans Saints v the Detroit Lions, 8 Nov 1970.

Longest pass completion ■ Pass completions for a touchdown of 99 yards were achieved by Frank Filchok to Andy Farkas, Washington Redskins v Pittsburgh Steelers, 15 Oct 1939; George Izo to Bobby Mitchell, Washington Redskins v Cleveland Browns, 15 Sep 1963; Karl Sweetan to Pat Studstill, Detroit Lions v Baltimore Colts, 16 Oct 1966; Sonny Jurgenson to Gerry Allen, Washington Redskins v Chicago Bears, 15 Sep 1968; Jim Plunkett to Cliff Branch, Los Angeles Raiders v Washington Redskins, 2 Oct 1983; Ron Jaworski to Mike Quick, Philadelphia Eagles v Atlanta Falcons, 10 Nov 1985.

Longest punt ■ 98 yards by Steve O'Neal for New York Jets v Denver Broncos, 21 Sep 1969.

Coaches ■ The most winningest coach in NFL history has been George Halas (1895–1983), whose Chicago Bears teams won 325 games (and 7 NFL titles) to 151 losses and 31 ties while he was coach 1920–29, 1933–42, 1946–55 and 1958–67. The highest winning percentage was ·736 achieved by Vince Lombardi (1913–70), 106 wins, 36 losses and 6 ties from the Green Bay Packers 1959–67 and Washington Redskins 1969.

THE SUPER BOWL

First held in 1967 between the winners of the NFL and the AFL. Since 1970 it has been contested by the winners of the National and American Conferences of the NFL. The most wins is four, by the Pittsburgh Steelers in 1975–76, 1979–80, coached by Chuck Noll on each occasion, and by the San Francisco 49ers in 1982, 1985, 1989 and 1990, coached by Bill Walsh (1982, 1985, 1989) and George Seifert (1990).

Most appearances ■ The most Super Bowl appearances is 5, by the Dallas Cowboys (2 wins, 3 losses), 1970, 1971, 1975, 1977–78 and by the Miami Dolphins (2 wins, 3 losses), 1971–73, 1982, 1984.

Highest scores ■ The highest aggregate score was 66 points when the Pittsburgh Steelers beat the Dallas Cowboys 35–31 on 21 Jan 1979. The highest team score and record victory margin was when the San Francisco 49ers beat the Denver Broncos 55–10 at New Orleans, LA on 28 Jan 1990. In their 42–10 victory over the Denver Broncos on 31 Jan 1988, the Washington Redskins scored a record 35 points in the second quarter.

Most valuable player ■ Joe Montana (b. 11 Jun 1956), quarterback of the San Francisco 49ers, has been voted the Super Bowl MVP on a record three occasions, 1982, 1985 and 1990.

COLLEGE FOOTBALL (NCAA)

The oldest collegiate series still contested is that between Yale and Princeton, first played in November 1873, three years before the formation of the Intercollegiate Football Association. The first Rose Bowl game was held at Pasadena, CA

MOST SEASON'S LEADING THE NFL

POINTS	5 Don Hutson (Green Bay Packers)	1940–44
	5 Gino Cappelletti (Boston Patriots)	1961, 1963–66
TOUCHDOWNS	8 Don Hutson (Green Bay Packers)	1935–38, 1941–44
FIELD GOALS	5 Lou Groza (Cleveland Browns)	1950, 1952–54, 1957
RUSHING	8 Jim Brown (Cleveland Browns)	1957–61, 1963–65
PASSING	6 Sammy Baugh (Washington Redskins)	1937, 1940 1943, 1945, 1947, 1949
PASS RECEPTIONS	8 Don Hutson (Green Bay Packers)	1936–37, 1939 1941–45

SUPER BOWL GAME & CAREER RECORDS

POINTS	18	Roger Craig (San Francisco 49ers)	1985
		Jerry Rice (San Francisco 49ers)	1990
Career	24	Franco Harris (Pittsburgh Steelers)	1975–6, 1979–80
		Roger Craig (San Francisco 49ers)	1985, 1989–90
		Jerry Rice (San Francisco 49ers)	1989–90
TOUCHDOWNS	3	Roger Craig (San Francisco 49ers)	1985
		Jerry Rice (San Francisco 49ers)	1990
Career	4	Franco Harris (Pittsburgh Steelers)	1975–6, 1979–80
		Roger Craig (San Francisco 49ers)	1985, 1989–90
		Jerry Rice (San Francisco 49ers)	1989–90
TOUCHDOWN PASSES	5	Joe Montana (San Francisco 49ers)	1990
Career	11	Joe Montana (San Francisco 49ers)	1982, 1985, 1989–90
HIGHEST PASSING PERCENTAGE (GAME)	·880	Phil Simms (New York Giants)	1987
YARDS GAINED PASSING	357	Joe Montana (San Francisco 49ers)	1989
Career	1,142	Joe Montana (San Francisco 49ers)	1982, 1985, 1989–90
YARDS GAINED RECEIVING	215	Jerry Rice (San Francisco 49ers)	1989
Career	364	Lynn Swann (Pittsburgh Steelers)	1975–6, 1979–80
PASSES COMPLETED	29	Dan Marino (Miami Dolphins)	1985
Career	83	Joe Montana (San Francisco 49ers)	1982, 1985, 1989–90
PASS RECEPTIONS	11	Dan Ross (Cincinnati Bengals)	1982
		Jerry Rice (San Francisco 49ers)	1989
Career	20	Jerry Rice (San Francisco 49ers)	1989–90
YARDS GAINED RUSHING	204	Timmy Smith (Washington Redskins)	1988
Career	354	Franco Harris (Pittsburgh Steelers)	1975–6, 1979–80
FIELD GOALS	4	Don Chandler (Green Bay Packers)	1968
		Ray Wersching (San Francisco 49ers)	1982
Career	5	Ray Wersching (San Francisco 49ers)	1982, 1985
LONGEST (yds)	48	Jan Stenerud (Kansas City Chiefs)	1970
		Rich Karlis (Denver Broncos)	1987
INTERCEPTIONS	3	Rod Martin (Oakland Raiders)	1981
MOST VALUABLE PLAYER	3	Joe Montana (San Francisco 49ers)	1982, 1985, 1990

on 1 Jan 1902, when Michigan beat Stanford 49–0. The National Collegiate Athletic Association began classifying college teams into divisions I, II and III in 1973. Five years later division I was subdivided into 1–A and 1–AA.

National College Football Champions
■ The most wins in the national journalists' poll to determine the college team of the year is eight by Notre Dame, 1943, 1946–47, 1949, 1966, 1973, 1977 and 1988.

Bowl Games ■ The oldest college bowl game is the Rose Bowl. First played on 1 Jan 1902 at Tournament Park, Pasadena, CA, where Michigan beat Stanford 49–0. The second game did not take place until 1916, and has been played continuously since. The University of Southern California (USC) has a record 19 wins in the Rose Bowl. The University of Alabama has made a record 42 bowl appearances and 23 wins. Most wins in the other 'big four' bowl games: Orange Bowl: 11 Oklahoma, Sugar Bowl: 7 Alabama, Cotton Bowl: 9 Texas.

Heisman Memorial Trophy ■ Awarded annually since 1935 by the Downtown Athletic Club of New York to the top college football

Longest field goal ● Rich Karlis booted a record-tying 48-yd field goal for the Denver Broncos v New York Giants in Super Bowl XXI on 25 Jan 1987. He equalled the mark set by Jan Stenerud (Kansas City Chiefs) in Super Bowl IV in 1970. (Photo: All-Sport/ Mike Powell)

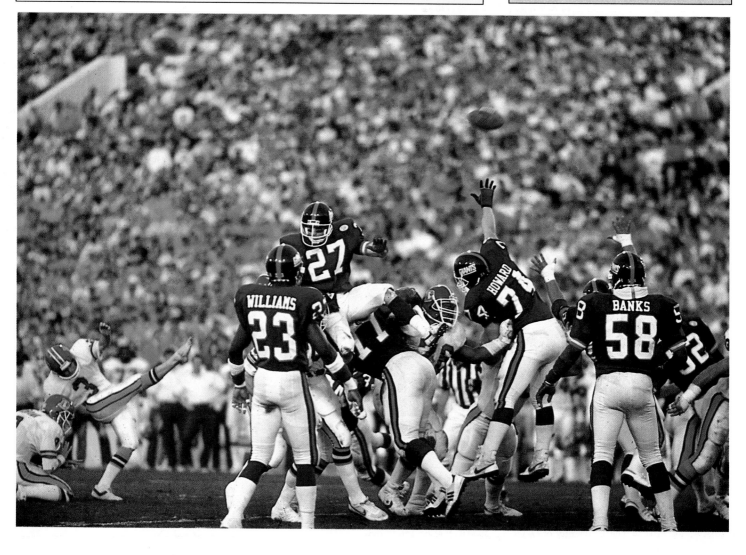

NCAA INDIVIDUAL RECORDS

POINTS	**43**	Jim Brown (Syracuse v Colgate; 6 touchdowns) .... 17 Nov 1956
Season	**234**	Barry Sanders (Oklahoma State) (39 touchdowns in 11 games) ... 1988
Career - 4 years	**394**	Anthony Thompson (Indiana) (kicking record, 73 field goals)..1986–89
Career - 3 years	**336**	Steve Owens (Oklahoma) (56 touchdowns) 1967–69
TOTAL YARDAGE	**625**	Scott Mitchell (Utah v Air Force) .... 15 Oct 1988
		631 passing, minus 6 rushing
Season	**4,627**	Jim McMahon (Brigham Young; 4,571 passing, 56 rushing) 1980
Career	**11,317**	Doug Flutie (Boston College; 10,579 passing, 738 rushing) 1981–84
YARDS GAINED RUSHING	**377**	Anthony Thompson (Indiana v Wisconcin) 1989
Season	**2,628**	Barry Sanders (Oklahoma State) 1988
		344 rushes in 11 games, record av. 238·9)
Career - 4 years	**6,082**	Tony Dorset (Pittsburgh; 1,074 rushes) 1973–76
Career - 3 years	**5,259**	Herschel Walker (Georgia; 994 rushes) 1980–82
YARDS GAINED PASSING	**631**	Scott Mitchell (Utah v Air Force completed 36 of 60) .... 15 Oct 1988
Season	**4,699**	Andre Ware (Houston) 1989
Career	**11,425**	Todd Santos (San Diego State; completed 910 of 1484) 1984–87
PASSES COMPLETED	**45**	Sandy Schwab (Northwestern v Michigan) .... 23 Oct 1982
		29 in second half)
Season	**365**	Andre Ware (Houston) 1989
Career - 4 years	**910**	Todd Santos (San Diego State; 1,484 attempts) 1984–87
TOUCHDOWN PASSES	**9**	Dennis Shaw, San Diego State v New Mexico State........ 15 Nov 1969
		(7 in first half)
Season	**47**	Jim McMahon (Brigham Young; in 12 games) 1980
Career	**84**	Jim McMahon (Brigham Young) 1977–8, 1980–81
PASS RECEPTIONS	**22**	Jay Miller (Brigham Young v New Mexico; 263 yards) .... 3 Nov 1973
Season	**142**	Emmanuel Hazard (Houston) 1969
Career - 4 years	**263**	Terance Mathis (New Mexico) 1985–87, 1989
Career - 3 years	**261**	Howard Twilley (Tulsa; 3,343 yards, record 10.0 per game) ...1963–65
YARDS GAINED RECEIVING	**349**	Chuck Hughes, UTEP v North Texas (caught 10) .... 18 Sep 1965
Season	**1,779**	Howard Twilley (Tulsa) (caught 134 in 10 games) 1965
Career	**4,254**	Terance Mathis (New Mexico) 1985–87, 1989
PASS INTERCEPTIONS	**5**	Dan Rebsch, Miami (Ohio) v Western Michigan.................. 4 Nov 1972
		88 yards; 5 three others with less yards
Season	**14**	Al Worley (Washington) (130 yards, in 10 games) 1968
Career	**29**	Al Brosky (Illinois) (356 yards, 27 games) 1950–52
TOUCHDOWNS (Receiving)	**6**	Tim Delaney (San Diego State) 1989
Season	**22**	Emmanuel Hazard (Houston) 1989
Career	**38**	Clarkston Hines (Duke) 1986–89
FIELD GOALS	**7**	Mike Prindle (West Michigan) 1984
		Dale Klein (Nebraska) 1985
Season	**29**	John Lee (UCLA) 1984
Career	**80**	Jeff Jaeger (Washington) 1983–86
Consecutive	**30**	Chuck Nelson (Washington) 1981–82
TOUCHDOWNS	**7**	Arnold Boykin (Mississippi) 1951
Season	**39**	Barry Sanders (Oklahoma State) 1988
Career	**65**	Anthony Thompson (Indiana) 1986–89

player as determined by a poll of journalists. It was originally called the D.A.C. Trophy but the name was changed in 1936. Its full title is the John W. Heisman Memorial Trophy and is named after the first athletic director of the Downtown Athletic club. The only double winner has been Archie Griffin of Ohio State, 1974–75. The University of Notre Dame has had more Heisman Trophy winners than any other school with seven selections.

Field goals ■ The NCAA record is seven field goals made in a game, by Dale Klein for Nebraska v Missouri on 19 Oct 1989 (7 attempts) and by Mike Prindle for Western Michigan v Marshall on 29 Sep 1989 (9 attempts). Eight field goals were scored in a 1–AA game by Goran Lingmerth for Northern Arizona University v Idaho on 25 Oct 1986, succeeding with all eight attempts.

Highest score ■ The most points ever scored in a college game is 222, by Georgia Tech v Cumberland College (0) of Lebanon, TN on 7 Oct 1916. Tech set records for 63 points in a quarter, 32 touchdowns, and 30 points after touchdown in a game.

Longest streak ■ The University of Oklahoma won 47 successive games from 1953 to 1957, when they were beaten 7–0 by Notre Dame. The longest unbeaten streak is 63 (59 won, 4 tied) by Washington from 1907 to 1917, ended by a 27–0 loss to California.

Coaches ■ The college coach achieving most victories at division one institutions has been Paul 'Bear' Bryant (1913–83), with 323 wins over 38 years: Maryland 1945, Kentucky 1946–53, Texas A&M 1954–57 and Alabama 1958–82. He led Alabama to five national titles and 15 bowl wins, including 7 Sugar Bowls. The best win percentage in division 1–A has been 0·881 by Knut Rockne (1888–1931), with 105 wins, 5 ties and 12 losses, 12,847 points for and 667 against, at Notre Dame 1918–30. Through 1989, Eddie Robinson compiled a 358–122–15 record at Gram bling State University, LA, the winningest coach in college football history.

Record attendances ■ The highest attendances at college football games were estimated crowds of 120,000 at Soldier Field, Chicago, IL on 26 Nov 1927 when Notre Dame beat Southern California 7–6 and on 13 Oct 1928 when Notre Dame beat Navy 7–0. The highest average attendance for home games is 105,498 for the six games played by Michigan in 1981.

Gaelic Football

Origins ■ The game developed from inter-parish 'free for all,' with no time limit, specific playing area or rules. The earliest reported match was Meath v Louth, at Slane in 1712. Standardization came with the formation of the Gaelic Athletic Association in Thurles, Ireland on 1 Nov 1884.

All-Ireland Championships ■ The greatest number of All–Ireland Championships won by one team is 30, by Ciarraidhe (Kerry) between 1903 and 1986.

The greatest number of successive wins is four, by Wexford (1915–18) and Kerry twice (1929–32, 1978–81).

The most finals contested by an individual is ten, including eight wins by the Kerry players Pat Spillane, Paudie O'Shea and Denis Moran, 1975–76, 1978–82, 1984–86.

The highest team score in a final was when Dublin, 27 (5 goals, 12 points), beat Armagh, 15 (3 goals, 6 points), on 25 Sep 1977.

The highest combined score was 45 points when Cork (26) beat Galway (19) in 1973. A goal equals three points.

The highest individual score in an All-Ireland final has been 2 goals, 6 points, by Jimmy Keaveney (Dublin) v Armagh in 1977, and by Michael Sheehy (Kerry) v Dublin in 1979.

Largest crowd ■ The record crowd is 90,556 for the Down v Offaly final at Croke Park, Dublin in 1961.

Most successful ● Gaelic football's principal championship is the All-Ireland Championship which is held annually on the third Sunday in September for the Sam Maguire Trophy. The most successful side is Kerry (shown here in action against Dublin who are in blue) who have won a record 30 times between 1903 and 1986. (Photo: All-Sport)

Gambling

Biggest win ■ The biggest individual gambling win is $40 million, by Mike Wittkowski in the Illinois State Lottery, announced on 3 Sep 1984. From $35 worth of 'Lotto' tickets bought by his family, the winning six numbers bring him $2 million for the next 20 years.

Largest casino ■ The Burswood Island Casino, Perth, Western Australia opened on 30 Dec 1985 has an area of 80,729 ft² and contains 200 video games and 142 gaming tables.

BINGO

Bingo is a lottery game which, as keno, was developed in the 1880s from lotto, whose origin is thought to be the 17th-century Italian game *tumbule*. The winner was the first to complete a random selection of numbers from 1 to 90. The United States version called Bingo differs in that the selection is from 1 to 75.

Largest house ■ The largest 'house' in bingo sessions was 15,756, at the Canadian National Exhibition, Toronto on 19 Aug 1983. Staged by the Variety Club of Ontario Tent Number 28, there was total prize money of $Cdn 250,000, with a record one-game payout of $Cdn 100,000.

Earliest and latest full house ■ A 'full house' call occurred on the 15th number by Norman A. Wilson at Guide Post Working Men's Club, Bedlington, United Kingdom on 22 Jun 1978; by Anne Wintle of Brynrethin, United Kingdom, on a coach trip to Bath on 17 Aug 1982; and by Shirley Lord at Kahibah Bowling Club, New South Wales, Australia on 24 Oct 1983.

'House' was not called until the 86th number at the Hillsborough Working Men's Club, Sheffield, South Yorkshire, United Kingdom on 11 Jan 1982. There were 32 winners.

HORSE RACING

Highest ever odds ■ The highest secured odds were 1,670,759 to 1, by George Rhodes of Aldershot, United Kingdom. For a 5 pence bet, with a 10 percent bonus for the ITV Seven, less tax, he was paid £86,024·42 by the William Hill Organisation on 30 Sep 1984.

Edward Hodson of Wolverhampton, West Mid-lands, United Kingdom landed a 3,956,748 to 1 bet for a 55 pence stake on 11 Feb 1984, but his bookmaker had a £3,000 payout limit.

The world record odds on a 'double' are 31,793 to 1 paid by the New Zealand Totalisator Agency Board on a five shilling tote ticket on Red Emperor and Maida Dillon at Addington, Christchurch in 1951.

Greatest payout ■ Anthony A. Speelman and Nicholas John Cowan (both from England) won $1,627,084·40, after federal income tax of $406,768·00 was withheld, on a $64 nine-horse accumulator at Santa Anita racetrack, CA on 19 Apr 1987. Their first seven selections won and the payout was for a jackpot, accumulated over 24 days.

Topmost tipster ■ The only recorded instance of a racing correspondent forecasting ten out of ten winners on a race card was at Delaware Park, Wilmington, DE on 28 Jul 1974, by Charles Lamb of the *Baltimore News American*.

SLOT MACHINES

The biggest beating handed to a 'one-armed bandit' was $6,814,823·48, by Cammie Brewer, 61, at the Club Cal-Neva, Reno, NV on 14 Feb 1988.

Gliding (Soaring)

Origins ■ Research by Isadore William Deiches has shown evidence of the use of gliders in ancient Egypt *c.* 2500–1500 B.C. Emanuel Swedenborg (1688–1772) of Sweden made sketches of gliders *c.* 1714. The earliest man-carrying glider was designed by Sir George Cayley (1773–1857) and carried his coachman (possibly John Appleby) about 500 yd across a valley in Brompton Dale, North Yorkshire, United Kingdom in the summer of 1853.

Most titles ■ The most World Individual Championships (instituted 1937) won is four, by Ingo Renner (Australia) in 1976 (Standard class), 1983, 1985 and 1987 (Open).

United States ■ The most titles won by a US pilot is two, by George Moffat, in the Open category, 1970 and 1974.

Women's altitude records ■ The women's single-seater world record for absolute altitude is 41,449 ft, by Sabrina Jackintell (US) in an Astir GS on 14 Feb 1979.

The height gain record is 33,506 ft, by Yvonne Loader (New Zealand) at Omarama, New Zealand on 12 Jan 1988.

HANG GLIDING

Origins ■ In the 11th century the monk Eilmer is reported to have flown from the 60-ft tower of Malmesbury Abbey, Wiltshire, United Kingdom. The earliest modern pioneer was Otto Lilienthal (1848–96; Germany), with about 2,500 flights in gliders of his own construction

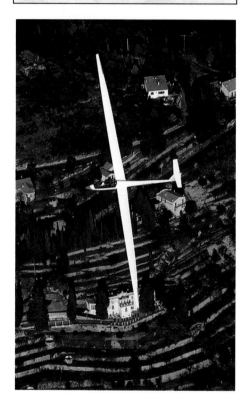

Most successful glider ● As the World gliding records table shows, one of the most successful crafts for setting records is the Nimbus. Seen here soaring over the French village of Tourettes is a Nimbus 3. (Photo: All-Sport/Vandystadt)

GLIDING WORLD RECORDS
(Single-seaters)

	DISTANCE	NAME	TYPE OF GLIDER	LOCATION	DATE	
STRAIGHT DISTANCE	907·7 miles	Hans-Werner Grosse (West Germany)	ASW-12	Lübeck, W. Germany to Biarritz, France	25 Apr	1972
DECLARED GOAL DISTANCE	779·4 miles	Bruce Drake (New Zealand)	Nimbus 2	Te Anau to Te Araroa, New Zealand	14 Jan	1978
		David Speight (New Zealand)	Nimbus 2	Te Anau to Te Araroa, New Zealand	14 Jan	1978
		S. H. 'Dick' Georgeson (New Zealand)	Nimbus 2	Te Anau to Te Araroa, New Zealand	14 Jan	1978
GOAL AND RETURN	1,023·2 miles	Tom Knauff (US)	Nimbus 3	Williamsport, PA to Knoxville, TN	25 Apr	1983
ABSOLUTE ALTITUDE	49,009 ft	Robert R. Harris (US)	Grob G102	California,	17 Feb	1986
HEIGHT GAIN	42,303 ft	Paul Bikle (US)	Schweitzer SGS1-23E	Mojave, CA,	25 Feb	1961

SPEED OVER TRIANGULAR COURSE

DISTANCE	SPEED KM/H	MPH	NAME	TYPE OF GLIDER	PLACE	DATE	
100 km	195·3	121·35	Ingo Renner (Australia)	Nimbus 3	Australia	14 Dec	1982
300 km	169·49	105·32	Jean-Paul Castel (France)	Nimbus 3	South Africa	15 Nov	1986
500 km	170·06	105·67	Beat Bunzli (Switzerland)	Nimbus 3	South Africa	18 Dec	1987
750 km	158·40	98·43	Hans-Werner Grosse (West Germany)	ASW-22	Australia	8 Jan	1985
1,000 km	145·32	90·29	Hans-Werner Grosse (West Germany)	ASW-17	Australia	3 Jan	1979
1,250 km	133·24	82·79	Hans-Werner Grosse (West Germany)	ASW-17	Australia	9 Jan	1980

Fastest hang glider ● Judy Leden, the current British, European and world champion, is the women's world record holder for the fastest speed achieved over 15 miles. At Forbes, Australia on 24 Jan 1990, she attained a speed of 11·185 mph. (Photos: All-Sport/Jon Nicholson)

between 1891 and 1896. In the 1950s Professor Francis Rogallo of the National Space Agency developed a flexible 'wing' from his space capsule reentry research.

World championships ■ The World Team Championships (officially instituted 1976) have been won most often by Great Britain (1981, 1985 and 1989).

WORLD RECORDS ■ The Fédération Aéronautique Internationale recognizes world records for rigid-wing, flex-wing and multiplace flex-wing. These records are the greatest in each category — all by flexwing gliders.

MEN: Greatest distance in straight line: 287·46 miles, Kevin Christopherson (US), Whiskey Peak, WY, 3 Aug 1989.

Height gain: 14,250 ft, Larry Tudor (US), Owens Valley, CA, 4 Aug 1985. Declared goal distance: 216·67 miles, Larry Tudor (US), Owens Valley, 30 Jan 1988.

Out and return distance: 192·818 miles, Larry Tudor (US) and Geoffrey Loyns (United Kingdom), Owens Valley, CA, 26 Jun 1988.

Triangular course distance: 100 miles, Drew W. Cooper (Australia), Kössen, Austria, 10 Jun 1989.

WOMEN: Greatest distance: 163·81 miles, Kathrine Yardley (US), Owens Valley, CA, 13 Jul 1989.

Height gain: 11,997 ft, Tover Buas-Hansen (Norway), Owens Valley, CA, 6 Jul 1989.

Out and return distance: 81·99 miles, Tover Buas-Hansen, Owens Valley, CA, 6 Jul 1989.

Declared goal distance: 124·97 miles, Liavan Mallin (Ireland), Owens Valley, CA, 13 Jul 1989.

Triangular course distance: Jenney Ganderton (Australia), 62·76 miles, Forbes, Australia, 22 Jan 1990.

Greatest descent ■ John Bird piloted a hang glider from a height of 39,000 ft when he was released from a hot-air balloon to the ground, landing in Edmonton, Alberta, Canada on 29 Aug 1982. He touched down 50 miles from his point of departure.

Golf

Origins ■ The Chinese Nationalist Golf Association claims the game is of Chinese origin (*ch'ui wan* – the ball hitting game) in the third or second century B.C. There were official ord-

inances prohibiting a ball game with clubs in Belgium and Holland from 1360. Gutta percha balls succeeded feather balls in 1848, and by 1902 were in turn succeeded by rubber-cored balls, invented in 1899 by Coburn Haskell (US). Steel shafts were authorized in the United States in 1925.

The first evidence of golf in the United States was that the game was played in Charleston, NC and in Virginia in the mid-18th century. The first club organized for the playing of golf in North America was in Canada, when the Royal Montreal Golf Club was formed on Nov 4 1873. Two golf clubs claim to be the first established in the United States: the Foxberg Golf Club, Clarion County, PA (1887) and St. Andrews Golf Club of Yonkers, NY (1888). The United States Golf Association (USGA) was founded in 1894 as the governing body of golf in the United States.

Oldest club ■ The oldest club of which there is written evidence is the Gentlemen Golfers (now the Honourable Company of Edinburgh Golfers) formed in March 1744—ten years prior to the institution of the Royal and Ancient Club of St Andrews, Fife, Scotland, United Kingdom. However, the Royal Burgess Golfing Society of Edinburgh claims to have been founded in 1735.

Highest course ■ The Tuctu Golf Club in Morococha, Peru, is 14,335 ft above sea level at its lowest point. Golf has, however, been played in Tibet at an altitude of over 16,000 ft.

Longest hole ■ The longest hole in the world is the 7th hole (par-7) of the Sano Course, Satsuki GC, Japan, which measures 909 yd.

Largest green ■ Probably the largest green in the world is that of the par-6 695 yd fifth hole at International GC, Bolton, MA, with an area greater than 228,000 ft^2.

Biggest bunker ■ The world's biggest bunker is Hell's Half Acre on the 585 yd seventh hole of the Pine Valley course, Clementon, NJ, built in 1912 and generally regarded as the world's most trying course.

WORLD'S MAJOR CHAMPIONSHIPS
MOST TITLES

The British Open	Harry Vardon (1870–1937)	6	1896, 1898–9, 1903, 11, 14
The British Amateur	John Ball (1861–1940)	8	1888, 90, 92, 94, 99, 1907, 1910, 12
US Open	Willie Anderson (1880–1910)	4	1901, 03–5
	Robert Tyre Jones Jr (1902–71)	4	1923, 26, 29–30
	William Ben Hogan (b. 13 Aug 1912)	4	1948, 50–51, 53
	Jack William Nicklaus (b. 21 Jan 1940)	4	1962, 67, 72, 80
US Amateur	Robert Tyre Jones Jr (1902–71)	5	1924–25, 27–28, 30
The PGA Championship	Walter Charles Hagan (1892–1969)	5	1921, 24–27
	Jack William Nicklaus	5	1963, 71, 73, 75, 80
The Masters	Jack William Nicklaus	6	1963, 65–66, 72, 75, 86
US Women's Open	Elizabeth 'Betsy' Earle-Rawls (b. 4 May 1928)	4	1951, 53, 57, 60
	'Mickey' Wright (b. 14 Feb 1935)	4	1958–59, 61, 64
US Women's Amateur	Glenna C. Vare (nee Collett; b. 20 Jun 1903)	6	1922, 25, 28–30, 35
British Women's Amateur	Charlotte Cecilia Pitcairn Leitch (1891–1977)	4	1914, 20–21, 26
	Joyce Wethered (b. 17 Nov 1901) (Now Lady Heathcoat-Amory)	4	1922, 24–25, 29

Note: Nicklaus is the only golfer to have won 5 different major titles (The British Open, US Open, Masters, PGA and US Amateur titles) twice and a record 20 all told (1959–86). In 1930 Bobby Jones achieved a unique 'Grand Slam' of the US and British Open and Amateur titles.

Longest course ■ The world's longest course is the par-77 8,325 yd International GC (see also above) from the 'Tiger' tees, remodeled in 1969 by Robert Trent Jones.

Floyd Satterlee Rood used the United States as a course, when he played from the Pacific surf to the Atlantic surf from 14 Sep 1963 to 3 Oct 1964 in 114,737 strokes. He lost 3,511 balls on the 3,397·7-mile trail.

Longest drives ■ In an officially regulated long driving contest over level ground the greatest distance recorded is 437 yd 2 ft 4 in by Jack L. Hamm on 25 Oct 1989 in Denver, CO. Corey Morley (US; b. 21 Sep 1961) won the 1989 Michelin National Long Driving Championship with a drive of 412 yd on 5 Aug 1989 in Albuquerque, NM at an altitude of 4,958 ft.

The longest recorded drive in a regulated competition at sea level is 411 yd 2 ft 8 in by Cary B. Schuman at the Navy Marine Course in Oahu, HI on 7 May 1989.

On an airport runway Liam Higgins (Ireland) drove a Spalding Top Flite ball 634·1 yd at Baldonnel Military Airport, Dublin, Republic of Ireland on 25 Sep 1984.

The women's record is held by Helen Dobson (United Kingdom), who drove a Titleist Pinnacle 531 yd at RAF Honnington, Suffolk, United Kingdom on 31 Oct 1987.

The greatest recorded drive on an ordinary course is one of 515 yd by Michael Hoke Austin (b. 17 Feb 1910) of Los Angeles, CA, in the US National Seniors Open Championship at Las Vegas, NV on 25 Sep 1974. Austin, 6 ft 2 in tall and weighing 210 lb, drove the ball to within a yard of the green on the par-4 450 yd fifth hole of the Winterwood Course and it rolled 65 yd past the flagstick. He was aided by an estimated 35 mph tailwind.

A drive of 2,640 yd (1½ miles) across ice was achieved by an Australian meteorologist named Nils Lied at Mawson Base, Antarctica in 1962.

Arthur Lynskey claimed a drive of 200 yd horizontal and 2 miles vertical off Pikes Peak, CO (14,110 ft) on 28 Jun 1968.

On the Moon the energy expended on a mundane 300 yd drive would achieve, craters permitting, a distance of 1 mile.

SCORES

Lowest 9 holes ■ Nine holes in 25 (4, 3, 3, 2, 3, 3, 1, 4, 2) was recorded by A. J. 'Bill' Burke in a round in 57 (32 + 25) on the 6,389 yd par-71 Normandie course at St Louis, MO on 20 May 1970.

The tournament record is 27, by Mike Souchak (US; b. 10 May 1927) for the second nine (par-35), first round of the 1955 Texas Open (see 72 holes); Andy North (US; b. 9 Mar 1950), for the second nine (par-34), first round, 1975 BC Open at En-Joie GC, Endicott, NY; José Maria Canizares (Spain; b. 18 Feb 1947), for the first nine, third round, in the 1978 Swiss Open on the 6,811 yd Crans GC, Crans-sur-Seine; and Robert Lee (Great Britain; b. 12 Oct 1961) first nine, first round, in the Monte Carlo Open on the 6,249 yd Mont Agel course on 28 Jun 1985.

Lowest 18 holes *Men* ■ At least four players have played a long course (over 6,561 yd) in a score of 58, most recently Monte Carlo Money (US; b. 3 Dec 1954), on the par-72, 6,607 yd Las Vegas Municipal GC, NV on 11 Mar 1981.

Alfred Edward Smith (1903–85) achieved an 18-hole score of 55 (15 under par 70) on his home course on 1 Jan 1936. The course measured 4,248 yd. The detail was 4, 2, 3, 4, 2, 4, 3, 4, 3 = 29 out, and 2, 3, 3, 3, 3, 2, 5, 4, 1 = 26 in.

The PGA tournament record for 18 holes is 59 (30 + 29), by Al Geiberger (b. 1 Sep 1937) in the second round of the Danny Thomas Classic, on the 72-par 7,249 yd Colonial GC course, Memphis, TN on 10 Jun 1977.

Other golfers to have recorded 59 over 18 holes in non-PGA tournaments include: Samuel Jackson 'Sam' Snead (b. 27 May 1912), in the third round of the Sam Snead Festival at White Sulphur Springs, WV on 16 May 1959; Gary Player (South Africa; b. 1 Nov 1935), in the second round of the Brazilian Open in Rio de Janeiro on 29 Nov 1974; David Jagger (Great Britain; b. 9 Jun 1949), in a Pro-Am tournament prior to the 1973 Nigerian Open at Ikoyi Golf Club, Lagos; and Miguel Martin (Spain), in the Argentine Southern Championship at Mar de Plata on 27 Feb 1987.

Women ■ The lowest recorded score on an 18-hole course (over 6,000 yd) for a woman is 62 (30 + 32) by Mary 'Mickey' Kathryn Wright (US; b. 14 Feb 1935) on the Hogan Park Course (par-71, 6,286 yd) at Midland, TX, in November 1964.

Wanda Morgan (b. 22 Mar 1910) recorded a score of 60 (31 + 29) on the Westgate and Birchington Golf Club course, Kent, United Kingdom over 18 holes (5,002 yd) on 11 Jul 1929.

Lowest 36 holes ■ The record for 36 holes is 122 (59 + 63), by Sam Snead in the 1959 Sam Snead Festival on 16–17 May 1959 (see above).

Horton Smith (1908–63), twice the Masters champion, scored 121 (63 + 58) on a short course on 21 Dec 1928 (see 72 holes).

Lowest 72 holes ■ The lowest recorded score on a first class course is 255 (29 under par) by Leonard Peter Tupling (Great Britain; b. 6 Apr 1950) in the Nigerian Open at Ikoyi Golf Club, Lagos in February 1981, made up of 63, 66, 62 and 64 (average 63·75 per round).

The lowest 72 holes in a PGA tour event is 257 (60, 68, 64, 65) by Mike Souchak in the 1955 Texas Open at San Antonio.

The 72 holes record on the European tour is 258 (64, 69, 60, 65) by David Llewellyn (b. 18 Nov 1951) in the Biarritz Open, France on 1–3 Apr 1988.

The lowest 72 holes in an open championship in Europe is 262 (67, 66, 66, 63) by Percy Alliss (United Kingdom; 1897–1975) in the 1932 Italian Open at San Remo, and by Lu Liang Huan (Taiwan; b. 10 Dec 1935) in the 1971 French Open at Biarritz.

Kelvin D. G. Nagle (b. 21 Dec 1920) of Australia shot 261 in the Hong Kong Open in 1961.

Trish Johnson scored 242 (64, 60, 60, 56) (21 under par) in the Bloor Homes Eastleigh Classic at the Fleming Park Course (4,402 yd) at Eastleigh, Hampshire, United Kingdom on 22–25 Jul 1987.

Horton Smith scored 245 (63, 58, 61 and 63) for 72 holes on the 4,700 yd course (par-64) at Catalina Country Club, CA, to win the Catalina Open on 21–23 Dec 1928.

World one-club record ■ Thad Daber (US), with a 6-iron, played the 6,037 yd Lochmore GC, Cary, NC in 70 to win the 1987 World One-club Championship.

Most shots for one hole ■ A woman player in the qualifying round of the Shawnee Invitational for Ladies at Shawnee-on-Delaware, PA, c. 1912, took 166 strokes for the short 130 yd 16th hole. Her tee shot went into the Binniekill River and the ball floated. She put out in a boat with her exemplary but statistically minded husband at the oars. She eventually beached the ball 1½ miles downstream but was not yet out of the woods. She had to play through one on the home run.

In a competition at Peacehaven, East Sussex, United Kingdom in 1890, A. J. Lewis had 156 putts on one green without holing out. The highest score for a single hole in the British Open is 21, by a player in the inaugural meeting at Prestwick in 1860. Double figures have been recorded on the card of the winner only once, when Willie Fernie (1851–1924) scored a ten at Musselburgh, Lothian, United Kingdom in 1883.

Ray Ainsley of Ojai, CA took 19 strokes for the par-4 16th hole during the second round of the US Open at Cherry Hills Country Club, Denver, CO on 10 Jun 1938. Most of the strokes were used in trying to extricate the ball from a brook. Hans Merell of Mogadore, OH took 19 strokes on the par-3 16th (222 yd) during the third round of the Bing Crosby National Pro-Am Tournament at Cypress Point Club, Del Monte, CA on 17 Jan 1959.

Fastest rounds *Individual* ■ With such variations in lengths of courses, speed records, even for rounds under par, are of little comparative value. The fastest round played when the golf ball comes to rest before each new stroke is 27 min 9 sec, by James Carvill (b. 13 Oct 1965) at Warrenpoint Golf Course, County Down, United Kingdom (18 holes, 6,154 yd) on 18 Jun 1987.

Team ■ Forty-eight players completed the 18-hole 7,108 yd Kyalami course, near Johannesburg, South Africa in 9 min 51 sec on 23 Feb 1988, using only one ball. They scored 73!

Slowest rounds ■ The slowest stroke-play tournament round was one of 6 hr 45 min, taken by South Africa in the first round of the 1972 World Cup at the Royal Melbourne GC, Australia. This was a four-ball medal round; everything holed out.

Most holes in 24 hours *On foot* ■ Ian Colston, 35, played 22 rounds and five holes (401 holes) at Bendigo GC, Victoria, Australia (par-73, 6,061 yd) on 27–28 Nov 1971.

Using golf carts ■ Charles Stock played 783 holes at Boston Hills GC, Hudson, OH (9 holes, 3,110 yd) on 20 Jul 1987.

Terry Zachary played 391 holes in 12 hours on the 6,706 yd course at Connaught Golf Club, Alberta, Canada on 16 Jun 1986.

Most holes played in a week ■ Steve Hylton played 1,128 holes at the Mason Rudolph Golf Club (6,060 yd), Clarkesville, TN from 25–31 Aug 1980. Using a buggy for transport, Colin Young completed 1,260 holes at Patshull Park Golf Club (6,412 yd), Pattingham, United Kingdom from 2–9 Jul 1988.

Most balls hit in one hour ■ The most balls driven in one hour, over 100 yds and into a target area, is 1,536 by Noel Hunt at Shrigley Hall, Pott Shrigley, Cheshire, United Kingdom on 2 May 1990.

MEN'S CHAMPIONSHIP RECORDS

Grand Slam ■ In 1930 Bobby Jones won the United States and British Opens and the United States and Amateur Championships. These four victories were christened the Grand Slam of golf. In 1960 the professional Grand Slam (the Masters, US Open, British Open and Professional Golfers Association [PGA] Championships), gained recognition when Arnold Palmer won the first two legs, the Masters and the US Open. However, he did not complete the set of victories, and the Grand Slam has still not been attained. The closest to succeed was Ben Hogan in 1951, when he won the first three legs, but he could not return to the United States from Britain in time for the PGA Championship.

The four grand slam events are also known as 'the majors.' Jack Nicklaus has won the most major championships with 18 professional titles (6 Masters, 4 US Opens, 3 British Opens and 5 PGA Championships). Additionally, Nicklaus has won two US Amateur titles, which are often included in calculating major championship victories.

The British Open (inaugurated 1860, Prestwick, Strathclyde)

Most wins ■ Harry Vardon won a record six titles, in 1896, 1898–99, 1908, 1911 and 1914. Tom Morris, Jr. is the only player to win four successive British Opens, from 1868 to 1872 (the event was not held in 1871).

LOWEST SCORE
Any round ■ 63, by: Mark Stephen Hayes (US;

b. 12 Jul 1949), at Turnberry, Strathclyde on 7 Jul 1977; Isao Aoki (Japan; b. 31 Aug 1942), at Muirfield, Lothian on 19 Jul 1980; Gregory John Norman (Australia; b. 10 Feb 1955) at Turnberry on 18 Jul 1986; and Paul Broadhurst (b. 14 Aug 1965), at St Andrews, Fife on 21 Jul 1990.

First 36 holes ■ Thomas Henry Cotton (1907–1987) at Royal St George's, Sandwich, Kent, completed the first 36 holes in 132 (67 + 65) on 27 Jun 1934. This was equaled by Nicholas Alexander 'Nick' Faldo (b. 18 Jul 1957) and Greg Norman at St Andrews on 19–20 Jul 1990. Faldo had a third round of 67 for a 54 holes record of 199.

Total aggregate ■ 268, (68, 70, 65, 65) by Thomas Sturges Watson (US; b. 4 Sep 1949) at Turnberry in July 1977.

US Open (inaugurated in 1895)

Most wins ■ Four players have won the title four times: Willie Anderson (1901, 1903–05), Bobby Jones (1923, 1926, 1929–30), Ben Hogan (1948, 1950–51, 1953) and Jack Nicklaus (b. 21 Jan 1940; in 1962, 1967, 1972, 1980). The only player to gain three successive titles was Willie Anderson from 1903 to 1905.

LOWEST SCORE
Any round ■ 63, by: Johnny Miller (b. 29 Apr 1947) on the 6,921 yd par-71 Oakmont Country Club course, PA on 17 Jun 1973; by Jack Nicklaus and Tom Weiskopf (US; b. 9 Nov 1942), both on 12 Jun 1980 at Baltusrol County Club, Springfield, NJ.

First 36 holes ■ 134, by: Jack Nicklaus (63, 71) at Baltusrol Country Club, Springfield, NJ, 12–13 Jun 1980; and Tze-Chung Chen (Taiwan) (65, 69) at Oakland Hills, Birmingham, MI in 1985.

Total aggregate ■ 272 (63, 71, 70, 68), by Jack Nicklaus on the lower course (7,015 yd) at Baltusrol Country Club, 12–15 Jun 1980.

The Masters (inaugurated on 6,980 yd Augusta National Golf Course, GA, 1934)

Most wins ■ Jack Nicklaus has won six green jackets (1963, 1965–66, 1972, 1975, 1986). Two players have won consecutive Masters; Jack Nicklaus (1965–66) and Nick Faldo (1989–90).

> **Consecutive wins ●** Nick Faldo (United Kingdom) celebrates winning the Masters for the second year running in 1990. Ironically, he won both titles in a play-off and at the second hole. He was the second player to have won back-to-back Masters, Jack Nicklaus (US) having won 1965–66. (Photo: All-Sport)

LOWEST SCORE
Any round ■ 63 by Nicholas Raymond Leige Price (Zimbabwe; b. 28 Jan 1957) in 1986.

First 36 holes ■ 131 (65, 66), by Raymond Loran Floyd (b. 4 Sep 1942) in 1976.

Total aggregate ■ 271, by: Jack Nicklaus (67, 71, 64, 69) in 1965 and Raymond Floyd (65, 66, 70, 70) in 1976.

Professional Golfers Association (PGA) Championship

Most wins ■ Two players have won the title five times: Walter Hagen (1921, 1924–27) and Jack Nicklaus (1963, 1971, 1973, 1975, 1980). Walter Hagen won a record four consecutive titles from 1924 to 1927.

LOWEST SCORE
Any round ■ 63, by Bruce Crampton (Australia; b. 28 Sep 1935), at Firestone CC, Akron, OH in 1975 and by Raymond Loran Floyd (b. 4 Sep 1942) at Southern Hills, Tulsa, OK in 1982.

First 36 holes ■ 131, by Hal Evan Sutton (b. 28 Apr 1958) at Riviera CC, Los Angeles, CA in 1983.

Total aggregate ■ 271, by Bobby Nicholls (64, 71, 69, 67) at Columbus CC, OH in 1964.

WOMEN'S CHAMPIONSHIP RECORDS

Grand Slam ■ The Grand Slam of women's golf has consisted of four tournaments since 1955. From 1955–66, the US Open, Ladies Professional Golfers Association (LPGA) Championship, Western Open and Titleholders Championship served as the 'majors.' From 1967–82 the Grand Slam events changed, as first the Western Open (1967) and then the Titleholders Championship (1972) were discontinued.

Since 1983, the US Open, LPGA Championship, du Maurier Classic and Nabisco Dinah Shore have been the major events. Patty Berg has won 15

professional Grand Slam events: US Open (1), Titleholders (7), Western Open (7). She also won one US Amateur title.

US Open ■ First held in 1946 at Spokane, WA at match-play, but at 72 holes of stroke-play annually on different courses from 1947. The most wins is four by Elizabeth Earle 'Betsy' Rawls (b. 4 May 1928), 1951, 1953, 1957 and 1960, and by Mary 'Mickey' Kathryn Wright (b. 14 Feb 1935), in 1958–59, 1961 and 1964. The biggest margin of victory is 14 strokes by Mae Louise Suggs (b. 7 Sep 1923) with an aggregate of 291 in 1949.

The oldest winner has been Fay Crocker at 40 yrs 11 months in 1955, and the youngest Catherine Lacoste (France; b. 27 Jun 1945) at 22 yrs 5 days in 1967. The lowest 72 holes aggregate is 279 by Pat Bradley (b. 24 Mar 1951) in 1981. The record for the lowest round is 65 by Sally Little (b. 12 Oct 1951 Cape Town, South Africa) in the fourth round in 1978 and by Judy Dickinson (b. 4 Mar 1950) in the third round in 1985.

Ladies Professional Golfers Association (LPGA) Championship (inaugurated 1955, Orchard Ridge Country Club, Fort Wayne, IN; since 1987 officially called the Mazda LPGA Championship)

Most wins ■ 4, by Mickey Wright in 1958, 1960–61 and 1963.

LOWEST CHAMPIONSHIP SCORES
18 holes ■ 63, by Patty Sheehan at the Jack Nicklaus Sports Center at Kings Island, OH in 1984.

72 holes ■ 272, by Patty Sheehan at the Jack Nicklaus Sports Center at Kings Island, OH in 1984.

Du Maurier Classic (inaugurated 1973, Royal Montreal Golf Club, Montreal, Canada; formerly called La Canadienne [1973] and the Peter Jackson Classic [1974–83])

Pat Bradley holds the record for most wins with three titles won in 1980, 1985–86. The lowest score for 18 holes is 64, by JoAnne Carner at the St. Georges Country Club, Canada in 1978.

72 holes ■ Pat Bradley and Ayako Okamoto share the record for the lowest score for 72 holes, 276, at the Board of Trade Country Club, Toronto, Canada in 1986.

Nabisco Dinah Shore (inaugurated 1972, Mission Hills Country Club, Rancho Mirage, CA, the permanent site)

The most wins is 2, shared by two players: Amy Alcott (1983, 1988) and Juli Inkster (1984, 1989).

Nancy Lopez holds the record for the lowest score for 18 holes, 64, in 1981. The lowest score for 72 holes is 274, by Amy Alcott in 1988.

US Women's Amateur Championship

■ First held in 1895, the most wins is six by Glenna Vare (nee Collett, 1904–89) in 1922, 1925, 1928–30 and 1935. The greatest winning margin in a final is 14 & 13, by which Anne Quast (later Decker, Welts, Sander, b. 31 Aug 1937) beat Phyllis Preuss in 1961. The oldest winner has been Dorothy Campbell Hurd (United Kingdom; 1883–1946) at 41 yrs 4 months in 1924 and the youngest Laura Baugh (b. 31 May 1955) at 16 yrs 82 days in 1971.

LOWEST TOUR SCORES

18 holes ■ Mickey Wright scored 62 on the Hogan Park course, Midland, TX in the first round of the 1964 Tall City Open, as did Vicki Fergon (b. 29 Sep 1955) at Almaden G&CC in the second round of the 1984 San Jose Classic.

36 holes ■ 129 (64–65), by Judy Dickinson at Pasadena Yacht & CC, St Petersburg, FL in the 1985 S&H Golf Classic.

72 holes ■ Nancy Lopez (b. 6 Jan 1957) scored 268 (66–67–69–66), at the Willow Creek GC, NC in the 1985 Henredon Classic.

TEAM COMPETITONS

Ryder Cup

■ The biennial Ryder Cup professional match between the United States and Europe (British Isles or Great Britain prior to 1979) was instituted in 1927. The United States has won 21 to 5 (with 2 tied) to date.

Arnold Palmer has the record of winning most Ryder Cup matches, with 22 from 32 played, with two halved and 8 lost. Christy O'Connor, Sr (Ireland; b. 21 Dec 1924) played in ten contests, 1955–73.

World Cup (formerly Canada Cup)

■ The World Cup (instituted as the Canada Cup in 1953) has been won most often by the United States, with 17 victories between 1955 and 1988. The only men to have been on six winning teams have been Arnold Palmer (b. 10 Sep 1929) in 1960, 1962–64, 1966–67 and Jack Nicklaus in 1963–64, 1966–67, 1971 and 1973. Only Nicklaus has taken the individual title three times (1963–64, 1971).

The lowest aggregate score for 144 holes is 544, by Australians Bruce Devlin (b. 10 Oct 1937) and Anthony David Graham (b. 23 May 1946), at San Isidro, Buenos Aires, Argentina from 12–15 Nov 1970. The lowest individual score has been 269 by Roberto de Vicenzo (Argentina; b. 14 Apr 1923), also in 1970.

Walker Cup

■ The series was instituted in 1921 (for the Walker Cup since 1922 and now held biennially). The United States has won 28, Great Britain & Ireland three (in 1938, 1971 and 1989) and the 1965 match was tied.

Jay Sigel (US; b. 13 Nov 1943) has won a record 14 matches, with five halved and eight lost, 1977–89. Joseph Boynton Carr (Great Britain & Ireland; b. 18 Feb 1922) played in ten contests, 1947–67.

Curtis Cup

■ The biennial ladies' Curtis Cup match between the United States and Great Britain and Ireland was first held in 1932. The United States has won 20, Great Britain & Ireland four (1952, 1956, 1986 and 1988) and two matches have been tied.

Anne Sander (nee Quast, later Decker, Welts; b. 31 Aug 1937) played in a US record eighth match in 1990, when at 52 years 332 days she became the oldest ever player in the series.

INDIVIDUAL RECORDS

Richest prize

■ The greatest first place-prize money ever won is $1 million, by the winners of the Sun City Challenge, Bophuthatswana, South Africa in 1987, Ian Woosnam (Wales; b. 2 Mar 1958), 1988, Fulton Allem (South Africa) and 1989, David Frost (South Africa).

The greatest total prize money is $2·5 million (including $450,000 first prize) for the Nabisco Championship of Golf at Hilton Head Island, SC on 26–29 Oct 1989.

Highest earnings *PGA and LPGA circuits*

■ The all-time professional money-winner is Tom Kite (US; b. 9 Dec 1949) with $5,933,190, to June 1990. He also holds the earnings record for a year on the PGA circuit, $1,395,278 in 1989.

The record career earnings for a woman is by Pat Bradley (b. 24 Mar 1951), with $3,210,547 to June 1990. The season's record is $654,132, by Betsy King (US) in 1989.

Most times leading money winner ■ Jack Nicklaus won eight times—1964–65, 1967, 1971–73, 1975–76.

Most tournament wins

■ John Byron Nelson (US; b. 4 Feb 1912) won a record 18 tournaments (plus one unofficial) in one year, including a record 11 consecutively from 8 Mar to 4 Aug 1945.

The LPGA record is 13 by Mickey Wright (1963).

She also holds the record for most wins in scheduled events, with four between August and September 1962 and between May and June 1963 and by Kathrynne 'Kathy' Ann Whitworth (b. 27 Sep 1939) between March and April 1969. Nancy Lopez won five successive tournaments between May and June 1978.

Sam Snead, who turned professional in 1934, won 84 official PGA tour events, 1936–65. The ladies' PGA record is 88 by Kathy Whitworth (b. 27 Sep 1939), from 1962 to 1985.

Most wins in a single event

■ Sam Snead won a record eight times at the Greater Greensboro Open — 1938, 1946, 1949–50, 1955–56, 1960 and 1965.

Biggest winning margin

■ The greatest margin of victory in a professional tournament is 21 strokes by Jerry Pate (US; b. 16 Sep 1953), who won the Colombian Open with 262, from 10–13 Dec 1981. Cecilia Leitch won the Canadian Ladies' Open Championship in 1921 by the biggest margin for a match-play title, 17 up and 15 to play.

Willie Smith won the US Open in 1899 by 11 strokes, with a score of 315. Jack Nicklaus won the Masters in 1965 with a 9-stroke margin, scoring 271. Arthur D'Arcy 'Bobby' Locke (South Africa; 1917–87) achieved the greatest winning margin in a PGA tour event by 16 strokes in the Chicago Victory National Championship in 1948.

Youngest and oldest champions
British Open ■ The youngest winner of the British Open was Tom Morris, Jr (1851–75) at Prestwick, Strathclyde, United Kingdom, in 1868 at age 17 yr 249 days.

The oldest Open champion was 'Old Tom' Morris (1821–1908), when he won at Prestwick in 1867, at age 46 yr 99 days. Oldest this century has been the 1967 champion, Roberto de Vicenzo, at 44 yr 93 days.

US Open ■ The oldest US Open champion was Hale Irwin (b. 3 Jun 1945), at 45 yr 15 days on 18 Jun 1990. The youngest winner was John J. McDermott, at 19 yr 317 days in 1911; this is also the record for the youngest winner of any PGA event in the United States.

The Masters ■ The oldest winner of the Masters was Jack Nicklaus, at the age of 46 years 81 days in 1986. Severiano Ballesteros (Spain) was the youngest player to win the Masters, at 23 yr 2 days in 1980.

PGA ■ The oldest winner of the PGA championship was Julius Boros (b. 3 Mar 1920) at the age of 48 yr 110 days in 1968. Eugene 'Gene' Sarazen (b. 27 Feb 1902) was the youngest PGA winner in 1922 at the age of 20 yr 170 days.

The oldest winner of a PGA tour event was Sam Snead at the age of 52 yr 312 days at the 1965 Greater Greensboro Open.

LPGA ■ The youngest LPGA tour event winner was Marlene Hagge (b. 16 Feb 1934) who won the 1952 Sarasota Open at the age of 18 yr 14 days. The oldest LPGA champion was Jo Anne Carter (nee Gunderson: b. 4 Apr 1939) at the 1985 Safeco Classic at the age of 46 yr 163 days.

Thuashni Selvaratnam (b. 9 Jun 1976) won the 1989 Sri Lankan Ladies Amateur Open Golf Championship, aged 12 yr 324 days, at Nuwara Eliya Golf Club on 29 Apr 1989. Angela Uzelli (b. 1 Feb 1940) won the English Women's Championship, aged 50 yr 114 days, at Rye, East Sussex on 26 May 1990.

NCAA Championships ■ The only golfer to win three NCAA titles is Ben Daniel Crenshaw (b. 11 Jan 1952) of the University of Texas in 1971–73, tying with Tom Kite in 1972.

Most club championships ■ Marjorie Edey (1913–81) was ladies champion at Charleswood Golf Club, Winnipeg, Manitoba, Canada 36 times between 1937 and 1980. The men's record is 34, by Bernard Charles Cusack (b. 24 Jan 1920), including 33 consecutive wins, at the Narembeen GC, Western Australia, between 1943 and 1982.

At different clubs, Peter Toogood (Australia; b. 11 Apr 1930) has won 35 championships: 2 at Huntingdale GC, Victoria, five at Riverside GC, 9 at Kingston Beach GC and 19 at Royal Hobart GC, all Tasmania. The American record for the most club championships at more than one club is 44, by Frances Miles-Maslon Hirsh, between 1951 and 1990.

Largest tournament ■ The Volkswagen Grand Prix Open Amateur Championship in the United Kingdom attracted a record 321,238 (206,820 men and 114,958 women) competitors in 1984.

HOLES IN ONE

Longest ■ The longest straight hole ever holed in one shot was, appropriately, at the tenth (447 yd) at Miracle Hil's Golf Club, Omaha, NE by Robert Mitera (b. 1944) on 7 Oct 1965. Mitera stood 5 ft 6 in tall and weighed 165 lb. He was a two handicap player who normally drove 245 yd. A 50 mph gust carried his shot over a 290 yd drop-off.

The longest 'dog-leg' hole achieved in one shot is the 480 yd fifth hole at Hope Country Club, AR by L. Bruce on 15 Nov 1962.

The women's record is 393 yd, by Marie Robie on the first hole of the Furnace Brook Golf Club, Wollaston, MA on 4 Sep 1949.

Consecutive ■ There are at least 17 cases of 'aces' being achieved in two consecutive holes, of which the greatest was Norman L. Manley's unique 'double albatross' on the par-4 330 yd seventh and par-4 290 yd eighth holes on the Del Valle Country Club course, Saugus, CA on 2 Sep 1964.

The first woman to record consecutive 'aces' was Sue Prell, on the 13th and 14th holes at Chatswood Golf Club, Sydney, Australia on 29 May 1977.

The closest to achieving three consecutive holes in one were the late Dr Joseph Boydstone on the third, fourth and ninth at Bakersfield GC, CA, on 10 Oct 1962 and the Rev Harold Snider (b. 4 Jul 1900), who aced the eighth, 13th and 14th holes of the par-3 Ironwood course, AZ on 9 Jun 1976.

Youngest and oldest ■ The youngest golfer recorded to have shot a hole-in-one is Coby Orr (5 years) of Littleton, CO on the 103 yd fifth at the Riverside Golf Course, San Antonio, TX in 1975.

The youngest American female to score an ace was Mrs Shirley Kunde (nee Caley) in August 1943, at age 13.

The oldest golfers to have performed this feat are: (men) 99 yr 244 days old Otto Bucher (Switzerland; b. 12 May 1885) on the 130 yd 12th at La Manga GC, Spain on 13 Jan 1985; (women) 95 yr 257 days old Erna Ross (b. 9 Sep 1890) on the 112 yd 17th at The Everglades Club, Palm Beach, FL on 23 Apr 1986.

The oldest player to score his age is C. Arthur Thompson (1869–1975) of Victoria, British Columbia, Canada, who scored 103 on the Uplands course of 6,215 yd at age 103 in 1973.

Greyhound Racing

Origins ■ The first greyhound meeting was staged at Hendon, London, United Kingdom, with a railed hare operated by a windlass, in September 1876. Modern greyhound racing originated with the perfecting of the mechanical hare by Owen Patrick Smith at Emeryville, CA, in 1919. St Petersburg Kennel Club, located in St Petersburg, FL, which opened on 3 Jan 1925, is the oldest greyhound track in the world still in operation on its original site.

Derby ■ The only two greyhounds to have won the American Derby, at Taunton, MA, twice are Real Huntsman in 1950–51 and Dutch Bahama in 1984–85.

Fastest greyhound ■ The highest speed at which any greyhound has been timed is 41·72 mph (410 yd in 20·1 sec) by The Shoe on the then straightaway track at Richmond, New South Wales, Australia on 25 Apr 1968. It is estimated that he covered the last 100 yd in 4·5 sec or at 45·45 mph.

US speed records ■ Tiki's Ace ran a distance of ⁵/₁₆ mile in 29·61 sec in Naples, Ft Myers, FL in 1988. The fastest ³/₈ mile time was 36·43 sec by P's Rambling in Hollywood, FL in 1987. Just Deb ran a ⁷/₁₆ mile track in 42·43 sec in Sanford, Orlando, FL in 1986.

Most wins ■ The most career wins is 143, by the American greyhound, JR's Ripper of Multnomah, Fairview, OR and Tuscon, AZ in 1982–86. The most wins in a year is 61, by Indy Ann in Mexico and the United States in 1966.

The most consecutive victories is 32 by Ballyregan Bob, owned by Cliff Kevern and trained by George Curtis, from 25 Aug 1984 to 9 Dec 1986, including 16 track record times. His race wins were by an average of more than nine lengths.

Joe Dump of Greenetrack, Eutaw, AL holds the US record, with 31 consecutive wins from 18 Nov 1978 to 1 Jun 1979.

Highest earnings ■ The career earnings record is held by Homespun Rowdy with $297,000, in the US, 1984–87.

The richest first prize for a greyhound race is $125,000, won by Ben G Speedboat in the Great Greyhound Race of Champions at Seabrook, NH on 23 Aug 1986.

Longest odds ■ Apollo Prince won at odds of 250–1 at Sandown GRC, Springvale, Victoria, Australia on 14 Nov 1968.

Most stakes victories ■ Real Huntsman achieved ten wins in 1949–51, including the American Derby twice.

Highest syndicated price ■ P's Rambling was syndicated for $500,000 in 1987.

Gymnastics

Origins ■ A primitive form of gymnastics was practiced in ancient Greece and Rome during the period of the ancient Olympic Games (776 B.C. to A.D. 393) but Johann Friedrich Simon was the first teacher of modern gymnastics at Basedow's School, Dessau, Germany in 1776.

World Championships *Women* ■ The greatest number of titles won in the World Championships (including Olympic Games) is 12 individual wins and five team, by Larisa Semyonovna Latynina (b. 27 Dec 1934) of the USSR, between 1956 and 1964. The USSR has won the team title on 19 occasions (ten world and nine Olympic).

Men ■ Boris Anfiyanovich Shakhlin (USSR; b. 27 Jan 1932) won ten individual titles between 1954 and 1964. He also had three team wins.

The USSR has won the team title a record 11 times (seven World Championships, four Olympics) between 1952 and 1989.

Youngest champions ■ Aurelia Dobre (Romania; b. 6 Nov 1972), won the women's overall world title at age 14 yr 352 days on 23 Oct 1987. Daniela Silivas (Romania) revealed in 1990 that she was born on 9 May 1971, a year later than previously claimed, so that she was age 14 yr 185 days when she won the gold medal for balance beam on 10 Nov 1985.

The youngest male world champion was Dmitriy Bilozerchev (USSR; b. 17 Dec 1966) at 16 yr 315 days, at Budapest, Hungary on 28 Oct 1983.

The most successful US gymnast has been Kurt Bittereaux Thomas (b. 29 Mar 1952), who won three gold medals: floor exercises 1978 and 1979, horizontal bar 1979.

Olympics ■ Japan has won the men's team title most often in 1960, 1964, 1968, 1972 and 1976.

Records are accepted for the most repetitions of the following activities within the given time span.

CHINS (CONSECUTIVE) 370 Lee Chin-yong (South Korea; b. 15 Aug 1925) at Backyon Gymnasium, Seoul, South Korea on 14 May 1988.

CHINS ONE ARM (FROM A RING)—**CONSECUTIVE** 22 Robert Chisnall (b. 9 Dec 1952) at Queen's University, Kingston, Ontario, Canada on 3 Dec 1982. (Also 18 two-finger chins, 12 one-finger chins).

PARALLEL BAR DIPS—1 HOUR 3,495 Simon Kent (United Kingdom) at Mablethorpe, United Kingdom on 31 Aug 1989.

PRESS-UPS (PUSH-UPS)—24 HOURS 37,350 Paddy Doyle (United Kingdom) at the Holiday Inn, Birmingham, United Kingdom on 1–2 May 1989.

PRESS-UPS IN A YEAR Paddy Doyle achieved a documented 1,500,230 press-ups of which the 24-hour record was a part, from October 1988 to October 1989.

PRESS-UPS (ONE ARM)—5 HOURS 5,260 Paddy Doyle at National Exhibition Centre, Birmingham, United Kingdom on 6 May 1990.

PRESS-UPS (FINGER TIP)—5 HOURS 5,570 Vince Manson (United Kingdom) at HM Gartree Prison, United Kingdom in December 1988.

PRESS-UPS (ONE FINGER)—CONSECUTIVE 100 Harry Lee Welch Jr at Durham, NC on 31 Mar 1985.

SIT-UPS—24 HOURS 60,405 Louis Scripa Jr (US) at Jack La Lanne's American Health & Fitness Spa, Sacramento, CA on 5–6 Aug 1985.

LEG RAISES—12 HOURS 41,788 Lou Scripa Jr at Jack La Lanne's American Health & Fitness Spa, Sacremento, CA on 2 Dec 1988.

SQUATS—1 HOUR 2,550 Ashrita Furman (US) at Philadelphia, PA on 3 Nov 1989.

SQUAT THRUSTS—1 HOUR 2,150 Paddy Doyle at the Pat Roach Health Centre, Birmingham, United Kingdom on 23 Feb 1990.

BURPEES—1 HOUR 1,551 Ashrita Furman at the Natural Physique Centre, NY on 13 Mar 1990.

PUMMEL HORSE DOUBLE CIRCLES—CONSECUTIVE 75 by Lee Thomas (United Kingdom) on the British Broadcasting Corporation television on 12 Dec 1985.

The USSR has won the women's title nine times (1952–80, 1988).

The most men's individual gold medals is six, by: Boris Shakhlin (USSR), one in 1956, four (two shared) in 1960 and one in 1964; and Nikolay Yefimovich Andrianov (USSR; b. 14 Oct 1952), one in 1972, four in 1976 and one in 1980.

Vera Caslavska-Odlozil (Czechoslovakia; b. 3 May 1942) has won most individual gold medals, with seven, three in 1964 and four (one shared) in 1968. Larisa Latynina won six individual gold medals and was on three winning teams from 1956–64, earning nine gold medals. She also won five silver and four bronze — 18 in all — an Olympic record.

The most medals for a male gymnast is 15, by Nikolai Andrianov (USSR), seven gold, five silver and three bronze, from 1972–80.

Aleksandr Nikolaievich Dityatin (USSR; b. 7 Aug 1957) is the only man to win a medal in all eight categories in the same Games, with three gold, four silver and one bronze at Moscow in 1980.

United States ■ The best US performances were in the 1904 Games. Anton Heida (b. 1878) won five gold medals and a silver, and George Eyser (b. 1871), who had a wooden leg, won three gold, two silver and a bronze medal. Mary Lou

Retton (b.24 Jan 1968) won a women's record five medals in 1984, gold at all-around, two silver and two bronze. The most medals won by a US male gymnast since 1904 is four, by Mitchell Jay 'Mitch' Gaylord (b. 10 Mar 1961), a team gold and a silver and two bronze in individual events in 1984, when both Bart Conner (b. 28 Mar 1958) and Peter Glen Vidmar (b. 3 Jun 1961) won two gold medals.

Highest score ■ Nadia Comaneci (Romania; b. 12 Nov 1961) was the first to achieve a perfect score (10·00) in the Olympics, and achieved seven in all at Montreal, Canada in July 1976.

World Cup ■ Gymnasts who have won two World Cup (instituted 1975) overall titles are three men, Nikolai Andrianov (USSR), Aleksandr Dityatin (USSR) and Li Ning (China; b. 8 Sep 1963), and one woman, Maria Yevgenyevna Filatova (USSR; b. 19 Jul 1961).

US championships ■ Alfred A. Jochim (1902–81) won a record seven men's all-round US titles, 1925–30 and 1933, and a total of 34 at all exercises between 1923 and 1934. The women's record is six all-round, 1945–46 and 1949–52, and 39 at all exercises, including 11 in succession at balance beam, 1941–51, by Clara Marie Schroth Lomady (b. 5 Oct 1920).

American Cup ■ The American Cup was created by the USGF in 1976. Since 1980 it has been called the McDonald's American Cup.

Most wins ■ Mary Lou Retton has won the title three times, more than any other gymnast, from 1983 to 1985. Kurt Thomas has also won three consecutive times (1978–80) making him champion of the men's division.

Youngest international ■ Pasakevi 'Voula' Kouna (b. 6 Dec 1971) was 9 yr 299 days at the start of the Balkan Games at Serres, Greece on 1 Oct 1981, when she represented Greece.

Modern rhythmic gymnastics ■ The most overall individual world titles in modern rhythmic gymnastics is three, by Maria Gigova (Bulgaria), in 1969, 1971 and 1973 (shared). Bulgaria has a record eight team titles in 1969, 1971, 1973, 1983, 1985, 1987, 1989 and 1989 (shared). Bianka Panova (Bulgaria; b. 27 May 1960) won all four apparatus gold medals, all with maximum scores, and won a team gold in 1987. Marina Lobach (USSR; b. 26 Jun 1970) won the 1988 Olympic title with perfect scores for all events. Lilia Ignatova (Bulgaria) has won both the individual World Cup titles that have been held, in 1983 and 1986.

Somersaults ■ Ashrita Furman performed 8,341 forward rolls in 10 hr 30 min over 12 miles 390 yards from Lexington to Charleston, MA on 30 Apr 1986. Shigeru Iwasaki (b. 1960) backwards somersaulted 54·68 yd in 10·8 sec at Tokyo, Japan on 30 Mar 1980.

Static wall 'sit' (or Samson's Chair) ■ Paddy Doyle stayed in an unsupported sitting position against a wall for 4 hr 40 min at The Magnet Centre, Erdington, West Midlands, United Kingdom on 18 Apr 1990.

Handball

Origins ■ Handball was first played *c.* 1895 in Germany. It was introduced into the Olympic Games at Berlin in 1936 as an 11-a-side outdoor game, with Germany winning, but when reintroduced in 1972 it was an indoor game with seven-a-side, the standard size of teams since 1952.

World records ● Paddy Doyle of Birmingham, United Kingdom has set numerous stamina records in gymnastics, most notably the most press-ups in a year. His versatility is also illustrated by being the current record holder in static wall sit and squat thrusts.

The International Handball Federation was founded in 1946. The first international match was held at Halle/Saale on 3 Sep 1925, when Austria beat Germany 6–3.

Most championships *Olympic* ■ The USSR has won four titles — men 1976 and 1988, women 1976 and 1980. Yugoslavia has also won two men's titles, in 1972 and 1984.

World Championship (instituted 1938) ■ Romania has won four men's and three women's titles (two outdoor, one indoor) from 1956 to 1974. East Germany has also won three women's titles, in 1971, 1975 and 1978.

Highest score ■ The highest score in an international match was recorded when the USSR beat Afghanistan 86–2 in the 'Friendly Army Tournament' at Miskolc, Hungary in August 1981.

Harness Racing

Origins ■ Trotting races were held in Valkenburg, the Netherlands in 1554. In the United Kingdom the trotting gait (the simultaneous use of the diagonally opposite legs) was known in the 16th century. The sulky first appeared in 1829. Pacers thrust out their fore and hind legs simultaneously on one side.

The sport became very popular in the United States in the 19th century, and the National Trotting Association was founded, originally as the National Association for the Promotion of the Interests of the Trotting Turf, in 1870. It brought needed controls to a sport that had been threatened by gambling corruption.

Most successful driver ■ The most successful sulky driver in North American harness racing history has been Herve Filion (b. 1 Feb 1940) of Québec, Canada, who had achieved 12,276 wins and prize earnings of $68,335,507 through 26 Jun 1990, including a record 814 wins in a year, 1989.

John D. Campbell (US; b. 8 Apr 1955) has the highest career earnings of $83,587,295 through 27 Jun 1990. This includes a season record of $11,148,565 in 1988, when he won 480 races.

Highest price ■ $19·2 million for Nihilator (a pacer), who was syndicated by Wall Street Stable and Almahurst Stud Farm in 1984.

The highest price paid for a trotter is $6 million,

for Mack Lobell, by John Erik Magnusson of Vislanda, Sweden in 1988.

Greatest winnings ■ For any harness horse the amount is $3,225,653, by the pacer Nihilator, who won 35 of 38 races in 1984–85. The greatest amount won by a trotting horse is $2,919,421, by Ourasi (France) to the end of 1988.

The single season records are $1,878,798, by trotter Mack Lobell in 1987, and $1,864,286, by pacer Nihilator in 1985.

The largest ever purse was $2,161,000, for the Woodrow Wilson two-year-old race over 1 mile at The Meadowlands, NJ on 16 Aug 1984. Of this sum a record $1,080,500 went to the winner, Nihilator, driven by William O'Donnell (b. 4 May 1948).

Hambletonian ■ The most famous trotting race in North America, the Hambletonian Stakes, run annually for three-year-olds, was first staged at Syracuse, NY in 1926. Since 1956 it has been run at Du Quoin, IL. The race is named after the great sire Hambletonian, born in 1849, from whom almost all harness horses track back in pedigree.

The race record time is 1 min 53·3 sec, by Mack Lobell, driven by John Campbell in 1987.

Little Brown Jug ■ Pacing's three-year-old classic has been held annually at Delaware, OH from 1946. The name honors a great 19th-century pacer. The race record time is 1 min 52·1 sec, by Nihilator, driven by Bill O'Donnell in 1985.

Horse Racing

Origins ■ Horsemanship was an important part of the Hittite culture of Anatolia, Turkey, dating from 1400 B.C. The 33rd ancient Olympic Games of 648 B.C. in Greece featured horse racing. Horse races can be traced in England from the third century. The first sweepstakes race was originated by the 12th Earl of Derby at his estate in Epsom in 1780. The Epsom Derby is still run today, and is the classic race of the English flat racing season.

Horses were introduced to the North American continent from Spain by Cortéz in 1519. In colonial America horse racing was common, Colonel Richard Nicholls, commander of English forces in New York, is believed to have staged the first organized race at Salisbury Plain, Long Island, NY in 1665. Thoroughbred racing was first staged at Saratoga Springs, NY in 1863.

The first Jockey Club to be founded was at Charleston, SC in 1734.

HORSES

Most successful ■ The horse with the best win-loss record was Kincsem, a Hungarian mare foaled in 1874, who was unbeaten in 54 races (1876–79) throughout Europe, including the Goodwood Cup of 1878.

Longest winning sequence ■ Camarero, foaled in 1951, was undefeated in 56 races in Puerto Rico from 19 Apr 1953 to his first defeat on 17 Aug 1955 (in his career to 1956, he won 73 of 77 races).

Career ■ Galgo Jr (foaled 1928) won 137 of 159 starts in Puerto Rico between 1930 and 1936; in

HARNESS RACING MILE RECORDS

TROTTING

World mile record	1:52·2	*Mack Lobell* (driver, John Campbell)	Springfield	21 Aug	1987

PACING

World	1:48·4	*Matt's Scooter* (driver, Michel Lachance)	Lexington	23 Sep	1988
World race record	1:49·6	*Nihilator* (driver, William O'Donnell)	East Rutherford	3 Aug	1985
	1:49·6	*Call For Rain* (driver, Clint Albraith)	Lexington	1 Oct	1988

Most wins ● Several jockeys have won a record eight races at a single meeting. The most recent and most notable was Pat Day, who achieved his successes from only nine rides. (Photo: All-Sport/Mike Powell)

1931 he won a record 30 races in one year.

Career — United States ■ The most wins is 89, by Kingston from 138 starts, 1886–94. This included 33 in stakes races, but the horse with the most wins in stake races in the US is Exterminator (foaled 1915), with 34 between 1918 and 1923. John Henry (foaled 1975) won a record 25 graded stake races, including 16 at Grade 1, 1978–84. On his retirement in 1984, his career prize money was $6,597,947, nearly twice as much as the next best. Of 83 races he won 39, he was second 15 times and third 9 times.

Same race ■ Doctor Syntax (foaled 1811) won the Preston Gold Cup on seven successive occasions, 1815–21.

Triple Crown winners ■ The American Triple Crown (Kentucky Derby, Preakness Stakes, Belmont Stakes) has been achieved 11 times, most recently by Affirmed in 1978.

The English Triple Crown (2,000 Guineas, Derby, St Leger) has been won 15 times, most recently by Nijinsky in 1970.

The fillies' equivalent (1,000 Guineas, Oaks, St Leger) has been won nine times, most recently by Oh So Sharp in 1985. Two of these fillies also won the 2,000 Guineas: Formosa (in a dead-heat) in 1868 and Sceptre in 1902.

Breeders' Cup ■ The highest prize money for a day's racing is $10 million, for the Breeders' Cup series of seven races staged annually since 1984. Included each year is a record $3 million for the Breeders' Cup Classic.

The jockey to have won the most Breeders' Cup races is Laffit Pincay, Jr, with five from 1985 to 1989, and the trainer with the most wins is D. Wayne Lukas, with ten.

Highest price ■ Enormous valuations placed on potential stallions may be determined from sales of a minority holding, but such valuations would, perhaps, not be reached on the open market.

The most paid for a yearling is $13·1 m on 23 Jul 1985 at Keeneland, KY, by Robert Sangster and partners for Seattle Dancer.

Greatest winnings ■ The career earnings record is $6,679,242, by the 1987 Kentucky Derby winner Alysheba (foaled 1984), from 1986–88. The most prize money earned in a year is $4,578,454, by Sunday Silence (foaled 1986) in 1989, with seven wins from nine races. His total included $1,350,000 from the Breeders' Cup Classic and a $1 million bonus for the best record in the Triple Crown races: he won the Kentucky Derby and Preakness Stakes and was second in the Belmont Stakes.

The leading money-winning mare is Lady's Secret (foaled 1982), with $3,021,325 in earnings from 1984 to 1987. The one race record is $2·6 million, by Spend A Buck (foaled 1982) for the Jersey Derby, Garden State Park, NJ on 27 May 1985, of which $2 million was a bonus for having previously won the Kentucky Derby and two preparatory races at Garden State Park.

Biggest weight ■ The biggest weight ever carried is 420 lb by both Mr Maynard's mare and Mr Baker's horse in a match won by the former over a mile at York, United Kingdom on 21 May 1788.

Oldest winners ■ The oldest horses to win on the Flat have been the 18-year-olds Revenge, at Shrewsbury, United Kingdom on 23 Sep 1790,

MAJOR RACE RECORDS

RACE (instituted)	RECORD TIME	MOST WINS			LARGEST FIELD
		Jockey	Trainer	Owner	
TRIPLE CROWN					
Kentucky Derby (1875) 1¼ miles Churchill Downs	1 min 59·4 sec *Secretariat* 1973	5–Eddie Arcaro 1938, 41, 45, 48, 52 5–Bill Hartack 1957, 60, 62, 64, 69	6–Ben Jones 1938, 41, 44, 48, 49, 52	8–Calumet Farm 1941, 44, 48, 49, 52, 57, 58, 68	23 (1974)
Preakness Stakes (1873) 1 mile 1½f Pimlico, Baltimore	1 min 53·2 sec *Tank's Prospect* 1985	6–Eddie Arcaro 1941, 48, 50, 51, 55, 57	7–Robert Wyndham Walden 1875, 78, 79, 80, 81, 82, 88	5–George Lorillard 1878, 79, 80, 81, 82	18 (1928)
Belmont Stakes (1867) 1½ miles Belmont Park, New York	2 min 24·0 sec *Secretariat* 1973 (By a record 31 lengths)	6–Jimmy McLaughlin 1882, 83, 84, 86, 87, 88 6–Eddie Arcaro 1941, 42, 45, 48, 52, 55	8–James Rowe Sr 1883, 84, 1901, 04, 07, 08, 10, 13	5–Dwyer Bros 1883, 84, 86, 87, 88 5–James R. Keene 1901, 04, 07, 08, 10 5–William Woodward Sr (Belair Stud) 1930, 32, 35, 36, 39	15 (1983)
FAMOUS INTERNATIONAL RACES					
Derby (1780) 1½ miles Epsom, United Kingdom	2 min 33·8 sec *Mahmoud* 1936 2 min 33·84 sec *Kahyasi* 1988 (Electronically timed)	9–Lester Piggott 1954, 57, 60, 68, 70, 72, 76, 77, 83	7–Robert Robson 1793, 1802, 09, 10, 15, 17, 23 7–John Porter 1868, 82, 83, 86, 90, 91, 99 7–Fred Darling 1922, 25, 26, 31, 38, 40, 41	5–3rd Earl of Egremont 1782, 1804, 05, 07, 26 5–HH Aga Khan III 1930, 35, 36, 48, 52	34 (1862)
Prix de l'Arc de Triomphe (1920) 1 mile 864 yd Longchamp, France	2 min 26·3 sec *Trempolino* 1987	4–Jacques Doyasbère 1942, 44, 50, 51 4–Frédéric 'Freddy' Head 1966, 72, 76, 79 4–Yves Saint-Martin 1970, 74, 82, 84 4–Pat Eddery 1980, 85, 86, 87	4–Charles Semblat 1942, 44, 46, 49 4–Alec Head 1952, 59, 76, 81 4–François Mathet 1950, 51, 70, 82	6–Marcel Boussac 1936, 37, 42, 44, 46, 49	30 (1967)
VRC Melbourne Cup (1861) 1 mile 1739 yd Flemington, Victoria, Australia	3 min 17·1 sec *Tawrrific* 1989	4–Bobby Lewis 1902, 15, 19, 27 4–Harry White 1974, 75, 78, 79	7–Bart Cummings 1965, 66, 67, 74, 75, 77, 79	4–Etienne de Mestre 1861, 62, 67, 78	39 (1890)
Grand National (1839) 4½ miles Aintree, Liverpool, United Kingdom	8 min 47·8 sec *Mr Frisk* 1990	5–George Stevens 1856, 63, 64, 69, 70	4–Fred Rimell 1956, 61, 70, 76	3–James Machell 1873, 74, 76 3–Sir Charles Assheton-Smith 1893, 1912, 13 3–Noel Le Mare 1973, 74, 77	66 (1929)

Marksman, at Ashford, Kent, United Kingdom on 4 Sep 1826 and Jorrocks, at Bathurst, Australia on 28 Feb 1851. At the same age Wild Aster won three hurdle races in six days in March 1919 and Sonny Somers won two steeplechases in February 1980.

World speed records ■ The highest race speed recorded is 43·26 mph by Big Racket, 20·8 sec for ¼ mile , at Mexico City, Mexico on 5 Feb 1945. The four-year-old carried 114 lb. The record for 1½ miles is 37·82 mph by 3-year-old Hawkster (carrying 121 lb) at Santa Anita Park, CA on 14 Oct 1989, with a time of 2 min 22·8 sec.

JOCKEYS

Most successful ■ William Lee 'Bill' Shoemaker (US; b. weighing 2½ lb, 19 Aug 1931), now weighing 97 lb and standing 4 ft 11 in, rode a record 8,833 winners from 40,350 mounts from his first ride on 19 Mar 1949 and first winner on 20 Apr 1949 to his retirement on 3 Feb 1990. Laffit Pincay, Jr (b. 29 Dec 1946; Panama City) has earned a career record $148,112,855 from 1964 to the end of 1989.

The most races won by a jockey in a year is 598 from 2,312 rides, by Kent Desormeaux (b. 27 Feb 1970) in 1989. The highest earnings won in a year is $14,877,298, by José Adeon Santos (US; b. 26 Apr 1961, Chile) in 1988.

Wins ■ The most winners ridden in one day is nine, by Chris Wiley Antley (US; b. 6 Jan 1966) on 31 Oct 1987. They consisted of four in the afternoon at Aqueduct, NY and five in the evening at The Meadowlands, NJ.

One card ■ The most winners ridden on one card is eight, by Hubert S. Jones, 17, from 13 rides at Caliente, CA on 11 Jun 1944; Oscar Barattuci, at Rosario City, Argentina on 15 Dec 1957; Dave Gall, from ten rides at Cahokia Downs, East St Louis, IL on 18 Oct 1978; Chris Loseth, from ten rides at Exhibition Park, Vancouver, BC, Canada on 9 Apr 1984; Robert Williams, from ten rides at Lincoln, NE on 29 Sep 1984; and Pat Day, from only nine rides at Arlington, IL on 13 Sep 1989.

Consecutive ■ The longest winning streak is 12, by: Sir Gordon Richards (1904–86) (one race at Nottingham, United Kingdom on 3 Oct, six out of six at Chepstow on 4 Oct and the first five races next day at Chepstow) in 1933; and by Pieter Stroebel at Bulawayo, Southern Rhodesia (now Zimbabwe), 7 Jun–7 Jul 1958.

TRAINERS

Jack Charles Van Berg (US; b. 7 Jun 1936) has the greatest number of wins in a year, 496 in 1976, and in a career, 5,389 from 1955 to the start of 1990. The greatest amount won in a year is $17,842,358, by Darrell Wayne Lukas (US; b. 2 Sep 1935) in 1988. The only trainer to saddle the first five finishers in a championship race is Michael William Dickinson (b. 3 Feb 1950), in the Cheltenham Gold Cup on 17 Mar 1983; he won a record 12 races in one day, 27 Dec 1982.

OWNERS

The most lifetime wins by an owner is 4,775, by Marion H. Van Berg (1895–1971), in North America in 35 years. The most wins in a year is 494, by Dan R. Lasater (US) in 1974. The greatest amount won in a year is $5,858,168, by Ogden Phipps (US) in 1988.

FLAT RACING

The Derby ■ The greatest of England's five Classics is the Derby Stakes, inaugurated on 4 May 1780, and named after Edward Stanley, 12th Earl of Derby (1752–1834). The distance was increased in 1784 from a mile to 1½ miles . The race has been run at Epsom Downs, Surrey, United Kingdom, except for the two war periods, when it was run at Newmarket, Cambridgeshire, United Kingdom, and is for three-year-olds only. Since 1884 the weights have been: colts 126 lb, fillies 121 lb. Geldings were eligible until 1904.

Largest and smallest winning margins ■ Shergar won the Derby by a record 10 lengths in 1981. There have been two dead-heats: in 1828 when Cadland beat The Colonel in the run-off, and in 1884 between St Gatien and Harvester (stakes divided).

JUMPING

Grand National ■ The first Grand National Steeple Chase may be regarded as the Grand Liverpool Steeple Chase of 26 Feb 1839, though the race was not given its present name until 1847. It became a handicap in 1843. Except for 1916–18 and 1941–45, the race has been run at Aintree, near Liverpool, United Kingdom, over 30 fences.

Most wins ■ The only horse to win three times is Red Rum (foaled 1965), in 1973, 1974 and 1977, from five runs. He came in second in 1975

and 1976. Manifesto (foaled 1888) ran a record eight times (1895–1904). He won in 1897 and 1899, came in third three times and fourth once.

Highest prize ■ The highest prize, and the richest ever over jumps in Great Britain, was £70,870·60, won by Mr Frisk on 7 Apr 1990.

Highest weight ■ The highest weight ever carried to victory is 79·4 kg by Cloister (1893), Manifesto (1899), Jerry M. (1912) and Poethlyn (1919).

Hurling

Origins ■ A game of very ancient origin, hurling was included in the Tailteann Games (instituted 1829 B.C.). It only became standardized with the formation of the Gaelic Athletic Association in Thurles, Ireland on 1 Nov 1884. The Irish Hurling Union was formed on 24 Jan 1879.

Most titles *All-Ireland* ■ The greatest number of All-Ireland Championships won by one team is 26, by Cork between 1890 and 1986. The greatest number of successive wins is four, by Cork (1941–44).

Most appearances ■ The most appearances in All-Ireland finals is ten, shared by Christy Ring (Cork and Munster) and John Doyle (Tipperary). They also share the record of All-Ireland medals, won with eight each. Ring's appearances on the winning side were in 1941–44, 1946 and 1952–54, while Doyle's were in 1949–51, 1958, 1961–62 and 1964–65. Ring also played in a record 22 inter-provincial finals (1942–63), and was on the winning side 18 times.

Highest and lowest scores ■ The highest score in an All-Ireland final (60 min) was in 1989, when Tipperary, 41 (4 goals, 29 points), beat Antrim, (3 goals, 9 points). The record aggregate score was when Cork, 39 (6 goals, 21 points), defeated Wexford, 25 (5 goals, 10 points), in the 80-minute final of 1970. A goal equals three points. The highest recorded individual score was by Nick Rackard (Wexford), who scored 7 goals and 7 points against Antrim in the 1954 All-Ireland semifinal. The lowest score in an All-Ireland final was when Tipperary (1 goal, 1 point) beat Galway (nil) in the first championship at Birr in 1887.

Longest hit ■ The greatest distance for a 'lift and stroke' is one of 129 yd credited to Tom Murphy of Three Castles, Kilkenny, in a 'long puck' contest in 1906.

Largest crowd ■ The largest crowd was 84,865 for the All-Ireland final between Cork and Wexford at Croke Park, Dublin in 1954.

Ice Hockey

Origins ■ There is pictorial evidence that a hockey-like game (*kalv*) was played on ice in the early 16th century in The Netherlands. The game was probably first played in North America on 25 Dec 1855 at Kingston, Ontario, Canada, but Halifax also lays claim to priority. The International Ice Hockey Federation was founded in 1908. The National Hockey League (NHL) of North America was inaugurated in 1917, and succeeded the National Hockey Association. The first league games were played on 19 Dec 1917. The NHL is now contested by 21 teams from Canada and the US, divided into two divisions within two conferences: Adams and Patrick Divisions in the Wales Conference; Norris and Smythe Divisions in the Campbell Conference.

STANLEY CUP

The top NHL teams play-off annually for the Stanley Cup, which was first presented in 1893 (original cost $ Cdn 48·67) by Lord Stanley of Preston, then Governor-General of Canada. From 1894 it was contested by amateur teams for the Canadian Championship. From 1910 it became the award for the winners of the professional league play-offs.

It has been won most times by the Montreal Canadiens with 23 wins in 1916, 1924, 1930–31, 1944, 1946, 1953, 1956–60, 1965–66, 1968–69, 1971, 1973, 1976–79, 1986, from a record 31 finals.

Most valuable player ■ The Conn Smythe Trophy for the most valuable player in the play-offs has been awarded annually from 1965. The only players to win it twice have been Robert Gordon 'Bobby' Orr (b. 20 Mar 1948) (Boston) 1970 and 1972, Bernard Marcel 'Bernie' Parent (b. 1945; Philadelphia) 1974–75, and Wayne Gretzky (b. 26 Jan 1961; Edmonton) 1985 and 1988.

Henri Richard played on a record 11 winning teams for the Montreal Canadiens between 1956 and 1973.

Most games played ■ Larry Robinson has played in 213 Stanley Cup playoff games for the Montreal Canadiens (1973–89) and the Los Angeles Kings (1990).

Scoring records ■ Wayne Gretzky (Edmonton Oilers and Los Angeles Kings) has scored a record 284 points in Stanley Cup games, 89 goals and a record 195 assists. His goal-scoring record was passed in 1990 by Jari Kurri (Finland; b. 18 May 1960), with 92 for Edmonton. Gretzky scored a playoff record 47 points (16 goals, record 31 assists) in 1985. The most goals in a playoff season is 19, by Reginald Joseph 'Reggie' Leach b. 23 Apr 1950) for Philadelphia Flyers in 1976 and Jari Kurri for Edmonton in 1985.

Five goals in a Stanley Cup game were scored by Maurice Richard (b. 14 Aug 1924) in Montreal's 5–1 win over the Toronto Maple Leafs on 23 Mar 1944; by Darryl Glen Sittler (b. 18 Sep 1950) for Toronto's 8–5 victory over Philadelphia on 22 Apr 1976; by Reggie Leach for Philadelphia's 6–3 victory over the Boston Bruins on 6 May 1976; and by Mario Lemieux (b. 1965) for the Pittsburgh Penguins 10–7 victory over Philadelphia on 25 Apr 1989.

A record six assists in a game were achieved by Mikko Leinonen (b. 15 Jul 1955) for the New York Rangers in their 7–3 victory over Philadelphia on 8 Apr 1982 and by Wayne Gretzky for Edmonton's 13–3 victory over Los Angeles on 9 Apr 1987, when his team set a Stanley Cup game record of 13 goals.

The most points in a game is eight, by Patrik Sundström, three goals and five assists, for the New Jersey Devils (10) *v* Washington Capitals (4) on 22 Apr 1988, and by Mario Lemieux, five goals and three assists, for Pittsburgh (10) *v* Philadelphia (7) on 25 Apr 1989. Lemieux scored four goals in the first period, to equal the record set by Tim Kerr in the second period for the Philadelphia Flyers *v* the New York Rangers at New York on 13 Apr 1985.

Goaltending ■ Jacques Plante holds the record for most shutouts in a playoff career, with 14, with the Montreal Canadiens (1953–63) and the St. Louis Blues (1969–70). The record for most victories in a playoff career is 88, by Billy Smith for the New York Islanders (1975–88).

NATIONAL HOCKEY LEAGUE (NHL) RECORDS

Most games played ■ Gordon 'Gordie' Howe (Canada; b. 31 Mar 1928) played in a record 1,767 NHL regular season games (and 157 play-off games), over a record 26 seasons, from 1946 to 1971 for the Detroit Red Wings and in 1979/80 for the Hartford Whalers. He also played 419 games (and 78 play-off games) for the Houston Aeros and for the New England Whalers in the World Hockey Association from 1973 to 1979, for a grand total of 2,421 major league games.

Most consecutive games played ■ From 8 Oct 1975–5 Apr 1987, Doug Jarvis played 962 consecutive NHL games for the Montreal Canadiens, Washington Capitals and the Hartford Whalers.

Fastest goals ■ In the NHL the fastest goal was after 4 sec by Joseph Antoine Claude Provost (b. 17 Sep 1933; Montreal Canadiens) *v* Boston Bruins in the second period on 9 Nov 1957, and by Denis Joseph Savard (b. 4 Feb 1961; Chicago Black Hawks) *v* Hartford Whalers in the third period at Chicago on 12 Jan 1986. From the opening whistle, the fastest is 5 sec, by Doug Smail (b. 2 Sep 1957; Winnipeg Jets) *v* St Louis Blues at Winnipeg on 20 Dec 1981, and by Bryan John Trottier (b. 17 Jul 1956; New York Islanders) *v* Boston Bruins at Boston on 22 Mar 1984. Bill Mosienko (b. 2 Nov 1921; Chicago Black Hawks) scored three goals in 21 sec *v* New York Rangers on 23 Mar 1952. Toronto scored eight goals in 4 min 52 sec *v* New York Americans on 19 Mar 1938.

Most goals *Team* ■ The NHL record is 21 goals when Montreal Canadiens beat Toronto St Patrick's, 14–7, at Montreal on 10 Jan 1920, and Edmonton Oilers beat Chicago Black Hawks, 12–9, at Chicago on 11 Dec 1985. The NHL single team record is 16, by Montreal Canadiens *v* Quebec Bulldogs 3, at Quebec City on 3 Nov 1920.

Most goals and points *Career* ■ The North American career record for goals is 1,071 (including a record 801 in the NHL) by Gordie Howe (b. 31 Mar 1928; Detroit Red Wings, Houston Aeros, New England Whalers and Hartford Whalers) from 16 Oct 1946 in 32 seasons ending in 1979/80. He took 2,204 games to achieve the 1,000th goal, but Robert Marvin 'Bobby' Hull (b. 3 Jan 1939; Chicago Black Hawks and Winnipeg Jets) scored his 1,000th in 1,600 games on 12 Mar 1978.

Wayne Gretzky (Edmonton Oilers 1979–88, Los Angeles Kings 1988–90) has the NHL record for assists of 1,302 and overall records for NHL and Stanley Cup play-offs for assists, 1,497 and total points, 2,263 (1979 NHL, 284 Stanley Cup). His 766 goals (677 + 89) have come from 985 games, scoring pace far in excess of his rivals.

Season ■ The most goals scored in a season in the NHL is 92 in the 1981/2 season by Wayne Gretzky (b. 26 Jan 1961) for the Edmonton Oilers. He scored a record 215 points, including a record 163 assists in 1985/6.

Game ■ The most goals in an NHL game is seven, by Michael Joseph 'Joe' Malone (b. 28 Feb 1890) in Québec's 10–6 win over Toronto St. Patricks at Québec City on 3¹ Jan 1920. The most assists in an NHL game is seven, by William

WAYNE GRETZKY

Ice hockey's most successful player

Wayne Gretzky (b. 26 Jan 1961, Brantford, Ontario) is probably the best player in the history of the National Hockey League (NHL). His NHL career began in 1979 and he soon established himself as a point-scoring machine. His prodigious ability is best shown when compared to the previous record holder, Gordie Howe. Howe took 26 seasons to accumulate his 1850 points in the NHL, whereas Gretzky scored his 1851st point on 15 Oct 1989, early in his 11th season. His consistency is shown by having won nine Hart Memorial Trophies (awarded for the League's most valuable player) and eight Art Ross Trophies (awarded to the leading point scorer in the regular season).

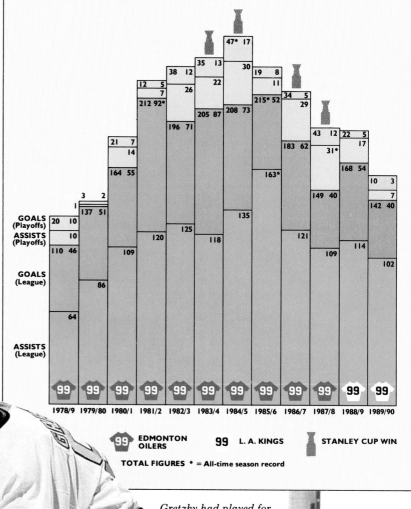

GOALS (Playoffs)
ASSISTS (Playoffs)
GOALS (League)
ASSISTS (League)

| 1978/9 | 1979/80 | 1980/1 | 1981/2 | 1982/3 | 1983/4 | 1984/5 | 1985/6 | 1986/7 | 1987/8 | 1988/9 | 1989/90 |

99 EDMONTON OILERS   99 L.A. KINGS   STANLEY CUP WIN

TOTAL FIGURES * = All-time season record

Gretzky had played for the Edmonton Oilers for nine years in the NHL before joining the L.A. Kings, so it was notable that he scored his record-breaking point against his old club.

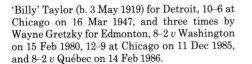

'Billy' Taylor (b. 3 May 1919) for Detroit, 10–6 at Chicago on 16 Mar 1947, and three times by Wayne Gretzky for Edmonton, 8–2 v Washington on 15 Feb 1980, 12–9 at Chicago on 11 Dec 1985, and 8–2 v Québec on 14 Feb 1986.

Consecutive games ■ Harry Broadbent scored in 16 consecutive games for Ottawa in the 1921–22 season.

Most hat tricks ■ The most hat tricks (three ore more goals in a game) in a career is 46, by Wayne Gretzky through the 1989–90 season for the Los Angeles Kings. Wayne Gretzky also holds the record for most hat tricks in a season, 10, in both the 1982 and 1984 seasons for the Edmonton Oilers.

Period ■ The most points in one period is six, by Bryan John Trottier (b. 18 Jul 1956), three goals and three assists in the second period, for the New York Islanders v New York Rangers (9–4) on 23 Dec 1978. Nine players have a record four goals in one period.

The record number of assists in one period is 5, by Dale Hawerchuk, for the Winnipeg Jets v the Los Angeles Kings on 6 Mar 1984.

Most points one game ■ The North American major league record for most points scored in one game is ten, by Jim Harrison (b. 9 Jul 1947) (three goals, seven assists) for Alberta, later Edmonton Oilers in a World Hockey Association match at Edmonton on 30 Jan 1973, and by Darryl Sittler (b. 18 Sep 1950; six goals, four assists) for Toronto Maple Leafs v Boston Bruins in an NHL game at Toronto on 7 Feb 1976.

Most consecutive points ■ The most consecutuive games scoring points was 51, by Wayne Gretzky from 5 Oct 1983–27 Jan 1984 for the Edmonton Oilers.

Goaltending *Career* ■ Terrance 'Terry' Gordon Sawchuk (1929–70) played a record 971 games as a goaltender, for the Detroit Red Wings, the Boston Bruins, the Toronto Maple Leafs, the Los Angeles Kings and the New York Rangers, from 1950 to 1970. He achieved a record 435 wins (to 337 losses, and 188 ties) and had a record 103 career shutouts. Jacques Joseph Ormer Plante (1929–86), with 434 NHL wins surpassed Sawchuk's figure by adding 15 wins in his one season in the WHA for a senior league total of 449 in 868 games.

Season ■ Bernie Parent achieved a record 47 wins in a season, with 13 losses and 12 ties, for Philadelphia in 1973/4.

Most successful goaltending ■ The most shutouts by a goaltender in an NHL career is 103, by Terrance 'Terry' Gordon Sawchuck (1929–70) of Detroit, Boston, Toronto, Los Angeles and New York Rangers, between 1949 and 1970. Gerry Cheevers (b. 2 Dec 1940), for the Boston Bruins, went a record 32 successive games without a defeat in 1971–72. George Hainsworth completed 22 shutouts for the Montreal Canadiens in 1929.

Alex Connell played 461 min 29 sec without conceding a goal for Ottawa in the 1928–29 season. Roy Worters saved 70 shots for the Pittsburgh Pirates v the New York Americans on 24 Dec 1925. Bernie Parent had 47 wins for the Philadelphia Flyers in 1974.

Team records ■ The Montreal Canadiens won a record 60 games and 132 points (with 12 ties) in 80 games played in 1976/7; their eight losses was also the least ever in a season of 70 or more games. The highest percentage of wins in a season was ·875% achieved by the Boston Bruins, with 30 wins in 44 games in 1929/30.

The longest undefeated run during a season, 35 games (25 wins and ten ties), was established by the Philadelphia Flyers from 14 Oct 1979 to 6 Jan 1980. The most goals scored in a season is 446, by the Edmonton Oilers in 1983/4, when they also achieved a record 1,182 scoring points. The most shutouts in a season is 22, in 1928/9 by the Montreal Canadiens, in just 44 games, all by George Hainsworth (b. 26 Jun 1895), who also achieved a record low for goals against percentage of 0.98 that season.

Longest match ■ The longest match was 2 hr 56 min 30 sec (playing time) when Detroit Red Wings beat Montreal Maroons 1–0 in the sixth period of overtime at the Forum, Montreal, at 2:25 A.M. on 25 Mar 1936. Norm Smith, the Red Wings goaltender, turned aside 92 shots for the NHL's longest single shutout.

Player awards ■ The Hart Trophy, awarded annually from the 1923/4 season by the Professional Hockey Writers Association as the Most Valuable Player award of the NHL, has been won a record nine times by Wayne Gretzky, 1980–87, 1989. Gretzky has also won the Art Ross Trophy a record eight times, 1981–87 and 1990; this has been awarded annually from 1947/8 to the NHL season's leading scorer. Bobby Orr of Boston won the James Norris Memorial Trophy, awarded annually from the 1953/4 season to the league's leading defenseman, a record eight times, 1968–75.

Coaches ■ Scotty Bowman coached his teams (St Louis 1967–71, Montreal 1971–79, Buffalo 1979–87) to a record 739 regular and 114 play-off wins in the NHL.

WORLD CHAMPIONSHIPS AND OLYMPIC GAMES

World Championships were first held for amateurs in 1920 in conjunction with the Olympic Games, which were also considered as world championships up to 1968. From 1977 World Championships have been open to professionals. The USSR won 22 world titles between 1954 and 1990, including the Olympic titles of 1956, 1964 and 1968. They have a record seven Olympic titles with a further four, 1972, 1976, 1984 and 1988. The longest Olympic career is that of Richard Torriani (Switzerland; 1911–88) from 1928 to 1948. The most gold medals won by any player is three, achieved by USSR players Vitaliy Semyenovich Davidov, Anatoliy Vasilyevich Firssov, Viktor Grigoryevich Kuzkin and Aleksandr Pavlovich Ragulin in 1964, 1968 and 1972, and by Vladislav Aleksandrovich Tretyak in 1972, 1976 and 1984.

Women ■ The first world championships were won by Canada, who beat the United States 5–2, at Ottawa, Canada on 24 Mar 1990.

Most goals ■ The greatest number of goals recorded in a world championship match was when Australia beat New Zealand 58–0 at Perth on 15 Mar 1987.

Fastest goals ■ In minor leagues, Per Olsen scored 2 seconds after the start of the match for Rungsted against Odense in the Danish First Division at Hørsholm, Denmark on 14 Jan 1990. Three goals in 12 seconds was achieved by Steve D'Innocenzo for Holliston v Westwood in a high school match in Massachusetts on 9 Jan 1982. The Skara Ishockeyclubb, Sweden, scored three goals in 11 seconds against Örebro IK at Skara on 18 Oct 1981. The Vernon Cougars scored five goals in 56 seconds against Salmon Arm Aces at Vernon, BC, Canada on 6 Aug 1982. The Kamloops Knights of Columbus scored seven goals in 2 min 22 sec v Prince George Vikings on 25 Jan 1980.

Ice Skating

Origins ■ The earliest reference to ice skating is in early Scandinavian literature referring to the second century, though its origins are believed, on archaeological evidence, to be ten centuries earlier still. The earliest English account of 1180 refers to skates made of bone. The earliest skating club was the Edinburgh Skating Club, United Kingdom formed in about 1742.

The first recorded race was from Wisbech to Whittlesey, Cambridgeshire, United Kingdom in 1763. The earliest artificial rink in the world was opened in London, United Kingdom on 7 Dec 1842, although the surface was not of ice. The first artificial ice rink was opened in London, United Kingdom on 7 Jan 1876. The International Skating Union was founded at Scheveningen, Netherlands in 1892.

FIGURE SKATING

In North America, the first national body was the Amateur Association of Canada, founded on 30 Nov 1887. The Skating Club of the United States was founded in Philadelphia, PA in 1887.

Most titles *Olympic* ■ The most Olympic gold medals won by a figure skater is three, by: Gillis Grafström (1893–1938) of Sweden in 1920, 1924 and 1928 (also silver medal in 1932); by Sonja Henie (1912–69) of Norway in 1928, 1932 and 1936; and by Irina Konstantinovna Rodnina (USSR; b. 12 Sep 1949) with two different partners, in the Pairs in 1972, 1976 and 1980.

World ■ The greatest number of men's individual world figure skating titles (instituted 1896) is ten, by Ulrich Salchow (1877–1949) of Sweden, in 1901–5 and 1907–11. The women's record (instituted 1906) is also ten individual titles, by Sonja Henie between 1927 and 1936. Irina Rodnina has won ten pairs titles (instituted 1908), four with Aleksey Nikolayevich Ulanov (b. 4 Nov 1947), 1969–72, and six with her husband, Aleksandr Gennadyevich Zaitsev (b. 16 Jun 1952), 1973–78. The most ice dance titles (instituted 1952) won is six, by Lyudmila Alekseyevna Pakhomova (1946–86) and her husband, Aleksandr Georgiyevich Gorshkov (USSR; b. 8 Oct 1946), 1970–74 and 1976. They also won the first ever Olympic ice dance title in 1976.

Richard 'Dick' Totten Button (b. 18 Jul 1929) set US records with two Olympic gold medals, 1948 and 1952, and five world titles, 1948–52. Five women's world titles were won by Carol Eliza beth Heise (b. 20 Jan 1940), 1956–60, as well as the 1960 Olympic gold.

United States ■ The US Championships were first held in 1914. The most titles won by an individual is nine, by Maribel Y. Vinson (1911–61), 1928–33 and 1935–37. She also won six pairs titles, and her aggregate of 15 titles is equaled by Therese Blanchard (nee Weld; 1893–1978) who won six individual and nine pairs titles between 1914 and 1927. The men's individual record is seven, by Roger Turner 1928–34 and by Dick Button, 1946–52. At age 16 in 1946, Button was the youngest ever winner.

Highest marks ■ The highest tally of maximum six marks awarded in an international championship was 29, to Jayne Torvill and Christopher Dean (United Kingdom) in the World Ice Dance Championships at Ottawa,

SPEED SKATING WORLD RECORDS

MEN

Metres	min sec	Name (Country)	Place	Date	
500	36·45	Uwe-Jens Mey (East Germany)	Calgary, Canada	14 Feb	1988
	36·23 u	Nick Thometz (US)	Medeo, USSR	26 Mar	1987
1,000	1:12·58	Igor Zhelozovsky (USSR)	Heerenveen, Netherlands	25 Feb	1989
	1:12·58 A	Pavel Pegov (USSR)	Medeo, USSR	25 Nov	1983
	1:12·05 u	Nick Thometz (US)	Medeo, USSR	27 Mar	1987
1,500	1:52·06	André Hoffmann (East Germany)	Calgary, Canada	20 Feb	1988
3,000	3:57·52	Johann Olav Koss (Norway)	Heerenveen, Netherlands	13 Mar	1990
	3:56·65 u	Sergey Martyuk (USSR)	Medeo, USSR	11 Mar	1977
5,000	6:43·59	Geir Karlstad (Norway)	Calgary, Canada	6 Dec	1987
10,000	13:48·20	Tomas Gustafsson (Sweden)	Calgary, Canada	21 Feb	1988

u *unofficial.* A *set at high altitude.*

WOMEN

Metres	min sec	Name (Country)	Place	Date	
500	39·10	Bonnie Blair (US)	Calgary, Canada	22 Feb	1988
1,000	1:17·65	Christa Rothenberg (now Luding; East Germany)	Calgary, Canada	26 Feb	1988
1,500	1:59·30	Karin Kania (East Germany)	Medeo, USSR	22 Mar	1986
3,000	4:11·94	Yvonne van Gennip (Netherlands)	Calgary, Canada	23 Feb	1988
5,000	7:14·13	Yvonne van Gennip (Netherlands)	Calgary, Canada	28 Feb	1988
10,000†	15:25·25	Yvonne van Gennip (Netherlands)	Heerenveen, Netherlands	19 Mar	1988

† Record not officially recognized for this distance.

WORLD SHORT TRACK SPEED SKATING RECORDS

MEN

Metres	min sec	Name (Country)	Place	Date	
500	44·46	Orazio Fagone (Italy)	Budapest, Hungary	16 Jan	1988
1,000	1:31·80	Tsutomu Kawasaki (Japan)	Amsterdam, Netherlands	17 Mar	1990
1,500	2:25·25	Michel Daignault (Canada)	Calgary, Canada	22 Feb	1988
3,000	5:04·24	Tatsuyoshi Ishihara (Japan)	Amsterdam, Netherlands	17 Mar	1985

WOMEN

Metres	min sec	Name (Country)	Place	Date	
500	47·77	Christina Sciolla (Italy)	Budapest, Hungary	16 Jan	1988
1,000	1:39·00	Li Yan (China)	Calgary, Canada	25 Feb	1988
1,500	2:34·85	Li Yan (China)	Calgary, Canada	23 Feb	1988
3,000	5:18·33	Maria-Rosa Candido (Italy)	Budapest, Hungary	17 Jan	1988

Canada on 22–24 Mar 1984. This comprised seven in the compulsory dances, a perfect set of nine for presentation in the set pattern dance and 13 in the free dance, including another perfect set from all nine judges for artistic presentation. They previously gained a perfect set of nine sixes for artistic presentation in the free dance at the 1983 World Championships in Helsinki, Finland and at the 1984 Winter Olympic Games in Sarajevo, Yugoslavia. In their career, Torvill and Dean received a record total of 136 sixes.

The most by a soloist is seven: by Donald George Jackson (Canada; b. 2 Apr 1940) in the World Men's Championship at Prague, Czechoslovakia in 1962; and by Midori Ito (Japan; b. 13 Aug 1969) in the World Championships at Paris, France in 1989.

Most midair rotations ■ Kurt Browning (Canada; b. 18 Jun 1966) was the first to achieve a quadruple jump in competition—a toe loop—in the World Championships at Budapest, Hungary on 25 Mar 1988. Midori Ito (Japan) was the first woman to complete a jump exceeding three rotations—a triple axel—in the World Championships at Paris, France on 18 Mar 1989.

Distance ■ Robin John Cousins (United Kingdom; b. 17 Aug 1957) achieved 19 ft 1 in in an axel jump and 18 ft with a back flip at Richmond Ice Rink, Surrey, United Kingdom on 16 Nov 1983.

Largest rink ■ The world's largest indoor ice rink is in the Moscow Olympic arena, which has an ice area of 86,800 ft². The five rinks at Fujikyu Highland Skating Center, Japan total 285,243 ft².

SPEED SKATING

Most titles *Olympic* ■ The most Olympic gold medals won in speed skating is six, by Lidiya Pavlovna Skoblikova (b. 8 Mar 1939) of Chelyabinsk, USSR, in 1960 (two) and 1964 (four). The male record is by Clas Thunberg (Finland; 1893–1973) with five gold (including one tied), and also one silver and one tied bronze, in 1924 and 1928. Eric Arthur Heiden (US; b. 14 Jun 1958) also won five gold medals, uniquely at one Games at Lake Placid, NY in 1980.

World ■ The greatest number of world overall titles (instituted 1893) won by any skater is five; by Oscar Mathisen (Norway; 1888–1954) in 1908–9 and 1912–14; and Clas Thunberg in 1923, 1925, 1928–29 and 1931. The most titles won in the women's events (instituted 1936) is five, by Karin Kania (nee Enke, East Germany; b. 20 Jun 1961) in 1982, 1984, 1986–88. Kania also won a record six overall titles at the World Sprint Championships, 1980–81, 1983–84, 1986–87. Eric Heiden won a men's record four men's sprint overall titles, 1977–80.

The record score achieved for the world overall title is 159·356 points, by Nikolay Gulyayev (USSR) at Heerenveen, Netherlands on 14–15 Feb 1987. The record low women's score is 171·630 points, by Jacqueline Börner (East Germany) at Calgary, Canada on 10–11 Feb 1990.

Eric Heiden won a US record three overall world titles 1977–79. His sister Elizabeth Lee 'Beth' Heiden (b. 27 Sep 1959) became in 1979 the only US woman's overall champion. She completed a unique double when the following year she became the first American woman to win the cycling road race world title. Later, at the University of Vermont, she took up cross-country skiing, and won the NCAA title.

World Short-track Championships
■ The most successful skater in these championships (instituted 1978) has been Sylvia Daigle (Canada; b. 1 Dec 1962) women's champion in 1979, 1983 and 1989–90.

Longest race ■ The 'Elfstedentocht' ('Tour of the Eleven Towns'), which originated in the 17th century, was held in the Netherlands from 1909–63, and again in 1985 and 1986, covering 124 miles 483 yd. As the weather does not permit an annual race in the Netherlands, alternative 'Elfstedentocht' take place at suitable venues. These venues have included Lake Vesijärvi, near Lahti, Finland; Ottawa River, Canada; and Lake Weissenssee, Austria. The record time for 200 km is: (men) 5 hr 40 min 37 sec, by Dries van Wijhe (Netherlands); and (women) 5 hr 48 min 8 sec, by Alida Pasveer (Netherlands), both at Lake Weissensee (altitude 3,609 ft), Austria on 11 Feb 1989. Jan-Roelof Kruithof (Netherlands) won the race eight times—1974, 1976–77, 1979–83. An estimated 16,000 skaters took part in 1986.

24 hours ■ Martinus Kuiper (Netherlands) skated 339·681 miles in 24 hr in Alkmaar, Netherlands on 12–13 Dec 1988.

Ice and Sand Yachting

Origins ■ The sport originated in the Low Countries from the year 1600 (earliest patent granted) and along the Baltic coast. The earliest authentic record is Dutch, dating from 1768. Land or sand yachts of Dutch construction were first reported on beaches (now in Belgium) in 1595. The earliest international championship was staged in 1914.

Largest yacht ■ The largest ice yacht was *Icicle*, built for Commodore John E. Roosevelt for racing on the Hudson River, NY in 1869. It was 68 ft 11 in long and carried 1,070 ft² of canvas.

Highest speeds *Ice* ■ The highest speed officially recorded is 143 mph by John D. Buckstaff in a Class A stern-steerer on Lake Winnebago, WI in 1938. Such a speed is possible in a wind of 72 mph.

Sand ■ The official world record for a sand yacht is 66·48 mph set by Christian-Yves Nau (France; b. 1944) in *Mobil* at Le Touquet, France on 22 Mar 1981, when the wind speed reached 75 mph. A speed of 88·4 mph was attained by Nord Embroden (US) in *Midnight at the Oasis* at Superior Dry Lake, CA on 15 Apr 1976.

Jai Alai (Pelota Vasca)

Origins ■ The game, which originated in Italy as *longue paume* and was introduced into

France in the 13th century, is said to be the fastest of all ball games. The glove or *gant* was introduced *c.* 1840 and the *chistera* was invented by Jean 'Gantchiki' Dithurbide of Ste Pée, France. The *grand chistera* was invented by Melchior Curuchague of Buenos Aires, Argentina in 1888. The world's largest *frontón* (enclosed stadium) is the World Jaı Alaı at Miami, FL, which had a record attendance of 15,052 on 27 Dec 1975.

World Championships ■ The Federacion Internacional de Pelota Vasca stage World Championships every four years (first in 1952). The most successful pair have been Roberto Elias and Juan Labat (Argentina), who won the *Trinquete Share* four times, in 1952, 1958, 1962 and 1966. Labat won a record seven world titles in all. The most wins in the long-court game *Cesta Punta* is three, by Hamuy of Mexico, with two different partners, in 1958, 1962 and 1966.

Highest speed ■ An electronically measured ball velocity of 188 mph was recorded by José Ramon Areitio at the Newport Jai Alai, RI on 3 Aug 1979.

Longest domination ■ The longest domination as the world's No. 1 player was enjoyed by Chiquito de Cambo (ne Joseph Apesteguy) (France; 1881–1955) from the beginning of the century until succeeded in 1938 by Jean Urruty (France; b. 19 Oct 1913).

Judo

Origins ■ Judo is a modern combat sport that developed out of an amalgam of several old Japanese martial arts, the most popular of which was ju-jitsu (jiu-jitsu), which is thought to be of Chinese origin. Judo has greatly developed since 1882, when it was first devised by Dr Jigoro Kano (1860–1938). The International Judo Federation was founded in 1951.

Most titles *World and Olympic* ■ World

Undefeated champion ● Yashiro Yamashita, undefeated in his competitive career and world champion four times, gives an exhibition of the skills that made him one of the top judo exponents. (Photo: All-Sport/John Gichigi)

Championships were inaugurated in Tokyo, Japan in 1956. Women's championships were first held in 1980 in New York. Yashiro Yamashita (b. 1 Jun 1957) won nine consecutive Japanese titles from 1977 to 1985: four world titles; Over 95 kg in 1979, 1981 and 1983; Open in 1981, and the Olympic Open category in 1984. He retired undefeated after 203 successive wins, between 1977 and 1985. Two other men have won four world titles: Wilhelm Ruska (Netherlands; b. 29 Aug 1940), Over 93 kg in 1967, 1971 and 1972; Olympic and Open titles, and Shozo Fujii (Japan; b. 12 May 1950), Under 80 kg in 1971, 1973 and 1975; Under 75 kg in 1979. The only men to have won two Olympic gold medals are Wilhelm Ruska (Netherlands), Over 93 kg and Open in 1972; Peter Seisenbacher (Austria; b. 25 Mar 1960), 86 kg in 1984 and 1988; and Hitoshi Saito (Japan; b. 2 Jan 1961), Over 95 kg in 1984 and 1988. Ingrid Berghmans (Belgium; b. 24 Aug 1961) has won a record six women's world titles (first held 1980): Open 1980, 1982, 1984 and 1986 and Under 72 kg in 1984 and 1989. She has also won three silver medals and a bronze. She also won the Olympic 72 kg title in 1988, when women's judo was introduced as a demonstration sport.

The only US judo players to win world titles have been Michael Swain (b. 21 Dec 1960), at men's 71 kg class in 1987, and Ann-Maria Bernadette Burns (b. 15 Aug 1958), at women's 56 kg in 1984.

Highest grades ■ The efficiency grades in judo are divided into pupil (*kyu*) and master (*dan*) grades. The highest awarded is the extremely rare red belt *judan* (10th dan), given to only 13 men so far. The Judo protocol provides for an 11th dan (*juichidan*) who also would wear a red belt, a 12th dan (*junidan*) who would wear a white belt twice as wide as an ordinary belt, and the highest of all, *shihan* (ductor), but these have never been bestowed, save for the 12th dan, to the founder of the sport Dr Jigoro

10 hours ■ The brothers Carl and Peter Udry

Most successful ● Since the introduction of a women's judo world championship in 1980, the most successful individual has been Belgian Ingrid Berghmans, winning six titles. She also won Olympic gold at the 1988 Games when women's judo was a demonstration sport. (Photo: All-Sport)

completed 18,779 judo throwing techniques in a ten-hour period at Hendra Sports Field, Truro, Cornwall, United Kingdom on 29 Aug 1987.

Jiu-Jitsu ■ The World Council of Jiu-Jitsu Organizations has staged World Championships biennially since 1984. The Canadian team has been the team winners on each occasion.

Karate

Origins ■ Based on techniques devised from the sixth century Chinese art of Shaolin boxing (kempo), karate was developed by an unarmed populace in Okinawa as a weapon against armed Japanese oppressors *c.* 1500. Transmitted to Japan in the 1920s by Funakoshi Gichin, this method of combat was refined into karate and organized into a sport with competitive rules. The five major styles of karate in Japan are: *shotokan, wado-ryu, goju-ryu, shito-ryu* and *kyokushinkai*, each of which places different emphasis on speed and power, etc. Other styles include *sankukai, shotokai* and *shukokai. Wu shu* is a comprehensive term embracing all Chinese martial arts. *Kung fu* is one aspect of these arts popularized by the movies.

World Championships ■ Great Britain has won a record five world titles (instituted 1970) at the kumite team event, in 1975, 1982, 1984, 1986 and 1988. Two men's individual kumite titles have been won by: Pat McKay (United Kingdom) at Under 80 kg, in 1982 and 1984; Emmanuel Pinda (France) at Open, in 1984; and Over 80 kg, in 1988; and Theirry Masci (France) at Under 70 kg, in 1986 and 1988. Four women's kumite titles have been won by Guus van Mourik (Netherlands), at Over 60 kg, in 1982, 1984, 1986 and 1988. Three individual kata titles have been won by men: Tsuguo Sakumoto (Japan), in 1984, 1986 and 1988; women: Mie Nakayama (Japan), in 1982, 1984 and 1986.

Top exponents ■ The leading exponents among karateka are a number of 10th dans in Japan.

Lacrosse

MEN
Origins ■ The game is of American Indian origin, derived from the inter-tribal game *bagga-*

taway, and was played before 1492 by Iroquois Indians in lower Ontario, Canada and upper New York State. The French named it after their game of *chouler à la crosse*, known in 1381. Lacrosse was included in the Olympic Games of 1904 and 1908, and featured as an exhibition sport in the 1928, 1932 and 1948 Games.

The first college team in the US was that of New York University in 1877, and the US Amateur Lacrosse Association was founded in 1879.

Most titles *World* ■ The United States has won five of the six World Championships, in 1967, 1974, 1982, 1986 and 1990. Canada won the other world title in 1978, beating the United States 17–16 after extra time — this was the first drawn international match.

United States ■ National champions were determined by committee from 1936, and they received the Wilson Wingate Trophy; from 1971 they have been decided by NCAA play-offs. Johns Hopkins University has the most wins overall: seven NCAA titles between 1974 and 1987, and six wins and five ties between 1941 and 1970.

Highest scores ■ The highest score in an international match is the US' 32–8 win over England at Toronto, Canada in 1986.

WOMEN

The first reported playing of lacrosse by women was in 1886. The game has evolved seperately from the men's game so that the rules now differ considerably.

World Championships / World Cup ■ The first World Cup was held in 1982, and the United States has won twice, in 1982 and 1989.

Microlighting

The Fédération Aéronautique Internationale have established two classes of aircraft for which records are accepted, C1 a/o and R 1-2-3, and the following are the overall best of the two classes (all in the C1 a/o class, except where shown).

World records ■ Distance in a straight line: 1,011·48 miles, Wilhelm Lischak (Austria), Volsau, Austria to Brest, France, 8 Jun 1988.

Altitude: 29,999 ft Eric S. Winton (Australia), Tyagarah Aerodrome, New South Wales, Australia, 11 Apr 1989 (R 1).

Distance in a closed circuit: 1,679·09 miles, Wilhelm Lischak (Austria), Wels, Austria, 18 Jun 1988.

Speed over a 100 km closed circuit: 185 mph, C. T. Andrews (US), 3 Aug 1982.

Speed over a 500 km closed circuit: 182 mph, C. T. Andrews (US), 3 Aug 1982.

Endurance ■ Eve Jackson flew from Biggin Hill, Kent, United Kingdom to Sydney, Australia from 26 Apr 1986 to 1 Aug 1987. The flight took 279 hr 55 min and covered 13,639 miles. From 1 Dec 1987 to 29 Jan 1988, Brian Milton (United Kingdom) flew from London to Sydney with a flying time of 241 hr 20 min and covered 13,650 miles. Vijaypat Singhania (India) flew from Biggin Hill to Delhi, India, a distance of 5,420 miles, in 87 hr 55 min, from 18 Aug to 10 Sep 1988.

Modern Pentathlon & Biathlon

Points scores in riding, fencing, cross-country, and hence overall scores, have no comparative

Most titles ● Franz-Peter Rötsch (East Germany) is one of two men to have won a record two Olympic individual Biathlon titles, winning both the 10 km and 20 km titles in 1988. He equaled the record of Magnar Solberg (Norway), who had won in 1968 and 1972. (Photo: All-Sport/Gray Mortimore)

value between one competition and another. In shooting and swimming (300 m) the scores are of record significance and the best achievements are shown.

The modern pentathlon (fencing, swimming, shooting, running and riding) was inaugurated into the Olympic Games at Stockholm in 1912. L'Union Internationale de Pentathlon Moderne (UIPM) was founded at Aldershot, Hampshire, United Kingdom on 3 Aug 1948. The administration of biathlon (cross-country skiing and shooting) was added in 1957, and the name modified accordingly, L'Union Internationale de Pentathlon Moderne et Biathlon (UIPMB). The first United States Modern Pentathlon Championship was held in 1955. The US Modern Pentathlon and Biathlon Association was established in 1971. In 1978 this body was split to create the US Modern Pentathlon Association.

MODERN PENTATHLON
Most titles *World* ■ András Balczó (Hungary; b. 16 Aug 1938) won the record

MODERN PENTATHLON HIGHEST SCORES
In major competition

SHOOTING
200/200 for 1,132 points: Charles Leonard (US; b. 23 Feb 1913)[1], Berlin, Germany, 3 Aug 1936. Daniele Masala (Italy; b. 12 Feb 1955), Jönkoping, Sweden, 21 Aug 1978. George Horvath (Sweden; b. 14 Mar 1960), Moscow, USSR, 22 Jul 1980.

SWIMMING
3 min 08·22 sec: John Scott (US; b. 14 Apr 1962), 1,368 points, London, United Kingdom, 27 Aug 1982.

[1] *points not given in 1936 Olympic Games.*

number of world titles (instituted 1949), six individual and seven team. He won the world individual title in 1963, 1965–67 and 1969 and the Olympic title in 1972. His seven team titles (1960–70) comprised five world and two Olympic. The USSR has won a record 14 world and four Olympic team titles. Hungary has also won a record four Olympic team titles and ten world titles.

Women's World Championships were first held in 1981. Great Britain won three team titles 1981–83, with Sarah Parker (b. 16 Jul 1956) a member of each of those teams. The only double individual champion has been Irina Kiselyeva (USSR), 1986–87. Wendy Johana Norman (b. 20 Feb 1965) won the individual title in 1982 and team golds in 1981–82. She also won the individual World Cup title in 1980 and Great Britain won three World Cup team titles, 1978–80.

The only US modern pentathletes to win world titles have been Robert Nieman (b. 21 Oct 1947), in 1979, when the men's team also won, and Lori Norwood (women's) in 1989.

Olympic ■ The greatest number of Olympic gold medals won is three, by András Balczó, a member of the winning team in 1960 and 1968 and the 1972 individual champion. Lars Hall (Sweden; b. 30 Apr 1927) has uniquely won two individual championships (1952 and 1956). Pavel Serafimovich Lednyev (USSR; b. 25 Mar 1943) won a record seven medals (two team gold, one team silver, one individual silver, three individual bronze), in 1968, 1972, 1976 and 1980. The only US individual Olympic medalist has been Robert Lee Beck, who won the bronze in 1960.

Probably the greatest margin of victory was by William Oscar Guernsey Grut (Sweden; b. 17 Sep 1914) in the 1948 Games, when he won three events and was placed fifth and eighth in the other two.

BIATHLON
The biathlon, which combines cross-country skiing and rifle shooting, was first included in the Olympic Games in 1960, and World Championships were first held in 1958. Since 1984 there has been a women's World Championship and a women's biathlon will be contested at the 1992 Olympics.

Most titles *Olympic* ■ Two Olympic individual titles have been won by: Magnar Solberg

World ■ Frank Ullrich (East Germany; b. 24 Jan 1958) has won a record six individual world titles, four at 10 km, 1978–81, including the 1980 Olympics, and two at 20 km, 1982–83. Aleksandr Tikhonov was in ten winning USSR relay teams, 1968–80, and won four individual titles.

The Biathlon World Cup (instituted 1979) was won four times by Frank Ullrich, in 1978 and 1980–82. He was second in 1979 and third in 1983.

Motorcycle Racing

Earliest race ■ The first motorcycle race was held over a mile on an oval track at Sheen House, Richmond, United Kingdom on 29 Nov 1897, won by Charles Jarrott (1877–1944) on a Fournier. The first important race in the United States was won by George Holden of Brooklyn, NY in 1903, recording 14 min 57·2 sec for 10 miles.

The oldest motorcycle races in the world are the Auto-Cycle Union Tourist Trophy (TT) series, first held on the 15·81 mile 'Peel' (St John's) course in the Isle of Man on 28 May 1907, and still run in the island on the 'Mountain' circuit.

Fastest circuits ■ The highest average lap speed attained on any closed circuit is 160·288 mph, by Yvon du Hamel (Canada; b. 1941) on a modified 903 cc four-cylinder Kawasaki Z1 at the 31-degree banked 2·5 mile Daytona International Speedway, FL in March 1973. His lap time was 56·149 sec.

The fastest road circuit was the Francorchamps circuit near Spa, Belgium, then 8·74 miles in length. It was lapped in 3 min 50·3 sec (average speed 137·150 mph) by Barry Stephen Frank Sheene (United Kingdom; b. 11 Sep 1950) on a 495 cc 4-cylinder Suzuki during the Belgian Grand Prix on 3 Jul 1977. On that occasion he set a record time for this ten-lap (87·74-mile) race of 38 min 58·5 sec (average speed 135·068 mph).

Longest race ■ The longest race was the Liège 24 hr, run on the old Francorchamps circuit. The greatest distance ever covered is 2,761·9 miles (average speed 115·08 mph) by Jean-Claude Chemarin and Christian Leon, both of France, on a 941 cc 4-cylinder Honda on the Francorchamps circuit on 14–15 Aug 1976.

Longest circuit ■ The 37·73-mile 'Mountain' circuit on the Isle of Man, over which the principal TT races have been run since 1911 (with minor amendments in 1920), has 264 curves and corners and is the longest used for any motorcycle race.

Most successful riders *World championships* ■ The most World Championship titles (instituted by the Fédération Internationale Motocycliste in 1949) won is 15, by Giacomo Agostini (Italy; b. 16 Jun 1942), seven at 350 cc, 1968–74, and eight at 500 cc in 1966–72, 1975. He is the only man to win two World Championships in five consecutive years (350 cc and 500 cc titles 1968–72).

Most successful ● The most successful exponent of the five discipline Modern Pentathlon is Hungarian András Balczó (b. 16 Aug 1938). During the 1960s and early '70s, he won six individual and seven team world titles, including a record three Olympic gold medals. (Photo: All-Sport/Don Morley)

(Norway; b. 4 Feb 1937), in 1968 and 1972; and by Franz-Peter Rötsch (East Germany; b. 19 Apr 1964) at both 10 km and 20 km in 1988. The USSR has won all six 4 × 7·5 km relay titles, from 1968 to 1988. Aleksandr Ivanovich Tikhonov (b. 2 Jan 1947), who was a member of the first four teams, also won a silver in the 1968 20 km.

Most wins ● Eddie Lawson (US) has won four world titles—the most by an American. He won his first 500 cc Grand Prix in 1984 , the year of his first World Championship, and he went on to win the 500 cc title in 1986, 1988 and 1989. (Photo: All-Sport/Pascal Rondeau)

Angel Roldan Nieto (Spain; b. 25 Jan 1947) won a record seven 125 cc titles, 1971–72, 1979, 1981–84 and he also won a record six titles at 50 cc, 1969–70, 1972, 1975–77. Klaus Enders (West Germany; b. 1937) won six world sidecar titles, 1967, 1969–70, 1972–74.

Agostini won 122 races (68 at 500 cc, 54 at 350 cc) in the World Championship series between 24 Apr 1965 and 25 Sep 1977, including a record 19 in 1970, also achieved by Mike Hailwood in 1966.

In 1985 Freddie Burdette Spencer (US; b. 20 Dec 1961), riding for Honda, became the first man ever to win the 250 cc and 500 cc titles in the same year.

The most world titles won by an American motorcyclist is four, by Eddie Lawson (b. 11Mar 1958), at 500 cc in 1984, 1986, 1988–89.

Moto-cross ■ Joël Robert (Belgium; b. 11 Nov 1943) won six 250 cc Moto-cross World Championships (1964, 1968–72). Between 25 Apr 1964 and 18 Jun 1972 he won a record fifty 250 cc Grand Prix. The youngest moto-cross world champion was Dave Strijbos (Netherlands; b. 9 Nov 1968), who won the 125 cc title at age 18 yr 296 days, on 31 Aug 1986. Eric Geboers (Belgium) has uniquely won all three categories of the Moto-cross World Championships, at 125 cc in 1983, 250 cc in 1987 and 500 cc in 1988.

Most successful machines ■ Japanese Yamaha machines won 39 World Championships between 1964 and 1989.

Youngest and oldest world champions ■ Alberto 'Johnny' Cecotto (Venezuela; b. 25 Jan 1956) is the youngest to win a World Championship. He was 19 yr 211 days when he won the 350 cc title on 24 Aug 1975. The oldest was Hermann-Peter Müller (1909–76) of West Germany, who won the 250 cc title in 1955 aged 46.

Mountaineering

Although Bronze-Age artifacts have been found on the summit of the Riffelhorn, Switzerland (9,605 ft), mountaineering as a sport has a continuous history dating back only to 1854. Isolated instances of climbing for its own sake exist back to the 13th century. The Atacamenans built sacrificial platforms near the summit of Llullaillaco (22,057 ft) in late pre-Columbian times c. 1490.

Mt Everest ■ Everest (29,078 ft) was first climbed at 11:30 A.M. on 29 May 1953, when the summit was reached by Edmund Percival Hillary (New Zealand; b. 20 Jul 1919) and Sherpa Tenzing Norgay (1914–86, formerly called Tenzing Khumjung Bhutia). The successful expedition was led by Col. (later Hon. Brigadier) Henry Cecil John Hunt (b. 22 Jun 1910).

Most conquests ■ Ang Rita Sherpa (b. 1947), with ascents in 1983, 1984, 1985, 1987, 1988 and 1990, has scaled Everest six times and all without the use of bottled oxygen.

Solo ■ Reinhold Messner (Italy; b. 17 Sep 1944) was the first to make the entire climb solo on 20 Aug 1980. Also, Messner, with Peter Habeler, (Austria; b. 22 Jul 1942), made the first entirely oxygen-less ascent on 8 May 1978.

First woman ■ Junko Tabei (Japan; b. 22 Sep 1939) reached the summit on 16 May 1975.

Oldest ■ Richard Daniel Bass (US; b. 21 Dec 1929) was 55 yr 130 days when he reached the summit on 30 Apr 1985.

Most successful expedition ■ The Mount Everest International Peace Climb, a team of American, Soviet and Chinese climbers, led by James W. Whittaker (US), in 1990 succeeded in putting the greatest number of people on the summit, 20, from 7–10 May 1990.

Sea level to summit ■ Timothy John Macartney-Snape (Australia; b. 1956) traversed Mount Everest's entire altitude from sea level to summit. He set off on foot from the Bay of Bengal near Calcutta, India on 5 Feb 1990 and reached the summit on 11 May, having walked approximately 745 miles.

All continents ■ The first person to climb the highest mountain in each of the seven continents (Africa: Kilimanjaro, 19,340 ft; Antarctica: Vinson Massif, 16,863 ft; Asia: Everest, 29,078 ft; Europe: El'brus, 18,510 ft; North and Central America: McKinley, 20,320 ft; South America: Aconcagua, 22,834 ft; and Australasia: Carstensz Pyramid, 16,502 ft) was Patrick Morrow (Canada; b.18 Oct 1952). He climbed the last of the seven mountains, Carstensz Pyramid, on 7 May 1986.

Mountaineer ■ Reinhold Messner was the first person to successfully scale all 14 of the world's mountains of over 26,250 ft, all without oxygen. With his ascent of Kanchenjunga in 1982, he became the first person to climb the world's three highest mountains, having earlier reached the summits of Everest and K2.

Greatest walls ■ The highest final stage in any wall climb is that on the south face of Annapurna I (26,545 ft). It was climbed by the British expedition led by Christian John Storey Bonington (b. 6 Aug 1934), when from 2 Apr to 27 May 1970, using 18,000 ft of rope, Donald Whillans (1933–85) and Dougal Haston scaled to the summit. The longest wall climb is on the Rupal-Flank from the base camp at 11,680 ft to the South Point at 26,384 ft of Nanga Parbat – vertical ascent of 14,704 ft. This was scaled by the Austro-German-Italian expedition led by Dr Karl Maria Herrligkoffer (b. 13 Jun 1916) in April 1970.

Europe's greatest wall is the 6,600 ft north face of the Eigerwand (Ogre wall), first climbed by Heinrich Harrer and Fritz Kasparek of Austria and Anderl Heckmair and Wiggerl Vörg of Germany from 21–24 Jul 1938. The northeast face of the Eiger had been climbed on 20 Aug 1932 by Hans Lauper, Alfred Zurcher, Alexander Graven and Josef Knubel. The greatest alpine solo climb was that of Walter Bonatti (Italy; b. 22 Jun 1930) of the southwest of the Dru, Montenvers, now called the Bonatti Pillar, with five bivouacs in 126 hr 7 min from 17–22 Aug 1955.

The most demanding free climbs in the world are those rated at 5·13, the premier location for these being in the Yosemite Valley, CA.

Highest bivouac ■ Four Nepalese summiters bivouacked at more than 28,870 ft in their descent from the summit of Everest on the night of 23 Apr 1990. They were Ang Rita Sherpa, on his record-breaking sixth ascent of Everest, Ang Kami Sherpa (b. 1952), Pasang Norbu Sherpa (b. 1963) and Top Bahadur Khatri (b. 1960).

Oldest ■ Teiichi Igarashi (Japan; b. 21 Sep 1886) climbed Mount Fuji (Fuji-yama) (12,388 ft) at the age of 99 yr 302 days on 20 Jul 1986.

Netball

The game was invented in the United States in 1891 and introduced into England in 1895 by Dr Toles.

Most titles *World* ■ Australia has won the World Championships (instituted 1963) a record five times, 1963, 1971, 1975, 1979 and 1983.

Highest scores ■ The World Tournament record score was in Auckland, New Zealand in 1975, when England beat Papua New Guinea 114 goals to 16. The record number of goals in the World Tournament is 402, by Judith Heath (England; b. 1942) in 1971.

Olympic Games

These records include the Games held at Athens in 1906.

The earliest celebration of the ancient Olympic Games, of which there is a certain record is that of July 776 B.C., when Coroibos, a cook from Elis, won the foot race, though their origin dates from perhaps as early as c. 1370 B.C. The ancient Games were terminated by an order issued in Milan in A.D. 393 by Theodosius I, 'the Great' (c. 346–95), Emperor of Rome. At the instigation of Pierre de Fredi, Baron de Coubertin (1863–1937), the Olympic Games of the modern era were inaugurated in Athens on 6 Apr 1896.

Ever present ■ Five countries have never failed to be represented at the 22 celebrations of the Summer Games: Australia, France, Greece, Great Britain and Switzerland. Of these only Great Britain has been present at all winter celebrations as well.

Most participants ■ The greatest number of competitors at a Summer Games celebration is 8,465 (6,279 men, 2,186 women), who represented a record 159 nations, at Seoul, South Korea in 1988. The greatest number at the Winter Games is 1,428 (1,113 men, 315 women), representing 57 countries, at Calgary, Canada in 1988.

Largest Crowd ■ The largest crowd at any Olympic site was 150,000, at the 1952 ski-jumping at the Holmenkollen, outside Oslo, Norway. Estimates of the number of spectators of the marathon race through Tokyo, Japan on 21 Oct 1964 ranged from 500,000 to 1·5 million. The total spectator attendance at Los Angeles in 1984 was given as 5,797,923 (see General Records).

Olympic Torch relay ■ The longest journey of the torch within one country was for the XV Olympic Winter Games in Canada in 1988. The torch arrived from Greece at St John's, Newfoundland on 17 Nov 1987 and was transported 11,222 miles (5,088 miles by foot, 4,419 miles by aircraft/ferry, 1,712 miles by snowmobile and 3 miles by dogsled) until its arrival at Calgary on 13 Feb 1988.

Most medals ■ In ancient Olympic Games victors were given a chaplet of wild olive leaves. Leonidas of Rhodos won 12 running titles 164–152 B.C. The most individual gold medals won by a male competitor in the modern Games is ten, by Raymond Clarence Ewry (US; 1874–1937) (see Track and Field Athletics). The female record is seven, by Vera Caslavska–Odlozil (Czechoslovakia) (see Gymnastics).

The most gold medals won by an American woman is four, by Patricia Joan McCormick (nee Keller, b. 12 May 1930), both in highboard and springboard diving, 1952 and 1956.

The most medals won by a US Olympian is 11, at shooting, by Carl Townsend Osburn (1884–1966), from 1912 to 1924, five gold, four silver, two bronze, and by Mark Andrew Spitz (b. 10 Feb 1950), at swimming, 1968–72, nine gold, one silver, one bronze.

The most medals won by an American woman is eight, by swimmer Shirley Babashoff (b. 31 Jan

MOST MEDALS

The total figures for medals for all Olympic events (including those now discontinued) for the Summer (1896–1988) and Winter Games (1924–88):

	Gold	Silver	Bronze	Total
USA.....................	788	607	509	1,904
USSR[1]	474	380	358	1,212
Germany[2]............	183	233	230	646
Great Britain[3].....	180	226	216	622

Excludes medals won in Official Art competitions in 1912–48.
[1] *Formerly Russia* [2] *Germany 1896–1964, West Germany from 1968* [3] *including Ireland to 1920*

1957), gold at 4 x 100 meters freestyle relay, 1972 and 1976, and six silver medals 1972–76, a record for any competitor in Olympic history.

The only Olympian to win four consecutive individual titles in the same event has been Alfred Adolph Oerter (US; b. 19 Sep 1936), who won the discus, in 1956–68. However, Raymond Clarence Ewry (US) won both the standing long jump and the standing high jump at four games in succession, 1900, 1904, 1906 and 1908. This is if the Intercalated Games of 1906, which were staged officially by the International Olympic Committee, are included. Also Paul B. Elvström (Denmark; b. 25 Feb 1928) won four successive gold medals at monotype yachting events, 1948–60, but there was a class change (1948 Firefly class, 1952–60 Finn class).

Swimmer Mark Andrew Spitz (US; b. 10 Feb 1950) won a record seven golds at one celebration, at Munich in 1972, including three in relays. The most won in individual events at one celebration is five, by speed skater, Eric Arthur Heiden (US; b. 14 Jun 1958) at Lake Placid, NY in 1980.

The only man to win a gold medal in both the Summer and Winter Games is Edward Patrick Francis Eagan (US; 1898–1967) who won the 1920 light-heavyweight boxing title and was a member of the winning four-man bob in 1932. Christa Luding (nee Rothenburger [East Germany]; b. 4 Dec 1959) became the first woman to win a medal at both the Summer and Winter Games when she won a silver in the cycling sprint event in 1988. She had previously won medals for speed skating, 500 m gold in 1984, and 1,000 m gold and 500 m silver in 1988.

Gymnast Larisa Latynina (USSR; b. 27 Dec 1934) won a record 18 medals (see Gymnastics). The record at one celebration is eight, by gymnast Aleksandr Dityatin (USSR; b. 7 Aug 1957) in 1980 (See Gymnastics).

Youngest and oldest gold medalist ■
The youngest ever winner was a French boy (whose name is not recorded), who coxed the Netherlands pair in 1900. He was 7–10 years old, and he substituted for Dr Hermanus Brockmann, who coxed in the heats but proved too

---

Longest span ● Paul B. Elvström (Denmark; b. 25 Feb 1928) is one of only four men to have competed in the Olympics over a span of 40 years. He first competed at yachting in the 1948 Games and made a record seventh Games appearance at Seoul in 1988. He also won a record four consecutive individual titles, at Olympic monotype yachting, 1948–60. Here he can be seen with his daughter, Trine (b. 6 Mar 1962), who also represented Denmark in yachting at the 1988 Olympics. (Photo: Per Kjærbye)

---

heavy. The youngest ever female champion was Marjorie Gestring (US; b. 18 Nov 1922, now Mrs Bowman), at age 13 yr 268 days, in the 1936 women's springboard event. Oscar Swahn was in the winning Running Deer shooting team in 1912 at age 64 yr 258 days, and in this event was the oldest medalist, bronze, at 72 yr 279 days in 1920.

The oldest US Olympic champion was retired minister Galen Carter Spencer (1840–1904), who assisted the Potomac Archers to an archery team medal two days after his 64th birthday in 1904. The oldest US medalist and Olympic participant was Samuel Harding Duvall (1836–1908), who was 68 yr 194 days when he was a member of the Cincinnati Archers silver medal team in 1904.

The youngest US medalist and participant was Dorothy Poynton (b.17 Jul 1915), who won the springboard diving bronze medal at 13 yr 23 days in 1928. She went on to win the highboard gold in 1932 and 1936 (by then Mrs Hill). The youngest male medalist was Donald Wills Douglas, Jr (b. 3 Jul 1917), with silver at 6-meter yachting in 1932, at 15 yr 40 days. He later became chief executive of the McDonnell-Douglas Corporation. The youngest US male gold medalist has been Jackie Fields, at 16 yr 161 days (see boxing).

Longest Span ■ The longest span of an Olympic competitor is 40 years, by: Dr Ivan Osiier (Denmark; 1888–1965), in fencing, 1908–32 and 1948; Magnus Konow (Norway; 1887–1972) in yachting, 1908–20, 1928 and 1936–48; Paul Elvström (Denmark), in yachting, 1948–60, 1968–72 and 1984–88; and Durward Randolph Knowles (Great Britain [1948], then Bahamas; b. 2 Nov 1917), in yachting, 1948–72 and 1988. Raimondo d'Inzeo (b. 8 Feb 1925) competed for Italy in equestrian events at a record eight

celebrations from 1948–76, gaining one gold, two silver and three bronze medals. This was equaled by Paul Elvström and Durward Knowles in 1988. The longest women's span is 28 years, by Anne Jessica Ransehousen (nee Newberry [US]; b. 14 Oct 1938), in dressage, 1960, 1964 and 1988. Fencer Kerstin Palm (Sweden; b. 5 Feb 1946) competed in a women's record seven celebrations, 1964–88.

The US record for longest span of Olympic competition is 28 years, by Jessica Ransehousen and by fencer Norman Cudworth Armitage (ne Cohn, 1907–72), who competed in the six Games between 1928 and 1956; he won a team bronze at saber in 1948. He was also selected for the Games of 1940, which were canceled. Four other Americans contested six games: Frank Davis Chapot (b. 24 Feb 1932), at show jumping, 1956–76, winner of two team silver medals; Lt Col William Willard McMillan (b. 29 Jan 1929), at shooting, 1952–76, missing 1956, gold medalist at rapid-fire pistol in 1960; Janice Lee York Romany (b. 6 Aug 1928), at fencing, 1948–68; and John Michael Plumb (b. 28 Mar 1940), at three-day event, 1960–84, winner of a gold and four silver medals. Plumb was also named for the 1980 Games, which the United States boycotted.

Orienteering

Origins ■ The first indications of orienteering as a competitive sport have been found in the Swedish army (1888) and the Norwegian army (1895). The first civilian competition seems to have been organized on 31 Oct 1897 (with eight participants) by the sport club Tjalve, outside Oslo, Norway. In spite of a number of other small events up to 1910, the sport died out in Norway but in Sweden survived World War I. On 25 Mar 1919, the first large competition with more than 200 participants was organized in the forest of Nacka, outside Stockholm. From there the sport spread rapidly throughout Sweden and later (about 1925) to Finland, Norway and (especially post-1945) to other countries in Europe and elsewhere. The initiator was Major Ernst Killander, who is known as 'The Father of Orienteering.' World Championships were instituted in 1966. The United States Orienteering Federation was founded in 1972.

Most titles *World* ■ The men's relay has been won a record seven times by Norway—1970, 1978, 1981, 1983, 1985, 1987 and 1989. Sweden has won the women's relay eight times—1966, 1970, 1974, 1976, 1981, 1983, 1985 and 1989. Three women's individual titles have been won by Annichen Kringstad-Svensson (Sweden; b. 15 Jul 1960), in 1981, 1983 and 1985. The men's title has been won twice by: Åge Hadler (Norway; b. 14 Aug 1944), in 1966 and 1972; Egil Johansen (Norway; b. 18 Aug 1954), in 1976 and 1978; and Øyvind Thon (Norway; b. 25 Mar 1958), in 1979 and 1981.

Most competitors ■ The most competitors at an event in one day is 22,510, on the first day of the Swedish O-Ringen at Småland on 18 Jul 1983.

Ski Orienteering ■ Seven World Championships in ski orienteering have been held. Sweden has won the men's relay four times (1977, 1980, 1982, 1984) and Finland has won the women's relay four times (1975, 1977, 1980, 1988).

Pétanque

The origins of pétanque or boules can be traced back over 2,000 years, but it was not until 1945 that the Fédération Française de Pétanque et Jeu Provençal was formed, and subsequently the Fédération Internationale (FIPJP).

World Championships ■ Winner of the most World Championships (instituted 1959) has been France, with ten titles to 1989. The first women's World Championships were held in 1988, when the winner was Thailand.

Highest score in 24 hours ■ Chris Walker (b. 16 Jan 1942) and his son Richard (b. 26 Dec 1966) scored a record 2,109 points in 24 hours (172 games) at the Gin Trap, Ringstead, Norfolk, United Kingdom on 24–25 Jun 1988.

Polo

Origins ■ Polo can be traced to origins in Manipur state *c.* 3100 B.C., when it was played as *sagol kangjei*. Other claims are of it being of Persian origin, having been played as *pulu c.* 525 B.C. The game was introduced to British officers at Cachar by the Manipur Maharaja, Sir Chandrakirti Singh, and the earliest club was the Cachar Club (founded in 1859) in Assam, India. The oldest club still in existence is the Calcutta Polo Club (1862). The game was introduced into England from India in 1869 by the 10th Hussars at Aldershot, Hampshire, United Kingdom, and the earliest match was one between the 9th Lancers and the 10th Hussars on Hounslow Heath, London, United Kingdom in July 1871. The earliest international match between England and the United States was in 1886.

Polo was introduced to the US by James Gordon Bennett in 1876, when he aranged for the first indoor game at Dickel's Riding Academy, NY. The United States Polo Association was formed in 1890. The United States Open Championship was inaugurated in 1904 and has been played continuously, with the exception of 1942–45, since 1919.

Highest handicap ■ The highest handicap based on eight 7½-min 'chukkas' is ten goals introduced in the United States in 1891 and in the United Kingdom and in Argentina in 1910. A total of 55 players have received ten-goal handicaps. A match of two 40-goal teams was staged, for the only time, at Palermo, Buenos Aires, Argentina in 1975.

Highest score ■ The highest aggregate number of goals scored in an international match is 30, when Argentina beat the United States 21–9 at Meadowbrook, Long Island, NY in September 1936.

Pool

Pool or championship pocket billiards with numbered balls began to become standardized *c.* 1890. The greatest exponents were Ralph Greenleaf (US; 1899–1950), who won the 'world' professional title 19 times (1919–37), and William Mosconi (US; b. 27 Jun 1913), who dominated the game from 1941 to 1957.

The longest consecutive run in an American straight pool match is 625 balls, by Michael Eufemia at Logan's Billiard Academy, Brooklyn, NY on 2 Feb 1960. The greatest number of balls pocketed in 24 hr is 16,009, by Paul Sullivan at Selby, North Yorkshire, United Kingdom on 8–9 Apr 1989.

The record times for potting all 15 balls in a speed competition are: (men) 37·9 sec, by Rob McKenna at Blackpool, Lancashire, United Kingdom on 7 Nov 1987, and (women) 44·5 sec, by Susan Thompson at Shrublands Community Centre, Gorleston, Norfolk, United Kingdom, on 20 Apr 1990.

A record break of 132 for 14–1 pool was set by Ross McInnes at Pontin's, Heysham, Lancashire, United Kingdom on 3 Oct 1984.

Powerboat Racing

A gasoline engine was first installed in a boat by Jean Joseph Etienne Lenoir (1822–1900) on the River Seine, Paris, France in 1865. Actual powerboat racing started in about 1900, the first prominent race being from Calais, France to Dover, Kent in 1903. International racing was largely established by the presentation of a Challenge Trophy by Sir Alfred Harmsworth in 1903. Thereafter, racing developed mainly as a 'circuit,' or short, sheltered course type competition. Offshore or sea-passage races also developed, initially for displacement (nonplaning) cruisers. Offshore events for fast (planing) cruisers began in 1958, with a 170-mile passage race from Miami, FL to Nassau, Bahamas. Outboard motor, i.e. the combined motor / transmission detachable propulsion unit type racing, began in the United States in about 1920. Both inboard and outboard motorboat engines are mainly gasoline fueled, but since 1950 diesel (compression ignition) engines have appeared and are widely used in offshore sport.

APBA Gold Cup ■ The American Power Boat Association (APBA) was formed in 1903, and held its first Gold Cup race at the Columbia Yacht Club on the Hudson River, NY in 1904, when the winner was *Standard*, piloted by C. C. Riotto at an average speed of 23·6 mph. The most wins by a pilot is eight by Bill Muncey, 1956–57, 1961–62, 1972, 1977–79. The most successful boat has been *Atlas Van Lines*, piloted by Muncey to victory in 1972, 1977–79, and by Chip Hanauer in 1982–84. Hanauer went on to complete a record seven successive victories to 1988.

Highest speeds ■ The highest speed recorded by a propeller-driven boat is 229 mph, by *The Texan*, a Kurtis Top Fuel Hydro Drag boat, driven by Eddie Hill (US) on 5 Sep 1982 at Chowchilla, CA. He also set a 440 yd elapsed time record of 5·16 sec in this boat at Firebird Lake, AZ on 13 Nov 1983. The official American Drag Boat Association record is 223·88 mph by *Final Effort*, a Blown Fuel Hydro boat driven by Robert T. Burns at Creve Coeur Lake, St Louis, MO on 15 Jul 1985 over a ¼ mile course.

The fastest speed recognized by the Union Internationale Motonautique for an outboard-powered boat is in Class (e): 177·61 mph by P. R. Knight in a Chevrolet-engined Lautobach hull on Lake Ruataniwha, New Zealand in 1986. Robert F. Hering (US) set the world Formula One record at 165·338 mph at Parker, AZ on 21 Apr 1986.

The fastest speed recognized for an offshore boat is 154·438 mph for one way and 148·238 mph for two runs by Tom Gentry (US), in his 49-ft catamaran, powered by four Gentry Turbo Eagle V8 Chevrolets.

The fastest speed recorded for a diesel (compression ignition) boat is 135·532 mph by the hydroplane *Iveco World Leader*, powered by an Aifo-Fiat engine, driven by Carlo Bonomi at Venice, Italy on 4 Apr 1985.

Highest race speeds ■ The highest speed recorded in an offshore race is 103·29 mph, by Tony Garcia (US) in a Class I powerboat at Key West, FL in November 1983.

Longest races ■ The longest offshore race

has been the Port Richborough London to Monte Carlo Marathon Offshore international event. The race extended over 2,947 miles in 14 stages from 10–25 Jun 1972. It was won by *H.T.S.* (United Kingdom), driven by Mike Bellamy, Eddie Chater and Jim Brooker in 71 hr 35 min 56 sec, for an average of 41·15 mph. The longest circuit race is the 24-hour race held annually since 1962 on the River Seine at Rouen, France.

Longest jetboat jumps ■ The longest ramp jump achieved by a jetboat has been 120 ft, by Peter Horak (US) in a Glastron Carlson CVX 20 Jet Deluxe with a 460 Ford V8 engine (takeoff speed 55 mph), for a documentary TV film, at Salton Sea, CA on 26 Apr 1980. The longest leap onto land is 172 ft, by Norm Bagrie (New Zealand), from the Shotover River on 1 Jul 1982 in the 1½-ton jetboat *Valvolene*.

Racquetball

Racquetball, using a 40 ft × 20 ft court, was invented in 1950 by Joe Sobek at the Greenwich YMCA, CT, originally as Paddle Rackets. The International Racquetball Association was founded in 1968 by Bob Kendler (US). It changed its name in 1980 to the American Amateur Racquetball Association.

US Titles ■ The governing body for the sport in the United States is the American Amateur Racquetball Association (AARA), whose championships were initiated in 1968. A record four men's open titles have been won by Ed Andrews of California, 1980–81 and 1985–86, and a record four women's open titles by Cindy Baxter of Pennsylvania, 1981, 1983, 1985–86.

Fastest powerboat ● The highest speed recorded by a propeller-driven boat is 229 mph by *The Texan*, a Kurtis Top Fuel Hydro Drag boat, driven by Eddie Hill (US) on 5 Sep 1982 at Chowchilla, CA. He also set a 440 yd elapsed time record of 5·16 sec in this boat at Firebird Lake, AZ on 13 Nov 1983. (Photo: Jim Welch)

Origins ● Although the game of rackets is now played on a closed court, it was originally played in open courts, becoming established in the mid-18th century. Such venues included the backyards of taverns, the school yard at Harrow and most notably Fleet debtor's prison, which Charles Dickens described in his novel *The Pickwick Papers* and which is shown in this etching by Theodore Lane. It was popular among the inmates of the prison, with Robert Mackay laying claim to the first world title in 1820. (Photo: E. T. Archive)

Rackets

There is record of the sale of a racket court at Southernhay, Exeter, Devon, United Kingdom dated 12 Jan 1798. The game, which is of 17th-century origin, was played by debtors in the Fleet Prison, London, United Kingdom in the middle of the 18th century, and an inmate, Robert Mackay, claimed the first 'world' title in 1820. The first closed court champion was Francis Erwood at Woolwich, London, United Kingdom in 1860.

World Championships ■ Of the 22 world champions since 1820 the longest reign is by Geoffrey Willoughby Thomas Atkins (b. 20 Jan 1927), who held the title, after beating the professional James Dear (1910–81) in 1954, until

retiring, after defending it four times, in April 1972.

The first American to be world champion was Jock Souter, and he had the longest span as champion, 1913–28.

Rodeo

Origins ■ Rodeo, which developed from 18th-century *fiestas*, came into being in the early days of the North American cattle industry. The sport originated in Mexico and spread from there into the cattle regions of the United States. Steer wrestling came in with Bill Pickett (1870–1932) of Texas in 1900, and a bronc-riding competition was held in Deer Trail, CO as early as 1869. Claims to the first held before paying spectators are many; The West of the Pecos Rodeo at Pecos, TX, first held in 1883 was the earliest documented, organized rodeo competition, and is now sanctioned by the Professional Rodeo Cowboys Association (PRCA), professional rodeo's largest organized association.

The largest rodeo in the world is the National Finals Rodeo, organized by the PRCA and Women's Professional Rodeo Association (WPRA). The top 15 money-earning cowboys in each of the six PRCA events and the top 15 WPRA barrel racers compete at the Finals. It was first held at Dallas, TX in 1959, and was held at Oklahoma City, OK for 20 years before moving to Las Vegas, NV in 1985. The 1989 Finals had a paid attendance of 165,467 for ten performances. In 1989 a record $2·2 million in prize money was offered for the event, staged in Las Vegas.

Most world titles ■ The record number of all-around titles (awarded to the leading money winner in a single season in two or more events) in the PRCA World Championships is six, by Larry Mahan (US; b. 21 Nov 1943) in 1966–70 and 1973, and, consecutively, 1974–79 by Tom Ferguson (b. 20 Dec 1950). Roy Cooper (b. 13 Nov 1955) has record career earnings of $1,184,325, 1976–89. Jim Shoulders (b. 13 May 1928) of Henrietta, TX won a record 16 World Championships at four events between 1949 and 1959. The record figure for prize money in a single season is $166,042, by Lewis Feild (b. 28 Oct 1956) in 1986. Feild won a record $75,219 for one rodeo ($47,449 for saddle bronc riding and $27,770 for bareback riding) at the 1987 National Finals Rodeo, Las Vegas, NV.

Youngest champions ■ The youngest winner of a world title is Anne Lewis (b. 1 Sep 1958), who won the WPRA barrel racing title in 1968, at 10 years of age. Ty Murray (b. 11 Oct 1969) is the youngest cowboy to win the PRCA All-Around Champion title, at age 20, in 1989.

Time records ■ Records for PRCA timed events, such as calf-roping and steer-wrestling, are not always comparable, because of the widely varying conditions due to the sizes of arenas and amount of start given the stock. The fastest time recorded for calf roping under the current PRCA rules is 6·7 sec, by Joe Beaver (b. 13 Oct 1965) at West Jordan, UT in 1986, and the fastest time for steer wrestling is 2·4 sec, by: James Bynum, at Marietta, OK in 1955; Carl Deaton at Tulsa, OK in 1976; and Gene Melton at Pecatonica, IL in 1976. The fastest team roping time is 3·7 sec, by Bob Harris and Tee Woolman at Spanish Fork, UT in 1986

Bull riding ■ Jim Sharp (b. 6 Oct 1965) of Kermit, TX became the first rider to ride all ten bulls at a National Finals Rodeo at Las Vegas in December 1988.

Largest attendance ● The 1989 National Rodeo Finals attracted a record paid attendance of 165,467 for ten performances and the prize money on offer was also a record for a rodeo. Seen here is action from the bull riding event. (Photo: PRCA)

The highest score in bull riding was 98 points out of a possible 100, by Denny Flynn on Red Lightning at Palestine, IL in 1979.

The top bucking bull Red Rock dislodged 312 riders, 1980–88, and was finally ridden to the 8-sec bell by Lane Frost (1963–89) (World Champion Bull Rider 1987) on 20 May 1988. Red Rock had retired at the end of the 1987 season but still continued to make guest appearances.

Saddle bronc riding ■ The highest scored saddle bronc ride is 95 out of a possible 100, by Doug Vold at Meadow Lake, Saskatchewan, Canada in 1979. Descent, a saddle bronc owned by Beutler Brothers and Cervi Rodeo Company, received a record six PRCA saddle bronc of the year awards, 1966–69, 1971–72.

Bareback riding ■ Joe Alexander of Cora, WY scored 93 out of a possible 100 at Cheyenne, WY in 1974. Sippin' Velvet, owned by Bernis

Johnson, has been awarded a record five PRCA bareback horse of the year titles between 1978 and 1987.

Roller Skating

The first roller skate was devised by Jean Joseph Merlin (1735–1803) of Huy, Belgium in 1760 and was demonstrated by him in London, United Kingdom, but with disastrous results. James L. Plimpton of New York produced the present four-wheeled type and patented it in January 1863. The first indoor rink was opened in the Haymarket, London, United Kingdom in about 1824.

Most titles *Speed* ■ The most world speed titles won is 18, by two women: Alberta Vianello (Italy), eight track and ten road 1953–65; and Annie Lambrechts (Belgium), one track and 17 road, 1964–81, at distances from 500 m to 10,000 m.

Figure ■ The records for figure titles are: five, by Karl Heinz Losch in 1958–59, 1961–62 and 1966; and four by Astrid Bader in 1965–68, both of West Germany. The most world pair titles is four, by Dieter Fingerle (West Germany) in 1959,

1965–67 with two different partners, and by John Arishita and Tammy Jeru (US) 1983–86.

Speed skating ■ The fastest speed put up in an official world record is 26·85 mph, when Luca Antoniel (Italy; b. 12 Feb 1968) recorded 24·99 sec for 300 m on a road at Gujan Mestras, France on 31 Jul 1987. The women's record is 25·04 mph by Marisa Canafoglia (Italy; b. 30 Sep 1965) for 300 m on the road at Grenoble, France on 27 Aug 1987. The world records for 10,000 m on a road or track are: (men) 14 min 55·64 sec, Giuseppe de Persio (Italy; b. 3 Jun 1959) at Gejun Mestras, France on 1 Aug 1988; (women) 15 min 58·022 sec, Marisa Canafogilia (Italy) at Grenoble, France on 30 Aug 1987.

Largest rink ■ The greatest indoor rink ever to operate was located in the Grand Hall, Olympia, London, United Kingdom. Opened in 1890 and closed in 1912, it had an actual skating area of 68,000 ft^2. The current largest is the main arena of 34,981 ft^2 at Guptill Roll-Arena, Boght Corner, NY. The total rink area is 41,380 ft^2.

Endurance ■ Theodore James Coombs (b. 1954) of Hermosa Beach, CA skated 5,193 miles from Los Angeles, CA to New York and back to Yates Center, KS from 30 May to 14 Sep 1979.

Rowing

The Sphinx Stela of Amenhotep (Amonophis) II (1450–1425 B.C.) records that he *stroked* a boat for some three miles. The earliest established sculling race is the Doggett's Coat and Badge, which was first rowed on 1 Aug 1716 from London Bridge to Chelsea, London, United Kingdom as a race for apprentices, and is still contested annually. Although rowing regattas were held in Venice in 1300 the first English regatta probably took place on the River Thames by the Ranelagh Gardens, near Putney, London, United Kingdom in 1775.

The first mention of rowing competition in the United States was in a New York newspaper in 1811, and the first regatta was probably that held on the Hudson River, off Peekskill, NY in 1848.

Most Olympic medals ■ Six oarsmen have won three gold medals: John Brenden Kelly (US; 1889–1960), father of the late HSH Princess Grace of Monaco and of John Brendan Kelly, Jr (b. 24 May 1927) who won bronze at single sculls in 1956, Single Sculls (1920) and Double Sculls (1920 and 1924); his cousin Paul Vincent Costello (US; b. 27 Dec 1894), Double Sculls (1920, 1924 and 1928); Jack Beresford, Jr (United Kingdom; 1899–1977), Single sculls (1924), Coxless Fours (1932) and Double Sculls (1936); Vyacheslav Nikolayevich Ivanov (USSR; b. 30 Jul 1938), Single Sculls (1956, 1960 and 1964); Siegfried Brietzke (East Germany; b. 12 Jun 1952), Coxless Pairs (1972) and Coxless Fours (1976, 1980); and Pertti Karppinen (Finland; b. 17 Feb 1953), Single Sculls 1976, 1980 and 1984.

World Championships ■ World rowing championships distinct from the Olympic Games were first held in 1962, at first four yearly, but from 1974 annually, except in Olympic years.

The most gold medals won at World Championships and Olympic Games is six, by the East German oarsmen twins; Bernd and Jörg Landvoigt (b. 23 Mar 1951); Joachim Dreifke (b. 26 Dec 1952); Karl-Heinz Bussert (b. 8 Jan 1955); Ulrich Diessner (b. 27 Dec 1954); Siegfried Brietzke (b. 12 Jun 1952); and Wolfgang Mager (b. 24 Aug 1952); at coxed pairs by the Italian brothers, Giuseppe (b. 24 Jul 1959) and Carmine (b. 5 Jan

Most successful ● The origins of the sport of roller hockey developed soon after the production of a four-wheel roller skate in the late nineteenth century. The most successful country in international competition is Portugal, seen here in action against Italy in the 1985 World Games. (Photo: All-Sport/ Michael King)

1962) Abbagnale; and at lightweight events by Italians Francesco Esposito (b. 4 Mar 1955) and Ruggero Verroca (b. 3 Jan 1961). At women's events Jutta Behrendt (nee Hahn; b. 15 Nov 1960) also won six gold medals.

The most wins at Single Sculls is five, by Peter-Michael Kolbe (West Germany; b. 2 Aug 1953), in 1975, 1978, 1981, 1983 and 1986, and by Pertti Karppinen, 1979 and 1985, with his three Olympic wins (above), and in the women's events by Christine Hahn (nee Scheiblich, [East Germany]; b. 31 Dec 1954), 1974–75, 1977–78 (and the 1976 Olympic title).

Boat Race ■ The earliest famous University Boat Race, between Oxford University and Cambridge University, was from Hambledon Lock,

Buckinghamshire to Henley Bridge, Oxfordshire, United Kingdom on 10 Jun 1829. Outrigged eights were first used in 1846. In the 136 races to 1990, Cambridge won 69 times, Oxford 66 times, and there was a dead heat on 24 Mar 1877.

Henley Royal Regatta ■ The annual regatta at Henley-on-Thames, Oxfordshire, United Kingdom was inaugurated on 26 Mar 1839. Since then the course, except in 1923, has been about 1 mile 550 yd, varying slightly according to the length of boat. In 1967 the shorter craft were 'drawn up' so all bows start level.

The most wins in the Diamond Challenge Sculls (instituted 1844) is six consecutively, by Stuart A. Mackenzie (Australia and Great Britain; b. 5 Apr 1937), 1957–62. The record time is 7 min 23 sec, by Vaclav Chalupa (Czechoslovakia; b. 7

Most titles ● Several rowers have won a record six World Championship titles and seen here in action are the Italian Abbagnale brothers, Giuseppe and Carmine, winning the coxed pairs in 1985. (Photo: All-Sport/Michael King)

Heaviest crew ● Oxford University lead Cambridge University just after Hammersmith Bridge, London, United Kingdom on their way to winning their 66th Boat Race. Oxford put out the heaviest crew ever for the 1990 race, weighing an average 208 lb per man, with Chris Heathcote, at 243 lb the heaviest ever individual. (Photo: All-Sport/Simon Bruty)

Dec 1967) on 2 Jul 1989. The record time for the Grand Challenge Cup (instituted 1839) event is 5 min 58 sec, by Hansa Dortmund, West Germany on 2 Jul 1989.

Highest speed ■ The highest recorded speed on non-tidal water for 2,000 m is by an American eight in 5 min 27·14 sec (13·68 mph) at Lucerne, Switzerland on 17 Jun 1984. A crew from Penn AC, was timed in 5 min 18·8 sec (14·03 mph) in the FISA Championships on the River Meuse, Liège, Belgium on 17 Aug 1930.

24 hours ■ The greatest distance rowed in 24 hours (upstream and downstream) by an eight is 130 miles, by members of the Renmark Rowing Club, South Australia on 20–21 Apr 1984.

Longest race ■ The longest annual rowing race is the annual Tour du Lac Leman, Geneva, Switzerland for coxed fours (the five-man crew taking turns as cox) over 99 miles. The record winning time is 12 hr 52 min, by LAGA Delft, Netherlands on 3 Oct 1982.

Rugby

Records are determined in terms of present-day scoring values, i.e. a try at 4 points; a dropped goal, penalty or goal from a mark at 3 points; and a conversion at 2 points. The *actual* score, in accordance with whichever of the eight earlier systems was in force at the time, is also given, in parentheses.

Although there are records of a game with many similarities to rugby dating back to the Roman occupation of Britain, the game is traditionally said to have originated from a breach of the rules of the soccer played in November 1823 at Rugby School, United Kingdom by William Webb Ellis (later the Rev.) (*c.* 1807–72). This handling code of soccer evolved gradually and was known to have been played at Cambridge University, United Kingdom by 1839. The Rugby Football Union was founded on 26 Jan 1871. The International Rugby Football Board (IRFB) was founded in 1886.

OLYMPIC GAMES

Held at four Games from 1900 to 1924, the only double gold medalist was the United States, which won in 1920 and 1924, defeating France in the final on both occasions.

WORLD CUP

The inaugural World Cup was contested in Australia and New Zealand by 16 national teams in 1987. The final in Auckland on 20 Jun 1987 was won by New Zealand, which beat France 29–9. The highest team score was New Zealand's 74–13 victory over Fiji at Christchurch, New Zealand on 27 May 1987. They scored 10 goals, 2 tries and 2 penalty goals. The individual match record was 30 (3 tries, 9 conversions), by Didier Camberabero (France; b. 9 Jan 1961) *v* Zimbabwe at Auckland, New Zealand on 2 Jun 1987. The leading scorer in the tournament was the New Zealand goal-kicker Grant James Fox (b. 6 Jun 1962), with 126 points.

HIGHEST TEAM SCORES

Internationals ■ The highest score in any full international was when New Zealand beat Japan by 106–4 at Tokyo, Japan on 1 Nov 1987. France beat Paraguay 106–12 at Asuncion, Paraguay on 28 Jun 1988.

HIGHEST INDIVIDUAL SCORES

Internationals ■ Phil Bennett (Wales; b. 24 Oct 1948) scored 34 points (2 tries, 10 conversions, 2 penalty goals) for Wales *v* Japan at Tokyo on 24 Sep 1975, when Wales won 82–6.

In all internationals Michael Patrick Lynagh (b.

Most appearances ● Seen here in the colors of the French Barbarians, Serge Blanco (b. 31 Aug 1958) has represented France a record 78 times, from his début on 8 Nov 1980 to 1 Jul 1990. (Photo: All-Sport/Mike Powell)

MOST INTERNATIONAL APPEARANCES

FRANCE	78†	Serge Blanco (b. 31 Aug 1958)	1980–90
IRELAND	69	Cameron Michael Henderson Gibson (b. 3 Dec 1942)	1964–79
NEW ZEALAND	55	Colin Earl Meads (b. 3 Jun 1936)	1957–71
WALES	55*	John Peter Rhys 'JPR' Williams (b. 2 Mar 1949)	1969–81
SCOTLAND	52	James Menzies 'Jim' Renwick (b. 12 Feb 1952)	1972–84
	52	Colin Thomas Deans (b. 3 May 1955)	1978–87
AUSTRALIA	51	Simon Paul Poidevin (b. 31 Oct 1958)	1980–89
ENGLAND	42	Anthony Neary (b. 25 Nov 1948)	1971–80
SOUTH AFRICA	38	Frederick Christoffel Hendrick Du Preez (b. 28 Nov 1935)	1960–71
	38	Jan Hendrik Ellis (b. 5 Jan 1943)	1965–76

Gareth Owen Edwards (b. 12 Jul 1947) made a record 53 consecutive international appearances, never missing a match throughout his career for Wales, 1967–78. Willie John McBride also had 53 consecutive appearances during his 63 games for Ireland.

† *France enumerate international appearances against all nations, whereas the figures for the seven members for the IRFB include only matches against each other. Blanco has played 58 matches v IRFB member nations.*

25 Oct 1963) scored a record 538 points in 41 matches for Australia, 1984–90.

Seven-a-sides ■ Seven-a-side rugby dates from 28 Apr 1883 when Melrose RFC Borders, in order to alleviate the poverty of a club in such a small town, staged a seven-a-side tournament. The idea was that of Ned Haig, the town's butcher.

Hong Kong Sevens ■ This, the world's most prestigious international tournament for seven-a-side teams, was first held in 1976. The record of five wins is held by Australia, 1979, 1982–83, 1985 and 1988.

Shooting

The Lucerne Shooting Guild (Switzerland) was formed *c.* 1466 and the first recorded shooting match was at Zurich in 1472.

Most Olympic medals ■ The record number of medals won is 11, by Carl Townsend Osburn (US; 1884–1966) in 1912, 1920 and 1924, consisting of five gold, four silver and two bronze. Six other marksmen have won five gold medals. The only marksman to win three individual gold medals has been Gudbrand Gudbrandsönn Skatteboe (Norway; 1875–1965) in 1906. Separate events for women were first held in 1984.

Six other marksmen have won five gold medals, including three Americans: Alfred P. Lane (b. 26 Sep 1891), 1912–20; Willis Augustus Lee, Jr (1888–194), all in 1920; and Morris Fisher (1890–1968), 1920–24. In 1920 a record seven medals were won by both Willis Lee, who also won a silver and bronze, and Lloyd S. Spooner (1884), four gold, a silver and two bronze.

The first US woman to win an Olympic medal was Margaret L. Murdock (nee Thompson; b. 25 Aug 1942), who took the silver at small-bore rifle three positions in mixed competition in 1976. The first to win an Olympic gold medal was Patricia Spurgin (b. 10 Aug 1965), at women's air rifle in 1984.

World record ■ The first world record by a woman at any sport for a category in direct and measurable competition with men was by Margaret Murdock, who set a world record for small-bore rifle (kneeling position) of 391 in 1967.

Clay pigeon ■ Most world titles have been won by Susan Nattrass (Canada; b. 5 Nov 1950) with six, 1974–75, 1977–79, 1981. The record number of clay birds shot in an hour is 2,312, by Colin Hewish at the Street and District Gun Club, Ivythorn, Somerset, United Kingdom on 8 May 1988.

The maximum 200/200 was achieved by Ricardo Ruiz Rumoroso at the Spanish Clay Pigeon

Championships at Zaragossa on 12 Jun 1983. Noel D. Townend achieved the maximum 200 consecutive down-the-line targets at Nottingham, United Kingdom on 21 Aug 1983.

Bench rest shooting ■ The smallest group on record at 1,000 yd is 4·375 in by Earl Chronister with a ·30-378 Weatherby Mag at Williamsport, PA on 12 Jul 1987.

Highest score in 24 hr ■ The Easingwold Rifle and Pistol Club team of John Smith, Edward Kendall, Phillip Kendall and Paul Duffield scored 120,242 points (averaging 95·66 per card) on 6–7 Aug 1983.

Skiing

The most ancient ski in existence was found well preserved in a peat bog at Hoting, Sweden, dating from *c.* 2500 B.C. The earliest recorded military use of skiing was at the Battle of Isen, near Oslo, Norway in 1200. The Trysil Shooting and Skiing Club, founded in Norway in 1861, claims it is the world's oldest. The oldest ski competitions are the Holmenkollen Nordic events, which were first held in 1866. The first downhill races were staged in Australia in the 1850s. The International Ski Federation (FIS) was founded on 2 Feb 1924, succeeding the International Skiing Commission, founded at Christiania (Oslo), Norway on 18 Feb 1910.

The first ski club in the United States was formed at Berlin, NH in January 1872, later known as the Nansen Ski Club. The US Ski Association was originally founded as the National Ski Association in 1905. In 1962 it was renamed the United States Ski Association, and was renamed US Skiing in May 1990.

Most titles *World/Olympic Championships-Alpine* ■ The World Alpine Championships were inaugurated at Mürren, Switzerland in 1931. The greatest number of titles won has been by Christel Cranz (b. 1 Jul 1914) of Germany, with seven individual—four slalom (1934, 1937–39) and three downhill (1935, 1937, 1939)—and five combined (1934–35, 1937–39). She also won the gold medal for the combined in the 1936 Olympics. The most won by a man is seven, by Anton 'Toni' Sailer (Austria; b. 17 Nov 1935), who won all four in 1956 (giant

SHOOTING–INDIVIDUAL WORLD RECORDS

In 1986, the International Shooting Union introduced new regulations for determining major championships and world records. Now the leading competitors undertake an additional round with a target sub-divided to tenths of a point for rifle and pistol shooting, and an extra 25 shots for trap and skeet. The table below shows the world records for the 13 Olympic shooting disciplines, giving in brackets the score for the number of shots specified plus the score in the additional round.

MEN

FREE RIFLE 50 m 3 × 40 shots	1,283·4	(1,183 + 100·4)	Petr Kurka (Czechoslovakia)	Seoul, South Korea	1 Oct 1987
FREE RIFLE 50 m 60 Shots Prone	704·9	(599 + 105·9)	Petr Kurka (Czechoslovakia)	Zürich, Switzerland	2 Jun 1987
	704·9	(598 + 106·9)	Goran Maksimović (Yugoslavia)	Munich, West Germany	21 Oct 1988
AIR RIFLE 10 m 60 shots	699·4	(596 + 103·4)	Rajmond Debevec (Yugoslavia)	Zürich, Switzerland	8 Jun 1990
FREE PISTOL 50 m 60 shots	671	(579 + 92)	Sergey Pyzhyanov (USSR)	Munich, West Germany	31 May 1990
RAPID-FIRE PISTOL 25 m 60 shots	698	(598 + 100)	Afanasiy Kuzmin (USSR)	Seoul, South Korea	23 Sep 1988
AIR PISTOL 10 m 60 shots	695·1	(593 + 102·1)	Sergey Pyzhyanov (USSR)	Munich, West Germany	Oct 1989
RUNNING GAME TARGET 50 m 30 + 30 shots	691	(594 + 97)	Sergey Luzov (USSR)	Suhl, East Germany	7 Sep 1986
	691	(596 + 95)	Nikolay Lapin (USSR)	Lahti, Finland	25 Jul 1987

WOMEN

STANDARD RIFLE 50 m 3 × 20 shots	691·6	(587 + 104·6)	Vessela Letcheva (Bulgaria)	Munich, West Germany	22 May 1987
AIR RIFLE 10 m 40 shots	504	(399 + 105)	Vessela Letcheva (Bulgaria)	Suhl, East Germany	30 May 1987
SPORT PISTOL 25 m 60 shots	696	(597 + 99)	Lulita Svetkova (USSR)	Mexico City, Mexico	10 Apr 1989
AIR PISTOL 10 m 40 shots	489·5	(389 + 100·5)	Jasna Sekaric (Yugoslavia)	Seoul, South Korea	21 Sep 1988

OPEN

TRAP 200 targets	224	(199 + 25)	Miloslav Bednarik (Czechoslovakia)	Suhl, East Germany	14 Sep 1986
SKEET 200 targets	224	(199 + 25)	Matthew Dryke (US)	Suhl, East Germany	8 Sep 1986
	224	(199 + 25)	Luca Scribani Rossi (Italy)	Bologna, Italy	11 Jun 1988
	224	(200 + 24)	Ole Riber Rasmussen (Denmark)	Bologna, Italy	11 Jun 1988

MOST OLYMPIC TITLES

MEN

ALPINE	3	Anton 'Toni' Sailer (Austria; b. 17 Nov 1935)	Downhill, slalom, giant slalom, 1956
	3	Jean-Claude Killy (France; b. 30 Aug 1943)	Downhill, slalom, giant slalom 1968
NORDIC	4[1]	Sixten Jernberg (Sweden; b. 6 Feb 1929)	50 km 1956; 30 km 1960; 50 km and 4 × 10 km 1964
	4	Gunde Svan (Sweden; b. 12 Mar 1962)	15 km and 4 × 10 km 1984; 50 km and 4 × 10 km 1988
	4	Thomas Wassberg (Sweden; b. 27 Mar 1956)	15 km 1980; 50 km 1984; 4 × 10 km 1984, 1988
Ski-jumping	4	Matti Nykänen (Finland; b. 17 Jul 1963)	70 m hill 1988; 90 m hill 1984, 1988; Team 1988

WOMEN

ALPINE	2	Andrea Mead-Lawrence (US; b. 19 Apr 1932)	Slalom, giant slalom 1952
	2	Marielle Goitschel (France; b. 28 Sep 1945)	Giant slalom 1964; slalom 1968
	2	Marie-Thérèse Nadig (Switzerland; b. 8 Mar 1954)	Downhill, giant slalom 1972
	2	Rosi Mittermaier (now Neureuther [West Germany]; b. 5 Aug 1950)	Downhill, slalom 1976
	2[2]	Hanni Wenzel (Liechtenstein; b. 14 Dec 1956)	Giant slalom, slalom 1980
	2	Vreni Schneider (Switzerland; b. 26 Nov 1964)	Giant slalom, slalom 1988
NORDIC	4[3]	Galina Kulakova (USSR; b. 29 Apr 1942)	5 km, 10 km and 3 ×5 km relay 1972; 4 ×5 km relay 1976
(individual)	3	Marja-Liisa Hämäläinen (Finland; b. 10 Aug 1955)	5 km, 10 km and 20 km 1984

[1] **Most medals** 9, Sixten Jernberg, four golds, three silver and two bronze
9, Raisa Smetanina, (USSR) three gold, five silver and one bronze at women's Nordic skiing 1976–88.
[2] *Wenzel won a silver in the 1980 downhill and a bronze in the 1976 slalom for a record four medals in Alpine skiing.*
[3] *Kulakova also won two silver and two bronze medals in 1968, 1976 and 1980 for a women's record eight medals.*

slalom, slalom, downhill and the non-Olympic alpine combination) and the downhill, giant slalom and combined in 1958.

The only US skier to win two Olympic gold medals has been Andrea Mead Lawrence (b. 19 Apr 1932), at slalom and giant slalom in 1952.

World / Olympic Championships-Nordic ■ The first World Nordic Championships were those of the 1924 Winter Olympics in Chamonix, France. The greatest number of titles won is ten, by Gunde Svan (Sweden; b. 12 Jan 1962), six individual—15 km 1989, 30 km 1985, 50 km 1985 and 1989, and Olympics, 15 km 1984, 50 km 1988—and four relays—4 × 10 km, 1987 and 1989, and Olympics, 1984 and 1988. The most titles won by a woman is nine, by Galina Alekseyevna Kulakova (USSR; b. 29 Apr 1942) in 1970–78. The most medals is 21, by Raisa Petrovna Smetanina (USSR; b. 29 Feb 1952) including six gold, 1974–88. Johann Grøttumsbraaten (1899–1942) of Norway also won six individual titles (two 18 km cross-country, four Nordic combined) in 1926–32. Ulrich Wehling (East Germany) has also won four Nordic combined, winning the World Championship in 1974 and the Olympic title, 1972, 1976 and 1980, the first skier to win the same event at three successive Olympics. The record for a jumper is five, by Birger Ruud (b. 23 Aug 1911) of Norway, in 1931–32 and 1935–37. Ruud is the only person to win Olympic events in each of the dissimilar Alpine and Nordic disci plines. In 1936 he won the Ski-jumping and the Alpine downhill (which was not then a separate event, but only a segment of the Combined event).

World Cup ■ The World Cup was introduced for Alpine events in 1967 and for Nordic events in 1981. The most individual event wins is 86 (46 giant slalom, 40 slalom) from a total of 287 races, by Ingemar Stenmark (Sweden; b. 18 Mar 1956) in 1974–89, including a men's record 13 in one season in 1978/9, of which 10 were part of a record 14 successive giant slalom wins from 18 Mar 1978, his 22nd birthday, to 21 Jan 1980. Franz Klammer (Austria; b. 3 Dec 1953) won a record 25 downhill races, 1974–84. Annemarie

Moser (nee Pröll, [Austria]; b. 27 Mar 1953) won a women's record 62 individual event wins, 1970–79. She had a record 11 consecutive downhill wins from Dec 1972 to Jan 1974. Vreni Schneider (Switzerland; b. 26 Nov 1964) in the 1988/89 season won a record 13 events and a combined, including all seven slalom events.

The most successful US skier has been Phillip Ferdinand Mahre (b. 10 May 1957), winner of the overall title three times, 1981–83, with two wins at giant slalom, and one at slalom. The most

successful woman has been Tamara McKinney (b. 16 Oct 1962), overall winner 1983, giant slalom 1981 and 1983, and slalom 1984.

The only American to win a Nordic skiing World Cup title has been William Koch (b. 7 Jun 1955), at cross-country in 1982.

Ski-jumping ■ The longest ski-jump ever recorded is one of 636 ft, by Piotr Fijas (Poland) at Planica, Yugoslavia on 14 Mar 1987. The women's record is 361 ft, by Tiina Lehtola (Finland; b. 3 Aug 1962) at Ruka, Finland on 29 Mar 1981. The longest dry ski-jump is 302 ft, by Hubert Schwarz (West Germany) at Berchtesgarten, West Germany on 30 Jun 1981.

Highest speed ■ The official world record, as recognized by the International Ski Federation, for a skier is 139·030 mph, by Michael Prufer (Monaco), and the fastest by a woman is 133·234 mph, by Tarja Mulari (Finland), both at Les Arcs, France on 16 Apr 1988. On the same occasion. Patrick Knaff (France) set a one-legged record of 115·309 mph.

The highest average speed in the Olympic downhill race was 64·95 mph, by William D. Johnson (US; b. 30 Mar 1960) at Sarajevo, Yugoslavia on 16 Feb 1984. The fastest in a World Cup downhill is 67·00 mph, by Harti Weirather (Austria; b. 25 Jan 1958) at Kitzbühel, Austria on 15 Jan 1982.

Highest speed—cross-country ■ Bill Koch (US; b. 13 Apr 1943) on 26 Mar 1981 skied ten times round a 3·11 mile loop on Marlborough Pond, near Putney, VT. He completed the course in 1 hr 59 min 47 sec, an average speed of 15·57 mph. A race includes uphill and downhill sections; the record time for a race in World Championships or Olympic Games is 2 hr 4 min 30·9 sec, by Gunde Svan (Sweden) in 1988, an average speed of 14·97 mph.

MOST WORLD CUP TITLES
ALPINE

MEN

OVERALL	4	Gustavo Thoeni (Italy)	1971–73, 1975
	4	Pirmin Zurbriggen (Switzerland)	1984, 1987–88, 1990
DOWNHILL	5	Franz Klammer (Austria)	1975–78, 1983
SLALOM	8	Ingemar Stenmark (Sweden)	1975–81, 1983
GIANT SLALOM	7	Ingemar Stenmark	1975–76, 1978–81, 1984
SUPER GIANT SLALOM	4	Pirmin Zurbriggen (Switzerland)	1987–90

Two men have won four titles in one year: Jean-Claude Killy (France; b. 30 Aug 1943) won all four possible disciplines (downhill, slalom, giant slalom and overall) in 1967; and Pirmin Zurbriggen (Switzerland; b. 4 Feb 1963) won four of the five possible disciplines (downhill, giant slalom, Super giant slalom [added 1986] and overall) in 1987.

WOMEN

OVERALL	6	Annemarie Moser (Austria)	1971–75, 1979
DOWNHILL	7	Annemarie Moser	1971–75, 1978–79
SLALOM	4	Erika Hess (Switzerland)	1981–83, 1985
GIANT SLALOM	3	Annemarie Moser	1971–72, 1975
	3	Lise-Marie Morerod (Switzerland)	1976–78
	3	Vreni Schneider	1986–87, 1989
SUPER GIANT SLALOM	2	Carole Merle (France)	1989–90

NORDIC

MEN

JUMPING	4	Matti Nykänen (Finland)	1983, 1985–86, 1988
CROSS-COUNTRY	5	Gunde Svan (Sweden)	1984–86, 1988–89

WOMEN

CROSS-COUNTRY	3	Marjo Matikainen (Finland)	1986–88

Closest verdict ■ The narrowest winning margin in a championship ski race was one hundredth of a second by Thomas Wassberg (Sweden) over Juha Mieto (Finland; b. 20 Nov 1949) in the Olympic 15-km cross-country race at Lake Placid, NY on 17 Feb 1980. His winning time was 41 min 57·63 sec.

Highest altitude ■ Jean Afanassieff and Nicolas Jaeger skied from 26,900 ft to 20,340 ft on the 1978 French expedition on Mt Everest.

Steepest descent ■ The steepest descents in alpine skiing history have been by Sylvain Saudan. At the start of his descent from Mont Blanc on the northeast side down the Couloir Gervasutti from 13,937 ft on 17 Oct 1967, he skied to gradients of *c.* 60°.

Longest run ■ The longest all-downhill ski run in the world is the Weissfluhjoch-Küblis Parsenn course, near Davos, Switzerland, which measures 7·6 miles. The run from the Aiguille du Midi top of the Chamonix lift (vertical lift 9,052 ft) across the Vallée Blanche is 13 miles.

Most competitors *Alpine* ■ 1,700 downhill skiers competed at Åre, Jämtland, Sweden on 30 Apr 1984.

Longest races ■ The world's greatest Nordic ski race is the Vasaloppet, which commemorates an event of 1521 when Gustav Vasa (1496–1560), later King Gustavus Eriksson, fled 53·3 miles from Mora to Sälen, Sweden. He was overtaken by loyal, speedy scouts on skis, who persuaded him to return eastwards to Mora to lead a rebellion and become the king of Sweden. The reenactment of this return journey is now an annual event at 55·3 miles. There were a record 10,934 starters on 6 Mar 1977 and a record 10,633 finishers on 4 Mar 1979. The fastest time is 3 hr 48 min 55 sec, by Bengt Hassis (Sweden) on 2 Mar 1986.

The Finlandia Ski Race, 46·6 miles from Hämeenlinna to Lahti, on 26 Feb 1984 had a record 13,226 starters and 12,909 finishers.

The longest downhill race is the Inferno in Switzerland, 9·8 miles from the top of the Schilthorn to Lauterbrunnen. The record entry was 1,401 in 1981 and the record time 15 min 26·44 sec, by Ueli Grossniklaus (Switzerland) in 1987.

Long-distance Nordic ■ In 24 hours Seppo-Juhani Savolainen covered 258·2 miles at Saariselkä, Finland on 8–9 Apr 1988. The women's record is 205·05 miles, by Sisko Kainulaisen at Jyväskylä, Finland on 23–24 Mar 1985.

In 48 hours Bjørn Løkken (Norway; b. 27 Nov 1937) covered 319 miles 205 yd on 11–13 Mar 1982.

Freestyle ■ The first World Championships were held at Tignes, France in 1986, titles being awarded in ballet, moguls, aerials and combined. A record two titles have been won by Lloyd Langlois (Canada), aerials, 1986 and 1989, and Jan Buchner (US), ballet, 1986 and 1989. The three seperate disciplines were included in the 1988 Olympics but only as demonstration events.

Longest lift ■ The longest gondola ski lift is 3·88 miles long at Grindelwald-Männlichen, Switzerland (in two sections, but one gondola). The longest chair lift in the world was the Alpine Way to Kosciusko Chalet lift above Thredbo, near the Snowy Mountains, New South Wales, Australia. It took from 45 to 75 min to ascend the 3·5 miles, according to the weather. It has now collapsed. The highest is at Chacaltaya, Bolivia, rising to 16,500 ft.

Ski-bob *Origins* ■ The ski-bob was the invention of J. C. Stevenson of Hartford, CT in 1891, and patented (No. 47334) on 19 Apr 1892 as a 'bicycle with ski-runners.' The Fédération Internationale de Skibob was founded on 14 Jan 1961 in Innsbruck, Austria, and the first World Championships were held at Bad Hofgastein, Austria in 1967.

The highest speed attained is 103·4 mph, by Erich Brenter (Austria; b. 1940) at Cervinia, Italy in 1964.

World Championships ■ The only ski-bobbers to retain a world championship are: men – Alois Fischbauer (Austria; b. 6 Oct 1951), 1973 and 1975, Robert Mühlberger (West Germany), 1979 and 1981; women – Gerhilde Schiffkorn (Austria; b. 22 Mar 1950), 1967 and 1969, Gertrude Geberth (Austria; b. 18 Oct 1951), 1971 and 1973.

GRASS SKIING

Grass skis were first manufactured by Josef Kaiser (West Germany) in 1963. World Championships (now awarded for Super G, giant slalom, slalom and combined) were first held in 1979. The most titles won is nine, by Ingrid Hirschhofer (Austria) 1979–87. The most by a man is seven, by Erwin Gansner (Switzerland) 1981–87.

The speed record is 53·99 mph, by Erwin Gansner at Owen, West Germany on 5 Sep 1982.

Skipping

10 Mile skip-run ■ Vadivelu Karunakaren (India) skipped 10 miles in 58 min at Madras, India, 1 Feb 1990.

Most turns *10 sec* ■ 128 by Albert Rayner (Great Britain; b. 19 Apr 1923), Stanford Sports, Birmingham, West Midlands, United Kingdom, 19 Nov 1982.

1 min ■ 425 by Robert Commers (US; b. 15 May 1950) at The Holiday Inn, Jamestown, NY, 23 Feb 1990.

One hour ■ 13,783 by Robert Commers (US), at Woodbridge, NJ, 13 May 1989.

On a single rope, team of 90 ■ 160, by students from the Nishigoshi Higashi Elementary School, Kumamoto, Japan, 27 Feb 1987.

On a tightrope ■ 58 (consecutive), by Bryan

Andro (ne Dewhurst), TROS TV, the Netherlands, 6 Aug 1981.

Most consecutive multiple turns *Double* ■ 10,709, by Frank Oliveri (US), at Rochester, NY, 7 May 1988.

Double (with cross) ■ 2,411, by Ken Solis (US), at North Shore-Elite Fitness and Racquets Club, Glendale, WI, 29 Mar 1988.

Treble ■ 423, by Shozo Hamada (Japan), at Saitama, Japan, 1 Jun 1987.

Quadruple ■ 51, by Katsumi Suzuki (Japan), at Saitama, Japan, 29 May 1975.

Quintuple ■ 6, by Hideyuki Tateda (Japan; b. 1968), at Aomori, Japan, 19 Jun 1982.

Most on a rope ■ (minimum 12 turns obligatory) 200, by a team at the International Rope Skipping Competition, Greeley, CO, 30 Jun 1989.

Sled Dog Racing

Racing between harnessed dog teams (usually huskies) had been practiced by the Inuits and the northern Indians of North America and in Scandinavia, but the first formal record of a race was in 1908, when the All-Alaskan Sweepstakes were contested on a run of 408 miles from Nome to Candle and back.

Iditarod Trail ■ Now established as the world's most prestigious race, the Iditarod has been raced annually since 1973 by dog teams, 1,158 miles from Anchorage to Nome, AK. The inaugural winner, Dick Wilmarth, took 20 days 49 min and 41 sec to complete the course, beating 33 other racers. The most wins is four, by Rick Swenson, 1977, 1979, 1981–82, and by Susan Butcher, 1986–88, 1990. In 1990 Butcher set the record time for the race of 11 days 1 hour 53 min 23 sec.

Snooker

Origins ■ Research shows that snooker was originated by Colonel Sir Neville Francis Fitzgerald Chamberlain (1856–1944) as a hybrid

of 'black pool,' 'pyramids' and billiards, in Jubbulpore, India in 1875. It did not reach England until 1885, where the modern scoring system was adopted in 1891. Championships were not started until 1916. The World Professional Championship was instituted in 1927.

Most world titles ■ The world professional title was won a record 15 times by Joe Davis, on the first 15 occasions it was contested, 1927–40 and 1946. The most wins in the Amateur Championships (instituted 1963) have been two by: Gary Owen (England) in 1963 and 1966; Ray Edmonds (England) 1972 and 1974; and Paul Mifsud (Malta) 1985–86.

World Championships *Youngest* ■ The youngest man to win a world title is Jimmy White (Great Britain; b. 2 May 1962), who was 18 yr 191 days when he won the World Amateur Snooker Championship in Launceston, Tasmania, Australia on 9 Nov 1980. Stephen Hendry (b. 13 Jan 1969) became the youngest World Professional champion, at 21 yr 106 days on 29 Apr 1990. He had been the youngest winner of a major title, at 18 yr 285 days, when he won the Rothmans Grand Prix on 25 Oct 1987.

Stacey Hillyard (Great Britain; b. 5 Sep 1969) won the Women's World Amateur Championship in October 1984 at the age of 15.

Highest breaks ■ Over 200 players have achieved the 'maximum' break of 147. The first to do so was E. J. 'Murt' O'Donoghue (New Zealand; b. 1901) at Griffiths, New South Wales, Australia on 26 Sep 1934. The first officially ratified 147 was by Joe Davis against Willie Smith, in London, United Kingdom on 22 Jan 1955. The first achieved in major tournaments were by John Spencer (b. 18 Sep 1935) at Slough, Berkshire, United Kingdom on 13 Jan 1979, but the table had oversized pockets, and by Steve Davis (b. 22 Aug 1957), who had a ratified break of 147 against John Spencer in the Lada Classic at Oldham, Greater Manchester, United Kingdom on 11 Jan 1982. The youngest to score a competitive maximum was Gary Hill (b. 29 Sep 1968), at 20 yr 249 days, during the World Junior Championship at Reykjavik, Iceland on 5 Jun 1989. Cliff Thorburn (Canada; b. 16 Jan 1948) has scored two tounament 147 breaks on 23 Apr 1983 (still the only one in the World Professional Championship) and 8 Mar 1989. Steve Duggan (b. 10 Apr 1958) made a break of 148 in a witnessed practice frame in Doncaster, South Yorkshire, United Kingdom on 27 Apr 1988. The break involved a free ball, which therefore created an 'extra' red, when all 15 reds were still on the table. In these very exceptional circumstances, the maximum break is 155.

The world amateur record break is 147, by Geet Sethi (India) in the Indian Amateur Championships on 21 Feb 1988.

Three consecutive century breaks were first compiled in a major tournament by Steve Davis: 108, 101 and 104 at Stoke-on-Trent, Staffordshire, United Kingdom on 10 Sep 1988. Doug Mountjoy (b. 8 Jun 1942) equaled the feat: 131, 106 and 124 at Preston, Lancashire, United Kingdom on 27 Nov 1988. Jim Meadowcroft (b. 15 Dec 1946) made four consecutive frame clearances of 105, 115, 117 and 125 at Connaught Leisure Centre, Worthing, West Sussex, United Kingdom on 27 Jan 1982.

The first century break by a woman in competitive play was 114, by Stacey Hillyard in a league match at Bournemouth, Dorset, United Kingdom on 15 Jan 1985. The highest break by a woman in competition is 116, by Allison Fisher in the British Open at Solihull, West Midlands, United Kingdom on 7 Oct 1989.

Soccer

For details of the FIFA World Cup see pages 284 and 285.

Major Indoor Soccer League (MISL) Founded in 1978, the most championships is six, by the San Diego Sockers, 1983, 1985–86, 1988–90.

Greatest crowds ■ The top attendance for a soccer match in the US was 101,799, for France's 2–0 Olympic final win over Brazil at the Los Angeles Coliseum, CA on 11 Aug 1984.

Softball

Origins ■ Softball, a derivative of baseball, was invented by George Hancock at the Farragut Boat Club of Chicago, IL in 1887. Rules were first codified in Minneapolis, MN in 1895 as kitten ball. The name softball was introduced by Walter Hakanson at a meeting of the National Recreation Congress in 1926. The name was adopted throughout the United States in 1930. Rules were formalized in 1933 by the International Joint Rules Committee for Softball and adopted by the Amateur Softball Association of America. The International Softball Federation was formed in 1950 as governing body for both fast pitch and slow pitch. It was reorganized in 1965.

Most titles ■ The United States has won the men's world championship (instituted 1966) five times, 1966, 1968, 1976 (shared), 1980 and 1988, and the women's title (instituted 1965) three times, in 1974, 1978 and 1986. The world's first slow-pitch championships for men's teams was held in Oklahoma City in 1987, when the winners were the United States.

US National Championships ■ The most wins in the fast pitch championships (first held in 1933) for men is 10, by the Clearwater (Florida) Bombers between 1950 and 1973, and for women is 20, by the Hi Ho (formerly Raybestos) Brakettes of Stratford, CT, between 1958 and 1988.

Slow pitch championships have been staged annually since 1953 for men and since 1962 for women. Three wins for men have been achieved by Skip Hogan A. C. of Pittsburgh, 1962, 1964–65 and by Joe Gatliff Auto Sales of Newport, KY, 1956–57, 1963. At super slow pitch three wins have been achieved by Howard's-Western Steer, Denver, CO, 1981, 1983–84, and by Steele's Silver Bullets, Grafton, OH, 1985–87. The Dots of Miami, FL have a record five women's titles, playing as the Converse Dots, 1969, Marks Brothers, N. Miami Dots, 1974–75 and Bob Hoffman Dots, 1978–79.

Speedway

Motorcycle racing on large dirt track surfaces has been traced back to 1902 in the United States. The first fully documented motorcycle track races were at the Portman Road Ground, Ipswich, Suffolk, United Kingdom on 2 Jul 1904. Two heats and a final were contested, F. E. Barker winning in 5 min 54·2 sec for three miles. Modern speedway has developed from the 'short track' races held at the West Maitland Agricultural Show (New South Wales, Australia) on 22 Dec 1923, by Johnnie Hoskins (New Zealand; 1892–1987).

Highest transfer fee ● Roberto Baggio, seen here in action for Italy in the 1990 World Cup, is soccer's most expensive player. In May 1990 he moved from Fiorentina to Juventus for a remarkable 16 thousand million lira ($12·3 million). (Photo: All-Sport/David Cannon)

World Championships ■ The World Speedway Championship was inaugurated at London, United Kingdom on 10 Sep 1936. The most wins have been six, by Ivan Mauger (New Zealand) in 1968–70, 1972, 1977 and 1979. Barry Briggs (New Zealand; b. 30 Dec 1934) made a record 17 consecutive appearances in the finals (1954–70) and won the world title in 1957–58, 1964 and 1966. He scored a record 201 points in world championship competition from 87 races.

The World Pairs Championships instituted 1968 have been won a record seven times, by England / Great Britain (1972, 1976–78, 1980 and 1983–84) and Denmark (1979, 1985–90). The most successful individual in the World Pairs has been Erik Gundersen (b. 8 Oct 1959), with five wins for Denmark, with Tommy Krudeen, in 1985 and with Hans Nielsen 1986–89. The World Team Cup (instituted 1960) has been won a record nine times by England / Great Britain (Great Britain 1968, 1971–73; England 1974–75, 1977, 1980, 1989). Hans Nielsen (Denmark) has ridden in a record eight Team wins.

Poland uniquely competed in 21 successive World Team Cup finals, 1960–80, and in a 22nd in 1984. Maximum points (then 30) were scored in the World Pairs Championship by: Jerzy Szczakiel (b. 28 Jan 1949) and Andrzej Wyglenda (Poland), at Rybnik, Poland in 1971; and Arthur Dennis Sigalos (b. 16 Aug 1959) and Robert Benjamin 'Bobby' Schwartz (US; b. 10 Aug 1956) at Liverpool, Australia on 11 Dec 1982.

Ivan Mauger also won four World Team Cups

(three for Great Britain), two World Pairs (including one unofficial) and three world long track titles. Ove Fundin (Sweden; b. 23 May 1933) won 12 world titles: five individual, one pairs, and six World Team Cup medals, in 1956–70. In 1985 Erik Gundersen (Denmark) became the first man to hold world titles at individual, pairs, team and long-track events simultaneously.

Tests *Maximum points* ■ The only rider to have scored maximum points in every match of a Test series was Arthur 'Bluey' Wilkinson (1911–40), in five matches for Australia *v* England in Sydney in 1937/8.

Squash

Although squash with a soft ball was played in 1817 at Harrow School, London, United Kingdom, there was no recognized champion of any country until John A. Miskey of Philadelphia, PA won the American Amateur Singles Championship in 1907.

The first organized game in the United States was held in 1882 at St Paul's School, Concord, NH.

World Championships ■ Jahangir Khan (Pakistan; b. 10 Dec 1963) won six World Open (instituted 1976) titles, 1981–85 and 1988, and the ISRF world individual title (formerly World Amateur, instituted 1967) in 1979, 1983 and 1985. Geoffrey B. Hunt (Australia; b. 11 Mar 1947) won four World Open titles, 1976–77 and 1979–80 and three World Amateur, 1967, 1969 and 1971.

Pakistan (1977, 1981, 1983, 1985 and 1987) and Australia (1967, 1969, 1971, 1973 and 1989) have each won five men's world titles. England won the women's title in 1985, 1987 and 1989, following Great Britain's win in 1979.

Most titles *Open Championship* ■ The most wins in the Open Championship held annually in Britain, is nine, by Jahangir Khan, in successive years, 1982–90. Hashim Khan (Pakistan; b. 1915) won seven times, 1950–55 and 1957, and also won the Vintage title six times in 1978–83.

The most British Open women's titles is 16, by Heather Pamela McKay (nee Blundell, [Australia]; b. 31 Jul 1941) from 1961 to 1977. She also won the World Open title in 1976 and 1979.

United States ■ The US amateur squash championships were first held for men in 1907 and for women in 1928; the most singles wins is six by Stanley W. Pearson, 1915–17 and 1921–23, and G. Diehl Mateer won a record eleven men's doubles titles between 1949 and 1966 with five different partners. Sharif Khan (Pakistan) won a record 13 North American Open Championships (inst. 1953), 1969–74 and 1976–82.

Unbeaten sequences ■ Heather McKay was unbeaten from 1962 to 1980. Jahangir Khan was unbeaten from his loss to Geoff Hunt at the British Open on 10 Apr 1981 until Ross Norman (New Zealand) ended his sequence in the World Open final on 11 Nov 1986.

Longest and shortest championship matches ■ The longest recorded competitive match was one of 2 hr 45 min, when Jahangir Khan beat Gamal Awad (Egypt; b. 8 Sep 1955) 9–10, 9–5, 9–7, 9–2, the first game lasting a record 1 hr 11 min, in the final of the Patrick International Festival at Chichester, West Sussex, United Kingdom on 30 Mar 1983. Lucy Soutter (Great Britain) beat Hugolein van Hoorn (Netherlands) in just 7½ min (9–0, 9–0, 9–0) in the British Under-21 Open Championship at Lamb's Squash Club, London, United Kingdom on 17 Jan 1988.

Highest speed ■ In tests at Wimbledon Squash and Badminton Club, United Kingdom in January 1988, Roy Buckland hit a squash ball by an overhead service at a measured speed of 144·6 mph over the distance to the front wall. This is equivalent to an initial speed at the racket of 150·8 mph.

Surfing

The traditional Polynesian sport of surfing in a canoe (*ehorooe*) was first recorded by Captain James Cook, (1728–79) on his first voyage at Tahiti in December 1771. Surfing on a board (*Amo Amo iluna ka lau oka nalu*) was first described as 'most perilous and extraordinary ... altogether astonishing and is scarcely to be credited' by Lt (later Capt) James King, in March 1779 at Kealakekua Bay, HI Island. A surfer was first depicted by this voyage's official artist, John Webber. The sport was revived at Waikiki by 1900. Hollow boards were introduced in 1929 and the light plastic foam type in 1956.

Most titles ■ World Amateur Championships were inaugurated in May 1964 at Sydney, Australia. The most titles is three, by Michael Novakov (Australia), who won the Kneeboard event in 1982, 1984 and 1986. A World Professional series was started in 1975. The men's title has been won five times, by Mark Richards (Australia), 1975 and 1979–82, and the women's title (instituted 1979) four times, by Freida Zamba (US), 1984–86, 1988.

Highest waves ridden ■ Waimea Bay, HI reputedly provides the most consistently high waves, often reaching the ridable limit of 30–35 ft. The highest wave ever ridden was the *tsunami* of 'perhaps 50 ft,' which struck Minole, HI on 3 Apr 1868, and was ridden to save his life by a Hawaiian named Holua.

Longest ride *Sea wave* ■ About four to six times each year, ridable surfing waves break in Matanchen Bay near San Blas, Nayarit, Mexico, that makes rides of *c.* 5,700 ft possible.

Swimming

In Japan, swimming in schools was ordered by imperial edict of Emperor Go-Yozei (1586–1611) in 1603, but competition was known from 36 B.C. Seawater bathing was fashionable at Scarborough, North Yorkshire, United Kingdom as early as 1660. The earliest pool was Pearless Pool, London, United Kingdom, opened in 1743.

Largest pools ■ The largest swimming pool in the world is the seawater Orthlieb Pool in Casablanca, Morocco. It is 1,574 ft long and 246 ft wide, and has an area of 8·9 acres. The largest land-locked swimming pool with heated water was the Fleishhacker Pool on Sloat Boulevard, near Great Highway, San Francisco, CA. It measured 1,000 × 150 ft and up to 14 ft deep and contained 7·5 million gal of heated water. It was opened on 2 May 1925 but has now been abandoned. The largest land-locked pool in current use is Willow Lake at Warren, OH. It measures 600 × 150 ft. The greatest spectator accommodation is 13,614, at Osaka, Japan.

Fastest swimmer ■ In a 25-yd pool, Tom Jager (US; b. 6 Oct 1964) achieved an average speed of 5·37 mph for 50 yards in 19.05 sec at Nashville, TN on 23 Mar 1990. The women's fastest is 4·48 mph, by Yang Wenyi (China) in her 50 m world record (see World Record table).

US Championships ■ Tracy Caulkins (b. 11 Jan 1963) won a record 48 US swimming titles and set 60 US records in her career, 1977–84. The men's record is 36 titles, by Johnny Weissmuller (ne Janos Weiszmuller; 1904–84), between 1921 and 1928.

Most world records ■ Men: 32, Arne Borg (Sweden; 1901–87), 1921–29. Women: 42, Ragnhild Hveger (Denmark; b. 10 Dec 1920), 1936–42. For currently recognized events (only metric distances in 50 m pools) the most is 26, by Mark Andrew Spitz (US; b. 10 Feb 1950), 1967–72, and 23 by Kornelia Ender (GDR; b. 25 Oct 1958), 1973–6. The most by a US woman is 15 by Deborah 'Debbie' Meyer (b. 14 Aug 1952) 1967–70.

Most world titles ■ In the World Championships (instinued 1973) the most medals won is ten, by Kornelia Ender, with eight gold and two

The *Fédération Internationale de Football Association* (FIFA), which was founded on 21 May 1904, instituted the first World Cup on 13 Jul 1930, in Montevideo, Uruguay. It is now held quadrennially. Three wins have been achieved by Brazil 1958, 1962 and 1970; Italy 1934, 1938 and 1982, and West Germany 1954, 1974 and 1990. Brazil, uniquely, have taken part in all 14 finals tournaments.

Appearances ■ Antonio Carbajal (Mexico) (b. 1923) is the only player to have appeared in five World Cup finals tournaments, keeping goal for Mexico in 1950, 1954, 1958, 1962 and 1966, playing 11 games in all. The most appearances in finals tournaments is 21 by: Uwe Seeler (West Germany) (b. 5 Nov 1936), 1958–70; and by Wladyslaw Zmuda (Poland) (b. 6 Jun 1954), 1974–86. Pelé is the only player to have been with three World Cup–winning teams, in 1958, 1962 and 1970. The youngest ever to play in the World Cup is Norman Whiteside, who played for Northern Ireland *v.* Yugoslavia aged 17 yr 42 days on 17 Jun 1982.

Goal scoring ■ Just Fontaine (b. Marrakesh, Morocco, 18 Aug 1933) of France scored 13 goals in six matches in the final stages of the 1958 competition in Sweden. Gerd Müller. (West Germany) (b. 3 Nov 1945) scored 10 goals in 1970 and four in 1974 for the highest aggregate of 14 goals. Fontaine, Jairzinho (Brazil) and Alcide Ghiggia (Uruguay) are the only three players to have scored in every match in a final series. Jairzinho scored seven in six games in 1970 and Ghiggia, four in four games in 1950 .

The most goals scored in a final is three by Geoff Hurst (b. 8 Dec 1941) for England *v.* West Germany on 30 Jul 1966. Three players have scored in two finals: Vava (real name Edwaldo Izito Neto) (Brazil) in 1958 and 1962, Pelé in 1958 and 1970; and Paul Breitner (West Germany) in 1974 and 1982. The fastest goal in World Cup competition was one in 27 sec by Bryan Robson (b. 11 Jan 1957) for England *v.* France in Bilbao on 16 Jun 1982.

The highest score in any match occurred in a qualifying match in Auckland on 15 Aug 1981 when New Zealand beat Fiji 13–0. The highest score during the final stages is 10, scored by Hungary in a 10–1 win over El Salvador at Elche, Spain on 15 Jun 1982. The highest match aggregate in the finals tournament is 12, when Austria beat Switzerland, 7–5, in 1954.

The best defensive record belongs to England, who in six matches in 1966 conceded only three goals.

Most goals in a finals series
Just Fontaine (France) 13 goals from six games

Leading scorer in 1990
Salvatore Schillaci (Italy) 6 goals from seven games

WORLD CUP

ITALIA '90 ■ The most notable record achieved during the the finals was West Germany's record-equaling third success. However, their 1-0 win over Argentina was the lowest scoring final in the history of the World Cup and marked the first time a team had failed to score in the final.

Argentina also achieved another first for a final by having a player sent-off (ejected from the game). In general the finals set undesirable records: the lowest scoring, with 115 goals in 52 matches for an average of 2·21; and discipline or lack of it, with 16 sendings-off and 170 bookings (warnings).

GROUP A

Italy v Austria	1 - 0
USA v Czechoslovakia	1 - 5
Italy v USA	1 - 0
Austria v Czechoslovakia	0 - 1
Italy v Czechoslovakia	2 - 0
Austria v USA	2 - 1

	P	W	D	L	F	A	Pts
ITALY	3	3	0	0	4	0	6
CZECHOSLOVAKIA	3	2	0	1	6	3	4
AUSTRIA	3	1	0	2	2	3	2
USA	3	0	0	3	2	8	0

GROUP B

Argentina v Cameroon	0 - 1
USSR v Romania	0 - 2
Argentina v USSR	2 - 0
Cameroon v Romania	2 - 1
Argentina v Romania	1 - 1
Cameroon v USSR	0 - 4

	P	W	D	L	F	A	Pts
CAMEROON	3	2	0	1	3	5	4
ROMANIA	3	1	1	1	4	3	3
ARGENTINA	3	1	1	1	3	2	3
USSR	3	1	0	2	4	4	2

GROUP C

Brazil v Sweden	2 - 1
Costa Rica v Scotland	1 - 0
Brazil v Costa Rica	1 - 0
Sweden v Scotland	1 - 2
Brazil v Scotland	1 - 0
Sweden v Costa Rica	1 - 2

	P	W	D	L	F	A	Pts
BRAZIL	3	3	0	0	4	1	6
COSTA RICA	3	2	0	1	3	2	4
SCOTLAND	3	1	0	2	2	3	2
SWEDEN	3	0	0	3	3	6	0

GROUP D

UAE v Colombia	0 - 2
West Germany v Yugoslavia	4 - 1
Yugoslavia v Colombia	1 - 0
West Germany v UAE	5 - 1
Yugoslavia v UAE	4 - 1
West Germany v Colombia	1 - 1

	P	W	D	L	F	A	Pts
WEST GERMANY	3	2	1	0	10	3	5
YUGOSLAVIA	3	2	0	1	6	5	4
COLOMBIA	3	1	1	1	3	2	3
UAE	3	0	0	3	2	11	0

GROUP E

Belgium v South Korea	2 - 0
Uruguay v Spain	0 - 0
Belgium v Uruguay	3 - 1
Spain v South Korea	3 - 1
Belgium v Spain	1 - 2
Uruguay v South Korea	1 - 0

	P	W	D	L	F	A	Pts
SPAIN	3	2	1	0	5	2	5
BELGIUM	3	2	0	1	6	3	4
URUGUAY	3	1	1	1	2	3	3
SOUTH KOREA	3	0	0	3	1	6	0

GROUP F

England v Republic of Ireland	1 - 1
Netherlands v Egypt	1 - 1
England v Netherlands	0 - 0
Republic of Ireland v Egypt	0 - 0
England v Egypt	1 - 0
Netherlands v Republic of Ireland	1 - 1

	P	W	D	L	F	A	Pts
ENGLAND	3	1	2	0	2	1	4
REPUBLIC OF IRELAND	3	0	3	0	2	2	3
NETHERLANDS	3	0	3	0	2	2	3
EGYPT	2	0	2	1	1	2	2

* WON ON PENALTIES

SECOND ROUND

ITALY	2
URUGUAY	0

REPUBLIC OF IRELAND *	0
ROMANIA	0

BRAZIL	0
ARGENTINA	1

SPAIN	1
YUGOSLAVIA	2

CAMEROON	2
COLOMBIA	1

ENGLAND	1
BELGIUM	0

CZECHOSLOVAKIA	4
COSTA RICA	1

WEST GERMANY	2
NETHERLANDS	1

QUARTER-FINALS

ITALY	1
REPUBLIC OF IRELAND	0

ARGENTINA *	0
YUGOSLAVIA	0

CAMEROON	2
ENGLAND	3

CZECHOSLOVAKIA	0
WEST GERMANY	1

SEMI-FINALS

ITALY	1
ARGENTINA *	1

ENGLAND	1
WEST GERMANY *	1

WORLD CUP FINAL

ARGENTINA	0
WEST GERMANY	1

3rd & 4th PLACE PLAYOFF

ITALY	2
ENGLAND	1

silver in 1973 and 1975. The most by a man is eight, by Ambrose 'Rowdy' Gaines (US; b. 17 Feb 1959), five gold and three silver, in 1978 and 1982. The most gold medals won is six (two individual and four relay), by James Paul Montgomery (US; b. 24 Jan 1955) in 1973 and 1975. The most medals won at a single championship is seven, by Matthew Nicholas Biondi (US; b. 8 Oct 1965), three gold, one silver, three bronze, in 1986.

The most gold medals by an American woman is five, by Tracy Caulkins (b. 11 Jan 1963), all in 1978, as well as a silver. The most medals is nine, by Mary Terstegge Meagher (b. 27 Oct 1964), two gold, five silver, two bronze, 1978–82.

OLYMPIC RECORDS
Most medals *Men* ■ The greatest number of Olympic gold medals won is nine, by Mark Spitz (US): 100 m and 200 m freestyle, 1972; 100 m and 200 m butterfly, 1972; 4 × 100 m freestyle, 1968 and 1972; 4 × 200 m freestyle, 1968 and 1972; 4 × 100 m medley, 1972. *All but one of these*

performances (the 4 × 200 m freestyle of 1968) were also new world records. He also won a silver (100 m butterfly) and a bronze (100 m freestyle) in 1968 for a record 11 medals. His record seven medals at one Games in 1972 was equaled by Matt Biondi (US) who took five gold, one silver and one bronze in 1988.

Women ■ The record number of gold medals won by a woman is six by Kristin Otto (East Germany; b. 7 Feb 1965) at Seoul in 1988: 100 m freestyle, backstroke and butterfly, 50 m free-

SHORT-COURSE SWIMMING WORLD BESTS (*set in 25 m pools*)

━━ MEN ━━

Event	Time	Name	Date	
FREESTYLE				
50 meters	21·76	Nils Rudolph (East Germany; b. 18 Aug 1965)	Bonn, West Germany	11 Feb 1990
100 meters	48·2†	Michael Gross (West Germany; b. 17 Jun 1964 — relay first leg)	Offenbach, West Germany	11 Feb 1988
	48·33	Tommy Werner (Sweden; b. 31 Mar 1966)	Malmö, Sweden	19 Mar 1989
200 meters	1:43·64	Giorgio Lamberti (Italy; b. 28 Jan 1969)	Bonn, West Germany	11 Feb 1990
400 meters	3:40·81	Anders Holmertz (Sweden; b. 1 Dec 1968)	Paris, France	4 Feb 1990
800 meters	7:38·75	Michael Gross (West Germany)	Bonn, West Germany	8 Feb 1985
1,500 meters	14:37·60	Vladimir Salnikov (USSR; b. 21 May 1960)	Göteberg, Sweden	19 Dec 1982
4 × 50 meters relay	1:27·95	West Germany	Bonn, West Germany	14 Feb 1988
4 × 100 meters relay	3:14·00	Sweden	Malmö, Sweden	19 Mar 1989
4 × 200 meters relay	7:05·17	West Germany	Bonn, West Germany	9 Feb 1986
BACKSTROKE				
50 meters	25·06	Mark Tewksbury (Canada; b. 2 Jul 1968)	Saskatoon, Canada	2 Mar 1990
100 meters	53·69	Mark Tewksbury (Canada)	Saskatoon, Canada	2 Mar 1990
200 meters	1:56·60	Tamás Darnyi (Hungary; b. 3 Jun 1967)	Bonn, West Germany	8 Feb 1987
BREASTSTROKE				
50 meters	27·15	Dmitriy Volkov (USSR; b. 3 Mar 1966)	Saint-Paul de la Réunion, France	30 Dec 1989
100 meters	59·30	Dmitriy Volkov (USSR)	Bonn, West Germany	11 Feb 1990
200 meters	2:08·82	Victor Davis (Canada; 1964–90)	Bonn, West Germany	7 Feb 1987
BUTTERFLY				
50 meters	24·07	Marcel Gery (Canada; b. 15 Mar 1965)	Leicester, United Kingdom	24 Feb 1990
100 meters	52·07	Marcel Gery (Canada)	Leicester, United Kingdom	23 Feb 1990
200 meters	1:54·78	Michael Gross (West Germany)	Bonn, West Germany	9 Feb 1985
MEDLEY				
200 meters	1:58·18	Pedro Pablo Morales (US; b. 5 Dec 1964)	Los Angeles, CA	26 Apr 1987
400 meters	4:09·64	Alex Baumann (Canada; b. Prague 21 Apr 1964)	Halifax, Canada	7 Mar 1987
4 × 50 meters relay	1:38·72	United States	Bonn, West Germany	14 Feb 1988
4 × 100 meters relay	3:36·66	University of Calgary (Canada)	Saskatoon, Canada	3 Mar 1990

━━ WOMEN ━━

Event	Time	Name	Date	
FREESTYLE				
50 meters	24·81	Livia Copariu (Romania; b. 1973)	Sibiu, Romania	8 Apr 1989
100 meters	53·48	Livia Copariu (Romania)	Sibiu, Romania	7 Apr 1989
200 meters	1:56·35	Birgit Meineke (East Germany; b. 4 Jul 1964)	Indianapolis, IN	7 Jan 1983
400 meters	4:02·05	Astrid Strauss (East Germany; b. 24 Dec 1968)	Bonn, West Germany	8 Feb 1987
800 meters	8:15·34	Astrid Strauss (East Germany)	Bonn, West Germany	6 Feb 1987
1,500 meters	15:43·31	Petra Schneider (East Germany; b. 11 Jan 1963)	Gainesville, FL	10 Jan 1982
4 × 50 meters relay	1:42·13	West Germany	Bonn, West Germany	13 Feb 1988
4 × 100 meters relay	3:38·77	East Germany	Monte Carlo, Monaco	12 Dec 1987
BACKSTROKE				
50 meters	28·91	Svenja Schlicht (West Germany; b. 26 Jun 1966)	Bonn, West Germany	8 Feb 1987
100 meters	59·89	Betsy Mitchell (US; b. 15 Jan 1966)	Los Angeles, CA	26 Apr 1987
200 meters	2:07·74	Cornelia Sirch (East Germany; b. 23 Oct 1966)	Indianapolis, IN	9 Jan 1983
BREASTSTROKE				
100 meters	1:07·05	Silke Hörner (East Germany; b. 12 Sep 1965)	Bonn, West Germany	8 Feb 1986
200 meters	2:22·92	Susanne Börnike (East Germany; b. 13 Aug 1968)	Bonn, West Germany	4 Feb 1989
BUTTERFLY				
50 meters	27·54	Jennifer Johnson (US; b. 11 Sep 1967)	Bonn, West Germany	12 Feb 1984
	27·54	Christiane Sievert (East Germany; b. 8 May 1972)	Bonn, West Germany	11 Feb 1990
100 meters	58·91*	Mary Terstegge Meagher (US; b. 27 Aug 1964)	Gainesville, FL	3 Jan 1981
200 meters	2:05·65	Mary Meagher (US)	Gainesville, FL	2 Jan 1981
MEDLEY				
200 meters	2:10·60	Petra Schneider (East Germany)	Gainesville, FL	8 Jan 1982
400 meters	4:31·36	Noemi Lung (Romania; b. 16 May 1968)	Paris, France	31 Jan 1987
4 × 50 meters relay	1:54·37	East Germany	Bonn, West Germany	14 Feb 1988
4 × 100 meters relay	4:02·85	East Germany	Indianapolis, IN	8 Jan 1983

* *slower than long-course bests.* † *hand timed.*

55·92 sec. In the 1972 men's 400 m individual medley, Gunnar Larsson (Sweden; b. 12 May 1951) beat Aleksander Timothy McKee (US; b. 14 Mar 1953) by just 2/1,000 th second, just 3 mm. Now timings are determined only to hundredths.

DIVING

Most Olympic medals ■ The most medals won by a diver is five, by: Klaus Dibiasi (Austria, [Italy]; b. 6 Oct 1947) (three gold, two silver), 1964–76; and Gregory Efthimios Louganis (US; b. 29 Jan 1960) (four golds, one silver), 1976, 1984–1988. Dibiasi is the only diver to win the same event (highboard) at three successive Games (1968, 1972 and 1976). Two divers have won the highboard and springboard doubles at two Games: Patricia Joan McCormick (nee Keller, [US]; b. 12 May 1930), 1952 and 1956, and Louganis, 1984 and 1988.

Most world titles ■ Greg Louganis (US) won a record five world titles, highboard in 1978, and both highboard and springboard in 1982 and

style, 4 × 100 m freestyle and 4 × 100 m medley. Dawn Fraser (Australia; b. 4 Sep 1937) is the only swimmer to win the same event, the 100 m freestyle, on three successive occasions (1956, 1960 and 1964).

The most gold medals won by a US woman is three by 14 swimmers.

The most medals won by a woman is eight, by: Dawn Fraser, four golds: 100 m freestyle, 1956, 1960 and 1964, 4 × 100 m freestyle, 1956 and four silvers: 400 m freestyle, 1956, 4 × 100 m freestyle, 1960 and 1964, 4 × 100 m medley, 1960; Kornelia Ender, four golds: 100 m and 200 m freestyle, 100 m butterfly and 4 × 100 m medley in 1976 and four silvers: 200 m individual medley, 1972, 4 × 100 m medley, 1972, 4 × 100 m freestyle, 1972 and 1976; and Shirley Babashoff (US; b. 3 Jan 1957), who won two golds (4 × 100 m freestyle, 1972 and 1976) and six silvers (100 m freestyle, 1972, 200 m freestyle, 1972 and 1976, 400 m and 800 m freestyle, 1976, 4 × 100 m medley, 1976).

Most individual gold medals ■ The record number of individual gold medals won is four, by: Charles Meldrum Daniels (US; 1884–1973) (100 m freestyle, 1906 and 1908, 220 yd freestyle 1904, 440 yd freestyle, 1904); Roland Matthes (East Germany; b. 17 Nov 1950) with 100 m and 200 m backstroke in 1968 and 1972; Mark Spitz and Kristin Otto; and the divers Pat McCormick and Greg Louganis (see below).

Closest verdict ■ The closest verdict in the Olympic Games was in Los Angeles, CA on 29 Jul 1984, when Nancy Lynn Hogshead (b. 17 Apr 1962) and Carrie Lynne Steinseifer (b. 12 Feb 1968), both of the United States, dead-heated for the women's 100 m freestyle gold medal in

SWIMMING—WORLD RECORDS (*set in 50 m pools*)

MEN

Event	Time	Name, country and date of birth	Place	Date
FREESTYLE				
50 meters	21·81	Thomas Jager (US; b. 6 Oct 1964)	Nashville, TN	24 Mar 1990
100 meters	48·42	Matthew Nicholas Biondi (US; b. 8 Oct 1955)	Austin, TX	10 Aug 1988
200 meters	1:46·69	Giorgio Lamberti (Italy; b. 28 Jan 1969)	Bonn, West Germany	15 Aug 1989
400 meters	3:46·95	Uwe Dassler (East Germany; b. 11 Feb 1967)	Seoul, South Korea	23 Sep 1988
800 meters	7:50·64	Vladimir Salnikov (USSR; b. 21 May 1960)	Moscow, USSR	4 Jul 1986
1,500 meters	14:54·76	Vladimir Salnikov (USSR)	Moscow, USSR	22 Feb 1983
	14:53·6 *	Glen Clifford Housman (Australia; b. 3 Sep 1971)	Adelaide, Australia	13 Dec 1989
4 × 100 meters relay	3:16·53	United States	Seoul, South Korea	23 Sep 1988
		(Christopher Jacobs, Troy Dalbey, Tom Jager, Matthew Nicholas Biondi)		
4 × 200 meters relay	7:12·51	United States	Seoul, South Korea	21 Sep 1988
		(Troy Dalbey, Matthew Cetlinski, Douglas Gjertsen, Matthew Nicholas Biondi)		

* not ratified as his finish was not recorded by the electronic touch pad.

Event	Time	Name, country and date of birth	Place	Date
BREASTSTROKE				
100 meters	1:01·49	Adrian David Moorhouse (Great Britain; b. 24 May 1964)	Bonn, West Germany	15 Aug 1989
	1:01·49	Adrian Moorhouse (Great Britain)	Auckland, New Zealand	25 Jan 1990
200 meters	2:11·53	Michael Barrowman (US; b. 4 Dec 1968)	Seattle, WA	20 Jul 1990
BUTTERFLY				
100 meters	52·84	Pedro Pablo Morales (US; b. 5 Dec 1964)	Orlando, FL	23 Jun 1986
200 meters	1:56·24	Michael Gross (West Germany; b. 17 Jun 1964)	Hannover, West Germany	28 Jun 1986
BACKSTROKE				
100 meters	54·51	David Berkoff (US; b. 30 Nov 1966)	Seoul, South Korea	24 Sep 1988
200 meters	1:58·14	Igor Polyanskiy (USSR; b. 20 Mar 1967)	Erfurt, East Germany	3 Mar 1985
MEDLEY				
200 meters	2:00·11	David Wharton (US; b. 19 May 1969)	Tokyo, Japan	20 Aug 1989
400 meters	4:14·75	Tamás Darnyi (Hungary; b. 3 Jun 1967)	Seoul, South Korea	21 Sep 1988
4 × 100 meters relay	3:36·93	United States	Seoul, South Korea	25 Sep 1988
		(David Berkoff, Richard Schroeder, Matthew Nicholas Biondi, Christopher Jacobs)		

WOMEN

Event	Time	Name, country and date of birth	Place	Date
FREESTYLE				
50 meters	24·98	Yang Wenyi (China; b. 11 Jan 1972)	Guangzhou, China	11 Apr 1988
100 meters	54·73	Kristin Otto (East Germany; b. 7 Feb 1965)	Madrid, Spain (relay first leg)	19 Aug 1986
200 meters	1:57·55	Heike Friedrich (East Germany; b. 18 Apr 1970)	East Berlin, East Germany	18 Jun 1986
400 meters	4:03·85	Janet B. Evans (US; b. 28 Aug 1971)	Seoul, South Korea	22 Sep 1988
800 meters	8:16·22	Janet B. Evans (US)	Tokyo, Japan	20 Aug 1989
1,500 meters	15:52·10	Janet B. Evans (US)	Orlando, FL	26 Mar 1988
4 × 100 meters relay	3:40·57	East Germany	Madrid, Spain	19 Aug 1986
		(Kristin Otto, Manuela Stellmach, Sabina Schulze, Heike Friedrich)		
4 × 200 meters relay	7:55·47	East Germany	Strasbourg, France	18 Aug 1987
		(Manuela Stellmach, Astrid Strauss, Anke Möhring, Heike Friedrich)		
BREASTSTROKE				
100 meters	1:07·91	Silke Hörner (East Germany; b. 12 Sep 1965)	Strasbourg, France	21 Aug 1987
200 meters	2:26·71	Silke Hörner (East Germany)	Seoul, South Korea	21 Sep 1988
BUTTERFLY				
100 meters	57·93	Mary Terstegge Meagher (US; b. 27 Oct 1964)	Milwaukee, WI	16 Aug 1981
200 meters	2:05·96	Mary Terstegge Meagher (US)	Milwaukee, WI	13 Aug 1981
BACKSTROKE				
100 meters	1:00·59	Ina Kleber (East Germany; b. 29 Sep 1964 — relay first leg)	Moscow, USSR	24 Aug 1984
200 meters	2:08·60	Betsy Mitchell (US; b. 15 Jan 1966)	Orlando, FL	27 Jun 1986
MEDLEY				
200 meters	2:11·73	Ute Geweniger (East Germany; b. 24 Feb 1964)	East Berlin, East Germany	4 Jul 1981
400 meters	4:36·10	Petra Schneider (East Germany; b. 11 Jan 1963)	Guayaquil, Ecuador	1 Aug 1982
4 × 100 meters relay	4:03·69	East Germany	Moscow, USSR	24 Aug 1984
		(Ina Kleber, Sylvia Gerasch, Ines Geissler, Birgit Meineke)		

1986, as well as four Olympic gold medals, in 1984 and 1988. Three gold medals at one event have also been won by Philip George Boggs (US; 1949–90), springboard, 1973, 1975 and 1978.

Highest scores ■ Greg Louganis achieved record scores at the 1984 Olympic Games in Los Angeles, CA, with 754·41 points for the 11-dive springboard event and 710·91 for the highboard. At the world championships in Guayaquil, Ecuador in 1984 he was awarded a perfect score of 10·0 by all seven judges for his highboard inward 1 ½ somersault in the pike position.

The first diver to be awarded a score of 10·0 by all seven judges was Michael Holman Finneran (b. 21 Sep 1948) in the 1972 US Olympic Trials, in Chicago, IL, for a backward 1 ½ somersault, 2 ½ twist, from the 10 m board.

LONG–DISTANCE SWIMMING
Channel Swimming ■ The first to swim the English Channel from shore to shore (without a life jacket) was the Merchant Navy captain Matthew Webb (1848–83), who swam from Dover, United Kingdom to Calais Sands, France, in 21 hr 45 min from 12:56 P.M. to 10:41 A.M., 24–25

Aug 1875. He swam an estimated 38 miles to make the 21 mile crossing. Paul Boyton (US) had swum from Cap Gris-Nez to the South Foreland in his patent life-saving suit in 23 hr 30 min on 28–29 May 1875. There is good evidence that Jean-Marie Saletti, a French soldier, escaped from a British prison hulk off Dover by swimming to Boulogne in July or August 1815. The first woman to succeed was Gertrude Caroline Ederle (US; b. 23 Oct 1906) who swam from Cap Gris-Nez, France to Deal, United Kingdom on 6 Aug 1926, in the then overall record time of 14 hr 39 min.

U.S NATIONAL RECORDS (set in 50 m pools)

——— MEN ———

Event	Time	Name and date of birth	Place	Date
FREESTYLE				
50 meters	21·81	Thomas Jager (b. 6 Oct 1964)	Nashville, TN	24 Mar 1990
100 meters	48·42	Matthew Nicholas Biondi (b. 8 Oct 1955)	Austin, TX	10 Aug 1988
200 meters	1:47·72	Matt Biondi	Austin, TX	8 Aug 1988
400 meters	3:48·06	Matthew Cetlinski (b. 4 Oct 1964)	Austin, TX	11 Aug 1988
800 meters	7:52·45	Sean Killion (b.24 Oct 1967)	Clovis, CA	27 Jul 1987
1,500 meters	15:01·51	George Thomas DiCarlo (b. 13 Jul 1963)	Indianapolis, IN	30 Jun 1984
4 × 100 meter relay	3:16·53	United States	Seoul, South Korea	23 Sep 1988
		(Christopher Jacobs, Troy Dalbey, Tom Jager, Matthew Nicholas Biondi)		
4 × 200 meter relay	7:12·51	United States	Seoul, South Korea	21 Sep 1988
		(Troy Dalbey, Matthew Cetlinski, Douglas Gjertsen, Matthew Nicholas Biondi)		
BREASTSTROKE				
100 meters	1:01·65	Steven K. Lundquist (b. 20 Feb 1961)	Los Angeles, CA	29 Jul 1984
200 meters	2:11·53	Michael Ray Barrowman (b. 4 Dec 1968)	Seattle, WA	20 Jul 1990
BUTTERFLY				
100 meters	52·84	Pedro Pablo Morales (b. 5 Dec 1964)	Orlando, FL	23 Jun 1986
200 meters	1:57·75	Pablo Morales	Los Angeles, CA	3 Aug 1984
BACKSTROKE				
100 meters	54·51	David Charles Berkoff (b. 30 Nov 1966)	Seoul, South Korea	24 Sep 1988
200 meters	1:58·86	Richard John 'Rick' Carey (b. 13 Mar 1963)	Indianapolis, IN	27 Jun 1984
MEDLEY				
200 meters	2:00·11	David Lee Wharton (b. 19 May 1969)	Tokyo, Japan	20 Aug 1989
400 meters	4:15·93	David Lee Wharton	Los Angeles, CA	2 Aug 1989
4 × 100 meter relay	3:36·93	United States	Seoul, South Korea	25 Sep 1988
		(David Berkoff, Richard Schroeder, Matthew Nicholas Biondi, Christopher Jacobs)		

——— WOMEN ———

Event	Time	Name and date of birth	Place	Date
FREESTYLE				
50 meters	25·50	Leigh Ann Fetter (b. 23 May 1969)	Austin, TX	13 Aug 1988
100 meters	55·30	Dara Grace Torres (b. 15 Apr 1967)	Orlando, FL (relay first leg)	25 Mar 1988
200 meters	1:58·23	Cynthia Woodhead (b. 7 Feb 1964)	Tokyo, Japan	3 Sep 1979
400 meters	4:03·85	Janet B. Evans (b. 28 Aug 1971)	Seoul, South Korea	22 Sep 1988
800 meters	8:16·22	Janet B. Evans	Tokyo, Japan	20 Aug 1989
1,500 meters	15:52·10	Janet B. Evans	Orlando, FL	26 Mar 1988
4 × 100 meter relay	3:43·43	United States	Los Angeles, CA	31 Jul 1984
		(Jenna Leigh Johnson, Carrie Steinseifer, Dara Torres, Nancy Lyn Hogshead)		
4 × 200 meter relay	8:02·12	United States	Madrid, Spain	17 Aug 1986
		(Betsy Mitchell, Mary Terstegge Meagher, Kim Brown, Mary Alice Wayte)		
BREASTSTROKE				
100 meters	1:08·91	Tracey McFarlane (b. 20 Jul 1966)	Austin, TX	11 Aug 1988
200 meters	2:29·58	Amy Shaw (b. 21 Sep 1971)	Brisbane, Australia	16 Aug 1987
BUTTERFLY				
100 meters	57·93	Mary Terstegge Meagher (b. 27 Oct 1964)	Brown Deer, WI	16 Aug 1981
200 meters	2:05·96	Mary Terstegge Meagher	Brown Deer, WI	13 Aug 1981
BACKSTROKE				
100 meters	1:01·20	Betsy Mitchell (b. 15 Jan 1966)	Orlando, FL	24 Jun 1986
200 meters	2:08·60	Betsy Mitchell	Orlando, FL	27 Jun 1986
MEDLEY				
200 meters	2:12·64	Tracy Anne Caulkins (b. 11 Jan 1963)	Los Angeles, CA	3 Aug 1984
400 meters	4:37·76	Janet B. Evans	Seoul, South Korea	19 Sep 1988
4 × 100 meter relay	4:06·94	United States	Seattle, WA	23 Jul 1990
		(Betsy Mitchell, Tracey McFarlane, Janel Jorgensen, Nicole Haislett)		

Fastest ■ The official Channel Swimming Association (founded 1927) record is 7 hr 40 min, by Penny Dean (b. 21 Mar 1955) of California, from Shakespeare Beach, Dover, United Kingdom to Cap Gris-Nez, France on 29 Jul 1978.

Longest swims ■ The greatest recorded distance ever swum is 1,826 miles down the Mississippi River between Ford Dam near Minneapolis, MN and Carrollton Ave, New Orleans, LA, by Fred P. Newton, (b. 1903) of Clinton, OK from 6 Jul to 29 Dec 1930. He was 742 hr in the water. The greatest distance covered in a continuous swim is 299 miles, by Ricardo Hoffmann (b. 5 Oct 1941), from Corrientes to Santa Elena, Argentina in the River Paraná, in 84 hr 37 min on 3–6 Mar 1981.

The longest ocean swim is one of 128·8 miles by Walter Poenisch, Sr (US; b. 1914) who started from Havana, Cuba, and arrived at Little Duck Key, FL (in a shark cage and wearing flippers) 34 hr 15 min later on 11–13 Jul 1978.

In 1966 Mihir Sen of Calcutta, India uniquely swam the Palk Strait from Sri Lanka to India (in 25 hr 36 min on 5–6 Apr); the Straits of Gibraltar (in 8 hr 1 min on 24 Aug), the length of the Dardanelles (in 13 hr 55 min on 12 Sep), the Bosphorus (in 4 hr on 21 Sep), and the length of the Panama Canal (in 34 hr 15 min on 29–31 Oct).

24 hours ■ Anders Forvass (Sweden) swam 63·3 miles at the 25-meter Linköping public swimming pool, Sweden on 28–29 Oct 1989. In a 50 meter pool, Evan Barry (Australia) swam 60·08 miles, at the Valley Pool, Brisbane, Australia on 19–20 Dec 1987.

The women's record is 51·01 miles, by Irene van der Laan (Netherlands) at Amersfoort, Netherlands on 20–21 Sep 1985.

Long-distance relays ■ The New Zealand national relay team of 20 swimmers swam a record 113·59 miles in Lower Hutt, New Zealand in 24 hours, passing 100 miles in 20 hr 47 min 13 sec on 9–10 Dec 1983. The 24-hour club record

by a team of five is 96·27 miles, by the City of Newcastle ASC on 16–17 Dec 1986. A women's team from the club swam 88·93 miles on the same occasion. The most participants in a one-day swim relay is 2,135, each swimming a length, organized by Syracuse YMCA in Syracuse, NY on 11 Apr 1986.

The longest duration swim relay was 233 hr 15 min, by a team of 15 from Maccabi Water Polo team at Sydney Football Stadium swimming pool, Sydney, Australia on 1–11 Dec 1988.

Underwater Swimming ■ Paul Cryne (United Kingdom) and Samir Sawan al Awami of Qatar swam 49·04 miles in a 24-hr period from Doha, Qatar to Umm Said and back on 21–22 Feb 1985 using sub-aqua equipment. They were swimming underwater for 95·5 percent of the time. A relay team of six swam 94·44 miles in a swimming pool at Olomouc, Czechoslovakia on 17–18 Oct 1987.

Table Tennis

Origins ■ The earliest evidence relating to a game resembling table tennis has been found in the catalogs of London sports goods manufacturers in the 1880s. The old Ping Pong Association was formed in 1902 but the game proved only a temporary craze until resuscitated in 1921. The International Table Tennis Federation was founded in 1926 and the United States Table Tennis Association was established in 1933. In 1971, a US table tennis team was invited to play in the People's Republic of China, thereby initiating the first officially sanctioned Chinese-American cultural exchange in almost 20 years.

Most American titles ■ US national championships were first held in 1931. Leah Neuberger (nee Thall) won a record 29 titles between 1941 and 1961: 9 women's singles, 12 women's doubles. Richard Mills won a record ten men's singles titles between 1945 and 1962.

Internationals ■ The youngest ever international was Joy Foster, who represented Jamaica in the West Indies Championships at Port of Spain, Trinidad in Aug 1958 at the age of 8.

World championships ■ The US won the Swaythling Cup in 1937 and the Corbillon Cup in 1937 and 1949. Ruth Aarons was the women's world champion in 1936 and 1937, sharing the title in the latter year. No American has won the men's world singles title, but James McClure won three men's doubles titles, with Robert Blattner in 1936–37 and with Sol Schiff in 1938.

Counter hitting ■ The record number of hits in 60 sec is 172, by Thomas Busin and Stefan Renold, both of Switzerland, on 4 Nov 1989. The women's record is 168, by the sisters Lisa (b. 9 Mar 1967) and Jackie (b. 9 Sep 1964) Bellinger, at Crest Hotel, Luton, Bedfordshire, United Kingdom on 14 Jul 1987. With a bat in each hand, Gary D. Fisher of Olympia, WA completed 5,000 consecutive volleys over the net in 44 min 28 sec on 25 Jun 1979.

Highest speed ■ No conclusive measurements have been published, but in a lecture M. Sklorz (West Germany) stated that a smashed ball had been measured at speeds up to 105·6 mph.

Taekwondo

Taekwondo is a martial art, with all activities based on defensive spirit, developed over 20 centuries in Korea. It was officially recognized as part of Korean tradition and culture on 11 Apr

---

TEAM AND INDIVIDUAL TABLE TENNIS CHAMPIONSHIPS

━━ MOST WINS IN WORLD CHAMPIONSHIPS ━━

Event	Name and Nationality	Times	Years
MEN			
Singles (St Bride's Vase)	G. Viktor Barna (Hungary; 1911–72)	5	1930, 1932–35
Doubles	G. Viktor Barna (Hungary)	8	1929–35, 1939
Mixed Doubles	Ferenc Sido (Hungary; b. 1923)	4	1949–50, 1952–53
WOMEN			
Singles (G. Geist Prize)	Angelica Rozeanu (Romania; b. 15 Oct 1921)	6	1950–55
Doubles	Maria Mednyanszky (Hungary; 1901–79)	7	1928, 1930–35
Mixed Doubles	Maria Mednyanszky (Hungary)	6	1927–28, 1930–31, 1933–34

G. Viktor Barna gained a personal total of 15 world titles, while 18 have been won by Maria Mednyanszky.
Note: With the staging of championships biennially the breaking of the above records would now be very difficult.

━━ MOST TEAM TITLES ━━

Event	Team	Times	Years
MEN (Swaythling Cup)	Hungary	12	1927–31, 1933–35, 1938, 1949, 1952, 1979
WOMEN (Marcel Corbillon Cup)	China	9	1965, eight successive 1975–89 (biennially)

1955. The first World Taekwondo Championships were organized by the Korean Taekwondo Association and were held at Seoul in 1973. The World Taekwondo Federation was then formed and has organized biennial championships.

Most titles ■ The most world titles won is four, by Chung Kook-hyun (South Korea), light middleweight, 1982–83, welterweight, 1985, 1987. Taekwondo was included as a demonstration sport at the 1988 Olympic Games.

Three American women won gold medals at the 1988 Olympics, one of whom, Lynette Love (b. 21 Sep 1957), at heavyweight (over 70kg), was also world champion in 1987.

Tennis

Origins ■ The modern game is generally agreed to have evolved as an outdoor form of the indoor game of tennis (see Tennis [Real]). 'Field tennis' is mentioned in an English magazine – *Sporting Magazine* – of 29 Sep 1793. The earliest club for such a game, variously called pelota or lawn rackets, was the Leamington Club founded in 1872 by Major Harry Gem. The earliest attempt to commercialize the game was by Major Walter Clopton Wingfield (1833–1912), who patented a form called 'sphairistike' on 23 Feb 1874. It soon became called lawn tennis. Amateur players were permitted to play with and against professionals in 'open' tournaments in 1968.

Grand Slam ■ The grand slam is to hold at the same time all four of the world's major championship singles: Wimbledon, the United States, Australian and French championships. The first man to have won all four was Frederick John Perry (Great Britain; b. 18 May 1909) when he won the French title in 1935. The first man to hold all four championships simultaneously was John Donald Budge (US; b. 13 Jun 1915) in 1938, and with Wimbledon and US in 1937; he won six successive grand slam tournaments. The first man to achieve the grand slam twice was Rodney George Laver (Australia; b. 9 Aug 1938) as an amateur in 1962 and again in 1969, when the titles were open to professionals.

Four women have achieved the grand slam and

the first three won six successive grand slam tournaments: Maureen Catherine Connolly (US; 1934–69), in 1953; Margaret Jean Court (nee Smith [Australia]; b. 16 Jul 1942) in 1970; and Martina Navrátilová (US; b. 18 Oct 1956) in 1983–84. The fourth was Stefanie Maria 'Steffi' Graf (West Germany; b. 14 Jun 1969) in 1988, when she also won the women's singles Olympic gold medal. Pamela Howard Shriver (US; b. 4 Jul 1962) with Navrátilová won a record eight successive grand slam tournament women's doubles titles and 109 successive matches in all events from April 1983 to July 1985.

The first doubles pair to win the grand slam were the Australians Frank Allan Sedgeman (b. 29 Oct 1927) and Kenneth Bruce McGregor (b. 2 Jun 1929) in 1951.

The most singles championships won in grand slam tournaments is 24, by Margaret Court (11 Australian, 5 US, 5 French, 3 Wimbledon), 1960–73. She also won the US Amateur in 1969 and 1970 when this was held as well as the US Open. The men's record is 12, by Roy Stanley Emerson (Australia; b. 3 Nov 1936) (6 Australian, 2 each French, United States, Wimbledon), 1961–67.

The most grand slam tournament wins by a doubles partnership is 20, by; Althea Louise Brough (US; b. 11 Mar 1923) and Margaret Evelyn Du Pont (nee Osborne, [US]; b. 4 Mar 1918), (12 US, 5 Wimbledon, 3 French), 1942–57; and by Martina Navrátilová and Pam Shriver, (7 Australian, 5 Wimbledon, 4 French, 4 US), 1981–89.

United States ■ The most singles wins in Grand Slam tournaments by a US player is 19 by Helen Newington Moody (nee Wills, later Mrs Roark; b. 6 Oct 1905): 8 Wimbledon, 7 US and 4 French. Martina Navrátilová (formerly of Czechoslovakia) has won a total of 52 Grand Slam titles, 18 singles, a world record 29 women's doubles and 5 mixed doubles. Billie-Jean King has the most of US-born players with 39 titles, 12 singles, 16 women's doubles and 11 mixed doubles.

OLYMPIC GAMES *United States ■* Four US players have won two Olympic gold medals: Beals Coleman Wright (1879–1961) in 1904, Vincent Richards (1903–59) and Helen Moody in 1924, all at both singles and doubles, and Hazel Virginia Hotchkiss Wightman (1886–1974), at ladies' and mixed doubles in 1924. Richards won a US record third medal, silver at mixed doubles (with Marion Jessup) in 1924.

WIMBLEDON CHAMPIONSHIPS

Most wins *Women* ■ Billie-Jean King (nee Moffit, [US]; b. 22 Nov 1943) won a record 20 titles between 1961 and 1979, six singles, ten women's doubles and four mixed doubles. Elizabeth Montague Ryan (US; 1892–1979) won a record 19 doubles (12 women's, 7 mixed) titles from 1914 to 1934.

Men ■ The greatest number of titles by a man has been 13, by Hugh Laurence Doherty (Great Britain; 1875–1919) with five singles titles (1902–6) and a record eight men's doubles (1897–1901, 1903–5) partnered by his brother Reginald Frank (1872–1910).

The most titles won by a US man is seven by John Patrick McEnroe (b. 16 Feb 1959), singles 1981, 1983 and 1984; men's doubles (all with Peter Fleming) 1979, 1981, 1983–84.

Singles ■ Martina Navrátilová won a record nine titles in 1978–79, 1982–87 and 1990. The most men's singles wins since the Challenge Round was abolished in 1922 is five consecutively, by Bjørn Borg (Sweden) in 1976–80. William Charles Renshaw (Great Britain; 1861–1904) won seven singles in 1881–86 and 1889.

Mixed doubles ■ The male record is four titles, shared by: Elias Victor Seixas (US; b. 30 Aug 1923) in 1953–56; Kenneth Norman Fletcher (Australia; b. 15 Jun 1940) in 1963, 1965–66, 1968; and Owen Keir Davidson (Australia; b. 4 Oct 1943) in 1967, 1971, 1973–74. The female record is seven, by Elizabeth Ryan (US) from 1919 to 1932.

Most appearances ■ Arthur William Charles 'Wentworth' Gore (Great Britain; 1868–1928) made a record 36 appearances at Wimbledon between 1888 and 1927. In 1964, Jean Borotra (b. 13 Aug 1898) of France made his 35th appearance since 1922. In 1977 he appeared in the Veterans' Doubles at age 78.

Youngest champions ■ The youngest champion was Charlotte 'Lottie' Dod (Great Britain; 1871–1960), who was 15 yr 285 days when she won in 1887. The youngest male champion was Boris Becker (West Germany; b. 22 Nov 1967), who won the men's singles title in 1985 at 17 yr 227 days. The youngest ever player at Wimbledon was reputedly Mita Klima (Austria) who was 13 yr in the 1907 singles competition. The youngest seed was Jennifer Capriatti (US; b. 29 Mar 1976) at 14 yr 89 days at the time of her first match on 26 Jun 1990. She won this match making her the youngest ever winner at Wimbledon.

Oldest champions ■ The oldest champion was Margaret Evelyn du Pont (nee Osborne, [US]; b. 4 Mar 1918) at 44 yr 125 days when she won the mixed doubles in 1962 with Neale Fraser (Australia). The oldest singles champion was Arthur Gore (Great Britain) in 1909 at 41 yr 182 days.

Greatest crowd ■ The record crowd for one day was 39,813 on 26 Jun 1986. The record for the whole championship was 403,706 in 1989.

US OPEN CHAMPIONSHIPS

Most wins ■ Margaret Evelyn du Pont (nee Osborne) won a record 25 titles between 1941 and 1960. She won a record 13 women's doubles (12 with Althea Louise Brough), nine mixed doubles and three singles. The men's record is 16, by William Tatem Tilden, including seven men's singles, 1920–25, 1929 – a record for singles

shared with: Richard Dudley Sears (1861–1943), 1881–87; William A. Larned (1872–1926), 1901–2, 1907–11, and at women's singles by: Molla Mallory (nee Bjurstedt; 1892–1959), 1915–16, 1918, 1920–22, 1926; and Helen Moody (nee Wills), 1923–25, 1927–29, 1931.

Youngest and oldest ■ The youngest champion was Vincent Richards (1903–59), who was 15 yr 139 days when he won the men's doubles with Bill Tilden in 1918. The youngest singles champion was Tracy Ann Austin (b. 12 Dec 1962), who was 16 yr 271 days when she won the women's singles in 1979. The oldest champion was Margaret du Pont, who won the mixed doubles at 42 yr 166 days in 1960. The oldest singles champion was William Larned, at 38 yr 242 days in 1911.

FRENCH OPEN CHAMPIONSHIPS
Most wins (from international status 1925) ■ Margaret Court won a record 13 titles, five singles, four women's doubles and four mixed doubles, 1962–73. The men's record is nine

by Henri Cochet (France) (1901–87), four singles, three men's doubles and two mixed doubles, 1926–30. The singles record is seven by Chris Evert, 1974–75, 1979–80, 1983, 1985–86. Bjørn Borg won a record six men's singles, 1974–75, 1978–81.

Youngest and oldest ■ The youngest doubles champions were the 1981 mixed doubles winners Andrea Jaeger (b. 4 Jun 1965), at 15 yr 339 days, and Jimmy Arias (b. 16 Aug 1964), at 16 yr 296 days. The youngest singles winners have been: Monica Seles (Yugoslavia; b. 2 Dec 1973) who won the women's title at 16 yr 169 days in 1990, and Michael Chang (US; b. 22 Feb 1972), men's singles winner at 17 yr 109 days in 1989. The oldest champion was Elizabeth Ryan, who won the 1934 women's doubles with Simone Mathieu (France) at 42 yr 88 days. The oldest singles champion was Andres Gimeno in 1972 at 34 yr 301 days.

AUSTRALIAN OPEN CHAMPIONSHIPS
Most wins ■ Margaret Jean Court (nee Smith; b. 16 Jul 1942) won the women's singles 11 times (1960–66, 1969–71 and 1973) as well as eight women's doubles and two mixed doubles, for a record total of 21 titles. A record six men's singles were won by Roy Stanley Emerson (Queensland; b. 3 Nov 1936), 1961 and 1963–67. Thelma Dorothy Long (nee Coyne; b. 30 May 1918) won a record 12 women's doubles and four mixed doubles for a record total of 16 doubles

titles. Adrian Karl Quist (b. 4 Aug 1913) won ten consecutive men's doubles from 1936 to 1950 (the last eight with John Bromwich) and three men's singles.

Longest span, oldest and youngest ■
Thelma Long won her first (1936) and last (1958) titles 22 years apart. Kenneth Robert Rosewall (b. 2 Nov 1934) won the singles in 1953, and in 1972 was, 19 years later, at 37 yr 62 days, the oldest singles winner. The oldest champion was (Sir) Norman Everard Brookes (1877–1968), who was 46 yr 2 months when he won the 1924 men's doubles. The youngest champions were Rodney W. Heath, aged 17, when he won the men's singles in 1905, and Margaret Smith, who won the women's singles at 17 yr 5 months in 1960.

GRAND PRIX MASTERS ■
The first Grand Prix Masters Championships were staged in Tokyo, Japan in 1970. They have been held in New York annually from 1977 to 1990. The 1991 Grand Prix Masters will be held in West Germany. Qualification to this annual event is by relative success in the preceding year's Grand Prix tournaments. A record five titles have been won by Ivan Lendl, 1982–83, two in 1986 (January and December) and 1987. He appeared in nine successive finals, 1980–88. James Scott Connors (US; b. 2 Sep 1952) uniquely qualified for 14 consecutive years, 1972–85. He chose not to play in 1975, 1976 and 1985, and won in 1977. He qualified again in 1987 and 1988, but did not play in 1988. A record seven doubles titles were won by John Patrick McEnroe (US; b. 16 Feb 1959) and Peter Fleming (US; b. 21 Jan 1955), 1978–84.

OLYMPIC GAMES ■
Tennis was re-introduced to the Olympic Games in 1988, having originally been included at the Games from 1896 to 1924. It was also a demonstration sport in 1968 and 1984.

A record four gold medals as well as a silver and a bronze, were won by Max Decugis (France) (1882–1978), 1900–20. A women's record five medals (one gold, two silver, two bronze) were won by Kitty McKane (later Mrs Godfree, [Great Britain]; b. 7 May 1897) in 1920 and 1924.

INTERNATIONAL TEAM
Davis Cup (instituted 1900) ■
The most wins in the Davis Cup, the men's international team championship, has been 28, by the United States. The most appearances for Cup winners is eight, by Roy Emerson (Australia), 1959–62, 1964–67. Bill Tilden (US) played in a record 28 matches in the final, winning a record 21, 17 out of 22 singles and 4 out of 6 doubles. He was in seven winning sides, 1920–26 and then four losing sides, 1927–30.

Nicola Pietrangeli (Italy; b. 11 Sep 1933) played a record 163 rubbers (66 ties), 1954 to 1972, winning 120. He played 109 singles (winning 78) and 54 doubles (winning 42).

Wightman Cup (instituted 1923) ■
The annual women's match was won 51 times by the United States and 10 times by Great Britain. The contest was suspended from 1990 after a series of whitewashes by the US team. Virginia Wade (Great Britain; b. 10 Jul 1945) played in a record 21 ties and 56 rubbers, 1965–85, with a British record 19 wins. Christine Marie Evert (US; b. 21 Dec 1954) won all 26 of her singles matches, 1971 to 1985 and including doubles achieved a record 34 wins from 38 rubbers played. Jennifer Capriatti became at 13 yr 168 days, the youngest ever Wightman Cup player when she beat Clare Wood (Great Britain) 6–0, 6–0 at Williamsburg, VA on 14 Sep 1989.

Federation Cup (instituted 1963) ■
The most wins in the Federation Cup, the women's international team championship, is 14, by the United States. Virginia Wade (Great Britain) played each year from 1967 to 1983, in a record 57 ties, playing 100 rubbers, including 56 singles (winning 36) and 44 doubles (winning 30). Chris Evert won her first 29 singles matches, 1977–86. Her overall record, 1977–89 is 40 wins in 42 singles and 16 wins in 18 doubles matches.

Longest span as national champion ■
Keith Gledhill (b. 17 Feb 1911) won the US National Boys' Doubles Championship with Sidney Wood in August 1926. Sixty-one years later, at Goleta, CA in August 1987, he won the US National 75 and over Men's Doubles Championship with Elbert Lewis.

Dorothy May Bundy-Cheney (US; b. September 1916) won 180 US titles at various age groups from 1941 to March 1988.

International contest *Longest span* ■
Jean Borotra (France; b. 13 Aug 1898) played in every one of the twice yearly contests between the International Club of France and the I.C. of Great Britain from the first in 1929 to his 100th match at Wimbledon on 1–3 Nov 1985. On that occasion he played a mixed doubles against Kitty Godfree (Great Britain; b. 7 May 1896). Both were former Wimbledon singles champions, and were 87 and 89 years respectively.

Highest earnings ■
Ivan Lendl (Czechoslovakia; b. 7 Mar 1960) won a men's season's record $2,344,367 in 1989 and had career earnings of $15,626,336 by end of 1989. The season's record for a woman is $2,173,556 in 1984 (including a $1 million Grand Slam bonus) by Martina Navrátilová. Earnings from special restricted events and team tennis are not included. Navrátilová's lifetime earnings by the end of 1989 reached $15,343,814.

The one-match record is $583,200, by Ivan Lendl (Czechoslovakia) when he beat Pat Cash (Australia; b. 27 May 1965) in the final of the four-man Stakes Match tennis exhibition at West Palm Beach on 30 Nov 1987. The highest total prize money was $4,371,500, for the 1988 US Open Championships.

Greatest crowd ■
A record 30,472 people were at the Astrodome, Houston, TX on 20 Sep 1973, when Billie-Jean King (nee Moffitt, [US]; b. 22 Nov 1943) beat Robert Larimore 'Bobby' Riggs (US; b. 25 Feb 1918). The record for an orthodox tennis match is 25,578 at Sydney, New South Wales, Australia on 27 Dec 1954, in the Davis Cup Challenge Round (first day) Australia v US.

Fastest service ■
The fastest service timed with modern equipment is 138 mph, by Steve Denton (US; b. 5 Sep 1956) at Beaver Creek, CO on 29 Jul 1984. The fastest *ever* measured was one of 163·6 mph, by William Tatem Tilden (US; 1893–1953) in 1931.

'Golden set' ■
The only known example of a 'Golden set' (to win a set 6-0 without dropping a single point, i.e. winning 24 consecutive points) in professional tennis was achieved by Bill Scanlon (US) against Marcos Hocevar (Brazil) in the first round of the WCT Gold Coast Classic at Del Ray, FL on 22 Feb 1983. Scanlon won the match, 6–2, 6–0.

Longest game ■
The longest known singles game was one of 37 deuces (80 points) between Anthony Fawcett (Rhodesia) and Keith Glass (Great Britain) in the first round of the Surrey Championships at Surbiton, Surrey, United Kingdom on 26 May 1975. It lasted 31 min. Noëlle van Lottum and Sandra Begijn

played a game lasting 52 min in the semifinals of the Dutch Indoor Championships at Ede, Gelderland on 12 Feb 1984.

The longest tiebreak was 26–24 for the fourth and decisive set of a first round men's doubles at the Wimbledon Championships on 1 Jul 1985. Jan Gunnarsson (Sweden) and Michael Mortensen (Denmark) defeated John Frawley (Australia) and Victor Pecci (Paraguay) 6–3, 6–4, 3–6, 7–6.

The longest rally in tournament play was one of 643 times over the net between Vicky Nelson and Jean Hepner at Richmond, VA in October 1984. The 6 hr 22 min match was won by Nelson 6–4, 7–6. It concluded with a 1 hr 47 min tiebreak, 13–11, for which one point took 29 minutes.

Will Duggan and Ron Kapp (both US) performed a rally of 6,202 strokes, which took 3 hr 33 min, at Santa Barbara Municipal Stadium, CA on 12 Mar 1988.

Tennis (Real / Royal)

The game originated as *jeu de paume* in French monasteries c. 1050. A tennis court is mentioned in the sale of the Hôtel de Nesle, Paris, bought by King Philippe IV of France in 1308. The oldest of the surviving active courts in Great Britain is that at Falkland Palace, Fife, United Kingdom, built by King James V of Scotland in 1539.

Most titles ■
Jay Gould, Jr (1888–1935) won his first US singles title in 1906, and retained the title until he retired from singles play in 1926. During his career he lost only one singles match. He also won 19 US doubles titles between 1909 and 1932.

World ■
The first recorded world tennis champion was Clerge (France) c. 1740. Jacques Edmond Barre (France; 1802–73) held the title for a record 33 yr from 1829 to 1862. Pierre Etchebaster (1893–1980), a Basque, holds the record for the greatest number of successful defenses of the title, with eight between 1928 and 1952.

The first two Women's World Championships in 1985 and 1987 were won by Judith Anne Clarke (Australia; b. 28 Dec 1954).

Track and Field

The earliest evidence of organized running was at Memphis, Eygpt c. 3800 B.C. The earliest accurately dated Olympic Games was in July 776 B.C., at which celebration Coroibos won the foot race. The oldest surviving measurements are a long jump of 23 ft 1 ½ in by Chioniz of Sparta in c. 656 B.C. and a discus throw of 100 cubits (about 152 ft) by Protesilaus.

Fastest speed ■
An analysis of split times at each 10 meters in the 1988 Olympic Games 100 m final in Seoul, South Korea on 24 Sep 1988 won by Ben Johnson (Canada) in 9·79 (average speed 22·85 mph but later disallowed as a world record due to his positive drugs test for steroids) from Carl Lewis (US) 9·92, showed that both Johnson and Lewis reached a peak speed (40 m–50 m and 80 m–90 m respectively) of 0·83 sec for 10 m, i.e. 26·95 mph.

Highest jump above own head ■
The greatest height cleared above an athlete's own head is 23 ¼ in, by Franklin Jacobs (US; b. 31 Dec 1957), who jumped 7 ft 7 ¼ in at New York City, on 27 Jan 1978. He is 5 ft 8 in tall. The greatest height cleared by a woman above her own head is 12 in, by Cindy John Holmes (US; b.

29 Aug 1960), 5 ft tall, who jumped 6 ft at Provo, UT on 1 Jun 1982.

Most Olympic gold medals ■ The most Olympic gold medals won is ten (an absolute Olympic record) by Raymond Clarence Ewry (US; 1874–1937) in the standing high, long and triple jumps in 1900, 1904, 1906 and 1908.

Women ■ The most gold medals won by a woman is four, shared by: Francina 'Fanny' E. Blankers-Koen (Netherlands; b. 26 Apr 1918), with 100 m, 200 m, 80 m hurdles and 4 × 100 m relay, 1948; Betty Cuthbert (Australia; b. 20 Apr 1938), with 100 m, 200 m, 4 × 100 m relay, 1956 and 400 m, 1964; and Bärbel Wöckel (nee Eckert, [GDR]; b. 21 Mar 1955), with 200 m and 4 × 100 m relay in 1976 and 1980.

Most wins at one Games ■ The most gold medals at one celebration is five by Paavo Johannes Nurmi (Finland; 1897–1973) in 1924: 1,500 m, 5,000 m, 10,000 m cross-country, 3,000 m team and cross-country team. The most at individual events is four, by Alvin Christian Kraenzlein (US; 1876–1928) in 1900: 60 m, 110 m hurdles, 200 m hurdles and long jump.

Most Olympic medals ■ The most medals won is 12 (nine gold and three silver) by Paavo Nurmi (Finland) in the Games of 1920, 1924 and 1928.

Women ■ The most medals won by a woman athlete is seven, by Shirley Barbara de la Hunty (nee Strickland, [Australia]; b. 18 Jul 1925), with three gold, one silver and three bronze in the 1948, 1952 and 1956 Games. A replay of the photo-finish indicates that she finished third, not fourth, in the 1948 200-meters event, thus unofficially increasing her medal haul to eight. Irena Szewinska (nee Kirszenstein, [Poland]; b. 24 May 1946) won three gold, two silver and two

bronze in 1964, 1968, 1972 and 1976, and is the only woman athlete to win a medal in four successive Games.

Most Olympic medals *United States* ■ The most Olympic medals won by a US female athlete is five, by Delorez Florence Griffith Joyner (b. 21 Dec 1959): 200m silver in 1984, gold at 100m, 200m and 4 x 100m relay, silver at 4 x 400m relay in 1988. Three gold medals have also been won by Wilma Glodean Rudolph (later Ward, b. 23 Jun 1940): 100m, 200m and 4 x 100m relay in 1960; by Wyomia Tyus (b. 29 Aug 1945):

First 8-foot high jump ● The first person to clear the elusive 8-foot high jump barrier was Javier Sotomayor (Cuba; b. 13 Oct 1967) at San Juan, Puerto Rico on 29 Jul 1989. Earlier in the year at Budapest, Hungary, on 4 Mar, he set a world indoor record of 7 ft 11 ½in. (Photo: All-Sport/Dan Smith)

World record ● Roger Kingdom on his way to setting a new 110-m hurdles world record of 12·92 sec at Zürich, Switzerland on 16 Aug 1989, improving the previous mark, set by Renaldo Nehemiah in the same meeting eight years earlier, by just one-hundreth of a second. (Photo: All-Sport/Bob Martin)

WORLD RECORDS MEN

World records for the men's events scheduled by the International Amateur Athletic Federation. Fully automatic electric timing is mandatory for events up to 400 meters.

RUNNING	min	sec	Name and country	Place	Date	
100 meters		9·92*	Frederick Carleton 'Carl' Lewis (US; b. 1 Jul 1961)	Seoul, South Korea	24 Sep	1988
200 meters		19·72A	Pietro Mennea (Italy; b. 28 Jun 1952)	Mexico City, Mexico	12 Sep	1979
400 meters		43·29	Harry Lee 'Butch' Reynolds, Jr (US; b. 8 Aug 1964)	Zürich, Switzerland	17 Aug	1988
800 meters	1:	41·73	Sebastian Newbold Coe (Great Britain; b. 29 Sep 1956)	Florence, Italy	10 Jun	1981
1,000 meters	2:	12·18	Sebastian Newbold Coe (Great Britain)	Oslo, Norway	11 Jul	1981
1,500 meters	3:	29·46	Saïd Aouita (Morocco; b. 2 Nov 1959)	West Berlin, West Germany	23 Aug	1985
1 mile	3:	46·32	Steven Cram (Great Britain; b. 14 Oct 1960)	Oslo, Norway	27 Jul	1985
2,000 meters	4:	50·81	Saïd Aouita (Morocco)	Paris, France	16 Jul	1987
3,000 meters	7:	29·45	Saïd Aouita (Morocco)	Cologne, West Germany	20 Aug	1989
5,000 meters	12:	58·39	Saïd Aouita (Morocco)	Rome, Italy	22 Jul	1987
10,000 meters	27:	08·23	Arturo Barrios (Mexico; b. 12 Dec 1963)	Berlin, West Germany	18 Aug	1989
20,000 meters	57:	18·4	Dionisio Castro (Portugal; b. 22 Nov 1963)	La Flèche, France	31 Mar	1990
25,000 meters	1 hr 13:	55·8	Toshihiko Seko (Japan; b. 15 Jul 1956)	Christchurch, New Zealand	22 Mar	1981
30,000 meters	1 hr 29:	18·8	Toshihiko Seko (Japan)	Christchurch, New Zealand	22 Mar	1981
1 hour		13·014 miles	Josephus Hermens (Netherlands)	Papendal, Netherlands	1 May	1976

* *Ben Johnson (Canada; b. 30 Dec 1961) ran 100 m in 9·79 sec at Seoul, South Korea on 24 Sep 1988, but was subsequently disqualified on a positive drugs test for steroids. He later admitted to having taken drugs over many years, and this invalidated his 9·83 sec at Rome, Italy on 30 Aug 1987.*
A *This record was set at high altitude—Mexico City 7,349 ft. Best mark at low altitude: 200 m: 19·75 sec, Carl Lewis, Indianapolis, IN, 19 Jun 1983 and Joseph Nathaniel DeLoach (US; b. 5 Jun 1967) at Seoul, South Korea on 28 Sep 1988.*

HURDLING

		sec	Name and country	Place	Date	
110 meters (3' 6")		12·92	Roger Kingdom (US; b. 26 Aug 1962)	Zürich, Switzerland	16 Aug	1989
400 meters (3' 0")		47·02	Edwin Corley Moses (US; b. 31 Aug 1955)	Koblenz, West Germany	31 Aug	1983
3,000 meters steeplechase	8:	05·35	Peter Koech (Kenya; b. 18 Feb 1958)	Stockholm, Sweden	4 Jul	1989

RELAYS

	min	sec	Name and country	Place	Date	
4 × 100 meters		37·83	United States	Los Angeles, CA	11 Aug	1984
			(Samuel Louis Graddy, Ronald James Brown, Calvin Smith, Carl Lewis)			
4 × 200 meters	1:	20·26†	Santa Monica Track Club (US)	Koblenz, West Germany	23 Aug	1989
			(Daniel Everett, Leroy Burrell, Floyd Heard, Carl Lewis)			
4 × 400 meters	2:	56·16A	United States	Mexico City, Mexico	20 Oct	1968
			(Vincent Edward Matthews, Ronald John Freeman, George Lawrence James, Lee Edward Evans)			
	2:	56·16	United States	Seoul, South Korea	1 Oct	1988
			(Daniel Everett, Steven Earl Lewis, Kevin Bernard Robinzine, Harry Lee 'Butch' Reynolds)			
4 × 800 meters	7:	03·89	Great Britain	London, United Kingdom	30 Aug	1982
			(Peter Elliott, Garry Peter Cook, Steven Cram, Sebastian Coe)			
4 × 1,500 meters	14:	38·8	West Germany	Cologne, West Germany	17 Aug	1977
			(Thomas Wessinghage, Harald Hudak, Michael Lederer, Karl Fleschen)			

† *Texas Christian University ran 1:20·20 at Philadelphia, PA on 26 Apr 1986. This time could not be ratified as their team was composed of different nationalities: Roscoe Tatum (US), Andrew Smith (Jamaica), Leroy Reid (Jamaica), Greg Sholars (US).*

FIELD EVENTS	m	ft	in	Name and country	Place	Date	
High Jump	2·44	8	0	Javier Sotomayor (Cuba; b. 13 Oct 1967)	San Juan, Puerto Rico	29 Jul	1989
Pole Vault	6·06	19	10 ½	Sergey Bubka (USSR; b. 4 Dec 1963)	Nice, France	10 Jul	1988
Long Jump	8·90A	29	2 ½	Robert Beamon (US; b. 29 Aug 1946)	Mexico City, Mexico	18 Oct	1968
Triple Jump	17·97	58	11	William Augustus 'Willie' Banks (US; b. 11 Mar 1956)	Indianapolis, IN	16 Jun	1985
Shot 16 lb	23·12	75	10 ¼	Eric Randolph 'Randy' Barnes (US; b. 16 Jun 1966)	Los Angeles, CA	20 May	1990
Discus 4 lb 8 oz	74·08	243	0	Jürgen Schult (East Germany; b. 11 May 1960)	Neubrandenburg, East Germany	6 Jun	1986
Hammer 16 lb	86·74	284	7	Yuriy Georgiyevich Sedykh (USSR; b. 11 Jun 1955)	Stuttgart, West Germany	30 Aug	1986
Javelin	90·98 †	298	6	Stephen Backley (Great Britain; b. 12 Feb 1969)	London, United Kingdom	20 Jul	1990

A *Set at high altitude; the low altitude best: 28 ft 10¼ in, Carl Lewis at Indianapolis, IN on 19 Jun 1983.*
†*With the new javelin, which has the centre of gravity moved back, introduced in 1986. The best performance with the old javelin was 343 ft 10 in by Uwe Hohn (East Germany; b. 16 Jul 1962) at East Berlin, East Germany on 20 Jul 1984.*

DECATHLON

8,847 points..........Francis Morgan 'Daley' Thompson (Great Britain; b. 30 Jul 1958)..........Los Angeles, CA..........8–9 Aug 1984

(1st day: 100 m 10·44 sec, Long Jump 26' 3 ½",
Shot Put 51' 7", High Jump 6' 8",
400 m 46·97 sec)

(2nd day: 110 m Hurdles 14·33 sec,
Discus 152' 9", Pole Vault 16' 4 ¾",
Javelin 214' 0", 1,500 m 4:35·00 sec)

---

100 m in 1968, 4 x 100m relay in 1964 and 1968; and by Valerie Ann Brisco (b. 6 Jul 1960) at 200 m, 400 m and 4 x 400 m relay. Rudolph and Tyus also won one silver medal each. Four gold medals at one Games were won by Alvin Kraenzlein (see above). Jesse Owens (1913–80) in 1936 and Frederick Carleton 'Carl' Lewis (b.1 Jul 1961) in 1984; both won four gold medals at one Games, both at 100 m, 200 m, long jump and the 4 x 100 m relay. Lewis won two more gold medals in 1988.

Olympic champions *Oldest & Youngest*
■ The oldest athlete to win an Olympic title was Irish-born Patrick Joseph 'Babe' McDonald (ne McDonnell, [US]; 1878–1954) who was aged 42 yr 26 days when he won the 56-lb weight throw at Antwerp, Belgium on 21 Aug 1920. The oldest female champion was Lia Manoliu (Romania; b. 25 Apr 1932), aged 36 yr 176 days when she won the discus at Mexico City, Mexico on 18 Oct 1968. The youngest gold medalist was Barbara Pearl Jones (US; b. 26 Mar 1937), who at 15 yr 123 days was a member of the winning 4 × 100 m relay team, at Helsinki, Finland on 27 Jul 1952. The youngest male champion was Robert Bruce Mathias (US; b. 17 Nov 1930), aged 17 yr 263 days when he won the decathlon at the London Games on 5–6 Aug 1948.

The oldest Olympic medalist was Tebbs Lloyd Johnson (1900–84), aged 48 yr 115 days when he was third in the 1948 50,000 m walk. The oldest woman medalist was Dana Zátopková (b. 19 Sep 1922), aged 37 yr 348 days when she was second in the javelin in 1960.

World championships ■ Quadrennial World Championships, distinct from the Olympic Games, were inaugurated in 1983, when they were held in Helsinki, Finland. The most

World record holders ● Left: Peter Elliott leads from Saïd Aouita. Elliott was a member of the world record 4 × 800 relay team and set the indoor 1,500 m world record of 3 min 34·21 sec at Seville, Spain on 27 Feb 1990 and Aouita holds four outdoor world records. (Photo: All-Sport/Bob Martin)

World record ● Right: Jürgen Schult (East Germany; b. 11 May 1960) illustrates the speed and power that is required to be a world-class discus thrower. He set the current world record with a throw of 243 ft at Neubrandenburg, East Germany on 6 Jun 1986. (Photo: All-Sport/Gray Mortimore)

medals won is five gold and one silver, by Carl Lewis; gold at 100 m, long jump, 4 × 100 m relay in 1983 and the latter two also in 1987, when he took the silver at 100 m.

World record breakers

Oldest & Youngest ■ For the greatest age at which anyone has broken a world record under IAAF jurisdiction.

The female record is 36 yr 139 days for Marina Styepanova (nee Makeieva, [USSR]; b. 1 May 1950) with 52·94 sec for the 400 m hurdles at Tashkent, USSR on 17 Sep 1986. The youngest individual record breaker is Wang Yan (China; b. 9 Apr 1971), who set a women's 5,000 m walk record at age 14 yr 334 days, 21 min 33·8 sec at Jian, China on 9 Mar 1986. The youngest male is 17 yr 198 days Thomas Ray (Great Britain; 1862–1904), when he pole-vaulted 11 ft 2¾ in on 19 Sep 1879 (prior to IAAF ratification).

WORLD RECORDS *WOMEN*

World records for the women's events scheduled by the International Amateur Athletic Federation. The same stipulation about automatically timed events applies in the six events up to 400 meters as in the men's list.

RUNNING

	min sec	Name and country	Place	Date	
100 meters	10·49	Delorez Florence Griffith Joyner (US; b. 21 Dec 1959)	Indianapolis, IN	16 Jul	1988
200 meters	21·34	Delorez Florence Griffith Joyner (US)	Seoul, South Korea	29 Sep	1988
400 meters	47·60	Marita Koch (East Germany; b. 18 Feb 1957)	Canberra, Australia	6 Oct	1985
800 meters	1:53·28	Jarmila Kratochvílová (Czechoslovakia; b. 26 Jan 1951)	Münich, West Germany	26 Jul	1983
1,000 meters	2:30·6	Tatyana Providokhina (USSR; b. 26 Mar 1953)	Podolsk, USSR	20 Aug	1978
1,500 meters	3:52·47	Tatyana Kazankina (USSR; b. 17 Dec 1951)	Zürich, Switzerland	13 Aug	1980
1 mile	4:15·61	Paula Ivan (Romania; b. 20 Jul 1963)	Nice, France	10 Jul	1989
2,000 meters	5:28·69	Maricica Puiča (Romania; b. 29 Jul 1950)	London, United Kingdom	11 Jul	1986
3,000 meters	8:22·62	Tatyana Kazankina (USSR)	Leningrad, USSR	26 Aug	1984
5,000 meters	14:37·33	Ingrid Kristiansen (nee Christensen [Norway]; b. 21 Mar 1956)	Stockholm, Sweden	5 Aug	1986
10,000 meters	30:13·74	Ingrid Kristiansen (Norway)	Oslo, Norway	5 Jul	1986

HURDLING

	min sec	Name and country	Place	Date	
100 meters (2' 9")	12·21	Yordanka Donkova (Bulgaria; b. 28 Sep 1961)	Stara Zagora, Bulgaria	20 Aug	1988
400 meters (2' 6")	52·94	Marina Styepanova (nee Makeyeva [USSR]; b. 1 May 1950)	Tashkent, USSR	17 Sep	1986

RELAYS

	min sec	Name and country	Place	Date	
4 × 100 meters	41·37	East Germany	Canberra, Australia	6 Oct	1985
		(Silke Gladisch [now Möller], Sabine Rieger [now Günther], Ingrid Auerswald [nee Brestrich], Marlies Göhr [nee Oelsner])			
4 × 200 meters	1:28·15	East Germany	Jena, East Germany	9 Aug	1980
		(Marlies Göhr [nee Oelsner], Romy Müller [nee Schneider], Bärbel Wöckel [nee Eckert], Marita Koch)			
4 × 400 meters	3:15·17	USSR	Seoul, South Korea	1 Oct	1988
		(Tatyana Ledovskaya, Olga Nazarova, Maria Pinigina [nee Kulchunova], Olga Bryzgina [nee Vladykina])			
4 × 800 meters	7:50·17	USSR	Moscow, USSR	5 Aug	1984
		(Nadezha Olizarenko [nee Mushta], Lyubov Gurina, Lyudmila Borisova, Irina Podyalovskaya)			

FIELD EVENTS

	m	ft in	Name and country	Place	Date	
High Jump	2·09	6 10¼	Stefka Kostadinova (Bulgaria; b. 25 Mar 1965)	Rome, Italy	30 Aug	1987
Long Jump	7·52	24 8¼	Galina Chistyakova (USSR; b. 26 Jul 1962)	Leningrad, USSR	11 Jun	1988
Triple Jump	14·52	47 7¾	Galina Chistyakova (USSR)	Stockholm, Sweden	3 Jul	1989
Shot 8 lb 13 oz	22·63	74 3	Natalya Lisovskaya (USSR; b. 16 Jul 1962)	Moscow, USSR	7 Jun	1987
Discus 2 lb 3 oz	76·80	252 0	Gabriele Reinsch (East Germany; b. 23 Sep 1963)	Neubrandenburg, East Germany	9 Jul	1988
Javelin 24 7 oz	80·00	262 5	Petra Felke (East Germany; b. 30 Jul 1959)	Potsdam, East Germany	9 Sep	1988

HEPTATHLON

		Name and country	Place	Date	
7,291 points		Jacqueline Joyner-Kersee (US; b. 3 Mar 1962)	Seoul, South Korea	23–24 Sep	1988
		(100 m hurdles 12·69 sec; High Jump 6 ft 1¼in; Shot 51 ft 10 in; 200 m 22·56 sec; Long Jump 23 ft 10 in; Javelin 149 ft 9 in; 800 m 2 min 08·51 sec)			

Most records in a day ■ Jesse Owens (US) (1913–80) set six world records in 45 min at Ann Arbor, MI on 25 May 1935, with a 9·4 sec 100 yd at 3:15 P.M., a 26 ft 8¼ in long jump at 3:25 P.M., a 20·3 sec 220 yd (and 200 m) at 3:45 P.M. and a 22·6 sec 220-yd low hurdles (and 200 m) at 4:00 P.M.

Most national titles ■ The most American national titles won at all events, indoors and out, is 65, by Ronald Owen Laird (b. 31 May 1938) at various walks events between 1958 and 1976. Excluding the walks, the record is 41, by Stella Walsh (nee Walasiewicz, 1911–80), who won women's events between 1930 and 1954: 33 outdoors and 8 indoors.

The most wins outdoors at one event in AAU/TAC history is 11, by James Sarsfield Mitchel (1864–1921) at 56 lb weight, in 1888, 1891–97, 1900, 1903, 1905; Stella Walsh, 220y/200m 1930–31, 1939–40, 1942–48 and long jump 1930, 1939–46, 1948 and 1951; Maren Seidler (b.11 Jun 1951) in shot 1967–68, 1972–80; Dorothy Dodson (b. 28 Mar 1919) in javelin 1939–49.

Most international appearances ■ The greatest number of international matches contested for any nation is 89, by shot-putter Bjørn Bang Andersen (b. 14 Nov 1937) for Norway, 1960–81.

Longest career ■ Duncan McLean (1884–1980) of Scotland set a world age (92) record of 100 m in 21·7 sec in August 1977, over 73 years after his best ever sprint of 100 yd in 9·9 sec in South Africa in February 1904.

Longest winning sequence ■ Iolanda Balas (Romania; b. 12 Dec 1936) won a record 140 consecutive competitions at high jump from 1956 to 1967. The record at a track event was 122, at 400 meters hurdles, by Edwin Corley Moses (US; b. 31 Jul 1955) between his loss to Harald Schmid (West Germany; b. 29 Sep 1957) at Berlin, West Germany on 26 Aug 1977 and that to Danny Lee Harris (US; b. 7 Sep 1965) at Madrid, Spain on 4 Jun 1987.

U.S NATIONAL RECORDS MEN

RUNNING	min sec	Name	Place	Date
100 meters	9·92	Frederick Carleton 'Carl' Lewis (b. 1 Jul 1961)	Seoul, South Korea	24 Sep 1988
200 meters	19·75	Carl Lewis	Indianapolis, IN	19 Jun 1983
	19·75	Joseph Nathaniel 'Joe' DeLoach (b. 5 Jun 1967)	Seoul, South Korea	28 Sep 1988
400 meters	43·29	Harry Lee 'Butch' Reynolds, Jr (b. 8 Aug 1964)	Zürich, Switzerland	17 Aug 1988
800 meters	1:42·60	John Lee 'Johnny' Gray (b. 19 Jun 1960)	Koblenz, West Germany	28 Aug 1985
1,000 meters	2:13·9	Richard Charles 'Rick' Wohlhuter (b. 23 Dec 1948)	Oslo, Norway	30 Jul 1974
1,500 meters	3:29·77	Sydney Maree (b. 9 Sep 1956)	Köln, West Germany	25 Aug 1985
1 mile	3:47·69	Steven Michael Scott (b. 5 May 1957)	Oslo, Norway	7 Jul 1982
2,000 meters	4:52·44	James C. 'Jim' Spivey (b. 7 Mar 1960)	Lausanne, Switzerland	15 Sep 1987
3,000 meters	7:33·37	Sydney Maree #	London, United Kingdom	17 Jul 1982
	7:35·84	Douglas Floyd Padilla (b. 4 Oct 1956)	Oslo, Norway	9 Jul 1983
5,000 meters	13:01·15	Sydney Maree	Oslo, Norway	27 Jul 1985
10,000 meters	27:20·56	Marcus James Nenow (b. 16 Nov 1957)	Brussels, Belgium	5 Sep 1986
15,000 meters	43:39·8	William Henry 'Bill' Rodgers (b. 23 Dec 1947)	Boston, MA	9 Aug 1977
20,000 meters	58:25·0	Bill Rodgers	Boston, MA	9 Aug 1977
25,000 meters	1 hr 14:11·8	Bill Rodgers	Saratoga, CA	21 Feb 1979
30,000 meters	1 hr 31:49	Bill Rodgers	Saratoga, CA	21 Feb 1979
1 hour	12 miles 135 yd	Bill Rodgers	Boston, MA	9 Aug 1977
Marathon	2 hr 08:52	Alberto Bauduy Salazar (b. 7 Aug 1958)	Boston, MA	19 Apr 1982

 # Prior to obtaining US citizenship

HURDLING				
110 meters	12·92	Roger Kingdom (b. 26 Aug 1962)	Zürich, Switzerland	16 Aug 1989
400 meters	47·02	Edwin Corley Moses (b. 31 Aug 1955)	Koblenz, West Germany	31 Aug 1983
3,000 meter steeplechase	8:09·17	Henry Dinwoodey Marsh (b. 15 Mar 1954)	Koblenz, West Germany	28 Aug 1985

RELAYS				
4 × 100 meters	37·83	National Team	Los Angeles, CA	11 Aug 1984
		(Samuel Louis Graddy, Ronald James Brown, Calvin Smith, Carl Lewis)		
4 × 200 meters	1:19·38	Santa Monica Track Club	Koblenz, West Germany	23 Aug 1989
		(Daniel Joe Everett, Leroy Russell Burrell, Floyd Heard, Carl Lewis)		
4 × 400 meters	2:56·16A	National Team	Mexico City, Mexico	20 Oct 1968
		(Vincent Edward Matthews, Ronald John Freeman, George Lawrence 'Larry' James, Lee Edward Evans)		
	2:56·16	National Team	Seoul, South Korea	1 Oct 1988
		(Daniel Everett, Steven Earl Lewis, Kevin Bernard Robinzine, Harry Lee 'Butch' Reynolds)		
4 × 800 meters	7:06·5	Santa Monica Track Club	Walnut, CA	26 Apr 1986
		(James Robinson, David Mack, Earl Jones, Johnny Gray)		
4 × 1,500 meters	14:46·3	National Team	Bourges, France	24 Jun 1969

A Set at high altitude

FIELD EVENTS	ft in			
High jump	7 10	Hollis Conway (b. 8 Jan 1967)	Norman, OK	30 Jul 1989
Pole vault	19 6½	Daniel Joe Dial (b. 26 Oct 1962)	Norman, OK	18 Jun 1987
Long jump	29 2½ A	Robert 'Bob' Beamon (b. 29 Aug 1946)	Mexico City, Mexico	18 Oct 1968
Triple jump	58 11½	William Augustus 'Willie' Banks (US) (b. 11 Mar 1956)	Indianapolis, US	16 Jun 1985
Shot	75 10¼	Earl Randolph 'Randy' Barnes (b.16 Jun 1966)	Westwood, LA	20 May 1990
Discus	237 4 *	Walter 'Ben' Plunknett (b. 13 Apr 1953)	Stockholm, Sweden	7 Jul 1981
Hammer	268 8	Judson Campbell Logan (b. 19 Jul 1959)	University Park, PA	22 Apr 1988
Javelin	280 1 †	Thomas Alan Petranoff (b. 8 Apr 1958)	Helsinki, Finland	7 Jul 1986

A Set at high altitude; the low altitude best: 28 ft 10¼ in, Carl Lewis at Indianapolis, IN on 19 Jun 1983.
* Ratified despite the fact that it was achieved after a positive drugs test.
† Petranoff has also thrown 283 ft 8 in at Port Elizabeth, South Africa on 5 Mar 1990.

DECATHLON

8,634 points	William Bruce Jenner (b. 29 Oct 1949)	Montreal, Canada	29–30 Jul 1976

(1st day: 100 m 10·94 sec, Long jump 23 ft 8 ¼in, Shot put 50 ft 4 ½in, High jump 6 ft 8 in, 400 m 47·51 sec)   (2nd day: 110 m hurdles 14·84 sec, Discus 164 ft 2 in, Pole vault 15 ft 9 in, Javelin 224 ft 10 in, 1,500 m 4:12·61 sec)

U.S NATIONAL RECORDS *WOMEN*

RUNNING	min sec	Name	Place	Date	
100 meters	10·49	Delorez Florence Griffith Joyner (b. 21 Dec 1959)	Indianapolis, IN	16 Jul	1988
200 meters	21·34	Florence Griffith Joyner	Seoul, South Korea	29 Sep	1988
400 meters	48·83	Valerie Ann Brisco (b. 6 Jul 1960)	Los Angeles, CA	6 Aug	1984
800 meters	1:56·90	Mary Thereza Slaney (nee Decker; b. 4 Aug 1958)	Berne, Switzerland	16 Aug	1985
1,000 meters	2:34·8	Mary Slaney	Eugene, OR	4 Jul	1985
1,500 meters	3:57·12	Mary Slaney	Stockholm, Sweden	26 Jul	1983
1 mile	4:16·71	Mary Slaney	Zürich, Switzerland	21 Aug	1985
2,000 meters	5:32·7	Mary Slaney	Eugene, OR	3 Aug	1984
3,000 meters	8:25·83	Mary Slaney	Rome, Italy	7 Sep	1985
5,000 meters	15:00·00	Patricia Susan 'Patti-Sue' Plumer (b. 27 Apr 1962)	Stockholm, Sweden	3 Jul	1989
10,000 meters	31:35·3	Mary Slaney	Eugene OR	16 Jul	1982
Marathon	2 hr 21:21	Joan Samuelson (nee Benoit; b. 16 May 1957)	Chicago, IL	20 Oct	1985

HURDLING		Name	Place	Date	
100 meters	12·61	Yolanda Gail Devers (now Roberts) (b. 19 Nov 1966)	Los Angeles, CA	21 May	1988
	12·61	Jacqueline Joyner-Kersee (b. 3 Mar 1962)	San Jose, CA	28 May	1988
400 meters	53·37	Sandra Marie Farmer-Patrick (b. 18 Aug 1962)	New York, NY	22 Jul	1989

RELAYS		Name	Place	Date	
4 × 100 meters	41·55	National Team	Berlin, West Germany	21 Aug	1987
		(Alice Regina Brown, Diane Williams, Florence Griffith, Pam Marshall)			
4 × 200 meters	1:32·57	Louisiana State University	Des Moines, IA	28 Apr	1989
		(Tananjalyn Stanley, Sylvia Brydson, Esther Jones, Dawn Sowell)			
4 × 400 meters	3:15·51	National Team	Seoul, South Korea	1 Oct	1988
		(Denean Howard, Diane Lynn Dixon, Valerie Brisco, Florence Griffith Joyner)			
4 × 800 meters	8:17·09	Athletics West	Walnut, CA	24 Apr	1983
		(Susan Addison, Lee Arbogast, Mary Decker, Chris Mullen)			

FIELD EVENTS	ft	in	Name	Place	Date	
High jump	6	8	Dorothy Louise Ritter (b. 18 Feb 1958)	Austin, TX	8 Jul	1988
	6	8	Louise Ritter	Seoul, South Korea	30 Sep	1988
Long jump	24	5 ½	Jacqueline Joyner-Kersee	Indianapolis, IN	13 Aug	1987
Triple jump	46	0 ¾	Sheila Hudson (b. 30 Jun 1967)	Durham, NC	2 Jun	1990
Shot	66	2 ½	Ramona Lu Pagel (nee Ebert) (b. 10 Nov 1961)	San Diego, CA	25 Jun	1988
Discus	216	10	Carol Therese Cady (b. 6 Jun 1962)	San Jose, CA	31 May	1986
Javelin	227	5	Kathryn Joan 'Kate' Schmidt (b. 29 Dec 1963)	Fürth, West Germany	11 Sep	1977

HEPTATHLON		Name	Place	Date	
7,291 points		Jacqueline Joyner-Kersee	Seoul, South Korea	23–24 Sep	1988

(100 m hurdles 12·69 sec; High jump 6 ft 1 ¼ in; Shot 51 ft 10 in; 200 m 22·56 sec; Long jump 23 ft 10 in; Javelin 149 ft 9 in; 800 m 2 min 08·51 sec)

World record ● Left: American Randy Barnes is the current world record holder for the shot, both indoors and outdoors. Here he can be seen setting the indoor record at Los Angeles in 1989. (Photo: All-Sport/Tim DeFrisco)

Longest throw ● Above: Steve Backley is the current world record holder for the javelin. His record throw surpassed the previous mark by 4·4 in and his personal best by 5·5 in. (Photo: All-Sport/Bob Martin)

WORLD INDOOR RECORDS

Track performances around a turn must be made on a track of circumference no longer than 200 meters.

Event	min:sec	Name and country	Place	Date
RUNNING				
50 meters	5·61*	Manfred Kokot (East Germany; b. 3 Jan 1948)	East Berlin, East Germany	4 Feb 1973
	5·61*	James Sanford (US; b. 27 Dec 1957)	San Diego, CA	20 Feb 1981
60 meters	6·50*	Lee McRae (US; b. 27 Dec 1957)	Indianapolis, IN	7 Mar 1987
200 meters	20·36	Bruno Marie-Rose (France; b. 20 May 1965)	Liévin, France	22 Feb 1987
400 meters	45·05	Thomas Schönlebe (East Germany; b. 6 Aug 1965)	Sindelfingen, West Germany	3 Feb 1988
	45·05#	Danny Everett (US; b. 1 Nov 1966)	Stuttgart, West Germany	4 Feb 1990
800 meters	1:44·84	Paul Ereng (Kenya; b. 22 Aug 1967)	Budapest, Hungary	4 Mar 1989
1,000 meters (2:16·4 officially)	2:16·62	Robert Druppers (Netherlands; b. 29 Apr 1962)	The Hague, Netherlands	20 Feb 1988
1,500 meters	3:34·20	Peter Elliott (Great Britain; b. 9 Oct 1962)	Seville, Spain	27 Feb 1990
1 mile	3:49·78	Eamonn Coghlan (Republic of Ireland; b. 21 Nov 1952)	East Rutherford, NJ	27 Feb 1983
3,000 meters	7:39·2	Emiel Puttemans (Belgium; b. 8 Oct 1947)	West Berlin, West Germany	18 Feb 1973
5,000 meters	13:20·4	Suleiman Nyambui (Tanzania; b. 13 Feb 1953)	New York, NY	6 Feb 1981
50 meters hurdles	6·25	Mark McKoy (Canada; b. 10 Dec 1961)	Kobe, Japan	5 Mar 1986
60 meters hurdles	7·36‡	Greg Foster (US; b. 4 Aug 1958)	Indianapolis, IN	16 Jan 1987
	7·37	Roger Kingdom (US; b. 26 Aug 1962)	Piraeus, Greece	8 Mar 1989

* Ben Johnson (Canada; b. 30 Dec 1961) ran 50 m in 5·55 sec at Ottawa, Cananda on 31 Jan 1987 and 60 m in 6·41 at Indianapolis, IN on 7 Mar 1987, but these were invalidated due to his admission of having taken drugs over many years, following his disqualification at the 1988 Olympics.
\# not recognised as run all the way in lanes and IAAF rules specify breaking from lanes after two turns.
‡ adjudged by observers to have been with a rolling start, but officially ratified.

RELAYS

4 × 200 meters	1:22·32	Italy	Turin, Italy	11 Feb 1984
		(Pierfrancesco Pavoni, Stefano Tilli, Giovanni Bongiorni, Carlo Simionato)		
4 × 400 meters	3:05·21	United States	Glasgow, United Kingdom	10 Mar 1989
		(Clarence Daniel, Charles 'Chip' Jenkins, Kenneth Lowery, Mark Rowe)		

WALKING

5,000 meters	18:11·41u	Ronald Weigel (East Germany; b. 8 Aug 1959)	Vienna, Austria	13 Feb 1988
	18:27·10	Mikhail Shchennikov (USSR; b. 24 Dec 1967)	Budapest, Hungary	5 Nov 1989

u *not officially recognised.*

FIELD EVENTS

Event	m	ft	in	Name and country	Place	Date
High Jump	2·43	7	11 ½	Javier Sotomayor (Cuba; b. 13 Oct 1967)	Budapest, Hungary	4 Mar 1989
Pole Vault	6·05	19	10	Sergey Bubka (USSR; b. 4 Dec 1963)	Donetsk, USSR	17 Mar 1990
Long Jump	8·79	28	10 ¼	Fredrick Carleton 'Carl' Lewis (US; b. 1 Jul 1961)	New York, NY	27 Jan 1984
Triple Jump	17·76	58	3 ¼	Michael Alexander Conley (US; b. 5 Oct 1962)	New York, NY	27 Feb 1987
Shot	22·66	74	4 ¼	Eric Randolph 'Randy' Barnes (US; b. 16 Jun 1966)	Los Angeles, CA	20 Jan 1989

HEPTATHLON	6,285 points	Christian Plaziat (France; b. 28 Oct 1963)	Nogent-sur-Oise, France	10–11 Feb 1990
		(60 m 6·78 sec; Long jump, 7·45 m; Shot, 14·42 m; High jump, 2·13 m; 60 m hurdles, 7·98 sec; Pole vault, 4·90 m; 1,000 m 2:47·24)		

WOMEN

Event	min:sec	Name and country	Place	Date
RUNNING				
50 meters	6·11†	Marita Koch (East Germany; b. 18 Feb 1957)	Grenoble, France	2 Feb 1980
60 meters	7·00	Nelli Cooman-Fiere (Netherlands; b. 6 Jun 1964)	Madrid, Spain	23 Feb 1986
200 meters	22·27	Heike Dreschler (East Germany; b. 16 Dec 1964)	Indianapolis, IN	7 Mar 1987
400 meters	49·59	Jarmila Kratochvílová (Czechoslovakia; b. 26 Jan 1951)	Milan, Italy	7 Mar 1982
800 meters	1:56·40	Christine Wachtel (East Germany; b. 6 Jan 1965)	Vienna, Austria	13 Feb 1988
1,000 meters	2:34·8	Brigitte Kraus (East Germany; b. 12 Aug 1956)	Dortmund, West Germany	19 Feb 1978
1,500 meters	4:00·27	Doina Melinte (Romania; b. 27 Dec 1956)	East Rutherford, NJ	9 Feb 1990
1 mile	4:17·13	Doina Melinte (Romania)	East Rutherford, NJ	9 Feb 1990
3,000 meters	8:33·82	Elly van Hulst (Netherlands; b. 9 Jun 1957)	Budapest, Hungary	4 Mar 1989
5,000 meters (mixed race)	15:19·84	Lesley Welch (now Lehane) (US; b. 12 Mar 1963)	Boston, MA	25 Jan 1986
	15:22·64	Lynn Jennings (US; b. 1 Jul 1960)	Hanover, NH	7 Jan 1990
50 meters hurdles	6·58	Cornelia Oschkenat (East Germany; b. 29 Oct 1961)	Berlin, East Germany	20 Feb 1988
60 meters hurdles	7·69	Lyudmila Narozhilenko (USSR)	Chelyabinsk, USSR	4 Feb 1990

† Angella Issajenko (nee Taylor [Canada]; b. 28 Sep 1958) ran 6·06 at Ottawa, Canada on 31 Jan 1987. This was accepted as a world record, but subsequently invalidated when she admitted steroid usage.

RELAYS

4 × 200 meters	1:32·55	S. C. Eintracht Hamm (West Germany)	Dortmund, West Germany	19 Feb 1988
		(Helga Arendt, Silke-Beate Knoll, Mechthild Kluth, Gisela Kinzel)		
4 × 400 meters	3:34·38	West Germany	Dortmund, West Germany	30 Jan 1981
		(Heide-Elke Gaugel, Christina Sussiek, Christiane Brinkmann, Gaby Bussmann)		

WALKING

3,000 meters	11:59·36	Beate Anders (East Germany; b. 4 Feb 1968)	Glasgow, United Kingdom	4 Mar 1990

FIELD EVENTS

Event	m	ft	in	Name and country	Place	Date
High jump	2·06	6	9 ¼	Stefka Kostadinova (Bulgaria; b. 25 Nov 1965)	Piraeus, Greece	20 Feb 1988
Long jump	7·37	24	2 ¼	Heike Dreschler (East Germany; b. 16 Dec 1964)	Vienna, Austria	13 Feb 1988
Triple jump	14·45	47	5	Galina Chistyakova (USSR; b. 26 Jul 1962)	Lipetsk, USSR	29 Jan 1989
Shot	22·50	73	9 ¾	Helena Fibingerová (Czechoslovakia; b. 13 Jul 1959)	Jablonec, Czechoslovakia	19 Feb 1988

PENTATHLON	4,705	Liliana Nastase (Romania; b. 1 Aug 1962)	Sofia, Bulgaria	25 Feb 1990
		(60 m hurdles 8·19 sec; High jump 1·72 m; Shot 13·71 m; Long jump 6·77 m; 800 m 2:16·60)		

Longest running race ■ The longest races ever staged were the 1928 (3,422 miles) and 1929 (3,665 miles) transcontinental races from New York City to Los Angeles, CA. The Finnish-born Johnny Salo (1893–1931) was the winner in 1929 in 79 days, from 31 Mar to 18 Jun. His elapsed time of 525 hr 57 min 20 sec (averaging 6·97 mph) left him only 2 min 47 sec ahead of Englishman Pietro 'Peter' Gavuzzi (1905–81).

The longest race staged annually is Australia's Westfield Run from Paramatta, New South Wales to Doncaster, Victoria (Sydney to Melbourne). The distance run has varied slightly, but the record is by Yiannis Kouros (Greece; b. 13 Feb 1956) in 5 days 2 hr 27 min 27 sec in 1989, when the distance was 658 miles.

Longest runs ■ The longest run by an individual is one of 11,134 miles around the United States, by Sarah Covington-Fulcher (US; b. 14 Feb 1962), starting and finishing in Los Angeles, CA, 21 Jul 1987–2 Oct 1988. Robert J. Sweetgall (US; b. 8 Dec 1947) ran 10,608 around the perimeter of the United States, starting and finishing in Washington D.C., Oct 1982–15 Jul 1983. Ron Grant (Australia; b. 15 Feb 1943) ran around Australia, 8,316 miles in 217 days 3 hr 45 min, 28 Mar–31 Oct 1983. Max Telford (New Zealand; b. Hawick, 2 Feb 1955) ran 5,110 miles from Anchorage, AK to Halifax, Nova Scotia, in 106 days 18 hr 45 min from 25 Jul to 9 Nov 1977.

The fastest time for the cross-America run is 46 days 8 hr 36 min, by Frank Giannino, Jr (US; b. 1952) for the 3,100 miles from San Francisco to New York from 1 Sep–17 Oct 1980. The women's trans-America record is 69 days 2 hr 40 min, by Mavis Hutchinson (South Africa; b. 25 Nov 1942) from 12 Mar–21 May 1978.

Greatest mileage ■ Douglas Alistair Gordon Pirie (Great Britain; b. 10 Feb 1931), who set five world records in the 1950s, estimated that he had run a total distance of 216,000 miles in 40 years to 1981.

Dr Ron Hill (b. 21 Sep 1938), the 1969 European and 1970 Commonwealth marathon champion, has not missed a day's training since 20 Dec 1964. Since then he has run twice a day, except once on Sundays and 23 Dec 1964. His meticulously compiled training log shows a total of 121,142·5 miles from 3 Sep 1956 to 15 Jun 1990. He has finished 112 marathons, all sub 2:52 and has raced in 50 nations.

The greatest competitive distance run in a year is 5,502 miles, by Malcolm Campbell (Great Britain; b. 17 Nov 1934) in 1985.

1,000 Hours ■ Trevor Harris (Australia) ran 1·7 miles within an hour, every hour, for 1,000 consecutive hours at Lake Burley Griffin, Canberra, Australian Capital Territory, Australia from 25 Apr–6 Jun 1989.

Mass relay records ■ The record for 100 miles by 100 runners from one club is 7 hr 53 min 52·1 sec, by Baltimore Road Runners Club, Towson, MD on 17 May 1981. The women's record is 10 hr 47 min 9·3 sec on 3 Apr 1977, by the San Francisco Dolphins Southend Running Club, CA. The record for 100 × 100 m is 19 min 14·19 sec by a team from Antwerp at Merksem, Belgium on 23 Sep 1989.

The longest relay ever run was 10,524 miles, by 2,660 runners at Trondheim, Norway from 26 Aug–20 Oct 1985. Twenty members of the Melbourne Fire Brigade ran 9,357 miles around Australia on Highway No. 1 in 43 days 23 hr 58 min, 10 Jul–23 Aug 1983. The most participants is 4,800, (192 teams of 25), in the Batavierenrace, 103·89 miles from Nijmegan to Enschede, Netherlands on 23 Apr 1983. The greatest distance covered in 24 hr by a team of ten is 264·459 miles by Gerrit Maritz High School at Johannesburg, South Africa on 28–29 Aug 1987.

Backwards running ■ Anthony 'Scott' Weiland, 27, ran the Detroit marathon backwards in 4 hr 7 min 54 sec on 13 Oct 1982. Donald Davis (US; b. 10 Feb 1960) ran 1 mile backwards in 6 min 7·1 sec at the University of Hawaii on 21 Feb 1983. Ferdie Ato Adoboe (Ghana) ran 100 yd backwards in 12·8 sec (100 m in 14·0 sec) at Amherst, MA on 28 Jul 1983.

Arvind Pandya of India ran backwards across America, Los Angeles to New York, in 107 days, 18 Aug–3 Dec 1984. He also ran backwards from John o' Groats to Land's End, 880 miles in 29 days 5 hr 39 min, 2–31 Oct 1985.

ULTRA LONG DISTANCE WORLD RECORDS

TRACK (Men)

Event	hr:min:sec	Name	Place	Date	
50 km	2:48:06	Jeff Norman (Great Britain)	Manchester, United Kingdom	7 Jun	1980
50 miles	4:51:49	Don Ritchie (Great Britain)	London, United Kingdom	12 Mar	1983
100 km	6:10:20	Don Ritchie (Great Britain)	London, United Kingdom	28 Oct	1978
100 miles	11:30:51	Don Ritchie (Great Britain)	London, United Kingdom	15 Oct	1977
200 km	15:11:10†	Yiannis Kouros (Greece)	Montauban, France	15–16 Mar	1985
200 miles	27:48:35	Yiannis Kouros (Greece)	Montauban, France	15–16 Mar	1985
500 km	60:23:00	Yiannis Kouros (Greece)	Colac, Australia	26–29 Nov	1984
500 miles	105:42:09	Yiannis Kouros (Greece)	Colac, Australia	26–30 Nov	1984
1,000 km	136:17:00	Yiannis Kouros (Greece)	Colac, Australia	26 Nov–1 Dec	1984

kilometres		Name	Place	Date	
24 hours	283·600	Yiannis Kouros (Greece)	Montauban, France	15–16 Mar	1985
48 hours	452·270	Yiannis Kouros (Greece)	Montauban, France	15–17 Mar	1985
6 days	1,023·200	Yiannis Kouros (Greece)	Colac, Australia	26 Nov–1 Dec	1984

ROAD (Men)

Where superior to track bests and run on properly measured road courses.

	hr:min:sec	Name	Place	Date	
50 km	2:43:38	Thompson Magawana (SAfrica)	Claremont–Kirstenbosch, South Africa	12 Apr	1988
50 miles	4:50:21	Bruce Fordyce (SAfrica)	London–Brighton, United Kingdom	25 Sep	1983
1,000 miles	10d 10hr 30min 35sec	Yiannis Kouros (Greece)	New York, NY	21–30 May	1988

kilometres					
24 hours	286·463	Yiannis Kouros (Greece)	New York, NY	28–29 Sep	1985
6 days	1,028·370	Yiannis Kouros (Greece)	New York, NY	21–26 May	1988

TRACK (Women)

	hr:min:sec	Name	Place	Date	
15 km	49:44·0	Silvana Cruciata (Italy)	Rome, Italy	4 May	1981
20 km	1:06:55·5	Rosa Mota (Portugal)	Lisbon, Portugal	14 May	1983
25 km	1:29:30	Karolina Szabo (Hungary)	Budapest, Hungary	23 Apr	1988
30 km	1:47:06	Karolina Szabo (Hungary)	Budapest, Hungary	23 Apr	1988
50 km	3:36:58	Ann Franklin (Great Britain)	Barry, United Kingdom	9 Mar	1986
50 miles	6:17:30†	Monika Kuno (West Germany)	Vogt, West Germany	8–9 Jul	1983
100 km	8:01:01	Monika Kuno (West Germany)	Vogt, West Germany	8–9 Jul	1983
100 miles	14:29:44	Ann Trason (US)	Santa Rosa, CA	18–19 Mar	1989
200 km	19:28:48	Eleanor Adams (Great Britain)	Melbourne, Australia	19–20 Aug	1989
200 miles	39:09:03	Hilary Walker (Great Britain)	Blackpool, United Kingdom	5–6 Nov	1988
500 km	77:53:46	Eleanor Adams (Great Britain)	Colac, Australia	13–15 Nov	1989
500 miles	134:01:59	Eleanor Adams (Great Britain)	Colac, Australia	13–19 Nov	1989

kilometres					
1 hour	18·084	Silvana Cruciata (Italy)	Rome, Italy	4 May	1981
24 hours	240·169	Eleanor Adams (Great Britain)	Melbourne, Australia	19–20 Aug	1989
48 hours	366·512	Hilary Walker (Great Britain)	Blackpool, United Kingdom	5–7 Nov	1988
6 days	866·360	Eleanor Adams (Great Britain)	Colac, Australia	13–19 Nov	1989

† *Timed on one running watch only.*

ROAD (Women)

Where run on properly measured road courses.

	hr:min:sec	Name	Place	Date	
30 km	1:38:27	Ingrid Kristiansen (Norway)	London, United Kingdom	10 May	1987
50 km	3:08:13	Frith van der Merwe (SAfrica)	Claremont-Kirstenbosch, South Africa	25 Mar	1989
40 miles	4:43:22	Marcy Schwam (US)	Chicago, IL	3 Oct	1982
50 miles	5:54:17	Ann Trason (US)	Duluth, MN	28 Oct	1989
100 km	7:18:57	Birgit Lennartz (W. Germany)	Hanua, West Germany	28 Sep	1989
100 miles	13:55:02	Ann Trason (US)	Queens, New York	16–17 Sep	1989
200 km	19:22:05	Ann Trason (US)	Queens, New York	16–17 Sep	1989
(indoors)	19:00:31	Elanor Adams (Great Britain)	Milton Keynes, United Kingdom	3–4 Feb	1990
24 hours	236·453 km	Hilary Walker (Great Britain)	Preston, United Kingdom	27–28 Aug	1988
1,000 miles	14d 20hr 18min 24sec	Suprabha Schecter (US)	New York, NY	20 Sep–5 Oct	1989

It should be noted that road times must be assessed with care as course conditions can vary considerably.

SEATTLE   21 Sep 1987

21 October 1987

21 Aug 1987

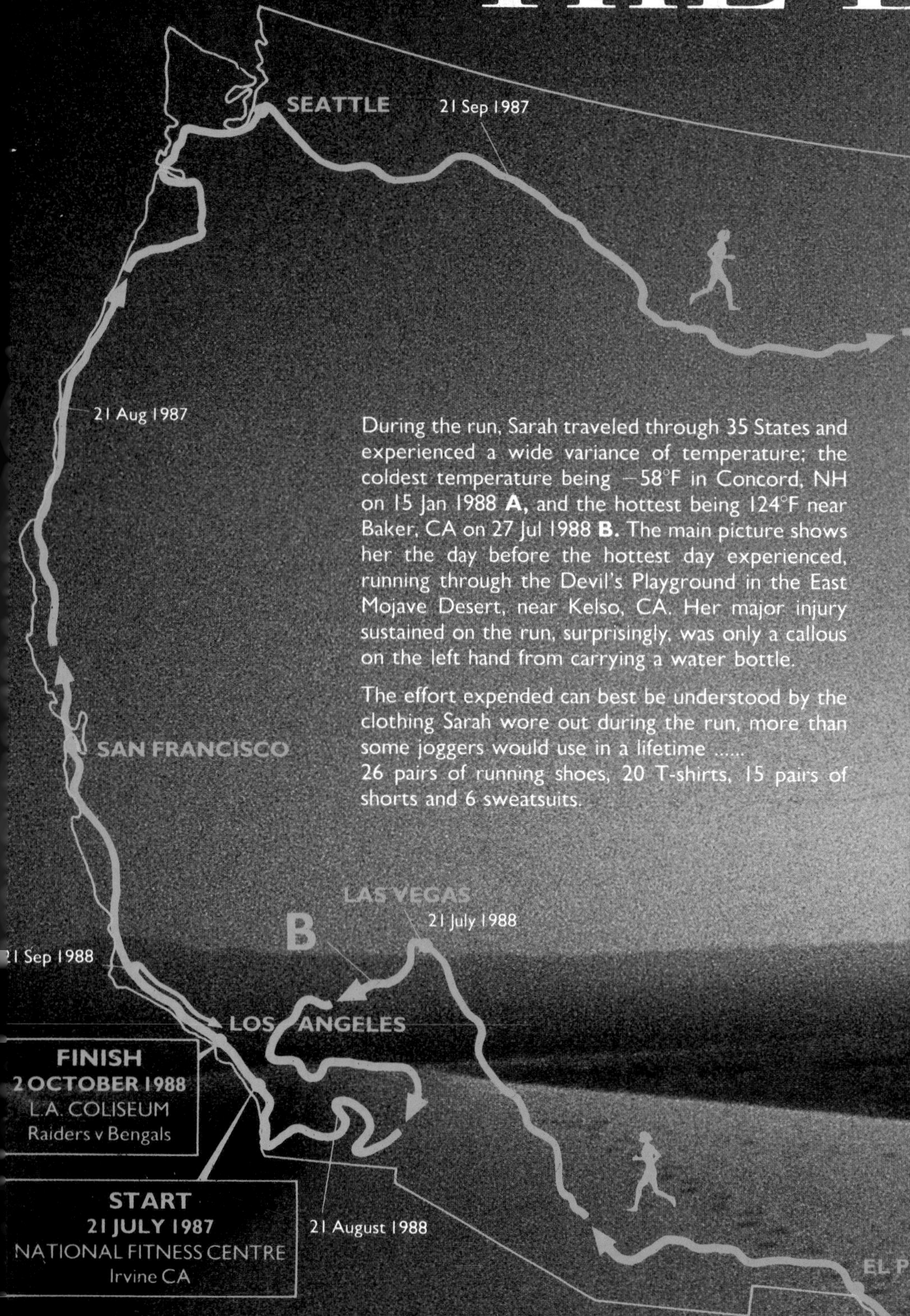

During the run, Sarah traveled through 35 States and experienced a wide variance of temperature; the coldest temperature being −58°F in Concord, NH on 15 Jan 1988 **A**, and the hottest being 124°F near Baker, CA on 27 Jul 1988 **B.** The main picture shows her the day before the hottest day experienced, running through the Devil's Playground in the East Mojave Desert, near Kelso, CA. Her major injury sustained on the run, surprisingly, was only a callous on the left hand from carrying a water bottle.

The effort expended can best be understood by the clothing Sarah wore out during the run, more than some joggers would use in a lifetime ......
26 pairs of running shoes, 20 T-shirts, 15 pairs of shorts and 6 sweatsuits.

SAN FRANCISCO

LAS VEGAS
21 July 1988

B

21 Sep 1988

LOS ANGELES

FINISH
2 OCTOBER 1988
L.A. COLISEUM
Raiders v Bengals

START
21 JULY 1987
NATIONAL FITNESS CENTRE
Irvine CA

21 August 1988

EL PASO   21 June 1988

OTHER LONG RUNS

Robert J. Sweetgall (USA; b. 8 Dec 1947) ran 10,608 miles around the perimeter of the United States, starting and finishing in Washington, D.C., 9 Oct 1982-15 Jul 1983. Ron Grant (Australia; b. 15 Feb 1943) ran around Australia, 8,316 miles in 217 days 3 hr 45 min, running every day from 28 Mar to 31 Oct 1983. Max Telford (New Zealand; b. 2 Feb 1935) ran 5,110 miles from Anchorage, AK to Halifax, Nova Scotia, Canada, in 106 days 18 hr 45 min from 25 Jul to 9 Nov 1977.

The fastest time for the cross-America run is 46 days 8 hr 36 min by Frank Giannino, Jr. (USA; b. 1952) for the 3,100 miles from San Francisco to New York from 1 Sep-17 Oct 1980. The women's trans-America record is 69 days 2 hr 40 min, by Mavis Hutchinson

RUN · · · · · · · · ·

The longest run by an individual is one of 11,134 miles around the United States, by Sarah Covington-Fulcher (US; b. 14 Feb 1962). She began at the United States Fitness Academy, Laguna Hills, CA on 21 Jul 1987 and then ran every day for the next 438 days (an average of 25·42 miles a day; the map shows her monthly progess) to finish at the Los Angeles Coliseum on 2 Oct 1988.

21 Jan 1988

MINNEAPOLIS

21 Nov 1987

NEW YORK

21 December 1987

21 February 1988

ATLANTA

21 March 1988

HOUSTON

21 April 1988

21 May 1988

MIAMI

(Inset Photo: Stan Honda Map: Rob and Rhoda Burns)

MARATHON

The marathon is run over a distance of 26 miles 385 yd. This distance was that used for the race at the 1908 Olympic Games, run from Windsor to the White City stadium, London, United Kingdom and which became standard from 1924. The marathon (40 km) was introduced to the 1896 Olympic Games to commemorate the legendary run of Pheidippides (or Philippides) from the battlefield of Marathon to Athens in 490 B.C. The 1896 Olympic marathon was preceded by trial races that year. The first Boston Marathon, the world's longest-lasting major marathon, was held on 19 Apr 1897 at 24 miles 1,232 yd, and the first national marathon championship was that of Norway in 1897.

The first championship marathon for women was organized by the Road Runners Club of America on 27 Sep 1970.

Fastest ■ There are as yet no official records for the marathon, and it should be noted that courses may vary in severity. The following are the best times recorded, all on courses whose distance has been verified: (men) 2 hr 6 min 50 sec, by Belayneh Dinsamo (Ethiopia; b. 28 Jun 1965) at Rotterdam, Netherlands on 17 Apr 1988, and (women) 2 hr 21 min 6 sec by Ingrid Kristiansen (nee Christensen, [Norway]; b. 21 Mar 1956) at London, United Kingdom on 21 Apr 1985.

Boston Marathon ■ First run by 15 men on 19 Apr 1897 over a distance of 24 miles 1,232 yards, the Boston Marathon is the world's oldest annual race. The full marathon distance was first run in 1927. It is run every year from Hopkinton, MA to Boston, MA on or about the 19th April, Patriot's Day, which honors the famed ride of Paul Revere through Boston.

World record ● Beate Anders (East Germany) on her way to victory over Kerry Saxby (Australia) in the 1989 World Race Walking Cup at Hospitalet, Spain. Saxby has set more than two dozen world records. Anders became the first to better 12 minutes for 3,000 meters when in 11:59·36 she won the European Indoor title at Glasgow, United Kingdom on 4 Mar 1990. (Photo: All-Sport/Dan Smith)

The most wins is seven, by Clarence DeMar (1888–1958), in 1911, 1922–24, 1927–28 and 1930.

Kathy Switzer (US) contested the race in 1967, although the race director tried to prevent her, but pioneering efforts helped force the acceptance of women runners, and they were admitted officially for the first time in 1972. Rosa Mota (Portugal; b. 29 Jun 1958) has a record three wins, 1987–88 and 1990, in the women's race.

The course record for men is 2 hr 8 min 19 sec, by Gelindo Bordin (Italy b. 2 Apr 1959), and for women is 2 hr 22 min 43 sec, by Joan Benoit (now Samuelson) in 1983.

New York Marathon ■ The race was run in Central Park each year from 1970 to 1976, when, to celebrate the US Bicentennial, the course was changed to a route through all five boroughs of the city. From that year, when there were 2,090 runners, the race has become one of the world's great sporting occasions, and in 1989 there were a record 24,588 finishers.

William Henry 'Bill' Rodgers (b. 23 Dec 1947) had a record four wins—1976–79, and Grete Waitz (nee Anderson, [Norway]: b. 1 Oct 1953) was the women's winner nine times — 1978–80, 1982–86 and 1988.

The course record for men is 2 hr 8 min 1 sec, by Juma Ikangaa (Tanzania: b. 19 Jul 1957), and for women is 2 hr 25 min 30 sec, by Ingrid Kristiansen (Norway) in 1990. On a course subsequently re-measured as about 170 yd short, Grete Waitz was the 1981 women's winner in 2 hr 25 min 29 sec.

Pancake race record ■ Dominic M. Cuzzacrea ran the Boston-New York Nissan Marathon while flipping a pancake in a time of 3 hours 6 min and 22 sec on 6 May 1990.

Most competitors ■ The record number of confirmed finishers in a marathon is 24,871 in the London Marathon, United Kingdom on 22 Apr 1990. A record 93 men ran under 2 hr 20 min at London in 1983, a record 35 under 2 hr 15 min in the World Cup marathon at Hiroshima, Japan on 14 Apr 1985, and a record six men ran under 2 hr 10 min at Fukuoka, Japan on 4 Dec 1983 and at London on 23 Apr 1989. A record nine women ran under 2 hr 30 min in the first Olympic marathon for women at Los Angeles, CA on 5 Aug 1984.

Most run by an individual ■ Sy Mah (US; 1926–88) ran 524 marathons of 26 miles 385 yd or longer from 1966 to his death in 1988. He paced himself to take 3½ hr each run.

Three in three days ■ The fastest combined time for three marathons in three days is 8 hr 22 min 31 sec by Raymond Hubbard (Belfast, Northern Ireland: 2 hr 45 min 55 sec, London: 2 hr 48 min 45 sec and Boston: 2 hr 47 min 51 sec) on 16–18 Apr 1988.

Highest altitude ■ The highest start to a marathon is the biennially held Everest Marathon, first run on 27 Nov 1987. It begins at Gorak Shep, 17,100 ft and ends at Namche Bazar, 11,300 ft. The fastest time to complete this race is 3 hr 59 min 4 sec, by Jack Maitland in 1989.

Oldest finishers ■ The oldest man to complete a marathon was Dimitrion Yordanidis (Greece), aged 98, in Athens, Greece on 10 Oct 1976. He finished in 7 hr 33 min. Thelma Pitt-Turner (New Zealand) set the women's record in August 1985, completing the Hastings, New Zealand Marathon in 7 hr 58 min at the age of 82.

WALKING

Most Olympic medals ■ Walking races have been included in the Olympic events since 1906. The only walker to win three gold medals has been Ugo Frigerio (Italy; 1901–68), with the 3,000 m in 1920, and 10,000 m in 1920 and 1924. He also holds the record of most medals, with four (he won the bronze medal at 50,000 m in 1932), a total shared with Vladimir Stepanovich Golubnichiy (USSR; b. 2 Jun 1936), who won gold medals for the 20,000 m in 1960 and 1968, the silver in 1972 and the bronze in 1964.

Longest race ■ The Paris–Colmar, until 1980 Strasbourg–Paris, event (instituted 1926 in the reverse direction), now about 325 miles, is the world's longest annual race walk.

24 hours ■ The greatest distance walked in 24 hr is 140 miles 1,229 yd, by Paul Forthomme (Belgium) on a road course at Woluwé, Belgium on 13–14 Oct 1984. The best by a woman is 125·7 miles by Annie van der Meer at Rouen, France on 30 Apr–1 May 1984 over a 1·185–km lap road course.

Backwards walking ■ The greatest ever exponent of reverse pedestrianism has been Plennie L. Wingo (b. 24 Jan 1895) then of Abilene, TX, who completed his 8,000 mile transcontinental walk from Santa Monica, CA to Istanbul, Turkey from 15 Apr 1931 to 24 Oct 1932. The longest distance recorded for walking backwards in 24 hr is 84·0 miles by Anthony Thornton (US) in Minneapolis, MN on 31 Dec 1985–1 Jan 1986.

Trampolining

Trampolines were used in show business at least as early as 'The Walloons' of the period 1910–12. The sport of trampolining (from the Spanish word *trampolin*, a springboard) dates from 1936, when the prototype 'T' model trampoline was developed by George Nissen (US).

Most titles ■ World Championships were instituted in 1964. A record five titles were won by Judy Wills (US; b. 1948) in the women's event, 1964–68. Five men have won two titles.

Somersaults ■ Christopher Gibson performed 3,025 consecutive somersaults at Shipley Park, Derbyshire, United Kingdom on 17 Nov 1989.

The most complete somersaults in one minute is 75, by Richard Cobbing of Lightwater, Surrey, United Kingdom, at British Broadcasting Corporation Television Centre, London for 'Record Breakers' on 8 Nov 1989. The most baranis in a minute is 78, by Zoe Finn of Chatham, Kent, United Kingdom at British Broadcasting Corporation Television Centre, London for 'Blue Peter' on 25 Jan 1988.

Triathlon

The triathlon combines long-distance swimming, cycling and running. Distances for each of the phases can vary, but for the best established event, the Hawaii Ironman (instituted 1978), competitors first swim 2·4 miles, then cycle 112 miles, and finally run a full marathon of 26 miles 385 yards. Record times for the Hawaii Ironman are: (men) 8 hr 9 min 16 sec, Mark Allen (US) ; (women) 9 hr 56 sec, by Paula Newby-Fraser (Zimbabwe), both on 15 Oct 1989. Dave Scott has won a record six races, 1980, 1982–84 and 1986–87.

World Championships ■ After earlier abortive efforts, a world governing body, L'Union Internationale de Triathlon (UIT), was founded at Avignon, France on 1 Apr 1989, staging the first official World Championships in August 1989.

A 'World Championship' race has been held annually in Nice, France from 1982; the distances 3,200 m, 120 km and 32 km respectively, with the swim increased to 4,000 m from 1988. Mark Allen (US) has won seven times, 1982–86, 1989–90.

Largest field ■ The largest field in a triathlon race has been 3,888 finishers, in the Bud Lite US Triathlon race at Chicago, IL in 1987. This series encompasses races over 1,500 m, 40 km and 10 km for the three phases.

Volleyball

The game was invented as *mintonette* in 1895 by William G. Morgan at the YMCA gymnasium at Holyoke, MA. The International Volleyball Association was formed in Paris, France in April 1947.

Most world titles ■ World Championships were instituted in 1949 for men and 1952 for women. The USSR has won six men's titles (1949, 1952, 1960, 1962, 1978 and 1982) and four women's (1952, 1956, 1960 and 1970).

Most Olympic titles ■ The sport was introduced to the Olympic Games for both men and women in 1964. The USSR has won a record three men's (1964, 1968 and 1980) and four women's (1968, 1972, 1980 and 1988) titles. The only player to win four medals is Inna Valeryevna Ryskal (USSR; b. 15 Jun 1944), who won women's silver medals in 1964 and 1976 and golds in 1968 and 1972. The record for men is held by Yuriy Mikhailovich Poyarkov (USSR; b. 10 Feb 1937) who won gold medals in 1964 and 1968 and a bronze in 1972, and by Katsutoshi Nekoda (Japan; b. 1 Feb 1944) who won gold in 1972, silver in 1968 and bronze in 1964.

The US were men's champions in 1984 and 1988. Three men played on each of those teams and on the only US teams to win the World Cup (1985) and World Championships (1986): Craig Buck (b. 24 Aug 1958), Charles 'Karch' Kiraly (b. 3 Nov 1960) and Stephen Timmons (b. 29 Nov 1958). David Saunders (b. 19 Oct 1960) was a reserve on the 1984 team and played on those of 1986 and 1988. 'Karch' Kiraly is the only player to win an Olympic gold medal and the World Championship of Beach Volleyball.

Water Polo

Water polo was developed in England as 'water soccer' in 1869 and first included in the Olympic Games in Paris, France in 1900.

Most Olympic titles ■ Hungary has won the Olympic tournament most often, with six wins, in 1932, 1936, 1952, 1956, 1964 and 1976.

Five players share the record of three gold medals: Britons George Wilkinson (1879–1946), in 1900, 1908, 1912; Paulo 'Paul' Radmilovic (1886–1968), and Charles Sidney Smith (1879–1951), in 1908, 1912, 1920; and Hungarians Deszö Gyarmati (b. 23 Oct 1927) and György Kárpáti (b. 23 Jun 1935), in 1952, 1956, 1964. Paul Radmilovic also won a gold medal for the 4 × 200 m freestyle swimming in 1908.

US teams took all the medals in 1904, but there were no foreign contestants. Since then their best result has been silver in 1984.

World Championships ■ First held at the World Swimming Championships in 1973. The USSR is the only double winner, 1975 and 1982. A women's competition was introduced in 1986, when it was won by Australia.

Most goals ■ The greatest number of goals scored by an individual in an international is 13, by Debbie Handley for Australia (16) *v* Canada (10) at the World Championship in Guayaquil, Ecuador in 1982.

Most international appearances ■ The greatest number of international appearances is 412, by Aleksey Stepanovich Barkalov (USSR; b. 18 Feb 1946), 1965–80.

Water Skiing

The origins of water skiing derive from walking on planks and aquaplaning. A 19th–century treatise on sorcerers refers to Eliseo de Tarentum who, in the 14th century, 'walks and dances' on the water. The first report of aquaplaning was on America's Pacific Coast in the early 1900s. At Scarborough, Yorkshire, United Kingdom on 15 Jul 1914, a single plank-gliding contest was won by H. Storry.

The present-day sport of water skiing was pioneered by Ralph W. Samuelson (1904–77) on Lake Pepin, MN, on two curved pine boards in the summer of 1922, although claims have been made for the birth of the sport on Lake Annecy (Haute-Savoie), France at about the same time. The first world organization, the Union Internationale de Ski Nautique, was formed in Geneva on 27 Jul 1946.

The American Water Ski Association was founded in 1939 and held the first national championships that year.

Most titles ■ World Overall Championships (instituted 1949) have been won four times by Sammy Duvall (US), in 1981, 1983, 1985 and 1987, and three times by two women, Willa McGuire (nee Worthington) of the United States, in 1949–50 and 1955 and Elizabeth 'Liz' Allan-Shetter (US), in 1965, 1969 and 1975. Liz Allan-Shetter has won a record eight individual championship events and is the only person to win all four titles — slalom, jumping, tricks and overall in one year, at Copenhagen, Denmark in 1969. The United States has won the team championship on 17 successive occasions, 1957–89.

United States ■ US national championships were first held at Marine Stadium, Jones Beach State Park, Long Island, NY on 22 Jul 1939. The

WATER SKIING
RECORDS

─── WORLD ───

SLALOM
MEN: 1 buoy on a 10·25 m line, Michael Kjellander (Sweden); Andrew Mapple (Great Britain; b. 3 Nov 1958), both at Lantana, FL on 30 Oct 1988.
WOMEN: 5 buoys on an 11·25 m line, Jennifer Leachman (US) at Fort Worth, TX on 29 Aug 1988.

TRICKS
MEN: 10,860 points, Cory Pickos (US) at Wapakoneta, OH on 17 Jul 1988.
WOMEN: 8,460 points, Tawn Larsen (US) at Sparta, NJ on 29 Aug 1988.

JUMPING
MEN: 205 ft, Sammy Duvall (US) at Shreveport, FL on 24 Jul 1988.
WOMEN: 156 ft, Deena Mapple (nee Brush; US) at Charlotte, NC on 9 Jul 1988.

World record ● Tawn Larsen (US) in action at the 1989 World Championships in Florida, where she won the women's tricks world title. She set a world record score of 8,640 points at Sparta, NJ on 29 Aug 1988. (Photo: All-Sport/Scott Halleran)

most overall titles is eight, by Willa Worthington McGuire, 1946–51 and 1954–55 and by Liz Allan Shetter 1968–75. The men's record is six titles, by Chuck Stearns 1957–58, 1960, 1962, 1965 and 1967.

Highest speed ■ The fastest water skiing speed recorded is 143·08 mph, by Christopher Michael Massey (Australia) on the Hawkesbury River, Windsor, New South Wales, Australia on 6 Mar 1983. His drag boat driver was Stanley Charles Sainty. Donna Patterson Brice (b. 1953) set a women's record of 111·11 mph at Long Beach, CA on 21 Aug 1977.

Longest run ■ The greatest distance traveled is 1,321·16 miles, by Steve Fontaine (US) on 24–26 Oct 1988 at Jupiter Hills, FL.

Most skiers towed by one boat ■ A record 100 water skiers were towed on double skis over a nautical mile by the cruiser *Reef Cat* at Cairns, Queensland, Australia on 18 Oct 1986. This feat, organized by the Cairns and District Powerboat and Ski Club, was then replicated by 100 skiers on single skis.

Barefoot ■ The first person to water ski barefoot is reported to be Dick Pope, Jr at Lake Eloise, FL on 6 Mar 1947. The barefoot duration record is 2 hr 42 min 39 sec, by Billy Nichols (US; b. 1964) on Lake Weir, FL on 19 Nov 1978. The backward barefoot record is 39 min, by Paul McManus (Australia).

The official barefoot speed record is 119·36 mph, by Scott Michael Pellaton (b. 8 Oct 1956) over a quarter-mile course at Chowchilla, CA on 4 Sep 1983. The fastest by a woman is 73·67 mph, by Karen Toms (Australia) on the Hawkesbury River, Windsor, New South Wales on 31 Mar 1984.

The fastest official speed backwards barefoot is 62 mph, by Robert Wing (Australia; b. 13 Aug 1957) on 3 Apr 1982.

The barefoot jump record is: (men) 72 ft 6 in, by Brett Sands (Australia) at Cohuna, Victoria, Australia on 29 Feb 1989 and (women) 47 ft 6¾ in, by Debbie Pugh (Australia) at Hellas Park, Australia on 5 Feb 1989.

Weightlifting

Competitions for lifting weights of stone were held in the ancient Olympic Games. The first championships entitled 'world' were staged at the Café Monico, Piccadilly, London, United Kingdom on 28 Mar 1891 and then in Vienna, Austria on 19–20 Jul 1898, subsequently recognized by the International Weightlifting Federation (IWF). Prior to that time, weightlifting consisted of professional exhibitions in which some of the advertized poundages were open to doubt.

The Fédération Internationalé Haltérophile et Culturiste, now the International Weightlifting Federation (IWF), was established in 1905, and its first official championships were held in Tallinn, Estonia on 29–30 Apr 1922.

There are two standard lifts: the 'snatch' and the 'clean and jerk' (or 'jerk'). Totals of the two lifts determine competition results. The 'press,' which was a standard lift, was abolished in 1972.

Most Olympic medals ■ Norbert Schemansky (US; b. 30 May 1924) won a record four Olympic medals: gold, middle heavyweight 1952; silver, heavyweight 1948; bronze, heavyweight 1960 and 1964.

Three US lifters won two gold medals: John Henry Davis, Jr (b. 12 Jan 1921), heavyweight 1948 and 1952; Tommy Tamio Kono (b. 27 Jun 1930), lightweight 1952, light heavyweight 1956; Charles Thomas 'Chuck' Vinci, Jr (b. 28 Feb 1933), bantamweight 1956 and 1960. Tommy Kono is the only lifter to have set world records in four different classes. The only American woman to win a world title has been Karyn Marshall, at 82 kg in 1987.

Most titles *World* ■ The most world title wins, including Olympic Games, is eight, by: John Henry Davis (US; 1921–84) in 1938, 1946–52; Tommy Kono (US; b. 27 Jun 1930) in 1952–59; and by Vasiliy Alekseyev (USSR; b. 7 Jan 1942), 1970–77.

United States ■ The most US national titles won is 13, by Anthony Terlazzo (1911–66), at 137lb, 1932 and 1936 and at 148lb, 1933, 1935, 1937–45.

Youngest world record holder ■ Naim Suleimanov (later Neum Shalamanov, [Bulgaria]; b. 23 Nov 1967) (now Naim Suleymanoğlü of Turkey) set 56-kg world records for snatch (130 kg) and total (290 kg) at age 15 yr 334 days, at Moscow, USSR on 23 Oct 1983.

Heaviest lift to body weight ■ The first man to clean and jerk more than three times his body weight was Stefan Topurov (Bulgaria), who lifted 396¾ lb at Moscow, USSR on 24 Oct 1983. The first man to snatch two-and-a-half times his own body weight was Naim Suleymanoğlü (Turkey), who lifted 330½ lb at Cardiff, South Glamorgan, United Kingdom on 27 Apr 1988. The first woman to clean and jerk more than two

WORLD WEIGHTLIFTING RECORDS

Bodyweight class	Lift	kg	lb	Name and country	Place	Date	
52 kg *114¹/₂lb*	Snatch	120·0	264 ¹/₂	Sevdalin Marinov (Bulgaria)	Seoul, South Korea	18 Sep	1988
FLYWEIGHT	Jerk	155·0	341 ³/₄	Ivan Ivanov (Bulgaria)	Athens, Greece	16 Sep	1989
	Total	272·5	600 ³/₄	Ivan Ivanov (Bulgaria)	Athens, Greece	16 Sep	1989
56 kg *123¹/₄lb*	Snatch	134·5	296 ¹/₂	Liu Shoubin (China)	Kemerovo, USSR	1 Mar	1989
BANTAMWEIGHT	Jerk	171·0	377	Neno Terziiski (Bulgaria)	Ostrava, Czechoslovakia	6 Sep	1987
	Total	300·0	661 ¹/₄	Naim Suleimanov (Bulgaria)	Varna, Bulgaria	11 May	1984
60 kg *132¹/₄lb*	Snatch	152·5	336	Naim Suleymanoğlü (Turkey)*	Seoul, South Korea	20 Sep	1988
FEATHERWEIGHT	Jerk	190·0	418 ³/₄	Naim Suleymanoğlü (Turkey)*	Seoul, South Korea	20 Sep	1988
	Total	342·5	755	Naim Suleymanoğlü (Turkey)*	Seoul, South Korea	20 Sep	1988
67·5 kg *148³/₄lb* †	Snatch	160·0	352 ³/₄	Israil Militosyan (USSR)	Athens, Greece	18 Sep	1989
LIGHTWEIGHT	Jerk	200·5	442	Mikhail Petrov (Bulgaria)	Ostrava, Czechoslovakia	8 Sep	1987
	Total	355·0	782 ¹/₂	Mikhail Petrov (Bulgaria)	Seoul, South Korea	5 Dec	1987
75 kg *165¹/₄lb*	Snatch	170·0	374 ³/₄	Angel Guenchev (Bulgaria)	Miskolc, Hungary	11 Dec	1987
MIDDLEWEIGHT	Jerk	215·5	475	Aleksandr Varbanov (Bulgaria)	Seoul, South Korea	5 Dec	1987
	Total	382·5	843 ¹/₄	Aleksandr Varbanov (Bulgaria)	Plovdiv, Bulgaria	20 Feb	1988
82·5 kg *181³/₄lb*	Snatch	183·0	403 ¹/₄	Asen Zlatev (Bulgaria)	Melbourne, Australia	7 Dec	1986
LIGHT-	Jerk	225·0	496	Asen Zlatev (Bulgaria)	Sofia, Bulgaria	12 Nov	1986
HEAVYWEIGHT	Total	405·0	892 ³/₄	Yurik Vardanyan (USSR)	Varna, Bulgaria	14 Sep	1984
90 kg *198¹/₄lb*	Snatch	195·5	431	Blagoi Blagoyev (Bulgaria)	Varna, Bulgaria	1 May	1983
MIDDLE-	Jerk	235·0	518	Anatoliy Khrapatiy (USSR)	Cardiff, South Glamorgan	29 Apr	1988
HEAVYWEIGHT	Total	422·5	931 ¹/₄	Viktor Solodov (USSR)	Varna, Bulgaria	15 Sep	1984
100 kg *220¹/₄lb*	Snatch	200·5	442	Nicu Vlad (Romania)	Sofia, Bulgaria	14 Nov	1986
	Jerk	242·5	534 ¹/₂	Aleksandr Popov (USSR)	Tallinn, USSR	5 Mar	1988
	Total	440·0	970	Yuriy Zakharevich (USSR)	Odessa, USSR	4 Mar	1983
110 kg *242¹/₂lb*	Snatch	210·0	462 ³/₄	Yuriy Zakharevich (USSR)	Seoul, South Korea	27 Sep	1988
HEAVYWEIGHT	Jerk	250·5	552 ¹/₄	Yuriy Zakharevich (USSR)	Cardiff, South Glamorgan	30 Apr	1988
	Total	455·0	1003	Yuriy Zakharevich (USSR)	Seoul, South Korea	27 Sep	1988
Over 110 kg *242¹/₂lb*	Snatch	216·0	476	Antonio Krastev (Bulgaria)	Ostrava, Czechoslovakia	13 Sep	1987
SUPER-	Jerk	266·0	586 ¹/₄	Leonid Taranenko (USSR)	Canberra, Australia	26 Nov	1988
HEAVYWEIGHT	Total	475·0	1,047	Leonid Taranenko (USSR)	Canberra, Australia	26 Nov	1988

* *Formerly Naim Suleimanov or Neum Shalamanov of Bulgaria*

† *Angel Guenchev (Bulgaria) achieved 160 kg snatch, 202·5 kg jerk for a 362·5 kg total at Seoul, South Korea on 21 Sep 1988 but was subsequently disqualified on a positive drugs test.*

Powerlifting feats ■ Lamar Gant (US) was the first man to deadlift five times his own body weight, lifting 661 lb when 132 lb in 1985.

The greatest powerlift by a woman is a squat of 628 lb by Lorraine Constanzo (US) at Dayton, OH on 21 Nov 1987. Cammie Lynn Lusko (US; b. 5 Apr 1958) became the first woman to lift more than her body weight with one arm, with 131 lb at a body weight of 128·5 lb, at Milwaukee, WI on 21 May 1983.

24-hr and 1-hr lifts ■ A deadlifting record of 5,519,634 lb in 24 hr was set by a team of ten from HM Prison Wandsworth, London, United Kingdom on 26–27 May 1990. The 24-hr deadlift record by an individual is 810,626 lb, by Paul Goodall at the Mayflower Leisure Centre, Plymouth, Devon, United Kingdom on 2–3 Dec 1989.

A bench press record of 8,529,565 lb was set by a nine-man team from the Hogarth Barbell Club, Chiswick, London on 18–19 Jul 1987. A squat record of 4,780,919 lb was set by a ten-man team from St Albans, United Kingdom Weightlifting Club and Ware Boys Club, Hertfordshire, United Kingdom on 20–21 Jul 1986. A record 133,380 arm-curling repetitions using three 48¹/₄-lb weightlifting bars and dumb-bells was achieved by a team of nine from Intrim Health and Fitness Club at Gosport, Hampshire, United Kingdom on 4–5 Aug 1989.

Michael Williams achieved 1,438 repetitions of his body weight (147·7 lb) in one hour by bench presses at Don Styler's Gymnasium, Gosport, Hampshire, United Kingdom on 17 Apr 1989.

World record ● A determined-looking Karyn Marshall (US) in the process of setting a women's world record in the 82·5 kg snatch at the 1989 World Championships, which were held in Manchester, United Kingdom. (Photo: All-Sport/Gray Mortimore)

times her own body weight was Cheng Jinling (China), who lifted 198 lb in the class of the World Championships at Jakarta, Indonesia in December 1988.

Women's World Championships ■ These are held annually, first at Daytona Beach, FL in October 1987. Women's world records have been ratified for the best marks at these champ ionships. The heaviest lift for any of the nine weight categories has been the 303 lb jerk by Han Changmei (China; b. 21 Dec 1965) for over 82·5 kg at Manchester, United Kingdom in November in 1989.

POWERLIFTING

The sport of powerlifting was first contested at national level in Great Britain in 1958. The first US Championships were held in 1964. The International Powerlifting Federation was founded in 1972, a year after the first, unofficial world championships were held. Offical championships have been held annually for men from 1973 and for women from 1980. The three standard lifts are squat, bench press and dead lift, the totals from the three lifts determining results.

Most world titles *World* ■ The winner of the most world titles is Hideaki Inaba (Japan), with 15, at 52 kg, 1974–83, 1985–89. The most by a women is six, by Beverley Francis (Australia; b. 15 Feb 1955) at 75 kg, 1980, 1982; 82·5kg 1981, 1983–85.

— WORLD POWERLIFTING RECORDS (All weights in kilograms) —

Class	Squat		Bench Press		Deadlift		Total	
MEN								
52 kg	243	Hideaki Inaba (Japan) 1986	146·5	Joe Cunha (US) 1982	237·5	Hideaki Inaba (Japan) 1987	587·5	Hideaki Inaba (Japan) 1987
56 kg	242·5	Hideaki Inaba (Japan) 1988	160·5	Hiroyuki Isagawa (Japan) 1989	289·5	Lamar Gant (US) 1982	625	Lamar Gant (US) 1982
60 kg	295	Joe Bradley (US) 1980	180	Joe Bradley (US) 1980	310	Lamar Gant (US) 1988	707·5	Joe Bradley (US) 1982
67·5 kg	300	Jessie Jackson (US) 1987	200	Kristoffer Hulecki (Swe) 1985	315	Daniel Austin (US) 1989	762·5	Daniel Austin (US) 1989
75 kg	328	Ausby Alexander (US) 1989	217·5	James Rouse (US) 1980	333	Jarmo Virtanen (Finland) 1988	850	Rick Gaugler (US) 1982
82·5 kg	379·5	Mike Bridges (US) 1982	240	Mike Bridges (US) 1981	357·5	Veli Kumpuniemi (Finland) 1980	952·5	Mike Bridges (US) 1982
90 kg	375	Fred Hatfield (US) 1980	255	Mike MacDonald (US) 1980	372·5	Walter Thomas (US) 1982	937·5	Mike Bridges (US) 1980
100 kg	422·5	Ed Coan (US) 1989	261·5	Mike MacDonald (US) 1977	378	Ed Coan (US) 1989	1,032·5	Ed Coan (US) 1989
110 kg	393·5	Dan Wohleber (US) 1981	270	Jeffrey Magruder (US) 1982	395	John Kuc (US) 1980	1,000	John Kuc (US) 1980
125 kg	412·5	David Waddington (US) 1982	278·5	Tom Hardman (US) 1982	387·5	Lars Norén (Sweden) 1987	1,005	Ernie Hackett (US) 1982
125 + kg	445	Dwayne Fely (US) 1982	300	Bill Kazmaier (US) 1981	406	Lars Norén (Sweden) 1988	1,100	Bill Kazmaier (US) 1981
WOMEN								
44 kg	142·5	Delcy Palk (US) 1988	75	Teri Hoyt (US) 1982	165	Nancy Belliveau (US) 1985	352·5	Marie-France Vassart 1985 (Bel)
48 kg	147·5	Keiko Nishio (Japan) 1987	82·5	Michelle Evris (US) 1981	182·5	Majik Jones (US) 1984	390	Majik Jones (US) 1984
52 kg	173·5	Sisi Dolman (Neth) 1989	95	Mary Ryan (US) 1984	197·5	Diana Rowell (US) 1984	427·5	Diana Rowell (US) 1984
56 kg	191	Mary Jeffrey (nee Ryan; US) 1989	115	Mary Jeffrey (US) 1988	200·5	Joy Burt (Canada) 1989	485	Mary Jeffrey (US) 1988
60 kg	200·5	Ruthi Shafer (US) 1983	105·5	Judith Auerbach (US) 1989	213	Ruthi Shafer (US) 1983	502·5	Vicki Steenrod (US) 1985
67·5 kg	230	Ruthi Shafer (US) 1984	117·5	Vicki Steenrod (US) 1989	244	Ruthi Shafer (US) 1984	565	Ruthi Shafer (US) 1984
75 kg	225	Sumita Laha (Ind) 1989	142·5	Liz Odendaal (Neth) 1989	230	Liz Odendaal (Neth) 1989	577·5	Liz Odendaal (Neth) 1989
82·5 kg	230	Juanita Trujillo (US) 1986	150	Beverley Francis (Aus) 1981	227·5	Vicky Gagne (US) 1981	577·5	Beverley Francis (Aus) 1983
90 kg	252·5	Lorraine Constanzo (US) 1988	130	Lorraine Constanzo (US) 1988	227·5	Lorraine Constanzo (US) 1988	607·5	Lorraine Constanzo (US) 1988
90 +kg	262·5	Lorraine Constanzo (US) 1987	137·5	Myrtle Augee (GB) 1989	237·5	Lorraine Constanzo (US) 1987	622·5	Lorraine Constanzo (US) 1987

Wrestling

The earliest depictions of wrestling holds and falls on wall plaques and a statue indicate that organized wrestling dates from c. 2750–2600 B.C. It was the most popular sport in the ancient Olympic Games, and victors were recorded from 708 B.C. The Greco-Roman style is of French origin and arose about 1860. The International Amateur Wrestling Federation (FILA) was founded in 1912.

Most titles *Olympic* ■ Three Olympic titles have been won by: Carl Westergren (Sweden; 1895–1958) in 1920, 1924 and 1932; Ivar Johansson (Sweden; 1903–79) in 1932 (two) and 1936; and Aleksandr Vasilyevich Medved (USSR; b. 16 Sep 1937) in 1964, 1968 and 1972. Four Olympic medals were won by: Eino Leino (b. 7 Apr 1891), at freestyle 1920–32; and by Imre Polyák (Hungary; b. 16 Apr 1932) at Greco-Roman in 1952–64.

The one US wrestler to win two Olympic freestyle titles was George Nicholas Mehnert (1881–1948), flyweight in 1904 and bantamweight in 1908. The first, and only, US men to win a Greco-Roman title were Steven Fraser (b. 23 Mar 1953) at light heavyweight and Jeffrey Blatnick (b. 27 Jul 1957) at super-heavyweight in 1984.

World ■ The freestyler Aleksandr Medved (USSR) won a record ten World Championships, 1962–64, 1966–72 at three weight categories. The only wrestler to win the same title in seven successive years has been Valeriy Grigoryevich Rezantsev (USSR; b. 2 Feb 1947) in the Greco-Roman 90 kg class in 1970–76, including the Olympic Games of 1972 and 1976.

United States ■ The most world titles won by a US wrestler is three, by Leroy Kemp (b. 24 Dec 1956), welterweight, 1978–79, 1982. Two world and one Olympic title have been won by Mark Schultz (b. 26 Oct 1960), middleweight 1984, 1985 and 1987, and by John Smith (b. 9 Aug 1965), featherweight 1987–89.

NCAA Division I Championship ■ Oklahoma State University were the first unoffi-

— US MEN'S WEIGHTLIFTING RECORDS —

Bodyweight class	Lift	kg	lb	Name and team	Place	Date	
52 kg 114½ lb	Snatch	95	209·0	Brain Okada (Hawaii)	Honolulu, HI	15 Feb	1986
	Jerk	115·0	253½	Brian Okada (Hawaii)	York, United Kingdom	10 Mar	1984
	Total	205·0	451½	Brian Okada (Hawaii)	York, United Kingdom	10 Mar	1984
56 kg 123¼ lb	Snatch	112·5	248	Albert Hood (Team US)	Los Angeles, CA	30 Jul	1984
	Jerk	135·0	297½	Albert Hood (Team US)	Colorado Springs, CO	3 Dec	1984
	Total	242·5	534½	Albert Hood (Team US)	Los Angeles, CA	30 Jul	1984
60 kg 132¼ lb	Snatch	115·0	253½	Phil Anderson (Team US)	Salonica, Greece	5 Nov	1979
	Jerk	152·5	336	Isaac Berger (Team US)	Tokyo, Japan	12 Oct	1964
	Total	260·0	573	Isaac Berger (Team US)	Tokyo, Japan	12 Oct	1964
67·5 kg 148¾ lb	Snatch	133·5	294	Michael Jacques (Coffee's Gym)	Winston-Salem, NC	22 Sep	1984
	Jerk	165·0	363½	Michael Jacques (Coffee's Gym)	Winston-Salem, NC	15 Jan	1983
	Total	297·5	655½	Michael Jacques (Coffee's Gym)	Winston-Salem, NC	21 Jan	1984
75 kg 165¼ lb	Snatch	152·5	336	Cal Schaks (Team US)	Atlantic City, NJ	3 Apr	1982
	Jerk	187·5	413	Roberto Urrutia (York Barbell)	Boca Raton, FL	15 Jul	1988
	Total	332·5	733	Roberto Urrutia (Team US)	Budapest, Hungary	12 Mar	1988
82·5 kg 181¾ lb	Snatch	157·5	347	Curt White (York Barbell)	Milwaukee, WI	28 Jan	1984
	Jerk	200·0	440½	Curt White (York Barbell)	Seekonk, MA	1 May	1983
	Total	355·0	782½	Curt White (York Barbell)	Seekonk, MA	1 May	1983
90 kg 198¼ lb	Snatch	167·5	369	Lee James (York Barbell)	York, United Kingdom	18 Feb	1978
	Jerk	205·0	451½	Curt White (Team US)	Sodertalje, Sweden	28 Aug	1985
	Total	365·0	804½	Curt White (Team US)	Sodertalje, Sweden	28 Aug	1985
100 kg 220¼ lb	Snatch	167·5	369	Jeff Michels (Team US)	Lille, France	19 Sep	1981
	Jerk	213·0	469½	Ken Clark (Sports Palace)	San Francisco, CA	9 Oct	1983
	Total	377·5	832	Ken Clark (Sports Palace)	San Francisco, CA	9 Oct 1983	
110 kg 242½ lb	Snatch	187·5	413	Jeff Michels (York Barbell)	Seekonk, MA	1 May	1983
	Jerk	227·5	501½	Mark Cameron (Team US)	Allentown, NH	13 Jan	1980
	Total	407·5	898	Jeff Michels (York Barbell)	Seekonk, MA	1 May	1983
Over 110 kg 242½ lb	Snatch	188·5	415½	Mario Martinez (Sports Palace)	Boca Raton, FL	16 Jul	1988
	Jerk	232·5	512½	Mario Martinez (Team US)	Seoul, South Korea	20 Sep	1988
	Total	415·0	914½	Mario Martinez (Sports Palace)	San Francisco, CA	24 Mar	1985

cial national champions in 1928. Including 5 unofficial titles Oklahoma State has won a record 29 NCAA titles, in 1928–31, 1933–35, 1937–42, 1946, 1948–49, 1954–56, 1958–59, 1961–62, 1964, 1966, 1968, 1971, 1989–90. The University of Iowa has won the most consecutive titles with 9 championships from 1978–86.

Longest bout ■ The longest recorded bout was one of 11 hr 40 min, when Martin Klein (Estonia representing Russia; 1885–1947) beat Alfred Asikáinen (Finland; 1888–1942) for the Greco-Roman 75 kg 'A' event silver medal in the 1912 Olympic Games in Stockholm, Sweden.

Heaviest heavyweight ■ The heaviest wrestler in Olympic history is Chris Taylor (1950–79), bronze medalist in the super-heavyweight class in 1972, who stood 6 ft 5 in tall and weighed over 420 lb. FILA introduced an upper weight limit of 286 lb for international competition in 1985.

SUMO WRESTLING

The sport's origins in Japan dates from *c.* 23 B.C. The heaviest ever *rikishi* is Samoan-American Salevaa Fuali Atisnoe of Hawaii, *alias* Konishiki, who in 1988 had a peak weight of 556 lb. He is also the first foreign *rikishi* to attain the second highest rank of *ozeki*, or champion.

Weight is amassed by over-alimentation with a high-protein stew called *chankonabe*.

The most successful wrestlers have been *yokozuna* Sadaji Akiyoshi (b. 1912), *alias* Futabayama, winner of 69 consecutive bouts in the 1930s; *yokozuna* Koki Naya (b. 1940), *alias* Taiho ('Great Bird'), who won the Emperor's Cup 32 times up to his retirement in 1971; and the *ozeki* Tameemon Torokichi, *alias* Raiden (1767–1825), who in 21 years (1789–1810) won 254 bouts and lost only ten for the highest ever winning percentage of 96·2. Taiho and Futabayama share the record of eight perfect tournaments without a single loss. The youngest of the 62 men to attain the rank of *yokozuna* (grand champion) was Toshimitsu Ogata (b. 16 May 1953), *alias* Kitanoumi, in Jul 1974 at age 21 yr and 2 months. He set a record in 1978, winning 82 of the 90 bouts that top *rikishi* fight annually, and had a record 804 wins in the top *Makunouchi* division.

Yokozuna Mitsugu Akimoto (b. 1 Jun 1955), *alias* Chiyonofuji, set a record for domination of one of the six annual tournaments by winning the Kyushu Basho for eight successive years, 1981–88. Hawaiian-born Jesse Kuhaulua (b. 16 Jun 1944), now a Japanese citizen named Daigoro Watanabe, *alias* Takamiyama, was the first

Top wrestler ● One of the top sumo wrestlers is *Yokozuna* Mitsugu Akimoto *alias* Chiyonofuji. He has recorded more career wins than any other wrestler and dominated the Kyushu Basho, winning for eight successive years, 1981–88. (Photo: Gerry Toff)

– US WOMEN'S WEIGHTLIFTING RECORDS –

Bodyweight class	Lift	kg	lb	Name and team	Place	Date
44 kg *97 lb*	Snatch	57·5	126 ½	Sibby Flowers (Team US)	Manchester, United Kingdom	24 Nov 1989
	Jerk	70·0	154	Sibby Flowers (Coffee's Gym)	Minnetonka, Papua New Guinea	29 Apr 1988
	Total	127·5	281	Sibby Flowers (Team US)	Manchester, United Kingdom	24 Nov 1989
48 kg *105 ½*	Snatch	67·5	148 ½	Robin Byrd (Team US)	Jakarta, Indonesia	4 Dec 1988
	Jerk	75·0	165	Robin Byrd (Team US)	Daytona Beach, FL	30 Oct 1987
	Total	140·0	308 ½	Robin Bryd (Team US)	Jakarta, Indonesia	4 Dec 1988
52 kg *114 ½ lb*	Snatch	65·0	143	Robin Byrd (Coffee's Gym)	Houston, TX	28 Apr 1989
	Jerk	85·0	187	Michelle Evris (West Park)	New Rochelle, NY	13 Apr 1985
	Total	145·0	319 ½	Michelle Evris (West Park)	New Rochelle, NY	13 Apr 1985
56 kg *123 ¼ lb*	Snatch	70·0	154	Melanie Getz (Sayre Park)	Amundsen Park	2 Dec 1989
	Jerk	96·0	211 ½	Michelle Evris (West Park)	Portland	1 Mar 1986
	Total	157·5	347	Colleene Colley (Coffee's Gym)	Atlanta, GA	5 May 1984
60 kg *132 ¼ lb*	Snatch	77·5	170 ½	Colleene Colley (Coffee's Gym)	Houston, TX	28 Apr 1989
	Jerk	102·5	225 ½	Colleene Colley (Coffee's Gym)	Houston, TX	28 Apr 1989
	Total	175·0	385 ½	Colleene Colley (Team US)	Jakarta, Indonesia	4 Dec 1988
67·5 kg *148 ¾ lb*	Snatch	87·5	192 ½	Arlys Kovach (Arizona Edge)	Chandler	18 Jun 1988
	Jerk	107·5	236 ½	Diana Fuhrman (Van Nuys WLC)	Houston, TX	7 Sep 1988
	Total	190·0	418 ½	Diana Fuhrman (Team US)	Manchester, United Kingdom	25 Nov 1989
75 kg *165 ¼ lb*	Snatch	92·5	203 ½	Arlys Kovach (Arizona Edge)	Houston, TX	28 Apr 1989
	Jerk	115·0	253 ½	Arlys Kovach (Arizona Edge)	Oklahoma City, OK	28 Jul 1989
	Total	207·5	457	Arlys Kovach (Arizona Edge)	Oklahoma City, OK	28 Jul 1989
82·5 kg *181 ¾ lb*	Snatch	102·5	225 ½	Karyn Marshall (Metrofir BBC)	Minnetonka, Papua New Guinea	30 Apr 1988
	Jerk	125·0	275 ½	Karyn Marshall (Team US)	Daytona Beach, FL	1 Nov 1987
	Total	225·5	497	Karyn Marshall (Metrofit BBC)	Minnetonka, Papua New Guinea	30 Apr 1988

non-Japanese to win an official top-division tournament, in Jul 1972 and in 1981 he set a record of 1,231 consecutive top-division bouts. He weighed in at 450 lb before his retirement in 1984.

Yukio Shoji (b. 14 Nov 1948), *alias* Aobajo, did not miss a single bout in his 22-year career, 1964–86, and contested a record 1,631 consecutive bouts. Kenji Hatano (b. 4 Jan 1948), *alias* Oshio, contested a record 1891 non-consecutive bouts in his 26-year career, 1962–88, the longest in modern sumo history. He holds the record for the most career wins with 1,017.

Yachting

Sailing as a sport dates from the seventeenth century. Originating in the Netherlands, it was introduced to England by Charles II, who participated in a 23 mile race along the River Thames in 1661. The oldest yacht club in the world is the Royal Cork Yacht Club which claims descent from the Cork Harbor Water Club, founded in Ireland in 1720. The oldest continuously existing yacht club in the United States is the New York Yacht Club, founded in 1844.

Olympic titles ■ The first sportsman ever to win individual gold medals in four successive Olympic Games was Paul B. Elvström (Denmark; b. 25 Feb 1928) in the Firefly class in 1948 and the Finn class in 1952, 1956 and 1960. He also won eight other world titles in a total of six classes. The lowest number of penalty points by the winner of any class in an Olympic regatta is three points (five wins, one disqualified and one second in seven starts) by *Superdocious* of the Flying Dutchman class (Lt. Rodney Stuart Pattisson, RN; b. 5 Aug 1943) and Iain Somerled Macdonald-Smith (b. 3 Jul 1945)) at Acapulco Bay, Mexico in October 1968.

United States ■ The only US yachtsman to have won two gold medals is Herman Frasch Whiton (1904–67), at 6 meter class, in 1948 and 1952.

America's Cup ■ The America's Cup was originally won as an outright prize by the schooner *America* on 22 Aug 1851 at Cowes, United Kingdom and was later offered by the New York Yacht Club as a challenge trophy. On 8 Aug 1870 J. Ashbury's *Cambria* (United Kingdom) failed to capture the trophy from *Magic*, owned by F. Osgood (US). The Cup has been challenged 27 times, the United States was undefeated, winning 77 races and only losing eight until 1983, when *Australia II*, skippered by John Bertrand and owned by a Perth syndicate headed by Alan Bond, beat *Liberty* 4–3, the narrowest series victory, at Newport, RI.

Longest race ● The longest sailing race in the world is the Whitbread Round the World Race, held every four years and which in 1989–90 covered 32,000 nautical miles, starting and finishing in Southampton, United Kingdom. *Steinlager*, skippered by New Zealander Peter Blake, won all six legs of the race. (Photo: All-Sport/Bob Martin)

The most times a single helmsman has steered a cup defender is in three separate series. This was achieved by Charlie Barr (US), who defended in 1899, 1901 and 1903, and again by Harold S. Vanderbilt (US) in 1930, 1934 and 1937. Dennis Walter Connor (US) has been helmsman of American boats four times in succession: in 1980, when he successfully defended; in 1983, when he steered the defender, but lost; in 1987, when American challenger regained the trophy, and in 1988, when he again successfully defended.

The largest yacht to have competed in the America's Cup was the 1903 defender, the gaff rigged cutter *Reliance*, with an overall length of 144 ft, a record sail area of 16,160 ft² and a rig of 175 ft high.

Admiral's Cup and ocean racing ■ The ocean racing series with the most participating nations (three boats allowed to each nation) is the Admiral's Cup, held by the Royal Ocean Racing Club. A record 19 nations competed in 1975, 1977 and 1979. Britain has a record nine wins.

Modern ocean racing (in moderate or small sailing yachts, rather than professionally manned sailing ships) began with a race from Brooklyn, NY to Bermuda, 630 nautical miles, organized by Thomas Fleming Day, editor of the magazine *The Rudder*, in June 1906. The race is still held today in every even numbered year, though the course is now Newport, RI to Bermuda.

The race still regularly run with the earliest foundation for any type of craft and either kind of water (fresh or salt) is the Chicago to Mackinac race on Lakes Michigan and Huron, first sailed in 1898. It was held again in 1904, then annually until the present day, except for 1917–20. The record for the course (333 nautical miles) is 1 day 1 hr 50 min (average speed 12·89 knots), by the sloop *Pied Piper*, owned by Dick Jennings (US) in 1987.

The current record holder of the elapsed time records for both the premier American and British ocean races (the Newport, RI to Bermuda race and the Fastnet race) is the sloop *Nirvana*, owned by Marvin Green (US). The record for the Bermuda race, 635 nautical miles, is 2 days 14 hr 29 min in 1982 and for the Fastnet race, 605 nautical miles, is 2 days 12 hr 41 min, in 1985, an average speed of 10·16 knots and 9·97 knots respectively.

Longest race ■ The world's longest sailing race is the Vendée Globe Challenge, the first of which started from Les Sables d'Olonne, France on 26 Nov 1989. The distance circumnavigated without stopping was 22,500 nautical miles. The race is for boats between 50–60 ft, sailed single-handed. The record time on the course is 109 days 8 hr 48 min 50 sec, by Titouan Lamazou (France; b. 1955) in the sloop *Ecureuil d'Aquitaine*, which finished at Les Sables on 19 Mar 1990.

The oldest regular sailing race around the world is the quadrennial Whitbread Round the World race (instituted August 1973), organized by the Royal Naval Sailing Association. It starts in England, and the course around the world and the number of legs with stops at specified ports are varied race to race. The distance for 1989–90 was 32,000 nautical miles from Southampton, United Kingdom and return, with stops and

restarts at Punta Del Este, Uruguay; Fremantle, Australia; Auckland, New Zealand; Punta del Este, Uruguay, and Fort Lauderdale, FL.

Highest speeds ■ The highest speed reached under sail on water by any craft over a 500-meter timed run is by a boardsailer Pascal Maka (France) at 42·91 knots at Saintes Maries de-la-Mer canal, Camargue, France on 27 Feb 1990. The women's record was set at the same venue by Brigitte Gimenez (France; b. 6 Oct 1961) who achieved 39·13 knots on 28 Oct 1989.

The sailing speed record prior to speeds achieved by boardsailers was 36·04 knots (41·50 mph) by the 73½ ft proa *Crossbow II* over a 500 m547 yd course in Portland Harbor, Dorset, United Kingdom, on 17 Nov 1980. The vessel (sail area 1,400 ft²) was designed by Rod McAlpine-Downie and owned and steered by Timothy Colman. In an unsuccessful attempt on the record in October 1978, *Crossbow II* is reported to have momentarily attained a speed of 45 knots (51 mph).

The American with the best time under sail over a 500m run is Jimmy Lewis with 38·68 knots at Saintes Maries-de-la-Mer in February 1988.

Most competitors ■ The most boats ever to start in a single race was 2,072 in the Round Zeeland (Denmark) race on 21 Jun 1984, over a course of 235 nautical miles. The greatest number to start in a race in Britain was 1,781 keeled yachts and multihulls on 17 Jun 1989 from Cowes in the Annual Round-the-Island Race. The fastest time achieved in this annual event is 3 hr 55 min 28 sec by the trimaran *Paragon*, owned and sailed by Michael Whipp on 31 May 1986.

The largest trans-oceanic race was the ARC (Atlantic Rally for Cruisers), when 204 boats of the 209 starters from 24 nations completed the race from Las Palmas de Gran Canaria, (Canary Islands) to Barbados in 1989.

Highest ■ The greatest altitude at which sailing has taken place is 16,109 ft on Laguna Huallatani, Bolivia, in Mirror Dinghy 55448, variously by Peter Williams, Gordon Siddeley, Keith Robinson and Brian Barrett, on 19 Nov 1977.

BOARDSAILING (Windsurfing)

The High Court ruled on 7 Apr 1982 that Peter Chilvers (when aged 12) had devised a prototype of a boardsailer in 1958 in England. In 1968 Henry Hoyle Schweitzer and Jim Drake pioneered the sport, often termed windsurfing, in California. World Championships were first held in 1973 and the sport was added to the Olympic Games in 1984 when the winner was Stephan van den Berg (Netherlands), who also won five world titles 1979–83.

Longest sailboard ■ The longest 'snake' of boardsails was set by 70 windsurfers in tandem at the 'Sailboard Show '89' event at Narrabeen Lakes, Manly, Australia on 21 Oct 1989.

The world's longest sail board, 165 ft, was constructed at Fredrikstad, Norway, and first sailed on 28 Jun 1986.

Highest altitude ■ Richard Franklin of Liverpool, United Kingdom boardsailed at a record height of 17,027 ft in an unnamed glacial meltwater near Cerro Wila Lloje, Bolivia in South America on 31 Jul 1988.